American Diversity, American Identity

American Diversity, American Identity

The Lives and Works of 145 Writers
Who Define the American Experience

John K. Roth, Editor

A Henry Holt Reference Book
HENRY HOLT AND COMPANY   NEW YORK

A Henry Holt Reference Book
Henry Holt and Company, Inc.
Publishers since 1866
115 West 18th Street
New York, New York 10011

Henry Holt® is a registered trademark of Henry Holt and Company, Inc.

Library of Congress Cataloging-in-Publication Data

American diversity, American identity : the lives and works of 145 writers who define
the American experience / John K. Roth, editor. — 1st ed.
    p.   cm. — (Henry Holt reference book)
  1. American literature—history and criticism.   2. national characteristics, American, in literature.   3. Pluralism (Social sciences) in literature.   4. United States—
Intellectual life.   5. Group identity in literature.   6. Authors, American—Biography.   7. Ethnic groups in literature.   8. Regionalism in literature.   I. Roth, John K.
II. Series.
PS169.N35A44   1995   94-38425
810.9—dc20   CIP

ISBN 0-8050-3430-7

First Edition—1995

Printed in the United States of American
All first editions are printed on acid-free paper. ∞

10 9 8 7 6 5 4 3 2 1

*. . . there is no longer any one typical American,
if there ever was . . . we need to expand our notion
of the typical American.*

—Gish Jen, *Typical American*, 1991

CONTENTS

CONTRIBUTING REVIEWERS

Timothy Dow Adams
Jacob H. Adler
Terry L. Andrews
Andrew J. Angyal
Marilyn Arnold
Jane L. Ball
Dan Barnett
Melissa E. Barth
Walton Beacham
Kate Begnal
Harold Branam
Gerhard Brand
Timothy Brennan
Carl Brucker
Domenic Bruni
Thomas Campbell
Allan Chavkin
Balance Chow
C. L. Chua
John L. Cobbs
John J. Conlon
David Cowart
Jeffery E. Cupp
Reed Way Dasenbrock
Bill Delaney
Lloyd N. Dendinger
K. Z. Derounian
Richard H. Dillman
Grace Eckley
Wilton Eckley
Bruce L. Edwards, Jr.
Robert P. Ellis
Thomas L. Erskine
Walter Evans
Howard Faulkner
Richard A. Fine
Sandra K. Fischer
Robert L. Gale
Scott Giantvalley
Jill B. Gidmark
James R. Giles

Richard F. Giles
Julian Grajewski
Daniel L. Guillory
Jay L. Halio
Donald Hall
David Mike Hamilton
Natalie Harper
Nelson Hathcock
Terry Heller
Jane Hill
Dennis Hoilman
William Hutchings
Helen Jaskoski
Shakuntala Jayaswal
Vera Jiji
Clarence O. Johnson
Deborah Kaplan
Anna B. Katona
William P. Kenney
Sue L. Kimball
Anne Mills King
James Reynolds Kinzy
Brooks Landon
Gregory W. Lanier
David Laubach
Norman Lavers
Leon Lewis
James L. Livingston
Robert Emmet Long
Perry D. Luckett
Philip A. Luther
Barbara A. McCaskill
Fred B. McEwen
Richard D. McGhee
Dennis Q. McInerny
Bryant Mangum
Patricia Marks
Peter Markus
Joseph R. Millichap
Kathleen Mills
Robert A. Morace

Robert E. Morsberger
Daniel P. Murphy
John M. Muste
William Nelles
Anne Newgarden
Evelyn S. Newlyn
Sally Osborne Norton
John G. Parks
David B. Parsell
Thomas D. Petitjean, Jr.
Karen Priest
Ron Querry
Edward C. Reilly
Rosemary M. Canfield Reisman
Mary Rohrberger
Carl Rollyson
Joseph Rosenblum
John K. Roth
Chaman L. Sahni
Barbara Kitt Seidman
D. Dean Shackelford
Frank W. Shelton
R. Baird Shuman
Genevieve Slomski
Nick David Smart
Katherine Snipes
Karen F. Stein
W. J. Stuckey
Catherine Swanson
Eleanor von Auw Berry
Edward E. Waldron
Nancy Walker
Qun Wang
Craig Werner
Dexter Westrum
Patricia A. R. Williams
Chester L. Wolford
Cynthia Wong
Jennifer L. Wyatt
Mary F. Yudin

PROLOGUE
Who Are We Americans?

America is woven of many strands; I would recognize them and let it so remain. . . . Our fate is to become one, and yet many—This is not prophecy, but description.

—Ralph Ellison, *Invisible Man*, 1952

When Ralph Ellison died at the age of eighty on April 16, 1994, the United States lost a national treasure, one of its most profound and gifted writers. True, his list of literary credits was briefer than those compiled by twentieth century American authors such as Saul Bellow and Willa Cather, Toni Morrison and Joyce Carol Oates, or Wallace Stegner and John Updike. Nor is it likely that Ellison can rank with nineteenth century literary giants such as Nathaniel Hawthorne, Emily Dickinson, or Herman Melville. Yet Ellison's *Invisible Man* is arguably the best novel ever written by an American.

In 1945, Ellison was working on a different narrative when what he called "blues-toned laughter" began to dominate his imagination. Eventually that laughter compelled him to give full expression to its voice, which belonged to the narrator of Ellison's classic, a young African American who in Ellison's words "had been forged in the underground of American experience and yet managed to emerge less angry than ironic." The result, *Invisible Man*, tells the story of that unnamed character's struggle to cope with the meanings of being black, male, American, and human—all at once—in a society that left him so "black and blue" that he could begin his life's narrative only by saying,

> I am an invisible man. No, I am not a spook like those who haunted Edgar Allan Poe; nor am I one of your Hollywood-movie ectoplasms. I am a man of substance, of flesh and bone, fiber and liquids—and I might even be said to possess a mind. I am invisible, understand, simply because people refuse to see me.

A month before Ellison's death in 1994, David Remnick hit the mark in the March 14 issue of *The New Yorker* when he described the appearance of *Invisible Man* as "something entirely new, lasting, and Ameri-can" and then observed that "in Ellison's view, America is not made up of separate, free-floating cultures but, rather, of a constant interplay and exchange." Written from the perspective of a black American whose individual identity had been denied by his native land, *Invisible Man* protested against the idea that there is a "free-floating" white American culture that deserves the privilege of dominating the "constant interplay and exchange." In a word, *Invisible Man* protested against *conformity*, against the assumption that there should be—or ever was—a "one-size-fits-all" pattern that answers the question "Who are we Americans?"

"Diversity is the word," Ellison insisted. To him that word, *diversity*, had a distinctive meaning for life in the United States. In an American context, the vast ethnic, cultural, and religious variety of the people would always make us many—pluralistic, different, and to some extent divided. But this same diversity, Ellison affirmed, was also bringing us together. Paradoxically, unexpectedly, ironically, even kicking and screaming and against our will, the diversity of American life would make the American people inexorably and distinctively one. That vision, Ellison also insisted, "is not prophecy, but description."

For Ellison, as Remnick's *New Yorker* article noted, "integration is not merely an aspiration but a given, a fact of cultural and political life." As Ellison knew, however, that fact remains as ambiguous as it is volatile, as much an occasion for frustration and rage as for encouragement and hope. Yes, it is true that American life is one, even integrated, in the sense that we Americans dwell together in a more or less shared geographical, political, and economic space. We Americans may debate the pros and cons of "multiculturalism" in the nation's schools, colleges, and universities, but the unavoidable fact is that American culture has long been multi-cultural. As Remnick pointed out, one has only to consider the music we hear, the games we play, the books we read, the clothes we wear, and the food we eat to find evidence of that. But the multi-cultural aspects of American life mean that the divisions among us are many, too. They run deep and seem to be running deeper. One has only to consider the divisions among the places we live, the schools we attend, the wealth we distribute, the homelessness we ignore, the racism we provoke, and the violence we unleash to find evidence of that. To the extent that American life is one life, the question is how bruised and bloody or how healing and caring it will be.

Ellison's invisible man says, "Now I know men are different and that all life is divided and that only in division is there true health." He was right about the first parts, but when he speaks about true health's being found only in division, the words bear watching. As Ellison knew, everything depends on the kinds of division, the styles of diversity, that find expression among us Americans. Ellison was not one who glorified the separatism of an "identity politics" that celebrates some particular "culture"—"white," "black," and so on—to the exclusion of a more inclusive vision of American life. On the other hand, the inclusion he championed had no place for invisibility. As Ellison understood, there can be no meaningful identity without particularity, but when particularity goes unrecognized and unappreciated, invisibility will not be far behind. At some level, all of us Americans understand such things—or at least we need to do so. Such considerations explain why Ellison could end *Invisible Man* credibly by having his narrator ask, "Who knows but that, on the lower frequencies, I speak for you?"

Ellison's ending to *Invisible Man* might be a question that all of the American authors discussed in this book put to their readers. That possibility exists because American literature is often preoccupied with American identities. Henry James, the nineteenth century novelist, summed up the reason when he observed, "It's a complex fate, being an American." So many factors make that fate complex. We Americans, for example, trace our roots to many different places. Our history is made up of histories. Those histories involve everything from ethnicity and religion to regional and class differences as well as gender distinctions and sexual preferences. Those particularities from the past give us memories and experiences that do not cohere easily.

There can never be one national narrative that tells every American story adequately. It takes an unfinished, unending multitude of stories to tell our story. In addition, while Americans have widespread agreement about the ideals that should govern our life together—for example, basic rights to life, liberty, and the pursuit of happiness, to name only the three most prominently proclaimed in the Declaration of Independence—we often differ sharply about how to interpret their meanings. As Abraham Lincoln said in an 1864 Civil War speech at Baltimore, Maryland, Americans "all declare for liberty; but in using the same *word* we do not all mean the same *thing*." American identities are marked, often scarred, by the fact that our agreement intensifies disagreement and our consensus inflames dissent.

The drama in these tensions runs high. So does the irony, for American life so often works against itself—abusing the land that we love, subverting the liberty we enjoy, deferring for others the American Dream we desperately want for ourselves. Authored by the novelists, poets, and playwrights represented in these pages, the nation's most brilliant literature takes that drama, especially the ironies of American experience, and artfully hands it back to us as readers and listeners. Thereby American literature helps us not only to grasp the complexity of our fate as Americans but also to revise and envision anew what American identity could mean for us—each and all—in a society that, if anything, is growing larger, more diverse, and increasingly complicated with every passing year.

Often exploring the particularities of time, place, circumstance, and experience, the voices of the great American writers discussed in this book raise the question "Who are we Americans?" They do so in ways that help us to see that the response must be an answering that is ongoing and of our own making. In that sense, this book is a microcosm of American life. Bound together in one volume are the lives, ideas, and stories of an amazingly rich chorus of American voices. Each has contributed something important to American life, something that no one else could have contributed. What these voices have to say sounds familiar to some of us, strange to others. Often, they perform the special service of making the familiar strange and the strange familiar. Vision sharpens, horizons open, understanding expands, and reading and listening improve when such transformations occur. Bound together, these writers are not saying the same thing, and certainly what they are saying is not said in the same way. But just as American experience has informed them all, each of them has written, at least in part, to inform us, to engage us in the future shaping of American experience and the multiple identities that quest involves. No one can say, once and for all, what their being together means, for any interpretation induces more and different ones. But here these writers are, together in this book, inviting us Americans to keep responding well to the question, "Who are we?"

Their presence, including the conversation we have with them, is interdependent, even (indeed, perhaps especially) when they disagree, because no novelists write alone any more than readers read or listeners listen by themselves. True, writing, reading, and listening often occur in solitude, but none of that activity happens entirely apart from the company of other people. Writers bring to their craft the instruction, sometimes the dissenting edge, that other writers have inspired. Readers and listeners, too, bring to their understanding the learning that comes only from social interaction.

Readers, listeners, and writers who take cues from Ralph Ellison's *Invisible Man* learn that its narrator's "world has become one of infinite possibilities." One way to understand what Ellison means is to note the endless variety of subjects and stories that literature must encompass to be fully American. That variety reflects both American history and what that history suggests about the future. To explain that point further, and to help set the scene for the rest of this book, consider a few more glimpses of the changing and expanding nature of the American people.

Having led his troops to victory in the American Revolution, George Washington served the first two terms of the American presidency. When he left office in 1796, he gave a now famous "Farewell Address." It was a plea for American unity. Washington urged his contemporaries to understand "the immense value of your national union to your collective and individual happiness." He also emphasized how the name "American" referred to a single people who had worked and fought together. With only "slight shades of difference," he added, "you have the same religion, manners, habits and political principles." Not only did Washington underestimate the nation's shades of difference. He could scarcely have imagined the variety they would come to contain. Homogeneity has never been a dominant American characteristic. Nor will it be. Unity will always be a rhetorical theme for American presidents—arriving, departing, or in between—because its depth and quality cannot be easily presumed.

Mandated by the Constitution of the United States, the first American census occurred in 1790, shortly after Washington became president, and it has continued at ten-year intervals ever since. That initial counting was comparatively simple. It included only free white males aged sixteen years or more, free white males under sixteen (to calculate how many men might be available for military duty), free white females, all other free persons (including Native Americans who paid taxes), and slaves. The census of 1790 placed the American population at about 3.9 million, including about 750,000 slaves (nearly 20 percent of the total).

Two centuries later, the figures for the 1990 census have been contested, particularly by municipal and state officials who argued that this census skipped people in urban areas, the poor, and minorities. Although the count may be off by a figure larger than the total for the 1790 census, Americans in 1990 numbered about 250 million, an increase of 10 percent from 1980. Nearly a million more American citizens could be found living abroad.

Currently the American people are the most diverse of any nation on earth. The next census, in 2000, will reveal increasing variety as the nation grows more complex and crowded. Meanwhile, Sam Roberts, urban affairs columnist for *The New York Times*, offers the following picture in *Who We Are: A Portrait of America Based on the Latest U.S. Census* (1993):

> Today, the average American is a 32.7-year-old white woman who lives in a mortgaged suburban home that has three bedrooms and is heated by natural gas. She is a married mother, with some German ancestry, on the cusp of the MTV generation—roughly the thirteenth to come of age since Benjamin Franklin's. She graduated from high school and holds a clerical job. She moves to a new home more frequently than residents of any other developed nation.

This typical American, Roberts hastens to add, is also mythical and, strictly speaking, nonexistent. As Roberts argues, the United States is too much a country of contrasts, it consists of too many parts, to let us speak meaningfully of *the* typical American. What can be said, as Roberts notes, is that "the nation's complexion changed more starkly in the 1980s than in any previous decade, and twice as fast as in the 1970s."

In 1990, whites still made up about 80 percent of the American population, but that majority is far from homogeneous, and it is shrinking. African Americans constitute about 12 percent of the population, an increase of 13 percent from 1980. Hispanics (a term used by the U.S. Census to refer to Latino citizens, who "may be of any race") increased by 53 percent during that same period and now account for about 9 percent of the total. Approximately 3 percent of the American population is Asian, a number that doubled between 1980 and 1990.

Significantly, the country's population is also aging. In 1990 one in five Americans was at least fifty-five and one in eight was at least sixty-five. The number of people over age sixty nearly equals the number under the age of fourteen. Moreover, "between 2010 and 2030," Roberts finds demographers predicting, "the number of Americans 65 and older will mushroom by 30 million as Baby Boomers turn the age pyramid upside down."

Language and religion tell similar stories of change and diversity. The number of people in the United States whose usual language or mother tongue is other than English rose from 28 million in 1976 to 34.7 million in 1990 and will likely reach 39.5 million by 2000. In Los Angeles, which is much more the microcosm of the nation than the Muncie, Indiana, that sociologists used to prefer, at least ninety languages can be heard in the public schools. Spanish will be increasingly important in the United States; Asian as well as other languages are becoming more prominent, too.

As for religion, although the Southern Baptist Convention has nearly 15 million members, making it the largest Protestant denomination, the days of the white Anglo-Saxon Protestant (WASP) hegemony in the United States are declining. Roman Catholics—55 million of them—are the largest Christian denomination. In addition, there are about 6 million Jews in the United States, a number now equaled by Muslims. In fact, there are more Muslims in the country than Mormons or than Presbyterians and Episcopalians combined. Meanwhile there is a resurgence of interest in Native American religious traditions, and the appearance of New Age spirituality combines with other so-called new religions and the increased influence of Asian religious practices, especially those of Buddhism, to expand the varieties of American religious experience even further.

In a chapter called "Why We Count," Sam Roberts' *Who We Are* observes that *census* is a word "derived from the French verb for 'to assess.'" Perhaps the most important reason for an American census/assessment

each decade, he reminds us, is "to make democracy more representative and responsive." Official census statistics can give us Americans a partial picture of who we are, but it takes stories told by writers like Ralph Ellison and appraisals like the ones in this book to make the picture more complete. Approached from that perspective, the essays in *American Diversity, American Identity* are part of an ongoing American census, too.

Ellison once expressed the wish that his writing could be "a raft of hope, perception and entertainment that might help keep us afloat as we tried to negotiate the snags and whirlpools that mark our nation's vacillating course toward and away from the democratic ideal." In that spirit, his voice can be heard to speak for all of the authors embraced by this volume. For in addition to showing the particularity and diversity of American experience, beyond disclosing where American life has been, the essays that follow, individually and collectively, suggest who we are becoming and where we are heading. They can be read as contributions that make our American democracy more representative and responsive.

While the 145 authors included in *American Diversity, American Identity* have painted a broad panorama of the American landscape, they do not and cannot, of course, do complete justice to the ever-increasing diversity of American identities. The writers presented in this volume have been selected not only because of their excellence in literary achievement but also because they are in some ways representative voices for their particular group. Readers interested in a fuller list of writers connected with the regional, ethnic, and other foci represented here can refer to the categorized listing of writers that appears at the end of this volume. It is followed by an index, for quick access to the writers and works discussed. Finally, the front matter to this volume contains a listing of "Contributing Reviewers," the academic specialists who prepared the essays within. Their assistance in the creation of this work is gratefully acknowledged.

—*John K. Roth*
Claremont McKenna College

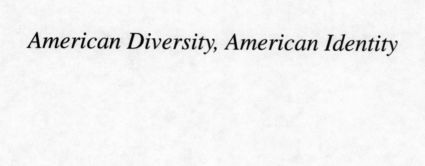

American Diversity, American Identity

I

DISCOVERIES OF AMERICA
Stories Told by Indian Voices

Every foot of what you proudly call America, not very long ago belonged to the Red Man. The Great Spirit gave it to us, there was room enough for all his tribes; all were happy in their freedom.
—Washakie, Shoshone chief, 1878

When Christopher Columbus blundered his way onto the shore of a small island in the Bahamas on Friday morning, August 3, 1492, believing he had reached India, he called the people who greeted his flotilla of three small ships "Indians." After five centuries of more or less uninterrupted use, and despite its misinformed coinage, the name Indian is the preferred collective one among most Indian people—this writer included—notwithstanding all the efforts of well-meaning but nonetheless misdirected overseers of politically correct terminology with their trendy labels of "Native American" and "indigenous people."

Early Indian cultures were preliterate, at least in the sense that, prior to 1821—when Sequoyah invented a syllabary for the Cherokee—no Indian tribe had a written language. Nevertheless, as literary scholar A. La-Vonne Ruoff has pointed out, while the writings of the seventeenth century English colonists have traditionally been considered—and are regularly taught—as the first works of American literature, the continent of North America already had a 28,000-year history of storytelling when John Smith and Anne Bradstreet first sat down to write of their experiences in the "new" world.

The texts of that long Indian history were oral and communal. Because of that fact, it is often assumed that Indians had no literature or, at the very least, that its oral quality made that literature inferior. Early on, however, their oral traditions gave Indian people a rich literary heritage, for, as anyone who is familiar with the *Iliad* or

the *Odyssey* can attest, oral literature is not necessarily inferior to that which is written.

It is entirely appropriate, then, that the first section of this survey of American literature is devoted to writers who trace their identities back to the voices of the continent's earliest storytellers. Unlike most of their ancestors, these contemporary Indian authors tell their stories in writing, but they continue an ancient tradition nonetheless. Like their ancestors, they tell distinctive stories about times and places that have shaped the identities of those who inhabit them. Like their ancestors, these modern storytellers provide challenging discoveries of America by showing what has happened here.

Nearly all of the authors considered in this chapter—eight out of nine—are living and working writers. This accent on contemporary Indian novelists is significant but not surprising because, prior to 1968, there were only nine published novels by six American Indian authors. If this book had been published less than three decades ago—that is, had this volume appeared in 1967—there would have been (indeed, *could* have been) only six American Indian novelists included. Consider, too, that seven of the nine Indian authors surveyed here have produced among them nearly two dozen novels. Of the other two, Lynn Riggs was at work on his first novel when he died in 1954, and it is surely only a matter of time before the multifaceted poet/essayist Joy Harjo will produce her first work of long fiction.

Before the publication in 1968 of Kiowa/Cherokee author N. Scott Momaday's fine novel *House Made of Dawn*, there had been a scarcity of long fiction produced by American Indian writers. Momaday's Pulitzer Prize-winning effort most certainly seems to have signaled the opening of a floodgate of Indian-authored books. The twenty-five years since the appearance of *House Made of Dawn* have seen the publication of no fewer than one hundred novels by American Indian writers.

What or who is an Indian? The question is not as strange as it may appear. In writing about the American Indian novel, Louis Owens points to the fact that people throughout the world have a strangely concrete sense of what a "real" Indian should be, a fact that adds to the confusion. Alan Velie, credited with having taught one of the first courses ever to be offered in American Indian literature (at the University of Oklahoma in 1971), maintains that, in spite of the movement toward pan-Indianism, "most Indians today identify themselves more readily as members of a particular tribe than they do as Indians"—which is to say that, while others may lump them together as Indians, and despite their acceptance of that term in its pantribal sense, they are more apt to describe themselves according to their tribal affiliations. Leslie Marmon Silko is more likely to say that she is Laguna than that she is Indian, James Welch that he is Blackfeet/Gros Ventre, Joy Harjo that she is Creek, and Louise Erdrich that she is Turtle Mountain Band Chippewa. (It must be added that the contemporary Indian writers here considered are, in every case, *mixedbloods* and that, furthermore, each has a high level of formal education.)

It is important to know that of all the ethnic, regional, and gender/sexual identities or groups included in *American Diversity, American Identity*, only American Indians are issued identification cards by the U.S. government—identification cards meant to prove that the bearer is, in fact, entitled to be called an Indian. Officially termed a Certificate of Degree of Indian Blood (CDIB), the card is issued by the Department of the Interior, Bureau of Indian Affairs, and testifies to the card holder's tribal affiliation and blood quantum.

Not to be left behind in matters of identification and certification of this politically sensitive segment of their populations, state legislatures too have adopted laws that define, with greater or lesser precision, exactly who among the state's citizenry is an Indian. The state of New Mexico (New Mexico State Bill 567, 1991), for example, officially considers an Indian to be (1) any person who is an enrolled member of an Indian tribe as evidenced by a tribal enrollment card or certified tribal records; or (2) any person who can meet the minimum qualifications for services offered by the United States government to Indians because of their special status as Indians as evidenced by a CDIB.

Moreover, tribes, from their legally held positions as sovereign entities, have the authority to determine membership, an authority that tribal governments take very seriously and attend to scrupulously, albeit from various points of view, depending upon the tribe.

Generally speaking, tribal membership is based upon one or some combination of four principal criteria: descendancy, blood quantum, residency, or birth to an enrolled parent. The Choctaw Nation of Oklahoma, for example, emphasizes provable descendancy. That is, persons directly and certifiably descended from individuals originally enrolled on the Dawes Commission Rolls of 1906 are eligible to apply for tribal membership. The Tohono O'Odham (formerly the Papago), on the other hand, emphasize residency and thus automatically grant tribal membership to all children born to members who reside on the reservation. And while some tribes require one-half or one-quarter or (as in the case of the Citizen Potawatomi Band) one-eighth tribal blood for qualification, others trace membership specifically through the mother or the father: Santa Clara Pueblo restricts membership to persons born to an enrolled father; the Seneca admit only individuals born to an enrolled mother.

What is American Indian literature, then? American Indian literature—that is, literature *by* Indians as opposed to that *about* them—has been categorized as falling into three areas: traditional, transitional, and modern literature. Traditional literature is defined as that which was composed in an Indian language for an Indian audience at a time when tribal cultures were intact and contact with whites was minimal. It was a literature made up of sacred stories, myths, legends, and songs. Transitional literature is generally represented by translations of the great Indian orators of the nineteenth century and by memoirs of the Indian experience as it related to white dominance. The literature that is examined in the work at hand falls into the area of modern literature—that is, modern works of fiction (both long and short), nonfiction, drama, and poetry, written in English by Indian Americans, most of whom speak no other language.

As pointed out earlier, with the exception of the dramatist Lynn Riggs, the Indian writers considered in this section are working writers. It is important that as readers we remember that the nine here considered are representative of a fast-growing number of American Indian writers who are today finding an equally fast-growing audience that they have not previously enjoyed. Publishers are drawn to contemporary Indian subjects and especially to Indian voices. One reason that we read literature, after all, is to discover truth. As readers, we are looking to learn how some aspect of the world that is beyond our immediate experience really works: how conflicts can be resolved, what values we might affirm, and what risks are involved in living from day to day.

—*Ron Querry*
Tucson, Arizona

PAULA GUNN ALLEN

Born: Cubero, New Mexico; October 24, 1939

Principal nonfiction

Studies in American Indian Literature: Critical Essays and Course Designs, 1983; *The Sacred Hoop: Recovering the Feminine in American Indian Traditions*, 1986; *Grandmothers of the Light: A Medicine Woman's Sourcebook*, 1991.

Other literary forms

Although Paula Gunn Allen's major impact has come through her academically oriented work as an editor, critic, and scholar in the field of Native American studies, she has also written a novel, *The Woman Who Owned the Shadows* (1983), and several chapbooks of poetry: *The Blind Lion* (1975), *Coyote's Daylight Trip* (1978), *Star Child* (1981), *A Cannon Between My Knees* (1981), *Shadow Country* (1982), *Wyrds* (1987), and *Skins and Bones* (1988).

Achievements

Allen has received considerable recognition for her writing and scholarship. She was chosen to be the project director for the 1977 Summer Seminar on American Indian Literature held at Northern Arizona University at Flagstaff and cosponsored by the Modern Language Association and the National Endowment for the Humanities. Other honors soon followed: a National Endowment for the Arts Creative Writing Fellowship in 1978, a postdoctoral fellowship in the Native American Scholars Fellowship program at the University of California at Los Angeles in 1980-1981, a postdoctoral Minorities Scholar Fellowship for research from the National Research Council and the Ford Foundation in 1984, and an appointment as an Associate Fellow for Humanities at Stanford University, also in 1984. In 1990 she was awarded the Native American Prize for Literature, and in the same year her anthology *Spider Woman's Granddaughters* (1989) won the American Book Award sponsored by the Before Columbus Foundation. Allen has also won the Susan Koppleman Award, sponsored by the Women's Caucus of the Popular and American Culture Associations.

Biography

Paula Gunn Allen was born on October 24, 1939, in Cubero, New Mexico, a Spanish land-grant town near the Laguna and Acoma (Keres) Indian reservations. Al-len's family background is ethnically diverse and multilingual. Her mother was of Laguna, Sioux, and Scots heritage; Allen says that her mother's significance to her work is incalculable and that "her life, her cast of mind, and her ways have provided me with the insights and experience of strong women, Indian women." Her father, a former lieutenant governor of New Mexico, Allen describes as a "cowboy, merchant, trader, steadfast friend and benefactor, and Lebanese storyteller supreme, who has spent hours teaching me how to string magic, memory, and observation into tales of life."

Allen's family, in addition to its variety of ethnicities and languages, is also quite talented. Her mother's uncle, John M. Gunn, collected traditional Laguna stories and published them under the title *Schat Chen: History, Traditions and Narratives of the Queres Indians of Laguna and Acoma* (1917); her sister, Carol Lee Sanchez, is a poet and painter; and the noted novelist Leslie Marmon Silko is a cousin. Allen attended schools in Cubero, San Fidel, and Albuquerque before entering Colorado Women's College. She transferred to the University of Oregon, where she earned a B.A. degree in English in 1966 and a M.F.A. degree in creative writing in 1968. She returned to the Southwest and completed her Ph.D. degree in American studies with an emphasis on Native American studies at the University of New Mexico in 1975. Her academic career includes teaching at Fort Lewis College, the University of New Mexico, the College of San Mateo, and San Francisco State University, where she was director of the American Indian Studies Program. Then she moved to the Department of Ethnic Studies at the University of California at Berkeley and from there to the Department of English at the University of California at Los Angeles.

Analysis

Allen's scholarly writings fall within that area of cultural studies for which Arnold Krupat has coined the term "ethnocriticism." As Krupat defines it, ethnocriticism is a multicultural critical perspective that emphasizes non-Western cultures and challenges the values of mainstream Euro-American culture, recognizing and validating "heterogeneity (rather than homogeneity) as the social and cultural norm." Basing her critical perspective on her Native American heritage and her research into traditional and contemporary Native American literatures, Allen describes her critical stance as both tribal-feminism and feminist-tribalism: "If I am dealing with feminism, I approach it from a strongly tribal posture, and when I am dealing with American Indian literature, history, culture, or philosophy I approach it from a strongly feminist one." It is as an interpreter of Native American ways of viewing the world and more especially as an interpreter of Native American women's traditions that Allen has made her greatest impact.

In all of her writing, Allen struggles with the sense of alienation and separation from both Indian and white culture that results from her mixed-blood heritage. Although her family did not follow a traditional Indian lifestyle, she grew up immersed in Indian culture. Thus, while her academic successes, scholarly reputation, and artistic recognition have all been achieved within white culture, ultimately her sense of her own personal identity is more closely related to the Keresan culture of Laguna Pueblo, the culture of her mother and grandmother, than to any of the other elements in her ethnic, educational, or professional background. Laguna itself is a place of considerable cultural diversity because of its location at a crossroads of Southwestern Indian cultures, its long history as a place of refuge for persons displaced from other pueblos and tribes, and the strong Catholic, Latino, and Anglo influences against which it has had to struggle for its cultural survival.

Allen's interest in feminism may perhaps be explained by the fact that Laguna culture is both matrilineal and matrilocal. According to Native American author Leslie Marmon Silko, who also grew up in Laguna: "In the Pueblo, the lineage of the child is traced through the mother. . . . The houses are the property of the woman, not the man. The land is generally passed down through the female side because the houses belong to the women." Allen herself notes that she began to study feminist thought and theory in the early 1970's, when she started to study and teach Native American literature.

In the Keresan culture of the Lagunas, the world was created by Thought Woman and the traditional religious beliefs were gynocentric and in harmony with the matrilineal nature of the culture. Allen argues that such beliefs were widespread among Indian cultures, and she explains that she has chosen such Indian women's traditions, which have long been ignored by white and Indian writers alike, as the major focus of her writing because "these traditions are the basis for much of the tribal society in the Americas." It is as a spokeswoman for this "gynocratic perspective" that she has played a leading role in the reassessment of American Indian cultures and in introducing tribal perspectives into the feminist movement.

Gynocracy, as Allen conceives it, is the woman-centered, woman-based, egalitarian principle of social organization that structured most of the tribal cultures of Native Americans prior to the coming of Europeans. It was a way of life tightly bound to ritual and based on spiritual understandings, in contrast to the patriarchal cultures that the Europeans brought with them, which were based on economic and political concepts.

Allen's scholarship has increasingly centered on the place of gay and lesbian lifestyles among both traditional and contemporary Native American communities. In traditional Indian communities, young women were frequently separated from men because of an array of menstrual rituals, because of the women's tilling and harvesting duties, and because the men were often absent for long periods of time on hunting or fishing expeditions or because of ritual and initiation practices. Thus, Allen argues, lesbianism and homosexuality were commonplace in tribal societies.

These ideas, which Allen developed over a period of some fifteen years in the 1970's and 1980's, can be found most conveniently in the essays written during that period of her life and collected under the title *The Sacred Hoop: Recovering the Feminine in American Indian Traditions*. This book, first published in 1986 and reissued in 1992, contains the major essays upon which Allen's scholarly reputation is based. In them Allen moves easily from literary analysis—chiefly of Native American writers and traditional tales, but with frequent reference to mainstream American literature—to historical analysis, to social commentary, and to personal history and insights. Because of her unique upbringing, she brings a rare expertise to her research that enables her to call not only upon the published sources in her field but also upon her own life experiences for insight and understanding.

In the years since the first publication of *The Sacred Hoop*, Allen has sought to demonstrate that gynocracy is not only a form of social organization superior to the Judeo-Christian patriarchal form imposed on the tribal peoples of North America by European invaders but also the structuring principle of the cosmos—a principle for which Allen has coined the term "cosmogyny" in her influential preface to *Grandmothers of the Light: A Medicine Woman's Sourcebook*. To Allen, the term implies "an ordered universe arranged in harmony with gynocratic principles," principles that value egalitarianism, personal autonomy, and communal harmony that structure a society in which individual and social good are mutually reinforcing rather than divisive, as they are in a patriarchy. Thus, gynocentric, gynocratic communities value peace, tolerance, sharing, relationship, balance, harmony, and a just distribution of goods. In *Grandmothers of the Light*, Allen retells traditional myths from many tribes in light of her understanding of gynocracy and cosmogyny, and in the concluding section she gathers stories that "testify to the pertinence today of the ways of power. They indicate that relations between human women and supernaturals are as viable and powerful in the present time as in days gone by."

Another central theme in Allen's scholarly writing, especially in *Grandmothers of the Light*, is that of "indianismo," the psychological, cultural, and spiritual attitude common to Native Americans. It is Allen's belief that the prevailing attitude among academic anthropologists stressing the diversity among tribes is just one more manifestation of the Euro-American policy of conquering native peoples by dividing them. While admitting that there is considerable diversity among native communities, especially with respect to their languages, Allen argues that the similarities among these communities are far greater and much more profound than mainstream scholarship admits. She believes that an emphasis on "indianismo" within Indian communities will lead naturally to a more viable and assertive Pan-Indian movement in the political arena, a movement that would "pose a grave threat to Western hegemony."

Allen's ideas have provoked considerable debate, not only among scholars in the academic community but also among writers, artists, and political activists within Indian communities. Allen's analysis of feminism in traditional Indian societies has been called a "sweeping exaggeration" by M. Annette Jaimes and Theresa Halsey, and many Indian women, among them Janet McCloud, Laura Waterman Wittstock, and Beverly Hungry Wolf, have rejected Allen's attempt to promote the cause of Indian women through alliance with the broader feminist and gay rights movements. Nevertheless, Allen continues to exert a powerful influence in the women's movement and the Native American community at large as well as in the academic discipline of Native American studies and the broader context of cultural studies.

Other major works

POETRY: *The Blind Lion*, 1975; *Coyote's Daylight Trip*, 1978; *Star Child*, 1981; *A Cannon Between My Knees*, 1981; *Shadow Country*, 1982; *Wyrds*, 1987; *Skins and Bones*, 1988.
LONG FICTION: *The Woman Who Owned the Shadows*, 1983.
EDITED TEXT: *Spider Woman's Granddaughters: Traditional Tales and Contemporary Writing by Native American Women*, 1989.

Bibliography

Bruchac, Joseph. *Survival This Way: Interviews with American Indian Poets*. Tucson: University of Arizona Press, 1987.
Hanson, Elizabeth I. *Paula Gunn Allen*. Boise State University Western Writers Series 96. Boise, Idaho: Boise State University, 1990.
Jaimes, Annette M., ed. *The State of Native America: Genocide, Colonization, Resistance*. Boston: South End Press, 1992.
Lincoln, Kenneth. *Indi'n Humor: Bicultural Play in Native America*. New York: Oxford University Press, 1993.
_____. *Native American Renaissance*. Berkeley: University of California Press, 1983.
Ruoff, A. LaVonne. *American Indian Literatures: An Introduction, Bibliographic Review, and Selected Bibliography*. New York: Modern Language Association, 1990.
Wiget, Andrew. *Native American Literature*. Boston: Twayne, 1985.

LOUISE ERDRICH

Born: Little Falls, Minnesota; June 7, 1954

Principal long fiction

Love Medicine, 1984, expanded edition 1993; *The Beet Queen*, 1986; *Tracks*, 1988; *The Crown of Columbus*, 1991 (with Michael Dorris); *The Bingo Palace*, 1994.

Other literary forms

Jacklight (1984) and *Baptism of Desire* (1989) are books of poetry (along with a few folktales) that present vivid North Dakota vignettes as well as personal reflections on Louise Erdrich's relationships to her husband and children.

Achievements

A poet and poetic novelist, Erdrich has drawn on her Chippewa and German-immigrant heritage to create a wide-ranging chronicle of Native American and white experience in twentieth century North Dakota. Since she began to publish her fiction and poetry in the early 1980's, her works have garnered high critical praise, and her three novels have been best-sellers as well. *Love Medicine*, Erdrich's first novel, won the National Book Critics Circle Award in 1984, and three of the stories gathered in that book were also honored: "The World's Greatest Fishermen" won the five-thousand-dollar first prize in the 1982 Nelson Algren fiction competition, "Scales" appeared in *Best American Short Stories, 1983* (1983), and "Saint Marie" was chosen for *Prize Stories 1985: The O. Henry Awards* (1985). Two of the stories included in the novel *Tracks* also appeared in honorary anthologies: "Fleur" in *Prize Stories 1987: The O. Henry Awards* (1987) and "Snares" in *Best American Short Stories, 1988* (1988).

Erdrich's works often focus on the struggle of Chippewa Indians for personal, familial, and cultural survival. Yet her treatment of white and mixed-blood characters also reveals an empathic understanding of the ways in which North Dakota people of all races long for closer connection with other people and the land.

Biography

Louise Erdrich grew up in Wahpeton, a small town in southeastern North Dakota. Her father, Ralph Erdrich, a German immigrant, taught in Wahpeton at the Indian boarding school. Her mother, Rita Journeau Erdrich, a three-quarters Chippewa, also worked at the school. Erdrich's mixed religious and cultural background provided a rich foundation for her later poetry and fiction.

Erdrich earned two degrees in creative writing, a B.A. from Dartmouth College in 1976 and an M.A. from The Johns Hopkins University in 1979. In 1981, she was married to Michael Dorris, a professor of anthropology and head of the Native American Studies Program at Dartmouth.

Erdrich and Dorris have devoted their lives to ambitious family, literary, and humanitarian goals. Like Erdrich, Dorris is three-eighths Indian, and years before his marriage to Erdrich he had adopted three Indian infants from Midwestern reservations. Dorris and Erdrich had several more children and reared their family in an eighteenth century farmhouse in Cornish, New Hampshire. Erdrich and her husband have said that they collaborate on virtually all the works that either one publishes—whether fiction, poetry, or nonfiction. Thus Erdrich acknowledges Dorris' important contribution to all of her fiction; similarly, she collaborated with him on his first novel, *A Yellow Raft in Blue Water* (1987), and on his study of fetal alcohol syndrome (FAS), *The Broken Cord* (1989). Erdrich and Dorris have donated money and campaigned for legislation to combat FAS, which afflicts the lives of many Native American children born to alcoholic mothers.

Analysis

In an 1985 essay entitled "Where I Ought to Be: A Writer's Sense of Place," Louise Erdrich states that the essence of her writing emerges from her attachment to her North Dakota locale. The ways in which Erdrich has brought this region to literary life have been favorably compared by critics to the methods and style of William Faulkner, who created the mythical Yoknapatawpha County out of his rich sense of rural Mississippi. Like Faulkner, Erdrich has created a gallery of diverse characters spanning several generations; she also uses multiple points of view and shifting time frames. Erdrich's fiction further resembles Faulkner's in that the experience of her characters includes a broad spectrum of experience "from the mundane to the miraculous," as one critic put it. Erdrich's stories generally begin with a realistic base of ordinary people, settings, and actions. As her tales develop, however, these people become involved in events and perceptions that strike the reader as quite extraordinary—as exaggerated or heightened in ways that may seem deluded or mystical, grotesque or magical, comic or tragic, or some strange mixture of these. Thus one critic has described Erdrich as "a sorceress with language" whose lyrical style intensifies some of the most memorable scenes in contemporary American fiction.

Love Medicine spans the years 1934 to 1984 in presenting members of five Chippewa and mixedblood families, all struggling in different ways to attain a sense of belonging through love, religion, home, and family. The novel includes fourteen interwoven stories; though the title refers specifically to traditional Indian magic in one story, in a broader sense "love medicine" refers to the different kinds of spiritual power that enable Erdrich's Chippewa and mixedblood characters to transcend, however momentarily, the grim circumstances of their lives. Trapped on their shrinking reservation by racism and poverty, plagued by alcoholism, disintegrating families, and violence, some of Erdrich's characters nevertheless discover a form of "love medicine" that helps to sustain them.

The opening story, "The World's Greatest Fishermen," begins with an episode of love medicine corrupted and thwarted. Though June Kashpaw was once a woman of striking beauty and feisty spirit, by 1981 she has sunk to the level of picking up men in an oil boomtown. Unfortunately, June fails in her last attempts to attain two goals that other characters will also seek throughout the novel: love and home. Yet though she appears only briefly in this and one other story, June Kashpaw is a central character in the novel, for she embodies the potential power of spirit and love in ways that impress and haunt the other characters.

Part 2 of "The World's Greatest Fishermen" introduces many of the other major characters of *Love Medicine*, as June's relatives gather several months after her death. Several characters seem sympathetic because of their closeness to June and their kind treatment of one another. Albertine Johnson, who narrates the story and remembers her Aunt June lovingly, has gone through a wild phase of her own and is now a nursing student. Eli

Kashpaw, Albertine's granduncle, who was largely responsible for rearing June, is a tough and sharp-minded old man who has maintained a traditional Chippewa existence as a hunter and fisherman. Lipsha Morrissey, who, though he seems not to know it, is June's illegitimate son, is a sensitive, self-educated young man who acts warmly toward Albertine. In contrast to these characters are others who are flawed or unsympathetic when seen through the eyes of Albertine, who would like to feel that her family is pulling together after June's death. These less sympathetic characters include Zelda and Aurelia (Albertine's gossipy mother and aunt), Nector Kashpaw (Albertine's senile grandfather), and Gordon Kashpaw (the husband whom June left, a hapless drunk). Worst of all is June's legitimate son King, a volatile bully. King's horrifying acts of violence—abusing his wife Lynette, battering his new car, and smashing the pies prepared for the family dinner—leaves Albertine with a dismayed sense of a family in shambles. *Love Medicine* then shifts back in time from 1981, and its thirteen remaining stories, which unfold chronologically from 1934 to 1984, continue to spotlight the largely flawed lives of these characters and their offspring.

Though in these earlier *Love Medicine* stories the positive powers of love and spirit are more often frustrated than fulfilled, in the last three stories several characters achieve breakthroughs that bring members of the different families together in moving and hopeful ways. In "Love Medicine," set in 1982, Lipsha Morrissey reaches out lovingly to his grandmother Marie and to the ghosts of Nector and June. In "The Good Tears," set in 1983, Lulu undergoes a serious eye operation and is cared for by Marie, who forgives her for being Nector's longtime extramarital lover. Finally, in "Crossing the Water," set in 1984, Lipsha helps his father, Gerry Nanapush, escape to Canada and comes to appreciate the rich heritage of love, spirit, and wiliness that he has inherited from his diverse patchwork of Chippewa relatives—especially from his grandmother Lulu, his aunt Marie, and his parents, June and Gerry.

In *The Beet Queen* Erdrich shifts her main focus from the Indian to the European-immigrant side of her background, and she creates in impressive detail the mythical town of Argus (modeled on Wahpeton, where she was reared, but located closer to the Chippewa reservation) in the years 1932 to 1972.

The opening scene of *The Beet Queen*, "The Branch," dramatizes two contrasting approaches to life that many characters will enact throughout the novel.

On a cold spring day in 1932, two orphans, Mary and Karl Adare, arrive by freight train in Argus. As they seek the way to the butcher shop owned by their Aunt Fritzie and Uncle Pete Kozka, Mary "trudge[s] solidly forward," while Karl stops to embrace a tree that already has its spring blossoms. When they are attacked by a dog, Mary runs ahead, continuing her search for the butcher shop, while Karl runs back to hop the train once again. As the archetypal plodder of the novel, Mary continues to "trudge solidly forward" throughout; she is careful, determined, and self-reliant in pursuit of her goals. Karl is the principal dreamer—impressionable, prone to escapist impulses, and dependent on others to catch him when he falls.

The Adare family history shows how Karl is following a pattern set by his mother, Adelaide, while Mary grows in reaction against this pattern. Like Karl, Adelaide is physically beautiful but self-indulgent and impulsive. Driven to desperation by her hard luck in the early years of the Depression, Adelaide startles a fairground crowd by abandoning her three children (Mary, Karl, and an unnamed newborn son) to fly away with the Great Omar, an airplane stunt pilot.

In Argus, Mary tangles with yet another beautiful, self-centered dreamer: her cousin Sita Kozka, who resents the attention that her parents, Pete and Fritzie, and her best friend, Celestine James, pay to Mary. Yet Mary prevails and carves a solid niche for herself among Pete, Fritzie, and Celestine, who, like Mary, believe in a strong work ethic and lack Sita's pretentious airs.

A number of episodes gratify the reader with triumphs for Mary and comeuppances for the less sympathetic characters Karl, Adelaide, and Sita. Mary becomes famous for a miracle at her school (she falls and cracks the ice in the image of Jesus), gains Celestine as a close friend, and in time becomes manager of the Kozka butcher shop. By contrast, Karl becomes a drifter who finds only sordid momentary pleasure in his numerous affairs. Meanwhile, Adelaide marries Omar and settles in Florida, but she becomes moody and subject to violent rages. Similarly, Sita fails in her vainglorious attempts to become a model and to establish a fashionable French restaurant; she escapes her first marriage through divorce and becomes insane and suicidal during her second.

Yet even as Erdrich charts the strange and sometimes grotesque downfalls of her flighty characters, she develops her more sympathetic ones in ways that suggest that the opposite approach to life does not guarantee happiness either. Mary fails in her attempt to attract Russell Kashpaw (the Chippewa half-brother of Celestine), and she develops into an exotically dressed eccentric who is obsessed with predicting the future and controlling others. Like Mary, Celestine James and Wallace Pfef are hardworking and successful in business, but their loneliness drives each of them to an ill-advised affair with Karl, and he causes each of them considerable grief. In addition, the union of Celestine and Karl results in the birth of Dot Adare (who grows up to be the ill-tempered lover of Gerry Nanapush in the *Love Medicine* story "Scales"); since Celestine, Mary, and Wallace all spoil the child, Dot turns out, in Wallace's words, to have "all of her family's worst qualities." As a teenager, Dot herself comes to grief when she is mortified to learn that Wallace has rigged the election for Queen of the Argus Beet Festival so that she, an unpopular and ludicrously unlikely candidate, will win.

Yet in addition to the defeats and disappointments that all the characters bear, Erdrich dramatizes the joy that they derive from life. The compensations of family and friendship—ephemeral and vulnerable as these may be—prove to be significant for all the characters at various times in the story, particularly at the end. The irrepressible vitality of these people, troublesome as they often are to one another, keeps the reader involved and entertained throughout the novel.

Tracks is Erdrich's most concentrated, intense, and mystical novel. It covers a time span of only twelve years and alternates between only two first-person narrators. This compression serves the story well, for the human stakes are high. At first, and periodically throughout the novel, the Chippewa characters fear for their very survival, as smallpox, tuberculosis, severe winters, starvation, and feuds with mixed-blood families bring them close to extinction. Later in the novel, government taxes and political chicanery threaten the Chippewas' ownership of their family homesteads. In response, Erdrich's Chippewa characters use all the powers at their command—including the traditional mystical powers of the old ways—to try to survive and maintain their control over the land.

Nanapush, one of the novel's two narrators, is an old Chippewa whom Erdrich names for the trickster rabbit in tribal mythology who repeatedly delivers the Chippewas from threatening monsters. In *Tracks*, Erdrich's Nanapush often does credit to his mythological model by wielding the trickster rabbit's powers of deliverance, wiliness, and humor. He saves Fleur Pillager, a seventeen-year-old girl who is the last of the Pillager clan, from starvation. Later he delivers young Eli Kashpaw from the sufferings of love by advising him how to win Fleur's heart. Also, Nanapush is instrumental in saving the extended family that forms around Fleur, Eli, and himself. This family grows to five when Fleur gives birth to a daughter, Lulu, and Eli's mother, Margaret Kashpaw, becomes Nanapush's bedmate. As these five come close to starvation, Nanapush sends Eli out to hunt an elk; in one of the most extraordinary passages of the novel, Nanapush summons a power vision of Eli hunting that the old man imagines is guiding Eli to the kill. Nanapush also demonstrates the humor associated with his mythological model in his wry tone as a narrator, his sharp wit in conversation, and the tricks that he plays on his family's mixed-blood antagonists: the Pukwans, Morrisseys, and Lazarres.

Foremost among these antagonists is the novel's other narrator, Pauline Pukwan. A "skinny big-nosed girl with staring eyes," Pauline circulates in Argus from the Kozkas' butcher shop to the Sacred Heart convent, and on the reservation from the Nanapush-Pillager-Kashpaw group to the Morrissey and Lazarre clans. At first attracted to Fleur by the beauty and sexual power that she herself lacks, Pauline later takes an envious revenge by concocting a love potion that seems to drive Fleur's husband, Eli, and Sophie Morrissey to become lovers. Ironically, though one side of her believes in a Catholic denial of her body, Pauline later gives birth out of wedlock to a girl named Marie, and at the end of her narrative Pauline enters the convent to become Sister Leopolda—the cruel nun who later torments her own daughter, Marie Lazarre, in *Love Medicine*.

If in some ways *Tracks* seems to conclude with a feeling of fragmentation and defeat, in other ways it strikes positive notes of solidarity and survival, especially when considered in relation to *Love Medicine* and *The Beet Queen*. Fleur disappears, leaving her husband and daughter, but Nanapush uses his wiliness to become tribal chairman and then to retrieve Lulu from a distant boarding school. At the end, the reader is reminded that Nanapush has addressed his entire narrative to Lulu: the old man hopes that his story will convince Lulu to embrace the memory of Fleur, "the one you will not call mother." Further, the reader familiar with *Love Medicine* will realize how this young girl, who becomes Lulu Lamartine, carries on the supernaturally powerful sexuality of her mother Fleur and the wily talent for survival of Nanapush, the old man who gave her his name and reared her.

In 1993, Henry Holt issued an expanded edition of *Love Medicine* that included five new sections. Erdrich believed that the new stories belonged with the earlier work. Then in 1994, she released *The Bingo Palace*, bringing the latest generation of her characters to adulthood. In the latter work, Lipsha Morrissey answers a mysterious call to return to his home on the Chippewa reservation, where he falls in love with and pursues Shawnee Toose, a talented tribal dancer and clothing designer. Lipsha seems gifted to become the reservation's traditional medicine man, the successor to Fleur Pillager, a powerful medicine woman who is his paternal great-grandmother and the oldest resident on the reservation.

Although the center of the novel is Lipsha's pursuit of Shawnee, *The Bingo Palace* is much more than a love story. Lipsha makes essentially the same discoveries about love that several of Erdrich's characters make in *Love Medicine*. He discovers that love is the essential medicine, the power that binds humanity together in the face of death. When, at the end of the novel, Lipsha faces death as an adult for the first time, he realizes fully that the human response is to hold on to others, to comfort and protect and receive comfort and protection. On his journey to this realization, he also learns that when he comprehends the finality of death, he is urgently impelled to love the world, all creation, without qualification or hesitation. In this novel, Erdrich's main efforts go into creating the rich and complex context within which Lipsha's courtship and learning take place. The meanings of the novel emerge from the interactions of Lipsha's self-discovery and learning about love with his and the reader's growing understanding of the tribal and familial web within which Lipsha lives.

The novel's title refers to the new Bingo Palace conceived by Lipsha's half uncle, Lyman Lamartine, who has developed a plan to bring wealth and comfort to the tribe. Lyman's most successful business venture has been the current Bingo Palace, a Quonset hut providing food, drink, and general entertainment, which includes gambling and features bingo. He envisions building an elaborate multipurpose resort on Matchimanito Lake. This complex will attract visitors from all over the region, bringing outside money to the reservation and improving life for the Chippewa. The problem is that the ideal site is sacred tribal land, an important portion of which is owned by Fleur Pillager. The main thing Lipsha learns while experiencing a vision is that this scheme can never work as Lyman envisions it, that it will lead to the destruction rather than the true enrichment of the tribe. The last chapter indicates that Lyman does complete the resort but suggests as well that thoughts about its last resident, Fleur, haunt all the Chippewa that frequent the resort, calling their lives into question.

To take in the book requires slow and patient reading and rereading. To solve the problems it poses and to be content with solutions that are imagined and not verified requires attuning oneself to the magical worldview that is the central thread of Chippewa tribal life and that is endangered by the new Bingo Palace on the sacred lakeshore. By requiring the reader to enter imaginatively into her world, Erdrich ensures a high degree of identification with her Chippewa. The reader thus comes to share her tribal conviction that Fleur Pillager's medicinal knowledge must be transferred to Lipsha; this thread of continuity must be preserved if the tribe is not to disappear back into its origins as Lipsha dreams it may during his vision quest. If Fleur's spiritual power

does not continue in Lipsha or someone of his ability, then the new resort threatens to absorb the Chippewa into the dominant materialistic culture, and so to make extinct another rich and beautiful, even though imperfect, way of negotiating humanity's relationship with the cosmos.

If Erdrich had been born two hundred years earlier, she might have become a traditional Chippewa storyteller, whose tales would have reminded her listeners of their unchanging relationship to the land and to the mythic and legendary characters who inhabited it. Now several generations removed from such a stable and undamaged culture, Erdrich nevertheless creates a richly neotribal view of people and place. Her novels testify to the profound interrelatedness of her characters—Indian and white, contemporaries and ancestors—both with one another and with their North Dakota homeland.

Other major works
POETRY: *Jacklight*, 1984; *Baptism of Desire*, 1989.

Bibliography
Bly, Robert. "Another World Breaks Through." *The New York Times Book Review* 92 (August 21, 1986): 2.
Erdrich, Louise. *Conversations with Louise Erdrich and Michael Dorris*. Edited by Allan Chavkin and Nancy Feyl Chavkin. Jackson: University Press of Mississippi, 1994.
——————. "Where I Ought to Be: A Writer's Sense of Place." *The New York Times Book Review* 91 (July 28, 1985): 1, 23-24.
Strouse, Jean. "In the Heart of the Heartland." *The New York Times Book Review* 94 (October 2, 1988): 1, 41-42.
Towers, Robert. "Roughing It." *The New York Review of Books* 35 (November 19, 1988): 40-41.
Wickenden, Dorothy. "Off the Reservation." *The New Republic* 195 (October 6, 1986): 46-48.

JOY HARJO

Born: Tulsa, Oklahoma; May 9, 1951

Principal poetry

The Last Song, 1975; *What Moon Drove Me to This?*, 1979; *She Had Some Horses*, 1983; *Scenes from the Center of the World*, 1989; *In Mad Love and War*, 1990.

Other literary forms

Joy Harjo collaborated with photographer Stephen Strom on *Secrets from the Center of the World* (1989), a critically acclaimed collection of images of the Navajo in the Four Corners area of the Southwest and Harjo's prose narrative poem. As a screenwriter, Harjo has written teleplays, public service announcements, and public broadcasting and educational television scripts.

Achievements

Harjo has been honored with the American Book Award from the Before Columbus Foundation, the American Indian Distinguished Achievement award, grants and fellowships, including one from the National Endowment for the Arts (NEA) in creative writing (1978), and an NEA summer stipend at the University of Arizona (1987). She has also received an Academy of American Poetry Award at the University of New Mexico and an Arizona Commission on the Arts Creative Writing Fellowship (1989). Her fourth book of poetry, *In Mad Love and War*, received the Poetry Society of America's William Carlos Williams Award, the Delmore Schwartz Memorial Poetry Prize from New York University, and the Pen Oak Josephine Miles Award.

Biography

Harjo was born to Allen W. and Wynema (Baker) Foster, in Tulsa, Oklahoma, on May 9, 1951. Her father's family members were Creek (Muscogee) Indians originally from Alabama and had been tribal leaders; Menawa led the Red Stick War during the presidency of Andrew Jackson. Harjo's mother was Cherokee and French Canadian.

At sixteen Harjo left home to attend boarding school at the Institute of American Indian Arts in Santa Fe, New Mexico. She then enrolled as an art student at the University of New Mexico to study painting. At twenty-two, however, Harjo began writing poetry, receiving her B.A. degree in poetry from the university in 1976. Harjo earned an M.F.A. degree in creative writing from the Writers' Workshop at the University of Iowa in 1978. From 1978 to 1979 she taught Native American literature and creative writing at the Institute of Native American Arts in Santa Fe; from 1980 to 1981 she taught creative writing and poetry part-time as an instructor at Arizona State University. She served as an assistant professor at the University of Colorado at Boulder from 1985 to 1988. Harjo then joined the faculty of the Department of English at the University of Arizona. In 1990 Harjo became a faculty member of the Department of English at the University of New Mexico. She has been a writer in residence at several universities, including the University of Montana and the State University of New York at Stony Brook. In addition to her university teaching, Harjo is active in the Artists-in-the-Schools program. She frequently travels to give readings, conduct workshops, and participate in literary festivals. Harjo has also worked as a filmmaker, artist, and scriptwriter for television.

Harjo sits on the boards of directors for the National Association for Third World Writers and the Native American Public Broadcasting Consortium and serves on the policy panel of the NEA. She has also been a member of the New Mexico Arts Commission as well as an NEA literature policy panel. Harjo is the poetry editor of *High Plains Literary Review* and a contributing editor for *Tyuonyi* and *Contact II*.

An avid musician, Harjo plays tenor saxophone and flute in rock, jazz, and big bands. She is the mother of two children, Phil Dayn and Rainy Dawn.

Analysis

Harjo's writing focuses on the pains, loves, and losses of contemporary Native American people, women in particular. Harjo's first book, the nine-poem chapbook *The Last Song*, was published only two years after she began writing poetry. These nine poems were subsequently made a part of *What Moon Drove Me to This?* The visual and emotional landscape of Harjo's poetry is bleak but sometimes hopeful; her personas live in cities, frequent bars, fail at love, lose their sense of tribe and history, and drive down empty interstate highways into a dark unknown.

A typical Harjo persona, Noni Daylight, figures in a number of works as her poetic alter ego. The first appearance of Noni, a troubled young Indian woman who drinks, takes drugs, and failed a suicide attempt, is in "The First Noni Daylight" (*What Moon Drove Me to This?*). Another poem, "Origin," describes Noni moving from the East into the unknown. As she drives, Noni remembers the Hopi account of the origin of all life, and she grapples with defining who she is, where she has come from, and in what direction she is headed. In "Someone Talking," Harjo places Noni in Oxford, Iowa, remembering Oklahoma Indian names: "Kickapoo, Creek,/ Sac and Fox." Despite Noni's recollections and focus on her Indian past, she remains rootless. In "Evidence," the final Noni Daylight poem of *What Moon Drove Me to This?*, Noni and an unnamed female friend drive aimlessly into the dark night, their only purpose to move from where they were. The Noni Daylight poems, as well as many of Harjo's other poems, examine the disjuncture between the traditions of the persona's tribal past, the unfulfilled rootedness implied by that past, and the impossible difficulties facing Indians who move within the dominant white/Anglo culture of the American cityscape.

Noni Daylight also appears in *She Had Some Horses* (1983), again struggling with her fears, isolated in an Anglo city. Noni watches trains rumble through town in "Kansas City"; she chooses self-destructive behavior and flight in "Heartbeat" by frequenting Albuquerque bars, picking up men, taking drugs, and finally departing in her car while awaiting a cleansing "fierce anger/ that will free her." Finally, in "She Remembers the Future," Noni addresses her "otherself," evidently looking for an answer that will provide the connection to the world she has been tracking, an answer that will be more than the impulse to violence that apparently has been Noni's frequent response. Noni wants "to know/ that we're alive/ we are alive."

In much of what Harjo writes, the past of an Indian culture, even the contemporary one left behind for the city, is interwoven with the alienating landscapes of urban life. In these inhospitable settings Harjo alludes to what has been left behind in the persona's attempt to assimilate into the white culture: life amid the wild landscapes of the Southwest, which contains the speaker's roots in Native American tradition and the tribal environment of the pueblo or reservation.

Harjo's most powerful pieces situate themselves in the urban landscape, the locus of white culture and the void into which so many Native Americans disappear. The alienation and anger expressed in this poetry circle back to the persona's homelands in an attempt to connect or reconnect with the person's roots. For example, "3AM" describes an early morning scene in Albuquerque in which the narrator and another individual try to find a flight out to Third Mesa, on ancient Hopi lands. Nowhere on the airport's departure board can they find their destination listed. Harjo makes clear the erasure of Native American culture and heritage by pointing out that no one in this white world realizes what Third Mesa represents: the center of the Hopi world, a site of origin for all that comes afterward. Bitterly, the poem makes it clear that, to the person behind the airline desk, the would-be travelers are merely two Indians. "3AM" underscores the bitterness and the alienation of the Native American swallowed up by a dominant Anglo culture that apparently cannot concern itself with learning about and respecting Indian history and traditions.

With few exceptions, the people in a Harjo poem fail to achieve community or rootedness; they remain buried inside an urban desert with the living world, the Indian world, somewhere out "there." This is the perspective taken in "Autobiography," in which Harjo accounts for her Creek roots, explaining her sense of difference as an Indian, the despair of the literally and psychologically "unhomed" reflected in early alcoholism. In this poem she meets her past, a derelict Indian from Jemez Pueblo whom she and friends encounter on a midnight street in an unnamed city in the Southwest, possibly Albuquerque. At twenty-one, the narrator tells us that in this man she sees herself, her heritage, her father. This street person figures as a talisman, as a positive vehicle for connecting with her own culture. His and her fractured pasts provide the persona with images that resonate for her at the poem's conclusion, and the poem opens outward from the desolate city street toward Muscogee tribal lands in springtime.

Harjo has said that she particularly identifies herself and her writing with the female, with the pains, sorrows, and victories of women. One of her strongest and most often-discussed poems, "The Woman Hanging from the Thirteenth Floor Window," examines suicide, fear, and detachment in an East Chicago slum. This woman serves as an emblem of the Indian trapped in the white city forced to the brink, perhaps pushed out onto that sill by an uncaring, unnoticing Anglo culture in a high-rise ironically built by Native American construction workers. Harjo has said that this poem is informed by her experience at the Chicago Indian Center. Mirroring contemporary Native American alienation in Anglo culture, this poem ends inconclusively. Harjo does not show the woman jumping or retreating inside: Both possibilities remain, leaving the unnamed Indian woman alone, isolated, and immobilized in a city that is not her own. Although this and many of Harjo's poems expressly speak to the pain of women, they also reflect a larger suffering, that of the dispossessed Native American of either gender. In many respects, the fears, joys, and needs of the poems' speakers transcend the boundaries of gender.

In the final poem of *She Had Some Horses*, "I Give You Back," Harjo deals directly with the fears she has explored in her earlier verse. No longer seeing fear as embodying the most important part of her self, the poem's persona disclaims any ties with her terrors of white oppression, including rape, displacement, the murder of children, and the countless other ways that the dominant culture has by implication brutalized the speaker and her people. As a capstone poem to this volume, "I Give You Back" claims ownership of such tyrannies as fearing her own anger, joy, love, hatred, and mixed racial background. Claiming herself back from fear, the persona understands the crippling nature of her fears while at the same time owning them as an integral part of her self. As the final poem in this collection, it addresses the issues Harjo's other poems have explored: the displacement, despair, and psychic immobility of the Indian people whose stories her poems have brought to life. In effect, *She Had Some Horses* ends on a cathartic note of refusal to break under the tyranny of a culture that has done its best to obliterate all that is important to the people about whom Harjo has written.

In *In Mad Love and War*, Harjo revisits the same themes. Divided into two sections—"The Wars" and "Mad Love"—the poems describe the alienation and anger that seem to affect and shape Harjo's sense of self, racial identity, and isolation. Divided as it is into these two sections, the book speaks to the divisions that Harjo had sought to bridge in "I Give You Back." Clearly, the wrestling with a divided self figures centrally in Harjo's work. In *In Mad Love and War*, however, Harjo turns her sights more firmly outward and begins examining issues reflected in the lives of others, persons who have been victims in circumstances similar to those she identifies as oppressing herself, her people, and the cultures of all Native Americans. In this volume, however, Harjo does not limit her poetry's scope to Indians; one poem, "Strange Fruit," describes the death of Jacqueline Peters, an African American activist lynched by the Ku Klux Klan in 1986. In Peters, Harjo discovers connections that transcend racial boundaries; the terror and brutality experienced by Peters are experiences shared by Harjo and the other Native Americans in her poems.

Music, particularly jazz and blues, plays an important role in much of what Harjo writes. These musical idioms—historically connected to and expressive of African Americans—seem to speak to Harjo's exploration of the displacement of late twentieth century Native Americans lost in urban landscapes. In one such poem, "Summer Night," Harjo describes the persona's impressions of a summer night spent waiting for a lover to come home. In an autobiographical piece published in *I Tell You Now: Autobiographical Essays by Native American Writers* (1987), Harjo wrote that she had wanted the poem to capture the feeling of a humid Oklahoma night and the impressions of her family's home. The poem's narrator talks of loneliness and what it feels like to be waiting in the dark on a humid, heavy summer night. Everyone else is sleeping, and it seems that they are all sleeping with someone: Even the night itself is cradled in the arms of day. The narrator sees herself as the only thing without a partner. Like a jazz piece improvising on a theme, the poem seems drowsy, languidly mirroring the sounds of a hot, sticky midsummer's night caught in the drifting, semifocused attention of someone sitting in the dark listening to the night sounds and waiting. Not only does the poem embody the tensions and laziness of the summer night, but Harjo also uses these impressions to make a powerful nonverbal statement about the speaker's isolation. Harjo's interest in and connection to blues is evident in this poem: The slow, languid musical rhythms of the lines drift from one topic to another in much the same way that the blues spill from harmony to harmony. Harjo gives a bluesy rhythm to her poetry by making use of numerous sentence fragments, a technique that mirrors musical phrasing. Each fragment is the equivalent of a tone, and the combination of these fragments establishes much of the poem's feeling of languor, isolation, and loneliness—in other words, the blues.

Bibliography

Bruchac, Joseph. "The Arms of Another Sky: Joy Harjo." In *The Sacred Hoop*, edited by Paula Gunn Allen. Boston: Beacon Press, 1986.

Crawford, John. "Notes Toward a New Multicultural Criticism." In *A Gift of Tongues: Critical Challenges in Contemporary American Poetry*, edited by Marie Harris and Kathleen J. Aguero. Athens: University of Georgia Press, 1987.

Crawford, John, and Patricia Clark Smith. "Joy Harjo." In *This Is About Vision: Interviews with Southwestern Writers*, edited by William Balassi, John F. Crawford, and Annie O. Eysturoy. Albuquerque: University of New Mexico Press, 1990.

Harjo, Joy. "A MELUS Interview with Joy Harjo." Interview by Helen Jaskoski. *MELUS* 16, no. 1 (1989/1990): 5-13.

——————. "Ordinary Spirit." In *I Tell You Now: Autobiographical Essays by Native American Writers*, edited by Brian Swann and Arnold Krupat. Lincoln: University of Nebraska Press, 1987.

——————. "The Story of All Our Survival: An Interview with Joy Harjo." Interview by Joseph Bruchac. In *Survival This Way: Interviews with American Indian Poets*, edited by Bruchac. Tucson: University of Arizona Press, 1987.

Lang, Nancy. "'Twin Gods Bending Over': Joy Harjo and Poetic Memory." *MELUS* 18, no. 3 (1993): 41-49.

Ruppert, Jim. "Paula Gunn Allen and Joy Harjo: Closing the Distance Between Personal and Mythic Space." *American Indian Quarterly* 7, no. 1 (1983): 27-40.

Scarry, John. "Representing Real Worlds: The Evolving Poetry of Joy Harjo." *World Literature Today* 66, no. 2 (Spring, 1992): 286-291.

Smith, Patricia Clark, and Paula Gunn Allen. "Earthly Relations, Carnal Knowledge: Southwestern American Indian Women Writers and Landscape." In *The Desert Is No Lady: Southwestern Landscapes in Women's Writing and Art*, edited by Vera Norwood and Janice Monk. New Haven, Conn.: Yale University Press, 1987.

LINDA HOGAN

Born: Denver, Colorado; July 16, 1947

Principal poetry

Calling Myself Home, 1978; *Daughters, I Love You*, 1981; *Eclipse*, 1983; *Seeing Through the Sun*, 1985; *Savings*, 1988; *Book of Medicines: Poems*, 1993.

Other literary forms

Linda Hogan has published critical and personal essays on Native American literature and culture in popular and academic periodicals and anthologies. A novel based on research initiated by Osage scholar Carol Hunter appeared in 1990. Her play *A Piece of Moon* was produced in 1981. She co-compiled the anthology *The Stories We Hold Secret: Tales of Women's Spiritual Development* (1987) and has authored short stories.

Achievements

The publication of books and securing of teaching positions in universities represent in themselves major achievements for a woman who has said that as a young girl she did not plan to attend college because she "didn't know what college was." Through what she might call a combination of love and defiance, Linda Hogan has overcome many of the oppressive conditions and obstacles placed in the way of those she characterizes as the less privileged of society. Her writing challenges accepted standards of literary taste, being deliberately aimed at an audience that may be without formal education or training in complex literary forms. Her achievement and potential have been recognized: *Seeing Through the Sun* received an American Book Award from the Before Columbus Foundation, and Hogan has been awarded grants from the National Endowment for the Arts (NEA) and the Minnesota State Arts Board.

Biography

Linda Hogan was born in Denver in 1947. Her ancestors include pioneer workers and farmers who had settled in Nebraska, as well as Winchester Colbert, nineteenth century head of the Chickasaw nation. She grew up in Colorado, in Denver and later in Colorado Springs, and also spent much of her childhood on her grandparents' farm in Oklahoma. The former experiences introduced Hogan to a multicultural, working-class environment, the latter to rural poverty and hard-

ship as well as the beauty of nature and strong ties to the land. Leaving school at fifteen to begin work as a nurse's aide, Hogan undertook a series of low-paying jobs before and during her first years in college. She earned a bachelor's degree and, in 1978, received an M.A. in creative writing from the University of Colorado.

During the period of her self-education and formal education, Hogan began to write, seeking to formulate her own sense of pattern and significance in her existence. Her first book of poems was published in 1978; it was followed by the publication of several essays on Native American and other writers. Hogan became active both as writer and as teacher, teaching in colleges and universities in Colorado and Minnesota and publishing poetry, fiction, nonfiction, and drama.

Politically active as well as articulate in her writing on issues relating to colonialism, human rights, and equitable treatment for working people, Hogan participated with her family in an antinuclear encampment in the Black Hills of South Dakota during 1980; the experience was later commemorated in the poems collected in *Daughters, I Love You* and reprinted in *Eclipse*.

Analysis

Hogan's poetry explores themes that are both universal in scope and unique to her Native American heritage. *Calling Myself Home*, Hogan's first collection of poems, showed the considerable promise of the young writer. The ambiguous title reflects the complexity of themes the author confronts: "calling myself home" signifies a journey back to origins, but it can mean, as well, that home is to be found only within the self. Both these meanings reverberate in the poems in this collection, even as the struggle between the two senses permeates all Hogan's work and her relationship with her family and ancestors. "Landless Indians" is how Hogan describes the Chickasaw and other Oklahoma Indians, typified by her grandparents and relatives, who lost their allotment lands to bank failures, swindlers, and periods of depressed economy. Thus returning "home" means awareness of loss in the act of restoring ties to the land, and plumbing one's inner resources to create a psychological and spiritual "homeland" that maintains individual and collective identity.

The ten poems of the first section are reflective meditations that turn to an arid and materially impoverished landscape, yet the poems present memories full of wonder and reverent attention to details of landscape, as well as awareness of connectedness to a historic and prehistoric past. The frequent references to the ancient turtle inhabiting the now-dry pond, for example, offer both an image of patient endurance and survival and an allusion to the great tortoise that, in many Native American mythologies, supports the world on its back. The title poem, "calling myself home," weaves these themes together in its imaginative re-creation of "old women/ who lived on amber" and danced to the rattles they created of turtle shell and pebble. The speaker goes on to express an identity between herself, her people, and the ancient ones: "we are plodding creatures/ like the turtle." Such affinity between people—especially women—and their land creates great strength. The generations of women forebears the author celebrates become part of the strength of the earth itself. Paradoxically, the speaker ends the poem on a note of farewell, stating that she has come to say goodbye, yet the substance of the poem indicates that the speaker, like the turtle, will carry her "home" with her always.

The second section includes sixteen poems meditating on Hogan's personal and family experience and also moves to larger themes of her heritage as a Chickasaw and as a Native American woman. The section's title poem, "Heritage," alludes specifically to events she has elsewhere described as happening to her great-grandparents and other relatives: a plague of grasshoppers that destroyed her great-grandfather's farm in Nebraska, her uncle who carved delicate wood and bone objects and passed on traditional Chickasaw lore, her silent grandfather, and the counsel and practice of her grandmother. She alludes to secret wisdom, suppressed knowledge, and the sense, again, of "never having a home."

Other poems in *Calling Myself Home* celebrate metamorphosis and transformation, pervasive themes and modes of writing throughout Hogan's work. The natural transformation in the birth of a colt is acknowledged in "Celebration: Birth of a Colt," while "The River Calls Them" offers close observation of the metamorphosis of tadpoles into frogs. In "Rain" metamorphosis be-

comes method as well as theme, as rainfall is portrayed as fish falling from the sky, while the actual fish revivified by the rain feed the exuberant children. In "Vapor Cave" the theme of metamorphosis extends to the speaker's reach beyond cultural past and identification with the earth itself. The vapor cave is a womblike hollow, both erotically steamy and innocently purifying; the speaker enters to be cleansed and restored and finds herself transmuting: "Legs and arms lose themselves/ lose their light boundaries of skin." The poem echoes the meditation in "Calling Myself Home" on women's bones transmuted into the calcified, tortoiselike skeleton of the earth itself.

Hogan's next major collection, *Eclipse*, moves outward from the grounding in personal memory and family history of *Calling Myself Home* to embrace wider philosophical issues and topical concerns. The first section groups poems affirming a sense of affinity and continuity with the natural world. Sometimes this affinity has the character of a spiritual, almost mystical union, as in these lines from "Landscape of Animals": "the birds/ fly through me/ a breath apart." Another poem, "Ruins," wonderfully evokes the atmosphere of vanished life within ruins of ancient peoples of the American Southwest: "the bare songs of a hundred flutes" are opened "out of stone/ to let themselves go/ with the wind." Another poem in this section, "Oil," reminds the reader of the fragility of the natural world: "The earth is wounded/ and will not heal." The last two sections of the book, "Small Animals at Night" and "Land of Exile," continue with poems on the theme of the continuity and interdependence the speaker perceives among herself, all human life, and the lives of animals.

In *Daughters, I Love You* Hogan comes to grips with the nuclear menace and with historical and imminent guilt, fear, and danger. Most of the poems in this section allude to the atomic bombing of Japan; at least one grew directly out of the experience of a peace encampment to protest the presence of nuclear missiles and bombs in the sacred Black Hills of South Dakota ("Black Hills Survival Gathering, 1980"). While they might loosely be categorized as poems of protest, the works in *Daughters, I Love You* are strongly unified in their underlying spiritual awareness, which Hogan sees as the most significant response she can make to the pure destructiveness represented by the dreams of power and poison with "a prayer that enters a house" to protect "the sleeping men and the gentle work/ of women."

The five poems grouped under the title "Who Will

Speak?" explore the history of Native American peoples in the United States. "A Place for the Eagle" evokes a sense of the ancient oral traditions, showing creation as the joint work of animal and spirit shapers. In "Stone Dwellers" the speaker gazes at a museum display of historic and prehistoric artifacts, reconstructing in her contemplation the vanished life of the people on the earth. Family history, including the astounding injustice and hardship of the removal of the five southern nations from their homelands in the south to the Oklahoma Indian Territory, is re-created in "Houses."

Seeing Through the Sun collects some fifty new poems grouped in four sections, titled "Seeing Through the Sun," "Territory of Night," "Daughters Sleeping," and "Wall Songs." The third section echoes and continues themes opened in the earlier *Daughters, I Love You* but focuses on a more personal vision of motherhood, moving at times into myth. "Tiva's Tapestry: La Llorona" is dedicated to a friend of the poet; the poem calls on the Mexican legend of La Llorona, the Weeping Woman, who is said to walk neighborhoods at dusk, weeping for her children, whom she has killed, and seeking to kidnap replacements. The voice in the poem speaks of the sewing or embroidering of a picture that suggests the tragic mother ("She comes dragging/ the dark river/ a ghost on fire"), who moves into a figure of cosmic dimension: "on the awful tapestry of sky/ just one of the mothers/ among the downward circling stars."

"Bees in Transit: Osage County" reflects Hogan's preoccupation for several years with *Mean Spirit*, published in 1990. The novel depicts life in Oklahoma during the 1920's, when a number of Native American holders of oil rights were murdered under suspicious circumstances; thorough investigations were not undertaken, and the killers were not brought to justice. The Osage murders, as they were called, were but an extreme manifestation of pervasive bigotry and oppression. A major theme of *Mean Spirit*, the suffering of women in those circumstances, emerges in "Bees in Transit: Osage County": "dark women, murdered for oil/ . . . still walk in numbers/ through smoky dusk." The poem combines Hogan's feeling for history with a spiritual outlook that has emerged more explicitly in *Seeing Through the Sun* and later works.

Savings, Hogan's next collection of poems, continues and expands themes initiated in the earlier works and provides a perspective on the development of the poet's work in the ten years since the publication of her first collection. The poems in *Savings* tend often to be more discursive than the tightly formulated associations of images in *Calling Myself Home*; many are longer, and there is some experimentation with form, as in the loose unrhymed couplets of "The New Apartment: Minneapolis."

Hogan's thematic preoccupations move from the sense of hardship endured and overcome in her personal, family, and tribal history to wider consideration of global issues of justice, care, and responsibility. Her characteristic method of building from image to image is sometimes grafted to more abstract expression, as in "The Legal System." In this poem the reader hears an ambiguous voice suggesting that the internalization of a "legal system" within the individual both reflects and predicts the judgments and prejudgments (literally, prejudices) of individual and society. Blame may be neither assigned nor denied.

The poems in *Savings* reach out from Chickasaw history and the Oklahoma landscape to embrace allusions to major contemporary injustices. Abuse of women, alcoholism, class hostility, the Holocaust, refugees from oppressive regimes, undocumented immigrants, poverty, and bigotry are all mentioned. The method in these poems differs somewhat from the focused topicality of the texts in *Daughters, I Love You*. In the earlier book the poet's strategy is to weave related images around a central theme; for example, in "Black Hills Survival Gathering, 1980," the image and feeling of sunrise is collated with historical memory of Hiroshima, the presence of a Buddhist monk protesting nuclear war, and the appearance of a bomber flying overhead. The method in *Savings*, by contrast, is often both more discursive and more allusive. In "The Other Voices" the speaker attempts to come to terms with an overpowering evil by contrasting unspecified refugees fleeing a police state with the commonplace, unthreatening lives of domestic animals such as chickens and horses. In "Workday" a speaker meditates through a workday—going to work, sitting in a meeting, riding the bus—on torture and mutilation happening elsewhere in the world, past losses of children, and pervasive poverty and drudgery.

Hogan's development as a poet shows continuing commitment to certain ethical and emotional themes: problems of justice and injustice, the beauty and significance of the lives of ordinary people, strong bonds of family love, and a nurturing care for the natural world. The poet's method moves from very tightly structured, imagistic lyrics, focused in personal expression and feeling, outward to embrace issues wider in a geopolitical or ideological sense.

Other major works

LONG FICTION: *Mean Spirit*, 1990.

SHORT FICTION: *That Horse*, 1984.

PLAY: *A Piece of Moon*, 1981.

ANTHOLOGY: *The Stories We Hold Secret: Tales of Women's Spiritual Development*, 1987 (with Carol Bruchac and Judith McDaniel).

MISCELLANEOUS: *Red Clay: Poems and Stories*, 1991.

Bibliography

Allen, Paula Gunn. *The Sacred Hoop: Recovering the Feminine in American Indian Traditions*. Boston: Beacon Press, 1986.

Bruchac, Joseph. *Survival This Way: Interviews with American Indian Poets*. Tucson: University of Arizona Press, 1987.

Crawford, John, William Balassi, and Annie O. Eysturoy. *This Is About Vision: Interviews with Southwestern Writers*. Albuquerque: University of New Mexico Press, 1990.

Hogan, Linda. "A Heart Made Out of Crickets: An Interview with Linda Hogan." Interview by Bo Scholer. *The Journal of Ethnic Studies* 16, no. 1 (1988): 107-117.

——————— . "The Story Is Brimming Around: An Interview with Linda Hogan." Interview by Carol Miller. *SAIL: Studies in American Indian Literatures*, 2d series, 2, no. 4 (1990): 1-9.

Jaskoski, Helen. Review of *Calling Myself Home. SAIL: Studies in American Indian Literatures* 6, no. 1 (1986): 9-10.

N. SCOTT MOMADAY

Born: Lawton, Oklahoma; February 27, 1934

Principal long fiction
House Made of Dawn, 1968; *The Ancient Child*, 1989.

Other literary forms
Best known for his novels and collections of Kiowa tales, N. Scott Momaday considers himself essentially a poet, having published several collections of verse. He is also the author of essays and several important prose works that are autobiographical in nature.

Achievements
Momaday's earliest recognition as a writer came in 1959, when he received the Stanford University Creative Writing Fellowship. An Academy of American Poets prize followed in 1962 in recognition of his poem "The Bear."

Three years after receiving the Ph.D. (1963) degree in English (1963), Momaday was awarded a Guggenheim Fellowship that enabled him to complete *House Made of Dawn*, which won the Pulitzer Prize in fiction for 1969. The National Institute of Arts and Letters awarded Momaday a grant in 1970, and in 1974, his collaboration with photographer David Muench, resulting in *Colorado* (1973), won a Western Heritage Award. Momaday was the recipient of Italy's Premio Letterario Internazionale "Mondelo" award in 1979 and the Distinguished Service Award of the Western Literary Association in 1983.

Biography
Navarre Scott Momaday spent much of his childhood in New Mexico's highlands, where his mother, Mayme Natachee Scott, and his father, Alfred Morris Momaday, worked as teachers on the Jemez Pueblo. Before his parents moved to New Mexico, they had lived among the father's Kiowa relatives in Oklahoma.

The mother's middle name was derived from her Cherokee great-grandmother. Mayme's father's background was Anglo-Saxon. Later, when she chose to adopt Native American ways and to dress accordingly, Natachee, as she was generally called, took a new name, Little Moon. While attending a Native American school in Kansas, Natachee met and married her Kiowa husband.

Both parents preferred the Native American lifestyle to that of the dominant white culture. Because English was the major language in his parents' household, Momaday does not speak Kiowa. From his father's branch of the family, however, he learned the importance of storytelling and the techniques Native Americans employ in weaving their tales. In his own writing, Momaday uses these techniques with facility, gracefully intermixing myth with historical fact, skillfully overcoming linear time-space constraints. His writing captures structurally the essence of Native American culture, transmuting its uniqueness into the art forms of the dominant culture.

At seventeen, Momaday went to Augusta Military Academy, after which he continued his education at the University of New Mexico, receiving the bachelor's degree in 1958. He continued his education at Stanford University, receiving the master's (1960) and Ph.D. (1963) degrees. In 1959, Momaday married Gay Mangold. Their union produced three daughters.

Upon receiving the doctorate, Momaday was appointed assistant professor of English at the University of California at Santa Barbara, where he taught until 1969. He left a tenured associate professorship there to become associate professor of English and comparative literature at the University of California at Berkeley, where he taught the first course in the country in Native American literature. Stanford hired him in 1973 as professor of English, a post he held until 1982, when he moved to the University of Arizona, where he serves as Regents Professor of English. In 1978, Momaday married Regina Heitzer, by whom he had one daughter.

An accomplished artist as well as a novelist and poet, Momaday has also exhibited his artwork. He serves as a trustee of the Museum of American Indian, Heye Foundation of New York City. Since 1970, Momaday has regularly been a consultant to the National Endowment for the Arts (NEA) and the National Endowment for the Humanities (NEH).

Analysis

Even though he does not speak the language of the Kiowa, Momaday captures in his writing the essence of Kiowa culture, demonstrating indisputably that he understands this culture as well as the broader Native American culture as it exists in contemporary society.

Momaday is unique among Native American writers because he does not concentrate on the tensions that exist between the Kiowa and the dominant culture. He chooses instead to present the experiences and customs of his heritage, using the English language to construct a physical environment, a striking Native American landscape, that captures the essence of Kiowa culture.

The Kiowa are members of a virtually extinct Indian tribe that, from the mid-1700's well into the 1870's, ruled supreme from Oklahoma and Texas nearly to the Canadian border. The devastation of the buffalo herds resulted in a diminution of the Kiowa. Their eventual crushing defeat at the Palo Duro Canyon in Texas marked the end of their supremacy. The leaders of the tribe surrendered to the United States Cavalry at Fort Sill, Oklahoma, and received long prison sentences.

That the tribe was devastated in this way, however, did not signal its total annihilation. Its ways lived on in people such as Momaday's father and grandmother, both of whom understood Kiowa culture. Momaday's grandmother, who lived well into his lifetime, was present at the last Sun Dance of the Kiowa in 1887.

Through family members, Momaday, who spent his earliest years among his Kiowa relatives on their farm in Oklahoma prior to his parents' moving to New Mexico, grew up knowing intimately the legends, myths, and history of his people. It is these materials that inform most of his writing.

Perhaps the book that best illustrates what Momaday aims to accomplish in his writing is *The Way to Rainy Mountain*. Although he writes in English, Momaday presents exquisitely and precisely the conventions of Kiowa storytelling, capturing the non-European thought patterns by telling his tales in snippets, much as Rolando Hinojosa does in many of the books that form his Klail City Death Trip series.

The Way to Rainy Mountain relates the history of the Kiowa, telling how the people emerged from darkness into light, entering the world, according to their mythology, through a hollow log. Momaday in *The Way to Rainy Mountain*, *House Made of Dawn*, and *The Ancient Child* recounts the mythic tale of how a Kiowa boy playing with his seven sisters was transformed into a great bear and then began to attack his sisters. In doing

so, he scored the bark of a tree they had climbed in terror. This caused the seven sisters to be transported into the sky, where they became fixed as the Big Dipper.

Momaday divides *The Way to Rainy Mountain* into three sections about equal in length, "The Setting Out," "The Going On," and "The Closing In." Within each section, on matched pairs of facing pages, he presents brief, single-paragraph vignettes, each distinguished by a different typeface. The first vignette is always a Kiowa myth or legend. The second relates a historical incident relating to the Kiowa. The third tells something about Momaday's uncovering some aspect of his Kiowa heritage.

The Way to Rainy Mountain is eighty-nine pages long. Its pages are not crammed with print but, rather, are printed upon sparingly. The entire physical arrangement of the book reflects the openness of the plains over which the Kiowa once had domain. The three-part arrangement of each set of vignettes reflects a Native American, nonlinear way of dealing with time and space. In the early pages of the book, the vignettes often seem disparate, but as the book continues, they more clearly become parts of a unified whole. Through this method, Momaday illustrates how the Native American worldview of harmony in the universe comes to fruition. Like the Kiowa, Momaday moves slowly, steadily, unrelentingly toward a unity so subtle as to be virtually incomprehensible.

In *House Made of Dawn*, as in much of his writing, Momaday's aim is to communicate the legends and myths of the Kiowa in a literary form foreign to the people who created and passed down these legends and myths, but without losing their authenticity. In this novel, the protagonist, Abel, has returned to his native pueblo at San Ysidro after serving in the United States Army during World War II. Abel, however, is a changed man who finds it difficult to recapture his roots.

Momaday writes reverently of the land and of all that it means to the Kiowa. Before long, Abel kills an albino Indian and is sentenced to a prison term. Finally, he wins his parole and is sent to a rehabilitation center in Los Angeles. He shares a room in Los Angeles with Ben, a Native American who has adapted more easily than Abel to living in the world of white people.

Abel, unable to cope with the pressures of his job, begins to drink heavily and to take part in ritualistic Native American religious ceremonies that involve the use of peyote. Abel is severely beaten by a policeman, after which Abel returns to the reservation, where he begins to recapture the ancient traditions of his people, looking after his grandfather, Francisco, and engaging in the traditional Kiowa death ceremonies as his grandfather's condition worsens.

As the novel ends, Abel is taking part in a ritual race against evil and death, traditionally run at dawn. This signifies that, as the novel's title suggests, a new day is dawning for Abel, who perhaps can find peace among his forebears. Despite the violence and dislocations in *House Made of Dawn*, the novel is upbeat and ends on an optimistic note.

In this book, Momaday creates a story that venerates the land, as much mainstream American literature does, while simultaneously developing a sacred text that is almost wholly Native American. Such has been Momaday's writing: His fiction and poetry both focus on how Native Americans try to relate to contemporary society without denying their ancient heritage.

In his autobiographical work *The Names: A Memoir*, Momaday probes deeply into a genealogy difficult to trace, given the dearth of written records. This book draws heavily upon the tales and folklore of Momaday's tribe and from his early boyhood memories of life among his father's Kiowa relatives in Oklahoma and later among the Jemez Indians of New Mexico.

Writing at a time when many minority groups were tracking down information about their identities, Momaday sought to rediscover himself much as James Joyce had more than a half century before in *A Portrait of the Artist as a Young Man* (1916). In *The Names*, Momaday uncovers the Native American mystique about naming things. (He himself had, as an infant, been given the Kiowa name Tsoaitalee, which had a sacred significance.) By giving Momaday this name, Pohdlohk, the aged Kiowa storyteller, implied that he (Pohdlohk) was passing on to the youth his tribal role.

In *The Names*, Momaday writes of his uncle James Mammedaty and of his grandmother. James, though a sympathetic character, is a drunk, while the grandmother is an elderly, self-assured Native American lady. The portrayal of the two is similar to Momaday's portrayal of Abel and his grandfather, Francisco, in *House Made of Dawn*.

Momaday's portrayal of the Jemez Pueblo, on which he lived as he was growing up, explains a great deal that occurs in his other writing. The Jemez tribe was on the decline when Momaday lived among its people; old rituals were dying or, at best, were looked upon benignly by the young as harmless curiosities. This theme of a culture lost pervades much of Momaday's work.

In *The Ancient Child*, Momaday captures his own feelings of what it is to become an accepted part of the dominant culture, as he certainly had become by his late teens. Locke Setman, the protagonist, is reared off the reservation and lives the life of an artist in San Francisco. Within him, however, is a nagging vacancy, a longing for a past that he vaguely intuits.

When Setman is called back to Oklahoma by the death of his Kiowa grandmother, whom he barely knew, he is reluctant to go. This return to his roots, however, awakens in him all the ancient mythology of his people. He meets Grey, the young medicine woman and visionary who has cared for his grandmother. Through her, Momaday introduces the legend of Billy, the Kid.

In *The Ancient Child*, as in his other work, Momaday scrupulously avoids linear representations of time and place. His episodes drift easily from place to place, from time to time. Setman's dream sequences and Grey's visions provide necessary flashbacks.

One episode in the final pages of *The Names* reflects well what Momaday tries to convey thematically in much of his writing. He faces a decisive break from his culture when his parents decide that he must attend Augusta Military Academy for his final year of high school. Hearing of their decision, the boy goes to his favorite mesa so that he can contemplate his future. When he turns to go home, he tries a path he has not used before and soon finds himself stuck between the top and the bottom. He can neither ascend nor descend. This is the fix in which, according to Momaday, many contemporary Native Americans find themselves. They chase after an identity, but being a part of neither world, they fail to find it.

The works of Momaday reflect that with which he identifies most vitally: the American Southwest and his Native American heritage and culture. His pioneering literary efforts in fiction, poetry, and autobiography have authentically rendered in English the beauty and power of Native American oral storytelling.

Other major works

POETRY: *Angle of Geese and Other Poems*, 1974; *The Gourd Dancer*, 1976.

NONFICTION: *The Way to Rainy Mountain*, 1969; *Colorado*, 1973 (photographs by David Muench); *The Names: A Memoir*, 1976.

EDITED TEXT: *The Complete Poems of Frederick Goddard Tuckerman*, 1965.

Bibliography

Antell, Judith A. "Momaday, Welch, and Silko: Expressing Feminine Principle Through Male Alienation." *The American Indian Studies Quarterly* 12 (Summer, 1988): 213-220.

Given, Bettye. "N. Scott Momaday: A Slant of Light." *MELUS* 12 (September, 1985): 79-87.

Kerr, Baine. "The Novel as Sacred Text: N. Scott Momaday's Myth-Making Ethic." *Southwest Review* 63 (Spring, 1978): 172-179.

Lattin, Vernon E. "The Quest for Mythic Vision in Contemporary Native American and Chicano Fiction." *American Literature* 50 (January, 1979): 625-640.

Lincoln, Kenneth. "Tai-me to Rainy Mountain: The Makings of American Indian Literature." *American Indian Quarterly* 10 (Spring, 1986): 101-117.

Meredith, Howard. "N. Scott Momaday: A Man of Words." *World Literature Today* 64 (Summer, 1990): 405-407.

Nicholas, Charles A. "N. Scott Momaday's Hard Journey Back." *The South Dakota Review* 13 (Winter, 1975/1976): 149-158.

Ramsey, Paul. "Faith and Form: Some American Poetry of 1976." *The Sewanee Review* 85 (Summer, 1977): 532-540.

Wild, Peter. "N. Scott Momaday: Gentle Maverick." *American West* 25 (February, 1988): 12-13.

Woodard, Charles L., ed. *Ancestral Voice: Conversations with N. Scott Momaday*. Lincoln: University of Nebraska Press, 1989.

LYNN RIGGS

Born: Claremore, Cherokee Nation (Oklahoma); August 31, 1899

Died: New York, New York; June 30, 1954

Principal drama

Knives from Syria, pr. 1925, pb. 1927 (one act); *Big Lake*, pr., pb. 1927; *Rancor*, pr. 1927; *A Lantern to See By*, pb. 1928, pr. 1930; *Sump'n Like Wings*, pb. 1928, pr. 1939; *Roadside*, pr., pb. 1930; *Green Grow the Lilacs*, pr., pb. 1931; *Russet Mantle*, pr., pb. 1936; *The Cherokee Night*, pr., pb. 1936; *A World Elsewhere*, pb. 1939; *The Year of Pilar*, wr. 1940, pb. 1947; *The Cream in the Well*, pr., pb. 1941; *Dark Encounter*, pb. 1947; *Laughter from a Cloud*, pr. 1947; *Hang on to Love*, pb. 1948; *Borned in Texas*, pr. 1950 (rev. of *Roadside*); *Toward the Western Sky*, pr., pb. 1951 (music by Nathan Kroll).

Other literary forms

Lynn Riggs was also the author of many poems, which appeared in such periodicals as *Poetry: A Magazine of Verse* (Harriet Monroe, editor), *The Smart Set* (H. L. Mencken, editor), and *The Nation*. A number of these poems were published in *The Iron Dish* (1930). Riggs also authored screenplays for Metro-Goldwyn-Mayer, including, perhaps most notably, *The Plainsman* (1936).

Achievements

Riggs achieved early recognition from such notable theatrical authorities as Barrett H. Clark and Arthur Hopkins, both of whom championed his work, although most later critics labeled him a minor regionalist. When Clark was speaking of Riggs's first full-length production for the commercial stage, *Big Lake*, he called Riggs "one of the few native dramatists who can take the material of our everyday life and mould it into forms of stirring beauty." Speaking of *Green Grow the Lilacs*, Hopkins said that "Riggs caught our fading glory and left it for posterity." It was this play and the comic *Russet Mantle* that were Riggs's greatest commercial successes for the stage during his lifetime, although he continued to write for the theater until 1951. His chief posthumous claim to fame has been as the author of *Green Grow the Lilacs*, which provided the basic text for the epoch-making Richard Rodgers and Oscar Hammerstein musical *Oklahoma!* (1943).

As noted by critic Richard Watts, Jr., Riggs's plays are "invariably rich and lyric folk [dramas, with] true feeling for atmosphere and period." "He wrote of people he had known," said his colleague Joseph Benton, "entwining their foibles, weaknesses and strengths, their garrulous chatterings and grass-roots wisdoms throughout his plays." Of Cherokee extraction, growing up the son of a farmer in Oklahoma in its earliest days as a state, Riggs wrote of the disappointed expectations and compromised human values that resulted among simple farm people from their conflicts with the changing values of American society. Perhaps his outstanding characteristics as an American playwright are his unwillingness to write cheap or empty plays, his facility with strong situations, his ability to write powerful two-person scenes, his appreciation for the genuine folk music of his region, and his gift for expressing the lyricism half-consciously felt and beautifully revealed in the lives of humble and ordinary people.

Biography

When Lynn Riggs was born in 1899, Claremore was still part of Indian Territory, which was later incorporated into the state of Oklahoma. Son of an Indian farmer, he enjoyed the simple amusements and "play parties" of his neighbors as well as their unselfconscious folk traditions. He did various odd jobs in his youth, first as an itinerant farmhand and cowpuncher and then as a singer at the local movie house. Later, he traveled around the country, working as a proofreader on a newspaper in San Francisco, as a clerk in the book section of Macy's department store in New York City, and as a newspaper reporter in Tulsa. At the age of twenty-one, Riggs enrolled at the University of Oklahoma as a music major, later changing his major to English so that he could qualify for a readership position. He continued to hold the position of second tenor in the quartet organized by the university, a group that toured in a professional summer Chautauqua and minstrel show. He had two farces, *Cuckoo* and *Honeymoon*, produced at school while he was still an undergraduate.

Riggs's dramatic successes at the university and his early one-act *Knives from Syria*, with its Ali Hakim-like peddler character, all showed originality and humor, and he was encouraged to continue playwriting. The production of the full-length *Big Lake* by the American Laboratory Theatre attracted some critical attention and won for Riggs a Guggenheim Fellowship. In 1928, Riggs resided in France, where he wrote *Green Grow the Lilacs* and much of *Roadside*, which was produced by Arthur Hopkins and starred Ralph Bellamy as Texas. At this point, Riggs was considered one of America's most promising playwrights, but critics qualified their praise. By 1936, when *Russet Mantle* succeeded as a comedy although it had been conceived as a serious work, reviewers were generalizing about Riggs's failure to master the needs of the theater in terms of plotting and characterization. They seemed to believe that Riggs's promise had somehow missed fire. During this period, Riggs was working with some success as a screenwriter.

Riggs was inducted into the United States Army in 1942, serving in the Army Air Corps, and his plays of the 1940's reflect his concern with the international chaos that rocked that era. His last work produced on Broadway was the 1950 *Borned in Texas*, a revision of the 1930 *Roadside*; in 1951, he wrote a "music play" on commission from Western Reserve University to celebrate the school's one hundred twenty-fifth anniversary. He was working on his first novel when he died of stomach cancer at the age of fifty-four. Riggs was survived by a sister and several brothers; there is no evidence that he ever married. A memorial for him was erected in the town of Claremore, Oklahoma, in 1958, and the library at Rogers University in Claremore has a collection of materials both by and about him.

Analysis

Riggs is known almost exclusively as a regional dramatist in the tradition of Susan Glaspell and Paul Green, but his work is more varied in both content and style than this label would suggest. For example, it is accurate to call Riggs an ethnic regionalist, but only if one includes the Cherokees in *The Cherokee Night*; the Latinos in *The Year of Pilar*, *A World Elsewhere*, and *Laughter from a Cloud*; the farmers and ranchers of *Green Grow the Lilacs*; and braggart frontiersmen in *Roadside* as ethnic groups associated with Riggs. A favorite theme deals with the attempts, in Arthur Hopkins' words, to show "beauty in rebellion . . . now

successful self-assertion, now frustration—usually girlhood or womanhood fighting for the right to self, for adventure, for love." This theme finds expression not only in the lightly sketched romance between Curly and Laurey in the well-known *Green Grow the Lilacs*, but also in almost all Riggs's other plays, which include tragedies, comedies, and two naturalistic studies of uneducated, lower-class women.

Riggs's plays demonstrate various kinds and strands of excellence, mixed with a number of structural problems. His poetic gift surfaces whenever the beauty of the natural world is invoked. This sensitivity to natural beauty, for example, resulted in the charming opening stage directions for *Green Grow the Lilacs*, which were translated into the lyrics of the title song in *Oklahoma!* In a number of his plays, Riggs uses songs and poetic diction in situations of heightened emotion. The same desire for lyricism finds expression in the effective use of scenic elements, such as the mountains in *Laughter from a Cloud*. In the play that Riggs himself considered his best, *The Cherokee Night*, a Cherokee burial ground looms in the background of each scene, dominating the stage action in an effective symbolic statement.

The Riggs protagonist searching for love is more often female than male, an emancipated woman, struggling to make some sort of active life for herself in which she will not be dependent on the superior strength or initiative of a man. It seems as though those plays end happily in which both the man and his "womern" agree on a common set of values—either mutually accepting the division into traditional, sharply defined masculine and feminine roles or both being willing to adjust to the newer emancipation of women—while those plays end unhappily in which some external condition or some restlessness within the characters forces an irresolvable confrontation over traditional values. It should not be assumed that Riggs was trying to assert the superiority of traditional values. He understood that the forces causing change were irresistible, and he was trying to chart what happened as people tried to accommodate such changes.

The first group of plays written by Riggs, dating from the 1925 *Knives from Syria* through the 1931 *Green Grow the Lilacs*, are studies of young people struggling to find themselves within the context of the kind of harsh farm environment made familiar by Eugene O'Neill in *Desire Under the Elms* (pr. 1924), which the early, tragic *A Lantern to See By* resembles. The issue of healthy versus neurotic sexuality underlies the seemingly simple *Green Grow the Lilacs*. The attraction of Curly and Laurey for each other, like the attraction of Texas and Hannie in *Roadside* (which seems to be a more broadly drawn caricature of some of the same themes as are found in *Green Grow the Lilacs*), is set in a context in which people pair off as a part of the fecund natural world. As the opening stage directions say, "men, cattle in a meadow, blades of the young corn, streams" give off "a visible golden emanation." Curly is associated with the outdoors and nature, both by his rhapsodic appreciation of natural beauty in several long speeches that serve no other dramatic function and by his job as a cowboy. Laurey, too, is part of nature. When Curly tells her he loves her, it is by describing how he saw her while she was growing up: first, "a little tyke" "pickin' blackberries"; next, riding "a little gray filly of Blue Starr's"; then, the year before, when she had been "out a-pickin' flowers" and "had a whole armful of Sweet Williams and wild roses and morning glories." In contrast, Jeeter, the hired hand on Aunt Eller's and Laurey's farm, lives "in a dark hole bent over a table a-fingerin' a pack of cards 's greasy 's a ole tin spoon." Laurey has made the mistake of being kind to Jeeter when he was ill, and his feelings of inferiority, along with his fascination with sadistic tales of sexual obsession, murder, and revenge, lead to his sexual advances on and threats to Laurey.

Laurey is afraid not to go to the play party with Jeeter, imagining that he might burn down her home in revenge, but when he goes too far at the play party, seizing and threatening her, she sends him off, relying on Curly. They soon agree to marry, but their wedding night is marred by the locals, who set on them to tease them in a "shivoree" (defined by Riggs as a bawdy, communitywide marriage celebration). Then Jeeter emerges from the crowd, setting fire to the haystack holding the young couple. He and Curly fight, and Jeeter is accidentally impaled on his own knife. Curly is arrested but breaks out of jail before the hearing that will determine his fate; in the play's last scene, he visits his bride, who assures him, "I'll put up with everything now. You don't need to worry about me no more." There is an implied happy ending, but there is not the onstage trial and freeing of Curly that occurs in *Oklahoma!*

In his introduction to the play, Riggs explained his intention to use "the simplest of stories." His play could have been subtitled "An Old Song," he wrote. He wanted to illustrate his characters' "quaintness, their sadness, their robustness, their simplicity, their hearty or bawdy humors, their sentimentalities, their melodrama, their touching sweetness." His success cannot be measured by the fate of the play. Although it was produced by the prestigious Theatre Guild with Franchot Tone as Curly, Helen Westley as Aunt Eller, June Walker as Laurey, and Lee Strasberg as the peddler, it ran for only sixty-four performances. In the musical version as *Oklahoma!*, however, it ran for more than five years and was one of the American theater's truly great events.

Russet Mantle, first produced in 1936, was Riggs's biggest hit. Ironically, although he intended it as a serious study of love versus convention and the materialistic values of American society, the minor character provided as comic relief came to dominate the play. It was produced as a comedy and thus provided an effective balance between Riggs's interests and Broadway standards. In the play, Kay Rowley and her mother visit Kay's retired aunt and uncle living in New Mexico. Kay spends her first night there in bed with a cowboy whom she has met that day. Kay's scandalized aunt and uncle try to discipline her, while Kay's mother, Effie, who is the comic creation largely responsible for the play's success, wants to know none of the details, so she will not have to be upset. The audience learns that the aunt did not marry the poor boy she loved in her youth but settled for financial security with her present husband. Their marriage, then, is an empty one, and their scandalized reaction to Kay's sexual aggressiveness may mask their own dissatisfaction.

A young poet named John comes to the farm seeking a job and is hired. He sees through Kay's pose of pseudosophistication, and the two have a love affair. When Kay's pregnancy is discovered, she refused to name the father, but John is delighted to acknowledge the child. Their hosts now threaten to throw them out into the harsh Depression world that has been evoked by John's job search and Kay's talk of "Riot squads, strikebreakers, nausea gas, bayonets and starvation! And voices crying out, for what? A little bread, a little sun, a little peace and delight." For their part, the young people are ready to go out into the world together, having affirmed the primacy of true love over convention. In the last line of the play, however, the aunt suggests that she and her husband talk things over before ejecting the young couple, implying that they may find a way to help their niece, even though they disapprove of her behavior.

Although not all Riggs's various concerns would captivate modern audiences, there is no question that he deserves a place in the history of American drama. Perhaps theater historian Alan S. Downer said it best when he praised Riggs for "the freshness and poetry of the speech and the warm humanity of the characters." His plays invoke the American tradition of love of nature, simplicity, and decency, at war with the complexities of modern life. The plays have value in helping to preserve that tradition.

Other major works

POETRY: *The Iron Dish*, 1930.

SCREENPLAYS: *Laughing Boy*, 1933; *Delay in the Sun*, 1935; *Garden of Allah*, 1936; *The Plainsman*, 1936 (with Waldemar Young and Harold Lamb).

Bibliography

Braunlich, Phyllis. *Haunted by Home: The Life and Letters of Lynn Riggs*. Norman: University of Oklahoma Press, 1988.

Brenton, Joseph. "Some Personal Reminiscences About Lynn Riggs." *Chronicles of Oklahoma* 34 (Autumn, 1956): 296-301.

Downer, Alan S. *Fifty Years of American Drama*. Chicago: Henry Regnery, 1951.

Erhard, Thomas. *Lynn Riggs: Southwest Playwright*. Austin: Steck-Vaughn, 1970.

Sper, Felix. *From Native Roots: A Panorama of Our Regional Drama*. Caldwell, Idaho: The Caxton Printers, 1948.

LESLIE MARMON SILKO

Born: Albuquerque, New Mexico; March 5, 1948

Principal long fiction
Ceremony, 1977; *The Almanac of the Dead*, 1991.

Other literary forms
Though she achieved major recognition with the publication of her first novel, Leslie Marmon Silko is a versatile writer whose short stories and poems are also well known. *Laguna Woman* (1974) is a collection of poems; *Storyteller* (1981) is an autobiographical collection of poems, short stories, photographs, and folktales. She has also written film and television scripts and has published correspondence.

Achievements
Silko is one of the most significant writers who draw upon various aspects of Native American tradition to create a contemporary literature. She brings to her work the sensibility and many of the structures inherent in the Laguna oral tradition. While placed within the context of her native Laguna culture, her works appeal to diverse readers for their insights into not only the marginal status of many nonwhite Americans but also the universal association between land and culture. Though the characters in her novels do not escape the rough fate of many Native Americans, they seek and find strength in ancient rituals. The emphasis on the survival of the Native American peoples through their traditions balances some of the inevitable bitterness about the effects of white society. Silko has also become a major voice in the analysis and understanding of contemporary Native American literature.

Silko has been honored in various ways. Several of her short stories have been anthologized. She won the *Chicago Review* Poetry Award in 1974 and the Pushcart Prize for Poetry in 1977. She has also been awarded major grants from the National Endowment for the Humanities (NEH) and the National Endowment for the Arts (NEA) for her efforts in both film and fiction, and she received a prestigious five-year fellowship from the MacArthur Foundation.

Biography
Leslie Marmon Silko is, like some of her characters, of mixed descent: Laguna Pueblo, Plains Indian, Mexican, and Anglo-American. Born in Albuquerque, New Mexico, in 1948, Silko was reared on the Laguna Pueblo Reservation and attended the schools run by the Bureau of Indian Affairs. In the fourth grade, she went to a private school, the Manzano Day School. Her great-grandmother and other members of her close, extended family passed along the Laguna legends and traditions that are the basis of so much of her writing, a legacy acknowledged in her dedication to both of her grandmothers and her two sons in her first novel. Her father, Lee H. Marmon, was an amateur photographer whose pictures became an integral part of her collection *Storyteller*.

Silko's interest in literature manifested itself during her college years, 1964 to 1969. During that time she published her first short story, "Tony's Story." She was graduated summa cum laude with a degree in English from the University of New Mexico the same year (1969) she published another short story, "The Man to Send Rain Clouds." While an undergraduate, she also married and had her first son, Robert William Chapman. From 1969 to 1971, she continued her studies at the university, this time attending law school; she also had her second son, Cazimir Silko, by former husband John Silko.

With the NEA grant, Silko decided to abandon law and pursue a writing career. She spent 1974 as artist-in-residence at the Rosewater-Foundation-on-Ketchikan Creek in Ketchikan, Alaska. Per Seyersted, a professor of American literature at the University of Oslo in Norway, reports that Silko started her first novel, *Ceremony*, as a form of therapy. While living in Alaska and very depressed to be so far from familiar territory, Silko started the short story that gradually evolved into the full-length novel that brought her national attention. In addition to holding writing residencies in fiction at several universities, she has taught at the Universities of New Mexico and Arizona.

Analysis

In *Ceremony* the main character, Tayo, lies in a hospital bed trying to survive the horrifying memories of war. His tension is expressed in the image of little threads all tangled together, getting more snagged and tangled as he tries to separate and untangle them. The novel is, in a sense, his story of going through the ceremony that helps him to untangle these different threads and understand how they are all part of his life.

Silko's body of work may be said to provide a similar untangling and recombining, both technically and thematically, resulting in publications that are hard to classify in traditional categories but are a stimulating addition to contemporary American literature. She is acknowledged to be one of the major voices emerging from the period in the 1970's sometimes referred to as the Native American Renaissance. What makes her work particularly thought-provoking is the number of different threads represented in her writing: the Native American tradition and the challenges associated with writing from an oral tradition; the contemporary interests in the dangers and values of narratives; the feminist point of view, forged in a dominantly white-female culture, brought to bear on a nonwhite culture.

The thematic need to untangle a knotted, problematic state of affairs, whether it be the affairs of an individual or a society, heeds no boundaries of form in Silko's writings. It is not merely that she is a versatile novelist, poet, and short-story writer; it is that she weaves prose and poetry, folktales and photographs, in her distinctive ways for her own purposes.

In an interview in 1986, Silko said that her writing is an attempt to translate onto a page the feeling, flavor, or sense of a story that has been told and heard, leading her to experiment with the way that words can be set on the page. For her, checklists of the differences between tragedy and comedy may be more valid in critiquing her work than checklists or strict boundary definitions of the differences between poetry and prose. She has referred, as an example, to the remarks on color written by the philosopher Ludwig Wittgenstein, citing them as some of the most beautiful poetry she has read, and so blurring for her the distinction between the prose of philosophy and poetry.

This idea of "translation" is a crucial one for writers, such as Silko, working out of an oral tradition. A key characteristic of stories that are transmitted orally is the combination of fixity and flexibility. The stories must have some stable features to be recognized as the same ones passed down through the ages. As Bernard A.

Hirsch notes, however, the difficulty of writing down such stories is that the printed page "freezes" the words, while in the oral tradition such stories change and grow; the printed word also ignores the context of the story, having removed the story from the place and the people who have helped it to change and grow.

So it is that the collection *Storyteller* is hard to classify, because Silko attempts to confront some of these translation problems by crossing the boundaries of genres. Again, as Hirsch observes, the photographs included in that volume are a means of re-creating some of the contextualization of oral storytelling: They show the reader the landscape and community of the Laguna tribe, as well as the specific members of Silko's family who have carried on the oral tradition. The reader is invited, as much as is possible in such a closed medium as a printed book, to "meet" the people and "be" in the environment that produced the stories. Hirsch's analysis of one section of the collection, a section dubbed the "Yellow Woman" section, suggests Silko's imaginative skill at translation. The central short story of the Yellow Woman is accompanied by four poems, two traditional stories retold, four reminiscences, four photographs, two more stories, and another poem called "Storytelling," which is also based on the same motif as the Yellow Woman stories. Again, the reader gets a glimpse of the great difference between reading a short story to understand it on its own versus reading a short story within the contextualization of a community, permutations and all.

"Yellow Woman" also illustrates another facet of Silko's appeal: her ability to adapt Native American stories to show their nurturing value for modern women. Various Yellow Woman stories are tales of abduction. In its simplest main features, it is the tale of a young woman carried away from her family, in some stories by a benign spirit, in others by an evil one, and forced to perform tasks to stay alive. She eventually returns to her family, either changed in some way or bringing a change to the community. The most fascinating aspect of the tale is that the abduction can be interpreted and understood in a positive light.

Silko's version exhibits the artistic command that re-creates this traditional oral folktale into a highly wrought literary story. First, instead of a narrator, she adopts the first-person viewpoint of the woman to tell the story. Immediately, this change focuses on the sensuality of the story; the nameless narrator's passionate attraction to the stranger becomes paramount, as it is her choice to leave with him. The setting is modernized, so that the stranger turns out to be a cattle rustler who is caught by one of the owners. Urged to flee the scene, she does, and so her return to the family seems less a matter of choice than of necessity, and she continues to yearn secretly for the stranger. The stranger evokes the Yellow Woman story, bringing the past and the present together for the narrator and thus the reader. The woman's confusion blurs the boundary of reality and dream, and that, too, turns her experience into another tale, another permutation of the Yellow Woman stories her grandfather loved to tell.

While *Storyteller*, and the "Yellow Woman" section in particular, may show Silko's virtuosity in discovering the technical means and weaving the different strands to suggest the richness of the Native American storytelling tradition, Silko's novel *Ceremony* may demonstrate the thematic value of such multiplicity. The novel is above all a paean to the importance and meaning of stories in our lives. Before the story of Tayo's journey starts, two poems alert the reader to the power of stories. The first poem, about the Thought-Woman, is a clue to the cosmic power of the thinking and naming that go into creating a story; the second, called "Ceremony," connects stories with rituals and with ceremony as a means of fighting evil.

Storytelling is central to *Ceremony* in that everyone needs stories as a means of survival. Interestingly, the kinds of stories that people choose to tell seem to fall into a natural hierarchy. At the bottom are stories of the truly lost souls of the other Native Americans who served in World War II. For those who survived to come home and tell the tale, the memories point to the bitter racism afflicting them. The war period seems to have been the one time that their uniform and patriotism in service made white society blind to their color. Back in their hometown bar, living off their veterans' checks, they drunkenly relive their days in the big city when they could have all the beer and blonde women they wanted and no one asked if they were Indian. For these veterans, such stories of the past, pathetic as they are, represent their glory days, from which they cannot move on.

Another level of storytelling is also a survival mechanism. A prostitute in the town asks mockingly, "Who listens to the stories wives tell?" Similarly, Tayo's grandmother, who lives with Tayo's aunt, the woman who reluctantly brings him up, is extremely sensitive to the family's position in the community because Tayo's mother had borne him by a Mexican father; hearing a gossipy story, she exclaims in triumph that as long as she has an even better story to tell about someone else, it does not matter what anyone says. Such stories as are commonly called gossip, then, used as tools of retaliation, also help people to survive.

At yet another level, the grandmother also tells the traditional stories that make the landscape come alive. Tayo's long process of healing involves his reconnecting back to the earth, to forget the mockery of the white people and the science teacher who told his class that the Indian tales were superstition. Slowly groping his way back to the past, he sees "a world made of stories, the long ago, time immemorial stories, as old Grandma called them."

Another productive level of storytelling in the novel comes from the unusual medicine man, Betonie, who does help Tayo. Betonie lifts Tayo from the morass of personal pain and loss, first by separating the story of evil from the story of white society. It was Indian witchery that made white people in the first place, Betonie says; a poem recounts this story of the evil witchery that brought death and destruction to the world.

Most important, Betonie reminds Tayo that stories, and the ceremonies that embody them, do not survive unchanged. Things that do not shift and grow, Betonie remembers, are dead things. For Tayo, this knowledge seems to be encapsulated in his insightful connection between the Japanese he was sent out to kill, his alarming perception during the war that his dead uncle was just like the Japanese enemy, and the used-up uranium mines once belonging to the Native Americans, which helped build the atom bomb. The story of the racism and violence that have destroyed so many of his peers and very nearly destroyed him, in short, has to change and shift for him to realize that these forces have also destroyed other people and the earth. Finally, his understanding of the living and loving nature of the earth and the connectedness of all living things helps him to overcome the violence and hatred in himself.

There are those who have criticized Silko for her unflattering portrayal of white society, especially in her second novel, *The Almanac of the Dead*. Her great strength as a storyteller, however, consists of her ability not to get stuck in simply retelling old or simplistic stories. Her personal vantage point as a woman brought up on different traditions woven together seems directly to influence her work technically and thematically. This multiplicity of printed forms and points of view provides an appealing and important contribution to contemporary American literature.

Other major works

POETRY: *Laguna Woman*, 1974.

SHORT FICTION: *Storyteller*, 1981.

PLAY: *Lullaby*, pr. 1976 (with Frank Chin).

NONFICTION: *The Delicacy and Strength of Lace: Letters Between Leslie Marmon Silko and James Wright*, 1986 (Anne Wright, ed.).

Bibliography

Allen, Paula Gunn. *The Sacred Hoop: Recovering the Feminine in American Indian Traditions*. Boston: Beacon Press, 1986.

—————————. *Spider Woman's Granddaughters*. Boston: Beacon Press, 1989.

Coltelli, Laura. "Leslie Marmon Silko." In *Winged Words: American Indian Writers Speak*. Lincoln: University of Nebraska Press, 1990.

Fisher, Dexter. "Stories and Their Tellers: A Conversation with Leslie Marmon Silko." In *The Third Woman: Minority Women Writers of the United States*. Boston: Houghton Mifflin, 1980.

Lincoln, Kenneth. *Native American Renaissance*. Berkeley: University of California Press, 1983.

Seyersted, Per. *Leslie Marmon Silko*. Boise: Boise State University, 1980.

—————————. "Two Interviews with Leslie Marmon Silko." *American Studies in Scandinavia* 13 (1981): 17-33.

GERALD VIZENOR

Born: Minneapolis, Minnesota; October 22, 1934

Principal long fiction

Darkness in Saint Louis Bearheart, 1978; *Griever: An American Monkey King in China*, 1987; *The Trickster of Liberty*, 1988; *The Heirs of Columbus*, 1991; *Dead Voices: Natural Agonies in the New World*, 1992.

Other literary forms

Gerald Vizenor began his writing career as a poet, writing mostly *haiku*. During the 1960's, he published seven books of verse. He contributed poetry to *Voices of the Rainbow* (1975), edited by Kenneth Rosen, and has edited a number of books relating to the Ojibwa Indians. He published autobiographical stories in *Growing up in Minnesota* (1976), edited by Chester Anderson, and *This Song Remembers* (1980), edited by Jane Katz. Vizenor's journalistic articles are collected in *Tribal Scenes and Ceremonies* (1976); his essays about his people appear in *Crossbloods: Bone Courts, Bingo, and Other Reports* (1990). Finally, the prolific Vizenor is the author of numerous short stories.

Achievements

In the twenty years between 1960 and 1980, Vizenor contributed prolifically to the literature of Native Americans, helping to establish the identity of the Ojibwa-Chippewa tribe in American history and letters. He preserved songs and stories, part of the rich oral tradition of Native Americans that could have been lost had he not collected them. Vizenor's major efforts during these two highly productive decades were directed toward preserving a culture, establishing the identity of that culture within the broader context of American letters, and writing creatively out of that rich cultural setting.

It was not until the 1980's that Vizenor came into his own as a novelist. His first novel, *Darkness in Saint Louis Bearheart*, attracted little critical attention when it was published in 1978, but his second novel, *Griever: An American Monkey King in China*, won the Fiction Collective Award of Illinois State University in 1986 and was published the following year. In 1988, this book, precisely right for its time because it reflected not only Native American culture but also the cultural upheaval in post-Maoist China, won the American Book Award. *The Trickster of Liberty* followed in 1988.

The Heirs of Columbus, a fanciful, somewhat histori-

cal novel, appeared in 1991 in time for the quincentenary of Christopher Columbus' voyage to the New World. The next year, Vizenor published *Dead Voices: Natural Agonies in the New World*, a highly experimental novel that, like most of his fiction, is nonlinear in its presentation of events. It is this nonlinear presentation of somewhat interrelated events that distinguishes Vizenor's fiction and that reflects the Native American mind-set and identity he depicts.

Biography

Gerald Vizenor invented the term "crossblood," which accurately describes his lineage. He was born into the Ojibwa nation, a crossblood member of the Chippewa tribe. His actual birth took place in Minneapolis, where his parents, Clement William and LaVerne Peterson Vizenor, were living.

Vizenor fulfilled his military obligation between 1952 and 1955. He was stationed for a part of his enlistment in Japan, where he became interested in and began to write *haiku*. Upon his discharge, he entered New York University, where he remained for a year before transferring to the University of Minnesota. He was awarded a bachelor's degree in 1960.

Having worked from 1957 to 1958 in the Ramsey County Corrections Authority of Saint Paul, Minnesota, Vizenor continued this line of work at the Minnesota State Reformatory in Saint Cloud during 1960 and 1961. He married Judith Helen Horns, an instructor at the University of Minnesota, in 1959 and began graduate studies there in 1962.

Through his work in penal institutions, Vizenor gained a considerable understanding of the kinds of tensions that exist between Native Americans and the dominant, white culture. His insights into this situation deepened between 1968 and 1970, when he was a staff writer for the *Minneapolis Tribune*.

Vizenor's marriage, which produced a son, Robert Thomas, ended in divorce in 1969. The following year, he left the newspaper and worked in teacher training for the Park Rapids Public Schools. He also taught at Bemidji State University and Lake Forest College prior to moving to the University of California at Berkeley in 1976, where he remained as a lecturer until 1980, when he returned to the University of Minnesota as a professor of American Indian studies. The following year, he married Laura Jane Hall.

Vizenor remained in Minneapolis until 1987, when he accepted a position as professor of literature and American studies at the University of California at Santa Cruz. He was also appointed a Fellow at Porter College, remaining in Santa Cruz until returning in the early 1990's to Berkeley as professor of ethnic studies.

Immediately preceding the Tiananmen Square uprising in the People's Republic of China, Vizenor spent several months as a visiting professor at the University of Tianjin. This experience resulted in *Griever: An American Monkey King in China*. Teaching in China helped Vizenor appreciate the universality of the Native American myths he had heard as a child.

Dedicated to preserving the Native American identity through literature and realizing the urgency of preserving this rapidly disappearing identity, Vizenor was among the founders of the American Indian Literature and Critical Studies Series of the University of Oklahoma Press and serves as its general editor. His *Dead Voices: Natural Agonies in the New World*, the second offering of this series, captures well the animistic nature of Ojibwa-Chippewa mythology, relating it to similar animistic crosscurrents in other mythologies, including those of the circumpolar natives of the Arctic regions.

Analysis

Vizenor ranks high among the most challenging contemporary writers. His work is important for its astute sociopolitical observations, for the subtlety of its content, and for its inventive and original use of language, an area in which Vizenor is still struggling and experimenting. One can classify Vizenor as a postmodern, poststructuralist writer whose emphasis is more on form and ideas than on individual characters. Vizenor's main focus is on broad cultural concerns in America and on the continuing conflict between the two societies with which he is primarily concerned.

It is best for readers new to Vizenor to read his first five novels in chronological order. Vizenor's characters recur from novel to novel and are referred to meaningfully in the later novels but in less detail. Unfamiliarity with the earlier novels reduces understanding of those

that follow. An exception to the value of a chronological reading is *The Trickster of Liberty*. It is unnecessary to read the various episodes of this novel sequentially because the chapters are often discrete pieces that can be read in any order without reducing comprehension and appreciation. The narrative frame between which these chapters fall, prologue and epilogue, reflects a pattern found in much of the older literature from which Vizenor sometimes borrows.

One of Vizenor's major emphases in all of his writing has been that of the trickster tradition in Native American culture. The trickster is a presence, sometimes lurking, sometimes prominent, in all Vizenor's novels, often resulting in incongruities that may confuse some readers unfamiliar with the contradictions and inconsistencies that necessarily occur when tricksters are at work in a narrative.

It is not easy for most mainstream American readers to understand the Native American frame of reference. Vizenor has not adapted his stories to the literary conventions of the dominant culture. Rather, he remains true to his own culture, depicting it as forthrightly and authentically as he can.

Vizenor, however, does not limit his writing to the oral sources through which most Native American culture has been conveyed. Employing his literary background studiously, he draws upon literary sources from various ages and cultures as he creates his stories. He wants more than merely to reproduce in written form the oral traditions of his forebears.

In the Western literatures with which most American readers are familiar, identifiable stimuli result in understandable actions and reactions. Vizenor often does not identify the stimuli from which the actions and reactions in his novels proceed, which results in some initial confusion for readers unfamiliar with the Native American mind-set.

The points of reference that most mainstream American writers provide for readers are often absent from Vizenor's fiction. Yet such references, were they provided, would not reflect the Native American way of dealing with reality. Vizenor's chief objective is to work toward developing new modes of expression that replicate as authentically as possible Native American modes of storytelling.

Darkness in Saint Louis Bearheart, which plays out in an apocalyptic setting some two or three decades in the future, is in a class with Doris Lessing's Canopus in Argus series, Margaret Atwood's *The Handmaid's Tale* (1985), and Ursula Le Guin's *A Wizard of Earthsea*

(1968) or *Tehanu: The Last Book of Earthsea* (1990). Vizenor's novel presages the environmental devastation of the United States accompanied by a total economic collapse.

This earliest of Vizenor's novels is a biting satire sustained by a penetrating irony of which Vizenor is obviously a master. By combining the social and political forces of mainstream culture with elements of his Native American culture, Vizenor produces a chilling prognostication of what lies in store for Americans. He reveals keen insights into the conundrums of life in contemporary Western society, especially when these issues are viewed from the perspective of Native Americans. These ironies pervade Vizenor's later novels and are perhaps most strenuously expounded in *The Trickster of Liberty*, in which the humor has an underlying element of sadness about it and in which the conflicting forces of contemporary civilization are clearly visible.

Critics have attacked Vizenor for the violence and sexuality that characterize much of his writing. He has countered such attacks by pointing out that he considers it unhealthy to suppress these elements of the human condition. In interviews, he has asserted that those who are not exposed to violence in literature are ill-equipped to deal with it in real life. The danger for such people is that they will allow unexpected violence to control them.

Certainly violence is not absent from the most significant and enduring literature that has ever been produced—from the early Greek and Roman tragedies to the plays of William Shakespeare, Thomas Kyd, and Christopher Marlowe to the fairy tales of the Brothers Grimm and the most significant plays and novels of such modern American writers as Tennessee Williams, William Inge, Edward Albee, Ernest Hemingway, William Faulkner, and John Steinbeck, all of whom have been attacked for the violence and brutality of some of their writing. The fact remains that violence is a fundamental part of human existence. In Vizenor's case, its depiction lends to his writing the verisimilitude that all serious writers hope to achieve.

One of Vizenor's major artistic quests has been to devise new, untried ways of working with language. He wants to shake loose the bonds of conventional grammar and push language to its most unimagined extremes. Although he has not yet achieved all that he hopes to in reinventing ways to structure language, he is moving strenuously and consciously to achieve unique ways of structuring the language in which he writes.

As part of this experimentation, he has intermingled tribal language with English. His collection of tales *Wordarrows* is an initial step in the direction of creating drastically new modes of expression, but much of that collection has baffled readers quite significantly. Although in *Griever* Vizenor at times commingles English and Chinese, the results there are somewhat more successful than those in *Wordarrows*, possibly because *Griever*, structurally, is Vizenor's most conventional novel to date.

In *The Heirs of Columbus*, Vizenor commingles fact and fiction in ways that have alarmed some readers and critics. This novel contains a great deal of factual history accurately reported, but it also distorts history to serve Vizenor's literary ends. Because it is difficult to separate truth from fiction in this novel, many readers have found the book quite bewildering, Vizenor's imaginative daring notwithstanding.

Other major works

SHORT FICTION: *Wordarrows: Indians and Whites in the New Fur Trade*, 1978; *Earthdivers: Tribal Narratives on Mixed Descent*, 1981.

POETRY: *Poems Born in the Wind*, 1960; *The Old Park Sleepers*, 1961; *Two Wings the Butterfly*, 1962; *South of the Painted Stone*, 1963; *Raising the Moon Vines*, 1964; *Seventeen Chirps*, 1964; *Empty Swings*, 1967.

NONFICTION: *Tribal Scenes and Ceremonies*, 1976; *Narrative Chance: Postmodern Discourse on Native American Indian Literatures*, 1989; *Crossbloods: Bone Courts, Bingo, and Other Reports*, 1990; *Interior Landscapes: Autobiographical Myths and Metaphors*, 1990.

MISCELLANEOUS: *Escorts to White Earth, 1868-1968: 100 Year Reservation*, 1968; *Thomas James White Hawk*, 1968; *The Everlasting Sky*, 1972; *Manifest Manners: Postindian Warriors of Survivance*, 1994.

EDITED TEXT: *Summer in the Spring: Ojibwe Lyric Poems and Tribal Stories*, 1981; *Touchwood: A collection of Ojibway Prose*, 1987.

Bibliography

Boyarin, Jonathan. "Europe's Indian, America's Jew: Modiano and Vizenor." *boundary 2* 19 (Fall, 1992): 197-222.

Bruchac, Joseph. *Survival This Way: Interviews with American Indian Poets*. Tucson: University of Arizona Press, 1987.

Hochbruck, Wolfgang. "Breaking Away: The Novels of Gerald Vizenor." *World Literature Today* 66 (Spring, 1992): 274-278.

Krupat, Arnold, and Brian Swann, eds. *Recovering the Word: Essays on Native American Literature*. Berkeley: University of California Press, 1987.

Martin, Calvin, ed. *The American Indian and the Problem of History*. New York: Oxford University Press, 1987.

Monaghan, Peter. "A Writer 'To Be Reckoned With.'" *Chronicle of Higher Education* 60 (July 13, 1994): A8, A12.

Vizenor, Gerald. "Head Water: An Interview with Gerald Vizenor." Interview by Larry McCaffrey and Tom Marshall. *Chicago Review* 39, nos. 3-4 (1993): 50-54.

_____ . *Interior Landscapes: Autobiographical Myths and Metaphors*. Minneapolis: University of Minnesota Press, 1990.

_____ . "An Interview with Gerald Vizenor." Interview by Neal Bowers and Charles P. Silet. *MELUS* 8 (Spring, 1981): 41-49.

Wiget, Andrew. "Narrative Chance: Postmodern Discourse on Native American Indian Literatures." *Modern Philology* 88 (May, 1991): 476-479.

JAMES WELCH

Born: Browning, Montana; November 18, 1940

Principal long fiction
Winter in the Blood, 1974; *The Death of Jim Loney*, 1979; *Fools Crow*, 1986; *Indian Lawyer*, 1990.

Other literary forms

Although it is for long fiction that James Welch is best known, he began his literary career as a poet; his first book, *Riding the Earthboy 40* (1971), is a collection of fifty-three poems. He has published very few poems since, but after finishing his third novel he expressed the intention to devote more time to poetry.

Achievements

Welch is widely regarded as among the most important Native American writers. In 1969, only two years after publishing his first poem, he received the first of several major awards for his literary accomplishments, a National Endowment for the Arts Fellowship in poetry. His first novel, *Winter in the Blood*, originally received mixed reviews but has steadily gained admirers and has come to be acknowledged as a comic masterpiece of contemporary Indian life. His second novel is generally regarded as less successful, but his third novel, *Fools Crow*, a historical re-creation of the Blackfeet Indian culture of the nineteenth century, won many important awards, most notably an American Book Award, a Pacific Northwest Booksellers' Award, and the *Los Angeles Times* Book Prize. In addition, Welch has held the Theodore Roethke Chair at the University of Washington, and, among only a handful of Native American writers, he has transcended the boundaries of ethnic and regional fiction to achieve mainstream status as indicated by the inclusion of his work in major anthologies of American literature.

Biography

James Welch is of mixed Irish and Native American heritage, with Blackfeet forebears in his father's family and Gros Ventre in his mother's. He was born on November 18, 1940, on the Blackfeet Indian Reservation in the small town of Browning, Montana, on the high plains just east of Glacier National Park. During World War II, while his father was away serving in the U.S. Army, James's mother moved with James and his older brother to Portland, Oregon, where she worked in a factory. After the war, both parents went to work for the Indian Service, spending three years in Alaska before returning to Montana, first to Browning and later to the Fort Belknap Reservation. Thus, during his most formative years young James lived on and around reservations, went to reservation schools, and absorbed the many details of his environment. With the exception of a few poems, all Welch's work deals with Indian themes and characters, reflecting his interest in and extensive knowledge of Indian culture.

On the Fort Belknap Reservation, the family tried ranching before moving to South Dakota and then to Minneapolis, where Welch graduated from high school. Finally, the family moved back to Montana, where he has lived more or less continuously since he was seventeen. He had begun writing poems in high school, and he continued writing poetry through his college years, first at the University of Minnesota and then at Northern Montana College, but only "as a diversion." It was not until he transferred to the University of Montana at Missoula and took a writing course from the noted poet Richard Hugo, whom he regards as his major literary influence, that Welch came to think of himself as a writer and began seriously to devote himself to poetry. In 1972, a year after the publication of *Riding the Earthboy 40*, Welch visited Greece, where he completed the manuscript of *Winter in the Blood*.

Returning to Montana, Welch settled on a ranch near Missoula, where his wife, Lois, teaches at the University of Montana. He has worked as a laborer, firefighter, and counselor, but he now devotes himself mostly to writing fiction. He occasionally teaches creative writing and contemporary American Indian literature at the University of Washington in Seattle, and in 1985 he went East to spend a year teaching at Cornell University in Ithaca, New York. Also important to his literary development were the ten years he served on the Montana State Board of Pardons, during which time he gained insights into prison life that are reflected in his fourth novel, *Indian Lawyer*.

Analysis

Welch has devoted himself to writing about a little-known group of people, the Blackfeet Indians, and a little-known geographical area, Blackfeet country in northwestern Montana, where he was born and now lives. He succeeds in crafting convincing characters about whom the reader comes to care, he presents their experiences with an unflinching realism, but also with great sensitivity, and he delineates the landscape sharply and with a keen eye for the precisely effective detail. Although the Native American experience and land are his subjects, he is not primarily a militant or protest writer; he is a chronicler of human experience and of the connections between human beings and the environment.

In many ways, *Winter in the Blood* is his masterpiece even though it is the most self-consciously "literary" of his novels and the one in which his literary influences are most apparent, growing as it does out of the confluence of literary surrealism, Freudian psychology, and existentialism. *Winter in the Blood* also demonstrates Welch at his tragicomic best, exploiting a vein of humor touched again in *Fools Crow* but largely absent from *The Death of Jim Loney* and *Indian Lawyer*. Even more central to the novel, however, is the theme of Indian identity and the importance of tradition, themes that are explored at greater length in *Fools Crow*.

The nameless narrator of *Winter in the Blood* suffers from the emotional condition suggested by the title—he is incapable of caring about anything or anyone, even himself. He feels alienated, distanced from everything: "But the distance I felt came not from country or people; it came from within me. I was as distant from myself as a hawk from the moon. And that was why I had no particular feelings toward my mother and grandmother. Or the girl who had come to live with me."

As the novel develops, the reader becomes aware through a series of fragmentary flashbacks that the narrator's emotions have been paralyzed and numbed by the repressed trauma of his older brother's death and the guilt he feels because of a misconceived sense of responsibility for it. At the same time, the narrator believes himself to be of mixed white and Blackfeet heritage and thus does not have a true sense of Indian identity. Thematically, Welch implies that the problems that beset his narrator—aimlessness, alcoholism, alienation, apathy—are those that beset Indian people in general. Moreover, the solution to these problems, if there is one, lies in facing up to the past, as the narrator eventually faces up to his brother's death, and in finding

an authentically Indian identity, as the narrator does when he discovers that he is actually a full-blood rather than the half-breed he had thought himself to be. As *Winter in the Blood* ends, the narrator seems to have begun a healing process that may eventually enable him to find a sense of self-respect and a purpose in life.

Although admitting that a summary of the plot "does not sound very funny," Alan R. Velie argues that *Winter in the Blood* is essentially a comic work in which the "humor varies from raucous farce to subtle satire" and "informs every corner of the novel." Most of the humor results from a combination of bleakness and absurdity, as in the final scene—the grandmother's funeral—when it turns out that the grave is not large enough for the coffin and the narrator's stepfather climbs down into the hole and jumps "up and down on the high end. It went down a bit more, enough to look respectable."

Humor is entirely absent from Welch's next novel, *The Death of Jim Loney*, which is in many ways an exploration of what would have happened to the narrator of *Winter in the Blood* if he had not discovered his Indian identity and found dignity and meaning in it. As Jim Loney's name suggests, he is also alienated, mostly because as a person of mixed blood he feels like an outsider in both the Indian and the white worlds. Loney unintentionally kills a hunting companion, is accused of murder, accepts his guilt in the shooting, and puts himself in a position to be killed by the police when he refuses to surrender to them. He wants to die and arranges things so that the police will kill him, thematically representing the bleak alternative to the healing achieved by the narrator in *Winter in the Blood*. As Lewis Owens points out, "In *The Death of Jim Loney* Welch turned his focus upon a mixedblood protagonist for whom the past was inexorably unknowable and irretrievable, making the future impossible."

In his third novel, *Fools Crow*, Welch re-creates the traditional Blackfeet way of life, emphasizing its spiritual dimensions and mysticism in the persons of the old medicine man Mik-api and the young warrior Fools Crow, who ultimately chooses to become Mik-api's apprentice. In this novel, Welch mixes historical characters with fictional ones, achieving an ethnologically accurate as well as fictionally convincing portrayal of the Blackfeet people. The daily lives of the tribe are balanced against the increasingly threatening and divisive incursions of the white men into Indian territory. The traditional way of life provides a source of spiritual strength, dignity, resolve, and purpose in the face of adversity for young Fools Crow, in dramatic contrast to the weakness and self-doubts of the central characters in the previous novels. Moreover, as in *Winter in the Blood*, within the serious framework there are many humorous scenes. Above all, in this novel Welch demonstrates the positive aspects of the traditional Blackfeet way of life, aspects that make preserving what can still be preserved of it worthwhile.

Welch's fourth novel, *Indian Lawyer*, returns to contemporary Indian life, but this time the central character, the young Blackfeet lawyer Sylvester Yellow Calf, who like Welch himself serves on the Montana Board of Pardons, is a success rather than an alienated loser like the central characters in *Winter in the Blood* and *The Death of Jim Loney*. In this novel, Welch develops the theme of the responsibility successful Indians have to their people and to themselves. Yellow Calf demonstrates a strength of character that shows him to be the contemporary counterpart of young Fools Crow in the previous novel. The former represents the modern embodiment of the traditional Blackfeet hero.

Since Welch's novels are set in the same rather restricted area, his central characters are young Blackfeet (or part Blackfeet) men, and his plots involve Indian heritage, it might seem that the appeal of his work would be rather limited, but this has not proved to be the case. His spare, terse, understated style, which reflects the same precision, clarity, and sharply defined imagery characteristic of his poetry, has attracted many readers, and his characters embody universal attitudes and emotions that make them interesting not only as Indians but also as recognizably familiar human beings.

Other major works

POETRY: *Riding the Earthboy 40*, 1971.
EDITED TEXT: *The Real West Marginal Way: A Poet's Autobiography*, 1986 (Lois Welch and Ridley Hugo, coeds.).

Bibliography

Bruchac, Joseph, ed. *Survival This Way: Interviews with American Indian Poets*. Tucson: University of Arizona Press, 1987.

Larson, Charles R. *American Indian Fiction*. Albuquerque: University of New Mexico Press, 1978.

Lincoln, Kenneth. *Native American Renaissance*. Berkeley: University of California Press, 1983.

Owens, Louis. *Other Destinies: Understanding the American Indian Novel*. Norman: University of Oklahoma Press, 1992.

Ruoff, A. LaVonne. *American Indian Literatures: An Introduction, Bibliographic Review, and Selected Bibliography*. New York: Modern Language Association, 1990.

_____ . *Literatures of the American Indian*. New York: Chelsea House, 1991.

Sands, Kathleen M. "Alienation and Broken Narrative in *Winter in the Blood*." *American Indian Quarterly* 4 (1978): 97-106. Reprinted in Andrew Wiget, ed., *Critical Essays on Native American Literature*. Boston: G. K. Hall, 1985.

Velie, Alan R. *Four American Indian Literary Masters*. Norman: University of Oklahoma Press, 1982.

Wiget, Andrew. *Native American Literature*. Boston: Twayne, 1985.

Wild, Peter. *James Welch*. Boise State University Western Writers Series 57. Boise, Idaho: Boise State University, 1983.

II

A CITY SET UPON A HILL
American Identities in the Northeast

The land was ours before we were the land's.
—Robert Frost, "The Gift Outright," 1936

Speaking in 1630 to the Puritans who would establish the Massachusetts Bay Colony, John Winthrop used the phrase "a city set upon a hill" to articulate his vision of what this new settlement was to be: visible to all, an emblem of the acceptance of God's sovereignty by the elect and an example of a community based on Christian piety. Three recurrent themes of American identity are implicit in Winthrop's declaration. The first is the theme of American newness; what is here represented has never before been known on earth. The second is the theme of the American destiny; these European settlers manifestly have been led here for a purpose. The third is the theme of American exceptionalism; in carrying out its sacred destiny, America will not fall prey to the forces that have made the fall of civilizations the great subject of history.

This was, to the Puritan mind, the American promise. It was, of course, a promise that would not be fulfilled. William Bradford's *History of Plymouth Plantation, 1620-47*, his account of the settlement begun ten years before the initiation of the Massachusetts Bay Colony, is a record of the failure of that settlement to realize its vision. By the end of the seventeenth century, the hold of Puritanism on the New England mind had dramatically weakened. Yet the themes and promises we ascertain in the words of the Puritans continue to reverberate in the American imagination, resting just below the surface of our consciousness, ever ready to emerge, to the present day. They are part of America's continuing rhetoric of crisis and resolution.

The discernment of the divine purpose, the Puritans believed, is the task imposed on God's elect. Because the corrupt human mind is incapable of knowing the divine nature directly, everything depends on a true understanding of the signs God has granted us. The first of these is the revelation transmitted through sacred scripture; these were people of the word. Further, uncompromising introspection may give us some hint of where we stand with God. Moreover, God makes himself known to humankind through the book of nature; God's created world reflects his essence and indicates his purposes for us.

The belief that the minute examination of nature will lead to the divine has remained constant in American literature. When the Puritan Anne Bradstreet, America's first considerable poet, tried to place her perceptions of everyday life in the colony in the context of ultimate truth, derived for her from the tenets of Puritanism, she inaugurated a recurrent concern of American writers.

That concern certainly informed the work of many of the writers whose coming to maturity in the middle of the nineteenth century has been celebrated as the American Renaissance. None of these writers was in any strict sense a Puritan. Ralph Waldo Emerson, the most important figure among them, found even the liberal Unitarian pulpit too confining. Why, he asked, must we look for revelation only in the records and observations of our ancestors? Can there not be a revelation original to ourselves?

That revelation could be found in nature. In the minute examination of nature, we arrive ultimately at the unifying vital principle that is the soul of nature itself, and that we might as well call God. The God Emerson announces is scarcely the God of the Puritans.

Yet the process of finding this God parallels the Puritan attempt to read aright the book of nature.

This same God may be located within the self. It is, in fact, what is deepest in the self. The notion that an exploration of the deepest recesses of the self is the way to God echoes the Puritan emphasis on introspection, even though, once again, the Emersonian God is a God of possibilities, of liberation, rather than the restrictive deity of the Puritan imagination.

It is because what is deepest in the self is God that we may, as Emerson tells us, rely on the self. In fact, self-reliance becomes an Emersonian imperative, and its rule is severe. In his address "The American Scholar," delivered to the Phi Beta Kappa society of Harvard College in 1837, Emerson celebrated the impending cultural independence of the New World from the Old; the address remains a key document in the evolution of a national literature. Yet even in that oration, and more explicitly in his essay "Self-Reliance," Emerson enunciated a still more radical notion of independence. If, as he insists, to be a man one must be a nonconformist, then the individual self must declare independence from America itself. But the rejection of conformity is not sufficient; we must also reject consistency. That is, we must not permit ourselves to be bound today by what we thought or said yesterday. We must be willing to declare our independence from the selves we have been, risking the spiritual isolation this suggests. For Emerson, the risk is exhilarating; for others, it could be terrifying. In any event, much of our American literature since Emerson has been devoted to the exploration of that risk, that exhilaration, and that terror; and to other themes—some, as we have seen, in clear continuity with the concerns of the Puritans—that Emerson brought to the center of the American imagination.

Just how central Emerson was is clear when we remember that writers of the stature of Henry David Thoreau, Margaret Fuller, Nathaniel Hawthorne, Herman Melville, Walt Whitman, and Emily Dickinson wrote much of their most important work in response or relation, however complex or ambivalent, to Emerson and to the Emersonian "Transcendentalism" that has become a constant of American literature. In the twentieth century as well, the Emersonian presence has continued to be felt in poets such as Robert Frost, Wallace Stevens, William Carlos Williams, and Allen Ginsberg. Documents of the Harlem Renaissance of the 1920's, and of the quest for a Black Aesthetic of the 1960's and after, suggest that the Emersonian spirit does not speak only to Americans of European ancestry. Ralph (Waldo) Ellison's *Invisible Man* (1952), a major work of African American fiction, can also be read as the greatest Transcendentalist novel America has yet produced.
anscendentalism

The Puritan and Transcendentalist traditions, both finding their origin in New England, define to a significant degree what we may call a New England identity and contribute to the formation of an American identity. But the great Transcendentalist impulse belongs to literary nationalism, a declaration of an American identity requiring something like an outright rejection of a European influence that might smother a literature still struggling to be born. Assurance that America had moved from cultural independence to cultural maturity required a reopening of literary relations with Europe. Here again, the Northeast played a significant role, although the emphasis shifted from New England to New York. A new cosmopolitanism, an assurance that America could enter into cultural commerce with Europe on an equal footing, finds expression in the fiction, criticism, and essays of Henry James.
anscendentalism

That James was ultimately to assume the role, not merely of cosmopolitan but of expatriate, is inescapably part of the story and accounts for his being included in this volume's section on expatriate writers, "Americans Abroad." For some, no writer is more American than James; surely no writer of fiction has been more obsessed with the struggle to define an American identity. Yet, from another point of view, James might seem to illustrate the alienation from the American mainstream that, for many, characterizes the artists of the Northeast, and especially of New York. In fact, of course, expatriates come from all over; Carl Sandburg waggishly described T. S. Eliot as the greatest English poet ever born in St. Louis, Missouri. Yet the sense that our Northeastern writers stand somehow apart from the heart of America has persisted. Perhaps the explanation lies in a matter of tone, which we may call the New Yorker attitude—or even the *New Yorker* attitude.

Many of the more recent writers most strongly associated with the Northeast have found an outlet for their work in *The New Yorker*, possibly the most important American literary magazine of the twentieth century. J. D. Salinger, John Cheever, and John Updike are among those who have appeared in its pages. The magazine has undergone changes in the course of its history, but every attempt to delineate that history reminds us that in its initial prospectus *The New Yorker* declared that it was not for the little old lady in Dubuque.

To a middle-American ear, and not just in Dubuque, that must sound like elitism. But if elitism is undeniably a part of the New York identity as it manifests itself in literary form, let us remember that New York is, in a way, a city set upon a hill. It is surely the most visible of American cities, and its literary community shares with the Puritan visionaries of the seventeenth century a sense of mission, of an obligation to stand as an example to the wilderness. That community also shares with the Transcendentalists a revulsion toward conformity, an insistence on the integrity of the self. And the cosmopolitan spirit represented by Henry James involves still a willingness to expose national pieties to the critique of international perspectives.

As the faith of America's Puritan settlers recedes, it becomes increasingly challenging to define just what the city is to be an example of. Few New York writers of the present day would, without irony, make the Emersonian claim that what is deepest within the self is nothing less than God. Toward the end of the twentieth century, population shifts, economic upheaval, industrial decline, and technological change have threatened to move New York, along with the rest of the Northeast, away from the culturally central position it has so long enjoyed. The region's sense of a special identity and a special destiny, the sense already articulated by the Puritans, has endured some telling blows, and from the regional perspective it may seem that the center cannot hold. Yet through all phases of American literature, no region of the country has contributed more to shaping an American identity.

—*W. P. Kenney*
Manhattan College

LOUIS AUCHINCLOSS

Born: Lawrence, New York; September 27, 1917

Principal long fiction

The Indifferent Children, 1947; *Sybil*, 1951; *A Law for the Lion*, 1953; *The Great World and Timothy Colt*, 1956; *Venus in Sparta*, 1958; *Pursuit of the Prodigal*, 1959; *The House of Five Talents*, 1960; *Portrait in Brownstone*, 1962; *The Rector of Justin*, 1964; *The Embezzler*, 1966; *A World of Profit*, 1968; *I Come as a Thief*, 1972; *The Partners*, 1974; *The Winthrop Covenant*, 1976; *The Dark Lady*, 1977; *The Country Cousin*, 1978; *The House of the Prophet*, 1980; *The Cat and the King*, 1981; *Watchfires*, 1982; *Exit Lady Masham*, 1983; *The Book Class*, 1984; *Honorable Men*, 1985; *Diary of a Yuppie*, 1986; *The Golden Calves*, 1988; *Fellow Passengers*, 1989; *The Lady of Situations*, 1990.

Other literary forms

While best known as a novelist, Louis Auchincloss has been a prolific and successful writer in a variety of other literary forms. Among his strongest collections of short fiction are *The Romantic Egoists* (1954), *Powers of Attorney* (1963), and *Tales of Manhattan* (1967), each of which presents stories linked by narration, characters, or theme in such a way as to resemble a novel. An accomplished critic, Auchincloss has published studies of a wide range of writers, from William Shakespeare to Edith Wharton; among his best-known critical works are *Reflections of a Jacobite* (1961) and *Reading Henry James* (1975). *Life, Law, and Letters: Essays and Sketches* (1979) consists chiefly of essays on literary subjects, while the autobiographical memoir *A Writer's Capital* (1974) provides valuable insight into the formation of Auchincloss' outlook. Finally, Auchincloss has published several heavily illustrated biographies or group biographies intended for a general readership; among these works are *Richelieu* (1972), *Persons of Consequence: Queen Victoria and Her Circle* (1979), *False Dawn: Women in the Age of the Sun King* (1984), and *The Vanderbilt Era: Profiles of a Gilded Age* (1989).

Achievements

During the 1950's, Auchincloss emerged as a strong social satirist and novelist of manners, rivaling in his best work the accomplishments of John Phillips Marquand and John O'Hara. Unlike those writers, however, Auchincloss was clearly an "insider" by birth and breeding, belonging without reservation to the social class and power structure that he so convincingly portrayed. With the waning of the tradition represented by figures such as Marquand and O'Hara, Auchincloss stands nearly alone as an American novelist of manners, unrivaled in his analysis of social and political power.

Freely acknowledging his debt to Henry James and Edith Wharton as well as to Marcel Proust and the Duc de Saint-Simon, Auchincloss continues to transform the stuff of success into high art, providing his readers with convincing glimpses behind the scenes of society and politics where top-level decisions are often made for the most personal and trivial of reasons. As a rule, his featured characters are credible and well developed, if often unsympathetic; Auchincloss' apparent aim is to describe what he has seen, even at the risk of alienating readers who care so little about his characters as not to wonder what will become of them. At the same time, Auchincloss' characteristic mode of expression leaves him open to accusations that he is an "elitist" writer, featuring characters who are almost without exception white, Anglo-Saxon, and Protestant. Such accusations, however, do little to undermine the basic premise that emerges from the body of Auchincloss' work: for good or for ill, the people of whom he writes are those whose decisions and behavior have determined the shape of the American body politic.

Biography

Louis Stanton Auchincloss was born September 27, 1917, in Lawrence, New York, where he spent his entire life except for his years of education and military service. A graduate of the prestigious Groton School, he entered Yale University in 1935 with plans to become a writer, only to withdraw several months short of graduation in 1939 after his initial efforts at publication had been rejected. Deciding instead to pursue a career in law, he received his LL.B. degree from the University of Virginia in 1941 and worked briefly for the firm of Sullivan and Cromwell in new York City before joining the Navy, from which he emerged in 1945 with the rank of lieutenant.

Returning to Sullivan and Cromwell after World War II, Auchincloss again tried his hand at creative writing, this time with demonstrable success. In 1951, he withdrew from the practice of law and devoted himself to writing full time, only to decide after some three years that law and literature were indeed compatible, even symbiotic, and that the writer's life excluding all other pursuits was a bore. In 1954, he returned to the practice of law with the Manhattan firm of Hawkins, Delafield, and Wood, of which he became a partner in 1958. The previous year, he had married the former Adele Lawrence, to whom he has since dedicated several of his publications. Three children were born to them: John Winthrop Auchincloss in 1958, Blake Leay Auchincloss in 1960, and Andrew Sloane Auchincloss in 1963. Auchincloss retired from Hawkins, Delafield, and Wood in 1986.

Analysis

For a writer with a full-time professional career, Louis Auchincloss has been astoundingly prolific, producing nearly one book of fiction or nonfiction each year since the age of thirty. Like that of many highly prolific writers, the quality of his work is decidedly uneven. At his best, however, Auchincloss meets and surpasses the standard set by J. P. Marquand and John O'Hara for twentieth century American social satire, displaying a resonant erudition that somehow eluded the two older writers even in their brightest moments. Even in the best of his novels, the results of Auchincloss' erudition are sometimes too conspicuous for the reader's comfort, but they can easily be overlooked in favor of the authenticity displayed by characters portrayed in convincing situations.

Auchincloss' reputation as a major writer rests primarily on novels written during the 1960's, a time somewhat past the vogue of social satire in the United States but coinciding neatly with the author's full maturity: The worst of his mistakes were behind him, and he had not yet experienced the temptation to repeat himself. In 1960, Auchincloss broke new ground with *The House of Five Talents*, ostensibly the memoirs, composed in 1948, of the septuagenarian Miss Gussie Millinder, heiress and survivor of an impressive nineteenth century New York fortune. The author's demonstrated skill at characterization and narration served

clear notice of his new, mature promise, soon to be fulfilled with *Portrait in Brownstone*, *The Rector of Justin*, and *The Embezzler*, any one of which would suffice to confirm Auchincloss' reputation as the successor to O'Hara and Marquand as a master observer of American society.

A New Yorker by proclivity as well as by birth, Auchincloss remains, above all, a New York novelist; his characters, like their author, spend most of their time in the metropolis, leaving it only for such traditional watering-places as Newport and Bar Harbor, or for higher civic duty in Washington, D.C. The author's sense of place serves to illustrate and to explain the dominant role traditionally played by New Yorkers in the shaping of American society.

In the first work of his "mature" period, *The House of Five Talents*, Auchincloss undertakes a personal record of upper-level Manhattan society through the still-perceptive eyes of one Augusta Millinder, age seventy-five, whose immigrant grandfather, Julius Millinder, founded one of the less conspicuous but more durable of the major New York fortunes. The Millinders had, by the time of Augusta's birth in 1873, established a position of quiet dominance, based upon diversified investments. The world in which Augusta and her more attractive elder sister Cora grew to maturity was thus one of easy movement and understated privilege, pursued frequently aboard yachts and in private railroad cars. As a memoirist, Augusta remains securely inside the closed world that she describes, yet she is privileged to have a gift for shrewd observation.

As the second and less attractive of two daughters, "Gussie" Millinder learned at an early age to view male admiration with a jaundiced eye. Indeed, the only man to whom she ever became engaged had proposed several years earlier to her vacuous sister Cora, who subsequently married a French prince. Although it seems likely that Lancey Bell, a rising young architect, has proposed to Gussie in good faith, she remains so skeptical that she breaks the engagement, having developed such inner resources that she no longer believes marriage to be necessary or desirable. In fact, the marriages in and around Gussie's family do little to encourage her faith in that institution. Soon after ending her engagement, Gussie becomes a reluctant participant in the dismantling of her own parents' marriage and household. Her father, aged sixty, has become enamored of a former actress half his age and wishes to marry her, supported in his folly by Gussie's older brother Willie and sister-in-law Julia.

Although the divorce and remarriage eventually take place as planned, Gussie has discovered in the meantime her own increasingly formidable talent for high-minded meddling. She has also begun to explore the extent of a freedom uniquely available to rich and well-read spinsters. Although dissuaded from attending college in her youth, she has taken enough courses at Columbia during her early adulthood to qualify her for part-time teaching in a private school. Later, around the age of forty, she becomes deeply involved in volunteer work. By 1948, when she at last addresses herself to her memoirs, she has led a life both independent and fulfilling, but not without its disappointments.

Appropriately, Gussie's greatest disappointments have less to do with spinsterhood than with her various relatives, many of whom seem to have a singular talent for ruining their lives, at least when measured by Gussie's demanding but forgiving standards. Gussie's personal favorite appears to have been her nephew Lydig, a versatile and talented former army flight instructor who tries his hand at various pursuits successfully but without commitment, only to seek fulfillment in a life of adventure. Having taken up mountain-climbing, he dies in an avalanche around the age of thirty, a year before the stock market crash of 1929.

The changes wrought by the Depression and its consequences upon the Millinders are recorded with a sympathetic but dispassionate eye by Gussie, whose own personal fortune is sufficiently great to sustain major loss without requiring more than minimal changes in her privileged life-style. Among the few things she is obliged to forfeit is her private railroad car, while the chauffeured limousine remains. To the others, Gussie remains a rock of stability in a river of change, able to avert disaster with a well-placed loan (or gift) and a bit of timely meddling. At seventy-five, however, she admits that her interventions have not always been the right ones, much as they may have seemed so at the time. Several marriages remain broken beyond all possible repair and certain of her cousins face congressional investigation for their leftist sympathies.

Self-aware, yet not too much so for credibility, Gussie Millinder remains one of Auchincloss' most engaging narrators and one of his most satisfying creations, combining in her large and slightly outrageous person the best qualities of observer and participant in the action that she records.

In *The Rector of Justin*, Auchincloss manages to broaden the appeal of the novel through his choice of subject matter, focusing upon the concept and execution of the American preparatory school. In analyzing the life and career of one Francis Prescott, founder of "Justin Martyr, an Episcopal boys' boarding school thirty miles west of Boston," Auchincloss provides through various viewpoint characters a thoughtful examination of a powerful American institution.

The main narrator is Brian Aspinwall, whose arrival at Justin coincides with the outbreak of World War II in Europe. Brian has recently returned to the United States after several years of study at Oxford, where doctors have diagnosed a heart murmur that renders him unfit for service in the British Army. Unsure as yet of his vocation to become an Episcopal priest, Brian welcomes the prospect of teaching at Justin as an opportunity to test his suitability for the priesthood as well as for teaching, another possibility. Drawn gradually deeper into the affairs of the school and its founder-headmaster, Brian records his observations and experiences in a journal that forms the backbone of the book. Later, as the idea of recording the school's history begins to take form in his mind, he includes the testimony—both oral and written—of Dr. Prescott's family, friends, and former students.

By the time of Brian's arrival, Francis Prescott is nearly eighty years of age and long overdue for retirement; as both founder and headmaster, however, he is such an institution that no one has given serious thought to replacing him. Brian vacillates between admiration and harsh criticism for the old man and his "muscular Christianity." To Brian's incredulity, the aging Prescott remains unfailingly democratic in pronouncements both public and private, seemingly unaware of the fact that he and his school have helped to perpetuate an American class system that Prescott personally deplores. This basic irony continues to animate the novel, providing as it does the subject matter for Brian's continuing research.

Early in the novel, Brian learns that Prescott, as a young man, took pains to examine at close range the British public-school system preparatory to founding a boarding school of his own; at no point does Prescott or anyone near him appear to have considered the difference between British aristocracy and American democracy. In fact, many of the questions raised in Brian's mind are left hanging, at least for the reader, calling attention to the anomalous role of private education in America. Prescott, for his part, continues to deny the existence of an American ruling class even when faced with evidence to the contrary from his own alumni rolls.

Brian's continuing research gradually uncovers a

wealth of conflicting evidence concerning Prescott's accomplishment. It is clear in any case that the realization of Prescott's lifelong dream has been achieved only at great personal cost. Brian finds the darker side of Justin's history both in a document penned by the long-dead son of the school's charter trustee, on whose behalf Prescott's efforts failed miserably, and in the spoken recollections of Prescott's youngest daughter, ironically named Cordelia. When Brian meets her, Cordelia is in her middle forties, an unreconstructed Greenwich Village bohemian with nymphomaniacal tendencies that, on one occasion, send Brian fleeing for his life. Prescott, it seems, did much to ruin not only her early first marriage but also a later liaison with a mortally wounded veteran of World War I. Cordelia ascribes much of her unhappiness to the fact that both men, as "old boys" of Justin Martyr, perceived a higher obligation to her father than to herself.

Ending with Prescott's death in retirement at age eighty-six, *The Rector of Justin* concludes much as it began, undecided as to the ultimate value of Prescott's achievement. Brian, however, has made a decision; now a fully ordained priest, he continues as a member of the faculty at Justin Martyr.

Together with *The House of Five Talents, The Rector of Justin* stands as one of Auchincloss' more impressive accomplishments; in few of his other novels are the interdependent questions of privilege and responsibility discussed with such thoughtfulness or candor. If the book has a major weakness it is that the characters, especially Prescott himself, are often stretched so flat as to strain the reader's belief; even then, it is possible to accept flatness in the case of a character who adamantly refuses to admit life's ambiguities.

Published some two years after *The Rector of Justin, The Embezzler* builds on the author's known strengths to provide a strong social satire. Recalling in its essentials one of the subplots in *The House of Five Talents*, wherein Gussie Millinder reluctantly covers the defalcations of a distant relative threatened with exposure. *The Embezzler* re-creates the heyday of high finance in America before, during, and after the crash of 1929.

The title character and initial narrator of *The Embezzler* is Guy Prime, writing in 1960 to set straight the record of his notoriety some twenty-five years earlier. His antagonist and eventual successor as narrator is Reginald (Rex) Geer, an erstwhile friend and associate since college days. The gathering tension between the two men, reflected in the conflict between their recollections of the same events, provides the novel with its major human interest. "Yes," reflects Guy Prime in the early pages of the novel,

> . . .they would all cut me dead in the street today, my old friends. Rex Geer, who might be a haberdasher in Vermont but for our Harvard friendship, would turn away his stony countenance and splash me with the wheels of his Rolls-Royce. Alphonse de Grasse, his partner, and one of my old golf foursome, might furtively nod as he hurried by, but only if he was sure that Rex's glassy eye was not upon him.

Throughout the novel, it is up to the reader to weigh conflicting testimony and to form his or her own considered judgments.

Grandson of a former Episcopal bishop of New York, Guy Prime has grown up less rich than other of Auchincloss' main characters. His breeding and Harvard education, however, qualify him to function competently at the upper reaches of Manhattan's financial establishment. His classmate Rex Geer, the son of a rural New England parson, is perhaps even better suited than Guy to the "art" of making money. Rex is not, however, a social climber; to interpret him as such, as a number of the characters do, is to oversimplify a personality of multiple and often conflicting motivations. Guy, for his part, is hardly less complex, an essentially humane man whose interactions with his fellow mortals are inevitably compounded by a flair for the dramatic and a tendency toward hero-worship.

From the start, the friendship of Guy Prime and Rex Geer is complicated by their interlocking relationships with women whom neither man quite understands. The first of these is Guy's wealthy cousin Alix Prime, a doll-like heiress with whom Rex falls suddenly and disastrously in love, quite to his own consternation. Although ambitious and industrious, Rex is immune to the blandishments of inherited wealth and quite undone by the common opinion that he covets Alix for her money. The second woman is Guy's wife Angelica, reared mainly in Europe by her expatriate mother. An affair in middle life between Rex and Angelica permanently alters the lives of all three characters, serving at least in part as Guy's justification for his ventures into thievery. To Guy's way of thinking, the affair between his wife and his best friend suffices to suspend his belief in permanent values; the fact remains, however, that Guy has already begun to borrow large sums of money from Rex to cover high-risk stock market activities. With the increase of risk, Guy "simply" begins to pledge the value of securities that have been left in trust with his firm.

Later testimony supplied by Rex (and by Angelica herself in a short concluding chapter) casts serious doubt upon some of the assertions made by Guy in the brief memoir that has been discovered following his death in 1962. Even so, there are few hard-and-fast answers to the questions that remain in the reader's mind. Auchincloss does not make any serious attempt to justify the plainly unethical conduct of his principal character; what he seeks, rather, is a credible re-creation of a significant moment in recent American history, leading immediately to the extensive financial reforms implemented by the administration of Franklin D. Roosevelt. To a far greater degree than in his earlier novels, Auchincloss presents characters caught and portrayed in all their understandably human ambiguity. Despite its limited scope and relative brevity, *The Embezzler* may well be the tightest and finest of Auchincloss' novels.

In his long and prolific career as a writer, Auchincloss has continued to explore the exercise of power and responsibility in American society. His reputation, however, rests primarily on his masterworks of the 1960's—*The House of Five Talents*, *The Rector of Justin*, *The Embezzler*—in which he achieved the fullest and most deftly nuanced expression of his characteristic themes.

Other major works

SHORT FICTION: *The Injustice Collectors*, 1950; *The Romantic Egoists*, 1954; *Powers of Attorney*, 1963; *Tales of Manhattan*, 1967; *Second Chance*, 1970; *Narcissa and Other Fables*, 1983; *Skinny Island: More Tales of Manhattan*, 1987; *False Gods*, 1992; *Three Lives*, 1993; *Tales of Yesteryear*, 1994; *The Complete Short Stories of Louis Auchincloss*, 1994.

NONFICTION: *Reflections of a Jacobite*, 1961; *Pioneers and Caretakers: A Study of Nine American Women Novelists*, 1965; *Motiveless Malignity*, 1969; *Edith Wharton: A Woman in Her Time*, 1971; *Richelieu*, 1972; *A Writer's Capital*, 1974; *Reading Henry James*, 1975; *Life, Law, and Letters: Essays and Sketches*, 1979; *Persons of Consequence: Queen Victoria and Her Circle*, 1979; *False Dawn: Women in the Age of the Sun King*, 1984; *The Vanderbilt Era: Profiles of a Gilded Age*, 1989; *J. P. Morgan: The Financier as Collector*, 1990; *The Style's the Man: Reflections on Proust, Fitzgerald, Wharton, Vidal, and Others*, 1994.

Bibliography

Bryer, Jackson R. *Louis Auchincloss and His Critics*. Boston: G. K. Hall, 1977.

Dahl, Christopher C. *Louis Auchincloss*. New York: Frederick Ungar, 1986.

Kane, Patricia. "Lawyers at the Top: The Fiction of Louis Auchincloss" *Critique: Studies in Modern Fiction* 7 (Winter, 1964-1965): 36-46.

Milne, Gordon. *The Sense of Society*. Rutherford, N.J.: Fairleigh Dickinson University Press, 1977.

Parsell, David D. *Louis Auchincloss*. Boston: Twayne, 1988.

ANNE BRADSTREET

Born: Northampton, England; 1612(?) **Died:** Andover, Massachusetts; September 16, 1672

Principal poetry

The Tenth Muse Lately Sprung Up in America, 1650; *Several Poems Compiled with Great Variety of Wit and Learning*, 1678.

Other literary forms

Anne Bradstreet's published collections in 1650 and 1678 consist entirely of poetry, and her reputation rests on her poems. She left in manuscript the prose "Meditations Divine and Morall" (short, pithy proverbs) and a brief autobiography written especially for her children.

Achievements

Bradstreet is one of the two foremost Colonial American poets (the other being Edward Taylor). One of Bradstreet's distinctive poetic strengths is her generic variety. She wrote epics, dialogues, love lyrics, public elegies, private elegies, a long meditative poem, and religious verse. Few other Puritan poets successfully tackled so many genres.

Although Bradstreet's contemporaries admired her early imitative poetry and the elegies, her later personal poetry is what endures (and endears). Poems included in *The Tenth Muse Lately Sprung Up in America* fall within an essentially Renaissance tradition, while those in *Several Poems Compiled with Great Variety of Wit and Learning* initiate a distinctive tradition of American literature. Bradstreet's love poems to her husband are admired for their wit, intricate construction, emotional force, and frank admission of the physical side of marriage. Bradstreet's personal elegies on her grandchildren skillfully dramatize the Puritans' unremitting battle between worldliness (grieving for the dead) and unworldliness (rejoicing in their salvation). But her masterpiece is probably her long meditative poem, "Contemplations," praised for its maturity, complexity, and lyricism. Her love poems, personal elegies, and "Contemplations" reveal the human side of Puritanism from a woman's vantage point.

Biography

Through her poetic voices, Bradstreet assumes a clear (but complex) presence, yet factual data about her are surprisingly scant. Joseph McElrath, editor of *The Complete Works of Anne Bradstreet* (1981), shows that even her birth date is uncertain. She was probably born in 1612 in Northampton, England, but may have been born as late as 1613, one of Thomas Dudley and Dorothy Yorke's six children.

In 1619 the family moved to Sempringham, where Dudley became steward to the earl of Lincoln. Both Dudley and his employer allowed the prospective poet an unusually good education for a woman. Scholars even speculate that she had access to the earl's library. There she may have read William Shakespeare, Sir Philip Sidney, Sir Walter Raleigh, Du Bartas, and Cervantes. In 1621, Simon Bradstreet joined the earl's household to assist Dudley; in 1624, the Dudleys moved to Boston, England, and Simon Bradstreet left to work for the countess of Warwick.

When Anne was about sixteen, as she records in her autobiographical prose, "the Lord layd his hand sore upon me & smott mee with the small pox." After her recovery in 1628, she and Simon Bradstreet married, and two years later, the Dudley and Bradstreet families left for America aboard the *Arbella*.

For Anne Bradstreet, the transition was not entirely smooth, and her prose autobiography speaks of "a new World and new manners at which my heart rose, But after I was convinced it was the way of God, I submitted to it & joined to the chh., at Boston." After brief spells in Salem, Boston, Cambridge, and Ipswich, Massachusetts, the Bradstreets moved to North Andover, where Anne Bradstreet reared eight children, wrote, and shared her husband's life as he rose from judge to governor of the colony. Although she was susceptible to many illnesses and was childless for several years, her supremely happy marriage compensated for, and helped her to overcome, these hardships.

As the governor's wife, Bradstreet enjoyed a socioeconomic status conducive to writing. In the mid-1640's, Bradstreet had completed the poems that appeared in her first collection. She herself did not supervise their printing; John Woodbridge, her brother-in-law, probably carried the manuscript to London, where it was published in 1650. Bradstreet expresses mixed feelings about its publication, largely because of the printing errors. The poem "The Author to Her Book" mildly chides "friends, less wise than true" who exposed the work "to publick view." Poems in the collection are mainly public in tone and content, while those in her second collection (published posthumously in 1678) are mainly private and personal.

Bradstreet was a known, respected, and loved poet in both the Old and the New worlds. Her death in 1672 called forth elegies and eulogies. These lines from the preface to *The Tenth Muse Lately Sprung Up in America*, probably written by Woodbridge, best convey Bradstreet's qualities: "It is the Work of a Woman, honoured, and esteemed where she lives, for her gracious demeanour, her eminent parts, her pious conversation, her courteous disposition, [and] her exact diligence in her place."

Analysis

Bradstreet wrote poetry from the 1640's to her death in 1672. The critic Kenneth Requa's distinction between her public and private poetic voices is a useful way to assess her poetic development. Her public voice, which dominates the early poetry, is eulogistic, imitative, self-conscious, and less controlled in metaphor and structure. Most of the poems in *The Tenth Muse Lately Sprung Up in America* illustrate these traits. Her private voice—more evident in *Several Poems Compiled with Great Variety of Wit and Learning*—is often elegiac, original, self-confident, and better controlled in metaphor and structure. Here it is convenient to consider representative elegies from three roughly chronological stages: "poetic" involvement, conventional involvement, and personal involvement.

Almost all the verse in her first collection conveys Bradstreet's public poetic involvement. Specifically, in secular poems such as the "Quaternions," "The Four Monarchies," and the elegies on famous Elizabethans, Bradstreet as professional poet or bard dominates and controls. "In Honour of Du Bartas" contains the typical Renaissance characteristics of public content, imitative style, classical allusions, and secular eulogy. The poem's content could hardly be more public, since it dutifully details the accomplishments of Bradstreet's mentor Du Bartas—his learning, valor, wit, and literary skill. The "Quaternions"—a quartet of long poems on the four elements, the four humors, the four ages of

humanity, and the four seasons—and the interminable rhymed history "The Four Monarchies" are similarly public in content.

An extension of public content and bardic involvement is imitative style. For example, "In Honour of Du Bartas" contains conventional images such as the simile comparing Bradstreet's muse to a child, the hyperbole declaring that Du Bartas' fame will last "while starres do stand," and the oxymoron in "senslesse Sences." In the three elegies on Du Bartas, Sidney, and Queen Elizabeth I, classical allusions are a conventional part of the Renaissance pastoral elegy, and in the "Quaternions" allusions imitate the medieval/Renaissance debates.

Finally, these lengthy early poems may contain secular eulogy, also a characteristic of the pastoral elegy, and hyperbole, common in the debate form. The opening lines of "In Honour of Du Bartas," for example, state that Du Bartas is "matchlesse knowne" among contemporary poets. In such a richly literary age, Bradstreet uses hyperbole and eulogy to emphasize Du Bartas' greatness for her.

The second phase—conventional involvement—includes religious poems within a public or orthodox context. A few poems (such as "David's Lamentations for Saul" and "Of the vanity of all worldly creatures") are from *The Tenth Muse Lately Sprung Up in America*; more are from her second collection (the elegies on Thomas and Dorothy Dudley and "The Flesh and the Spirit," for example). In this poetry, Bradstreet moves closer to mainstream Puritan verse. The elegies on her parents are conventionally formal and fit the pattern of the New England funeral elegy, whose hallmark was public praise of the dead one's life and virtues to overcome personal grief. "The Flesh and the Spirit," "As weary pilgrim, now at rest," and "Of the vanity of all worldly creatures" treat the theme of worldliness versus unworldliness generally and impersonally to reach unorthodox conclusions.

Standard, often biblical, imagery is another distinct aspect of the second phase. While this imagery is to some extent present in the earlier and later phases, it is particularly evident in the middle stage. In the first stage, Bradstreet's images are traditionally Renaissance, and in the third stage, they are biblical but infused with emotive and personal force. The elegy on Thomas Dudley illustrates the traditionally biblical images found in phase two: Dudley has a "Mansion" prepared above; like a ripe shock of wheat, he is mown by the sickle Death and is then stored safely. The other orthodox poems also use biblical images almost exclusively. Appropriately, in these poems, Bradstreet generally excludes the personal voice. Only "As weary pilgrim, now at rest," the theme of which is the heaven-bound soul housed within the "Corrupt Carcasse," succeeds in combining the general and individual situations.

Universality and individuality form the special strength of Bradstreet's masterpiece, "Contemplations." This thirty-three-verse meditative poem fits best into the second stage because of its spiritual content. Bradstreet skillfully evokes a dramatic scene—she walks at dusk in the countryside—then uses it to explore the relationships among man, God, and nature. In stanzas 1-7, the poet acknowledges nature's potency and majesty by looking first at an oak tree and then at the sun. If they are glorious, she muses, how much more glorious must their creator be? Stanzas 8-20 recall humanity's creation and fall, extending from Adam and Eve to Cain and Abel and finally to Bradstreet's own day. The answer to humanity's misery, however, is not nature worship. Instead, humanity must acknowledge that God made it alone for immortality. In stanzas 21-28, the poet considers the amoral delight of nature—the elm, the river, the fish, and the nightingale—incapable of the tortures of free will. Stanzas 29-33 show that beyond the natural cycle, only humanity ("This lump of wretchedness, of sin and sorrow," as the poet states) can be resurrected within the divine cycle.

"Contemplations" contains some of Bradstreet's most original and inspired poetry within the three-part structure of the seventeenth century meditation. These parts correspond to the mental faculties of memory, understanding, and will. In the first part, the person creates or recalls a scene; in the second part, he analyzes its spiritual significance; and last, he responds emotionally *and* intellectually by prayer and devotion. Clearly, these are the three basic structural elements of "Contemplations." Although Bradstreet ultimately returns to orthodoxy, this poem is no mere religious exercise; it is "the most finished and musical of her religious poems."

The third phase of Bradstreet's poetry includes love lyrics, elegies on grandchildren and a daughter-in-law, and other works inspired by private matters (the burning of Bradstreet's house, the publication of her first collection, the poet's eight children). Yet, unlike the poems of the previous stage, which are overwhelmingly spiritual, the poems of the third phase are primarily secular. If they deal with religious matters—as the elegies do, for example—it is within a personal context. One critic calls Bradstreet "the worldly Puritan," and these late poems show the material face of Puritanism. Bradstreet's personal involvement affects structure, tone, rhythm, and metaphor. "In memory of my dear grand-child Elizabeth Bradstreet" illustrates many of these changes.

A marked difference in the poetry of the third phase is its tone. Instead of sounding self-conscious, bookish, derivative, over-ambitious, or staunchly orthodox, Bradstreet's later poetry is poised, personal, original, modest, and unwilling to accept orthodoxy without question. Another tonal change is subtlety, which the elegy on Elizabeth illustrates well. Throughout the poem Bradstreet hovers between the worldly response of grief and the unworldly one of acceptance. This uneasy balance, finally resolved when Bradstreet accepts God's will, makes the elegy especially poignant. The poet's other late elegies on her grandchildren Anne and Simon and her daughter-in-law Mercy are also poignant. The secular love poetry that Bradstreet wrote to her husband—often while he was away on business—conveys playfulness, longing, and, above all, boundless love. The tone of Bradstreet's late poetry tends to be more varied and complex than the tone of her early poetry, the only notable exception being "Contemplations," placed in phase two.

Bradstreet's rhythm reflects her increased poetic self-confidence. Gone are the strained lines and rhythms characteristic of the "Quaternions" and "The Four Monarchies"; instead, the opening lines of Bradstreet's elegy on Elizabeth show how private subject matter lends itself to natural, personal expression: "Farewel dear babe, my hearts too much content,/ Farewel sweet babe, the pleasure of mine eye,/ Farewel fair flower that for a space was lent,/ Then ta'en away unto Eternity." The delicate antithesis in lines 1-3 and the repetition of "Farewel" add emotional force to the content and emphasize Bradstreet's difficulty in accepting Elizabeth's death. The other late elegies are rhythmically varied and use antithesis to underscore life's everpresent duality: worldliness/unworldliness, flesh/ spirit. For example, within the elegy on three-year-old Anne, Bradstreet conveys her problem in coming to terms with yet another grandchild's death when she uses this forced, monosyllabic rhythm, "More fool then I to look on that was lent./ As if mine own, when thus impermanent." The love poetry is also written with special attention to rhythmic variety.

Bradstreet's poetry has always been known, but now,

more than ever, critics agree on her importance as one of the two foremost Colonial poets. Until recently, scholarship focused on biographical and historical concerns. Modern criticism, on the other hand, concentrates on structure, style, theme, and text. This move toward aesthetic analysis has deepened scholarly appreciation of Bradstreet's talent. In addition, the rise of women's studies ensures her place as a significant female voice in American poetry.

Other major works

MISCELLANEOUS: *The Complete Works of Anne Bradstreet*, 1981 (Joseph R. McElrath and Allan P. Robb, eds.).

Bibliography

Cowell, Pattie, and Ann Stanford, eds. *Critical Essays on Anne Bradstreet*. Boston: G. K. Hall, 1983.

Hammond, Jeffrey A. *Sinful Self, Saintly Self: The Puritan Experience of Poetry*. Athens: University of Georgia Press, 1993.

Martin, Wendy. *An American Triptych: Anne Bradstreet, Emily Dickinson, Adrienne Rich*. Chapel Hill: University of North Carolina Press, 1984.

Piercy, Josephine K. *Anne Bradstreet*. New York: Twayne, 1965.

Requa, Kenneth A. "Anne Bradstreet's Poetic Voices." *Early American Literature* 9 (1974): 3-18.

Rich, Adrienne. "Anne Bradstreet and Her Poetry." Foreword to *The Works of Anne Bradstreet*. Cambridge, Mass.: The Belknap Press of Harvard University Press, 1967.

Rosenmeier, Rosamond. *Anne Bradstreet Revisited*. Boston: Twayne, 1991.

Stanford, Ann. *Anne Bradstreet: The Worldly Puritan*. New York: Burt Franklin, 1974.

Tyler, Moses C. *A History of American Literature During the Colonial Period*. New York: G. P. Putnam's Sons, 1897.

White, Elizabeth Wade. *Anne Bradstreet: The Tenth Muse*. New York: Oxford University Press, 1971.

JOHN CHEEVER

Born: Quincy, Massachusetts; May 27, 1912   **Died:** Ossining, New York; June 18, 1982

Principal short fiction

The Way Some People Live, 1943; *The Enormous Radio and Other Stories*, 1953; *The Housebreaker of Shady Hill and Other Stories*, 1958; *Some People, Places and Things That Will Not Appear in My Next Novel*, 1961; *The Brigadier and the Golf Widow*, 1964; *The World of Apples*, 1973; *The Stories of John Cheever*, 1978; *Thirteen Uncollected Stories by John Cheever*, 1994.

Other literary forms

Believing that "fiction is our most intimate and acute means of communication, at a profound level, about our deepest apprehension and intuitions on the meaning of life and death," John Cheever devoted himself to the writing of stories and novels. Although he kept voluminous journals, he wrote only a handful of essays and even fewer reviews, and only one television screenplay, *The Shady Hill Kidnapping*, which aired January 12, 1982, on the Public Broadcasting Service (PBS). A number of Cheever's works have also been adapted by other writers, including several early short stories such as "The Town House" (play, 1948), "The Swimmer" (film, 1968), "Goodbye, My Brother" as *Children* (play, 1976), and "O Youth and Beauty," "The Five-Forty-Eight," and "The Sorrows of Gin" (teleplays, 1979). Benjamin Cheever has edited selections of his father's correspondence, *The Letters of John Cheever* (1988), and journals, *The Journals of John Cheever* (1991).

Achievements

A major twentieth century novelist, Cheever has achieved even greater fame as a short-story writer. He published his first story, "Expelled," in *The New Republic* when he was only eighteen. Reviewers of his first collection, *The Way Some People Live*, judged Cheever to be a promising young writer. Numerous awards and honors followed: two Guggenheim grants (1951, 1961), a Benjamin Franklin award for "The Five-Forty-Eight" (1955), an O. Henry Award for "The Country Husband" (1956), election to the National Institute of Arts and Letters in 1957, elevation to the American Academy in 1973, a National Book Award in 1958 for *The Wapshot Chronicle* (1957), the Howells Medal in 1965 for *The Wapshot Scandal* (1964), cover stories in *Time* (1964) and *Newsweek* (1977), the Edward MacDowell Medal in 1979, a Pulitzer Prize and a National Book Critics Circle award (both in 1978), an American Book Award (1979) for *The Stories of John Cheever*, and the National Medal for Literature (1982). Cheever's achievements, however, cannot be measured only in terms of the awards and honors that he has received (including the honorary doctorate bestowed on this high school dropout), for his most significant accomplishment was to create, with the publication of *The Stories of John Cheever*, a resurgence of interest in, and a new respect for, the short story on the part of public and publishers alike.

Biography

The loss of his father's job in 1930, followed by the loss of the family home and the strained marital situation, caused, Cheever believed, by his mother's growing financial and emotional dependence, all had a lifelong effect on Cheever. When he was expelled from Thayer Academy at the age of seventeen, he was already committed to a writing career. His career, however, would do little to assuage his sense of emotional and economic insecurity. Although he liked to claim that "fiction is not crypto-autobiography," from the beginning his stories were drawn from his personal experiences. They have even followed him geographically: from New England to New York City through his military service to the suburbs (first Scarborough, then Ossinging), with side trips to Italy (1956-1957), the Soviet Union (on three government-sponsored trips), and Sing Sing prison, where he taught writing (1971-1972). The stories have more importantly followed Cheever over hazardous emotional terrain, transforming personal obsessions into published fictions: alcoholism, bisexuality, self-doubts, strained marital relations, and the sense of "otherness." The stories also evidence the longing for stability and home that manifested itself in three of the most enduring relationships of his fifty-year career: with the Yaddo writers colony in Saratoga Springs, New York (beginning in 1934); with *The New Yorker* (which began publishing his work in 1935); and with his wife Mary Winternitz Cheever (whom he met in 1939 and married two years later, and with whom he bickered over the next forty years).

Cheever did not become free of his various fears and dependencies—including his nearly suicidal addiction to alcohol—until the mid-1970's. After undergoing treatment for alcoholism at Smithers Rehabilitation Center, he transformed what might well have become his darkest novel into his most affirmative. *Falconer* (1977) was both a critical and a commercial success. Like its main character, Cheever seemed for the first time in his lie free, willing at least to begin talking about the private life that he had so successfully guarded, even mythified before, when he had played the part of country squire. The triumph was, however, short-lived: two neurological seizures in 1980, a kidney operation and the discovery of cancer in 1981, and, shortly after the publication of his fifth novel, the aptly and perhaps whimsically titled *Oh What a Paradise It Seems* (1982), his death on June 18, 1982.

Analysis

In 1988, Scott Donaldson, author of the first substantial biography of John Cheever, observed that his novels and stories "tell us more about people in the American middle class during that half century [1930-1980] than any other writer's work has done or can do." Cheever has justly been praised as a master chronicler of a way of life that he both celebrates and satirizes in stories that seem at once conventional and innovative, realistic and fantastic. The stories offer a series of brilliant variations on a number of basic, almost obsessive themes, of which the most general and the most recurrent as well as the most important is the essential conflict between his characters' spiritual longings and social and psychological (especially sexual) nature. "What I wanted to do," one of his narrator-protagonists says, is "to grant my dreams, in so incoherent a world, their legitimacy," "to celebrate," as another claims, "a world that lies spread out around us like a bewildering and stupendous dream." Their longings are tempered not only by the incoherence of their world but also by a doubt concerning whether what they long for actually exists or is rather only an illusion conjured out of nothing more substantial than their own ardent hopes for something or some place or someone other than who, what, and where they presently are.

Whether treated comically or tragically, Cheever's characters share a number of traits. Most are male, married, white-collar workers. All—despite their Sutton Place apartments or, more often, comfortable homes in affluent Westchester communities—feel confused, dispossessed, lost; they all seem to be what the characters in Cheever's Italian stories actually are: expatriates and exiles. Physical ailments are rare, emotional ones epidemic. Instead of disease, there is the "dis-ease" of "spiritual nomadism." They are as restless as any of Cheever's most wayward plots and in need of "building a bridge" between the events in their lives as well as between those lives and their longings. Trapped in routines as restricting as any prison cell and often in marriages that seem little more than sexual battlefields, where even the hair curlers appear "bellicose," his characters appear poised between escaping into the past in a futile effort to repeat what they believe they have lost and aspiring to a lyrical future that can be affirmed, even "sung," though never quite attained. Even the latter can be dangerous. "Dominated by anticipation" (a number of Cheever's characters hope excessively), they are locked in a state of perpetual adolescence, unwilling to grow up, take responsibility, and face death in any form. Although their world may lie spread out like a bewildering and stupendous dream, they find it nevertheless confining, inhospitable, even haunted by fears of emotional and economic insecurity and a sense of personal inadequacy and inconsequentiality. Adrift in an incoherent world and alone in the midst of suburbs zoned for felicity, they suffer frequent blows to their already fragile sense of self-esteem, seeing through yet wanting the protection of the veneer of social decorum and ceremoniousness that is the outward and visible sign of American middle-class aspiration and which Cheever's characters do not so much court as covet.

The thinness of that veneer is especially apparent in "The Enormous Radio," a work that shows little trace of the Hemingway style that marks many of Cheever's earlier stories. The story begins realistically enough. Jim and Irene Westcott, in their mid-thirties, are an average couple in all respects but one: their above-average interest in classical music (and, one assumes, in the harmony and decorum that such music represents). When their old radio breaks down, Jim generously buys an expensive new one to which Irene takes an instant dislike. Like their interest in music, which they indulge as if a secret but harmless vice, this small disruption in their harmonious married life seems a minor affair, at least at first. The radio, however, appearing "like an aggressive intruder," shedding a "malevolent green light," and possessing a "mistaken sensitivity to discord," soon becomes a divisive, even diabolical presence, but the evil in this story, as in Nathaniel Hawthorne's "Young Goodman Brown," to which it has often been compared, comes from within the characters, not from without (the radio). When the radio begins to broadcast the Westcotts' neighbors' quarrels, lusts, fears, and crimes, Irene becomes dismayed, perversely entertained, and finally apprehensive; if she can eavesdrop on her neighbors' most intimate conversations, she thinks that perhaps they can listen in on hers. Hearing their tales of woe, she demands that her husband affirm their happiness. Far from easing her apprehensiveness, his words only exacerbate it as he first voices his own previously well-guarded frustrations over money, job prospects, and growing old, and as he eventually exposes his wife's own evil nature. As frustration explodes into accusation, the illusion of marital happiness that the Westcotts had so carefully cultivated shatters.

"O Youth and Beauty" makes explicit what virtually all Cheever's stories imply, the end of youth's promise. Thus it seems ironically apt that "O Youth and Beauty" should begin with a long (two-hundred-word) Whitmanesque sentence, which, in addition to setting the scene and establishing the narrative situation, subtly evokes that Transcendental vision that Walt Whitman both espoused and, in his distinctive poetic style, sought to embody. Beginning "at the tag end of nearly every long, large Saturday night party in the suburb of Shady Hill," it proceeds through a series of long anaphoric subordinate clauses beginning with the word "when" and ending with "then Trace Bearden would begin to chide Cash Bentley about his age and thinning hair." The reader is thus introduced to what, for the partygoers, has already become something of a suburban ritual: the perfectly named Cash Bentley's hurdling of the furniture as a way of warding off death and reliving the athletic triumphs of the youth that he refuses to relinquish. When Cash, now forty, breaks his leg, the intimations of mortality begin to multiply in his morbid mind. Although he may run his race alone, and although the Lawrentian gloominess that comes in the wake of the accident may make him increasingly isolated from his neighbors and friends, Cash is not at all unique, and his fears are extreme but nevertheless representative of a fear that pervades the entire community and that evidences itself in his wife's trying to appear younger and slimmer than she is and her "cutting out of the current copy of *Life* those scenes of mayhem, disaster, and violent death that she felt might corrupt her chil-

dren." It is rather ironic that a moment later she should accidentally kill her husband in their own living room with the starter's pistol as he attempts to recapture the past glories of all those other late Saturday night races against time and self when he was a young track star. The track is in fact an apt symbol for Cash's circular life, in which, instead of progress, one finds only the horror of Nietzschean eternal recurrence.

Upon first reading, "The Five-Forty-Eight" seems to have little in common with the blackly humorous "O Youth and Beauty." A disturbed woman, Miss Dent, follows Blake, whose secretary she had been for three weeks and whose lover she was for one night, some six months earlier. She trails him from his office building to his commuter train. Threatening to shoot him, she gets off at his stop and forces him to kneel and rub his face in the dirt for having seduced and abandoned her six months earlier. One of Cheever's least likable characters, Blake gets what he deserves. Having chosen Miss Dent as he has chosen his other women (including, it seems, his wife) "for their lack of self-esteem," he not only had her fired the day after they made love but also took the afternoon off. Miss Dent fares considerably better, for in choosing not to kill Blake she discovers "some kindness, some saneness" in herself that she believes she can put to use. Blake too undergoes a change insofar as he experiences regret for the first time and comes to understand his own vulnerability, which he has heretofore managed to safeguard by means of his "protective" routines and scrupulous observance of Shady Hill's sumptuary laws. Whether these changes will be lasting remains unclear; he is last seen picking himself up, cleaning himself off, and walking home, alone.

"The Five-Forty-Eight" is one of Cheever's darkest stories; only the dimmest of lights and the faintest of hopes shine at its end. Although it too ends at night, "The Housebreaker of Shady Hill" is one of Cheever's brightest and most cheerful works, full of the spiritual phototropism so important in *Falconer*, the novel *Newsweek* hailed as "Cheever's triumph." The housebreaker is thirty-six-year-old Johnny Hake, kindly and comical, who suddenly finds himself out of work, at risk of losing his house, his circle of friends, and the last shreds of his self-esteem. Desperate for cash, he steals nine hundred dollars from a neighbor, a theft that transforms his vision of the world. Suddenly, he begins to see evil everywhere and, of course, evidence that everyone can see him for what he now is. The "moral bottom" drops out of his world but in decidedly comic fashion:

Even a birthday gift from his children—an extension ladder—becomes an acknowledgment of his wrong-doing (and nearly cause for divorce). Chance, however, saves Johnny. Walking to his next victim's house, he feels a few drops of rain fall on his head and awakens from his ludicrous nightmare, his vision of the world restored. Opting for life's simple pleasures (he is after all still unemployed), he returns home and has a pleasant dream in which he is seventeen years old. Johnny cannot get his youth back, but he does get his job (and he does return the money he has stolen). The happy endings proliferate as the story slips the yoke of realism and romps in the magical realm of pure fairy tale, where, as Cheever puts it far more sardonically in his third novel, *Bullet Park* (1969), everything is "wonderful wonderful wonderful wonderful."

Comic exaggeration and hyperbolically happy endings characterize many of the stories of the late 1950's and early 1960's. In "The Housebreaker of Shady Hill," it is losing his job that starts Johnny Hake on his comical crime spree; in "The Country Husband," it is nearly losing his life that sends Francis Weed on an ever more absurdly comical quest for love and understanding. Weed has his brush with death when his plane is forced to make an emergency landing in a field outside Philadelphia. The danger over, his vulnerability (like Blake's) and mortality (like Cash Bentley's) established, the real damage begins when Weed can find no one to lend a sympathetic ear—not his friend, Trace Bearden, on the commuter train, not even his wife, Julia (too busy putting dinner on the table), or his children (the youngest are fighting and the oldest is reading *True Romance*). With his very own True Adventure still untold, Weed goes outside, where he hears a neighbor playing "Moonlight Sonata," *rubato*, "like an outpouring of tearful petulance, lonesomeness, and self-pity—of everything it was Beethoven's greatness not to know," and everything it will now be Weed's comic misfortune to experience as he embarks upon his own True Romance with the rather unromantically named Anne Murchison, his children's new teenage babysitter.

Playing the part of a lovesick adolescent, the middle-aged Weed acts out his midlife crisis and in doing so jeopardizes his family's social standing and his marriage. The consequences are potentially serious, as are the various characters' fears and troubles (Anne's alcoholic father, Julia's "natural fear of chaos and loneliness," which leads to her obsessive partygoing). What is humorous is Cheever's handling of these fears in a story in which solecisms are slapstick, downfalls are pratfalls, and pariahs turn out to be weeds in Cheever's suburban Garden of Eden. When Francis finally decides to overcome his Emersonian self-reliance, to confide in and seek the help of a psychiatrist (who will do what neither friends nor family have thus far been willing to do—that is, listen), the first words Weed tearfully blurts out are, "I'm in love, Dr. Harzog." Since "The Country Husband" is a comedy, Weed is of course cured of his "dis-ease" and able to channel his desires into more socially acceptable occupations (conjugal love and, humorously enough, woodworking). The story ends with a typically Cheeveresque affirmation of F. Scott Fitzgerald-like romantic possibilities, no less apparent in Shady Hill than in the West Egg of *The Great Gatsby* (1925). It is an affirmation, however, tempered once again by the tenuousness of the characters' situation in a "village that hangs, morally and economically, from a thread."

For all the good cheer, hearty advice, biblical quotations, comical predicaments, and lyrical affirmations, there lies at the center of Cheever's fiction the fear of insufficiency and inadequacy—of shelters that will not protect, marriages that will not endure, jobs that will be lost, threads that will not hold. That the thread does not hold in "The Swimmer," Cheever's most painstakingly crafted and horrific work, is especially odd, for the story begins as comedy, a lighthearted satire, involving a group of suburban couples sitting around the Westerhazys' pool on a beautiful midsummer Sunday afternoon talking about what and how much they drank the night before. Suddenly Neddy Merrill, yet another of Cheever's middle-aged but youthfully named protagonists, decides to swim home, pool to pool. More than a prank, he intends it as a celebration of the fineness of the day, a voyage of discovery, a testament to life's romantic possibilities. Neddy's swim will cover eight miles, sixteen pools, in only ten pages (as printed in *The Stories of John Cheever*). The story and its reader move as confidently and rapidly as Neddy, but then there are a few interruptions: a brief rain shower that forces Neddy to seek shelter, a dry pool at one house, and a for-sale sign inexplicably posted at another. Midway through both journey and story, the point of view suddenly and briefly veers away from Neddy, who now looks pitifully exposed and foolishly stranded as he attempts to cross a divided highway. His strength and confidence ebbing, he seems unprepared for whatever lies ahead yet unable to turn back. Like the reader, he is unsure when his little joke turned so deadly serious. At the one public pool on his itinerary, he is assaulted by crowds, shrill sounds, and harsh odors. After being very nearly stalled for two pages, the pace quickens ever so slightly but only to leave Neddy still weaker and more disoriented. Each "breach in the succession" exposes Neddy's inability to bridge the widening gap between his vision of the world and his actual place in it. He is painfully rebuffed by those he had previously been powerful enough to mistreat—a former mistress, a socially inferior couple whose invitations he and his wife routinely discarded. The apparent cause of Neddy's downfall begins to become clear to the reader only as it begins to become clear to Neddy—a sudden and major financial reversal—but Neddy's situation cannot be attributed to merely economic factors, nor is it susceptible to purely rational analysis. Somewhere along Neddy's and the reader's way, everything has changed: the passing of hours becomes the passage of whole seasons, perhaps even years, as realism gives way to fantasy,

humor to horror as the swimmer sees his whole life pass before him in a sea of repressed memories. Somehow Neddy has awakened into his own worst dream. Looking into his empty house, he comes face to face with the insecurity that nearly all Cheever's characters fear and the inadequacy that they all feel.

The stories (and novels) that Cheever wrote during the last two decades of his life grew increasingly and innovatively disparate in structure. "The Jewels of the Cabots," for example, or "The President of the Argentine" matches the intensifying disunity of the author's personal life. Against this narrative waywardness, however, Cheever continued to offer and even to extend an affirmation of the world and his protagonists' place in it in a lyrically charged prose at once serene and expansive ("The World of Apples," *Falconer*). In other words, he continued to do during these last two decades what he had been doing so well for the previous three: writing a fiction of celebration and incoherence.

Other major works

NOVELS: *The Wapshot Chronicle*, 1957; *The Wapshot Scandal*, 1964; *Bullet Park*, 1969; *Falconer*, 1977; *Oh What a Paradise It Seems*, 1982.

SCREENPLAY: *The Shady Hill Kidnapping*, 1982.

NONFICTION: *The Letters of John Cheever*, 1988; *The Journals of John Cheever*, 1991; *Glad Tidings: A Friendship in Letters, the Correspondence of John Cheever and John D. Weaver, 1945-1982*, 1993.

Bibliography

Bosha, Francis J. *John Cheever: A Reference Guide*. Boston: G. K. Hall, 1981.

——————— , ed. *The Critical Response to John Cheever*. Westport, Conn.: Greenwood Press, 1993.

Byrne, Michael D. *Dragons and Martinis: The Skewed Realism of John Cheever*. San Bernardino, Calif.: Borgo Press, 1993.

Cheever, Susan. *Home Before Dark*. Boston: Houghton Mifflin, 1984.

Collins, Robert G., ed. *Critical Essays on John Cheever*. Boston: G. K. Hall, 1982.

Donaldson, Scott, ed. *Conversations with John Cheever*. Jackson: University Press of Mississippi, 1987.

Donaldson, Scott. *John Cheever: A Biography*. New York: Random House, 1988.

Hunt, George. *John Cheever: The Hobgoblin in Company of Love*. Grand Rapids, Mich.: Wm. B. Eerdmans, 1983.

O'Hara, James E. *John Cheever: A Study of the Short Fiction*. Boston: Twayne, 1989.

JAMES FENIMORE COOPER

Born: Burlington, New Jersey; September 15, 1789   **Died:** Cooperstown, New York; September 14, 1851

Principal long fiction

Precaution: A Novel, 1820; *The Spy: A Tale of the Neutral Ground*, 1821; *The Pioneers: Or, The Sources of the Susquehanna*, 1823; *The Pilot: A Tale of the Sea*, 1824; *Lionel Lincoln: Or, The Leaguer of Boston*, 1825; *The Last of the Mohicans: A Narrative of 1757*, 1826; *The Prairie: A Tale*, 1827; *The Red Rover: A Tale*, 1827; *The Wept of Wish-Ton-Wish: A Tale*, 1829; *The Water-Witch: Or, The Skimmer of the Seas*, 1830; *The Bravo: A Tale*, 1831; *The Heidenmauer: Or, The Benedictines—A Tale of the Rhine*, 1832; *The Headsman: Or, The Abbaye des Vignerons*, 1833; *The Monikens*, 1835; *Homeward Bound: Or, The Chase*, 1838; *Home as Found*, 1838; *The Pathfinder: Or, The Inland Sea*, 1840; *Mercedes of Castile: Or, The Voyage to Cathay*, 1840; *The Deerslayer: Or, The First Warpath*, 1841; *The Two Admirals: A Tale*, 1842; *The Wing-and-Wing: Or, Le Feu-Follet*, 1842; *Wyandotté: Or, The Hutted Knoll*, 1843; *Le Mouchoir: An Autobiographical Romance*, 1843 (also known as *Autobiography of a Pocket Handkerchief*); *Afloat and Ashore: A Sea Tale*, 1844; *Miles Wallingford: Sequel to Afloat and Ashore*, 1844; *Satanstoe: Or, The Littlepage Manuscripts a Tale of the Colony*, 1845; *The Chainbearer: Or, The Littlepage Manuscripts*, 1845; *The Redskins: Or, Indian and Injin, Being the Conclusion of the Littlepage Manuscripts*, 1846; *The Crater: Or, Vulcan's Peak, a Tale of the Pacific*, 1847; *Jack Tier: Or, The Florida Reef*, 1848; *The Oak Openings: Or, The Bee Hunter*, 1848; *The Sea Lions: Or, The Lost Sealers*, 1849; *The Ways of the Hour*, 1850.

Other literary forms

Although James Fenimore Cooper was primarily a novelist, he also tried his hand at short stories, biography, and a play. Among these works, only the biographies are considered significant. He also wrote accounts of his European travels, history, and essays on politics and society. Cooper was an active correspondent. Many of his letters and journals have been published, but large quantities of material remain in the hands of private collectors.

Achievements

Though he is best known as the author of the Leatherstocking Tales, Cooper has come to be recognized as America's first great social historian. The Leatherstocking Tales—*The Pioneers*, *The Last of the Mohicans*, *The Prairie*, *The Pathfinder*, and *The Deerslayer*—are those novels in which the frontier hunter and scout Natty Bumppo is a central character. Along with *The Spy* and *The Pilot*, two novels of the American Revolution, the Leatherstocking Tales are familiar to twentieth century readers, and critics agree that these are Cooper's best novels. Less well-known are the novels he began writing during his seven-year residence in Europe, his problem and society novels. In these books, he works out and expresses a complex social and political theory and a social history of America seen within the context of the major modern developments of Euro-

pean civilization. They remain, as Robert Spiller argues, among the most detailed and accurate pictures available of major aspects of American society and thought in the early nineteenth century.

Cooper achieved international reputation with *The Spy*, his second novel, which was translated into most European languages soon after its publication. With this work, he also invented a popular genre, the spy novel. He is credited with having invented the Western in the Leatherstocking Tales and the sea adventure with *The Pilot*, another popular success. In his thirty-year writing career, he wrote more than thirty novels, the naval history, several significant social works, and many other works as well. Howard Mumford Jones credits Cooper with early American developments of the international theme, the theme of the Puritan conscience, the family saga, the utopian and dystopian novel, and the series novel. By general agreement, Cooper stands at the headwaters of the American tradition of fiction; he contributed significantly to the themes and forms of the American novel.

Biography

Cooper was born in Burlington, New Jersey, on September 15, 1789, the twelfth of thirteen children of William and Elizabeth Cooper. He added "Fenimore" in 1826 in memory of his mother's family. Elizabeth Fenimore was an heiress whose wealth contributed to William Cooper's success in buying and developing a large tract of land on which he founded Cooperstown, New York. The Coopers moved to Cooperstown in 1790, and Cooper grew up there as the son of the community's developer and benefactor, a gentleman who eventually became a judge and a Federalist congressman. Cooper's conservative Enlightenment views of the frontier, of American culture, and of democracy had their roots in his Cooperstown youth.

Like many sons of the wealthy gentry, Cooper had some difficulty deciding what to do with his life. In his third year at Yale, he was dismissed for misconduct. In 1806, he began a naval career that led to a commission in the U.S. Navy in 1808, where he served on Lake Ontario, scene of *The Pathfinder*. In 1809, his father died from a blow delivered from behind by a political opponent, and Cooper came into a large inheritance. In 1811, he married Susan Augusta DeLancy, of an old and respectable Tory family, and resigned from the Navy. For eight years he lived the life of a country gentleman, eventually fathering seven children. By 1819, however, because of the financial failures and deaths of all his brothers, which left him responsible for some of their families, Cooper found himself in financial difficulty. Cooper began writing at this time, not with the hope of making money—there was no precedent for achieving even a living as an author—but in response to a challenge from his wife to write a better novel than one he happened to be reading to her. Once he had begun, Cooper found in various ways the energy and motivation to make writing his career. Susan's support and the family's continued domestic tranquillity inspired Cooper's writing and protected him from what he came to see as an increasingly hostile public.

The success of *The Spy* and of his next four novels made him secure enough in 1826 to take his family to Europe, where he hoped to educate his children and to improve the foreign income from his books. While living in Paris and London and traveling at a leisurely pace through most of Europe, Cooper involved himself in French and Polish politics and published several works. Before his return to the United States in 1833, he met Sir Walter Scott, became intimate with Marie de La Fayette, aided the sculptor Horatio Greenough in beginning his career, and maintained his lifelong friendship with Samuel Morse. This period of travel was another turning point in his life. In *Notions of the Americans* (1828), Cooper wrote an idealized defense of American democracy that offended both his intended audiences,

the Americans and the English. When he went on to publish a series of novels set in Europe (1831-1833), Cooper provided American reviewers with more reasons to see him as an apostate. Upon his return to America, he tended to confirm this characterization by announcing his retirement as a novelist and publishing a group of travel books, satires, and finally a primer on republican democracy, *The American Democrat* (1838). When he returned to writing novels with *Homeward Bound* and *Home as Found* in 1838, he indicated that he had found America much decayed on his return from Europe. The promises of a democratic republic he had expressed in *Notions of the Americans* were fading before the abuse of the Constitution by demagogues and the increasing tyranny of the majority. *The American Democrat* was, in part, a call to return to the original principles of the republic.

Having resettled in Cooperstown in 1833, Cooper soon found himself embroiled in controversies over land title and libel, controversies which the press used to foster the image of Cooper as a self-styled aristocrat. He is credited with establishing important legal precedents in the libel cases he won against editors such as Thurlow Weed and Horace Greeley. By 1843, Cooper's life had become more tranquil. He had settled down to the most productive period of his life, producing sixteen novels in ten years. Many of these are marred by obtrusive discussions of political and social issues; several, however, are considered American classics, such as *The Pathfinder* and *The Deerslayer*, the last two of the Leatherstocking Tales. His last five novels show evidence of increasing interest in religious ideas. Though Cooper had been active in religious institutions all his life and though all his novels express Christian beliefs, he was not confirmed as an Episcopalian until the last year of his life. He died at Cooperstown on September 14, 1851.

Analysis

James Fenimore Cooper was a historian of America. His novels span American history, dramatizing central events from Christopher Columbus' discovery (*Mercedes of Castile*) through the French and Indian Wars and the early settlement (the Leatherstocking Tales) to the Revolution (*The Spy* and *The Pilot*) and the contemporary events of the Littlepage and the Miles Wallingford novels. In some of his European novels, he examined major intellectual developments, such as the Reformation, which he thought important to American history, and in many of his novels, he reviewed the whole of American history, attempting to complete his particular vision of America by inventing a tradition for the new nation.

In his *Studies in Classic American Literature* (1923), D. H. Lawrence argued that Cooper's myth of America is centered in the friendship between Natty Bumppo and his Indian friend Chingachgook and in the order of composition of the Leatherstocking Tales. Of the friendship, Lawrence says, Cooper "dreamed a new human relationship deeper than the deeps of sex. Deeper than property, deeper than fatherhood, deeper than marriage, deeper than love. . . . This is the nucleus of a new society, the clue to a new epoch." Of the order of writing, he says that the novels "go backwards, from old age to golden youth. That is the true myth of America. She starts old, old and wrinkled in an old skin. And there is a gradual sloughing of the old skin, towards a new youth." These insightful statements have been elaborated by critics who have looked deeply into Cooper's works, but who have concentrated most of their attention on the Leatherstocking Tales in order to find in Cooper affinities with Herman Melville, Mark Twain, and others who seem to find it necessary, like Natty Bumppo, to remain apart from social institutions to preserve their integrity. Because these critics tend to focus on Leatherstocking and mythic elements in the tales, they may be better guides to American myth than to Cooper. While Cooper contributes images and forms to what became myths in the hands of others, his own mind seems to have been occupied more with making American society than with escaping it.

Another, more traditional mythic pattern pervades all of his works, including the Leatherstocking Tales. Several critics have called attention to a key passage in *The Last of the Mohicans* when Natty describes the waterfall where the scout and his party take refuge from hostile Indians. The pattern of a unified flow falling into disorder and rebellion only to be gathered back again by the hand of Providence into a new order not only is descriptive of the plot of this novel but also suggests other levels of meaning that are reflected throughout Cooper's work, for it defines Cooper's essentially Christian and Enlightenment worldview, a view he found expressed in Alexander Pope's *Essay on Man* (1733-1734).

In *The American Democrat*, Cooper often echoes Pope's *Essay on Man* as he explains that human life in this world is a fall into disorder where the trials exceed the pleasures; this apparent disorder, however, is a merciful preparation for a higher life to come. Many of

Cooper's novels reflect this pattern; characters leave or are snatched out of their reasonably ordered world to be educated in a dangerous and seemingly disordered one, only to be returned after an educational probation into a more familiarly ordered world, there to contribute to its improvement. This pattern of order, separation, and reintegration pervades Cooper's thought and gives form to his conscious dream of America. He came to see America as moving through the anarchic and purifying phase of the Revolution toward a new society that would allow the best that is in fallen humanity to realize itself. This dream is expressed, in part, in *The Pioneers*.

The Pioneers is Cooper's first great novel, the first he composed primarily to satisfy himself. The popular success of *The Spy* increased both his freedom and his confidence, encouraging him to turn to what proved to be his richest source of material, the frontier life of New York State. The seasonal ordering of events brings out the nature of the community at Templeton at this particular point in its development. Templeton is shown to be suspended between two forms of order. Representing the old order are the seventy-year-old Natty Bumppo, the Leatherstocking, and his aged Indian friend, John Mohegan, whose actual name is Chingachgook. The forest is their home and their mediator with divine law. Natty, through his contact with Chingachgook and his life in the forest, has become the best man that such a life can produce. He combines true Christian principles with the skills and knowledge of the best Indian civilization. Natty and the Indian live an ideal kind of life, given the material circumstances of their environment, but that environment is changing. Otsego Lake is becoming settled and civilized. Chingachgook remains because he wishes to live where his ancestors once dwelt. Natty stays with his friend. Their presence becomes a source of conflict.

The new order is represented at first by Judge Temple, but the form of that order remains somewhat obscure until the revealing of motives and identities at the end of the novel. Temple's main function in the community is moral. He is important as the owner and developer of the land. He has brought settlers to the land, helped them through troubled times, and, largely at his own expense, has built the public buildings and established the institutions of Templeton. During the transition to civilization, Temple is a center of order, organization, and—most important—restraint. The settlers need restraint; Judge Temple feels in himself the desire to overharvest the plentiful natural resources of Templeton and knows firsthand the importance of restraining laws that will force the settlers to live by an approximation of the divine law by which Natty lives.

The central conflict in the seasonal ordering of the novel is between Natty, who lives by the old law, the natural law of the forest that reflects the divine law, and the settlers, who are comparatively lawless. This conflict is complicated as the new restraining civil laws come into effect and the lawless members of the community exploit and abuse those laws in order to harass Natty. Natty becomes a victim of the very laws designed to enforce his own highest values, underlining the weakness of human nature and illustrating the cyclical pattern of anarchy, order, and repression and abuse of the law. Subsequently, he announces his intent to move west into the wilderness, which is his proper home.

The conflict between the old order and the new is resolved only in part by Natty's apparent capitulation and retreat into the wilderness. Before Natty leaves, he performs a central function in an important land transfer plot, a function that infuses the values of the old order into the new order. The land to which Judge Temple holds title was given to Major Effingham by a council of the Delaware chiefs at the time of the French and Indian Wars. In recognition of his qualities as a faithful and brave warrior, Effingham was adopted into the tribe as a son of Chingachgook. In this exchange, the best of Native American civilization recognized its own qualities in a superior form in Effingham, a representative of the best of European Christian civilization. This method of transfer is crucial because it amounts to a gentleman's agreement ratified by family ties; the transfer is a voluntary expression of values and seems providentially ordained.

The Pioneers is a hopeful novel, for in it Cooper reveals a confidence in a providential ordering of history which will lead to the fulfillment of his ideas of a rational republic. This novel resolves the central anarchic displacements of the native inhabitants and of the traditional European ruling class by asserting that the American republic is the fruition of these two traditions.

The Last of the Mohicans is the best known of the Leatherstocking Tales, probably because it combines Cooper's most interesting characters and the relatively fast-paced adventure of *The Spy* and *The Pilot*. Set in the French and Indian Wars, this novel presents Natty and Chingachgook in their prime. Chingachgook's son, Uncas, is the last of the Mohican chiefs, the last of the line from which the Delaware nation is said to trace its origin. Although the novel moves straightforwardly through two adventures, it brings into these adventures a number of suggestive thematic elements.

The two main adventures are quests, with filial piety as their motive. Major Duncan Heyward attempts to escort Cora and Alice Munro to their father, commander of Fort William Henry on Horican Lake (Lake George). Led astray by Magua, an Indian who seeks revenge against Munro, the party encounters and enlists the help of Natty and his Indian companions. This quest is fully successful. Magua joins the Hurons who are leagued with the besieging French forces at William Henry and captures the original party, which is then rescued by Natty and his friends to be delivered safely to the doomed fort. This adventure is followed by an interlude at the fort in which Heyward obtains Munro's permission to court Alice and learns, to his own secret pain, that Cora has black blood. Also in this interlude, Munro learns he will get no support from nearby British troops and realizes that he must surrender his position. Montcalm allows him to remove his men and equipment from the fort before it is destroyed, but the discontented Indians, provoked by Magua, break the truce and massacre the retreating and exposed people for booty and scalps. Magua precipitates the next quest by capturing Alice and Cora and taking them north toward Canada. The second quest is the rescue mission of Natty, Chingachgook, Uncas, Heyward, and Munro. This attempt is only partly successful, for both Cora and Uncas are killed.

The first meeting of Heyward's party with Natty's party in the forest has an allegorical quality that looks forward to the best of Nathaniel Hawthorne and begins the development of the theme of evil, which—in Cooper's vision—can enjoy only a temporary triumph. Lost in the forest, misled by the false guide, Magua, this party from civilization has entered a seemingly anarchic world in which they are babes "without the knowledge of men." This meeting introduces two major themes: the conception of the wilderness as a book one must know how to read if one is to survive, and the conception of Magua and his Hurons as devils who have tempted Heyward's party into this world in order to work their destruction. Magua has most of the qualities of the good men: courage, cunning, the ability to organize harmoniously talent and authority, and highly developed skills at reading the book of Nature. He differs from Natty and his Indian companions, however, in that he allows himself to be governed by the evil passion of revenge rather than by unselfish rationality. Of his kind, the unselfishly rational men must be constantly suspicious. Montcalm's failure to control his Indian forces demonstrates that only the most concerted efforts can prevent great evil. The novel's end shows that ultimately only divine providence can fully right the inevitable wrongs of this world.

Throughout his career, Cooper worked within a general understanding of human history as a disordered phase of existence between two orders, and a particular vision of contemporary America as a disordered phase between the old aristocratic order and the new order to be dominated by the American gentleman. In the first three of the Leatherstocking Tales, Cooper reveals a desire to naturalize the aristocratic tradition through exposure to the wilderness and its prophet, the man who reads God's word in the landscape. The result of this process would be a mature natural order which, though far form divine perfection, would promise as much happiness as is possible for fallen humankind. In all of these works, Cooper continues to express his faith in the possibility of a high American civilization.

Other major works

NONFICTION: *Notions of the Americans*, 1828; *A Letter to His Countrymen*, 1834; *Sketches of Switzerland*, 1836; *Gleanings in Europe: France*, 1837; *Gleanings in Europe: England*, 1837; *Gleanings in Europe: Italy*, 1838; *The American Democrat*, 1838; *Chronicles of Cooperstown*, 1838; *The History of the Navy of the United States of America*, 1839 (2 vols.); *Ned Meyers: Or, A Life Before the Mast*, 1843; *Lives of Distinguished American Naval Officers*, 1845; *New York*, 1851; *The Letters and Journals of James Fenimore Cooper*, 1960-1968 (J. F. Beard, editor, 6 vols.).

Bibliography

Clark, Robert, ed. *James Fenimore Cooper: New Critical Essays*. London: Vision, 1985.

Fields, W., ed. *James Fenimore Cooper: A Collection of Critical Essays*. Boston: G. K. Hall, 1979.

Franklin, Wayne. *The New World of James Fenimore Cooper*. Chicago: University of Chicago Press, 1982.

Long, Robert Emmett. *James Fenimore Cooper*. New York: Continuum, 1990.

Motley, Warren. *The American Abraham*. Cambridge, England: Cambridge University Press, 1987.

Ringe, Donald A. *James Fenimore Cooper*. 2d ed. New York: Twayne, 1988.

EMILY DICKINSON

Born: Amherst, Massachusetts; December 10, 1830   **Died:** Amherst, Massachusetts; May 15, 1886

Principal poetry

The Poems of Emily Dickinson, 1955 (Thomas H. Johnson, ed., 3 vols.); *The Complete Poems of Emily Dickinson*, 1960 (Thomas H. Johnson, ed.); *The Manuscript Books of Emily Dickinson*, 1981 (Ralph Franklin, ed., 2 vols.).

Other literary forms

In addition to her poetry, Dickinson left behind voluminous correspondence. Because she was so rarely out of Amherst—and in her later life so rarely left her house—much of her contact with others took place through letters, many of which include poems. Like her poetry, the letters are witty, epigrammatic, and often enigmatic.

Achievements

As surely as William Faulkner and Ernest Hemingway, different as they were, brought American fiction into the twentieth century, so Walt Whitman and Emily Dickinson brought about a revolution in American poetry. By the mid-nineteenth century, American lyric poetry had matured to an evenly polished state. Edgar Allan Poe, Ralph Waldo Emerson, and Herman Melville were creating poetry of both power and precision, but poetry in the United States was still hampered by certain limiting assumptions about the nature of literary language, about the value of regular rhythm, meter, and rhyme, and about imagery as ornamental rather than organic. Were the medium not to become sterile and conventionalized, poets had to expand the possibilities of the form.

Into this situation came Dickinson and Whitman, poets committed to writing a personalized poetry unlike anything the nineteenth century had thus far read. Whitman rid himself of the limitations of regular meter entirely. Identifying with the common man, Whitman attempted to make him a hero who could encompass the universe. He was a poet of the open road; Whitman journeyed along, accumulating experience and attempting to unite himself with the world around him. For him, life was dynamic and progressive. Dickinson, however, was the poet of exclusion, of the shut door. She accepted the limitations of rhyme and meter and worked endless variations on one basic pattern, exploring the nuances that the framework would allow. No democrat, she constructed for herself a set of aristocratic images. No

traveler, she stayed at home to examine small fragments of the world she knew. For Dickinson life was kinesthetic; she recorded the impressions of experience on her nerves and on her soul. Rather than being linear and progressive, it was circular: "My business is circumference," she wrote, and she often described the arcs and circles of experience.

Different as they were, however, they are America's greatest lyric poets. Although Dickinson was barely understood or appreciated in her own lifetime, she now seems a central figure—at once firmly in a tradition and, at the same time, a breaker of tradition, a revolutionary who freed American poetry for modern thought and technique.

Biography

"Renunciation is a piercing virtue," wrote Emily Dickinson, and her life can be seen as a series of renunciations. Born in 1830 of a prominent Amherst family, she rarely left the town, except for time spent in Boston and trips to Washington and Philadelphia. She attended the Amherst Academy and Mount Holyoke Female Seminary. Although she was witty and popular, she set herself apart from the other girls by her refusal to be converted to the conventional Christianity of the town. Her life was marked by a circle of close friends and of family: a stern and humorless father; a mother who suffered a long period of illness and whom Emily took care of; her sister Lavinia, who likewise never married and remained in the family home; and her brother Austin, who married Sue Gilbert Dickinson and whose forceful personality, like that of his wife, affected the family while Emily Dickinson lived, and whose affair with Mrs. Todd, the editor of the poems, precipitated family squabbles that affected their publication.

Additionally, there was a series of men—for it almost seems that Dickinson took what she called her "preceptors" one at a time—who formed a sort of emotional resource for her. The first of these was Samuel

Bowles, the editor of the neighboring Springfield, Massachusetts, *Republican*, which published some of her poetry. Charles Wadsworth was the minister of a Philadelphia church; a preacher famous for his eloquence, he preached one Sunday when Dickinson was in Philadelphia, and afterward they corresponded for several years. In 1862, however, he and his family moved from Philadelphia to the West Coast. Dickinson immediately sent four of her poems to Thomas Wentworth Higginson, at the *Atlantic Monthly*, for his advice, and they began a long friendship; although Higginson was never convinced that Dickinson was a finished poet, he was a continuing mentor. Finally, late in life, Dickinson met Judge Otis Lord, and for a time it seemed as if they were to be married; this was her one explicitly romantic friendship, but the marriage never took place. There were also less intense friendships with women, particularly Mabel Todd, who, despite her important role in Dickinson's life, never actually met her, and the writer Helen Hunt Jackson, one of the few to accept Dickinson's poetry as it was written.

The nature of the relationships with the "preceptors" and their effect on the poetry is a matter of much controversy. It is complicated by three famous and emotional "Master" letters that Dickinson wrote between 1858 and 1862 (the dates are partly conjectural). Who the master was, is uncertain. For Johnson, Dickinson's editor, the great influence was Wadsworth, and although their relationship was always geographically distant, it was he who was the great love, his moving to California the emotional crisis that occasioned the great flood-years of poetry—366 poems in 1862 alone, according to Johnson. For Richard B. Sewall, author of the standard biography, Bowles was the master.

Whatever the case, it is true that after 1862, Dickinson rarely left her house, except for a necessary visit to Boston, where she was treated for eye trouble. She wore white dresses and with more and more frequency refused to see visitors, usually remaining upstairs, listening to the conversations and entering, if at all, by calling down the stairs or by sending in poems or other tokens of her participation. She became known as the "Myth of Amherst," and from this image is drawn the popular notion of the eccentric old maid that persists in the imagination of many of her readers today. Yet it is clear that whatever the limits of her actual experience, Dickinson lived life on the emotional level with great intensity. Her poetry is dense with vividly rendered emotions and observations, and she transformed the paucity of her outward life into the richness of her inner life.

Richard Wilbur has suggested that Dickinson suffered three great deprivations in her life: of a lover, of publication and fame, and of a God in whom she could believe. Although she often questioned a world in which such deprivations were necessary, she more frequently compensated, as Wilbur believes, by calling her "privation good, rendering it positive by renunciation." That she lived in a world of distances, solitude, and renunciation her biography makes clear; that she turned that absence into beauty is the testimony of her poetry.

Analysis

Dickinson's mastery of the short lyric poem is indisputable. The subjects of her verse, expressed in personalized, often epigrammatic figures of speech, include love, death, nature, and God. Her voluminous poems and letters reveal both a passionate, witty woman and a writer in full command of her craft. As one of America's preeminent lyric poets, Dickinson was an innovator who helped to free American poetry from becoming sterile and conventional.

During her lifetime, only seven of Dickinson's poems were published, most of them edited to make them more conventional. After Dickinson's death, her sister Lavinia discovered about nine hundred poems, half of the 1,775 poems that now compose the Dickinson canon. She took these to a family friend, Mrs. Mabel Loomis Todd, who, with Dickinson's friend Thomas Wentworth Higginson, published 115 of the poems in 1890. Together they published a second group of 166 in 1891, and Mrs. Todd alone edited a third series in 1896. Unfortunately, Mrs. Todd and Col. Higginson continued the practice of revision that had begun with the first seven published poems, smoothing the rhymes and meter, revising the diction, and generally regularizing the poetry.

In 1914, Dickinson's niece, Martha Dickinson Bianchi, published the first of several volumes of the poetry she was to edit. Although she was more scrupulous about preserving Dickinson's language and intent, several editorial problems persisted, and the body of Dickinson's poetry remained fragmented and often altered. In 1950, the Dickinson literary estate was given to Harvard University, and Thomas H. Johnson began his work of editing, arranging, and presenting the text. In 1955, he produced the variorum edition, 1,775 poems arranged in an attempt at chronological order, given such evidence as handwriting changes and incorporation of the poems in letters, and including all variations of the poems. In 1960, he chose one form of each poem as the final version and published the resulting collection as *The Complete Poems of Emily Dickinson*. Johnson's text and numbering system are accepted as the standard. His job was thorough, diligent, and imaginative. This is not to say, however, that his decisions about dates or choices among variants must be taken as final. Many scholars have other opinions, and since Dickinson herself apparently did not make final choices, there is no reason to accept every decision Johnson made. In 1981, an invaluable two-volume facsimile edition of Dickinson's poems, *The Manuscript Books of Emily Dickinson*, was published by Harvard University Press.

One of Dickinson's poems (#1129) begins, "Tell all the Truth but tell it slant," and the oblique and often enigmatic rendering of Truth is the theme of Dickinson's poetry. Its motifs often recur: love, death, poetry, beauty, nature, immortality, the self; but such abstractions do not indicate the broad and rich changes that Dickinson obliquely rings on the truths she tells.

Dickinson's truth is, in the broadest sense, a religious truth. Formally, her poetry plays endless variations on the Protestant hymn meters that she knew from her youthful experiences in church. Her reading in contemporary poetry was limited, and the form she knew best was the iambic of hymns: common meter (with its alternating tetrameter and trimeter lines), long meter (four lines of tetrameter), and short meter (four of trimeter) became the framework of her poetry. That static form, however, could not contain the energy of her work, and the rhythms and rhymes are varied, upset, and broken to accommodate the feeling of her lines. The predictable patterns of hymns were not for Dickinson, who delighted in off-rhyme, consonance, and, less frequently, eye-rhyme.

Dickinson is a religious poet more than formally, but her thematic sense of religion lies not in her assurance but in her continual questioning of God, in her attempt to define his nature and that of his world. Although she is always a poet of definition, straightforward definition was too direct for her: "The Riddle we can guess/ We speedily despise," she wrote. Her works often begin, "It was not" or "It was like," with the poem being an oblique attempt to define the "it." "I like to see it lap the Miles" (#585) is a typical Dickinson riddle poem. Like many, it begins with "it," a pronoun without an antecedent, so that the reader must join in the process of discovery and definition. The riddle is based on an extended metaphor; the answer to the riddle, a train, is compared to a horse; but in the poem both tenor (train)

and vehicle (horse) are unstated. Meanwhile, what begins with an almost cloying tone, the train as an animal lapping and licking, moves through subtle gradations of attitude until the train stops at the end "docile and omnipotent." This juxtaposition of incongruous adjectives, like the coupling of unlikely adjective and noun, is another of Dickinson's favorite devices; just as the movement of the poem has been from the animal's (and train's) tame friendliness to its assertive power, so these adjectives crystallize the paradox.

Thus, one sees many of Dickinson's typical devices at work: the tightly patterned form, based on an undefined subject, the riddlelike puzzle of defining that subject, the shifting of mood from apparent observation to horror, the grotesque images couched in emotionally distant language. All this delineates that experience, that confrontation—with God, with nature, with the self, with one's own mind—that is the center of Dickinson's best poetry. Whether her work looks inward or outward, the subject matter is a confrontation leading to awareness, and part of the terror is that for Dickinson there is never any mediating middle ground; she confronts herself in relation to an abyss beyond. There is no society, no community to make that experience palatable in any but the most grotesque sense of the word, as in the awful "tasting" of uncontrollable fear.

Dickinson often questions the nature of the universe; she senses that God is present only in one's awareness of his absence. She shares Robert Frost's notion that God has tricked humankind, but while for Frost God's trick is in the nature of creation, for Dickinson it is equally in God's refusal to answer our riddles about that creation. She writes of the "eclipse" of God, and for Dickinson, it is God himself who has caused the obscurity. The customary movement in her explicitly religious poetry is from apparent affirmation to resounding doubt. Poem #338 begins with the line, "I know that He exists." While Dickinson rarely uses periods even at the ends of her poems, here the first line ends with one: a short and complete affirmation of God's existence, but an affirmation that remains unqualified for only that one line. God is not omnipresent but exists "Somewhere—in Silence"; Dickinson then offers a justification for God's absence: His life is so fine that he has hidden it from humans who are unworthy. The second stanza offers two more justifications: He is playing with people, and one will be that much happier at the blissful surprise one has earned. Yet the play, in typical Dickinson fashion, is a "fond Ambush," and both the juxtaposition of incongruous words and the reader's understanding that only villains engage in ambush indicate how quickly and how brutally the tone of the poem is changing.

Other overtly religious poems, such as #501 ("This World is not Conclusion"), likewise begin with a clear statement followed by a period and then move rapidly toward doubt. Here God is a "Species" who "stands beyond." Humans are shown as baffled by the riddle of the universe, grasping at any "twig of Evidence." They ask "a Vane, the way," indicating the inconstancy of that on which humankind relies and punning on "in vain." Whatever answer humanity receives is only a narcotic, which "cannot still the Tooth/ That nibbles at the soul."

Dickinson also persistently questions nature, which was for her an equivocal manifestation of God's power and whims. Although there are occasional poems in which her experience of nature is exuberant ("I taste a liquor never brewed," for example, #214), in most of her work the experience is one of terror. Whenever Dickinson looks at nature, the moment becomes a confrontation. Although she is superficially within the Puritan tradition of observing nature and reading its message, Dickinson differs not only in the chilling message that she reads, but also because nature refuses to remain passive; it is not simply an open book to be read—for books remain themselves—but active and aggressive; personification suggests its assertive malevolence. For Dickinson's nineteenth century opposite, Whitman, the world was one of possibilities, of romantic venturing forth to project oneself onto the world and form an organic relationship with it. For Dickinson, the human and the natural give way to the inorganic; nature is, if like a clock, not so in its perfect design and workings but in its likeliness to wind down and stop.

One of Dickinson's finest poems, #1624 ("Apparently with no surprise"), a poem from late in her career, unites her attitudes toward nature and God. Even as Frost does in "Design," Dickinson examines one destructive scene in nature and uses it to represent a larger pattern; with Frost, too, she sees two possibilities for both microcosm and macrocosm: accident or dark design. The first two lines of her short poem describe the "happy Flower." The personified flower is unsurprised by its sudden death: "The Frost beheads it at its play—/ In accidental power—/ The blonde Assassin passes on—." In common with many American writers, she reverses the conventional association of white with purity; here the killer, the frost, is blonde. While she suggests that the power may be accidental, in itself not a consoling thought, the two lines framing that assertion

severely modify it, for beheading is rarely accidental, nor do assassins attain their power by chance. Whichever the case, accident or design, there is finally little significant difference, for nothing in the world pays attention to what has happened. "The Sun proceeds unmoved," an unusual pun, since unmoved has the triple meaning of unconcerned, stationary, and without a prime mover; it measures off the time for a God who does approve.

When Dickinson concentrates her vision upon external reality, then, the results are often horrific and appalling. The alternative for her is to direct her gaze within, at her own self—but what she finds there is as chaotic and chilling as what she finds without. Exemplifying such internal confusion is poem #435, "Much Madness is divinest Sense," which makes the familiar assertion that, although the common majority have enough power to label nonconformists as insane and dangerous, often what appears as madness is sense, "divinest Sense—/ To a discerning Eye." Usually, however, her poetry of the mind is more unsettling, her understanding more personal. The awareness of one's tenuous grasp on reason seems clearest in #280, "I felt a Funeral, in my Brain," one of her most piercing poems about the death of reason, for there the funeral is explicitly "in," although not necessarily "of," the speaker's brain. The metaphor is developed through a series of comparisons with the funeral rites, each introduced by "and," each arriving with increasing haste. At first the monotony of the mourners' tread almost causes sense to break through, but instead the mind reacts by going numb. Eventually the funeral metaphor gives way to that of a shipwreck—on the surface, an illogical shift, but given the movement of the poem, a continuation of the sense of confusion and abandonment. The last stanza returns to the dominant metaphor, presenting a rapid series of events, the first of which is "a Plank in Reason" breaking, plunging the persona—and the reader—back into the funeral imagery of a coffin dropping into a grave. The poem concludes with, "And Finished knowing—then," an ambiguous finish suggesting the end both of her life and of her reasoning, thus fusing the two halves of the metaphor. Alternatively, the last line suggests that the poet, even at the moment of her death, possesses awareness—for Dickinson, that most terrifying of experiences.

Death, incidentally, is not merely metaphorical for Dickinson—it is the greatest subject of her work. Perhaps her finest lyrics are on this topic, which she surveyed with a style at once laconic and acute, a tone of quiet terror conveyed through understatement and indirection. Her power arises from the tension between her formal and tonal control and the emotional intensity of what she writes. She approaches death from two perspectives, adopts two stances: the persona as the grieving onlooker, attempting to continue with life, her own faith tested by the experience of watching another die; and the persona as the dying person.

By consensus the greatest of all Dickinson's poems, "Because I could not stop for Death" (#712), explores death from the second perspective. The poem unites love and death, for death comes to the persona in the form of a gentleman caller. Her reaction is neither haste to meet him nor displeasure at his arrival. She has time to put away her "labor and . . . leisure"; he is civil. The only hint in the first two stanzas of what is really occurring is the presence of Immortality, and yet that presence, although not unnoticed, is as yet unfelt by the persona. The third stanza brings the customary metaphor of life as a journey and the convention of one's life passing before one's eyes at the moment of death: from youth through maturity to sunset.

As is common in Dickinson, the poem is hinged by a coordinate conjunction in the exact middle. This time the conjunction is "Or," as the speaker realizes not that she is passing the sun but that "He passed us." The metaphoric journey through life continues; it is now night, but the emotions have changed from the calm of control to fright. The speaker's "Zero at the Bone" is literal, for her clothing, frilly and light, while appropriate for a wedding, is not so for the funeral that is occurring. The final stop is before the grave, "a House that seemed/ A Swelling of the Ground." The swelling ground also suggests pregnancy, but this earth bears death, not life. The last stanza comments that even though the persona has been dead for centuries, all that time seems shorter than the one moment of realization of where her journey must ultimately end. Death, Dickinson's essential metaphor and subject, is seen in terms of a moment of confrontation. Absence thus becomes the major presence, confusion the major ordering principle.

Dickinson's stature in American literature, only established decades after her death, is partly historical: With Whitman she changed the shape and direction of American poetry, creating and fulfilling poetic potentials that make her a poet beyond her century. Her importance, however, is much greater than that. The intensity with which she converted emotional loss and intellectual questioning into art, the wit and energy of her work, mark the body of her poetry as among the finest America has yet produced.

Other major works

NONFICTION: *The Letters of Emily Dickinson*, 1958 (Thomas H. Johnson and Theodora Ward, eds., 3 vols.).

Bibliography

Boruch, Marianne. "Dickinson Descending." *The Georgia Review* 40 (1986): 863-877.

Cameron, Sharon. *Choosing Not Choosing: Dickinson's Fascicles.* Chicago: University of Chicago Press, 1992.

Carruth, Hayden. "Emily Dickinson's Unexpectedness." *Ironwood* 14 (1986): 51-57.

Dickenson, Donna. *Emily Dickinson.* Oxford, England: Berg, 1985.

Farr, Judith. *The Passion of Emily Dickinson.* Cambridge, Mass.: Harvard University Press, 1992.

Ferlazzo, Paul, ed. *Critical Essays on Emily Dickinson.* Boston: G. K. Hall, 1984.

Howe, Susan. *My Emily Dickinson.* Berkeley, Calif.: North Atlantic Books, 1985.

Juhasz, Suzanne, ed. *Feminist Critics Read Emily Dickinson.* Bloomington: Indiana University Press, 1983.

MacNeil, Helen. *Emily Dickinson.* New York: Pantheon Books, 1986.

Miller, Cristanne. *Emily Dickinson: A Poet's Grammar.* Cambridge, Mass.: Harvard University Press, 1987.

Robinson, John. *Emily Dickenson: Looking to Canaan.* Winchester, Mass.: Faber & Faber, 1986.

RALPH WALDO EMERSON

Born: Boston, Massachusetts; May 25, 1803

Died: Concord, Massachusetts; April 27, 1882

Principal poetry

Poems, 1847; *May-Day and Other Pieces*, 1867; *Selected Poems*, 1876; *Collected Poems and Translations*, 1994.

Other literary forms

Ralph Waldo Emerson's *Journals*, written over a period of fifty-five years (1820-1875), were ultimately the source of everything else he wrote. These have been edited in ten volumes by Edward W. Emerson and Waldo Emerson Forbes (1909-1914). Emerson was a noted lecturer in his day, although many of his addresses and speeches were not collected and published until after his death. Emerson's voluminous correspondence has also been published, as have his uncollected writings (essays and reviews, for example) and other miscellaneous papers.

Achievements

Although Emerson's poetry was but a small part of his overall literary output, he thought of himself as very much a poet—even in his essays and lectures—and he stands as a major influence on the subsequent course of American poetry. As scholar, critic, and poet, Emerson was the first to define the distinctive qualities of American verse. In "The American Scholar" he called for a distinctive American poetry, and in his essay "The Poet" he provided the theoretical framework for American poetics. Scornful of imitation, he demanded freshness and originality from his verse, even though he did not always achieve in practice what he sought in theory.

"The Poet" rejects fixed poetic form in favor of a freer, more open verse. For Emerson, democratic poetry would be composed with variable line and meter, with form subordinated to expression. The poet in a democracy is thus a "representative man," chanting the poetry of the common, the ordinary, and the low. Although Emerson pointed the way, it took Walt Whitman to master this new style of American poetry with his first edition of *Leaves of Grass* (1855), which Emerson recognized and praised for its originality. Whitman thus became the poet whom Emerson had called for in "The American Scholar"; American poetry had come of age.

Biography

Born in Boston on May 25, 1803, Ralph Waldo Emerson was the second of five sons in the family of William and Ruth Emerson. His father was a noted Unitarian minister of old New England stock whose sudden death in 1811 left the family to struggle in genteel poverty. Although left without means, Emerson's mother and his aunt, Mary Moody Emerson, were energetic and resourceful women who managed to survive by taking in boarders, accepting the charity of relatives, and teaching their boys the New England values of thrift, hard work, and mutual assistance within the family. Frail as a child, Emerson attended Boston Latin School and Harvard, from which he was graduated without distinction in 1821. Since their mother was determined that her children would receive a decent education, each of her sons taught after graduation to help the others through school. Thus Emerson taught for several years at his brother's private school for women before he decided to enter divinity school. His family's high thinking and plain living taught young Emerson self-reliance and a deep respect for books and learning.

With his father and step-grandfather, the Reverend Ezra Ripley of Concord, as models, Emerson returned to Harvard to prepare for the ministry. After two years of intermittent study at the Divinity School, Emerson was licensed to preach in the Unitarian Church. He was forced to postpone further studies, however, and travel south during the winter of 1826 because of poor health. The next two years saw him preaching occasionally and serving as a substitute pastor. One such call brought him to Concord, New Hampshire, where he met his future wife, Ellen Louisa Tucker. After his ordination in March, 1829, Emerson married Ellen Tucker and accepted a call as minister of the Second Church, Boston, where his father had also served. The position and salary were good, and Emerson was prepared to settle into a respectable career as a Boston Unitarian clergyman. Unfortunately his wife was frail, and within a year and a half she died of tuberculosis. Grief-stricken, Emerson found it difficult to continue with his duties as pastor and resigned from the pulpit six months after his wife's death. Private doubts had assailed him, and he found he could no longer administer the Lord's Supper in good conscience. His congregation would not allow him to dispense with the rite, so his resignation was reluctantly accepted.

With a small settlement from his wife's legacy, he sailed for Europe in December, 1832, to regain his health and try to find a new vocation. During his winter in Italy he admired the art treasures in Florence and Rome. There he met the American sculptor Horatio Greenough (whose "organic aesthetic" would later inspire Emerson) and the English writer Walter Savage Landor. The following spring, Emerson continued his tour through Switzerland and into France. Paris charmed him with its splendid museums and gardens and he admired the natural history exhibits at the Jardin des Plantes. Crossing to England by August, he met Samuel Taylor Coleridge in London, then traveled north to visit Thomas Carlyle in Craigenputtock and William Wordsworth at Rydal Mount. His meeting with Carlyle resulted in a lifelong friendship.

After returning to Boston in 1833, Emerson gradually settled into a new routine of study, lecturing, and writing, filling an occasional pulpit on Sundays and assembling ideas in his journals for his essay "Nature." Lydia Jackson, a young woman from Plymouth, New Hampshire, heard Emerson preach in Boston and became infatuated with him. Within a year they were married and settled in a house on the Boston Post Road near the Old Manse of Grandfather Ripley. Emerson was now thirty-two and about to begin his life's work.

The next decade marked Emerson's intellectual maturity. "Nature" was completed and published as a small volume in 1836. In its elaborate series of correspondences between humanity and nature, Emerson established the foundations of his idealistic philosophy. "Why should not we also enjoy an original relation to the universe?" he asked. Humanity could seek revelations firsthand from nature, rather than having them handed down through tradition. A year later Emerson gave his "The American Scholar" address before the Harvard Phi Beta Kappa Society, an event that Oliver Wendell Holmes later called "our intellectual Declaration of Independence." In his address, Emerson called for a distinctively American style of letters, free from European influences. Invited in 1838 to speak before the graduating class of Harvard Divinity School, Emerson affirmed in his address that the true measure of religion resided within the individual, not in institutional or historical Christianity. If everyone had equal access to the Divine Spirit, then inner experience was

all that was needed to validate religious truth. For this daring pronouncement he was attacked by Harvard president Andrews Norton and others for espousing "the latest form of infidelity." In a sense each of these important essays was an extension of Emerson's basic doctrine of self-reliance, applied to philosophy, culture, and religion.

Emerson's self-reliance served him equally well in personal life, even as family losses haunted him, almost as if to test his hard-won equanimity and sense of purpose. Besides losing his first wife, Ellen Tucker, Emerson saw two of his brothers die and a third become so feeble-minded that he had to be institutionalized. Worst of all, his first-born and beloved son, Waldo, died in 1841 of scarlet fever at the age of six.

During these years, Emerson found Concord a congenial home. He established a warm and stimulating circle of friends there and enjoyed the intellectual company of Nathaniel Hawthorne, Henry David Thoreau, and Bronson Alcott. As his fame as a lecturer and writer grew, he attracted a wider set of admirers, including Margaret Fuller, who often visited to share enthusiasms and transcendental conversations. Emerson edited *The Dial* for a short time in 1842, but for the most part he remained aloof from, although sympathetic to, the Transcendentalist movement that he had so largely inspired.

Emerson continued to lecture widely and write, and his essays touched an entire generation of American writers. Thoreau, Whitman, and Emily Dickinson responded enthusiastically to the appeal of Emerson's thought, while even Hawthorne and Herman Melville, although rejecting it, still felt compelled to acknowledge his intellectual presence. Emerson spent his last few years in Concord quietly and died in the spring of 1882. Of his life it can be said that perhaps more than any of his contemporaries he embodied the qualities of the American spirit—its frankness, idealism, optimism, and self-confidence.

Analysis

Expression mattered more than form in poetry, according to Emerson. His ideas often closely parallel those of Alexis de Tocqueville on the nature of poetry in America. Both men agreed that the poetry of a democratic culture would embrace the facts of ordinary experience rather than celebrate epic themes. It would be a poetry of enumeration rather than elevation, of fact rather than eloquence.

Writing poetry was not for Emerson a smooth, continuous act of composition. Nor did he have a set formula for composition; instead, he trusted inspiration to allow the form of the poem to be determined by its subject matter. This "organic" theory of composition shapes many of Emerson's best poems, including "The Snow-Storm," "Hamatreya," "Days," and "Ode." These poems avoid a fixed metrical or stanzaic structure and allow the sense of the line to dictate its poetic form.

In "The Poet," Emerson announced that "it is not metres, but metre-making argument that makes a poem." His representative American poet would be a namer and enumerator, not a rhymer or versifier. The poet would find inspiration from the coarse vigor of American vernacular speech and in turn reinvigorate poetic language by tracing root metaphors back to their origins in ordinary experience, avoiding stilted or artificial poetic diction in favor of ordinary speech. This meant sacrificing sound to sense, however, since Emerson's "metre-making arguments" were more often gnomic than lyrical. As a result, his poems are as spare as their native landscape. They are muted and understated rather than rhapsodic and—with the exception of his Orientalism—tempered and homey in their subject matter.

Emerson's poems fall into several distinct categories, the most obvious being his nature poems; his philosophical or meditative poems, which often echo the essays; his autobiographical verse; and his occasional pieces. Sometimes these categories may overlap, but the "organic" aesthetic and colloquial tone mark them as distinctly Emersonian.

"Days" has been called the perfect Emerson poem, and while there is a satisfying completeness about the poem, it resolves less than might appear at first reading. The poem deals with what was for Emerson the continuing problem of vocation or calling. How could he justify his apparent idleness in a work-oriented culture? "Days" thus contains something of a self-rebuke, cast in terms of an Oriental procession of Days, personified as daughters of Time, who pass through the poet's garden bringing various gifts, the riches of life, which the poet too hastily rejects in favor of a "few herbs and apples," emblematic of the contemplative life. The Day scorns his choice, presumably because he has squandered his time in contemplation rather than having measured his imbibition against worthier goals. The Oriental imagery employed here transforms a commonplace theme into a memorable poem, although the poet never responds to the implied criticism of his life; nor does he identify the "morning wishes" that have been abandoned for the more sedate and domestic "herbs and apples," although

these images do suggest meanings beyond themselves.

A thematically related poem is "The Problem," in which Emerson tries to justify his reasons for leaving the ministry, which he respects and admires but cannot serve. Perhaps because he was more poet than priest, Emerson preferred the direct inspiration of the artist to the inherited truths of religion. Alternatively, it may have been that, as a romantic, he found more inspiration in nature than in Scripture. The third stanza of "The Problem" contains one of the clearest articulations of Emerson's "organic" aesthetic, of form emerging from expression, in the image of the artist who "builded better than he knew." The temples of nature "art might obey, but not surpass."

This organized theory of art reached its fullest expression in "The Snow-Storm," which still offers the best example in Emerson's poetry of form following function and human artistry imitating that of nature. Here the poem merges with what it describes. The first stanza announces the arrival of the storm and the second stanza evokes the "frolic architecture" of the snow and the human architectural forms that it anticipates. Nature freely creates, and humanity imitates through art. Wind and snow form myriad natural forms that humanity can only "mimic in slow structures" of stone. As the wind-sculpted snowdrifts create beauty from the materials at hand, the poem rounds upon itself in the poet's implicit admiration of nature's work.

Religious myth is also present in the poem "Uriel," which Robert Frost called "the greatest Western poem yet." Even if Frost's praise is overstated, this is still one of Emerson's most profound and complex poems. Again it deals with the reconciliation of opposites, this time in the proposed relativity of good and evil. Borrowing the theme of the primal revolt against God by the rebellious archangels, Emerson uses the figure of the angel Uriel as the prototype of the advanced thinker misunderstood or rejected by others. Uriel represents the artist as the rebel or prophet bearing unwelcome words, roles that Emerson no doubt identified with himself and the hostile reception given his "Divinity School Address" in 1838 by the Harvard theological faculty. Uriel's words,

> "Line in nature is not found;
> Unit and universe are round;
> In vain produced, all rays return;
> Evil will bless, and ice will burn."

speak with particular force to our age, in which recent discoveries in theoretical physics and astronomy seem to have confirmed Emerson's intuitions about the relativity of matter and energy and the nature of the physical universe.

Emerson's muse most often turned to nature for inspiration, so it is no accident that his nature poems contain some of his best work. "The Rhodora" is an early poem in which Emerson's attention to sharp and precise details of his New England landscape stands out against his otherwise generalized and formal poetic style. The first eight lines of the poem, in which Emerson describes finding the rhodora, a Northern azalea-like flower, blooming in the woods early in May of the New England spring, before other plants have put out their foliage, seem incomparably the best. Unfortunately, the second half of the poem shifts from specific nature imagery to a generalized homily on the beauty of the rhodora, cast in formal poetic diction. This division within "The Rhodora" illustrates some of Emerson's difficulties in breaking away from the outmoded style and conventions of eighteenth century English landscape poetry to find an appropriate vernacular style for American nature poetry. Here the subject matter is distinctly American, but the style—the poem's manner of seeing and feeling—is still partially derivative.

Emerson's "Ode" is a much more unconventional piece, written in terse, variable lines, usually of two or three stresses, and touching upon the dominant social and political issues of the day—the Mexican War, the Fugitive Slave Law of 1850, the threat of secession in the South, and radical Abolitionism in the North. This open form was perhaps best suited to Emerson's oracular style, which aimed to leave a few memorable lines with the reader. His angry muse berates Daniel Webster for having compromised his principles by voting for the Fugitive Slave Law, and it denounces those materialistic interests, in both the North and the South, that would profit from wage or bond slavery. Emerson's lines "Things are in the saddle,/ And ride mankind" aptly express his misgivings about the drift of American affairs that seemed to be leading toward a civil war. His taut lines seem to chant their warning like a Greek chorus, foreseeing the inevitable but helpless to intervene. By the 1850's Emerson had become an increasingly outspoken opponent of the Fugitive Slave Law, and on occasion he risked his personal safety in speaking before hostile crowds.

Despite his commitment to a new American poetry based upon common diction and ordinary speech, Emerson's poetry never quite fulfilled the promise of his call, in "The American Scholar" and "The Poet," for a new poetics. Emerson wanted to do for American poetry what William Wordsworth had accomplished for English lyrical poetry, to free it from the constraints of an artificial and dead tradition of sensibility and feeling. Emerson could envision a new poetics, but he could not sustain in his poetry a genuine American vernacular tradition. That had to wait for Whitman and Dickinson.

Emerson's greatness resides in the originality of his vision of a future American poetry, free and distinct from European models. It can be found in the grace of his essays and the insights of his journals, and it appears in those select poems in which he was able to match vision and purpose, innovation and accomplishment.

Other major works

NONFICTION: *Nature*, 1836; "The American Scholar," 1837; *An Address Delivered Before the Senior Class in Divinity College, Cambridge . . .*, 1838; *Essays: First Series*, 1841; *Orations, Lectures and Addresses*, 1844; *Essays: Second Series*, 1844; *Addresses and Lectures*, 1849; *Representative Men: Seven Lectures*, 1850; *English Traits*, 1856; *The Conduct of Life*, 1860; *Representative of Life*, 1860; *Society and Solitude*, 1870; *Works and Days*, 1870; *Letters and Social Aims*, 1876; *Lectures and Biographical Sketches*, 1884; *Miscellanies*, 1884; *Natural History of Intellect*, 1893; *The Journals of Ralph Waldo Emerson*, 1909-1914 (E. W. Emerson and W. E. Forbes, eds., 10 vols.); *The Heart of Emerson's Journals*, 1926 (Bliss Perry, ed.); *The Letters of Ralph Waldo Emerson*, 1939- (Ralph L. Rusk and Elinor M. Tilton, eds.); *The Journals and Miscellaneous Notebooks*, 1960-1982 (16 vols.); *The Complete Sermons of Ralph Waldo Emerson*, 1989-1992 (Albert J. Von Frank, ed., 4 vols.); *The Topical Notebooks of Ralph Waldo Emerson*, 1990- (Ralph H. Orth, ed.).

MISCELLANEOUS: *Uncollected Writings: Essays, Addresses, Poems, Reviews, and Letters*, 1912.

Bibliography

Bloom, Harold. *Figures of Capable Imagination*. New York: Seabury Press, 1976.
Burkholder, Robert E. *Ralph Waldo Emerson: An Annotated Bibliography of Criticism, 1980-1991*. Westport, Conn.: Greenwood Press, 1994.

Burkholder, Robert E., and Joel Myerson, eds. *Critical Essays on Ralph Waldo Emerson*. Boston: G. K. Hall, 1983.

Cameron, Kenneth Walter. *Firstlings of Emerson the Writer: A Study in Background and Sources*. Hartford, Conn.: Transcendental Books, 1992.

Jacobson, David. *Emerson's Pragmatic Vision: The Dance of the Eye*. University Park: Pennsylvania State University Press, 1993.

Neufelt, Leonard. *The House of Emerson*. Lincoln: University of Nebraska Press, 1982.

Robinson, David. *Emerson and the Conduct of Life: Pragmatism and Ethical Purpose in the Later Work*. Cambridge, England: Cambridge University Press, 1993.

Thurin, Erik Ingvar. *Emerson as Priest and Pan: A Study in the Metaphysics of Sex*. Lawrence: University Press of Kansas, 1981.

Von Frank, Albert J. *An Emerson Chronology*. New York: G. K. Hall, 1993.

Waggoner, Hyatt Howe. *Emerson as Poet*. Princeton, N.J.: Princeton University Press, 1974.

West, Cornel. *The American Evasion of Philosophy: A Genealogy of Pragmatism*. Madison: University of Wisconsin Press, 1989.

Yanella, Donald. *Ralph Waldo Emerson*. Boston: Twayne, 1982.

ROBERT FROST

Born: San Francisco, California; March 26, 1874

Died: Boston, Massachusetts; January 29, 1963

Principal poetry

A Boy's Will, 1913; *North of Boston*, 1914; *Selected Poems*, 1923; *New Hampshire: A Poem with Notes and Grace Notes*, 1923; *West-Running Brook*, 1928; *Collected Poems*, 1930; *A Further Range*, 1936; *Collected Poems*, 1939; *A Witness Tree*, 1942; *A Masque of Reason*, 1945; *Steeple Bush*, 1947; *A Masque of Mercy*, 1947; *Complete Poems*, 1949; *How Not to Be King*, 1951; *In the Clearing*, 1962; *The Poems of Robert Frost*, 1969.

Other literary forms

Although the majority of Robert Frost's published work is poetry, he published a one-act play in 1929. His only other literary publications include letters, particularly to his friend Louis Untermeyer, and lectures in which he discusses in detail his own work and poetic theory. He recorded many of his poems on records and film.

Achievements

Perhaps the most successful of American poets, Frost reached a large and diversified readership almost immediately after the publication of *North of Boston*. He sustained both popular and critical acclaim throughout his career, which spanned fifty years. He won the Pulitzer Prize in poetry four times and was nominated for the Nobel Prize in 1950 upon publication of the *Complete Poems*. Much of Frost's contribution to American literature has come from his ability to speak in poetic but plain language to both common people and scholars and to observe ordinary occurrences with irony and wit. If modern American poetry began with Walt Whitman and Emily Dickinson and evolved through Edgar Lee Masters, Robinson Jeffers, and Edward Arlington Robinson, Frost's poetry is the culmination, combining all elements of poetic craft and modern themes. Frost liberated American poets by proving the potential success of traditional forms, even during a period when form was giving way to free verse under the influence of Eliot and Ezra Pound. Frost's most important contribution may be as the model for a clearly identifiable twentieth century *American* poet. Unlike the expatriate Americans, Frost never lost touch with American persistence, folk humor, plain speech, and attachment to the land. His pragmatic, clever intelligence never became pedantic, abstract, condescending, or introverted but remained full of mischief and horseplay. In both his poetry and his public image, Frost embodied the American ideals of rugged gentleness, quiet reflection, and an unconquerable spirit. His poetry is compassionate without falling into sentimentality, positive without being naïve.

Biography

A native of New Hampshire and a graduate of Harvard University, Robert Lee Frost's father, William Prescott Frost, moved to San Francisco in 1873 to escape post-Civil War bitterness against the South. Shortly before his untimely death at thirty-five, William Prescott requested that he be buried in New England. Fulfilling this request, Robert, his sister Jeanie Florence, and their mother accompanied the casket across the country to Massachusetts. Because they could not afford the return trip, the Frosts settled in Salem, New Hampshire, when Robert was eleven years old. In 1892 Robert Frost was graduated as covaledictorian from Lawrence High School and entered Dartmouth College to study law. He dropped out, however, before completing his first semester, spending the following two years working at odd jobs and writing poetry. In 1894 he published his first poem, "My Butterfly," and became engaged to Elinor White, with whom he had shared the valedictorian honor. After his marriage in 1895, Frost helped his mother run a small private school, studied for two years at Harvard, then moved to Derry, New Hampshire, for a life of farming. Between 1900 and 1905 Frost raised poultry and wrote most of the poems that would constitute his first two volumes; after 1905 he taught school in Plymouth, New Hampshire, and in 1912 he sailed for England with Elinor and his two children, where he collected and published *A Boy's Will* and *North of Boston*. British reviewers responded so enthusiastically to these volumes that three American publishers expressed interest in bringing out U.S. editions. While in England Frost became acquainted with poets Ezra Pound, Edward Thomas, W. W. Gibson, T. E. Hulme, Lascelles Abercrombie, and others. After the onset of World War I, Frost and his family returned to the United States, in early 1915, just when his first two books were being published in New York. The Frosts moved to a small farm at Franconia, New Hampshire. *North of Boston*, meanwhile, became an enormous critical and popular success, and Frost spent 1916, and indeed most of his life, in the limelight giving readings and lectures. He taught at Amherst College from 1916 to 1920 and 1923 to 1925. He was Ralph Waldo Emerson Fellow of Poetry at Harvard from 1939 until 1943, when he left to become Ticknor Fellow in the Humanities at Dartmouth College, remaining there until 1949.

Because Frost is so strongly identified as a New England poet whose poems are inextricably rooted in the land of New Hampshire and Vermont, readers expect a high correlation between the events of his life and the resultant poetry. While Frost certainly invested most of his life in New England, there is a surprisingly dichotomy between his biography and his poetic themes. His family life was tragic because premature death beset many of its members. His father died of tuberculosis, his mother of cancer. He lost his sister; two of his children died in infancy; his married daughter died in childbirth; and his son committed suicide. During cancer surgery, his wife died of a heart attack. In spite of his long wait for recognition and the private disasters that befell him, Frost's poetry is free from bitterness and from any direct personal references. His official biographer, Lawrance Thompson, unveiled many shocking characteristics of Frost's personality— including jealousy and vindictiveness—but, much to Frost's credit, his art rises above these frailties and speaks not of pettiness but of deep matters of the heart.

Analysis

The most distinctive characteristic of Frost's work is elusiveness. Frost operates on so many levels that to interpret his poems confidently on a single level frequently causes the reader to misunderstand them completely. Because Frost's poems operate on so many levels, it is possible for almost everyone to find his own beliefs about life reflected in his poetry. Optimists can argue that Frost understands the complexities of life while still affirming humanity's ability to make creative choices that determine the future. Realists can argue that Frost is not an optimist, although, having acknowledged that doubt is more prevalent than faith, he still derives pleasure from the process of living life in the present. Skeptics can point out Frost's irony, noting that

he affirms nothing but the dualities and contradictions of life and human nature. Each type of reader has interpreted Frost correctly; one must consider all levels of Frost's poems before being certain of any particular meaning. Because Frost writes about familiar experiences in what appears to be conversational language, the overwhelming impulse is to accept what he says at face value.

The place to begin an explication of Frost's poetry is with the narrative persona and dramatic situation, for it is here that Frost draws the reader into the poems and begins his illusions. Only a few of his poems have no dramatic context, the device that offers the surest chance of discovering Frost's themes. In "After Apple-Picking," for example, a great deal can be established about the dramatic situation, the dramatic moment, and the narrative persona. The reader knows that the narrator has been harvesting apples, perhaps in great numbers, and that he is now "done" with apple-picking. He has collected his apples in barrels, one of which remains unfilled, and the narrator speculates that there may be a few apples left unpicked, although he does not know for certain. His ladder, long and two-pointed, is in the tree where he has left it, and it points "toward heaven still."

In these first six lines, Frost has already begun his sleight of hand by introducing some facts within the dramatic situation that seem extraneous to the poem's development. For example, why does he describe a "two-pointed" ladder when it does not make any difference what kind of ladder it is as long as the narrator can reach the apples with it? Why does he say that it is "sticking" toward heaven? These details help to bring the poem alive, but as part of the dramatic situation they add implications far beyond their descriptive use. The empty barrel is similarly suggestive: Readers want to know whether it is empty because somebody miscalculated the number of barrels needed, whether the narrator simply quit before the job was "done," or whether there is a more sinister suggestion that something that should have been filled is empty. Both the ladder and the barrel are facts within the dramatic situation, but they are more than simple details because they raise questions that fall outside the realm of the poem. Readers should be careful to recognize that these questions arise only if they read the ladder and barrel as suggestive. Clearly, however, Frost did not place them in the poem by accident, and therefore they are important.

Complicating the dramatic moment, the narrator tells some things about himself that help to explain why he has left the barrel empty. Readers know that the time is late fall because it is the end of apple-picking season and the beginning of winter sleep. Readers also know that the narrator is tired as he remembers visions that he saw "this morning through a pane of glass" and as he recognizes what form his dreaming is about to take. The morning world of "hoary grass" was strange to him, and as the ice pane melted, the narrator intentionally let it fall and break. Now, at the end of the day, he is embarking upon a nightmare of apples; his ladder sways precariously as the boughs bend. He is no longer safe in the apple tree, where he had once been certain of his purpose; now, it is the source of his fears. Too many apples "rumble" into the cellar, a place beneath the earth, in the opposite of that direction in which the ladder is pointing. What worries the narrator most is that some of the good apples "not bruised or spiked" will end up in the "cider-apple heap," a place that offends the narrator's sense of justice. Even as readers want to know why the barrel was left unfilled, the narrator asks why good apples that he let fall by accident are sent to the heap. If readers can understand why he is so troubled by this, they will know a great deal more about the poem's meaning.

With his typical magic, however, Frost sets readers up to accept the easy explanation as he tempts them to explain the narrator's anxieties merely as a fear of failure to do his job properly. Frost has planted a host of potentially misleading elements that encourage conventional interpretations. The ladder, with its image of outstretched arms, implores heaven, perhaps even suggesting Jacob's ladder. Because apples have such a strong traditional association with the story of the Garden of Eden, one might also conclude that apples represent the narrator's fall into mortal existence—his banishment from the grace of God. He has not, himself, sinned but carries the burden of original sin, and even though he has done the best he can with his life—he has dutifully picked apples until the very end—he is still plagued by nightmares. He knows that he has let slip from his grasp some apples that went undeservedly to the cider-apple heap; it is he who has condemned them to unworthy destruction by the apple grinder, and it occurs to him that his destiny might be similar to one of the good apples that is banished to destruction by chance. The narrator, then, is plagued by two doubts: The first is his own failure to fulfill all of his earthly obligations, knowing that time is running out for him ("essence of winter sleep is on the air"); the second is a fear that there is no ultimate mercy—fallen apples like fallen humanity are disposed of indiscriminately. The

hoary world he saw through the pane of glass (with its biblical allusion: "for now we see through a glass, darkly; but then face to face") was the image of life and death, and of his own mortality.

Frost has gone to considerable trouble to establish this as the proper reading: The narrator is frightened by the thought of death because he is uncertain whether he has satisfied his earthly duties. A simple moralistic conclusion might be that people should work harder before finding themselves, like the narrator, on the verge of death without salvation. Frost first offered the reader those suggestive objects, then presented a narrator filled with visions, dreams, and sleep, and finally, he produced a dozen highly recognizable and traditional biblical symbols.

Why should "After Apple-Picking" (and "Stopping by Woods on a Snowy Evening," for that matter) not be interpreted as a poem about the virtues of steadfastness and singleness of purpose? Yet, one cannot read the poem only at that level—Frost has effected a sleight of hand. The narrator inserts a telling clue in line 37—"one can see what will trouble this sleep of mine"—"one" meaning none other than the reader. All along, the reader has been thinking that the narrator is troubled about his sleep because he is unprepared for death, but now the reader begins to suspect that this interpretation is incorrect. "This sleep of mine" is not the sleep the reader originally understood, and the narrator corrects the misconception by adding, "whatever sleep it is." The reader believed it was death, and for good reason: Again trickled into it, the reader has fallen into the poem's message.

The "one" who can see the narrator's sleep is not the reader but the woodchuck who could "say" whether "it's like his long sleep or just some human sleep." In reality, the woodchuck could not say anything, nor could the woodchuck fear death because of any failure to fulfill religious obligations. The narrator can speak of and fear death, unsure of salvation, but not the woodchuck. Even more trickily, the narrator projects or imagines what the woodchuck's long sleep is ("as I describe its coming on"); so readers have the woodchuck, who cannot possess human vision, telling the narrator only what the narrator imagines and ascribes to the animal. It is through imagination that humanity conceives death, even as the reader has used his or her imagination to create the symbols in the poem. So moments of life may be misinterpreted to create concepts of death. For Frost, human imagination is the trickster, not death, and people often use it to torment themselves about a mortality that they have fabricated. This theme of "After Apple-Picking" reflects Frost's larger worldview and helps to account for the frequent misreading of his poems. Even though "After Apple-Picking" seems to be concerned with death, Christian fate, redemption, and the virtuous life—abstract ideas about the afterlife—Frost is much more concerned with earthly existence.

More important than the technical devices for discovering Frost's irony and major themes is the presence of "opposites," which set up patterns of reversal. Frost frequently presents "pairs" of contrasting personae, ideas, images, or symbols, perhaps most famously in "Mending Wall," where narrator and neighbor, pine and apple trees, civilized being and savage, father and son, light and dark, ego and alter ego square off against each other with yet another barrier—the wall—between them.

Most of the "opposite" poems use some kind of physical barrier to identify territory, and the wall in "Mending Wall" has been consciously constructed in violation of nature, which "doesn't love a wall." To the narrator, the wall serves no useful purpose and is only an annoying reminder of his neighbor's foolish platitudes and the inability of the neighbors to communicate except once a year at spring mending time. Before the narrator built a wall, he would want to know what he "was walling in or walling out," but there is a more important question implied: If there were no wall, would he and his neighbor still be opposites? Because the narrator knows that the answer is "yes," and because he is deliberately antagonistic ("Spring is the mischief in me, and I wonder/ If I could put a notion in his head"), the presence of the wall is a purely academic argument for the narrator. The wall is unnatural—nature wants it down and topples it every winter. There is "Something" that does not love a wall. The persistence of "unnatural" barriers reminds the narrator that he cannot explain the existence of contraries any more than his neighbor can explain why good fences make good neighbors, but he does know that in contraries lie the secrets of living, that through the self-conscious process of witnessing contraries one is most likely to discover one's own life forces rather than any profound secrets of life.

Unlike the English Romantic poets and "nature poets" with whom he is frequently compared, Frost does not look to nature for an affirmation of life, for solace, or for a road to self-discovery. For Frost, humanity is alone in the world, unable to answer questions about God and death but having some control over its earthly destiny. For Frost, who is not a fatalist or a determinist, who believes things happen neither for good nor for evil but simply occur, who does not fear death or embrace promises of heaven, the only way is "to go by contraries," making creative choices, accepting paradoxes, questioning walls.

In "Fire and Ice," the entire doctrine of "opposites" and irony is at work, and this poem, perhaps most directly of all his work, illustrates Frost's themes and techniques. Arranged as a single stanza of nine lines (in framed segments), the poem establishes the opposites of fire and ice, hot and cold, love and hate, and centers on the middle (fifth) line of the poem. Fire is presented in the first four lines, ice in the last four. The center line asks, "But *if* it had to perish twice," and that becomes the ironic key. Whether the world will be destroyed a second time makes no difference to Frost's narrator; it is a moot question reserved for the gullible reader who interprets "After Apple-Picking" as a Christian manifesto. Frost is much more concerned with the power of hate, an opposite of love, which he says "will suffice," but one must not be tricked by that simple explanation either, to conclude that man is beset by hate any more than he is pursued by death. It "would suffice," if readers wanted it to, just as the woodchuck "would say" if he were asked, but the world does not have to "perish twice" except as one fears destruction, and readers do not have to ask the woodchuck, and one does not have to stoop to hate. "Some day the world will end in fire," but not Frost.

During an age when the thrust of literature has been to question illusion and reality, and to lament the lonely plight and desperation of the isolated human being in an overwhelming universe, Frost presents a more positive vision, rooted in the American search for the good life. Human beings may struggle to discover their tormented spirit, but they are also capable of creative choices and of accepting contraries and uncertainties. Frost delights in the mysteries of life without being burdened by debilitating responsibilities for them, and while human beings might not become the conquerors of the universe, neither are they suppressed by it, and in that Frost rejoices.

Other major works

PLAY: *A Way Out*, 1929.

NONFICTION: *The Letters of Robert Frost to Louis Untermeyer*, 1963 (with a commentary by Louis Untermeyer);

The Record of a Friendship, 1963 (Margaret Bartlett, ed.); *Selected Letters of Robert Frost*, 1964 (Lawrance Thompson, ed.); *Selected Prose*, 1966 (Hyde Cox and Edward C. Lathem, eds.).

Bibliography

Burnshaw, Stanley. *Robert Frost Himself*. New York: George Braziller, 1986.

Gerber, Philip L. *Robert Frost*. Rev. ed. Boston: Twayne, 1982.

Lathem, Edward Connery. *Robert Frost: A Biography*. New York: Holt, Rinehart and Winston, 1981.

Poirier, Richard. *Robert Frost: The Work of Knowing*. New York: Oxford University Press, 1977.

Potter, James L. *The Robert Frost Handbook*. University Park: Pennsylvania State University Press, 1980.

Pritchard, William H. *Frost: A Literary Life Reconsidered*. 2d ed. Amherst: University of Massachusetts Press, 1993.

NATHANIEL HAWTHORNE

Born: Salem, Massachusetts; July 4, 1804

Died: Plymouth, New Hampshire; May 19, 1864

Principal long fiction

Fanshawe: A Tale, 1828; *The Scarlet Letter*, 1850; *The House of the Seven Gables*, 1851; *The Blithedale Romance*, 1852; *The Marble Faun*, 1860; *Septimius Felton*, 1872 (fragment); *The Dolliver Romance*, 1876 (fragment); *The Ancestral Footstep*, 1883 (fragment); *Doctor Grimshawe's Secret*, 1883 (fragment).

Other literary forms

Many of Nathaniel Hawthorne's short stories were originally published anonymously in such magazines as the *Token* and the *New England Magazine* between 1830 and 1837. Hawthorne also wrote stories for children. As a favor to Franklin Pierce, he wrote a biography for the presidential campaign. Hawthorne's last completed work was *Our Old Home* (1863), a series of essays about his sojourn in England. At the time of his death, he left four unfinished fragments.

Achievements

Few other American authors, with the possible exception of Henry James, have engaged in so deliberate a literary apprenticeship as Hawthorne. After an initial period of anonymity during his so-called solitary years from 1825 to 1837, he achieved an unfaltering reputation as an author of short stories, romances, essays, and children's books. He is remembered not only for furthering the development of the short-story form but also for distinguishing between the novel and the romance. The prefaces to his long works elucidate his theory of the "neutral ground"—the junction between the actual and the imaginary—where romance takes place. He is noted for his masterful exploration of the psychology of guilt and sin; his study of the Puritan heritage contributed to the emerging sense of historicity that characterized the American Renaissance of the mid-nineteenth century. Hawthorne is unrivaled as an allegorist, especially as one whose character typologies and symbols achieve universality through their psychological validity. While he has been faulted for sentimentality, lapses into archaic diction, and Gothicism, Hawthorne's works continue to evoke the "truth of the human heart" that is the key to their continuing appeal.

Biography

Nathaniel Hawthorne was born in Salem, Massachusetts, on July 4, 1804. On his father's side, Hawthorne was descended from William Hathorne, who settled in Massachusetts in 1630 and whose son John was one of the judges in the 1692 Salem witchcraft trials. Hawthorne's father, a sea captain, married Elizabeth Clarke Manning in 1801. After his father's death, Hawthorne, his sisters Elizabeth Manning and Maria Louisa, and his mother moved into the populous Manning household. He attended school, explored the forests surrounding his home, and spent long afternoons reading such favorite authors as Edmund Spenser, John Bunyan, and William Shakespeare. Back in Salem, he began in 1820 to be tutored for college by the lawyer Benjamin Lynde Oliver, working, in the meantime, as a bookkeeper for his Uncle Robert, an occupation that foreshadowed Hawthorne's later business ventures. The first member of his family to attend college, he was sent to Bowdoin, where he was graduated eighteenth in a class of thirty-eight. His fellow students at Bowdoin included Henry Wadsworth Longfellow and Franklin Pierce, who later was elected president of the United States.

Hawthorne had determined early on to pursue a career in letters. Returning to Salem upon graduation, he began a self-imposed apprenticeship, the so-called solitary years. During this time, Hawthorne privately published *Fanshawe* (a work that he would so thoroughly repudiate that his wife, Sophia, knew nothing of it). He published many short stories anonymously and unsuccessfully attempted to interest publishers in several of his collections. As a means of support he edited the *American Magazine of Useful and Entertaining Knowledge* and compiled *Peter Parley's Universal History*. Not until the publication of *Twice-Told Tales* under the secret financial sponsorship of his friend Horatio Bridge did Hawthorne's name become publicly known. During this time Hawthorne met Sophia Peabody. For Hawthorne, Sophia was the key by which he was released from "a life of shadows" to the "truth of the human heart."

They were married on July 19, 1842. His financial difficulties were exacerbated by the birth of Una in 1844; finally, in 1846, when his son Julian was born and *Mosses from an Old Manse* was published, he was appointed surveyor of the Salem Custom House, a post he held from 1846 to 1849, when a political upset cost him his job. With more time to write and with the pressure to support a growing family, Hawthorne began a period of intense literary activity; his friendship with Herman Melville dates from that time. *The Scarlet Letter*, whose ending sent Sophia to bed with a grievous headache, was finished in February, 1850. *The House of the Seven Gables* appeared in 1851, the year Hawthorne's daughter Rose was born; by the end of the next year, Hawthorne had completed *The Blithedale Romance*; two volumes of children's tales; *The Life of Franklin Pierce*; and a collection of stories, *The Snow-Image and Other Twice-Told Tales*.

From 1853 to 1857, Hawthorne served as United States consul at Liverpool, England, a political appointment under President Pierce. After four years of involvement with the personal and financial problems of stranded Americans, Hawthorne resigned and lived in Rome and Florence from 1857 to 1858, where he acquired ideas for his last romance, *The Marble Faun*. After returning with his family to the United States, Hawthorne worked on four unfinished romances, *Doctor Grimshawe's Secret*, *Septimius Felton*, *The Dolliver Romance*, and *The Ancestral Footstep*, in which two themes are dominant: the search for immortality and the American attempt to establish title to English ancestry. His carefully considered essays on the paucity of American tradition, the depth of British heritage, and the contrast between democracy and entrenched class systems were first published in *The Atlantic* and then collected as *Our Old Home*. After a lingering illness, he died at Plymouth, New Hampshire, on May 19, 1864, during a trip with Franklin Pierce. He was buried at Sleepy Hollow Cemetery in Concord, Massachusetts.

Analysis

Hawthorne's reading in American colonial history confirmed his basically ambivalent attitude toward the American past, particularly the form that Puritanism took in the New England colonies. Sin and guilt preoccupied him, as they did his Puritan ancestors. In his move from Salem to Concord, Hawthorne encountered what he considered the facile dismissal of the problem of evil by the Concord intellectuals. As a result, he developed a deeply ambivalent attitude that colored the situations and characters of his fiction.

Central to Hawthorne's romances is his idea of a "neutral territory," described in the Custom House sketch that precedes *The Scarlet Letter* as a place "somewhere between the real world and fairy-land, where the Actual and the Imaginary may meet, and each imbue itself with the nature of the other." A romance, according to Hawthorne, is different from the novel, which maintains a "minute fidelity . . . to the probable and ordinary course of man's experience." In the neutral territory of romance, however, the author may make use of the "marvellous" to heighten atmospheric effects, if he also presents "the truth of the human heart." As long as the writer of romance creates characters whose virtues, vices, and sensibilities are distinctly human, he may place these individuals in an environment that is out of the ordinary—or that is, in fact, allegorical. Thus, for example, while certain elements—the stigma of the scarlet letter or Donatello's faun ears—are fantastical in conception, they represent a moral stance that is true to nature. Dimmesdale's guilt at concealing his adultery with Hester Prynne is, indeed, as destructive as the wound on his breast, and Donatello's pagan nature is expressed in the shape of his ears.

A number of recurring thematic patterns and character types appear in Hawthorne's novels and tales. These repetitions show Hawthorne's emphasis on the effects of events on the human heart rather than on the events themselves. One common motif is concern for the past, or, as Hawthorne says in the preface to *The House of the Seven Gables*, his "attempt to connect a bygone time with the very present that is flitting away from us." Hawthorne's interest in the Puritan past was perhaps sparked by his "discovery," as a teenager, of his Hathorne connections; it was certainly influenced by his belief that progress was impeded by inheritance, that "the wrong-doing of one generation lives into the successive ones, and . . . becomes a pure and uncontrollable mischief." For Hawthorne, then, the past must be reckoned with and then put aside; the eventual decay of aristocratic families is not only inevitable but also desirable.

Hawthorne's understanding of tradition is illustrated in many of his works. In *The Scarlet Letter*, for example, he explores the effect of traditional Puritan social and theological expectations on three kinds of sinners—the adultress (Hester), the hypocrite (Dimmesdale), and the avenger (Chillingworth)—only to demonstrate that the punishment they inflict on themselves far outweighs the public castigation. Hester, in fact, inverts the rigid

Puritan system, represented by the scarlet letter, whose meaning she changes from "adultress" to "able." Probably the most specific treatment of the theme, however, is found in *The House of the Seven Gables*, in which the Pyncheon family house and fortune have imprisoned both Hepzibah and Clifford, one in apathy and one in insanity; only Phoebe, the country cousin who cares little for wealth, can lighten the burden, not only for her relatives but also for Holgrave, a descendant of the Maules who invoked the original curse.

Another recurring theme is that of isolation. Almost every character that Hawthorne created experiences some sense of isolation, sometimes from a consciousness of sin, sometimes from innocence itself, or sometimes from a deliberate attempt to remain aloof. According to Hawthorne, this kind of isolation, most intense when it is self-imposed, frequently comes from a consciousness of sin or from what he calls the "violation of the sanctity of the human heart." For Hawthorne, the "unpardonable sin" is just such a violation, in which one individual becomes subjected to another's intellectual or scientific (rather than emotional) interest. Chillingworth is a good example; as Hester's unacknowledged husband, he lives with Dimmesdale, deliberately intensifying the minister's hidden guilt.

In the prefatory essay to the book, Hawthorne establishes the literalism of the scarlet letter, which, he says, he has in his possession as an old, faded, tattered remnant of the past. Just as Hawthorne contemplates the letter, thus generating the novel, so the reader is forced to direct attention to the primary symbol, not simply of Hester's adultery or of her ability but also of the way in which the restrictions of the Puritan forebears are transcended by the warmth of the human heart. Through this symbol, then, and through its living counterpart, Pearl, the daughter of Hester and Dimmesdale, Hawthorne examines the isolating effects of a sense of sin, using as his psychological setting the Puritan ethos.

With Hester's first public appearance with the infant Pearl and the heavily embroidered scarlet letter on her breast, the child—Hester's "torment" and her "joy"—and the letter become identified. Hester's guilt is a public one; Dimmesdale's is not. To admit to his share in the adultery is to relinquish his standing as the minister of the community, and so, initially too weak to commit himself, he pleads with Hester to confess her partner in the sin. She does not do so, nor does she admit that Chillingworth, the doctor who pursues Dimmesdale, is her husband. Three solitary people, then, are inexorably bound together by the results of the sin but are unable to communicate with one another.

The Puritan intention of bringing the sinner into submission has the opposite effect upon Hester, who, with a pride akin to humility, tenaciously makes a way for herself in the community. As an angel of mercy to the suffering, the sick, and the heavy of heart, she becomes a living model of charity that the townspeople, rigidly enmeshed in their Puritan theology, are unable to emulate. In addition, she exercises a talent for fine embroidery, so that even the bride has her clothing embellished with the sinner's finery. Hester's ostracization hardens her pride until, as she says to Dimmesdale in the forest, their act has a "consecration of its own." The adultery, in short, achieves a validation quite outside the letter of the Puritan law, and Hester finds no reason not to suggest that Dimmesdale run away with her in a repetition of the temptation and the original sin.

In the meantime, Dimmesdale has not had the relief of Hester's public confession. As veiled confessions, his sermons grow in intensity and apparent sincerity, gaining many converts to the church. Under Chillingsworth's scrutiny, however, Dimmesdale's concealed guilt creates a physical manifestation, a scarlet letter inscribed in his flesh. While Hester's letter has yet to work its way inward to repentance, Dimmesdale's is slowly working its way outward. Chillingworth himself, initially a scholar, becomes dedicated to the cause of intensifying the minister's sufferings. Although Chillingworth eventually takes partial responsibility for Hester's sin, admitting that as a scholarly recluse he should not have taken a young wife, he inexorably causes his own spiritual death. He becomes the lowest in the hierarchy of sinners, for while Hester and Dimmesdale have at least joined in passion, Chillingworth is isolated in pride.

The scaffold scenes are central to the work. For Dimmesdale, public abnegation is the key: Standing as a penitent on the scaffold at midnight is insufficient, for his act is illuminated only by the light of a great comet. His decision to elope with Hester is also insufficient to remove his guilt; what he considers to be the beginning of a "new life" is a reenactment of the original deed. In the end, the scaffold proves the only real escape from the torments devised by Chillingworth, for in facing the community with Hester and Pearl, the minister faces himself and removes the concealment that is a great part of his guilt. His "new life" is, in fact, death, and he offers no hope to Hester that they will meet again, for to do so would be to succumb to temptation again. Only Pearl, who married a lord, leaves the community permanently; as the innocent victim, she in effect returns to her mother's home to expiate her mother's sin.

As Hawthorne notes in his preface to *The House of the Seven Gables*, he intends to show the mischief that the past does when it lives into the present, particularly when coupled with the question of an inheritance. The family curse that haunts Hepzibah and Clifford Pyncheon, the hidden property deed, and even Hepzibah's dreams of an unexpected inheritance are so centered on the past that the characters are unable to function in the present. In fact, says Hawthorne, far more worrisome than the missing inheritance is the "moral disease" that is passed from one generation to the next.

This "moral disease" results from the greed of the family progenitor, Colonel Pyncheon, who coveted the small tract of land owned by one Matthew Maule. Maule's curse—"God will give him blood to drink"— comes true on the day the new Pyncheon mansion, built on the site of Maule's hut, is to be consecrated. The colonel dies, presumably from apoplexy but possibly from foul play, and from that day, Hawthorne says, a throwback to the colonel appears in each generation— a calculating, practical man, who, as the inheritor, commits again "the great guilt of his ancestor" in not making restoration to the Maule descendants. Clifford, falsely imprisoned for the murder of his Uncle Jaffrey Pyncheon, the one Pyncheon willing to make restitution, is persecuted after his release by Judge Pyncheon, another of Jaffrey's nephews and Jaffrey's real murderer, for his presumed knowledge of the hiding place of the Indian deed giving title to their uncle's property.

In contrast to these forces from the past, Hawthorne poses Phoebe, a Pyncheon country cousin with no pretensions to wealth but with a large fund of domesticity and a warm heart. Almost certainly modeled on Sophia, Phoebe possesses an unexpected power, a "homely witchcraft." Symbolically, as Frederick Crews suggests, she neutralizes the morbidity in the Pyncheon household and eventually stands as an "ideal parent" to Hepzibah and Clifford. Indeed, Phoebe brings her enfeebled relatives into the circle of humanity.

If Phoebe represents the living present, Holgrave, the daguerreotypist and descendant of the Maules, represents the future. Like Clifford, however, who is saved by his imprisonment from an aesthetic version of the unpardonable sin, Holgrave runs the risk of becoming merely a cold-blooded observer. Like Hawthorne, Holgrave is a writer, boarding at the House of the Seven Gables to observe the drama created as the past spills into the present and turning Pyncheon history into fiction. He is, nevertheless, a reformer. In an echo of Hawthorne's preface, he would have buildings made of impermanent materials, ready to be built anew with each generation; likewise, he would merge old family lines into the stream of humanity. While Holgrave's progressive views become mitigated once he marries Phoebe, he is rescued from becoming a Chillingworth by his integrity, his conscience, and his reverence for the human soul. Although he unintentionally hypnotizes Phoebe by reading her his story of Matthew Maule's mesmerism of Alice Pyncheon, he eschews his power, thereby not only saving himself and her from a Dimmesdale/Chillingworth relationship but also breaking the chain of vengeance that was in his power to perpetuate. The chain of past circumstances is also broken by the death of Judge Pyncheon, who, unlike Holgrave, intended to exercise his psychological power to force Clifford to reveal where the Indian deed is hidden. Stricken by apoplexy (or Maule's curse), however, the judge is left in solitary possession of the house as Clifford and Hepzibah flee in fear.

Holgrave's integrity and death itself thus prevent a reenactment of the original drama of power and subjection that initiated the curse. As Holgrave learns, the judge himself murdered his bachelor uncle and destroyed a will that gave the inheritance to Clifford. Although exonerated, Clifford's intellect cannot be recalled to its former state, and so he remains a testimonial to the adverse effects of "violation of the human heart."

During Hepzibah and Clifford's flight from the scene of the judge's death, Phoebe, representing the present, and Holgrave, the future, pledge their troth, joining the Pyncheon and Maule families. In marrying Holgrave, Phoebe incorporates Pyncheon blood with the "mass of the people," for the original Maule was a poor man and his son a carpenter.

The Scarlet Letter and *The House of the Seven Gables* remain classic studies of the psychology of sin and guilt. The cultural significance of these "symbolic romances" is enriched by Hawthorne's great skill at placing his characters squarely within the context of the American colonial past, thus adding imaginatively not only to the readers' sense of an important period in the American past but also our insight into some of the deeply rooted sensibilities that have helped form the American present.

Other major works

SHORT FICTION: *Twice-Told Tales*, 1837, expanded 1842; *Mosses from an Old Manse*, 1846; *The Snow-Image and Other Twice-Told Tales*, 1851.

NONFICTION: *The Life of Franklin Pierce*, 1852; *Our Old Home*, 1863.

CHILDREN'S LITERATURE: *Grandfather's Chair*, 1841; *Biographical Stories for Children*, 1842; *True Stories from History and Biography*, 1851; *A Wonder-Book for Boys and Girls*, 1852; *Tanglewood Tales for Boys and Girls*, 1853.

EDITED TEXT: *Peter Parley's Universal History*, 1837.

MISCELLANEOUS: *Complete Works*, 1850-1882 (13 vols.); *The Complete Writings of Nathaniel Hawthorne*, 1900 (22 vols.).

Bibliography

Baym, Nina. *The Shape of Hawthorne's Career*. Ithaca, N.Y.: Cornell University Press, 1977.

Bloom, Harold, ed. *Nathaniel Hawthorne*. New York: Chelsea House, 1986.

Charvat, William, et al., eds. *The Centenary Edition of the Works of Nathaniel Hawthorne*. Columbus: Ohio State University Press, 1963-   .

Colacurcio, Michael J. *The Province of Piety: Moral History in Hawthorne's Early Tales*. Cambridge, Mass.: Harvard University Press, 1984.

Crews, Frederick. *The Sins of the Fathers: Hawthorne's Psychological Themes*. New York: Oxford University Press, 1966.

Doubleday, Neal Frank. *Hawthorne's Early Tales: A Critical Study*. Durham, N.C.: Duke University Press, 1972.

Fogle, Richard Harter. *Hawthorne's Fiction: The Light and the Dark*. Rev. ed. Norman: University of Oklahoma Press, 1964.

Fossum, Robert H. *Hawthorne's Inviolable Circle: The Problem of Time*. Deland, Fla.: Everett/Edwards, 1972.

Herbert, T. Walter. *Dearest Beloved: The Hawthornes and the Making of the Middle-Class Family*. Berkeley: University of California Press, 1993.

Mellow, James R. *Nathaniel Hawthorne and His Times*. Boston: Houghton Mifflin, 1980.

Miller, Edward Havilland. *Salem Is My Dwelling Place: A Life of Nathaniel Hawthorne*. Iowa City: University of Iowa Press, 1991.

Newman, Lea Bertani Vozar. *A Reader's Guide to the Short Stories of Nathaniel Hawthorne*. Boston: G. K. Hall, 1979.

Stoehr, Taylor. *Hawthorne's Mad Scientists*. Hamden, Conn.: Archon Books, 1978.

Waggoner, Hyatt. *Hawthorne: A Critical Study*. Rev. ed. Cambridge, Mass.: Harvard University Press, 1963.

JOHN IRVING

Born: Exeter, New Hampshire; March 2, 1942

Principal long fiction

Setting Free the Bears, 1969; *The Water-Method Man*, 1972; *The 158-Pound Marriage*, 1974; *The World According to Garp*, 1978; *The Hotel New Hampshire*, 1981; *The Cider House Rules*, 1985; *A Prayer for Owen Meany*, 1989; *A Son of the Circus*, 1994.

Other literary forms

Unlike many contemporary fiction writers, John Irving has published very few short stories, and several of these were later incorporated into his novels. The exceptions include "Lost in New York" and "Almost in Iowa," both published in Esquire in 1973; "Brennbar's Rant," published in Playboy in 1974; and "Interior Space," written in 1974 and published in Fiction in 1980.

Achievements

When *The World According to Garp* became a best-seller in 1978, prompting the reissue of his three previous novels, Irving captured the attention of literary critics as well as of the popular audience. His life and works were profiled in *Time*, *Saturday Review*, and *Rolling Stone*, and his novels entered what he calls in *The World According to Garp* "that uncanny half-light where 'serious' books glow, for a time, as also 'popular' books."

Various aspects of Irving's work appeal to different audiences, making him difficult to classify as either "serious" or "popular." The sometimes ribald, occasionally grotesque humor and the explicit sexuality of the novels give them a sensational appeal and have made Irving—and his novelist character T. S. Garp—cult heroes for the American public.

On the other hand, Irving's representation of random violence in the modern world, his emphasis on love and family responsibilities, and his use of writers as major characters have prompted serious examination of his work among academic critics. He has proven himself a figure to be reckoned with in contemporary American fiction, in part because of his confrontation with issues that occupy public attention, such as abortion and the morality of war. This blend of contemporary issues, bizarre yet believable characters, and an old-fashioned devotion to good storytelling distinguishes Irving's novels.

Biography

John Winslow Irving was born on March 2, 1942, in Exeter, New Hampshire, to F. N. and Frances Winslow Irving. His father taught Russian history at Exeter Academy, where Irving attended prep school. At Exeter, he developed two lifelong interests, writing and wrestling, and became convinced that both required the same skills: practice and determination. Though not an outstanding student, he developed an appreciation of hard, steady work and a love of literature. After being graduated from Exeter at the age of nineteen, Irving spent a year at the University of Pittsburgh, where the wrestling competition convinced him that writing was a better career choice.

In 1962, Irving enrolled at the University of New Hampshire, where he began to work with authors Thomas Williams and John Yount, but a desire to see more of the world caused him to drop out. After an intensive summer course in German at Harvard University, he left for Vienna, where he enrolled at the Institute of European Studies. During his two years in Vienna, Irving married Shyla Leary, a painter whom he had met at Harvard, studied German, and became seriously devoted to writing. Living in an unfamiliar place sharpened his powers of observation. He returned to the University of New Hampshire, worked again with Thomas Williams, and was graduated cum laude in 1965. From there, with his wife and son, Colin, Irving went to the University of Iowa Writers' Workshop, where he earned an M.F.A. degree in creative writing in 1967. During his time at Iowa, Irving continued wrestling with Dan Gable, the Iowa coach who won a medal at the 1976 Munich Olympics. Irving also completed his first published novel, *Setting Free the Bears*, which is set in Austria.

Setting Free the Bears was well received by critics and sold well (6,228 copies) for a first novel. Irving moved his family back to New England. After a brief period of teaching at Windham College, he taught at

Mount Holyoke College until 1972, and for 1971-1972 he was awarded a Rockefeller Foundation grant. *The Water-Method Man*, published in 1972, did not sell as well as *Setting Free the Bears*, but Irving was invited to be a writer-in-residence at the University of Iowa from 1972 to 1975, and for 1974-1975 he received a fellowship from the National Endowment for the Arts. During that time, Irving published his third novel, *The 158-Pound Marriage*, which was set in Iowa City. Sales of *The 158-Pound Marriage* were poor, and Irving returned to New England to begin a second period of teaching at Mount Holyoke.

The turning point in Irving's career came in 1978, with the publication of *The World According to Garp*. Discouraged by the seeming reluctance of Random House to promote his novels, he moved to E. P. Dutton and the guidance of Henry Robbins, its editor-in-chief. Although Dutton promoted the novel in ways that normally disenchant the serious reviewer (bumper stickers, T-shirts), the critical reaction was good and the public reception overwhelming; combined hardback and paperback sales reached three million in the first two years. In 1982, *The World According to Garp* was made into a film, with Irving playing a bit part as a wrestling referee. The success of the novel allowed Irving to devote more of his time to writing, and in 1981 Dutton published his fifth novel, *The Hotel New Hampshire*. Although some critics expressed disappointment in the novel, it was a best-seller and a Book-of-the-Month Club selection, and it was filmed in 1984. The author of *The World According to Garp* had become a household word.

Irving's two later novels of the 1980's—*The Cider House Rules* and *A Prayer for Owen Meany*—were also best-sellers and book-club selections. He is increasingly the subject of scholarly study; articles about and reviews of his work have been published in journals as diverse as *Novel, The Sewanee Review*, and the *Journal of the American Medical Association*.

Analysis

Irving's major contribution to the American novel is the creation of truly memorable characters who struggle to cope with the fragilities and ambiguities of contemporary existence. His fiction is distinguished by a highly personal fusion of seemingly incongruous elements. Irving's settings, actions, and characters are often bizarre, sometimes violent, yet infused with humor. The world he presents is frequently chaotic and unpredictable, full of sudden death and apparently meaningless collisions of people, values, ideologies, and objects. Among his characters are the Ellen Jamesians (*The World According to Garp*), who cut out their tongues to protest the rape and mutilation of a little girl; a blind bear-trainer named Freud (*The Hotel New Hampshire*); and a motorcyclist who locks a zoo attendant in a cage with an anteater (*Setting Free the Bears*). Characters die in excruciating ways: stung to death by thousands of bees, killed in airplane crashes, assassinated in parking lots. Irving himself has referred to *The World According to Garp* as "an X-rated soap opera." Balancing the sensational and pessimistic elements of the novels, however, is a core of humane values. Irving posits not a violent and arbitrary world but one in which violence and havoc are present in sufficient quantities to demand constant vigilance. His characters may behave strangely, but their motives are usually pure. Infidelity exists, but so does real love; children deserve protection; human kindness is paramount. Many issues with which his novels deal are quite contemporary: feminism, sex-change operations, political assassination. Of equal importance, however, are romantic impulses such as freeing the animals in a zoo, rescuing the afflicted, and guarding one's loved ones against harm. Underlying the bizarre in Irving's novels is often a deep vein of humor arising from the incongruities and relieving the tension between tradition and novelty, reverence and blasphemy, contributing to the singularity of Irving's work.

The humor in Irving's novels serves both to make the bizarre and violent elements more acceptable and to reinforce the duality of his vision. No contemporary novelist better exemplifies Dorothy Parker's requisites for humor: "a disciplined eye and a wild mind." Early in his career, Irving relied heavily on slapstick comedy. Increasingly, he has turned to irony and wit as major devices of humor, but all the novels have a strong element of fantasy; dreams or nightmares become reality. Comedy and tragedy are woven closely together. Irving, always sensitive to public opinion, built into *The World According to Garp* a defense against those who would accuse him of treating serious subjects too lightly. A reader writes to T.S. Garp, the novelist-protagonist, to accuse him of finding other people's problems funny; Garp replies that he has "nothing but sympathy for how people behave—and nothing but laughter to console them with." By insisting that life is both comically absurd and inevitably tragic, Irving espouses an acceptance of extremes.

By far Irving's most successful novel, *The World*

According to Garp is the best example of his ability to wed the bizarre and the commonplace, the tragic and the comic. The novel deals with the extremes of human experience, embodying that dualism of vision which is Irving's greatest strength as a writer. Titled in the working draft *Lunacy and Sorrow*, it has been called "a manic, melancholic carnival of a book," and Irving manages to keep the reader poised between laughter and tears. The seriousness of *The World According to Garp* lies in its thematic concerns: the elusive nature of reality and the human need to find or impose order on existence. The "lunacy" in the novel derives from the extremes to which people will go to achieve order and meaning; the "sorrow' arises from the ultimate human inability to control destiny. The last line—"in the world according to Garp we are all terminal cases"—conveys the stoic acceptance of misfortune and disaster that Irving posits as necessary for survival, yet the lightly ironic tone of this concluding sentence also reflects the novel's utter lack of sentimentality or melodrama.

T. S. Garp, the main character, is an unlikely hero. On the one hand he is a fairly typical twentieth century man, a husband and father who worries about his children, pursues his career, jogs regularly, and has a penchant for young female baby-sitters. He loves his wife, is good to his mother, and has a few close friends. These bare facts, on the other hand, do not explain Garp, nor, Irving suggests, would such a sketch be adequate to represent most people. Garp is the son of Jenny Fields, nurse, daughter of a wealthy family, author of an autobiography, and finally sponsor of a haven for women with special needs. Garp's father, a fatally injured ball turret gunner during World War II, enters the picture only long enough to impregnate Jenny Fields. Jenny then rears the boy at the Steering School, where she is the school nurse. After Garp is graduated from Steering, mother and son go to Vienna, where Jenny writes her autobiography, *A Sexual Suspect*, and Garp writes "The Pension Grillparzer." *A Sexual Suspect*, the beginning and end of Jenny Fields's writing career, catapults her to fame as a feminist writer and finally leads to her assassination by a reactionary gunman during a political rally. "The Pension Grillparzer" launches Garp on a career as a writer and also makes possible his marriage to Helen Holm, daughter of the wrestling coach at Steering, with whom he has two sons, Duncan and Walt. Because of his mother's fame, Garp becomes a close friend of Roberta Muldoon, a transsexual who was formerly Robert Muldoon, tight end for the Philadelphia Eagles. Garp also encounters the Ellen Jamesians,

a radical feminist group that protests rape with self-mutilation. After an automobile accident that kills Walt and blinds Duncan in one eye, Garp and Helen adopt the real Ellen James, who eventually becomes a writer. Garp himself is killed at the age of thirty-three by an Ellen Jamesian angered by Garp's rejection of the group's extremist practices.

Despite this grim outline, *The World According to Garp* is often humorous and occasionally wildly comic. The humor usually grows out of human foibles: Dean Bodger catching a dead pigeon as it falls from the Steering infirmary roof and mistaking it for the body of young Garp; Jenny Fields failing to recognize a well-dressed woman as a prostitute on the streets of Vienna; Garp sprinting down the streets of his neighborhood to overtake astonished speeders who endanger the lives of his children or dressing as a woman to attend the "feminist funeral" of his mother. When the comic and tragic merge, the result is black humor in the tradition of Nathanael West. At the climax of the novel, for example, when Garp's car crashes into that of Michael Milton, Helen, in the act of performing oral sex on Milton, bites off his penis, effectively ending the affair that she has been trying to conclude and providing an ironic counterpoint to the tonguelessness of the Ellen Jamesians.

Humor and tragedy may coexist because the nature of reality is always in question. The title of the novel suggests that the world presented in the novel may be only Garp's idiosyncratic version of reality. The short stories and the fragment of Garp's novel *The World According to Bensenhaver* are different versions of reality—those created by T. S. Garp the novelist. Ultimately, of course, the novel presents a version of the world according to John Irving. That things are not always what they seem is further evidenced in many of the novel's details. Garp's name is not really a name at all. The initials T. S. though echoing those of T. S. Eliot, do not stand for anything, and "Garp" is merely a sound made by Garp's brain-damaged father. Roberta Muldoon is occasionally uncertain whether to behave as a female or male. Jenny Fields does not set out to be a feminist but is regarded as one by so many people that she takes up the cause. Given this confusion between reality and illusion, order is difficult to achieve. As a novelist, Garp can control only the worlds of his fiction; he cannot protect his family and friends from disaster.

Shortly before T. S. Garp is killed in *The World According to Garp*, he has begun a new novel called *My Father's Illusions*, an apt title for *The Hotel New*

Hampshire. Like *The World According to Garp*, *The Hotel New Hampshire* deals with illusion and reality—specifically, with one man's dreams for his family. Win Berry is a man with improbable hopes. As his son John, the narrator, says of him, "the first of my father's illusions was that bears could survive the life lived by human beings, and the second was that human beings could survive a life led in hotels." The Berry family lives in three hotels during the course of the novel, which spans the period from 1920, when Win Berry meets Mary Bates, to 1980, when the surviving Berry children are grown and have become successful at various pursuits. (Egg, the youngest, is killed in a plane crash along with his mother; Lilly, the smallest, commits suicide.) All the Berry children are marked by a childhood spent in the hotels created by their father's dreams: first a converted school in Dairy, New Hampshire; than a dubious *pension* in Vienna. Finally, Win Berry, by this time blind—as he in some ways has been all his life—returns to the Maine resort where he first met Mary Bates, shielded by his children from the knowledge that it has become a rape crisis center. The familiar Irving motifs and images are prominent in *The Hotel New Hampshire*: Win Berry's father, Iowa Bob, is a wrestling coach whose strenuous view of life contrasts sharply with his son's dreaminess; bears appear in both actual and simulated form. Near the beginning of the novel, Win Berry buys a bear named State O'Maine from a wanderer named Freud, who eventually lures Win and his family to the second Hotel New Hampshire in Vienna; there they meet Susie-the-bear, a young American who wears a bear suit as a protection against reality.

Although the tone of *The Hotel New Hampshire* is gentler than that of *The World According to Garp*, Irving presents many of the same social problems and situations: rape (which Irving has called "the most violent assault on the body and the head that can happen simultaneously"), murder, race relations, sex roles, and the modern family. The difference between this fifth novel and those that preceded it is that Irving seems to have become reconciled to the need for illusion as a means of survival. No longer are dreams only irresponsible fantasies or terrible nightmares; they are what enable most people, in the refrain of the novel, to "keep passing the open windows" rather than taking a suicidal plunge. By treating contemporary anxieties with the traditional devices of the storyteller, Irving conveys an age-old message about the purpose of art: It can provide an illusion of order that may be more important—and is

certainly more readily attained—than order itself.

John Irving's two novels following *The Hotel New Hampshire* deal more insistently with moral and ethical issues, although they also contain the bizarre characters and situations that have become hallmarks of his fiction. *The Cider House Rules* concerns, as the title suggests, the rules by which people are to conduct their lives, but just as the list of rules posted in the cider house ("Please don't smoke in bed or use candles") is consistently ignored, so Dr. Wilbur Larch, one of the novel's central characters, breaks the rules by performing abortions in rural Maine in the 1920's. As he dealt with the issue of rape in *The World According to Garp*, Irving here approaches the issue of abortion inventively: Wilbur Larch is no back-alley abortionist, but a skilled obstetrician who also runs an orphanage for the children whose mothers prefer to give birth, and he seeks to have the children adopted.

As *The Cider House Rules* is set against the political and social realities of the first half of the twentieth century, *A Prayer for Owen Meany* chronicles American political and social realities in the latter half of the twentieth century—from the escalation of the Vietnam War to the advent of heavy-metal rock music, and from the early spread of television culture to the presidency of Ronald Reagan. In its overtly religious imagery, the novel posits the need for some kind of salvation during these turbulent years. The novel features the quick juxtapositions of violence and comedy of Irving's earlier work and is ambitious in its creation of an unlikely Christ figure.

A Prayer for Owen Meany details the friendship—from childhood in the 1950's to Owen Meany's death in the 1960's—of two boys who grow up in Gravesend, New Hampshire, at opposite ends of the social scale: Owen's reclusive family owns the local granite quarry, whereas John Wheelwright's family boasts of Mayflower origins and functions as the local gentry. Their roles are reversed and confused, however, in the course of the narrative: Owen, a diminutive boy who even as an adult is never more than five feet tall, and whose voice—rendered by Irving in capital letters—is a prepubescent squeak, becomes a Christ figure with powers over life and death, whereas John leads a rather uneventful adult life as a schoolteacher in Toronto, even remaining a virgin, as Owen does not.

Yet *A Prayer for Owen Meany* is far from being a solemn theological tract. Irving's characteristically ebullient humor erupts throughout the novel in slapstick scenes, in boyish pranks, and even in the ironic contrast between Owen's small voice and the large print in which it leaps authoritatively from the page. Religious imagery permeates but does not overwhelm the novel, which takes its tone from the narrator's somewhat self-mocking stance and his obvious delight in recalling the "miracle" of Owen Meany. Like Irving's work in general, *A Prayer for Owen Meany* is a mixture of realism and fabulism, of commentary on contemporary American culture and evocation of the magic of childhood and friendship.

Bibliography

Burgess, Anthony. "A Novel of Obstetrics." *The Atlantic* 98 (July, 1985): 98-100.

Carton, Evan. "The Politics of Selfhood: Bob Slocum, T. S. Garp, and Auto-American-Biography." *Novel* 20 (Fall, 1986): 41-61.

Davenport, Gary. "The Contemporary Novel of Sensibility." *The Sewanee Review* 94 (Fall, 1986): 672-677.

French, Sean. "Pleasures of Plot." *The New Statesman and Society* 2 (May 12, 1989): 35-36.

Haller, Scot. "John Irving's Bizarre World." *Saturday Review* 8 (September, 1981): 30-34.

Harter, Carol C., and James R. Thompson. *John Irving*. Boston: Twayne, 1986.

Kazin, Alfred. "God's Own Little Squirt." *The New York Times Book Review*, March 12, 1989, 1, 30.

King, Stephen. "The Gospel According to John Irving." *Washington Post Book World*, March 5, 1989, 1, 14.

Miller, Gabriel. *John Irving*. New York: Frederick Ungar, 1982.

Priestley, Michael. "Structure in the Worlds of John Irving." *Critique* 23, no. 1 (1981): 82-96.

Reisenberg, Donald E., and Morris Fishbein Fellow. "Rules." *Journal of the American Medical Association*, January 3, 1986, 97-98.

Ruppersburg, Hugh M. "John Irving." In *American Novelists Since World War II*. Vol. 6, 2d ser. *Dictionary of Literary Biography*, edited by James E. Kilber, Jr. Detroit, Mich.: Gale, 1980.

Wymard, Eleanor B. "'A New Version of the Midas Touch': *Daniel Martin* and *The World According to Garp*." *Modern Fiction Studies* 27 (Summer, 1981): 284-286.

WASHINGTON IRVING

Born: New York, New York; April 3, 1783

Died: Tarrytown, New York; November 28, 1859

Principal short fiction

The Sketch Book of Geoffrey Crayon, Gent., 1819-1820; *Bracebridge Hall*, 1822; *Tales of a Traveller*, 1824; *The Alhambra*, 1832; *Legends of the Conquest of Spain*, 1835.

Other literary forms

Washington Irving distinguished himself in a variety of genres. His finest and most typical book, *The Sketch Book of Geoffrey Crayon, Gent.*, blends essay, sketch, history, travel, humor, and short story. *A History of New York* (1809), his first best-seller, was a satire. In collaboration with American dramatist John Howard Payne, he wrote plays. Irving devoted the latter and most prolific part of his career to books of travel and especially of history.

Achievements

Irving was America's first internationally recognized author. While he achieved national notoriety with *A History of New York*, his fame abroad was made with *The Sketch Book of Geoffrey Crayon, Gent.* Irving's masterpiece, the work has a historical importance few American books can match. No previous American book had achieved such significant popular and critical success in England, the only arena of opinion that then mattered; Irving demonstrated that an American could write not only well but also brilliantly even by British standards. In fact, throughout the nineteenth century English as well as American schoolboys studied Irving's book as a model of graceful prose. Irving was a prolific writer throughout his life, from his first collaborations with his brother William and friend James Kirke Paulding, to his many biographies of well-known historical figures, including George Washington. Among his most successful works were his collections of sketches and tales, a distinction then made between realistic and imaginative types of fiction. His sketches often make use of historical sources, while the tales usually derive from traditional folktales. His best-known stories, "Rip Van Winkle" and "The Legend of Sleepy Hollow," although largely copied from German folktales, still maintain an originality through their American settings and Irving's own gently humorous style.

Biography

The eleventh and last child of a successful merchant, Washington Irving, somewhat frail and indulged as he was growing up, was the favorite child of his Anglican mother and Presbyterian minister father. As a young man, Irving studied law in the office of Josiah Ogden Hoffman, to whose daughter he was attracted, and enjoyed the social and cultural advantages of New York City as something of a gentleman-playboy. At this time he dabbled in satirical writing in serial publications. He gained a certain amount of cosmopolitan sophistication with a tour of Europe in 1804-1806, during which he kept a journal.

Irving was admitted to the New York bar at the age of twenty-three and nominally began to work as a lawyer on Wall Street, although he practiced little. Instead, he wrote serial essays with his brother and James Kirke Paulding for a periodical they called *Salmagundi*, modeled on Joseph Addison's *Spectator*, "to instruct the young, reform the old, correct the town, and castigate the age." This amounted to making light fun of fashion and social mores in high society, although occasionally they made jabs at Thomas Jefferson's "logocratic" democracy.

"Diedrich Knickerbocker's" *A History of New York* followed in 1809; originally intended as a parody of a pretentious New York guidebook, it had become instead a comic history of the Dutch in New York. When Matilda Hoffman died in the same year, Irving, distraught, stopped writing for a time. He moved in 1811 to Washington (D.C.) to lobby for the Irving brothers' importing firm. Still affected by Matilda's death, he drifted into several different occupations, lost the brothers' firm to bankruptcy, yet benefitted from his literary contacts to the point where he began to pursue writing with renewed effort. By the time he published *The Sketch Book of Geoffrey Crayon, Gent.* in 1819, he was on his way to supporting himself through his writing. In order to find original materials for his sketches, he made various trips through Europe and America, including a ministry to Spain; he returned to New York finally in 1832. His long absence, reminiscent of Rip Van Winkle's, provided him with a new perspective on the United States, whose western frontier was beginning to open; he packed again, this time for the West, and wrote many of his books out of the experience. He finally returned home to the Hudson, ensconced in family and friends, where he died in 1859.

Analysis

Irving's early career coincided with the rise of Romanticism, and the movement strongly influenced his greatest book, *The Sketch Book of Geoffrey Crayon, Gent.*, in which he displayed by turns his facility for imaginative storytelling, whimsicality, satire, sentimentality, factual and fictional sketches. Irving's travels are reflected in this collection as well, which contains both Old and New World reflections—notably evident in "English Writers on America," an essay examining the reasons that British and American writers looked askance at each other. In many ways, that nexus is the essence of Irving as an American writer: He occupied the America of a post-Colonial generation that was coming into its own culturally as well as politically, and he functioned as a literary ambassador, articulating and legitimating a purely American form of writing that took the best of the Old World and married it to the New. In a society that had not fully extracted itself from its European progenitors (not only British but notably, in Irvings New York, Dutch), this was no mean feat. Irving is therefore regarded as the "father of the American short story"—as much for his accident of time and birth as for his literary gifts. His stories reflect the regions and characters of the new Republic's Northeast delightfully and memorably.

In "The Spectre Bridegroom," the title character triumphs not through strength, physical skills, or intelligence but through manipulating the imaginations of those who would oppose his aims. The story's first section humorously describes a bellicose old widower, the Baron Van Landshort, who has gathered a vast audience, consisting mostly of poor relatives properly cognizant of his high status, to celebrate his only daughter's marriage to a young count whom none of them has ever seen. In the story's second part, the reader learns that as the count and his friend Herman Von Starkenfaust journey to the castle, they are beset by bandits; the outlaws mortally wound the count who, with his last breath, begs Von Starkenfaust to relay his excuses to the wedding party. The story's third part returns to the castle

where the long-delayed wedding party finally welcomes a pale, melancholy young man. The silent stranger hears the garrulous baron speak on, among other matters, his family's longstanding feud with the Von Starkenfaust family; meanwhile the young man wins the daughter's heart. He shortly leaves, declaring he must be buried at the cathedral. The next night the daughter's two guardian aunts tell ghost stories until they are terrified by spying the Spectre Bridegroom outside the window; the daughter sleeps apart from her aunts for three nights, encouraging their fears the while, and finally absconds. When she returns with her husband, Von Starkenfaust, who had pretended to be the Spectre, they both are reconciled with the Baron and live happily ever after.

By becoming in one sense themselves, Herman and his bride both manipulate the imaginations of the baron, the aunts, and the entire wedding party to make their courtship and elopement possible; here, happily, the dupees lose nothing and share the ultimate happiness of the dupers. There are at least three dimensions to "The Spectre Bridegroom." As it is read, one can imaginatively identify with the duped family and believe the Spectre genuine; or one can, alternatively, identify with the young couple innocently manipulating their elders. A third dimension enters when the reader recalls the personality of the frame's Swiss taleteller, occasionally interrupting himself with "a roguish leer and a sly joke for the buxom kitchen maid" and himself responsible for the suggestive antlers above the prospective bridegroom's head at the feast.

The narrative perspectives informing Irving's most famous achievement, "Rip Van Winkle," radiate even greater complexities. At the simplest level the core experience is that of Rip himself, a good-natured idler married to a termagant who drives him from the house with her temper. While hunting in the woods, Rip pauses to assist a curious little man hefting a keg; in a natural amphitheater he discovers dwarfish sailors in archaic dress playing at ninepins. Rip drinks, falls asleep, and awakens the next morning alone on the mountainside. In a subtle, profound, and eerily effective sequence, Irving details Rip's progressive disorientation and complete loss of identity. The disintegration begins mildly enough—Rip notices the decayed gun, his dog's absence, some stiffness in his own body— each clue is emotionally more significant than the last, but each may be easily explained. Rip next notices changes in nature—a dry gully has become a raging stream, a ravine has been closed by a rockslide; these are more dramatic alterations, but still explainable after a long night's sleep.

Upon entering the village, Rip discovers no one but strangers and all in strange dress; he finds his house has decayed, his wife and children have disappeared; buildings have changed as well as the political situation and even the very manner and behavior of the people. In a terrible climax, when Irving for once declines to mute the genuine horror, Rip profoundly questions his own identity. When Rip desperately asks if anyone knows poor Rip Van Winkle, fingers point to another ragged idler at the fringe, the very image of Rip himself as he had ascended the mountain. After a moment of horror, Irving's sentimental good humor immediately reasserts itself. Rip's now-adult daughter appears and recognizes him; the ragged idler turns out to be his son, Rip, Jr. Rip himself hesitates for a moment but, upon learning that his wife has died "but a short time since," declares his identity and commences reintegrating himself into the community, eventually to become an honored patriarch, renowned for recounting his marvelous experience.

Thus is the nature of the core narrative, which is almost all most people ever read. The reader values the story for its profound mythic reverberations; after all, throughout Western civilization Irving's Rip has become an archetype of time lost. The reader may also appreciate Irving's amoral toying with lifestyles; although the Yankee/Benjamin Franklin lifestyle Rip's wife advocates and which leads to her death (she bursts a blood vessel while haggling) fails to trap Rip, he triumphs by championing the relatively unambitious, self-indulgent lifestyle Irving identifies with the Dutch. Still, many people feel tempted to reject the piece as a simplistic fairy tale dependent on supernatural machinery for its appeal and effect. This is a mistake.

Those who read the full story as Irving wrote it will discover, in the headnote, that Irving chose to relate the story not from the point of view of an omniscient narrator but from the point of view of Diedrich Knickerbocker, the dunderheaded comic persona to whom years earlier he had ascribed the burlesque *A History of New York*. The presence of such a narrator—and Irving went to some trouble to introduce him—authorizes the reader to reject the supernatural elements and believe, as Irving tells us many of Rip's auditors believed, that in actuality Rip simply tired of his wife, ran away for twenty years, and concocted a cock-and-bull story to justify his absence. Looking closer, the reader discovers copious hints that this is precisely what happened: Rip's reluctance to become Rip again until he is sure his wife

is dead; the fact that when his neighbors hear the story they "wink at each other and put their tongues in their cheeks"; the fact that, until he finally established a satisfactory version of the events, he was observed "to vary on some points every time he told it." In the concluding footnote, even dim Diedrich Knickerbocker acknowledges the story's doubtfulness but provides as evidence of its truth the fact that he has heard even stranger supernatural stories of the Catskills. To authenticate the story, he adds, Rip signed a certificate in the presence of a justice of the peace. Irving clearly intends to convince his closest readers that Rip, like the couple in "The Spectre Bridegroom," triumphed over circumstances by a creative manipulation of imagination.

In "The Legend of Sleepy Hollow" our source is again Diedrich Knickerbocker, and again, creatively manipulating the imaginations of others proves the key to success. The pleasant little Dutch community of Sleepy Hollow has imported a tall, grotesquely lanky Yankee as schoolmaster, Ichabod Crane. Although he is prey to the schoolboys' endless pranks, he himself ravenously and endlessly preys on the foodstuffs of the boys' parents. Ichabod finally determines to set his cap for the pretty daughter of a wealthy farmer, but Brom Bones, the handsome, Herculean local hero, has likewise determined to court the girl. The climax comes when the principals gather with the entire community at a dance, feast, and "quilting frolic" held at Katrina Van Tassel's home. Brom fills the timorous and credulous Ichabod full of tales of a horrible specter, the ghost of a Hessian soldier beheaded by a cannonball, who inhabits the region through which Ichabod must ride that night to return home. As he makes his lonely journey back, Ichabod encounters the dark figure, who carries his head under his arm rather than on his neck and who runs him a frightful race to a bridge. At the climax the figure hurls his head and strikes Ichabod, who disappears, never to be seen in the village again. Brom marries Katrina, and years later the locals discover that Ichabod turned lawyer, politician, newspaperman, and finally became a "justice of the Ten Pound Court." Again it is the character who creatively manipulates the imagination who carries the day; the manipulatee wins only the consolation prize. Again the Dutch spirit triumphs over the Yankee.

In this story there is something quite new, however; for the first time in American literature there is, in the characterization of Brom Bones, the figure of the frontiersman so important to American literature and American popular culture: physically imposing, self-confident, rough and ready, untutored but endowed with great natural virtues, gifted with a rude sense of chivalry, at home on the fringes of civilization, and incorporating in his own being the finer virtues of both the wilderness and the settlements. Irving here brilliantly anticipated both the essence of Southwestern humor and of James Fenimore Cooper's seminal Westerns.

Irving is variously considered the first American man of letters, the father of American literature, and the inventor of the short story. He is renowned for his influential prose style, native American humor, and creation of memorable characters such as those that appear in *The Sketch Book of Geoffrey Crayon, Gent.*, his greatest literary success.

Other major works

NONFICTION: *A History of New York*, 1809; *Biography of James Lawrence*, 1813; *A History of the Life and Voyages of Christopher Columbus*, 1828; *A Chronicle of the Conquest of Granada*, 1829; *Voyages and Discoveries of the Companions of Columbus*, 1831; *A Tour of the Prairies*, 1835; *Astoria*, 1836; *The Adventures of Captain Bonneville*, 1837; *The Life of Oliver Goldsmith*, 1849; *The Life of George Washington*, 1855-1859 (5 vols.).

Bibliography

Bowden, Mary Weatherspoon. *Washington Irving*. Boston: Twayne, 1981.

McFarland, Philip. *Sojourners*. New York: Atheneum, 1979.

Myers, Andrew B., ed. *A Century of Commentary on the Works of Washington Irving*. Tarrytown, N.Y.: Sleepy Hollow Restorations, 1976.

Rubin-Dorsky, Jeffrey. *Adrift in the Old World: The Psychological Pilgrimage of Washington Irving*. Chicago: University of Chicago Press, 1988.

Tuttleton, James W. *Washington Irving: The Critical Reaction*. New York: AMS Press, 1993.

Wagenknecht, Edward. *Washington Irving: Moderation Displayed*. New York: Oxford University Press, 1962.

Williams, Stanley T. *The Life of Washington Irving*. 2 vols. New York: Oxford University Press, 1935.

SARAH ORNE JEWETT

Born: South Berwick, Maine; September 3, 1849   **Died:** South Berwick, Maine; June 24, 1909

Principal short fiction

Deephaven, 1877; *Old Friends and New*, 1879; *Country By-Ways*, 1881; *The Mate of the Daylight, and Friends Ashore*, 1884; *A White Heron*, 1886; *The King of Folly Island, and Other People*, 1888; *Tales of New England*, 1890; *Strangers and Wayfarers*, 1890; *A Native of Winby*, 1893; *The Life of Nancy*, 1895; *The Queen's Twin*, 1899; *Stories and Tales*, 1910; *The Uncollected Short Stories of Sarah Orne Jewett*, 1971.

Other literary forms

Sarah Orne Jewett wrote four novels: *A Country Doctor* (1884), *A Marsh Island* (1885), *The Country of the Pointed Firs* (1896), and *The Tory Lover* (1901). She also published popular books for children, including *Play Days* (1878) and *Betty Leicester* (1890). Her main work of nonfiction was a history, *The Story of the Normans* (1887).

Achievements

Jewett is best known as a local colorist who captured with fidelity the life of coastal Maine in the late nineteenth century in sensitive and moving portraits, primarily of women's lives. When she was young she decided to devote her writing to documenting the fast-disappearing traditions of life in this region of America, and she succeeded in chronicling the manners, traditions, and details surrounding the people of this unique region of the Northeast with insight, with humor, and without resorting to sentimentality. During her lifetime, she was considered one of America's best short-story writers. Most of her stories appeared first in popular magazines such as *The Atlantic*, under the editorship of William Dean Howells, and *Harper's*. American literary historian F. O. Matthiessen said in his 1929 study of Jewett that she and Emily Dickinson were the two best women writers America had produced. Willa Cather offered Jewett similar praise and credited her with positively changing the direction of her literary career in a brief but rich acquaintance near the end of Jewett's life.

Biography

Jewett spent most of her life in South Berwick on the Maine coast, where she was born on September 3, 1849. Daughter of a country doctor, she aspired to medicine herself but moved toward writing because of early ill health (which led her father to take her on his calls for fresh air), the special literary education encouraged by her family, and her discovery as a teenager of her "little postage stamp of soil" in reading Harriet Beecher Stowe's *The Pearl of Orr's Island* (1862). Her father, especially, encouraged her to develop her keen powers of observation, and her grandfathers stimulated her interest in storytelling. After the death of her father in 1878, she began a lifelong friendship with Annie Fields that brought her into contact with leading writers in America and Europe, such as Henry James and George Eliot. The two friends traveled together in Europe, the Caribbean, and the United States, and after the death of Mr. Fields, they lived together for extended periods.

Jewett began writing and publishing at the age of nineteen. During her career she developed and maintained the purpose of helping her readers to understand and love the ordinary people of her native Maine, and later she told stories about other misunderstood people such as the Irish and Southern whites. In her career, she produced more than twenty volumes of fiction for children and adults, history, prose sketches, and poetry. Her short stories show rapidly increasing subtlety and power. Her early books were well received, but beginning with *The Mate of the Daylight, and Friends Ashore*, reviewers routinely praised her collections highly. It was not unusual for a reviewer to be a little puzzled by how much he or she liked Jewett's stories. A frequent response was that the stories seemed to lack plot and action and yet at the same time were absorbing and charming. Late twentieth century critics, notably feminist critics, have suggested that Jewett was developing a kind of storytelling in opposition to the popular melodramas with their fast-paced romance or adventure plots. Jewett's stories came more and more to focus on intimate relations of friendship, especially between older women but eventually in one way or another between all kinds of people.

By the time Jewett wrote her masterpiece, the novella *The Country of the Pointed Firs*, she had fully developed a form of narration that pointed toward the James Joyce of *Dubliners* (1914). This novella, and a number of her best stories such as "Miss Tempy's Watchers" and "The Queen's Twin," would set up a problem of tact, of how to overcome barriers to communion between two or more people, and then through a subtle process of preparation would make overcoming these barriers possible. The story would end with an epiphany that involved communion between at least two people. Though she wrote a variety of other kinds of stories in her career, this type of development was probably her major accomplishment, and it achieved its fullest realization in *The Country of the Pointed Firs*.

In 1901, Jewett became the first woman to receive an honorary degree from Bowdoin College. A tragic carriage accident on her birthday in 1902 left her in such pain that she gave up fiction writing and devoted herself to her friends. In the fall of 1908, she met Willa Cather, to whom she wrote several letters that inspired Cather to write about Nebraska. Cather recognized Jewett's help by dedicating to Jewett her first Nebraska novel, *O Pioneers!* (1913). Jewett died at her South Berwick home on June 24, 1909.

Analysis

When a young reader wrote to Jewett in 1899 to express admiration of her stories for girls, Jewett encouraged her to continue reading: ". . . you will always have the happiness of finding friendships in books, and it grows pleasanter and pleasanter as one grows older. And then the people in books are apt to make us understand 'real' people better, and to know why they do things, and so we learn sympathy and patience and enthusiasm for those we live with, and can try to help them in what they are doing, instead of being half suspicious and finding fault."

Here Jewett states one of the central aims of her fiction, to help people learn the arts of friendship. Chief among these arts is tact, which Jewett defines in *The Country of the Pointed Firs* as a perfect self-forgetfulness that allows one to enter reverently and sympathetically the sacred realms of the inner lives of others. In her stories, learning tact is often a major element, and those who are successful are often rewarded with epiphanies, moments of visionary union with individuals or with nature, or with communion, the feeling of oneness with another person that for Jewett is the ultimate joy of friendship.

"A White Heron," which first appeared in *A White Heron*, is often considered Jewett's best story, perhaps because it goes so well with such American classics as Nathaniel Hawthorne's *The Scarlet Letter* (1850), Herman Melville's *Moby Dick* (1851), and William Faulkner's "The Bear" (1942). With these works, the story shares a central, complex symbol in the white heron and the major American theme of a character's complex relationship with the landscape and society. As a story about a young person choosing between society and nature as the proper spiritual guide for a particular time in her life, however, "A White Heron" is atypical for Jewett. One main feature that marks the story as Jewett's, however, is that the main character, Sylvia, learns a kind of tact during her adventure in the woods, a tact that grows out of an epiphany and that leads to the promise of continuing communion with nature that the story implies will help this somewhat weak and solitary child grow into a strong adult.

Sylvia, a young girl rescued by her grandmother, Mrs. Tilley, from the overstimulation and overcrowding of her city family meets a young ornithologist, who fascinates her and promises her ten dollars if she will tell him where he can find the white heron he has long sought for his collection. Childlishly tempted by this magnificent sum and her desire to please the hunter, who knows so much of nature yet kills the birds, she determines to climb at dawn a landmark pine from which she might see the heron leave its nest. She succeeds in this quest but finds she cannot tell her secret to the hunter. The story ends with the assertion that she could have loved the hunter as "a dog loves" and with a prayer to the woodlands and summer to compensate her loss with "gifts and graces."

Interesting problems in technique and tone occur when Sylvia climbs the pine. The narrative tone shifts in highly noticeable ways. As she begins her walk to the tree before dawn, the narrator expresses personal anxiety that "the great wave of human interest which flooded for the first time this dull little life should sweep away the satisfactions of an existence heart to heart with nature and the dumb life of the forest." This statement seems to accentuate an intimacy between reader and narrator; it states the position the narrative rhetoric has implied from the beginning and, in effect, asks if the reader shares this anxiety. From this point until Sylvia reaches the top of the tree, the narrator gradually merges with Sylvia's internal consciousness. During the climb, Jewett builds on this intimacy with Sylvia. Both narrator and reader are aware of sharing in detail Sylvia's subjective impressions of her climb and of her view, and this merging of the subjectivities of the story (character, narrator, and reader) extends beyond the persons to objects as the narrator unites with the tree and imagines its sympathy for the climber. The merging extends further yet when Sylvia, the reader, and the narrator see with lyric clarity the sea, the sun, and two hawks that, taken together, make all three observers feel as if they could fly out over the world. Being atop the tallest landmark pine, "a great mainmast to the voyaging earth," one is, in a way, soaring in the cosmos as the hawks soar in the air. At this point of clarity and union, the narrative tone shifts again. The narrator speaks directly to Sylvia, commanding her to look at the point where the heron will rise. The vision of the heron rising from a dead hemlock, flying by the pine, and settling on a nearby bough is a kind of colloquy of narrator and character and, if the technique works as it seems to intend, of the reader, too. This shift in "place" involves a shift in time to the present tense that continues through Sylvia's absorption of the secret and her descent from the tree. It seems clear that the intent of these shifts is to transcend time and space, to unite narrator, reader, character, and the visible scene that is "all the world." This is virtually the same technical device that is the central organizing device of Walt Whitman's "Crossing Brooklyn Ferry," and the intent of that device seems similar as well. The reader is to feel a mystical, "transcendental" union with the cosmos that assures one of its life and one's participation in that life.

A purpose of this union is to make justifiable and understandable Sylvia's choice not to give the heron's life away because they have "watched the sea and the morning together." The narrator's final prayer makes sense when it is addressed to transcendental nature on behalf of the girl who has rejected superfluous commodity in favor of Spirit, the final gift of Ralph Waldo Emerson's nature in his essay, "Nature." Though this story is atypical of Jewett insofar as it offers a fairly clearly transcendental view of nature and so presents a moment of communion with the nonhuman, it is characteristic of Jewett in that by subtly drawing reader and narrator into the epiphany, the story creates a moment of human communion.

More typical of Jewett's best work is "The Only Rose," which was first published in *The Atlantic* in January, 1894, and was then collected in *The Life of Nancy*. This story is organized by three related epiphanies, each centering on the rose and each involving a blooming.

In the first "miracle of the rose," Mrs. Bickford and Miss Pendexter are hypnotized into communion by contemplating the new bloom on Mrs. Bickford's poor rose bush. In this epiphany, Miss Pendexter enters into spiritual sympathy with Mrs. Bickford, realizing that Bickford's silence this time is unusual, resulting not from having nothing to say but from "an overburdening sense of the inexpressible." They go on to share the most intimate conversation of their relationship. The blooming flower leads to a blooming in their friendship. It also leads, however, to Mrs. Bickford's dilemma: On which of her three dead husbands' graves should she place this single rose? Her need to answer this question points to a deeper need to escape from her comparatively isolated and ineffectual life by shifting from an ethic of obligation to an ethic of love. Her heart has been frozen since her first husband's death, and it is long past time now for it to thaw and bloom again. Miss Pendexter understands something of this and tactfully leaves Mrs. Bickford to work it out for herself.

The second miracle of the rose occurs almost at the end of the story, when John confesses his love for Lizzie to his Aunt Bickford as he drives the latter to the graveyard. The symbolic rose of young and passionate love moves him to speak, even though he is unsure of the propriety of speaking up to the wealthy aunt from whom he hopes to inherit. His story of young love and hope, however, takes Mrs. Bickford out of herself, and she forgets her troubles in sharing his joy. As a result, he blooms, blushing a "fine scarlet."

The final miracle is that while John is taking the flowers to the graves, Bickford realizes which of her husbands should have the rose. At the same time that John is taking the rose for his Lizzie, Mrs. Bickford is giving it in her heart to Albert, the first husband whom she loved so passionately in her youth. Her realization of this event makes her blush "like a girl" and laugh in self-forgetfulness before the graveyard as she remembers that the first flower Albert gave her was just such a rose.

In the overall movement of the story, Mrs. Bickford is lifted out of herself and prepared for a richer and deeper communion with her friends and relatives. The single rose blossom seems mysteriously to impose an obligation upon her, but probably it really awakens the ancient spring of love within her that was perhaps covered over by grief at losing Albert so young and by the difficult life that followed his loss. When she finally struggles free of the weight of the intervening years, she recovers her hidden capacity for friendship and joy, for forgetting herself and joining in the happiness of others.

She has epiphanies, rediscovers tact, and begins again to experience communion.

"Martha's Lady" first appeared in *The Atlantic* in October, 1897, and was then collected in *The Queen's Twin*. This story illustrates Jewett's mature control over her technique and material. She represents a kind of sainthood without falling into the syrupy sentimentality of popular melodrama.

Into a community beginning to show the effects of a Puritan formalism comes Helena Vernon, a young city woman who is unself-consciously affectionate and beautiful and, therefore, a pleasure to please. She delights her maiden cousin, Harriet Pyne, charms the local minister, who gives her a copy of his *Sermons on the Seriousness of Life*, and transforms Martha, Harriet's new and awkward servant girl. In fact, Helena transforms to some extent everyone she meets in the village of Ashford, taking some of the starch out of their stiff and narrow way of life. After Helena leaves to marry, prosper, and suffer in Europe, Martha carries her memory constantly in her heart: "To lose out of sight the friend whom one has loved and lived to please is to lose joy out of life. But if love is true, there comes presently a higher joy of pleasing the ideal, that is to say, the perfect friend." This is the ideal of sainthood that the narrative voice asks the reader to admire. Thanks largely to Martha's living this ideal of always behaving so as to please Helena, she and Harriet live a happy life together for forty years. Helena returns to visit, worn but with the same youthful spirit, and to reward with a kiss what she recognizes as Martha's perfect memory of the services Helena enjoyed as a girl. This recognition acknowledges Martha's faithfulness to her ideal and creates that moment of communion that is the ultimate reward for such faithfulness.

What prevents this story from dissolving into mush? Nearly all the special features of Jewett's technical facility are necessary. She avoids overelaboration. It is not difficult for an alert reader to notice the parallel to the Christ story type; a liberating figure enters a legalistic society to inspire love in a group of followers, which results in an apotheosis after her departure. The disciple remains true to the ideal until the liberator comes again to claim the disciple. Jewett could have forced this analogy on the reader, but she does not. Only a few details subtly suggest the analogy—character names, calling Martha a saint, and her relics—but these need not compel the reader in this direction, which, in fact, adds only a little to the story's power. While avoiding overelaboration, Jewett also avoids internal views. On the whole, the story is made of narrative summary and brief dramatic scenes. Emotion is revealed through action and speech; this technical choice produces less intensity of feeling than, for example, the intimate internal view of Sylvia in "The White Heron." The result is a matter-of-factness of tone that keeps Martha's sainthood of a piece with the ordinary world of Ashford. This choice is supported by nearly every other technical choice of the story—the attention to detail of setting, the gentle but pointed humor directed against religious formalism, and the emergence of Martha from the background of the story. Jewett's intention seems to be on the one hand to prevent the reader from emoting in excess of the worth of the object, but on the other hand to feel strongly and warmly the true goodness of Martha's faithfulness to love. Another purpose of this narrative approach is to demonstrate tact. In "A White Heron," both Sylvia and the reader enter the quest for the heron with mixed motives, but the nature of the journey—its difficulties, its joys, the absorption it requires—tends to purify motives and to prepare the spirit for epiphany. Sylvia's vision from atop the pine culminates in communion with the wild bird, a vision she has earned and that she may repeat if she realizes its value.

Jewett's light touch, her own tact in dealing with such delicate subjects, is one of her leading characteristics, and it flowers magnificently in the fiction of the last ten years of her writing career. While the stories discussed above illustrate Jewett's most powerful and moving storytelling, they do not illustrate so fully another of the main characteristics of her stories—humor. Humor is often present in her stories and can be found in more abundance than might be expected in "The Only Rose" and "Martha's Lady." She also wrote a number of funny stories that discriminating readers such as Cather would not hesitate to compare with the work of Mark Twain. "The Guests of Mrs. Timms," though more similar to the stories of Jane Austen than Twain, is a popular story of the humorous ironies that result when a socially ambitious widow calls on another widow of higher status without announcing her visit in advance. Among her best humorous stories are "Law Lane," "All My Sad Captains," "A Winter Courtship," and "The Quest of Mr. Teaby," but there are many others that are a delight to read.

Other major works

NOVELS: *A Country Doctor*, 1884; *A Marsh Island*, 1885; *The Country of the Pointed Firs*, 1896; *The Tory Lover*, 1901.

POETRY: *Verses: Printed for Her Friends*, 1916.

NONFICTION: *The Story of the Normans*, 1887; *Letters of Sarah Orne Jewett*, 1911 (Annie Fields, ed.); *Sarah Orne Jewett Letters*, 1956 (Richard Cary, ed.).

CHILDREN'S LITERATURE: *Play Days: A Book of Stories for Children*, 1878; *Betty Leicester: A Story for Girls*, 1890.

MISCELLANEOUS: *Novels and Stories*, 1994.

Bibliography

Cary, Richard, ed. *Appreciation of Sarah Orne Jewett: Twenty-nine Interpretive Essays*. Waterville, Maine: Colby College Press, 1973.

_____ . *Sarah Orne Jewett*. New York: Twayne, 1962.

Donovan, Josephine. *Sarah Orne Jewett*. New York: Frederick Ungar, 1980.

Matthiessen, F. O. *Sarah Orne Jewett*. Boston: Houghton Mifflin, 1929.

Nagel, Gwen L., ed. *Critical Essays on Sarah Orne Jewett*. Boston: G. K. Hall, 1984.

Nagel, Gwen L., and James Nagel. *Sarah Orne Jewett: A Reference Guide*. Boston: G. K. Hall, 1978.

Roman, Margaret. *Sarah Orne Jewett: Reconstructing Gender*. Tuscaloosa: University of Alabama Press, 1992.

Silverthorne, Elizabeth. *Sarah Orne Jewett: A Writer's Life*. Woodstock, N.Y.: Overlook Press, 1993.

Weber, Clara Carter, and Carl J. Weber. *A Bibliography of the Published Writings of Sarah Orne Jewett*. Waterville, Maine: Colby College Press, 1949.

WILLIAM KENNEDY

Born: Albany, New York; January 16, 1928

Principal long fiction

The Ink Truck, 1969; *Legs*, 1975; *Billy Phelan's Greatest Game*, 1978; *Ironweed*, 1983; *The Albany Cycle*, 1985 (includes *Legs*, *Billy Phelan's Greatest Game*, and *Ironweed*); *Quinn's Book*, 1988; *Very Old Bones*, 1992.

Other literary forms

Like his novels, William Kennedy's nonfiction *O Albany! An Urban Tapestry* (1983), pamphlets for the New York State Library, Empire State College, and the *Albany Tricentennial Guidebook* (1985) largely center on his native Albany, New York. He wrote the screenplays for *The Cotton Club* (1984), with Francis Coppola and Mario Puzo, and *Ironweed* (1987), adapted from his novel of the same title. Kennedy collaborated with his son, Brendan, on a children's book, *Charlie Malarkey and the Belly Button Machine* (1986).

Achievements

Kennedy's first books—*The Ink Truck*, *Legs*, and *Billy Phelan's Greatest Game*—drew some notice but sold sluggishly, so *Ironweed* was rejected by thirteen publishers until Saul Bellow, Kennedy's teacher and mentor, persuaded Viking to reconsider. Viking reissued the previous two novels along with *Ironweed* as *The Albany Cycle*, and *Ironweed* won the National Book Critics Circle Award in 1983 and the Pulitzer Prize in fiction in 1984. Kennedy received a MacArthur Foundation Fellowship in 1983. This unsolicited "genius" award freed him for creative work; he used part of the proceeds to start a writers' institute in Albany, later funded by New York State with him as director. His novels' characters are drawn from the world of bums and gangsters and have been compared in brilliance to those of James Joyce and William Faulkner. *The Albany Cycle*, with its interlocking characters and spirit of place, has been compared to Faulkner's Yoknapatawpha stories and Joyce's *Dubliners* (1914) and *Ulysses* (1922). Kennedy's style has won praise as a combination of naturalism and surrealism, yet critics have faulted what they call his overwriting and pandering to the public's demand for violence, explicit sex, and scatological detail. Critics generally agree that *Ironweed* is also Kennedy's best novel, fusing the style, characterization, attention to detail, and mysticism of the others and focusing them with mastery. Kennedy has said

The Albany Cycle will continue to grow with future books.

Biography

William Kennedy was born in Albany, New York, on January 16, 1928. He was graduated from Siena College in 1949 and went to work for the Glens Falls, New York, *Post Star*, as sports editor and columnist, followed by a stint as reporter on the Albany *Times Union* until 1956. He went to Puerto Rico to work for the *Puerto Rico World Journal*, then for the *Miami Herald* (1957), returning to Puerto Rico as founding managing editor of the San Juan *Star* from 1959 to 1961. Deciding to make fiction writing his career and Albany his literary source and center, he returned to the Albany *Times Union* as special writer and film critic from 1963 to 1970, while he gathered material and wrote columns on Albany's rich history and its often scabrous past. Upon the success of *Ironweed*, he was promoted to Professor of English at State University of New York (SUNY) Albany in 1983. The university and the city sponsored a "William Kennedy's Albany" celebration in September, 1984.

Analysis

Kennedy's fiction is preoccupied with spirit of place, language, and style, and a mystic fusing of characters and dialogue. The place is Albany, New York, the capital city, nest of corrupt politics, heritor of Dutch, English, and Irish immigrants, home to canallers, crooks, bums and bag ladies, aristocrats, and numbers-writers. Albany, like Boston, attracted a large Irish Catholic population, which brought its churches, schools, family ties, political machine, and underworld connections. Albany, according to Kennedy, is "centered squarely in the American and human continuum."

Legs is the first novel in the series of novels for which Kennedy is best known, *The Albany Cycle*. Kennedy demonstrates the truth of his 1975 novel's epigraph, "People like killers," a quote from Eugène Ionesco, through his portrayal of John "Jack" Diamond, also known as "Legs," an idolized, flamboyant underworld figure, a liquor smuggler during Prohibition, a careless killer, and a tough womanizer. Finally brought to justice by New York governor Franklin D. Roosevelt, Jack was mysteriously executed gangland style in Albany in December, 1931.

The story begins in a seedy Albany bar, where four of the book's characters meet in 1974 to reminisce about the assassination of their gangster-hero, Jack "Legs" Diamond. The novel is a fictionalization of Jack's life, superimposing fictional characters, fictional names for real people, and Kennedy's imagination on real events. Three of the four in the frame story are minor, therefore surviving, members of Jack's entourage. The fourth member of the group is Marcus Gorman, Jack's attorney, mouthpiece, and friend, who gave up a political career to lend respectability and a capacity for legal chicanery to Jack. Marcus is the narrator of the novel, providing a less-than-intimate portrait, yet one filtered through a legal mind accustomed to the trickery of the profession as it was practiced then in Albany.

Jack Diamond became a mythical imaginative popular hero, a "luminous" personality who appealed to the crowds, and remained their darling even in his final trials. He survived assassination attempts, though his murder is foretold from the beginning. Finally, Jack comes to trial over his torture of a farmer in the matter of a still. The farmer complains, and a grand jury is called by Roosevelt. Though acquitted of the assault on the farmer, a federal case against him nearly succeeds because of the testimony of an aide Jack betrayed. Following this, Jack is shot and killed in a rooming house in Albany.

Kennedy's manic touch is evident in his portrayal of scenes on an ocean liner as Jack and Marcus try to conclude a drug deal, scenes in the Kenmore bar in Albany in its art deco heyday, and of the singing of "My Mother's Rosary" at the Elk's Club bar in Albany. The final coda is a lyrically written, but puzzling, apotheosis: Jack, dead, gradually emerges from his body, in a transfiguration worthy of a Seigfried or a Njall of Nordic sagas.

Kennedy's next novel, *Billy Phelan's Greatest Game*, tells the story of another of Albany's historical crimes—the real kidnaping of the political boss Dan O'Connell's nephew—through the framework of a series of games of chance played by a young hanger-on of the city's underside. He is Billy Phelan, son of an absent

father, Francis, who will be the protagonist of *Ironweed*. The other consciousness of the book is Martin Daugherty, old neighbor of the Phelans and a newspaperman. The time frame covers several days in late October, 1938, the time of the greatest game—the kidnaping.

Family interrelationships loom importantly in this novel. Billy Phelan has lost his father, Francis, by desertion twenty-two years before; Martin's father, a writer with an insane wife and a lovely mistress, now lies senile in a nursing home. The politically powerful McCall family almost loses their only heir, the pudgy, ineffectual Charlie. Martin lusts after his father's mistress, who plays sexual games with him. Similarly, Billy's lady friend, Angie, cleverly outwits him by pretending to be pregnant, to see what Billy will do. They have never, she says, really talked about anything seriously. Billy reminisces about rowing down Broadway in a boat, during a flood in 1913, with his father and uncle. Soon, he finds his father in a seedy bar, along with his companion Helen, and gives Helen his last money for his father.

The same time frame and some of the same characters appear in *Ironweed*, the third book of the cycle and the Pulitzer Prize-winner. *Ironweed* takes place immediately after the events in *Billy Phelan's Greatest Game*, on Halloween and All Saint's Day, 1938, just after the radio broadcast of Orson Welles's adaptation of H. G. Wells's *The War of the Worlds* (1898). The dates are not randomly chosen: the story, though on the surface the saga of a failed, homeless man, is actually a religious pilgrimage toward redemption from sin. Ironweed is described in an epigraph as a tough-stemmed member of the sunflower family, and Francis, like the weed, is a survivor. These analogies, like the Welles broadcast, hinge on a question of belief important to this novel.

Unlike Kennedy's previous books, *Ironweed* has no narrator or central consciousness. The main character, Francis Phelan, first left home after he killed a man during a transit strike by throwing a stone during a demonstration against the hiring of scab trolley drivers. Subsequently he returned, but left for long periods when he played professional baseball. Later, he disappeared for twenty-two years after he dropped his infant son while diapering him; the child died, yet Francis' wife, Annie, never told anyone who dropped Gerald. Francis and another bum, Rudy, dying of cancer, get jobs digging in St. Agnes' Cemetery, where Gerald and other relatives are buried.

Reason and fact are supremely important in the book,

yet within one page Francis' mother, a disagreeable hypocrite, twitches in her grave and eats crosses made from weeds, and the infant Gerald converses with his father and wills him to perform acts of expiation, as yet unknown, that will cease his self-destructiveness and bring forgiveness. Francis has killed several people besides the scab driver, yet it is not for these crimes that he needs forgiveness but for deserting his family. The rest of the book chronicles his redemption. Throughout, shifts to fantasy occur, triggered by passages of straight memory and detailed history. Ghosts of the men Francis killed ride the bus back to Albany, yet they do not seem as horrible to Francis as a woman he finds near the mission, freezing in the cold. He drapes a blanket around her, yet later he finds her dead, mangled and eaten by dogs.

During the night, Francis meets with his hobo "wife," Helen, a gently educated musician (she once went to Vassar) with enough energy, though dying of a tumor, to sing proudly in a pub on their rounds. In the mission, Francis gets a pair of warm socks; on the street, Helen is robbed of the money given to her by Francis' son Billy. Then follows a nightmare search through the cold streets for shelter for the delicate Helen. In desperation, Francis goes to a friend's apartment, where he washes his genital region in the toilet and begs a clean pair of shorts. The friend refuses them shelter, so Francis leaves Helen in an abandoned car with several men, though he knows she will be molested sexually.

The next day, Francis gets a job with a junkman. While making his rounds, he reads in a paper about his son Billy getting mixed up in the McCall kidnaping. Making the rounds of old neighborhoods, buying junk from housewives, releases a flood of memories for Francis: He sees his parents, his neighbors the Daughertys in their house, now burned, where one day the mad Katrina Daugherty walked out of her house naked to be rescued by the seventeen-year-old Francis. Because of this memory, he buys a shirt from the ragman to replace his filthy one. While he is buying the shirt, Helen goes to Mass, then listens to records in a record store (stealing one). Retrieving money she has hidden in her bra, Helen redeems her suitcase at the hotel. In her room, she recalls her life, her beloved father's suicide, her mother's cheating her of her inheritance, her exploiting lover/employer in the music store. Washing herself and putting on her Japanese kimono, she prepares to die.

Francis, meanwhile, revisits his family, bringing a turkey bought with his earnings from the day's job. He bathes, dresses in his old clothing his wife has saved, looks over souvenirs, meets his grandson, gets his daughter's forgiveness as well as his wife's, and is even invited to return. He leaves, however, finds Rudy, and together they look for Helen. Finding Helen registered at Palumbo's Hotel, Francis leaves money with the clerk for her. The final violent scene occurs in a hobo jungle, as it is being raided by Legionnaires. Francis kills Rudy's attacker with his own baseball bat and carries the fatally injured Rudy to the hospital. Returning to the hotel, Francis discovers Helen dead and leaves swiftly in a freight car.

The ending, typical of Kennedy's novels, is inconclusive. The reader can assume either that Francis leaves on a southbound freight or that he returns to Annie's house and lives hidden in the attic. The use of the conditional in narration of this final section lends the necessary vagueness. Nevertheless, in *Ironweed*, the intricacy of poetry combines with factual detail and hallucinatory fugues to create a tight structure, the most nearly perfect of *The Albany Cycle*. The parallelism, for example, of a discussion of the temptations of Saint Anthony with the name of the Italian Church of St. Anthony, where Helen hears Mass on her last day of life, shows the craftsmanship of the author. The interconnections of theme, plot, and character in the Albany novels, their hallucinatory fantasies, their ghostly visitations ennoble the lowest of the low into modern epic heroes.

Kennedy continues *The Albany Cycle* in *Very Old Bones*, recalling names, characters, and events from the previous works and carrying the story forward into the 1950's. The story is narrated by Francis Phelan's nephew, Orson Purcell, son of Peter Purcell and his mistress Claire. Loved by his father but never publicly acknowledged as his son, Orson can both observe the Phelan family and participate in its destiny. His life intersects with characters previously introduced in the *Cycle*, revealing nuances of the family's history which contribute to this multigenerational saga. His own life adds to the family's tragedy but also offers hope for regeneration: His German wife announces that she is pregnant at the end of the novel.

Kennedy has suggested that the Phelan story will continue in his next book, requiring each of the previous books to be reinterpreted by readers. As Faulkner's Compsons defined the twentieth century Southern identity through their lives, so Kennedy's Phelan family reveals the tragedy and hope which have forged a modern Northeastern American identity. His evocative depiction of Albany focuses intensely on the culture, politics, and ethnic identity of the city, the place of history, myth, memory, and fantasy at the center of Irish American life.

Other major works

SHORT FICTION: "The Secrets of Creative Love," 1983; "An Exchange of Gifts," 1985; "A Cataclysm of Love," 1986.
SCREENPLAY: *The Cotton Club*, 1984 (with Francis Coppola and Mario Puzo): *Ironweed*, 1987.
NONFICTION: *Getting It All, Saving It All: Some Notes by an Extremist*, 1978; *O Albany! An Urban Tapestry*, 1983; *Albany and the Capital*, 1986; *Riding the Yellow Trolley Car: Selected Nonfiction*, 1993.
CHILDREN'S LITERATURE: *Charlie Malarkey and the Belly Button Machine*, 1986 (with Brendan Kennedy).

Bibliography

Allen, Douglas R., and Mona Simpson. "The Art of Fiction CXI: William Kennedy." *The Paris Review* 31 (Winter, 1989): 34-59.
Clarke, Peter P. "Classical Myth in William Kennedy's *Ironweed*." *Critique: Studies in Modern Fiction* 27 (Spring, 1986): 167.
Cloutier, Candace. "William Kennedy." In *Contemporary Authors*, edited by Linda Metzger. New Revision Series. Detroit, Mich.: Gale Research, 1987.
Nichols, Loxley F. "William Kennedy Comes of Age." *National Review* 27 (August 9, 1985): 78-79.

ROBERT LOWELL

Born: Boston, Massachusetts; March 1, 1917   **Died:** New York, New York; September 12, 1977

Principal poetry

Land of Unlikeness, 1944; *Lord Weary's Castle*, 1946; *Poems 1938-1949*, 1950; *The Mills of the Kavanaughs*, 1951; *Life Studies*, 1959; *Imitations*, 1961; *For the Union Dead*, 1964; *Near the Ocean*, 1967; *Notebook 1967-68*, 1969; *Notebook*, 1970; *The Dolphin*, 1973; *History*, 1973; *For Lizzie and Harriet*, 1973; *Selected Poems*, 1976, 1977; *Day by Day*, 1977.

Other literary forms

Besides his free translations or rewritings of poems by writers from Homer to Boris Pasternak that constitute *Imitations* and the similar translations of Roman poems in *Near the Ocean*, Robert Lowell translated plays by the French playwright Jean Baptiste Racine and the ancient Greek dramatist Aeschylus. *The Old Glory*, a trilogy of plays (*Endecott and the Red Cross*, *My Kinsman, Major Molineux*, and *Benito Cereno*) based on stories by Nathaniel Hawthorne and Herman Melville, was originally published in 1965; the latter two plays premiered at the American Place Theater in 1964, winning for Lowell an Obie Award. Lowell also published a number of reviews and appreciations of writers; his *Collected Prose* was published in 1987.

Achievements

Lowell's poetry gives uniquely full expression to the painful experience of living in modern America; he speaks personally of his own experience as son, husband, lover, father, and mentally troubled individual human being and publicly of American policy and society as a morally and spiritually troubled inheritor of Western cultural and Christian spiritual values. All the diverse kinds of poetry that Lowell wrote over a career in which he repeatedly transformed his art—religious, confessional, public—share a high degree of formal interest, whether written in traditional metrical forms or in free verse. Indeed, it was Lowell's ceaseless formal invention that enabled him to articulate, in so many different voices, the experience of modernity. *Lord Weary's Castle* won the Pulitzer Prize in poetry in 1947, *Life Studies* the National Book Award in poetry in 1959, *Imitations* the Bollingen poetry translation prize, and *The Dolphin* the Pulitzer Prize in poetry in 1974.

Biography

Robert Traill Spence Lowell, Jr., the only child of Commander Robert Traill Spence Lowell, a naval officer, and Charlotte Winslow Lowell, was joined by birth to a number of figures variously prominent in the early history of Massachusetts Bay and in the cultural life of Boston. On his mother's side he was descended from Edward Winslow, who came to America on the *Mayflower* in 1620. His Lowell ancestors included Harvard president A. Lawrence Lowell and astronomer Percival Lowell, as well as the poets James Russell Lowell and Amy Lowell. His sense of his family's direct involvement in the shaping of American history and culture was conducive to the fusing of the personal and public that is one of the distinguishing features of his poetry.

Lowell attended Brimmer School in Boston and St. Mark's Boarding School in Southborough, Massachusetts. His parents had limited means relative to their inherited social position, and his ineffectual father and domineering mother filled the home with their contention. Richard Eberhart, then at the beginning of his poetic career, was one of Lowell's English teachers at St. Mark's, and at Eberhart's encouragement he began to write poetry, some of which was published in the school magazine. In 1935 Lowell entered Harvard, intent on preparing himself for a career as a poet. He was disheartened by the approach to poetry of his Harvard professors, however, and frustrated in his search for a mentor. He then met writer Allen Tate, who was to be a formative influence. His intimacy with Tate led to Lowell's immersion in the world and values of the traditionalist Southern agrarian poets who constituted the Fugitive group. After spending the summer of 1937 at the Tates' home, Lowell transferred from Harvard to Kenyon College to study with John Crowe Ransom, who had recently been hired at Kenyon, which he would turn into a center of the New Criticism. At Kenyon, Lowell met Randall Jarrell, with whom he began a personal and literary friendship that ended with Jarrell's suicide in

1965. While apprenticing himself as a poet, Lowell studied Classics, graduating summa cum laude in 1940.

Also in that year, Lowell married the young Catholic novelist Jean Stafford and converted to Roman Catholicism. He did a year's graduate work in English at Louisiana State University, studying under Cleanth Brooks and Robert Penn Warren, and then worked as an editorial assistant at Sheed and Ward, a Catholic publishing house in New York City. Then he and his wife spent a year with the Tates, a year in which Lowell and Allen Tate both did a great deal of writing under each other's inspiration. For Lowell, the year's output became the poems of his first book, *Land of Unlikeness* (1944), about half of which were subsequently revised and included in *Lord Weary's Castle* (1946), the book that launched his poetic career, winning for him the Pulitzer Prize in poetry in 1947. Also during this period Lowell, having earlier tried to enlist in the U.S. Army, refused to serve in protest against Allied bombing of civilian populations and served time in prison for this failure to comply with the Selective Service Act. In 1948, Lowell's marriage to Jean Stafford ended in divorce, and the following year he married essayist and fiction writer Elizabeth Hardwick.

The late 1940's saw the reemergence of Lowell's respect for William Carlos Williams' free verse. Lowell admired the unpoetical language of Williams' "American idiom," and he developed a close friendship with the older poet, who succeeded Tate as his mentor. The impact of Williams' work and ideas is reflected in the free-verse form of the poems in the last of the four sections of *Life Studies* (1959). From 1950 to 1953, Lowell and his wife were in Europe. Returning to the United States in 1953, he taught at the University of Iowa, where one of his students was W. D. Snodgrass; the younger poet, along with the older Williams, helped Lowell to develop the "confessional" mode pioneered in *Life Studies* and in Snodgrass' *Heart's Needle* (1959). From 1954 to the end of the decade, Lowell and his wife lived in Boston while he taught at Boston University. His students included Sylvia Plath and Anne Sexton. His daughter Harriet was born in 1957. In 1959, *Life Studies* won Lowell the National Book Award in poetry, while Snodgrass' *Heart's Needle* took the Pulitzer Prize.

In 1960, Lowell moved with his wife and daughter to New York City. *Life Studies* was followed in 1961 by *Imitations*. From 1963 to 1977 he taught at Harvard. During the 1960's Lowell became active in the movement against American involvement in Vietnam. In June, 1965, in an open letter to President Lyndon Johnson, published in *The New York Times*, he refused an invitation to participate in the White House Festival of the Arts in protest against American foreign policy. He participated in the Pentagon March protesting American bombing and troop activities in Vietnam in October, 1967, and was active in Eugene McCarthy's campaign for the Democratic nomination for the Presidency in 1967-1968, becoming a warm personal friend of McCarthy. His political experiences are recorded in *Notebook 1967-68* and the subsequent revisions of that book.

At the beginning of the 1970's, Lowell moved to England. He was a Visiting Fellow at All Soul's College, Oxford, in 1970, and taught at Essex University from 1970 to 1972. His book *The Dolphin* records the breakdown of his marriage of more than twenty years to Elizabeth Hardwick and his developing relationship with the English novelist Caroline Blackwood. In 1972 he was divorced from Hardwick and married to Blackwood. By the late 1970's, Lowell was commuting back and forth between Ireland, where he and Caroline had a house, and America, where he was teaching a term each year at Harvard. He died of a heart attack in a taxicab in New York City in September of 1977.

Analysis

American and European history and historical figures—military, political, and religious—and other writers and their works were very much present in Lowell's consciousness. This influence is reflected in all of his poetry, although the learning is worn more lightly after *The Mills of the Kavanaughs*. As evident in his poetry as his awareness of literary tradition is the intensity of his mental and emotional life, expressed indirectly through the vehicles of historical and fictional personae in his early poetry and in undisguised, if more or less fictionalized, autobiography, beginning with *Life Studies*. Lowell's is a poetry in the symbolist tradition; its symbols, whether used to convey religious significance (as in his first two books) or to express psychological realities (as in his subsequent works) are remarkable for their irreducible ambiguity. Ambiguity is indeed an essential feature of Lowell's mature vision. Symbolic resonance is accompanied in his work by a wealth of named particulars of the represented world; Norman Mailer has aptly described Lowell's language as "particular, with a wicked sense of names, details, places."

Lowell's voice in *Lord Weary's Castle* is that of a Catholic convert raging against the spiritual depravity of the Protestant and secular culture of New England, of which his own family was so much a part, and that of a conscientious objector decrying the waging of war. A note reveals that the book's title comes from an old ballad that tells of "Lambkin," a good mason who "built Lord Weary's castle" but was never paid for his work; in Lowell's poems, the mason Lambkin becomes a figure for Christ and Lord Weary for the people who wrong God in their lives.

Of the poems in this book, "The Quaker Graveyard in Nantucket," an elegy for Lowell's cousin Warren Winslow, whose ship had disappeared at sea in the war, has been the most frequently anthologized and extensively discussed. The poem is in seven parts. Part I is a dramatic account of the recovery and sea burial of the drowned sailor's body. It presents the sea as implacable in its power and the loss of life as irrevocable. Parts II and IV elaborate on the power of the sea and view the newly dead sailor as joining dead generations of Quaker whalers who foolishly dared the sea's and the whale's might; Lowell takes his imagery from Herman Melville's *Moby Dick* (1851) and associates the fatal presumption of the Quaker sailors with Ahab's obsessive and fatal quest of the white whale. The whale in whose pursuit the earlier generations of sailors lost their lives has more than one symbolic association—at once the wrathful, inscrutable Jehovah of the Old Testament and the merciful Christ of the New.

Lowell's dead cousin, who joins the whalers in their "graveyard," is implicated in their guilt, together with the war-waging society of which he was a member. Part IV closes with the question, "Who will dance/ The mast-lashed master of Leviathans/ Up from this field of Quakers in their unstoned graves?"—ambiguously alluding at once to Ahab and to the Christ whom the whalers are seen as having crucified again in their slaughter of the whale, as contemporary soldier/sailors do in their killing in war. Part V presents a horrific scene of whale-butchering as a sort of vision of apocalypse; drawing on the exegetical tradition that sees Jonah as a prefiguration of Christ, Lowell concludes this section with a prayer to the hacked, ripped whale, in the richness of its symbolic associations, "Hide,/ Our steel, Jonas Messias, in Thy side." The scene then switches abruptly from the violence of the sea to the pastoral serenity of the Catholic shrine of Our Lady of Walsingham in England, destroyed in the Reformation but recently restored. The final part returns the reader to the death-dealing sea, closing with a vision of Creation in which, even as "the Lord God formed man from the sea's slime," "blue-lung'd combers lumbered to the kill." After this formulation of the implacability and inscrutability of God's will, the poem closes with the line, "The Lord survives the rainbow of His will," offering, despite its recollection of the covenant at the end of the flood, no reassurance to the individual human creatures who sin and die, but only an assertion of an ultimate abiding that may or may not prove gracious to them.

After an eight-year silence, Lowell published *Life Studies*. The book is in four parts. The fourth, which gives the book its title, "Life Studies," contains the poems that drew the epithet "confessional."

"Skunk Hour" is the poem that closes the book. The eight six-line stanzas of "Skunk Hour" carry the speaker from detached, amusingly sharp observations of the foibles and failings of fellow residents of his New England summer resort town and the "illness" of its season, to direct, mordantly sharp confessions of his own neurotic behavior and his mind's and spirit's illness, and finally to the richly ambiguous image of vitality and survival in the face of the town's enervation, the season's fading, and the speaker's despair that concludes *Life Studies*. The first four stanzas are devoted to social observation—of "Nautilus Island's hermit/ heiress" who is "in her dotage" and "buys up all/ the eyesores facing her shore,/ and lets them fall"; of the disappearance of the "summer millionaire,/ who seemed to leap from an L. L. Bean/ catalogue," and the sale of his yacht; of the "fairy/ decorator [who] brightens his shop for fall" but finds "no money in his work" and would "rather marry." Significantly, where the first person pronoun appears, it is in the plural ("our summer millionaire," "our fairy decorator"); the poet speaks as a townsman, one of a community (albeit a derelict one). By the fifth stanza, however, he has ceased to be one of the people; now, apart from them, he tells the reader that he "climbed the hill's skull," where "I watched for love-cars." In a scene of anguished isolation he declares, "My mind's not right." By the end of the sixth stanza, his voice has come to echo that of Milton's Satan: "I myself am hell;/ nobody's here." From this nadir, his attention swings to be arrested, in the final two stanzas, by "a mother skunk with her column of kittens" that "march[es] . . . up Main Street," "swills the garbage pail . . . / and will not scare." If her crassness is appalling, her vitality is indeed a "rich air" against the town's stale atmosphere and the speaker's self-constructed cell. The significance of the image is as intractable in its ambiguity as its subject is stubborn in her determination to feed on the sour cream in the garbage.

In *For the Union Dead*, Lowell's poetry continues to speak in the personal voice that emerged in *Life Studies*. There is, moreover, a new element in this book: The poet deals with contemporary society and politics, not, as he had in *Lord Weary's Castle*, in Christian terms, as features of a world for which apocalypse was imminent, but with the same keen, painful observation and moral concern he had, since *Life Studies*, been bringing to bear on his personal life; he deals with them, indeed, as part and parcel of his personal experience.

The title poem, "For the Union Dead," revisits the old Boston Aquarium that the poet had visited as a child, even as "The Public Garden" revisits that old "stamping ground" of Lowell and his wife. The difference is that while in the latter "[t]he city and its cruising cars surround" a private failure to "catch fire," in "For the Union Dead" the Aquarium is presented not as part of a personal landscape only but, closed, its fish replaced by "giant finned cars," as emblematic of the course of Boston's, New England's, and America's culture. The other complex emblem in the poem is the monument to Colonel Shaw, friend and in-law to the poet's Lowell ancestors, who led the first regiment of free blacks in an attack on a fort defending Charleston harbor, in which he and about half of his black soldiers were killed. As the Aquarium's fish have been replaced by finned cars, the monument to the Civil War hero is now "propped by a plank splint" as support against the "earthquake" produced by excavation for a parking garage, and it has come to "stick like a fishbone/ in the city's throat." In a city of giant cars and parking garages, the martyred leader, "lean/ as a compass-needle," who "seems to wince at pleasure," is "out of bounds"; such firm sense of direction and such ascetisim are no longer virtues the populace is comfortable contemplating or moved to emulate.

The poem is not, however, a sentimental one of pure nostalgia for an earlier period of the society's life or of the poet's, for the heroism of war before the World Wars or for the lost Aquarium and the child's pleasure in it. The fish that lived in the Aquarium tanks are described as "cowed, compliant," and the child's eagerness was "to burst the bubbles/ drifting from their noses." Colonel Shaw is said to have enjoyed "man's lovely,/ peculiar power to choose life and die." Indeed, the attractiveness of martyrdom, as Lowell presents it, may not be that far removed from the appeal of fish behind glass or steamshovels behind barbed wire: "I often sigh still," says the poem's speaker, "for the dark downward

and vegetating kingdom/ of the fish and reptile."

A striking feature of *Near the Ocean* is that it consists partly of original poems, partly of translations—which Lowell said enabled him to express ideas that he himself would never dare to write. The title sequence of *Near the Ocean* includes the critically esteemed "Waking Early Sunday Morning." "Waking Early Sunday Morning" has its meaning in relation to another poem, Wallace Stevens' "Sunday Morning." While the poet of "Sunday Morning" was content that earth should turn out to "Seem all of paradise that we shall know," the poet of "Waking Early Sunday Morning" finds no "heavenly fellowship/ Of men that perish and of summer morn" (Stevens) to supersede the failed fellowship of "the Faithful at Church," where the Bible is "chopped and crucified/ in hymns we hear but do not read." Lowell finds instead that "Only man thinning out his kind/ sounds through the Sabbath noon," and instead of the vision of earth as a paradisal garden with deer, whistling quail, ripening berries, and flocks of pigeons that closes Stevens' poem, Lowell sees the planet as a joyless "ghost/ orbiting forever lost," its people "fall[ing]/ in small war on the heels of small/ war." The world of Lowell's poem is a more complicated one than that of Stevens in that it has a political aspect; the state with its monstrous militarism and the vulgarity of its leader, which is seen as "this Sunday morning, free to chaff/ his own thoughts with his bear-cuffed staff,/ swimming nude, unbuttoned, sick/ of his ghost-written rhetoric," is part of what the speaker here must assimilate.

Notebook 1967-68, Lowell's next collection, both effects a striking formal transformation, being a series of fourteen-line pieces in blank verse, and registers events of what became one of the most socially revolutionary periods of American history. Because Lowell was at the center of opposition to the Vietnam War, through public activism as well as in his poems, this collection is particularly significant as part of the redefinition of identity—or, rather, identities—inaugurated during that era. Here Lowell records his preoccupations with his marriage, family, love affairs, and dreams; with the Vietnam War, the Pentagon March, Eugene McCarthy's campaign for the Democratic presidential nomination, and other political events; and with other writers, both contemporaries and predecessors. Both the heterogeneity of material treated as readers move from poem to poem, section to section, and the quick shifts within individual poems create an impression of a mind besieged by an unremitting succession of experiences, both external and internal. In two poems on the Pentagon March, Lowell expresses his ambivalence toward pacifism and the military—he was a pacifist yet admired military valor—which so polarized Americans during the 1960's; in the book's final poem, "Obit," Lowell looks toward the ending of this flux of experience and emotion in death: "After loving you so much, can I forget/ you for eternity, and have no other choice?" the speaker asks; the accumulated context of his poem and the whole preceding book of poems suggests that his intellect would answer yes, his inclination, no.

History draws on the historical poems from *Notebook 1967-68*, with additional new poems, in chronological sequence. The book has a thematic focus for which ordering of the poems in accord with the dates of their subject matter is appropriate. The personal poems from *Notebook* were transformed into *For Lizzie and Harriet*, whose theme is continued in *The Dolphin*. Here, however, the poems are differentiated by the use of a central symbol, accreting in complexity and ambiguity over the course of the book. The dolphin and its variants (mermaid, "baby killer whale") and attributes (it is graceful, a playful swimmer, a powerful predator) is associated with Caroline, who is progressively mythicized until she becomes a gigantic, ambiguous, and disturbing character set forth in the image of a dolphin, while Elizabeth, the wife Lowell is waveringly leaving, becomes an ever clearer, more human voice.

Lowell's last collection, *Day by Day*, abandons the fourteen-line blank-verse form begun in *Notebook 1967-68* for a looser, free-verse form. Here the central theme is age, fear of aging and pain, and the prospect of death. The bulk of the book stays close to a journal's day-by-day record of events and emotions. It moves from poems of summer's fullness with Caroline, her daughters, and Lowell's son by her to wrenching memories of self-chastisement, illness, mental breakdown, and a resulting nostalgia for his lost Catholic faith. Driven by his consciousness of mortality, these poems finally resolve into gentle memories of Caroline's love, recovery, and an apologia for abandoning "those blessed structures, plot and rhyme," which served his other books.

Although his work and his significance go far beyond his poems of the 1960's, Robert Lowell in many ways epitomizes the experience of Americans who came of age during that turbulent decade, examining the issues and sounding the moral ambiguities that preoccupied that era. Much more than an antiwar poet, Lowell will nevertheless be remembered in part for articulating, in both personal and public terms, the concerns of a generation at the forefront of social revolution. Not surprisingly, his later poetry—focused as it is on death and a search for spiritual values—still speaks to the postwar, baby-boom generation as it continues to age.

Other major works

PLAYS: *Phaedra*, 1961 (trans.); *The Old Glory*, 1965 (*Endecott and the Red Cross, My Kinsman, Major Molineux,* and *Benito Cereno*); *Prometheus Bound*, pr. 1967, pb. 1969; *The Oresteia of Aeschylus*, 1979 (trans.).
NONFICTION: *Collected Prose*, 1987.

Bibliography
Cosgrave, Patrick. *The Public Poetry of Robert Lowell*. New York: Taplinger, 1970.
Hamilton, Ian. *Robert Lowell: A Biography*. New York: Random House, 1982.
Mariani, Paul. *Lost Puritan: A Life of Robert Lowell*. New York: W. W. Norton, 1994.
Perloff, Marjorie G. *The Poetic Art of Robert Lowell*. Ithaca, N.Y.: Cornell University Press, 1973.
Rudman, Mark. *Robert Lowell: An Introduction to the Poetry*. New York: Columbia University Press, 1983.
Wallingford, Katherine. *Robert Lowell's Language of the Self*. Chapel Hill: University of North Carolina Press, 1988.
Williamson, Alan. *Pity the Monsters: The Political Vision of Robert Lowell*. New Haven, Conn.: Yale University Press, 1974.
Witek, Terri. *Robert Lowell and Life Studies: Revising the Self*. Columbia: University of Missouri Press, 1993.

MARY McCARTHY

Born: Seattle, Washington; June 21, 1912

Died: New York, New York; October 25, 1989

Principal long fiction

The Oasis, 1949; *The Groves of Academe*, 1952; *A Charmed Life*, 1955; *The Group*, 1963; *Birds of America*, 1971; *Cannibals and Missionaries*, 1979.

Other literary forms

First known as a book reviewer, drama critic, and essayist, Mary McCarthy also wrote short stories. Her drama criticism is collected in *Sights and Spectacles: 1937-1956* (1956) and in *Mary McCarthy's Theatre Chronicles, 1937-1962* (1963). *Venice Observed* (1956) and *The Stones of Florence* (1959) are books of travel and art history. *The Writing on the Wall* (1970) and *Ideas and the Novel* (1980) are literary essays and lectures. *On the Contrary: Articles of Belief* (1961) contains autobiographical essays and literary criticism. *Memories of a Catholic Girlhood* (1957) and *How I Grew* (1987) are memoirs of her childhood and youth.

Achievements

From the appearance of her first book reviews, when she was barely out of college, to the time of her death, McCarthy was one of the leading figures on the American literary scene. In her novels as much as in her essays and reviews, she was above all a critic, a sharp observer of contemporary society. For students of twentieth century American culture, her work is indispensable. McCarthy was awarded Guggenheim Fellowships in 1949-1950 and 1959-1960. In honor of her extraordinary contributions to the field of literature, she received the National Medal of Literature and the Edward MacDowell Medal in 1984. She was, in addition, elected to the National Institute of Arts and Letters and the American Academy of Arts and Letters.

Biography

Born into an affluent family of mixed Irish and Jewish heritage on June 21, 1912, in Seattle, Washington, Mary Therese McCarthy had a segmented childhood. After six years of what she called a "fairy-tale" existence of happiness, both parents died of influenza in 1918 during a move to Minneapolis. Mary and her three younger brothers, placed with their grandaunt and uncle, then entered a bleak phase of intense, strict Catholicism, which Mary described in *Memories of a Catholic Girlhood*. In 1923, Mary's grandparents moved her to a convent school in Seattle for the seventh and eighth grades; she spent her ninth grade year in a public school and then her remaining high school years at the Annie Wright Seminary in Tacoma, from which she was graduated in 1929 at the top of her class. In the same year of her graduation as a Phi Beta Kappa from Vassar College in 1933, she married Harold Johnsrud, a marriage that lasted three years. She reviewed novels and biographies for *The New Republic* and *The Nation*, worked for the left-wing publisher Covici Friede, and, in 1937, involved herself in Trotskyite politics. In 1937, she became drama editor for the *Partisan Review*.

The next year, McCarthy married Edmund Wilson and gave birth to a son, Reuel Wilson; also, at Wilson's urging, she wrote her first fiction, a short story. Thereafter, the stories she wrote for *Southern Review*, *Partisan Review*, and *Harper's Bazaar* were collected in 1942 in the book *The Company She Keeps*. She separated from Edmund Wilson in 1945, the same year that she was teaching literature at Bard College; in 1946, she married Bowden Broadwater. In 1948, she taught one semester at Sarah Lawrence College and, in 1949, was a Guggenheim Fellow, an award that was repeated in 1959. Also in 1949, she received the *Horizon* literary prize from the publishers of her novel *The Oasis*. In 1961, she was divorced from Broadwater, married James Raymond West—a State Department official assigned to Paris—and went to live with West in France.

Two events dominated the 1960's for McCarthy. The first was the enormous popular success of her novel *The Group*, which became a number-one best-seller. The second was the Vietnam War; she was an outspoken critic of United States policy in Vietnam. In the 1970's she published two novels with social and political themes: *Birds of America* in 1971 and *Cannibals and Missionaries* in 1979; the latter, she said, would be her last novel.

In 1980, an offhand remark on *The Dick Cavett Show*

embroiled McCarthy in a prolonged legal battle that became a *cause célèbre* in the literary community. McCarthy said of Lillian Hellman that "every word she writes is a lie, including 'and' and 'the.'" Hellman sued. The resulting legal maneuvering was costly for McCarthy (in contrast, the wealthy Hellman did not count the cost), ending only in 1984, when, after Hellman's death, the suit was dropped before going to trial. Meanwhile, legal issues aside, the controversy brought several of Hellman's autobiographical works under close scrutiny, and the consensus was that McCarthy's judgment, clearly stated in hyperbolic terms, was vindicated.

In 1987, McCarthy published *How I Grew*, the first installment in what was projected to be a multivolume intellectual autobiography. In general, critics found it inferior to *Memories of a Catholic Girlhood*, which had covered some of the same territory from a different perspective. McCarthy died in New York on October 25, 1989.

Analysis

A keenly observant critic of modern American culture, and armed with a rapier wit, McCarthy uses satire to expose the folly of the intelligentsia and other elite classes of the Northeast. She is noted for her pungent commentaries on issues concerning marriage, sexual expression, and the role of the emancipated woman in contemporary urban America. Her novels often feature herself, with an assumed name, as protagonist; she also exploited her husbands and other people close to her for fictional purposes. Her characters generally have a superior education and/or intellect so that citations and quotations from learned sources—mainly classical or artistic—spring into their conversations. In the close conceptual unity of McCarthy's novels, lengthy paragraphs of extensive character analyses frequently fill several pages without interruption. As a result, the technique of several speakers in one paragraph seems to support the general schema. It supports, also, the paradigm of the group. Structurally, the novels preceding *The Group* develop around separate chapters, each presenting the viewpoints and the consciousness of the different characters; their point of unity is the common awareness of the social group. A protagonist, often a reflection of the author, generally emerges from among these peripheral persons, but the effect of each chapter remains that of the portrait or sketch.

The dominant quality of McCarthy's work is satire, and much of it is achieved by exaggeration and generalization. The dominant organization is the pairing of a separate character with each chapter, infused with an occasional chorus of viewpoints. McCarthy compared the technique to ventriloquism: The author throws her voice into various characters who speak for her. The long paragraphs of explication or character analysis tend to minimize plot; the concentration is on the psychological effects of what are frequently trivial incidents—as in *The Oasis*, when a couple illegally picking berries on the group's farm destroys the group.

The themes of McCarthy's novels generally concern the social failures of a group—of Utopian communities in *The Oasis*, of progressive education in *The Groves of Academe*, or of cultural progress in *The Group*. The interest in group attitudes can be best observed in the political content of McCarthy's novels, many of which feature a person who had some affiliation with the Communist party and defected or failed to become a member. Her work also shows a persistent aversion to the efforts of Senator Joseph McCarthy to eradicate Communists in the United States.

The Groves of Academe is set in a small Pennsylvania college called Jocelyn, which resembles Bard College. Directing its satire at progressive education, this novel pits the progressive against the classical, satirizes the small college in general, and exposes the evils of McCarthyism, focused in Senator McCarthy's House Committee on Un-American Activities. The group here is the English department faculty, from which Professor Henry Mulcahy finds himself dismissed. He rallies the faculty to his support, although he is a poor academician and deserves dismissal, and gains it through an appeal for sympathy for his wife and children. McCarthyism brought him to the position—the president of the college hired Mulcahy because the latter had been unjustly accused of being a Communist sympathizer—and, finally, it accounts for his retention. Mulcahy loses his chief faculty supporter when she discovers that he lied about his wife's illness, but he gains another weapon through a visiting poet who recognizes him from Communist party meetings. At the climax of the novel, the McCarthy scare is shown at its most evil: Protecting the college, the well-meaning president conducts an interview into Mulcahy's past, which results in the administrator being charged with libel. The unstable Mulcahy triumphs and secures his position at Jocelyn—certain to continue bullying students and colleagues alike—and the president resigns.

In *A Charmed Life*, Martha Sinnott returns to a group of artistic people at New Leeds, a small New England village based on Wellfleet, Cape Cod, where she had lived with her former husband (much as Mary McCarthy had lived at Wellfleet and returned with a second husband). Martha returns determined to be different from and independent of the New Leedsians who live a charmed life of many accidents, none of which kills them. Here, time, which signifies the mortal, is askew and awry, as indicated by the many problems with clocks and calendars. Part of Martha's anxiety about her return to New Leeds is the possibility of meeting her former husband (based on Edmund Wilson) with his new wife and child and the fear that he will reestablish domination over her. When he seduces her and she later finds herself pregnant, she cannot remember the date well enough to determine whether her former or present husband is the father. Her moral decision to have an abortion because she cannot live a lie results in her death; returning from borrowing money for the abortion, she drives on the right side of the road, contrary to New Leeds custom, and meets another car head-on. The charmed life of New Leeds goes on, but Martha lives and dies an outsider.

McCarthy called this novel a fairy tale. As in "Sleeping Beauty," Sinnott pricks her hand at the beginning of the novel, lives in self-doubt on the fringes of the immortality of New Leeds (the timelessness of a century of sleep), and is awakened to the new existence of pregnancy and decision. The prince who wakens her with a kiss (the seduction), however, is an evil prince.

With a theme of the failure of modern progress, *The Group* was published in November, 1963. At that time, Betty Friedan's *Feminine Mystique* (1962) and other feminist writings had focused on the problems of women, and the public was responsive to works focused on the problems of the emancipated woman. Although the novel is set in the seven years from 1933 to 1940, the progressiveness of the eight *cum* nine young Vassar women seemed to be the progress that was engulfing women of the 1960's. Like gleanings from an alumnae bulletin, the random appearances, different voices, and loose ends are not expected to be resolved. The undistinguished occupations of the group, also, confirm the alumnae magazine reports of most women graduates, but somehow more is expected of Vassar women. Not only the money but also increased competition for admission meant that, by 1963, most women could not get into Vassar. For the general public, there is some comfort in the failure of the culturally advantaged.

The novel begins with the wedding of Kay Strong in 1933 and ends with her death seven years later at the age of twenty-nine. Of the eight members of the group who had lived in the same dormitory, plus one outsider, Kay seemed to be most forward-looking and progressive. Like McCarthy, she comes from the West, and, immediately upon graduation, she marries her lover of some time, a mostly unemployed playwright, Harald Petersen, who resembles Harold Johnsrud. Part of McCarthy's personality is dispersed among the other characters, especially Libby MacAusland, a woman of formidable intellect who writes book reviews and becomes a literary agent.

The elegant, beautiful, and wealthy Elinor Eastlake disappears into Europe and reemerges a lesbian prior to Kay's death. Polly Andrews becomes attached to a married man who is obviously well adjusted except that he pays twenty-five dollars a week for psychiatric counseling. Working in a hospital, Polly becomes engaged to another man, a psychiatrist who has defected from the profession and thus augments the satiric attack on psychiatry. Helena Davison, in Cleveland, remains the stable rich girl, highly intelligent and analytic. Priss Hartshorn marries a pediatrician and, attempting to breast-feed her son and train him by modern theories, provides the satire on this aspect of progressivism. Pokey Prothero, from a household organized and represented by an invaluable butler, plans to become a veterinarian.

Kay, during a fight with Harald, gets a black eye and finds herself committed to a mental hospital. Despite Harald's admission that she does not belong there, she decides to stay for a rest and then disappears from the story until she reemerges after a divorce and a year in the West. Back East, ready to start a career again, she falls to her death while spotting planes from her window and becomes the first casualty of the war.

Representing a culmination of the group philosophy and the disjointed voices of the earlier novels, *The Group* with its timely feminist content earned for McCarthy a great deal of money and many appearances on talk shows and in magazines. Some Vassar alumnae were recognizable in it, and the film version omitted the name of the college. This novel established McCarthy as a popular writer.

Cannibals and Missionaries continues McCarthy's early interest in Communism and employs her familiar group structure with separate narrative voices. The group of *Cannibals and Missionaries*, originally formed as a committee of six to fly by Air France to Iran to investigate reports to the Shah of Iran's torturing of prisoners, expands, by the time the plane is hijacked to

Holland, to twenty-four hostages and eight terrorists. Set during the administration of President Gerald Ford, the novel takes its title from the puzzle in which three cannibals and three missionaries must cross a river in a boat that will hold only two people, but if the cannibals outnumber the missionaries, they might eat the missionaries. In the novel, however, there is no clear indication as to which group represents the cannibals and which the missionaries.

In one passage of explication, McCarthy points out that the terrorists' demands accomplish nothing but the reabsorption into the dominant society of whatever they demanded; prisoners released, for example, are eventually returned to prison. Confined in a Dutch farmhouse, hostages learn of their terrorists' demands from television: one and a quarter million dollars, Holland's withdrawal from NATO, the breaking of relations with Israel, and the release of "class war" prisoners from Dutch jails. Like the other groups in McCarthy's fiction, the members of this group are pulled together in a common cause; even though divided between hostages and terrorists, the hostages willingly aid the terrorists in some efforts and feel triumphant in the successful completion of a task, such as hiding the helicopter that brought them to the farmhouse. At the novel's conclusion, however, all but four are killed, one of whom claims that she has not been changed by the experience.

While *The Groves of Academe* is still highly esteemed as an example of the academic novel, and *The Group* is read by students of popular fiction and women's issues, McCarthy's novels considered by themselves do not make up a lasting body of work. Rather, they derive their lasting significance from their place in the life and work of an exemplary woman of letters.

Other major works

SHORT FICTION: *The Company She Keeps*, 1942; *Cast a Cold Eye*, 1950; *The Hounds of Summer and Other Stories*, 1981.

NONFICTION: *Sights and Spectacles: 1937-1956*, 1956; *Venice Observed*, 1956; *Memories of a Catholic Girlhood*, 1957; *The Stones of Florence*, 1959; *On the Contrary: Articles of Belief*, 1961; *Mary McCarthy's Theatre Chronicles, 1937-1962*, 1963; *Vietnam*, 1967; *Hanoi*, 1968; *The Writing on the Wall and Other Literary Essays*, 1970; *Medina*, 1972; *The Seventeenth Degree*, 1974; *The Mask of State*, 1974; *Ideas and the Novel*, 1980; *Occasional Prose*, 1985; *How I Grew*, 1987; *Intellectual Memoirs: New York, 1936-1938*, 1993; *Between Friends: The Correspondence of Hannah Arendt and Mary McCarthy, 1949-1975*, 1994.

Bibliography

Auchincloss, Louis. *Pioneers and Caretakers: A Study of Nine American Novelists*. Minneapolis: University of Minnesota Press, 1961.

Bennett, Joy. *Mary McCarthy: An Annotated Bibliography*. New York: Garland, 1992.

Brightman, Carol. *Writing Dangerously: Mary McCarthy and Her World*. New York: Clarkson Potter, 1992.

Gelderman, Carol, ed. *Conversations with Mary McCarthy*. Jackson: University Press of Mississippi, 1991.

_____ . *Mary McCarthy: A Life*. New York: St. Martin's Press, 1988.

Grumbach, Doris. *The Company She Kept*. New York: Coward, McCann, 1967.

Munroe, Gretchen Himmele. "Mary McCarthy." In *American Novelists Since World War II*, edited by Jeffrey Helterman and Richard Layman. Vol. 2 in *Dictionary of Literary Biography*. Detroit: Gale Research, 1978.

Stock, Irvin. *Mary McCarthy*. Minneapolis: University of Minnesota Press, 1968.

HERMAN MELVILLE

Born: New York, New York; August 1, 1819

Died: New York, New York; September 28, 1891

Principal long fiction

Typee: A Peep at Polynesian Life, 1846; *Omoo: A Narrative of Adventures in the South Seas*, 1847; *Mardi and a Voyage Thither*, 1849; *Redburn: His First Voyage*, 1849; *White-Jacket: Or, The World in a Man-of-War*, 1850; *Moby Dick: Or, The Whale*, 1851; *Pierre: Or, The Ambiguities*, 1852; *Israel Potter: His Fifty Years of Exile*, 1855; *The Confidence Man: His Masquerade*, 1857; *Billy Budd, Foretopman*, 1924.

Other literary forms

After the financial failure of *Moby Dick* and *Pierre*, Herman Melville, as if turning a new corner in his literary career, began a series of short stories. Published between 1853 and 1856, either in a collection (*The Piazza Tales*, 1856) or individually in journals such as *Putnam's Monthly Magazine* and *Harper's Monthly Magazine*, the tales present an enigmatic addition to Melville's artistry. Melville had difficulty with the short forms, and he seemed unable to work out the plot and characters in the space required. His best stories are novella-length; "Benito Cereno," "The Encantadas," and "Bartleby the Scrivener" are among the best stories in the language.

Melville also wrote poetry, which suffers from the same unevenness that plagues his short fiction. A handful of poems are worthy of being anthologized with the best poetry of the nineteenth century. "Hawthorne and His Mosses," Melville's only serious attempt at criticism and analysis, is important as an assessment of Hawthorne's first important sketches.

Achievements

Melville's achievements, before the discovery of *Billy Budd, Foretopman*, and the subsequent revival of Melville studies, were viewed simply as writings from "a man who lived among the cannibals." He was remembered only for *Typee* and *Omoo*, his slight but extremely popular South Seas adventures. Only with the publication of *Billy Budd, Foretopman* and the critical scrutiny that its publication encouraged were *Moby Dick*, *Pierre*, and the rest reassessed and Melville's reputation as a leader among giants affirmed.

Apart from introducing the South Seas tale to the American public, *Pierre* is arguably the first important work of psychological realism; *Moby Dick* is a masterpiece of metaphysics, allegory, philosophy, and literary greatness that has never been surpassed in American fiction. The assessment of Melville's work was not realized until years after his death and almost seventy years after Melville had given up the novel form for the quick money of short stories, the personal introspection of poetry, and the security of a government post in the New York customs office. Melville was never psychologically or ideologically attuned to the demands of his public, and thus popularity eluded him in his lifetime.

Biography

Melville was born in New York City, August 1, 1819, the third child of a modestly wealthy family. His father, a successful merchant, traced his lineage back to Major Thomas Melville, one of the "Indians" (disguised colonists) at the Boston Tea Party. His mother, Maria Gansevoort Melville, was the only daughter of General Peter Gansevoort, also a revolutionary war hero. Melville had a happy childhood in a home where there was affluence and love. He had access to the arts and books, and he was educated in some of the city's finest private institutions. His father, however, considered young Melville to be somewhat backward, despite his son's early penchant for public speaking, and marked him for a trade rather than law or a similar professional pursuit.

The prosperity that the Melvilles enjoyed from before Herman's birth came to an end in the economic panic of 1830. Unable to meet creditors' demands, Melville's father lost his business and was forced into bankruptcy. After attempts to save the business, he moved the family to Albany and assumed the management of a fur company's branch office. The move seemed to settle the Melville's financial problems until the cycle repeated itself in 1831. Melville's father, again, suffered a financial reversal, went into physical and mental decline, and died on January 28, 1832.

After his father's death, Melville became, successively, a bank clerk and accountant, a farm worker, a schoolteacher, and, after another economic failure, an unemployed, but genteel, young man seeking employment in New York City. With the aid of his brothers, Melville secured a berth on a Liverpool packet and thus launched his sea career and, indirectly, his literary fortunes. After one cruise, however, Melville returned to schoolteaching. When the school closed for lack of funds, he and a friend determined to go West to visit Melville's uncle in Illinois, hoping to find some type of financially satisfying arrangement there. Failing to find work, Melville returned to New York City and signed aboard the *Acushnet*, a new whaler making her maiden voyage. From 1841 to 1844, Melville was to participate in seafaring adventures that would change American literature.

On his return to New York in 1844, he found his family's fortunes somewhat improved. He also found that the stories he had to tell of his travels were enthusiastically received by his friends and relatives. Finally persuaded to write them, he produced *Typee* and published it in 1846. The immediate success and acclaim that followed the publication assured Melville that he had finally found his place in life. He followed *Typee* with its sequel, *Omoo*, achieved a similar success, and resolutely set out to make his living by his pen. He found the financial return of two popular novels was not sufficient to support him, however, and he applied for a government position but was rejected. Melville married Elizabeth Shaw, moved to New York City with most of his family, and started a third novel that became *Mardi and a Voyage Thither*.

The visionary and allegorical structure of *Mardi and a Voyage Thither* did not appeal to the readers of his previous successes, and its failure frustrated Melville. In need of ready funds, he began two "potboilers" in order to produce those funds. After the publication and success of *Redburn* and *White-Jacket*, Melville moved his family to a farm in the Berkshires, which he dubbed "Arrowhead" because of Indian artifacts he found there, and assumed the life of a country gentleman and a member of the loosely knit literary society that included Oliver Wendell Holmes and Nathaniel Hawthorne and others living in the vicinity of Pittsfield, Massachusetts.

How Hawthorne and Melville met is not known, but that they met is witnessed by the production of *Moby Dick*. It was likely that Hawthorne encouraged Melville to write as he saw fit, not as the public demanded. Their correspondence reveals an intense, cordial friendship that was of immense value to Melville during this time

of his greatest personal, emotional, and artistic development. Hawthorne was one of the first, not to mention the few, to praise Melville's whaling story. Despite Hawthorne's praise, *Moby Dick* was a financial and critical failure. *Pierre*, the "rural bowl of milk" that followed *Moby Dick*, defied Melville's predictions for its success and was also a failure. The dual failure caused Melville considerable pain and bitterness. As a result of the failures and the debt to his publishers, Melville turned away from the novel to the short-story form.

Melville was to publish two more novels in his lifetime, but neither was commercially successful. Melville began writing poetry in addition to the short story, but his poetry was even more introspective than his fiction, and by the time he was appointed to the customs office of New York City in 1866, he had virtually stopped publishing for public consumption.

The security of the customs office eliminated Melville's need for the slim financial return of publication, and he no longer felt compelled to write for an unwilling public. Yet, he continued to write. At his death, he left a box full of manuscripts of his unpublished work during the years from 1866 to his death (he had published some poetry). When the box was opened, it was found to contain one more novel. *Billy Budd, Foretopman* was the final piece of Melville's frustration. He never finished it and never attempted to publish it, but since its discovery and publication in 1924 it has been recognized as one of Melville's masterpieces. When Melville died in 1891, his obituaries recalled him not only as a man who wrote novels of adventure, but also as one who had "fallen into a literary decline." It was left for another generation to appreciate and revere him.

Analysis

Melville's career as a novelist breaks down, somewhat too neatly, into a three-part voyage of frustration and disappointment. The first part of his career is characterized by the heady successes of *Typee* and *Omoo*, the second by the frustrating failure of, among other works, *Moby Dick*, and the third by his increasing withdrawal from publication and the final discovery of and acclaim for *Billy Budd, Foretopman*, three decades after Melville's death. After the initial successes of *Typee* and *Omoo*, Melville never again achieved anything approaching popular success, but it was the acclaim over those two novels that assured Melville that he should attempt to make his way as a novelist. It probably did not occur to Melville at the time, but he was introducing a new genre into American literature.

Typee struck the American public like a ray of sunshine falling into a darkened room. The fresh descriptions and intriguing narrative of an American sailor trapped among the natives of the Marquesas Islands were hailed on both sides of the Atlantic, and its sequel, *Omoo*, was received even more enthusiastically. The problems inherent in Melville's harsh treatment of missionaries and imperialism and the general disbelief of the veracity in the author's tale aside, the works satiated a public thirst for exotic places. That *Typee* and *Omoo* have survived in the estimation of critics is testimony to Melville's art even in those early stages of his development.

Whether it is the simple narrative or the dramatic suspense of impending doom which holds the reader, *Typee* offers a flowing romantic atmosphere of timeless days, pointless endeavor, and mindless existence. The Happy Valley in which Melville's Tommo finds himself trapped is an idyllic setting for the lovely Fayaway and Tommo to live and love. In *Typee* there is none of the agonizing speculation on life, man, philosophy, or the cosmos, which readers later came to expect of Melville. With only slight exaggeration and minimal research, Melville created the picture of a world beyond the ken of his readers but which would never die in his memories.

Omoo, a sequel to *Typee*, is only an extension of that idyll. There is a basic difference between *Typee* and *Omoo*, however. *Typee* is a tightly woven dramatic narrative, incorporating the day-to-day suspense of whether Tommo would be the Marquesan cannibals' next meal. *Omoo* is a more picaresque representation of the events, the charm in *Omoo* depending solely on the loosely tied chain of events encountered by the narrator and his companion, Dr. Long Ghost, among the natives of Tahiti. There is no threat hanging over them, as in *Typee*, and there is no necessity for escape. *Omoo* also differs in that it takes place in a tainted paradise. Tahiti has been, in *Omoo*, Christianized and settled and, thus, the natives are familiar with the white sailor and his games. This reduction of innocence colors *Omoo* in a way not reflected in *Typee*.

There is an inescapable glow of romance throughout Melville's two Polynesian novels. The record of missionary abuse and the encroachment of civilization does not make an overbearing appearance, but it does lay the groundwork for the reflections of Melville's despair and convoluted indictments of man and his world in later, more mature works.

Mardi, *Redburn*, and *White-Jacket* rapidly followed Melville's early successes. *Mardi*, opening like a continuation of *Typee* and *Omoo*, shocked readers when it lapsed into philosophical allegory. *Mardi's* subsequent failure prompted Melville, in search of fame and funds, to return to sea-narrative in *Redburn* and *White-Jacket*, but despite their modest successes, Melville reviled them as hackwork.

There is evidence that Melville initially intended *Moby Dick* to be little more than a factual account of the whale fisheries in the South Pacific detailed with first-hand tales of adventures on a whaler. When completed two years after its beginning, it was a puzzling, intricately devised literary work in which a white whale is the central character. Around this central figure, Melville weaves symbolism, speculation, philosophy, and allegory on life, God, humanity, and the human condition. In short, Melville had created an epic romance that stood at the brink of becoming mythology.

The plot of *Moby Dick*, when not interrupted by authorial asides and digressions, is relatively direct. A young man, Ishmael, comes to the sea seeking a berth on a whaling ship. He finds the *Pequod*; falls into a friendship with the cannibal harpooner Queequeg; discovers that the ship is captained by a madman, Ahab, who is driven to wreak vengeance on the white whale that took his leg off on a previous voyage; finds himself in a crew that is a microcosm of the world's peoples; watches as Ahab drives the ship and crew in pursuit of Moby Dick; and is the sole survivor when Ahab is killed in a direct confrontation with the whale. By itself, the plot is thrilling but does not have the ingredients of greatness. The layers of fiction—the levels that the reader must traverse in order to rend the novel for all its substance—make the work magnificent. To the surface adventure, Melville adds gleanings from volumes of cetological and marine lore, his own observations on the psychology of humanity, and, finally, his ultimate speculations on good and evil—the basic morality of humanity and of humanity's place in the universe.

In describing Ahab, his ship and crew, Melville employs a nonnarrative form of characterization, where each individual is the subject of an inquiry or is an example of a human type. Of the major characters, Ahab is the most complex, but the others form a society in which that complexity can best be displayed. For example, Ahab feels compelled to explain the real reasons behind his insane search for the white whale only to Starbuck, the conscientious, scrupulous first mate. Rather than simple revenge, as Starbuck supposes it to be, Ahab proposes to strike through the "pasteboard masks" of reality by striking at the whale. In his reasoning with Starbuck, Ahab demonstrates a side of himself that is otherwise hidden; there is purpose, calculation, and preparation in his madness. Ahab's insanity, thereby, becomes a divine sort of madness, and he transcends mere earthly logic to become an epic madman jousting with Creation.

Ahab becomes more than a simple villain when viewed against the backdrop of Starbuck and the other characters. He becomes a monolithic character testing a universe that he sees as perverse and unkind toward humanity's existence. He dares to confront Nature itself and to challenge it to single combat. Yet humanity and its science cannot stand against Nature and hope to survive. It is Ahab's hamartia to believe that he can survive; his belief is the final sign of his ultimately evil nature. Ahab would, he tells Starbuck, "strike the sun if he offended me," and the captain considers himself as the equal of any other force in Nature. He forgets that he is limited by human frailty—or he believes he is no longer subject to the laws of temporal existence or his own physical shortcomings. He is, in one sense, a blighted Prometheus who can offer nothing but his vision to his fellow humans, and they blindly accept it. Ahab's greatest evil is the corruption of his relatively innocent world, and its ultimate destruction is his sole responsibility.

The last of Melville's attempts in the novel form, *Billy Budd, Foretopman*, has come to be recognized as Melville's final word on the great problems with which he first grappled in *Moby Dick*. The tale is a masterful twisting of historical event into fiction in order to maintain the tension of a gripping story. While so doing, Melville explores the stirring, but somewhat less exciting, problems of the conflict between humanity, good and evil, and the law. Melville uses a blend of the historically significant British mutinies of the *Nore* and at Spithead in 1797, and the 1842 execution of three alleged mutineers of the United States ship *Somers*, to mold the setting and motive for his story leading to the trial and execution of the "handsome sailor."

There is a slightly melodramatic air about the principal characters in *Billy Budd, Foretopman*. Claggart, by shrewd characterization and description, is the evil master-at-arms who is in direct conflict with the innocent, pure, guileless Billy Budd. Melville never makes clear why Claggart develops his seemingly perverse prejudice against Billy, but a definite line of good and evil is drawn between the two men. The evil is magni-

fied by the mysterious impetus for Claggart's antipathy toward Billy; the good is intensified by Billy's naïve ignorance of Claggart's malice, even though the entire crew seems to know of it and understand the reasons for it, and by his cheerful mien not only in the face of Claggart's bullying but also in spite of the circumstances that brought him to the *Indomitable*.

Billy is wronged from the beginning when he is impressed from the American *Rights of Man* to the British *Indomitable* (the names of the ships being a sly piece of Melville commentary on the British navy, the War of 1812, and Billy Budd's predicament, among other things). Billy is instantly recognized and accepted by his new mates on board the *Indomitable* and becomes a full and useful member of the crew and a good shipmate. Claggart, who has the unenviable job of policing a British man-of-war and administering the queen's maritime justice, seems to extend himself to bring charges against the new man. When Billy is implicated in a mutiny rumor, Claggart seizes the opportunity to bring him before a drumhead courtmartial. At the hearing, Claggart concentrates all of his inexplicable venom against Billy Budd in false charges, innuendo, and lies calculated to ensure a guilty verdict for which Billy will be hanged.

The wonder of Billy Budd and Claggart is that Melville, while portraying the two extremes of human morality in human forms, avoids creating flat caricatures. Billy and Claggart seemingly are real people operating in a real world, and they develop in very believable ways, even given Claggart's behavior toward Billy. At the climax of the trial, perhaps the most fantastic moment in the novel, there is no appreciable relaxation of the verisimilitude Melville creates, even though Billy strikes Claggart dead with one crashing blow of his fist. The other major character of the novel fills the momentary gap in the credibility of the story after Claggart's death. Captain Vere commands not only the *Indomitable* but also the trial, and it is he who pushes the novel through its climactic scene and who, in essence, takes the message of the novel from Billy Budd and develops it to its fruition.

Edward Fairfax ("Starry") Vere appears at length only from the trial to the end of the novel, but, despite the title character and his antagonist, Vere is the heart of the novel. He is everything Billy and Claggart are not. He is a complex character—a philosophical ship's captain—and a man who is caught between many pressures as he decides the fate of a man whom he evidently likes. Faced with the precedent of the historical mutinies that

Melville introduces into the novel's background, Vere feels the necessity of creating Billy Budd as an example to other prospective mutineers. Seeing Billy's innocence, and understanding at least part of Claggart's fulsome character, Vere is loathe to condemn a man who probably was within his moral right to strike his superior. Even so, the need for order and the maritime sense of justice force Vere to send Billy to the yardarm. Vere, more than anyone, recognizes that he is sacrificing an innocent man for the good of his ship, its crew, and, ultimately, for his society. He sentences Billy under the prescription of law, but he begs his forgiveness as a moral human being.

The sacrifice of the innocent is a theme that pervades Western literature, but in *Billy Budd, Foretopman*, Melville confronts the struggle between chaos and order, law and morality, humanity and society. There is no clear decision as Vere dies in battle; Billy haunts him to his end. Yet, the society, the system for which Billy was sacrificed, survives and prevails. Vere remains incomprehensible except to the man he condemns. Billy Budd understands but does not have the capacity or the will to exert himself in order to save himself. He is reminiscent, in some respects, of the Christ-figure he has universally been called. In the final analysis, Vere, Claggart, and Billy are all sacrificed, and the initial skirmishes between good and evil become almost trivial when compared to the moral and philosophical riddles Melville poses.

Melville's significance as a writer who helped shape an "American" identity is twofold: Most obviously, his depiction of the seagoing Northeast is evoked in several of his novels; his evocation of contemporary sociopolitical concerns, such as the 1842 executions, also plays a part. More important, however, was Melville's ability to weave these settings and issues into a broader fabric: the relationships of the individual to others and to the universe at large, complete with the attendant implications for good and evil. Melville had his causes and injected them into his stories, but he is primarily interested in the human condition. He inspects all facets of each character ruthlessly and meticulously, without judgment and without prejudice, and he allows the results of his inspection to speak for themselves without gratuitous commentary. Since the revival of Melville studies with the discovery of *Billy Budd, Foretopman*, Melville's reputation as one of America's most significant authors is secure.

Other major works

SHORT FICTION: *The Piazza Tales*, 1856; *The Apple-Tree Table and Other Sketches*, 1922.

POETRY: *Battle-Pieces and Aspects of the War*, 1866; *Clarel: A Poem and Pilgrimage in the Holy Land*, 1876; *John Marr and Other Sailors*, 1888; *Timoleon*, 1891.

NONFICTION: *Journal Up the Straits*, 1935; *Journal of a Visit to London and the Continent*, 1948; *Correspondence*, 1993.

Bibliography

Berthoff, Warner. *The Example of Melville*. Princeton, N.J.: Princeton University Press, 1962.

Bryant, John, ed. *A Companion to Melville Studies*. Westport, Conn.: Greenwood Press, 1986.

Dillingham, William D. *An Artist in the Rigging*. Athens: University of Georgia Press, 1972.

_____ . *Melville's Later Novels*. Athens: University of Georgia Press, 1986.

_____ . *Melville's Short Fiction, 1853-1856*. Athens: University of Georgia Press, 1977.

Garner, Stanton. *The Civil War World of Herman Melville*. Lawrence: University Press of Kansas, 1993.

Karcher, Carolyn L. *Shadow Over the Promised Land: Slavery, Race, and Violence in Melville's America*. Baton Rouge: Louisiana State University Press, 1980.

Kirby, David K. *Herman Melville*. New York: Continuum, 1993.

Olson, Charles. *Call Me Ishmael*. San Francisco: City Lights Books, 1947.

Rosenberry, Edward H. *Melville*. Boston: Routledge & Kegan Paul, 1979.

Sherrill, Rowland A. *The Prophetic Melville: Experience, Transcendence, and Tragedy*. Athens: University of Georgia Press, 1979.

Young, Philip. *The Private Melville*. University Park: Pennsylvania State University Press, 1993.

JOHN O'HARA

Born: Pottsville, Pennsylvania; January 31, 1905

Died: Princeton, New Jersey; April 11, 1970

Principal long fiction

Appointment in Samarra, 1934; *Butterfield 8*, 1935; *A Rage to Live*, 1949; *The Farmer's Hotel*, 1951; *Ten North Frederick*, 1955; *A Family Party*, 1956; *From the Terrace*, 1958; *Ourselves to Know*, 1960; *Sermons and Soda Water*, 1960; *The Big Laugh*, 1962; *Elizabeth Appleton*, 1963; *The Lockwood Concern*, 1965; *The Instrument*, 1967; *Lovely Child: A Philadelphian's Story*, 1969; *The Ewings*, 1972.

Other literary forms

John O'Hara was a prolific writer of short stories. Scattered through the short-story collections are most of O'Hara's works in the novella form; the only novellas to be separately published are the three in *Sermons and Soda Water*. The play version of the story "Pal Joey" was published in 1952. O'Hara's last complete play, *Far from Heaven* (1962), was first published posthumously in 1979 along with an unproduced original screenplay, *The Man Who Could Not Lose* (1959), under the title *Two by O'Hara*. O'Hara wrote and collaborated on film scripts from the 1930's through the 1950's, and several of his novels were made into films during his lifetime. He was several times a newspaper columnist. Two collections of his columns were published: *Sweet and Sour*—columns written for the Trenton *Sunday Times-Advertiser*—and *My Turn*, a series of syndicated columns written for *Newsday*. A collection of O'Hara's speeches, essays, and interviews, *An Artist Is His Own Fault*, appeared in 1977.

Achievements

Often dismissed as a popular novelist with tendencies toward sensationalism, or as a "social historian," O'Hara has nevertheless secured a faithful following among many literary critics for his skill at storytelling and his evocation of times, places, and manners in American society in the first half of the twentieth century. Matthew J. Bruccoli is probably most accurate in calling O'Hara a "novelist of manners," in the sense that O'Hara was primarily concerned with the accurate depiction of a social matrix and its effect on human behavior and potential. Like William Faulkner and other twentieth century American novelists, O'Hara turned the realities of his hometown experience into a fictional world; unlike Faulkner, he probed this milieu with a dedication to social realism rather than elevating it to mythic status. In addition to his native eastern Pennsylvania, O'Hara used New York and Hollywood as frequent settings for his fiction. Although he lived and worked in both places, he is most clearly identified with the "Region" of Pennsylvania on which he brings to bear an insider's perceptions.

Biography

John Henry O'Hara was born on January 31, 1905, in Pottsville, Pennsylvania. The town of Pottsville became the "Gibbsville" of his fiction, and the surrounding eastern Pennsylvania anthracite coal-mining area, known to residents as the Region, was the locale of his major novels and stories. The author's father, Patrick O'Hara, was a doctor whose father had settled in the area during the Civil War, and his mother, Katharine Delaney O'Hara, was the daughter of a prosperous businessman in nearby Lykens, which became O'Hara's fictional Lyons. Patrick O'Hara was a respected surgeon, necessarily specializing in injuries resulting from mining accidents, and he was seriously disappointed at his firstborn son's refusal to study medicine. Rather than inspiring a dedication to the medical profession, O'Hara's travels with his father to the scenes of medical emergencies provided him with regional lore that found its way into his writing.

Living on Pottsville's "best" street, Mahantongo ("Lantenengo" in the fictional Gibbsville), was a sign of the O'Hara family's relative affluence and provided O'Hara with an awareness of the rigid economic and ethnic stratification of the town. Until his father's early death in 1925, O'Hara led a fairly privileged existence, and his dream of attending Yale was thwarted less by lack of funds than by O'Hara's dismissals from three prepatory schools for low grades and disregard of discipline. The alternative to college was a job as a reporter on the Pottsville *Journal* in 1924, which effectively launched O'Hara's career as a writer.

In 1928, O'Hara left Pottsville for New York, where he worked briefly for the *Herald-Tribune* and *Time* and began to contribute stories to *The New Yorker*, which eventually published more than two hundred of his short stories; accordingly, some have attributed to O'Hara the creation of that sub-genre the "*New Yorker* story." During these early years in New York, O'Hara established friendships with Franklin P. Adams (F.P.A.)—to whose New York *World* column "The Conning Tower" he sometimes contributed—Robert Benchley, Dorothy Parker, and F. Scott Fitzgerald. In 1931, he married Helen Ritchie Petit ("Pet"), but his heavy drinking and frequent unemployment led to a divorce in 1933.

Appointment in Samarra, the first of O'Hara's fifteen novels, was published in 1934, and his first collection of short stories, *The Doctor's Son*, appeared the following year. In 1937, O'Hara married a second time, to Belle Mulford Wylie, who would become the mother of his only child, Wylie Delaney O'Hara (born in 1945). Although he intermittently aspired to be a playwright, O'Hara's only successful play was *Pal Joey*, based on a series of stories in *The New Yorker*, which ran on Broadway between 1940 and 1941 and made into a film in 1957.

Although he was not financially secure for some time, O'Hara was growing in reputation as a fiction writer and for the next several years lived alternately on the East Coast and in Hollywood, where he wrote screenplays. The O'Haras moved to Princeton, New Jersey, in 1949; in 1953 a serious ulcer condition prompted O'Hara to quit drinking permanently. Following Belle's death in 1954, O'Hara married Katharine Barnes Bryan ("Sister") in 1955, and the family moved two years later to "Linebrook," a home in Princeton that O'Hara and Sister had designed.

For the next fifteen years, until his death, O'Hara lived a more settled, productive life than ever before. In 1964, the American Academy of Arts and Letters presented O'Hara with its Gold Medal Award of Merit. O'Hara died at Linebrook on April 11, 1970, while working on a sequel to *The Ewings*.

Analysis

O'Hara was committed throughout his career to providing accurate records of the decades and places in which he lived. The novels and novellas that resulted from this commitment are uneven in quality as examples of the art of fiction, but they provide an unmatched portrait of segments of American society in the first half of the twentieth century. The central characters of much of his fiction are wealthy, prominent people, whether they are the leading citizens of "Gibbsville," Pennsylvania, or Hollywood film stars, yet O'Hara frequently illuminates their circumstances by juxtaposing them with members of other socioeconomic groups: servants, tradesmen, laborers. The result is a panoramic social canvas, consonant with O'Hara's conception of the traditional novel form.

One of O'Hara's major themes is power—not only the power of money, though that is a central metaphor, but also the power inherent in talent, morality, and sexuality. O'Hara shared with F. Scott Fitzgerald a fascination with wealth and social prestige, but O'Hara's treatment of their influence is far more analytical. His novels typically trace the establishment of a family dynasty, as in *The Lockwood Concern*, or the progress of an individual's aspirations for himself or herself, as in *Ten North Frederick* and *Elizabeth Appleton*—always within the constraints of a social web rendered palpable by realistic settings and dialogue. O'Hara is concerned particularly to show the limits of human power, not in the face of an overwhelming fate but as the result of miscalculation, error, or simple human frailty. When Julian English throws a drink in the face of Harry Reilly in *Appointment in Samarra*, or when George Lockwood, in *The Lockwood Concern*, builds a wall around his mansion, neither can foresee the fatal consequences, but both have made choices that dictate inevitable results.

As money is a metaphor for power in O'Hara's fiction, sexuality is an ambivalent metaphor for love. Though he was accused of sensationalism and bad taste in his relatively explicit depiction of sexual relationships, O'Hara was primarily interested in showing the potential for manipulation in the human sexual relationship. Women as well as men are portrayed as captive to sexual desire, and both sexes frequently mistake love for possession or sex for love. From Grace Caldwell Tate's injudicious couplings in *A Rage to Live* to the tender relationship between Jim Malloy and Charlotte Sears in *The Girl on the Baggage Truck*, the possibility of true romantic love seems remote in O'Hara's fiction. His realistic approach assumes a basic human egotism and desire for power which renders such love rare.

The structures of O'Hara's novels and novellas reinforce the sense of inevitability of consequence. His novels frequently begin with an apparently small but significant event or action that spins out in mystery-story fashion to create the web that catches the characters and demonstrates their ultimate powerlessness. Yet, he avoids the predictability of formulaic fiction by using multiple points of view and a wealth of complex, believable characters to play out the drama. In the novellas, the structure is frequently circular, the story beginning at a moment of culmination and then tracing the events that have brought the characters to that point. Common too, especially in the novellas, is O'Hara's use of a narrator, usually Jim Malloy, a journalist whose background and attitudes resemble those of O'Hara. Although these structural devices were not original with O'Hara, he used them skillfully to suit his fictional purposes.

Character is of supreme importance in O'Hara's fiction. The majority of them inhabit the Pennsylvania "Region" in which he spent his youth, and the fictional canon provides a vivid picture of relationships among people of various social levels over time. The reappearance of certain characters in many works reinforces the sense of a coherent world within which the codes of morality and propriety dictate the shape of both society and individual human lives.

Appointment in Samarra is set in the Region and has strong autobiographical elements. The novel deals starkly and dramatically with the themes of power and fate and demonstrates O'Hara's understanding of individual human destiny as a delicate balance between necessity and accident. The novel's title derives from a quotation from W. Somerset Maugham; the "appointment in Samarra" is an inescapable appointment with death, yet Julian English, O'Hara's main character, is doomed by his own actions—his tragedy is of his own making.

The story of Julian English is set against a richly detailed social and geographical background. O'Hara takes pains to provide the reader with the flavor of the early Depression years: the names of popular songs, the intricacies of the bootlegger's profession, and the subdued desperation of both rich and poor. To tie the novel to an era even further, there are topical references; Julian English mentions having recently read Ernest Hemingway's *A Farewell to Arms* (1929), and Irma Fleigler counts on President Herbert Hoover's promise that next year will be better for everyone, so that she and her husband can join the country club to which the Englishes belong. The club, and the town and region of which it is the social pinnacle, are treated with the same careful detail. O'Hara devotes several pages to the peculiarities of the anthracite coal region and the social hierarchy of Gibbsville, making clear that no per-

son or action is independent of the social context. Despite the anxieties of what was called in 1930 a "slump," Gibbsville and its inhabitants are filled with self-importance, and none more so than Julian English, the doctor's son.

To dramatize his perception that the individual is inextricably bound up in his social context, O'Hara deftly shifts the point of view in the novel from interior to exterior views of Julian English, emphasizing the extent to which one person becomes the object of others' scrutiny. The novel covers the last three days of Julian's life, from the moment he throws a drink in Harry Reilly's face at the country-club Christmas party until he commits suicide by carbon monoxide poisoning, yet the narrative begins and ends with the observations of Luther and Irma Fleigler, a middle-class couple whose solid respectability and loving relationship contrasts sharply with the weakness and manipulation of the far wealthier Julian and Caroline English. Julian's action is, in itself, insignificant—a social error from which all parties could have recovered in time—but it becomes symbolic of Julian's misperception of his own strength and power. With the inevitability of Greek tragedy, social ostracism follows Julian's throwing of the drink; he becomes an outsider to his own group, and he fails in all his efforts to pick up the pieces of his life.

O'Hara presents, one by one, the sources of comfort to which twentieth century individuals turn in times of personal trouble and shows them all to be ineffective. Family, sex, work, drink, religion, even a simple apology—none provides solace to Julian, who is the isolated twentieth century man, left with nothing in which to believe. If Julian does not understand the motivation for his action, neither does anyone else around him, and neither his father, Dr. English, nor his wife can respond adequately to his anguish. Work fails as an escape because, as the president of a Cadillac dealership, Julian is dependent upon precisely the good will of potential customers that his action has temporarily denied him, and drink leads to either self-pity or further belligerence. Monsignor Creedon, to whom Julian, a Protestant, feels obscurely drawn, confesses that he has sometimes wished he had chosen a different life's work; lacking a true vocation, Creedon cannot provide a spiritual solution to Julian's guilt and loneliness.

Ten North Frederick was the first novel after *Appointment in Samarra* to deal with the "Region," and it marked a new phase of O'Hara's work as well as a new, alcohol-free stage of his life. Whereas *Appointment in Samarra* demonstrates that the power of individuals over their own lives is limited by the influence of society and the intervention of chance, *Ten North Frederick* introduces great wealth and ambition into the equation and demonstrates how that power is equally restricted by such factors.

Ten North Frederick chronicles the failure of Joe Chapin, the central character, to achieve his ambitions. Those ambitions are far from modest. Chapin wants nothing less than to leave each of his children a million dollars upon his death and to become president of the United States. That he achieves neither goal is in part the result of circumstances (the Depression reduces his financial assets) and in part of errors in judgment, such as his attempting to circumvent the local political system managed by Mike Slattery. Despite the magnitude of his hopes, Chapin is neither grasping nor overwhelmingly egotistical. Though he makes some ill-considered decisions about the lives of others—notably his daughter's abortion and the dissolution of her marriage to an Italian musician—he is not a power-hungry schemer. Instead, he is unaware that his own power has limits. Reared to believe in the privileges of wealth and status and trained in the proprieties of social forms, Chapin is merely inflexible. Rules and forms have taken precedence over human responsiveness, and his one extramarital affair, late in his life, seems to be the only spontaneous action of which he is capable.

Chapin's life thus has an opaque surface that prevents even his closest Gibbsville associates from knowing him well. At Chapin's funeral, one of his cousins remarks, "I could never figure Joe out," to which Slattery replies, "We knew exactly what Joe wanted us to know. And believe me, that wasn't much." Coming at the beginning of the novel, this exchange might have foreshadowed the revelation of a secret life that Chapin had hidden carefully from his friends, but O'Hara's intention instead is to show that the reality of Chapin's life is one with its facade. Behind the mask of respectability is a life that is precisely as sterile as the mask would suggest. With the exception of minor scandals such as his daughter's elopement and pregnancy, Chapin's experience has been one of single-minded devotion to the accumulation of wealth and status.

The major strength of *Ten North Frederick*, as of most of O'Hara's fiction, is its characterization. The novel deals with three generations of the Chapin family, beginning with Joe Chapin's parents, though instead of a straight chronological narrative O'Hara uses a flashback technique, weaving past and present together to emphasize the effect of family—especially women—

on the formation of character and ambition. Both Joe's mother, Charlotte, and his wife, Edith, have plans for his life; both are women for whom love means power and ownership, and for whom sex is a form of manipulation. Edith Chapin articulates this persistent theme of O'Hara's novels as she thinks, on her wedding night, "It was not Love; Love might easily have very little to do with it; but it was as strong a desire as Love or Hate and it was going to be her life, the owning of this man." As clearly as anywhere in his fiction, O'Hara here portrays women who, because they are denied most masculine forms of power, participate vicariously by requiring their men to succeed in their stead.

Yet Joe Chapin is a failure. If there is a "secret" in his life, it is the depth of his desire for high political office. On the surface a personable, respected pillar of Gibbsville, highly regarded by most of its leading citizens, Chapin nurses the ambition for which his mother has groomed him, but he is not willing to play the political games required to gain the backing of Mike Slattery's organization, nor can money buy him the office he seeks. After he is forced to withdraw from the political arena, only his brief affair with his daughter's friend Kate Drummond gives his life meaning, and when that ends he slowly begins to commit suicide by drinking heavily.

Many of O'Hara's own feelings about accomplishment and aging informed his creation of Joe Chapin. O'Hara was fifty when the novel was completed. Like Chapin, he had gained the respect of many of his contemporaries, but certain measures of "success" had eluded him: in particular, recognition as a first-rate novelist. Both O'Hara and his character had suffered frightening indications of poor health; Chapin ignored the warning that alcohol was killing him, but O'Hara did not. Time had become precious to him, and he reflects on this in the final paragraph of *Ten North Frederick*: "There is always enough to do while the heart keeps pumping. There is never, never enough time to do it all." O'Hara was rewarded for his persistence when *Ten North Frederick* received the National Book Award for 1955. The award citation read in part: "Tough-minded as usual, Mr. O'Hara has written a novel of emotional depth and moral conviction."

Of the novels written during O'Hara's last decade, *The Lockwood Concern* is particularly interesting as a culmination of many aspects of his career. During this period he used a variety of settings for his fiction, but in *The Lockwood Concern* he returned again to the "Region." The book's theme is consistent with much of

O'Hara's other work, reaching back to *Appointment in Samarra*: the ultimate powerlessness of the individual against the forces of circumstance. The attempts of Abraham and George Lockwood, the second and third generations of the Lockwood family of Swedish Haven (based on Schuylkill Haven, near Pottsville), to establish a family dynasty break down in the fourth generation when George's son and daughter reject the town and family. The "concern" of the title is a Quaker concept, denoting an overwhelming sense of mission. Abraham, in the late nineteenth century, has secularized and corrupted this religious concept into a vision of increasing wealth and prestige. His son George has adopted that vision, and his children will be the first generation to enjoy full acceptance by elite society—a fulfillment of a variation of the American Dream. Ironically, however, the accoutrements of this success—such as the walled mansion George is having built near Swedish Haven and the death of a neighboring farm boy who becomes impaled on the spikes that top the wall—bespeak the exclusivity that the Lockwoods have fought to overcome, and herald the crumbling of their new-found dynasty. George ultimately falls to his death down a secret staircase in his still-incomplete mansion.

The Lockwood Concern is a summation of much that O'Hara sought to accomplish during his thirty years of writing. Though not his best novel, it is one of his most ambitious and provides a history of the "Region" from the time of his ancestors to the time when he left it for New York, showing its growth from a backwoods settlement to a thriving coal-mining and farming area that could afford to send its sons to Princeton and Harvard. In many ways, this novel encapsulates not only the themes that run throughout O'Hara's work but also the material, and at times failed personal, aspirations of many Americans who have inhabited the Northeast (and North America in general) for several generations.

Although O'Hara rejected the terms "social realist" and "social historian," these are appropriate characterizations of his best work. His sense of history, his precise rendering of detail and dialogue, and his command of narrative technique make him one of the most significant chroniclers of American life in the first half of the twentieth century.

Other major works

SHORT FICTION: *The Doctor's Son and Other Stories*, 1935; *Hope of Heaven*, 1938; *Files on Parade*, 1939; *Pal Joey*, 1940; *Pipe Night*, 1945; *Hellbox*, 1947; *Assembly*, 1961; *The Cape Cod Lighter*, 1962; *The Hat on the Bed*, 1963; *The Horse Knows the Way*, 1964; *Waiting for Winter*, 1966; *And Other Stories*, 1968; *The O'Hara Generation*, 1969; *The Time Element and Other Stories*, 1972; *Good Samaritan and Other Stories*, 1974.
PLAYS: *Five Plays*, 1961; *Two by O'Hara*, 1979 (*Far from Heaven* and *The Man Who Could Not Lose*).
NONFICTION: *Sweet and Sour*, 1954; *My Turn*, 1966; *A Cub Tells His Story*, 1974, *An Artist Is His Own Fault*, 1977.

Bibliography

Bruccoli, Matthew. *John O'Hara: A Descriptive Bibliography*. Pittsburgh: University of Pittsburgh Press, 1978.
_____. *The O'Hara Concern: A Biography of John O'Hara*. New York: Random House, 1975.
Eppard, Philip B. ed. *Critical Essays on John O'Hara*. New York: G. K. Hall, 1994.
Grebstein, Sheldon Norman. *John O'Hara*. New York: Twayne, 1966.
McShane, Frank. *The Life of John O'Hara*. New York: E. P. Dutton, 1980.
Shannon, William V. *The American Irish*. New York: Macmillan, 1963.

EUGENE O'NEILL

Born: New York, New York; October 16, 1888   **Died:** Boston, Massachusetts; November 27, 1953

Principal drama

Chris Christophersen, wr. 1919, pb.1982 (rev. as *Anna Christie*); *Beyond the Horizon*, pr. 1920, pb. 1921; *The Emperor Jones*, pr. 1920, pb. 1921; *Anna Christie*, pr. 1921, pb. 1923; *The Hairy Ape*, pr. 1922, pb. 1923; *All God's Chillun Got Wings*, pr., pb. 1924; *Complete Works*, pb. 1924 (2 vols); *Desire Under the Elms*, pr. 1924, pb. 1925; *The Great God Brown*, pr., pb. 1926; *Lazarus Laughed*, pb. 1927, pr. 1928; *Strange Interlude*, pr., pb. 1928; *Mourning Becomes Electra*, pr., pb. 1931 (includes *Homecoming*, *The Hunted*, *The Haunted*); *Nine Plays*, pb. 1932; *Ah, Wilderness!*, pr., pb. 1933; *Plays*, pb. 1941 (3 vols), pb. 1955 (rev.); *The Iceman Cometh*, pr., pb. 1946; *A Moon for the Misbegotten*, pr. 1947, pb. 1952; *Long Day's Journey into Night*, pr., pb. 1956; *Later Plays*, pb. 1967; *The Calms of Capricorn*, pb. 1981 (with Donald Gallup); *The Complete Plays*, pb. 1988 (3 vols.).

Other literary forms

Although primarily known for his plays, Eugene O'Neill also wrote poetry and a large amount of correspondence, collected in several volumes and published posthumously. A volume of his previously unpublished or unfamiliar writings appeared in 1988.

Achievements

O'Neill has been called, rightly, the father of modern American drama, not only because he was the first major American playwright but also because of the influence of his work on the development of American theater and on other dramatists. In addition to achieving both popular success and critical acclaim in America, O'Neill has achieved an international reputation; produced throughout the world, his plays are the subject of countless critical books and articles. In many of his plays, O'Neill employed traditional themes such as the quest, while in others he treated subjects that had gone largely unexamined on the American stage, particularly subjects concerning human psychology. In addition to breaking new ground in theme and subject matter, O'Neill was innovative in his use of technical elements of the theater; he experimented with such devices as masks, "asides," and even the stage itself as vehicles to further theme. Moreover, in an effort to achieve for the drama the broad temporal spectrum of the novel, he experimented with static time, presenting two of his works in trilogies of nine acts each. His plays continue to be widely produced throughout the world, both on the stage and on film, because they speak to the human experience that is shared by all.

Biography

Eugene Gladstone O'Neill's parents were James O'Neill, an actor imprisoned by the material success of his role as the Count of Monte Cristo, and Ellen Quinlan O'Neill, a romantic and idealistic woman similarly trapped for much of her life by an addiction to morphine. The complex psychologies of O'Neill's parents and his brother, and the relationships among all the family members, figure significantly as subjects of many of O'Neill's best plays, particularly *Long Day's Journey into Night*.

Educated in Catholic schools, O'Neill entered Princeton University in 1906 but left before a year was over. His travels in 1910 and 1911 to South America and England provided background for his early plays of the sea, several of which he wrote during a six-month hospitalization for tuberculosis in 1912. The following year, he participated in George Pierce Baker's Workshop 47 at Harvard University, where he formally studied playwrighting. O'Neill was married three times: to Kathleen Jenkins in 1909, to Agnes Boulton in 1918, and to Carlotta Monterey in 1929. He had three children, Eugene, Jr., who was born to the first marriage and who committed suicide in 1950, and Shane and Oona, who were born to the second marriage. O'Neill won four Pulitzer Prizes for his plays: in 1920 for *Beyond the Horizon*, in 1922 for *Anna Christie*, in 1928 for *Strange Interlude*, and in 1957 for *Long Day's Journey into Night*. In 1936, he was awarded the Nobel Prize in Literature. Although ill for the last seventeen years of his life, O'Neill wrote several of his finest plays during that period.

118

Analysis

O'Neill was initially criticized for his choice of characters, for their aberrant psychologies, and for their emotionalism. His approach to drama might be said to be "anti-dramatic" to the extent that the struggles of his characters frequently take place within themselves, leaving little real action to be performed but the external staging of these struggles in symbolic settings and relatively static dialogue. One critic once wryly noted the contrast between the stage directions one finds in an O'Neill play—elaborate paragraphs explaining the precise state of a character's mind along with detailed specifications of props and their arrangement—with the essential theatricalness of a typical stage direction in a Shakespeare play: *Enter, Hamlet.* Such a contrast, if hyperbolic and somewhat misleading, serves to point up O'Neill's preoccupation with psychological realism.

O'Neill's first real success was *The Emperor Jones*, produced by the Provincetown Players in 1920. Devoted to the final hours in the life of Brutus Jones, an ex-convict who, in the course of two years, comes to be emperor of an island in the West Indies, O'Neill's expressionist play won immediate acclaim, both popular and critical.

The movement of the play is a journey from the civilized world into the primitive world of the forest and of the mind, and a journey for Jones to self-knowledge and to death. The play's expository opening scene reveals that Jones, who arrived on the island two years earlier as a stowaway and who has come to rule the island, has exploited the natives; has enriched himself by manipulation, thievery, and cruel taxation; and has, as a consequence, become so hated that the natives have withdrawn into the hills to stage a revolution. Jones has, moreover, created among the islanders a mystique and a mythology for himself; distancing himself completely from the natives, whom he terms "bush niggers" and to whom he feels vastly superior, Jones has propagated the myth that he is magically protected from lead bullets and can be killed only by one of silver. He has made for himself a silver bullet that he carries as the sixth in his gun. Having learned that the natives are rebelling, he makes his way to the forest through which he must go in order to meet the boat that will take him to safety.

When, in the second scene, Jones reaches the edge of the forest, the audience begins to see some of O'Neill's experimental techniques. The edge of the forest, O'Neill tells the audience, is a "wall of darkness dividing the world," a point at which Jones begins to understand the uselessness of his precautions: He cannot find his store of food, and, more important, he is not even sure where he is, exactly. When the little Formless Fears appear, amorphous, black, child-size shapes which, with low sounds of laughter, advance writhingly toward him, he is terrified and fires a shot at them.

This first forest scene and the five that follow present a series of vignettes that derive both from Jones's own life and mind and from the racial memory, or collective unconscious. He comes next upon Jeff, the Pullman porter he killed with a razor in a fight over a crap game and for whose death he went to prison; both furious and terrified, Jones fires his second bullet into the ghost. By the fourth scene, his outer appearance is beginning to deteriorate, his glorious uniform torn and dirty. He is nearly paralyzed with fright when he sees another apparition, a chain gang with a guard who forces Jones to join the prisoners. Jones, reenacting his actual break from prison, fires a bullet into the guard's back.

These first three forest scenes serve to make Jones aware of the evil to which he has committed himself and are important stages in his journey to self-knowledge. Moreover, they indicate, beyond a doubt, the true criminality of his nature. The following scenes, concerned with aspects of his racial memory, reveal some of the cultural forces that have made him what he is.

In the fifth scene, in a clearing in the forest, Jones comes upon a dead stump that looks like an auction block. His appearance further deteriorating, his pants torn and ragged, he removes his battered shoes; the outer symbols of his exalted position, and of his difference from the natives, are virtually gone. As he sends an agonized prayer to Jesus, admitting his wrongdoing and acknowledging that as Emperor he is getting "mighty low," he is suddenly surrounded by a group of Southern aristocrats of the 1850's awaiting a slave auction. To Jones's utter horror, the auctioneer compels Jones to stand on the auction block; as the sale is made, Jones, suddenly coming to life and resisting this treatment, angrily pulls out his gun and fires at both the auctioneer and his purchaser, using his last two lead bullets.

The sixth scene goes back to a time preceding the fifth; Jones finds himself in a clearing so overhung by trees that it appears as the hold of a ship. By this time, Jones's clothes have been so torn that he is wearing only a loincloth. Discovering that he is among two rows of blacks who moan desolately as they sway back and forth, Jones finds himself inadvertently joining in their chorus of despair, crying out even more loudly than they. Having used all of his lead bullets, he has nothing with which to dispatch them, since he needs his silver bullet for luck, for self-preservation. He is obliged, then, as he was obliged to recommit his crimes, to enter into the racial experience of slavery, to feel the grief and desperation of his ancestors. Unable to disperse this scene, Jones simply walks into the seventh and last of the forest scenes, which takes him to an even earlier time. Coming upon an ancient altar by the river, Jones instinctively bows, even as he wonders why he does so. Although he prays for the Christian God's protection, what appears is a witch doctor whose dance and incantations hypnotize Jones and force his participation in an ancient and mysterious ritual. O'Neill's stage directions indicate that Jones is expected at this point to sacrifice himself to the forces of evil, to the forces that have governed his life and that are now represented by a huge crocodile emerging from the river. Urged onward by the witch doctor and unable to stop himself from moving toward the crocodile, Jones, in a last act of desperate defiance, shoots the crocodile with his last bullet—the silver bullet.

The last act at the edge of the forest, an act that serves as an epilogue, is almost anticlimactic, describing how the natives enter the forest to kill the dazed Jones, who has wandered back (full circle) to the spot where he entered. The audience knows, however, that Jones has symbolically killed himself, destroying with his own silver bullet his evil and his identity.

The journey into the forest has been for Jones a journey to death, but it has also been a journey to understanding. He has come not only to understand the evil of his own life but also to destroy it symbolically by destroying the crocodile with the bullet that affirms his identity. He has also come, however, to understand both his membership in his race and his connection with those natives to whom he felt so superior; by being forced to undergo the primitive experiences of his people, he is able to move from individuation into the group, into an awareness of the experiences common to his race. He is able to return, by means of this backward and inward journey, to his essential self, the self he had denied out of greed and egotism.

A play differing considerably in kind is *Desire Under the Elms*, first performed by the Provincetown Players in 1924 and perhaps one of O'Neill's most representative works. It reflects a number of the influences that worked significantly upon him, including the Bible and classical mythology. It treats several of his favorite subjects, including the tension-ridden family, antimaterialism, and individuals' participation in creating their own fate. Although the play was initially received with

considerable skepticism and disapproval, its critical reputation and its popular acceptance have steadily increased with time, and it continues to be produced for appreciative contemporary audiences.

The play is set on a New England farm in the midnineteenth century, a thematically important setting. Just as the New England land is rocky, unyielding, and difficult to manage, so is old Ephraim Cabot, who owns the farm, and so is the Puritan ethos that governs the lives of this patriarch and those around him. Accompanying this symbolism of hardness and coldness in the land and in Ephraim is the emotional symbolism associated with the farmhouse: O'Neill's set directions specify that the farmhouse is flanked by "two enormous elms" that "brood oppressively over the house," that "appear to protect and at the same time subdue," and that possess "a sinister maternity in their aspect, a crushing, jealous absorption." Clearly symbolic of Ephraim's dead second wife, and typifying both her physical and mental exhaustion and her unavenged spirit, the elms are also symbolic of the restrictive nature of New England farm life; in signifying that restriction, they are symbolic also of Ephraim, who exercises a jealous and unrelenting selfish control over everything and everyone within his reach.

When the play opens, Ephraim is away from the farm on a trip, during which he marries Abbie Putnam, a young widow. By means of the marriage, Ephraim can prove his continuing virility and vigor and, he believes, achieve his paramount desire: to perpetuate his power and his hold over the land. His three grown sons, Simeon and Peter, children of Ephraim's first wife, and the sensitive Eben, son of Ephraim's second wife, dislike and distrust their father and recognize that his marriage to Abbie ensures that none of them will satisfy their desire to inherit the farm. Ephraim, who sees himself as an extension of the Old Testament God, desires to maintain his power forever; Abbie, who marries because of her initial desire for security, comes later to desire love instead, as does Eben, who initially desires revenge upon his father for working his mother to death.

The play establishes in the first act the many violent tensions existing between father and son. Blaming his father for the death of his mother, Eben also believes his father is cheating him out of the farm. Both father and son are governed by strong emotions: Both are quick to anger, stubborn, vengeful, proud, and hard, and both are the victims of seething animal passions that are covered by only a thin veneer of civilization. The psychologically normal conflict between any father and son is thus intensified by their temperamental similarities, and when Abbie, the catalyst, appears as the stepmother who is closer in age to son than to father, the stage is indeed set for a depiction of violent emotions that result in great tragedy.

Because they both desire the farm, Abbie and Eben initially hate and mistrust each other, but their harsh and cruel behavior toward each other is counterpointed by a growing physical desire between them, a reflection, perhaps, of O'Neill's interest in the classical myths of Oedipus and Phaedra. O'Neill's use of a divided set permits the audience to watch this desire growing as they see simultaneously into the bedroom of Eben, as he moves half-unconsciously toward the wall beyond which Abbie stands, and into the bedroom of Ephraim and Abbie, who continue to hope for the son who will fulfill Ephraim's desire and ensure Abbie's security. As the obvious but unspoken passion between Abbie and Eben mounts and the house grows correspondingly cold, Ephraim is driven to find solace in the barn, among the animals, where it is warm—an opportunity that Abbie uses to seduce Eben in the parlor, where the restless spirit of Eben's mother seems to be concentrated.

Among the motives for Abbie that O'Neill leaves uncertain is her need to produce a son for Ephraim; it is one of the fine ambiguities of the play that we are unable to decide whether Abbie seduces Eben out of greed for the land, out of maternal caring, out of physical lust, or out of genuine love for him. Eben is moved by similarly discordant motives, by both a real desire for Abbie and a desire to avenge his mother by taking his father's woman; he senses his mother's spirit leaving the house and returning to her grave, finally at peace. Eben indicates his understanding of and his satisfaction with the retributive nature of this act the next morning when he offers his hand to his father, remarking to the uncomprehending Ephraim that they are now "quits."

Yet, despite the deliberate calculation with which this love affair begins, Abbie and Eben come in time genuinely to love each other. What was initially, at least in part, a mutually self-serving and opportunistic seduction results in the first warm human relationship the farm has seen. There is, however, no way for the drama to end happily, even though, at the beginning of the third act, all have attained what they at one time desired: Ephraim has a son to prove his virility, Abbie has earned the farm by providing that son, and Eben has avenged

his mother. These desires are, to Abbie and Eben, at least, no longer of prime importance, and the party Ephraim gives to celebrate the birth of "his" son serves as an ironic backdrop to the play's tragic climax.

Ephraim, flushed with liquor and pride at producing a son at seventy-six and oblivious to the knowing sneers of the townspeople, in a brutal physical and emotional confrontation with Eben gloats that Abbie wanted a child only to preempt Eben's claim to the farm. Believing that Abbie has seduced him only in order to become pregnant and cheat him, Eben turns violently against her, telling her that he hates her and wishes their son dead. The half-crazed Abbie, hysterically wishing to restore the time when Eben loved her and confusedly identifying the child as the cause of Eben's present hate, smothers the child in its cradle in an appalling inversion of the myth of Medea: Whereas Medea murders her children as an act of revenge against her faithless husband, Abbie murders her child in order to recapture the lost love of Eben. Eben, however, does not respond with love, but with horror and revulsion, and he runs for the sheriff to arrest her. Returning before the sheriff, Eben in a change of heart acknowledges his own guilt and reaffirms his love for Abbie. The play ends with their mutual expression of love as they are taken off by the sheriff.

The play seems, then, to be unmitigatedly naturalistic and pessimistic as the lovers go off to be hanged and as Ephraim is left alone with his farm. Yet O'Neill poses the possibility of a spiritual victory in the play: Although the desire to possess has dominated their lives, Abbie and Eben are freed of that desire at the end—even though their victory is to be short-lived. It is also possible to see a victory over the forces of evil embodied in Puritanism and in the New England patriarchal society, because, even though Eben reacts initially to his father's announcement and to the baby's murder with all the violent self-righteousness one would expect of Ephraim, Eben comes to transcend this attitude and to acknowledge both his love for Abbie and his own guilt. Although Abbie and Eben have lost everything in the worldly sense, in finding love and faith in each other they do perhaps escape, however briefly and symbolically, from the brooding, confining New England elms.

In this play, O'Neill seems to return to the naturalism that informed his early plays of the sea. His characters are presented as bewildered, struggling beings, blown about like leaves in the gutter, compelled by the external forces of fate, chance, and environment and by the internal workings of their physical nature. It is indeed difficult for these characters to win, but for O'Neill, the salient point is that, in struggling, his characters can transcend their fate.

The critics, who had difficulty with *Desire Under the Elms* because of its objectionable subject matter, were also troubled by *The Iceman Cometh*, but for different reasons; many considered the latter play unhealthy, pessimistic, and morbid in its depiction of the wasted lives of the habitués of Harry Hope's New York saloon, modeled after those in which O'Neill spent considerable time in 1911 and in 1914-1919. A key theme in the play, and a recurring theme in O'Neill's dramas, is the power and the necessity of illusion to give meaning to life. O'Neill develops this theme through expository conversation and monologues, since there is very little onstage action during the two-day period that the play's four acts encompass. Containing both comic and tragic elements, the play, set in 1912, takes place entirely in the back room of Harry Hope's bar, where the regulars gather.

The play opens upon a gathering of regulars to await the arrival of Hickey, a hardware salesman who is the most successful among them and who comes to the bar for periodic drunks, particularly on the occasion of Harry Hope's birthday, when he funds a great drunken party for the regulars. Himself unfaithful to his wife, Hickey maintains a running gag that his apparently saintly wife must, in his absence, be having an affair with the iceman. Hickey and all the other characters live in a world of illusion, a world which ignores today: They all look backward to yesterday, to what they once were, or to what their rosy rewriting of history now tells them they once were, just as they look forward to an equally rosy and improbable tomorrow. The illusion that they all have a future is part of the pipe dream each has, a pipe dream essential to their lives which helps them "keep up the appearances of life." Although these people really have, in Robert Frost's words, "nothing to look backward to with pride" and "nothing to look forward to with hope," they somehow manage to live, to survive in the bleak, drunken world they inhabit, because they possess the illusion that they have a yesterday about which they can feel pride and a tomorrow about which they can hope. That illusion enables them to ignore the dark reality that is their today. Moreover, because they understand one another's illusions and accept them, they can be sympathetic and tolerant of one another's failings as well as of their own.

Although many of these regulars stay up all night in the saloon to await Hickey, his arrival is disappointing and strangely troubling: When he finally appears, he is not the same as before. For one thing, he fails to make his usual joke about his wife and the iceman, and for another, he no longer drinks; he explains that he no longer needs it since he threw away "the damned lying pipe dream" that had made him feel miserable. Moreover, he wants very much to save his friends by persuading them to be honest, to stop lying about themselves, and to stop kidding themselves about their tomorrows. He believes that by giving up their illusions, they can attain peace and contentment, and he systematically embarks on a campaign to make them admit the truth. Then, Hickey believes, his friends will have peace, as he does. As a result of his campaign, however, the friendly and tolerant atmosphere of the bar wears dangerously thin as the friends, stripped of their protective illusions and their defense mechanisms, become not only sober but also nervous, irritable, and belligerent with one another.

Hickey is genuinely puzzled by these results, since his expectation was that, once they had "killed tomorrow," they would have "licked the game of life." The play's fourth act centers upon Hickey's revelation of his new philosophy and how he acted out this philosophy in his marriage, finally murdering his wife. Juxtaposed to Hickey's story of love and guilt is Parritt's parallel narrative disclosing his betrayal of his mother. The two stories reach a climax when Parritt confesses that he betrayed the movement because he hated his mother as Hickey confesses that after killing his wife he laughed and called her a "damned bitch." Unable to live with what he has admitted, Hickey seizes upon the explanation that he must have been insane—insane, that is, to laugh at his wife's death, because everyone surely knows that he has always loved her, and if he laughed at her death, then he must have been insane.

The other characters seize upon this explanation as well, because it means they can disregard what he has said before, reestablish their illusions, and thereby once again live with one another and themselves. Don Parritt, however, apparently unable to live with his betrayal of his mother and the reality that his betrayal was motivated by hate, commits suicide by jumping off the fire escape, as, in a sense, does Hickey by calling the police to come for him. He and Parritt, facing the reality about themselves, must destroy themselves because of the pain of that reality. In truth, Hickey hated his wife because she represented his conscience, because although she always forgave him, she also always expected him to try to be better, which he simply did not wish to do. When for one brief moment he admits the truth, that he wanted and was glad to be free of the burden of this conscience, he is unable to live with that truth and he immediately rationalizes that he must have been insane. He thus proves that illusion is, in fact, necessary, in order to accept oneself and in order to live not only with others in the world but also with the reality that death, the iceman, does indeed "cometh." O'Neill suggests that, in order for life to exist, there must be hope—and hope, very often, is created from illusion.

At a time when the discoveries of Sigmund Freud were making their way into the popular consciousness, O'Neill explored a wide range of tragic figures and situations, often drawn from his personal experiences, and often from the Northeastern milieus which he inhabited much of his life. In dramatizing human emotions—earlier explored in the novel by Herman Melville and brought to high art by Henry James—O'Neill took a more public step toward exposing human beings to themselves.

Other major works

POETRY: *Poems, 1912-1944*, 1979 (Donald Gallup, ed.).

NONFICTION: *"The Theatre We Worked For": The Letters of Eugene O'Neill to Kenneth MacGowan*, 1982 (Jackson R. Bryer and Ruth M. Alvarez, eds.); *"Love and Admiration and Respect": The O'Neill-Commins Correspondence*, 1986 (Dorothy Commins, ed.); *"As Ever, Gene": The Letters of Eugene O'Neill to George Jean Nathan*, 1987 (Nancy L. Roberts and Arthur W. Roberts, eds.); *Selected Letters of Eugene O'Neill*, 1988 (Travis Bogard and Jackson R. Bryer, eds.).

MISCELLANEOUS: *The Unknown O'Neill: Unpublished or Unfamiliar Writings of Eugene O'Neill*, 1988 (Travis Bogard, ed.).

Bibliography

Alexander, Doris. *Eugene O'Neill's Creative Struggle: The Decisive Decade, 1924-1933*. University Park: Pennsylvania State University Press, 1992.

Bloom, Harold, ed. *Eugene O'Neill*. New York: Chelsea House, 1987.

Floyd, Virginia, ed. *Eugene O'Neill: A World View*. New York: Frederick Ungar, 1979.

Moorton, Richard F., Jr., ed. *Eugene O'Neill's Century*. New York: Greenwood Press, 1991.

Ranald, Margaret Loftus. *The Eugene O'Neill Companion*. Westport, Conn.: Greenwood Press, 1984.

Robinson, James A. *Eugene O'Neill and Oriental Thought: A Divided Vision*. Carbondale: Southern Illinois University Press, 1982.

Sheaffer, Louis. *O'Neill*. 2 vols. Boston: Little, Brown, 1968-1973.

Wainscott, Ronald H. *Staging O'Neill: The Experimental Years, 1920-1934*. New Haven, Conn.: Yale University Press, 1988.

J. D. SALINGER

Born: New York, New York; January 1, 1919

Principal long fiction

The Catcher in the Rye, 1951.

Other literary forms

Several collections of J. D. Salinger's short fiction have been published. There has been one film adaptation of his work, produced by Samuel Goldwyn and adapted by Julius J. and Philip G. Epstein from Salinger's "Uncle Wiggily in Connecticut," renamed *My Foolish Heart* (1950) and starring Susan Hayward and Dana Andrews. Salinger was so upset by the screen version that he banned all further adaptations of his work into any other medium.

Achievements

In the post-World War II years, Salinger was unanimously acclaimed by both the literate American youth and the critical establishment. His only novel has sold steadily since its publication, and not only does it still generate high sales but it also generates intense discussion as to its appropriateness for classroom use. Although his productivity has been slow, his popularity in terms of both sales and critical articles and books written about him has continued unabated since the early 1950's.

The Catcher in the Rye has been cited as one of the most read and influential postwar novels and has entered the culture as a statement of youth's view of the complex world. The novel has been translated into German, Italian, Japanese, Norwegian, Swedish, French, Dutch, Danish, Hebrew, Czechoslovakian, Yugoslavian, and Russian and has been highly successful. It has been favorably compared to Mark Twain's *The Adventures of Huckleberry Finn* (1884) in terms of its portrayal of the "phoniness" of society, the coming of age of a young man, and its use of colloquial language.

Biography

Jerome David Salinger was born in New York, New York, on January 1, 1919, the second child and only son of Sol and Miriam (Jillich) Salinger. Salinger's father was born in Cleveland, Ohio, the son of a rabbi, but he drifted far enough away from orthodox Judaism to become a successful importer of hams and to marry a gentile, the Scotch-Irish Marie Jillich, who changed her name soon after to Miriam to fit in better with her husband's family.

Salinger attended private schools on Manhattan's upper West Side, doing satisfactory work in all subjects except arithmetic. In September of 1934, his father enrolled him at Valley Forge Military Academy in Pennsylvania. Following graduation Salinger returned to New York and enrolled in Whit Burnett's famous course in short-story writing at Columbia University. Salinger's first story, "The Young Folks," was impressive enough to be published in the March, 1940, issue of *Story*, edited by Burnett.

After publishing in a magazine famous for discovering new talent, Salinger spent another year writing without success until, at age twenty-two, he broke into the well-paying mass circulation magazines with a "short, short story" in *Collier's* and a "satire" in *Esquire*; he even had a story accepted by *The New Yorker*, which delayed publication of "Slight Rebellion off Madison," until after the war. This story proved to be one of the forerunners to *The Catcher in the Rye*.

During 1941, Salinger worked as an entertainer on the Swedish liner *M. S. Kungsholm*. Upon his return to the United States, he was inducted into the military but continued to write whenever he found the opportunity, publishing again in *Collier's Story*, and at last in the well-paying and highly celebrated *Saturday Evening Post*. One of the *Saturday Evening Post* stories marks the first mention of the central character in *The Catcher in the Rye*, Holden Caulfield. Meanwhile, landing in Europe just hours after the start of the D-Day invasion, Salinger was a special agent responsible for security of the Twelfth Infantry Regiment. There is an unsupported story that Salinger had an audience with author and war correspondent Ernest Hemingway, who shot off the head of a chicken either to impress Salinger or to demonstrate the effectiveness of a German Luger. This incident has been used to explain why Salinger has written about Hemingway in a bad light in his stories and has

Holden Caulfield in *The Catcher in the Rye* detest Hemingway's *A Farewell to Arms* (1929). There are also reports that during the war Salinger married a French woman, Sylvia, who was a doctor, possibly a psychiatrist. The two returned together to the United States after the war, according to biographer Ian Hamilton, but the marriage did not last long.

After the war, Salinger decided to make a living by selling stories to the so-called slicks, publishing again in the *Saturday Evening Post* and *Collier's*, which issued "I'm Crazy" in its Christmas issue. "I'm Crazy" featured the long-delayed debut of Holden Caulfield, who had been mentioned as missing in action in several of Salinger's wartime stories. *Mademoiselle*, *Good Housekeeping*, and *Cosmopolitan* also published Salinger's work.

After the disastrous film version of "Uncle Wiggily in Connecticut" and stories in *Harper's* and *World Review*, Salinger settled down with a contract to produce stories exclusively for *The New Yorker*. At that time, Salinger was also his most public: He lived in Tarrytown, New York, and even visited a short-story class at Sarah Lawrence College. Although he seemed to enjoy the conversation and interaction, he never repeated it. It was during that period that he decided to avoid all public appearances and concentrate on writing.

The Catcher in the Rye finally made its appearance on July 16, 1951, although years earlier Salinger successfully had submitted and then withdrawn a much shorter version. It was not an immediate hit, but it did gain Salinger enormous critical praise and respect. The novel was successful enough to cause Salinger to have his picture removed from the dust jacket of the third edition and all subsequent editions; annoyed by the letters, autograph seekers, and interviewers that sought him, he apparently sailed to Europe to keep his composure and avoid publicity.

In 1952, Salinger moved to Cornish, New Hampshire, where he settled permanently. In 1955, he returned to print in *The New Yorker* with the publication of "Franny," the first of the Glass Family series that occupied all of his forthcoming stories. He supposedly dedicated it to his new bride, Claire Douglas, whom he married in Barnard, Vermont, on February 17, 1955. On December 10 of that year, the Salingers became the parents of their first child, Margaret Ann; on February 13, 1960, his only son, Matthew, was born. Thereafter, Salinger concentrated his efforts on rearing his family and documenting the Glass family. Little has been heard or read from Salinger since the 1965 publi-

cation of "Hapworth 16, 1924" in *The New Yorker*. He was divorced from his wife in November, 1967.

The reclusive Salinger, dubbed "the Greta Garbo of American letters" by *People Weekly*, was thrust into the media limelight in the mid-1980's because of disputes over the content of a biography being published by Ian Hamilton that included the use of Salinger's unpublished letters. Eventually, a U.S. Court of Appeals ruling decreed that the letters were indeed Salinger's property and could not be quoted, or even paraphrased, without his permission. The Supreme Court declined to hear an appeal, and Salinger returned to his seclusion. Hamilton's book *In Search of J. D. Salinger*, minus the content of the letters but filled out with a detailed account of the controversy, was finally published in 1988.

Analysis

Salinger's works have attracted much critical and popular acclaim. Those readers especially influenced by them were the post-World War II generation of American college students who recognized in them an expression of their disenchantment with the values and aspirations of their elders. Populated by a cast of complex characters struggling with the pursuit of innocence, goodness, and truth in an increasingly corrupt and artificial world, his novels and stories served to articulate that generation's rejection of materialism and regimentation. Much of his work depicts individuals fighting to preserve or recapture the honesty and spontaneity of childhood in a world of adult hypocrisy and conformity.

Salinger's characters are always extremely sensitive young people who are trapped between two dimensions of the world: love and "squalor." The central problem in most of his fiction is not finding a bridge between these two worlds but bringing some sort of indiscriminate love into the world of squalor: to find a haven where love can triumph and flourish. Some characters, such as the young, mixed-up Holden Caulfield, adopt indiscriminate love to aid them in their journey through the world of squalor, while others, such as Seymour Glass, achieve a sort of perfect love, or satori, and are destroyed, in Seymour's case by a bullet through his head. Each of these characters is metropolitan in outlook and situation and is introverted: Their battles are private wars of spirit, not outward conflicts with society. The characters' minds struggle to make sense of the dichotomy between love and squalor, often reaching a quiet peace and transcending their situation through a small act.

All Salinger's work has a strong focus on the family; it is held up as an ideal, a refuge, and a raft of love amid a sea of squalor. Although the family does not provide the haven that Salinger suggests it might be, it is through coming home that the characters flourish, not by running away. Holden Caulfield, in *The Catcher in the Rye*, never realistically considers running away, for he realizes that the flight cannot help him. At the critical moment his family may not be ready to grant him the salvation that he needs, but it is his only security. If the world is a place of squalor, perhaps it is only through perfect love within the family unit that an individual can find some kind of salvation. It is important to notice that the family unit is never satirized in Salinger's fiction.

The basic story of *The Catcher in the Rye* follows the adventures of sixteen-year-old Holden Caulfield, during a forty-eight-hour period after he has been expelled from Pencey, the latest in a long line of expulsions for Holden. After a few confrontations with various fellow students at Pencey, he goes to New York City, his hometown, to rest before confronting his parents with the news. During the trip he tries to renew some old acquaintances, has an adventure or two, and tries to come to grips with the headaches that he has been having lately. Eventually, after two meetings with his younger sister, Phoebe, he returns home. At the book's opening, he is somewhere in California recovering from an illness (it is not clear if it is physical or mental) and has reconciled himself to his lot by returning to the bosom of his family. The entire story is told through the first-person narration of Holden, who uses adolescent phrasings and profanity as he tries to reconstruct his "crazy" period of the previous year.

Holden Caulfield is a normal sixteen-year-old, no better and no worse than his peers, except that he is slightly introverted, a little sensitive, and willing to express his feelings openly. His story can be seen as a typical growing process. As he approaches and is ready to cross the threshold into adulthood, he begins to get nervous and worried. His body has grown, but his emotional state has not. He is gawky, clumsy, and not totally in control of his body. He tries to find some consolation, some help, during this difficult time but finds no one. The school cannot help him, his peers seem oblivious to his plight, his parents are too concerned with other problems (his mother's nerves and his father's business activities as a corporate lawyer). His girlfriend, Sally Hayes, is no help, and his favorite teacher merely lectures him drunkenly. The only people with whom he can communicate are the two young boys

at the museum, the girl with the skates at the park, and Phoebe: All of them are children, who cannot help him in his growing pains but remind him of a simpler time, one to which he wishes he could return. Eventually, he does cross the threshold (his fainting in the museum) and realizes that his worries were unfounded. He has survived. At the end of the book, Holden seems ready to reintegrate himself into society and accept the responsibilities of adulthood.

Through Holden's picaresque journeys through New York City, he grows spiritually. He slowly begins to recognize the "phoniness" around him and the squalor that constantly presses down on him. Although he castigates himself for doing some of the phony things, lying especially, Holden does realize that what he is doing is incorrect: This understanding sets him above his fellows; he knows what he is doing. Holden never hurts anyone in any significant way; his lies are small and harmless. Conversely, the phony world also spins lies, but they are dangerous since they harm people. For example, Holden mentions that Pencey advertises that it molds youth, but it does not. He is angry with motion pictures because they offer false ideals and hopes. Yet his lies help a mother think better of her son. Like Huck Finn, he lies to get along, but not to hurt, and also like Huck, he tries to do good.

By the end of the book, Holden has accepted a new position—an undiscriminating love for all humankind. He even expresses that he misses all the people who did wrong to him. Although not a Christ-figure, Holden does acquire a Christlike position—perfect love for all humankind, good and evil. He is not mature enough to know what to do with this love, but he is mature enough to accept it. In this world, realizing what is squalor and what is good, and loving it all, is the first step in achieving identity and humanity: Compassion is what Holden learns.

Recalling all the suffering and pain that he has witnessed, Holden develops a profound sense of the human condition and accepts Christ's ultimate commandment. In the passage regarding Holden's argument with his Quaker friend, Holden argues that Judas is not in hell because Jesus would have had the compassion and love not to condemn Judas to hell. Also, Jesus did not have time to analyze who would be perfect for his Disciples; thus, they were not perfect and would have condemned Judas if they had had the chance. In this discussion, Holden points out his own dilemma, not having time to analyze his decisions, and his belief in the perfect love that he embraces at the end of the book. Although not a would-be saint, Holden does become a fuller human being through his experiences.

The title symbol of the novel comes from Holden's misreading of a line from a song. His wish, as expressed to his sister, is that he wishes to be a catcher in the rye, standing beneath a cliff waiting to catch any child that falls over the cliff: He wants to spare children the pain of growing up and facing the world of squalor. He also wishes to provide some useful, sincere activity in the world. The catcher-in-the-rye job is a dream, a hope, and a job that Holden realizes is impractical in the world as it is. Only by facing the world and loving it indiscriminately can anyone hope to live fully within it and have any hope of changing it.

In the novel, Holden is also constantly preoccupied with death. He worries about the ducks freezing in the winter, the Egyptian mummies, and his dead brother Allie. He cries to Allie not to let him disappear. This symbolizes Holden's wish not to disappear into society as another cog in the great machine and not to lose what little of himself he feels that he has. To Holden, the change from childhood to adulthood is a kind of death, a death he fears because of his conviction that he will become other than he is. This fear proves groundless by the end of the book. His name also provides a clue: Holden—hold on. His quest is to hold on to his adolescent self and to save other children from the pain of growth. His quest fails, but his compassion and the growth of his humanity provide him with better alternatives.

In terms of sex, Holden is often puritanical. His trouble lies in the fact that he begins to feel sorry for the girls he dates, and he has too much compassion for them to defile their supposed virtue. This problem ties in with his compassion: He tries to see people as they are and not as types. He looks quickly and may make rash judgments, but once he talks to or acquaints himself with someone, he sees him or her as an individual. His mentioning of the boring boy he knew in school who could whistle better than anyone is the perfect example: Holden cannot help but confront people as individuals. Again, this shows his growing compassion and indiscriminate love. He sympathizes with the girl's position, which is a very mature quality for a teenager, and with anyone's position once he gets to know that person.

Salinger more fully develops the contrast between squalor and love in the world and reintroduces various elements of his Caulfield family saga in his grand design of charting the story of the Glass family. The compassion, the satire, the heights of perfect love, the love of the family unit, and the use of brilliant conversational language that characterized *The Catcher in the Rye* will continue to set his fiction apart.

Other major works

SHORT FICTION: *Nine Stories*, 1953; *Franny and Zooey*, 1961; *Raise High the Roof Beam, Carpenters, and Seymour: An Introduction*, 1963.

Bibliography

Belcher, William F., and James W. Lee, eds. *J. D. Salinger and the Critics*. Belmont, Calif.: Wadsworth, 1962.

French, Warren. *J. D. Salinger*. New York: Twayne, 1963.

Gwynn, Frederick L., and Joseph L. Blotner. *The Fiction of J. D. Salinger*. Pittsburgh: University of Pittsburgh Press, 1958.

Hamilton, Ian. *In Search of J. D. Salinger*. New York: Vintage, 1988.

Laser, Marvin, and Norman Furman, eds. *Studies in J. D. Salinger: Reviews, Essays, and Critiques of "The Catcher in the Rye" and Other Fiction*. New York: Odyssey Press, 1963.

Lundquist, James. *J. D. Salinger*. New York: Frederick Ungar, 1979.

HENRY DAVID THOREAU

Born: Concord, Massachusetts; July 12, 1817

Died: Concord, Massachusetts; May 6, 1862

Principal nonfiction

A Week on the Concord and Merrimack Rivers, 1849; *Walden*, 1854; *Consciousness in Concord*, 1858; *Excursions*, 1863; *The Maine Woods*, 1864; *Cape Cod*, 1864; *The Writings of Henry David Thoreau*, 1906; *Journal*, 1981, 1984 (2 vols.).

Other literary forms

Although Thoreau is known today principally for the prose works in which he expounded his views as a Transcendentalist and social philosopher, he also published poetry. His attitude toward that form, however—characteristic of the Transcendentalists' emphasis on life over art—was that the value of the poem lay not in its form but in the act of writing itself. Moreover, Thoreau came to speak of both good verse and good prose as "poetry" and so at times blurred the distinction between the latter and other of his works. In general, his poetry is seldom considered first-rate. Nevertheless, it is historically significant in that it demonstrates the problems American poets faced in freeing themselves artistically from European influences and because it provides some fresh insights (not fully apparent in Thoreau's prose) into some of the deepest problems in Thoreau's life—especially his attempts to cope with the problems of love and friendship and his own role as an artist.

Achievements

During his own lifetime, Thoreau met with only modest literary success. His early poems and essays published in *The Dial* were well known and appreciated in Transcendentalist circles but were generally unknown to popular audiences. As a lecturer, his talks were appreciated by the most liberal of his audiences but were generally found to be obscure or even dangerous by more conservative listeners. *Walden* garnered favorable reviews and good sales, winning for him some fame with popular audiences and creating a small but devoted number of disciples who occasionally visited him in Concord. After the success of that book, Thoreau found it easier to publish his essays in mainstream periodicals.

Thoreau's literary reputation rose steadily after his death. During the 1960's he became something of an icon of political radicalism (especially with reference to "Civil Disobedience"), and beginning in the 1970's his writings on the relationship of human beings to their environment (particularly as expounded in *Walden*) established him as an early bellwether of environmental concerns. It is largely as an exponent of such philosophies, perceived as American, that Thoreau is remembered today.

Biography

Henry David Thoreau (christened David Henry Thoreau) was born in Concord, Massachusetts, on July 12, 1817, the third of four children of John and Cynthia Thoreau. His father was a quiet man whose seeming lack of ambition had led to a series of unsuccessful attempts to establish himself as a shopkeeper prior to his finally establishing a very successful pencil factory in Concord. His mother was an outgoing, talkative woman who took in boarders to supplement the family's income. Both parents were fond of nature and could often be seen taking the children picnicking in the Concord woods.

Thoreau received a good grammar school education at the Concord Academy and seems to have had an essentially pleasant and typical boyhood. He attended Harvard College from 1833 to 1837. Upon being graduated near the top of his class, he took a teaching job in the Concord public schools, but after a few weeks he resigned in protest over the school board's insistence that he use corporal punishment to discipline his students. Unable to find another position, Thoreau opened a private school of his own and was eventually joined by his older brother John. John's cheerful disposition together with Henry's high academic standards made the school very successful until it was closed in 1841 because of John's prolonged illness.

During these years as a teacher, Thoreau traveled to Maine, took, with his brother, the famous excursion on the Concord and Merrimack rivers that eventually became the subject of his first book, delivered his first lecture, and published his first essay and his first poetry in *The Dial*. Through one of his students, Edmund Sewall (whom he praises in one of his best-known poems, "Lately, Alas, I Knew a Gentle Boy"), he met Ellen Sewall, the only woman to whom he seems to have been romantically attracted in any serious way. Ellen seems to have been the subject or recipient of a number of Thoreau's poems of 1839 and 1840, but his brother John was the more forward of the two in courting Ellen, and it was after John's proposal to Ellen had failed that Henry also proposed, only to be rejected as John had been.

After the closing of the school, Thoreau was invited to live with Ralph Waldo Emerson's family as a handyman; he stayed two years, during which time he continued to contribute to, and occasionally help Emerson edit, *The Dial*. In 1842, John died suddenly of a tetanus infection, leaving Thoreau so devastated that he himself briefly exhibited psychosomatic symptoms of the disease. The following year, a brief stint as a tutor to William Emerson's family on Staten Island confirmed his prejudice against cities, so Thoreau returned to Concord, where in 1844 he and a companion accidentally set fire to the Concord Woods, thus earning some rather long-lasting ill will from some of his neighbors and some long-lasting damage to his reputation as a woodsman.

Thoreau built a one-room cabin and moved in on July 4, thus declaring his intention to be free to work on his writing and on a personal experiment in economic self-reliance. He continued to use the cabin as his main residence for two years, during which time he wrote *A Week on the Concord and Merrimack Rivers* and much of *Walden*, raised beans, took a trip to the Maine Woods, and spent his famous night in the Concord jail for nonpayment of taxes. The fruits of his stay at the pond finally began to appear in 1849, when *A Week on the Concord and Merrimack Rivers* and his essay on "Resistance to Civil Government" (later renamed "Civil Disobedience") were both published.

Throughout the 1840's, Thoreau had become increasingly interested in the natural sciences, and he began to spend much time gathering and measuring specimens, often at the expense of his writing, so that by 1851 he had reason to complain in his journal, "I feel that the character of my knowledge is from year to year becoming more distinct and scientific; that, in exchange for views as wide as heaven's scope, I am being narrowed down to the field of the microscope." His scientific and mechanical abilities had benefits for the family's pencil-making business, however, because in 1843 he had developed a more effective means of securing the graphite in the pencils and was later to improve the quality of pencils still further. The publication of *Walden* in 1854 brought him both renewed encouragement and a small but devoted group of admirers.

Throughout the 1850's Thoreau made several excursions to Canada, the Maine Woods, and Cape Cod that culminated in travel essays in popular periodicals. He also traveled to New Jersey and to Brooklyn, where he met Walt Whitman, with whom he was favorably impressed. Thoreau's admiration for Whitman's raw genius was surpassed only by his admiration for John Brown, the abolitionist, whom he first met in 1857 and whose cause he vigorously supported in lectures and published essays.

In 1860, Thoreau caught a bad cold that eventually developed into tuberculosis. Advised to seek a different climate, Thoreau took a trip to Minnesota in 1861, a trip that provided him with some brief glimpses of "uncivilized" Indians but with no relief from his illness. After returning to Concord, his health continued to deteriorate, and he died at home on May 6, 1862.

Analysis

Thoreau is a major figure in the American Transcendental movement and in what F. O. Matthiessen calls the American Renaissance of the 1840's and 1850's, when American literature came of age. Undogmatic and unsystematic, Transcendentalism was in part a heritage from Puritanism but in larger part a rebellion against it. Its American leader was Emerson, who resigned from his Unitarian ministry because even it was too dogmatic for him. Transcendentalism rejected organized religion, biblical authority, and Original Sin in favor of pantheism and a belief in the daily rebirth of God in the individual soul. An eclectic faith rather than a systematic philosophy, it derived in part from Platonic idealism, German mysticism, French utopianism, and the Hindu scriptures. Part of the Romantic movement's reaction against the Age of Reason, it stressed the instinct rather than the intellect. As Thoreau wrote, "We do not learn by inference and deduction and the application of mathematics to philosophy, but by direct intercourse and sympathy."

At first Thoreau was Emerson's disciple, but soon he became his own man. Emerson complained that Thoreau had no new ideas: "I am very familiar with all his thoughts," Emerson wrote, "they are my own quite originally drest." Formulating new ideas did not interest Thoreau. Emerson wrote largely in abstractions, but Thoreau did not care for abstract ideas and theorizing, stating, "Let us not underrate the value of a fact; it will only day flower in a truth." His friend Ellery Channing said that "metaphysics was his aversion." Thus F. O. Matthiessen observes that "Thoreau does not disappear into the usual transcendental vapour." Thoreau had to test his ideas by living them and then communicating his experiences instead of declaiming abstractions. "How can we expect a harvest of thought who have not had a seed time of character?" he asked. His actions were not entirely original; Alcott had earlier refused to pay his poll tax, and Stearns Wheeler had lived in a shanty on Flint's Pond, but they did not write about these experiences in the pithy way Thoreau did, nor did they offer his profound criticism of materialism, which prevented people from realizing their own potential. Thoreau insisted that "if one advances confidently in the direction of his dreams, and endeavors to live the life which he has imagined, he will meet with a success unexpected in common hours" and will thus transcend his lower self and his society. Doing so requires what Emerson called self-reliance, which Thoreau exemplified in his own life, writing that "if a man does not keep pace with his companions, perhaps it is because he hears a different drummer. Let him step to the music which he hears, however measured or far away."

Thoreau's first book, *A Week on the Concord and Merrimack Rivers*, is the account of a two-week boat and hiking trip he made with his brother John in 1839. Shortly thereafter, Thoreau sold the boat to Nathaniel Hawthorne. Thoreau worked on the manuscript for ten years, intending it, after John's death in 1842, to be a tribute to him. Thoreau wrote most of the work while living at Walden (writing it was part of the "private business" he planned to transact there) but continued revising it for two more years. Despite its being promoted by Emerson, publishers would not print it unless the author underwrote the cost. James Munroe & Co. printed a thousand copies but bound only 450.

Despite generally favorable reviews at home and in England, the book did not sell, and Thoreau, stuck with the unsold copies, lamented in 1853, "I have now a library of nearly nine hundred volumes, over seven hundred of which I wrote myself." A second edition came out posthumously in 1867, with additions and corrections, and the book has remained in print ever since.

In part, the work is an elegy to Thoreau's brother, who, in the elegiac tradition, is never named. Following an introductory essay, there are seven chapters—one for each day of the week. About 40 percent consists of travel narrative; the rest is a combination of essays, poems, anecdotes, quotations, translations, philosophical observations on life and nature, and numerous digressions. James Russell Lowell complained that so little of it is about the trip itself, noting, "We were bid to a river party—not to be preached at."

Carl Bode somewhat agrees with Lowell, noting that "the scholar is much more apparent than the traveler, for the original narrative has been weighted down with learned allusions and quotations." While the book does contain many of Thoreau's philosophical musings, however, it is by no means all preaching. Thoreau celebrates the sounds and silences, the light and shadows, of the natural world. Drifting along in their boat, he and his brother find a freedom like that of Huckleberry Finn on his raft. There are word paintings of the river and the landscape through which it flows that make it a verbal correspondence to some of the landscape paintings of the time.

Thoreau celebrates the variety and vitality of nature and wildlife, "such healthy natural tumult as proves the last day is not yet at hand." He presents part of what he elsewhere calls "The Natural History of Massachusetts" in his incisive picture of river birds, fish and fishermen, trees and wildflowers. As Robert Frost would later, Thoreau often details a scene of nature and then draws a moral or philosophical reflection from it. A neoplatonist, he sometimes sees "objects as through a thin haze, in their eternal relations," wondering "who set them up, and for what purpose." At times, "he becomes immortal with her [nature's] immortality." Yet he also has a Darwinian awareness of the suffering in nature, the tragic end of creatures of the wild. Sometimes he recounts historical vignettes called to mind by passing locations. The book lacks the unity of *Walden* but anticipates it in many of Thoreau's concerns—a mystical relationship with nature and the life spirit, a love for wildness in nature and independence in people, and the belief that people can redirect their lives in simpler and more fulfilling ways.

In 1845, when he was twenty-seven years old, Thoreau built a one-room cabin on Emerson's land in the woods on the shore of Walden Pond, less than two miles from Concord. He borrowed an axe, bought the boards from an Irish railroad worker's shanty, and erected a ten-by-fifteen-foot building. He moved into his new abode on the symbolic date of Independence

Day. There he lived austerely, working about six weeks a year growing beans and doing odd jobs, living on a simple diet, and spending less than nine dollars for food during the first eight months. His plan was to simplify his life, to "live free and uncommitted," working about six weeks a year in order to have the remaining forty-six weeks free to read, write, live in intimate relationship to nature, "affect the quality of the day," and demonstrate the Transcendental belief in "the unquestionable ability of man to elevate his life by a conscious endeavor." He summed up his experiment by writing:

> I went to the woods because I wished to live deliberately, to front only the essential facts of life, and see if I could not learn what it had to teach, and not, when I came to die, discover that I had not lived. . . . I wanted to live deep and suck out all the marrow of life, to live so sturdily and Spartan-like as to put to rout all that was not life, to cut a broad swath and shave close; to drive life into a corner, and reduce it to its lowest terms, and, if it proved to be mean . . . to get the whole and genuine meanness of it, and publish its meanness to the world; or if it were sublime, to know it by experience, and be able to give a true account of it.

Feeling that most people live hurried, complicated "lives of quiet desperation," "frittered away by detail," he urged them to simplify. Citing the case of an Indian craftsman whose baskets people would no longer buy, Thoreau set an example for poor students and for would-be artists who fear being unable to make a living by their writing, painting, music, or sculpture. Believing that many people were enslaved too much by working at unfulfilling jobs to provide themselves with material objects, he showed that if they will do with less, they can find the freedom to pursue their heart's desire. Like Thomas Carlyle, the English Transcendentalist friend of Emerson, Thoreau urged people to lower their denominator—to enrich the spiritual quality of their lives by reducing their dependence on the material by choosing "the vantage point of what we should call voluntary poverty," for "a man is rich in proportion to the number of things which he can afford to let alone."

Walden functions on several levels. As autobiography, it resembles Walt Whitman's "Song of Myself" (1855), for like Whitman, Thoreau wrote, "I should not talk so much about myself if there were anybody else whom I knew so well." Leon Edel places *Walden* among the literature of imaginary voyages. On the autobiographical and documentary level, it has affinities with Robinson Crusoe's solitary and self-reliant life on his island; its documentary detail also resembles Herman Melville's accounts of South Seas culture and of whaling, while on another level it is like the voyage of the *Pequod* in his *Moby Dick* (1851) as a quest for ultimate spiritual reality. Emerson complained of Thoreau's fondness for leading huckleberry parties, and as a "drop-out" from "the chopping sea of civilized life," Thoreau resembles Huckleberry Finn fleeing from "sivilization," the Walden cabin and Huck's raft both symbolizing freedom from conformity. As a work of social criticism, *Walden* challenges the abuses of capitalist materialism, for Thoreau observes that wage slaves such as the Fitchburg railroad workers laboring sixteen hours a day in poverty have no freedom to develop the artistic and spiritual side of their lives. Full of close observation of the seasons, of flora and fauna, *Walden* is finally a testament to the renewing power of nature, to the need to respect and preserve the environment, to a belief that "in wildness is the salvation of the world"—a statement that has become a doctrine of the Sierra Club.

Thoreau never expected his readers to follow his example and live alone in a one-room hut. Such a life would make marriage difficult if not impossible (indeed, Thoreau remained a bachelor). He himself stayed at Walden only long enough to prove that his experiment could work, after which he returned to Concord. In some ways, *Walden* is misleading. In form, it consists of eighteen essays loosely connected, in which Thoreau condenses his twenty-six-month sojourn at Walden into the seasons of a single year. In addition, he draws upon experiences there before and after his residence at the pond.

Thoreau was not as solitary, austere, or remote as *Walden* suggests. Walden was not a wilderness, nor was Thoreau a pioneer; his hut was within two miles of town, and while at Walden, he made almost daily visits to Concord and to his family, dined out often, had frequent visitors, and went off on excursions. Thoreau did not expect his readers literally to follow his example but to find applications to their own lives so that they can live more freely and intensively, with their eyes and ears more keenly attuned to the world around them, whatever it may be, and with their spirit closer to the life force behind nature.

Thoreau wrote "Civil Disobedience," first entitled "Resistance to Civil Government" when it was published in the periodical *Aesthetic Papers*, in response to questions about why he had gone to jail. As an abolitionist, he had objected to the Massachusetts poll tax and refused to pay it as a protest against slavery. When the Mexican War broke out in 1846, he protested against it as an aggressive war of conquest aimed in part at adding new slave territories to the nation, and for this reason as well, he refused to pay the tax. For several years, the authorities ignored Thoreau's nonpayment, but in July of 1846, Concord constable Sam Staples ordered Thoreau to pay up; when he still failed to comply, Staples arrested him on July 23 or 24 and imprisoned him in the Middlesex County jail. That evening some unknown person paid Thoreau's fine, but Staples kept Thoreau in jail until after breakfast and then released him. Emerson called Thoreau's action "mean and skulking, and in bad taste," and there is an apocryphal story that Emerson, visiting Thoreau in prison, asked, "Henry David, what are you doing in there?" to which he replied, "Ralph Waldo, what are you doing out there?" Bronson Alcott, however, called Thoreau a good example of "dignified noncompliance with the injunction of civil powers."

In the essay, Thoreau argues that laws, because they are created by human beings, are not infallible, that there is a higher divine law, and that when those laws conflict, one must obey the higher law. Hence slavery, no matter how legal (and it remained legal until 1865), was always unjust in its violation of the integrity and divine soul of the enslaved. So long as the American government upheld slavery, Thoreau said, one "cannot without disgrace be associated with it. I cannot for an instant recognize that political organization as my government which is the slave's government also." Carrying to extremes the logic of the Declaration of Independence, Thoreau argues in effect that each individual should declare independence from unjust laws, that citizens must never surrender their conscience to the legislator, and that "it is not desirable to cultivate a respect for the law, so much as for the right." Most people, he feared, served the state as soldiers do, like unthinking machines.

Thoreau does not, however, argue for violent revolution; he advocates nonviolent resistance. (Later, Thoreau contradicted himself in three essays championing John Brown, who endorsed and practiced violence.) The disobedient must be prepared to accept punishment if necessary: "Under a government which imprisons any unjustly, the true place for a just man is also a prison." Thoreau concludes:

The authority of government . . . must have the sanction and consent of the governed. It can have no pure right over my person and property but what I conceded to it. . . . There will never be a really free and enlightened State until the State comes to recognize the individual as a higher and independent power, from which all its own power and authority are derived, and treats him accordingly.

One problem with Thoreau's doctrine is that it is not always easy to determine whether a law is just or unjust. Thoreau never intended the indiscriminate breaking of laws; civil disobedience applies only in cases of fundamental moral principle. Not all individuals are necessarily right in defying the government. For example, during the Civil Rights movement of the 1960's, some Southern governors defied court orders, arguing instead that segregation was the will of God. Frequently, it is liberals who endorse civil disobedience, but in the late 1980's, members of the conservative Iran-Contra conspiracy defended their breaking of laws and lying to Congress on the grounds that they were serving a higher law. Similarly, opponents of abortion have argued that a higher law requires them to break laws that prohibit them from harassing proponents of abortion. Thus the debate continues; through it all, Thoreau's essay remains a key document in American history and a potent shaper of Americans' view of themselves.

Attacked by hostile critics such as James Russell Lowell for his nonconformity, Thoreau in some ways anticipated what came to be called the "counterculture." Despite his criticism of a materialistic society, he did not "propose to write an ode to dejection, but to brag as lustily as chanticleer in the morning, standing on his roost, if only to wake my neighbors up" to the Transcendental belief that they can elevate themselves to a fuller, simpler, more intense life. America's greatest nature writer, Thoreau is a forefather of John Muir, Edward Abbey, and Aldo Leopold. Politically, he influenced William Morris and leaders of the British labor movement in the late nineteenth century. Leo Tolstoy called *Walden* one of the great books, and Robert Frost wrote that it "surpasses everything we have in America." Frank Lloyd Wright spoke of its positive impact on American architecture, and President John F. Kennedy spoke of "Thoreau's pervasive and universal influence on social thinking and political action." Thoreau unquestionably wrote one of the indispensable classics of American literature.

Other major works

POETRY: *Poems of Nature*, 1895; *Collected Poems of Henry David Thoreau*, 1943, 1964 (Carl Bode, ed.).

Bibliography

Dillman, Richard. *Essays on Henry David Thoreau: Rhetoric, Style, and Audience*. West Cornwall, Conn.: Locust Hill Press, 1993.

Fink, Steven. *Prophet in the Marketplace: Thoreau's Development as a Professional Writer*. Princeton, N.J.: Princeton University Press, 1992.

Harding, Walter. *The Days of Henry Thoreau*. New York: Alfred A. Knopf, 1965.

Harding, Walter, and Michael Meyer. *The New Thoreau Handbook*. New York: New York University Press, 1980.

Howarth, William. *The Book of Concord: Thoreau's Life as a Writer*. New York: Viking Press, 1982.

Milder, Robert. *Reimagining Thoreau*. Cambridge, England: Cambridge University Press, 1994.

Richardson, Robert D. *Henry Thoreau: A Life of the Mind*. Berkeley: University of California Press, 1986.

Scharnhorst, Gary. *Henry David Thoreau: A Case Study in Canonization*. Columbia, S.C.: Camden House, 1993.

Shugard, Alan. *American Poetry: The Puritans Through Walt Whitman*. Boston: Twayne, 1988.

JOHN UPDIKE

Born: Shillington, Pennsylvania; March 18, 1932

Principal long fiction

The Poorhouse Fair, 1959; *Rabbit, Run*, 1960; *The Centaur*, 1963; *Of the Farm*, 1965; *Couples*, 1968; *Bech: A Book*, 1970; *Rabbit Redux*, 1971; *A Month of Sundays*, 1975; *Marry Me: A Romance*, 1976; *The Coup*, 1978; *Rabbit Is Rich*, 1981; *Bech Is Back*, 1982; *The Witches of Eastwick*, 1984; *Roger's Version*, 1986; *S.*, 1988; *Rabbit at Rest*, 1990; *Memories of the Ford Administration: A Novel*, 1992; *Brazil*; 1994.

Other literary forms

Since publishing his first story in *The New Yorker* in 1954, Updike has written in virtually every literary genre—poetry, short fiction, novel, essay, drama, art criticism, and autobiography.

Achievements

One of the major figures to emerge in American fiction after World War II, John Updike is widely acclaimed as one of the most accomplished stylists and prolific writers of his generation. Showing remarkable versatility and range, his fiction represents a penetrating chronicle in the realist mode of the changing morals and manners of American society. Updike's work has met both critical and popular success. His first novel, *The Poorhouse Fair*, was awarded the Rosenthal Award of the National Institute of Arts and Letters in 1960. In 1964, he received the National Book Award for *The Centaur*. He was elected in the same year to the National Institute of Arts and Letters. A number of his short stories have won the O. Henry Prize for best short story of the year and have been included in the yearly volumes of *Best American Short Stories*. In 1977, he was elected to the prestigious American Academy of Arts and Letters. In 1981, his novel *Rabbit Is Rich* won the Pulitzer Prize in fiction and the American Book Award. In that same year, he was awarded the Edward Mac-Dowell Medal for literature. More honors followed for *Rabbit at Rest*: the 1991 Pulitzer Prize and the National Book Critics Circle Award.

Biography

The only child of Wesley and Linda Grace (née Hoyer) Updike, John Updike spent the first thirteen years of his life living with his parents and grandparents in his maternal grandparents' home in Shillington, Pennsylvania, in rather strained economic conditions. In 1945, the Updikes had to move to the family farm in Plainville, ten miles away from Shillington. Updike's father supported the family on his meager salary as a mathematics teacher at the high school. His mother had literary aspirations of her own and later became a freelance writer. A number of short stories, such as "Flight," and the novels *The Centaur* and *Of the Farm* drew upon this experience. As a youth, Updike dreamed of drawing cartoons and writing for *The New Yorker*, an ambition he fulfilled in 1955. Updike went to Harvard University in 1950 on a full scholarship, majoring in English. He was editor of the Harvard *Lampoon* and was graduated in 1954 with highest honors. In 1953, he married Radcliffe student Mary Pennington, the daughter of a Unitarian minister; they were to have four children.

After a year at Oxford, England, where Updike studied at the Ruskin School of Drawing and Fine Art, he returned to the United States to a job offered him by E. B. White as a staff writer with *The New Yorker*, for which he wrote the "Talk of the Town" column. In April of 1957, fearing the city scene would disturb his development as a writer, Updike and his family left New York for Ipswich, Massachusetts, where he would live for the next seventeen years and which would serve as the model for the settings of a number of stories and novels. During this time, Updike was active in Ipswich community life and regularly attended the Congregational Church. In 1974, the Updikes were divorced. In 1977, Updike remarried, to Martha Bernhard, and settled in Georgetown, Massachusetts.

During the late 1950's and early 1960's, Updike faced a crisis of faith prompted by his acute consciousness of death's inevitability. The works of such writers as Søren Kierkegaard and, especially, Karl Barth, the Swiss orthodox theologian, helped Updike come to grips with this fear and to find a basis for faith. Religious and theological concerns pervade Updike's fiction. In a real sense, like Nathaniel Hawthorne's more than one hundred years earlier, Updike's fiction explores for his time the great issues of sin, guilt, and grace—of spiritual yearnings amid the entanglements of the flesh.

Analysis

In a compendious study of American fiction since 1940, Frederick R. Karl offers a useful overview of Updike: "Updike's fiction is founded on a vision of a compromised, tentative, teetering American, living in suburban New England or in rural Pennsylvania; an American who has broken with his more disciplined forebears and drifted free, seeking self-fulfillment but uncertain what it is and how to obtain it." While this rather global description fairly represents the recurring condition in most of Updike's novels, it does not do justice to the complex particularities of each work. Nevertheless, it does point to the basic predicament of nearly all Updike's protagonists—that sense of doubleness, of the ironic discrepancy of the fallen creature who yet senses, or yearns for, something transcendent. Updike's people are spiritual amphibians—creatures in concert with two realms yet not fully at home in either. Updike employs an analogous image in *The Centaur*— here is a creature that embodies the godly with the bestial, a fitting image of the human predicament in Updike's fiction. His fiction depicts the ambiguity of the "yes-but" stance toward the world, similar to the paradox of the "already and the not-yet." In his fine story "The Bulgarian Poetess" (1966), Updike writes: "Actuality is a running impoverishment of possibility." Again there is a sense of duplicity, of incompleteness. In such a world, problems are not always solved; they are more often endured if not fully understood. Yet even the curtains of actuality occasionally part, unexpectedly, to offer gifts, as Updike avers in his preface to *Olinger Stories* (1964)—such gifts as keep alive a vision of wholeness in an often lost and fragmented world.

Updike's first novel, *The Poorhouse Fair*, may seem anomalous in comparison with the rest of his work. In fact, the novel depicts the collision of values that runs throughout Updike's work. As in so much of Updike's fiction, the novel is concerned with decay, disintegration, a loss or abandonment of vital traditions, of values, of connection to a nurturing past. This opposition is embodied in the two principal characters: ninety-four-year-old John Hook, former teacher and resident of the poorhouse, and Stephen Conner, the poorhouse's pre-

fect. The novel is set in the future, sometime in the late 1970's, where want and misery have virtually been eliminated by a kind of humanistic socialism. Such progress has been made at a price: sterility, dehumanization, spiritual emptiness, regimentation. In a world totally run by the head, the heart dies. Hook tells Conner, in response to the prefect's avowed atheism: "There is no goodness, without belief." Conner's earthly paradise is a false one, destroying what it would save. The former prefect, Mendelssohn, sought, as his name would suggest, to fulfill the old people's spiritual needs in rituals and hymn singing.

Out of frustration with Conner's soulless administration, the old people break into a spontaneous "stoning" of Conner in the novel's climax. In effect, Conner is a corrupt or perverted martyr to the new "religion" of godless rationalism. The incident symbolizes the inherent desire and need for self-assertion and individualism. Conner's rationalized system is ultimately entropic. The annual fair is symbolic of an antientropic spirit in its celebration of the fruits of individual self-expression—patchwork quilts and peach-pit sculptures. In its depiction of an older America—its values of individuality, personal dignity, and pride—being swallowed up by material progress and bureaucratic efficiency, the novel is an "old" and somber book for a young author to write. In effect, Updike depicts an America become a spiritual "poorhouse," though materially rich. It is Hook, one of the last links to that lost America, who struggles at the end for some word to leave with Conner as a kind of testament, but he cannot find it.

The Centaur is arguably Updike's most complex novel, involving as it does the complicated interweaving of the myth of Chiron the centaur with the story of an adolescent boy and his father one winter in 1947. The novel is part *Bildungsroman*, a novel of moral education, and part *Künstlerroman*, a novel of an artist seeking identity in conflict with society. Operating on different levels, temporally and spatially, the nine chapters of the novel are a virtual collage, quite appropriate for the painter-narrator, nearly thirty, self-described as a "second-rate abstract expressionist," who is trying to recover from his past some understanding that might clarify and motivate his artistic vocation. Peter Caldwell, the narrator, reminisces to his African American mistress in a Manhattan loft about a three-day period in the winter of 1947, fourteen years earlier. On the realistic level, Peter tells the story of his self-conscious adolescence growing up an only child, living on a farm with his parents and Pop Kramer, his grandfather. His father is the high school biology teacher and swim coach, whose acts of compassion and charity embarrass the boy. On the mythic level, the father is depicted as Chiron the centaur, part man and part stallion, who serves as mentor to the youthful Greek heroes. As such, he suffers for his charges. By moving back and forth between the mythic and the realistic levels, Peter is able to move to an understanding of his father's life and death and to a clarification of his own vocation.

Just as Chiron sacrifices his immortality—he accepts death—so that Prometheus may be free to live, so too does George give his life for his son. While George is obsessed with death, it is doubtful that his sacrifice takes the form of death. Rather, his sacrifice is his willingness to go on fulfilling his obligations to his family. In reflecting upon this sacrifice by his father, Peter, feeling a failure in his art, asks: "Was it for this that my father gave up his life?" In the harsh reappraisal his memory provides, Peter is learning what he could not know as an adolescent. Love, guilt, and sacrifice are somehow inherent in the very structure of life. It is this that his mythicized father reveals to him in the very act of his narrating the story. For many critics, George Caldwell's sacrificial act frees the son to resume his artistic vocation with courage. For others, the novel is a mock epic showing in Peter the artist, the son of a scientist father and the grandson of a preacher, a loss of the metaphoric realm that makes great art possible and that leaves Peter diminished by his confinement to the earth alone. However the end is taken, the mythic element of the narrative richly captures the doubleness of human existence so pervasive in Updike's fictions.

The "Rabbit" novels (four through 1994) are a kind of gauge of the changes occurring in American culture. For *Rabbit, Run*, Updike quotes from philosopher Blaise Pascal for an epigraph: "The motions of Grace, the hardness of heart; external circumstances." Updike has commented that those three things describe our lives. In a real sense, those things also describe the basic movements and conflicts in the Rabbit novels. From *Rabbit, Run* to *Rabbit at Rest*, as the titles themselves suggest, Rabbit's life has been characterized by a series of zigzag movements and resistances and yearnings, colliding, often ineffectually, with the external circumstances of a fast-paced and changing world. *Rabbit, Run* takes place in a small city in Pennsylvania in the late 1950's, when Harry Angstrom, a former high school basketball great nicknamed "Rabbit," at twenty-six finds himself in a dead-end life: with a job selling items

in a dime store and a marriage to a careless and boozie woman. Wounded by the stifling boredom of everyday life and the cloying pressures of conforming and adapting to his environment, so characteristic of the 1950's, Harry wonders, confusedly, what has happened to his life. The disgust he feels about his present life is aggravated by his memories of when he was "first-rate at something" as a high school basketball great. Out of frustration, Rabbit bolts from his life-stifling existence, feeling that something out there wants him to find it. The novel is the study of this nonhero's quest for a nonexistent grail. Rabbit's zigzagging or boomeranging movements from wife Janice to mistress Ruth, the part-time prostitute, wreaks havoc: Janice accidentally drowns the baby; Ruth is impregnated and seeks an abortion. Pursued by the weak-faithed, do-gooder minister Eccles and failed by his old coach Tothero, Rabbit has no one to whom he can turn for help. Rabbit, like so many of Updike's protagonists, is enmeshed in the highly compromised environment of America, locked in the horizontal dimension yet yearning for something transcendent, the recovery of the vertical dimension. For Rabbit, the closest he can come to that missing feeling is sex, the deep mysteries of the woman's body replacing the old revelations of religion. Rabbit, though irresponsible, registers his refusal to succumb to such a world through movement, his running replacing the lost territories of innocent escape.

Ten years later, in *Rabbit Redux*, Rabbit has stopped running. He is back home with Janice and works as a typesetter. It is the end of the 1960's, and Rabbit watches the Moon landing on television as well as the upheavals of civil rights, campus demonstrations, and the Vietnam War. Rabbit feels that the whole country is doing what he did ten years earlier. As Janice moves out to live with her lover Stavros, Rabbit and his son Nelson end up as hosts to Jill, a runaway flower-child, and a bail-jumping Vietnam veteran and African American radical named Skeeter. This unlikely combination allows Updike to explore the major cultural and political clashes of the 1960's. This time Rabbit is more a passive listener-observer than an activist searcher. Skeeter's charismatic critiques of the American way of life challenge Rabbit's unquestioning patriotism and mesmerize him. As a result, Rabbit is helpless when disaster comes—his house is set on fire and Jill dies inside. Rabbit helps Skeeter escape. Fearing for her lover's heart, Janice returns to Rabbit. Unlike the restless figure of the first novel, Rabbit now seems to have capitulated or resigned himself to those powerful "external circumstances" from which he once sought escape. Rabbit bears witness, numbingly, to a disintegrating America, even as it puts a man on the Moon. America's spiritual landscape is as barren as that on the Moon. The novel ends with Rabbit and Janice asleep together. Perhaps they can awake to a new maturity and sense of responsibility for what they do in the world.

In the first two Rabbit novels, Rabbit was out of step with the times—running in the placid 1950's, sitting in the frenetic 1960's. In *Rabbit Is Rich*, he is running again, but this time in tune with the rhythms of the 1970's. Rabbit now jogs, which is in keeping with the fitness craze that began in the 1970's. He and Janice are prospering during the decade of inflation and energy crises. They own a Toyota dealership and are members of a country club. Rabbit plays golf and goes to Rotary Club lunches. Instead of newspapers, as in *Rabbit Redux*, he reads *Consumer Reports*, the bible of his new status. The ghosts of his past haunt him, however: the drowned baby, the child he did or did not have with Ruth, memories of Jill and Skeeter. The chief reminder of the sins of his past is his son Nelson, returning home, like something repressed, to wreak havoc on the family's new affluent complacency. Like his father of old but lacking Rabbit's conscience and vision, Nelson's quest for attention practically wrecks everything that he touches: his father's cars, his relationships. Rabbit can see himself in Nelson's behavior and tries to help him avoid recapitulating Rabbit's mistakes, but communication is difficult between them. With Skylab falling and Americans held hostage by Iranians, the present is uneasy and anxious, the future uncertain. Characteristically, Rabbit turns to sex to fill the spiritual void. He and Janice make love on top of their gold Krugerrands. Rabbit lusts for the lovely Cindy, but in a wife-swapping escapade during their Caribbean holiday, Rabbit gets Thelma Harrison instead and is introduced to anal sex—a fitting image of the sense of nothingness pervading American culture at the end of the "Me Decade." Updike does not end there. He leaves Rabbit holding his granddaughter, "another nail in his coffin," but also another chance for renewal, perhaps even grace, a richness unearned.

The sense of exhaustion—of a world "running out of gas" in so many ways—that pervades *Rabbit Is Rich* becomes more serious, even terminal, in *Rabbit at Rest*. The fuzzy emptiness and mindlessness of the 1980's pervade the novel, even as so much is described in such vivid detail. Rabbit and Janice now winter in Florida and Nelson runs the car dealership. Rabbit sustains

himself on junk food and endless television viewing, images of the emptiness of American life under Ronald Reagan. He suffers a heart attack and undergoes an angioplasty procedure. His son's cocaine addiction and embezzlement of $200,000 from the business shock the family. Yet this often coarse and unsympathetic man continues to compel the reader's interest. He wonders about the Dalai Lama then in the news. As the Cold War dissipates, Rabbit asks: "If there's no Cold War, what's the point of being an American?" The man called "Mr. Death" in *Rabbit, Run* now must face death in his own overblown body and contemplate it in relation to a world he has always known but that now is no more. Can such a man find peace, an acceptance and understanding of a life lived in such struggle and perplexity? In *Rabbit Is Rich*, Harry confesses to Janice the paradox of their lives: "Too much of it and not enough. The fear that it will end some day, and the fear that tomorrow will be the same as yesterday." In intensive care in Florida, at the end of *Rabbit at Rest*, Rabbit says, "Enough." Is this the realization and acceptance of life's sufficiency or its surplus? A confession of his own excesses and indulgences, or a command of sorts that he has had enough? These are only a few of the questions raised by the Rabbit novels.

Many critics praise Updike for being the premier American novelist of marriage. Nearly all of his fiction displays the mysterious as well as commonplace but ineluctable complexities and conflicts of marriage. It is one of Updike's major concerns to explore the conditions of love in our time.

Couples, Marry Me: A Romance, and *The Witches of Eastwick* each try to answer the question, "After Christianity, what?" Human sexuality is liturgy and sacrament of the new religion emerging in America in the 1960's—a new end of innocence in a "post-pill paradise." The three novels make an interesting grouping because all deal with marriages in various states of deterioration, and all explore the implications of "sex as the emergent religion, as the only thing left," Updike says.

Updike's concern with love, marriage, and adultery in so much of his fiction links him to Nathaniel Hawthorne's great novel *The Scarlet Letter* (1850), America's first great treatment of the complex social and religious consequences of adulterous love. Three novels in particular treat different dimensions of that adulterous triangle of Hawthorne's novel—*A Month of Sundays, Roger's Version*, and *S*. Hawthorne's Dimmesdale is updated in the figure of the Reverend Tom

Marshfield, the exiled protagonist of *A Month of Sundays*. Roger Lambert of *Roger's Version*, the professor of theology specializing in heresies, is Updike's treatment of Hawthorne's Roger Chillingworth. Sarah Worth of *S.* is a contemporary depiction of Hawthorne's Hester, the truly noble and strong character of *The Scarlet Letter*.

With the astonishing variety and richness of his narratives, John Updike's fiction constitutes a serious exploration and probing of the spiritual conditions of American culture in the late twentieth century. The fate of American civilization is seen in the condition of love—its risks and dangers as well as its possibility for gracious transformation.

Other major works

SHORT FICTION: *The Same Door*, 1959; *Pigeon Feathers and Other Stories*, 1962; *Olinger Stories: A Selection*, 1964; *The Music School*, 1966; *Museums and Women and Other Stories*, 1972; *Problems and Other Stories*, 1979; *Too Far to Go: The Maples Stories*, 1979; *Trust Me*, 1987.

PLAYS: *Three Texts from Early Ipswich: A Pageant*, 1968; *Buchanan Dying*, 1974.

POETRY: *The Carpentered Hen, and Other Tame Creatures*, 1958; *Telephone Poles and Other Poems*, 1963; *Midpoint and Other Poems*, 1969; *Tossing and Turning*, 1977; *Facing Nature*, 1985; *Collected Poems, 1953-1993*, 1993.

NONFICTION: *Assorted Prose*, 1965; *Picked-Up Pieces*, 1975; *Hugging the Shore: Essays and Criticism*, 1983; *Just Looking: Essays on Art*, 1989; *Self-Consciousness*, 1989; *Odd Jobs: Essays and Criticism*, 1991.

Bibliography

Burchard, Rachel C. *John Updike: Yea Sayings*. Carbondale: Southern Illinois University Press, 1971.

Detweiler, Robert. *John Updike*. Boston: Twayne, 1984.

Greiner, Donald J. *Adultery in the American Novel: Updike, James, and Hawthorne*. Columbia: University of South Carolina Press, 1985.

_____ . *John Updike's Novels*. Athens: Ohio University Press, 1984.

Hamilton, Alice, and Kenneth Hamilton. *The Elements of John Updike*. Grand Rapids, Mich.: Wm. B. Eerdman's, 1970.

Hunt, George W. *John Updike and the Three Secret Things: Sex, Religion, and Art*. Grand Rapids, Mich.: Wm. B. Eerdman's, 1980.

Markle, Joyce B. *Fighters and Lovers: Theme in the Novels of John Updike*. New York: New York University Press, 1973.

Uphaus, Suzanne Henning. *John Updike*. New York: Frederick Ungar Publishing Co., 1980.

Vargo, Edward P. *Rainstorms and Fire: Ritual in the Novels of John Updike*. Port Washington, N.Y.: Kennikat Press, 1973.

Wood, Ralph C. *The Comedy of Redemption: Christian Faith and Comic Vision in Four American Novelists*. Notre Dame, Ind.: University of Notre Dame Press, 1988.

EDITH WHARTON

Born: New York, New York; January 24, 1862   **Died:** St.-Brice-sous-Forêt, France; August 11, 1937

Principal long fiction

The Touchstone, 1900; *The Valley of Decision*, 1902; *Sanctuary*, 1903; *The House of Mirth*, 1905; *Madame de Treymes*, 1907; *The Fruit of the Tree*, 1907; *Ethan Frome*, 1911; *The Reef*, 1912; *The Custom of the Country*, 1913; *Summer*, 1917; *The Marne*, 1918; *The Age of Innocence*, 1920; *The Glimpses of the Moon*, 1922; *A Son at the Front*, 1923; *Old New York*, 1924; *The Mother's Recompense*, 1925; *Twilight Sleep*, 1927; *The Children*, 1928; *Hudson River Bracketed*, 1929; *The Gods Arrive*, 1932; *The Buccaneers*, 1938.

Other literary forms

In addition to her novels, of which several had appeared serially in *Scribner's*, *The Delineator*, and *The Pictorial Review*, Edith Wharton published eleven collections of short stories and three volumes of poetry as well as a variety of nonfiction works. She wrote an early and influential book on interior decorating, *The Decoration of Houses* (1897); a short book on the art of narrative, *The Writing of Fiction* (1925), published originally in *Scribner's*; and a delightful if highly selective autobiography, *A Backward Glance* (1934). Wharton, an indefatigable traveler, recorded accounts of her travels in *Italian Villas and Their Gardens* (1904), *Italian Backgrounds* (1905), *A Motor Flight Through France* (1908), and *In Morocco* (1920). During World War I, she wrote numerous pamphlets and letters to inform Americans about French and Belgian suffering and to enlist sympathy and support. Articles she wrote to explain the French people to American soldiers were later collected in the volume *French Ways and Their Meanings* (1919), and accounts of her five tours of the front lines were published under the title *Fighting France from Dunkerque to Belfort* (1915). Wharton also published a great many short stories, articles, and reviews that have never been collected. A number of her stories and novels have been adapted for the stage, motion pictures, and television and have also been translated into French, Italian, Spanish, German, Danish, Finnish, and Japanese.

Achievements

Wharton managed to attract a large audience of general readers and at the same time command the interest of critics and fellow writers. Among her admirers were Sinclair Lewis and F. Scott Fitzgerald; Bernard Berenson, the art critic; and Percy Lubbock. Wharton's popularity remained high almost to the end of her career in the 1930's, but critical enthusiasm began to diminish after 1920, when the quality of her fiction declined. Wharton's major talent was for social observation. She filled her novels with precise accounts of the decoration of houses, of dress and of dinner parties, describing them often down to the cut of a waistcoat and the contents of the soup tureen. This is not to say that such details were signs of superficiality, but rather that Wharton's fiction depended heavily on the notation of manners and were the result of direct observation.

Wharton's fiction is significantly autobiographical—many of the issues treated in her works stem from her own restrictive upbringing and unhappy marriage.

Wharton's major work was written between 1905, the year *The House of Mirth* was published, and 1920, when *The Age of Innocence* appeared. Interesting novels were still to come: *The Mother's Recompense*, *The Children*, and *The Buccaneers*, which has the best qualities of her earlier fiction; but the major works of the 1930's, *Hudson River Bracketed* and *The Gods Arrive*, betray a serious falling off of energy and of talent. Despite this later decline, however, and despite the undeniable influence of Henry James on some of her early work, Wharton produced a considerable body of original fiction, high in quality and superior to most of what was being published at the time. Her fiction also influenced other, younger American writers, notably Lewis and Fitzgerald. After a long decline in readership and a period of critical indifference, there has been a renewal of interest in her writing, by critics of the American novel, by scholars of turn-of-the-century American society and manners, and by feminist scholars interested in extraliterary issues. This interest laid claim to the popular imagination in the 1993 feature film *The Age of Innocence*, based on Wharton's novel of the same name.

Biography

Edith Wharton was born Edith Newbold Jones on January 24, 1862, in New York City. Her parents, George Frederic and Lucretia Rhinelander Jones, were descendants of early English and Dutch settlers and belonged to the pre-Civil War New York aristocracy, families whose wealth consisted largely of Manhattan real estate and who constituted in their common ancestry, landed wealth, and traditional manners a tightly knit, closed society. With the industrial expansion that occurred during and immediately after the Civil War, the old society was "invaded" by a new class of self-made rich men such as John Jacob Astor and Cornelius Vanderbilt. Whereas the old society had lived unostentatiously, observing, outwardly at least, a strict code of manners—the women presiding over a well-regulated social life and the men making perfunctory gestures at pursuing a profession—the new rich spent lavishly, built expensive, vulgar houses, and behaved in ways the old order found shockingly reprehensible. With its energy, its money, and its easier morality, the new order inevitably triumphed over the old, and this displacement of New York society constituted one of the chief subjects of Wharton's fiction, particularly in *The House of Mirth* and *The Custom of the Country*.

Jones was educated at home by governesses and tutors, and it was expected that she would assume the role young women of her class were educated to play, that of wife, mother, and gracious hostess. From an early age, however, she showed intellectual and literary talents that, along with an acute shyness, kept her at the edge of conventional social life and later threatened to consign her at the age of twenty-three to a life of spinsterhood—the worst fate, so it was thought, that could befall a young woman of her class. Jones eventually married a man twelve years her senior, Edward ("Teddy") Robbins Wharton, a socially prominent Bostonian and friend of her brother, and moved into a house in Lenox, Massachusetts. After revelations of his mismanagement of her estate and his adulterous affairs, she divorced Teddy in 1913. In his research for the biography of Wharton, Lewis uncovered the fact that she herself had had a brief but intense affair in 1908 with American journalist Morton Fullerton, and that that relationship had a profound influence on her fiction.

In 1903, Wharton met Henry James in England, beginning an important friendship. Like James, and for somewhat the same reasons, Wharton became in time an expatriate, giving up the newer, rawer life of America for the rich, deeply rooted culture of Europe. She felt at home in the salons and drawing rooms of Paris and London, where art and literature and ideas were discussed freely, where women were treated by men as equals, and where life itself was more pleasing to the senses and to the contemplative mind. Wharton also felt that in Europe, respect for the family, for manners, for learning, and for culture, even among the poorer classes, was very much alive.

When World War I broke out, Wharton remained in Paris and devoted her time, energy, and money to the relief of French and Belgian refugees; in 1916, she was officially recognized for her services to her adopted country by being made a Chevalier of the Legion of Honor. After the war, she bought a house not far from Paris and, later, another in the south of France. She made only one more trip home, in 1923, to receive an honorary degree at Yale. The remainder of her life was spent abroad.

According to those who knew her well, Wharton was a highly intelligent, well-read, brilliant conversationalist. She read and spoke Italian and French fluently, and her salons in both Paris and Saint Claire were gathering places for literary, artistic, and social luminaries of the time. Wharton continued to write regularly, turning out novels and short stories and articles, most of which sold well and brought her a considerable sum of money. She suffered a slight stroke in 1935; two years later, she died at her home in St.-Brice-sous-Forêt, August 11, 1937. Her body was buried in a cemetery at Versailles.

Analysis

The premier American novelist of manners as well as one of America's most admired women writers, Edith Wharton is known best for realistic works that depict the lives of the upper classes of late nineteenth and early twentieth century New York society. At the same time, her novels move beyond mere observation of surface manners and expectations to expose universal truths about individuals in relation to the larger society.

Wharton's fiction is significantly autobiographical—many of the issues treated in her works stem from her own restrictive upbringing and her unhappy marriage. Marriage was one of her principal subjects and provided her with a way of exploring and dramatizing her two main themes: the entrapment of an individual and the attempt by an outsider, often a vulgar, lower-class individual, to break into an old, aristocratic society. Blake Nevius points out how the entrapment theme is implicit in the principal relationships among characters in many of the novels, in which a superior nature is caught in a wasteful and baffling submission to an inferior nature. It was a situation that Wharton herself must have experienced, not only with a mother who was obsessed with fashion and propriety but also in a society given up to the pursuit of pleasure. It was a situation in which she later found herself in her marriage to Teddy, who disliked and resented her interest in social and intellectual life. In novel after novel, one sees this same situation treated—superior individuals trapped in relationships with their inferiors and prevented from extricating themselves by a finer sensibility.

In *The House of Mirth*, Lily Bart is impoverished by the bankruptcy and later the death of her father and is obliged to recoup her fortune in the only way open to her, by attempting to marry a rich man. Lily's situation was not Wharton's, but the social pressures on her must have been similar: to make a suitable marriage, with social position certainly, and, if possible, money as well. In the novel, Lily is given a choice that Wharton apparently did not have: an offer of marriage from Selden, an emancipated young lawyer of her own class. Wharton chose a passionless marriage with Teddy; Lily was not allowed that solution. Selden deserts Lily at the crucial moment, and she dies of an overdose of sleeping medicine.

In her autobiography, *A Backward Glance*, Wharton stated that her subject in *The House of Mirth* was to be the tragic power of New York society in "debasing people and ideas" and that Lily Bart was created in order to give that power dramatic scope. Lily's entrapment by society and her eventual destruction are not the final story. Lily overcomes the limitations of her upbringing and aspirations and acts on principle. She has in her possession a packet of letters that could be used to regain her social position, but the letters would involve the reputation of Selden. She also has a ten-thousand-dollar inheritance that could be used to establish herself in a profitable business, but she burns the letters and uses the money to repay a debt of honor. Lily dies, but in choosing death rather than dishonor, she has escaped entrapment.

In *The Age of Innocence*, published fifteen years after *The House of Mirth*, the underlying conflict is the same, though the tone of the novel and the nature of the entrapment are somewhat different. Here, the trapped individual is a man, Newland Archer, a young lawyer who is engaged to marry May Welland, a pretty and shallow young woman of respectable old New York society of the 1870's and 1890's. This is the world of Wharton's young womanhood, a society that is narrow and rigid and socially proper. Into this limited and self-contained world, she brings Ellen Olenska, a cousin of May, who belongs to this world by birth but left it years before and has since married a Polish count. Ellen has now separated from her husband, who has been notoriously unfaithful, and has returned to the bosom of her family for support and comfort. Archer is engaged by the family to help her in her quest for a divorce settlement. The inevitable happens. Archer and Ellen fall in love. Archer is attracted by Ellen's European sophistication, her freedom of thought and manners, and her refusal to take seriously the small taboos of New York society. Archer considers breaking with May and marrying Ellen. The family, sensing his defection, contrive with other members of the society to separate the lovers and reunite Archer with May, his conventional fiancé. Social pressure forces Ellen to return to Europe, and Archer is again thinking of pursuing Ellen; then May announces that she is expecting a baby. Archer is finally and permanently trapped.

As though to drive home the extent to which Archer has been defeated, Wharton takes him to Paris years later. His son is grown, his wife dead, and Ellen Olenska is now a widow living alone. Archer makes an appointment to see Ellen but gets only as far as a park bench near her apartment. At the last minute, he decides to send his son to see her, while he remains seated on the bench, telling himself that it would be more real for him to remain there than to go himself to see Ellen. The trap has done its work.

While one can see resemblances between Ellen and Wharton—the expatriation, the charm, the liberated views, perhaps even the slight French accent with which Ellen speaks—Archer is also Wharton, or that side of her that could never entirely escape the past. *The Age of Innocence* was thought by some reviewers to be a glorification of the past, which it clearly is not. Wharton does evoke with some nostalgia the old New York of her youth, but she also sets forth with delicate but cutting irony that society's limitations and its destructive narrowness. Archer has led an exemplary life, one is led to believe, but the happiness he might have had was gently but firmly denied him. Whereas a more popular novelist might have allowed Archer to be reunited with Ellen at the end of the novel, Wharton insists that that would be unreal; for her, personal happiness in the real world is the exception rather than the rule.

Two of Wharton's best novels—also two of her shortest, some critics preferring to call them novellas—

both deal with protagonists trapped by passionless marriages. The earliest of these, *Ethan Frome*, is about a Massachusetts farmer married to an older, neurasthenic wife, whose pretty young cousin, Mattie, has come to work for her. The inevitable again happens. Ethan falls in love with Mattie and dreams about running away with her. Ethan's jealous wife, however, arranges for Mattie to be sent away, and Ethan is obliged to escort her to the train station. It is winter, and the lovers stop for a brief time together. They embrace, realize the inevitability of separation, and decide to kill themselves by coasting on a sled down a steep hill into a great elm tree. During the ride down the steep hill, Ethan accidentally swerves the sled; a crash occurs in which the lovers are seriously injured but survive. Mattie becomes a whining invalid, while Zeena, the neurotic wife, takes over the running of the household, and Ethan, who is severely disfigured, feels himself like a handcuffed convict, a prisoner for life.

As R. W. B. Lewis has pointed out, the situation in *Ethan Frome* is very much like the situation in Wharton's own life at the time. If one shifts the sexes, Frome is Wharton trapped in a loveless marriage with the neurasthenic Teddy and passionately in love with a younger man who shared her interests and feelings, Morton Fullerton. The violent ending may be seen as Wharton's passionate statement about her own desperate situation. The success of *Ethan Frome*, however, does not depend on making such biographical connections; the book is a brilliantly realized work of realistic fiction that owes its power not to some abstractly conceived pessimistic philosophy of life but to Wharton's successful transposition of her own emotional life into the language of fiction.

The Custom of the Country deals with the destruction of an aristocracy by the invasion of uncivilized materialists. The protagonist of the novel, Undine Spragg, is a handsome young woman from Apex, a city in the American Middle West. Undine's father made a great deal of money in Apex and now has come East to try his hand in New York City. The Spraggs move into an expensive, vulgar hotel, and the parents would be content to exist on the fringes of New York society, but Undine, who is as ambitious as she is vulgar, manages to meet and then marry Ralph Marvel, an ineffectual member of old New York society. When life with Marvel grows boring, Undine becomes the mistress of a richer and more aggressive New York aristocrat, Peter Van Degen; when Van Degen drops her, she manages to snare the son of an old aristocratic French family, the

Marquis de Chelles. Undine marries de Chelles, but she has learned nothing, being without taste, manners, or ideas; her sole interest is in amusing and gratifying herself. As soon as she gets what she thinks she wants, she becomes dissatisfied with it and wants something she decides is better. She grows tired of having to fit herself to the demands of the feudal aristocracy into which she has married; when she attempts to sell family heirlooms, whose value she does not understand, her husband divorces her. Her third husband is a perfect match, a hard-driving vulgar materialist from Apex, Elmer Moffat, whose chief interest is in buying up European art. Moffat also aspires to an ambassadorial post, but is barred because he is married to Undine, a divorced woman. Undine represents everything that Wharton detested in the America of 1912, and, at a deeper and vaguer level, perhaps also expressed Wharton's fear and resentment at the displacement of her own class by more energetic and less cultivated outsiders. Measured against books such as *The House of Mirth*, *Ethan Frome*, *Summer*, and *The Reef*, *The Custom of the Country* is crude and unconvincing. Nevertheless, its stereotypes gave expression to the changing face of America at the beginning of the twentieth century, and to the deep social divisions that lay behind that transition.

Fortunately, the last of Wharton's novels, *The Buccaneers*, published the year after her death, was a return to the territory of her earlier fiction, old New York of the 1870's. The novel was unfinished at her death and lacks the coherence of her best early work, but she could still write with the sharpness and scenic fullness that had characterized *The House of Mirth* and *The Age of Innocence*.

Wharton was a novelist of manners, then, not a chronicler of large social movements, and her real subject was the entrapment of superior individuals who keenly feel the pull of moral responsibility. Her talents for social observation, for noting subtleties of dress and decoration, for nuance of voice and phrase, and for language—precise and yet expressive—were essential instruments in the creation of her novels. Wharton has been unduly charged with pessimism; her characteristic tone is ironic, the product of a sensibility able to see and feel the claims on both sides of a human dilemma. If her voice faltered in her later years and she conceded too much to the popular taste for which she increasingly wrote, she nevertheless produced some of the finest American fiction published in the first two decades of the twentieth century.

Other major works

SHORT FICTION: *The Greater Inclination*, 1899; *Crucial Instances*, 1901; *The Descent of Man*, 1904; *The Hermit and the Wild Woman*, 1908; *Tales of Men and Ghosts*, 1910; *Xingu and Other Stories*, 1916; *Here and Beyond*, 1926; *Certain People*, 1930; *Human Nature*, 1933; *The World Over*, 1936; *Ghosts*, 1937; *The Collected Short Stories of Edith Wharton*, 1968.

POETRY: *Verses*, 1878; *Artemis to Actoeon*, 1909; *Twelve Poems*, 1926.

NONFICTION: *The Decoration of Houses*, 1897 (with Ogden Codman, Jr.); *Italian Villas and Their Gardens*, 1904; *Italian Backgrounds*, 1905; *A Motor Flight Through France*, 1908; *Fighting France from Dunkerque to Belfort*, 1915; *French Ways and Their Meaning*, 1919; *In Morocco*, 1920; *The Writing of Fiction*, 1925; *A Backward Glance*, 1934; *The Letters of Edith Wharton*, 1988.

Bibliography

Ammons, Elizabeth. *Edith Wharton's Argument with America*. Athens: University of Georgia Press, 1980.

Auchincloss, Louis. *Pioneers and Caretakers: A Study of Nine American Novelists*. Minneapolis: University of Minnesota Press, 1965.

Fryer, Judith. *Felicitous Space: The Imaginative Structures of Edith Wharton and Willa Cather*. Chapel Hill: University of North Carolina Press, 1986.

Gimbel, Wendy. *Edith Wharton: Orphancy and Survival*. New York: Praeger, 1984.

Lewis, R. W. B. *Edith Wharton: A Biography*. 2 vols. New York: Harper & Row, 1975.

Lindberg, Gary H. *Edith Wharton and the Novel of Manners*. Charlottesville: University Press of Virginia, 1975.

Lyde, Marilyn Jones. *Edith Wharton: Convention and Morality in the Work of a Novelist*. Norman: University of Oklahoma Press, 1959.

Nevius, Blake. *Edith Wharton: A Study of Her Fiction*. Berkeley: University of California Press, 1953.

Vita-Finzi, Penelope. *Edith Wharton and the Art of Fiction*. New York: St. Martin's Press, 1990.

Wertshoven, Carol. *The Female Intruder in the Novels of Edith Wharton*. Rutherford, N.J.: Fairleigh Dickinson University Press, 1982.

III

SECULAR RABBIS
Jewish American Voices

"The disorder is here to stay." ... *And so it is—rich, baffling, agonizing, and diverse.*

—Saul Bellow, *Humboldt's Gift*, 1975

Whether the writers included in this section of *American Diversity, American Identity* are Jews who happen to be American or Americans who happen to be Jews, all respond in their individual ways to the tension between religion and the secular world, between past and present. From these tensions have come some of the greatest examples of twentieth century literature, as evidenced by two Nobel laureates (Isaac Bashevis Singer and Saul Bellow) as well as recipients of the Pulitzer Prize, the New York Drama Critics Circle Award, and the National Book Award. These writers have energized twentieth century writing and enriched American identities by drawing from the wells of Jewish and American literature at the same time that they have contributed to those sources.

They also reflect the full range of Jewish responses to the American experience. Nelson Algren stands at one extreme of this spectrum, representing the assimilationist tendency. Algren's grandfather, Nels Ahlgren, in his religious zeal changed his name to Isaac Ben Abraham. Nelson Algren, however, dropped the Abraham from his name and considered himself "neither Jew nor Gentile, neither Aryan nor Semite." His first published story, "So Help Me" (1932), deals with anti-Semitism. The villain, Luther, exploits and finally kills David, and Luther's partner in crime, Homer, tells the district attorney that he would "never have picked up with [David] if I'd knowed" the young man was Jewish. This theme of anti-Semitism later vanished from Algren's fiction. Indeed, Algren's attack on New York in *Who Lost an American?* (1962) can itself be seen as an expression of anti-Semitism. The main characters in Algren's story "Design for Departure," published in *The New Wilderness* (1946), are Mary and Christy. As these names indicate, the story draws on Christian symbolism. *Never Come Morning* (1942) and *The Man with the Golden Arm* (1949) recount the immigrant experience in Chicago, but that experience is rendered through a depiction of Polish American ghetto life. Algren's concern for the oppressed underclass owes more to Stephen Crane, Theodore Dreiser, and Richard Wright than to Abraham Cahan, and the philosophical underpinnings of Algren's work derive from Simone de Beauvoir and Jean-Paul Sartre.

In *Who Lost an American?* Algren attacked Norman Mailer, satirizing him as "Norman Manlifellow." Yet Mailer and Algren both seek to abandon a Jewish for an American identity. Mailer has said that in his literary career he has tried to reject "the one personality he found absolutely insupportable—the nice Jewish boy from Brooklyn." Like Algren, Mailer has explored subjects generally excluded from Jewish American fiction, including orgy, rape, murder, suicide, and insanity. Mailer, again like Algren, has taken as his literary models American writers of social protest, in Mailer's case John Dos Passos, James T. Farrell, and John Steinbeck, rather than Jewish or Jewish American authors. Mailer's heroes generally are WASPs or assimilated Jews. His Jewish characters often are unsympathetic: The movie mogul Herman Teppis in *The Deer Park* (1955) is vulgar and rapacious; Denise Gondelman in "The Time of Her Life" (1959) is a "proud, aggressive, vulgar, tense, stiff and arrogant Jewess" who attempts to dominate the Aryan hero of the story, Sergius O'Shaughnessy. In *The Armies of the Night* (1968) Mailer contrasts his own Jewish bungling with the dignified heroism of the WASP poet Robert Lowell, and Mailer also rejects his Jewish modesty for the arrogant, oppressive side that he equates with true manliness. The critic Leslie Fiedler regarded *Ancient Evenings* (1983) as another manifestation of Mailer's lifelong rejection of Judaism, "in which [Mailer] is able to project once more his lifelong fantasy of becoming the 'Golden Goy.'" Mailer's writings about Marilyn Monroe, the blond icon of American femininity, once more demonstrate his allegiance to his American rather than his Jewish identity.

Isaac Bashevis Singer stands at the opposite end of the Jewish American spectrum. In his work, the American themes are less important than the Jewish ones even when his work is set in the New World. His models include Rabbi Nachman of Bratzlav and Singer's brother Israel Joshua; his writings are a dialogue with the Jewish philosopher Baruch Spinoza and the Kabbala. Singer writes about characters like Algren and Mailer, Jews alienated from their tradition. This condition is not unique to America. When Asa Heshel Bannet in *Die Familie Muskat* (1950; *The Family Moskat*) comes to Warsaw, he buys a new wardrobe that prompts Abram Shapiro to remark that Asa looks like a Gentile. Jekuthiel in that novel reads German philosophy and rejects religion. Ezriel Babad in *Der Hoyf* (1953-1955; *The Manor*, 1967, and *The Estate*, 1969), a work again set in Singer's native Poland, is a rationalist, and his sister converts to Catholicism. Though most of Singer's novels are set in Europe and though all of his work was written in Yiddish before it was translated for Anglophones, many of his short stories treat the Jewish immigrant experience. *A Crown of Feathers and Other Stories* (1973) contains as many pieces about life in the United States as it does about pre-World War II Poland. These stories depict the decay of Yiddish culture in America even as they reveal that culture to audiences unfamiliar with it.

Singer used the Jewish world he knew to portray universal themes. Bernard Malamud also used the Jewish experience to discuss these issues. The son of Russian-Jewish immigrants, Malamud grew up in Brooklyn, the setting of many of his works, including *The Assistant* (1957), a novel that explores the nature of Judaism and the conflict between religion and the American ethos that emphasizes financial success.

Much of Malamud's fiction is rooted in nineteenth century Yiddish depictions of the schlemiel, like Sholom Aleichem's Tevye, translated to America. For Malamud the schlemiel is redeemed through an acceptance of community, especially the Jewish community. Malamud recognized the temptation, again not limited to America, to seek freedom through denial of one's identity, but that path leads only to self-destruction. Neither Singer nor Malamud argues for orthodox Judaism or even for formal religion, but their values derive from the Jewish tradition and their fiction from Jewish models.

Chaim Potok has described the theme of his novels as "the interplay of the Jewish tradition with the secular twentieth century." Potok's first book, *The Chosen* (1967), introduced American readers to the Hasidic world of the Crown Heights-Williamsburg section of Brooklyn. The novel shows the conflict between that world and that of modern orthodoxy. *The Promise* (1969), a sequel to *The Chosen*, extends Potok's anatomy of American Judaism by examining rifts between Orthodox and Conservative believers, and *In the Beginning* (1975), set in a multiethnic Bronx neighborhood, explores hostilities between Jew and Gentile.

The antagonisms in Philip Roth's fiction often are internal. Potok does not ignore the psyche of his characters, but for Roth the central confrontations concern his characters' desire to be American even as they remain aware of their roots. *Portnoy's Complaint* (1969) offers a vision of growing up Jewish in America, a *Catcher in the Rye* of the Jewish American experience. The complaint of the title is not only the typical Yiddish kvetching; it is also a brief against what Portnoy sees as an oppressive cultural heritage. Here and elsewhere in his fiction Roth articulates Jewish guilt, the ambivalence of desire to escape into the imagined freedom of the gentile world, the lingering loyalty to traditional values, the longing for individual expression, and the yearning for community. The autobiographical Nathan Zuckerman indicates how these conflicts impinge upon the Jewish American writer.

Tension also underlies the work of Cynthia Ozick, most of whose fiction concerns American Jews torn between Pan and Moses, the pagan and the Jewish. Those who choose the pagan in Ozick's fiction are destroyed. Yet Ozick recognizes that art itself may be pagan. In her writing and life, she wrestles with the dichotomy of being a Jewish writer in secular America.

According to Alan Guttman's *The Jewish Writer in America* (1971), Saul Bellow epitomizes the figure in the title. Bellow insists that he is an American writer: "I did not go to the public library to read the Talmud." Still, his prose reflects the Yiddish rhythms he heard at home in the immigrant communities of Lachine, Canada, and Chicago. His subjects include Eastern European immigrants, and he writes of alienation and what Alfred Kazin described as "the unreality of this world as opposed to God's." Asa Leventhal in *The Victim* (1947) offers a case study of the Jewish mind; *The Adventures of Augie March* (1953) retells the quintessential American myth, *Huckleberry Finn*, from a Jewish perspective. *Seize the Day* (1956) suggests that the attempt to deny one's identity is self-destructive, and only in a union with one's past can one find salvation. Bellow's *To Jerusalem and Back* (1976) and his coverage of the Six-Day War (1967) for *Newsday* demonstrate his continuing attachment to his heritage, while his fiction fuses tradition with the modern American idiom.

Grace Paley's stories often present the Jewish immigrant experience, though her characters may be second- or third-generation Americans. Her subjects are herself, the daughter of Jewish immigrants, her parents, and the New York City world where she has spent almost all her life. She presents the world of the sweatshops, the legacy of the Holocaust, and pressures of assimilation. With Bellow and Arthur Miller, she resides in the middle of the Jewish American spectrum, drawing on Jewish ideas, history, beliefs, and literary tradition but writing as an American.

Arthur Miller's *Death of a Salesman* (1949) and *The Crucible* (1953) are quintessential American dramas, representing American economics and history. *A View from the Bridge* (1955) is set in an Italian American community in Brooklyn. Other of Miller's works address Jewish concerns. His novel *Focus* (1945) and play *Incident at Vichy* (1964) deal with anti-Semitism. His earliest plays and again *Broken Glass* (1994) put the Jewish family on stage. Perhaps the most evident manifestation of Miller's Jewish heritage is his emphasis on moral responsibility, the recognition—which Von Berg achieves at the end of *Incident at Vichy*—that no one can deny his ties to others. In one way or another, all of the Jewish American writers discussed in this section wrestle with their own versions of that theme—baffling, agonizing, and diverse.

—Joseph Rosenblum
Greensboro, North Carolina

146

NELSON ALGREN
Nelson Ahlgren Abraham

Born: Detroit, Michigan; March 28, 1909   **Died:** Sag Harbor, New York; May 9, 1981

Principal long fiction

Somebody in Boots, 1935; *Never Come Morning*, 1942; *The Man with the Golden Arm*, 1949; *A Walk on the Wild Side*, 1956; *The Devil's Stocking*, 1983.

Other literary forms

Nelson Algren wrote short stories—*The Neon Wilderness* (1947) has been called one of the best collections of short stories published in the 1940's. *Chicago: City on the Make* (1951) is a prose poem variously described as a social document and a love poem to the city that serves as the center of Algren's fictional world. Similar nonfiction writings include *Who Lost an American?* (1963), a self-described "guide to the seamier sides" of several cities, including Chicago, and *Notes from a Sea Diary: Hemingway All the Way* (1965); both books combine travel writing and personal essays. What little poetry Algren wrote that is not included in his novels is included in *The Last Carousel* (1973), along with some unpublished stories and sketches.

Achievements

While Algren's first novel, *Somebody in Boots*, failed commercially, it drew the attention of serious literary critics, who were even more impressed by his second novel, *Never Come Morning*, which won for Algren in 1947 one thousand dollars from the American Academy of Arts and Letters. Also in 1947, he received a grant from the Newberry Library to assist him in the writing of *The Man with the Golden Arm*, which subsequently received the National Book Award in 1950. Since many of the stories in *The Neon Wilderness* had previously appeared in the O. Henry Memorial collections or in *Best American Stories*, Algren's stature as a first-class writer of fiction was assured by 1950. *The Man with the Golden Arm* and *A Walk on the Wild Side* were made into films, in 1955 and 1962, respectively.

Maxwell Geismar has termed Nelson Algren a "neo-naturalist" with roots in the American realistic tradition of Stephen Crane, Theodore Dreiser, and Ernest Hemingway. Algren's chief preoccupation is with what critic George Bluestone has called the "world's derelicts." The focus of Algren's fiction is on the victims of the

American Dream, those losers customarily associated with the Depression. From 1945 to 1960, he was among America's most acclaimed writers because of his focus and his vision, both of which were compatible with post-World War II America.

Biography

Nelson Ahlgren Abraham was born in Detroit, Michigan, on March 28, 1909, to second-generation Chicagoans, who moved back to Chicago when Algren was three years old. From 1912 until 1928, Algren absorbed the Chicago environment that was to become the center of his fictional world. After receiving his journalism degree from the University of Illinois in 1931, he began traveling across the Southwest, working at odd jobs (as a door-to-door coffee salesman in New Orleans, migrant worker, co-operator of a gasoline station in Texas, and carnival worker) and gathering the raw material that he later transformed into his fiction, particularly *A Walk on the Wild Side*. After serving time for stealing a typewriter, he returned to Chicago, where he continued his "research" on the Division Street milieu and began to write short stories, poems, and his first novel, *Somebody in Boots*, a Depression tale about the Southwest that became, after extensive revision, *A Walk on the Wild Side*.

After World War II (he served three years in the Army), Algren legally shortened his name, returned to Chicago, and within five years enjoyed a reputation as one of America's finest fiction writers. *The Man with the Golden Arm* received the National Book Award, and several stories were also recognized for their excellence. *A Walk on the Wild Side* and its subsequent filming, as well as the cinematic adaptation of *The Man with the Golden Arm*, brought Algren to the height of his popularity during the 1950's and 1960's, but aside from some travel books and his last novel, his writing career essentially ended in 1956. In his later years, he taught creative writing, before spending his last years on *The Devil's Stocking*, a thinly veiled fictional treatment of the trial and imprisonment of Reuben "Hurricane" Carter, a middleweight boxer. The "novel" did little to restore Algren's literary reputation.

Analysis

Whether the setting is Chicago or New Orleans, Algren's characters live, dream, and die in an environment alien to most Americans, many of whom have achieved the financial success and spiritual failure endemic to the American Dream. His characters are, at their best, losers in the quest for success; at their worst, they are spectators, not even participants, in that competitive battle. While his protagonists do aspire to escape from their environments, to assume new identities, and to attain that American Dream, they are so stunted by their backgrounds and so crippled with their own guilt that their efforts are doomed from the start and their inevitable fate often involves the punishment that their guilt-ridden souls have unconsciously sought. In *Never Come Morning*, Bruno cannot escape his guilt for allowing Steffi to be raped by his gang and almost welcomes his punishment for the murder of another man; in *The Man with the Golden Arm*, Frankie Machine cannot escape his guilt for the accident that incapacitates his wife and can end his drug addiction only by hanging himself; in *A Walk on the Wild Side*, Dove cannot escape his guilt for having raped Terasina, to whom he returns after having been blinded in a fight. In all three novels, the guilt that the man experiences from having abused a woman leads to a self-destructive impulse that negates his attempt to escape from his environment and produces the punishment he seeks.

Never Come Morning is Algren's first major novel. As the chronicle of a young man's passage from boyhood to manhood, *Never Come Morning* is another, albeit more cynical, American initiation novel, in which Bruno Bicek's initiation leads to his death. Like many young men, Bruno dreams of escaping from the ghetto through professional sports, either boxing or baseball ("Lefty" Bicek is a pitcher), but Algren quickly indicates, through similar chapter headings, that Bruno shares a "problem" with Casey Benkowski, his idol, whose defeat in the ring foreshadows Bruno's eventual defeat in life. Bruno's dreams are illusory, the product of the media: He reads *Kayo* magazine, sees pictures of boxers on matchbook covers, and watches Jimmy Cagney movies. His dream of becoming a "modern

Kitchel," a former Polish American boxing champion, reflects his desire to become someone else, to define his success in terms of other people, not himself. To become a successful man, he seeks status as the president and treasurer of the Warriors, his street gang, but his allegiance to the gang reflects his childish dependence on the group, not his adult leadership of it. His "other-directedness" also affects his relationship with Steffi, whom he seduces partly in order to gain status from the Warriors, who subsequently assert their own sexual rights to her. Rather than defend her and reveal the very "softness" that wins the readers' respect, he yields to the Warriors, thereby forsaking independence and manhood and incurring the guilt that eventually destroys him.

Images of imprisonment pervade the novel, which is concerned with the institutions that house inmates. When Bruno first serves time, Algren digresses to describe prison life, even as he does when he recounts Steffi's life at the brothel, where she is no less a prisoner. While she is there, she dreams of a "great stone penitentiary" and of the "vault" that is the barber's room. The prison and the brothel are appropriate institutions for a city that Algren compares to a madhouse. (Algren also sees the prostitutes as inmates of an insane asylum.) There is no escape for Steffi or Bruno, just as there is no real morning in this somber tale of darkness and night. Algren's Chicago is America in microcosm: As madhouse, prison, and brothel, it is an insane, entrapping world where people "sell out," prostituting themselves.

In *The Man with the Golden Arm*, also set in Polish American Chicago, Algren reiterates many of the themes, images, and character types that exist in *Never Come Morning*. Although the novel's controversial theme of drug addiction has received much attention, Algren is concerned not with drug addiction per se but with the forces, external and internal, that lead to the addictive, dependent personalities that render people unable to cope with their environments or escape from them. Once again, Algren's characters are life's losers, "the luckless living soon to become the luckless dead." The "hunted who also hope" in *Never Come Morning* become the "pursued" in *The Man with the Golden Arm*, which also relies on naturalistic metaphors comparing people and animals.

Since the characters are themselves victims of a system that excludes them, it seems ironic that they should experience guilt, but Algren's protagonist, Frankie Machine, is trapped by the guilt he feels at having been responsible for the car accident that has paralyzed Sophie, his wife. (Since Sophie has induced the paralysis—there is nothing physically wrong with her—his guilt is even more ironic.) Sophie uses Frankie's guilt to "hook" (a word suggesting addiction) him, punish him, and contribute to their self-destructive mutual dependence.

Sin and guilt permeate this novel, which belabors religious imagery, particularly that concerning the Crucifixion. The controlling metaphor in the novel is Sophie's "luminous crucifix," which she uses to enslave Frankie. Sophie states, "My cross is this chair. I'm settin' on *my* cross. . . . I'm *nailed* to mine." When her friend Violet suggests that she is driving in her own "nails," Sophie evades the issue because her "crucifixion," while voluntary, is not selfless but selfish. Algren observes the parallels between Sophie and Christ—both have been betrayed and bleed for the sins of others—but Sophie lacks love. In another parody of the crucifixion, Sparrow protests to Bednar, "You're nailin' me to the cross, Captain"; Bednar responds, "What the hell you think they're [the politicians] doin' to me?" Although they have enough religious teaching to mouth biblical allusions, Algren's characters use Christianity only as popular culture, as a source, like advertising and the movies, of reference to their own ego-centered worlds. Although Algren suggests that "God had forgotten His own," at least in Frankie's case, it is at least equally true that, as Sophie confesses, she and Frankie have forgotten God. Sophie's pathetic, self-centered musing about God having gone somewhere and keeping His distance indicates that He has no place in the world of Division Street. Surely Algren's allusion to the gamblers' God, who watches Sparrow's "fall," reflects the post-Christian modern world.

In Algren's naturalistic world, the characters are seen as caged animals waiting to be slaughtered. At the beginning of the novel, Frankie, who waits for justice from Bednar, watches a roach drowning in a bucket and is tempted to help it, but the roach dies before he intercedes; Frankie also dies without anyone interceding for him.

Prison inmates are the focus once again in *A Walk on the Wild Side*, a reworking of *Somebody in Boots*. The time is the Depression, the setting New Orleans rather than Chicago. The story concerns prison inmates, whose "kangaroo court" justice is superior to the justice they receive "outside," and on prostitutes, who also "serve their time" and are compared to caged birds (the brothel is an "aviary"). Despite their situation and their pasts, they are "innocent children" in their naïveté and illusions, and one of them is the means by which the hero is redeemed.

A parody of the Horatio Alger myth of the American Dream, *A Walk on the Wild Side* concerns an ambitious young man who "wants to make something of himself" and leaves the farm to find fame and fortune in the city. The protagonist's journey is "educational," in terms of the reading instruction he receives and the culture he acquires, as well as the "lessons" he learns about capitalism and life in general. At the beginning of the novel, the protagonist, Dove Linkhorn, is an "innocent," as his name suggests, but that "innocence" is not sexual—he rapes Terasina, the Earth Mother who is also his first "mentor"—but experiential, in that he believes in the "Ladder of Success" with "unlimited opportunities" for "ambitious young men." His subsequent experiences, however, illustrate the illusory offerings of capitalism and particularly the tenuous nature of life at the top.

Before he achieves his greatest success as a "salesman" of sex, Dove works, appropriately, in a condom manufacturing plant, which also sells sex. In his role as "Big Stingaree" in Finnerty's brothel, he is paid to perform an art that involves the "deflowering" of "virgins," who are played by prostitutes. In effect, the brothel, the primary setting in the novel, also serves as the symbolic center since Algren presents a society that has sold itself, has "prostituted" itself to survive. Ironically, the prostitutes in the brothel are morally superior to the "prostitutes" in mainstream American society, the "Do-Right Daddies," the powerful people who crusade against sin but also sin within the laws they create.

Hallie Breedlove, a prostitute, "sins," but she is capable of love and compassion, first with Schmidt and then with Dove, with whom she leaves the brothel. The "escape" is futile, however, for her subsequent pregnancy, in the light of her black "blood," threatens their future, and she believes that she can have her child only if she returns to her past, the mulatto village where she was born. Dove lacks her insight and in his attempt to find her is jailed, released, and then loses his sight in a battle with Schmidt. Metaphorically, however, in searching for her, he finds himself, and in losing his vision, he gains insight. Having learned that the "loser's side of the street" is superior to the "winners'," Dove abandons his quest for success and returns to his Texas hometown to be reconciled to Terasina. Unlike Bruno and Frankie, Dove not only survives but also resolves to deal constructively with the guilt caused by his sin against his woman.

Despite the qualified optimism of *A Walk on the Wild Side*, Algren's novels end to paint a negative image of capitalistic American society with its nightmarish American Dream. Chicago and New Orleans become microcosms of America, a country marked by images of madness, imprisonment, and prostitution. In that world, virtue, such as it is, resides on the "loser's side of the street," in the prisons and the brothels. Constricted by their backgrounds, Algren's male protagonists typically strive to escape and assume a new identity, sin against a woman (thereby incurring guilt that compounds their problems), serve time in prison (presented as a place of refuge), and pursue a self-destructive course that leads inevitably to death or mutilation.

Other major works

SHORT FICTION: *The Neon Wilderness*, 1947; *The Last Carousel*, 1973 (also includes sketches and poems).

NONFICTION: *Chicago: City on the Make*, 1951; *Who Lost an American?*, 1963; *Conversations with Nelson Algren*, 1964; *Notes from a Sea Diary: Hemingway All the Way*, 1965.

ANTHOLOGY: *Nelson Algren's Own Book of Lonesome Monsters*, 1962.

Bibliography

Corrington, John William. "Nelson Algren Talks with NOR's Editor-at-Large." *New Orleans Review* 1 (Winter, 1969): 130-132.

Cox, Martha Heasley, and Wayne Chatterton. *Nelson Algren*. Boston: Twayne, 1975.

Donohue, H. E. F., with Nelson Algren. *Conversations with Nelson Algren*. New York: Hill & Wang, 1964.

Drew, Bettina. *Nelson Algren: A Life on the Wild Side*. New York: Putnam, 1989.

Giles, James Richard. *Confronting the Horror: The Novels of Nelson Algren*. Kent, Ohio: Kent State University Press, 1989.

Karl, Frederick R. *American Fictions: 1940-1980*. New York: Harper & Row, 1983.

Pitts, Mary Ellen. "Algren's El: Internalized Machine and Displaced Nature." *South Atlantic Review* 52 (November, 1987): 61-74.

SAUL BELLOW

Born: Lachine, Quebec, Canada; June 10, 1915

Principal long fiction

Dangling Man, 1944; *The Victim*, 1947; *The Adventures of Augie March*, 1953; *Seize the Day*, 1956; *Henderson the Rain King*, 1959; *Herzog*, 1964; *Mr. Sammler's Planet*, 1970; *Humboldt's Gift*, 1975; *The Dean's December*, 1982; *More Die of Heartbreak*, 1987; *A Theft*, 1989; *The Bellarosa Connection*, 1989.

Other literary forms

In addition to his many novels, Saul Bellow has published short stories, plays, and a variety of nonfiction. His stories have appeared in *The New Yorker*, *Commentary*, *Partisan Review*, *Hudson Review*, *Esquire*, and other periodicals. Throughout his career, Bellow has also written numerous articles on a variety of topics.

Achievements

Often described as America's best living novelist, Bellow has enjoyed enormous critical praise and a wide readership as well. His popularity is, perhaps, surprising, because his novels do not contain the ingredients one expects to find in best-selling fiction—suspense, heroic figures, and graphic sex and violence. In fact, his novels are difficult ones that wrestle with perplexing questions. One of America's most erudite novelists, Bellow often alludes to the work of philosophers, psychologists, poets, anthropologists, and other writers in his fiction. He has stated that the novelist should not be afraid to introduce complex ideas into his work. He finds nothing admirable about the anti-intellectualism of many modern writers and believes that most of them have failed to confront the important moral and philosophical problems of the modern age. Opposed to the glib pessimism and the "complaint" of the dominant tradition of modern literature, Bellow has struggled for affirmation at a time when such a possibility is seen by many writers as merely an object of ridicule.

Bellow's many honors include the National Book Award (1954, 1965, 1971), the Pulitzer Prize (1976), and the Nobel Prize in Literature (1976). He received a special literary medal from the National Book Foundation in 1990. A master of narrative voice and perspective, Bellow is a great comic writer (perhaps the best in America since Mark Twain), and a fine craftsman whose remarkable control of the language allows him to move easily from the highly formal to the colloquial.

Most important, he writes novels that illuminate the dark areas of the psyche and that possess immense emotional power. Bellow has complained that many contemporary authors and critics are obsessed with symbolism and hidden meanings. A literary work becomes an abstraction for them, and they contrive to evade the emotional power inherent in literature. Bellow's novels do not suffer from abstraction; they deal concretely with passion, death, love, and other fundamental concerns: He is able to evoke the whole range of human emotions in his readers.

Biography

Saul Bellow was born in Lachine, Quebec, Canada, on June 10, 1915, the youngest of four children. Two years before, his parents, Abraham and Liza (Gordon) Bellow, had immigrated to Canada from St. Petersburg, Russia. The family lived in a very poor section of Montreal, where Bellow learned Yiddish, Hebrew, French, and English. When he was nine, the family moved to Chicago.

In 1933, he entered the University of Chicago but two years later transferred to Northwestern University, where he received a bachelor's degree. In 1937, he entered the University of Wisconsin at Madison to study anthropology but left school in December to marry and to become a writer. He was employed briefly with the Works Progress Administration Writers' Project and then led a bohemian life, supporting himself with teaching and odd jobs. During World War II, he served in the merchant marine and published his first novel, *Dangling Man*. After publishing his second novel, *The Victim*, he was awarded a Guggenheim Fellowship in 1948, which enabled him to travel to Europe and work on *The Adventures of Augie March*. This third novel won the National Book Award in fiction in 1954 and established Bellow as one of America's most promising novelists.

After Bellow's return from Europe in 1950, he spent

a large part of the next decade in New York City and Dutchess County, New York, teaching and writing before moving back to Chicago to publish *Herzog*. While *Seize the Day* and *Henderson the Rain King* did not receive the critical attention they deserved, *Herzog* was an enormous critical and financial success, even becoming a best-seller for a period of time.

The next two novels, *Mr. Sammler's Planet* and *Humboldt's Gift*, helped increase Bellow's reputation but also created some controversy. *Mr. Sammler's Planet* was critical of the excesses of the late 1960's, and some complained that Bellow had become a reactionary. Although Bellow opposed the Vietnam War, he found it difficult to identify with the "counterculture." *Humboldt's Gift* disturbed some critics, who complained that Bellow's interest in the ideas of Rudolf Steiner indicated that he was becoming an escapist; it was a mistaken assumption. An ardent supporter of Israel, Bellow traveled to that country in 1975 and published an account of his journey, *To Jerusalem and Back*. In 1976 he was awarded the Nobel Prize in Literature.

Bellow has been married four times and has three sons by his first three wives. At present, he lives in Chicago, where he prefers to shun the publicity that other writers cultivate.

Analysis

Bellow is acclaimed for his witty depictions of the modern urban individual, estranged from society but not destroyed in spirit. Drawing upon inspiration supplied by his rich Jewish heritage, he plumbs the depths of the modern human condition, addressing the disorder of the modern age and the role of the intellectual in such a world. The heroes of Bellow's greatest novels are Jewish intellectuals whose environment, peopled by energetic and incorrigible realists, tempers their moral speculations. Reared in a Jewish household and fluent in Yiddish, Bellow is representative of the Jewish American writers whose works rose to the forefront of American literature in the period following World War II.

Bellow's mature fiction can be considered as a conscious challenge to modernism, the dominant literary tradition of the age. Modernist literature reveals a horror of life and considers humanist values useless in a bleak, irrational world. Modernism assumes that the notion of the individual self, which underlies the great tradition of the novel, is an outmoded concept, and that modern civilization is doomed.

Bellow has never accepted the idea that humankind has reached its terminal point. The first full expression of this anti-modernist rebellion occurred with *The Adventures of Augie March*, an open-ended picaresque narrative with flamboyant language and an exuberant hero who seeks to affirm life and the possibility of freedom. While the environment has a profound influence upon Joseph and Asa Leventhal, Augie refuses to allow it to determine his fate. During the course of many adventures, a multitude of Machiavellians seek to impose their versions of reality upon the good-natured Augie, but he escapes from them, refusing to commit himself. Unlike the modernists, who denigrate the concept of the individual, Bellow believes in the potential of the self and its powerful imagination that can redeem ordinary existence and affirm the value of freedom, love, joy, and hope.

If *The Adventures of Augie March* presents Bellow's alternative to a "literature of victimization," his subsequent novels can be regarded as probing, exploratory studies in spiritual survival in a hostile environment. *Herzog*, Bellow's best and most difficult novel, is a retrospective meditation by a middle-aged professor who seeks to understand the reasons for his disastrous past. Bellow's method enables the reader to see how Herzog's imagination recollects and assembles the fragments of the past into a meaningful pattern.

Distraught over his recent divorce from his second wife, Madeleine, Herzog has become obsessed with writing letters to everyone connected with that event as well as to important thinkers, living and dead, who concern him. He associates his domestic crisis with the cultural crisis of Western civilization, and therefore he ponders the ethics of Friedrich Nietzsche as well as those of his psychiatrist, Dr. Edvig. His letter-writing is both a symptom of his psychological disintegration and an attempt to meditate upon and make sense of suffering and death.

At his home in the Berkshires, Herzog recalls and meditates upon the events of his recent past; the five-day period of time that he recalls reveals the severity of his psychological deterioration. His mistress Ramona believes that a cure for his nervous state can be found in her Lawrentian sexual passion, but he considers her "ideology" to be mere hedonism; impulsively, he decides to flee from her to Martha's Vineyard, where he has friends. After arriving there, the unstable professor leaves almost immediately and returns to New York. The next evening he has dinner with Ramona and spends the night with her, waking in the middle of the night to write another letter. The following morning he visits a courtroom while waiting for a meeting with his lawyer to discuss a lawsuit against Madeleine. Hearing a brutal child-abuse and murder case causes the distraught professor to associate Madeleine and her lover with the brutal child-murderers; he flies to Chicago to murder them. As he spies upon them, he realizes his assumption is absurd and abandons his plan. He eventually returns to his run-down home in the Berkshires, and the novel ends where it began.

Interspersed within these recollections of the immediate past are memories of the more distant past. By piecing these together, one learns the sad story of Herzog's domestic life. Feeling a vague dissatisfaction, the successful professor divorced his first wife Daisy, a sensible Midwestern woman, and began affairs with a good-natured Japanese woman, Sono, and the beautiful, bad-tempered Madeleine. After marrying Madeleine, Herzog purchased a house in the Berkshires, where he intended to complete his important book on the Romantics. Soon they returned to Chicago, however, where both saw a psychiatrist, and Madeleine suddenly announced that she wanted a divorce. The shocked Herzog traveled to Europe to recuperate, only to return to Chicago to learn that Madeleine had been having an affair with his best friend and confidante the whole time their marriage had been deteriorating.

Herzog's grim past—his disastrous marriages and the other sad events of his life that he also recalls—becomes emblematic of the pernicious influence of cultural nihilism. Herzog is devoted to basic humanist values but wonders if he must, as the ubiquitous "reality-instructors" insist, become another mass man devoted to a brutal "realism" in the Hobbesian jungle of modern society. His antipathy for the cynicism of these "wastelanders" is strong, but he knows his past idealism has been too naïve. Repeatedly, the "reality instructors" strive to teach ("punish") Herzog with lessons of the "real"—and the "real" is always brutal and cruel. Sandor Himmelstein, Herzog's lawyer and friend, proudly announces that all people are "whores." It is an accurate description not only of Himmelstein but also of his fellow reality instructors. Their cynical view is pervasive in modern society, in which people play roles, sell themselves, and seduce and exploit others for their own selfish ends.

The turning point of the novel is Herzog's revelation in the courtroom episode. Intellectually, he has always known about evil and suffering, but emotionally he has remained innocent. His hearing of the case in which a mother mistreats and murders her son while her lover apathetically watches is too much for him to bear; here is a monstrous evil that cannot be subsumed by any intellectual scheme. In a devastating moment the professor is forced to realize that his idealism is foolish.

At the end of the novel, Herzog has achieved a new consciousness. He recognizes that he has been selfish and excessively absorbed in intellectual abstractions. A prisoner of his private intellectual life, he has cut himself off from ordinary humanity and everyday existence. He sees that his naïve idealism and the wastelanders' cruel "realism" are both escapist and therefore unacceptable attitudes; they allow the individual to evade reality by wearing masks of naïve idealism or self-serving cynicism. The exhausted Herzog decides to abandon his compulsive letter-writing and to stop pondering his past. The threat of madness has passed, and he is on the road to recovery.

Mr. Sammler's Planet is a meditative novel of sardonic humor and caustic wit. The "action" of the novel centers upon the protagonist's recollection of a brief period of time in the recent past, though there are recollections of a more distant past, too. Once again the mental state of the protagonist is Bellow's main concern. Like Herzog, Artur Sammler has abandoned a scholarly project because he finds rational explanations dissatisfying; they are unable to justify suffering and death. The septuagenarian Sammler is yet another of Bellow's survivors, a lonely humanist in a society populated by brutal "realists."

Sammler had been reared in a wealthy, secular Jewish family in Krakow. As an adult, he became a haughty, cosmopolitan intellectual, useless to everyone, as he readily admits. On a visit to Poland in 1939, when the Germans suddenly attacked, he, his wife, and others were captured and ordered to dig their own graves as the Nazis waited to murder them. Although his wife was killed in the mass execution, miraculously he escaped by crawling out of his own grave. After the war ended, Sammler and his daughter Shula were rescued from a displaced persons camp by a kind nephew, Dr. Elya Gruner, who became their patron.

The experience of the Holocaust destroyed what little religious inclination Sammler possessed, but in his old age he has become concerned with his spiritual state. Unfortunately, it is difficult to pursue spiritual interests in a materialistic society hostile to them. The basic conflict in the novel is between Sammler's need to ponder the basic questions of existence—a need accentuated by the dying of the noble Gruner—and the distractions of contemporary society. In the primary action of the novel, Sammler's main intention is to visit the dying Gruner, who finds Sammler a source of great comfort. Several "accidents" distract Sammler from his goal, and on the day of his nephew's death, he arrives too late.

The "accidents" that encumber Sammler reveal clearly the "degraded clowning" of contemporary society. Sammler is threatened by a pickpocket who corners the old man and then exposes himself. In the middle of a lecture Sammler is shouted down by a radical student who says that Sammler is sexually defective. Shula steals a manuscript from an Indian scholar, and Sammler must waste precious time to recover it.

Opposed to Gruner, who is part of the "old system" that esteems the family, the expression of emotion, and the traditional humanist values, is the contemporary generation, a kind of "circus" characterized by role-playing, hedonism, amorality, self-centeredness, and atrophy of feeling. Despite its flaws, Bellow sympathizes with the "old system." The novel concludes after Sammler, despite the objections of the hospital staff, goes into the post-mortem room and says a prayer for Gruner's soul.

As in Bellow's previous novels, the tension and the humor of *Humboldt's Gift* have their origin in the protagonist's attempt to free himself from the distractions of contemporary society and pursue the needs of his soul. The protagonist Charlie Citrine strives to define for himself the function of the artist in contemporary America. He tries to come to terms with the failure and premature death of his one-time mentor, Von Humboldt Fleisher, who had the potential to be America's greatest modern poet but achieved very little. Charlie wonders if the romantic poet can survive in a materialistic society; he wonders, too, if he can overcome his fear of the grave and exercise his imagination. A writer who has squandered his talent, Charlie has intimations of terror of the grave but also intimations of immortality and reincarnation.

The primary nemesis of Charlie's spiritual life is Ronald Cantabile, a small-time criminal. Renata, Charlie's voluptuous mistress, Denise, his ex-wife, and Pierre Thaxter, a confidence man, are also major distractions. When Charlie, on the advice of a friend, refuses to pay Cantabile the money he owes him from a poker game, the criminal harasses him. In fact, the proud, psychopathic Cantabile refuses to leave Charlie alone even after he agrees to pay him the money. He continually humiliates Charlie and even tries to involve

him in a plot to murder the troublesome Denise.

Denise, Renata, and Thaxter also distract Charlie from pondering the fate of Humboldt and meditating upon fundamental metaphysical questions. Hoping Charlie will return to her, Denise refuses to settle her support suit and continues to demand more money. When Charlie is forced to put up a two-hundred-thousand-dollar bond, he is financially ruined, and the loss of his money results in the loss of the voluptuous Renata, who decides to marry a wealthy undertaker. A third disillusioning experience involves Thaxter, who has apparently conned Charlie. Charlie had invested a small fortune in a new journal, *The Ark*, which was supposed to restore the authority of art and culture in the United States. Thaxter, the editor of *The Ark*, never publishes the first issue and has, it appears, stolen the money. His confidence game symbolizes America's lack of respect for art and culture, impractical subjects in a practical, technological society.

Charlie does, however, overcome these "distractions." Humboldt's posthumously delivered letter, accompanied by an original film sketch (his "gift") and a scenario that the two had written at Princeton years before, provides the genesis for Charlie's salvation. The original film idea and the scenario of their Princeton years enable Charlie to attain financial security, but more important, Humboldt's letter provides the impetus for Charlie's decision at the end of the novel to repudiate his past empty life and to pursue the life of the imagination. Humboldt's ideas, bolstered by the poetry of William Blake, William Wordsworth, and John Keats, enable Charlie to avoid the fate of the self-destructive artist. He decides to live in Europe and meditate upon the fundamental questions—in short, to take up a different kind of life. When, at the end of the novel, Charlie gives Humboldt and the poet's mother a proper burial, Bellow suggests that Charlie's imagination is ready to exert itself and wake him from his self-centered boredom and death-in-life. The final scene of the novel promises Charlie's spiritual regeneration.

In these and subsequent novels—notably *The Dean's December* and *The Bellarosa Connection* (the latter an examination of how the assimilation of Jews into American life corrupts their values and poses a threat even greater than the Nazi Holocaust)—the Bellow protagonist is a sensitive, thinking individual at war against the forces of society that kill the spirit. While often a suffering victim and a spiritual alien in a materialistic world, Bellow's heroes eventually demonstrate uncommon dignity, sympathy, compassion—and hope.

Other major works

SHORT FICTION: *Mosby's Memoirs and Other Stories*, 1968; *Him with His Foot in His Mouth and Other Stories*, 1984 (includes short novels).

PLAYS: *The Wrecker*, pb. 1954; *The Last Analysis*, pr. 1964, pb. 1965; *A Wen*, pb. 1965; *Under the Weather*, pr. 1966 (includes *Out from Under*, *A Wen*, and *Orange Soufflé*).

NONFICTION: *To Jerusalem and Back: A Personal Account*, 1976; *It All Adds Up: From the Dim Past to the Uncertain Future, a Nonfiction Collection*, 1994.

ANTHOLOGY: *Great Jewish Short Stories*, 1963.

Bibliography

Chavkin, Allan. "The Problem of Suffering in the Fiction of Saul Bellow." *Comparative Literature Studies* 21, no. 2 (1984): 161-174.

Cronin, Gloria L., and L. H. Goldman. *Saul Bellow in the 1980's: A Collection of Critical Essays*. East Lansing: Michigan State University Press, 1989.

Cronin, Gloria L., and Blaine H. Hall. *Saul Bellow: An Annotated Bibliography*. 2d ed. New York: Garland, 1987.

Fuchs, Daniel. *Saul Bellow: Vision and Revision*. Durham, N.C.: Duke University Press, 1984.

Goldman, Liela, ed. *Saul Bellow Journal*, 1982 to present.

Harris, Mark. *Saul Bellow, Drumlin Woodchuck*. Athens: University of Georgia Press, 1980.

Hyland, Peter. *Saul Bellow*. New York: St. Martin's Press, 1992.

Kiernan, Robert. *Saul Bellow*. New York: Continuum, 1988.

Miller, Ruth. *Saul Bellow: A Biography of the Imagination*. New York: St. Martin's Press, 1991.

NORMAN MAILER

Born: Long Branch, New Jersey; January 31, 1923

Principal long fiction

The Naked and the Dead, 1948; *Barbary Shore*, 1951; *The Deer Park*, 1955; *An American Dream*, 1965; *Why Are We in Vietnam?*, 1967; *The Armies of the Night: History as a Novel, the Novel as History*, 1968; *Marilyn*, 1973; *The Executioner's Song*, 1979; *Of Women and Their Elegance*, 1980; *Ancient Evenings*, 1983; *Tough Guys Don't Dance*, 1984; *Harlot's Ghost*, 1991.

Other literary forms

Beginning with *The Armies of the Night*, Norman Mailer has published several works that cross the conventional boundaries of fiction and nonfiction: a "novel biography," *Marilyn*; a "true life novel," *The Executioner's Song*; and an "imaginary memoir," *Of Women and Their Elegance*. Because of his sophisticated handling of style, structure, point of view, and characterization, much of Mailer's journalism and reportage approaches the novel's complexity of language and form: *Miami and the Siege of Chicago: An Informal History of the Republican and Democratic Conventions of 1968* (1969), *Of a Fire on the Moon* (1970), *The Prisoner of Sex* (1971), *St. George and the Godfather* (1972), and *The Fight* (1975). His essays, interviews, short stories, and poems have been collected in *Advertisements for Myself* (1959), *Deaths for the Ladies and Other Disasters* (1962), *The Presidential Papers* (1963), *Cannibals and Christians* (1966), *The Short Fiction of Norman Mailer* (1967), *The Idol and the Octopus: Political Writings on the Kennedy and Johnson Administrations* (1968), *Existential Errands* (1972), and *Pieces and Pontifications* (1982). His work in drama and literary criticism appears in *The Deer Park: A Play* (1967) and *Genius and Lust: A Journey Through the Major Writings of Henry Miller* (1976).

Achievements

With the appearance of *The Naked and the Dead* in 1948, Mailer was hailed by many critics as one of the most promising writers of the postwar generation. Since his early acclaim, Mailer's reputation has risen and fallen repeatedly—in part because of the unevenness of his writing, and in part because of his intense participation in the causes and quarrels of his age. More important, however, his work has often been misunderstood because of its remarkably changing character and its innovative procedures, for Mailer has been restlessly searching throughout his career for the style and structure that would most effectively express his ambition to make "a revolution in the consciousness of our time."

By whatever standard Mailer is judged, it is already clear that several of his books have a secure place not only in postwar literary history but also in the canon of significant American literary achievements. *The Naked and the Dead* and *The Armies of the Night* continue to receive attention as masterpieces, and in recent years his other novels have begun to benefit from the serious exploration accorded to the finest works of fiction. *The Executioner's Song*—very favorably reviewed when it first appeared—may eventually rank with Mailer's greatest writing because it contains a complexity of point of view and characterization rivaled only by *The Naked and the Dead*, *An American Dream*, and *Why Are We in Vietnam?*

In addition to receiving several literary honors and distinctions—including the National Book Award, the Pulitzer Prize, and election to the National Institute of Arts and Letters—Mailer has been the subject of more than a dozen book-length studies and hundreds of articles. His work is an essential part of college syllabi in contemporary literature, not only because he has addressed crucial events, concerns, and institutions such as World War II, the Cold War, Hollywood, Vietnam, the Pentagon, and capital punishment but also because he has treated all of his important themes in the light of a deeply imaginative conception of literary form.

Biography

Norman Mailer grew up in Brooklyn, New York, and attended Harvard University (1939-1943), where he studied aeronautical engineering and became interested in writing. After he was graduated from Harvard, he married Beatrice Silverman and was inducted into the U.S. Army, serving with the 112th Cavalry out of San

Antonio, Texas. He was overseas for eighteen months in Leyte, Luzon, and with occupation forces in Japan. His varied experience as a Field Artillery surveyor, clerk, interpreter of aerial photographs, rifleman, and cook undoubtedly contributed to the comprehensive portrayal of the military in *The Naked and the Dead*.

After his discharge from the army in May, 1946, Mailer immediately began work on *The Naked and the Dead* and completed it within fifteen months. In the next two years (1948-1950), he traveled in Europe, studied at the Sorbonne, wrote articles and delivered speeches, campaigned for the election of Henry Wallace, worked briefly as a screenwriter in Hollywood, and finished his second novel, *Barbary Shore*, which was poorly received—in part because of his sympathetic engagement with Marxist ideas and his aggressive exploration of shifting political attitudes in the postwar years.

For the next ten years, Mailer was beset by various personal and professional traumas which he slowly surmounted. He divorced his first wife—they had one daughter—in 1952. He married Adele Morales in 1954; he stabbed her with a penknife on November 19, 1960, after a party organized to launch his New York City mayoral campaign. The couple was divorced in 1962. During this period, Mailer had difficulty getting his third novel, *The Deer Park*, published, while he simultaneously struggled to complete another novel. At the same time, his second and third daughters were born, and he married Lady Jeanne Campbell, who gave birth to his fourth daughter in 1962. With the publication of *Advertisements for Myself*, he began to find a way of rescuing the fragments and dead-ends of his career, and with his essay, "Superman Comes to the Supermarket" (1960), he evolved a supple way of dramatizing and musing on social and political issues that freed him from the constraints of his not entirely successful first-person narrators in *Barbary Shore* and *The Deer Park*.

In many ways, the 1960's were Mailer's most productive years. Not only did he publish his two most sophisticated novels, *An American Dream* and *Why Are We in Vietnam?* and adapt *The Deer Park* for the stage but also he directed and acted in three films—*Wild 90* (January, 1968), *Beyond the Law* (October, 1968), and *Maidstone* (1971)—which provoked him to write important essays on the nature of film and prepared him for his innovative "novel biography," *Marilyn*. He was an active journalist during this period, covering political conventions and the landing of a man on the Moon, and out of his reportage he created a book, *The Armies of the Night*, that transcends the immediate occasion of its conception—a protest march on the Pentagon—in order to probe the shaping processes of history and fiction and their mutuality as human constructs. In 1963, Mailer divorced Lady Jeanne Campbell and married the actress Beverly Bentley, with whom he had two sons. He campaigned unsuccessfully for mayor of New York City in 1969 and fathered a fifth daughter by Carol Stevens in 1971. His sixth wife is Norris Church.

In the 1970's and 1980's, Mailer continued to write nonfiction while working on his Egyptian novel, *Ancient Evenings*. Although he began in the mid-1970's to withdraw from public attention, his appearance in the film *Ragtime* (1981) and his defense of Jack Abbott, a writer-convict who committed a murder shortly after his release from prison, revived the image of a controversial, embattled author. As several reviewers pointed out, both *Ancient Evenings* and *Tough Guys Don't Dance* have first-person narrators who bear considerable resemblance to Mailer. His controversial tenure as president of the U.S. chapter of PEN (International Association of Poets, Playwrights, Editors, Essayists and Novelists), along with the film of *Tough Guys Don't Dance* (1987), which Mailer wrote and directed, once again focused public attention on him. *Harlot's Ghost* was published in 1991.

Analysis

Mailer has achieved literary renown as a flawed yet brilliant chronicler of American life. He employs a skillful blend of fiction and nonfiction to dissect public events, which become metaphors that exemplify and clarify the issues he views as significant, apocalyptic, or destructive about modern America. Finding within his own personal concerns a reflection of the national crisis and of the conflicts he observes as being at the heart of the American identity, Mailer has become the heir to a tradition of American visionaries.

The Naked and the Dead is far more than a war novel, more than a political novel, for it examines the way human experience is shaped and interpreted, and it establishes the ground out of which human character and belief arise. Part 1, "Wave," concerns preparations for the invasion of Anopopei, an island held by the Japanese during World War II. The first wave of troops will assault the beaches by riding through the surf and charging ashore. One wave against another, humanity against the nature of its own enterprise, is one of the dominant themes of the novel. Much of what makes the novel fascinating is its persistent aligning of the interface between planning and probability; each soldier tries to gauge what his chances are of surviving—or, in Sergeant Croft's and General Cummings' cases, dominating—the war, although almost every man, like Martinez, has at least one moment of fear, of total vulnerability, when he feels "naked" and almost certainly dead under fire. Part 2, "Argil and Mold," shifts from the reactions of the combat soldiers to war to the grand strategy of General Cummings, who plans on shaping his army to fit his master design. For Cummings, the war—like history itself—must have a pattern, one that he can follow and channel in his direction. He disclaims the operations of chance; seeming accidents, he contends, are actually a result of a person's failure to capitalize on the opportunities life affords. If Cummings does not yet know the precise trajectory of history, he is confident that he will be percipient enough to discover it eventually.

In the course of his conflict with his resistant subordinate Lieutenant Hearn, Cummings reveals his disdain for the liberal's "exaggerated idea of the rights due" to persons as individuals. In the general's reading of history, it is the development not of individuality but of power concentrations that counts in evaluating the causes of the war. As a result, he violates the integrity of much of the experience that is portrayed in the novel, for each character—including the general—is given a unique biography, a singularity of purpose that defies the notion that individuals can be permanently fashioned as part of a power bloc. Each of the principal characters in the novel behaves not only in terms of his background and his participation in a platoon but also in terms of the power argument between Cummings and Hearn. That is why it is inevitable that Hearn will ultimately be placed at the head of Sergeant Croft's platoon, for Croft has often kept his men together by the force of his own will, by an invincible belief in the rightness of his position that is virtually identical to Cummings' self-assurance.

Like Cummings, Croft contends with a geographical and ethnic cross section of soldiers: Red Valsen, "the wandering minstrel" from Montana, who distrusts all permanent relationships; Gallagher, "the revolutionary reversed," an Irish Catholic from Boston who seems perpetually angry at the way the more privileged or the more conniving have deprived men of their dignity but who is also profoundly prejudiced against other groups, especially the Jews; Julio Martinez, the Mexican American, who desperately asserts his loyalty, his integrity, by taking pride in courageously executing Croft's dangerous orders; Joey Goldstein, who from his "cove in Brooklyn" tries to ingratiate himself in a world inhospitable to Jews; and Wilson, the affable Southerner who traffics easily with women and the world and who is without much sense of life's disparities and of how he has hurt as well as charmed others with his "fun." These characters and others are meant to convey the multiplicity of experience that Croft crushes in disciplining his platoon.

In one of the most telling scenes in the novel, Croft allows a captured Japanese soldier time to recover his composure, to express his humanity, to plead for his life, and to sense that he is in the presence of other compassionate human beings, before brutally shooting him in the very moment of his happiness. Croft's cruelty is the most extreme extension of Cummings' declaration that individuals do not count, that single lives are valued too highly.

Part 3 confronts the question of human nature, which is unanswerable; human beings are divided creatures, both body and mind, and neither side of that nature can entirely suppress the other even in the shrewdest of individuals. In the novel, men live and die as thinking and feeling beings who are bound by the conditions of nature and by the consequences of their own actions, over which they often have surprisingly little control. Men are truncated, their lives are suddenly cut off, even as their thoughts appear to extend their hold over events. Thus, Hearn drives his men to the other side of the island so that they can reconnoiter the possibility of an invasion behind Japanese battle lines. He suffers from weariness, from the men's resistance, from his own self-doubt, but he reasserts himself:

> As they moved along out of the hollow he felt good; it was a new morning, and it was impossible not to feel hopeful. The dejection, the decisions of the previous night seemed unimportant. He was enjoying this, but if he was, so much the better.
> A half hour later, Lieutenant Hearn was killed by a machine gun bullet which passed through his chest.

Part 4, "Wake," is retrospective, a brief review of the invasion wave of Part 1. The reality of the invasion has not conformed to expectations. Even after the fact, Major Dalleson deludes himself about the significance of the campaign, supposing that the forces Cummings finally deployed with naval support behind Japanese lines were decisive. Even more self-conscious characters such as Hearn and Cummings catch themselves in self-deceptions. Hearn believes that he is rebelling against Cummings by crushing a cigarette on the general's immaculate floor when in fact he is playing his superior officer's game, getting himself into a position where Cummings is able to employ Hearn as merely another pawn in his military strategy. Cummings, in turn, bitterly admits to himself that Hearn has a way of depriving him of his sense of command, for Hearn (who is something like a wayward son) represents the intractability of the fighting force Cummings wants to regard as an extension of himself. Mailer brilliantly reveals the ironies of Cummings' command in the general's discovery of the cigarette butt "mashed into the duckboards in a tangled ugly excrement of black ash, soiled paper, and brown tobacco." Cummings has been having bouts of diarrhea; what he sees on the floor is a manifestation of his lack of control, his inability to make his body, like his men, obey his rigorous schedule. In this encyclopedic novel—Mailer's attempt to write the equivalent of Leo Tolstoy's *War and Peace* (1865-1869) in his generation, to show that, like Napoleon, Cummings fails to reduce history to the curve of his desire—no character can claim mastery over himself or the world, for the interplay between individuals and events is too complex, too contingent, to be predictable.

An American Dream, by its very title, points to Mailer's fascination with the notion that America is a complex fiction, a drama of reality that is captured in the dynamic language of its narrator, Steven Rojack, Mailer's hipster hero *par excellence*, a war hero, a college chum of John Kennedy, a congressman, college professor, psychologist, television personality, and actor. All of Rojack's actions have to be viewed within the existential requirements of reality in the novel rather than within rigid moral codes applied by readers who want to keep "concepts firmly in category." For some readers, the novel's sense of absolute relativity, of moral fluidity, is repugnant, and *An American Dream* has been rejected out of hand as Mailer's most disturbing work, since Rojack as hipster does not merely live close to violence; he purges and cleanses himself through murdering his wife, Deborah. Virtually the entire novel is written in a style that dramatizes Rojack's search for a new basis on which to live. After considering suicide, Rojak does away with his wife. He then goes on to find a lover, confronts his former wife's father, loses his lover to murder, again considers suicide, and finally departs for Guatemala on his metaphoric trip toward selfhood.

The measure of Mailer's progress as a writer can be taken in *Why Are We in Vietnam?*, a novel that invites deliberate comparison with Faulkner. Mailer deftly describes a bear hunt, as does Faulkner in "The Bear," that explores the fundamental meanings of American identity inherent in the conquest of animals and environment. Men must prove themselves no matter how much they override the intimate connections between humankind and nature. Rusty, the narrator D. J.'s father, "is fucked unless he gets that bear, for if he don't, white men are fucked more and they can take no more." This kind of reasoning leads to Vietnam, Mailer implies, just as the hunting of bear leads to slavery and other forms of subjugation in Faulkner. Both D. J. and Faulkner's Ike McCaslin come to identify with the animals whose lives they take and with the nature they usurp, so that they must also commune with their feeling of solidarity with life itself.

However close Mailer comes to Faulkner in terms of style and theme, *Why Are We in Vietnam?* is still an insistently original novel. In the passage quoted above, for example, the point of view is wholly that of D. J., of the Texan teenager who has never encountered the raw elements of life, who is a disc jockey in his ventriloquizing of many voices in the manner of a radio rock-music personality. Although the prose has Faulkner's relentless flow, its flippant and frenetic beat suggests the repetitive rhythms of technology that heat up D. J.'s talk.

Mailer's playful sport with his narrator's identity is striking. Is D. J. "a Texas youth for sure or is he a genius of a crippled Spade up in Harlem making all this shit up?" Or is D. J. imitating a "high I.Q. Harlem Nigger"? "There is no security in this consciousness," he maintains, since much of what one takes to be reality is an American dream, or rather a "dream field," a "part of a circuit" with "you swinging on the inside of the deep mystery." Inevitably, one is reminded of Ralph Ellison's *Invisible Man* (1952) narrated by a shifting persona, a man of many guises who impersonates others, who like D. J. follows many channels, as if he is broadcasting to the world at large, a world he has somehow subsumed in his supple prose. D. J. brashly appropriates and transforms the styles of others; whereas Ellison's narrator mellowly hints that on the "lower frequencies" he speaks for "you," D. J. commands: "Goose your frequency"—in other words, rev up your sensibility, your reception of the totality D. J. imagines.

As in *An America Dream*, the tendency for the language to turn mystical is checked, even substantiated, by scatological images and metaphors. Some readers find the style offensive, but it is absolutely at the heart of Mailer's vision, since he wants to show on a visceral level how the ideology of consumption works. Because he believes that "the secrets of existence, or some of them anyway, are to be found in the constructions of language" ("The Metaphysics of the Belly"), his style must go to the scatological site of those secrets. To extend D. J.'s remark, the world is "shit" made up by human beings, and in America such "shit" prevails because of the incredible amount of resources that are used, turned into waste products, into refuse which Americans refuse to see; as Mailer sums it up in "The Metaphysics of the Belly": "Ambitious societies loathe scatological themes and are obsessed with them." The last words of the novel, "Vietnam, hot dam," reflect D. J.'s anticipation; here is still another frontier on which to test himself, another territory for him to explore like Huckleberry Finn, to whom he compares himself at the beginning of the novel. D. J., "disc jockey to America," echoes the country's heated urge to dominate, to damn itself. Or is the minority voice mimicking the majority's will? "Which D. J. white or black would possibly be worse of a genius if Harlem or Dallas is guiding the other, and who knows which?" All the jive talk keeps the channels of possibility open at the end of *Why Are We in Vietnam?*, so that the question of the title has been answered in some ways but is still open-ended, like the identity of the narrator. The reader is left perfectly pitched between alternative readings, once again in the grip of the existential reality that Mailer has faultlessly articulated.

The Armies of the Night climaxed a period of impressive creativity for Mailer in the mid-1960's. A culmination of the self-review he began in *Advertisements for Myself* and *Cannibals and Christians*, it is a definitive portrait of himself as writer and actor, a discovery of his nonfiction aesthetic, and a subtle amalgam of documentary notation and novelistic interpretation that convincingly captures the complexity and ambiguity of the march on the Pentagon. The book's authority is established by its point of view: Mailer's assessment of himself in the third person, sticking close to his own consciousness. Thus, Mailer is able to preserve the spontaneity of historic moments in which he is free to act like a fool or a philosopher while reserving the right as an aloof narrator to judge himself and others with the benefit of hindsight and later research. The Mailer of the march is at various times "the Beast," "the Historian," "the Participant," "the Novelist," and "the Ruminant," all of which emphasize the many different guises he assumes depending upon the evolving context of his actions.

The book shuttles from such intimate dialogue and precise character delineation to panoramic sweeps of the crowds of the Pentagon march. Book 2, "History as a Novel," portrays Mailer as actor in order to show that history is understood only through a deep appreciation of the intersection of very personal feelings and public affairs. No episode, no idea, no impression remains unqualified by the circumstances out of which it arises, and chapter titles constantly emphasize the way in which the literary imagination shapes historical experience.

Book 2, "The Novel as History," goes even further than book 1 in suggesting that history as a whole can make sense only when the interpreter employs all the "instincts of the novelist," for the record of the march is contradictory, fragmentary, and skewed by various viewpoints. Only an act of profound imagination, a reading of the significance of the event itself, can possibly make its constituent parts coalesce, and Mailer convincingly shows that he has studied the record and found it wanting. History is essentially interior and intuitive, he avers. He then proceeds to elaborate a complex re-creation of events that concretely exposes the factitiousness of newspaper accounts.

Beyond the immediate causes and consequences of the march on the Pentagon, Mailer sees the event as a rite of passage for the young marchers, especially the ones who refuse to flee when their fellows are brutally beaten into submission in one of the most riveting and frightening pages in all Mailer's writing. The coming of knowledge, of a historical fatalism, creeps into both Mailer's prose and his characters' weary postures as he recites events from America's past that reveal that it was founded on a rite of passage. It is as if these young people are suddenly imbued with historical consciousness, although Mailer's ruminations and their agony are kept separate on the page. Nevertheless, in his coda he suggests that if the march's end took place in the "isolation in which these last pacifists suffered naked in freezing cells, and gave up prayers for penance, then who was to say they were not saints? And who to say that the sins of America were not by their witness a tithe remitted?" His final words balance an earlier passage where he describes the marchers' opponents, "the gang of Marshals" who in their "collective spirit" emit "little which was good," and one of whom "paid tithe to ten parallel deep lines rising in ridges above his eye brows." Mailer achieves a harmony of form and an equilibrium of language that make the novel's ending seem as complex as the history it imagines and as moving in its depiction of ignorance and confusion as the Matthew Arnold poem "Dover Beach," from which Mailer's title is taken.

While they are satisfactory in sections, *Of a Fire on the Moon*, *The Fight*, and Mailer's other writings from the late 1960's to the mid-1970's do not equal *Marilyn*, his follow-up study of the ambiguities of fiction and history so magnificently explored in *The Armies of the Night*. *Marilyn* has a twofold purpose: to measure faithfully and evaluate the obstacles that bar the biographer's way to a full understanding of his subject's life, and to suggest tentatively a biographical method which will aim at re-creating the whole person even though conceding that the search for wholeness is elusive and problematical.

Furthermore, Monroe ranks with Mailer's other major characters, such as General Cummings. Just as Cummings works to make himself an instrument of his own policy, so Monroe paints herself into the camera lens as an instrument of her own will. She is Napoleonic and yet divided against herself, a Dreiserian character who traverses the continent in quest of her true self in much the same way as Lovett, O'Shaugnessy, and Rojack do, detecting voids in themselves and voyaging to find their genuine identities. Much of Mailer's work in film, and his discussions of film in "Some Dirt in the Talk" and "A Course in Film-Making" (both collected in *Existential Errands*), lead directly to his perception of Monroe's disrupted sense of self. Although his more recent "imaginary memoir," *Of Women and Their Elegance*, in which Monroe recalls her last years, seems less substantial than *Marilyn*, he carries his concern with "twin personalities" a step further by integrating his narrative with Milton Greene's provocative photographs, which are studies in the doubling of personalities in a divided world.

Set against the background of his reflexive writing of the 1960's and 1970's, *The Executioner's Song* is a startling book. Its sentences are simple and clear, with an occasionally striking but not elaborate metaphor. Absent from the narrative is Mailer's characteristic sentence or paragraph, which is long and comprehensive—an encyclopedic attempt to gather all of reality in one magnificent statement. There is no intrusive voice to sum up the life of Gary Gilmore, a convicted and executed murderer, and the age in which Gilmore grows to kill. Mailer does not explicitly explore a theory of biography, and does not comment, except in his afterword, on his interactions with the life he has written. His book seems keyed to a new aesthetic.

In spite of its 1,056 pages, *The Executioner's Song* is not a garrulous work; it is a quiet book punctuated by myriad silences and a spare style. There is a double space following nearly every paragraph of the book, indicating the gap between events, the momentary pause that intervenes even in events that seemingly follow one another swiftly and smoothly. Reality is defined by these frequent intervals of silence, periods of stillness that intimate how much is left unsaid and how many characters fail to connect with one another. Gilmore is the most solitary character of all, cut off in large part from humanity and therefore able to murder.

Reading such sparely created scenes, one is tempted to comb through the details over and over again in order to search for the pertinent clue that will point to the meaning of Gilmore's story, but as Joan Didion points out in her review in *The New York Times Book Review* (October 7, 1979), "the very subject of *The Executioner's Song* is that vast emptiness at the center of the Western experience, a nihilism antithetical not only to literature but to most other forms of human endeavor, a dread so close to zero that human voices fade out, trail off, like skywriting."

Mailer is a keen observer of the American scene. His reports on public events become panoramic discussions of individuals in confrontation with society.

Other major works

SHORT FICTION: *New Short Novels* 2, 1956; *The Short Fiction of Norman Mailer*, 1967.

PLAY: *The Deer Park: A Play*, 1967.

POETRY: *Deaths for the Ladies and Other Disasters*, 1962.

NONFICTION: *The White Negro*, 1957; *The Presidential Papers*, 1963; *Cannibals and Christians*, 1966; *The Bullfight*, 1967; *The Idol and the Octopus: Political Writings on the Kennedy and Johnson Administrations*, 1968; *Miami and the Siege of Chicago: An Informal History of the Republican and Democratic Conventions of 1968*, 1969; *Of a Fire on the Moon*, 1970; *The Prisoner of Sex*, 1971; *The Long Patrol: 25 Years of Writing from the Work of Norman Mailer*, 1971 (Robert Lucid, ed.); *Existential Errands*, 1972; *St. George and the Godfather*, 1972; *The Faith of Graffiti*, 1974 (with Mervyn Kurlansky and Jon Naar); *The Fight*, 1975; *Some Honorable Men: Political Conventions 1960-1972*, 1975; *Genius and Lust: A Journey Through the Major Writings of Henry Miller*, 1976;

Pieces and Pontifications, 1982; *Pablo and Fernande: Portrait of Picasso as a Young Man, an Interpretive Biography*, 1994.

MISCELLANEOUS: *Advertisements for Myself*, 1959.

Bibliography

Adams, Laura, ed. *Will the Real Norman Mailer Please Stand Up?* Port Washington, N.Y.: Kennikat Press, 1974.

Braudy, Leo, ed. *Norman Mailer: A Collection of Critical Essays*. Englewood Cliffs, N.J.: Prentice-Hall, 1972.

Bufithis, Philip H. *Norman Mailer*. New York: Ungar, 1978.

Gordon, Andrew. *An American Dreamer: A Psychoanalytic Study of the Fiction of Norman Mailer*. Rutherford, N.J.: Fairleigh Dickenson University Press, 1980.

Lennon, J. Michael, ed. *Conversations with Norman Mailer*. Jackson: University Press of Mississippi, 1988.

_____ . *Critical Essays on Norman Mailer*. Boston: G. K. Hall, 1986.

Lucid, Robert F., ed. *Norman Mailer: The Man and His Work*. Boston: Little, Brown, 1971.

Manso, Peter, ed. *Mailer: His Life and Times*. New York: Simon & Schuster, 1985.

Merrill, Robert. *Norman Mailer*. Boston: Twayne, 1978.

Mills, Hilary. *Norman Mailer: A Biography*. New York: Empire Books, 1982.

Poirier, Richard. *Norman Mailer*. New York: Viking Books, 1972.

Solotaroff, Robert. *Down Mailer's Way*. Urbana: University of Illinois Press, 1974.

Wenke, Joseph. *Mailer's America*. Hanover, N.H.: University Press of New England, 1987.

BERNARD MALAMUD

Born: Brooklyn, New York; April 26, 1914   **Died:** New York, New York; March 18, 1986

Principal short fiction

The Natural, 1952; *The Assistant*, 1957; *A New Life*, 1961; *The Fixer*, 1966; *The Tenants*, 1971; *Dubin's Lives*, 1979; *God's Grace*, 1982; *The People*, 1989.

Other literary forms

While acknowledging his significant achievements as a novelist, many critics believe that Bernard Malamud's most distinctive and enduring contributions to American fiction are to be found in his short stories, particularly those collected in *The Magic Barrel* (1958) and *Idiots First* (1963).

Achievements

With novelists such as Saul Bellow and Philip Roth, Malamud is among the most distinguished of a number of Jewish American writers who did much to set the tone of postwar American fiction. In his eight novels and numerous short stories, Malamud transcends the Jewish experience so ably chronicled by the so-called Jewish literary renaissance writers by using Jewish life as a metaphor for universal human experience. By detailing the plight of his Jewish characters in tales that blend both the real and the symbolic, he reveals the common humanity of all people.

Both a traditionalist and an experimenter in his fiction, Malamud won rave reviews, literary plaudits, and many awards. *The Magic Barrel* brought a National Book Award in 1959. In 1967, *The Fixer* won for him a second National Book Award as well as a Pulitzer Prize. In addition, he was president of the International Association of Poets, Playwrights, Editors, Essayists, and Novelists (PEN Club) from 1979 to 1981.

Biography

Bernard Malamud was born in Brooklyn to Russian immigrant parents. His father, like Morris Bober in *The Assistant*, was a small grocer, the family moving around Brooklyn as business dictated. When Malamud was nine years old, he had pneumonia and began a period of intensive reading. Later, encouraged by his teachers, he also began writing short stories.

From 1932 to 1936, Malamud was a student at the City College of New York. He later began work on an M.A. degree at Columbia University, and, while teaching night school at Erasmus Hall, his own alma mater, he started writing in earnest. He married Ann de Chiara in 1945, and four years later, he and his family moved to Corvallis, Oregon, where for twelve years Malamud taught English at Oregon State. A son was born before he left for Corvallis, a daughter after he arrived. While there, he published his first four books; after leaving, he wrote his satire of academic life in an English department, *A New Life*. Returning to the East in 1961, Malamud taught for many years at Bennington College in Vermont. He received numerous awards for his fiction, including two National Book Awards and a Pulitzer Prize. Malamud died in New York on March 18, 1986.

Analysis

Malamud's singular achievement is to have captured the experience of Jews in America at a point of transition between cultures. His characters—not only the Jews but also their Gentile counterparts—are not yet quite a part of American culture, nor have they fully abandoned the old culture of which they are no longer members. Out of this sense of dislocation and the struggle to create a new life, Malamud created most of his early stories and novels. Although not all the novels have Jewish protagonists—the first two in fact do not—the dilemma is constant; the Gentile characters are as displaced and alienated as the Jewish ones.

In *The Natural*, Iris Lemon tells the protagonist that all people have two lives, "the life we learn with and the life we live with after that. Suffering is what brings us toward happiness." Although her statement requires qualification, it is a suggestive summary of the major theme of Malamud's work: the journey toward a new life, a journey marked by suffering, which may or may not be redemptive. In fact, however, Malamud's characters usually have three lives: one from which they have not learned and which they are attempting to leave behind, a life the reader sees in flashbacks and confessions as well as in brief opening scenes; a middle life, the learning life, which is the substance of the books; and the new life promised to successful characters at the end. Malamud's novels, then, are in the tradition of the *Bildungsroman*, but they have older protagonists than do most American novels of education. What Malamud depicts in each of his novels is a renewed attempt to find new life and convert suffering to meaning, a second journey toward knowledge.

Malamud's novels usually begin with a journey away from a past life. Whether European Jews coming to America or moving from their *shtetl* to Kiev, or whether American Jews traveling from New York to Oregon or baseball players leaving the country for the big city, Malamud's protagonists are always travelers, uneasy with their past, uncertain of their future. What all Malamud's characters must learn, however, is that they have to accept responsibility for their past actions. Acceptance of the law, curbing one's appetite, is the first lesson. Yet law alone is not enough, and Malamud's questers must pass a second test as well for their journeys to be successful: the test of love, of dream, of acceptance of life in its fullness and ambiguity.

Malamud's first novel, *The Natural*, is a fanciful combination of American baseball lore with the myth of the wasteland. Here, the wasteland is a New York baseball team, the Knights, whose coach, Pop Fisher, is the fisher king of the legend. The quester and protagonist of the novel is Roy Hobbs; his name meaning "rustic king," Roy undergoes a double-edged test to see if he can bring life to the baseball team, but the center of the novel is what Roy himself does—or does not—learn from the tests, the chance of a new life for the quester. Though *The Natural* is in many ways the least Jewish of Malamud's novels, it is the prototype for the rest of his fiction; the story it tells and the patterns it uses are those that persist through Malamud's work.

The pregame section of the novel, the brief history of the past life in which Hobbs does not learn and that he will attempt to leave behind, opens with the image of Hobbs staring at his own reflection in the train window. This inability to look beyond himself, his egocentric view of the world, is Hobbs's undoing. Both parts of Roy's testing are also prefigured in this section, which is a microcosm of the novel as a whole. In the public test, Roy, a pitcher, is challenged by an established batting king, whom Roy strikes out as Malamud draws the mythic parallels. The cost of that success is that Roy slays his first father-figure; his mentor, who catches the pitches without adequate chest protection, is injured and dies.

If Roy is at least partially successful in his physical challenge, he is not at all so in the world of moral choice. In the pregame section, he is questioned by the first of the women in the novel, Harriet Bird. The episode is based on the real-life shooting of a ballplayer. Harriet invites Roy up to her hotel room. She tests him with a series of questions about the value of his ambitions, but when Roy's self-centered answers reveal the limits of his aspirations—he plays only for his own glory—his unalloyed confidence is rewarded with a bullet.

The nine inninglike sections of the novel that follow repeat more spaciously the double test the quester has to undertake to revitalize the team and prove himself worthy of a new life. When Roy arrives, everything is dismal; the Knights are losing, the players are dispirited, Pop Fisher is ailing. Even the drinking fountain produces only rusty water. Once Roy begins to play, however, the team's luck changes. Armed with his mythic bat, Wonder Boy, Roy hits five home runs and energizes the team. Rain falls, and the process of restoring life-giving water to the land begins. Roy, however, gets his chance to play only when another player, Bump Baily, is injured. Again, Roy's success depends on the suffering of another, suffering on which Roy is too willing to capitalize. Roy and Bump are doubles, Bump a darker projection of many of Roy's faults. As the fans and team members point out, they share a common limitation: They play for themselves rather than for the team. The high point of Roy's career is Roy Hobbs Day, an event that occurs in the middle of this symmetrical novel. He is given a white Mercedes, a symbolic lancer on which he proudly rides around the stadium.

Roy's acceptance speech has only one theme, his own greatness, and from this triumph, Roy's downward path, indicated by his batting slump, begins. Although there are short times of solid hitting, as when Roy agrees to play for another, the on-field slump is accompanied by Roy's involvement with the illegal off-the-field dealings of the team's owner, who is setting up the throwing of the league playoffs, a fictive event modeled on the notorious "Black Sox" scandal of the 1919 World Series. Roy is in a world beyond his experience. Baffled by the owner's oily, cliché-ridden speeches, Roy participates in the fix. Although at the end of the playoff game Roy tries to play well to reverse the evil he has already done, it is too late; he can no longer free himself and strikes out. The story that begins with Roy striking out an aging star comes full circle with a new young pitcher striking out Roy.

In the private half of the test, Roy once again fails. As he earlier made the wrong choice with Harriet Bird, he once again makes the wrong moral choices in this section of the novel. He becomes involved with the dark lady, Memo Paris, and they drive off together to a beach, even though the sign cautions danger, warning them of polluted water. There can be no symbolic cleansing here. Memo tries to explain the values she has learned from the suffering in her past, but what she has learned is solely to look out for herself. Roy wants to say something comparable about his own life, but he can think of nothing except more boasting about his future. When he returns to the ballfield after this episode, his grim future is apparent and his lack of control is magnified.

Memo's counterpart, the redemptive lady of the lake, is Iris Lemon. Like Memo and Harriet, she is associated with birds, flowers, and water, and as with Memo, the key scene involves a journey to the lake; Iris' role, however, is as potential savior of Roy. They drive together to a lake sheltered from the outside world, and it is there that Iris, too, questions Roy about his values, but she tries to lead him beyond boasting. She begins a confession of her own life. Although she is a grandmother at thirty-three, she has learned from her suffering, has transformed it into meaning. Roy is thirty-four, but something about Iris' confession repels him. They make love and Iris becomes pregnant—she is the only fruitful woman in the novel—but Roy finally rejects her. In the last game of the playoffs, he sees her in the stands, but he is intent on trying to hit a dwarf who habitually heckles him from the bleachers. The ball instead hits Iris, who has stood to cheer for Roy. In the final scene between them, Iris tells Roy that she is pregnant, that he has created a new life for another at least, and she asks Roy to hit one for their child. It is too late, and Roy strikes out. He thinks of all the wrong choices he has made and wants to undo them, but he cannot.

In Malamud's second novel, *The Assistant*, the surface of the myth is quite different. The pastoral world of baseball gives way to an urban business setting. The rustic king gives way to the petty thief, and the myth of heroic action on which the fate of many depends is replaced by the legend of a saint.

These differences sketched, however, *The Assistant* remains another telling of Malamud's basic myth. For most critics, it is his most successful; the fusion of romance and realism, of surface accuracy with poetic evocation, is seamless and compelling. Like Roy Hobbs, Frankie Alpine, the protagonist of *The Assistant*, is without parents. Both find older men from whom to learn, and both are partially responsible for their deaths. When the lessons they encounter involve renunciation, a check on their passions, they refuse to heed the wisdom. Both learn the wrong lessons from their suffering, at least for a time, and both cheat for financial gain. The two novels are stories of their protagonists' education, and they both open with a glimpse of the old life: Frankie Alpine and a friend rob Morris Bober, the Jewish shopkeeper to whom Alpine apprentices himself. That old life indicated, Malamud settles into the central concern of his books: the middle life, the learning life, where suffering may promise the characters a new and better future.

Frankie returns to the scene of his robbery and begins to help Morris Bober in the grocery store. The relationship between the two is one of father and son, typically cast as master-assistant, an educational apprenticeship. There are three pairs of natural fathers and sons in the novel, and they contrast with Frankie and Morris in their inadequacy. The most promising of these is that of Nat Pearl, one of Frankie's rivals for Helen Bober's affection, with his father. Nat becomes a lawyer, but although he rises financially, he is shallow compared to Alpine, and his treatment of Helen is unkind. Less successful is the relationship of the loutish Louis Karp with his father, who is trying to arrange a marriage between Louis and Helen. The worst is that between Detective Minogue, who investigates the burglary, and his son Ward, who, with Frankie, has perpetrated it.

What Frankie must learn from his surrogate father is stated in a crucial scene in which Frankie asks Morris why Jews suffer so much. Morris first answers that suffering is a part of human existence: "If you live, you suffer." He goes on, though, to indicate that suffering can be meaningful if one suffers not only *from* but also *for*. "I think if a Jew don't suffer for the Law, he will suffer for nothing." Frankie's question is ironically self-directed, for it is Alpine himself, the non-Jew, who is suffering more than he has to: He is suffering not only the existential guilt that comes with living but also the contingent guilt that comes from his own stealing. Like Roy Hobbs, Alpine cannot check his appetite, and he continues to steal from Morris even while trying to atone for the earlier robbery. Though he steals only small amounts, though he promises himself he will repay Bober, and though he assures himself that he is really a good man, Alpine continues to violate the law, and he suffers unnecessarily for this violation. At the end of the novel, Alpine becomes a Jew and replaces Bober in the store—an acknowledgment of guilt for the suffering Alpine has imposed on others and on himself and the resolve to be like a Jew in suffering for something, in making suffering meaningful.

Alpine must learn more than simply law, however, for human needs are more complex than that. When Helen Bober meets Nat Pearl on the subway, he is carrying a thick law book; her own book seems to her protection, and when he asks what it is, she replies, *Don Quixote*. Like Quixote, she is a dreamer, unsatisfied with her life as it is, and it is this quality that she will share with Frankie and that draws them together. The dialectic that informs Malamud's work is represented here: the law book, from a discipline that recognizes human limitations and demands human attention to the responsibilities of this world, and *Don Quixote*, the book that allows one to look beyond these limits and provides a model for noble action. Helen rejects Nat Pearl because the law is insufficient by itself. Her action is not a rejection of the law, for she rejects Alpine, too, when he lives in a world of dreams, unbound by law, for his dreams lead him into actions the law forbids. The generative force is a synthesis of the two.

Helen is, then, the other person from whom Frankie will learn. That he has the capacity for knowledge and for gentle action—as well as for the lawlessness that has marked his life—is shown by his constant identification with St. Francis. Frankie is from San Francisco, and his name resembles that of the saint. He looks at pictures of and dreams about St. Francis, striving for his quality of goodness. With Helen, too, though, Frankie must learn to moderate his passions; with her, too, he violates the law. He climbs an airshaft to watch her showering, a voyeur, like so many Malamud characters. The mirror having been replaced by a glass, the glass remains itself a partition, separating the dreamer from the object of his desires. More serious is his rape of Helen in the park. It is the low point of the novel: Morris fires Frankie; his business is failing and Morris tries to commit suicide. Frankie looks at himself in the mirror, finds himself trapped inside a prisonlike circle, and hates himself for always having done the wrong thing. He returns to the store and resolves to bring it back to life for the hospitalized Morris. Although Helen and her mother do not like Frankie's return, they have little choice but to accept him, and although Frankie occasionally backslides, he makes firmer progress at controlling his passions.

Unlike *The Natural*, with its unambiguously pessimistic ending, *The Assistant* ends on a note of hope. Morris has died and Frankie has taken his place, and there is a suggestion that Frankie may be entrapped by the small grocery and poverty of the Bobers' life, but there is also, in his conversion to Judaism and in his gradual winning of Helen's trust, a more powerful suggestion that he has learned the lessons of love and law, of dream and check, and that this middle life, for all its suffering, may indeed bring him toward happiness and offer him the promise of new life.

The Fixer is Malamud's most ambitious novel, both because the reality he creates to embody his myth—the historical trial of a Russian Jew accused of murdering a Christian boy—is the most distant from his own experience and because the purpose of the tale, its philosophic underpinnings, is the most explicit and has the most scope.

As usual the novel opens with a journey. The main character, Yakov Bok, sees his travels, the leaving of his *shtetl* for a new life in Kiev, as an escape from his past. Bok attempts to strip away his Jewishness: He shaves his beard and cuts his earlocks; on the ferry across the river to his new hell, he drops his prayer things into the water. In this version of Malamud's story, Bok is betrayed by both men (his adoptive father figure) and women, including being falsely imprisoned for the rape and murder of a young village boy.

Most of the novel takes place after the discovery of the murdered child's body and the imprisonment of Bok. The prison is a consistent metaphor in Malamud for the confined lives of his characters; Bok has left a figurative prison for a literal one. Malamud allows Bok escape through the agency of his mind, especially in his dreams. Like those of most of Malamud's characters, however, Yakov's dreams are full of bitterness and terror. If they provide him with a vision and a remembrance of life beyond the prison, they also remind him of the limits of his existence.

A second relief for Bok is that one of the Russian prosecutors, Bibikov, knows of Bok's innocence, and they share a philosophical discussion, its base in Spinoza, throughout the novel. Bok emphasizes that Spinoza, although he is a philosopher who asserts human freedom, recognizes that humankind is limited; his name for that restrictive force is Necessity. The accumulated suffering in *The Fixer* is a powerful documentation of Necessity, and forces outside human control play a more significant role in this novel than in any other of Malamud's works.

If Necessity is so powerful, asks Bibikov, where does

freedom enter? Bok replies that freedom lies within the mind: Individuals rise to God when they can think themselves into nature. Bok also learns from one sympathetic guard, who quotes to him from the Bible that whoever endures to the end will be saved. Yakov learns to endure, and he does so through the freedom his mind creates. He learns also that thoughtful endurance is not enough, for neither Bibikov nor the guard, Kogin, is allowed even to survive: Bibikov takes his own life; Kogin is murdered.

Bibikov has explained to Bok that there is in Spinoza's philosophy something Bok has missed, another kind of freedom, more limited but nonetheless real: "a certain freedom of political choice, similar to the freedom of electing to think." It is this freedom that Bok finally affirms. He has undergone the extreme suffering that Necessity entails. For most of the novel there is hope that in his mind he is at least free and can create new worlds, and there is hope that he will endure. The novel ends with a more political hope. Bok, at least in his dreams, elects to shoot the tsar. He has created political freedom by electing to think of himself as free. Again he cites Spinoza: If "the state acts in ways that are abhorrent to human nature, it's the lesser evil to destroy it."

In Malamud's fictional world, a blend of both the real and the symbolic, evil, and the suffering that inevitably ensues point the way to ultimate redemption and, therefore, true contentment. The complex moral experience of universal human suffering, responsibility, and love—of which his Jewish protagonists are the embodiment—is the transcending theme of his work.

Other major works

SHORT FICTION: *The Magic Barrel*, 1958; *Idiots First*, 1963; *Pictures of Fidelman: An Exhibition*, 1969; *Rembrandt's Hat*, 1973; *The Stories of Bernard Malamud*, 1983; *The People, and Uncollected Stories*, 1989.

Bibliography

Abramson, Edward A. *Bernard Malamud Revisited*. New York: Twayne, 1993.

Astro, Richard, and Jackson J. Benson, eds. *The Fiction of Bernard Malamud*. Corvallis: Oregon State University Press, 1977.

Berger, Alan L. *Crisis and Covenant: The Holocaust in American Jewish Fiction*. Albany: State University of New York Press, 1985.

Ducharme, Robert. *Art and Idea in the Novels of Bernard Malamud: Toward "The Fixer."* The Hague: Mouton, 1974.

Field, Leslie A., and Joyce W. Field, eds. *Bernard Malamud: A Collection of Critical Essays*. 1970. Rev. ed. Englewood Cliffs, N.J.: Prentice-Hall, 1975.

Kosofsky, Rita N. *Bernard Malamud: A Descriptive Bibliography*. New York: Greenwood Press, 1991.

Lasher, Lawrence M. *Conversations with Bernard Malamud*. Jackson: University Press of Mississippi, 1991.

Ochshorn, Kathleen G. *The Heart's Essential Landscape: Bernard Malamud's Hero*. New York: P. Lang, 1990.

Richman, Sidney. *Bernard Malamud*. Boston: Twayne, 1966.

Salzberg, Joel, ed. *Critical Essays on Bernard Malamud*. Boston: G. K. Hall, 1987.

Solotaroff, Robert. *Bernard Malamud: A Study of the Short Fiction*. Boston: Twayne, 1989.

ARTHUR MILLER

Born: New York, New York; October 17, 1915

Principal drama

The Man Who Had All the Luck, pr. 1944, pb. 1989; *All My Sons*, pr., pb. 1947; *Death of a Salesman*, pr., pb. 1949; *An Enemy of the People*, pr. 1950, pb. 1951 (adaptation of Henrik Ibsen's play); *The Crucible*, pr., pb. 1953; *A Memory of Two Mondays*, pr., pb. 1955; *A View from the Bridge*, pr., pb. 1955 (one-act version); *A View from the Bridge*, pr. 1956, pb. 1957 (two-act version); *Collected Plays*, pb. 1957 (includes *All My Sons*, *Death of a Salesman*, *The Crucible*, *A Memory of Two Mondays*, *A View from the Bridge*); *After the Fall*, pr., pb. 1964; *Incident at Vichy*, pr. 1964, pb. 1965; *The Price*, pr., pb. 1968; *The Creation of the World and Other Business*, pr. 1972, pb. 1973; *The American Clock*, pr. 1980, pb. 1982; *Arthur Miller's Collected Plays, Volume II*, pb. 1981 (includes *The Misfits, After the Fall, Incident at Vichy, The Price, The Creation of the World and Other Business, Playing for Time*); *The Archbishop's Ceiling*, pr., pb. 1984; *Two-Way Mirror*, pb. 1984; *Danger: Memory!*, pb. 1986, pr. 1988; *The Ride Down Mt. Morgan*, pr., pb. 1991; *Last Yankee*, pb. 1991, pr. 1993; *Broken Glass*, pr., pb. 1994.

Other literary forms

Although Arthur Miller's major reputation is as a playwright, he has published reportage, novels, works for both the screen and television, short stories, and book-length photo essays in collaboration with Inge Morath, his wife. He has proved himself remarkably adept at blending reportage, autobiography, and dramatic reflection in his later essay-length books, such as *"Salesman" in Beijing* (1984) and *Spain* (1987). All the important themes of his plays are explored in his nondramatic work, which also contains considerable comment on the nature of drama. *The Theater Essays of Arthur Miller* (1978) and *Conversations with Arthur Miller* (1987) are essential to an understanding of Miller's theory of drama, his career in the theater, his political views, and his work as a whole; as is his autobiography, *Timebends* (1987).

Achievements

Miller has been acclaimed as America's most distinguished dramatist since the death in 1953 of Eugene O'Neill, the father of modern American drama. Because of Miller's direct engagement with the political issues of his day and with the theoretical concerns of contemporary drama, he has often been treated as one of the most significant spokesmen of his generation of writers. His plays continue to be performed all over the world, and his place in the American college curriculum is secure.

Unlike O'Neill, Miller will endure not as a great innovator in dramatic form but as a superb synthesizer of diverse dramatic styles and movements in the service of his capacious understanding that a play ought to embody a delicate balance between the individual and society, between the singular personality and the polity, and between the separate and the collective elements of life. His achievements as a dramatist have been recognized with numerous awards, including Tony Awards in 1947, 1949, and 1953 for, respectively, *All My Sons*, *Death of a Salesman*, and *The Crucible*. *Death of a Salesman* won the Pulitzer Prize in 1949 and made Miller's reputation as a great playwright. The work's main character, Willy Loman, has become a classic American figure, and the play itself has become a fixture of the American literary canon. Miller also received the New York Drama Critics Circle Award in 1947 and 1949 and a Peabody Award for television playwriting in 1981. In 1984, he was honored with the John F. Kennedy Award for Lifetime Achievement.

Biography

Arthur Miller grew up in New York City with an older brother and a younger sister. His father was a prosperous businessman until the Crash of 1929, after which the family suffered through the Depression, a period that had a major impact on Miller's sense of himself, his family, and his society and one that figures prominently in many of his dramas, essays, and stories. During the Depression, Miller drove trucks, unloaded cargoes, waited on tables, and worked as a clerk in a warehouse. These jobs brought him close to the kind of working-class characters who appear in his plays. His observation of his father's fall from financial security and of the way the people immediately around him had to struggle for even a modicum of dignity placed Miller in a position to probe individuals' tenuous hold on their place in society.

Although Miller had been a poor student in school, he was inspired by Fyodor Dostoevski's implacable questioning of individual impulses and societal rules in *The Brothers Karamazov* (1879-1880), and eventually he was able to persuade the University of Michigan to admit him. Almost immediately, he began to write plays that were to receive several Hopwood awards. If Miller was not exactly a Marxist during his college years (1934-1938), he was certainly a radical insofar as he believed that American society had to be made over, to be made fair to the masses of people who had been ruined by the Depression.

Miller's early student plays contain sympathetic portrayals of student militants and union organizers as well as compassionate characterizations of small businessmen and other professional people caught in the economic and political tyranny of capitalism. In the fall of 1938, after his graduation from the University of Michigan with a bachelor of arts degree in English language and literature, Miller joined the Federal Theatre Project in New York City, for which he wrote numerous radio plays and scripts until 1943. Some of these works express his irrepressible interest in social and political issues.

From Miller's earliest student plays to *Death of a Salesman*, there is an evolution in his treatment of individuals in conflict with their society, a gradual realization of conflicts within individuals that both mirror the larger conflicts in society and define a core of singularity in the characters themselves. Undoubtedly, Miller's intense involvement in public affairs in the 1940's and 1950's—his support of various liberal and radical causes and his subsequent testimony about his political commitments before the House Committee on Un-American Activities in 1956 are two examples—reflected and reinforced his need to write social plays.

Miller's marriage to Marilyn Monroe in 1956, far from being the perplexing and amusing sideshow the press made of it, had a significant impact on his writing, not only by encouraging him to focus on female characters in ways he had not done before but also by stimulating him to enlarge on and reconsider the theme of innocence that he had adumbrated in earlier plays. After his divorce from Monroe in 1960, he wrote some of his finest plays and continued to participate in local, national, and international affairs—including two terms

as international president of the International Association of Poets, Playwrights, Editors, Essayists and Novelists (PEN). He was a delegate to the Democratic conventions of 1968 and 1972. Miller married Inge Morath, a photojournalist, in 1962, and the couple collaborated on several travel books. After serving as a lecturer at the University of Michigan in the mid-1970's, Miller retired to a large Connecticut estate, where he continued to write and where he indulged in such hobbies as carpentry and gardening.

Analysis

Miller's plays concern primarily the individual's relationship to society and the issues of personal identity and human dignity. His masterpiece, *Death of a Salesman*, measures the enormous gap between America's promise of inevitable success and the devastating reality of one's concrete failure. Commitment to the false values perpetuated by society blinds one to the true values of human life—personal relationships, family and friendship, love.

In *Death of a Salesman*—originally entitled "The Inside of His Head"—Miller brilliantly solves the problem of revealing his main character's inner discord, rendering Willy Loman as solid as the society in which he tries to sell himself. Indeed, many critics believe that Miller has never surpassed his achievement in this play, which stands as his breakthrough work, distinguished by an extremely long Broadway run, by many revivals, and by many theater awards, including the Pulitzer Prize in 1949. *Death of a Salesman* remains an American classic and a standard text in American classrooms.

Willy Loman desperately wants to believe that he has succeeded, that he is "well liked" as a great salesman, a fine father, and a devoted husband. That he has not really attracted the admiration and popularity at which he has aimed is evident, however, in the weariness that belabors him from the beginning of the play. At the age of sixty-three, nearing retirement, Willy dreads confronting the conclusion that his life has gone offtrack, just like the automobile he cannot keep from driving off the road. His mind wanders because he has lost control: He has trouble keeping up with the bills; he feels hemmed in at home by huge, towering apartment buildings; his sales are slipping drastically; and his sons have thwarted his hope for their success.

Willy is not easily categorized; he is both simple and complex. On the one hand, he has all the modern conveniences that stamp him as a product of American society; on the other hand, he is not content to be simply another social component. As he tells Linda, his wife, who tries to soothe his sense of failure, "some people accomplish something." "A man has got to add up to something," he assures his brother, Uncle Ben. Willy resists the idea that his life has been processed for him—like the processed American cheese he angrily rejects for Swiss, his favorite. Still, he wonders, "How can they whip cheese?" and thus he can be diverted from self-scrutiny to the trivialities of postwar consumer society. Willy worries that he talks too much, that he is fat and unattractive, but he also brags about his persuasive abilities, his knack for knowing how to please people. Similarly, he alternately regards his son Biff as a bum and as having "greatness"; Willy's automobile is alternately the finest of its kind and a piece of junk. Willy is a mass of contradictions who asks why he is "always being contradicted." He has never been able to sort himself out, to be certain of his course in life. He is insulted when his friend Charley offers him a job, because the job offer and Charley's self-assured demeanor—he keeps asking Willy when will he grow up—remind Willy of Uncle Ben. Ben is a man who is "utterly certain of his destiny" and who once extended to Willy a tremendous opportunity in Alaska, an opportunity Willy rejected with regret in favor of a salesman's career. He lives with the might-have-been of the past as though it were his present and even confuses Charley with Ben; as a result, scenes from Willy's past and present follow—and indeed pursue—one another successively in a fuguelike fashion that shows his awareness of his failure to progress. There is a grandeur in Willy's dreams of success; his self-deceptions are derived from his genuine perceptions of life's great possibilities, which are like the big sales he has always hoped to make.

When the play is read aloud, there is an uncanny power in some of its simplest and seemingly pedestrian lines, lines that capture the nuances and innuendos of colloquial language. This subtly effective dialogue is enhanced by a powerful use of human gesture that distinguishes *Death of a Salesman* as a completely realizable stage drama. Toward the end of the play, after Biff, "at the peak of his fury," bluntly tells Willy, "Pop, I'm nothing!" Biff relents, breaks down, sobs, and holds on to Willy, "who dumbly fumbles for Biff's face." This brief intimate encounter encapsulates everything that can be learned about Willy and Biff and about the play's import, for the son renounces the father's ridiculous belief in the son's superiority even as the son clings to the father for support. While Biff rejects Willy, he em-

braces him and has to explain himself to Willy, who is "astonished" and at first does not know how to interpret his son's holding on to him. Willy does not understand why Biff is crying. Willy has always been blind to Biff's needs, has always "fumbled" their relationship, yet—as so often—Willy transforms Biff's words of rejection into an affirmation. The Biff who leans on him is the son who "likes me!" Willy exclaims, after their close but momentary contact. This fleeting instance of family solidarity, however, cannot overcome the abiding family conflicts and misunderstandings, epitomized by Willy's delusion that the insurance money accrued from his suicide will finally make him the good provider, the furtherer of his son's magnificent future.

As American society was experiencing an explosive consumerism and a shift toward conformism, *Death of a Salesman* arrived with astonishing force. Domestically, the country seemed to be in no mood to tolerate individuality or dissent. If that play is about the failure of the American Dream, *The Crucible*, produced four years later, is about the value of human dignity and individuality and the kind of justice one can expect from a majority culture. In this work Miller again probes the corrosive effects of society on the individual.

Miller has connected the origins of *The Crucible*, which is specifically about the Salem witch trials of 1692, with McCarthyism—the national paranoia, hysteria, and general immorality that characterized the anticommunist witch-hunts of the 1950's, spearheaded by Senator Joseph McCarthy. The play bitterly attacks the society that encourages the suppression of individual freedom for the sake of "right" and "conformity." With incisive historical summaries, Miller characterizes the community of Salem, Massachusetts, in 1692, which has been beset by property disputes, by a slackening in religious fervor and an increasing lack of trust among its citizens. Rather than face their inner turmoil, certain of Salem's citizens search for scapegoats, for persons who can take on the society's sense of defeat and frustration, who can be punished, and who can carry away by means of their execution of society's burden of guilt. In short, the Puritans seek signs of the Devil and Devil-worship in their midst in order to dissolve their own dissension. John Proctor speaks against his community's blindness to the true causes of its corruption. Proctor eventually opposes the witch-hunt, because he accepts his own part in having made that hysterical clamor for scapegoats possible. He knows that he has not acted quickly enough to expose Abigail, the chief instigator of the witch-hunt, because he has feared his own exposure as an adulterer. What finally exercises his conscience is not simply that he had previously given way to his lust for Abigail but that he had deluded himself into thinking he no longer cared for her and had even reprimanded his wife, Elizabeth, for failing to forgive him. Elizabeth is unbending but not without cause, for she intuits her husband's tender feelings toward Abigail and suspects that he refuses to know his own mind. Proctor almost relinquishes his good name by confessing to witchery, until he realizes that however deep his guilt and responsibility may be for the community's corruption, he cannot surrender his integrity, his cherished individuality. Like Willy Loman, Proctor reaffirms his own name—"I am John Proctor!"—and prefers his own crucible to his society's severe test of him for its redemption.

The Crucible is not only Proctor's play, however, and as important as its moral and political implications are—it was first received as a parable on McCarthyism and the 1950's hysteria over Communism in America—it deserves analysis as a dramatic whole in the same way that *Death of a Salesman* does. In Miller's superb creation of scenes that require a company of carefully choreographed actors and actresses, he is able to dramatize an entire society and to show the interplay of individual and group psychology.

Miller's plays are a blend of social awareness inherited from the 1930's and a searching concern for their characters' inner lives. His heroes are common, ordinary people in relentless pursuit of their firm convictions or their misguided illusions. In these stories of individuals in conflict with their society, the conflicts that afflict the protagonists mirror conflicts typical of American society as a whole.

Other major works

NOVELS: *Focus*, 1945; *The Misfits*, 1961.

SHORT FICTION: *I Don't Need You Any More*, 1967.

NONFICTION: *Situation Normal*, 1944; *In Russia*, 1969 (photo essay with Inge Morath); *In the Country*, 1977 (photo essay with Morath); *The Theater Essays of Arthur Miller*, 1978 (Robert A. Martin, ed.); *Chinese Encounters*, 1979 (photo essay with Morath); *"Salesman" in Beijing*, 1984; *Conversations with Arthur Miller*, 1987 (Matthew C. Roudané, ed.); *Spain*, 1987; *Timebends: A Life*, 1987; *Arthur Miller and Company*, 1990 (Christopher Bigsby, ed.).

SCREENPLAYS: *The Misfits*, 1961; *Everybody Wins*, 1990.

TELEPLAY: *Playing for Time*, 1980.

Bibliography

Bigsby, C. W. E. *File on Miller*. New York: Methuen, 1987.

Bloom, Harold, ed. *Arthur Miller*. New York: Chelsea House, 1987.

——————— , ed. *Arthur Miller's "Death of a Salesman."* New York: Chelsea House, 1988.

Koon, Helene Wickham, ed. *Twentieth Century Interpretations of "Death of a Salesman."* Englewood Cliffs, N.J.: Prentice-Hall, 1983.

Schleuter, June, and James K. Flanagan. *Arthur Miller*. New York: Frederick Ungar, 1987.

CYNTHIA OZICK

Born: New York, New York; April 17, 1928

Principal short fiction

The Pagan Rabbi and Other Stories, 1971; *Bloodshed and Three Novellas*, 1976; *Levitation: Five Fictions*, 1982; *The Shawl*, 1989.

Other literary forms

Cynthia Ozick is the author of poems, articles, reviews, and essays, as well as short stories. She has also published several novels. Her poems have appeared in journals such as *Epoch*, *Commentary*, *The Literary Review*, and *Judaism*. Her other short works have been published frequently in journals such as those mentioned above and also in a wide variety of others.

Achievements

Often characterized as difficult and involved in syntax and idea, Ozick's works have, nevertheless, received many awards. The short fiction especially has been judged prizeworthy, winning for her such prestigious awards and honors as the Best American Short Stories award (five times), the National Book Award, the American Academy of Arts and Letters Award, the O. Henry Award, the PEN/Faulkner Award, and the Jewish Book Council Award. Immediately consequent to the publication of "Rosa," one of her prizewinning stories, Ozick was invited to deliver the Phi Beta Kappa oration at Harvard University, and she became the first person to receive the Michael Rea Award for career contribution to the short story. In 1988 she was one of ten cultural figures elected to the American Academy and Institute of Arts and Letters.

In spite of her many commendations, however, Ozick has been bothered through most of her career by the question of whether an authentic Jew can or should write imaginative works that call attention to themselves as art forms. Literary artists involved in such activity, Ozick came to believe, are in great danger of becoming worshipers of themselves or, by extension of the thought, proponents of idolatry. Ozick seemed to believe that art existing entirely to delight and satisfy the senses can be argued to be inverted, narcissistic, and finally perverse. In the 1980's, however, Ozick began to realize that creative writers need to use the highest powers of imagination to posit an incorporeal god, as exists in the Jewish faith, and to put forth a vision of moral truth rooted in the history, traditions, and literature of the Jewish people. Ozick's success in this endeavor is manifested not only in her identification as a Jewish American author but also in the number of awards she has received from representatives of the Jewish people. Perhaps most important, however, is her own satisfaction that in her writing she is serving the cause of moral truth according to Mosaic law.

Biography

Born of Russian immigrants who took up residence in the Bronx borough in New York, Cynthia Ozick and her parents and siblings worked in the family drugstore, which kept them in comfort and relative prosperity even through the years of the Great Depression. As a female child, Ozick was not marked for extensive education by her family and community. Nevertheless, she was enrolled at the age of five and a half in a Yiddish-Hebrew school so she could take religious instruction, and her family insisted that she be allowed to stay. The rabbi giving the instruction soon found that she had what he called a "golden head." Successful as she was in religious instruction, however, her public school experiences were difficult and humiliating. It was not until her entrance into Hunter College High School in Manhattan that she was once again made to feel part of an intellectual elite. Her years at New York University, where she earned a B.A. degree in 1949, were followed by attendance at Ohio State University, where she received her M.A. degree in 1951.

In 1952, she married Bernard Hallote. One daughter, Rachel, was born in 1965. Early in her career, Ozick became interested in the Jewish textual tradition, and over the years she became an expert in it. In fiction and nonfiction, she has argued with passion concerning the vital role Judaism has played in Western culture, and she has become for many a spokesperson for the importance of art and artists in the Jewish tradition and for the role of women in Jewish culture.

Analysis

In her essays as well as her fiction, Cynthia Ozick has consistently returned to a handful of themes associated with being Jewish American in a secular society. Her works evince a strong concern with the modern Jew's connection with Jewish culture and morals—particularly the cultural and ethical burdens afflicting generations of Jewish Americans in the wake of the Holocaust. It is impossible, Ozick maintains, to separate modern Judaism from the devastation that Jewish culture endured during World War II. In her use of self-referential devices and other dazzling postmodern presentations of the fantastic, the irreverent, and the grotesque, Ozick—tapping the powers of the creative imagination— conveys the traditions and teachings of Judaism, where magic, dreams, and fantasies are ways to express truth.

"The Pagan Rabbi" is a case in point. It is the story of Isaac Kornfeld, a pious and intelligent man who one day hangs himself from the limb of a tree. Isaac's story is told by a friend who has known Isaac since they were classmates in the rabbinical seminary and who is a parallel character to Isaac. In the same way that the narrator and Isaac are counterparts, the fathers of both men are set up as opposites who agree on one thing only—that philosophy is an abomination that must lead to idolatry. Though the fathers are rivals, the sons accept the apparent differences in their own personalities and remain friends. In time, their different ambitions and talents separate them. The narrator leaves the seminary, marries a Gentile, and becomes a furrier; Isaac continues his brilliant career in the seminary and achieves the peak of his renown at the time of his death, when he has almost reached the age of thirty-six. The narrator, now a bookseller separated from his wife, learns that Isaac has hanged himself with his prayer shawl from a tree in a distant park. Immediately, the narrator takes a subway to the site of the suicide, since Isaac's behavior seems totally alien to his character and personality.

In the remainder of the story, Ozick attempts to explain the odd circumstances of Isaac's death and, by means of the parallelisms, inversions, and doublings, to point to the ramifications of leaving the intellectual path for the mysteries and seductions of the unknown world of fantasy, magic, and dreams. Apparently Isaac, shortly after his marriage, began to seek different kinds of pleasure that may have been associated with the marriage bed and beautiful Scheindel. In line with marriage customs, Scheindel covers her lustrous black hair after the wedding ceremony and subsequently bears Isaac

seven daughters, one after another. As he fathers each daughter, Isaac invents bedtime stories for them, relating to such aberrations as speaking clouds, stones that cry, and pigs with souls. At the same time, Isaac shows an inordinate interest in picnics in strange and remote places.

As Isaac behaves in odder and odder ways for a rabbi, exhibiting unhealthy (because excessive) interest in the natural world, Scheindel becomes more and more puzzled and estranged, since she has no interest in old tales of sprites, nymphs, gods, or magic events. Scheindel's refusal to countenance anything magical is in counterpoint to her escape from the electrified fences in the concentration camp, which seemed a miracle of chance. Isaac's notebook offers little explanation for his behavior, though it is filled with romantic jottings, quotations from lyric poets, and a strange reference to his age, using the means of counting rings as for a tree. Below this unusual computation, Isaac has written a startling message: "Great Pan lives."

The narrator begins to understand more as Scheindel reads a letter written by Isaac and left tucked in his notebook. The letter makes clear that Isaac has eschewed deeply held Jewish beliefs to accept a kind of animism or pantheism, where all matter has life and, moreover, soul. All except humans can live separate from their souls, and thus they are able to know everything around them. Humans, however, cannot live separate from their souls and thus are cursed with the inability to escape from their bodies except through death. Isaac concludes that there may be another route to freedom—exaltation and ecstasy by means of coupling with a freed soul. The idea, once conceived, needs a trial, and Isaac's efforts are subsequently rewarded by the appearance of a dryad, the soul of a tree. The dryad's lovemaking brings Isaac to marvels and blisses that no man, it is said, has experienced since Adam. Isaac errs, however, in trying to trap the dryad into his own mortal condition. In so doing, he loses his own soul. His soul free, Isaac's body is doomed to death. More important, however, the soul retains the visage of the rabbi, who has been and will be the one who walks indifferently through the beauties of the fields, declaring that the sounds, smells, and tastes of the law are more beautiful than anything to be found in the natural world.

Scheindel's repugnance toward, and lack of charity for, her husband's folly surprises the narrator and turns him away from her. The narrator is able to appreciate the subtlety of the rabbi's thinking and the bravery of the pursuit. Yet it is Scheindel who guarded the Mosaic law with her own wasted body during the Holocaust, and Scheindel is the issue here—not intellectual subtlety—she who seemed doomed to death when she was seventeen years old, she who traded her youth and vitality for marriage to a Jewish rabbi. After his conversation with Scheindel, and as an ironic afterthought, the narrator goes home to clear his house of his three paltry houseplants. His gesture next to Isaac's forthright penetration into the forest, however, indicates something of the struggle of every Jew seduced by the pleasures of the beautiful but charged to interpret and guard the laws instead.

By the time of the publication of "The Shawl" in *The New Yorker* and "Rosa," also in *The New Yorker*, Ozick had come to articulate fairly clearly her recognition that imagination need not be a negative, leading to idolatry (the worship of false gods), but a positive, allowing Jews to imagine a god without image. These stories are of exceptional importance and significance in the Ozick canon. In them, Ozick deals directly with the horror of the Holocaust. Rosa is the focal character of both stories.

In "The Shawl," Rosa is a young woman with a baby in her arms wrapped in a shawl that serves not only to shelter the child, Magda, but also to hide her, to muffle her cries, and to succor her. With Rosa is her young niece, Stella, who is jealous of Magda and craves the shawl for her own comfort. Deprived of her shawl, the baby begins to cry and crawl around on the ground. Rosa's dilemma must be excruciatingly painful. She understands that her adolescent niece took the shawl, trying to cling to her own life, and she understands that if she chances getting the baby without the shawl to cover it up, she is likely to lose both her life and Magda's. She chooses to go after the shawl first, and the fatal moment arrives too soon. A German officer finds the child wandering about and hurls her against the electrified fence.

Complicating the issue is the question of who is Magda's father. Early in the story, it is suggested that the father is no Jew, since Magda has blue eyes and blond hair and seems a pure Aryan, a situation that causes Stella to react even more bitterly. As in any nightmare, the dreaded occurs. Stella steals the shawl; the baby cries, wanders about, and is killed. Rosa survives the horrible ordeal as she has survived others, including repeated rapes by German soldiers. She knows that any action will result in her death, so she stuffs the shawl in her own mouth and drinks Magda's saliva to sustain herself. After Rosa and Stella are rescued from the camps, Rosa brings Stella to the United States, where Stella gets a job and Rosa opens an antique shop.

"Rosa" resumes the story some thirty-five years after the occurrences described in "The Shawl." Rosa is still very angry with Stella for her role in Magda's death and is able to get little personal satisfaction working in the antique shop. Apparently, her customers do not want to listen to the stories she has to tell, and one day, extremely angry and apparently insane, Rosa destroys her shop. To escape institutionalization, she agrees to move to what appears to be a poverty-stricken retirement hotel in Miami Beach. Life is difficult for her. The intense heat makes it hard for her to get out into the sunlight in order to shop. When she does eat, she scavenges or makes do with tiny portions, such as a cracker with grape jelly or a single sardine. The condition of her clothes seems to indicate that she has nothing to wear. One morning, however, Rosa makes her way to a supermarket, and there, she meets Simon Persky. Persky is not a person in the ordinary mold. He notices Rosa on a personal level and insists that she respond to him. While Rosa's relationship with Simon Persky is developing, Ozick establishes two parallel plot lines having to do with Rosa's request of Stella that she send Magda's shawl and a request from a Dr. Tree asking Stella to help him conduct research on Rosa's reaction to her imprisonment and ill treatment.

These three plot lines weave about one another, providing the matrices for the action. Rosa is, of course, responsible for saving Stella's life in the concentration camp and bringing her to the United States, and Stella is indirectly responsible for Magda's death, perhaps the single most horrible thing that happened to Rosa in a life full of horrors—the internment, the death of family and friends, assaults and rape by brutal Nazis, near starvation, and, finally, Magda's execution by electric shock. Since Magda's death, Rosa has teetered on the brink of insanity, managing to hold herself together by working and by the creative act of writing letters to an imaginary Magda who, in Rosa's fantasy, has survived and become a professor of Greek philosophy at Columbia University. Stella too has survived in Rosa's imagination in another guise—as a thief, a bloodsucker, evil personified, and the Angel of Death.

The shawl, which Stella agrees to send to Rosa and which finally arrives, acted in Poland during the worst years as an umbrella covering the three people—Rosa, prepubescent Stella, and baby Magda—and providing (illusionary) sustenance and security. After Magda's death, the shawl becomes for Rosa an icon; "idol," "false god," Stella says, since Rosa worships it and prays to it.

Dr. Tree is another threat to Rosa; he is a kind of parasite, living to feed off the horrors attached to other people's lives. He wants to interview Rosa for a book that he is writing on survivors of the Holocaust. His letter to Rosa calling her a survivor is replete with jargon, with clinical terms naming the horrible conditions with neutral language and hiding the grotesque reality under the name of his own Institute for Humanitarian Context. Rosa objects to being called "a survivor" because the word dehumanizes her and every other person on the planet. Persky, by contrast, offers Rosa an actual friendship, a human relationship in concrete, not abstract, terms. Thus he emerges as winner of Rosa's attention, with Dr. Tree dismissed and memories of Magda put on hold for a while.

Discussions of Cynthia Ozick's fiction often include the descriptors "uncompromising," "demanding," and "difficult," characteristics that can diminish a writer's popularity, and consequently, status. For Ozick, however, no such diminution has taken place. Indeed, her reputation has grown steadily and strongly, her writings gaining more attention and herself more rewards. The phenomenon is not, after all, that surprising. If her protestations are stronger than those of other Jewish American writers, her demands are based more clearly in moral imperatives of the Jewish tradition. Yet there is another tradition of which she is a part—an American literary heritage that includes Nathaniel Hawthorne, Herman Melville, Edgar Allan Poe, William Faulkner, writers who clearly work like Ozick, in a realm where the "power of blackness" wrestles with us all.

Other major works

NOVELS: *Trust*, 1966; *The Cannibal Galaxy*, 1983; *The Messiah of Stockholm*, 1987.

NONFICTION: *Art and Ardor*, 1983; *Metaphor and Memory: Essays*, 1989; *What Henry James Knew: And Other Essays*, 1993.

POETRY: *Epodes: First Poems*, 1992.

Bibliography

Bloom, Harold, ed. *Cynthia Ozick: Modern Critical Views*. New York: Chelsea House, 1986.

Burstein, Janet Handler. "Cynthia Ozick and the Transgressions of Art." *American Literature: A Journal of Literary History, Criticism, and Bibliography* 59 (March, 1987): 85-101.

Cohen, Sarah Blacher. *Cynthia Ozick's Comic Art: From Levity to Liturgy*. Bloomington: Indiana University Press, 1994.

Fisch, Harold. "Introducing Cynthia Ozick." *Response* 22 (1974): 27-34.

Friedman, Lawrence S. *Understanding Cynthia Ozick*. Columbia: University of South Carolina Press, 1991.

Kauvar, Elaine M. *Cynthia Ozick's Fiction: Tradition and Invention*. Bloomington: Indiana University Press, 1993.

Lowin, Joseph. *Cynthia Ozick*. New York: Twayne, 1988.

Ozick, Cynthia. "An Interview with Cynthia Ozick." Interview by Elaine M. Kauvar. *Contemporary Literature* 26 (Winter, 1985): 375-401.

Pinsker, Sanford. *The Uncompromising Fiction of Cynthia Ozick*. Columbia: University of Missouri Press, 1987.

GRACE PALEY

Born: New York, New York; December 11, 1922

Principal short fiction

The Little Disturbances of Man: Stories of Men and Women in Love, 1959; *Enormous Changes at the Last Minute,* 1974; *Later the Same Day,* 1985; *The Collected Stories,* 1994.

Other literary forms

In addition to her short fiction, Grace Paley has published collections of poetry and coedited *A Dream Compels Us: Voices of Salvadoran Women* (1989). She has also contributed uncollected short stories to *The New Yorker* and essays on teaching to various journals.

Achievements

Despite her small literary output, Paley's innovative style and the political and social concerns she advocates in her work have enabled her to generate significant critical attention. To speak out is a basic theme in Paley's stories, and it reflects her own life and political principles. The women in her stories are like her; they are political activists who speak on nuclear energy, the environment, and on all conditions that affect the world into which their children are born. This intermingling of politics and art brought Paley mixed reviews, but she has continued to stretch the limits of the short story, in both form and content. In 1970, she received an award for short fiction from the National Academy of Arts and Letters. She was elected to the American Academy and Institute of Arts and Letters in 1980, and in 1988 and 1989 she received the Edith Wharton Award. Paley is also the recipient of a Guggenheim Fellowship and a National Council of the Arts grant. She was named state author of New York in 1986. Her other prizes include the $25,000 Rea Award for the Short Story in 1992.

Biography

The daughter of Russian immigrant parents, Grace Paley was born and raised in New York City. Both her parents, Mary (Ridnyik) Goodside and Isaac Goodside, a physician, were political exiles in their early years and passed on their political concern to their daughter. At home they spoke Russian and Yiddish as well as English, exposing their daughter to both old and new cultures. Grace studied in city schools and after graduation attended Hunter College in 1938 and later New York University. She was not, however, interested in formal academic study and dropped out of college. She had begun to write poetry and in the early 1940's studied with W. H. Auden at the New School for Social Research. In 1942 she married Jess Paley, a motion picture cameraman. The couple had two children and separated three years later but were not legally divorced for twenty years. In the 1940's and 1950's, Paley worked as a typist while raising her children and continuing to write. At this time she began her lifelong political involvement by participating in New York City neighborhood action groups.

After many rejections, Paley's first collection of eleven stories, *The Little Disturbances of Man,* was published in 1959. Even though the book was not widely reviewed, critics admired her work. In the meantime, she had begun to teach, and in the early 1960's, she taught at Columbia University and Syracuse University and also presented summer workshops. She also began writing a novel, a project that she did not complete. She increased her political activism, participating in nonviolent protests against prison conditions in New York City and the government's position on the war in Vietnam. A prominent member of the peace movement, she participated in a 1969 mission to Hanoi to negotiate for the release of prisoners of war. In 1973, she was a delegate to the World Peace Conference in Moscow. In 1974, her second collection of stories appeared. It received sporadic condemnation from reviewers, partially because of her political views but also because the writing was termed uneven in quality.

In the 1970's and 1980's, Paley continued her political activism as well as her writing and teaching. She joined with other activists in condemning the Soviet repression of human rights, was a leader in the 1978 demonstrations in Washington against nuclear weapons, and in 1985, along with campaigning against American government policy in Central America, visited Nicaragua and El Salvador. This trip resulted in *A Dream Compels Us: Voices of Salvadoran Women,* published in 1989. Her stories have appeared in *The Atlantic*, *Esquire*, *Accent*, and other magazines. She continues to teach in the New York City area, particularly at Sarah Lawrence College. Paley settled in Greenwich Village in New York City with her second husband, poet, playwright, and landscape architect Robert Nichols.

Analysis

Paley's stories treat traditional themes, focusing on the lives of women and the experiences of love, motherhood, and companionship that bind them together. She presents these themes, however, in inventive rather than traditional structures. Her stories are frequently fragmented and open-ended, without conventional plot and character development. Paley believed these structural innovations made her work more true to life. The stories gain their vitality by Paley's use of distinctive language—the voice, idiom, tone, and rhythms of the New York City locale. She writes best when rendering the razor-tongued Jewish American urban female, with an ironic wit, who does not hesitate to voice her opinions.

"Goodbye and Good Luck," the first story in *The Little Disturbances of Man*, shows her characteristic style and theme. The story begins, "I was popular in certain circles, says Aunt Rose. I wasn't no thinner then, only more stationary in the flesh." Aunt Rose knows what her sister—Lillie's "mama"—does not, that time rushes by relentlessly, that the old generation is quickly forgotten as the new generation supplants it, and that mama's life of stodgy domesticity (the "spotless kitchen") has meant little to her or anyone else as her life slips away. Mama, however, feels sorry for "poor Rosie" because Aunt Rose has not married and led a virtuous life. As a young girl, she could not stand her safe but boring job in a garment factory and took instead a job selling tickets at the Russian Art Theatre, which put on Yiddish plays. The man who hired her said, "Rosie Lieber, you surely got a build on you!" These attributes quickly gained the attention of the Yiddish matinee idol Volodya Vlashkin, "the Valentino of Second Avenue."

Although he was much older than her and had a wife and family elsewhere, Vlashkin set her up in an apartment. Their affair went on—and off—over the years while he had many other lovers, but Rose was not lonely herself when he was gone. She never complained but worshipped him when she had him and was philosophical about his infidelities: An actor needs much practice if he is to be convincing on the stage. While she never asked anything from him, "the actresses . . . were only interested in tomorrow," sleeping lovelessly with wealthy producers for advancement. They got their advancement; now they are old and forgotten. Vlashkin himself is old and retired, and Aunt Rose fat and fifty, when his wife divorces him for all of his past adulteries. He comes back to Rosie, the only woman who never asked anything of him, and they decide to get married. She has had her warm and love-filled life, and now she will have a bit of respectability, a husband—"as everybody knows, a woman should have at least one before the end of the story."

The theme is seen most clearly when Rose contrasts her life with her own mother's. Her mother had upbraided her when she moved in with Vlashkin, but her mother had "married who she didn't like. . . . He never washed. He had unhappy smell . . . he got smaller, shriveled up little by little, till goodbye and good luck." Rosie, therefore, "decided to live for love." No amount of respectability, no husband, advancement, or wealth will save one from imminent change, decay, and death; so live for love, Aunt Rose would say, and you will have the last laugh.

The characters and tone may change in other stories, but the theme remains the same. In "The Pale Pink Roast" Anna sees her former husband and asks him to help her move into her new apartment. He is in "about the third flush of youth," a handsome, charming, but "transient" man. In the midst of hanging her curtains, he stops and makes love to her. Then, admiring her fancy apartment and stylish clothes, he asks archly who is paying for it. "My husband is," is her reply. Her former husband is furious with her. The new husband, she tells him, is a "lovely" man, in the process of moving his business here. Why did you do it, then, her former husband wants to know: "Revenge? Meanness? Why?" "I did it for love," she says.

Over and over Paley's female characters must choose between the safe and boring man and the charming but worthless lover. In "An Interest in Life" the girl has her secure but dull boyfriend yet dreams of the husband who deserted her. In "Distance," Paley tells the same story over again, but this time from the point of view of another character in the story, a bitter old woman full of destructive meanness. She was wild in youth but then opted for the safe, loveless marriage, and it has so soured her life that she has tried to force everyone into the same wrong pattern. Her own very ordinary son is the boring boyfriend of the girl who dreams of her deserter husband. At heart, the old woman understands the young girl, and this is her redeeming humanity.

In a slight variation of theme, "Wants" demonstrates why the love relationship between man and woman must be transitory. The desirable man wants everything out of life; the loving woman wants only her man. "You'll always want nothing," the narrator's former husband tells her bitterly, suggesting a sort of ultimate biological incompatibility between the sexes. The result assuredly is sadness and loneliness, but with islands of warmth to make it endurable. In "Come On, Ye Sons of Art," Kitty is spending Sunday morning with her boyfriend ("Sunday was worth two weeks of waiting"). She is pregnant by him and already has a houseful of children by other fathers. She takes great pleasure in the fine morning she can give her boyfriend. The boyfriend, a traveling salesman, delights in his skill as a salesman. He only regrets he is not more dishonest, like his sister who, ignoring human relationships, has devoted herself to amassing an immense fortune by any means. Kitty's boyfriend wistfully wishes that he too were corrupt, high, and mighty. They are listening to a beautiful piece of music by Purcell on the radio, which the announcer says was written for the queen's birthday; in reality, the music was written not for the queen but for Purcell's own delight in his art, in the thing he did best, and no amount of wealth and power equals that pleasure.

In her later stories, Paley has struck out in new directions, away from the inner-city unwed mothers and the strongly vernacular idiom, to sparse, classical, universal stories. The theme, however, that there is no safe harbor against change and death, and that the only salvation is to live fully, realistically, and for the right things, has not changed. "In the Garden" has, essentially, four characters who appear to be in some country in the West Indies. Lush gardens of bright flowers and birds surround them, suggesting a particularly bountiful nature. One character is a beautiful young woman whose children were kidnapped eight months ago and now are certainly dead. She cannot, however, face this fact, and her talk is constantly about "when they come home." Her husband is a rich landlord who did not give the kidnappers their ransom money; he shouts constantly in a loud voice that everything is well. There is

a vacationing Communist renting one of the landlord's houses, who, out of curiosity, asks the neighbors about the case. He learns that the landlord had once been poor, but now is rich and has a beautiful wife; the landlord could not believe that anything had the power to hurt his luck, and he was too greedy to hand over the ransom money. It is known that it was "his friends who did it." There is an elderly neighbor woman who is dying of a muscle-wasting disease. She had spent much time with the beautiful woman listening to her talk about when the children would return, but now she is fed up with her and cannot stand the husband's shouting. For a while, since the old woman is too wasted to do much more, she follows with her eyes the movements of the Communist, but "sadly she had to admit that the eyes' movement, even if minutely savored, was not such an adventurous journey." Then "she had become interested in her own courage."

At first it may appear that nothing happens in the story, but it is all there. The garden is the world. The young woman with her beauty has won a rich husband; the landlord, through aggressiveness, has clawed his way to the top. Both these modes—beauty and aggressiveness—have succeeded only for a while, but inevitably whatever is gained in the world is lost because all human beings are mortal. The Communist—by being a Communist, "a tenderhearted but relentless person"—suggests someone who will try to find a political way to stave off chance and mortality, but in fact he merely leaves, having done nothing. The old woman, who realizes the fecklessness of trying to help and who has found mere observation of process insufficient, becomes more interested in the course of her own courage in facing up to inevitable change. She and her husband are the only ones who admit to change, and this seems the right position, the tragic sense of life that makes life supportable.

Through the unique and very personal voice of her short stories, Paley vividly, humorously, and emphatically expresses the characters and social concerns of her time. As a result, these works present a delightful, provocative, and moving depiction of a segment of society, a collection of individuals trying to better their lives and their world.

Other major works

POETRY: *Leaning Forward*, 1985; *New and Collected Poems*, 1992.

MISCELLANEOUS: *Long Walks and Intimate Talks*, 1991.

EDITED TEXT: *A Dream Compels Us: Voices of Salvadoran Women*, 1989 (Paley and the staff of New Americas Press, eds.).

Bibliography

Arcana, Judith. *Grace Paley's Life Stories: A Literary Biography*. Champaign-Urbana: University of Illinois Press, 1993.

Baumbach, Jonathan. "Life Size." *Partisan Review* 42, no. 2 (1975): 303-306.

DeKoven, Marianne. "Mrs. Hegel-Shtein's Tears." *Partisan Review* 48, no. 2 (1981): 217-223.

Iannone, Carol. "A Dissent on Grace Paley." *Commentary* 80 (August, 1985): 54-58.

Isaacs, Neil David. *Grace Paley: A Study of the Short Fiction*. Boston: Twayne, 1990.

Marchant, Peter, and Earl Ingersoll, eds. "A Conversation with Grace Paley." *The Massachusetts Review* 26 (Winter, 1985): 606-614.

Paley, Grace. "Grace Paley: Art Is on the Side of the Underdog." Interview by Harriet Shapiro. *Ms.* 11 (May, 1974): 43-45.

Taylor, Jacqueline. *Grace Paley: Illuminating the Dark Lives*. Austin: University of Texas Press, 1990.

CHAIM POTOK

Born: New York, New York; February 17, 1929

Principal long fiction

The Chosen, 1967; *The Promise*, 1969; *My Name Is Asher Lev*, 1972; *In the Beginning*, 1975; *The Book of Lights*, 1981; *Davita's Harp*, 1985; *The Gift of Asher Lev*, 1990; *I Am the Clay*, 1992.

Other literary forms

Wanderings: Chaim Potok's History of the Jews (1978) is a personal reconstruction of four thousand years of Jewish history. Potok has also written essays and book reviews for Jewish and popular periodicals and newspapers. In January, 1988, his stage adaptation of *The Chosen* opened as a short-lived Broadway musical, with music by Philip Springer and lyrics by Mitchell Bernard.

Achievements

Critical acceptance and public acclaim have greeted Potok's novelistic explorations of the conflict between Orthodox Judaism and secular American culture. Potok received the Edward Lewis Wallant Award and a National Book Award nomination for *The Chosen*, his first novel. He received the Athenaeum Award for its sequel, *The Promise*. His sympathetic (critics would say sentimental) portrayal of Jewish fundamentalism and those who choose to leave it highlights the poignancy of an individual's break with tradition. Indeed, Potok's novels test the ability of traditional communities to contribute to the modern world without themselves being assimilated. His evocation of Jewish life in New York in the latter two-thirds of the twentieth century has universal appeal and disturbing implications.

Biography

Born of Orthodox Jewish parents in the Bronx in 1929, Chaim Potok was reared in a fundamentalist culture. Potok's father, Benjamin Potok, was a Polish émigré and no stranger to the pogroms of Eastern Europe. The young Potok was taught that the profound suffering of the Jews would one day transform the world. Yet, as Potok suggests in *Wanderings*, his service as a Jewish chaplain with the United States Army in Korea (1956-1957) confronted him with a world of good and evil that had never heard of Judaism. His attempt to come to terms with this larger world led Potok to a critical investigation of his own Jewish heri-

tage and the limitations of the fundamentalist perspective. Though he had been ordained a Conservative rabbi in 1954, attracted by doctrines more liberal than those of strict Jewish Orthodoxy, Potok has continued his struggle to reconcile fundamental Judaism with the findings of science (as historiography and textual criticism shed new light on ancient traditions). *The Chosen* inaugurated his public search for a voice with which to speak to his heritage as well as to the larger world.

In the early 1960's, Potok taught at the Jewish Theological Seminary in New York, edited *Conservative Judaism*, and in 1965 became an editor with the Jewish Publication Society of Philadelphia. He was married to Adena Mosevitzky in 1958, with whom he would reside in Merion, Pennsylvania. The Potoks would have three children: Rena, Naama, and Akiva.

Analysis

In his novels, Potok returns again and again to the story of a young protagonist coming of age in a culture (usually Jewish) at once mysterious, beautiful, sad, and somehow inadequate. Usually told in the first person, Potok's stories surround the reader with forebodings of the larger, evil world (news of pogroms in Europe, the Holocaust, the first atom bomb) into which his characters are plunged. Potok creates a microcosm of feeling and reaction to events that shake the world. His sentences are simple and reportorial, at times almost a parody of the staccato style of Ernest Hemingway. The stories develop chronologically, though they are frequently invaded by dreams, visions, or voices from the "Other Side."

In each of his stories, Potok sets for himself a question to be answered and reworks his own experiences until he is satisfied with at least a provisional resolution. Controlling metaphors help shape the questions. In *The Chosen*, the baseball game symbolizes the competition between two Jewish cultures, the very strict Hasidic and a more openly assimilationist one, content to become integrated into mainstream American society. What happens to those caught in between those two traditions? The vision of pups being born in *The Book of Lights* represents the entrance of fertile Cabala mysticism into a world of strict Jewish law. How can Jewish mysticism enrich Orthodoxy? Asher Lev's dreams of his mythical ancestor foreshadow the young artist's confrontation with his own culture. What happens when art brings great hurt? The sound of a little door harp symbolizes the transforming power of the imagination for Ilana Davita Chandal of *Davita's Harp*. What is the place of the imagination in Jewish Orthodoxy? What is the place of women? (Davita is Potok's first female protagonist.)

The Chosen recounts the story of Danny Saunders, brilliant son of a Hasidic rabbi, chosen by tradition to succeed his father one day as leader of the fundamentalist community in Brooklyn, New York. Yet Danny is less interested in studying the Talmud (Jewish law) than in probing the works of Sigmund Freud and other secular psychologists. The story closes with the inevitable confrontation between Danny and his father, which is mediated by Danny's friend Reuvan Malter. In the climactic scene in Reb Saunders' office, the old rabbi turns to his son and addresses him as a father for the first time. (For years, Danny had been reared in silence, except for time of Talmud study.) With fatherly tears, Reb Saunders explains that the years of silence created a soul of compassion within his brilliant son. Though he may well leave the Hasidic community for secular studies, Danny will always carry with him the legacy of Jewish suffering. That legacy will provide the moral force to change the world.

Reuvan, son of a Talmud scholar of the new school of textual criticism, chooses to become a rabbi. The choices, for Reuvan and for Danny, do not, however, come easily. Reuvan faces ostracism by the Hasidic community for suggesting that some Talmudic texts were of inferior quality and subject to misinterpretation. Danny must seemingly turn against his father if he is to pursue secular studies and abandon his leadership obligations.

The Promise continues the exploration of Reuvan's choice to receive his rabbinate from an Orthodox seminary and his refusal to become a secular Jew. Yet Reuvan is uneasy with the traditional method of Talmud study advanced by Rav Kalman, one of his teachers. If the Talmud is the sacred oral tradition of the Jews in written form, contradictory commentaries from rabbis down through the centuries must always be reconciled by newer interpretations, so as not to call God's Word into question. For Reuvan, there is another possibility; a corrupt text could be the source of confusion. Any correction, however, would mean violence to sacred scripture. Reuvan will become a rabbi so that he might debate Rav Kalman and the others from within a common tradition.

Reuvan's father, David Malter, is the voice of quiet wisdom throughout both books. Though a proponent of the new Talmud studies, he is sympathetic toward those whose tightly knit culture is being threatened. As he tells Reuvan in *The Promise*, "We cannot ignore the truth. At the same time, we cannot quite sing and dance as they do.... That is the dilemma of our time, Reuvan. I do not know what the answer is." Earlier, Reuvan's father had challenged his son to make his own meaning in the world. Those who had committed themselves to the Hasidic traditions had kept the faith alive through incomprehensible persecution. Now Reuvan must also choose with the greatest seriousness and fervency, for he, too, must make a mark on the world and endure hardship of his own.

Potok picks up this theme in his third novel, *My Name Is Asher Lev*. Covering the period of the late 1940's through the late 1960's, the book is an apologia for the artist. The Orthodox Jewish surroundings are familiar, but this time the controversy is not over textual criticism but rather representational art. Painting is not strictly forbidden to the Orthodox Jew, but it is regarded as useless, as foolishness, as a waste of time better devoted to the study of the Torah, the five books of Moses. Moreover, certain pictures could come close to violating the commandment forbidding graven images. Asher Lev is a born painter, however, and throughout the novel, as he develops his talent, he is increasingly isolated from his family and culture. Asher is born in Crown Heights in Brooklyn in 1943. His father travels extensively for the local Rebbe in an effort to establish Ladover Hasid communities throughout Europe and to aid families emigrating to the United States.

Metaphors of things unfinished and things completed permeate the novel. Asher's father is continually on the move because of the great unfinished work of the Ladover. Asher himself finds that he must bring some kind of completeness to the world by painting not only what he sees with his eyes but also what his inner vision reveals to him. Those visions are not always beautiful; his paintings can be like knives, plunging the reality of evil into the soul of the onlooker. The wise Rebbe, sensing Asher's vast talent, entrusts him to Jacob Kahn, himself an artistic genius and a nonobservant Jew. Kahn forces Asher to absorb the work of Pablo Picasso, especially *Guernica* (1937), a painting inspired by the German bombing of the Basque capital during the Spanish Civil War. In time, Asher begins to surpass his teacher.

Asher becomes virtually a stranger to his father. At the end of the novel, Asher's parents stare with mixed rage and amazement at the two crucifixions he has painted. Both are of his mother, looking in abstract fashion at Asher the stranger on one side and the always-traveling husband on the other. The image of the cross for Asher has become the supreme symbol of suffering, devoid of any Christian preoccupation. The image, however, is too much for his parents, Orthodox Jews. As the Rebbe tells him, "You have crossed a boundary. I cannot help you. You are alone now. I give you my blessings."

There is a marked contrast between Asher's sensitive paintings (an effort to say what must be said about the evil in the world) and his selfish behavior toward his parents. He is one of the least sympathetic of Potok's protagonists because he struggles less with his own anguish than with his need to express his artistic gift at whatever cost. Jacob Kahn's advice, "Be a great painter, Asher Lev. . . . That will be the only justification for all the pain your art will cause," seems too facile. Asher is determined to remain an observant Jew, but he will do so on his own terms. The commandment about honoring one's parents must be radically reinterpreted. The book suffers from the technical difficulty that Asher Lev must be identified as a genius early in the story in order for Potok to create the kind of tension he needs to interest a reader. A mediocre artist who causes pain is merely self-indulgent.

Yet the book reveals something of Potok's larger purpose. Art must be true to itself even if that means surprise or hurt. The artist, painter, or writer must speak from the heart; anything else is mere propaganda. Potok is seeking to provide a rationale for his novelistic critiques of fundamentalist communities.

Potok introduces something else into Asher's story: Asher often dreams of his "mythic ancestor," a Jew who served a nobleman only to have the nobleman unleash evil upon the world. Even as Asher envisioned that ancient Jew traveling the world, seeking to redress the wrong in which he had a part, so must the artist reshape evil into art and so bring the kind of balance to the world. Asher's visions are forerunners of Potok's use of mysticism or imaginative visions themselves as ways of coming to terms with a world gone crazy.

The Book of Lights, narrated in the third person, uses the technique of mystical reconciliation for a universal purpose. If the Master of the Universe truly exists, how is a believer to accept the death light of the twentieth century, the atomic bomb? Potok's answer is that through the imaginative use of Jewish mysticism, the spark of God can be found in an evil world. The story departs from Potok's previous novels, which traced the childhood of the protagonist. Only a few pages are devoted to Gershon Loran's early life before his seminary days and subsequent chaplaincy in Korea. Those first pages, however, are significant. Gershon witnesses the birth of some pups on a rooftop in the midst of his rundown neighborhood; he is awed by the presence of life even amid wreckage.

In seminary, Gershon is introduced to the study of the Cabala and its *Zohar*, a Jewish mystical work from the thirteenth century. The *Zohar* is the book of lights of the novel's title, describing the creation of the world through the emanations of God. There are places where God has withdrawn his light; that has enabled humankind to come on the scene but it has also ushered in great evil. Now the mystic is called to ascend through those emanations to find God. Such mystical tradition is complex and even contradictory. For Gershon, however, it is the pounding heart of a living faith. Gershon's quiet moments of reverie serve him well during his chaplaincy. Though Potok paints a detailed picture of Gershon's activities in Korea, the crucial story is elsewhere. Gershon's seminary friend, Arthur Leiden, travels with him to Kyoto and Hiroshima. At the Hiroshima monument, Arthur reads from the Psalms and pleads to God in vain for some kind of atonement. Arthur's father had worked with other scientists in developing the atom bomb, and Arthur is haunted by the memory. Later, Arthur is killed in a plane crash; Gershon, visiting Arthur's parents, hears a portion of one of Arthur's letters: "All the world, it seems, is a grayish sea of ambiguity, and we must learn to navigate in it or be drowned."

That is Potok's message in the novel; "Loran" is itself a navigational acronym. If Judaism were merely the law, the faith would break on the shoals of the gritty world. Its mystical tradition infuses the faith with the ambiguity of real life. It does not explain but rather affirms the nature of God's creation. The *Zohar* is an imaginative understanidg of the nature of God; in it, God enfolds both good and evil. It is a light by which to view a decaying civilization, a light that will survive the death light. In his final mystical vision of his old Cabala teacher, Gershon learns that the mystical light will help mend the world so that it can be broken again in yet new acts of creation.

It is the "mending power" of imagination that is at the heart of *Davita's Harp*. The harp referred to is a small instrument that fits on a door, with little balls that strike piano wires when the door is opened or closed. Here Potok returns to the first-person narrative, tracing the childhood of Ilana Davita Chandal, his first female lead character. She is the daughter of a nonbelieving Jewish mother and a nonbelieving Christian father. Spanning the years from the mid-1930's to 1942, the novel relates Davita's growing up in New York, her family's frequent moves, the constant singing of the door harp as people come and go, and her parents' efforts on behalf of the Communist revolutionaries during the Spanish Civil War. Davita endures the death of her father in that war and the sexism of her own culture when her Jewish high school (yeshiva) refuses to grant her the Akiva Award because, she is told, she is a woman. It is 1942. Another student is selected for the award but learns the truth and refuses it. He is Reuvan Malter, first introduced in *The Chosen*. In the end, Davita will go on to public school, angry with "sacred discontent." In an interview, Potok explained that Davita's experience was based on that of his wife, who was passed over as valedictory speaker because of her sex. *Davita's Harp* is a new exploration for Potok, that of Orthodoxy and feminism.

The novels of Chaim Potok give dramatic form to the problem of finding a viable Orthodox faith that embraces ancient beliefs yet remains open to the best of secular American culture. His works are offered as a gift of imagination to the Orthodox world and to all who are children of a restrictive past. The gift is risky, but it may well infuse new life into old ways or serve as a beacon for those who must plunge into the world in their search for meaning.

Other major works

NONFICTION: *Wanderings: Chaim Potok's History of the Jews*, 1978; *Tobiasse: Artist in Exile*, 1986.

Bibliography

Abramson, Edward A. *Chaim Potok*. Boston: Twayne, 1986.

Guttman, Allen. *The Jewish Writer in America: Assimilation and the Crisis of Identity*. New York: Oxford University Press, 1971.

Potok, Chaim. "An Interview with Chaim Potok." Interview by Elaine M. Kauvar. *Contemporary Literature* 27 (Fall, 1986): 290-317.

_____ . "Judaism Under the Secular Umbrella." Interview by Cheryl Forbes. *Christianity Today* 22 (September 8, 1978): 14-21.

Studies in American Jewish Literature 4 (1985). Special issue on Potok.

PHILIP ROTH

Born: Newark, New Jersey; March 19, 1933

Principal long fiction

Letting Go, 1962; *When She Was Good*, 1967; *Portnoy's Complaint*, 1969; *Our Gang*, 1971; *The Breast*, 1972, rev. 1980; *The Great American Novel*, 1973; *My Life as a Man*, 1974; *The Professor of Desire*, 1977; *The Ghost Writer*, 1979; *Zuckerman Unbound*, 1981; *The Anatomy Lesson*, 1983; *Zuckerman Bound*, 1985 (includes *The Ghost Writer, Zuckerman Unbound, The Anatomy Lesson*, and *Epilogue: The Prague Orgy*); *The Counterlife*, 1986; *Deception*, 1990; *Operation Shylock: A Confession*, 1993.

Other literary forms

Five of Philip Roth's short stories are collected along with his novella *Goodbye, Columbus* in a volume bearing that title (1959). A number of his essays, interviews, and autobiographical pieces appear in *Reading Myself and Others* (1975). An unproduced screenplay, *The Great American Pastime*, was anthologized in 1968, and two of his works, *Goodbye, Columbus* and *Portnoy's Complaint*, have been made into films by others. In 1975, Roth began editing a series called "Writers from the Other Europe" for Penguin Books, to which he contributed several introductions. *The Facts: A Novelist's Autobiography* appeared in 1988. The nonfictional *Patrimony: A True Story*, appeared in 1991.

Achievements

Ever since Roth's first published book, *Goodbye, Columbus*, won the National Book Award in 1960, he has been acclaimed as a leading Jewish American writer along with Saul Bellow and Bernard Malamud. All three are vitally interested in the social and moral dilemmas facing modern people, particularly Jewish Americans. Like Bellow, Roth has become increasingly absorbed in the problematic nature of love relationships, not only between man and woman but also between father and son, brother and brother, neighbor and neighbor. In addition, he has taken as his special concern the relation between a writer and his critics, or between a writer and the society in which he lives. His fictional accounts of Jewish family relationships and illicit love affairs involving Jews in his early work made him notorious among the conservative Jewish establishment, although subsequently the notoriety seems to have died down. In his later work, Roth has brilliantly presented the fascinating relationship between fiction and autobiography, using fictional surrogates, such as Nathan Zuckerman, to explore what he calls "counter-

lives," or the idea of an alternative existence to one actually lived.

Throughout his fiction, Roth exhibits the abilities of a master comedian. He has arguably the best ear of any contemporary writer, capturing the spoken voice in a wide variety of accents, intonations, and cadences, but his facility with dialogue has sometimes led critics to miss the serious undercurrents of his work. As a satirist, Roth works in a variety of modes, from the social (*Portnoy's Complaint*) to the political (*Our Gang*) to the literary and academic (*The Professor of Desire*). Whatever mode he adopts, he presents the objects of his satire or comedy in vivid and compelling fashion.

Once referred to as preeminently a social realist (as in *Goodbye, Columbus*), Roth has transcended that mode successfully in such works as *The Counterlife* and *Deception*, which show him, as ever, both a consummate craftsman and a tireless experimenter with his medium. For the body of his work, Roth won the Medal of Honor for Literature from the National Arts Club in 1991. For the nonfictional *Patrimony: A True Story* (1991), he received a National Book Critics Circle Award in 1992.

Biography

Born in the Weequahic section of Newark, New Jersey, on March 19, 1933, Philip Roth learned very early what it was like to grow up Jewish in a lower-middle-class neighborhood of a large metropolitan area. His parents were Beth Finkel and Herman Roth, a salesman for the Metropolitan Life Insurance Company. After he was graduated from Weequahic High School in 1950, Roth worked for a while at the Newark Public Library and attended Newark College of Rutgers University. A year later, he transferred to Bucknell University. Although the family could ill afford the expense of a private college, Herman Roth determined that if his son wanted to go there, he would go. At Bucknell, Roth began writing stories and edited the school's literary magazine. He also had his first love affairs, from which he drew incidents for his novels. He received his B.A. in English, magna cum laude, in 1954, and he accepted a teaching fellowship at the University of Chicago for graduate work in English.

After receiving his M.A. in English from Chicago, Roth enlisted in the United States Army, but a back injury suffered during basic training resulted in an early discharge. He returned to Chicago to pursue doctoral studies in English but continued writing short stories, which had begun to get published as early as the fall of 1954 in small literary journals such as the *Chicago Review* and *Epoch*. Several of his stories were anthologized in Martha Foley's *Best American Short Stories* and in *The O. Henry Prize Stories*. These awards, the success of his first published volume, *Goodbye, Columbus*, a Houghton Mifflin Literary Fellowship, and a Guggenheim Fellowship persuaded Roth to leave graduate work in English for a career as a creative writer.

While a graduate student and instructor at the University of Chicago, Roth met and later married Margaret Martinson Williams. The relationship was never a happy one, and after a few years they separated, Margaret steadfastly refusing to agree to a divorce. Meanwhile, they spent one year of their marriage (1960) at the Writers' Workshop at the University of Iowa, where Philip served on the faculty. After his first full-length novel, *Letting Go*, was published in 1962, he became writer-in-residence at Princeton University. He later taught English literature at the University of Pennsylvania. His experiences as an academic provided much material for novels, many of which have a university setting or are otherwise peopled by academics.

The publication of *Portnoy's Complaint* in 1969, a year after his estranged wife was killed in an automobile accident, launched Roth's greatest notoriety, especially among the conservative Jewish community in America, and assured his fame as a novelist. He became an increasingly prolific writer, spending part of the year in his Connecticut home and part in London in an apartment near his writing studio. He married British actress Claire Bloom in April, 1990. In 1970 he was elected to the National Academy of Arts and Letters.

Analysis

Roth came into his own as a novelist beginning with *Portnoy's Complaint*, which reveals a unique voice in American literature. His first novels are set squarely in his native land: in Newark, where he was born and reared; in the great Midwest, where he went to graduate school; and in New York and Philadelphia, where he lived, wrote, and taught literature at several universities. The protagonists of his later fiction travel abroad to Western and Eastern Europe and as far as Hong Kong. His novels are thus the product of a growing cosmopolitanism along with a deepening interest in basic human concerns and predicaments.

Chief among those predicaments is the endless struggle between the id and the superego, or, in less Freudian terms, between the drive for sensual gratification and the drive for moral uprightness. On the one hand, pulling at his protagonists (all but one of whom are men) is the powerful desire for sexual conquest; on the other hand is the almost equally powerful desire to lead a morally self-fulfilling and decent life. These drives, conflicting at almost every turn, nearly tear his protagonists apart.

Indeed, Roth's heroes, if we can call such unlikely characters by that term, all seem doomed in one way or another. Their pervasive sense of disaster, however, does not destroy Roth's comedy; it deepens it. The sense of the absurd, of the incongruities of human experience, also pervades Roth's novels and is the source of much rich humor. Moreover, his protagonists usually are fully self-aware; if (more often than not) they are utterly baffled in trying to find a solution to their dilemmas, they at least understand their predicaments with uncommon self-perception. Again, their awareness and frustration combine to make the reader laugh, though the reader must be careful not to let the laughter obscure or nullify the compassion that is also the character's due.

The hook on which Roth's later protagonists wriggle is the dilemma between commitment and freedom. Thus, in *Portnoy's Complaint*, Alexander Portnoy finds himself torn between his desire to maintain his position as New York's Assistant Commissioner for Human Opportunity, a job of considerable responsibility as well as prestige, and his desire to enjoy the full sexual freedoms heralded by the 1960's. For a while he seems to manage both, until his affair with Mary Jane Reed develops into something else: Mary Jane's wish to get married. Her sexual adroitness—she is called "the Monkey"—has kept them together for more than a year, but this demand for full commitment proves too much for Alex, who abandons her in Athens during a trip to Europe in which they have experienced the ultimate of their sexual adventures. Alex flees to Israel, the land of his forefathers, only to find that when he tries to make love there he is impotent. The experience drives him to seek help from Dr. Otto Spielvogel, a New York psychiatrist.

The novel, in fact, is told as a series of confessions, or therapy sessions, and derives its title from the name Spielvogel gives to his patient's illness. "Portnoy's Complaint" is "a disorder in which strongly felt ethical and altruistic impulses are perpetually warring with extreme sexual longings, often of a perverse nature." The symptoms of the illness, Spielvogel believes, can be traced to the mother-child relationship, and indeed Portnoy's boyhood has been fraught with problems, often hilarious ones as he recounts them, occasioned by his stereotypical Jewish mother. Sophie Portnoy is a domineering, overprotective mother who frequently drives her young son to distraction, as he tries in vain to understand her demands upon him and her suffocating affection. Jack Portnoy, his father, long-suffering (mostly from constipation) and hardworking, seems unable to mitigate the family relationship, exacerbating Alex's quandary. No wonder Alex grows up as he does, afflicted with the dilemma, or the condition, Spielvogel describes. By the end of the novel, after the long unfolding of his tales of woe, all Alex hears from his therapist is, "Now vee may perhaps to begin. Yes?"

Nathan Zuckerman, the protagonist of the *Zuckerman Bound* trilogy and epilogue, is clearly Roth's alter ego. The major events in Zuckerman's life—growing up in Newark, attending the University of Chicago, and then embarking on a literary career, for example—certainly mirror those in Roth's. Again, as in *My Life as a Man*, Roth borrows from autobiography while continuing his literary experimentation with fictional "counterlives." In Zuckerman, Roth found the perfect vehicle for exploring the conflicts that have plagued all of his characters since *Goodbye, Columbus*. These conflicts—between conformity and rebellion, ethnic solidarity and personal identity, public image and private desires, ethical and artistic ideals and mundane realities—underlie each part of the trilogy and determine its overall movement.

Roth has described the subject of *Zuckerman Bound* as "the moral consequences of the literary career of Nathan Zuckerman," or "the unintended consequences of art." In *The Ghost Writer*, the first of the series that make up this *Bildungsroman*, Nathan Zuckerman is at the beginning of a promising career as a writer. He has published a few short stories and is now staying at an artist's colony, trying to write more. Since he is not far from the home of E. I. Lonoff, a writer he much admires, he visits and is welcomed by the older writer and his wife. Zuckerman is surprised by them in many ways: first by Lonoff's austere life as a writer, spent endlessly turning his sentences around, and then by Hope Lonoff's conviction that her husband would be better off without her. By birth and upbringing far different from him—she is a New England Yankee as opposed to his immigrant origins—she is temperamentally unsuited to the kind of life they have led for many years. She is convinced, moreover, that Lonoff would be better off living with a younger woman, like Amy Bellette, a former student from the nearby women's college where Lonoff teaches, who obviously adores him. Lonoff refuses, however, to entertain any such thoughts of abandoning Hope or realizing his fantasy of living abroad in a villa in Italy with a younger woman.

Nathan is persuaded to stay the night, especially after meeting Amy Bellett, who is also staying there on a brief visit. Nathan has his own fantasy that evening, that Amy is really Anne Frank, author of the famous diary, who has miraculously survived the death camps. They fall in love, get married, and thus show his parents and other relatives that, despite what they may think from some of his stories, he is a good Jewish man, the worthy husband of the famous Jewish heroine. As a tribute to Roth's skill as a writer, the account of Amy's survival is quite credible; moreover, it shows Roth's understanding of compassion for the suffering in the death camps. At the same time, it supports Nathan Zuckerman's qualifications as a writer, justifying Lonoff's praise and encouragement of the young man.

Lonoff's belief in Nathan is borne out in *Zuckerman Unbound*, the second novel in the trilogy. By now Zuckerman is the author of several novels, including the notorious "Carnovsky." This novel is to Zuckerman what *Portnoy's Complaint* was to Philip Roth, and *Zuckerman Unbound* recounts experiences similar to those Roth must have had, such as the notoriety that involved mistaking his fictional characters for his real mother and father. Zuckerman is accosted in the streets, on the telephone, and apparently everywhere he goes by people who think they know him because they mistake his confessional novel for actual autobiography. Yet fiction and autobiography are at best distant relatives; for example, unlike Zuckerman's father, who is extremely upset by his son's novel and turns on him at his death, Roth's parents remained proud of their son's accomplishments and never took offense at what he wrote, notwithstanding the uproar in the Jewish establishment.

Zuckerman is beset by would-be hangers-on, such as Alvin Pepler, the Jewish marine, once a quiz-show winner but deprived of full fame by a scam reminiscent of the Charles Van Doren scandal. Zuckerman's brief affair (actually, no more than one-night stand) with the Irish actress Caesara O'Shea is a comic treatment of the adventures attributed to Roth by columnists such as Leonard Lyons, who insisted that Roth was romantically involved with Barbra Streisand, though actually Roth at that time had not so much as met her. Finally, Zuckerman's trip to Miami with his brother, Henry, which ends with their estrangement on the way home after their father dies of a stroke, is totally different from actual events in Roth's life. All these incidents are, after all, "counterlives," imaginative renderings of what might have or could have happened, not what did.

Similarly, in *The Anatomy Lesson*, the third novel in the series, Roth borrows from incidents in his life but fictionalizes them so that no one-to-one equivalence can be made. Now, some years later, Zuckerman is afflicted with a strange ailment that causes him intense pain, from which he gets temporary relief only from vodka or Percodan. He can no longer write, but four different women tend to his other needs, including his sexual ones. Among them are a young Finch College student, who also works as his secretary; his financial adviser's wife; an artist in Vermont who occasionally descends from her mountaintop to visit; and a Polish émigré, whom Zuckerman meets at a trichological clinic (in addition to everything else, Zuckerman is losing his hair).

In despair of his life and his calling, Zuckerman decides to give up writing and become a doctor. He flies to Chicago, where he hopes his old friend and classmate, Bobby Freytag, will help him get admitted to medical school. En route on the plane and later from the airport, Zuckerman impersonates Milton Appel, a literary critic modeled on Irving Howe, who early praised Roth's work and then turned against it. In this impersonation, however, Zuckerman pretends that Appel is a pornography king, editor and publisher of *Lickety Split* and an impresario of houses of pleasure. The impersonation is triggered by Appel's appeal, delivered through an intermediary, to Zuckerman to write an op-ed piece on behalf of Israel.

Zuckerman as the porn king Appel provides plenty of material for those who like to see Roth as antifeminist but who thereby miss the point of his fiction. It is a tour de force, a persona adopting a persona—miles away from the real Roth. At his office in the hospital, Bobby Freytag reminisces with Zuckerman for a bit and then tries to talk him out of his scheme. Only the next day when, under the influence of too much Percodan and vodka, Zuckerman falls and fractures his jaw does the healing begin, in soul as well as body. Zuckerman learns what real pain and loss are, as he walks the corridors of the hospital watched over by his friend, who also weans him from his drug addiction. At the end, Zuckerman is a chastened and more altruistic individual, though still deluded into thinking he could change into a more radically different person from who he is.

The epilogue, *The Prague Orgy*, shows Zuckerman not as a doctor but as a famous novelist undertaking an altruistic mission on behalf of an émigré Czech writer whose father had written some excellent, unpublished stories in Yiddish. Unfortunately, the Czech's estranged wife holds the stories but will not release them, and it is Zuckerman's task to fetch them. In the event, he manages to do so without having to sleep with her, despite her pleas, but the stories are immediatley confiscated by the police, who then escort him out of the country (this is pre-1989 Czechoslovakia). Zuckerman thus learns to accept his limitations and to become reconciled to them. To become "transformed into a cultural eminence elevated by the literary deeds he performs" does not seem to be his fate, and he accepts that.

In *The Counterlife*, Nathan and his brother are briefly reunited, mainly so that Roth can explore alternative versions of a fate that first befalls one and then the other. The plot thus doubles back on itself more than once and is too complex for summary treatment. Despite its complexity, the novel is not difficult to follow and is full of surprises that intellectually stimulate as they also amuse the reader. Particularly interesting are the episodes in Israel, where Henry has fled to start a new life, bringing Nathan after him to discover what is going on. Much is going on, including a considerable amount of discussion from characters on the political left and right, with Nathan clearly in the middle. The latter part of the novel finds Nathan in London, married to an English divorcee with a child and trying to come to grips with British anti-Semitism, including some of his wife's family. Throughout the novel, Roth implicitly and sometimes explicitly raises questions about the nature of fiction and the characters that inhabit it.

Surveying the corpus of Roth's longer fiction, one may conclude that here is a novelist who rarely repeats himself, even as he reworks ideas, issues, dilemmas, or reintroduces characters and locales. This is the essence of the "counterlife" motif that has been present in Roth's work from the start but becomes explicit only later on, where its fascination has grown even as Roth's techniques and maturity as a writer have also grown.

Other major works

SHORT FICTION: *Goodbye, Columbus*, 1959.

NONFICTION: *Reading Myself and Others*, 1975; *The Facts: A Novelist's Autobiography*, 1988; *Patrimony: A True Story*, 1991.

Bibliography

Appelfeld, Aron. *Beyond Despair: Three Lectures and a Conversation with Philip Roth.* New York: Fromm International, 1994.

Halio, Jay L. *Philip Roth Revisited.* New York: Twayne, 1992.

Lee, Hermione. *Philip Roth.* London: Methuen, 1982.

Milbauer, Asher Z., and Donald G. Watson, eds. *Reading Philip Roth.* New York: St. Martin's Press, 1988.

Pinsker, Sanford. *The Comedy That "Hoits": An Essay on the Fiction of Philip Roth.* Columbia: University of Missouri Press, 1975.

_____ , ed. *Critical Essays on Philip Roth.* Boston: G. K. Hall, 1982.

Pughe, Thomas. *Comic Sense: Reading Robert Coover, Stanley Elkin, Philip Roth.* Boston: Birkhauser Verlag, 1994.

Rodgers, Bernard F., Jr. *Philip Roth.* Boston: Twayne, 1978.

ISAAC BASHEVIS SINGER

Born: Leoncin, Poland; July 14, 1904

Died: Surfside, Florida; July 24, 1991

Principal short fiction

Gimpel the Fool and Other Stories, 1957; *The Spinoza of Market Street*, 1961; *Short Friday and Other Stories*, 1964; *The Séance and Other Stories*, 1968; *A Friend of Kafka and Other Stories*, 1970; *A Crown of Feathers and Other Stories*, 1973; *Passions and Other Stories*, 1975; *Old Love*, 1979; *The Collected Stories*, 1982; *The Image and Other Stories*, 1985; *The Death of Methuselah and Other Stories*, 1988.

Other literary forms

Singer is as well known for his long fiction as for his short stories. *Sotan in Goray* (1935; *Satan in Goray*, 1955) first appeared, like all of his subsequent novels (and his short stories), in Yiddish. Most of these novels explore the Jewish experience in Poland, though *Enemies: A Love Story* (1972), which was made into a film in 1989, is set in America. Not all Singer's novels were translated into English during his lifetime, so that his work, such as *The Certificate* (1992), continues to appear posthumously.

In his sixties Singer began writing for children, and he published extensively in this genre over a twenty-year period. His first book for children, *Zlateh the Goat and Other Stories* (1966), won a Newbery Medal and was included in the American Library Association's list of notable children's books. *A Day of Pleasure* (1969) won the National Book Award, only the second work for children so honored. Others of his children's books have also enjoyed critical acclaim and extensive sales in a variety of languages.

In addition to fiction Singer published several autobiographical volumes, beginning with *Mayn Tatn's Besdin Shtub* (1956; *In My Father's Court*, 1966). He also wrote plays, of which *Yentl, the Yeshiva Boy* (1974), co-authored with Leah Napolin, is the best known because of the 1983 film starring Barbra Streisand.

Achievements

The Nobel Prize in Literature, presented to Singer in 1978, capped a series of awards. In addition to the recognition given to his children's books, Singer received the National Book Award for his 1973 collection of stories, *A Crown of Feathers*. In 1964 he was elected to the National Institute of Arts and Letters. Although he wrote of a vanished world in a vanishing language, his works continue to strike a responsive chord in readers because he explores with humor, sympathy, and wisdom the foibles, joys, and tragedy of the human condition.

Biography

Isaac Bashevis Singer was born in Leoncin, Poland, on July 14, 1904, to Rabbi Pinchas Mendel and Bathsheba (Zylberman) Singer. When Isaac was four his family moved to nearby Warsaw, where they resided at 10 Krochmalna Street. Here in the midst of the capital city was a small Jewish village that Singer would describe repeatedly in his fiction as well as in his autobiography.

During World War I Singer, his younger brother, Moshe, and his mother moved to the village of Bilgoray (1917), near Austria, an experience that bore fruit in Singer's first novel. Here Singer first encountered the Haskalah, the Jewish Enlightenment. Though the movement had begun in Germany in the eighteenth century, Polish Jewry had remained largely unaffected by its modernist outlook. In Bilgoray, too, Singer read Hillel Zeitlin's *The Problem of Good and Evil* (1898), which argues that God remains aloof from human suffering. Only human sympathy can unite individuals with one another and with the divine; this is one of the principal tenets of Singer's fiction.

Although Singer enrolled in the Tachkemoni Rabbinical Seminary (Warsaw) at his father's insistence (1921), he remained only a year before returning to Bilgoray. He then joined his father at Dzikow, where the elder Singer was serving as rabbi. In 1923 Singer returned to Warsaw to work as a proofreader for his older brother's Yiddish literary magazine, *Literarische Bletter*, and in 1925 Singer published his first story there ("Oyf der Elter," meaning "in old age"). Israel Joshua Singer later arranged for his brother's immigration to the United States in 1935. In 1940 Singer married Alma Haimann Wasserman, and in 1942 he joined the staff of the *Jewish Daily Forward*, one of New York City's Yiddish newspapers. The publication of *The Family Moskat* in English in 1950, following Yiddish serialization, and Saul Bellow's masterful 1953 translation of "Gimpl Tam" (1945) as "Gimpel the Fool" established Singer's reputation among American readers. As his literary awards indicate, he achieved an international reputation. His death in 1991 was a loss not only to his Yiddish readers but also to world literature.

Analysis

In the "Author's Note" to *A Crown of Feathers and Other Stories* Singer wrote,

> As the reader can see, there are in this collection as many stories dealing with life in the United States as stories about pre-war Poland. Because I have now lived in this country longer than in Poland, I have developed roots here too. Just the same, my American stories deal only with Yiddish-speaking immigrants from Poland so as to ensure that I know well not only their present way of life but *their* roots—their culture, history, ways of thinking and expressing themselves.

Most of Singer's stories set in America deal not only with people like him; the narrator or central character usually is the author, thinly disguised. Thus, "A Day in Coney Island" recounts the experiences in 1935 of a thirty-year-old Polish writer who has recently come to America. In "The Lecture" the narrator is a successful Yiddish writer who goes to Montreal to deliver an optimistic assessment of the future of the Yiddish language, Singer's own view of the subject. Though "The Letter Writer" is told from the third-person point of view, here, too, the protagonist, Herman Gombiner, is in many ways a Singer double: A vegetarian like Singer, Herman works as an editor, proofreader, and translator for a Yiddish publication.

The stories that Singer tells about himself and his fellow transplanted Jews belong to the genre of Magical Realism, for which Singer is indebted partly to the Kabalah and partly to Rabbi Nachman of Bratzlav (1772-1810), whose work, pervaded with mysticism, Singer encountered in 1922 at Dzikow. Much of Singer's American fiction could easily be transported to Poland, and at times it is. When the narrator of "The Lecture" boards the train in New York City, he remarks on the contrast between American trains and those he knew in Eastern Europe. Here he sees "no bundles, no high fur hats, no sheepskin coats, no boxes. . . . Nobody was eating bread and lard. Nobody drank vodka from a bottle." All is orderly, warm, and clean. As the train journeys through the wintry landscape, these distinctions fade. The cars grow cold; the floors become muddy. Passengers begin to drink and eat bread and sausage if not bread and lard, like their Polish counterparts; the train halts in the middle of a wood that could as easily be in Poland as in upstate New York.

The narrator reaches his destination in the middle of the night, to be greeted only by an old lady and her daughter. The former "was wrinkled, disheveled, like an old woman in Poland. . . . Her clothes also reminded me of Poland." The daughter's accent is Polish as well. The street in which they live suggests to the narrator a village in his homeland, and the smells in their apartment are European.

Even more mysterious events follow. The narrator loses the text of the lecture he is supposed to deliver, and his sleep is disturbed by sounds that seem to emanate from a mythical beast. When he finally dozes off, the daughter awakens him with the news that her mother has died; she had willed herself to live only until she could meet the narrator, whose work had, after World War II, lifted the darkness from her heart.

These nightmarish experiences typify the mysticism, the inexplicable role of the divine—or the demonic—in Singer's fiction. The transformation of the narrator similarly is characteristic of Singer's work, showing the power of love. At the beginning of the story, the narrator is alone. Other passengers use the bad weather as a pretext for starting conversations, but the narrator reads. As he admits, "I exclude myself from society." When he tries to look outside, he sees only "the reflection of the interior of the car," and he expresses agreement with "the solipsistic philosophy of Bishop Berkeley." Since he has a bottle of cognac and a box of crackers, he does not care whether or not the train remains stranded.

The old woman who meets him observes, "All the troubles come from people being deaf and blind. They don't see the next man and so they torture him." She thus precisely describes the state of the narrator. Although the old woman has told him of her horrific experiences in Nazi concentration camps and of the deaths of her three sons and her husband in the war, the narrator can think only of the loss of his manuscript. He regards this event as "a real catastrophe!" worthy of an exclamation point, even though he did not like what he had written. While his accommodations are uncomfortable, his comparing them to Treblinka is excessive. When Binele, the daughter, tells him of her mother's death, he thinks about how old he is and asks, "What can I do? I can't see anything," a comment that identifies him with the deaf and blind people whom the old women had mentioned.

Binele leaves the narrator to seek help; alone with the corpse he is afraid, and when she returns with a neighbor the narrator is for the first time glad to be with another person. At the end of the story the narrator embraces Binele and promises not to abandon her. His physical and metaphysical chill has yielded to warmth, symbolized in the story by melting snow. Singer writes in the penultimate paragraph, "Life had returned." "The Lecture" provides a perfect *mise en scène* of Singer's belief, expressed in the "Author's Note" to *The Image and Other Stories*: "Literature is the story of love and fate, a description of the mad hurricane of human passions and the struggle with them." The narrator has undertaken a quest, journeying from the familiar to the unknown, the secure to the terrifying, to find himself.

"The Letter Writer," which, like "The Lecture," was collected in *The Séance and Other Stories*, again illustrates the inexplicable nature of the world and the redemptive power of love. Herman Gombiner, like other Singer characters who move from the Old World to the New, has Americanized his Hebrew name, Hayim David, but he remains faithful to old beliefs. As a result, his employer regards him as "a superstitious greenhorn," but Singer's verdict is more sympathetic: "Herman Gombiner had long ago arrived at the conclusion that modern man was as fanatic in his non-belief as ancient man had been in his faith. The rationalism of the present generation was itself an example of preconceived ideas.". Certainly the world of "The Letter Writer" defies rational explanation. Gombiner prays for a taxi, and one instantly appears. He has premonitions that someone is ill or that his publisher will close down, and his intuition is almost never wrong.

Like the narrator of "The Lecture," Gombiner lives in a mysterious world, and he lives in it alone. He corresponds with many women, whose names he finds in magazines devoted to the occult, but he selects people who live far away because he does not want to meet them. He has rejected marriage and has long been attracted to cemeteries. His thoughts dwell on the dead; to him sleep is more real than waking. He does not weep when he learns that his family has been destroyed in the Holocaust, another indication of his lack of human sympathy. His one love is a mouse, Hulda, that he feeds regularly.

Gombiner falls ill, and only the unexpected appearance of Ruth Beechman, one of his distant correspon-

dents, saves his life. She has been directed to visit him by the spirit of her dead grandmother, yet another instance of the inexplicable at work in the story. She nurses Gombiner back to physical health, and spiritual health as well. Upon his recovery he first thinks of Hulda; and when she emerges to drink the milk he has asked Ruth to set down for her, he feels a joy he has seldom known. He weeps generous tears and feels love for both Hulda and the woman who has saved both their lives. When Ruth asks whether he wants her to stay with him, he replies affirmatively. He has returned literally and figuratively from the dead. In the last paragraph Singer invokes the image of Noah's dove bearing the promise of new life, as a pigeon flies into the breaking dawn and sounds of life fill Gombiner's long-silent apartment.

"The Bishop's Robe" exemplifies another facet of Singer's examination of the Jewish American experience, the movement away from one's roots and the consequences of that spiritual (and, in this story, physical) migration. Bessie Feingevirtz was born in Pishnitz, Poland, worked in the New York garment district, married, and became rich. In her late sixties she remarries; she and her second husband, Jacob Getzelles, move from New York to the diaspora of California, buying a home in the Hollywood Hills. Here Jacob grows lazy and silent; like the Jews of Babylon he cannot write or speak in this alien world.

In California Bessie meets Phyllis Gurdin, another East Coast Jew who had been married to the spiritualist leader Thomas Delano Gurdin, whose mantle she assumed after his death. Although she remembers some Yiddish and recites Hebrew prayers on her parents' graves, her congregation worships God, Jesus, and her, and it prays in an unknown tongue. Gurdin declares that Jacob Getzelles is the reincarnation of her former husband, a metamorphosis even her gullible followers cannot believe because the two men look and sound so different. Tragic delusion and comic absurdity meet in this new faith when Jacob puts on Gurdin's robes, which, though altered, still make him look like "a schlemiel."

Phyllis Gurdin's true religion proves to be greed. She persuades Bessie to share her wealth and her husband. Ultimately, she absconds with Bessie's fortune, and the couple commits suicide. An audit reveals that they still had about $400,000, and a lawyer comments, "She [Bessie] certainly did not die from want." He fails to understand that the want that drove Bessie and Jacob to suicide was spiritual, an insufficiency not of funds but of love and tradition.

The Swedish Academy, which awarded Singer the Nobel Prize, praised "his impassioned narrative art which . . . brings universal human conditions to life." Although his stories deal with Eastern European Jews in their native towns or translated to America, his message is universal. His stories present the ongoing struggle between good and evil. They speak of the need for love, the moral responsibility of the individual in a world in which God is silent and meaning is elusive. They warn that the greatest credulity is the belief in nothing.

Other major works

LONG FICTION: *Sotan in Goray*, 1935 (*Satan in Goray*, 1955); *Di Familie Muskat*, 1950 (*The Family Moskat*, 1950); *Der Hoyf*, 1953-1955 (*The Manor*, 1967, and *The Estate*, 1969); *Der Kunstnmakher fun Lublin*, 1959 (*The Magician of Lublin*, 1960); *Der Knecht*, 1961 (*The Slave*, 1962); *Sonim, de Geshichte fun a Liebe*, 1966 (*Enemies: A Love Story*, 1972); *Neshome Ekspeditsyes*, 1974 (*Shosha*, 1978); *Der Bal-Tshuve*, 1974 (*The Penitent*, 1983); *Der Kenig vun di Felder*, 1988 (*The King of the Fields*, 1988); *Scum*, 1991; *The Certificate*, 1992; *Meshugah*, 1994.

PLAYS: *The Mirror*, 1973; *Yentl, the Yeshiva Boy*, 1974 (with Leah Napolin); *Schlemiel the First*, 1974; *Teibele and Her Demon*, 1978.

NONFICTION: *Mayn Tatn's Bes-din Shtub*, 1956 (*In My Father's Court*, 1966); *A Little Boy in Search of God: Mysticism in a Personal Light*, 1976; *A Young Man in Search of Love*, 1978; *Lost in America*, 1980.

CHILDREN'S LITERATURE: *Zlateh the Goat and Other Stories*, 1966; *The Fearsome Inn*, 1967; *Mazel and Shlimazel: Or, The Milk of a Lioness*, 1967; *When Schlemiel Went to Warsaw and Other Stories*, 1968; *A Day of Pleasure: Stories of a Boy Growing Up in Warsaw*, 1969; *Elijah the Slave*, 1970; *Joseph and Koza: Or, The Sacrifice to the Vistula*, 1970; *Alone in the Wild Forest*, 1971; *The Topsy-Turvy Emperor of China*, 1971; *The Wicked City*, 1972; *The Fools of Chelm and Their History*, 1973; *Why Noah Chose the Dove*, 1974; *A Tale of Three Wishes*, 1975; *Naftali the Storyteller and His Horse, Sus, and Other Stories*, 1976; *The Power of Light: Eight Stories*, 1980; *The Golem*, 1982; *Stories for Children*, 1984.

Bibliography

Alexander, Edward. *Isaac Bashevis Singer*. Boston: Twayne, 1980.

Allentuck, Marcia, ed. *The Achievement of Isaac Bashevis Singer*. Carbondale: Southern Illinois University Press, 1969.

Berger, Alan. *Crisis and Covenant: The Holocaust in American Jewish Fiction*. Albany: State University of New York Press, 1985.

Lee, Grace Farrell. *From Exile to Redemption: The Fiction of Isaac Bashevis Singer*. Carbondale: Southern Illinois University Press, 1987.

Malin, Irving, ed. *Critical Views of Isaac Bashevis Singer*. New York: New York University Press, 1969.

_____ . *Isaac Bashevis Singer*. New York: Frederick Ungar, 1972.

Studies in American Jewish Literature, 1 (1981). A special issue devoted entirely to the works of Singer.

IV

THE PRESENCE OF THE PAST
American Identities in the South

The poet's voice need not merely be the record of man, it can be one of the props to help him endure and prevail.
—William Faulkner, Nobel lecture, 1950

Although more than fifty years have passed since W. J. Cash brought out his brilliant book *The Mind of the South* (1941), most Southerners would still agree with his assertion that, in spite of marked differences between the various areas of the South, the region as a whole is unified by what Cash calls "a complex of established relationships and habits of thought, sentiments, prejudices, standards and values." Cash was aware that many believed the Old South was gone forever, replaced by a New South whose commercial values reflected the industrial basis of its economy. However, Cash found that even those Southerners who were most committed to the concept of the New South firmly believed in a unique Southern identity.

Four decades later, in his introduction to the Louisiana State University Press's monumental *History of Southern Literature* (1985), Louis D. Rubin, Jr., insisted that despite current attempts to de-regionalize literary studies, "the Southern identity is important because it is." What Rubin identified as the key quality in imaginative literature written by both black and white Southerners is "History, as a mode for viewing one's experience and one's identity." As the critic Lewis P. Simpson has frequently pointed out, it is no accident that the cynic in Robert Penn Warren's novel *All the King's Men* (1946) is named Jack Burden, for only when he agrees to take up the "burden" of history can Jack discover who and what he is. Southerners, black and white, rural and urban, still deeply believe that to be truly human, one must claim a family, a place, and a history. More than any other element, the Southern

insistence on the presence of the past is responsible for the richness of twentieth century Southern literature and its continuing power to affect the senses of American identity.

Because Southerners have always had great respect for tradition, they have also been peculiarly susceptible to myths. One of the most influential of these was the myth of the Old South, which was largely derived from romantic stories of feudal society, such as Sir Walter Scott's *Ivanhoe* (1819). In fact, as Southern historians have pointed out, most Southern white men were not the owners of huge plantations but small farmers, who owned few slaves or none, or poor tenants, who had difficulty scratching out a living from the soil. In the nineteenth century, however, novelists such as Augusta Evans Wilson liked to show Southern white gentlemen as feudal lords and chivalrous heroes, willing to die for love and honor. So persuasive was Wilson's writing that during the Civil War a Union general ordered all the copies of her book *Macaria, or Altars of Sacrifice* (1864) to be burned, for fear that reading it would weaken the resolve of his troops. Like Wilson, Margaret Mitchell found an enthusiastic audience in the North as well as in the South. The enormous popularity of *Gone with the Wind* (1936) proved that the myth of the Old South was as permanent a part of the American heritage as the similarly fanciful myth of the Wild West—which, too, was rooted in the romantic version of the medieval world.

However, if there was scant basis for the myth of the Old South, there were valid reasons for Southerners to be preoccupied with history. Theirs was the only section of the United States ever to be invaded, defeated, and occupied by an enemy force. Those Confederate soldiers who lived to return home found their fields neglected, their women destitute, and themselves disenfranchised. Faced with a ruined economy, they found it difficult even to survive, much less to rebuild. What is sometimes forgotten is that African Americans shared with white Americans in the hardships of those years. The novel *Jubilee* (1966), by black writer Margaret Walker, shows clearly how desperate conditions were for all Southerners during the Reconstruction period, and because it is based on the life of the author's great-grandmother, it also illustrates the importance of history, not myth, in the Southern literary imagination.

If black Southern writers contemplating history have to deal with their anger, white Southern writers have to come to terms with their guilt. Once they have rejected the idea that the Old South was an idyllic place to live, they must admit that, slave holders or not, the ancestors of whom they are so proud were defending an indefensible institution. This changed perspective can be seen in such works as William Styron's historical novel *The Confessions of Nat Turner* (1967), which shows the leader of the 1831 slave rebellion both as a viction of oppression and, finally, as a visionary hero and prophet. In his own family history, however, the novelist William Faulkner found a basis for ambivalence. On one hand, he firmly believed that the existence of slavery had left an ineradicable curse on the South; on the other hand, he knew from his own family that in the society which had been destroyed there were many who adhered to a code of honor, based on uncompromising idealism. In the New South that was arising from the ashes of the Old, Faulkner was troubled to see no allegiance to any code, no motivation but selfish greed.

In Faulkner's ambivalent vision, one can see evidence of a basic preoccupation in Southern life and a major theme in Southern literature, the struggle between good and evil. Whether they are African Americans steeped in the spirit, whites of Scots-Irish descent reared in the Calvinistic tradition, or quietly devout Anglicans or Roman Catholics, Southerners are a religious lot, unwilling to believe that life has no meaning. Instead, they see both private and public life in terms of spiritual and moral conflict. The effect on literature could not be more beneficial, for, like John Milton composing his great poem about the fall of man (*Paradise Lost*, 1667), Southern writers find the battle lines in place, tension assured, and the steady movement of the plot inevitable. In some cases, as in the short stories of Flannery O'Connor, the emphasis is on the evil within one human heart; in others, as in Robert Penn Warren's novel *All the King's Men* (1946), an entire state becomes corrupted. Whatever the setting, the antagonists are the same—put simply, God and the Devil.

For one group of Southern intellectuals, the Nashville Agrarians gathered at Vanderbilt University, the largely rural South constituted a bulwark against the general decay of moral values, which they saw as the result of urbanization. In 1930, the Agrarians jointly published *I'll Take My Stand*, a "Southern Manifesto," in which they urged Southerners to defy dehumanizing materialistic industrialism in favor of a life close to nature and imbued with spiritual values. Among those represented in the book were the important poets and novelists John Crowe Ransom, Donald Davidson, Allen Tate, Robert Penn Warren, and Andrew Lytle. As individuals and as members of the group, they were to have an important influence, if not on the march of what the New South termed "progress," at least on intellectual history, undoubtedly providing an impetus for the environmental movement.

The most effective opposition to the Agrarians came from other writers. Seeing yet another myth in the making, they decided to oppose it with a healthy dose of realism. Walker Evans' haunting photographs of hollow-eyed white tenant families in Alabama and James Agee's prose account of their daily lives, which were united in the documentary book *Let Us Now Praise Famous Men* (1941), showed how difficult it is to retain a sense of human dignity when one is struggling merely to survive. Such novels as *Tobacco Road* (1932) and *God's Little Acre* (1933), by Georgia-born Erskine Caldwell, went much further. Instead of being ennobled by their rural surroundings, Caldwell's characters seemed to be interested primarily in outdoing their animals in bestial behavior.

The fact that well-known Southern writers have such different perceptions of their world is an indication of a profound truth. Despite their strong streak of conservatism, or at least their reverence for tradition, Southerners do recognize that human life is complex and varied. Therefore they find it possible to make room for individual differences. The tormented souls of Edgar Allan Poe, the grotesques of Faulkner and Caldwell, and the appealing eccentrics of Eudora Welty can still be found in small Southern towns, or in cities, for that matter. Their actions may provide the occasion for a leisurely analysis of family history, but because they can lay claim to a common past, they are not expelled from their communities but instead are regarded as an integral part of them. In fact, such natives are accepted more fully than the most respectable immigrants without recognizable bloodlines, who are likely to be told to "come see us" by people who would be horrified if they accepted the invitation.

It seems that only in paradoxes can one define the South. At one and the same time it believes in myths and debunks them, preaches goodness and indulges in evil, glorifies the country and settles in the city, argues con-

servative conformity and shields eccentricity, offers hospitality and denies it. Perhaps the most paradoxical fact of all is that even while they argue about the differences between one state and another—even the superiority of one area over another—Southerners agree on one point: that they have a common history and a vital unifying source for their multiple identities.

—Rosemary M. Canfield Reisman
Troy State University

JAMES AGEE

Born: Knoxville, Tennessee; November 27, 1909   **Died:** New York, New York; May 16, 1955

Principal long fiction

The Morning Watch, 1951; *A Death in the Family*, 1957.

Other literary forms

James Agee's earliest published book, *Permit Me Voyage* (1934), is a collection of poems; his second, a nonfiction account of Alabama sharecroppers in the Depression. He and photographer Walker Evans lived with their subjects for eight weeks in 1936 on a *Fortune* magazine assignment, with a number of critics hailing the resulting book, *Let Us Now Praise Famous Men* (1941), as Agee's masterpiece.

From 1941 through 1948, Agee wrote film reviews and feature articles for *Time* and *The Nation*; thereafter, he worked on film scripts in Hollywood, his most notable screenplay being his 1951 adaptation of C. S. Forester's novel *The African Queen* (1935). He also wrote an esteemed television script on Abraham Lincoln for the *Omnibus* series in 1952. *Letters of James Agee to Father Flye* (1962) contains his thirty-year correspondence with an Episcopalian priest who had been his teacher.

Achievements

The prestigious Yale Series of Younger Poets sponsored Agee's first book, Archibald MacLeish contributing its introduction. Agee went on to gain an unusual degree of literary fame for a man who published only three books, two of them slim ones, in his lifetime. Sometimes accused of wasting his talent on magazine and film hack work, Agee lavished the same painstaking attention on film reviews as on his carefully crafted books. His film work was highly prized by director John Huston, and their collaboration on *The African Queen* resulted in a film classic. His greatest fame developed posthumously, however, when his novel *A Death in the Family* won a 1958 Pulitzer Prize. Three years later, Tad Mosel's dramatization of the novel, *All the Way Home* (1960), earned another Pulitzer. The continued popularity of Agee's work attests his vast human sympathy, his unusual lyrical gift, and his ability to evoke the tension and tenderness of family life in both fiction and nonfiction.

Biography

Born in Knoxville, Tennessee, on November 27, 1909, James Rufus Agee was the son of Hugh James Agee, from a Tennessee mountain family, and Laura Whitman Tyler, the well-educated and highly religious daughter of a businessman. His father sang mountain ballads to him, while his mother passed on to him her love of drama and music. Hugh Agee's death in an automobile accident in the spring of 1916 profoundly influenced young Rufus, as he was called.

Agee received a first-rate education at St. Andrew's School, near Sewanee, Tennessee, where he developed a lifelong friendship with Father James Harold Flye; at Phillips Exeter Academy, Exeter, New Hampshire; and at Harvard College, where in his senior year he edited the *Harvard Advocate*. Upon his graduation in 1932, he went immediately to work for *Fortune* and later its sister publication, *Time*. Over a sixteen-year period, he did a variety of staff work, reviewing and writing feature stories while living in the New York metropolitan area.

From 1950 on, Agee spent considerable time in California working mostly with John Huston, but his health deteriorated. Highly disciplined as a writer, Agee exerted less successful control over his living habits, with chronic insomnia and alcoholism contributing to a succession of heart attacks beginning early in 1951. Agee was married three times and had a son by his second wife and three more children by his third, Mia Fritsch, who survived him. He succumbed to a fatal heart attack in a New York taxicab on May 16, 1955, at the age of forty-five.

Analysis

Neither James Agee's novella *The Morning Watch* nor his novel *A Death in the Family* offers much in the way of plot. The former covers a few hours of a boy's Good Friday morning at an Episcopalian boys' school, the latter a few days encompassing the death and funeral of a young husband and father. In depicting the people, traditions, and sensibilities of the American South,

Agee's fiction develops a remarkable lyric intensity, however, and dramatizes with sensitivity the consciousness of children. He presents the minutiae of life as experienced by his characters at times of maximum awareness and thereby lifts them out of the category of mere realistic detail into the realm of spiritual discovery.

Agee was a writer who stayed close to home in his work. His fiction, autobiographically based, displays no trace of the two-thirds of his life spent mainly in New England, New York, and California. As is so often the case with Southern writers, Agee's work is imbued with a sense of his origins, of folk traditions viewed in their own right and in competition with the emerging urban culture. The South, with its insistence on the primacy of personal and familial relationships, was in his bones. In keeping to his earliest and most vividly felt years, Agee created a convincing context in which experiences of universal significance can unfold.

At the beginning of *The Morning Watch*, a preadolescent boy and several of his classmates are awakened in the wee hours of Good Friday morning to spend their assigned time in an overnight vigil in the school chapel as part of the Maundy Thursday and Good Friday devotions. While his friends fumble and curse in the darkness, Richard prepares for adoration. Once in the chapel before the veiled monstrance, he strives to pray worthily despite the inevitable distractions of potentially sinful thoughts, the dangers of spiritual pride, and the torture of the hard kneeling board. Richard wonders whether he can make a virtue of his discomfort: To what extent is it proper for him to suffer along with the crucified Savior? Agee brings Richard intensely alive and conveys the power and the puzzlement of mighty spiritual claims at this stage of life.

The narrative also develops from the start Richard's sense of his relationships with the other boys, most of whom, he realizes, lack his delicate spiritual antennae. After the stint in the chapel is over, he and two classmates do not return to the dormitory as expected but decide to take an early-morning swim. Their adventure is presented in a heavily symbolic way. Richard dives into deep water at their swimming hole, stays down so long that his friends begin to worry, and emerges before his lungs give out. The boys torture and kill a snake, with Richard (who, like Agee himself, cannot bear to kill) finishing the job. He debates in his mind whether the snake is poisonous and whether to wash the slime from his hand, deciding finally in the negative. He carries back to the school a locust shell he has found on

the way. The snake, which seemingly cannot be killed, suggests both ineradicable evil and, in its victimization, Christ; the locust shell, which he holds next to his heart, seems to represent suffering in a purer form. Richard's dive into the water and subsequent resurfacing obviously symbolize his own "death" and "resurrection" in this Christian Holy Week.

The novel upon which Agee's reputation as an important American novelist primarily rests, however, and which he did not quite complete before his early death, is *A Death in the Family*. As he left it, the story begins at the supper table of the Follet household in Knoxville, Tennessee, in about 1915, and ends soon after Jay Follet's funeral on the third day following. The novel has no single protagonist. The family members include Jay and Mary Follett and their children, Rufus and Catherine. Jay Follet, strong, tall, and taciturn, is described most specifically, at one point being compared to Abraham Lincoln, though apparently he is more handsome. He appears in five of the novel's six scenes and remains the main object of the other characters' thoughts in the last two parts of the narrative. At various stages, each important family member reflects on him—no point of view outside the family circle intrudes. Throughout the novel, Agee juxtaposes the tensions and tendernesses of domestic life. The reader is constantly made to feel not only how much the family members love one another but also how abrasive they can be. Recognizing that a family does not succeed automatically, Agee portrays a continual struggle against external divisive pressures and selfishness within.

Jay and Mary's marriage has withstood a number of strains. First of all, their origins differ greatly. Mary's people are the citified, well-educated Lynches; the Follets are Tennessee mountain folk. The couple's ability to harmonize their differences is exemplified in the second of the six scenes. Rufus notes that when singing together, his father interprets music flexibly, "like a darky," while his mother sings true and clear but according to the book. Rufus particularly admires his father's sense of rhythm. Sometimes, the boy observes, his mother tries to sing Jay's way and he hers, but they soon give up and return to what is natural.

Another source of marital discord is Mary's opinion of Jay's father, her antipathy toward him being known to all the Follets. Mary is similarly distressed over Jay's alcoholism, a Follet weakness. Jay dies while visiting his father, who reportedly was very ill. It is on the return trip that a mechanical defect in Jay's car causes the crash that kills him instantly. A little later Mary learns that his drunken driving may have caused the crash.

Religion is another divisive issue. Jay does not appear to be a denominational Christian, while Mary is, like Agee's own mother, a fervent Episcopalian. The men on both sides of the family are either skeptics or thoroughgoing unbelievers. A devotee of Thomas Hardy's fiction, Mary's father, Joel, has little use for piety or what he calls "churchiness." Although he originally disapproved of Mary's marriage to Jay, he has come to terms with Jay, whom he views as a counterweight to Mary's religiosity. Mary's brother Andrew carries on open warfare with the Christian God. When he first hears of Jay's accident, Mary senses that he is mentally rehearsing a speech about the folly of belief in a benevolent deity. Even young Rufus is a budding skeptic. Told that God has let his father "go to sleep," he ferrets out the details and concludes that the concussion he has heard about, "not God," has put his father to sleep. When he hears that his father will wake up at the Final Judgment, he wonders what good that is. The women accept the inscrutable as God's will, but the men take an agnostic stance and fear the influence of the Church. Father Jackson, the most unpleasant person in the novel, ministers to Mary in her bereavement. Rufus quickly decides that the priest's power is malevolent and that, were his real father present, the false father would not be allowed into his home.

Some hours after the confirmation of Jay's death, Mary feels his presence in the room, and though Andrew and Joel will not concede any kind of spiritual visitation, they acknowledge that they too felt "something." Later, Andrew tells Rufus of an event he considers "miraculous": the settling of a butterfly on Jay's coffin in the grave and the creature's subsequent flight, high into the sunlight. The men recognize the possibility of a realm beyond the natural order, but they bitterly oppose the certified spiritual agent, Father Jackson, as too self-assured and quick to condemn.

To counter the estrangements brought on by cultural and religious conflicts in the family, reconciliations dot the narrative. Rufus senses periodic estrangements from his father and then joyful feelings of unity. Jay frequently feels lonely, even homesick. Crossing the river between Knoxville and his old home, he feels restored. To go home is impracticable, bound up with a vanished childhood. In one of the scenes, the family visits Rufus' great-great-grandmother. It is a long, winding journey into the hills and into the past. It is apparent that none of the younger generations of Folletts has gone to see the old woman in a long time. Rufus,

who has never been there, comes home in a way impossible to his father. The old woman, more than a hundred years old, barely acknowledges any of her numerous offspring, but she clasps Rufus, the fifth-generation descendant, who is joyful to her. On other occasions, Jay, by imaginative identification with Rufus, can feel as if he is his "own self" again.

Much of the talk following Jay's death is irritable and nerve-shattering. Andrew dwells thoughtlessly on the one-chance-in-a-million nature of Jay's accident, for which his father rebukes him. Mary begs Andrew to have mercy and then hysterically begs his forgiveness, upon which her aunt censures her for unwarranted humility. Both Mary and Andrew are enduring crises, however, and are hardly responsible for what they say. She is resisting the temptation to despair of God's mercy; he is trying to come to terms with a possibly meaningless universe.

The truest communication exists between Jay and Mary. When he is not silent, he can be sullen or wrathful. As he prepares to set forth on his journey to his father's, Mary dreads the "fury and profanity" she can expect if, for example, the car will not start, but this sometimes harsh husband stops in the bedroom to recompose their bed so it will look comfortable and inviting when she returns to it. She disapproves of his drinking strong coffee, but she makes it very strong on this occasion because she knows he will appreciate it. By dozens of such unobtrusive deeds, Jay and Mary express their love, which prevails over the numerous adverse circumstances and personal weaknesses that threaten it.

Long before he began work on *A Death in the Family*, Agee expressed his intention to base a literary work on his father's death. The novel is thus deeply meditated and very personal. At the same time, it attains universality by means of its painstaking precision. In the Folletts can be seen any family that has striven to harmonize potentially divisive differences or has met a sudden tragedy courageously. At the end, Andrew, for the first time in his life, invites Rufus to walk with him. Sensing the negative feelings in his uncle, Rufus nevertheless is afraid to ask him about them. Walking home with this man who can never replicate his father but who will fill as much of the void as possible, Rufus comes to terms with his father's death in the silence that in Agee's fiction communicates beyond the power of words. In this reconstruction of his own most momentous childhood experience, Agee portrays the most difficult reconciliation of all.

Other major works

SHORT FICTION: "A Mother's Tale," 1952; *Four Early Stories by James Agee*, 1964; *The Collected Short Prose of James Agee*, 1968.

SCREENPLAYS: *The Red Badge of Courage*, 1951 (based on Stephen Crane's novel); *The African Queen*, 1951 (based on the novel by C. S. Forester); *The Bride Comes to Yellow Sky*, 1952 (based on Crane's short story); *Noa Noa*, 1953; *White Mane*, 1953; *Green Magic*, 1955; *The Night of the Hunter*, 1955; *Agee on Film: Five Film Scripts*, 1960.

POETRY: *Permit Me Voyage*, 1934; *The Collected Poems of James Agee*, 1968.

NONFICTION: *Let Us Now Praise Famous Men*, 1941; *Agee on Film: Reviews and Comments*, 1958; *Letters of James Agee to Father Flye*, 1962.

Bibliography

Barson, Alfred. *A Way of Seeing: A Critical Study of James Agee*. Amherst: University of Massachusetts Press, 1972.

Bergeen, Laurence. *James Agee: A Life*. New York: E. P. Dutton, 1984.

Kramer, Victor A. *Agee and Actuality: Artistic Vision in His Work*. Troy, N.Y.: Whitston, 1991.

_____ . *James Agee*. Boston: Twayne, 1975.

Lofaro, Michael A. *James Agee: Reconsiderations*. Knoxville: University of Tennessee Press, 1992.

Lowe, James. *The Creative Process of James Agee*. Baton Rouge: Louisiana State University Press, 1994.

Madden, David, ed. *Remembering James Agee*. Baton Rouge: Louisiana State University Press, 1974.

Moreau, Geneviève. *The Restless Journey of James Agee*. Translated by Miriam Kleiger. New York: William Morrow, 1977.

Ohlin, Peter H. *Agee*. New York: I. Obolensky, 1966.

Seib, Kenneth. *James Agee: Promise and Fulfillment*. Pittsburgh: University of Pittsburgh Press, 1968.

WENDELL BERRY

Born: Henry County, Kentucky; August 5, 1934

Principal poetry

November Twenty-six, Nineteen Hundred Sixty-three, 1963; *The Broken Ground*, 1964; *Openings*, 1968; *Findings*, 1969; *Farming: A Hand Book*, 1970; *The Country of Marriage*, 1973; *An Eastward Look*, 1974; *To What Listens*, 1975; *Horses*, 1975; *Sayings and Doings*, 1975; *The Kentucky River: Two Poems*, 1976; *There Is Singing Around Me*, 1976; *Three Memorial Poems*, 1976; *Clearing*, 1977; *The Gift of Gravity*, 1979; *A Part*, 1980; *The Wheel*, 1982; *Collected Poems: 1957-1982*, 1985; *Sabbaths*, 1987; *Traveling at Home*, 1989; *Sabbaths 1987-90*, 1992.

Other literary forms

In addition to poetry, Berry has written fiction, essays, and a biography of Harland Hubbard.

Achievements

Wendell Berry has achieved regional prominence as a poet, essayist, and novelist who writes about the common tobacco farmers of his fictional Port William community in northern Kentucky. As a poet, Berry has published widely since 1957 in small magazines, poetry volumes, private printings, and a collected edition of his verse in 1985.

Biography

Born in Henry County, Kentucky, on August 5, 1934, Wendell Berry grew up in a family of strong-willed, independent-minded readers and thinkers. His father, John M. Berry, was an attorney and a leader of the Burley Tobacco Growers Association. After attending the University of Kentucky for his bachelor's and master's degrees, Berry was married and taught for a year at Georgetown College in Kentucky. He then accepted a Wallace Stegner Fellowship in creative writing (1958-1959) at Stanford University. A Guggenheim Foundation award allowed him to travel to Europe in 1962 before he returned to teach English at New York University from 1962 to 1964. Berry wrote a moving elegy for President John F. Kennedy that won critical praise, and his first poetry volume, *The Broken Ground*, appeared in 1964.

Berry and his family returned to Kentucky in 1964, when he was appointed to the English Department at the University of Kentucky in Lexington. He purchased Lane's Landing Farm in Port Royal in 1965 and moved back to his native county, settling there with his wife and children. There he continued to farm and write. Berry also became a contributing editor to Rodale Press.

Analysis

Berry is considered one of the most important modern American nature poets, perhaps the best of his generation. He also ranks among the leading American regional writers: His poetic world is first the physical and social world of his native Kentucky region and its farming communities.

Berry is, moreover, a poet of deep conviction. Like Henry David Thoreau, he has felt a need to reestablish himself from the ground up by articulating the ecological and economic principles by which he would live and by trying to live and write in accordance with those principles. He has striven to achieve a rigorous moral and aesthetic simplicity in his work by reworking the same basic themes and insights: the proper place of human life in the larger natural cycle of life, death, and renewal; the dignity of work, labor, and vocation; the central importance of marriage and family commitments; the articulation of the human and natural history of his native region; and precise, lyrical descriptions of the native flora and fauna of his region, especially of the birds, trees, and wildflowers. Expanding on these basic themes, he has included elegies to family members and friends, topical and occasional poems (especially anti-war poems expressing his strong pacifist convictions), didactic poems expressing his environmental beliefs, and a surprising number of religious poems expressing a deeply felt but nondenominational faith.

One finds in Berry's verse a continual effort to unify life, work, and art within a coherent philosophy or vision. Put simply, that vision includes a regional sensibility, a farming avocation, a poetic voice of the farmer-husband-lover-environmentalist, and a strong commitment to a localized environmental ethic. From childhood, Berry always hoped to become a farmer, and his verse celebrates the life of the land. His vision, however, is that of diminishment: of the land, of the community, and even of his art. One senses in Berry's poetry a keen awareness of living in a fallen world, to be redeemed, if at all, through hard work, disciplined self-knowledge, and a gradual healing of the land.

Although Berry had been publishing poems in literary magazines and journals since the mid-1950's, his first critical recognition followed the publication of *November Twenty-six, Nineteen Hundred Sixty-three*, his elegy for John F. Kennedy, which first appeared in the December 21, 1963, issue of *The Nation*, and *The Broken Ground*, Berry's first poetry volume. *The Broken Ground* is a collection of thirty-one free-verse lyrics with a distinctly regional flavor, twenty of which were later included in his *Collected Poems*. This early collection introduces the Berry voice and some of his major themes: the cycle of life and death, a sensitivity to place, pastoral subject matter, and recurring images of water, the Kentucky River, and the hilly, pastoral landscape of north-central Kentucky. These poems bespeak his love of farming and the rhythms of physical labor: its purposefulness, its physicality, and its tangible rewards.

There is a mythic vision in Berry's poems of a lost, primeval paradise, a fall from grace, and a guarded hope in work, discipline, and renewal. "Paradise might have appeared here," he announces in "The Aristocracy," but instead he finds a wealthy old dowager airing her cat. Like Robert Frost's pastoral world of a diminished New England landscape, Berry's Kentucky River Valley has suffered from neglect and abuse. The moments of grace are few—bird songs, the return of spring, the cycle of the seasons, glimpses of the natural order—and death is always present. Like Frost, Berry has chosen to make a "strategic retreat" to a pastoral world in which the poet-farmer can take stock of his resources. For Berry the sense of loss comes from environmental despoilation of the Cumberland plateau, first by careless farming practices and later by timber interests and the big coal companies.

Collected Poems contains Berry's best poetry. Among his best early work was the sequence of three long poems from *Findings*. "The Design of a House" is a poem about beginnings and intentions, the conscious fabrication of a dwelling and a marriage relationship that had previously existed merely as a vague dream or desire, and a wish to reestablish roots in one's native place. It becomes a nuptial poem, the speaker's dedication of his love to his wife, Tanya, and his daughter, Mary, and the continuation of their life together. The design of their house comes to signify the design of their family relationship.

The second poem in *Findings*, "The Handing Down," continues this theme of family and place, this time in terms of an old man's memories and reflections, his sense of satisfaction with the life he has led, as expressed through conversations with his grandson. The poem concerns an old man's preparations for death, his gradual letting go of life through the memories that run through his mind. The third part of *Findings*, "Three Elegiac Poems," commemorates the death of the old man, which the speaker hopes will occur quietly at home, away from the sterile coldness and isolation of hospital wards and the indifference of physicians.

Openings, *Farming: A Hand Book*, *The Country of Marriage*, and *Clearing* celebrate his return to Kentucky and the satisfaction he found in taking up farming. After living in California, Europe, and New York City, he came to appreciate the possibilities of writing about his native region. Berry was particularly impressed with the hill farms of Tuscany, around Florence, which showed him that such "marginal land" might remain productive for many centuries with the proper care and attention. The quality of these farms led him to rethink the possibilities of hill farming in his native Kentucky. As he indicates in the autographical title essay in *The Long-Legged House* (1969), he kept feeling himself drawn back home, particularly to the small cabin built on the Kentucky River by his uncle Curran Matthews. After it was flooded, Berry moved this house farther up the riverbank and rebuilt it to create his writer's study.

Berry's poems in these middle volumes show a new depth of craft and responsiveness to nature. They celebrate the values of land and nature, family and community, marital love and devotion. They are quietly attentive to the cycle of seasons, of the organic cycles of growth and decay, of the subtle beauty of the native flora and fauna. As philosopher, visionary, and political activist, his "Mad Farmer" persona speaks out against war, wastefulness, and environmental destruction. He dreams of a new, gentler orientation to the land that will encourage people to cherish and preserve their natural heritage. He finds deep spiritual sustenance as he reflects on the beauty and fitness of the natural order and the richness of the present moment.

Berry's poems are broadly pastoral in orientation, but they reflect the Kentucky frontier tradition of pioneer homesteading and yeoman farming rather than artificial literary tradition. Some pastoral themes evident in his work include an idealization of the simple life, an implied city-country contrast, a yearning for a past "golden age" of rural life, a celebration of the seasonal tasks of farming life, a strong affirmation of small-scale, organic farming, and an identification of the poet with his native region.

Berry's relationship with his wife and children has been central to his task of renewal as a pastoral poet. Berry has written many poems to his wife on the anniversaries of their marriage or to express his gratitude for their common life. For his children, too, Berry has written poems on their births, comings of age, and marriages, and on the births of grandchildren. In "The Country of Marriage," farming and marriage serve as complementary and inseparable extensions of each other. Husbandry and marriage are recurring tropes in Berry's poetry, illustrated in clearing fields, sowing crops, planting a garden, tending livestock, mowing hay, and taking in the harvest. He celebrates farming as a labor of love, the work of regeneration and fecundity that is at once vital and procreative.

The poems in *Clearing* articulate Berry's sense of region and place. "Where" is a long pastoral meditation on the history and ownership of the fifty-acre farm, Lane's Landing, which the Berrys purchased between 1965 and 1968. The history of the farm provides a case study in attitudes toward stewardship and land use, from the earliest settlers to the developer from whom Berry purchased the farm. The transition from wilderness to settlement to worn-out land rehearses an ecological myth of the fall from primeval abundance to reckless waste and decay. Berry presents the history of his farm as a parable of the American frontier and an indictment of the reckless habits that quickly exhausted the land's natural richness and abundance. "Where" is both a personal credo and a contemporary ecological statement of what needs to be done, in terms of both land management and changing cultural attitudes toward the land.

The Wheel reflects Berry's deepening ecological awareness. This collection is a book of elegies of remembrance and praise, celebrating the continuities of birth, growth, maturity, death, and decay. "Elegy," one of Berry's finest poems, appears in this collection. A pastoral elegy, it is one of a series of three poems dedicated to Owen Flood, whom Berry honors as a teacher and friend. The first poem, "Requiem," announces his passing, though his spirit remains in the fields he had tended. "Elegy" pays tribute to the quality of Flood's life in eight sections, invoking the spirits of the dead to reaffirm the traditional values that Flood embodied: duty, loyalty, perseverance, honesty, hard work, endurance, and self-reliance. It reaffirms the continuity of the generations within a permanent, stable agricultural order. There is a sense of recycling human life, as nature recycles organic materials back into the soil to create the fertile organic humus of the soil. The poem also celebrates human permanences: marriage, work, friendship, love, fidelity, and death. The dominant image is of life as a dance within the circle of life, implying closure, completeness, and inclusion. "Elegy" affirms farm labor as an honorable calling, true to the biblical injunction to live by the sweat of one's brow. The opening line of the poem reaffirms an implicit purpose in all Berry's work: "To be at home on its native ground."

Sabbaths is more overtly religious in its sensibility than previous works. There are quiet, restrained, almost metaphysical meditations that incorporate a number of lines from Scripture. Here Berry makes use of traditional rhyme and meter. These poems show a deep, nonsectarian religious sensibility, akin to the personal faith of the New England Transcendentalist poets—especially Emily Dickinson. Like Dickinson, Berry applies Christian tropes to nature to imply a natural religion. The many allusions to Eden, Paradise, worship, hymns, song, grace, gift, Maker, heaven, resurrection, darkness, and light invoke a kind of prophetic vision of a new earth, healed and reborn—a paradise regained. Berry again describes the primal fertility and richness of the Kentucky landscape before it was ruined by the rapacious settlers. His poems combine a moral awareness of a deep wrong done to the earth by human greed and ignorance with an ecological awareness of the need for a change that can come only from within. His poems offer a dichotomized moral vision of nature as basically innocent and human nature as the source of evil.

The overall theme of *Sabbaths* is the need for rest and renewal—both within human hearts and in the natural world. Berry calls for the cultivation of a different kind of sensibility—less inclined to impose human will on nature and more inclined to appreciate the natural world on its own terms, as a kind of heaven on earth. Berry weaves many scriptural allusions into his poems, quoting from the Psalms, the Old Testament prophets, and the New Testament. The poems manage to convey a deep meditative sensibility without making any formal religious affirmations except by implication. One finds in *Sabbaths* a new blend of spiritual and ecological awareness, a sense of life, of the earth, of the land, as worthy of the deepest veneration.

Wendell Berry's poetry marks him as one of the most

important contemporary American nature poets. His sense of the sacredness and interdependence of all life places him within the tradition of Ralph Waldo Emerson, Walt Whitman, and Henry David Thoreau. He is also one of the foremost American regional writers, insisting that his poetry be firmly rooted in a sense of place. His poetry reflects the same deep concern for the natural environment and for sound conservation and farming practices that is evident in his essays and fiction. His emphasis on marriage, family, and community allows him to affirm these necessary human bonds. His poems reflect his loyalty to his native region, his love of farming, his view of marriage as a sacrament, and his deep awareness of the beauty and wonder of the natural world.

Other major works

LONG FICTION: *Nathan Coulter*, 1960, rev. 1985; *A Place on Earth*, 1967, rev. 1983; *The Memory of Old Jack*, 1974; *Remembering*, 1988.

SHORT FICTION: *The Wild Birds*, 1986; *Fidelity: Five Stories*, 1992; *Watch with Me*, 1994.

NONFICTION: *The Long-Legged House*, 1969; *The Hidden Wound*, 1970; *The Unforeseen Wilderness*, 1971; *A Continuous Harmony*, 1972; *The Unsettling of America*, 1977; *Recollected Essays, 1965-1980*, 1981; *The Gift of Good Land*, 1981; *Standing by Words*, 1983; *Home Economics*, 1987; *What Are People For?*, 1990; *Harland Hubbard: Life and Work*, 1990; *Standing on Earth: Selected Essays*, 1991; *Sex, Economy, Freedom and Community*, 1993.

Bibliography

Cornell, Daniel. "*The Country of Marriage:* Wendell Berry's Personal Political Vision." *Southern Literary Journal* 16 (Fall, 1983): 59-70.

Hicks, Jack. "Wendell Berry's Husband to the World: *A Place on Earth*." *American Literature* 51 (May, 1979): 238-254.

Morgan, Speer. "Wendell Berry: A Fatal Singing." *The Southern Review* 10 (October, 1974): 865-877.

Nibbelink, Herman. "Thoreau and Wendell Berry: Bachelor and Husband of Nature." *The South Atlantic Quarterly* 84 (Spring, 1985): 127-140.

Weiland, Steven. "Wendell Berry: Culture and Fidelity." *Iowa Review* 10 (Winter, 1979): 99-104.

ERSKINE CALDWELL

Born: White Oak, Georgia; December 17, 1903

Died: Paradise Valley, Arizona; April 11, 1987

Principal long fiction

The Bastard, 1929; *Poor Fool*, 1930; *Tobacco Road*, 1932; *God's Little Acre*, 1933; *Journeyman*, 1935; *Trouble in July*, 1940; *All Night Long: A Novel of Guerrilla Warfare in Russia*, 1942; *Tragic Ground*, 1944; *A House in the Uplands*, 1946; *The Sure Hand of God*, 1947; *This Very Earth*, 1948; *Place Called Estherville*, 1949; *Episode in Palmetto*, 1950; *A Lamp for Nightfall*, 1952; *Love and Money*, 1954; *Gretta*, 1955; *Claudelle Inglish*, 1958; *Jenny by Nature*, 1961; *Close to Home*, 1962; *The Last Night of Summer*, 1963; *Miss Mamma Aimee*, 1967; *Summertime Island*, 1968; *The Weather Shelter*, 1969; *The Earnshaw Neighborhood*, 1972; *Annette*, 1974.

Other literary forms

Erskine Caldwell's first published work was "The Georgia Cracker," a 1926 article. Other pieces were printed in "little" magazines, and then in *Scribner's Magazine*. For several decades, he regularly wrote articles for magazines and newspapers. He produced several nonfiction books, some in collaboration with photojournalist Margaret Bourke-White (at one time his wife), and collections of short stories.

Achievements

More than 64 million copies of Caldwell's books have been published in thirty-four countries, with 320 editions released in such languages as Croatian, Chinese, Slovene, Turkmenian, Arabic, Danish, Hebrew, Icelandic, Russian, and Turkish. He has been called the best-selling writer in America.

In 1933, Caldwell received the *Yale Review* award for fiction for his short story "Country Full of Swedes." Between 1940 and 1955, he was editor of twenty-five volumes of a regional series, *American Folkways*. His novel *Tobacco Road* was adapted for the stage in 1934 and ran seven and a half years on Broadway, a record run. It was made into a motion picture in 1941. *Claudelle Inglish* became a film in 1961. *God's Little Acre*, possibly his best-known novel, sold more than eight million copies in paperback in the United States alone and became a film in 1959.

Biography

Erskine Caldwell was the son of Ira Sylvester Caldwell, a preacher, and Caroline "Carrie" Preston (Bell) Caldwell. At the time Erskine was born, on December 17, 1903, the Reverend Caldwell was minister in Newman, Georgia, in Coweta County, forty miles from Atlanta. His wife, active in helping her husband in his ministry, also ran a small school. She taught Caldwell through much of his elementary and secondary education, both in her school and at home. He actually spent only one year in public school and one in high school.

Between 1906 and 1919, the Caldwells moved several times as the ministry dictated. This not-quite-nomadic existence and the straitened circumstances under which the family lived were probably influential in molding Caldwell into early self-reliance and in fostering a wanderlust that persisted throughout his youth and adult life. Caldwell left home at fourteen, roaming about the Deep South, Mexico, and Central America. He did return home, however, to complete his high school education.

In 1920, Caldwell enrolled in Erskine College in Due West, South Carolina. From 1923 to 1924, he attended the University of Virginia on a scholarship; in 1924, he studied for two terms at the University of Pennsylvania. In 1925, he returned to the University of Virginia for an additional term, but he was never graduated.

While attending the University of Virginia, Caldwell married Helen Lannegan, and it was at this time that he decided to write for a living. With his wife and growing family of three children, he lived in Maine between 1925 and 1932 while he wrote and earned a living at odd jobs; seven years of writing elapsed before any of his work was published. In his lifetime, Caldwell had experience as a mill laborer, cook, cabdriver, farmhand, stonemason's helper, soda jerk, professional football player, bodyguard, stagehand at a burlesque theater, and once even a hand on a boat running guns to a Central American country in revolt.

Caldwell published his first article in 1926. Soon Maxwell Perkins, the legendary editor at Charles Scribner's Sons, discovered some of his works and was enthusiastic and encouraging about his talent. Subsequently, Perkins published *American Earth* and *Tobacco Road*, which brought Caldwell his first real recognition.

Divorced from his first wife in 1938, Caldwell married the photojournalist Margaret Bourke-White. They collaborated on several successful books, but the marriage ended in divorce in 1942. The same year, he married June Johnson, with whom he had one son, Jay Erskine. In 1957, after divorcing his third wife, he married Virginia Moffett Fletcher.

Active as a writer and lecturer, Caldwell toured Europe in the 1960's under the auspices of the U.S. State Department. In the 1970's, he made a series of speeches in Georgia, promoting the paperback reprint of his 1937 book *You Have Seen Their Faces*. He used this opportunity to decry the remaining poverty in the South despite its industrialization.

Analysis

Caldwell is the chronicler of the poor Southern white. He has told the story of the diversions and disasters of this figure with more detail and sympathetic attention than any other American writer of his time. In doing so, he has created memorable characters and unforgettable episodes and has provoked scandalized eyebrow-raising at his language, his imagery, and his view of American life in the Depression years.

The most prominent and lasting quality of Caldwell's fiction—the one that has made *Tobacco Road* a minor classic and several other of his earlier novels important literary pieces—is comic grotesquerie. Caldwell conveys a kind of ludicrous horror that becomes more horrible when the reader realizes that hyperbole does not negate the truth behind the most ridiculous episodes: The poor people of the South were deprived to the point of depravity. Writing in a naturalistic style, Caldwell allows the reader to observe the day-to-day activities of poor white families whose impoverished condition has created tragicomic eccentricities.

Those impoverished conditions are the key to understanding Caldwell's main thrust in nearly all of his earlier novels. Living in hopeless hunger, illiterate, and essentially cut off from the world of progress, ambition, and culture, Caldwell's characters seem not quite human. The veneer of civilized attitudes and activities has been ground away by the endless struggle to satisfy the daily hunger and to find some hope, in a vast vista of barren prospects, of a better day tomorrow.

Caldwell was deeply concerned that this segment of society he chose to depict in his work had been repressed by ignorance and poverty as an almost direct result of society's indifference. There are seldom any "bad guys" in Caldwell's novels, no dastardly villains. The villain is society, which allows abject poverty, ignorance, hunger, and hopelessness to exist without trying to correct the circumstances that caused them. His characters, victims of society, flounder into tragic situations without knowing how to save themselves.

In the case of *Tobacco Road*, tragedy strikes as unpredictably as lightning and the characters accept their lot as though it were a natural, unalterable phenomenon. This book, perhaps his best-known work, is the story of a family of ignorant poor white Georgians who at the outset are at the depths of degradation. They have no food, no prospects, and no apparent opportunity to get either. They have settled into a bleak routine, planning to plant a crop in the vague future and hoping for something to happen to change their lot. Jeeter Lester, the patriarch, has the last trace of a noble love of the land and a strong inherent need to farm his land and produce a crop, yet he cannot or will not do any of the practical things that must be done for serious, life-saving farming. He has no money and no credit, and he will not leave his farm to find work in the town to get the money for seed and fertilizer. Thus, he drifts from day to day with good intentions but takes no positive action. Survival for him and his family has reached an "every man for himself" level. His mother is treated with less consideration than a dog: When any food is acquired, as when Jeeter steals a bag of turnips from his son-in-law, the old mother is not given any. The others in the family—Jeeter's wife Ada and the two remaining children, Ellie Mae and Dude—are equally unfeeling.

These people seem to be as far down the scale of humanity as anyone can get, yet the story relates a series of episodes that carry them progressively toward degeneracy and death. The most inhuman and inhumane episode involves the death of Mother Lester, who is hit by the car in the Lester yard. After being knocked down and run over, she lies there, unaided by any of the family. The old woman struggles a bit, every part of her body in agonizing pain, and manages to turn over. Then she is still. When Jeeter at last decides something must be done with his old mother, he looks down and moves one of her arms with his foot, and says, "She aint stiff yet, but I don't reckon she'll live. You help me tote her out in the field and I'll dig a ditch to put her in."

When Caldwell depicts the indifference of the family

members to Mother Lester's slow, painful death, he is really depicting the degeneracy of people whom society has deprived of all "human" feeling. Thus, when in the last chapter the old Lester house catches fire and burns the sleeping occupants without their ever waking, the reader may well feel that poetic justice has been served: The Lesters have lived a subhuman existence, and their end is fittingly subhuman. Yet, one does not entirely blame the Lesters for their lack of humanity; Caldwell moves his readers to wonder that a rich, progressive country such as the United States could still harbor such primitive conditions.

The comic quality that is so much a part of Caldwell's work saves *Tobacco Road* from utter grimness. There is, for example, a particular comic quality in Jeeter's serious pronouncements, which bespeak a completely unrealistic creature out of touch with himself and his true condition. Yet the enduring ridiculousness of Jeeter and his family is undercoated with a pathos that is obvious to the thoughtful reader. The condition and ultimate end of Jeeter and Ada are perhaps atypical but are still symptomatic of the condition and ultimate end of the many others like them living in the destitute areas of the South.

God's Little Acre tells the story of Ty Ty Walden, a Georgia dirt farmer who for fifteen years has been digging enormous holes in his land looking for gold. Ty Ty, who is in most other respects a man with considerable mother wit, has a curious tunnel vision where this quest for gold is concerned. Because of it, he neglects his farming to the point of endangering his livelihood and that of his family. Worse yet, he fails to see the peril in the growing tension among the members of his family living on the farm with him.

The inevitable tragedy results from the fact that he has two beautiful daughters and an even more beautiful daughter-in-law, Griselda. Ty Ty himself praises Griselda so much to anyone who will listen that he is largely instrumental in encouraging the fatal allurement she has for the other men in the family. When these men—a son, Jim Leslie, and a son-in-law, Will Thompson—make advances toward Griselda, her husband Buck understandably becomes enraged. He is thwarted in his revenge against Will Thompson by another calamity—Will, a mill worker, is killed during a strike action—but Jim Leslie does not escape his brother Buck's wrath, nor does the tragedy stop there, for Buck's action is harshly punished.

Caldwell's comic style is once again in evidence. The infighting and escapades of Ty Ty's clan are brought to life in richly comic scenes that create a humorously cockeyed view of the Georgia poor white. Yet the novel is, in fact, a serious story about people who in their daily lives do things that seem comic to those who observe them from a distance. Caldwell begins with a feckless existence that gradually becomes tragic; the comical episodes of Ty Ty's clan assume a grim inevitability.

Ty Ty has set aside one acre of his land for God. His intent is to farm the land, raise a crop, and give the proceeds to God through the church. Ty Ty has been digging for gold all over his farm, however, and there is very little land left that can still be farmed. Because he needs to raise a crop to feed his family and the two black families who tenant-farm for him, Ty Ty must constantly shift the acre for God from place to place. He readily admits that he will not dig for gold on God's little acre because then he would be honorbound to give the gold to the church. He has no compunctions about doing God out of what he has declared is God's due. Later in the story, however, when he learns of Will Thompson's death, he has a sudden need to bring the acre closer to the homestead:

> He felt guilty of something—maybe it was sacrilege or desecration—whatever it was, he knew he had not played fair with God. Now he wished to bring God's little acre back to its rightful place beside the house where he could see it all the time. . . . He promised himself to keep it there until he died.

After this decision, however, blood is shed on God's little acre: Buck kills his own brother, Jim Leslie. The bloodletting on God's ground is almost a ceremonial sacrifice wherein Ty Ty, albeit involuntarily, atones for a life spent giving only lip-service to God. This ironic justice has the tragicomic grotesquerie characteristic of Caldwell's best work. The fall of his protagonists is both inevitable and absurd, utterly lacking in dignity.

Tobacco Road and *God's Little Acre* are the novels by Caldwell that are most likely to endure. Still, Caldwell is considered to be among the significant twentieth century writers produced by the South. His major contribution was his naturalistic comedic approach to his subjects. His best work depicts, with admirable craftsmanship, the harsh life of the sharecropper and tenant farmer through painful explicitness and comic vigor, juxtaposing social issues to the grotesque.

Other major works

SHORT FICTION: *American Earth*, 1931; *Mama's Little Girl*, 1932; *Message for Genevieve*, 1933; *We Are the Living: Brief Stories*, 1933; *Kneel to the Rising Sun and Other Stories*, 1935; *Southways: Stories*, 1938; *Jackpot: The Short Stories of Erskine Caldwell*, 1940; *Georgia Boy*, 1943; *Stories by Erskine Caldwell: 24 Representative Stories*, 1944; *Jackpot: Collected Short Stories*, 1950; *The Courting of Susie Brown*, 1952; *Complete Stories*, 1953; *Gulf Coast Stories*, 1956; *Certain Women*, 1957; *When You Think of Me*, 1959; *Men and Women: 22 Stories*, 1961; *Stories of Life: North and South*, 1983; *The Black and White Stories of Erskine Caldwell*, 1984.

NONFICTION: *Tenant Farmer*, 1935; *Some American People*, 1935; *You Have Seen Their Faces*, 1937 (with Margaret Bourke-White); *North of the Danube*, 1939 (with Bourke-White); *Say! Is This the U.S.A.?*, 1941 (with Bourke-White); *All-Out on the Road to Smolensk*, 1942 (with Bourke-White; also known as *Moscow Under Fire: A Wartime Diary*, 1941); *Russia at War*, 1942 (with Bourke-White); *The Humorous Side of Erskine Caldwell*, 1951; *Call It Experience: The Years of Learning How to Write*, 1951; *Around About America*, 1964; *In Search of Bisco*, 1965; *In the Shadow of the Steeple*, 1967; *Deep South: Memory and Observation*, 1968; *Writing in America*, 1968; *Afternoons in Mid-America*, 1976; *With All My Might*, 1987; *Conversations with Erskine Caldwell*, 1988.

CHILDREN'S LITERATURE: *Molly Cottontail*, 1958; *The Deer at Our House*, 1966.

MISCELLANEOUS: *The Caldwell Caravan: Novels and Stories*, 1946.

Bibliography

Cook, Sylvia Jenkins. *Erskine Caldwell and the Fiction of Poverty: The Flesh and the Spirit*. Baton Rouge: Louisiana State University Press, 1991.

Devlin, James. *Erskine Caldwell*. Boston: Twayne, 1984.

Gray, R. J. "Southwestern Humor, Erskine Caldwell, and the Comedy of Frustration." *Southern Literary Journal* 8, no. 1 (1975): 3-26.

Klevar, Harvey L. *Erskine Caldwell: A Biography*. Knoxville: University of Tennessee Press, 1993.

Korges, James. *Erskine Caldwell*. Minneapolis: University of Minnesota Press, 1969.

MacDonald, Scott. *Critical Essays on Erskine Caldwell*. Boston: G. K. Hall, 1981.

Pembroke Magazine 11 (1979). Special issue on Caldwell.

KATE CHOPIN

Born: St. Louis, Missouri; February 8, 1851

Died: St. Louis, Missouri; August 22, 1904

Principal long fiction

At Fault, 1890; *The Awakening*, 1899.

Other literary forms

In addition to her novels, Kate Chopin wrote nearly fifty poems, approximately one hundred stories and vignettes, and a small amount of literary criticism. Chopin's most important work, apart from her novels, lies in her short stories, many of which are included in the two volumes published during her lifetime—*Bayou Folk* (1894) and *A Night in Acadie* (1897). All the stories and sketches have now been made available in *The Complete Works of Kate Chopin* (1969). Had she never written *The Awakening*, these stories alone, the best of which are inimitable and gemlike, would ensure Chopin a place among the notable writers of the 1890's.

Achievements

Chopin's reputation today rests on three books—her two short-story collections, *Bayou Folk* and *A Night in Acadie*, and her mature novel, *The Awakening*. *Bayou Folk* collects most of her fiction of the early 1890's set in Natchitoches Parish. Three of the stories in this volume—"Beyond the Bayou," "Désirée's Baby," and "Madame Célestin's Divorce"—are among her most famous and most frequently anthologized. *A Night in Acadie* collects Chopin's stories from the middle and late 1890's. It differs from *Bayou Folk* somewhat in the greater emphasis it gives to the erotic drives of its characters.

Chopin's authority in this aspect of experience, and her concern with the interaction of the deeply inward upon the outward life, set her work apart from other local-color writing of the time. In her early novel *At Fault*, she had not as yet begun to probe deeply into the psychology of her characters. After she had developed her art in her stories, however, she was able to bring her psychological concerns to perfection in *The Awakening*, her greatest work. In *Bayou Folk*, *A Night in Acadie*, and *The Awakening*, Chopin gave to American letters works of enduring interest—the interest not so much of local color as of a strikingly sensuous psychological realism.

Biography

Kate Chopin was born Katherine O'Flaherty on February 8, 1851, in St. Louis, Missouri, into a socially prominent family with roots in the French past of both St. Louis and New Orleans. Her father, Thomas O'Flaherty, an emigrant to America from Ireland, had lived in New York and Illinois before settling in St. Louis. Kate was one of three children and the only one to live to mature years. In 1855, tragedy struck the O'Flaherty family when the father, a director of the Pacific Railroad, was killed in a train wreck. In 1860, she entered the St. Louis Academy of the Sacred Heart, a Catholic institution where French history, language, and culture were stressed—as they were, also, in her own household. Such an early absorption in French culture would eventually influence Chopin's own writing, an adaptation in some ways of French forms to American themes.

Chopin was graduated from the Academy of the Sacred Heart in 1868 and two years later was introduced to St. Louis society, becoming one of its ornaments, a vivacious and attractive girl known for her cleverness and talents as a storyteller. The following year, she made a trip to New Orleans, and it was there that she met Oscar Chopin, whom she married in 1871. The couple moved to New Orleans, where Chopin's husband was a cotton factor (a businessman who financed the raising of cotton and transacted its sale). By all accounts, the Chopin marriage was an unusually happy one, and in time Kate became the mother of six children. This period in Kate's life ended, however, in 1883 with the sudden death, from swamp fever, of her husband. A widow at thirty, she moved to St. Louis, where she remained for the rest of her life. She began to write in 1888, while still rearing her children, and in the following year she made her first appearance in print. As her writing shows, her marriage to Oscar Chopin proved to be much more than an "episode" in her life, for it is from this period in New Orleans and Natchitoches Parish that she drew her best literary material and her strongest inspiration. She knew this area personally, and yet as an "outsider" she was also able to observe it with a freshness of detachment.

Chopin had published her first novel, *At Fault*, by 1890. She then wrote a second novel that was never published. Subsequently, she concentrated on the shorter forms of fiction, writing forty stories, sketches, and vignettes during the next three years. By 1894, her stories had begun to find a reception in Eastern magazines, notably in *Vogue*, *The Atlantic Monthly*, and *Century*. In the same year, her first short-story collection, *Bayou Folk*, was published by Houghton Mifflin to favorable reviews. *A Night in Acadie* was brought out by a relatively little-known publisher in Chicago in 1897. Although having achieved some reputation as an author of what were generally perceived to be local-color stories set in northern Louisiana, Chopin was still far from having established herself as a writer whose work was commercially profitable. Under the advice of editors that a longer work would have a broader appeal, she turned again to the novel form, publishing *The Awakening* in 1899. *The Awakening*, however, received uniformly unfavorable reviews and in some cities was banned from library shelves. In St. Louis, Chopin was cut off by friends and was refused membership in a local fine arts club. Chopin had never expected such a storm of condemnation, and, although she withstood it calmly, she was, according to those who knew her best, deeply hurt by the experience. She wrote little thereafter and never published another book. In 1904, after attending the St. Louis World's Fair, she was stricken with a cerebral hemorrhage and died two days later.

Analysis

Acclaimed for her literary naturalism and feminism, Chopin, against the restrictive backdrop of nineteenth century America, challenged conventional roles for women and addressed other controversial themes, such as human sexual awakening. In her vivid re-creation of the world of the Louisiana bayou region, she stressed the power of individuals to determine the course of their own lives.

When Chopin began to publish, local-color writing, which had come into being after the Civil War and crested in the 1880's, had already been established. A late arriver to the scene, Chopin was at first, as her stories show, uncertain even of her locale. *At Fault*, her first novel, was a breakthrough for her in the sense that she found her rural Louisiana "region." The novel is set in the present, a setting that is important to its sphere of action. Place-du-Bois, the plantation, represents conservative, traditional values that are challenged by new,

emergent ones. David Hosmer, from St. Louis, obtains lumber rights on Place-du-Bois, and with him comes conflict. *At Fault* deals with divorce but beyond that with the contradictions of nature and convention. Place-du-Bois seems at times idyllic, but it is shadowed by the cruelties of its slaveholding past, abuses created by too rigidly held assumptions. St. Louis is almost the opposite, a world as much without form as Hosmer's pretty young wife, who goes to pieces there and again at Place-du-Bois.

At Fault looks skeptically at nature but also at received convention. It raises a question that will appear again in *The Awakening*: Is the individual responsible to others or to himself?

Apart from its two settings, *At Fault* does not seem autobiographical. It has the form of a "problem novel," reminiscent of the novels of William Dean Howells. As in certain of Howells's novels, a discussion takes place at one point that frames the conflict that the characters' lives illustrate. In this case it is the conflict between nature and convention, religious and social precept versus the data of actual experience. The proprietor of Place-du-Bois, Thérèse Lafirme, although a warm and attractive woman, is accustomed to thinking about human affairs abstractly. When she learns that David Hosmer, who owns a sawmill on her property, is divorced from his young wife, a weak and susceptible woman who drinks, she admonishes him to return to her and fulfill his marriage pledge to stand by and redeem her. Hosmer admires Thérèse to such an extent that, against his own judgment, and most reluctantly, he returns to St. Louis and remarries Fanny Larimore. They then return to the plantation to live, and in due course history repeats itself. Despite Hosmer's dutiful attentions and her acceptance into the small social world of Place-du-Bois, Fanny begins to drink and to behave unreasonably. Near the end of the novel, having become jealous of Thérèse, Fanny ventures out in a storm and, despite Hosmer's attempt to rescue her, dies in a river flood.

Running parallel to this main plot is a subplot in which Hosmer's sister Melicent feels a romantic attraction to Thérèse's impetuous young nephew Grégoire but decides on the most theoretical grounds that he would not be suitable for a husband. When he becomes involved in a marginal homicide, she condemns him utterly, literally abandoning him. He then returns to Texas, where he goes from bad to worse and is eventually killed in a lawless town. At the end, a year after these events, Hosmer and Thérèse marry and find the happiness they had very nearly lost through Thérèse's preconceptions. It is clear to her that Fanny never could have been redeemed, and that her plan to "save" her had brought suffering to all parties concerned—to Hosmer, to herself, and to Fanny as well. Left open, however, is the question of Melicent's responsibility to Grégoire, whom she had been too quick to "judge." *At Fault* appears to end happily, but in some ways it is pessimistic in its view of nature and convention.

Comparable in kind to Gustave Flaubert's *Madame Bovary* (1857), *The Awakening* is Chopin's largest exploration of feminine consciousness and her most elaborate orchestration of the theme of bondage and illusion. Edna Pontellier, its heroine, is always at the center of the novel, and nothing occurs that does not in some way bear upon her thoughts or developing sense of her situation. As a character who rejects her socially prescribed role as a wife and mother, Edna has a certain affinity with the "New Woman," much discussed in the 1890's, but Edna's special modeling and the type of her experience suggest a French influence. Before beginning the novel, Chopin translated eight of Guy de Maupassant's stories. Two of these tales, "Solitude" and "Suicide," share with *The Awakening* the theme of illusion in erotic desire and the inescapability of the solitary self. At the same time, *The Awakening* seems to have been influenced by *Madame Bovary*. Certain parallels can be noticed in the experience of the two heroines— their repudiation of their husbands, estrangement, and eventual suicides. More important, Flaubert's craftsmanship informs the whole manner of Chopin's novel—its directness, lucidity, and economy of means; its steady use of incident and detail as leitmotif. The novel also draws upon a large fin-de-siècle background concerned with a hunger for the exotic and the voluptuous, a yearning for the absolute. From these diverse influences, Chopin has shaped a work that is strikingly, even startlingly, her own.

The opening third section of *The Awakening*, the chapter set at Grand Isle, is particularly impressive. Here one meets Edna Pontellier, the young wife of a well-to-do Creole *negociant* and mother of two small boys. Mrs. Pontellier, an "American" woman originally from Kentucky, is still not quite accustomed to the sensuous openness of this Creole summer colony. She walks on the beach under a white parasol with handsome young Robert Lebrun, who befriends married Creole women in a way that is harmless, since his attentions are regarded as a social pleasantry, nothing more. Edna and Lebrun have returned from a midday swim in the ocean, an act undertaken on impulse and perhaps not entirely prudent, in view of the extreme heat of that hour and the scorching glare of the sun. When Edna rejoins her husband, he finds her "burnt beyond recognition." Léonce Pontellier is a responsible husband who gives his wife no cause for complaint, but his mind runs frequently on business and he is dull. He is inclined to regard his wife as "property," but by this summer on Grand Isle she has begun to come to self-awareness, suppressed by her role as a "mother-woman." Emboldened by her unconventional midday swim, she goes out swimming alone that night and with reckless exhilaration longs to go "further out than any woman had ever swum before." She quickly tires, however, and is fortunate to have the strength to return to the safety of the shore. When she returns to their house, she does not go inside to join her husband but drowses alone in a porch hammock, lost in a long moonlit reverie that has the voluptuous effulgence of the sea.

As the novel proceeds, it becomes clear that Edna has begun to fall in love with Lebrun, who decides suddenly to go to Mexico, following which the Pontelliers themselves return to their well-appointed home in New Orleans. There Edna begins to behave erratically, defying her husband and leading as much as possible an independent existence. After moving to a small house nearby by herself, she has an affair with a young roué. Alcée Arobin; Lebrun returns from Mexico about the same time and, although in love with her, does not dare to overstep convention with a married woman and the mother of children. Trapped once again within her socially prescribed role, Edna returns to the seashore and goes swimming alone, surrendering her life to the sea.

The imagery of the sea expresses Edna's longing to reach a state in which she feels her own identity and where she feels passionately alive. In this "enfolding" touch of the sea, however, Edna discovers her own solitude, and she loses herself in "mazes of inward contemplation." Yet Edna is no thinker; she is a dreamer who, in standing apart from conditioned circumstance, can only embrace the rhapsodic death lullaby of the sea. At the end of her life, she returns to her childhood, when, in protest against the aridness of her Presbyterian father's Sunday devotions, she had wandered aimlessly in a field of tall meadow grass that made her think of the sea. She had married her Catholic husband despite her father's objection or rather, one thinks, because of his objection. Later, discovering the limitations that her life with her husband imposes upon her, she rebels once again, grasping at the illusion of an idealized Robert Lebrun.

The final irony of *The Awakening*, however, is that even though Edna is drawn as an illusionist, her protest is not quite meaningless. Never before in a novel published in America was the issue of a woman's suppressed erotic nature and need for self-definition, apart from the single received role of wife and mother, raised so forcefully. *The Awakening* is a work in which the feminist protest of the modern age had already been memorably imagined.

In the mid-1950's, Van Wyck Brooks described *The Awakening* as a "small perfect book that mattered more than the whole life work of many a prolific writer." Chopin was not prolific; all but a few of her best stories are contained in *Bayou Folk* and *A Night in Acadie*, and she produced only one mature novel, but these volumes have the mark of genuine quality. Lyric and objective at once, deeply humane and yet constantly attentive to illusion in her characters' perception of reality, these volumes reveal Chopin as a psychological realist of magical empathy, a writer having the greatness of delicacy.

Other major works

SHORT FICTION: *Bayou Folk*, 1894; *A Night in Acadie*, 1897.
MISCELLANEOUS: *The Complete Works of Kate Chopin*, 1969 (Per Seyersted, ed., 2 vols.).

Bibliography

Bloom, Harold, ed. *Modern Critical Views: Kate Chopin*. New York: Chelsea House, 1987.

Bonner, Thomas, Jr. *The Kate Chopin Companion*. New York: Greenwood Press, 1988.

Boren, Lynda S., and Sara deSaussure Davis. *Kate Chopin Reconsidered: Beyond the Bayou*. Baton Rouge: Louisiana State University Press, 1992.

Ewell, Barbara, *Kate Chopin*. New York: Frederick Ungar, 1986.

Koloski, Bernard, ed. *Approaches to Teaching Chopin's "The Awakening."* New York: Modern Language Association of America, 1988.

Martin, Wendy, ed. *New Essays on "The Awakening."* New York: Cambridge University Press, 1988.

Seyersted, Per. *Kate Chopin: A Critical Biography*. Baton Rouge: Louisiana State University Press, 1969.

Skaggs, Peggy. *Kate Chopin*. Boston: Twayne, 1985.

Toth, Emily. *Kate Chopin*. New York: William Morrow, 1990.

WILLIAM FAULKNER

Born: New Albany, Mississippi; September 25, 1897   **Died:** Oxford, Mississippi; July 6, 1962

Principal long fiction

Soldiers' Pay, 1926; *Mosquitoes*, 1927; *Sartoris*, 1929; *The Sound and the Fury*, 1929; *As I Lay Dying*, 1930; *Sanctuary*, 1931; *Light in August*, 1932; *Pylon*, 1935; *Absalom, Absalom!*, 1936; *The Unvanquished*, 1938; *The Wild Palms*, 1939; *The Hamlet*, 1940; *Go Down, Moses*, 1942; *Intruder in the Dust*, 1948; *Requiem for a Nun*, 1951; *A Fable*, 1954; *The Town*, 1957; *The Mansion*, 1959; *The Reivers*, 1962; *Flags in the Dust*, 1973 (original version of *Sartoris*).

Other literary forms

William Faulkner published two volumes of poetry and several volumes of short stories. Most of his best stories appear in *Knight's Gambit* (1949), *Collected Short Stories of William Faulkner* (1950), and the posthumous *Uncollected Stories of William Faulkner* (1979). His early journalistic and prose pieces have been collected and published as have his interviews and a number of his letters. Later years saw the publication of several interesting minor works, including a fairy tale, *The Wishing Tree* (1964), and a romantic fable, *Mayday* (1976). New Faulkner material is steadily seeing print, much of it in the annual Faulkner number of *Mississippi Quarterly*. Scholars are making public more information on Faulkner's screenwriting in Hollywood, where he collaborated on such major successes as *To Have and Have Not* (1944) and *The Big Sleep* (1946). Several of his works have been adapted for television and film; notably successful were film adaptations of *Intruder in the Dust* and *The Reivers*.

Achievements

When Faulkner received the Nobel Prize in Literature in 1949, he completed an emergence from comparative obscurity that had begun three years before. After the Nobel Prize, honors came steadily. He was made a member of the French Legion of Honor, received two National Book Awards for *A Fable* and *Collected Short Stories of William Faulkner*, and received two Pulitzer Prizes for *A Fable* and *The Reivers*. He traveled around the world for the United States State Department in 1954. During 1957, he was writer-in-residence at the University of Virginia. Recognition and financial security, while gratifying, neither diminished nor increased his output. He continued writing until his death.

Faulkner has achieved the status of a world author. His works have been painstakingly translated into many languages. Perhaps more critical books and articles have been written about him in recent times than about any other writer with the exception of William Shakespeare. Critics and scholars from all over the world have contributed to the commentary. Faulkner's achievement has been compared favorably with that of Henry James, Honoré de Balzac, and Charles Dickens; many critics regard him as the preeminent novelist of the twentieth century.

Biography

William Cuthbert Faulkner was born in New Albany, Mississippi, on September 25, 1897. His ancestors had emigrated from Scotland in the eighteenth century. The oldest son of Maud and Murry Falkner, William Cuthbert later became the head of the family. He began to take this responsibility seriously, struggling most of his life to care for those whom, whether by blood or moral commitment, he considered members of his family. In 1924, he changed the spelling of his family name to Faulkner.

Faulkner discovered his storytelling gifts as a child, but his writing career did not really begin until after his brief training for the Royal Air Force in Canada, shortly before the World War I armistice in 1918. He attended the University of Mississippi for one year, worked at odd jobs, and published a volume of poetry, *The Marble Faun* (1924). He began to take writing more seriously, with encouragement from Sherwood Anderson, while living in New Orleans in 1925.

The early novels are interesting, but Faulkner began to show his powers as a prose stylist and as a creator of psychologically deep and interesting characters in *Sar-*

toris, which he had originally written as *Flags in the Dust*. Beginning with *The Sound and the Fury* and up through *Go Down, Moses*, Faulkner wrote the major novels and stories of his Yoknapatawpha series. Of the ten novels he published in these thirteen years, five are generally considered to be masterpieces: *The Sound and the Fury*, *As I Lay Dying*, *Light in August*, *Absalom, Absalom!*, and *Go Down, Moses*. At least two others, *Sanctuary* and *The Hamlet*, are widely studied and admired. The entire series of novels set in the mythical Yoknapatawpha County, Faulkner's "little postage stamp of native soil," is sometimes considered as a great work in its own right, especially when all of the Snopes trilogy (*The Hamlet*, *The Town*, *The Mansion*) is included with the above-named masterpieces. Stories from his two collections of the 1929-1942 period regularly appear in anthologies; "Old Man" and "The Bear," which are parts of *The Wild Palms* and *Go Down, Moses*, respectively, are perhaps his best-known novellas.

Faulkner's personal life was difficult and has provoked much critical interest in tracing relationships between his life and his work. The family-arranged and unhappy marriage to Estelle Oldham in 1929 ended in divorce. Both Faulkner and his wife were subject to alcoholism; he carried on a virtually continuous struggle against debt, resentful and unhappy over the necessity of working in Hollywood in order to keep his family solvent. Though Faulkner was a fiercely loyal husband and father, he was also capable of philandering.

Faulkner preferred to work at home in Mississippi. Still, he traveled a great deal, first for education, later to deal with publishers and to work in Hollywood, and finally as a goodwill ambassador for the United States. He met and formed acquaintances with several important contemporaries, notably Nathanael West, Sherwood Anderson, and Howard Hawkes.

Faulkner died of a heart attack on July 6, 1962, after entering the hospital to deal with one of his periodic drinking bouts.

Analysis

Faulkner's prolific and imaginative body of work, particularly the series of novels known as the "Yoknapatawpha" cycle, developed as a fable of the American South and, more universally, of human destinies everywhere. Within the confines of the mythical Mississippi county, he discovered the themes that engaged him and triggered the creation of his greatest fiction. Among his more notable concerns are the search for meaning, racism, the intricate association between the past and the present, and the social and moral burdens afflicting the South as it entered modernity.

The history and people of the South become, in the Faulkner canon, a fertile source of drama, pathos, and humor. At the same time, Faulkner, in his cast of unique and distinctive characters, sought a depiction of the region that was realistic and stripped of all false and harmful idealizations tied to the genteel, aristocratic Southern past.

Lewis P. Simpson argues that Faulkner, like the greatest of his contemporaries, dramatizes in most of his novels some version of the central problem of modern humanity in the West, how to respond to the recognition that one has no certain knowledge of a stable transcendent power that assures the meaning of human history. Panthea Broughton makes this view of Faulkner more concrete: In Faulkner's world, people struggle to find or make meaning, exposing themselves in various ways to the danger of spiritual self-destruction, of losing their own souls in the effort to find a way of living in a universe that does not provide meaning. Broughton also demonstrates that the Faulknerian universe is characterized essentially by motion. Human beings need meaning; they need to impose patterns on the motion of life. Out of this need spring human capacities for mature moral freedom as well as for tragic destructiveness.

Faulkner's novels generally contain juxtapositions of attitudes, narrative lives, voices, modes of representation, and emotional tones. He was particularly interested in the juxtaposition of voices. His career as a novelist blossomed when he juxtaposed the voices and, therefore, the points of view of various characters.

The technique of juxtaposition, like Faulkner's characteristic style, reflects his concern with the problems of living meaningfully within the apparently meaningless flow of time. Because life will not stand still or even move consistently according to patterns of meaning, it becomes necessary to use multiple points of view to avoid the complete falsification of his subject. Faulkner's most tragic characters are those who feel driven to impose so rigid a pattern upon their lives and on the lives of others as to invite destruction from the overwhelming forces of motion and change. These characters experience the heart in conflict with itself as the simultaneous need for living motion and meaningful pattern.

The Sound and the Fury is divided into four parts to which an appendix was added later—all of which is related by a series of multiple narrators. The effect of reading these juxtapositions may be described as similar to that of putting together a puzzle, the whole of which cannot be seen until the last piece is in place.

The novel concerns the tragic dissolution of the Compson family. The decline dates decisively from the marriage of Candace (Caddy), the only daughter of Jason Compson III and Caroline Bascomb. Caddy's marriage is not the sole cause of the family's decline; rather, it becomes symbolic of a complex of internal and external forces that come to bear on this Mississippi family early in the twentieth century. Caddy becomes pregnant by Dalton Ames, a romantic, heroic, and apparently devoted outsider. Her mother then seeks out Sydney Herbert Head as a respectable husband for her. After the marriage, Herbert finds he has been gulled and divorces Caddy. These events deprive all the Compson men of their center of meaning. Quentin, the oldest son who loves Caddy not as a sister but as a woman, commits suicide. Jason III drinks himself to death, having lost the children upon whom his meaning depended. Jason IV seeks petty and impotent revenge on Caddy's daughter, also named Quentin, because he believes the failure of Caddy's marriage has deprived him of a chance to get ahead. Benjy, the severely retarded youngest brother, suffers the absence of the only real mother he ever had. Control of the family passes to Jason IV, and the family ceases finally to be a place where love is sustained, becoming instead, despite the efforts of the heroic and loving black servant, Dilsey, a battleground of petty scheming, hatred, and revenge.

This general picture emerges from the internal monologues of Benjy, Quentin (male), and Jason IV, from a third-person narrative centering on Dilsey and Jason IV, and from the final appendix. As the portrait of the family's decline emerges from these juxtaposed sections, their tragic significance becomes apparent.

Benjamin Compson's internal monologue consists of images, most of which are memories. At the center of his memory and of his stunted life is Caddy, whose "hair was like fire" and who "smelled like trees." Every experience of Benjy, which evokes these images or which resembles any experience he has had with Caddy, automatically triggers his memory. As a result, Benjy lives in a blending together of past and present in which memory and present experience are virtually indistinguishable. The spring of his suffering is that for him the experience of losing Caddy is continuous; the memory of her presence is perfect and the experience of her absence is constant.

Quentin's section also proceeds largely by the juxtaposition of memory and present experience. Quentin's memories are triggered by present events and he is sometimes unable to distinguish between memory and external reality. Perhaps the major irony of Quentin's suicide is that the state of being that he desires is in many ways like the state in which his youngest brother suffers. Quentin wishes to be free of time, to end all motion. His grief, of which every event reminds him, is unbearable. He wishes to keep Caddy as she was and to deny the repetitions that force him to remember her loss. Though he sees such a transcendent state in many images in his world, he can only imagine himself in that state, for it is impossible in life. Suicide seems his only alternative.

Jason's section reveals that he desires power above all things. He delights in the power to be cruel, to make others fear him. Jason tells primarily about his troubles bringing up Caddy's daughter, Quentin. The girl has been left in the care of the family while the divorced Caddy makes her way in the world. Quentin becomes the central instrument of Jason's revenge against Caddy for the failure of her marriage and the disappointment of his hope. Jason is so fixed on his need to exercise cruel power that he is unable to restrain himself sufficiently to keep the situation stable. He drives Quentin out of the family, losing the monthly checks from Caddy that he has been appropriating, the hoard he has collected in part from this theft, and the one person on whom he can effectively take his revenge.

"I've seed de first en de last," says Dilsey. She refers to the beginning and the end of the doom of the Compson family, to Caddy's wedding and Quentin's elopement. The importance of Dilsey's section is that she sees a pattern of human meaning in the events that threaten an end to meaning for so many. Her part in these events has been a heroic struggle to bind the family together with her love and care, a doomed but not a meaningless struggle, for she can still see pattern, order, meaning in all of it. The events of Easter morning, in which Dilsey figures, suggest that at least one source of that power to mean and to love is her community at the black church service, a community that, in the contemplation of the Christian symbols of transcendence, attains an experience of communion that partakes of the eternal even though it is temporary. Dilsey's church is a model of the family. The Compson family, by contrast, has somehow lost this experience. As the appendix suggests, all the Compsons, except perhaps for Benjy, are damned, for they have all, in various ways, come to see themselves as "dolls stuffed with sawdust." *The Sound and the Fury* is in part an exploration of the loss of the Christian worldview.

In *The Sound and the Fury*, Faulkner thought of himself as trying to tell the whole story and finding that he had to multiply points of view in order to do so. In *Absalom, Absalom!* the story is only partly known; it is a collection of facts, not all of which are certain, which seem to those who know them profoundly and stubbornly meaningful. The various characters who try their formulae for bringing those facts together into a meaningful whole are the historians of the novel. Faulkner has written a novel about writing novels, about giving meaning to the flow of events. *Absalom, Absalom!* dramatizes so effectively the processes of and obstacles to creating a satisfying structure for events and offers such an ideal wedding of structure, content, technique, and style, that many critics regard it as Faulkner's greatest achievement. With *The Sound and the Fury* this novel shares characters from the Compson family and a degree of difficulty which may require multiple readings.

The central concern of the narrative is the life of Thomas Sutpen and his family. Sutpen has appeared out of nowhere to build a vast plantation near Jefferson, Mississippi, in the early nineteenth century. Apparently without much wealth, he nevertheless puts together the greatest establishment in the area, marries Ellen Coldfield, a highly respectable though not a wealthy woman, and fathers two children by her. When Sutpen's son, Henry, goes to college, he meets and befriends Charles Bon. Charles and Sutpen's daughter, Judith, fall in love and plan to marry. For no apparent reason Sutpen forbids the marriage and Henry leaves his home with Charles. During the Civil War, Ellen dies. Near the end of the war, Henry and Charles appear one day at the plantation, Sutpen's Hundred, and Henry kills Charles. After the war, Sutpen becomes engaged to Rosa Coldfield, Ellen's much younger sister, but that engagement is suddenly broken off. A few years later, Sutpen fathers a daughter with Milly Jones, the teenage daughter of his handyman, Wash Jones. When Sutpen refuses to marry Milly, Jones kills him. Then Sutpen's daughter, Judith, and his slave daughter, Clytie, live together and, somewhat mysteriously, care for the descendants of Charles Bon by his "marriage" to an octoroon.

Though not all the known facts, these constitute the outline of the story as it is generally known in Jefferson. The major mysteries stand out in this outline. Why did Sutpen forbid the marriage? Why did Henry side with Charles and then kill him? Why did Rosa agree to marry Sutpen and then refuse? Why did Sutpen get a squatter's daughter pregnant and abandon her, bringing about his own death? Why did Judith take responsibility for Bon's family? These are the questions to which Rosa Coldfield, Jason Compson III and his father General Compson, and Quentin Compson and his Harvard roommate Shreve McCannon address themselves.

The novel's climax comes when Shreve and Quentin "discover" through intense imaginative identification with Henry and Charles a meaning latent in the facts they have gathered. Their discovery implies that Sutpen prevented the marriage and alienated Henry by revealing that Charles and Henry were half brothers. The substance of their discovery is that the first wife whom Sutpen put aside, the mother of Charles, was a mulatto. Sutpen reserves this information as his trump card in case Henry comes to accept an incestuous marriage. Only this revelation could have brought Henry to kill Charles rather than allow him to marry Judith. The means by which the boys arrive at this conclusion reveal much about the meanings of the novel. Not least among these meanings is the revelation of a sickness at the "prime foundation" of the South, the sickness of a planter society that prevents one from loving one's own children.

There is no way for the boys to *prove* this solution. Their discovery is above all an imaginative act, yet it has the ring of truth. Only through the most laborious process do Quentin and Shreve gather the facts together from the narratives of their elders and a few documents. Informants such as Rosa and Jason III have chosen simple truths to which they make all their experiences conform. Rosa's portrait of Sutpen grows almost entirely out of Sutpen's proposal that they produce a child before they marry. Jason III's portrait of Charles Bon is an idealized self-portrait. Even eyewitnesses such as General Compson and Rosa have faulty memories and biased points of view. In the world of this novel, the truth is difficult to know because the facts on which it is based are hard to assemble.

When the facts are assembled, they are even harder to explain. Jason realizes that he has "just the words, the symbols, the shapes themselves." Quentin and Shreve are able to explain, not because they find the facts, but because they use their imaginations so effectively as to find themselves in the tent with Sutpen and Henry in 1865 and in the camp when Charles tells Henry that even though they are brothers, Charles is the "nigger" who is going to marry his sister. Quentin and Shreve have felt Thomas Sutpen's motives, his reasons for opposing the marriage. They have felt Charles's reasons for insisting on the marriage and Henry's victimization as an instrument of his father. They have entered into the heart's blood, the central symbolic image of the novel, the symbol of the old verities which touch the heart and to which the heart holds as truth. Sutpen's honor is embodied in the design that will crumble if he accepts Charles as his son or allows the marriage. The love of sons for fathers and of brothers for sisters becomes a tragic trap within that design. If love, honor, courage, compassion, and pride are found at the center of these inexplicable events, then the boys have discovered "what must be true."

In order for Quentin and Shreve to complete this act of imagination, they must come to understand Sutpen more fully than anyone does.

Because of Sutpen's failure, many children stand before doors, which they cannot pass. Only an act of sympathetic imagination can get one past the symbolic doors of this novel, but most of the children are so victimized that they are incapable of imaginative sympathy. Even Quentin would not be able to pass his door, the subject of incest and a sister's honor, without help from Shreve. Without Quentin's passion and knowledge, Shreve would never have seen the door. Their brotherhood is a key "ingredient" in their imaginative power.

Many significant elements of this complex novel must remain untouched in any brief analysis. One other aspect of the novel, however, is of particular interest: In *Absalom, Absalom!*, Faulkner suggests the possibility of seeing the Yoknapatawpha novels as a saga, a unified group of works from which another level of significance emerges. He chooses to end *Absalom, Absalom!* with a map of Yoknapatawpha County. This map locates the events of all the preceding Yoknapatawpha novels and some that were not yet written, though the relevant Snopes stories had appeared in magazines. Reintroducing the Compson family also suggests that Faulkner was thinking of a unity among his novels in addition to the unity of the individual works. It seems especially significant that Shreve McCannon, an outsider, neither a Compson nor a Southerner nor an American, makes the final imaginative leap which inspirits Sutpen's story with the heart's truth. In this way, that truth flows out of its narrow regional circumstances to a world which shares in the same heart's blood. With *Absalom, Absalom!*, Faulkner may have seen more clearly than before how his novels could be pillars to help people "endure and prevail" by reminding them of those "old verities," the central motives which bind humankind and the Yoknapatawpha novels together.

Other major works

SHORT FICTION: *These 13*, 1931; *Doctor Martino and Other Stories*, 1934; *The Portable Faulkner*, 1946, 1967; *Knight's Gambit*, 1949; *Collected Short Stories of William Faulkner*, 1950; *Big Woods*, 1955; *Three Famous Short Novels*, 1958; *Uncollected Stories of William Faulkner*, 1979.

SCREENPLAYS: *Today We Live*, 1933; *To Have and Have Not*, 1944; *The Big Sleep*, 1946; *Faulkner's MGM Screenplays*, 1982.

POETRY: *The Marble Faun*, 1924; *A Green Bough*, 1933.

NONFICTION: *New Orleans Sketches*, 1958; *Faulkner in the University*, 1959; *Faulkner at West Point*, 1964; *Essays, Speeches and Public Letters*, 1965; *The Faulkner-Cowley File: Letters and Memories, 1944-1962*, 1966 (Malcolm Cowley, ed.); *Lion in the Garden*, 1968; *Selected Letters*, 1977.

MISCELLANEOUS: *The Faulkner Reader*, 1954; *William Faulkner: Early Prose and Poetry*, 1962; *The Wishing Tree*, 1964; *Mayday*, 1976.

Bibliography

Blotner, Joseph. *Faulkner: A Biography*. 2 vols. New York: Random House, 1974.

Brodhead, Richard H., ed. *Faulkner: New Perspectives*. Englewood Cliffs, N.J.: Prentice-Hall, 1983.

Brodsky, Louis Daniel. *William Faulkner: Life Glimpses*. Austin: University of Texas Press, 1990.

Cox, Leland H., ed. *William Faulkner: Biographical and Reference Guide*. Detroit: Gale Research, 1982.

_____, ed. *William Faulkner: Critical Collection*. Detroit: Gale Research, 1982.

Dowling, David. *William Faulkner*. New York: St. Martin's Press, 1989.

Karl, Frederick Robert. *William Faulkner, American Writer: A Biography*. New York: Weidenfeld & Nicolson, 1989.

Kinney, Arthur F. *Critical Essays on William Faulkner: The Compson Family*. Boston: G. K. Hall, 1982.

Vickery, Olga W. *The Novels of William Faulkner*. Baton Rouge: Louisiana State University Press, 1959.

Volpe, Edmond L. *A Reader's Guide to William Faulkner*. New York: Noonday Press, 1964.

Weinstein, Philip M. *Faulkner's Subject: A Cosmos No One Owns*. Cambridge, England: Cambridge University Press, 1992.

Williamson, Joel. *William Faulkner and Southern History*. New York: Oxford University Press, 1993.

ELLEN GLASGOW

Born: Richmond, Virginia; April 22, 1873

Died: Richmond, Virginia; November 21, 1945

Principal long fiction

The Descendant, 1897; *Phases of an Inferior Planet*, 1898; *The Voice of the People*, 1900; *The Battle-Ground*, 1902; *The Deliverance*, 1904; *The Wheel of Life*, 1906; *The Ancient Law*, 1908; *The Romance of a Plain Man*, 1909; *The Miller of Old Church*, 1911; *Virginia*, 1913; *Life and Gabriella*, 1916; *The Builders*, 1919; *One Man in His Time*, 1922; *Barren Ground*, 1925; *The Romantic Comedians*, 1926; *They Stooped to Folly*, 1929; *The Sheltered Life*, 1932; *Vein of Iron*, 1935; *In This Our Life*, 1941.

Other literary forms

Ellen Glasgow wrote a book of short stories, a book of poems, a book on her views of fiction-writing (concerned primarily with her own works), *A Certain Measure* (1943), and an autobiography, *The Woman Within* (1954). She also wrote a number of articles on fiction for various periodicals and magazines. Her letters were published in 1958.

Achievements

Although Glasgow never felt that she had received the critical acclaim she deserved, she played an important part in the development of Southern letters. A significant figure in the so-called Southern Renascence, she provided in her novels a new picture of the South, a region reluctantly ushered into the modern world. Against a sentimentalized view of the Old South, Glasgow advocated an acceptance of the inevitability of change.

The publication of *Barren Ground* solidified Glasgow's literary reputation. That novel made the 1925 *Review of Review* list of twenty-five outstanding novels of the year. *The Sheltered Life* was a best-seller and likewise greatly enhanced her reputation. *Vein of Iron* and *In This Our Life*, which received the Pulitzer Prize in 1942, helped to ensure her position as a writer of major significance.

Biography

Born in Richmond, Virginia, in 1873, Ellen Glasgow came from a combination of stern Scots-Irish pioneers on her father's side and Tidewater, Virginia, aristocratic stock on her mother's side. Francis Glasgow was an ironworks executive, an occupation well suited to his Puritan temperament and character. Ellen Glasgow had little positive to say about her father. Her mother, by contrast, was a cultivated, gracious, and humane woman. These divergent influences provided the crucible from which Glasgow's writings were to emerge.

The next to the youngest in a family of four sons and six daughters, Glasgow experienced a more-or-less lonely childhood. Because of fragile health and a nervous temperament that precluded adjustment to formal schooling, her isolation was increased, and most of her education came from her father's extensive library. Glasgow grew up in the period that followed the Civil War, during Reconstruction (1865-1877). As she matured she gradually rejected the harsh Calvinism of her father and the bloodless social graces of Richmond society and retreated even further into a life of the mind. Glasgow's growing sense of alienation and rebelliousness has been seen by critics as the wellspring of her literary vision.

By 1890, Glasgow had produced some four hundred pages of a novel, "Sharp Realities" (unpublished). Putting that effort aside, she began writing *The Descendant* in 1891. Two years later, however, upon the death of her mother, with whom she had great affinity, she destroyed a good part of what she had written. Another two years passed before she returned to the novel and completed it.

With the anonymous publication of *The Descendant* in 1897, Glasgow was launched on her prolific career, a career that saw novels appearing every two years or so. Writing became and remained her role in life, and she was ever mindful of the growth of her literary reputation, changing publishers when she felt it to her advantage and making sure that critics were fully aware of her books.

Presumably while on a trip to Europe in 1899, Glasgow fell in love with an older, married man with a wife and children. Another serious love affair was with Henry Watkins Anderson, a Richmond lawyer. He and

Glasgow met in 1915 and were engaged in 1917. In July of the next year, Glasgow attempted suicide when she learned that Anderson, who was working with the Red Cross in the Balkan states, was attracted to Queen Marie of Romania. This turbulent love affair between Glasgow and Anderson was broken about 1920. In two novels, *The Builders* and *One Man in His Time*, Glasgow incorporated aspects of her relationship with Anderson.

As Glasgow began receiving the critical recognition for which she longed, her health began to fail. A heart condition worsened, and she died on November 21, 1945, in Richmond, Virginia.

Analysis

Turning away from a romanticized view of her own Virginia, Glasgow became a part of the revolt against the elegiac tradition of Southern letters. Although she rejected romance, she did not turn to realism; rather, she saw herself as a "verist": "The whole truth," she said, "must embrace the interior world as well as external appearances." In this sense, she strove for what she called "blood and irony"—blood because the South had grown thin and pale and was existing on borrowed ideas, copying rather than creating, and irony because it is the surest antidote to sentimental decay. Certain that life in the South was not as it had been pictured by previous writers, she produced a series of novels that recorded the social history of Virginia through three generations, picturing sympathetically the social and industrial revolution that was transforming the romantic South. A central theme in this record is that of change— change brought about by the conflict between the declining agrarian regime and the rising industrial system. Glasgow argued that, as a matter of survival, such change must be accepted and even welcomed.

The theme of change gives a mythic quality to Glasgow's work, expressed through her sense of what Henry Canby calls "a tragedy of frustration—the waste of life through maladjustment of man to his environment and environment to its men." Often, too, Glasgow's works picture nobility cramped by prejudice, or beauty gone wrong through an inability to adjust to the real, or a good philosophy without premises in existing experience. A good example of the latter theme can be found in the character of John Fincastle in *Vein of Iron*. A man of deep thought, he is viewed "as a dangerous skeptic, or as a man of simple faith, who believed that God is essence, not energy, and that blessedness, or the life of the spirit, is the only reality." Fincastle is a part of the constant change in the world, but he himself does not fully realize the implications of the dynamic society in which he lives. He sees nothing of any potential value in the machine age and is unable to reconcile his own philosophy to the reality of the times.

Barren Ground marks Glasgow's emergence not only from a period of despondency regarding her social life but also as a novelist who has moved without question from apprentice to master. Certainly her finest work to that time, *Barren Ground* was to Glasgow the best of all of her novels. One of her country novels, and set in the Shenandoah Valley of Virginia, it deals with that class of people often referred to as "poor whites." Glasgow herself refutes this appellation, preferring instead to call them "good people," a label that distinguishes them from the aristocratic "good families." Lineal descendants of the English yeoman farmer, these people were the ones who pushed the frontier westward. In this novel, they stand as a "buffer class between the opulent gentry and the hired labourers."

Dorinda Oakley, the heroine, is the offspring of a union of opposites: her father, Joshua, a landless man whose industry and good nature do not compensate for his ineffectuality, and her mother, Eudora, the daughter of a Presbyterian minister, with a religious mania of her own. This background, says Glasgow, has kept Dorinda's heart "in arms against life." More important, however, Dorinda has also inherited a kinship with the earth. This kinship enables her to make something positive out of "barren ground."

Dorinda falls in love with Jason Greylock, a young doctor, seeing in him the promise of something more than the grinding poverty she has known. They plan to marry, but Jason cannot go against his father's wishes, and he marries Geneva Ellgood instead. Pregnant by Jason, Dorinda flees to New York, where, after being struck by a taxi, she loses the baby. She works as a nurse for a Dr. Faraday until she learns that her father is dying. She returns home with enough money borrowed from Faraday to start a dairy farm. Back on the land, she becomes a tough-minded spinster and makes a success of the farm. Although she marries Nathan Pedlar, a storekeeper, she remains the head of the family. After his death in a train wreck, she is again alone but happy, rearing Nathan's child by a previous marriage and managing the farm. Jason, in the meantime, has lost his wife by suicide and is forced to sell his farm to Dorinda. Because he is ill and an alcoholic, she unwillingly provides him with food and shelter. After a few months, he dies, and once more she is alone. When a local farmer

219

asks Dorinda to marry him, she responds, "I am thankful to have finished with all that."

A tragic figure of sorts, Dorinda sees herself trapped by fate, "a straw in the wind, a leaf on a stream." Even so, she is not content to be simply a passive victim of that fate. Unlike Jason, who through his inherited weakness succumbs to the forces that beset him, Dorinda looks upon the land as a symbol of that fate against which she must struggle. Hardened by adversity and with a deep instinct for survival, she refuses to surrender.

Although Dorinda's life may be compared to barren ground because it has been emotionally unfulfilled, it nevertheless is a successful life in that she does master herself and in turn masters the land. Even as the broom sedge must be burned off the land, so must romantic emotions be purged from Dorinda's soul. In giving her life to the land, she, in a sense, gains it back—and is thus, ironically, both victim and victor.

Following *Barren Ground*, Glasgow turned to the novel of manners with *The Romantic Comedians*. The first of a trilogy—the subsequent works being *They Stooped to Folly* and *The Sheltered Life*—this novel has been regarded by some critics as Glasgow's finest.

The novel exhibits a high spirit of comedy with tragic overtones. Judge Gamaliel Bland Honeywell, the protagonist, "is a collective portrait of several Virginians of an older school," says Glasgow, "who are still unafraid to call themselves gentlemen." Living in Queenborough (Richmond, Virginia), he seeks female companionship after his wife of thirty-six years dies. At age sixty-five, he is expected to marry a former sweetheart, Amanda Lightfoot. Disdaining such expected decorum, however, he falls in love and marries Annabelle Upchurch, a young cousin of his wife. Annabelle marries him not so much for love as to heal the pain of being jilted by Angus Blount. As one might suspect in such a marriage, Annabelle is soon looking for greener pastures, finding them in Delaney Birdsong, with whom she goes to New York. Unable to win her back, the judge, ill and disillusioned, believes that life holds nothing more for him. With the coming of spring, however, he looks upon his attractive young nurse and muses, "Spring is here, and I am feeling almost as young as I felt last year." Judge Honeywell, like many of Glasgow's women, is of another tradition; more than age separates him from Annabelle.

In *The Sheltered Life*, the last novel of her trilogy on manners, Glasgow employs two points of view—that of youth and that of age, in this case a young girl and an old man. Against the background of a "shallow and aimless society of happiness hunters," she presents more characters of Queenborough as they are revealed through the mind and emotions of Jenny Blair and her grandfather, General David Archbald.

Glasgow intended General Archbald as the central character in the novel—a character who "represents the tragedy, wherever it appears, of the civilized man in a world that is not civilized." General Archbald sees before him a changing world, a world that is passing him by. Thus, he holds to the social traditions of the nineteenth century, which have provided little shelter for him. He was never a man for his time. A sensitive person who had wanted to be a poet, he was ridiculed in his earlier years. Poetry had been his one love in life; it was lost before it could be realized. He married his wife only because of an accidental, overnight sleigh ride that, in tradition-bound Queenborough, demanded marriage to save appearances.

Jenny, too, unknowingly is caught in the patterned existence of the Archbald heritage. A willful girl, she has been sheltered from the real world by culture and tradition and can see things only in terms of her own desires. At eighteen, she falls in love with an older married man, George Birdsong. George's wife, Eva, eventually finds them in each other's arms. Jenny flees the scene, only to learn later that Eva has killed George.

Eva Birdsong is another perfect image of Southern womanhood, beautiful and protected all her life. A celebrated belle prior to her marriage to George, she has striven to achieve a perfect marriage. Over the years, George has been a bit of a *roué*, seeking pleasure where he could find it. In the end, Eva is left with the realization that what women "value most is something that doesn't exist."

When Jenny realizes what she has done, she flies to the general's understanding and sheltering arms, crying, "Oh, Grandfather, I didn't mean anything. . . . I didn't mean anything in the world." Ironically enough, she is right: She did not mean anything.

The Sheltered Life is more a tragicomedy than simply a comedy of manners. It is also, perhaps, Glasgow's best work, the novel toward which its predecessors were pointed. Symbol, style, characterization, and rhythm all combine to make *The Sheltered Life* a poignant and penetrating illustration of the futility of clinging to a tradition that has lost its essential meaning.

Glasgow's goal in all of her writing is perhaps stated best in *A Certain Measure*, when she says in reference to her last novel, *In This Our Life*, that she was trying to show "the tragedy of a social system which lives, grows, and prospers by material standards alone." One can sense in such a statement a conservative regard for tradition; even though Glasgow and many of her characters struggled against a shallow romanticism, a yearning for a genuine tradition was never far from her own artistic vision. The land seems to be the single sustaining factor in all of Glasgow's novels—it was the land that gave rise to and nourished the so-called Southern tradition and that provides the "living pulse of endurance" to so many of her characters.

Other major works

SHORT FICTION: *The Shadowy Third and Other Stories*, 1923; *The Collected Stories of Ellen Glasgow*, 1963.
POETRY: *The Freeman and Other Poems*, 1902.
NONFICTION: *A Certain Measure*, 1943; *The Woman Within*, 1954; *Letters of Ellen Glasgow*, 1958.

Bibliography

Godbold, E. Stanly, Jr. *Ellen Glasgow and the Woman Within*. Baton Rouge: Louisiana State University Press, 1972.
Inge, M. Thomas, ed. *Ellen Glasgow: Centennial Essays*. Charlottesville: University Press of Virginia, 1976.
McDowell, Frederick P. W. *Ellen Glasgow and the Ironic Art of Fiction*. Madison: University of Wisconsin Press, 1960.
Raper, Julius Rowan. *From the Sunken Garden: The Fiction of Ellen Glasgow, 1916-1945*. Baton Rouge: Louisiana State University Press, 1980.
Thiébaux, Marcelle. *Ellen Glasgow*. New York: Frederick Ungar, 1982.

CORMAC McCARTHY

Born: Providence, Rhode Island; July 20, 1933

Principal long fiction

The Orchard Keeper, 1965; *Outer Dark*, 1968; *Child of God*, 1973; *Suttree*, 1979; *Blood Meridian: Or, The Evening Redness in the West*, 1985; *All the Pretty Horses*, 1992; *The Crossing*, 1994.

Other literary forms

Cormac McCarthy has produced several dramatic works, including *The Gardener's Son*. First broadcast in January, 1977, this teleplay was scripted for the *Visions* series shown on national public television.

Achievements

McCarthy has consistently been praised for his carefully crafted work, his unflinching, dark vision, his immense range of vocabulary, and his powers of observation and description. These qualities have also won for him rich recognition in the form of prizes and grants. *The Orchard Keeper* won the 1965 William Faulkner Foundation Award as the best first novel by an American writer and helped win for McCarthy an American Academy of Arts and Letters traveling fellowship to Europe in 1965-1966. The following years, as more of McCarthy's work appeared, brought him grants from the Rockefeller, Guggenheim, Lyndhurst, and MacArthur foundations. McCarthy has been compared to Faulkner, Edgar Allan Poe, and Mark Twain. *All the Pretty Horses*, the first volume of the Border Trilogy, won the National Book Award in fiction in 1992. The second book of the trilogy, *The Crossing*, was critically acclaimed at the time of publication.

Biography

Cormac McCarthy is the product of a middle-class Catholic family—about as far as one can get from the background of most of his characters (with the notable exception of Suttree). He was born in Providence, Rhode Island, in 1933. When McCarthy was four, his family moved to the Knoxville, Tennessee, area, where his father was chief legal counsel to the Tennessee Valley Authority (TVA). There, McCarthy grew up, attending parochial school, Catholic High School, and the University of Tennessee. He dropped out of the university after one year, traveled for a year, and then joined the United States Air Force, in which he served for four years. Afterward, he attended the University of

Tennessee for three more years but finally left in 1959 without getting a degree.

McCarthy did discover his writing vocation at the University of Tennessee, where he began work on a novel. After the publication of *The Orchard Keeper*, he traveled in Europe for three years, living in London and Paris and on the Spanish island of Ibiza. While in Europe, he married Anne de Lisle of Hamble, England. Later, they lived on a small farm in Rockford, Tennessee, on the outskirts of Knoxville. McCarthy moved to El Paso, Texas, during the time he was writing *Blood Meridian*.

As *Blood Meridian* and his East Tennessee novels show, McCarthy is influenced by the landscape around him and is good at absorbing local talk, color, and tradition. Whether he was more directly influenced by his father's work with the TVA is an interesting question. For many families who had been living in the mountain valleys for generations, the TVA was their first contact with big government—a traumatic one that has still not been forgiven. The permanent flooding of their land by TVA projects, despite "compensation," resulted in massive dislocations within the traditional mountain culture. One of the more gruesome aspects was transferring the contents of cemeteries to higher ground—a scene of the restless dead that seems to be echoed repeatedly in McCarthy's work, as is the theme of the government's bringing of change.

Analysis

McCarthy's earliest novels are rooted in the geography and experience of the eastern Tennessee region, and McCarthy is reluctant to develop any optimistic themes. He is also reluctant about stating his themes, although some of his titles offer strong hints. For the most part, he merely tells his stories and leaves it up to the reader to interpret their meanings. As a result, one critic has judged McCarthy to be nihilistic, but surely this judgment is incorrect. McCarthy's reluctance to preach about the good news masks a profoundly moral sensibility that is forced to face the worst in human nature and to recognize the power of evil.

There is also a softer, more modern side to McCarthy's morality. Few writers identify so thoroughly with people beyond the pale—the poor, the homeless and dispossessed, the criminal and degenerate, the outcasts. He manages to find some humanity even in the worst of these and to ascribe their conditions partly to contingency, bad luck, or the operations of respectable society. Their nemesis (besides themselves) is often the law and its officers, who, for them, become additional embodiments of the death and destruction that pursue everyone. McCarthy's refusal to avert his sympathies from the outcasts thus raises some complex social and theological issues.

McCarthy's first novel, *The Orchard Keeper*, introduces the outcasts as members of the disappearing mountain culture of East Tennessee. Young Marion Sylder lives by bootlegging, and in self-defense he kills a man and disposes of the body in an abandoned peach orchard that symbolizes the dying culture. Old Arthur Ownby, who fondly watches over the orchard, finds the body, but he does not report it. He lets it rest in peace for seven years. The old man also believes in his own peace and privacy, and when these are disturbed by a government holding tank erected on a nearby hill, he shoots his *X* on the tank's side. Both the men live by old mountain codes which, by definition, are outside the law of the intruding modern world. Yet the enforcers of the law, who finally arrest and beat Sylder and send the old man to a mental institution, seem degenerate in comparison.

The episodic converging stories and italicized flashbacks of *The Orchard Keeper* recall Faulkner's narrative techniques, and McCarthy's second novel, *Outer Dark*, also owes a debt to Faulkner. The novel takes place in some vaguely Deep South setting early in the twentieth century and deals with the horrible consequences of incest between Culla and Rinthy Holme, brother and sister. Rinthy delivers a baby boy, and Culla abandons it in the woods, where a passing tinker finds and takes it. Culla tells Rinthy that the baby died, but Rinthy digs up the shallow grave, discovers his lie, and intuitively goes in search of the tinker. Culla goes after Rinthy to bring her back. Their wanderings on the roads recall those of Lena Grove and Joe Christmas in Faulkner's *Light in August* (1932). Everyone Rinthy encounters befriends her, but Culla meets nothing except suspicion and trouble.

McCarthy's most original and unforgettable creation in *Outer Dark* is a set of three avenging angels, or devils, who rove about the landscape murdering people. On a realistic level, they are lawless, asocial drifters who have gone totally beyond the pale into the "outer dark." They have lost all caring. Appropriately, Culla meets this unholy trio of blood brothers near the novel's end. The three hang the tinker and dispose of the baby (now symbolically scarred as in a Nathaniel Hawthorne story) before Culla's eyes: One slits the baby's throat and another sucks its blood.

If *Outer Dark* does not contain horror enough, McCarthy followed it with *Child of God*, which returns to a rural East Tennessee setting. Here, mountain man Lester Ballard loses his farm for failure to pay taxes; embittered and alone, he sinks gradually into necrophilia and then murder. His degeneration is marked by movement from the farm to an abandoned shack and a cave where he stores his supply of dead women. He is finally captured, dies in a state mental hospital, and is dissected in a medical laboratory. His neighbors, whose choruslike, folksy comments are interspersed throughout the story, always thought him a bit strange, with bad blood. McCarthy suggests that all Lester ever needed, however, was a home and love. Lester was only "a child of God much like yourself perhaps."

A short, tightly unified work, *Child of God* contrasts with McCarthy's next novel, *Suttree*, usually considered his masterpiece. *Suttree* displays the variety and range of McCarthy's talent. Set in Knoxville during the 1950's, the novel is a long, rambling work rich in incident, character, language, and mood, including some surprisingly amusing, bawdy humor. Yet *Suttree* has certain features in common with *Child of God*. Misery and unhappiness also predominate here, and instead of one child of God, *Suttree* has hundreds—drunks, prostitutes, perverts, petty criminals, and the poor generally, black and white—all dumped together in a slum known as McAnally Flats. The characters have such names as Gatemouth, Worm, Hoghead, and Trippin Through the Dew, and their dialogue is spiced with slang and expletives.

The central character is Cornelius "Buddy" Suttree, scion of a prominent local family. He has deliberately chosen to live in this slum on a houseboat moored in the Tennessee River, from whose filthy waters he catches a few carp and catfish to sell. Why he has made this strange choice gradually becomes clear. On the one hand, he has made a mess of his life. He and his parents are no longer on speaking terms, and his wife left him long ago, taking their child (who dies in the novel). Suttree sank to drink and served a term in the prison workhouse. Now he lives in McAnally Flats because, on the other hand, he feels at home there. There, he can find the company of likeminded, fun-loving pals who can help him avoid involvement in the pain of life. There he sits, the fisher king in his wasteland, and with dread and longing he awaits the oblivion of death.

A happy flaw in Suttree's character, however, prevents his nihilistic scheme from taking effect: compassion. He cannot avoid feeling compassion for the people around him, such as the ignorant but irrepressible Gene Harrogate, a country boy who serves a term in the workhouse for having sex with a farmer's watermelons and who dynamites the city's sewer system down on himself trying to rob a bank (the "country mouse," as he is first called, soon becomes the "city rat"). Further involvement with people leads to further pain for Suttree—a girl he falls in love with is killed, his long affair with a rich prostitute breaks up, and most of his pals are killed or imprisoned. Deeper emotional commitment on Suttree's part, however, might have saved both the girl and the affair with the prostitute. After a solitary retreat to the Great Smoky Mountains and a near-fatal illness, Suttree decides to embrace life—pain and all—and to leave Knoxville. He leaves as the McAnally Flats are being torn down to make room for an expressway. His parting words of advice concern the hounds of death: "Fly them."

McCarthy's fifth book, *Blood Meridian*, is a historical novel set in the American Southwest and northern Mexico around the middle of the nineteenth century and provides the transition between his "Southern" and his "Southwestern" novels. The novel's protagonist is a nameless character known only as "the kid" (with suggested parallels perhaps to Billy the Kid), who runs away from his Tennessee home when he is fourteen and heads west. His story might be that of Huck Finn after Huck "lit out for the Territory" and left civilization behind. After repeated scrapes, always moving west, the kid joins a band of scalping bounty hunters who hunt the Apaches when the Apaches are not hunting them. The massacres go on endlessly, all duly noted in the running summaries that head each chapter.

In some ways, *Blood Meridian* provides a useful retrospective view of McCarthy's early work. It returns to the horrors of his earlier novels but seems to relate these to the social themes of *Suttree*. The scalp hunters are, after all, the advance guard of Western civilization. They suggest a terrible moral ambiguity at the heart of civilization, as in the hearts of individuals, that enables it to stamp out Apaches and backward mountaineers and to create such slums as McAnally Flats. Judge Holden, the repulsive and evil philosopher of *Blood Meridian*, argues that God made man thus, that morality is irrelevant, and that superior violence shall triumph. The naked judge finally embraces the kid with an apparent death hug inside a jakes behind a whorehouse in Fort Griffin, Texas. Readers can probably find a warning in this to flee such philosophers.

With *All the Pretty Horses* and *The Crossing*, McCarthy has abandoned his Southern roots and adopted his new home in the Southwest. The first two novels in his Border Trilogy find the same type of wanderers, cut adrift from geographical and emotional moorings, who appear in his Southern novels. However, here he displays his ability to capture the tempo of a different American identity, one sharply observed, characterized by more tenderness, wistfulness, and comedy than in his earlier works. This new direction gives further evidence of McCarthy's true talent as one of our most creative contemporary novelists.

Other major works

TELEPLAY: *The Gardener's Son*, 1977.
PLAY: *The Stonemason: A Play in Five Acts*, 1994.

Bibliography

Arnold, Edwin T., and Dianne C. Luce, eds. *Perspectives on Cormac McCarthy*. Jackson: University Press of Mississippi, 1993.
Bell, Vereen M. *The Achievement of Cormac McCarthy*. Baton Rouge: Louisiana State University Press, 1988.
_____. "The Ambiguous Nihilism of Cormac McCarthy." *Southern Literary Journal* 15 (Spring, 1983): 31-41.
Ditsky, John. "Further into Darkness: The Novels of Cormac McCarthy." *The Hollins Critic* 18 (April, 1981): 1-11.
Longley, John Lewis, Jr. "Suttree and the Metaphysics of Death." *The Southern Literary Journal* 17 (Spring, 1985): 79-90.

Schafer, William J. "Cormac McCarthy: The Hard Wages of Original Sin." *Appalachian Journal* 4 (Winter, 1977): 105-119.

Sepich, John Emil. *Notes on "Blood Meridian."* Louisville, Ky.: Bellarmine College Press, 1993.

Sullivan, Walter. "Model Citizens and Marginal Cases: Heroes of the Day." *Sewanee Review* 87 (Spring, 1979): 337-344.

CARSON McCULLERS

Born: Columbus, Georgia; February 19, 1917

Died: Nyack, New York; September 29, 1967

Principal long fiction

The Heart Is a Lonely Hunter, 1940; *Reflections in a Golden Eye*, 1941; *The Member of the Wedding*, 1946; *The Ballad of the Sad Café*, 1951; *Clock Without Hands*, 1961.

Other literary forms

Carson McCullers published a number of short stories, some of which are included in the volume containing *The Ballad of the Sad Café* and in *The Mortgaged Heart* (1971). The latter also contains some magazine articles and notes on her writing. McCullers wrote two plays, including an adaptation of *The Member of the Wedding* for the stage in 1950 (a film version appeared in 1952). Her poetry is published in *The Mortgaged Heart* and in a children's book, *Sweet as a Pickle and Clean as a Pig* (1964).

Achievements

Several of McCullers' works received critical acclaim. "A Tree. A Rock. A Cloud," a short story sometimes compared in theme to Samuel Taylor Coleridge's "The Rime of the Ancient Mariner," was chosen for the O. Henry Memorial Prize in 1942. The dramatic version of *The Member of the Wedding* was extremely successful, running on Broadway continuously for nearly fifteen months, and it was named for both the Donaldson Award and the New York Drama Critics Circle Award in 1950. In addition, McCullers was a Guggenheim Fellow in 1942 and 1946, and she received an award from the American Academy of Arts and Letters in 1943.

Biography

Carson McCullers was born Lula Carson Smith on February 19, 1917, in Columbus, Georgia. Marguarite Smith, McCullers' mother, was very early convinced that her daughter was an artistic genius and sacrificed herself and, to some extent, McCullers' father, brother, and sister, to the welfare of her gifted child. McCullers announced early in life that she was going to be a concert pianist and indeed displayed a precocious talent in that direction. Smith placed her daughter under the tutelage of Mary Tucker, a concert musician, who agreed that McCullers was talented. McCullers came to love Mrs. Tucker and her family with an all-consuming passion, a pattern she was to follow with a number of other close friends during her life. Consequently, she lapsed into deep despair when the Tuckers moved away from her hometown. She seemed to experience every break in human contact as personal betrayal or tragedy.

Writing was also an early enthusiasm of McCullers. As a child, she created shows to be acted by herself and her siblings in the sitting room. Early in life she became enthralled by the great Russian writers Fyodor Dostoevski, Anton Chekhov, and Leo Tolstoy—a fascination she never outgrew. Years later, she was to suggest, with considerable cogency, that modern Southern writing is most indebted to the Russian realists.

The Smith household, while never wealthy, was not so hard pressed for money as McCullers sometimes later pretended. Lamar Smith, her father, was a respected jeweler in Columbus, Georgia, and a skilled repairer of clocks and watches. There was enough money, at least, to send the seventeen-year-old McCullers to New York City to attend the famous Juilliard School of Music. By the time she came home following the end of he school term, she had begun to write in earnest, and the dream of being a concert pianist was entirely displaced by the vision of becoming a great writer. She had launched her publishing career by selling two short stories to *Story* magazine: "Wunderkind" and "Like That." Her first novel, *The Heart Is a Lonely Hunter*, was in its formative stages.

Back home, McCullers met handsome young soldier Reeves McCullers, who shared her ambitions of living in New York and of becoming a writer. In 1936, Reeves left the army and traveled to New York to be with McCullers. Later he escorted her back home to Georgia to help her recover from one of her many serious illnesses.

In 1937, Carson and Reeves were married, although Reeves was financially in no condition to support a wife. Though idyllically happy at the first, their marriage became increasingly troubled. While McCullers' first novel, published when she was twenty-two, brought her immediate recognition in the literary world of New York, her husband met with continual frustration in his own ambitions.

Their problems did not derive simply from the professional dominance of McCullers. Both she and her husband were sexually ambivalent. The repressed homosexuality and odd love triangles that are so characteristic of McCullers' fiction had some correlation to real-life situations. McCullers had a disconcerting tendency to fall in love with either men or women, and to suffer inordinately when such attentions were repulsed. As her fiction suggests, she believed that one of the central problems of living was to love and be loved in equal measure.

McCullers often left Reeves to his own devices when professional opportunities or invitations came her way. She was offered a fellowship, for example, in the prestigious Bread Loaf Writers Conference, where she consorted with such literati as Robert Frost, Louis Untermeyer, John Marquand, and Wallace Stegner. That same summer, McCullers also met Erika and Klaus Mann, Thomas Mann's children, and Annemarie Clarac-Schwartzenbach, a prominent Swiss journalist and travel-writer. McCullers fell deeply in love with the stunning Annemarie. When Annemarie left the country, it was another terrible "desertion" for McCullers. *Reflections in a Golden Eye*, McCullers' second novel, was dedicated to Annemarie.

McCullers eventually divorced Reeves. Although they later remarried, Reeves became increasingly despondent. He was eventually found dead in a Paris hotel.

McCullers' last years were a nightmare of pain, though she continued to maintain a fairly cheerful social life while partially paralyzed and often bedridden. She had two strokes, underwent several operations on her paralyzed left arm, leg, and hand, had a cancerous breast removed, broke her hip and elbow in a fall, and finally died after another massive stroke. She was fifty years old.

Analysis

Like William Faulkner, McCullers has literary kinship with those older, midnight-haunted writers— Edgar Allan Poe, Nathaniel Hawthorne, and Herman Melville, among them—who projected in fable and with symbol the story of America's unquiet mind. Against her Southern background she created a world of symbolic violence and tragic reality, indirectly

lighted by the cool Flaubertian purity of her style. Of the writers of her generation, none was more consistent or thorough in achieving a sustained body of work. Her fiction has a childlike directness, a disconcerting exposure of unconscious impulses in conjunction with realistic detail. She is like the candid child who announces that the emperor in his new clothes is really naked. She sees the truth, or at least a partial truth of the human psyche, then inflates or distorts that truth into a somewhat grotesque fable that is sometimes funny but always sad.

McCullers explained her technique for fusing objective reality with symbolic, psychic experience in "The Russian Realists and Southern Literature" (reprinted in *The Mortgaged Heart*), responding to the charge of cruelty in her fiction and that of other Southern writers, such as William Faulkner:

No single instance of "cruelty" in Russian and Southern writing could not be matched or outdone by the Greeks, the Elizabethans, or, for that matter, the creators of the Old Testament. Therefore it is not the specific "cruelty" itself that is shocking, but the manner in which it is presented. And it is in this approach to life and suffering that the Southerners are so indebted to the Russians. The technique briefly is this: a bold and outwardly callous juxtaposition of the tragic with the humorous, the immense with the trivial, the sacred with the bawdy, the whole soul of a man with a materialistic detail.

All of McCullers' stories deal with the metaphysical isolation of individuals and their desperate need to transcend this isolation through love. Love provides the alchemy for a magnificent transformation of leaded existence into gold, but the exalted state is doomed because love is so seldom reciprocated. By projecting this terrible sense of unrequited love into all kinds of human relationships (except that between mother and daughter), McCullers successfully universalizes the state of metaphysical isolation as a perennial human condition.

Her first novel, *The Heart Is a Lonely Hunter*, has as its child character Mick Kelly, who clings to John Singer, the deaf-mute, who, she fancies, understands and sympathizes with her problems. McCullers' own definition of the character in "Author's Outline of 'The Mute'" (*The Mortgaged Heart*) reveals an almost transparent self-dramatization: "Her story is that of the violent struggle of a gifted child to get what she needs from an unyielding environment." Only metaphorically is Mick's struggle "violent," but even when McCullers presents physical violence in fiction it often seems to function as the objective correlative to mental anguish.

McCullers casts Jake Blount, the ineffectual social agitator, as a would-be Marxist revolutionary, but he may seem more like an overgrown frustrated child. Her outline says, "His deepest motive is to do all that he can to change the predatory, unnatural social conditions existing today. . . . He is fettered by abstractions and conflicting ideas. . . . His attitude vacillates between hate and the most unselfish love." Dr. Benedict Copeland is the more believable character, representing the peculiar plight of the educated African American in the South, who has internalized the white man's condemnation of black cultural traits. His daughter's black dialect and careless posture embarrass him, and he frowns on what he considers the irresponsible fecundity and emotionality of the black youth. What McCullers calls his "passionate asceticism" has driven away even his own family. Biff Brannon, the proprietor of the local restaurant, is the dispassionate observer of humanity, sympathetic, in a distant way, with all human oddities. Like Mick, he seems almost a part of McCullers, a grown-up version of the child who sat silently in the corners of stores watching people, who loved to listen to the voices of blacks, and who paid her dimes repeatedly to see the freaks in the side shows. Brannon is also sexually impotent, with homosexual leanings. He is cold and withdrawn with his wife and has a repressed attraction for Mick in her tomboyish prepuberty—an impulse that fades as soon as she shows sexual development.

All of these characters pivot around the deaf-mute, John Singer, who is the central symbol of humankind's metaphysical isolation. They take his silence as wisdom and pour out their hearts to his patient, but unreceptive, ears. He does lipread, so he knows what they are saying, but he has no way to communicate with them in reply. Moreover, the experiences they confide to him seem so alien to his own that he does not really understand. Mick talks about music, which he has never heard; Jake Blount rants about the downtrodden working classes; Dr. Copeland speaks of his frustrations as a racial leader without any followers; and Biff Brannon simply looks on with no project of his own.

Yet, John Singer shares their universal need to love and communicate with a kindred soul. The object of his adoration is another mute, a sloppy, retarded Greek named Antonopoulos, who loves nothing but the childish pleasure of a full stomach. When the Greek dies in an institution, Singer commits suicide. The whole pyramid of illusion collapses.

This bleak tale suggests that the beloved is created in the lover's mind out of the extremity of the latter's need and projected upon whomever is available. Singer drew the love of these desperate souls on account of his polite tolerance of their advances coupled with an essential blankness. They looked into his eyes and saw their own dreams reflected there, even as Singer himself read a secret sympathy and understanding in the blank round face of Antonopoulos, who was actually incapable of such sentiments.

McCullers' next novel, *Reflections in a Golden Eye*, caused considerable shock in conservative Southern communities. Americans generally were not prepared for a fictional treatment of homosexuality. A perceptive reader might suspect the latent homosexuality in Biff Brannon, but there is no doubt about Captain Penderton's sexual preferences. Moreover, the sadomasochism, the weird voyeurism, and the Freudian implications of horses and guns are unmistakable. If *The Heart Is a Lonely Hunter* is about love, *Reflections in a Golden Eye* is about sex and its various distortions. These are lonely, isolated people driven by subconscious impulses. The story concerns two army couples, a houseboy, a rather primitive young man, all of them somewhat abnormal, and a horse. One suspects the horse is akin to a dream symbol for the ungovernable libido.

Captain Penderton is impotent with his beautiful wife Leonora but is drawn to her lover, Major Langdon. The major's wife is sickly and painfully aware of her husband's affair with Leonora. Mrs. Langdon is solicitously attended by a Filipino houseboy, who is also maladjusted. The other character is Private Williams, an inarticulate young man who seems to be a fugitive from somebody's unconscious (probably Penderton's). He has a mystical affinity for nature, and he is the only person who can handle Leonora's high-spirited stallion, Firebird. Penderton is afraid of the horse, and he both loves and hates Private Williams.

The silent Private Williams enacts a psychodrama that repeats, in different terms, the sexual impotence of Penderton. Having seen Leonora naked through an open door, he creeps into the Penderton house each night to crouch silently by her bedside, watching her sleep. When Penderton discovers him there, he shoots him. The scene in the dark bedroom beside the sleeping woman is loaded with psychological overtones. Not a word is spoken by either man. In one sense, the phallic gun expresses the captain's love-hate attraction to the private; in another sense, Penderton is killing his impotent shadow-self.

Reflections in a Golden Eye is objective and non-judgmental—like the impersonal eye of nature in which it is reflected. McCullers was perfecting the kind of perception and style she spoke of in her essay on the Russian realists, presenting human action starkly without editorial comment.

McCullers' subsequent work, *The Ballad of the Sad Café*, was a more successful treatment of archetypal myth, with its psychodramatic overtones tempered this time by humor. Like the true folk ballad, it is a melancholy tale of unrequited love and of betrayal. The setting is an isolated Southern village—little more than a trading post with a few dreary, unpainted buildings. The most prominent citizen is known as Miss Emelia, a strong, mannish, cross-eyed woman with a sharp business sense. She runs the general store and operates a still that produces the best corn liquor for miles around. There is nothing to do for entertainment in town except drink her brew, follow the odd career of this sexless female, and listen to the melancholy singing of the chain gang, which suggests a universal entrapment in the dreary reality of one's life.

The story concerns a temporary hiatus from boredom when Miss Emelia and the observing townspeople become a real community. Love provides the means for a temporary transcendence of Miss Emelia's metaphysical isolation and, through her, sheds a reflected radiance on all. Like John Singer, Miss Emelia chooses an odd person to love, a homeless dwarf who straggles into town, claiming to be her cousin and hoping for a handout. Although Miss Emelia had thrown out the only man who had ever loved her because he expected sexual favors when they were married, she unaccountably falls in love with this pathetic wanderer. She takes "Cousin Lymon" in and, because he likes company, begins a restaurant, which becomes the social center of the entire community. All goes well until the despised husband, Marvin Macy, is released from the penitentiary and returns to his hometown, bent on revenge for the monstrous humiliation Miss Emelia had visited upon him.

Another unusual threesome develops when Cousin Lymon becomes infatuated with Marvin Macy. The competition between Macy and Miss Emelia for the attention of Cousin Lymon comes to a tragicomic climax in a fistfight between the rivals. Miss Emelia, who has been working out with a punching bag, is actually winning when the treacherous Cousin Lymon leaps on her back, and the two men give her a terrible drubbing. Macy and Cousin Lymon flee after they vandalize Miss Emelia's store and her still. Miss Emelia is left in a more desolate isolation than she has ever known and becomes a solitary recluse thereafter. The coda at the end recalls again the mournful song of the chain gang.

This story is surely McCullers' most successful treatment of unrequited love and betrayal. Besides the satire on all crude American substitutes for the duel of honor, this story calls to mind Faulkner's famous gothic tale, "A Rose for Emily," about the genteel aristocratic lady who murdered her lover to keep him in her bed. Miss Emelia is certainly the absolute opposite of all conventions about the beautiful but fragile Southern belle, who is entirely useless.

The Member of the Wedding is possibly the most popular of McCullers' novels. The protagonist, a motherless adolescent girl named Frankie Addams, is the central quester for human happiness, foredoomed to disappointment. In the isolation and boredom of Frankie's life, the only exciting event is the upcoming marriage of her older brother. Frankie conceives of the dream that will sustain her in the empty weeks of the long, hot summer: She will become a member of the wedding and join her brother and his bride on their honeymoon and new idyllic life of love and communion.

This impossible dream is the central issue of those long conversations in the kitchen where the girl is flanked by a younger cousin, John Henry, who represents the childhood from which Frankie is emergining, and the black maid, Berenice, who tries to reason with Frankie without stripping her of all solace. Ignorant as she is of the dynamics of sexual love, what Frankie aspires to is not a love so self-seeking as eros or one quite so all-encompassing as agape. She envisions an ideal love that establishes a permanent and free-flowing communication among the members of a small, select group. This imagined communion seems to express an unvoiced dream of many, situated sometimes in a visionary future or in an equally visionary past. Berenice, for all her gentle earthiness, shows that her vision of a golden age is in the past, when she was married to her first husband. She admits that after that man died, her other two marriages were vain attempts to recapture the rapport she had known with her first husband.

A curious irony of the story is that Frankie, with her persistent goal of escaping her isolated personal identity in what she calls the "we of me," actually comes closest to that ideal in the course of these endless conversations with the child and the motherly black woman. This real communion also passes away, as surely as the imagined communion with the wedded pair never materializes.

John Henry dies before the end of the story, symbolic perhaps of the passing of Frankie's childhood. Reality and banality seem to have conquered in a world unsuited to the dreams of sensitive human beings.

In her last novel, *Clock Without Hands*, McCullers made an attempt to move beyond the not-quite-adult problems of adolescence with the story of a terminally ill man, J. T. Malone, who, all too late, has discovered that moral dignity requires some commitment to action. To redeem his otherwise meaningless life, he refuses to accept the community's order to bomb the home of a black person who had dared to move into a white neighborhood. McCullers' description of Judge Clane,

Malone's aging friend, reveals the peculiar combination of sentimentality and cruelty that characterizes conventional white racism of the Old Southern variety.

Despite this last effort, McCullers' legacy will be of fiction with a special talent for describing the in-between world before a child becomes an adult, the no-man's-land of repressed homosexuality, the irrational demands of love in the absence of any suitable recipient of love. Somehow the "child genius" never quite achieved maturity. Nevertheless, all people are immature or maimed in some way, and in that sense every reader must admit kinship with McCullers' warped and melancholy characters.

Other major works

SHORT FICTION: *The Mortgaged Heart*, 1971 (M. G. Smith, ed.).
PLAYS: *The Member of the Wedding*, 1950; *The Square Root of Wonderful*, 1957.
CHILDREN'S LITERATURE: *Sweet as a Pickle and Clean as a Pig*, 1964.

Bibliography

Bradbury, John M. *Renaissance in the South: A Critical History of the Literature, 1920-1960*. Chapel Hill: University of North Carolina Press, 1963.

Carr, Virginia Spencer. *The Lonely Hunter: A Biography of Carson McCullers*. Garden City, N.Y.: Anchor Press, 1975.

_____ . *Understanding Carson McCullers*. Columbia: University of South Carolina Press, 1990.

Evans, Oliver. *The Ballad of Carson McCullers: A Biography*. New York: Coward, McCann, 1966.

_____ . "The Theme of Spiritual Isolation in Carson McCullers." In *South: Modern Southern Literature in Its Cultural Setting*, edited by Louis D. Rubin, Jr., and Robert D. Jacobs. Westport, Conn.: Greenwood Press, 1961.

Graver, Lawrence. *Carson McCullers*. Minneapolis: University of Minnesota Press, 1969.

McDowell, Margaret B. *Carson McCullers*. Boston: Twayne, 1980.

FLANNERY O'CONNOR

Born: Savannah, Georgia; March 25, 1925   **Died:** Milledgeville, Georgia; August 3, 1964

Principal short fiction
A Good Man Is Hard to Find, 1955; *Everything That Rises Must Converge*, 1965; *The Complete Stories*, 1971.

Other literary forms
In addition to writing thirty-one short stories, Flannery O'Connor wrote two short novels. *Mystery and Manners* (1969) collects her essays and occasional prose. *The Habit of Being* (1979) contains much of her correspondence. O'Connor also wrote book reviews, largely for the Catholic press; these are collected in *The Presence of Grace* (1983).

Achievements
The fiction of O'Connor has been highly praised for its unrelenting irony, its symbolism, and its unique comedy. Today, O'Connor is considered one of the most important American writers of the short story, and she is frequently compared with William Faulkner as a writer of short fiction.

For an author with a relatively small literary output, O'Connor has received an enormous amount of attention. More than twenty-five books devoted to her have appeared beginning in the early 1960's, when significant critics worldwide began to recognize O'Connor's gifts as a fiction writer. Almost all critical works have emphasized the bizarre effects of reading O'Connor's fiction, which, at its best, powerfully blends the elements of southwestern humor, the Southern grotesque, Catholic and Christian theology and philosophy, atheistic and Christian existentialism, realism, and romance. Most critics have praised and interpreted O'Connor from a theological perspective and have noted how unusual her fiction is, as it unites the banal, the inane, and the trivial with Christian, though fundamentally humorous, tales of proud Georgians fighting battles with imaginary or real agents of God sent out to shake some sense into the heads of the protagonists.

As an ironist with a satirical bent, O'Connor may be compared with some of the best in the English language, such as Jonathan Swift and George Gordon, Lord Byron. It is the comic irony of her stories that probably attracts most readers—from the orthodox and religious to the atheistic humanists whom she loves to ridicule in some of her best fiction. Thus, as a comedian,

O'Connor's achievements are phenomenal, since through her largely Christian stories, she is able to attract readers who consider her beliefs outdated and quaint.

In her lifetime, O'Connor won recognition, but she would be surprised at the overwhelming response from literary critics that her fiction has received since her death. O'Connor won O. Henry Awards for her stories "The Life You Save May Be Your Own," "A Circle in the Fire," "Greenleaf," "Everything That Rises Must Converge," and "Revelation." *The Complete Stories*, published posthumously in 1971, won the National Book Award for Fiction. O'Connor received many other honors, including several grants and two honorary degrees.

Biography
Flannery O'Connor's relatively short life was, superficially, rather uneventful. O'Connor was born on March 25, 1925, in Savannah, Georgia, to Regina Cline and Edward Francis O'Connor, Jr. She was their only child. O'Connor's father worked in real estate and construction, and the family lived in Savannah until 1938, when the family moved to Atlanta. In that year, Edward O'Connor became a zone real estate appraiser for the Federal Housing Administration (FHA). Shortly thereafter, O'Connor and her mother moved to Milledgeville, Georgia, and her father became so ill that he had to resign from his job in Atlanta and move to Milledgeville. On February 1, 1941, Edward O'Connor died.

In her youth, O'Connor was diagnosed with the same disease that had killed her father when she was almost sixteen. Her short life would end tragically from complications related to disseminated lupus, a disease that attacks the body's vital organs. From the fall of 1938 until her death, O'Connor spent most of her life in Milledgeville, except for brief hiatuses. After graduating from the experimental Peabody High School in 1942, O'Connor entered Georgia State College for Women (now Georgia College) in Milledgeville, where she majored in sociology and English, and was graduated with an A.B. degree in June, 1945. While in college, she was gifted both in drawing comic cartoons and in writing. In September, 1945, O'Connor enrolled at the State University of Iowa with a journalism scholarship, and in 1946, her first story, "The Geranium" (later revised several times until it became "Judgement Day," her last story), was published in *Accent*. In 1947, she received the master of fine arts degree and enrolled for postgraduate work in the prestigious Writers' Workshop. She was honored in 1948 by receiving a place at Yaddo, an artists' colony in Saratoga Springs, New York.

Planning never to return to the South, O'Connor lived briefly in New York City in 1949 but later moved to Ridgefield, Connecticut, to live with Robert and Sally Fitzgerald. Robert Fitzgerald is best known as a classics scholar and a translator of such works as the *Odyssey* and *The Theban Plays*. City life was too much for O'Connor, but she became quickly acclimated to life in slower-paced Ridgefield. In January, 1950, she underwent an operation while visiting her mother during Christmas. She remained in Milledgeville until she returned to Ridgefield in March.

In December, 1950, O'Connor became extremely ill en route to Milledgeville for Christmas. At first, it was believed that she was suffering from acute rheumatoid arthritis, but in February, after being taken to Emory University Hospital in Atlanta, O'Connor was diagnosed with disseminated lupus erythematosus. As a result of her illness, O'Connor would remain under the care of her mother for the rest of her life, and in March, 1951, she and her mother moved from the former governor's mansion in Milledgeville to Andalusia, the Cline family's farm, which was on the outskirts of town. O'Connor's mother, a Cline, was part of a family who had played a significant part in the history of the town of Milledgeville and the state of Georgia. Like many O'Connor protagonists, her mother, using hired help probably very often similar to the "white trash" and black field hands of O'Connor's fiction, ran Andalusia as a dairy farm.

Meanwhile, O'Connor continued to write when she was not too weak. During the rest of her lifetime, she wrote fiction and befriended many people, some, such as the woman referred to in the collected letters as "A," through correspondence, others through frequent trips to college campuses for lectures, and still others through their visits to see her at Andalusia. Though her illness restricted her life considerably, she was able to achieve greatness as a writer, with a literary output that had already become a permanent part of the canon of American literature since World War II.

Physicians were able to control the effects of lupus for years through the use of cortisone and other drugs, but in early 1964, O'Connor, suffering from anemia, was diagnosed with a fibroid tumor. The operation to rid her of the tumor reactivated the lupus, and O'Connor died of kidney failure in August, 1964. In her last months, most of which were spent in hospitals, O'Connor worked slowly but conscientiously on the fiction that was to appear in her second (and posthumously published) collection of short stories, *Everything That Rises Must Converge*.

Analysis

In creating a fiction that questions the modern disbelief in the mysteries of Christianity, O'Connor blends theological themes and ideas with comically realistic characters drawn from her native American South. Her work is secure in its Christian conviction that the core issue of human existence is salvation through Christ.

O'Connor is best remembered for nearly a dozen works of short fiction. These major stories may be classified as typical O'Connor short stories for a number of reasons. Each story concerns a proud protagonist, usually a woman, who considers herself beyond reproach and is boastful about her own abilities, her Christian goodness, and her property and possessions. Each central character has hidden fears that are brought to the surface through an outsider figure, who serves as a catalyst to initiate a change in the protagonist's perception. O'Connor's primary theme, from her earliest to her last stories, is hubris—that is, overweening pride and arrogance—and the characters' arrogance very often takes on a spiritual dimension.

Closely connected with the theme of hubris is the enactment of God's grace (or Christian salvation). In an essay entitled "A Reasonable Use of the Unreasonable," O'Connor states that her stories are about "the action of grace in territory held largely by the devil" and points out that the most significant part of her stories is the "moment" or "action of grace," when the protagonist is confronted with her own humanity and offered, through an ironic agent of God (an outsider) and usually through violence, one last chance at salvation. O'Connor's protagonists think so highly of themselves that they are unable to recognize their own fallenness because of Original Sin, so the characters typically are brought to an awareness of their humanity (and their sinfulness) through violent confrontations with outsider figures.

O'Connor's most famous story may be the title story of *A Good Man Is Hard to Find*, her first collection of short fiction. This story deals with a Georgia family on its way to Florida for vacation. As the story opens, the main character, the grandmother, tries to convince her son, Bailey, to go to East Tennessee because she has recently read about an escaped convict, The Misfit, who is heading to Florida. The next day, the family, including the nondescript mother, a baby, the other children, John Wesley and June Star, and Pitty Sing, the grandmother's cat, journeys to Florida. They stop at Red Sammy's Famous Barbeque, where the proprietor discusses his views of the changing times, saying "A good man is hard to find" to the grandmother, who has similar views.

The seemingly comic events of the day turn to disaster as the grandmother, upsetting the cat, causes the family to wreck, and The Misfit and two men arrive. The grandmother recognizes The Misfit and, as a result, brings about the death of the entire family. Before she dies, however, the grandmother, who has been portrayed as a self-centered, judgmental, self-righteous, and hypocritical Protestant, sees the humanity of The Misfit and calls him "one of my babies." This section of the story represents what O'Connor calls "the action or moment or grace" in her fiction. Thematically, the story concerns religious hypocrisy, faith and doubt, and social and spiritual arrogance. The Misfit, who strikes comparison with Hazel Motes of *Wise Blood* (1952), is a "prophet gone wrong" (from "A Reasonable Use of the Unreasonable"), tormented by doubt over whether Christ was who he said he was.

Another important story, "The Life You Save May Be Your Own," portrays a drifter named Tom T. Shiftlet, a one-armed man who idolizes the automobile of a widow named Lucynell Crater and marries her daughter, a deaf-mute, in order to obtain it. He tells the mother that he is a man with "a moral intelligence." Shiftlet, who is searching for some explanation for the mystery of human existence, which he cannot quite comprehend, reveals himself to be completely the opposite: one with amoral intelligence. An outsider figure who becomes the story's protagonist, Shiftlet leaves his wife, also named Lucynell, at a roadside restaurant, picks up a hitchhiker, and flies away to Mobile as a thunderstorm approaches. The story's epiphany concerns the irony that Shiftlet considers the hitchhiker a "slime from this earth," when in reality it is Shiftlet who fits this description. In rejecting his wife, he rejects God's grace and,

the story suggests, his mother's valuation of Christianity.

The next major tale, "The Artificial Nigger," is one of O'Connor's most important and complex. It has been subjected to many interpretations, including the suggestion by some critics that it contains no moment of grace on the part of Mr. Head and Nelson, the two main characters. The most Dantesque of all O'Connor stories, "The Artificial Nigger" concerns a journey to the city (hell), where Nelson is to be introduced to his first black person. As O'Connor ridicules the bigotry of the countrified Mr. Head and his grandson, she also moves toward the theological and philosophical. When Nelson gets lost in the black section of Atlanta, he identifies with a big black woman and, comparable to Saint Peter's denial of Christ, Mr. Head denies that he knows him. Nevertheless, they are reunited when they see a statue of an African American, which represents the redemptive quality of suffering and as a result serves to bring about a moment of grace in the racist Mr. Head. The difficulty of this story, other than the possibility that some may see it as racist itself, is that O'Connor's narrative is so ironic that critics are unsure whether to read the story's epiphany as a serious religious conversion or to assume that Mr. Head is still as arrogant and bigoted as ever.

Of all O'Connor's stories—with the possible exceptions of "The Life You Say May Be Your Own" and "Good Country People"—"The Artificial Nigger" most exemplifies the influence of the humor of the Old Southwest, a tradition that included authors such as Augustus Baldwin Longstreet, Johnson Jones Hooper, and George Washington Harris. In "The Artificial Nigger," the familiar motif of the country bumpkin going to the city, which is prevalent in southwestern humor in particular and folk tradition in general, is used.

The next important story, "Good Country People," concerns another major target of O'Connor's satirical fictions: the contemporary intellectual. O'Connor criticizes modern individuals who are educated and who believe that they are capable of achieving their own salvation through the pursuit of human knowledge. Hulga Hopewell, who holds a Ph.D. in philosophy and is an atheistic existentialist, resides with her mother, a banal woman who cannot comprehend the complexity of her daughter. Hulga has a weak heart and has had an accident that caused her to lose one leg.

Believing herself to be of superior intellect, Hulga agrees to go on a picnic with a young Bible salesman and country bumpkin named Manley Pointer, hoping that she can seduce him, her intellectual inferior. Ironically, he is a confidence man with a peculiar affection for the grotesque comparable to characters in the humor of the Old Southwest. As he is about to seduce Hulga, he speeds away with her wooden leg and informs her, "I been believing in nothing since I was born," shattering Hulga's illusion that she is sophisticated and intelligent and that her atheism makes her special. As the story ends, Hulga is prepared for a spiritual recognition that her belief system is as weak and hollow as the wooden leg on which she has based her entire existence. Pointer, whose capacity for evil has been underestimated by the logical positivist Mrs. Hopewell but not by her neighbor Mrs. Freeman, crosses "the speckled lake" in an ironic allusion to Christ's walking on water.

The second collection of O'Connor's short fiction, *Everything That Rises Must Converge*, shows the author's depth of vision as she moved away from stories rooted primarily in the tradition of southwestern humor to heavily philosophical, though still quite humorous, tales of individuals in need of a spiritual experience. Most apparent is the influence of Pierre Teilhard de Chardin, the French paleontologist and Catholic theologian who argued that through the course of time, and even in the evolution of the species, that there was an inevitable process of moving toward convergence with God.

This idea, though perhaps used ironically, appears as the basis for "Everything That Rises Must Converge," which is considered one of O'Connor's greatest works. O'Connor once said that this story was her only one dealing with the racial issue; even so, the tale transcends social and political commentary. The main character, Julian, is another typical O'Connor protagonist. Arrogant and unjust to his more conventional Southern and racist mother, the adult college graduate Julian angrily hopes that his mother will be given a lesson in race relations by having to sit next to a black woman wearing the same hat that she is wearing. Outwardly friendly to the black woman's child, Julian's mother converges with the oppressed black race after she offers a penny to Carver, the child. After the black woman hits Julian's mother with her purse, Julian is as helpless, lost, and innocent as Carver is. He recognizes that his mother is dying and enters the world of "guilt and sorrow." Through this story, O'Connor reflects on the rising social status of blacks and connects this rise with a spiritual convergence between the two races.

"Greenleaf," also a major work, portrays still another woman, Mrs. May, attempting to run a dairy farm. Her two ungrateful bachelor sons refuse to take her self-imposed martyrdom seriously when she complains of the Greenleafs and their bull, which, at the beginning of the story, is hanging around outside her window. The Greenleafs are lower-class tenant farmers whose grown children are far more productive and successful than the bourgeois Mrs. May's. O'Connor moves to pagan mythology as she characterizes the bull as a god (a reference to the Greek god Zeus in one of his myriad disguises) and unites the Greenleaf bull symbolically with peculiarly Christian elements. The coming of grace in this story is characteristically violent. Mrs. May is gored by a bull, who, like the ancient Greek gods, is both pagan lover and deity (although a Christian deity).

The next significant story in the collection, "The Lame Shall Enter First," strikes comparison with the novel *The Violent Bear It Away* (1960), for the main character, Rufus Johnson, a sociopathic teenage criminal, reminds readers of Francis Marion Tarwater, the hero of the novel. There is also Sheppard, the intellectual social worker who, like Tarwater's Uncle Rayber, is a secular humanist and believes that if he takes away the biblical nonsense that the adolescent protagonist has been taught, he will be saved.

Ironically, Sheppard spends all of his time trying to analyze and improve Rufus while at the same time neglecting his own son, Norton. While Rufus is clearly a demonic figure, he nevertheless believes in God and the devil and convinces the child that he can be with his dead mother through Christian conversion. The child, misunderstanding, kills himself, and Sheppard is left to recognize the emptiness of his materialist philosophy. O'Connor's attitude toward the secular humanist is again satirical; without a divine source, there can be no salvation.

"Revelation," one of the greatest pieces of short fiction in American literature, is O'Connor's most complete statement concerning the plight of the oppressed. While her fiction often uses outsiders, she seldom directly comments on her sympathies with them, but through Ruby Turpin's confrontation with the fat girl "blue with acne," who is named Mary Grace, O'Connor is able to demonstrate that in God's Kingdom the last shall be first. Mary Grace calls Mrs. Turpin, who prides herself on being an outstanding Christian lady, a "wart hog from hell," a phrase that Mrs. Turpin cannot get out of her mind. Later, Mrs. Turpin goes to "hose down" her hogs, symbols of unclean spirits, and has a vision of the oppressed souls entering heaven ahead of herself and her husband (Claud). Critical disagreement has centered largely on whether Mrs. Turpin is redeemed after her vision or whether she remains the same arrogant, self-righteous, bigoted woman she has been all of her life.

O'Connor's fiction uses a powerful blend of southwestern humor, the Southern grotesque, and Christian theology to express a Christian worldview. In contrast to the religious disbelief pervading so much of American life are divine grace and redemption—for O'Connor the central facts of human life.

Other major works

NOVELS: *Wise Blood*, 1952; *The Violent Bear It Away*, 1960.

NONFICTION: *Mystery and Manners*, 1969; *The Habit of Being: Selected Letters of Flannery O'Connor*, 1979; *The Presence of Grace*, 1983; *The Correspondence of Flannery O'Connor and Brainard Cheneys*, 1986.

MISCELLANEOUS: *The Complete Works of Flannery O'Connor*, 1988; *Collected Works*, 1988.

Bibliography

Asals, Frederick. *Flannery O'Connor: The Imagination of Extremity*. Athens: University of Georgia Press, 1982.

Bacon, Jon Lance. *Flannery O'Connor and Cold War Culture*. Cambridge, Mass.: Cambridge University Press, 1993.

Brinkmeyer, Robert H., Jr. *The Art and Vision of Flannery O'Connor*. Baton Rouge: Louisiana State University Press, 1989.

Desmond, John F. *Risen Sons: Flannery O'Connor's Vision of History*. Athens: University of Georgia Press, 1987.

Feeley, Kathleen. *Flannery O'Connor: Voice of the Peacock*. New Brunswick, N.J.: Rutgers University Press, 1972.

Giannone, Richard. *Flannery O'Connor and the Mystery of Love*. Urbana: University of Illinois Press, 1989.

Hendin, Josephine. *The World of Flannery O'Connor*. Bloomington: Indiana University Press, 1970.

Orvell, Miles. *Flannery O'Connor: An Introduction*. Jackson: University Press of Mississippi, 1991.

Paulson, Suzanne Morrow. *Flannery O'Connor: A Study of the Short Fiction*. Boston: Twayne, 1988.

Walters, Dorothy. *Flannery O'Connor*. Boston: Twayne, 1973.

Westling, Louise Hutchings. *Sacred Groves and Ravaged Gardens: The Fiction of Eudora Welty, Carson McCullers, and Flannery O'Connor*. Athens: University of Georgia Press, 1985.

WALKER PERCY

Born: Birmingham, Alabama; May 28, 1916   **Died:** Covington, Louisiana; May 10, 1990

Principal long fiction

The Moviegoer, 1961; *The Last Gentleman*, 1966; *Love in the Ruins: The Adventures of a Bad Catholic at a Time Near the End of the World*, 1971; *Lancelot*, 1977; *The Second Coming*, 1980; *The Thanatos Syndrome*, 1987.

Other literary forms

Walker Percy wrote more than fifty reviews and essays on many of the same topics that inform his novels: existential philosophy, language theory, modern scientific method, contemporary American culture, the South, and literature. With one or two exceptions, the most important of these essays are collected in *The Message in the Bottle* (1975).

Achievements

Percy is perhaps most easily described as a Catholic-Existentialist-American-Southern novelist, a baggy phrase that at least has the virtue of identifying the various currents that are blended together in his distinctive works. In Percy's fiction, Mark Twain's Huck Finn from the novel *The Adventures of Huckleberry Finn* (1884) and Jean-Paul Sartre's Antoine Roquentin from *Nausea* (1938) meet in a single character adrift in a world where, despite the formless sprawl of mass society, the possibility of grace still exists. Percy's fiction is readily identifiable by its distinctive narrative voice. That voice—laconic yet disarmingly honest and filled with wonder—has gained for Percy both critical respect and a dedicated readership. Percy received the National Book Award for *The Moviegoer*, the *Los Angeles Times* Book Award for *The Second Coming*, and the St. Louis Literary Award for *Lost in the Cosmos*. Among his other literary honors were memberships in the National Institute of Arts and Letters and the American Academy of Arts and Sciences.

Biography

Walker Percy was born in Birmingham, Alabama, on May 28, 1916. When his father, lawyer Leroy Percy, committed suicide in 1929, the widow and her three sons moved to Greenville, Mississippi, where they lived with Leroy's bachelor cousin, William Alexander Percy, who adopted the boys in 1931, following their mother's death in an automobile accident. The Greenville home served as something of a local cultural cen-

ter; the uncle, the author of several works, including an autobiographical memoir of the South entitled *Lanterns on the Levee* (1941), entertained such houseguests as William Faulkner, Carl Sandburg, Langston Hughes, David Cohn, and Harry Stack Sullivan. In the early 1930's, Percy attended Greenville High School, where he wrote a gossip column and became the close friend of Shelby Foote, who was by then already committed to a literary career. At the University of North Carolina, which was noted for its school of behaviorism, Percy majored in chemistry and received a B.S. degree in 1937. He then enrolled in Columbia's College of Physicians and Surgeons (M.D., 1941), where, in addition to his studies, Percy underwent psychoanalysis and became a frequent moviegoer. The turning point in his life came in early 1942 when, as a resident at Bellevue Hospital in New York, Percy contracted tuberculosis. During his two-year convalescence at Saranac Lake, he began reading extensively in philosophy and literature (Sartre, Albert Camus, Søren Kierkegaard, Gabriel Marcel, Fyodor Dostoevski, Nikolai Gogol, Leo Tolstoy, Franz Kafka). What he discovered was that as a medical doctor he knew much about man but had no idea what a man really is.

Following a relapse and further convalescence in 1944, Percy seemed sure of only two things: He was a doctor who did not wish to practice medicine, and he was literally as well as existentially homeless (his uncle having died in 1942). In 1945, he traveled with Foote to New Mexico and then stayed on alone for a time. On November 7, 1946, he married Mary Bernice Townsend, and less than a year later they both converted to Catholicism. Soon after, the Percys moved from Sewanee, Tennessee, to New Orleans, Louisiana, where Percy continued his contemplative life, financially secure, thanks to his uncle's estate, and intellectually rich. His landlord, Julius Friend, a professor of philosophy, introduced him to the writings of Charles Saunders Peirce, whose triadic theory of language formed the basis of Percy's own linguistic speculations.

In the 1950's, Percy began publishing essays in such journals as *Thought, Commonweal*, and *Philosophy and Phenomenological Research*. After discarding two early novels, he began writing *The Moviegoer* in 1959, revising it four times before its publication two years later. Until his death on May 10, 1990, Percy lived quietly in Covington, Louisiana, a serious and meditative novelist who was also a Catholic, an existentialist, and a Southerner, pondering the world in thought, fiction, and an occasional essay.

Analysis

As perhaps the preeminent Christian "novelist of ideas" during the second half of the twentieth century, Percy invented the American existentialist novel. In his fiction, the modern American South—the last authentic refuge of American religious faith—becomes the setting for characters attempting to reconcile the alienation and hostility of the modern world with the conflicting demands of community and tradition. Only by recognizing a transcendent order, according to Percy, will humankind recapture a unified vision of the world.

Percy acknowledged that Kierkegaard's writings provided him with "a theoretical frame of reference," and one of the most important ideas which he adapted from this frame is Kierkegaard's devotion to a subjective and intensely passionate commitment on the part of the individual. In Percy's view, modern science in general and the social sciences in particular have mistakenly and indiscriminately adopted the behaviorist, or biological, method and have consequently defined humankind reductively and abstractly. Existentialism, including the existential novel, by contrast, presents an alternative to behaviorism: a "concrete" phenomenological approach whose aim is the recovery of humanity's uniqueness.

In classifying humankind as a biological organism acting in accordance with rules applicable to all biological organisms, the behaviorist method fails to deal with what is distinctly human in individuals: their nonbiological goals. Denying the Fall, modern science makes the Gnostic mistake; it attempts to build Eden, the secular city, where humankind's guilt and anxiety are conditioned away, where all of humanity's biological needs are met, and where human existence is certified by experts.

Percy rejects this "brave new world" and calls instead for a "radical anthropology" that can account for the ontological as well as the biological aspects of human existence. Guilt and anxiety, he points out, are not symptoms of maladjustment to be gotten rid of so that the individual (as human organism) can live the life of the satisfied consumer; rather, these signs of estrangement serve to summon humanity not to self-fulfillment but to authentic existence. Individuals are on earth not to have their needs met but to be saved, and that necessitates consciousness of their situation as castaways.

As Robert Coles has pointed out, Percy's novels trace the protagonist's movement from lofty observation to active participation in the openness of life—its possibilities and the necessity of making choices. Each of Percy's major characters feels estranged "from being, from his own being, from the being of other creatures in the world, from the transcendent being. He has lost something, but what he does not know; he only knows that he is sick to death with the loss of it." Since this quest for being is a quest for God, it involves the hero's progress through Kierkegaard's three stages: the aesthetic (the pursuit of pleasure; the self becomes an uncommitted ironic spectator detached from himself and from others); the ethical (living within a general human code, such as marriage); the religious (requiring an entirely personal and, Kierkegaard would say, absurd leap of faith). The hero's search for being begins only when he becomes conscious of his despair and tries either to understand it or to alleviate it in one of two ways: rotation or repetition. Rotation, the quest for new experiences to offset "everydayness," makes up the comic substance of Percy's novels. Repetition, the return to the past, may be rendered comically, but more often it serves a darker purpose, for Percy's heroes are, like William Faulkner's, haunted by the past; as a result, they do not live fully in the present. Only when they confront the past directly and become conscious of it can they break its spell and become sovereign wayfarers.

John Bickerson Bolling, "Binx," is the narrator and main character of *The Moviegoer* and the first of Percy's spiritually "sick" protagonists. At age twenty-nine, he is a successful broker in a modern world where the Church has been replaced by the brokerage house. Although financially secure, Binx feels uneasy; although adept at planning his client's futures, he has trouble living his own life from day to day, fearful that he may at any moment succumb to that worst of all plagues, the malaise of "everydayness." To counter its effects, Binx becomes a moviegoer, partly because movies project a "heightened . . . resplendent reality," albeit temporarily, and partly because movies provide Binx with accepted role-models, whom he impersonates. Impersonation can never fully satisfy the moviegoer, however, who must eventually face the fact that the reality of his own life can never attain the heightened illusion of the star's gestural perfection. Moviegoing serves Binx in two additional ways: It enables him to view his world through the perspective of the films he has seen and, more important, to observe the world as if it were itself a movie and he the passive audience.

Binx's detachment is both a virtue and a vice. As the detached spectator, he observes those around him closely and accurately, thus exposing the roles they have unknowingly adopted. Appropriately, the novel's temporal setting is the week before Mardi Gras, the period of rehearsals for New Orleans' citywide impersonation. Instead of recognizing their situation as castaways, these others feel serenely at home in the world, whereas in fact they are, as Binx understands, "dead." Neither virtuous nor sinful, they ar merely "nice"; they speak, but in clichés; they ask questions but neither expect nor desire answers. Binx, who fears becoming invisible—losing his identity—is right to keep his distance from these shadowy others. At the same time, however, he longs to be like them, to have his identity certified for him by such spurious means as movies, identity cards, *Consumer Reports*, newspaper advice columns, and radio shows such as *This I Believe*, which broadcasts the meaningless affirmations of abstracted religionists to a half-believing, half-skeptical Binx.

If it is his ironic detachment that saves Binx from the unreflective life of mass humanity, then it is his "search" that most clearly characterizes his longing for authenticity and being. "To become aware of the possibility of the search is to be onto something," Binx says. "Not to be onto something is to be in despair." While Binx is indeed "onto something," his search takes a purely aesthetic form. To ease "the pain of loss," he pursues money and women, but the pursuit leads only to boredom and depression because the novelty of his possessions quickly wears off and everydayness inevitably returns to remind him of his inauthenticity and his position as a castaway.

Binx's search begins with the fact of his own "invincible apathy" and eventually leads, after many wrong turns, to authenticity and intersubjective relationships with his fourteen-year-old half-brother, Lonnie Smith, and his twenty-five-year-old cousin, Kate Cutrer. There exists a "complicity" between Binx and the dying Lonnie, who faces life with true serenity because he understands it religiously. Like the other dying children in Percy's novels, Lonnie represents the paradox of unmerited suffering in a world ruled by a supposedly benevolent God, a paradox Percy resolves by depicting their spiritual victory in a "world full of God's grace where sorrow and death do not have the final word." Binx attends to the "good news" that Lonnie embodies because, in part, Lonnie's monotonous way of talking makes his words fresh and therefore meaningful, "like a code tapped through a wall."

Kate, unlike Lonnie, lives in pure anxiety, swinging wildly between various extremes. Although she lacks Binx's degree of awareness as well as his ironic detachment and is more prone to impersonation that he, Kate, like Binx, is aware of her dis-ease, which others can understand only in psychological terms. She correctly points out that in his search Binx may be overlooking something "obvious." She requests that Binx be her God—by which she means he is to tell her what to do. Significantly, her other suitors play the part of intersubjective God rather badly: One wants to send her to a high-priced psychoanalyst; the other promises an interminable vista of "niceness" and everydayness.

Binx's leap from nominal Catholic existing in despair to sovereign wayfarer and authentic being occurs very late in the novel and is effected by what, in a parallel context, Percy calls "some dim dazzling trick of grace." In crucial situations, Binx has invariably chosen to "default," to "exit." Yet, in the final pages, it is clear that Binx will do so no longer. Neither, however, will he play the part his aunt has chosen for him: Southern stoic. He will go to medical school, not because she wants him to but because now he knows what to do: to observe and to serve others.

The Second Coming was, as Percy noted, his "first unalienated novel." Here the author celebrates the unequivocal victory of love over death. Such a conclusion is consistent with Percy's religious vision and his flexible aesthetic with its various tones and broad range of narrative structures: the novelist's version of God's plenty.

The novel picks up the life of Will Barrett some twenty years after *The Last Gentleman* (Percywhere he first appears). At age forty-three, Will is a retired lawyer, a wealthy widower living in Linwood, North Carolina, and recent recipient of the Rotary's man-of-the-year award; yet, he is still a sick man, subject to dizzy spells and tricks of memory. What troubles Will is not the loss of his wife Marion but the sudden realization that he has wasted his life and been "only technically alive." At the brink of the abyss, he sees himself as a total stranger; only two percent of himself, he sets out to find the missing ninety-eight percent. His search takes him in a number of directions. One is back to his father, or more specifically to the only "event" in his life. This is a hunting accident that he comes to realize was no accident at all but instead the father's attempt to kill his son and then himself and so free them both from lives not worth living.

Like his father, Will rejects the "death in life" that characterizes modern believers as well as unbelievers. Will also rejects his father's solution, suicide, because it proves nothing. Instead, he devises the "ultimate scientific experiment" which will, he believes, provide conclusive proof of either God's existence or His non-existence and noninvolvement. Will plans to hide in a cave and fast until God gives him a sign of His existence. Yet Will is looking for God in the wrong place. While waiting in the cave for "a clear yes [The Second Coming ()or] no," he misses the unambiguous beauty of Indian summer; while he assails God's "unavailability," his own "fade outs," such as the cave experiment, preclude the very intersubjective relationships through which God manifests Himself to people. The sign he does receive, a toothache, is a "muddy maybe" that cuts short the experiment and sends Will howling in pain out of the wilderness of self and into a world that, while not physically new, can be seen in an original way.

The person who changes Will's angle of vision is Allison Huger, who has recently escaped her own cave, a mental hospital, and begun a new life in an abandoned greenhouse. She resembles Will in that she feels uncomfortable around other people, as well she should, for the Allison they see is the mentally disturbed organism for whom they can imagine nothing better than "the best-structured environment money can buy." Although she wants to live an entirely self-reliant life, each afternoon about four o'clock she experiences a sense of loss or emptiness. What she feels is identical to one of the symptoms of Will's disease (Hausmann's syndrome), which the doctors call "inappropriate longing." There is a pill to control Will's disease, but there is only one way to satisfy the longing, and that is by loving Allison, by finding his being in her just as she finds hers in him.

When, in the novel's concluding scene, Will Barrett confronts Father Weatherbee, an old priest,

> his heart leapt with joy. What is it I want from her and him, he wondered, not only want but must have? Is she a gift and therefore a sign of the giver? Could it be that the Lord is here, masquerading behind this simple holy face? Am I crazy to want both, her and Him? No, not want, must have. And will have.

The Thanatos Syndrome, Percy's sixth and last novel, ends a bit differently, which is to say less insistently. The novel picks up the life and times of Tom More (Percywho first appears in *Love in the Ruins*) in the mid-1990's, a short while after his release from federal prison, where he has served a two-year term for illegally selling drugs. A brilliant diagnostician, More describes himself as "a psyche-iatrist, an old-fashioned physician of the soul" who believes that it is better, psychologically and spiritually speaking, to be sick (anxious, even terrified) than well, for dis-ease is prolapsarian humanity's natural state. Many of the people around him are, he realizes, anything but anxious. They are, instead, content: without inhibitions, without anxiety, without anything more than rudimentary language skills, and, most important, without a sense of self. More discovers "Blue Boy," a clandestinely funded pilot project that involves introducing heavy sodium into the local water supply in order to stem the tide of social deterioration (crime, teenage pregnancy, even autoimmune deficiency syndrome).

Director of Blue Boy is the ironically "graceful" Bob Comeaux (née Robert D'Angelo Como), who calls Blue Boy "our Manhattan Project." He tries to cajole, seduce, bribe, and threaten More into complicity, all to no avail. Comeaux would make everyone happy, at the cost of his or her freedom as well as self-awareness as a distinctly human being: a creature caught in the malaise, lost in the cosmos, in need of something other than heavy sodium, self-help, or talk-show hosts. *The Thanatos Syndrome* expresses More's faith (in there being "more" than Comeaux allows) in the form of a doubt concerning the modern belief that the causes and cures of humankind's problems are invariably physical.

Other major works

NONFICTION: *The Message in the Bottle*, 1975; *Lost in the Cosmos: The Last Self-Help Book*, 1983; *Conversations with Walker Percy*, 1985; *Signposts in a Strange Land*, 1991; *More Conversations with Walker Percy*, 1993.

Bibliography

Allen, William Rodney. *Walker Percy: A Southern Wayfarer*. Jackson: University Press of Mississippi, 1986.

Baker, Lewis. *The Percys of Mississippi*. Baton Rouge: Louisiana State University Press, 1983.

Broughton, Panthea Reid, ed. *The Art of Walker Percy: Strategies for Being*. Baton Rouge: Louisiana State University Press, 1979.

Ciuba, Gary M. *Walker Percy: Books of Revelations*. Athens: University of Georgia Press, 1991.

Coles, Robert. *Walker Percy: An American Search*. Boston: Little, Brown, 1978.

Crowley, J. Donald, and Sue Mitchell Crowley. *Critical Essays on Walker Percy*. Boston: G. K. Hall, 1989.

Gretlund, Jan Norby, and Karl-Heinz Westarp, eds. *Walker Percy: Novelist and Philosopher*. Jackson: University Press of Mississippi, 1991.

Hardy, John Edward. *The Fiction of Walker Percy*. Urbana: University of Illinois Press, 1987.

Lawson, Lewis A. *Following Percy: Essays on Walker Percy's Work*. Troy, N.Y.: Whitston, 1988.

Tharpe, Jac. *Walker Percy*. Boston: Twayne, 1983.

——————, ed. *Walker Percy: Art and Ethics*. Jackson: University Press of Mississippi, 1980.

Tolson, Jay. *Pilgrim in the Ruins: A Life of Walker Percy*. New York: Simon & Schuster, 1992.

EDGAR ALLAN POE

Born: Boston, Massachusetts; January 19, 1809   **Died:** Baltimore, Maryland; October 7, 1849

Principal short fiction

Tales of the Grotesque and Arabesque, 1840; *The Prose Romances of Edgar Allan Poe*, 1843; *Tales*, 1845; *The Short Fiction of Edgar Allan Poe*, 1976 (Stuart and Susan Levine, eds.).

Other literary forms

During his short literary career, Edgar Allan Poe produced a large quantity of writing, most of which was not collected in book form during his lifetime. He published one novel and several volumes of poetry, the most famous of which is *The Raven and Other Poems* (1845). Poe earned his living mainly as a writer and as an editor of magazines, for which he wrote reviews, occasional essays, meditations, literary criticism, and a variety of kinds of journalism, as well as poetry and short fiction.

Achievements

During his life, Poe was a figure of controversy and so became reasonably well known in literary circles. Two of his works were recognized with prizes: "Manuscript Found in a Bottle" and "The Gold Bug." "The Raven," his most famous poem, created a sensation when it was published and became something of a best-seller. After his death, Poe's reputation grew steadily—though in the United States opinion remained divided—until by the middle of the twentieth century he had clear status as an author of worldwide importance. Poe's achievements may be measured in terms of what he has contributed to literature and of how his work influenced later culture.

Poe was accomplished in fiction, poetry, and criticism, setting standards in all three that distinguish him from most of his American contemporaries. In fiction, he is credited with inventing the conventions of the classic detective story, beginning the modern genre of science fiction, and turning the conventions of gothic fiction to the uses of high art in stories such as "The Fall of the House of Usher." He was also an accomplished humorist and satirist. In poetry, he produced a body of work that is respected throughout the world and a few poems that, in part because of their sheer verbal beauty, have persistently appealed to the popular imagination, such as "The Bells" and "Annabel Lee." In criticism, Poe is among the first to advocate and demonstrate

methods of textual criticism that came into their own in the twentieth century, notably in his essay "The Philosophy of Composition," in which he analyzed with remarkable objectivity the process by which "The Raven" was built in order to produce a specific effect in its readers.

Poe's influence on later culture was pervasive. Nearly every important American writer after Poe shows signs of his influence, especially those working in the gothic mode or with grotesque humor. The French, Italians, and writers in Spanish and Portuguese in the Americas acknowledge and demonstrate their debts to Poe in technique and vision. Only to begin to explore Poe's influence on twentieth century music and film would be a major undertaking. In terms of his world reputation, Poe stands with William Faulkner and perhaps T. S. Eliot as one of the most influential authors of the United States.

Biography

Edgar Allan Poe was born in Boston on January 19, 1809. His parents, David and Elizabeth Arnold Poe, were actors at a time when the profession was not widely respected in the United States. David was making a success in acting when alcohol addiction brought an end to his career. He had deserted his family a year after Edgar's birth; Elizabeth died a year later in 1811, leaving Edgar an orphan in Richmond, Virginia. There, he was taken in by John Allan, who educated him well in England and the United States. Poe was a sensitive and precocious child; during his teens, his relations with his foster father declined. Stormy relations continued until Allan's first wife died and his second wife had children. Once it became unlikely that he would inherit anything significant from the wealthy Allan, Poe, at the age of twenty-one, having already published a volume of poetry, began a literary career.

From 1831 to 1835, more or less dependent on his Poe relatives, he worked in Baltimore, writing stories and poems, a few of which were published. In 1835, he secretly married his cousin, Virginia Clemm, when she was thirteen. From 1835 to 1837, he was assistant editor of *The Southern Literary Messenger*, living on a meager salary, tending to drink enough to disappoint the editor, publishing his fiction, and making a national reputation as a reviewer of books. When he was fired, he moved with his wife (by then the marriage was publicly acknowledged) and her mother to New York City, where he lived in poverty, selling his writing for the next two years. Though he published *The Narrative of Arthur Gordon Pym* in 1838, it brought him no income. He moved to Philadelphia that same year and for several months continued to live on only a small income from stories and other magazine pieces. In 1839, he became coeditor of *Burton's Gentleman's Magazine*. Before drinking led to his losing this job, he wrote and published some of his best fiction, such as "The Fall of the House of Usher." He took another editing position with *Graham's Magazine* that lasted about a year. He then lived by writing and working at occasional jobs. In 1844, he went with his family back to New York City. His wife, Virginia, had been seriously ill, and her health was declining. In New York, he wrote for newspapers. In 1845, he published "The Raven" and *Tales*, both of which were well received ("The Raven" was a popular success), though again his income from them was small. In the early nineteenth century, an author could not easily earn a satisfactory income from writing alone, in part because of the lack of international copyright laws. He was able to purchase a new weekly, *The Broadway Journal*, but it failed in 1846.

After 1845, Poe was famous, and his income, though unstable, was a little more dependable. His life, however, did not go smoothly. He was to some extent lionized in literary circles, and his combination of desperation for financial support with alcoholism and a combative temper kept him from dealing well with being a "star." Virginia died in 1847, and Poe was seriously ill for much of the next year. In 1849, he found himself in Richmond, and for a few months he seemed quite well. His Richmond relatives received and cared for him kindly, and he stopped drinking. In October, however, while on a trip, he paused in Baltimore, became drunk, was found unconscious, and was carried to a local hospital, where he died on October 7, 1849.

Analysis

The variety of Poe's short fiction cannot be conveyed fully in a short introduction. Though he is best known for his classics of gothic horror such as "The Fall of the House of Usher" and his portraits of madmen and grotesques such as "The Tell-Tale Heart" and "The Cask of Amontillado," he is also the author of detective stories, "The Purloined Letter,"; science fiction, *The Narrative of Arthur Gordon Pym*; parodies, "The Premature Burial"; satires, "The Man That Was Used Up"; social and political fiction, "The System of Dr. Tarr and Prof. Fether"; and a variety of kinds of humor, "Diddling Considered as One of the Exact Sciences" and "Hop-Frog."

Three stories that illustrate some of this variety while offering insight into Poe's characteristic themes are "A Descent into the Maelström," "The Purloined Letter," and "The Fall of the House of Usher." Among Poe's central themes is an emphasis on the mysteries of the self, of others, of nature, and of the universe. His stories usually function in part to undercut the kinds of easy optimism and certainty that were characteristic of popular thought in his time.

"A Descent into the Maelström" opens with a declaration of mystery in which Poe announces several motifs for the story that follows. One of these is the mystery of how God acts and, therefore, may be revealed in nature. Another is inadequacy of humanly devised models for explaining nature or God's presence in nature. Yet another is the idea of the multiple senses of depth, not merely the physical depth of a well or a maelstrom but also the metaphorical depths of a mystery, of God, of nature, of God's manifestation in nature.

The story is relatively simple in its outline, though interestingly complicated by its frame. In the frame, the narrator visits a remote region of Norway to observe the famous maelstrom, an actual phenomenon described in contemporary reference books that were Poe's sources. There, he encounters an apparently retired fisherman, who guides him to a view of the whirlpool and who then tells the story of how he survived being caught in it. In the main body of the story, the guide explains how a sudden hurricane and a stopped watch caused him and his two brothers to be caught by the maelstrom as they attempted to return from a routine, if risky, fishing trip. He explains what the experience was like—an unexplainable, supernatural event—and how he managed to survive.

As the maelstrom forms, the narrator sees it as more than a natural phenomenon. Unable to accept the naturalistic account of it offered by the *Encyclopædia Britannica*, he is instead drawn by the power that it exerts over his imagination to see it as a manifestation of occult powers, an eruption of supernatural power into the natural world. This view forms the context within which the guide tells his tale.

An important feature of the guide's story is the contrast between his sense of chaotic threat and his repeated perceptions that suggest an ordered purpose within this chaos. For the fisherman, it was good fortune, assisted perhaps by a kind Providence, that allowed him to find a means of escape once his fishing boat had been sucked into the gigantic whirlpool. Even as the boat is blown into the whirlpool by the sudden and violent hurricane, a circle opens in the black clouds, revealing a bright moon that illuminates the scene of terror. An inverted funnel of clouds ascends to an opening where the moon appears, over a funnel of whirling seawater descending into an obscured opening where a rainbow appears. This view of a tremendous overarching cosmic order composing a scene of mortal chaos produces other kinds of order that help to save the fisherman.

Bewitched by the beauty that he sees in this scene, the fisherman, like the narrator on the cliff-top, gains control of himself, loses his fear, and begins to look around, merely for the sake of enjoying it: "I began to reflect how magnificent a thing it was to die in such a manner . . . in view of so wonderful a manifestation of God's power." No longer terrified, the fisherman begins to understand how the whirlpool works. Finally, he is borne up until the maelstrom stops and he finds himself again in comparatively calm water.

"The Purloined Letter," one of Poe's best detective stories, places a greater emphasis on the nature and importance of intelligence, while still pointing at the mysteries of human character. The narrator and his friend C. Auguste Dupin are approached by the comical Monsieur G——, the prefect of the Paris police. The prefect has come to Dupin with a troubling problem. He eventually explains that the Minister D—- has managed, in the presence of an important lady, presumably the queen, to steal from her a compromising letter with which he might damage her severely by showing it to her husband. The minister has since been using the threat of revealing the letter to coerce the queen's cooperation in influencing policy. As the prefect repeats, to Dupin's delight, getting the letter back without publicity ought to be simple for an expert policeman—yet the letter has not been found. After several fruitless searches by the police, Dupin manipulates the prefect into declaring what he would pay to regain the letter, instructs him to write Dupin a check for that amount, and gives him the letter. The prefect is so astonished and

gratified that he runs from the house, not even bothering to ask how Dupin has managed this feat.

The second half of the story consists of Dupin's explanation to the narrator, with a joke or two at the prefect's expense, of how he found and obtained the letter. One key point is the importance of poetic imagination to the process of solution. Most of Dupin's explanation of his procedure has to do with how one goes about estimating the character and ability of one's opponent, for understanding what the criminal may do is ultimately more important to a solution than successful deduction. While a "mere" mathematician can make competent deductions from given ideas, as the prefect has done, it requires a kind of poet to penetrate the criminal's mind. It takes a combination of poet and mathematician—in short, Dupin—to solve such a crime dependably. The prefect has greatly underestimated the minister because the latter is known to be a poet and the prefect believes poets are fools. Dupin says that the police often fail because they assume that the criminal's intelligence mirrors their own, and therefore over- or underestimate the criminal's ability. Having established that the minister is a very cunning opponent who will successfully imagine the police response to his theft, Dupin is able to deduce quite precisely how the minister will hide the letter, by placing it very conspicuously, so as not to appear hidden at all, and by disguising it. Dupin's deduction, of course, proves exactly right, and by careful plotting, he is able to locate and regain it.

The two main portions of the story, presenting the problem and the solution, illustrate the nature and powers of human reason. The end of the story emphasizes mystery by raising questions about morality—and about Dupin, whose detecting occurs in a morally ambiguous world. The end of the story calls attention repeatedly to the relationship between Dupin and the Minister D—: They could be brothers, and Dupin claims intimate acquaintance and frequent association with the minister. They disagree, however, politically. Dupin, in leaving a disguised substitute for the regained letter, has arranged for the minister's fall from power and may even have endangered his life.

By providing this kind of information at the end, Poe raises moral and political questions, encouraging the reader to wonder whether Dupin's brilliant detection serves values of which the reader might approve. In this way, Dupin's demonstration of a magnificent human intellect is placed in the context of moral mystery, quite unlike the tales of Sherlock Holmes and related classical detectives. While Poe invented what became major conventions in detective fiction—the rational detective, his less able associate, the somewhat ridiculous police force, the solution scene—his detective stories show greater moral complexity than those of his best-known followers.

"The Fall of the House of Usher" has everything a Poe story is supposed to have according to the popular view of him: a gothic house, a terrified narrator, live burial, madness, and horrific catastrophe. The narrator journeys to the home of his boyhood chum, Roderick Usher. Usher has been seriously ill and wishes the cheerful companionship of his old friend. The house and its environs radiate gloom, and though Usher alternates between a kind of creative mania and the blackest depression, he tends also on the whole to radiate gloom. Usher confides that he is upset in part because his twin sister, Madeline, is mortally ill. It develops, however, that the main reason Usher is depressed is his suspicion that his house is a living organism that is driving him toward madness. Madeline dies, and, to discourage grave robbers, Usher and the narrator temporarily place her in a coffin in a vault beneath the house. Once Madeline is dead, Usher's alternation of mood ceases, and he remains always deeply gloomy.

On his last evening at Usher, the narrator witnesses several events that seem to confirm Usher's view that the house is driving him mad. Furthermore, these confirmations seem to suggest that the house is merely one in a nest of Chinese boxes, in a series of closed, walled-in enclosures that make up the physical and spiritual universe. This oft-repeated image is represented most vividly in one of Usher's paintings, what appears to be a burial vault unnaturally lit from within. This image conveys the idea of the flame of human consciousness imprisoned, as if buried alive in an imprisoning universe. The terrifying conviction of this view is one of the causes of Usher's growing madness. On the last evening, a storm seems to enclose the house as if it were inside a box of wind and cloud, on which the house itself casts an unnatural light. The narrator tries to comfort both himself and Usher by reading a story, but the sound effects described in the story are echoed in reality in the house. Usher, as his reason crumbles, interprets these sounds as Madeline, not really dead, breaking

through various walls behind which she has been placed—her coffin and the vault—until finally, Usher claims, she is standing outside the door of the room where they are reading. The door opens, perhaps supernaturally, and there she stands. The narrator watches the twins fall against each other and collapse; he rushes outside only to see the house itself collapse into its reflection in the pool that stands before it, this last event taking place under the unnatural light of a blood-red moon.

One of the main difficulties in interpreting the story is the way that the narrator tells his story. He is represented as telling the story of this experience some time after the events took place. He insists that there are no supernatural elements in his story, that everything that happened at the House of Usher can be accounted for in a naturalistic way. In this respect, he is like the narrator of "A Descent into the Maelström." The latter "knows" that the natural world operates according to regular "natural" laws, but when he actually sees the whirlpool, his imagination responds involuntarily with the conviction that this is something supernatural. Likewise, the narrator of "The Fall of the House of Usher" is convinced that the world can be understood in terms of natural law and, therefore, that what has happened to him at Usher either could not have happened or must have a natural explanation.

Perhaps "The Fall of the House of Usher" is a kind of trap, set to enmesh readers in the same sort of difficulty in which the narrator finds himself. If this is the case, then the story functions in a way consistent with Poe's theme of the inadequacy of models constructed by human intelligence to explain the great mysteries of life and the universe. The narrator says he has had an experience that he cannot explain and that points toward an inscrutable universe, one that might be conceived as designed to drive humans mad if they find themselves compelled to comprehend it. Likewise, in reading the story, the reader has an experience that finally cannot be explained, that seems designed to drive a reader mad if he or she insists upon achieving a final view of its wholeness. The story itself may provide an experience that demonstrates the ultimate inadequacy of human reason to the mysteries of Creation.

Other major works

NOVEL: *The Narrative of Arthur Gordon Pym*, 1838.
PLAY: *Politician*, 1835-1836.
POETRY: *Tamerlane and Other Poems*, 1827; *Al Aaraaf, Tamerlane, and Minor Poems*, 1829; *Poems*, 1831; *The Raven and Other Poems*, 1845; *Eureka: A Prose Poem*, 1848; *Poe: Complete Poems*, 1959.

NONFICTION: *The Letters of Edgar Allan Poe*, 1948; *Literary Criticism of Edgar Allan Poe*, 1965; *Essays and Reviews*, 1984.

MISCELLANEOUS: *The Complete Works of Edgar Allan Poe*, 1902 (17 vols.); *Collected Works of Edgar Allan Poe*, 1969, 1978 (3 vols.).

Bibliography

Bittner, William. *Poe: A Biography*. Boston: Little, Brown, 1962.

Buranelli, Vincent. *Edgar Allan Poe*. 2d ed. Boston: Twayne, 1977.

Carlson, Eric, ed. *Critical Essays on Edgar Allan Poe*. Boston: G. K. Hall, 1987.

_____ , ed. *The Recognition of Edgar Allan Poe*. Ann Arbor: University of Michigan Press, 1966.

Howarth, William L. *Twentieth Century Interpretations of Poe's Tales*. Englewood Cliffs, N.J.: Prentice-Hall, 1971.

Hyneman, Esther K. *Edgar Allan Poe: An Annotated Bibliography of Books and Articles in English, 1827-1973*. Boston: G. K. Hall, 1974.

LeVert, Suzanne. *Edgar Allan Poe*. New York: Chelsea House, 1992.

May, Charles E. *Edgar Allan Poe: A Study of the Short Fiction*. Boston: Twayne, 1991.

Meyers, Jeffrey. *Edgar Allan Poe: His Life and Legacy*. New York: Charles Scribner's Sons, 1992.

Quinn, Arthur Hobson. *Edgar Allan Poe*. New York: D. Appleton-Century, 1941.

Silverman, Kenneth, ed. *New Essays on Poe's Major Tales*. Cambridge, England: Cambridge University Press, 1993.

KATHERINE ANNE PORTER

Born: Indian Creek, Texas; May 15, 1890   *Died:* Silver Spring, Maryland; September 18, 1980

Principal short fiction

Flowering Judas and Other Stories, 1930; *Hacienda*, 1934; *Noon Wine*, 1937; *Pale Horse, Pale Rider: Three Short Novels*, 1939; *The Leaning Tower and Other Stories*, 1944; *The Old Order*, 1944; *The Collected Stories of Katherine Anne Porter*, 1965.

Other literary forms

Katherine Anne Porter wrote one novel, *Ship of Fools* (1962), and essays of various kinds, some of which she published under the title of one of them, *The Days Before* (1952). Porter was a reporter with unsigned journalism for the Fort Worth weekly newspaper *The Critic* in 1917 and the Denver *Rocky Mountain News* in 1918-1919. Early in her career, she worked on a critical biography of Cotton Mather, which she never finished; she did, however, publish parts in 1934, 1940, 1942, and 1946. Her few poems and most of her nonfictional prose have been collected in *The Collected Essays and Occasional Writings* (1970). Her memoir of the Sacco and Vanzetti trial, *The Never-Ending Wrong*, was published in 1977 on the fiftieth anniversary of their deaths. She was a prodigious writer of personal letters, many of which have been published.

Achievements

Porter is distinguished by her small literary production of exquisitely composed and highly praised short fiction. Although she lived to be ninety years old, she produced and published only some twenty-five short stories and one long novel. Nevertheless, her work was praised early and often from the start of her career; some of her stories, such as "Flowering Judas," "Pale Horse, Pale Rider," and "Old Mortality," have been hailed as masterpieces. Sponsored by Edmund Wilson, Allen Tate, Kenneth Burke, and Elizabeth Madox Roberts, Porter won a Guggenheim Fellowship in 1931 and went to Berlin and Paris to live while she wrote such stories as "The Cracked Looking-Glass" and "Noon Wine," for which she won a Book-of-the-Month Club award in 1937. After publication of the collection *Pale Horse, Pale Rider: Three Short Novels* in 1939, she received a gold medal for literature from the Society of Libraries of New York University, in 1940. Elected a member of the National Institute of Arts and Letters in 1943, Porter was also appointed as writer-in-residence at Stanford University in 1949, and, in the same year, she received an honorary degree, doctor of letters, from the University of North Carolina. In 1959 she received a Ford Foundation grant, in 1962 the Emerson-Thoreau gold medal from the American Academy of Arts and Sciences, and in 1966-1967 the National Book Award for Fiction, the Pulitzer Prize in fiction, and the Gold Medal for fiction, National Institute of Arts and Letters.

Biography

There are conflicting reports of dates from Katherine Anne Porter's life, partly because Porter herself was not consistent about her biography. Nevertheless, the main events are fairly clear. Her mother, Mary Alice, died less than two years after Katherine Anne's birth. Subsequently, her grandmother, Catherine Anne Porter, was the most important adult woman in her life, and after the death of her grandmother in 1901, Katherine Anne was sent away by her father to an Ursuline convent in New Orleans, then in 1904 to the Thomas School for Girls in San Antonio. She ran away from her school in 1906 to marry John Henry Kroontz, the twenty-year-old son of a Texas rancher. She remained with him seven years (some reports say her marriage lasted only three years), and in 1911 she went to Chicago to earn her own way as a reporter for a weekly newspaper and as a bit player for a film company. From 1914 to 1916, she traveled through Texas, earning her way as a ballad singer. Then she returned to journalism, joining the staff of the Denver *Rocky Mountain News* in 1918. At about this time, Porter was gravely ill, and she thought she was going to die. Her illness was a turning point in the development of her character, and it was the basis for her story "Pale Horse, Pale Rider," which she finished twenty years later.

After she recovered her health, Porter lived briefly in New York and then Mexico, where she studied art while observing the Obregón revolution in 1920. Her experiences in Mexico provided material for Porter's earliest published stories, "María Concepción" and "The Martyr" in 1922 and 1923. She married and promptly divorced Ernest Stock, a young English art student in New York, in 1925. Soon after, she participated in protests against the trial of Nicola Sacco and Bartolomeo Vanzetti, and then, in 1928, she began work on her biography of Mather, which was never completed. Porter traveled often during these years, but she wrote some of her greatest stories at the same time, including "He," "The Jilting of Granny Weatherall," "Theft," and "Flowering Judas."

After publication of her collection *Flowering Judas and Other Stories* in 1930, Porter was awarded a Guggenheim Fellowship to support her while living in Berlin and Paris, from 1931 to 1937. While in Europe, she composed "The Leaning Tower" and "The Cracked Looking-Glass," and she wrote an early draft of "Noon Wine." In 1933, she married Eugene Pressly, whom she divorced to marry Albert Erskine in 1938, when she returned to the United States to live with her new husband in Baton Rouge, Louisiana. At that time, she became a friend of Tate and his family.

In 1941, Porter appeared on television with Mark Van Doren and Bertrand Russell; in 1944, she worked on films in Hollywood; and in 1947, she undertook a lecture tour of several Southern universities. The novel that she began as a story, "Promised Land," in 1936, was finally published in 1962 as *Ship of Fools* to mixed reviews. Apart from her work on this long fiction, Porter wrote little except for occasional essays and reviews, some of which she published as *The Days Before* in 1952. Porter spent most of her life after 1950 lecturing, traveling, buying and selling property, and slowly composing her novel along with her biography of Mather. In October, 1976, she read her essay "St. Augustine and the Bullfight" at the Poetry Center in New York City, and in 1977, she published a memoir of Sacco and Vanzetti, whose trials of injustice had haunted her for fifty years. When she died, in 1980, in Silver Spring, Maryland, she left behind a small canon of fiction and a great achievement of literary art.

Analysis

Katherine Ann Porter's fiction is noted for its sophisticated use of symbolism, complex exploitation of point of view, challenging variations of ambiguously ironic tones, and profound analyses of psychological and social themes. While her works are not obviously autobiographical, they clearly are based on people and places familiar to her. In a portion of her fiction, the American South and Southwest form the backdrop against which assorted individuals and their relationships are drawn.

From 1922 to 1935, Porter's fiction is concerned with the attempts of women to accommodate themselves to, or to break the bounds of, socially approved sexual roles. They usually fail to achieve the identities that they seek; instead, they ironically become victims of their own or others' ideas of what they ought to be. Violeta of "Virgin Violeta" fantasizes about her relationship with her cousin Carlos, trying to understand it according to the idealistic notions that she has learned from church and family; when Carlos responds to her sensual reality, she is shocked and disillusioned. The ironies of Violeta's situation are exploited more fully, and more artfully, in "María Concepción." As the heroine, María manages, through violence, to assert her identity through the social roles that she is expected to play in her primitive society; she kills her sensual rival, María Rosa, seizes the baby of her victim, and retrieves her wandering husband.

Images of symbolic importance organize the ironies of such stories as "Flowering Judas" and "The Cracked Looking-Glass." "Flowering Judas," one of Porter's most famous stories, develops the alienated character of Laura from her resistance to the revolutionary hero Braggioni to her refusal of the boy who sang to her from her garden and finally to her complicity in the death of Eugenio in prison. At the center of the story, in her garden and in her dream, Laura is linked with a Judas tree in powerfully mysterious ways: as a betrayer, as a rebellious and independent spirit. Readers will be divided on the meaning of the tree, as they will be on the virtue of Laura's character.

The same ambivalence results from examining the symbolic function of a cracked mirror in the life of Rosaleen, the point-of-view character in "The Cracked Looking-Glass." This middle-aged Irish beauty sees herself as a monster in her mirror, but she cannot replace the mirror with a new one any more than she can reconcile her sexual frustration with her maternal affection for her aged husband, Dennis. This story twists the May-December stereotype into a reverse fairy tale of beauty betrayed, self deceived, and love dissipated. Rosaleen treats young men as the sons she never had to rear, and she represses her youthful instincts to nurse her impotent husband in his old age. She does not like what she sees when she looks honestly at herself in the mirror, but she will not replace the mirror of reality, cracked as she sees it must be.

In the middle period of her short fiction, Porter's characters confront powerful threats of illusion to shatter their tenuous hold on reality. Romantic ideals and family myths combine to shape the formative circumstances for Miranda in "Old Mortality." Divided into three parts, this story follows the growth of the young heroine from 1885, when she is eight, to 1912, when she is recently married against her father's wishes. Miranda and her older sister, Maria, are fascinated by tales of their legendary Aunt Amy, their father's sister whose honor he had risked his life to defend in a duel, and who died soon after she married their Uncle Gabriel. The first part of the story narrates the family's anecdotes about Aunt Amy and contrasts her with her cousin Eva, a plain woman who participated in movements for women's rights. Part 2 of the story focuses on Miranda's disillusionment with Uncle Gabriel, whom she meets at a racetrack while she is immured in a church school in New Orleans; he is impoverished, fat, and alcoholic, remarried to a bitter woman who hates his family, and insensitive to the suffering of his winning race horse.

Part 3 describes Miranda's encounter with cousin Eva on a train carrying them to the funeral of Uncle Gabriel. Here, Miranda's romantic image of Aunt Amy is challenged by Eva's skeptical memory, but Miranda refuses to yield her vision entirely to Eva's scornful one. Miranda hopes that her father will embrace her when she returns home, but he remains detached and disapproving of her elopement. She realizes that from now on she must live alone, separate, and alienated from her family. She vows to herself that she will know the truth about herself, even if she can never know the truth about her family's history. The story ends, however, on a note of critical skepticism about her vow, suggesting its hopefulness is based upon her ignorance.

Love and death mix forces to press Miranda through a crisis of vision in "Pale Horse, Pale Rider." This highly experimental story mixes dreams with waking consciousness, present with past, and illness with health. Set during World War I, it analyzes social consequences of a military milieu, and it uses that setting to suggest a symbolic projection of the pressures that build on the imagination and identity of the central character. Miranda is a writer of drama reviews for a newspaper; her small salary is barely enough to support herself, and so when she balks at buying Liberty Bonds, her patriotism is questioned. This worry preoccupies her thoughts and slips into her dreaming experience. In fact, the opening of the story seems to be an experience of a sleeper who is slowly coming awake from a dream of childhood in which the adult's anxieties about money are mixed. Uncertainty about the mental state of Miranda grows as she mixes her memories of past with present, allowing past feelings to affect present judgments.

Miranda meets a young soldier, Adam, who will soon be sent to battle. They both know that his fate is sealed, since they are both aware of the survival statistics for soldiers who make assaults from trenches. Miranda becomes gravely ill shortly before Adam leaves for the war front, and he nurses her through the earliest days of her sickness. Her delirium merges her doctor with Adam, with the German enemy, and with figures of her dreams. By this process, Miranda works through her attractions to Adam, and to all men, and survives to assert her independence as a professional artist. The climax of her dream is her refusal to follow the pale rider, who is Death. This feature of her dream is present at the beginning of the story, to anticipate that Miranda will have to contend with this, to resolve her inner battle, even before the illness that constitutes her physical struggle with death. The men of her waking life enter her dreams as Death, and so when Adam actually dies in battle, Miranda is symbolically assisted in winning her battle for life. The story makes it seem that her dreaming is the reality of the men, that their lives are figments of her imagination. Her recovery of health is a triumph, therefore, of her creative energies as well as an assertion of her independent feminine identity.

In the final, sustained period of her work in short fiction, from 1935 to 1942, Porter subjects memories to the shaping power of creative imagination, as she searches out the episodes that connect to shape the character of Miranda, and as she traces the distorting effects of social pressures on children, wives, and artists in the remaining stories of the third collection. The crucial, shaping episodes of Miranda's childhood constitute the core elements of several stories in the collection called *The Leaning Tower and Other Stories*. Two of the stories of this collection, "The Circus" and "The Grave," are examples of remarkable compression and, particularly in "The Grave," complex artistry.

Miranda cries when she sees a clown perform highwire acrobatics in "The Circus." Her fear is a child's protest against the clown's courtship with death. There is nothing pleasurable about it for Miranda. In fact, she seems to see through the act to recognize the threat of death itself, in the white, skull-like makeup of the clown's face. The adults enjoy the spectacle, perhaps insensitive to its essential message or, alternatively, capable of appreciating the artist's defiance of death. In any event, young Miranda is such a problem that her father sends her home with one of the servants, Dicey. The point of poignancy is in Miranda's discovery of Dicey's warm regard for her despite the fact that Dicey had keenly wanted to stay at the circus. When Miranda screams in her sleep, Dicey lies beside her to comfort her, to protect her even from the dark forces of her nightmares. This sacrifice is not understood by the child Miranda, though it should be to the adult who recalls it. "The Grave" is more clear about the function of time in the process of understanding. Miranda and her brother Paul explore open graves of their family while hunting. They find and exchange a coffin screw and a ring, then skin a rabbit that Paul killed, only to find that the rabbit is pregnant with several young that are "born" dead. The experience of mixing birth with death, of sexual awareness with marriage and death, is suddenly illuminated for Miranda years later when she recalls her brother on that day while she stands over a candy stand in faraway Mexico.

Other stories in *The Leaning Tower* contain elements of the Southern gothic reminiscent of Flannery O'Connor or even Poe. The strange story of little Stephen in "The Downward Path to Wisdom" provides painful insights concerning a young boy who grows to hate his father, mother, grandmother, and uncle; although the family members are concerned, his hatred is understandable, since no one really reaches out to love and help him. He articulates his hatred in a song to which the mother shows no alarm; she may think that he really does not mean what he sings, or she may not really hear

what he is trying to say through his art. A similar theme of hatred is treated in the heartless marital problems of Mr. and Mrs. Halloran of "A Day's Work," in which the emotional violence is borne physically and which ends in a fight to the death—but whose, the reader remains uncertain. In a later story, "The Fig Tree," Miranda is revived, burying a dead baby chicken beneath a fig tree. When she thinks she hears it, cheeping from beneath the earth, she becomes frantic but is unable to rescue it because her grandmother forces her to leave with the family for the country. In "Holiday," the narrator spends a long holiday with German immigrants in the backlands of Texas. The Müllers appear to have a servant, Ottilie, who is disabled and mentally retarded; the narrator gradually comes to realize that Ottilie is a member of the family who is ignored, even to the point of leaving her behind during the mother's funeral. When the narrator desperately attempts to transport Ottilie to the funeral, she realizes that the girl has no interest in acknowledging death; the narrator comes to accept the radical difference that separates her from Ottilie, and from all other human beings, resigning herself to the universal condition of alienation.

In such ways, Porter's fiction educates the patiently naïve reader into radical paths of maturity. Whether one sees her as a voice of the Southern experience per se or as a voice articulating visions of an alienated human condition in general—and at some level she is both—the subtleties of technique, patterned symbolism, and synthesis of past and present feeling in Porter's stories will repay careful reading.

Other major works

NOVEL: *Ship of Fools*, 1962.

NONFICTION: *My Chinese Marriage*, 1921; *Outline of Mexican Popular Arts and Crafts*, 1922; *What Price Marriage*, 1927; *The Days Before*, 1952; *A Defence of Circe*, 1954; *A Christmas Story*, 1967; *The Collected Essays and Occasional Writings*, 1970; *The Selected Letters of Katherine Anne Porter*, 1970; *The Never-Ending Wrong*, 1977; *Letters of Katherine Anne Porter*, 1990; *This Strange, Old World and Other Book Reviews*, 1991.

MISCELLANEOUS: *Uncollected Early Prose of Katherine Anne Porter*, 1993.

Bibliography

Bloom, Harold, ed. *Katherine Anne Porter: Modern Critical Views*. New York: Chelsea House, 1986.

Brinkmeyer, Robert H. *Katherine Anne Porter's Artistic Development: Primitivism, Traditionalism, and Totalitarianism*. Baton Rouge: Louisiana State University Press, 1993.

DeMouy, Jane Krause. *Katherine Anne Porter's Women: The Eye of Her Fiction*. Austin: University of Texas Press, 1983.

Givner, Joan. *Katherine Anne Porter: A Life*. Rev. ed. Athens: University of Georgia Press, 1991.

Hardy, John Edward. *Katherine Anne Porter*. New York: Frederick Ungar, 1973.

Hartley, Lodwick, and George Core, eds. *Katherine Anne Porter: A Critical Symposium*. Athens: University of Georgia Press, 1969.

Hendrick, Willene, and George Hendrick. *Katherine Anne Porter*. Rev. ed. Boston: Twayne, 1988.

Hilt, Kathryn, and Ruth M. Alvarez. *Katherine Anne Porter: An Annotated Bibliography*. New York: Garland, 1990.

Liberman, M. M. *Katherine Anne Porter's Fiction*. Detroit: Wayne State University Press, 1971.

Nance, William L. *Katherine Anne Porter and the Art of Rejection*. Chapel Hill: University of North Carolina Press, 1964.

Stout, Janis P. *Strategies of Reticence: Silence and Meaning in the Works of Jane Austen, Willa Cather, Katherine Anne Porter, and Joan Didion*. Charlottesville: University Press of Virginia, 1990.

Unrue, Darlene Harbour. *Understanding Katherine Anne Porter*. Columbia: University of South Carolina Press, 1988.

REYNOLDS PRICE

Born: Macon, North Carolina; February 1, 1933

Principal long fiction

A Long and Happy Life, 1962; *A Generous Man*, 1966; *Love and Work*, 1968; *The Surface of Earth*, 1975; *The Source of Light*, 1981; *Mustian: Two Novels and a Story*, 1984 ; *Kate Vaiden*, 1986; *Good Hearts*, 1988; *The Tongues of Angels*, 1990; *The Foreseeable Future: Three Long Stories*, 1991; *Blue Calhoun*, 1992.

Other literary forms

Price has published poetry, short fiction, and plays. *Things Themselves: Essays and Scenes* (1972) and *A Common Room: Essays 1954-1987* (1987) contain his most salient essays on writing. Among Price's retellings of biblical stories are *Presence and Absence: Versions from the Bible* (1973), *Oracles: Six Versions from the Bible (1977), and A Palpable God: Thirty Stories Translated from the Bible with an Essay on the Origins and Life of Narrative* (1978). The autobiographical *Clear Pictures: First Loves, First Guides* was published in 1989.

Achievements

Focusing on a single region of North Carolina just south of the Virginia border, Reynolds Price has moved beyond the limitations one sometimes finds in regional writers and in his work has dealt with universal themes, particularly with those that concern original sin and free choice; biological determinism, particularly as it is reflected in heredity; and the meanings of and relationships between life and death. In Price's novels, children inherit the burden of sin passed on by their parents, and, try as they will, they cannot escape this burden. Price's many honors include the William Faulkner Foundation prize for a first novel (*A Long and Happy Life*), fellowships from the Guggenheim Foundation and the National Endowment for the Arts (NEA), and the National Book Critics Circle Award in fiction for *Kate Vaiden*.

Biography

Born on February 1, 1933, in the rural North Carolina town of Macon, the son of William Solomon and Elizabeth Rodwell Price, Edward Reynolds Price was a child of the Depression. Although because of the closeness of his family structure his welfare was not seriously threatened by it, the boy was aware of the social dislocations around him and had what his biographer, Constance Rooke, calls Dickensian terrors of abandonment and destitution. His parents, hard pressed economically, lost their house when the father could not raise a fifty-dollar mortgage payment.

Upon graduation from Needham-Broughten High School in Raleigh, Price became an English major at Duke University in 1951, where he came under the influence of William Blackburn, who taught creative writing. Through Blackburn, he met Eudora Welty, who respected his work and ten years later was instrumental in helping to get Price's first book, *A Long and Happy Life*, published.

Upon receiving the bachelor's degree from Duke, Price attended Merton College, Oxford, as a Rhodes Scholar; there he received the bachelor of letters degree in 1958. He returned to Duke University in that year as an assistant professor of English and, except for brief intervals, continued to teach there. In 1977, he became James B. Duke Professor of English at that institution, where he taught courses in creative writing and on the poetry of John Milton.

Price burst on the literary scene auspiciously when *Harper's Magazine* devoted the whole of its April, 1962, issue to printing *A Long and Happy Life*, which was being released in hardcover at about the same time. The critical reception of this first novel was enthusiastic and brought Price the prestigious Faulkner Foundation Award for a first novel.

In 1963, Price visited England, and in the same year a collection of his short stories, *The Names and Faces of Heroes*, was released. This collection included "Michael Egerton," the short story that had first impressed Eudora Welty when she gave a reading at Duke in the early 1950's. The title story, told from the perspective of a young boy, is an especially sensitive study in point of view.

Price's second novel, *A Generous Man*, appeared in 1966 and focused on the Mustian family, as had his first book. In 1977, Price produced a play, *Early Dark*, based on the Mustian cycle, and, in 1984, *Mustian: Two Nov-*

els and a Story was issued, consisting of the first two novels and "The Chain of Love," a short story.

Love and Work and the loosely woven collection *Permanent Errors* (1970) both explore matters of heredity and its effect upon people. Neither received overwhelming praise, although they had support among some critics. Price, however, was busy with a much larger project, an ambitious saga of the Kendal-Mayfield family through four generations. The first novel of this story, *The Surface of Earth*, was received with skepticism by some critics when it appeared in 1975, but few could deny the creative zeal it reflected. The second volume of the Kendal-Mayfield story was published in 1981 under the title *The Source of Light*, and it, too, received mixed reviews.

A turning point in Price's life came in 1984, when he was in the middle of writing *Kate Vaiden*. He was stricken with spinal cancer, and the surgery that saved his life also left him a paraplegic. Pain drove Price to seek the help of a psychiatrist who specialized in hypnosis, in the hope that hypnosis might be a key to controlling his pain. Little did he suspect that through hypnosis he would be put in touch with a distant past that he had not realized existed. Suddenly details of his earliest childhood and of his family surfaced. When *Kate Vaiden* was published in 1986, it was, because of these unexpected insights, a quite different novel from what Price had originally projected.

Price's hypnosis unlocked the memories from which his autobiography, *Clear Pictures: First Loves, First Guides*, published in 1989, evolved. *The Tongues of Angels*, a novel published in 1990, is also a product of Price's hypnotic communication with his past.

Analysis

Woven throughout Price's intimate portraits of rural life in his native North Carolina is the framing idea of the family, a theme that pervades much of Southern literature. He considers the family unit to be the fundamental organism within which society operates. More precisely, much of his fiction explores the link between heredity and the biblical concept of Original Sin. Price notes, moreover, that throughout all of Christian faith are inherent paradoxes. These contradictions exist, in his vision, in the whole of Southern culture and are personified in family relationships.

Any reading of all Price's novels quickly demonstrates that Price, throughout his career as a novelist, has been grappling with puzzling questions. Preeminent among these questions is the effect that families have on

communities and on the broader societies outside the isolated communities that provide Price with his microcosms.

Price's consuming interest in the family as the fundamental unit of society is found in his first novel, *A Long and Happy Life*, and pervades his future writing. The work has to do with the Mustian family, which lives in Macon, North Carolina, the town on the Virginia border in which Price was born and reared. *A Long and Happy Life* revolves around the romance between twenty-year-old Rosacoke Mustian and her boyfriend of six years, Wesley Beavers, two years her senior.

Wesley motorcycles to his native Macon to visit Rosacoke whenever he can take a weekend away from the naval base in Norfolk, 130 miles to the northeast. Wesley is sexually experienced, but Rosacoke is a virgin, when the story opens in July. On a scorching day, Rosacoke rides on the back of Wesley's motorcycle to the black church from which her friend Mildred Sutton is to be buried. Mildred has died while giving birth to her child Sledge.

Wesley roars up to the church, deposits Rosacoke, and stays outside polishing his bike. The church moans in ecstasies of religious transport. One woman cries, "Sweet Jesus," and Wesley, hearing her cry, is transported to a sweaty bed in Norfolk, where one of his many women uttered an identical cry at a crucial point in their lovemaking.

Reminded of this, Wesley zooms off in a cloud of red dust so dry and thick that reading about it almost makes one want to wash it off. Wesley has to get ready for the afternoon, for the church picnic that he and Rosacoke will attend. Price's descriptions in this portion of the book are masterful and memorably comic, although the import of what is being communicated is deadly serious and universally significant.

At the church picnic, Wesley tries to seduce Rosacoke, but she resists him, as she always has in the past. The picnic itself is a jolly affair. As the picnickers are about to sit down to their meals, Uncle Simon discovers that his false teeth are missing. Those who have not already begun to consume their barbecued pork and Brunswick stew help Simon look for his teeth. Someone asks him when he last remembers having them.

Simon, after due deliberation, proclaims that he took them out while he was stirring the large kettle of Brunswick stew. With this revelation, all eating comes to an abrupt halt. Still, the eating never quite gets back to normal because of the general uncertainty about where the lost dentures are. It is vignettes such as this that help

Price to convey a deeply philosophical message to readers without immersing them in specialized terminology or in abstruse and abstract thinking.

Price's artistic vision is considerably more complex in the first volume of the Kendal-Mayfield saga, *The Surface of Earth*. It constitutes the first half of a sprawling family saga with heavy biblical overtones, that has to do fundamentally with Original Sin, guilt, conflicted race relations, incestuous feelings, incredibly frequent suicides, and much that is a common part of rural Southern experience. Southern families such as the two Price writes about in the Kendal-Mayfield novels are smothering families. Their members sometimes try to escape, but the magnetic pull back into the decaying bosom of the family is too strong for them to resist. In that respect, this saga is not unlike William Faulkner's *The Sound and the Fury* (1929), in which the Compsons can never escape their heredity and all that it has predestined for them.

The beginning of the Kendal family history is Bedford Kendal's rendition to his children of their grandparents' tragedy. Their grandmother died in giving birth to their mother. Their grandfather, considering himself responsible for his wife's death, killed himself, leaving his newborn daughter (like Price's own mother) an orphan. Bedford, having married this orphan when she grew to adulthood, soon realized that she was consumed by guilt and that she had a strong aversion to sex, all tied up with the guilt she suffered at the thought of having, through her birth, killed her own mother and driven her father to suicide.

Bedford's children, hearing this story, build up their own guilt feelings and their own aversions to sex. His daughter Eva, the strongest student of thirty-two-year-old Latin teacher Forrest Mayfield, elopes with him. Forrest is looking for family ties and thinks that he has found them among the Kendals, who, on the surface, seem to be an enviable family. Yet his marrying Eva disrupts the family's delicate balance, so all that Forrest hopes for in the marriage is not available to him.

The title of book 1 in the novel, "Absolute Pleasures," seems to be both an irony and a warning. Eva has her absolute pleasure, her unremitting sexual release on her wedding night, but then guilt possesses her. She dreams an Electra dream of her father stretched out over her body, and she is never able to enjoy sex again. She passes on her sexual aversion to her children, suggesting to her son Rob that he masturbate rather than become ensnared in love relationships with women.

Eva, like many of Price's women, barely survives the birth of her son Rob, and in this difficult birth, which also severely threatens the life of the infant, one sees an entire cycle recurring. The mother, with her cargo of guilt about sex and about her mother's death in childbirth, has a difficult delivery that will increase her aversion to sex and that will impose upon her newborn child the same guilt with which she has lived.

Book 2 of *The Surface of Earth*, the real heart of the novel, is the story of Eva and Forrest's son, Rob Mayfield. Rob, now seventeen, is leaving the family nest, but the family surges within him. He has no more hope of leaving it than did any of the Kendals before him. There is no escape from either the biological heredity or the strong pull of memory and custom that families impose.

Rob, obsessed with oedipal feelings since the onset of puberty, hopes that contact with other women will help him to overcome the shameful feelings that disturb his equilibrium. He tries to seduce his date for the senior prom, but she denies him, whereupon he sheds her. Like Milo in *A Generous Man*, his sexual thoughts are only of his own gratification, and his masturbation gives him an independence when he is rebuffed.

Rob seeks to overcome his problems by marrying Rachel. Not in love with Rachel, Rob wavers in his commitment to marry her, and he goes—as his father before him had gone to the first Rob—to his father for counsel. Forrest is now living in a heterodox arrangement with Polly, a woman with whom he makes love only ten times a year, fearing that more frequent contact would jeopardize what they have struggled to achieve. Having seen his father's relationship, Rob can now return to Rachel and marry her. Rachel dies giving birth to Hutch, however, whose story becomes the next portion of the saga.

In *The Source of Light*, the sequel to *The Surface of Earth*, both Hutch and Rob seem to have reached an accord in their lives, to have matured into acceptance of what seems for them inevitable. The pull of the family and the inevitability of their heredity are both still operative, but they are less oppressive than they were in the earlier book.

Throughout his writing, Price is concerned with showing that people cannot outrun their past. At the center of his vision are the related themes of family, irresistible heredity, and intergenerational guilt. Undergirding these themes, Price's intimate knowledge of Southern rural life has enabled him to produce some of the most accurate and authentically rendered descriptions in print of northern North Carolina.

Other major works

SHORT FICTION: *The Names and Faces of Heroes*, 1963; *Permanent Errors*, 1970; *The Collected Stories*, 1993.

PLAYS: *Early Dark*, 1977; *Private Contentment*, 1984; *House Snake*, 1986 (teleplay); *New Music: A Trilogy*, 1990 (includes *August Snow, Night Music, Better Days*); *Night Dance*, 1990; *Full Moon and Other Plays*, 1993.

POETRY: *Late Warning: Four Poems*, 1968; *Lessons Learned: Seven Poems*, 1977; *Nine Mysteries (Four Joyful, Four Sorrowful, One Glorious)*, 1979; *Vital Provisions*, 1982; *The Laws of Ice*, 1986; *The Use of Fire*, 1990.

NONFICTION: *Things Themselves: Essays and Scenes*, 1972; *A Common Room: Essays 1954-1987*, 1987; *Clear Pictures: First Loves, First Guides*, 1989; *A Whole New Life*, 1994.

TRANSLATIONS: *Presence and Absence: Versions from the Bible*, 1973; *Oracles: Six Versions from the Bible*, 1977; *A Palpable God: Thirty Stories Translated from the Bible with an Essay on the Origins and Life of Narrative*, 1978.

Bibliography

Brown, Rosellen. "Travels with a Dangerous Woman." *The New York Times Book Review*, June 29, 1981, 40-41.

Kreyling, Michael. "Reynolds Price." In *The History of Southern Literature*, edited by Louis D. Rubin et al. Baton Rouge: Louisiana State University Press, 1985.

Oates, Joyce Carol. "Portrait of the Artist as Son, Lover, and Elegist." *The New York Times Book Review*, April 26, 1981, 3, 30.

Price, Reynolds. "A Conversation with Reynolds Price." Interview by Wallace Kaufman. *Shenandoah* 17 (Summer, 1966): 3-25.

_____ . *Conversations with Reynolds Price*. Edited by Jefferson Humphries. Jackson: University Press of Mississippi, 1991.

_____ . "Reynolds Price on Writing." Interview by Ashby Bland Crowder. *Southern Review* 22 (Spring, 1986): 329-341.

Rooke, Constance. *Reynolds Price*. Boston: Twayne, 1983.

Sadler, Lynn Veach. "Reynolds Price and Religion: The 'Almost Blindingly Lucid' Palpable World." *Southern Quarterly* 26 (Winter, 1988): 1-11.

WILLIAM STYRON

Born: Newport News, Virginia; June 11, 1925

Principal long fiction

Lie Down in Darkness, 1951; *The Long March*, 1952 (serial), 1956; *Set This House on Fire*, 1960; *The Confessions of Nat Turner*, 1967; *Sophie's Choice*, 1979; *A Tidewater Morning: Three Tales from Youth*, 1993.

Other literary forms

Known principally for his novels, William Styron has published collections of essays and short fiction and a play. *Darkness Visible: A Memoir of Madness* appeared in 1990. A candid and insightful recounting of his personal battle with severe clinical depression, it was an immediate popular success.

Achievements

Until the publication of *The Confessions of Nat Turner* in 1967, Styron was well known in literary circles as a young novelist of great talent but largely unrealized potential. *The Confessions of Nat Turner*, riding the crest of a wave of social activism in the late 1960's and capitalizing on a national interest in African American literature and history, gave Styron a major popular reputation as well as making him the center of a vitriolic controversy between academic and literary critics on the one hand, who tended to see the novel as an honest attempt to come to terms with history, and a small group of strident black critics on the other hand, who questioned, often abusively, the ability of any white writer to deal with the black experience and who called Styron's portrait of Nat Turner unflattering and inaccurate. The book and the debate it engendered made Styron a major voice in twentieth century fiction.

Despite the twelve-year hiatus between the publication of *The Confessions of Nat Turner* and that of *Sophie's Choice*, Styron's reputation grew, particularly in terms of his role as an interpreter of the South. *Lie Down in Darkness* had been recognized as one of the finest presentations in fiction of the modern Southern family, haunted by memory, guilt, and time, and *The Confessions of Nat Turner* came to be seen as representative of the concern of Southern writers with the burden of history. *The Confessions of Nat Turner* was accepted as a rhetorically beautiful evocation of the past, whatever its historical inaccuracies.

The publication of *Sophie's Choice* in 1979 cemented Styron's position as one of the major figures of contemporary literature. Although several major critics had reservations about the novel, its ambitious confrontation of a moral theme of enormous implication—the Holocaust—and Styron's compelling, lyrical prose made the novel the literary event of the year. With *Sophie's Choice*, some of Styron's lifelong concerns as a novelist become clearer: the unanswerable problem of pain and suffering, the elusive nature of memory, the ambiguous legacy of history.

Styron's many awards include the American Academy Prix de Rome in 1952 for *Lie Down in Darkness*, the Pulitzer Prize in 1968 for *The Confessions of Nat Turner*, the American Book Award in 1980 for *Sophie's Choice*, and the MacDowell Medal in 1988 for lifetime achievement in letters. He was elected a member of the American Academy of Arts and Letters and a Commander in France's Legion of Honor, both in 1987.

Biography

William Styron was born June 11, 1925, in Newport News, Virginia, which he later called "a very Southern part of the world." His mother, Pauline Margaret Abraham Styron, was from the North, but his father, William Clark Styron, a shipyard engineer, came from an old, if not aristocratic, land-poor Virginia family, and Styron remembers his grandmother telling him as a little boy of the days when the family owned slaves, a memory he was to incorporate years later into *Sophie's Choice*. Styron's father was a "Jeffersonian gentleman," liberal in his views for a Southerner, who implanted in his son much of the philosophical curiosity that would characterize the young Styron's novels. His mother, a gentling influence, died when Styron was twelve after a long, painful siege by cancer, an experience that was also to leave a mark on his fiction in the form of an almost obsessive concern with physical pain and suffering and the vulnerability of the flesh.

Styron's stint in Officer Candidate School during World War II marked the beginning of his writing career, for while there, he enrolled in a creative writing course at Duke University under William Blackburn, whom Styron acknowledges as the most powerful formative influence on his work. One early story, about a Southern lynching, similar in tone and execution to William Faulkner's "Dry September," appeared in a student anthology, Styron's first published fiction. At the tail end of the war, Styron was commissioned and sent to the Pacific, arriving on the island of Okinawa after the fighting was over. Styron was to speak later of his sense of guilt at not having seen action, as well as his feeling of horror at the waste and destruction of the war and the terrible, almost casual way in which life could be lost. Back in America, Styron resumed his program at Duke and was graduated in 1947. He took a job in New York as an associate editor in the book division at McGraw-Hill. His senior editor and immediate superior was Edward C. Aswell, the august second editor of Thomas Wolfe and an eminence rivaling Maxwell Perkins; Aswell was to appear grotesquely as "The Weasel" in an autobiographical passage in *Sophie's Choice* nearly thirty years later. The callow young Styron found McGraw-Hill humorless and confining, and after six months he was fired.

Living in a Brooklyn boardinghouse on a tiny legacy from his grandmother, Styron took another creative writing course, this time from Hiram Haydn at the New School for Social Research. Styron began work on his first novel, *Lie Down in Darkness*, the story of a star-crossed upper-middle-class Southern family whose failure to find love and meaning in life drives the sensitive daughter, Peyton Loftis, to insanity and suicide. The complex treatment of time in the novel and its high Southern rhetoric showed the influence of Faulkner, whom Styron had been reading intensely, but *Lie Down in Darkness* was manifestly the work of a powerful and original talent. Styron found that the writing of the book, although exhausting, went surprisingly fast, and he finished it and saw it accepted for publication by Bobbs-Merrill before he was recalled by the Marines for service in the Korean War.

Lie Down in Darkness was an immediate critical success and a moderate popular one, winning the prestigious Prix de Rome in 1952. At that time, Styron had decamped to Paris and had fallen in with a young crowd of American expatriate intellectuals, many of whom would later make names for themselves in literature. In 1952 and 1953, the group began compiling a literary magazine, *The Paris Review*, which was to become one of the most influential literary periodicals of the post-war period. Styron served as an advisory editor of the publication from its inception. In 1953, he used the money from his Prix de Rome to travel in Italy. During this time he met Rose Burgunder, a Jewish poet with some family money from Baltimore, whom he soon married. They returned to America, settling in Roxbury, Connecticut.

The Confessions of Nat Turner took years to research and write, and true to Styron's expectations, it was immediately acclaimed as a masterpiece. For years, Styron had had his mind on Nat Turner's 1831 slave rebellion as a subject for fiction. It had taken place close to his own Tidewater, Virginia, home, and Styron saw the suffering, the violence, and the misunderstanding of the revolt as emblematic both of the South's guilt and pain and of his personal concerns as a writer. *Sophie's Choice* was five difficult years in the writing, but Styron was richly rewarded when it was finally published in 1979. The gratifyingly large sales were capped by a spectacular sale of the film rights. In 1983, Meryl Streep won an Academy Award for Best Actress for her portrayal of Sophie in that film.

In 1985, Styron was hospitalized with acute clinical depression. His struggle to overcome his suicidal feelings and to return to health are recounted in his memoir *Darkness Visible*, published five years later.

Analysis

Styron's subjects are radically diverse—a doomed Southern family, the intellectual jet set of American expatriates, a historical slave revolt, the horror of the Holocaust. Strongly underlying all of his novels is a concern with the past, not so much in the form of the passage of time but rather an awareness that it is either lost or potentially reclaimable. Each of Styron's major novels moves from the present to the past in an attempt to explain or understand how things came to be as they are. *Lie Down in Darkness*, with its relentless burrowing in the Loftis family past, looks backward to explain Peyton's death. Both *The Confessions of Nat Turner* and *Sophie's Choice* are historical novels concerned with the actual past and with what Robert Penn Warren called "the awful burden of history."

Styron's fiction is historical, but in an intensely personal and psychological way. Each of Styron's characters lives on the verge of apocalyptic catastrophe, always on the edge of mental breakdown. Perhaps the most representative Styron "hero" is Cass Kinsolving of *Set This House on Fire*, the only protagonist who is a philosopher as well as a sufferer. Cass's madness derives from his contemplation of the horror of human life and misery, and he staggers drunkenly around postwar Italy demanding a teleological answer for the chaos of existence in which God is silent; "you can shake the whole universe and just get a snicker up there."

This is Styron's theme—the absence of God and the meaninglessness of life. Consistently, he approaches it through a single technique, the presentation and contemplation of pain and suffering. Styron's novels are a catalog of the slings and arrows of outrageous fortune, some physical, some mental, and some simply the result of an empathic identification with the suffering state of humankind.

Lie Down in Darkness is the story of how and why Peyton Loftis becomes insane and kills herself, tracing the roots of her tortured madness to her father's weakness and her mother's inability to love. Peyton's father, Milton, showers her with an excessive adoration that is one facet of his alcoholic self-indulgence; he smothers his daughter with a sloppy, undemanding adulation that counterpoints his wife Helen's psychotic frigidity. Helen is able to show love only in terms of compulsive formal discharge of parental obligations, bitterly resentful of the martyr role she has chosen to play. Eventually, Peyton instinctively rejects both her father's almost unnatural affection and her mother's unnatural lack of it. By the time Peyton cuts herself loose, however, she has been emotionally crippled, unable to accept any genuine love from a series of lovers, including the Jewish artist she marries and who might have brought her peace. She retreats deeper and deeper inside herself, watching first other people and finally the real world recede before her disintegrating mind. The last major section of the novel is her tormented, insane monologue, a brilliant tour de force reminiscent of the Benjy sections of Faulkner's *The Sound and the Fury* (1929).

When *Lie Down in Darkness* was published, it was widely hailed as a significant addition to the "Southern" school of writing led by Faulkner, Ellen Glasgow, Flannery O'Connor, and Thomas Wolfe. Thematically, *Lie Down in Darkness* is not a markedly "Southern" novel. Although the Loftis family is from Tidewater, Virginia, and some mannerisms described in the book are definitively Southern, Milton Loftis' weakness, his wife's cold rage, and their daughter's breakdown are in no way regional. What is distinctive about the tragedy of the Loftises is how much it is exclusively their own rather than a product of the dictates of fate or society. In this respect, the novel differs from Styron's later works, in which he increasingly attributes human suf-

ferings to forces beyond the individual.

Styron called *The Confessions of Nat Turner* "a meditation on history." Its subject is not only the character of Nat but also the meaning of slavery itself— what it does to people and to society. Like Styron's previous novels, the book is a contemplation of horror, with a protagonist who becomes a victim of that horror, but in this case the horror is not a purely personal one. Significantly, unlike the Loftises and Cass Kinsolving, Nat does not deteriorate but grows through the course of the book as his comprehension of society and life grows. Nat Turner is the richest and most psychologically complex of Styron's characters, and the historical subject matter of the work is filtered through his sensitive consciousness to produce a visionary "meditation" on the world of slavery, dreamlike in quality and poetic in execution. Southern Virginia of the 1830's, the novel's world, is very much a projection of Nat's mind—a mind produced by that world and savaged by it.

Nat's mind ranges with astonishing virtuosity over his universe—the natural world, the complexities of human relations, the elusive mysteries of God, and the bitterness of mortality. An enormously sophisticated narrative persona, Nat moves fluidly across time, contemplating the painful mystery of the past, represented by his long-dead African grandmother, and of the future, represented by his own forthcoming death. Nat narrates the entire story in flashback, remembering his abortive slave rebellion and the personal and historical events leading up to it, constantly trying to cipher out the meaning of those events. The novel is a study of the growth of knowledge and of the growth of Nat's mind. In the introspective isolation of his anguished imprisonment, he reconstructs his lifelong struggle to understand the meaning of existence. He recalls his progression from childhood, when he had no comprehension of what slavery meant, to an early adult period when he accepted his condition either bitterly or philosophically, to a final understanding of slavery in personal, societal, and moral terms. Ironically, as Nat becomes more morally and aesthetically sensitive, he becomes more insensitive in human terms, gravitating toward an acceptance of the violence that finally characterizes his revolt. Only a sudden, visionary conversion to a God of love at the end of the novel saves him from closing the book as an unrepentant apostle of retributory cruelty.

In the process of expanding his knowledge and developing his terrible vision of deliverance from slavery by violence, Nat becomes the spokesman for two familiar Styron themes: the complexity of human psychology and the mystery of human suffering. The most self-searching of Styron's characters, Nat recognizes in his own emotional turmoil personal depths that he can plumb with only partial understanding. His psychology is the battleground of conflicting feelings, symbolized by his powerful attraction to his master's gentle daughter and his vitriolic hatred for all she represents. When he eventually kills her, neither he nor the reader can discriminate his motives. She dies imploring, "Oh, Nat, it hurts so!" and his realization of her pain is the climax of his apprehension of the myriad pains of all humankind, particularly those of his own people. In this concern, he is representative of all Styron's protagonists.

Styron's novel *Sophie's Choice* was some twelve years in the works, if somewhat less in the writing. Having dealt in earlier novels with suicide, physical agony, existential despair, and slavery, Styron chose the Holocaust as the logical next state of human misery suitable for artistic contemplation. The narrator of *Sophie's Choice*, a young Southerner named "Stingo," is, for all intents and purposes, indistinguishable from the young Styron. A young artist *manqué* in New York, Stingo meets and is fascinated by a beautiful survivor of a Nazi concentration camp, Sophie, who is permanently psychologically scarred by the horror she has undergone, the most ghastly aspect of which was being forced to decide which of her two children would live and which would die. Stingo is the ultimate naïf: sexually, emotionally, morally, and artistically immature. As he comes to know Sophie, he comes to know himself.

Whereas the emotional pain of Peyton Loftis is alienation from family and love and Nat Turner's ultimate pain derives from his isolation from all humankind and God, Sophie and Stingo suffer the pain of guilt. Stingo believes he has not "paid his dues," suffered as others have suffered, and he learns of Sophie's anguished life with a guilty voyeurism. Sophie's guilt has a specific origin in her hideous choice to doom one of her children. She also feels ashamed that in Auschwitz she somehow "suffered less" since she was the commandant's mistress and finally survived when others died. Constantly and compulsively, her mind plays over

the fates of those dead—her little girl, her tortured friends, and the gassed millions whom she never knew. The knowledge that she did what she had to do to survive gives no relief. She says, "I see that it was—beyond my control, but it is still so terrible to wake up these many mornings with the memory of that, having to live with it . . . it makes everything unbearable. Just unbearable." Soon, she will kill herself to stop the pain.

After Sophie's death, the shattered Stingo, who had just become her lover, walks on the beach trying to find some sort of personal resolution and acceptance of a world in which horror and anguish such as Sophie's exist. Her message, though, has been clear: There is no resolution. Madness and suffering of the magnitude represented by the Holocaust can be neither accepted nor understood. Sophie, like Herman Melville's Ishmael, realizes that "there is a wisdom that is woe, and there is a woe that is madness." Stingo has come to know it, too.

With the death of Sophie, Styron seems to have come full circle in his exploration of human suffering and his search for meaning in a flawed and painful world. Both Sophie and Peyton Loftis find death to be the only release from lives so agonizing and painful as to be unbearable. In both his first novel and this one, Styron leads the reader to the edge of the grave and points to it as the goal of life—"therefore it cannot be long before we lie down in darkness, and have our light in ashes." The crucial difference between *Sophie's Choice* and *Lie Down in Darkness*, however, is the character of Stingo, who like Ishmael escapes to tell the tale. The earlier novel leaves the reader in desolation, but the latter, through Stingo, holds forth the possibility of an alternative existence, one not horribly haunted by the knowledge of pain. Stingo's life is hardly one of euphoria, but it is a tenable existence compared to Sophie's untenable one. To some degree, Stingo has paid his dues through her; he has come to know pain and evil through her sacrifice, and therefore he is sadder and wiser, but not destroyed as she is. His survival counterpoints her destruction; the novel that Stingo will write grows out of her ashes and becomes her immortality.

Other major works

PLAY: *In the Clap Shack*, 1972.
NONFICTION: *This Quiet Dust*, 1982; *Darkness Visible: A Memoir of Madness*, 1990.
SHORT FICTION: *A Tidewater Morning: Three Tales from Youth*, 1993.

Bibliography

Clarke, John Henrik, ed. *William Styron's Nat Turner: Ten Black Writers Respond*. Boston: Beacon Press, 1968.

Cologne-Brookes, Gavin. *The Novels of William Styron: From Harmony to History*. Baton Rouge: Louisiana State University Press, 1994.

Coale, Samuel. *William Styron Revisited*. Boston: Twayne, 1991.

Crane, John Kenny. *The Root of All Evil: The Thematic Unity of William Styron's Fiction*. Columbia: University of South Carolina Press, 1984.

Fossom, Robert H. *William Styron: A Critical Essay*. Grand Rapids, Mich.: Wm. B. Eerdmans, 1968.

Friedman, Melvin J. *William Styron*. Bowling Green, Ohio: Bowling Green University Popular Press, 1974.

Friedman, Melvin J., and Irving Malin, eds. *William Styron's "The Confessions of Nat Turner": A Critical Casebook*. Belmont, Calif.: Wadsworth, 1970.

Morris, Robert K., and Irving Malin, eds. *The Achievement of William Styron*. Athens: University of Georgia Press, 1975.

Pearce, Richard. *William Styron*. Minneapolis: University of Minnesota Press, 1971.

Ratner, Marc L. *William Styron*. New York: Twayne, 1972.

Serlin, Rhoda. *William Styron's "Sophie's Choice": Crime and Self-Punishment*. Ann Arbor, Mich.: Research Press, 1990.

Ruderman, Judith. *William Styron*. New York: Ungar, 1987.

West, James L. W., III, ed. *Conversations with William Styron*. Jackson: University Press of Mississippi, 1985.

ROBERT PENN WARREN

Born: Guthrie, Kentucky; April 24, 1905   **Died:** Stratton, Vermont; September 15, 1989

Principal long fiction

Night Rider, 1939; *At Heaven's Gate*, 1943; *All the King's Men*, 1946; *World Enough and Time*, 1950; *Band of Angels*, 1955; *The Cave*, 1959; *Wilderness: A Tale of the Civil War*, 1961; *Flood: A Romance of Our Times*, 1964; *Meet Me in the Green Glen*, 1971; *A Place to Come To*, 1977.

Other literary forms

Robert Penn Warren wrote successfully in so many genres that Charles Bohner called him "the pentathlon champion of American literature." In addition to his novels, he published short stories, numerous volumes of poetry, and a considerable amount of nonfiction. Warren's fiction and his poetry often consider the same philosophical themes: humankind's fall from innocence and the difficulty of establishing moral ideals in a fallen world.

Warren's concerns over history and morality are also evident in his earliest, nonfiction works. Warren's neo-orthodox insistence on man's fallen nature and his skepticism about the possibilities of pure idealism, both of which are reflected in his novels, led him to accept the traditionalist attitudes of the Southern intellectuals who made up the "Fugitive Group," and he contributed to the Agrarian Manifesto, *I'll Take My Stand* (1930). Warren did, however, espouse a more liberal attitude toward racial matters in his later nonfiction works *Segregation: The Inner Conflict in the South* (1956) and *Who Speaks for the Negro?* (1965).

Warren's social criticism ultimately proved less influential than his literary criticism. His *Selected Essays* (1958) contains perceptive studies of Samuel Taylor Coleridge's *The Rime of the Ancient Mariner*, Joseph Conrad's *Nostromo* (1904), William Faulkner, Ernest Hemingway, and Katherine Anne Porter. These essays are important not only for what they say about these authors but also for what they reveal about Warren's own work. Even more important than these essays, however, was Warren's collaboration with Cleanth Brooks. Their textbooks, *Understanding Fiction* (1943, 1959) and *Understanding Poetry* (1938, 1950, 1960), helped to change substantially the way literature was taught in the United States.

Warren continued to publish literary criticism at intervals throughout his life; indeed, *New and Selected Essays* appeared in the year of his death, 1989. Yet with a poetry-writing career that spanned fifty years, he was at least equally well known as a craftsman in that genre. His poems have been widely anthologized, and he is recognized as one of the United States' foremost twentieth century poets.

Achievements

With a body of work spanning more than three decades, Warren is undoubtedly one of the most honored men of letters in American history. Many believe that his greatest acclaim is as a poet and literary critic. In the latter capacity his landmark works on the tenets of the New Criticism influenced generations of readers in their perceptions of literature and literary interpretation. Among his novels, *All the King's Men* is considered his best; made into an Oscar-winning film in 1949, it is also his best-known work overall. Warren's short story "Blackberry Winter" has also been highly praised and widely anthologized. Among his numerous honors and awards were Pulitzer Prizes for *All the King's Men* in 1947, *Promises: Poems 1954-1956* (1957) in 1958 (thereby becoming the only person to have won the prize for both fiction and poetry), and *Now and Then: Poems 1976-1978* (1978) in 1979. He won the National Medal for Literature in 1970 and the Presidential Medal of Freedom in 1980. The following year he was among the first to receive a MacArthur Foundation "genius" grant. In 1986 he was named the first poet laureate of the United States, serving in that distinguished capacity until age and ill health forced him to resign the next year.

Biography

Robert Penn Warren's background and experience had a tremendous impact upon the thematic concerns of his fiction. He demonstrated the need, common to so many Southern writers, to cope with the burden of the past. His recurring subject was the peculiar experience of the South; a love-hate relationship with a dying heritage runs throughout his work.

Born to Robert Franklin and Anna Ruth Penn Warren on April 24, 1905, in the tiny Kentucky town of Guthrie, Warren grew up in an almost classic Southern situation. His father, a banker and businessman struggling to support a large family, did not initially fire the young Warren's imagination as his grandfather did. The emotional bond between Warren and his maternal grandfather, Gabriel Thomas Penn, ripened during long summers spent on his grandfather's tobacco farm. Here, Warren experienced the pastoral charms of agrarian life, soaked up the nostalgic glow of the American Civil War from his grandfather, and absorbed the rhetoric and humor that permeates Southern storytelling.

In spite of the contribution to his early imaginative development by his grandfather and his agrarian milieu, the influence of Warren's father was subtle and pervasive, perhaps more significant in the long run to the human relationships explored in his novels. Ambiguous father-son relationships appear over and over in such novels as *All the King's Men*, *The Cave*, *At Heaven's Gate*, and *A Place to Come To*. None is modeled after Warren's actual relationship to his own father, but they reflect a combination of admiration, guilt, and mystery that suggests some deep personal involvement in the issues they raise.

Warren has often admitted to an odd sense of guilt about "stealing his father's life." Robert Franklin Warren had wanted to be a lawyer and a poet but had become a businessman instead, because of financial responsibilities not only to his own family but also to a family of half brothers and sisters left without a provider when his father died. One of Warren's favorite reminiscences was about finding a book with some poems written by his father in it and carrying it with delight to him. His father summarily confiscated the book, and his son never saw it again. Warren thought perhaps his father had been embarrassed or pained at this reminder of a goal long since set aside. According to Warren, his father never regretted the obligations that dictated the terms of his life. Indeed, he took joy in them. Warren speaks with an admiration bordering on awe of the seemingly effortless rectitude of his father, and the ideal relationship between his father and mother.

As the result of an accident when he was fifteen years old, Warren lost his sight in one eye and was thus prevented from pursuing a career as a naval officer, as he had planned. Warren went, instead, to Vanderbilt University and came under the influence of John Crowe Ransom and the Fugitives, a group of academics and townspeople who met regularly to discuss philosophy and poetry. Ransom soon recognized Warren's unusual ability and encouraged him to write poetry.

Warren was graduated summa cum laude from Vanderbilt in 1926 and pursued an M.A. at the University of California at Berkeley. While there, he became an ardent student of Elizabethan and Jacobean drama, which perhaps struck a responsive chord in an imagination already steeped in the violence and melodrama of Southern history. He started to work on a doctorate at Yale University but left for Oxford, England, as a Rhodes scholar, where he received a bachelor of letters degree in 1930.

During this period, Warren wrote his first book, *John Brown: The Making of a Martyr*. To some extent, this book grew out of an impulse shared with a number of his Vanderbilt friends and other writers of the so-called Southern Renascence. They were concerned about the exclusively Northern bias of most historians dealing with events leading up to and during the Civil War and its aftermath. Certainly, Warren presents a jaundiced view of the radical abolitionist. Brown seems to have provided a nucleus for Warren's meditations about the effects of power and the misuses of altruism which were to be explored in a number of later novels, especially *Night Rider* and *All the King's Men*. Warren also wrote his first fiction while at Oxford, a short story called "Prime Leaf," about the impact of the Kentucky tobacco war on an old man, his son, and his grandson. The old man has a role similar to that of the elder Todd in *Night Rider*, the wise man who bows out of the organization when it resorts to vigilante tactics.

Warren taught at a number of universities, including Louisiana State, where he lived in the legendary ambience of the Southern demagogue Huey Long, whose presence lies behind the fictional Willie Stark of *All the King's Men*. The years from 1944 to 1950, though a dry period for poetry, were productive ones for fiction and literary criticism. Besides *All the King's Men*, he produced *At Heaven's Gate*, about the unscrupulous liaison between government and industry, and *World Enough and Time*, about a nineteenth century murder case. When Warren was poetry consultant for the Library of Congress in 1944-1945, Katherine Anne Porter, who was fiction consultant that year, threw on his desk the confession of Jeroboam Beauchamp, hanged for murder in Kentucky in 1826. Porter announced cryptically that she was giving him a novel. This was, indeed, the germ for his most complex novel, *World Enough and Time*.

Warren's dry period in poetry eventually ended after he divorced his first wife, Emma Brescia, married the writer Eleanor Clark, and fathered two children. He began writing excellent poetry and produced several more novels. A long association with Yale University began in 1950.

Warren continued his distinguished career as teacher, poet, novelist, critic, editor, and lecturer virtually to the end of his long life. In 1986 Warren was named the United States' first poet laureate, a post he held for two years. He died of cancer in 1989, at his summer home in Stratton, Vermont.

Analysis

In both his poetry and his fiction, Warren often explores the same philosophical themes: the meaning of history, the loss of innocence and the recognition of evil in a fallen world, and the difficulty of finding a moral balance in a world in which traditional Christian values seem to be faltering. His abiding interest in the history and culture of his native American South brings an added dimension to the more personal elements that appear in his writings. Warren's thematic concerns reflect those of so many Southern writers: the need to reconcile the burdens of the past.

Often, what Warren said about other writers provides an important insight into his own works. This is especially true of Warren's perceptive essay "The Great Mirage: Conrad and *Nostromo*" in *Selected Essays*, in which he calls *Nostromo* "a study in the definition and necessity of illusion." This phrase could also describe most of Warren's works of fiction. Like Conrad, Warren sees the world as naturalistic but recognizes that an individual must live in two worlds, the world of facts and the world of ideas, which he or she alone creates. Warren's notion of submission to the realm of ideas is analogous, perhaps, to Ernest Hemingway's code of the hunter, the fisherman, the bullfighter, or the soldier, which provides existential meaning in a meaningless world.

Warren's early novels, particularly *Night Rider*, *All the King's Men*, and *World Enough and Time*, which critics generally agree are his best, trace a pattern of increasing complexity in the theme of human vacillation between the fantasy of dreams and the reality of facts. His protagonists are often initially passive persons whose emptiness is filled by other, more dynamic personalities. Having acquired a somewhat fictitious self under such influence, they proceed to act in the real world as though that dream were true—often with tragic results. Thus, Mr. Munn seems an innocuous, ordinary young lawyer when he first appears in *Night Rider*, but he is drawn irresistibly to his more dynamic friend, Mr. Christian, who has a legitimate concern for the plight of the tobacco growers at the mercy of the price-controlling tobacco company. Munn learns to savor his new role as labor leader. He is ripe, then, for indoctrination by more conniving, professional agitators, Professor Ball and Dr. MacDonald, who preach a secret society that will scrape the fields of uncooperative growers and punish backsliders who dare to violate the embargo. What begins as a lawful strike by the downtrodden majority becomes a lawless vigilante group that destroys crops, burns warehouses, and commits murder. In the case of Munn, the crisis of this psychic change in direction comes when he realizes that his assigned task to assassinate the tobacco farmer Bunk Trevelyon, whom he once defended in court on a murder charge, not only is his "duty" to the group but also satisfies something very personal in himself that he has not yet recognized. Trevelyon had committed the murder of which he was once accused, and the black man who was hanged for that murder was innocent. Trevelyon thus becomes the symbol for Munn's half-conscious cooperation in framing the other man, or, to use another favorite term of Warren, for Munn's original sin. In this ritual of retribution, the shared myth of community justice fuses with Munn's private myth of killing the shadow-self, an act of self-condemnation and of deliberate concealment of a secret crime.

After this private confrontation and ritual killing of his shadow-self, Munn makes no more moral objections to anything Ball and MacDonald want to do. The three lead a concerted assault on the company warehouses, which results in a number of casualties.

Munn's subsequent flight to the West to escape prosecution for a murder he did not commit might have resulted in redemption, but it does not. Despite a period of withdrawal and contemplation, within a moral vacuum in which traditional values have been eliminated in a society concerned primarily with power and wealth, he is not transformed.

The polarity of idea and fact receives more explicit development in *All the King's Men*. Again, an essentially passive person, Jack Burden, feeds emotionally on a more dynamic personality, Willie Stark. Burden calls himself—somewhat cynically—an idealist, but his idealism consists mostly of a fastidious preference for not getting his hands dirty with some of Stark's more questionable political maneuvers. Stark is good-naturedly tolerant of Burden's moral preferences, since he has Tiny Duffy to do his dirty work.

Burden considers himself a good judge of character and motives, but when a cherished image about the purity and goodness of his former girlfriend, Anne Stanton, is proven to be false, he is devastated and lost in self-doubt. Anne, who is quite a passive, unfulfilled person herself, has become Stark's mistress. Burden's first impulse is to flee, to escape, to drown, to fall into what he calls the Great Sleep. From this symbolic death, Burden is born again into a bleak but emotionally insulating belief in the Great Twitch—an understanding of the world as completely amoral and mechanistic, wherein no one has any responsibility for what happens. Here, indeed, Burden has stepped out of the fantasy of dreams into the reality of facts.

Burden can now consent to let Stark use the information he has uncovered concerning Judge Irwin's long-forgotten political crime. Burden soon discovers how brutal the world of fact can be, when Judge Irwin's suicide reveals that the judge was actually Burden's own father. Hardly recovered from this blow, Burden recognizes a measure of responsibility for the deaths of Willie Stark and his best friend, Adam Stanton, who is shot by Willie's bodyguard after the assassination. Through his passivity and noninvolvement, Jack Burden had virtually handed over Anne Stanton to his more dynamic boss and thus set the stage for assassination.

The novel is a fascinating study of symbiotic relationships, of which the most striking is that between Willie Stark, the practical politician, and Adam Stanton, the puritanical idealist and perfectionist. Warren also suggests a politically symbiotic relationship between the demagogue and the people he represents. In social terms, the world of *All the King's Men* is more complex than that of *Night Rider*. Munn's career is essentially that of the tragic hero, the good but not exclusively good man who is corrupted by power. Willie Stark, hwoever, is sustained not only by his own drive for power but also by the concerted will of his constituency, who feel themselves to be socially and politically helpless. He is probably more significant as an antidote to their depression than as an answer to their physical needs. Even though Willie wants to change the world of facts for their benefit—build roads, bridges, a free hospital—it is for his psychological impact, exemplifying the triumph of the common person over the privileged elite, that he

is beloved. Thus, even the man of facts floats in the symbolic sea of ideas.

If the relationship between dream and reality is complicated in *All the King's Men*, in *World Enough and Time* it becomes intricately complex. Seldom have human aspirations been so relentlessly exposed, one after another, as frail illusions.

Jeremiah Beaumont, the orphaned son of an unsuccessful Kentucky farmer in the early nineteenth century, becomes the loved protégé of Colonel Cassius Fort, a well-known lawyer and statesman of the region. Jerry's exalted view of Colonel Fort receives a cruel blow from his dashing friend Wilkie Barron, a popular man-about-town and dabbler in politics. Wilkie tells Jerry of a beautiful woman he once loved in vain, who was seduced by an older man who had come to console her when her father died. When the young woman, Rachel Jordan, had a stillborn child, the older man abandoned her. The knave who wronged her was the unimpeachable Colonel Fort.

The persuasive Wilkie succeeds in promoting in a somewhat passive Jerry a romantic vision of wronged womanhood. From this point on, Jerry creates his own drama of love and revenge, though Wilkie continues to manipulate him in ways Jerry never understands until near the end of his life. Jerry repudiates Colonel Fort, his surrogate father, and woos and eventually wins the lovely Rachel, who is in a neurotic state of depression, not because of the supposed perfidy of Colonel Fort but because of her baby's death. Jerry, blind to the real source of her despondency, hounds her into commanding him to defend her honor. Fort refuses a duel with Jerry, however, and the honorable vengeance seems destined to fizzle. Rachel is again pregnant, and Jerry is fitting into the comfortable role of country squire. An unknown messenger brings to Rachel a slanderous handbill in which Colonel Fort, presumably denying to his political opponents his affair with Rachel, claims that Rachel had slept with a slave. Fort had gallantly claimed paternity of the child as a chivalric gesture. This shocking document, which is actually a forgery written by Wilkie Barron, precipitates Rachel's labor, and Jerry's child is also born dead. Jerry, in remorse, kills Fort—not openly in a duel, as he planned, but secretly, letting it appear to be a political assassination.

Jerry's trial is a bewildering process where deceit and truth become inextricably mixed. Wilkie Barron appears, however, and reveals Jerry's vow to kill Fort, the reaction Wilkie had himself orchestrated even before Jerry had met the wronged lady. All is lost, and Jerry is sentenced to hang. The unpredictable Wilkie appears at the last minute, after the lovers have unsuccessfully tried to commit suicide by drinking laudanum. Wilkie rescues them and sends them west to live in the desolate island refuge of a notorious bandit. This is a return to nature, but a nature devoid of its original innocence, incapable of healing the scars of "civilization." Jerry sinks into a bestial pattern and Rachel into insanity, eventually killing herself. Jerry, who finds out that the slanderous handbill came from Wilkie Barron, is himself murdered as he seeks to find his way back to the hangman, resigned now to the most austere prize of all—neither love nor honor but simply knowledge.

Perhaps this tortured journey through innocence and experience should arrive at some reconciliation of op-posites, but, if so, that too seems more dream than reality. "There must be a way whereby the word be-comes flesh," muses Jerry in his last days. Even so, "I no longer seek to justify. I seek only to suffer." If this is not a particularly lucid analysis of philosophical possi-bilities, it may nevertheless be true psychologically to the mental and moral confusion in which men live.

Warren's fictional world shows its creator's fascina-tion with what he called, in his Conrad essay, "the Great Mirage." It is a dark vision that sees all human values as illusions, yet insists—with the passion that fueled six decades of creative work—that such illusions are nec-essary, and that humankind must continue to invent itself.

Other major works

SHORT FICTION: *Blackberry Winter*, 1946; *The Circus in the Attack and Other Stories*, 1947.

PLAY: *All the King's Men*, 1958.

POETRY: *Thirty-six Poems*, 1935; *Eleven Poems on the Same Theme*, 1942; *Selected Poems 1923-1943*, 1944; *Brother to Dragons: A Tale in Verse and Voices*, 1953; *Promises: Poems 1954-1956*, 1957; *You, Emperors, and Others: Poems 1957-1960*, 1960; *Selected Poems: New and Old, 1923-1966*, 1966; *Incarnations: Poems 1966-1968*, 1968; *Audubon: A Vision*, 1969; *Homage to Theodore Dreiser on the Centennial of His Birth*, 1971; *Or Else—Poem/ Poems 1968-1974*, 1974; *Selected Poems: 1923-1975*, 1976; *Now and Then: Poems 1976-1978*, 1978; *Brother to Dragons: A New Version*, 1979; *Being Here: Poetry 1977-1980*, 1980; *Ballad of a Sweet Dream of Peace*, 1980 (with Bill Komodore); *Rumor Verified: Poems 1979-1980*, 1981; *Chief Joseph of the Nez Percé*, 1983; *New and Selected Poems, 1923-1985*, 1985.

NONFICTION: *John Brown: The Making of a Martyr*, 1929; *An Approach to Literature: A Collection of Prose and Verse with Analysis and Discussions*, 1936 (with Cleanth Brooks and John Thibaut Purser); *Understanding Poetry: An Anthology for College Students*, 1938, 1950, 1960 (with Cleanth Brooks); *Understanding Fiction*, 1943, 1959 (with Brooks); *Modern Rhetoric*, 1949 (with Brooks; also as *Fundamentals of Good Writing: A Handbook of Modern Rhetoric*); *Segregation: The Inner Conflict in the South*, 1956; *Selected Essays*, 1958; *The Legacy of the Civil War: Meditations on the Centennial*, 1961; *Who Speaks for the Negro?*, 1965; *Faulkner: A Collection of Critical Essays*, 1966; *Randall Jarrell, 1914-1965*, 1967 (with Robert Lowell and Peter Taylor); *American Literature: The Makers and the Making*, 1974 (with R. W. B. Lewis); *Democracy and Poetry*, 1975; *Portrait of a Father*, 1988; *New and Selected Essays*, 1989; *Talking with Robert Penn Warren*, 1990.

Bibliography

Bohner, Charles. *Robert Penn Warren*. 1964. Rev. ed. Boston: Twayne, 1981.

Casper, Leonard. *Robert Penn Warren: The Dark and Bloody Ground*. Seattle: University of Washington Press, 1960.

Clark, William Bedford. *The American Vision of Robert Penn Warren*. Lexington: University Press of Kentucky, 1991.

—————— . *Critical Essays on Robert Penn Warren*. Boston: G. K. Hall, 1981.

Gray, Richard, ed. *Robert Penn Warren: A Collection of Critical Essays*. Englewood Cliffs, N.J.: Prentice-Hall, 1980.

Justus, James. *The Achievement of Robert Penn Warren*. Baton Rouge: Louisiana State University Press, 1981.

Runyon, Randolph. *The Braided Dream: Robert Penn Warren's Late Poetry*. Lexington: University Press of Kentucky, 1990.

Strandberg, Victor. *The Poetic Vision of Robert Penn Warren*. Lexington: University Press of Kentucky, 1977.

Walker, Marshall. *Robert Penn Warren: A Vision Earned*. New York: Barnes & Noble Books, 1979.

EUDORA WELTY

Born: Jackson, Mississippi; April 13, 1909

Principal short fiction

A Curtain of Green and Other Stories, 1941; *The Wide Net and Other Stories*, 1943; *The Golden Apples*, 1949; *The Bride of the Innisfallen and Other Stories*, 1955; *The Collected Stories of Eudora Welty*, 1980; *Moon Lake and Other Stories*, 1980; *Retreat*, 1981.

Other literary forms

Eudora Welty has published novels, essays, reviews, an autobiography, a fantasy story for children, and a volume of photographs of Mississippi during the Depression, taken during her stint as photographer and writer for the Works Progress Administration (WPA).

Achievements

Welty possesses a distinctive voice in Southern, and indeed in American, fiction. Her vibrant, compelling evocation of the Mississippi landscape, which is her most common setting, has led to comparisons between her work and that of other eminent Southern writers such as William Faulkner, Carson McCullers, and Flannery O'Connor. Welty's graceful, lyrical fiction, however, lacks the pessimism that characterizes much of established Southern writing, and though her settings are distinctly Southern, her themes are universal and do not focus on uniquely Southern issues.

The honors and awards that Welty has amassed throughout her long career are so many as to defy complete listing in a short space. Among her major achievements are four O. Henry Awards for her short stories (first prizes in 1942, 1943, and 1968, and a second prize in 1941); two Guggenheim Fellowships (1942, 1949); honorary lectureships at Smith College (1952) and the University of Cambridge (1955); election to the National Institute of Arts and Letters (1952) and to the American Academy of Arts and Letters (1971); honorary LL.D. degrees from the University of Wisconsin (1954) and Smith College (1956); a term as Honorary Consultant to the Library of Congress (1958-1961); the William Dean Howells Medal of the American Academy of Arts and Letters for *The Ponder Heart* (1954); the Gold Medal for Fiction of the National Institute of Arts and Letters (1972); the Pulitzer Prize in fiction (awarded in 1973 for her 1972 novel *The Optimist's Daughter*); the National Medal for Literature and the Presidential Medal of Freedom (1980); the National Medal of Arts (1987); and the naming of the Jackson Public Library in her honor (1986). She was awarded the National Book Foundation Medal for Distinguished Contribution to American Letters in 1991.

Biography

Eudora Welty was born on April 13, 1909, in Jackson, Mississippi. In the Welty household, reading was a favorite pastime, and Welty recalls in her autobiography, *One Writer's Beginnings* (1984), both being read to often as a young child and becoming a voracious reader herself. Her recollections of her early life are of a loving and protective family and of a close, gossip-prone community in which she developed her lifelong habit of watching, listening to, and observing closely everything around her. Her progressive and understanding parents encouraged her in her education, and in 1925, she enrolled at the Mississippi State College for Women. After two years there, she transferred to the University of Wisconsin and was graduated with a B.A. degree in English in 1929.

Welty subsequently studied advertising at the Columbia University Business School; her father had recommended to her that if she planned to be a writer, she would be well advised to have another skill to which she could turn in case of need. During the Depression, however, she had little success finding employment in the field of advertising. She returned to Mississippi and spent the next several years working variously as a writer for radio and as a society editor. In 1933, she began working for the Works Progress Administration (WPA), traveling throughout Mississippi, taking photographs, interviewing people, and writing newspaper articles. She later credited this experience with providing her with much material for her short stories as well as sharpening her habits of observation. During these working years, she wrote short stories and occasionally traveled to New York in an effort to interest publishers in her work, with little success. Her first short story, "Death of a Traveling Salesman," was published in 1936 by a "little" magazine called *Manuscript*. Her ability as a writer soon attracted the attention of Robert Penn Warren and Cleanth Brooks, editors of *The Southern Review*, and over the next years her writing appeared in that magazine as well as *The New Yorker*, *The Atlantic Monthly*, and *The Sewanee Review*.

Welty's first collection of short stories, *A Curtain of Green and Other Stories*, appeared in 1941, with a preface by Katherine Anne Porter. Welty's reputation as an important Southern writer was established with this first volume, and, at the urging of her editor and friend John Woodburn, who encouraged her to write a longer work of fiction, she followed it with her fabular novel *The Robber Bridegroom* in 1942. Thenceforth, she continued with a fairly steady output of fiction, and with each successive publication, her stature as a major American writer grew. Although fiction became her primary field, she wrote many essays and critical reviews and dabbled in the theater. In addition to stage adaptations of *The Robber Bridegroom* and *The Ponder Heart*, she collaborated on a musical (never produced) entitled *What Year Is This?* and wrote several short theatrical sketches. In 1984, her autobiography, *One Writer's Beginnings*, appeared and quickly became a best-seller.

Welty has spent most of her life living in, observing, and writing about Jackson and the Mississippi Delta country. Her frequent visits to New York and her travels in France, Italy, Ireland, and England (where she participated in a conference on American studies at the University of Cambridge in 1955) have provided her with material for those few stories that are set outside her native Mississippi. From time to time, she has lectured or taught but in general has preferred the quiet and privacy of her lifelong home of Jackson.

Analysis

Although some dominant themes and characteristics appear regularly in Eudora Welty's fiction, her work resists categorization. The majority of her stories are set in her beloved Mississippi Delta country, of which she paints a vivid and detailed picture, but she is equally comfortable evoking such diverse scenes as a Northern city or a transatlantic ocean liner. Thematically, she concerns herself both with the importance of family and community relations and, paradoxically, with the strange solitariness of human experience. Elements of myth and symbol often appear in her work, but she uses

them in shadowy, inexplicit ways. Perhaps the only constant in Welty's fiction is her unerring keenness of observation, both of physical landscape and in characterization, and her ability to create convincing psychological portraits of an immensely varied cast of characters.

One of her earliest stories, "Death of a Traveling Salesman," tells of a commercial traveler who loses his way in the hill country of Mississippi and accidentally drives his car into a ravine. At the nearest farm dwelling, the salesman finds a simple, taciturn couple who assist him with his car and give him a meal and a place to stay for the night. The unspoken warmth in the relationship of the couple is contrasted with the salesman's loneliness, and he repeatedly worries that they can hear the loud pounding of his heart, physically weakened from a recent illness and metaphorically empty of love. When he leaves their house in the morning, his heart pounds loudest of all as he carries his bags to his car; frantically he tries to stifle the sound and dies, his heart unheard by anyone but himself.

Another relatively early story, "A Worn Path," recounts an ancient black woman's long and perilous journey on foot from her remote rural home to the nearest town. The frail old woman, called Phoenix, travels slowly and painfully through a sometimes hostile landscape, described in rich and abundant detail. She overcomes numerous obstacles with determination and good humor. Into the vivid, realistic description of the landscape and journey, Welty interweaves characteristically lyrical passages describing Phoenix's fatigue-induced hallucinations and confused imaginings. When Phoenix reaches the town, she goes to the doctor's office, and it is revealed that the purpose of her journey is to obtain medicine for her chronically ill grandson. A poignant scene at the story's close confirms the reader's suspicion of Phoenix's extreme poverty and suggests the likelihood that her beloved grandson will not live long; old Phoenix's dignity and courage in the face of such hardship, however, raise the story from pathos to a tribute to her resilience and strength of will. Like her mythical namesake, Phoenix triumphs over the forces that seek to destroy her.

"Why I Live at the P.O." is a richly comic tale of family discord and personal alienation, told in the first person in idiomatic, naturalistic language that captures the sounds and patterns of a distinctive Southern speech. It is one of the earliest examples of Welty's often-used narrative technique, what she calls the "monologue that takes possession of the speaker." The

4

4444444

story recounts how Sister, the intelligent and ironic narrator, comes to fall out with her family over incidents arising from her younger sister Stella-Rondo's sudden reappearance in their small Southern town, minus her husband and with a two-year-old "adopted" child in tow. Welty's flair for comedy of situation is revealed as a series of bizarrely farcical episodes unfolds. Through the irritable Stella-Rondo's manipulative misrepresentations of fact and Sister's own indifference to causing offense, Sister earns the ire of her opinionated and influential grandfather Papa-Daddy, her gullible, partisan mother, and her short-tempered Uncle Rondo. Sister responds by removing all of her possessions from communal use in the home and taking up residence in the local post office, where she is postmistress. Inability to communicate is a recurrent theme in Welty's short fiction; in this case, it is treated with a controlled hilarity that is chiefly comic but that nevertheless reveals the pain of a family's disunity. This story is one of the best examples of Welty's gift for comic characterization, her gentle mockery of human foibles, and her ear for Southern idiom and expression.

"The Wide Net" is a fabular tale of the mysteries of human relationships and the potency of the natural world. Young William Wallace returns home from a night on the town to find a note from his pregnant wife saying that she has gone to drown herself in the river. William Wallace assembles a motley collection of men and boys to help him drag the river. The river's power as a symbol is apparent in the meaning that it holds for the many characters: To youngsters Grady and Brucie it is the grave of their drowned father; to the rough, carefree Malones, it is a fertile source of life, teeming with catfish to eat, eels to "rassle," and alligators to hunt; to the philosophical and somewhat bombastic Doc, it signifies that "the outside world is full of endurance." It is also, the river-draggers discover, the home of the primeval "king of the snakes."

Throughout the story, Welty deliberately obscures the nature of William Wallace's relationship with his wife, the history behind her threat, and even whether William Wallace truly believes his wife has jumped into the river. Characteristically, Welty relies on subtle hints and expert manipulation of tone rather than on open exposition to suggest to her readers the underpinnings of the events that she describes. This deliberate vagueness surrounding the facts of the young couple's quarrel lends the story the quality of a fable or folktale. The young lover must undergo the test of dragging the great river, confronting the king of snakes and experiencing

a kind of baptism, both in the river and in the cleansing thunderstorm that drenches the searchers, before he is worthy of regaining his wife's love. Like a fable, the story has an almost impossibly simple and happy ending. William Wallace returns from the river to find his welcoming wife waiting calmly at home. They have a brief, affectionate mock quarrel that does not specifically address the incident at all, and they retire hand in hand, leaving the reader to ponder the mystery of their bond.

"Livvie" has a lyrical, fabular quality similar to that of "The Wide Net." Livvie is a young black woman who lives with her elderly husband, Solomon, on a remote farm far up the old Natchez Trace. The strict old husband is fiercely protective of his young bride and does not allow her to venture from the yard or to talk with— or even see—other people. The inexperienced Livvie, however, is content in Solomon's comfortable house, and she takes loving care of him when his great age finally renders him bedridden. One day, a white woman comes to her door, selling cosmetics. Livvie is enchanted with the colors and scents of the cosmetics but is firm in her insistence that she has no money to buy them. When the saleswoman leaves, Livvie goes into the bedroom to gaze on her ancient, sleeping husband. Desire for wider experience and a more fulfilling life has been awakened in her, and as her husband sleeps, she disobeys his strictest command and wanders off down the Natchez Trace. There, she comes upon a handsome, opulently dressed young man named Cash, whom she leads back to Solomon's house. When Solomon awakes and sees them, he is reproachful but resigned to her need for a younger man, asking God to forgive him for taking such a young girl away from other young people. Cash steals from the room, and as Livvie gazes on the frail, wasted body of Solomon, Solomon dies. In a trancelike shock, Livvie drops Solomon's sterile, ticking watch; after momentary hesitation, she goes outside to join Cash in the bright light of springtime.

"Livvie" is almost like a fairy tale in its use of simple, universal devices. The beautiful young bride, the miserly old man who imprisons her, the strange caller who brings temptation, and the handsome youth who rescues the heroine are all familiar, timeless characters. Welty broadens the references of her story to include elements of myth and religion. Young Cash, emerging from the deep forest dressed in a bright green coat and green-plumed hat, could be the Green Man of folklore, a symbol of springtime regeneration and fertility. In contrasting youth with age and old with new, Welty subtly employs biblical references. Old Solomon thinks rather than feels but falls short of his Old Testament namesake in wisdom. Youthful Cash, redolent of spring, tells Livvie that he is "ready for Easter," the reference ostensibly being to his new finery but suggesting new life rising to vanquish death. The vague, dreamy impressionism of "Livvie," which relies on image and action rather than dialogue to tell the story (except in the scenes featuring the saleswoman), adds to this folktalelike quality.

"Moon Lake" is from the collection *The Golden Apples*, the stories of which are nearly all set in or around the mythical community of Morgana, Mississippi, and feature a single, though extensive, cast of characters. Thematically, it shares with "A Still Moment" the sense of the paradoxical oneness and interconnectedness of the human condition. The story describes a sequence of events at a camp for girls at the lake of the story's title. The characteristically lushly detailed landscape is both beautiful and dangerous, a place where poisonous snakes may lurk in the blackberry brambles and where the lake is a site for adventure but also a brown-watered, bugfilled morass with thick mud and cypress roots that grasp at one's feet. The story highlights the simultaneous attraction and repulsion of human connection. Antipathies abound among the group assembled at the lake: The lake's Boy Scout lifeguard, Loch, feels contempt for the crowd of young girls; the Morgana girls look down on the orphan girls as ragged thieves; rivalry and distrust crops up among individual girls. The sensitive Nina yearns for connection and freedom from connection at the same time; she envies the lonely independence of the orphans and wishes to be able to change from one persona to another at will, but at the same time she is drawn to Easter, the "leader" of the orphans, for her very qualities of separateness and disdain for friendship.

Nina and her friend Jinny Love follow Easter to a remote part of the lake in an unsuccessful attempt to cultivate her friendship, and when they return to where the others are swimming, Easter falls from the diving platform and nearly drowns. The near-drowning becomes a physical acting out of the story's theme, the fascinating and inescapable but frightening necessity of human connection. Without another's help, Easter would have died alone under the murky water, but Loch's lengthy efforts to resuscitate the apparently lifeless form of Easter disgust the other girls. The quasisexual rhythm of the resuscitation is made even more disturbing to the girls by its violence: Loch pummels Easter with his fists, and blood streams from her mudsmeared mouth as he flails away astride her. The distressing physical contact contrasts with the lack of any emotional connection during this scene. One orphan, a companion of Easter, speculates that if Easter dies she will get her winter coat, and gradually the other girls grow bored of the spectacle and resent the interruption of their afternoon swim. Jinny Love's mother, appearing unexpectedly at the camp, is more concerned with the lewdness that she imputes to Loch's rhythmic motions than with Easter's condition and she barks at him, "Loch Morrison, get off that table and shame on you." Nina is the most keenly aware of the symbolic significance of the incident and of the peril of connection; she reflects that "Easter had come among them and had held herself untouchable and intact. Of course, for one little touch could smirch her, make her fall so far, so deep."

"Where Is the Voice Coming From?" was originally published in *The New Yorker*, and it remained uncollected until the appearance of the complete *The Collected Stories of Eudora Welty* in 1980. In it, Welty uses a fictional voice to express her views on the Civil Rights struggle in the South. The story, written in 1963 in response to the murder of Medgar Evers in Welty's hometown of Jackson, is told as a monologue by a Southern white man whose ignorance and hate for African Americans are depicted as chillingly mundane. He tells how, enraged by black activism in the South, he determines to shoot a local Civil Rights leader. He drives to the man's home late on an unbearably hot summer night, waits calmly in hiding until the man appears, and then shoots him in cold blood. The callous self-righteousness of the killer and his unreasoning hate are frighteningly depicted when he mocks the body of his victim, saying "Roland? There was only one way left for me to be ahead of you and stay ahead of you, by Dad, and I just taken it. . . . We ain't never now, never going to be equals and you know why? One of us is dead. What about that, Roland?" His justification for the murder is simple: "I done what I done for my own pure-D satisfaction." His only regret is that he cannot claim the credit for the killing.

Unlike most of Welty's fiction, "Where Is the Voice Coming From?" clearly espouses a particular viewpoint, and the reader is left with no doubt about the writer's intention in telling the story. The story, however, embodies the qualities that typify Welty's fiction: the focus on the interconnections of human society; the full, sharp characterization achieved in a minimum of space; the detailed description of the physical landscape that powerfully evokes a sense of place; the ear for speech and idiom; and the subtle floating symbolism that insinuates rather than announces its meaning.

Other major works

NOVELS: *The Robber Bridegroom*, 1942; *Delta Wedding*, 1946; *The Ponder Heart*, 1954; *Losing Battles*, 1970; *The Optimist's Daughter*, 1972.

NONFICTION: *Place in Fiction*, 1957; *Three Papers on Fiction*, 1962; *One Time, One Place: Mississippi in the Depression, A Snapshot Album*, 1971; *The Eye of the Story: Selected Essays and Reviews*, 1978; *One Writer's Beginnings*, 1984; *Eudora Welty: Photographs*, 1989; *A Writer's Eye: Collected Book Reviews*, 1994.

CHILDREN'S LITERATURE: *The Shoe Bird*, 1964.

Bibliography

Appel, Alfred, Jr. *A Season of Dreams: The Fiction of Eudora Welty*. Baton Rouge: Louisiana State University Press, 1965.

Evans, Elizabeth. *Eudora Welty*. New York: Frederick Ungar, 1981.

Prenshaw, Peggy Whitman, ed. *Conversations with Eudora Welty*. Jackson: University Press of Mississippi, 1984.

Vande Kieft, Ruth M. *Eudora Welty*. 1962. Rev. ed. Boston: Twayne, 1987.

Westling, Louise. *Sacred Groves and Ravaged Gardens: The Fiction of Eudora Welty, Carson McCullers, and Flannery O'Connor*. Athens: University of Georgia Press, 1985.

TENNESSEE WILLIAMS
Thomas Lanier Williams

Born: Columbus, Mississippi; March 26, 1911   **Died:** New York, New York; February 25, 1983

Principal drama

Battle of Angels, pr. 1940, pb. 1945; *This Property Is Condemned*, pb. 1941, pr. 1946 (one act); *I Rise in Flame, Cried the Phoenix*, wr. 1941, pb. 1951, pr. 1959 (one act); *The Lady of Larkspur Lotion*, pb. 1942 (one act); *The Glass Menagerie*, pr. 1944, pb. 1945; *Twenty-seven Wagons Full of Cotton*, pb. 1945, pr. 1955 (one act); *You Touched Me*, pr. 1945, pb. 1947 (with Donald Windham); *Summer and Smoke*, pr. 1947, pb. 1948; *A Streetcar Named Desire*, pr., pb. 1947; *American Blues*, pb. 1948 (collection); *Five Short Plays*, pb. 1948; *The Long Stay Cut Short: Or, The Unsatisfactory Supper*, pb. 1948 (one act); *The Rose Tattoo*, pr., pb. 1951; *Camino Real*, pr., pb. 1953; *Cat on a Hot Tin Roof*, pr., pb. 1955; *Orpheus Descending*, pr. 1957, pb. 1958 (revision of *Battle of Angels*); *Suddenly Last Summer*, pr., pb. 1958; *The Enemy: Time*, pb. 1959; *Sweet Bird of Youth*, pr., pb. 1959 (based on *The Enemy: Time*); *Period of Adjustment*, pr. 1959, pb. 1960; *The Night of the Iguana*, pr., pb. 1961; *The Milk Train Doesn't Stop Here Anymore*, pr. 1963, pb. 1976 (revised); *The Eccentricities of a Nightingale*, pr., pb. 1964 (revision of *Summer and Smoke*); *Slapstick Tragedy: The Mutilated and The Gnädiges Fräulein*, pr. 1966, pb. 1970 (one acts); *The Two-Character Play*, pr. 1967, pb. 1969; *The Seven Descents of Myrtle*, pr., pb. 1968 (as *Kingdom of Earth*); *In the Bar of a Tokyo Hotel*, pr. 1969, pb. 1970; *Confessional*, pb. 1970; *Dragon Country*, pb. 1970 (collection); *The Theatre of Tennessee Williams*, pb. 1971-1981 (7 vols.); *Out Cry*, pr. 1971, pb. 1973 (revision of *The Two-Character Play*); *Small Craft Warnings*, pr., pb. 1972 (revision of *Confessional*); *Vieux Carré*, pr. 1977, pb. 1979; *A Lovely Sunday for Creve Coeur*, pr. 1979, pb. 1980; *Clothes for a Summer Hotel*, pr. 1980; *A House Not Meant to Stand*, pr. 1981.

Other literary forms

Besides his plays, Tennessee Williams produced short stories (many of which appear in collections), two volumes of poetry, a collection of essays, several screenplays, two novels, and a volume of memoirs.

Achievements

By consensus, Williams ranks second—after Eugene O'Neill—among American dramatists. His major plays are performed all over the world, in spite of the fact that their usual locale, the American South, might seem too specialized for international appreciation. In this respect, Williams may be compared to Anton Chekhov, who is in many ways his master and whose plays have also gained worldwide appreciation in spite of their intensely local ambience. Williams was unquestionably the most important American disciple of Chekhov—the most obvious resemblance lies in Williams' frequently superb use of symbol. His portrayal of frail characters in a cold and alien world is another immediate reminder of Chekhov. Like Chekhov's, Williams' characters are often repeated types—the gentleman caller, the helpless young woman, the witch-of-an-older-woman—but at their best, they are also highly individual and indeed unforgettable. Other characteristics which his plays share with Chekhov's are an apparent (though not actual) lack of structure, the use of settings and sound effects for atmospheric and thematic purposes, and poetic language. Yet what Williams drew from Chekhov he made distinctively his own.

Biography

Tennessee Williams was born Thomas Lanier Williams in 1911 in Columbus, Mississippi, the son of Cornelius Coffin Williams and Edwina Dakin Williams. He lived his early years in the home of his grandparents, for whom he felt great affection. His grandfather was a minister, while Williams' father was a traveling salesman, apparently at home infrequently. In about 1919, his father accepted a nontraveling position at his firm's headquarters in St. Louis. The move from a more or less traditional Southern environment to a very different metropolitan world was extremely painful both for Williams and for his older sister, neither of whom ever really recovered from it.

The Glass Menagerie is clearly a play about the Williams family and its life in St. Louis, though Williams' *Memoirs* (1975) and other known facts make it clear that the play is by no means a precise transcription of actuality. On the other hand, *The Glass Menagerie* is by no means the only one of Williams' plays with biographical elements. His father, his mother, and his sister (who became mentally ill) are reflected in his characters in various plays. Williams' homosexuality, which he examines in some detail in his *Memoirs*, is also an important element in a number of his plays, including *A Streetcar Named Desire*, *Cat on a Hot Tin Roof*, and *Suddenly Last Summer*.

Williams attended the University of Missouri and Washington University and was graduated in 1938 from the University of Iowa. His adult life involved considerable wandering, with periods in such places as Key West, New Orleans, and New York. After various attempts at writing, some of which gained helpful recognition, Williams first won acclaim with *The Glass Menagerie*. Most of his plays from that point through *The Night of the Iguana* were successful, either on first production or later. He won Pulitzer Prizes for *A Streetcar Named Desire* and *Cat on a Hot Tin Roof*, and New York Drama Critics Circle Awards for those two and for *The Glass Menagerie* and *The Night of the Iguana*. The many plays that he wrote in the last twenty years of his life, however, achieved almost no success, either in the United States or abroad. Depending on one's point of view, either Williams' inspiration had run out or he was writing a kind of play for which neither the public nor most critics were yet ready. Williams died in New York on February 25, 1983, having choked on a foreign object lodged in his throat.

Analysis

Williams was a penetrating dramatist whose best plays depict tortured human relationships played out against a backdrop of sex and violence yet modulated by an atmosphere of Southern romantic gentility. One of America's greatest playwrights, he was the poet laureate of the outcast.

The Glass Menagerie opens on a near-slum apartment, with Tom Wingfield setting the time (the Depression and Spanish-Civil-War 1930's). Tom works in a shoe warehouse, writes poetry, and feels imprisoned by the knowledge that his hateful job is essential to the family's financial survival. His relationship with his mother is a combination of love, admiration, frustration, and acrimony, with regular flare-ups and reconciliations. His relationship with his sister is one of love and sympathy. Laura is physically crippled as well as with-

drawn from the outside world. She is psychologically unable to attend business college and lives in a world of her phonograph records and fragile glass animals. Amanda, a more complex character than the others, is the heart of the play: a constantly chattering woman who lives in part for her memories, perhaps exaggerated, of an idealized antebellum Southern girlhood and under the almost certain illusion that her son will amount to something and that her daughter will marry. Yet she also lives very positively in the real world, aware of the family's poverty, keeping track of the bills, scratching for money by selling magazine subscriptions. Amanda must accept the fact that a job for Laura is out of the question, and she therefore starts planning for the other alternative, marriage. Scene 1 introduces a second symbol (the menagerie being the first) in a nickname that Laura says a boy gave her in high school: "Blue Roses." Roses are delicate and beautiful, like Laura and like her glass menagerie, but blue roses, like glass animals, have no real existence.

At Amanda's urging, Tom invites Jim O'Connor, a friend from the warehouse, home to dinner, in the hope that the "gentleman caller" will be attracted to Laura. Scene 6 shows the arrival of the guest and his attempt to accept Amanda's pathetic and almost comical Southern-belle behavior and elaborate "fussing" and Laura's almost pathological fright and consequent inability to come to the dinner table. By Amanda's inevitable machinations after dinner, Jim and Laura are left alone. Jim—who has turned out to be the "Blue Roses" boy from high school, the boy with whom Laura was close to being in love—is a sympathetic and understanding person who, even in the short time they are alone together, manages to get more spontaneous and revealing conversation out of Laura than her family ever has and even persuades her to dance. Clearly, here is a person who could bring to reality Amanda's seemingly impossible dreams, a man who could lead Laura into the real world (as he symbolically brought her glass unicorn into it by unintentionally breaking off its horn), a man who would make a good husband. Later, however, Jim tells Laura that he is already engaged, and Laura's life is permanently in ruins. What might have happened will never happen. When Amanda learns the truth from Jim just before he leaves, the resulting quarrel with Tom convinces Tom to leave home permanently, abandoning his mother and sister to an apparently hopeless situation.

Williams' next successful play, *A Streetcar Named Desire*, is generally regarded as his best. Initial reaction was mixed, but there would be little argument now that it is one of the most powerful plays in the modern theater. Like *The Glass Menagerie*, it concerns, primarily, a man and two women and a "gentleman caller." As in *The Glass Menagerie*, one of the women is very much aware of the contrast between the present and her Southern aristocratic past; one woman (Stella) is practical if not always adequately aware, while the other (Blanche), her sister, lives partly in a dream world and teeters on the brink of psychosis.

The setting of *A Streetcar Named Desire* is the two-room slum apartment of Stanley and Stella Kowalski. As the play opens, Blanche is coming to visit. She has never before seen Stella's apartment or met her sister's husband. To mark her progress through New Orleans to get to the apartment, Blanche has to transfer from a streetcar called "Desire" to one called "Cemeteries" in order to arrive in the slum, called "Elysian Fields." Blanche's progress in the play is from a wide range of desires (for culture, security, sex, and money) to a sort of living death, and while the slum may be an Elysian Fields for Stanley and Stella, it is a Tartarus for her.

The audience learns about the sisters' past, about Blanche's hostile attitude toward her environment, about the grim string of family illnesses and deaths, about the loss of the family plantation. The loss of the plantation angers Stanley, especially after he examines Blanche's trunk and finds it full of expensive clothes and furs.

In scene 3, Stanley has had too much to drink and is becoming verbally violent. Blanche encounters Stanley's friend Mitch at the apartment, and they are clearly attracted to each other. Stanley, meanwhile, becomes physically violent and (offstage) hits Stella. Blanche, horrified, takes Stella to the upstairs apartment. Stanley realizes what has happened, sobs, and screams for Stella, who presently joins him on the outside stairs. They fall into a sexual embrace, and he carries her inside. Clearly, this series of events has occurred before; clearly, this is the usual outcome, and it is one of the attractions that Stanley has for Stella.

In scene 4, Blanche returns from upstairs the next morning and is shocked to learn that Stella accepts all that has happened and wants no change in her marital situation. With some justice, Blanche describes Stanley as an uncultured animal in a world where culture is essential—a speech which Stanley overhears. He comes in, and to Blanche's horror, Stella embraces him. Later, Blanche and Stella agree that marrying Mitch is the solution to Blanche's problem, and Blanche is left

alone. A young newsboy comes to collect money, and Blanche comes very close to trying, consciously and cynically, to seduce him. Clearly, sex, like alcohol, has been both a cause of and a response to her situation. In a subsequent scene, Blanche tells Mitch about her dead husband, whom she encountered one evening in an embrace with an older man, and who later commits suicide.

In scene 7, several months later, with Blanche still there and with the marriage idea apparently no further advanced, Stanley tells Stella of his now detailed and verified knowledge of Blanche's sordid sexual past, including her having seduced a seventeen-year-old student. As a result of this last action, Blanche lost her job, and Stanley, as he explains to Stella, has told Mitch the whole story. Blanche eventually loses Mitch as well.

In scene 10, the climactic scene, Stanley comes back. Blanche has been drinking and is desperately upset. With Stanley, she tries to retreat into fanciful illusions—Mitch has returned and apologized, a rich boyfriend has invited her on a Caribbean tour. Stanley exposes her lies, and her desperation grows. Their confrontation reaches a climax, and, after she tries to resist, he carries her off to bed. In scene 11, some weeks later, one learns that Blanche has told Stella that Stanley raped her, that Stella must believe that the rape is merely one of Blanche's psychotic illusions if her life with Stanley is to survive, and that Stella has made arrangements to place Blanche in a state institution. A doctor and nurse come to get her. Blanche is terrified. The nurse is cold and almost brutal, but the doctor gains Blanche's confidence by playing the role of a gentleman, and she leaves on his arm, clearly feeling that she has found what she has been seeking, a man to protect her.

Cat on a Hot Tin Roof concerns the lives of Brick and Margaret (Maggie) Pollitt. Its setting is in the plantation mansion of Brick's father, Big Daddy, on his twenty-eight-thousand-acre estate in the Mississippi delta. Maggie, like Amanda and Blanche before her, is a loquacious and desperate woman who may be fighting for the impossible; unlike her predecessors, she lives entirely in the present and without major illusions, and hence she fights more realistically. She wants Brick to return to her bed: She is a cat on a hot tin roof, sexually desperate but interested only in her husband. Maggie tells Brick the news that his father is dying of cancer. Formerly an important athlete, a professional football player, and then a sports announcer, he has given up everything and lapsed into heavy drinking. Mae and her husband, Brick's older brother Gooper, a lawyer in

Memphis, are visiting in the hope, as Maggie correctly guesses, of Big Daddy's signing a will in Gooper's favor, because, while Brick is Big Daddy's favorite, the latter will want the estate to go to a son who has offspring. Maggie is from a society background in Nashville, though her immediate family had been poor because of her father's alcoholism. Big Daddy himself is a Mississippi redneck who has worked his way to great wealth. Formerly, according to Maggie, an excellent lover, Brick has made Maggie agree that they will stay together only if she leaves him alone. Unable to bear the frustration, Maggie is ready to break the agreement and fight to get Brick back.

The roots of Brick and Maggie's conflict are fitfully revealed when Maggie begins to speak of Skipper, their dead friend, any mention of whom greatly upsets Brick. In Maggie's version of the story, from college on, Brick's greatest loyalty was to Skipper. She says that Brick's standards of love and friendship were so pure as to have been frustrating to both Skipper and Maggie; that on an out-of-town football weekend when Brick had been injured and could not go, Maggie and Skipper, out of their common frustration, went to bed together; that Skipper could not perform, and that Maggie therefore, but in no condemnatory sense, assumed that he was unconsciously homosexual, though she believes that Brick is not. Maggie told Skipper that he was actually in love with her husband, and she now believes that it was this revelation that prompted Skipper to turn to liquor and drugs, leading to his death. Maggie now tells Brick that she has been examined by a gynecologist, that she is capable of bearing children, and that it is the right time of the month to conceive.

Big Daddy is a loud, vulgar, apparently insensitive man. Near the end of his famous talk with Brick in act 2, with great difficulty Big Daddy expresses the love he has for him. The motivation for the long father-and-son talk is that Big Daddy, hugely relieved at having been told, falsely, that he does not have cancer, wants to find out why Brick has given up working, given up Maggie and turned to heavy drinking. Big Daddy finally brings himself to make the climactic statement that the problem began when Skipper died. He makes painfully clear that the very idea of homosexuality disgusts him. The relationship, he believes, was simply an unusually profound friendship, though he is finally forced to grant the likelihood that, from Skipper's point of view, though emphatically not his own, sexual love existed. (Whether Brick is himself bisexual is left uncertain, but it is clear that he could not face this idea if it were true.) He grants

that liquor has been his refuge from a fact that Big Daddy (who has no prejudice against homosexuals) makes him face: that Brick's unwillingness to believe in the possibility of a homosexual reaction in Skipper, and to help Skipper recognize and accept it, is the major cause of Skipper's death. Brick then makes his father face the truth as his father has made him face it: The father is in fact dying of cancer.

In the original version, in act 3 the doctor tells Big Mama the truth of Big Daddy's condition. Gooper tries to get Big Mama to agree to a plan he has drawn up to take over the estate as trustee. Big Mama will have it run by nobody but Brick, whom she calls her only son. She remarks what a comfort it would be to Big Daddy if Brick and Maggie had a child. Maggie announces that she is pregnant. Whether this lie is planned or spontaneous, one has no way of knowing, but Brick does not deny it. A loud cry of agony fills the house: Big Daddy is feeling the pain the doctor has predicted. Maggie thanks Brick for his silence, asserts that she is in control, and declares that she will not return his liquor until he has gone to bed with her. Maggie reiterates that she is in charge and tells Brick she loves him. Brick, in the last speech of the play, says exactly what Big Daddy had said earlier when Big Mama said she loved him: "Wouldn't it be funny if that was true." Apparently, he has yielded. The curtain falls. One can only assume that Brick will "perform," that the result will be a pregnancy, and that the eventual effect of Maggie's use of force and of Big Daddy's shock tactics may be Brick's return to "normality."

Williams went on to write many more plays, notably *The Night of the Iguana*, his last successful play and his first to end optimistically. He has been accused of pseudopoeticism, ineffective ambiguity, overly obvious use of symbolism, extremes of violence, and sentimentality, and at his worst, the blame is justified. At his best, however, he was one of the most dramatically effective and profoundly perceptive playwrights in the modern theater. Williams' finest characterizations approach the archetypal; such figures as Blanche Dubois, Stanley Kowalski, and Big Daddy seem destined to join the enduring characters of world theater.

Williams, a true poet of the American stage, was noted for the tension of his brilliantly crafted dialogue. His characters, vivid and memorable, exhibit strong passions and overwhelming frustrations. Yet beneath the surface of his plays' genteel Southern settings and characterizations exist troubled and often violent people.

Other major works

NOVELS: *The Roman Spring of Mrs. Stone*, 1950; *Moise and the World of Reason*, 1975.

SHORT FICTION: *One Art and Other Stories*, 1948; *Hard Candy: A Book of Stories*, 1954; *The Knightly Quest: A Novella and Four Short Stories*, 1967; *Eight Mortal Ladies Possessed: A Book of Stories*, 1974; *Collected Stories*, 1985.

POETRY: *In the Winter of Cities*, 1956; *Androgyne, Mon Amour*, 1977.

NONFICTION: *Memoirs*, 1975; *Where I Love: Selected Essays*, 1978; *Conversations with Tennessee Williams*, 1986; *Five O'Clock Angel: Letters of Tennessee Williams to Maria St. Just, 1948-1982*, 1990.

SCREENPLAYS: *The Glass Menagerie*, 1950 (with Peter Berneis); *A Streetcar Named Desire*, 1951 (with Oscar Saul); *The Rose Tattoo*, 1955 (with Hal Kanter); *Baby Doll*, 1956; *The Fugitive Kind*, 1960 (with Meade Roberts, based on *Orpheus Descending*); *Suddenly Last Summer*, 1960 (with Gore Vidal); *Stopped Rocking and Other Screenplays*, 1984.

Bibliography

Bloom, Harold, ed. *Tennessee Williams*. New York: Chelsea House, 1987.

Rader, Dotson. *Tennessee: Cry of the Heart*. Garden City, N.Y.: Doubleday, 1985.

Spoto, Donald. *The Kindness of Strangers: The Life of Tennessee Williams*. Boston: Little, Brown, 1985.

Williams, Dakin, and Shepherd Mead. *Tennessee Williams: An Intimate Biography*. New York: Arbor House, 1983.

Williams, Tennessee. *Tennessee Williams' Letters to Donald Windham, 1940-1965*. Edited by Donald Windham. New York: Holt, Rinehart and Winston, 1977.

THOMAS WOLFE

Born: Asheville, North Carolina; October 3, 1900   **Died:** Baltimore, Maryland; September 15, 1938

Principal long fiction

Look Homeward, Angel, 1929; *Of Time and the River*, 1935; *The Web and the Rock*, 1939; *You Can't Go Home Again*, 1940; *The Short Novels of Thomas Wolfe*, 1961.

Other literary forms

During his lifetime Thomas Wolfe published four major works: two novels, *Look Homeward, Angel* and *Of Time and the River*; a collection of short stories, *From Death to Morning* (1935); and his description of his life as a creative artist, *The Story of a Novel* (1936). In addition to his major works, he composed poems and also sold a few lengthy stories to magazines; *Scribner's Magazine* published "A Portrait of Bascom Hawke" (April, 1932) and "The Web of Earth" (July, 1939). Both of these have since been republished as short novels in *The Short Novels of Thomas Wolfe*. Wolfe began his career (unsuccessfully) as a playwright with *The Mountains*, which he wrote in 1920 but which was not published until 1970. *Thomas Wolfe's Purdue Speech* (1964), delivered by Wolfe in 1938, is a statement of his development as an artist. Wolfe's letters and notebooks have also been published, allowing for firsthand insight into his personal and creative life.

Achievements

Wolfe captured the essence of what it meant to be young in his time with the publication of *Look Homeward, Angel*. He further influenced readers of the Depression-plagued 1930's with stories he published in magazines such as *The New Yorker*, *Harper's Bazaar*, *Redbook*, *Scribner's Magazine*, and the *Saturday Evening Post*. Widely read in America and abroad, Wolfe was a well-respected author during his lifetime, a man who in a very real sense lived the part of the driven artist. His achievement is especially remarkable when one considers that his literary life spanned little more than a decade. Wolfe's reputation as an important figure in twentieth century American literature is secure.

Biography

Born on October 3, 1900, in Asheville, North Carolina, Thomas Wolfe was the youngest of the seven surviving children of Julia Elizabeth Westall and William Oliver Wolfe. Of Pennsylvania Dutch-German stock, Wolfe's father was a man of intense vitality, a stonecutter who instilled in Wolfe a love of language, whether it was the high rhetoric of Elizabethan poetry or the low vernacular of the mountain people surrounding Asheville. Wolfe's mother was more attuned than her husband to the values of commerce (she was forever speculating in real estate). In fact, one biographer has termed the match an "epic misalliance." Domestic relations in the Wolfe household were often strained; young Wolfe grew up a witness to his father's drunken rampages and his mother's ensuing resentment. From this family cauldron came much of the autobiographical material Wolfe poured forth in *Look Homeward, Angel*.

In September of 1912, Wolfe entered the North State Fitting School, where he came under the influence of his teacher, Margaret Roberts (Margaret Leonard in *Look Homeward, Angel*). Roberts encouraged Wolfe's voracious appetite for reading by introducing him to the best of English literature. In 1916, at the precocious age of fifteen, Wolfe entered the University of North Carolina at Chapel Hill. Six feet tall and still growing (he would eventually reach six feet six inches), Wolfe was a skinny, long-legged youth, sensitive to the criticism of his older classmates. Wolfe's first year at Chapel Hill was unremarkable, but he eventually made a name for himself as an excellent student and a campus literary figure. In March of 1919, *The Return of Buck Garvin*, a play Wolfe had written in a dramatic writing course, was performed by the Carolina Playmakers, with Wolfe performing in the title role.

After graduating in 1920, Wolfe entered Harvard University to pursue his interests as a playwright. He was especially attracted by the famous workshop given by playwright George Pierce Baker (whom he would later depict as Professor Hatcher in *Of Time and the River*). Wolfe hoped to make a literary name for himself, but after a series of setbacks, he accepted an appointment as an instructor in English at the Washington Square College of New York University and began teaching in February of 1924, continuing to do so intermittently until 1930.

In October of 1924, Wolfe made his first trip to Europe. Many of his experiences there he later incorporated into *Of Time and the River*. Returning to New York in August of 1925, Wolfe met Aline Bernstein, a wealthy married woman who was involved in the theater world of New York. For the next seven years, Wolfe participated in a stormy on-and-off affair with Bernstein, who was seventeen years his elder. She was the mother-mistress Wolfe seemed to need; certainly, she inspired *Look Homeward, Angel*, which he commenced while abroad with Bernstein in July of 1926.

The popular image of Wolfe as a literary lion is in part caused by the critical success he achieved with *Look Homeward, Angel* but is based mostly in his personal appearance and habits. Often dressed in shabby clothes, he was known to prowl the streets of Brooklyn, where he had settled after another trip abroad in 1931. One night while wandering the streets, he was overheard to say, "I wrote ten thousand words today! I wrote ten thousand words today!" Although Wolfe resented efforts to publicize his eccentricities, it was inevitable that his behavior and fame would make him a legendary figure.

In December of 1933, Wolfe began work on what was to become *Of Time and the River*. It was also during this period that Maxwell Perkins, Wolfe's editor at Scribner's, worked closely with the author on the formation of the novel. Wolfe incorporated his experiences at Harvard, in Europe, and with Bernstein into *Of Time and the River*, which picks up the Eugene Gant story where *Look Homeward, Angel* concludes. In 1937, after critics had raised questions concerning Perkins' influence on his work, Wolfe left Scribner's for Harper and Brothers. His editor at Harper's was Edward C. Aswell, and Wolfe left two large crates containing nearly a million words of manuscript with him before leaving on a tour of the West in May of 1938. In July, Wolfe fell ill with pneumonia and was hospitalized near Seattle. In September, having been transferred to The Johns Hopkins Hospital in Baltimore, he underwent brain surgery for complications he suffered from tuberculosis. He died on September 15, 1938.

Analysis

Wolfe's self-professed intention as a novelist was to create an American mythology. Pursuant to this vision, the core themes of his work are the record of a lonely individual, the isolated artist lost in the flux of time, forever exploring the diversity of life in a search for self-discovery and the true meaning of the American experience. Calling upon characters and events drawn from the time of his youth and early adulthood, he evoked a timeless picture of life in the American South, its ethos and spirit.

Look Homeward, Angel, Wolfe's first and most significant novel, made use of extensive autobiographical material. In many ways, it is the story of his own life, the life of his family, his neighbors, and the region in which he lived. For those who know something of Wolfe's background, there are unmistakable connections between the fictional characters in *Look Homeward, Angel* and the real people among whom Wolfe grew up in Asheville, North Carolina.

Wolfe departed from the development of a traditional plot in *Look Homeward, Angel* and instead made use of impressionistic realism to tie events and characters together. The narrator moves in and out of the consciousness of the principal characters, giving readers impressions of their inner feelings and motivations. As much as anything else, *Look Homeward, Angel* is the story of a quest, a search for self-knowledge and for lasting human interaction. The subtitle of the novel is *A Story of the Buried Life*, and much of what Wolfe depicts concerns itself with the inner lives of the characters in the novel—what they really think and feel as well as how isolated and alienated they are from one another. In this sense, the novel explores the relationship of time, change, and death as elements which will always frustrate the human desire for happiness and fulfillment.

Look Homeward, Angel was initially entitled *O Lost* and then *Alone, Alone*. The title on which Wolfe finally settled comes from "Lycidas," John Milton's poem in which the archangel Michael is asked to look back toward England to mourn a young man's death and all the unfulfilled potential it signifies. Eugene Gant, is, like most of Wolfe's protagonists, the isolated and sensitive artist in search of meaning and companionship in a hostile world.

The novel covers the first twenty years of Gant's life—his adolescence, his four years at the private school of Margaret Leonard, and his four years at the university. A pattern of potential fulfillment destroyed by frustration is personified in Eugene's parents, Eliza and Oliver, who are modeled after Wolfe's own mother and father. Oliver Gant is a stonecutter who passionately desires to create something beautiful, to carve an angel's head. He is an unfulfilled artist, a man of intense vitality who desires a full and sensuous life. His intensity, his capacity for life, is checked by his wife, Eliza, who is his antithesis: parsimonious, cold, and materialistic. This pattern of frustrated potential recurs throughout the novel. In one example, after spending his first year at the university and losing his innocence in a brothel, Eugene returns home to spend the summer at Dixieland, his mother's boardinghouse. There he meets and falls in love with Laura James (based on his own first love, Clara Paul). In his descriptions of the young, passionate love that develops between them, Wolfe's prose becomes a lyrical celebration that turns to tragic frustration as Eugene learns that Laura is engaged to marry another young man back home, that she will never be a part of his life again. Thus, potential (in this example, physical and spiritual union between Eugene and Laura) is checked by reality (separation and isolation). This pattern manifests itself in varying ways throughout the novel. The story of a youth coming of age by initiation into experience, *Look Homeward, Angel* is a comprehensive account of the inner life of a sensitive and artistic youth.

Composed of eight sections, each of which is named after some epic or mythic figure, *Of Time and the River* exceeds nine hundred pages in length and spans two continents, continuing the story of Thomas Wolfe as personified in the character of Eugene Gant. Wolfe continues the story with Eugene's departure from Altamont for study at Harvard. He stated his ambitious theme for *Of Time and the River* in *The Story of a Novel*; his central idea was to depict the search for a father, not only in a literal but also in a figurative sense. While trying to exemplify his theme, Wolfe also struggled to form *Of Time and the River* out of the vast amount of manuscript he had written (a detailed discussion of that struggle is related in *The Story of a Novel*). In *The Story of a Novel*, Wolfe describes how he wrote one scene that ran to eighty thousand words (about two hundred pages). He was attempting to capture "the full flood and fabric" of four people simply talking to one another for four continuous hours. This scene, as good as he thought it was, eventually was cut, but it illustrates the massive amount of writing he did for the novel as well as the extensive amount of cutting he did to get it into publishable form.

While working out his central theme of a search for a father, Wolfe developed a three-part vision of time: time present, time past, and time eternal. The first, time present, is the time in which the actual events in the novel take place, the time of reality. The second, time past, represents all of the accumulated experience that

affects time present. The third, time eternal, stands for the lasting time of oceans, forests, and rivers, of things that form the permanent backdrop for man's experiences. These three levels of time allow Wolfe to contrast, in a vast and symbolic scale, the relationship of past present, and eternal experience with the experience of Eugene Gant. The result is an intensely personal search for meaning, an attempt to reconcile opposites, to find something lasting and meaningful.

Wolfe discards Gant in favor of a new protagonist, George "Monk" Webber, in *The Web and the Rock*. Like Gant, Webber bears a close resemblance to Wolfe himself. Indeed, *The Web and the Rock* is quite similar to Wolfe's earlier works: Its first half parallels *Look Homeward, Angel*, while its second half stands as a sequel to *Of Time and the River*.

One of the strongest chapters in the novel is enlightening insofar as it illustrates how Wolfe continually reshaped past material to meet a present need. "The Child by Tiger" was first published in 1937 as a short story, but in the eighth chapter of *The Web and the Rock*, Wolfe reworks the story with changes in character and point of view. It is a moving story about the nature of good and evil, innocence and experience. Dick Prosser, a black man, is the object of the racial prejudice that was so pronounced in the South during the early part of the twentieth century. He is a man who befriends several young white boys; he teaches them how to throw a football, how to box, and how to make a fire. In short, he becomes a kindly father-figure who initiates them into experience. There is, however, another side to Prosser. Driven to the point of madness by prejudicial treatment, by his own apocalyptic brand of religion, and by his involvement with a woman, he goes on a shooting spree one night, killing blacks and whites alike. Eventually shot by the mob formed to hunt him down, his bullet-riddled body is hung up for display in the window of the undertaker's parlor. In the course of these events, the young men who were Prosser's friends are initiated into a world full of violence and death. For the first time in their lives, they experience profound loss, and they witness evil as it is personified in the bloodthirsty mob. Woven within the story are stanzas from William Blake's poem "The Tiger," from which the chapter title is derived.

In what makes up the second half of the novel, Wolfe deals with his own experiences in New York City. He explores his relationship with Bernstein, depicting her as a sophisticated mistress and himself as a brilliant but egocentric genius. Their relationship is described in detail—from their lovemaking and eating to their quarrels and reconciliations. These segments are remarkable for their candor and intriguing because of the insight they provide into the tempestuous relationship between the two. Webber's past experiences, the environment in which he was reared, and his ancestry symbolically form the web in which he is snared, and, as Esther Jack becomes a part of that web, he escapes to Germany. His search for the rock, the strength and beauty of vision that is represented by the father-figure for whom he longs, is interrupted by his realization at the end of the novel that "you can't go home again." In short, he knows that he must look to the future to escape the past.

Continuing the chronicle of George Webber's life and artistic development, *You Can't Go Home Again* metaphorically develops the theme that Webber cannot go "home," cannot return to past places, old ideas, and former experiences, because time and change have corrupted them. In this sense, "home" is an idealized vision of America as it appeared to George in his youth. These youthful visions come into abrupt contact with reality, and the resulting clash allows Wolfe to explore the very fabric of American society.

The novel begins approximately six months after *The Web and the Rock* ends. Webber has returned home to America, and, against his better judgment, he decides to resume his relationship with Esther Jack. He also resumes work on his novel "Home to Our Mountains" (*Look Homeward, Angel*) and finds a publisher, James Rodney & Co. (Scribner's), as well as a sympathetic editor and father-figure, Foxhall Edwards (Maxwell Perkins). Before his book is published, however, he returns home for the first time in years to attend the funeral of his Aunt Maw. Home in this novel is Libya Hill (like the Altamont of *Look Homeward, Angel*, the locale still represents Asheville, North Carolina). On the train trip home, he meets his childhood friend Nebraska Crane, a one-time big-league baseball star. Crane, a Cherokee Indian, is now satisfied to lead the simple life of a family man and part-time tobacco farmer, standing in contrast to Webber, whose intellectual drive and literary ambition make him a driven "city" man.

Also on the train is Judge Rumford Bland, a blind syphilitic whose corruption serves to symbolize the corruption in Libya Hill toward which Webber is traveling. Upon his arrival, Webber finds that his quiet boyhood town has become crazed from a land-boom mentality that has everyone making huge paper fortunes in real estate (these events parallel those immediately preceding the Depression). Thus, his idealized expectations of home are shattered by the corruption and madness running rampant throughout Libya Hill.

After the publication of his novel, Webber receives abusive letters from the residents of Libya Hill. Typically, Wolfe incorporated his own experiences into his fiction. In this instance, he drew upon his unpleasant memories of what happened after he published *Look Homeward, Angel*. An entire book in the novel ("The World That Jack Built") is devoted to the wealthy lives of Esther and Frederick Jack (the Bernsteins). Writing about his own breakup with Aline Bernstein, Wolfe describes Webber's move to Brooklyn and the end of his relationship with Esther Jack. In Brooklyn, Webber learns to love the low-life characters who inhabit the streets—the prostitutes, the derelicts, and the petty criminals—for they are very much a part of the American experience. To ignore them—or worse yet, to explain them away somehow—would be to deny the underbelly of America that Webber (and Wolfe) found so compelling.

After his years in Brooklyn (with scenes devoted to his relationship with Foxhall Edwards, his editor), Webber tires of New York and sails for Europe. In Germany, he is welcomed with the fame and notoriety he has sought for so long, but he also witnesses the darker side of Nazi Germany. The novel is the story of one man's pilgrimage, a search for a faith that will endure within a society so corrupt that each individual is destroyed by it. *You Can't Go Home Again* is not an entirely cynical book, however, for it concludes with a sense of hope and faith in the future.

Throughout his novels, Wolfe explored isolation, death, and the changes wrought by time—themes that exemplify his interest in the darker elements of life. In his attempts to capture the essence of a moment, he often overlooked the artistic demands that the novel imposes upon any writer. He was not a craftsman of the novel because he often sacrificed form, unity, and coherence to capture experience. His reputation is linked directly to his ambitious attempts to say it all, and *Look Homeward, Angel*, although only the beginning of the story Wolfe desired to tell, stands as his most satisfying and fully realized work.

Other major works

SHORT FICTION: *From Death to Morning*, 1935; *The Hills Beyond*, 1941; *The Complete Short Stories of Thomas Wolfe*, 1987.

PLAYS: *Mannerhouse*, 1948; *Welcome to Our City*, 1962 (published only in Germany as *Willkommen in Altamont*); *The Mountains*, 1970.

POETRY: *The Face of a Nation: Poetical Passages from the Writings of Thomas Wolfe*, 1939; *A Stone, a Leaf, a Door: Poems by Thomas Wolfe*, 1945.

NONFICTION: *The Story of a Novel*, 1936; *Thomas Wolfe's Letters to His Mother*, 1943; *The Portable Thomas Wolfe*, 1946; *The Letters of Thomas Wolfe*, 1956; *Thomas Wolfe's Purdue Speech*, 1964; *The Notebooks of Thomas Wolfe*, 1970; *The Thomas Wolfe Reader*, 1982; *Beyond Love and Loyalty: The Letters of Thomas Wolfe and Elizabeth Nowell*, 1983; *My Other Loneliness: Letters of Thomas Wolfe and Aline Bernstein*, 1983; *The Autobiography of an American Novelist*, 1983.

Bibliography

Donald, David Herbert. *Look Homeward*. Boston: Little, Brown, 1987.

Evans, Elizabeth. *Thomas Wolfe*. New York: Frederick Ungar, 1984.

Field, Leslie A., ed. *Thomas Wolfe: Three Decades of Criticism*. New York: New York University Press, 1968.

Holman, C. Hugh. *The World of Thomas Wolfe*. New York: Charles Scribner's Sons, 1962.

Kennedy, Richard S. *The Window of Memory: The Literary Career of Thomas Wolfe*. Chapel Hill: University of North Carolina Press, 1962.

Nowell, Elizabeth, ed. *The Letters of Thomas Wolfe*. New York: Charles Scribner's Sons, 1956.

Rubin, Louis D., Jr., ed. *Thomas Wolfe: A Collection of Critical Essays*. Englewood Cliffs, N.J.: Prentice-Hall, 1973.

V

CONSIDER ME
Bearers of the
African American Tradition

But someday somebody'll
Stand up and talk about me,
And write about me—
. . . .
I reckon it'll be
Me myself!

—Langston Hughes,
"Note on Commercial Theatre," 1949

The diverse and distinguished body of writing that is African American literature presents some of the best examples of the American investigation of the question of identity. From the early days of the Republic, when a slave was counted as only three-fifths of a person, to Frederick Douglass' adoption of a fictional character's name as his last name as a free man, to Ralph Ellison's postulation of the African American persona as an "invisible man," identity has been a central concern of African American fiction, nonfiction, poetry, and drama. Perhaps more than any other grouping of American texts, African American literature is also characterized by a dialogical structure that is both internally and externally directed.

According to the noted African American scholar Henry Lewis Gates, Jr., African American literary dialogue often takes the form of "signifying," or verbal gamesmanship, a tradition that he traces back to African folktales featuring the signifying monkey, a trickster figure prominent in Yoruban mythology. Set against this playfulness and exuberance of language is the often grim history and oppressive social reality experienced by many African American writers. Internally, this liter-

ary dialogue mirrors the political and aesthetic debates within African American culture. Externally, the question of the nature or even the possibility of dialogue with the predominantly white and European culture of the United States occupies a place of primary importance. A simple, single African American identity, in this instance, is impossible to define; African American identity is instead best thought of as a composite of the differing voices present in the dialogue, each contributing her or his own perspective on a question that remains critically important in African American culture.

The tension created by the distance between an eloquent oral tradition and an oppressive reality often finds its way into the debate between the two distinct strands in the fabric of African American literature, the cyclically popular realist "protest" movement and the vernacular tradition, with its emphasis on a distinctive and often joyful identity. More often than not, however, these two traditions can be seen competing in a single text, in a manner that Soviet literary critic Mikhail Bakhtin termed "dialogic," or partaking of the nature of a dialogue. The best example of this structure is found in Ralph Ellison's *Invisible Man* (1952), which combines numerous generic modes over its epic length. The narrator, an otherwise unnamed "I," tells in a number of voices the story of his formal education in the South and his informal indoctrination into the ways of Harlem and New York City. The narrator's search for an identity leads him to incorporate the many voices he hears, or has heard, in the course of his theoretical and real-world education. He repeats bits of speeches from famous African Americans such as Booker T. Washington, and dreams folktales and bits of songs. His experience ultimately leads him to conclude that he has become the speaker for all those who are in search of an identity.

Against this symbolic representation of the African American search for an identity one finds the realistic and naturalistic expression of the lives of African Americans in the United States, beginning in fiction with the novels of Paul Laurence Dunbar. The ultimate expression of this form is Richard Wright's novel *Native Son* (1940), justifiably among the most celebrated works of American naturalism. The protagonist of *Native Son*, Bigger Thomas, dreams of escaping the South Side Chicago ghetto where he has spent the majority of his young life. He finds, however, that, like the boundaries of the ghetto, his life has been circumscribed by the white world and all avenues of escape have been cut off. Increasingly frantic in his search for a satisfactory identity, Bigger accidentally kills a white girl, the daughter of his wealthy employer. Stereotyped immediately by the media as a cunning predator and rapist, Bigger becomes the subject of an intense manhunt and, when caught, is sentenced to death for his crime. *Invisible Man* and *Native Son* together form two of the poles within which the dialogue concerning the nature of African American tradition is contained. Other significant writers of the twentieth century have added their own commentaries, either realistic or fabulous, though often a combination of the two.

Within this paradigmatic structure, the "realist" vein of the African American tradition has been the specialty of numerous novelists and poets, both in their favorite genres and in a number of significant works of nonfiction and autobiography. Other writers of important realistic and naturalistic novels include Ernest J. Gaines, Terry McMillan, Gloria Naylor, John Edgar Wideman, Alice Walker, and 1993 Nobel laureate in literature Toni Morrison. While the dominant mode in many of these novelists' works may be realism, contemporary novelists also continue in the tradition of Ralph Ellison, including his narrative innovations in otherwise realist works. The poetry of Dunbar, Langston Hughes, and Gwendolyn Brooks shares this interest in representing the realities of everyday life, often in a vernacular form. Brooks's first volume of poetry, *A Street in Bronzeville* (1945), established the South Side of Chicago as a poetic landscape as well as the home of hard-boiled fictional characters. The most realistic genre of all, of course, is nonfiction—much of it, in this case, highly autobiographical. Most famous among these works are Richard Wright's *Black Boy* (1945), Wright's autobiography concerning growing up in the segregated South, and the long-suppressed sequel *American Hunger* (1977), not published until seventeen years after Wright's death; James Baldwin's *Notes of a Native Son* (1955), part of his rejection of the literary tradition begun by Wright; John Edgar Wideman's memoir *Brothers and Keepers* (1984), the story of Wideman's brother's incarceration for murder and the writer's own estrangement from the African American community; and Alice Walker's many significant literary essays, among them the often-anthologized "In Search of Our Mothers' Gardens," in which Walker discusses the "womanist" tradition in African American culture. Walker theorizes that African American women have used various nonliterary outlets for their creative talents, including her mother's famous mid-Georgia gardens.

Perhaps the writer most responsible for popularizing and helping maintain the signifying tradition is anthropologist and novelist Zora Neale Hurston, a notable member of the Harlem Renaissance of the 1920's. Hurston's works fell into disrepute during the heyday of Wright and other naturalist writers, and they were not rediscovered and reprinted until the 1970's. Her most famous novel, *Their Eyes Were Watching God* (1937), is the story of Janie Crawford, a young woman who, in the words of the narrator, is in search of a bee for her bloom. The poetic rendering and romantic questing structure of the novel place it alongside Jean Toomer's *Cane* (1923) as one of the most lyrical works in the canon of African American literature. Hurston's novel has also served as an important influence in the writing of the current generation of African American women novelists, including Walker and Morrison. Likewise, the very different works of novelist Charles Johnson and poet Rita Dove bear some relation to the questing structure apparent in Hurston's work. Johnson's novel *Middle Passage* (1990), winner of a National Book Award, concerns the quest of a manumitted slave who struggles to find a satisfactory place in society. Dove's widely varied poetry presents individualized characters in a usually lyric form, with a range of historical examples unparalleled by any writer since Ellison.

The three contemporary writers who best exemplify the continuation of the various African American traditions are Ishmael Reed, August Wilson, and Toni Morrison. Reed's narratives, usually mythic and theological in proportion, feature African traditions transplanted into an American context. *Mumbo Jumbo* (1972) tells the story of PaPa LaBas' quest for the key document of the Jes Grew movement, a sacred HooDoo text that affirms life against the death-worshiping Judeo-Christian culture. Even the name Jes Grew is part of Reed's signifying on American literary tradition, "jes grew" being the answer given by the slave child Topsy in Harriet Beecher Stowe's *Uncle Tom's Cabin* (1851) to the catechistic question "Where did you come from?" Playwright August Wilson has captured both the realistic and the signifying traditions in a series of critically acclaimed plays, most notably *Fences* (1985) and *The Piano Lesson* (1987), parts of a projected cycle of plays whose purpose is to document and explain African American experience in twentieth century America. Troy Maxson, the protagonist in *Fences*, was a star slugger in the Negro Leagues who was never allowed a chance to the enjoy the prosperity of his white counterparts. *The Piano Lesson*, like Morrison's *Beloved*, features a ghost, Sutter, the white former owner of the two protagonists' great-grandmother. The ghost is a figuration of the burden of African American history and tradition, a heritage that can be either celebrated and remembered or repressed and forgotten. Berniece, the heroine of the play, regains her heritage only when she begins to play an inherited piano for the first time in many years. Like all culture, Wilson argues, African American culture is kept alive only when its identity can be fully realized through continuing practice.

Toni Morrison stands as perhaps the most prominent exemplar of these combined traditions, and enjoys as well both a wide readership among the general public and inclusion in the literary curricula of many high schools and universities. Her work ranges from the psychological realism of *Sula* (1973), which chronicles the decline and destruction of a fictional Ohio town, to the experimental *Beloved* (1987), which tells in realistic detail of the haunting of a slave mother by the ghost of her daughter Beloved, whom the mother killed with a handsaw rather than allowing her to return to slavery. The first African American woman to win the Nobel Prize in Literature (1993), Morrison stands as a major figure of American "mainstream" literature, combining the concerns of African Americans, black women, and Americans in general. She skillfully incorporates into her works of fiction the elements of Wrightian naturalistic protest literature and the lyricism and universality more commonly associated with the works of Zora Neale Hurston, Ralph Ellison, and James Baldwin. Morrison is the preeminent figure in the current generation of African American writers; as a writer who best exhibits the diversity of the American search for an identity, her work will be discussed in the final section of this volume, "Epilogue: Renewing Visions of America."

—Jeffery Cupp
The University of Charleston

JAMES BALDWIN

Born: New York, New York; August 2, 1924   *Died:* St. Paul de Vence, France; November 30, 1987

Principal long fiction

Go Tell It on the Mountain, 1953; *Giovanni's Room*, 1956; *Another Country*, 1962; *Tell Me How Long the Train's Been Gone*, 1968; *If Beale Street Could Talk*, 1974; *Just Above My Head*, 1979.

Other literary forms

Before he published his first novel, James Baldwin had established a reputation as a talented essayist and reviewer. Many of his early pieces, later collected in *Notes of a Native Son* (1955) and *Nobody Knows My Name: More Notes of a Native Son* (1961), have become classics; his essays on Richard Wright, especially "Everybody's Protest Novel" (1949) and "Many Thousands Gone" (1951), occupy a central position in the development of "universalist" African American thought during the 1950's. *The Fire Next Time* (1963), an extended meditation on the relationship of race, religion, and the individual experience in America, is the culmination of Baldwin's early prose. *The Price of the Ticket: Collected Nonfiction 1948-1985* (1985) includes Baldwin's essay collections as well as a number of previously uncollected pieces.

Baldwin also wrote children's fiction, verse, and drama. Although he published little short fiction after 1965, Baldwin was an acknowledged master of the novella form. "Sonny's Blues" (1957), the story of the relationship of a jazz musician to his "respectable" narrator-brother, anticipates many of the themes of Baldwin's later novels and is widely recognized as one of the great American novellas.

Achievements

Baldwin's public role as a major African American racial spokesman of the 1950's and 1960's guarantees his place in American cultural history. Though not undeserved, this reputation more frequently obscures than clarifies the nature of his literary achievement, which involves his relationship to African American culture, existential philosophy, and the moral tradition of the world novel. More accurate, though ultimately as limited, is the view of Baldwin primarily as an exemplar of the African American presence in the of the American literary tradition. Grouped with Ralph Ellison as a major "post-Wright" black novelist, Baldwin represents, in this view, the generation that rejected "protest litera-

ture" in favor of "universal" themes. This view emphasizes the craftsmanship of Baldwin's early novels and his treatment of themes such as religious hypocrisy, father-son tensions, and sexual identity.

The deepest level of Baldwin's literary achievement, whatever his immediate political focus or fictional form, are his penetrating moral insights. Refusing to lie about the reality of pain, he provided realistic images of the moral life possible in the inhospitable world that encompasses the streets of Harlem and the submerged recesses of the mind.

Biography

James Baldwin once dismissed his childhood as "the usual bleak fantasy." Nevertheless, the major concerns of his fiction consistently reflect the social context of his family life in Harlem during the Depression. The dominant figure of Baldwin's childhood was clearly his stepfather, David Baldwin, who worked as a manual laborer and preached in a storefront church. Clearly the model for Gabriel Grimes in *Go Tell It on the Mountain*, David Baldwin had moved from New Orleans to New York City, where he married Emma Berdis. The oldest of what was to be a group of nine children in the household, James assumed a great deal of the responsibility for the care of his half-brothers and sisters. Insulated somewhat from the brutality of Harlem street life by his domestic duties, Baldwin, as he describes in *The Fire Next Time*, sought refuge in the Church. At age fourteen in 1938, he underwent a conversion experience similar to that of John in *Go Tell It on the Mountain*. Baldwin preached as a young minister for the next several years. At the same time, he began to read, immersing himself in works such as *Uncle Tom's Cabin* (1852) and the novels of Charles Dickens. Both at his Harlem junior high school, where the African American poet Countée Cullen was one of his teachers, and at his predominantly white Bronx high school, Baldwin contributed to student literary publications. The combination of family tension, economic hardship, and religious vocation provides the focus of much of Baldwin's greatest writing, most notably *Go Tell It on the Mountain*, *The Fire Next Time*, and *Just Above My Head*.

If Baldwin's experience during the 1930's provided his material, his life from 1942 to 1948 shaped his characteristic approach to that material. After he was graduated from high school in 1942, Baldwin worked for a year as a manual laborer in New Jersey, an experience that increased both his understanding of his stepfather and his insight into America's economic and racial systems. Moving to Greenwich Village in 1943, Baldwin worked during the day and wrote at night for the next five years; his first national reviews and essays appeared in 1946. The major event of the Village years, however, was Baldwin's meeting with Richard Wright in the winter between 1944 and 1945. Wright's interest helped Baldwin secure first a Eugene F. Saxton Memorial Award and then a Rosenwald Fellowship, enabling him to move to Paris in 1948.

After his arrival in France, Baldwin experienced more of the poverty that had shaped his childhood. Simultaneously, he developed a larger perspective on the psychocultural context conditioning his experience, feeling at once a greater sense of freedom and a larger sense of the global structure of racism, particularly as reflected in the French treatment of North Africans. In addition, he formed many of the personal and literary friendships that contributed to his later public prominence. Baldwin's well-publicized literary feud with Wright, who viewed the younger writer's criticism of *Native Son* (1940) as a form of personal betrayal, helped establish Baldwin as a major presence in African American letters. Although Baldwin's first novel, *Go Tell It on the Mountain*, was well-received critically, it was not so financially successful that he could devote his full time to creative writing. As a result, Baldwin continued to travel widely, frequently on journalistic assignments, while writing *Giovanni's Room*, which is set in France and involves no black characters.

Returning to the United States as a journalist covering the Civil Rights movement, Baldwin made his first trip to the American South in 1957. The essays and reports describing that physical and psychological journey propelled Baldwin to the position of public prominence which he maintained for more than a decade. During the height of the movement, Baldwin lectured widely and was present at major events such as the March on Washington and the voter registration drive in Selma, Alabama. In addition, he met with most of the

major African American activists of the period, including Martin Luther King, Jr., Elijah Muhammad, James Meredith, and Medgar Evers. Attorney General Robert Kennedy requested that Baldwin bring together the most influential voices in the black community, and, even though the resulting meeting accomplished little, the request testifies to Baldwin's image as a focal point of black opinion. In addition to this political activity, Baldwin formed personal and literary relationships—frequently tempestuous ones—with numerous white writers, including William Styron and Norman Mailer. A surge in literary popularity, reflected in the presence of *Another Country* and *The Fire Next Time* on the best-seller lists throughout most of 1962 and 1963, accompanied Baldwin's political success and freed him from financial insecurity for the first time. He traveled extensively throughout the decade, and his visits to Puerto Rico and Africa were to have a major influence on his subsequent political thought.

Partly because of Baldwin's involvement with prominent whites and partly because of the sympathy for homosexuals evinced in his writing, several black militants, most notably Eldridge Cleaver, attacked Baldwin's position as "black spokesman" beginning in the late 1960's. As a result, nationalist spokesmen such as Amiri Baraka and Bobby Seale gradually eclipsed Baldwin in the public literary and political spotlights. He died in St. Paul de Vence, France, on November 30, 1987.

Analysis

Baldwin was both a major African American writer and a racial spokesperson for his generation. Through his novels, essays, plays, and poetry, he boldly and articulately explored the moral dimensions of race in American society.

Uncompromising in his demand for personal and social integrity, Baldwin from the beginning of his career charged the individual with full responsibility for his or her moral identity. Both in his early individualistic novels and in his later political fiction, he insisted on the inadequacy of received definitions as the basis for self-knowledge or social action. Never denying the possibility of transcendent moral power—which he frequently imaged as the power of love—he simply insisted that human conceptions must remain flexible enough to allow for the honest perception of experience. Fully recognizing the reality of existential pain and despair, Baldwin invoked honesty and self-acceptance as the necessary supports for the love capable of generating individual communication and at least the groundwork for political action.

Baldwin's social vision, reflecting his experience in a racist culture, acknowledges the forces militating against self-knowledge and moral responsibility. Each of his novels portrays a series of evasive and simplifying definitions built into religious, economic, and educational institutions. These definitions, which emphasize the separation of self and other, control the immediate contexts of individual experience. As a result, they frequently seem to constitute "human nature," to embody the inevitable limits of experience. While sympathizing with the difficulty of separating the self from context without simultaneously denying experience, Baldwin insists that acquiescing to the definitions inevitably results in self-hatred and social immorality. The individual incapable of accepting his or her existential complexity flees to the illusion of certainty provided by the institutions which assume responsibility for directing moral decisions. This cycle of institutional pressure encouraging existential evasion ensuring further institutional corruption recurs in each of Baldwin's novels.

Such elements endorse William Blake's vision of morality as a movement from innocence through experience to a higher innocence. Beginning with an unaware innocence, individuals inevitably enter the deadening and murderous world of experience, the world of the limiting definitions. Those who attempt to deny the world and remain children perish. Only those who plunge into experience, recognize its cruelty, and resolve to forge an aware innocence can hope to survive morally. Specifically, Baldwin urges families to pass on a sense of the higher innocence to their children by refusing to simplify the truth of experience. This painful honesty makes possible the commitment to love despite the inevitability of pain and isolation. It provides the only hope, however desperate, for individual or social rejuvenation.

Go Tell It on the Mountain centers on the religious conversion and family relationships of John Grimes, whose experience parallels that of Baldwin during his youth. Growing up under the influence of his hypocritical and tyrannical stepfather, preacher Gabriel Grimes, John alternately attempts to please and transcend him. Gabriel expends most of his emotional energy on his openly rebellious son Ray, whose immersion in the violent life of the Harlem streets contrasts sharply with John's involvement with the "Temple of the Fire Baptized," the storefront church where John's conversion takes place.

A victim of the institutional context of his youth, Gabriel, in turn, victimizes his family by attempting to force them into narrowly defined roles. The roots of Gabriel's character lie in the "temple-street" dichotomy of his Southern childhood. Encouraged by his religious mother to deny his sensuality, Gabriel undergoes a conversion experience and immerses himself in the role of preacher. As a result, he enters into a loveless asexual marriage with his mother's friend Deborah. Eventually, Gabriel's repressed street self breaks out, and he fathers a son by the sensual Esther. Again attempting to deny his sensuality, Gabriel refuses to acknowledge this son, Royal. Like John's half-brother Roy, Royal immerses himself in the street life that Gabriel denies; Royal dies in a Chicago barroom brawl. Gabriel fears that Roy will share Royal's fate, but his attempt to crush his second son's street self merely strengthens the resulting rebellion. Faced with the guilt of Royal's death and the sense of impending doom concerning Roy, Gabriel retreats into a solipsism that makes a mockery of his Christian vocation. Far from providing a context for moral responsibility, the Church is depicted as a source of the power needed to destroy the innocence of others.

Against this backdrop, John's conversion raises a basic question that will recur in slightly different circumstances in each of Baldwin's novels: Can an individual hope to break the cycle of evasion that has shaped his personal and social context?

Confronted with the issue of self-identity, John progresses from a sense of isolation to a vision of the dispossessed with whom he shares his agony and his humanity. John's vision of the multitude whose collective voice merges with his own suggests suffering as the essential human experience, one obliterating both the safety and the isolation of imposed definitions. Significantly, this vision leads John to Jesus the Son rather than God the Father, marking an implicit rejection of Gabriel's Old Testament vengeance in favor of the New Testament commitment to an all-encompassing love. The son metamorphoses from symbol of limitation to symbol of liberation. Near the end of his vision, John explicitly rejects the separation of opposites—street and temple, white and black—encouraged by his social context. Returning to his immediate environment from the depths of his mind, John responds not to the call of Gabriel but to that of Elisha, a slightly older member of the congregation with whom he has previously engaged in a sexually suggestive wrestling match. John's salvation, then, may bring him closer to an acceptance of his own sensuality, to a definition of himself encompassing both temple and street. Baldwin ends the novel with the emergence of the newly "saved" John onto the streets of Harlem. His fate hinges on his ability to move ahead to the higher innocence suggested by his vision of the dispossessed rather than submitting to the experiences that have destroyed and deformed the majority of the saints.

Another Country, Baldwin's greatest popular success, analyzes the effects of this deforming pressure on a wide range of characters, black and white, male and female, homosexual and heterosexual. To accommodate these diverse consciousnesses, Baldwin employs the sprawling form usually associated with political rather than psychological fiction, emphasizing the diverse forms of innocence and experience in American society.

Casting a Melvillean shadow over the novel is the black jazz musician Rufus Scott, who is destroyed by an agonizing affair with Leona, a white Southerner recently arrived in New York at the time she meets him. Unable to forge the innocence necessary for love in a context which repudiates the relationship at every turn, Rufus destroys Leona psychologically. After a period of physical and psychological destitution, he kills himself by jumping off a bridge. His sister Ida, an aspiring singer, and his friend Vivaldo Moore, an aspiring white writer, meet during the last days of Rufus' life and fall in love as they console each other over his death. Struggling to overcome the racial and sexual definitions that destroyed Rufus, they seek a higher innocence capable of countering Ida's sense of the world as a "whorehouse." In contrast to Ida and Vivaldo's struggle, the relationship of white actor Eric Jones and his French lover Yves seems Edenic. Although Baldwin portrays Eric's internal struggle for a firm sense of his sexual identity, their shared innocence at times seems to exist almost entirely outside the context of the pressures that destroyed Rufus. The final major characters, Richard and Cass Silenski, represent the cost of the "American dream." After Richard "makes it" as a popular novelist, their personal relationship decays, precipitating Cass's affair with Eric. Their tentative reunion after Richard discovers the affair makes it clear that material success provides no shortcut to moral responsibility.

Baldwin examines each character and relationship in the context of the institutional pressures discouraging individual responsibility. Baldwin opens *Another Country* with the image of Rufus, who "had fallen so low, that he scarcely had the energy to be angry." Both an exceptional case and a representative figure, Rufus embodies the seething anger and hopeless isolation rendering Baldwin's America a landscape of nightmare. Forcing the reader to recognize the social implications of Rufus' situation, Baldwin emphasizes that his specific situation originates in his own moral failure with Leona. Where Gabriel Grimes remained insulated from his immorality by arrogance and pride, Rufus feels the full extent of his self-enforced damnation. Ironically and belatedly, his destitution clarifies his sense of the extent of his past acceptance of the social definitions that destroy him.

Wandering the streets of Manhattan, Rufus feels himself beyond human contact. Desperately in need of love, he believes his past actions render him unfit for even minimal compassion. His abuse of Leona, who as a white woman represents both the "other" and the source of the most obvious social definitions circumscribing his life as a black male, accounts for his original estrangement from family and friends, who find his viciousness uncharacteristic. All, including Rufus, fail to understand soon enough that his abuse of Leona represents both a rebellion against and an acceptance of the role dictated by racial and sexual definitions. Separated from the psychological source of his art—jazz inevitably rejects the substructure of Euro-American definitions of reality—Rufus falls ever further into a paranoia that receives ample reinforcement from the racist context. Largely by his own choice, he withdraws almost entirely from both his black and his white acquaintances. Once on the street following Leona's breakdown, he begins to recognize not only his immediate but also his long-term acceptance of destructive definitions. Thinking back on a brief homosexual affair with Eric to which he submitted out of pity rather than love, Rufus regrets having treated his friend with contempt. Having rejected the other in Eric and Leona, Rufus realizes he has rejected a part of himself. He consigns himself to the ranks of the damned, casting himself beyond human love with his plunge off the bridge.

Baldwin's turbulent and passionate life informs all of his works. In his fiction he turned to autobiographical events, issues, and characters in constructing a world that in its overt racism has inhibited the development not so much of black identity as of a truly integrated and fulfilled American identity.

Other major works

SHORT FICTION: *Going to Meet the Man*, 1965

PLAYS: *The Amen Corner*, 1954; *Blues for Mister Charlie*, 1964; *One Day, When I Was Lost: A Scenario Based on the Autobiography of Malcolm X*, 1972.

POETRY: *Jimmy's Blues: Selected Poems*, 1983.

NONFICTION; *Notes of a Native Son*, 1955; *Nobody Knows My Name: More Notes of a Native Son*, 1961; *The Fire Next Time*, 1963; *Nothing Personal*, 1964 (with Richard Avedon); *No Name in the Street*, 1971; *A Rap on Race*, 1971 (with Margaret Mead); *A Dialogue*, 1975 (with Nikki Giovanni); *The Devil Finds Work*, 1976; *The Evidence of Things Not Seen*, 1985; *The Price of The Ticket: Collected Nonfiction 1948-1985*, 1985; *Conversations with James Baldwin*, 1989.

CHILDREN'S LITERATURE: *Little Man, Little Man*, 1975.

Bibliography

Kinnamon, Keneth, ed. *James Baldwin*. Englewood Cliffs, N.J.: Prentice-Hall, 1974.

Kollhofer, Jakob, ed. *James Baldwin: His Place in American Literary History and His Reception in Europe*. New York: P. Lang, 1991.

Leeming, David. *James Baldwin: A Biography*. New York: Alfred A. Knopf, 1994.

Macebuh, Stanley. *James Baldwin: A Critical Study*. New York: Third Press, 1973.

Standley, Fred L., and Nancy N. Burt, eds. *Critical Essays on James Baldwin*. Boston: G. K. Hall, 1988.

Sylvander, Carolyn Wedin. *James Baldwin*. New York: Frederick Ungar, 1980.

Weatherby, W. J. *James Baldwin: Artist on Fire*. New York: Donald I. Fine, 1989.

GWENDOLYN BROOKS

Born: Topeka, Kansas; June 7, 1917

Principal poetry

A Street in Bronzeville, 1945; *Annie Allen*, 1949; *The Bean Eaters*, 1960; *Selected Poems*, 1963; *In the Mecca*, 1968; *Riot*, 1969; *Family Pictures*, 1970; *Aloneness*, 1971; *Beckonings*, 1975; *Primer for Blacks*, 1980; *To Disembark*, 1981; *The Near-Johannesburg Boy*, 1986; *Blacks*, 1987; *Gottschalk and the Grand Tarantelle*, 1988; *Winnie*, 1991.

Other literary forms

In addition to the poetry on which her literary reputation rests, Gwendolyn Brooks has published a novel, *Maud Martha* (1953); a book of autobiographical prose, *Report from Part One* (1972); and volumes of children's verse. She has written introductions to, and edited anthologies of, the works of younger African American writers. These introductions frequently provide insight into her own work. Several recordings of Brooks reading her own work have been made.

Achievements

Working comfortably in relation to diverse poetic traditions, Brooks has been widely honored. Early in her career, she received numerous major literary awards, including the Pulitzer Prize in poetry in 1950 for *Annie Allen*. She became Poet Laureate of Illinois in 1969 and has received more than fifty honorary doctorates. Equally significant, numerous writers associated with the Black Arts movement recognize her as an inspirational figure linking the older and younger generations of African American poets. Brooks's ability to appeal both to poetic establishments and to a sizable popular audience, especially among younger blacks, stems from her pluralistic voice, which echoes a wide range of precursors while remaining unmistakably African American.

This integrity of vision and voice assumes special significance in the context of African American writing of the 1950's and 1960's. A period of "universalism" in black literature, the 1950's brought prominence to such poets as Brooks, Amiri Baraka (then LeRoi Jones), and Robert Hayden, all of whom provided clear evidence that African American poets matched the technical and intellectual range of their white counterparts. During this period of intellectual and aesthetic integration, Brooks never abandoned her social and racial heritage to strive for the transcendent (and deracinated) universalism associated by some African American critics

with T. S. Eliot. Responding to William Carlos Williams' call in *Paterson* (1946-1951) to "make a start out of particulars and make them general," Brooks demonstrates unambiguously that an African American writer need not be limited in relevance by concentrating on the black experience.

The 1960's, conversely, encouraged separatism and militancy in African American writing. Even while accepting the Black Arts movement's call for a poetry designed to speak directly to the political condition of the black community, Brooks continued to insist on precision of form and language. While Jones changed his name to Amiri Baraka and radically altered his poetic voice, Brooks accommodated her new insights to her previously established style.

Brooks was appointed to the Presidential Commission on the National Agenda for the Eighties; she was the first African American woman elected to the National Institute of Arts and Letters. She was named Consultant in Poetry to the Library of Congress for 1985-1986.

Biography

Gwendolyn Brooks's poetry bears the strong impress of Chicago, particularly of the predominantly black South Side, where she has lived most of her life. Although she was born in Topeka, Kansas, Brooks was taken to Chicago before she was a year old. In many ways she has devoted her career to the physical, spiritual, and, more recently, political exploration of her native city.

Brooks's life and writings are frequently separated into two phases, with her experience at the 1967 Black Writers' Conference at Fisk University in Nashville serving as a symbolic transition. Prior to the conference, Brooks was known primarily as the first African American to win a Pulitzer Prize in poetry. Although not politically unaware, she held to a somewhat cautious attitude. The vitality she encountered at the conference crystallized her sense of the insufficiency of universalist attitudes and generated close personal and artistic friendships with younger black poets such as Madhubuti, Walter Bradford, and Knight. Severing her ties with the mainstream publishing firm of Harper and Row, which had published her first five books, Brooks transferred her work and prestige to the black-owned and -operated Broadside Press of Detroit, Third World Press of Chicago, and Black Position Press, also of Chicago. Her commitment to black publishing houses remains unwavering.

Educated in the Chicago school system and at Wilson Junior College, Brooks learned her craft under Inez Cunningham Stark (Boulton), a white woman who taught poetry at the South Side Community Art Center in the late 1930's and 1940's. Brooks's mother, who had been a teacher in Topeka, had encouraged her literary interests from an early age. Her father, a janitor, provided her with ineffaceable images of the spiritual strength and dignity of "common" people. Brooks married Henry Blakely in 1939, and her family concerns continued to play a central role in shaping her career. The eleven-year hiatus between the publication of *Annie Allen* and *The Bean Eaters* resulted at least in part from her concentration on rearing her two children, born in 1940 and 1951. Her numerous poems on family relationships reflect both the rewards and the tensions of her own experiences. Her children grown, Brooks concentrated on teaching, supervising poetry workshops, and speaking publicly. These activities brought her into contact with a wide range of younger black poets, preparing her for her experience at Fisk. As Poet Laureate of Illinois, a position she has held since 1969, she continues to encourage the development of younger poets through personal contact and formal competitions.

The division between the two phases of Brooks's life should not be overstated. She evinced a strong interest in the Civil Rights movement during the 1950's and early 1960's; her concern with family continued in the 1980's. Above all, Brooks continues to live with and write of and for the Chicagoans whose failures and triumphs she sees as deeply personal, universally resonant, and specifically black.

Analysis

The image of Gwendolyn Brooks as a readily accessible poet is at once accurate and deceptive. Capable of capturing the experiences and rhythms of African American street life, she frequently presents translucent surfaces that give way suddenly to reveal ambiguous depths. Equally capable of manipulating traditional poetic forms such as the sonnet, rhyme royal, and heroic couplet, she employs them to mirror the uncertainties of characters or personae who embrace conventional attitudes to defend themselves against internal and external chaos. Whatever form she chooses, Brooks consistently focuses on the struggle of people to find and express love, usually associated with the family, in the midst of a hostile environment. In constructing their defenses and seeking love, these persons typically experience a disfiguring pain. Brooks devotes much of her energy to defining and responding to the elusive forces, variously psychological and social, that inflict this pain. Increasingly in her later poetry, Brooks traces the pain to political sources and expands her concept of the family to encompass all black people. Even while speaking of the social situation of blacks in a voice crafted primarily for blacks, however, Brooks maintains the complex awareness of the multiple perspectives relevant to any given experience. Her ultimate concern is to encourage every individual, black or white, to "Conduct your blooming in the noise and whip of the whirlwind" ("The Second Sermon on the Warpland").

A deep concern with the everyday circumstances of black people living within the whirlwind characterizes many of Brooks's most popular poems, in which she focuses on characters whose experiences merge the idiosyncratic and the typical. She frequently draws on black musical forms to underscore the communal resonance of a character's outwardly undistinguished life. By tying the refrain of "Swing Low Sweet Chariot" to the repeated phrase "Plain black boy," Brooks transforms the character of De Witt Williams into an Everyman figure. Brooks describes his personal search for love in the poolrooms and dance halls but stresses the representative quality of his experience by starting and ending the poem with the musical allusion.

"We Real Cool," perhaps Brooks's single best-known poem, subjects a similarly representative experience to an intricate technical and thematic scrutiny, at once loving and critical. The poem is only twenty-four words long, including eight repetitions of the word "we." It is suggestive that the subtitle of "We Real Cool" specifies the presence of only seven pool players at the "Golden Shovel." The eighth "we" suggests that poet and reader share, on some level, the desperation of the group-voice that Brooks transmits. The final sentence, "We/ die soon," restates the *carpe diem* motif in the vernacular of Chicago's South Side.

On one level, "We Real Cool" appears simply to catalog the experiences of a group of dropouts content to "sing sin" in all available forms. A surprising ambiguity enters into the poem, however, revolving around the question of how to accent the word "we," which ends every line except the last one, providing the beat for the poem's jazz rhythm. Brooks has said that she intended that the "we" not be accented. Read in this way, the poem takes on a slightly distant and ironic tone, emphasizing the artificiality of the group identity that involves the characters in activities offering early death as the only release from pain. Conversely, the poem can be read with a strong accent on each "we," affirming the group identity. Although the experience still ends with early death, the pool players metamorphose into defiant heroes determined to resist the alienating environment. Their confrontation with experience is felt, if not articulated, as existentially pure. Pool players, poet, and reader cannot be sure which stress is valid.

Brooks crafts the poem, however, to hint at an underlying coherence in the defiance. The intricate internal rhyme scheme echoes the sound of nearly every word. Not only do the first seven lines end with "we," but the penultimate words of each line in each stanza also rhyme (cool/school, late/straight, sin/gin, June/soon). In addition, the alliterated consonant of the last line of each stanza is repeated in the first line of the next stanza (Left/lurk, Strike/sin, gin/June) and the first words of each line in the middle two stanzas are connected through consonance (Lurk/strike, Sing/thin). The one exception to this suggestive texture of sound is the word "Die," which introduces both a new vowel and a new consonant into the final line, breaking the rhythm and subjecting the performance to ironic revaluation. Ultimately, the power of the poem derives from the tension between the celebratory and the ironic perspectives on the lives of the plain black boys struggling for a sense of connection.

A similar struggle informs many of Brooks's poems in more traditional forms, including "The Mother," a powerful exploration of the impact of an abortion on the woman who has chosen to have it. Brooks states that the mother "decides that *she*, rather than her world, will kill her children." Within the poem itself, however, the motivations remain unclear. Although the poem's position in Brooks's first book, *A Street in Bronzeville*, suggests that the persona is African American, the poem neither supports nor denies a racial identification. Along with the standard English syntax and diction, this suggests that "The Mother" was designed to speak directly of an emotional, rather than a social, experience, and to be as accessible to whites as to blacks. Re-creating the anguished perspective of a persona unsure whether she is victim or victimizer, Brooks directs her readers' attention to the complex emotions of her potential Everywoman.

"The Mother" centers on the persona's alternating desire to take and to evade responsibility for the abortion. Resorting to ambiguous grammatical structures, the persona repeatedly qualifies her acceptance with "if" clauses ("If I sinned," "If I stole your births"). She refers to the lives of the children as matters of fate ("Your luck") and backs away from admitting that a death has taken place by claiming that the children "were never made." Her use of the second person pronoun to refer to herself in the first stanza reveals her desire to distance herself from her present pain. This attempt, however, fails. The opening line undercuts the evasion with the reality of memory: "Abortions will not let you forget." At the start of the second stanza, the pressure of memory forces the persona to shift to the more honest first-person pronoun. The first stanza's end-stopped couplets, reflecting the persona's simplistic attempt to recapture an irrevocably lost mother-child relationship through an act of imagination, give way to the intricate enjambment and complex rhyme scheme of the second stanza, which highlight the mother's inability to find rest.

The rhyme scheme—and Brooks can rival both Robert Frost and W. B. Yeats in her ability to employ various types of rhyme for thematic impact—underscores her struggle to come to terms with her action. The rhymes in the first stanza insist on her self-doubt, contrasting images of tenderness and physical substance with those of brutality and insubstantiality (forget/get, hair/air, beat/sweet). The internal rhyme of "never," repeated four times, and "remember," "workers," and "singers" further stresses the element of loss. In the second stanza, Brooks provides no rhymes for the end words "children" in line 11 and "deliberate" in line 21. This device draws attention to the persona's failure to answer the crucial questions of whether her children did in fact exist and of whether her own actions were in fact deliberate (and perhaps criminal). The last seven lines of the stanza end with hard *d* sounds as the persona struggles to forge her conflicting thoughts into a unified perspective. If Brooks offers coherence, though, it is emotional rather than intellectual. Fittingly, the *d* rhymes and off-rhymes focus on physical and emotional pain (dead/instead/made/afraid/said/died/cried). Brooks provides no easy answer to the anguished question: How is the truth to be told?" The persona's concluding cry of "I loved you/ All" rings with desperation. It is futile but it is not a lie. To call "The Mother" an antiabortion poem distorts its impact. Clearly portraying the devastating effects of the persona's action, it by no means condemns her or lacks sympathy. Like many of Brooks's characters, the mother is a person whose desire to love far outstrips her ability to cope with her circumstances and serves primarily to heighten her sensitivity to pain.

Perhaps the most significant change in Brooks's poetry involves her analysis of the origins of this pervasive pain. Rather than attributing the suffering to some unavoidable psychological condition, Brooks's later poetry indicts social institutions for their role in its perpetuation. The final poem of *Annie Allen*, "Men of Careful Turns," intimates that the defenders of a society that refuses to admit its full humanity bear responsibility for reducing the powerless to "grotesque toys." Despite this implicit accusation, however, Brooks perceives no "magic" capable of remedying the situation. She concludes the volume on a note of irresolution typical of her early period: "We are lost, must/ Wizard a track through our own screaming weed." The track, at this stage, remains spiritual rather than political.

Although the early volumes include occasional poems concerning articulate political participants such as "Negro Hero," her later work frequently centers on specific black political spokespersons such as Malcolm X, Paul Robeson, John Killens, and Don L. Lee. Beginning in the early 1960's, a growing anger informs poems as diverse as the ironic "The Chicago *Defender* Sends a Man to Little Rock," the near-baroque "The Lovers of the Poor," the imagistically intricate "Riders to the Blood-Red Wrath," and the satiric "Riot." This anger originates in Brooks's perception that the social structures of white society value material possessions and abstract ideas of prestige more highly than individual human beings. The anger culminates in Brooks's brilliant narrative poem "In the Mecca," concerning the death of a young girl in a Chicago housing project, and in her three "Sermons on the Warpland."

The "Warpland" poems mark Brooks's departure from the traditions of Euro-American poetry and thought represented by T. S. Eliot's *The Waste Land* (1922). The sequence typifies her post-1967 poetry, in which she abandons traditional stanzaic forms, applying her technical expertise to a relatively colloquial free verse. This technical shift parallels her rejection of the philosophical premises of Euro-American culture. Brooks refuses to accept the inevitability of cultural decay, arguing that the "waste" of Eliot's vision exists primarily because of our "warped" perceptions. Seeing white society as the embodiment of these distortions, Brooks embraces her blackness as a potential counterbalancing force.

The first "Sermon on the Warpland" opens with Ron Karenga's black nationalist credo: "The fact that we are black is our ultimate reality." Clearly, in Brooks's view, blackness is not simply a physical fact; it is primarily a metaphor for the possibility of love. As her poem "Two Dedications" indicates, Brooks sees the Euro-American tradition represented by the Chicago Picasso as inhumanly cold, mingling guilt and innocence, meaningfulness and meaninglessness, almost randomly. This contrasts sharply with her inspirational image of the Wall of Heroes on the South Side. To Brooks, true art assumes meaning from the people who interact with it. The Wall helps to redefine black reality, rendering the "dispossessions beakless." Rather than contemplating the site of destruction, the politically aware black art that Brooks embraces should inspire the black community to face its pain and, with renewed determination, to remove its sources. The final "Sermon on the Warpland" concludes with the image of a black phoenix rising from the ashes of the Chicago riot. No longer content to accept the unresolved suffering of "The Mother," Brooks forges a black nationalist politics and poetics of love.

Brooks's poetry vividly captures the essence of African American street life in her native Chicago, in language and images—in a poetic voice—crafted principally for a black audience. Her works attempt both to expose the elusive sources of the oppressive pain inflicted upon black Americans and to arouse these individuals to face and, if possible, eradicate such sources.

Other major works

NOVEL: *Maud Martha*, 1953.
NONFICTION: *Report from Part One*, 1972; *Young Poet's Primer*, 1980.
CHILDREN'S LITERATURE: *Bronzeville Boys and Girls*, 1956; *The Tiger Who Wore White Gloves*, 1974; *Very Young Poets*, 1983.

ANTHOLOGY: *Jump Bad: A New Chicago Anthology*, 1971.
MISCELLANEOUS: *The World of Gwendolyn Brooks*, 1971.

Bibliography

Baker, Houston A., Jr. *The Journey Back: Issues in Black Literature and Criticism*. Chicago: University of Chicago Press, 1980.

Kent, George E. *A Life of Gwendolyn Brooks*. Lexington: University Press of Kentucky, 1990.

Melhem, D. L. *Gwendolyn Brooks: Poetry and the Heroic Voice*. Lexington: University Press of Kentucky, 1987.

Miller, R. Bazter, ed. *Black American Poets Between Worlds, 1940-1960*. Tennessee Studies in Literature 30. Knoxville: University of Tennessee Press, 1986.

Mootry, Maria K., and Gary Smith, eds. *A Life Distilled: Gwendolyn Brooks: Her Poetry and Fiction*. Urbana: University of Illinois Press, 1987.

Shaw, Harry B. *Gwendolyn Brooks*. Twayne, 1980.

RITA DOVE

Born: Akron, Ohio; August 28, 1952

Principal poetry

The Yellow House on the Corner, 1980; *Museum*, 1983; *Thomas and Beulah*, 1986; *Grace Notes*, 1989; *Selected Poems*, 1993.

Other literary forms

Rita Dove has published both long and short fiction, including the novel *Through the Ivory Gate (1991)*.

Achievements

Dove's literary honors include grants and fellowships from the National Endowment for the Arts (NEA), the Academy of American Poets, the Guggenheim Foundation, and the General Electric Foundation. She spent 1988-1989 as a Senior Mellon Fellow at the National Humanities Center in North Carolina. In 1987 her collection *Thomas and Beulah* made her the first African American woman since Gwendolyn Brooks to win the Pulitzer Prize. She was named the U.S. poet laureate in 1993.

Biography

Born in 1952 in Akron, Ohio, Rita Dove is the daughter of Ray and Elvira (Hord) Dove. She received a B.A. degree in 1973 from Miami University (Ohio) and then, on a Fulbright Fellowship, attended the University of Tübingen in Germany, where she studied modern European literature. She returned to the United States to earn an M.F.A. degree at the highly regarded University of Iowa Writers' Workshop in 1977. Having held a number of teaching posts and traveled widely in Europe and the Middle East, she became a professor of English at the University of Virginia.

Dove married Fred Viebahn, a writer, in 1979.

Analysis

In a period when much American poetry is condemned as being merely an exercise in solipsistic navel gazing, and when African American poetry more specifically seems to have lapsed into hibernation after the vigorous activity of the Black Arts movement, Rita Dove has stepped forth with a body of work that answers such criticism resoundingly. Hers is a poetry characterized by discipline and technical proficiency, surprising breadth of reference, a willingness to approach emotionally charged subjects with aesthetic objectivity, and a refusal to define herself only in terms of blackness. She combines a novelist's eye for action and gesture with the lyric poet's exalted sense of language.

The startling scope of Dove's learning opens for her poetry a correspondingly vast range of topics and concerns, but the most persistent topic, and the one that most distinguishes her work from that of poets in the 1970's and 1980's, is history. She is constantly laboring to bring into focus the individual struggle in the ebb and flow of the historical tide. A second major concern is cultural collision, the responses of an outsider to a foreign culture, and she pursues this theme in a number of travel poems. Dove also plumbs the circumstances of her life as a way of confronting the puzzle of her own identity—as an African American, as a woman, as a daughter, as a parent—but manages self-dramatization without self-aggrandizement.

Dove's first two volumes, *The Yellow House on the Corner* and *Museum*, both provide a balance between the personal or individual and the social or cultural. *Museum* is the more consciously organized, with its sections pointedly titled and each dealing with a central topic—history and myth, art and artifact, autobiography and the personal past, life in the modern world. *Thomas and Beulah* represents Dove's coming-of-age critically, a step into the position of a leading African American poet. It allows her to extend her continual dissertation on the single person striving in the midst of historical flux; at the same time she can pursue her abiding interest in her own family romance, the question of heritage. Still availing itself of a variety of themes, *Grace Notes* is by far the most intensely autobiographical of her works, becoming a study in limitation and poignant regret. How, she seems to ask here, does one grant to daily life that ornament or variation that magically transforms it?

Poems in *The Yellow House on the Corner* often depict the collision of wish with reality, of the heart's desire with the dictates of the world. This collision is made tolerable by the working of the imagination, and the result is, for Dove, "magic," or the existence of an unexplainable occurrence. It is imagination and the art it produces that allow the speaker in "This Life" to see that "the possibilities/ are golden dresses in a nutshell." "Possibilities" have the power to transform this life into something distinct and charmed. Even the woman driven mad with grief over the loss of her son (or husband?) in "The Bird Frau" becomes a testament to possibility in her desire to "let everything go wild!" She becomes a bird-woman as a way of reuniting with her lost airman, who died in the war over France. While her condition may be perceived as pathetic, Dove refuses to indulge sentimentality, instead seeing her madness as a form of undying hope.

Some of the most compelling poems in Dove's first book are in a group of vignettes and portraits from the era of American slavery. These poems not only reveal her historical awareness but also allow her to engage the issue of race from a distance. Dove wants her poetry to produce anger, perhaps, but not to be produced only by anger. One example of this aesthetic distance from emotion might be "The Abduction," a brief foray in the voice of Solomon Northrup. Northrup is a free black lured to Washington, D.C., by "new friends" with the promise of good work and then kidnapped and sold into bondage. Dove dwells on the duplicity of these men and Northrup's susceptibility to them. Yet no pronouncements are made. The poem ends with the end of freedom, but that ending has been foreshadowed by the tightly controlled structure of the poem itself, with each stanza shortened as the scope of the victim's world constricts to this one-line conclusion: "I woke and found myself alone, in darkness and in chains." The indignation and disgust that such an episode could call forth are left entirely to the reader.

Museum is as the title suggests, a collection of historical and aesthetic artifacts. The shaping impulse of the book seems to be retrospective, a looking back to people and things that have been somehow suspended in time by legend, by historical circumstance, by all-too-human emotional wish. Dove intends to delve beneath the publicly known side of these stories—to excavate, in a sense, and uncover something forgotten but vital. The book is filled with both historical and mythical figures, all sharing the single trait of muted voice. In "The Hill Has Something to Say," the poet speculates on the buried history of Europe, the cryptic messages that a culture sends across time. In one sense, the hill is

a metaphor for this book, a repository of signs and images that speak only to that special archaeologist, the reader.

In the section titled "In the Bulrush" Dove finds worthy subjects in unlikely places and draws them from hiding. "Banneker" is another example of her flair for evoking the antebellum world of slavery, where even the free man is wrongly regarded because of his race. In the scientist Benjamin Banneker she finds sensitivity, eloquence, and intelligence, all transformed by prejudice into mere eccentricity. Banneker was the first African American man to devise an almanac and served on Thomas Jefferson's commission to lay out the city of Washington, D.C., but the same qualities that lifted him to prominence made him suspect in the eyes of white society. Dove redeems this crabbed conception of the man in an alliterative final passage that focuses attention on his vision:

> Lowering his eyes to fields
> sweet with the rot of spring, he could see
> a government's domed city
> rising from the morass and spreading
> in a spiral of lights . . .

In the final section, "Primer for the Nuclear Age," Dove includes what is one of her most impressive performances. Although she has not shown herself to be a poet of rage, she is certainly not inured to the social and political injustice she observes. Her work is a way of channeling and controlling such anger; as she says in "Primer for the Nuclear Age": "if you've/ got a heart at all, someday/ it will kill you." "Parsley," the final poem of *Museum*, summons up the rank insanity of Rafael Trujillo, dictator of the Dominican Republic, who, on October 2, 1957, ordered twenty thousand black Haitians killed because they could not pronounce the letter *r* in *perejil*, Spanish for "parsley." The poem is divided into two sections: The first is a villanelle spoken by the Haitians; the second describes General Trujillo on the day of his decision. The second section echoes many of the lines from the Haitians' speech, drawing murderer and victim together, suggesting a disturbing complicity among all parties in this episode of unfettered power. Even though Dove certainly wants to draw attention to this event, the real subject here is the lyric poet's realm—that point at which language intersects with history and actually determines its course.

Thomas and Beulah garnered the Pulitzer Prize, but it is more important for the stage it represents in Dove's poetic development. Her first two books reveal a lyric poet generally working within the bounds of her medium. The lyric poem denies time, process, change. It becomes a frozen moment, an emotion reenacted in the reading. In *Thomas and Beulah* she pushes at the limitations of the form by stringing together, "as beads on a necklace," a whole series of these lyric moments. As the poems begin to reflect upon one another, the effect is a dramatic unfolding in which the passing of time is represented, even though the sequence never establishes a conventional plot. To accomplish this end Dove creates a two-sided book: Thomas' side ("Mandolin," twenty-one poems) followed by Beulah's ("Canary in Bloom," twenty-one poems). The narrative moves from Thomas' riverboat life and the crucial death of his friend Lem to his arrival in Akron and marriage, through the birth of children, jobs, illness, and death. Beulah's part of the book then begins, moving through her parents' stormy relationship, her courtship with Thomas, marriage, pregnancy, work, and death. These two lives transpire against the historical backdrop of the great migration, the Depression, World War II, and the March on Washington; however, these events are practically the only common elements in the two sides of the story. Thomas and Beulah seem to live separate lives. Their communication with each other is implicit in the survival of the marriage itself. Throughout, Dove handles the story through exacting use of imagery and character.

Thomas emerges as a haunted man, dogged by the death of Lem, which occurs in the opening poem, "The Event." Thomas drunkenly challenges Lem to swim from the deck of the riverboat to an island in the Mississippi. Lem drowns in the attempt to reach what is probably a mirage, and Thomas is left with "a stinking circle of rags/ the half-shell mandolin." In "Courtship" he begins to woo Beulah, but the poem implies that the basis of their relationship will be the misinterpreted gesture and that Thomas' guilt has left him with a void. He casually takes a yellow silk scarf from around his neck and wraps it around her shoulders; "a gnat flies/ in his eye and she thinks/ he's crying." Thomas' gift, rather than a spontaneous transfer of warmth, is a sign of his security in his relative affluence. The show of vulnerability and emotional warmth is accidental. The lyric poet in Dove allows her to compress this range of possibility in the isolated gesture or image. Beulah's life is conveyed as a more interior affair, a process of attaining the wisdom to understand her world rather than to

resist it openly. In "The Great Palace of Versailles," Beulah's reading becomes her secret escape from the nastiness of the whites for whom she works in Charlotte's Dress Shoppe. As she lies dying in the final poem, "The Oriental Ballerina," her contemplation of the tiny figurine seems a similar invitation to fantasy, but her sensibilities have always been attuned to seeing the world as it is, as it has to be, and the poem ends in a brief flurry of realistic details and an air of acceptance; there is "no cross, just the paper kiss/ of a kleenex above the stink of camphor,/ the walls exploding with shabby tutus. . . ."

Grace Notes marks Dove's return to the purely lyric mode, but an autobiographical impulse dominates the work to an unprecedented degree. More than in any of her previous collections, the poet can be seen as actor in her own closet drama, whether as a young child learning a rather brutal lesson in the Southern black school of survival ("Crab-Boil") or as a mother groping for a way to reveal feminine mysteries to her own little girl ("After Reading *Mickey in the Night Kitchen* for the Third Time Before Bed"). The willingness to become more self-referential carries with it the danger of obscurity, the inside joke that stays inside. Dove, however, seems to open herself to a kind of scrutiny and challenge that offer no hiding place, and that assay extends to her own poetic practice. In "Dedication," a poem in the manner of Czesław Miłosz, Dove seems to question the veracity of her own technical expertise: "What are music or books if not ways/ to trap us in rumors? The freedom of fine cages!" In the wickedly ironic "Ars Poetica" she places herself on the literary chain of being with what might pass for self-deprecation. Her ambition is to make a small poem, like a ghost town, a minute speck on the "larger map of wills." "Then you can pencil me in as a hawk:/ a traveling x-marks-the-spot." Yet in the very next poem in the book, the aptly titled "Arrow," she exposes the sexism and racism of an "eminent scholar" in all of its condescending glory.

Rita Dove's distinguishing feature is her ability to turn a cold gaze on the larger world with which she has to interact as a social being and as an African American woman. That gaze is filtered through an aesthetic sensibility that regards poetry as a redemptive force, a transformational power. Her attention to the craft of poetry gives to her work a clarity, elegance, and naturalness that promise great things to come.

Other major works

NOVEL: *Through the Ivory Gate*, 1991.
SHORT FICTION: *Fifth Sunday*, 1985.

Bibliography

Dove, Rita. "Coming Home." Interview by Steven Schneider. *The Iowa Review* 19 (Fall, 1989): 112-123.

_____ . Interview by Judith Kitchen and others. *Black American Literature Forum* 20 (Fall, 1986): 227-240.

McDowell, Robert. "The Assembling Vision of Rita Dove." *Callaloo: A Black South Journal of Arts and Letters* 9 (Winter, 1986): 61-70.

Rampersad, Arnold. "The Poems of Rita Dove." *Callaloo: A Black South Journal of Arts and Letters* 9 (Winter, 1986): 52-60.

Shoptaw, John. Review of *Thomas and Beulah. Black American Literature Forum* 21 (Fall, 1987): 335-341.

PAUL LAURENCE DUNBAR

Born: Dayton, Ohio; June 27, 1872   **Died:** Dayton, Ohio; February 9, 1906

Principal poetry

   Oak and Ivy, 1893; *Majors and Minors*, 1895; *Lyrics of Lowly Life*, 1896; *Lyrics of the Hearthside*, 1899; *Lyrics of Love and Laughter*, 1903; *Lyrics of Sunshine and Shadow*, 1905; *Complete Poems*, 1913; *The Collected Poetry of Paul Laurence Dunbar*, 1993.

Other literary forms

   Paul Laurence Dunbar's achievements in fiction include four volumes of short stories and four novels. Criticism of his short fiction suggests that the stories contained in *Folks from Dixie* (1898) represent his best accomplishment in this literary form. His novels *The Uncalled* (1898) and *The Sport of the Gods* (1902) acquired more critical acclaim than his other two novels, *The Love of Landry* (1900) and *The Fanatics* (1901). Dunbar wrote an assortment of lyrics and libretti for a variety of theatrical productions. He also wrote essays for newspapers and attempted to establish a periodical of his own.

Achievements

   Dunbar's literary career was brilliant, extending roughly across two decades. He can be credited with several first-time accomplishments: He was the first to use dialect poetry as a medium for the true interpretation of African American character and psychology, and he was the first African American writer to earn national prominence. In range of style and form, Dunbar remains the most versatile of African American writers.

Biography

   Paul Laurence Dunbar was born to former slaves Joshua and Matilda J. Murphy Dunbar on June 27, 1872. He spent his early childhood in Dayton, Ohio, where he attended Central High School. Dunbar began to write at age sixteen and gained early patronage for his work, and he was introduced to the Western Association of Writers in 1892.

   The next few years of Dunbar's life found him in the presence of great African American leaders. He met Frederick Douglass, Mary Church Terrell, and Ida B. Wells at the World's Columbian Exposition in Chicago in 1893. He met W. E. B. Du Bois in 1896 and Booker T. Washington in 1897. These encounters influenced Dunbar's literary tone and perspective significantly. He blended the creative perspective of Washington with the social philosophy of Du Bois in order to present a valid scenario of African Americans after the Civil War.

   Major James B. Pond, a Dunbar enthusiast, sponsored a trip to England for the writer that extended from February to August of 1897. Upon his return to the United States, Dunbar married Alice Moore and decided to earn his living as a writer. Between 1898 and 1903, Dunbar wrote essays for newspapers and periodicals, addressing primarily the issues of racial equality and social justice in America. He attempted to establish his own journalistic voice in 1890 through a periodical that he named the *Dayton Tattler*. This effort failed.

   During the latter years of his life, Dunbar wrote lyrics, including those for the school song for Tuskegee Institute. Dunbar died in Dayton on February 9, 1906.

Analysis

   The body of poetry produced by Dunbar illustrates some of the best qualities found in lyrical verse. Writing in all the major lyrical forms—idyll, hymn, sonnet, song, ballad, ode, and elegy—Dunbar established himself as one of the most versatile poets in American literature. The more than four hundred poems written by Dunbar are varied in style and effect. It is clear, however, that his dominant aim was to create an empathetic poetic mood resulting from combinations of elements such as meter, rhyme, diction, sentence structure, characterization, repetition, imagery, and symbolism.

   Dunbar's commitment to speak to the black people of America through his verse is reflected in his dialect poetry. His *Lyrics of Love and Laughter* is not the best of his collections, but it contains some remarkable dialect verse. "A Plea" provides an example of this aspect of his reputation. Speaking of the unsettling feelings experienced by one overcome with love, Dunbar exhorts a lover's love object to "treat him nice."

I ain't don a t'ing to shame,
Lovahs all ac's jes de same:
Don't you know we ain't to blame?
  Treat me nice!

Rendering a common experience in the African American idiom, Dunbar typifies the emotionally enraptured lover as one who has no control over his behavior:

Whut a pusson gwine to do,
W'en he come a-cou'tin' you
All a-trimblin' thoo and thoo?
  Please be nice.

The diction in this poem is not pure dialect. Only those portions that describe the emotions and behavior of the lover are stated in dialect, highlighting the primary emotions and enhancing the pathetic mood, which is apparently Dunbar's principal intent. Typical of Dunbar's love lyrics, "A Plea" is rooted in the experience of a particular culture yet remains universal in its themes. Through his use of diction, meter, and stanzaic form, Dunbar captures fundamental human emotions and renders them with intensity and lyrical compassion.

Reflective lyrics form a large segment of Dunbar's poetry. Some of his best poems of this type are found in *Lyrics of Lowly Life*, including the long stanzaic poem "Ere Sleep Comes Down to Soothe the Weary Eyes." This poem utilizes one sensory impression as a focal point for the lyrical evolution in the style of Keats. The sleep motif provides an avenue through which the persona's imagination enters the realm of reflection.

Through sleep's dream the persona is able to "make the waking world a world of lies—/ of lies palpable, uncouth, forlorn." In this state of subconscious reflection, past pains are revisited as they "come thronging through the chambers of the brain." As the poem progresses, it becomes apparent that the repetitive echo of "ere sleep comes down to soothe the weary eyes" has some significance. This refrain begins and ends each stanza of the poem except the last. In addition to serving as a mood-setting device, this expression provides the channel of thought for the literary journey, which is compared with the "spirit's journeying." Dunbar's audience is thus constantly reminded of the source of his revelations.

Dunbar reveals his poetic thesis in the last stanza. He uses images from the subconscious state of life, sleep, to make a point about death. Prior to making this point, Dunbar takes the reader to the realm of reflective introspection: "So, trembling with the shock of sad surprise,/

The soul doth view its awful self alone." There is an introspective confrontation of the soul with itself, and it resolves:

When sleep comes down to seal the weary eyes,
. . . .
Ah, then, no more we heed
the sad world's cries,
Or seek to probe th' eternal mystery,
Or fret our souls at long-withheld replies.

The escape from pain and misery is death; there is no intermediary state which will eradicate that fact of life. Dunbar presents this notion with sympathy and sincerity. His metaphorical extensions, particularly those relative to the soul, are filled with compassion. The soul is torn with the world's deceit; it cries with "pangs of vague inexplicable pain." The spirit, an embodiment of the soul, forges ahead to seek truth as far as Fancy will lead. Questioning begins then, and the inner sense confronts the inner being until Truth emerges. Dunbar's presentation of the resolution is tender and gentle.

Dunbar wrote reflective lyrics in the vernacular as well. Espousing the philosophy of Divine intention. Dunbar wrote "Accountability," a poem also found in *Lyrics of Lowly Life*. In this poem, the beliefs and attitudes of the persona are revealed in familiar language.

Folks ain't got no right to
  censuah othah
    folks about dey habits;
. . . .
We is all constructed diff'ent,
  d'ain't no two of
    us de same;
. . . .
But we all fits into places dat
  no othah ones
    could fill.

Each stanza in this poem presents a thesis and develops that point. The illustrations from the natural world support a creationist viewpoint. The persona obviously accepts the notion that everything has a purpose. The Creator gave the animals their members shaped as they are for a reason and so, "Him dat giv' de squr'ls de bushtails made de bobtails fu' de rabbits." The variations in nature are by design: "Him dat built de gread big mountains hollered out de little valleys"; "Him dat made de streets an' driveways wasn't shamed to make de alley." The poet establishes these notions in three quatrains, concluding in the fourth quatrain: "When you come to think about it, how it's all planned out it's splendid./ Nuthin's done er evah happens, dout hit's somefin' dat's intended." The persona's position that Divine intention rules the world is thereby sealed.

The subjects of love and death are treated in Dunbar's lyrics of melancholy. "Yesterday and To-morrow," in *Lyrics of Sunshine and Shadow*, is one example. The mood of this poem is in the tradition of the British Romantic poets, particularly that of William Wordsworth. Dunbar treats the melancholy feelings in this poem with tenderness and simplicity. The persona expresses disappointment with the untimeliness of life's events and the uncertainties of love. This scenario intimates a bleak future.

"Yesterday and To-morrow" is developed in three compact quatrains. Each quatrain envelopes a primary emotion. The first stanza unfolds yesterday's contentment in love. The lover remembers the tender and blessed emotion of closeness with his lover: "And its gentle yieldingness/ From my soul I blessed it." The second stanza is reminiscent of the metaphysical questionings and imagery of John Donne: "Must our gold forever know/ Flames for the refining?" The lovers' emotions are compared with precious metal undergoing the fire of refinement: Their feelings of sadness are released in this cynical question.

In the third quatrain, Dunbar feeds the sad heart with more cynicism. Returning to the feelings of disappointment and uncertainty, the persona concludes: "Life was all a lyric song/ Set to tricksy meter." The persona escapes in cynicism, but the poem still ends on a hopeless note.

"Communion," which is collected in *Lyrics of the Hearthside*, is another of Dunbar's melancholy lyrics and focuses on the theme of love and death. The situation in the poem again evokes a cynical attitude, again reminiscent of Donne. The poem presents a struggle between life's memories and death. Life's memories are primarily of the existence of the love relationship, and death symbolizes its demise. This circumstance unfolds in a dramatic narrative in the style of Browning.

The first two stanzas of the poem introduce the situation, and the mood begins to evolve in stanza 3. The poet uses images from nature to create the somber mood. The "breeze of Death," for example, sweeps his lover's soul "Out into the unsounded deeps." On one hand, the Romantic theme of dominance of nature and humanity's helplessness in the face of it creeps through; on the other hand, faith in love as the superior experience resounds. The conflict between conquering Death,

symbolized in Nature, and Love creates tension in the poem. Consequently, though the breeze of Death has swept his bride away, the persona announces that "Wind nor sea may keep me from/ Soft communing with my bride." As these quatrains of iambic pentameter unfold, the poem becomes somewhat elegiac in tone.

The persona solemnly enters into reflective reminiscence in the fifth stanza and proclaims: "I shall rest my head on thee/ As I did long days of yore." Continuing in stanza 6, he announces: "I shall take thy hand in mine,/ And live o'er the olden days." Leading up to the grief-stricken pledge of eternal love, the melancholic feeling is intensified. The mourner details his impression as follows:

> Tho' the grave-door shut between,
> Still their love lights o'er me steal.
>
> I can see thee thro' my tears,
> As thro' rain we see the sun.

The comfort which comes from such memories brings a ray of light; the lover concludes:

> I shall see thee still and be
>   Thy true lover evermore,
> And thy face shall be to me
>   Dear and helpful as before.

The drama cannot end unless the persona interacts with his audience. The audience is therefore included in the philosophical conclusion: "Death may vaunt and Death may boast,/ But we laugh his pow'r to scorn." Dunbar illustrates in his lyrics an ability to overcome the causes of melancholy.

"In Summer," from *Lyrics of the Hearthside*, and "The Old Apple-Tree," from *Lyrics of Lowly Life*, are representative of Dunbar's nature lyrics. "In Summer" captures a mood of merriment that is stimulated by nature. The common individual is used as a model of one who possesses the capacity to experience this natural joy. Summer is a bright, sunny time; it is also a time for ease, as presented in the second stanza. Introducing the character of the farmer boy in stanza 3, Dunbar presents a model embodiment of the ease and merriment of summer. Amid the blades of green grass and as the breezes cool his brow, the farmer boy sings as he plows. He sings "to the dewy morn" and "to the joys of life." This behavior leads to some moralizing, to which the last three stanzas of the poem are devoted. The poet's point is made through a contrast:

O ye who toil in the town.
  And ye who moil in the mart,
Hear the artless song, and your faith made strong
  Shall renew your joy of heart.

Dunbar admonishes the reader to examine the behavior of the farm boy. Elevation of the simple, rustic life is prevalent in the writings of early British Romantic poets and postbellum African American writers alike. The admonition to reflect on the rustic life, for example, is the same advice Wordsworth gives in "The Old Cumberland Beggar." Both groups of writers agree that there are lessons to be learned through an examination of the virtues of the rustic life. In this vein, Dunbar advises: "Oh, poor were the worth of the world/ If never a song were heard." He goes further by advising all to "taunt old Care with a merry air."

The emphasis on the rustic life is also pervasive in "The Old Apple-Tree." The primary lyrical quality of the poem is that the poetic message evolves from the poet's memory and imagination. Image creation is the medium through which Dunbar works here: His predominant image, dancing in flames of ruddy light, is an orchard "wrapped in autumn's purple haze."

Dunbar creates a nature scene that provides a setting for the immortalization of the apple tree. Memory takes the persona to the scene, but imagination re-creates events and feelings. The speaket admits that it probably looks ugly "When you look the tree all over/ Unadorned by memory's glow." The tree has become old and crooked, and it bears inferior fruit. Thus, without the nostalgic recall, the tree does not appear special at all.

Utilizing the imaginative frame, the speaker designs features of the simple rustic life, features that are typically British Romantic and peculiarly Wordsworthian. The "quiet, sweet seclusion" realized as one hides under the shelter of the tree and the idle dreaming in which one engages dangling in a swing from the tree are primary among these thoughts. Most memorable to the speaker is the solitary contentment he and his sweetheart found as they courted beneath the old apple tree.

Now my gray old wife is Hallie,
  An I'm grayer still than she,
But I'll not forget our courtin'
  'Neath the old apple-tree.

The poet's ultimate purpose, to immortalize the apple tree, is fulfilled in the last stanza. The old apple tree will never lose its place in nature or its significance, for the speaker asks:

But when death does come a-callin',
  This my last request shall be,—
That they'll bury me an' Hallie
  'Neath the old apple-tree.

The union of humanity and nature at the culmination of physical life approaches a notion expressed in Wordsworth's poetry. This tree has symbolized the ultimate in goodness and universal harmony; it symbolizes the peace, contentment, and joy in the speaker's life. Here Dunbar's indebtedness to the Romantic traditions that inform his entire oeuvre is most profoundly felt.

Other major works

NOVELS: *The Uncalled*, 1898; *The Love of Landry*, 1900; *The Fanatics*, 1901; *The Sport of the Gods*, 1902.

SHORT FICTION: *Folks from Dixie*, 1898; *The Strength of Gideon and Other Stories*, 1900; *In Old Plantation Days*, 1903; *The Heart of Happy Hollow*, 1904.

Bibliography

Brawley, Benjamin, *Paul Laurence Dunbar: Poet of His People*. Port Washington, N.Y.: Kennikat Press, 1967.

Gayle, Addison, Jr. *Oak and Ivy: A Biography of Paul Laurence Dunbar*. Garden City, N.Y.: Doubleday, 1971.

Lawson, Victor. *Dunbar Critically Examined*. Washington, D.C.: Associated Publishers, 1941.

Martin, Jay, ed. *A Singer in the Dawn: Reinterpretations of Paul Laurence Dunbar*. New York: Dodd, Mead, 1975.

Okeke-Ezigbo, Emeka. "Paul Laurence Dunbar: Straightening the Record." *California Library Association Journal* 24 (1980-1981): 481-496.

Revell, Peter. *Paul Laurence Dunbar*. Boston: Twayne, 1979.

Wagner, Jean. "Paul Laurence Dunbar." In *Black Poets of the United States from Paul Laurence Dunbar to Langston Hughes*, translated by Kenneth Douglas. Urbana: University of Illinois Press, 1973.

Wiggins, Lida Keck. *The Life and Works of Paul Laurence Dunbar: Containing His Complete Poetical Works, His Best Short Stories, Numerous Anecdotes and a Complete Biography of the Famous Poet*. Nashville, Winston-Derek, 1992.

RALPH ELLISON

Born: Oklahoma City, Oklahoma; March 1, 1914   **Died:** New York, New York; April 16, 1994

Principal long fiction

Invisible Man, 1952.

Other literary forms

Ralph Ellison's reputation rests primarily on *Invisible Man*, but *Shadow and Act* (1964), a collection of nonfiction prose, established him as a major force in the critical theory of pluralism and in African American aesthetics. Arranged in three thematically unified sections, the essays, most of which appeared originally in journals such as *Antioch Review*, *Partisan Review*, and *The New Republic*, emphasize the importance of folk and popular (especially musical) contributions to the mainstream of American culture. Several of the essays from *Shadow and Act* are recognized as classics, notably "Richard Wright's Blues," "Change the Joke and Slip the Yoke," and "The World and the Jug." In addition, Ellison published several excellent short stories, including "Flying Home" and "Did You Ever Dream Lucky?" At long intervals, several sections of an unfinished work, a second novel, appeared in periodicals. A new collection of essays, *Going to the Territory*, was published in 1986.

Achievements

Ellison occupies a central position in the development of African American literature and of contemporary American fiction. He was the first African American writer to attain recognition as a full-fledged artist rather than as an intriguing exotic. Where Euro-American critics had previously, and unjustly, condescended to black American writers such as Langston Hughes, Zora Neale Hurston, and Richard Wright, most granted Ellison the respect given Euro-American contemporaries such as Norman Mailer and Saul Bellow. A 1965 *Book World* poll identifying *Invisible Man* as the most distinguished postwar American novel simply verified a consensus already reflected in the recurrence of the metaphor of invisibility in countless works by both Euro-Americans and African Americans during the 1950's and 1960's.

Within the African American tradition itself, Ellison occupies a similarly prominent position, although his mainstream acceptance generates occasional reserva-

tions among some black critics, particularly those committed to cultural nationalism. In the later decades of the twentieth century, both Euro-American and African American critics recognized Ellison's synthesis of the oral traditions of black culture and the literary traditions of both his black and his white predecessors.

Ellison's most profound achievement, his synthesis of modernist aesthetics, American Romanticism, and black folk culture, embodies the aspirations of democratic pluralists such as Walt Whitman, Mark Twain, and Langston Hughes. His vernacular modernism has earned Ellison an international reputation while exerting a major influence on the contemporary mainstream. With a reputation resting almost entirely on his first novel, Ellison's career is among the most intriguing in American literary history. He served as Honorary Consultant in American Letters to the Library of Congress from 1966 to 1972 and received the National Book Award in 1953 for *Invisible Man*, the Presidential Medal of Freedom in 1969, and the National Medal of Arts in 1985.

Biography

Despite Ralph Waldo Ellison's steadfast denial of the autobiographical elements of *Invisible Man* and his insistence on the autonomy of the individual imagination, both the specific details and the general sensibility of his work clearly derive from his experience of growing up in a Southern family in Oklahoma City, attending college in Alabama, and residing in New York City during most of his adult life. Ellison's parents, whose decision to name their son after Ralph Waldo Emerson reflects their commitment to literacy and education, moved from Southern Carolina to the comparatively progressive Oklahoma capital several years before their son's birth. Reflecting on his childhood, which was characterized by economic hardship following his father's death in 1917, Ellison emphasizes the unusual psychological freedom provided by a social structure that allowed him to interact relatively freely with both whites and blacks. Encouraged by his mother Ida, who was active in socialist politics, Ellison developed a frontier sense of a world of limitless possibility rather than the more typically Southern vision of an environment filled with dangerous oppressive forces.

During his teenage years, Ellison developed a serious interest in music, both as a trumpet player and as a composer/conductor. Oklahoma City offered access both to formal classical training and to jazz, which was a major element of the city's nightlife. The combination of Euro-American and African American influences appears to have played a major role in shaping Ellison's pluralistic sensibility. After he was graduated from high school in 1933, Ellison accepted a scholarship to the Tuskegee Institute, founded by Booker T. Washington, where he remained for three years, studying music and literature, until financial problems forced him to drop out. Although he had originally planned to finish his studies, his subsequent relocation in New York City marked a permanent departure from the South.

Arriving in the North in 1936, Ellison established contacts with black literary figures, including Langston Hughes and Richard Wright, who encouraged him to develop his knowledge of both the black literary world and Euro-American modernism, especially that of T. S. Eliot and James Joyce. Never as deeply involved in leftist politics as Wright, Ellison nevertheless began developing his literary ideas in reviews and stories published in radical magazines such as *New Masses*. In 1938, Ellison, who had previously supported himself largely as a manual laborer, worked for the Federal Writers' Project, which assigned him to collect urban folklore, providing direct contact with Northern folk culture to complement his previous knowledge of Southern folkways. Ellison's short fiction began appearing in print in the late 1930's and early 1940's. After a short term as managing editor of *Negro Quarterly* in 1942, he briefly left New York, serving in the merchant marine from 1943 to 1945. Awarded a Rosenwald Fellowship to write a novel, Ellison returned to New York and married Fanny McConnell in 1946.

Invisible Man, which took Ellison nearly seven years to write, was published in 1952, bringing him nearly instantaneous recognition as a major young writer. The novel won the National Book Award in 1953, and its reputation has continued to grow. From 1952, Ellison taught at Bard College, Rutgers University, New York University, and other institutions. In addition, he delivered public lectures, wrote essays, and worked on a second novel. Less inclined to direct political involve-ment than contemporaries such as Amiri Baraka and James Baldwin, Ellison participated in the Civil Rights movement in a relatively quiet manner. He nevertheless attracted political controversy during the rise of the African American nationalist movements in the mid-1960's.

Refusing to endorse any form of cultural or political separatism, Ellison was attacked as a European aesthetically and a reactionary politically, especially after accepting appointments to the American Institute of Arts and Letters (1964) and to the National Council on the Arts and Humanities, acts that were interpreted as support for the Johnson Administration's Vietnam policy. During the mid-1970's, however, these attacks abated as nationalist critics such as Larry Neal rose to Ellison's defense and a new generation of African American writers turned to him for aesthetic inspiration.

Retired from full-time teaching, during the 1980's Ellison continued to work on his second novel, which was delayed both by his own perfectionism and by events such as a house fire that destroyed part of the manuscript during the 1960's. He died on April 16, 1994, in New York.

Analysis

Invisible Man ranks among the finest achievements in contemporary American fiction and as one of the most complete statements of the African American experience. The underlying theme in Ellison's writing is the search for identity, a quest he finds at the heart of American life. His best novel depicts this quest for self-definition in the lives of not only African Americans but also the nation as a whole. The book stands as a single, complex vision of the universal search for identity.

A masterwork of American pluralism, *Invisible Man* insists on the integrity of individual vocabulary and racial heritage while encouraging a radically democratic acceptance of diverse experiences. Ellison asserts this vision through the voice of an unnamed first-person narrator who is at once heir to the rich African American oral culture and a self-conscious artist who, like T. S. Eliot and James Joyce, exploits the full potential of his written medium. Intimating the potential cooperation between folk and artistic consciousness, Ellison confronts the pressures that discourage both individual integrity and cultural pluralism. The narrator of *Invisible Man* introduces Ellison's central metaphor for the situation of the individual in Western culture in the first paragraph: "I am invisible, understand, simply because people refuse to see me." As the novel develops, Ellison extends this metaphor: Just as a man can be rendered invisible by the willful failure of others to acknowledge his presence, so by taking refuge in the seductive but ultimately specious security of socially acceptable roles, he can fail to see himself, fail to define his own identity. Ellison envisions the escape from this dilemma as a multifaceted quest demanding heightened social, psychological, and cultural awareness.

In many ways a classic *Künstlerroman*, the main body of the novel traces the protagonist from his childhood in the deep South through a brief stay at college and then to the North, where he confronts the American economic, political, and racial systems. This movement parallels what Robert B. Stepto in *From Behind the Veil* (1979) calls the "narrative of ascent," a constituting pattern of black culture. With roots in the fugitive slave narratives of the nineteenth century, the narrative of ascent follows its protagonist from physical or psychological bondage in the South through a sequence of symbolic confrontations with social structures to a limited freedom, usually in the North.

This freedom demands from the protagonist a "literacy" that enables him to create and understand both written and social experiences in the terms of the dominant Euro-American culture. Merging the narrative of ascent with the *Künstlerroman*, which also culminates with the hero's mastery of literacy (seen in creative terms), *Invisible Man* focuses on writing as an act of both personal and cultural significance. Similarly, Ellison employs what Stepto calls the "narrative of immersion" to stress the realistic sources and implications of his hero's imaginative development. The narrative of immersion returns the "literate" hero to an understanding of the culture he symbolically left behind during the ascent. Incorporating this pattern in *Invisible Man*, Ellison emphasizes the protagonist's links with the African American community and the rich folk traditions that provide him with much of his sensibility and establish his potential as a conscious artist.

Two interrelated progressions, one social and the other psychological, guide the narrative development. The social pattern, essentially that of the narrative of ascent, closely reflects the historical experience of the African American community as it shifts from rural Southern to urban Northern settings. Starting in the deep South, the invisible man first experiences invisibility as a result of casual but vicious racial oppression. His unwilling participation in the "battle royal" underscores the psychological and physical humiliation vis-

ited upon Southern blacks. Ostensibly present to deliver a speech to a white community group, the invisible man is instead forced to engage in a massive free-for-all with other blacks, to scramble for money on an electrified rug, and to confront a naked white dancer who, like the boys, has been rendered invisible by the white men's blindness. Escaping his hometown to attend a black college, the invisible man again experiences humiliation when he violates the unstated rules of the Southern system—this time imposed by blacks rather than whites—by showing the college's liberal Northern benefactor, Mr. Norton, the poverty of the black community. As a result, the black college president, Dr. Bledsoe, expels the invisible man. Having experienced invisibility in relation to both blacks and whites and still essentially illiterate in social terms, the invisible man travels north, following the countless Southern blacks involved in the "Great Migration."

Arriving in New York, the invisible man first feels a sense of exhilaration resulting from the absence of overt Southern pressures. Ellison reveals the emptiness of this freedom, however, stressing the indirect and insidious nature of social power in the North. The invisible man's experience at Liberty Paints, clearly intended as a parable of black American involvement in the American economic system, emphasizes the underlying similarity of Northern and Southern social structures. On arrival at Liberty Paints, the invisible man is assigned to mix a white paint used for government monuments. Labeled "optic white," the grayish paint turns white only when the invisible man adds a drop of black liquid. The scene suggests the relationship between government and industry, which relies on black labor. More important, however, it points to the underlying source of racial blindness/invisibility: the white need for a black "other" to support a sense of identity. White becomes white only when compared to black.

The symbolic indirection of the scene encourages the reader, like the invisible man, to realize that social oppression in the North operates less directly than that in the South; government buildings replace rednecks at the battle royal. Unable to mix the paint properly, a desirable "failure" intimating his future as a subversive artist, the invisible man discovers that the underlying structure of the economic system differs little from that of slavery.

Ellison creates a much more complex political vision when the invisible man moves to Harlem. The political alternatives available in Harlem range from the Marxism of the "Brotherhood" (loosely based on the American Communist party of the late 1930's) to the black nationalism of Ras the Exhorter (loosely based on Marcus Garvey's Pan-Africanist movement of the 1920's). The Brotherhood promises complete equality for blacks and at first encourages the invisible man to develop the oratorical talent ridiculed at the battle royal. As his effectiveness increases, however, the invisible man finds the Brotherhood demanding that his speeches conform to its "scientific analysis" of the black community's needs.

Neither political option has fulfilled the invisible man's search for identity—both, in fact, reinforce the invisible man's feelings of invisibility by refusing to see basic aspects of his character. After a riot breaks out in Harlem, the invisible man escapes into an underground burrow. Separated from the social structures, which have changed their façade but not their nature, the invisible man begins the arduous process of reconstructing his vision of America while symbolically subverting the social system by stealing electricity to light the 1,369 light bulbs on the walls of the burrow and to power the record players blasting out the pluralistic jazz of Louis Armstrong.

The second major progression in *Invisible Man* focuses on the narrator's psychological development. As he gradually gains an understanding of the social forces that oppress him, the invisible man simultaneously discovers the complexity of his own personality. Throughout the central narrative, he accepts various definitions of himself, mostly from external sources. Ultimately, however, all definitions that demand he repress or deny aspects of himself simply reinforce his sense of invisibility. Only by abandoning limiting definitions altogether, Ellison implies, can the invisible man attain the psychological integrity necessary for any effective social action.

Ellison rejects both acceptance of external definitions and abandonment of all definitions as viable means of attaining literacy. Ultimately, he endorses the full recognition and measured acceptance of the experience, historical and personal, that shapes the individual. The invisible man must therefore learn to accept his African American heritage, the primary imperative of the narrative of immersion. Initially, he attempts to repudiate or to distance himself from the aspects of the heritage associated with stereotyped roles. He shatters and attempts to throw away the "darky bank" he finds in his room at Mary Rambro's. His failure to lose the pieces of the bank reflects Ellison's conviction that the stereotypes, major aspects of the black social experi-

ence, cannot simply be ignored or forgotten. As an element shaping individual consciousness, they must be incorporated into, without being allowed to dominate, the integrated individual identity. Symbolically, in a scene in which the invisible man meets a yam vendor shortly after his arrival in Harlem, Ellison warns that one's racial heritage alone cannot provide a full sense of identity. After first recoiling from yams as a stereotypic Southern food, the invisible man eats one, sparking a momentary epiphany of racial pride. When he indulges the feelings and buys another yam, however, he finds it frost-bitten at the center.

The invisible man's heritage, placed in proper perspective, provides the crucial hints concerning social literacy and psychological identity that allow him to come provisionally to terms with his environment. Speaking on his deathbed, the invisible man's grandfather offers cryptic advice that lies near the essence of Ellison's overall vision: "Live with your head in the lion's mouth. I want you to overcome 'em with yeses, undermine 'em with grins, agree 'em to death and destruction, let 'em swoller you till they vomit or bust wide open." Similarly, an ostensibly insane veteran echoes the grandfather's advice, adding an explicit endorsement of the Machiavellian potential of masking:

> Play the game, but don't believe in it—that much you owe yourself. Even if it lands you in a strait jacket or a padded cell. Play the game, but play it your own way—part of the time at least. Play the game, but raise the ante, my boy. Learn how it operates, learn how *you* operate.... that game has been analyzed, put down in books. But down here they've forgotten to take care of the books and that's your opportunity. You're hidden right out in the open—that is, you would be if you only realized it. They wouldn't see you because they don't expect you to know anything.

The vet understands the "game" of Euro-American culture, while the grandfather directly expresses the internally focused wisdom of the African American community.

The invisible man's quest leads him to a synthesis between these forms of literacy in his ultimate pluralistic vision. Although he at first fails to comprehend the subversive potential of his position, the invisible man gradually learns the rules of the game and accepts the necessity of the indirect action recommended by his grandfather. Following his escape into the underground burrow, he contemplates his grandfather's advice from a position of increased experience and self-knowledge.

Ellison's revolution seeks to realize a pluralist ideal,

a true democracy recognizing the complex experience and human potential of every individual. Far from presenting his protagonist as a member of an intrinsically superior cultural elite, Ellison underscores his shared humanity in the concluding line: "Who knows but that, on the lower frequencies, I speak for you?"

Other major works

NONFICTION: *The Writer's Experience*, 1964 (with Karl Shapiro); *Shadow and Act*, 1964; *Going to the Territory*, 1986.

Bibliography

Benston, Kimberly, ed. *Speaking for You: The Vision of Ralph Ellison*. Washington, D.C.: Howard University Press, 1987.

Bloom, Harold, ed. *Ralph Ellison*. New York: Chelsea House, 1986.

Nadel, Alan. *Invisible Criticism: Ralph Ellison and the American Canon*. Iowa City: University of Iowa Press, 1988.

O'Meally, Robert G. *The Craft of Ralph Ellison*. Cambridge, Mass.: Harvard University Press, 1980.

_____ , ed. *New Essays on "Invisible Man."* New York: Cambridge University Press, 1988.

Trimmer, Joseph F., ed. *A Casebook on Ralph Ellison's "Invisible Man."* New York: Thomas Y. Crowell, 1972.

ERNEST J. GAINES

Born: Oscar, Louisiana; January 15, 1933

Principal long fiction

Catherine Carmier, 1964; *Of Love and Dust*, 1967; *The Autobiography of Miss Jane Pittman*, 1971; *In My Father's House*, 1978; *A Gathering of Old Men*, 1983; *A Lesson Before Dying*, 1993.

Other literary forms

Ernest J. Gaines published a collection of short stories, *Bloodline*, in 1968. One story from that collection, "A Long Day in November," was published separately in a children's edition in 1971.

Achievements

For thirty years, Gaines has been a serious and committed writer of fiction. He has always worked slowly, frustratingly slowly to his admirers, but that is because of his great devotion to and respect for the craft of fiction. His five novels are all set in rural Louisiana, north of Baton Rouge: Gaines, like William Faulkner, has created a single world in which all of his works are centered. Even though Gaines has written during a time of great racial turmoil and unrest, he has resisted becoming involved in political movements, believing that he can best serve the cause of art and humanity by devoting himself to perfecting his craft. This does not mean that he has remained detached from political realities. Taken together, his novels cover the period of 1865 to 1980, reflecting the social movements that have affected black Americans during that time. Gaines has said again and again, however, that he is primarily interested in people; certainly it is in his depiction of people that his greatest strength lies. His focus is on the universals of life: love, pride, pity, hatred. He aspires thus not to have an immediate political impact with his writing but to move people emotionally. His supreme achievement in this regard is *The Autobiography of Miss Jane Pittman*. With its publication—and with the highly acclaimed 1974 television film based on the novel—Gaines achieved the recognition he had long deserved. In recognition of his achievements over the course of three decades, he was awarded a 1993 MacArthur grant. *A Lesson Before Dying* won the National Book Critics Circle Award for fiction in 1994.

Biography

From birth until age fifteen, Ernest J. Gaines lived in rural Louisiana with his parents. As a boy, he often worked in the plantation fields and spent much of his spare time with his aunt, Miss Augusteen Jefferson. He moved to Vallejo, California, in 1948 to live with his mother and stepfather, and he attended high school and junior college there before serving in the Army. After his military service, he earned a B.A. degree at San Francisco State College. On the basis of some stories written while he was a student there, he was awarded the Wallace Stegner Creative Writing Fellowship in 1958 for graduate study at Stanford University. Since that time, he has lived, impermanently, by his own testimony, in or near San Francisco, believing that living elsewhere enables him to gain a perspective on his Southern material that would be unavailable to him were he to live in the South full-time. By making yearly trips back to Louisiana, where he holds a visiting professorship in creative writing at the University of Southwestern Louisiana in Lafayette, he retains contact with his native region.

Analysis

While Gaines has physically left the South, he has never left emotionally. His ties remain with the South, and his works remain rooted there. When he first began reading seriously, Gaines gravitated toward those writers who wrote about the soil and the people who lived close to it, among them William Faulkner, John Steinbeck, Willa Cather, and Ivan Turgenev. Gaines was disappointed to discover that few black writers had dealt with the black rural Southern experience. Thus, Gaines began his career with the conscious desire to fill a void.

This fact helps explain why his novels always concentrate on rural settings and on the "folk" who inhabit them. One of the great strengths of his work is voice; the sound of the voice telling the story is central to its meaning. Among his works, *Of Love and Dust, The Autobiography of Miss Jane Pittman*, and all the stories in *Bloodline* are told in the first person by rural black characters. The voices of the storytellers, especially Miss Jane's, express the perspective not only of the individual speakers but also in some sense of the entire black community, and it is the community on which Gaines most often focuses his attention.

Several themes recur in the Gaines canon, and together they create the total effect of his work. Generally, he deals with the relationship between past and present and the possibility of change, both individual and social. Using a broad historical canvas in his works, especially in *The Autobiography of Miss Jane Pittman*, Gaines treats the changes in race relations over time, but he is most interested in people, in whether and how they change as individuals. The issue of determinism and free will is therefore a central question in his work. Gaines has been very interested in and influenced by Greek tragedy, and in his fiction, a strain of environmental determinism is evident. In his works prior to and including *The Autobiography of Miss Jane Pittman*, a growing freedom on the part of his black characters can be seen, but the tension between fate and free will always underlies his works.

The Autobiography of Miss Jane Pittman is among Gaines's major contributions to American literature. Except for an introduction written by "the editor," it is told entirely in the first person by Miss Jane and covers approximately one hundred years, from the Civil War to the Civil Rights movement of the 1960's. Basing the novel on stories he heard while a child around his aunt, Augusteen Jefferson, and using the format of oral history, Gaines created a "folk autobiography" that tells the story of people who are not in the history books. While the work is the story of Miss Jane, she is merely an observer for a substantial portion of its length, and the story becomes that of black Americans from slavery to the present. Gaines's mastery of voice is especially important here, for Miss Jane's voice is the voice of her people.

From the very beginning of the novel Miss Jane is courageous and in the best sense of the word "enduring." In her character and story, many of the dichotomies that run through Gaines's work are unified. The differing roles of men and women are important elements in the book. Women preserve and sustain—a role symbolized by Miss Jane's longevity. Men, by contrast, feel the need to assert their manhood in an active way. Three black men are especially important in Miss Jane's life, beginning with Ned, whom she rears from childhood after his mother is killed and who becomes in

effect a "son" to her. Ned is a rebel, but his rebellion is concentrated in the political arena. Returning to Louisiana after the start of the twentieth century, he attempts to lead his people to freedom. Though he is murdered by whites, his legacy and memory are carried on by Miss Jane and the people in the community. Later, in the 1960's, Jimmy Aaron, another young man who tries to encourage his people to take effective political action, appears. Again the members of the older generation hang back, fearful of change and danger, but after Jimmy is killed, Jane unites old and young, past and present by her determination to go to Bayonne and carry on Jimmy's work. The third man in Jane's life is Joe Pittman, her husband. A horsebreaker, he is committed to asserting and proving his manhood through his work. Although he too dies, killed by a wild horse he was determined to break, Jane in her understanding and love of him, as well as in her affection for all her men, bridges the gap between man and woman. In her character, the opposites of old and young, past and present, and man and woman are reconciled.

Miss Jane's strength is finally the strength of the past, but it is directed toward the future. When Jimmy returns, he tells the people that he is nothing without their strength, referring not only to their physical numbers but also to the strength of their character as it has been forged by all the hardships they have undergone through history. Even though the people seem weak and fearful, the example of Miss Jane shows that they need not be. They can shake off the chains of bondage and determinism, assert their free spirit through direct action, and effect change. The change has only begun by the conclusion of *The Autobiography of Miss Jane Pittman*, but the pride and dignity of Miss Jane and all those she represents suggest that ultimately they will prevail.

A Gathering of Old Men is also set in Gaines's characteristic rural setting and continues the optimism with which *The Autobiography of Miss Jane Pittman* ended. Once again, it is up to the old among the black community to lead the struggle for change, this time primarily because there are no young men left to lead. All of them have escaped to towns and cities that promise more of a future than does rural Louisiana.

In this small corner of Louisiana, however, Cajuns are encroaching on the land, replacing men with machines and even threatening to plow up the old graveyard where generations of blacks have been buried. When Beau Boutan, son of the powerful Cajun Fix Boutan, is shot to death in the quarters of Marshall plantation, the old black men who have lived there all their lives are faced with one last chance to stand up and be men. They stand up for the sake of Matthu, the only one of them who ever stood up before and thus the most logical suspect in the murder. They prove one last time that free action is possible when eighteen or more of them, all in their seventies and eighties, arm themselves with rifles of the same gauge used in the shooting and face down the white sheriff, Mapes, each in his turn claiming to be the killer.

As shut off as the quarters are from the rest of the world, it is easy to forget that the events of the novel take place as recently as the late 1970's. Beau Boutan's brother Gil, however, represents the change that has been taking place in the world outside Marshall. He has achieved gridiron fame at Louisiana State University by working side by side with Cal, a young black man. Youth confronts age when Gil returns home and tries to persuade his father not to ride in revenge against Beau's murderer. He convinces his father to let the law find and punish Beau's murderer, but he pays a heavy price when his father disowns him. He cannot stop other young Cajuns, led by Luke Will, who are not willing to change but would rather cling to the vigilantism of the Old South.

In spite of their dignity and pride, the old men at Marshall risk looking rather silly because after all these years they stand ready for a battle that seems destined never to take place once Fix Boutan decides not to ride on Marshall. Sheriff Mapes taunts them with the knowledge that they have waited too late to take a stand. Ironically, they are ultimately able to maintain their dignity and reveal their growth in freedom by standing up to the one person who has been most valiant in her efforts to help them: Candy Marshall, niece of the landowner. In her effort to protect Matthu, who was largely responsible for rearing her after her parents died, Candy has gone so far as to try to take credit for the murder herself. What she fails to realize is that the days are long past when black men need the protection of a white woman. She is stunned to realize that she too has been living in the past and has been guilty of treating grown black men like children.

The novel does eventually end with a gunfight, because Luke Will and his men refuse to let the murder of a white man by a black one go unavenged. It is fitting that the two men who fall in the battle are Luke Will, the one who was most resistant to change, and Charlie Biggs, the real murderer. Charlie's body is treated like a sacred relic as each member of the black community,

from the oldest to the youngest, touches it, hoping that some of the courage that Charlie found late in life will rub off. Apparently, it already has.

In *A Lesson Before Dying*, Gaines approaches the theme of determinism and free will from the personal level. His novel is again set in Louisiana, this time in 1948. Jefferson, a barely literate young black man, was an unfortunate bystander at the murder of a white man. He has been charged with murder, and the prosecution seeks the death penalty. His attorney argues that since Jefferson is closer to an animal than a man and cannot possibly be held accountable for his actions, he should be spared the death penalty. This defense fails, and Jefferson is sentenced to die in the electric chair.

Miss Emma, Jefferson's elderly godmother, enlists the aid of her friend Tante Lou to help Jefferson gain knowledge of his own self-worth before he dies. They approach Lou's nephew, Grand Wiggins, to help Jefferson discover his dignity and humanity. Grant is a university-educated teacher who has returned to the black quarter, where he was raised, to teach the children who live there. His personal doubts about whether it is possible to teach the children of the quarter, much less a man condemned to die, make him reluctant to help the two elderly women. They use all of their powers to persuade Grant, and then turn their attention to the white officials whose approval they need in order for Grant to enter the prison. Here Gaines returns to his theme of the role played by black women in the South. The women, after years of service to whites, possess both humility and strength, knowing how to extract favors according to the unspoken rules of race relations in this environment.

Once they gain visiting rights for Grant, the process of self-discovery begins, but it cannot change the law. Jefferson must die in the electric chair on the designated day. At Grant's suggestion, Jefferson has kept a diary, and its message affirms the success of the process he and Grant have gone through together: "tell them im a man."

Only when Miss Emma and Tante Lou persuade Jefferson and Grant to rise above their self-doubt is each man able to rise above his own situation and find hope. Jefferson goes to his death knowing what a man is; Grant regains the hope that he can make a difference in other people's lives.

Gaines's novels depict in the world of Southern blacks the core concerns of his fictional world: concern for the common people, reverence for the everyday, love of the land, and the power of dignity and self-knowledge. He does not create simplistic formulas for change in the racially divided South, but he does hope these virtues for personal change will also slowly enact social change. In Gaines's fictional South, the relation-ship between past and present and the hope that both personal and social change are possible stems from the pride and dignity that inform his characters.

Other major works

SHORT FICTION: *Bloodline*, 1968; *A Long Day in November*, 1971.

Bibliography

Gaines, Ernest J. "A Conversation with Ernest Gaines." Interview by Ruth Laney. *Southern Review* 10 (Winter, 1974): 1-14.

_____ . *Porch Talk with Ernest Gaines: Conversations on the Writer's Craft*. By Marcia Gaudet and Carl Wooton. Baton Rouge: Louisiana State University Press, 1990.

_____ . "Talking with Ernest J. Gaines." Interview by Monica Gaudet and Carl Wooton. *Callaloo* 11 (Spring, 1988): 229-243.

_____ . "A Very Big Order: Reconstructing Identity." *Southern Review* 26 (Spring, 1990): 245-253.

Hudson, Theodore R. "Ernest J. Gaines." In *The History of Southern Literature*, edited by Louis D. Rubin, Jr., et al. Chapel Hill: University of North Carolina Press, 1985.

Shelton, Frank W. "*In My Father's House:* Ernest Gaines After Jane Pittman." *Southern Review* 17 (Spring, 1981): 340-345.

Stoelting, Winifred L. "Human Dignity and Pride in the Novels of Ernest Gaines." *College Language Association Journal* 14 (March, 1971): 340-358.

LANGSTON HUGHES

Born: Joplin, Missouri; February 1, 1902

Died: New York, New York; May 22, 1967

Principal poetry

The Weary Blues, 1926; *Fine Clothes to the Jew*, 1927; *Dear Lovely Death*, 1931; *The Negro Mother*, 1931; *The Dream Keeper and Other Poems*, 1932; *Scottsboro Limited*, 1932; *A New Song*, 1938; *Shakespeare in Harlem*, 1942; *Jim Crow's Last Stand*, 1943; *Lament for Dark Peoples*, 1944; *Fields of Wonder*, 1947; *One Way Ticket*, 1949; *Montage of a Dream Deferred*, 1951; *Selected Poems of Langston Hughes*, 1959; *Ask Your Mama: Or, 12 Moods for Jazz*, 1961; *The Panther and the Lash: Or, Poems of Our Times*, 1967; *The Collected Poems of Langston Hughes*, 1994.

Other literary forms

Langston Hughes wrote, translated, edited, or collaborated on works in a number of other genres. He wrote two novels, volumes of short stories, translations, biographies of African Americans, and histories for both young people and adults. In addition he published two autobiographies. A volume of his correspondence appeared in 1980.

Hughes wrote the libretti for several operas, plays, a screenplay, radio scripts, and song lyrics. His most famous contribution to musical theater, however, was the lyrics he wrote for Kurt Weill and Elmer Rice's musical adaptation of Rice's *Street Scene* (1947).

Over the years, Hughes also wrote several nonfiction articles, focused mainly on his role as a poet and his love of African American music—jazz, gospel, and the blues. Perhaps his most important article was his first: "The Negro Artist and the Racial Mountain," published in *The Nation* on June 23, 1926, in defense of the idea of an African American literary style, voice, and subject matter. An anthology of his works was published in 1958.

Achievements

All Hughes's works illustrate the depth of his commitment to a celebration of African American life in all its forms and make immediately evident the reason why he has been proclaimed "The Poet Laureate of Black America." As a young poet he won prizes in contests sponsored by *The Crisis* and *Opportunity*, and his first two volumes of poetry, *The Weary Blues* and *Fine Clothes to the Jew*, won critical acclaim. Hughes also won a Harmon Gold Award for his novel *Not Without Laughter*, as well as a Rosenwald Fund Fellowship in the early 1930's, which enabled him to make his first cross-country reading tour.

Hughes's stature as a humorist grew from his creation of Jesse B. Semple, also known as Simple, a Harlem barstool philosopher in the tradition of American folk humor ranging from Davy Crockett to Mr. Dooley. Hughes wrote about Simple in columns published in the *Chicago Defender*, begun in the 1940's and continuing into the 1960's. His Simple columns also appeared in the *New York Post* between 1962 and 1965. Publication of his five books of Simple sketches increased the readership of that sage of Harlem with his views on life in white America.

Although Hughes never had any one big seller, his efforts in so many fields of literary endeavor earned for him the admiration and respect of readers in all walks of life. Certainly, too, Hughes is a major poetic figure of his time and perhaps the best African American poet.

Biography

James Mercer Langston Hughes (the first two names were soon dropped) was born in Joplin, Missouri, on February 1, 1902. His parents, James Nathaniel and Carrie Mercer Langston Hughes, separated when Hughes was young. Hughes began writing poetry during his grammar school days in Lincoln, Illinois. While attending Cleveland's Central High School (1916-1920), Hughes wrote his first short story, "Mary Winosky," and published poems in the school's literary publications. The first national publication of his work came in 1921, when *The Crisis* published "The Negro Speaks of Rivers." The poem had been written while Hughes was taking a train on his way to see his father in Mexico City, a visit that the young man dreaded making. His hatred for his father, fueled by his father's contempt for poor people who could not make anything of themselves, actually led to Hughes's being hospitalized briefly in 1919.

Hughes's father did, however, send his son to Columbia University in 1921. Although Hughes did not stay at Columbia, his experiences in Harlem laid the groundwork for his later love affair with the city within a city. Equally important to Hughes's later work was the time he spent at sea and abroad during this period of his life. His exposure to American blues and jazz players in Paris nightclubs and his experiences in Europe and especially Africa, although brief, provided a rich source of material that he used over the next decades in his writing.

The years between 1919 and 1929 have been variously referred to as the Harlem Renaissance, the New Negro Renaissance, and the Harlem Awakening. Whatever they are called, they were years of rich productivity within the black artistic community, and Hughes was an important element in that renaissance. While working as a busboy in the Wardman Park Hotel in Washington, D.C., in 1925, Hughes showed some of his poems ("Jazzonia," "Negro Dancers," and "The Weary Blues") to Vachel Lindsay, who read them during one of his performances that same evening. The next day, Hughes was presented to the local press as "the busboy poet." With that introduction, and with the aid of people such as writer Carl Van Vechten and Walter White of the National Association for the Advancement of Colored People (NAACP), Hughes's popularity began to grow. He published *The Weary Blues* in 1926 and entered Lincoln University in Pennsylvania, where he completed his college education. The 1920's also saw the publication of his second volume of poems, *Fine Clothes to the Jew*, and the completion of his first novel, *Not Without Laughter*.

During much of the early 1930's, Hughes traveled abroad. He went to Cuba and Haiti during 1931-1932 and joined a group of young writers and students from Harlem on a film-making trip to Russia in 1932-1933. Publishing articles in Russian journals enabled him to extend his own travels in the Far East; he also began to write short stories during that time. By 1934, he had written the fourteen stories that he included in *The Ways of White Folks*. During the mid-1930's, several of Hughes's plays were produced. He also started the Harlem Suitcase Theatre (1938), the New Negro Theatre in Los Angeles (1939), and the Skyloft Players of Chicago (1941).

When America entered World War II, Hughes produced material for the war effort, ranging from "Defense Bond Blues" to articles on black participation in the war. In addition, during the 1940's, he began work on his translations of the poetry of Nicolás Guillén, wrote essays for such diverse magazines as the *Saturday Review of Literature* and *Negro Digest*, wrote the lyrics for *Street Scene*, and published three volumes of poetry: *Shakespeare in Harlem*, *Fields of Wonder*, and *One Way Ticket*.

Also in the 1940's, Hughes "discovered" Jesse B. Semple. Drawing inspiration from a conversation he had in a bar with a worker from a New Jersey war plant, Hughes developed the framework for his Simple stories. He combined his own authorial voice, the voice of Simple's learned interrogator (eventually named Boyd), and the voice of Simple himself to weave a mixture of folk humor that has direct ties back to the "old southwest" humor of Mark Twain and his contemporaries.

The next decades saw continued production of poetry and other writing by Hughes. He continued his public readings, often accompanied by piano and/or jazz orchestra—a prototype of the Beat poets. His second volume of autobiography, *I Wonder as I Wander*, was published in 1956, and *The Langston Hughes Reader*, an extensive collection of his work in several genres, appeared two years later. The last two volumes of his poetry, *Ask Your Mama* and *The Panther and the Lash*, continued his experimentation with incorporating jazz and folk elements in his poetry. Hughes spent the last years of his life living and working in Harlem, where he died on May 22, 1967.

Analysis

The work of Hughes explores the humor and the pathos, the exhilaration and the despair, of African American life in ways that are sometimes conventional and sometimes unique. He explored the blues as a poetic form, and he peopled his poems with Harlem dancers, as well as with a black mother trying to explain her life to her son. He worked with images of dreams and of "dreams deferred"; he looked at life in the middle of America's busiest black city and at the life of the sea and of exploration and discovery. Always, too, Hughes examined the paradox of being black in mostly white America, of being not quite free in the land of freedom.

Hughes's first collection of poetry, *The Weary Blues*, contains samples of many of the poetic styles and themes of his poetry in general. The collection begins with a celebration of blackness ("Proem") and ends with an affirmation of the African American's growing sense of purpose and equality ("Epilogue: I, Too, Sing

America"). In between, there are poems that sing of Harlem cabaret life and poems that sing the blues. Some of the nonblues poems also sing of a troubled life, as well as an occasional burst of joy. Here, too, are the sea poems drawn from Hughes's traveling experiences. All in all, the sparkle of a love of life in these poems was that which caught the attention of many early reviewers.

The titles of some of the poems about cabaret life suggest their subject: "Jazzonia," "Negro Dancers," "The Cat and the Saxophone (2 a.m.)," and "Harlem Night Club." "The Cat and the Saxophone (2 a.m.)" is especially intriguing because it intersperses a conversation between two "jive" lovers with the first chorus of "Everybody Loves My Baby," producing the effect of a jazz chorus within the song's rhythmic framework.

Part of the controversy that flared in the black community during the Harlem Renaissance involved whether an artist should present the "low-life" elements or the more conventional middle-class elements in African American life. Hughes definitely leaned toward the former as the richer, more exciting to portray in his poetry.

Because the blues tradition is more tied to the common folk than to the middle-class, Hughes's interest in the possibilities of using the blues style in his poetry is not surprising. He took the standard three-line blues stanza and made it a six-line stanza to develop a more familiar poetic form; the repetition common in the first and second lines in the blues becomes a repetition of the first/second and third/fourth lines in Hughes's poems. As in the traditional blues, Hughes varies the wording in the repeated lines—adding, deleting, or changing words. For example, here is a stanza from "Blues Fantasy":

> My man's done left me,
> Chile, he's gone away.
> My good man's left me,
> Babe, he's gone away.
> Now the cryin' blues
> Haunts me night and day.

Often exclamation points are added to suggest more nearly the effect of the sung blues.

There are not as many blues poems in this first collection as there are in later ones such as *Fine Clothes to the Jew* and *Shakespeare in Harlem*. (The latter contains a marvelous seven-poem effort entitled "Seven Moments of Love," which Hughes subtitled "An Un-Sonnet Sequence in Blues.") The title poem of his first collection, "The Weary Blues," is an interesting vari-

ation because it has a frame for the blues that sets up the song sung by a blues musician. The poet recalls the performance of a blues singer/pianist "on Lenox Avenue the other night" and describes the man's playing and singing. Later, the singer goes home to bed, "while the Weary Blues echoed through his head." Over the years, Hughes wrote a substantial number of blues poems and poems dealing with jazz, reflecting clearly his love for the music that is at the heart of the black experience.

Some of the poems in *The Weary Blues* are simple lyrics. They are tinged with sadness ("A Black Pierrot") and with traditional poetic declarations of the beauty of a loved one ("Ardella"). The sea poems are also, by and large, more traditional than experimental. Again, their titles reflect their subject matter: "Water-Front Streets," "Port Town," "Sea Calm," "Caribbean Sunset," and "Seascape."

A few of these early poems reflect the gentle but insistent protest that runs through Hughes's poems; they question the treatment of African Americans and search for a connection with the motherland, Africa. The last section of the book is entitled "Our Land," and the first poem in the section, "Our Land: Poem for a Decorative Panel," explores the idea that blacks should live in a land of warmth and joy instead of in a land where "life is cold" and "birds are grey." Other poems in the section include "Lament for Dark Peoples," "Disillusion," and "Danse Africaine." Perhaps the most poignant poem in the book is also in this last section: "Mother to Son." The poem is a monologue in dialect in which a mother encourages her son to continue the struggle she has carried on, which she likens to climbing a rough, twisting staircase: "Life for me ain't been no crystal stair./ It's had tacks in it . . . And places with no carpet on the floor—/ Bare." The collection's final poem, "Epilogue" ("I, Too, Sing America"), raises the hope that some day equality will truly be reached in America for the "darker brother" who is forced "to eat in the kitchen/ When company comes." Taken together, the poems of *The Weary Blues* make an extraordinary first volume of poetry and reveal the range of Hughes's style and subject matter.

The next two principal volumes of poetry, *Fine Clothes to the Jew* and *The Dream Keeper and Other Poems*, present more of Hughes's blues poems (the latter volume is primarily in that genre) and more poems centering on Harlem's night life. The final two volumes, *Ask Your Mama* and *The Panther and the Lash*, continue the experiment of combining musical elements with poetry and offer some of Hughes's strongest protest poetry.

Ask Your Mama is dedicated to "Louis Armstrong— the greatest horn blower of them all." In an introductory note, Hughes explains that "the traditional folk melody of the 'Hesitation Blues' is the leitmotif for this poem." The collection was designed to be read or sung with jazz accompaniment, "with room for spontaneous jazz improvisation, particularly between verses, when the voice pauses." Hughes includes suggestions for music to accompany the poetry. Sometimes the instructions are open ("delicate lieder on piano"), and sometimes they are more direct ("suddenly the drums roll like thunder as the music ends sonorously"). There are also suggestions for specific songs to be used, including "Dixie" ("impishly"), "When the Saints Go Marchin' In," and "The Battle Hymn of the Republic." As a final aid, Hughes includes at the end of his collection "Liner Notes" for, as he says, "the Poetically Unhep."

Throughout, the poems in *Ask Your Mama* run the current of protest against "the shadow" of racism that falls over the lives of the earth's darker peoples. Shadows frequently occur as images and symbols, suggesting the fear and the sense of vague existence created by living in oppression. "Show Fare, Please" summarizes the essence of the poet's feeling of being left out because he has not got "show fare," but it also suggests that "the show" may be all illusion anyway. Not all the poems are so stark; the humor of Hughes's earlier work is still very much in evidence. In "Is It True," for example, Hughes notes that "everybody thinks that Negroes have the *most* fun, but, of course, secretly hopes they do not—although curious to find out if they do."

The poetry of Langston Hughes is charged with life and love, even when it cries out against the injustice of the world. He was a poet who loved life and loved his heritage. More than any other black American writer, he captured the essence of the complexity of a life that mixes laughter and tears, joy and frustration, and still manages to sing and dance with the spirit of humanity.

Other major works

NOVELS: *Not Without Laughter*, 1930; *Tambourines to Glory*, 1958.

SHORT FICTION: *The Ways of White Folks*, 1934; *Simple Speaks His Mind*, 1950; *Laughing to Keep from Crying*, 1952; *Simple Takes a Wife*, 1953; *Simple Stakes a Claim*, 1957; *The Best of Simple*, 1961; *Something in Common and Other Stories*, 1963; *Simple's Uncle Sam*, 1965.

PLAYS: *Mulatto*, 1935; *Little Ham*, 1936; *Don't You Want to Be Free?*, 1938; *Freedom's Plow*, 1943; *Simply Heavenly*, 1957; *Black Nativity*, 1961; *Tambourines to Glory*, 1963; *Five Plays*, 1963; *Jerico-Jim Crow*, 1964; *The Prodigal Son*, 1965.

NONFICTION: *The Big Sea: An Autobiography*, 1940; *The First Book of Negroes*, 1952; *The First Book of Rhythms*, 1954; *Famous American Negroes*, 1954; *Famous Negro Music Makers*, 1955; *The First Book of Jazz*, 1955; *The First Book of the West Indies*, 1955; *A Pictorial History of the Negro in America*, 1956 (with Milton Meltzer); *I Wonder as I Wander: An Autobiographical Journey*, 1956; *Famous Negro Heroes of America*, 1958; *The First Book of Africa*, 1960; *Fight for Freedom: The Story of the NAACP*, 1962; *Black Magic: A Pictorial History of the Negro in American Entertainment*, 1967 (with Meltzer); *Arna Bontemps–Langston Hughes Letters*, 1980.

TRANSLATIONS: *Masters of the Dew*, 1947; *Cuba Libre*, 1948; *Gypsy Ballads*, 1951; *Selected Poems of Gabriela Mistral*, 1957.

MISCELLANEOUS: *Troubled Island*, c. 1930 (opera libretto); *Popo and Fijina: Children of Haiti*, 1932 (with Arna Bontemps); *Street Scene*, 1947 (lyrics); *The Langston Hughes Reader*, 1958; *Simply Heavenly*, c. 1959 (opera libretto).

EDITED TEXT: *The Poetry of the Negro, 1746-1949*, 1949 (with Arna Bontemps); *The Book of Negro Folklore*, 1959 (with Bontemps); *New Negro Poets: U.S.A.*, 1964; *The Book of Negro Humor*, 1966; *The Best Short Stories by Negro Writers: An Anthology from 1899 to the Present*, 1967.

Bibliography

Berry, Faith. *Langston Hughes: Before and Beyond Harlem*. Westport, Conn.: Lawrence Hill, 1983.

Bloom, Harold, ed. *Langston Hughes*. New York: Chelsea House, 1989.

Emanuel, James A. *Langston Hughes*. Boston: Twayne, 1967.

Gates, Henry Louis, Jr., and K. A. Appiah. *Langston Hughes: Critical Perspectives Past and Present*. New York: Amistad, 1993.

Miller, R. Baxter. *The Art and Imagination of Langston Hughes*. Lexington: University Press of Kentucky, 1989.

Mullen, Edward J., ed. *Critical Essays on Langston Hughes*. Boston: G. K. Hall, 1986.

Onwuchekwa, Jemie. *Langston Hughes: An Introduction to the Poetry*. New York: Columbia University Press, 1976.

Rampersad, Arnold. *The Life of Langston Hughes, 1902-1941: I, Too, Sing America*. Vol. 1. New York: Oxford University Press, 1986.

ZORA NEALE HURSTON

Born: Eatonville, Florida; January 7, 1891

Died: Fort Pierce, Florida; January 28, 1960

Principal long fiction

Jonah's Gourd Vine, 1934; *Their Eyes Were Watching God*, 1937; *Moses, Man of the Mountain*, 1939; *Seraph on the Suwanee*, 1948.

Other literary forms

Zora Neale Hurston produced two collections of folklore, *Mules and Men* (1935) and *Tell My Horse* (1938), and an autobiography, *Dust Tracks on a Road* (1942). Hurston also published plays, short stories, and essays in anthologies and in magazines as diverse as *Opportunity*, and *Journal of Negro History*, the *Saturday Evening Post*, *Journal of American Folklore*, and *American Legion Magazine*. Finally, she wrote several articles and reviews for such newspapers as the *New York Herald Tribune* and the *Pittsburgh Courier*.

Achievements

Hurston was the best and most prolific African American woman writer of the 1930's. All of her novels were highly praised. Even so, Hurston never made more than one thousand dollars in royalties on even her most successful works, and when she died in 1960, she was penniless and forgotten. Hurston's career testifies to the difficulties of a black woman writing for a mainstream white audience whose appreciation was usually superficial and racist and for a black audience whose responses to her work were, of necessity, highly politicized.

Hurston achieved recognition at a time when, as Langston Hughes declared, "the Negro was in vogue." The Harlem Renaissance, the African American literary and cultural movement of the 1920's, created an interracial audience for her stories and plays. Enthusiasm for her work extended through the 1930's, although that decade also marked the beginning of critical attacks. Hurston did not portray blacks as victims, stunted by a racist society. Such a view, she believed, implies that black life is only a defensive reaction to white racism. Black and left-wing critics, however, complained that her unwillingness to represent the oppression of blacks and her focus, instead, on an autonomous, unresentful black folk culture served to perpetuate minstrel stereotypes and thus fueled white racism. The radical, racial protest literature of Richard Wright, one of Hurston's strongest critics, became the model for black literature in the 1940's, and publishers on the lookout for protest works showed less and less interest in Hurston's manuscripts. Yet when she did speak out against American racism and imperialism, her work was often censored. Her autobiography, published in 1942, as well as a number of her stories and articles were tailored by editors to please white audiences. Caught between the attacks of black critics and the censorship of the white publishing industry, Hurston floundered, struggling through the 1940's and 1950's, to find other subjects. She largely dropped out of public view in the 1950's, though she continued to publish magazine and newspaper articles. The African American and feminist political and cultural movements of the 1960's and 1970's provided the impetus for the rediscovery and renewed appreciation of her work.

Biography

Zora Neale Hurston was born on January 7, 1891. Her family lived in the all-black Florida town of Eatonville, in an eight-room house with a five-acre garden. Her father, the Reverend John Hurston, mayor of Eatonville for three terms and moderator of the South Florida Baptist Association, wanted to temper his daughter's high spirits, but her intelligent and forceful mother, Lucy Potts Hurston, encouraged her to "jump at de sun." When Hurston was about nine, her mother died. That event and her father's rapid remarriage to a woman his daughter did not like prematurely ended Hurston's childhood. In the next few years, she lived only intermittently at home, spending some time at a school in Jacksonville and some time with relatives. Her father withdrew all financial support during this period, forcing her to commence what was to be a lifelong struggle to make her own living.

When Hurston was fourteen, she took a job as a wardrobe girl to a repertory company touring the South. Hurston left the troupe in Baltimore eighteen months later and finished high school there at Morgan Academy. She went on to study part-time at Howard University in 1918, taking jobs as a manicurist, a waitress, and a maid in order to support herself. At Howard, her literary talents began to emerge. She was admitted to a campus literary club formed by Alain Locke, a Howard professor and one of the forces behind the Harlem Renaissance. Locke brought Hurston to the attention of Charles S. Johnson, another key promoter of the Harlem Renaissance. Editor of *Opportunity: A Journal of Negro Life*, he published one of her stories and encouraged her to enter the literary contest sponsored by his magazine.

With several manuscripts but little money, Hurston moved to New York City in 1925, hoping to make a career of her writing. Her success in that year's *Opportunity* contest—she received prizes for a play and a story—won her the patronage of Fanny Hurst and a scholarship to complete her education at Barnard College. She studied anthropology there under Franz Boas, leading a seemingly schizophrenic life in the next two years as an eccentric, iconoclastic artist of the Harlem Renaissance on the one hand and a budding, scholarly social scientist on the other.

The common ground linking these seemingly disparate parts of Hurston's life was her interest in black folk culture. Beginning in 1927 and extending through the 1930's, she made several trips to collect black folklore in the South and in the Bahamas, Haiti, and Jamaica. Collecting trips were costly, however, as was the time to write up their results. Charlotte Osgood Mason, a wealthy domineering white patron to a number of African-American artists, supported some of that work, as did the Association for the Study of Negro Life and History and the Guggenheim Foundation. Hurston also worked intermittently during the 1930's as a drama teacher at Bethune Cookman College in Florida and at North Carolina College, as a drama coach for the Works Progress Administration (WPA) Federal Theatre Project in New York, and as an editor for the Federal Writers' Project in Florida.

Mules and Men and several scholarly and popular articles on folklore were the products of Hurston's collecting trips in the late 1920's and early 1930's. In 1938, she published *Tell My Horse*, the result of trips to Haiti and Jamaica to study hoodoo. As a creative writer, Hurston, devised other outlets for her folk materials. Her plays, short stories, and first three novels make use of folklore. She also presented folk materials in theatrical revues, but even though the productions were enthu-

siastically received, she could never generate enough backing to finance commercially successful long-term showings.

Hurston's intense interest in black folklore prevented her from sustaining either of her two marriages. She could not reconcile the competing claims of love and work. She married Herbert Sheen, a medical student, in 1927 but separated from him a few months later. They were divorced in 1931. She married Albert Price III in 1939, and they too parted less than a year later.

In the 1940's, Hurston lost her enthusiasm for writing about black folk culture. She wrote her autobiography and in 1948 published *Seraph on the Suwanee*, a work that turns away from black folk culture entirely. The last decade of her life took a downward turn. Falsely accused of committing sodomy with a young boy, Hurston, depressed, dropped out of public view. Through the 1950's, she lived in Florida, struggling for economic survival. She barely managed to support herself by writing newspaper and magazine articles, many of which expressed her increasing political conservatism, and by working as a maid, a substitute teacher, and a librarian. In 1959, she suffered a stroke. Too ill to nurse herself, she was forced to enter a welfare home. She died there on January 28, 1960.

Analysis

For much of her career, Hurston was dedicated to the presentation of African American folk culture. She introduced readers to hoodoo, folktales, lying contests, spirituals, the blues, sermons, children's games, riddles, playing the dozens, and, in general, a highly metaphoric folk idiom. Although she represented black folk culture in several genres, Hurston was drawn to the novel form because it could convey folklore as communal behavior. Hurston knew that much of the unconscious artistry of folklore appears in the gestures and tones in which it is expressed and that it gains much of its meaning in performance. Even *Mules and Men*, the folklore collection she completed just before embarking on her first novel (although it was published after *Jonah's Gourd Vine*), "novelizes" what could have been an anthology of disconnected folk materials. By inventing a narrator who witnesses, even participates in the performance of folk traditions, she combated the inevitable distortion of an oral culture by its textual documentation.

Hurston's motives for presenting black folklore were, in part, political. She wanted to refute contemporary claims that African Americans lacked a distinct culture of their own. Her novels depict the unconscious creativity of the African American proletariat or folk. They represent community members participating in a highly expressive communication system that taught them to survive racial oppression and, moreover, to respect themselves and their community. At the beginning of Hurston's second novel, for example, the community's members are sitting on porches. "Mules and other brutes had occupied their skins" all day, but now it is night, work is over, and they can talk and feel "powerful and human" again: "They became lords of sounds and lesser things. They passed nations through their mouths. They sat in judgment." By showing the richness and the healthy influence of black folk culture, Hurston hoped not only to defeat racist attitudes but also to encourage racial pride among blacks. Why should African Americans wish to imitate a white bourgeoisie? The "Negro lowest down" had a richer culture.

Hurston also had a psychological motive for presenting black folk culture. She drew the folk materials for her novels from the rural Southern black life she had known as a child and subsequently recorded in folklore collecting trips in the late 1920's and 1930's. She had fond memories of her childhood in the all-black town of Eatonville, where she did not experience poverty or racism. In her autobiographical writings, she suggests that she did not even know that she was "black" until she left Eatonville. Finally, in Eatonville, she had a close relationship with and a strong advocate in her mother. In representing the rich culture of black rural Southerners, she was also evoking a happier personal past.

Hurston knew that black folk culture was composed of brilliant adaptations of African culture to American life. She admired the ingenuity of these adaptations but worried about their preservation. Would a sterile, materialistic white world ultimately absorb blacks, destroying the folk culture they had developed? Her first two novels demonstrate the disturbing influence of white America on black folkways.

Jonah's Gourd Vine portrays the tragic experience of a black preacher caught between black cultural values and the values imposed by his white-influenced church. The novel charts the life of John Pearson, laborer, foreman, and carpenter, who discovers that he has an extraordinary talent for preaching. With his linguistic skills and his wife Lucy's wise counsel, he becomes pastor of the large church Zion Hope and, ultimately, moderator of a Florida Baptist convention. His sexual promiscuity, however, eventually destroys his marriage and his career.

Though Pearson's verbal skills make him a success while his promiscuity ruins him, the novel shows that both his linguistic gifts and his sexual vitality are part of the same cultural heritage. His sexual conduct is pagan and so is his preaching. In praying, according to the narrator, it was as if he "rolled his African drum up to the altar, and called his Congo Gods by Christian names." Both aspects of his cultural heritage speak through him. Indeed, they speak through all members of the African American community, if most intensely through John. A key moment early in the novel, when John crosses over Big Creek, marks the symbolic beginning of his life and shows the double cultural heritage he brings to it. John heads down to the Creek, "singing a new song and stomping the beats." He makes up "some words to go with the drums of the Creek," with the animal noises in the woods, and with the hound dog's cry. He begins to think about the girls living on the other side of Big Creek: "John almost trumpeted exultantly at the new sun. He breathed lustily. He stripped and carried his clothes across, then recrossed and plunged into the swift water and breasted strongly over."

To understand why two expressions of the same heritage have such different effects on John's life, one has to turn to the community to which he belongs. Members of his congregation subscribe to differing views of the spiritual life. The view most often endorsed by the novel emerges from the folk culture. As Larry Neal, one of Hurston's best critics, explains, that view belongs to "a formerly enslaved communal society, non-Christian in background," which does not strictly dichotomize body and soul. The other view comes out of a white culture. It is "more rigid, being a blend of Puritan concepts and the fire-and-brimstone imagery of the white evangelical tradition." That view insists that John, as a preacher, exercise self-restraint. The cultural conflict over spirituality pervades his congregation. While the deacons, whom Hurston often portrays satirically, pressure him to stop preaching, he still has some loyal supporters among his parishioners.

Pearson ultimately falls. His sexual conduct destroys his marriage and leads to an unhappy remarriage with one of his mistresses, Hattie Tyson. He is finally forced to stop preaching at Zion Hope. Divorced from Hattie, he moves to another town, where he meets and marries Sally Lovelace, a woman much like Lucy. With her support, he returns to preaching. On a visit to a friend, however, he is tempted by a young prostitute and, to his dismay, succumbs. Although he has wanted to be faithful to his new wife, he will always be a pagan preacher, spirit and flesh. Fleeing back to Sally, he is killed when a train strikes his car.

In its presentation of folklore and its complex representation of cultural conflict, *Jonah's Gourd Vine* is a brilliant first novel, although Hurston does not always make her argument sufficiently clear. It was not until she wrote her next novel, *Their Eyes Were Watching God*, that she learned to control point of view and presented a solution to the problem of white influences on black culture.

The life of Janie Crawford, the heroine of *Their Eyes Were Watching God*, is shaped by bourgeois values—white in origin. She finds love and self-identity only by rejecting that life and becoming a wholehearted participant in black folk culture. Her grandmother directs Janie's entrance into adulthood. Born into slavery, the older woman hopes to find protection and materialistic comforts for Janie in a marriage to the property-owning Logan Killicks. Janie, who has grown up in a different generation, does not share her grandmother's values. When she finds she cannot love her husband, she runs off with Jody Stark, who is on his way to Eatonville, where he hopes to become a "big voice," an appropriate phrase for life in a community that highly values verbal ability. Jody becomes that "big voice" as mayor of the town, owner of the general store, and head of the post office. Stark lives both a bourgeois and a folk life in Eatonville. He constructs a big house—the kind white people have—but wanders out to the porch of the general store whenever he wants to enjoy the perpetual storytelling that takes place there. Even though Janie has demonstrated a talent for oratory, however, he will not let her join these sessions. "He didn't," the narrator suggests, "want her talking after such trashy people."

For several years, Janie has no voice in the community or in her private life. One day, after Stark insults her in front of customers in the store, however, she speaks out and, playing the dozens, insults his manhood. The insult causes an irreconcilable break between them.

After Jody's death, Janie is courted by Tea Cake Woods, a laborer with little money. Though many of her neighbors disapprove of the match, Janie marries him. The marriage lowers her social status but frees her from her submissive female role, from her shadow existence. Refusing to use her money, Tea Cake takes her down to the Everglades, where they become migrant workers. She picks beans with him in the fields, and he helps her prepare their dinners. With Tea Cake, she also enters into the folk culture of the Everglades, and that more than anything else enables her to shed her former submissive identity. Workers show up at their house every night to sing, dance, gamble, and, above all, to talk, like the folks in Eatonville on the front porch of the general store. Janie learns how to tell "big stories" from listening to the others, and she is encouraged to do so.

This happy phase of Janie's life ends tragically as she and Tea Cake attempt to escape a hurricane and the ensuing flood. Although Tea Cake dies, she retains her strong self-identity and returns to Eatonville, self-reliant and wise. Tea Cake, she knows, will live on in her thoughts and feelings—and in her words. She tells her story to her friend Pheoby—this storytelling event frames the novel—and allows Pheoby to bring it to the other members of the community. As the story enters the community's oral culture, it will influence it beneficially.

Janie does not find happiness until she gives up a life governed by white values and enters into the verbal ceremonies of black folk culture. Loving celebrations of a separate black folklife were Hurston's effective political weapon; racial pride was one of her great gifts to American literature.

Other major works

SHORT FICTION: *Spunk: The Selected Short Stories of Zora Neale Hurston*, 1985.

NONFICTION: *Mules and Men*, 1935; *Tell My Horse*, 1938; *Dust Tracks on a Road*, 1942; *The Sanctified Church*, 1981.

MISCELLANEOUS: *I Love Myself When I Am Laughing . . . and Then Again When I Am Looking Mean and Impressive: A Zora Neale Hurston Reader*, 1979.

Bibliography

Gates, Henry Louis, Jr. *The Signifying Monkey: A Theory of Afro-American Literary Criticism*. New York: Oxford University Press, 1988.

Gates, Henry Louis, Jr., and K. A. Appiah, eds. *Zora Neale Hurston: Critical Perspectives Past and Present*. New York: Amistad, 1993.

Hemenway, Robert. *Zora Neale Hurston*. Urbana: University of Illinois Press, 1977.

Howard, Lillie P., ed. *Alice Walker and Zora Neale Hurston: The Common Bond*. Westport, Conn.: Greenwood Press, 1993.

——————. *Zora Neale Hurston*. Boston: Twayne, 1980.

Johnson, Barbara. *A World of Difference*. Baltimore: The Johns Hopkins University Press, 1987.

Washington, Mary Helen. *Invented Lives: Narratives of Black Women, 1860-1960*. Garden City, N.Y.: Anchor Press, 1987.

Willis, Susan. *Specifying*. Madison: University of Wisconsin Press, 1987.

CHARLES JOHNSON

Born: Evanston, Illinois; April 23, 1948

Principal long fiction
Faith and the Good Thing, 1974; *Oxherding Tale*, 1982; *Middle Passage*, 1990.

Other literary forms

Charles Johnson has published more than one thousand satirical comic drawings and two books of socially relevant cartoons, *Black Humor* (1970) and *Half-Past Nation Time* (1972). Two of the eight short stories in *The Sorcerer's Apprentice* (1986) are award winners: "Popper's Disease" (receiving the 1983 *Callaloo* Creative Writing Award) and "China" (receiving the 1984 Pushcart Prize Outstanding Writer citation); the highly acclaimed "Exchange Value" appeared in an anthology of the best American short stories of 1982.

Among Johnson's documentary drama and his screenplays are the award-winning *Me, Myself, Maybe* (a 1982 Public Broadcasting System *Up and Coming* episode), one of the first scripts to deal with the issue of the married African American woman's process of self-determination.

Johnson has also published *Being and Race: Black Writing Since 1970* (1988), a controversial critical analysis and winner of the 1989 Governors Award for Literature, the product of Johnson's twenty-year exploration into the makings of black fiction.

Achievements

With several international editions of his novels as well as numerous grants and awards and professional and public recognition of his affirmative philosophical approach to the chaotic dualities of the Western world, Johnson's profound belief in the inexhaustible capacities of humankind is unquestionable. He has been the recipient of a 1977 Rockefeller Foundation Grant, a 1979 National Endowment for the Arts Creative Writing Fellowship, and a 1988 Guggenheim Fellowship. His screenplay *Booker* alone received four awards: against strong network competition, the 1985 Writers Guild Award for outstanding children's show script; the distinguished 1985-1987 Prix Jeunesse (International Youth Prize); the 1984 Black Film Maker's Festival Award; and the 1984 National Education Film Festival Award for Best Film in the social studies category. In addition, *Oxherding Tale* was given the 1983 Governors

Award for Literature, and *The Sorcerer's Apprentice* was one of the 1987 final nominees for the prestigious PEN/Faulkner Award. In 1989, Johnson was named by a University of California study as one of the ten best American short-story writers. In 1990, his *Middle Passage* was honored with a National Book Award.

Biography

In 1948, Charles Richard Johnson was born to Ruby Elizabeth (Jackson) and Benjamin Lee Johnson of Evanston, Illinois. Both parents had emigrated from the South, specifically Georgia and North Carolina. Johnson's mother, an only child (as is Johnson himself), had wanted to be a schoolteacher but could not because of her health. Instead, she pursued her artistic and aesthetic passions in the Johnson home. His father's education was cut short by the Depression, a time when all able-bodied males worked in the fields.

Johnson describes his early years as a "benign upbringing" in a progressive town of unlocked doors and around-the-clock safety. Schools had been integrated by the time Johnson became a student; therefore, he did not encounter serious racism during his childhood or adolescence. His first two short stories, "Man Beneath Rags" and "50 Cards 50" (which he also illustrated), as well as many cartoons (one award-winning), were published at Evanston Township High School, then one of the best high schools in the country. While in high school, Johnson began to work with Laurence Lariar, a cartoonist and mystery writer. In 1965, he sold his first drawing to a Chicago magazine's catalog for illustrated magic tricks. From 1965 to 1973, Johnson sold more than one thousand drawings to major magazines.

After high school graduation, Johnson had planned to attend a small art school rather than a four-year college. Nevertheless, as the first person in his extended family to attend college, he felt some obligation to fulfill his parents' hopes. The concern, combined with his art teacher's recommendation that he attend a four-year college for practical reasons, was enough to motivate Johnson to register at Southern Illinois University at Carbondale as a journalism major (with a compelling interest in philosophy). A cartoonist for the *Chicago Tribune* from 1969 to 1970, Johnson wrote and aired fifty-two fifteen-minute PBS episodes of *Charlie's Pad*, a how-to show on cartooning in 1970.

During his senior year in college, Johnson began writing novels. From 1970 to 1972, he wrote six; three are naturalistic, while three are in the style of the Black Arts movement. Although his fourth novel was accepted for publication, Johnson withdrew it after talking with John Gardner about the implications of precipitate first publication. All six apprentice novels were filed, unread, in a drawer. Johnson credits Gardner's tutelage on *Faith and the Good Thing* with saving him six additional years of mistakes.

In 1973, Johnson was awarded his master's degree in philosophy from Southern Illinois University. Following three years of doctoral work at the State University of New York at Stony Brook, Johnson began teaching at the University of Washington as well as serving as fiction editor of the *Seattle Review*. Under a 1977-1978 Rockefeller Foundation Grant, he joined the WGBH New Television Workshop as writer-in-residence. In 1982, he became a staff writer and producer for the last ten episodes of KQED's *Up and Coming* series.

From 1985 to 1987, Johnson worked on the text for *Being and Race: Black Writing Since 1970*, a project he began while guest lecturing for the University of Delaware. His 1983 draft of the first two chapters in *Middle Passage* came quickly, but Johnson worked on the novel sporadically from 1983 to 1987 before finally giving it his full attention for nine months. The *Los Angeles Times* began publishing his monthly reviews in 1987.

Johnson was director of the University of Washington's Creative Writing Program for three years (1987-1990). On September 21, 1990, he was awarded an endowed chair, the first Pollock Professorship in Creative Writing at the University of Washington.

Johnson was married to Joan New in 1970. The couple have two children: Malik, a son born in 1975, and a daughter, Elizabeth, born in 1981. His life is chronicled in Joan Walkinshaw's PBS documentary "Spirit of Place," which aired in Seattle.

Analysis

Johnson's fictional world contains an assortment of African American characters who are forced to examine the nature of self and who must repeatedly confront major philosophical issues. Before they can attain self-identification, however, they must come to terms with their environment and social surroundings. This issue, the question of black American identity, is the heart of Johnson's prose.

Johnson constructs fictional universes that elucidate integral life experiences in the universal search for personal identity. Even though Johnson has dedicated himself to the evolution of "a genuinely systematic philosophical black American literature" and most frequently creates his *Lebenswelt* (life-world) within a black context, he sees the racial details as qualifiers of more universal questions. Moreover, the multiplicity of consciousness embodied by his characters seeks to strip the preconceptions from his readers so that they may "re-experience the world with unsealed vision." Consequently, the unrelenting integrity of his fictional vision resolutely reaffirms humanity's potential to live in a world without duality and in the process also reveals Johnson's own indefatigable regard for the unfathomable, moment-by-moment mystery of humankind.

Written from the fall of 1972 to the early summer of 1973 under the tutelage of John Gardner, *Faith and the Good Thing* is the metaphysical journey of eighteen-year-old Faith Cross, who believes that she is following her mother's deathbed instructions and the werewitch Swamp Woman's advice by searching the external world for the "Good Thing." This quest for the key that will release her and everyone else from servitude leads from Hatten County, Georgia, to Chicago, Illinois, and home again. Despite limitations inherent in the narrative form itself, occasional lapses in viewpoint, and infrequent verbal artifice, Johnson has created a magical novel of legendary characters and metaphysical import.

The diverse characters who people Faith's life enrich her explorations on both ordinary and extraordinary levels of existence, yet none can lead her to her Good Thing. Faith's mystical odyssey, remembered with relish by a third-person narrator addressing his listeners "children," commits every individual to his own search and, through reflection, to the potential alteration of individual consciousness. Despite identifiable elements of naturalism, romanticism, allegory, the *Bildungsroman*, and black folktales, of far greater importance is that *Faith and the Good Thing* creates its own genre of philosophical fiction in which the metaphysical and the real are integrated into a healing totality of being.

Oxherding Tale, inspired by Eastern artist Kakuan-Shien's "Ten Oxherding Pictures," is Andrew Hawkins' rite of passage, an often-humorous, metaphysical search for self through encounters that culminate in his non-dualistic understanding of himself and the world. The narrator, born to the master's wife and the master's butler as the fruit of a comic one-night adventure, sees himself as belonging to neither the fields nor the house. Although Andrew lives with his stepmother and his father (recently demoted to herder), George and Mattie Hawkins, Master Polkinghorne arranges his classical education with an eccentric Eastern scholar. An excellent student, Andrew nevertheless expresses his recognition of the dualism when he protests that he can speak in Latin more effectively than in his own dialect. As Andrew opens his mind to the learning of the ages, George Hawkins becomes progressively more paranoid and nationalistic, This delicate counterbalance is sustained throughout the novel until, at the end, the assimilated Andrew learns that his father was shot to death as an escaped slave.

At twenty, Andrew wishes to marry the Cripplegate plantation seamstress, Minty. Instead, he is sold to Flo Hatfield, a lonely woman who considers her eleven former husbands subhuman and who has the reputation of sexually using each male slave until, discarding him to the mines or to his death, she replaces him with another. Believing that he is earning the funds for his own, his family's, and Minty's manumission, Andrew cooperates. He finds himself quickly satiated, however, with the orgiastic physical pleasures Flo demands to conceal her psychic lifelessness.

Andrew proceeds to seek out Reb, the Allmuseri coffinmaker in whose Buddhist voice he finds comfort, friendship, and enlightenment. Flo's opposite, Reb (neither detached nor attached) operates not from pleasure but from duty, acting without ulterior motives simply because something needs to be done. Together, the two escape Flo's sentence to her mines along with Bannon the Soulcatcher, a bounty hunter, with Andrew posing as William Harris, a white teacher, and Reb posing as his gentleman's gentleman. When Reb decides to leave Spartanburg for Chicago because of Bannon, Andrew, emotionally attached to the daughter of the town doctor, decides that Reb's path is not appropriate for him to follow. Instead, his dharma (Eastern soul-sustaining law of conduct) is to be a homemaker married to Peggy.

The final chapter, "Moksha," like the last of Kakuan-Shien's ten pictures, reveals the absolute integration between self and universe. "Moksha" is the Hindu concept of ultimate realization, perpetual liberation, beyond dualities, of self with the Great Spirit. In an illegal slave auction, the mulatto Andrew discovers and buys his dying first love, Minty. He, Peggy, and Dr. Undercliff unite to ease her transition from this world. Thus, the three move beyond self to *arete*, "doing beautifully what needs to be done," and begin the process of healing their world. In *Oxherding Tale*, Johnson offers the experience of affirmation and renewal. Through the first-person universal voice of Andrew Hawkins, he constructs a tightly interwoven, well-honed portrait of self-actualization. Once again, the search does not belong solely to Johnson's characters; the search belongs to everyone who chooses to free himself of "self-inflicted segregation from the Whole."

Johnson deliberately depersonalized his third novel's working title, "Rutherford's Travels," to *Middle Passage*, a multiple literary allusion, to "emphasize the historical event rather than the character" and to enhance the novel's provocative content. Johnson had already used members of the Allmuseri, a mystical African tribe reputed to be the origin of the human race, in *Oxherding Tale*, as well as in two short stories, yet never before had he so masterfully drawn the portrait of this compelling tribe of Zen sorcerers.

Recently manumitted Rutherford Calhoun, a land-lubbing twenty-three-year-old picaro, stows away aboard the slave ship *Republic* in order to avoid a marriage forced by his prospective bride. Discovered but allowed to remain as chef's helper by the dwarflike captain, Ebenezer Falcon, the first-person universal narrator candidly records human brutality during the forty-one-day voyage to Bangalang for forty captive Allmuseri and their living god. Later revealed as a duty assigned by the suicidal Falcon, Calhoun's log becomes a primary tool by which he processes his responses to his shipmates and to the ship's adventures.

Following an eerie storm, the Allmuseri revolt and capture the ship. Yet, this tribe believes that each individual is responsible for the creation of his own universe and that even the most minute action has eternal repercussions. Therefore, that human death was involved in their freedom is a source of great sorrow, particularly for their leader, Ngonyama. Despite ceremonies of atonement, the *Republic* sinks, aided by a storm and the Allmuseri renegade Diamelo.

Of captors and captives, only five survive until the *Juno*, a floating pleasure palace, rescues them: Rutherford Calhoun, his friend Josiah Squibb, and three Allmuseri children including Rutherford's female tribal ward, Baleka. On board *Juno* is Isadora Bailey, Rutherford's forceful fiancé, now scheduled to marry an underworld figure who profits by betraying his race. Instead, a transformed Rutherford convinces the Créole gangster that marrying Isadora would not be in his best interest; now Rutherford can marry Isadora himself.

Against a backdrop of sea adventure, the poignancy of the characters' startling self-revelations becomes even more deeply moving. Falcon, the remorseless captain to whom human life has no value other than the price he can pocket, collects his treasures to fulfill his dead mother's dream. The first mate, Peter Cringle, who responds from his heart to others' victimization, escapes his wealthy family's mistreatment of him by offering his body as food for the *Republic*'s last survivors. Nathaniel Meadows, who murdered his own family, is so fiercely loyal to Falcon that he conditions the ship's dogs to attack those persons he believes most likely to lead a mutiny. Conversely, Diamelo, the Allmuseri insurrectionist, is so spiritually consumed by his own anger that he blinds himself to the good of his people and destroys them. Yet Ngonyama, grieving over the loss of his tribe's metaphysical connectedness to the Whole, is able to heal Rutherford before lashing himself to the helm in propitiation for the deaths that his tribe's freedom has cost.

Rutherford, self-proclaimed liar and petty thief, finds that instead of hungering for new sensory experiences, he is finally content to experience the present with acceptance and gratitude. Faced with material choices, such as those having to do with food or bed linens, he can no longer comprehend their relevance. Instead of taking, he seeks opportunities for sharing himself without expectations and in universal love. He has taken full possession of his life. He no longer needs; he simply responds.

Charles Johnson's innate belief in the essential goodness of humankind and his intuitive grasp of the metaphysical empower him to create living fiction with the potential to alter human consciousness. Employing a precise awareness of human motivation, Johnson structures his writing nonlinearly to evince tantalizing pieces of the human mystery, but he withholds consummate revelation until the metaphysical world of philosophical fiction surrounding his characters is fully realized.

Other major works

SHORT FICTION: *The Sorcerer's Apprentice*, 1986.
TELEPLAYS: *Charlie Smith and the Fritter Tree*, 1978; *Me, Myself, Maybe*, 1982; *Booker*, 1984.
NONFICTION: *Being and Race: Black Writing Since 1970*, 1988.
MISCELLANEOUS: *Black Humor*, 1970; *Half-Past Nation Time*, 1972.

Bibliography

Davis, Arthur P. "Novels of the New Black Renaissance, 1960-1977: A Thematic Survey." *CLA (College Language Association) Journal* 21 (June, 1978): 457-491.

Harris, Norman. "The Black Universe in Contemporary Afro-American Fiction." *CLA (College Language Association) Journal* 30 (September, 1986): 1-13.

Johnson, Charles. Interview by Nicholas O'Connell. In *At the Field's End: Interviews with Twenty Pacific Northwest Writers*. Seattle: Madrona, 1987.

_____ . "Reflections on Film, Philosophy, and Fiction." Interview by Ken McCullough. *Callaloo* 1 (October, 1978): 118-128.

Olderman, Raymond M. "American Fiction 1974-1976: The People Who Fell to Earth." *Contemporary Literature* 19 (Autumn, 1978): 497-527.

TERRY McMILLAN

Born: Port Huron, Michigan; October 18, 1951

Principal long fiction

Mama, 1987; *Disappearing Acts*, 1989; *Waiting to Exhale*, 1992.

Other literary forms

Terry McMillan edited a collection of short stories by African American writers in 1990. *Breaking Ice: An Anthology of Contemporary African-American Fiction* brought the attention of critics and of the public to fifty-seven outstanding African American authors, many of them previously unpublished or relatively unknown.

Achievements

McMillan's meteoric rise to fame and fortune has been largely dependent on her own efforts. The year after *Mama* was published, she received a fellowship from the National Endowment for the Arts. Although full acceptance by the American literary establishment has been slow to arrive, she has won praise from novelist Ishmael Reed, her college mentor, and noted playwright Ntozake Shange, and such reviewers as novelist Valerie Sayers have called her one of the outstanding talents of her generation. McMillan is admired for her realism, her accurate use of language, her gift for comedy, her skill in creating character, and her understanding of contemporary African American women. She is also given much of credit for developing a new reading public among middle-class African Americans, who in McMillan have found someone who writes brilliantly both for them and about them.

Biography

Terry McMillan was born on October 18, 1951, in Port Huron, Michigan. Her father, Edward Lewis McMillan, was a sanitation worker; her mother, Madeline Tillman McMillan, performed domestic work or held jobs in various factories. The family was always hard-pressed financially, but after Madeline divorced her alcoholic, abusive husband, their life became even more difficult. As the oldest of five children, Terry had to help support the family. Fortunately, one of her jobs was in a public library; it was there she discovered that African Americans, like white Americans, could write books and get them published.

When Terry was seventeen, she went to Los Angeles, got a secretarial job, and began taking courses at Los Angeles City College, including some that featured literary works by African Americans. Her own first work, a poem, was merely a response to disappointment in love; however, after experiencing the joy of creation, she rapidly moved from words to sentences and finally, after transferring to the University of California at Berkeley, to fiction. In 1976, novelist and editor Ishmael Reed was responsible for the publication of her first short story.

After graduation, McMillan moved to New York, with the intention of studying screenwriting. She dropped out of Columbia University, however, and, addicted to cocaine and alcohol, abandoned her writing. On her thirtieth birthday, McMillan says that she finally faced the fact she was an addict and decided to take control of her life. She stopped taking drugs and gave up drinking. Then, some nine months after the birth of her son Solomon, she decided that she would not take the kind of physical abuse her mother had endured. McMillan walked out on her boyfriend, a cocaine dealer, taking their baby with her.

McMillan's first novel was the result of a suggestion made by friends in the Harlem Writers' Guild. After she had read one of her short stories to the group, someone commented that she ought to make it into a novel. The result was *Mama*.

Accepting a teaching position at the University of Wyoming in Laramie, McMillan began writing *Disappearing Acts*, which was inspired by her own experiences in New York. When it was published in 1989, the work was a popular and critical success. In 1990, McMillan brought out her collection of fiction by African American writers. During the academic year of 1990-1991, she was teaching at the University of Arizona in Tucson. Meanwhile, McMillan's former lover had filed a lawsuit against the author and her publishers, alleging that the character of Franklin Swift in *Disappearing Acts* was based on him. The case was, however, decided in McMillan's favor.

In 1991, McMillan took a leave of absence from the university and moved to Danville, California, near San Francisco. The following year, her third novel appeared. Not only was *Waiting to Exhale* praised by many critics, but upon the announcement that the paperback rights to the novel had been sold for $2.64 million, it was evident that the reading public was no less enthusiastic than the reviewers. Within the short space of five years, McMillan had published three successful novels and was generally recognized as a major African American writer.

Analysis

McMillan has been criticized by other African Americans, such as writer Thulani Davis, because the evil of racism is not the dominant theme of McMillan's novels. What frustrates McMillan's characters in their typically American pursuit of happiness is not an oppressive establishment but the unwillingness of other individuals to see life as they do. This pattern is evident in the lives of the black women who, with one notable exception, are McMillan's major characters. While they have normal sexual desires, they want more from a man than an occasional night of passionate activity; they also desire kindness, honesty, and a monogamous commitment. Most of the available men, however, are polygamous and hedonistic by nature. They see a woman primarily as a sex object, though sometimes they will use her as a source of income to support a drug or alcohol addiction or fund an affair with someone else.

Such inequities have much to do with the plight of Mildred Peacock, the protagonist of *Mama*, who lives with her husband, Crook, and their five children in a working-class community near Detroit. Further compounding the problem, as McMillan points out, is that most of the black men living in Point Haven in the 1960's cannot find jobs, and even when they are hired, their wages are minimal. Unhappy with their present lives and deprived of hope for the future, they drink, drive around in big cars, which are their status symbol and often their homes, and prove their masculinity by beating up their girlfriends and their wives.

McMillan's sympathy for the plight of uneducated African American men is indicated by the fact that she dedicated *Waiting to Exhale* to her father, Edward Lewis McMillan, who died at the age of thirty-nine, only three years after her mother had divorced him. Yet although McMillan can understand why poor men, persuaded that their future is bleak, might feel driven to seek release from their frustrations, during her own childhood the novelist also had firsthand experience of the unhappiness that their self-centered behavior could cause their wives and children. It is significant that McMillan dedicated her first novel to her mother, Madeline Tillman, "whose love and support made everything possible."

Those words point to what McMillan shows as a major difference between African American women and men. While in *Mama* her women characters are committed to their families, most of her men are preoccupied with themselves. Thus while Mildred works to buy food for her children and even a car for her husband, Crook spends his wages on getting drunk or supporting his longtime mistress. When he does turn up at home, Crook gets jealous and beats up his wife; as even the children realize, the only way that Mildred can then escape further abuse is to divert him into intercourse.

The relationship between Crook and Mildred also illustrates how dissimilarly men and women view parenthood. For Crook, becoming a father is proof of masculinity and therefore a source of pride. Supporting the children he has produced is not, however, one of his priorities. Even if there is no food on hand, even if the light and heat have been cut off because the bills have not been paid, Crook will still take his money and go off to his mistress. In stark contrast, Mildred delights in her pregnancies and devotes herself to her children, in whom she sees a hope for the future. Even when her son becomes addicted to heroin and takes to burglary to finance his habit, Mildred never abandons hope. Knowing that her blood courses in his veins, she has to believe that her strength, passed down to him, will someday enable him to change his life for the better.

McMillan does not show Mildred, or any of her other female characters, as a flawless victim. The fact that she is capable of violence is indicated in the riveting first sentence of *Mama*, which describes Mildred's hiding an ax under a mattress as part of her plan to get revenge on Crook for beating her the previous night. Fortunately, Mildred gives up the ax, the lye, and the butcher knives in favor of a quick divorce.

Mildred also has a weakness for good-looking, no-good men. As she explains to her daughter Freda, the sexual urge is not connected to the brain, nor is it diminished by age. In other ways, too, Mildred is less than perfect. For example, while she does try to be financially responsible, when she is desperate she will evade her most insistent creditors. Moreover, like

Crook, Mildred seems always to have a drink in her hand; in addition, she cannot live without her cigarettes, and she pops "nerve pills" like candy. At one point in the novel, her beer, her cigarettes, and her nerve pills are not enough to keep her going, and Mildred has a nervous breakdown. Nevertheless, while a man might consider this a good excuse to quit trying, Mildred is so motivated by her love for her children that she pulls herself together and comes back to her family responsibilities.

Unlike *Mama*, in which the world is seen through the eyes of two women, the protagonist and her daughter, McMillan's second novel, *Disappearing Acts*, gives equal time to the male viewpoint. This love story, set in New York, is told alternately by Zora Banks, a well-educated music teacher and would-be singer, and Franklin Swift, an uneducated but intellectually curious construction worker. Surprisingly, the two have much in common; Franklin feels the same way about his woodworking as Zora does about her music. Their flaws, however, reflect the same kind of gender differences that McMillan had pointed out in her earlier novel. For example, Zora is so keenly aware of the male habit of wandering that she is afraid to be honest with Franklin for fear she might lose him. First, she conceals her epilepsy from him, and then she has an abortion without ever having informed him that she was pregnant. Ironically, the wisdom of her second decision seems to be borne out by later events; when she becomes pregnant again and decides to have the baby, Franklin, who by then is unemployed, cannot deal with the situation. Even though in good times he is a responsible person, when he is under pressure he acts like the men in Point Haven: He beats Zora, walks out on her, and finally resorts to cocaine. Yet Franklin's own narrative shows that he has both a loving nature and a capacity for self-examination, and that after his lapse he has worked very hard to remedy his faults. Franklin may well have changed. At any rate, since most critics agree that Franklin is a more fully developed character than Zora, *Disappearing Acts* proved that McMillan could present a male version of reality.

With *Waiting to Exhale*, McMillan returns to the female viewpoint. The four protagonists of this complex novel are all successful women in their thirties, living in Phoenix, Arizona. They have good jobs, nice cars, pleasant homes, and plenty of spending money. They are, however, repeatedly disappointed by men. Savannah Jackson's married doctor keeps talking about a divorce but never gets one; Robin Stokes's boyfriend keeps saying that he is not ready for marriage; and Bernadine Harris' well-to-do husband has been transferring his assets for months so that he can divorce his wife without having to contribute much child support or alimony.

At times, all these women wonder if the fourth member of their group, Gloria Matthews, has the right idea. Having long ago given up on men, Gloria devotes herself to motherhood, work, and food. In the course of the novel, some decent, unattached men do turn up, including one for Gloria. In *Waiting to Exhale*, as in her previous novels, McMillan leaves open the possibility of a happy marriage. Yet she also points out that there are other satisfactions in life. Mildred, Zora, Bernadine, Gloria, and even the newly pregnant Robin all admit that, resident male or not, women find fulfillment in having children. In addition, McMillan stresses the power of women to sustain one another, whether they are mother and daughter, as in *Mama*, or friends, as in *Waiting to Exhale*.

No one denies that the women in McMillan's novels are vividly drawn or that her stories, episodic though they may be, are almost impossible to put down. It is her language that has drawn the most criticism—specifically, her excessive use of profanity. McMillan's answer to this criticism is simply that she is a realist, and that what she writes is what she hears. Her popularity among young, middle-class black women and even black men bears out the author's contention, voiced in the preface of her anthology, that the writers of a new era must speak in new voices, reflecting the life around them. Evidently, her readers believe that she has succeeded.

Other major works

EDITED TEXT: *Breaking Ice: An Anthology of Contemporary African-American Fiction*, 1990.

Bibliography

Davis, Thulani. "Don't Worry, Be Buppie: Black Novelists Head for the Mainstream." *Village Voice Literary Supplement* 85 (May, 1990): 26-29.
Isaacs, Susan. "Chilling Out in Phoenix." *The New York Times Book Review*, May 31, 1992, p. 12.

Randolph, Laura B. "Black America's Hottest Novelist: Terry McMillan Exhales and Inhales in a Revealing Interview." *Ebony* 48, no. 7 (May, 1993): 23-28.

Smith, Wendy. "Terry McMillan: The Novelist Explores African American Life from the Point of View of a New Generation." *Publishers Weekly* 239, no. 22 (May 11, 1992): 50-51.

Trescott, Jacqueline. "The Urban Author, Straight to the Point: Terry McMillan, Pulling Together the Urgent Fiction of Black Life." *The Washington Post*, November 17, 1990, p. D1+.

GLORIA NAYLOR

Born: New York, New York; January 25, 1950

Principal long fiction

The Women of Brewster Place: A Novel in Seven Stories, 1982; *Linden Hills*, 1985; *Mama Day*, 1988; *Bailey's Cafe*, 1992.

Other literary forms

In 1986, Gloria Naylor wrote a column, *Hers*, for *The New York Times*. She has also published nonfiction, a number of screenplays, short stories, and articles for various periodicals. She is known primarily, however, for her novels.

Achievements

Enjoying both critical and popular acclaim, Naylor's work has reached a wide audience. *The Women of Brewster Place* won the 1983 American Book Award for best first novel and was later made into a television miniseries. Naylor's other awards include a National Endowment for the Arts Fellowship in 1985 and a Guggenheim Fellowship in 1988.

Surveying the range of African American life in America, from poor ghetto to affluent suburb to Southern offshore island, Naylor's work examines questions of black identity and, in particular, celebrates black women. In the face of enormous problems and frequent victimization, black women are shown coping through their sense of community and their special powers. Although written from a feminist perspective, her depictions of courage, community, and cultural identity have universal appeal.

Biography

The oldest child of African American parents who had migrated from Mississippi, Gloria Naylor was born and reared in New York City. After graduation from high school, she spent seven years as a missionary for the Jehovah's Witnesses in New York, North Carolina, and Florida. She eventually found missionary life too strict, but her original zeal apparently carried over into her later feminism. Although her writings are not religious, a fundamentalist pattern of thinking still pervades them. She tends to separate her characters into the sheep and the goats (mostly men), the saved and the damned, with one whole book, *Linden Hills*, being modeled after Dante's *Inferno* (c. 1320).

In high school Naylor read widely in the nineteenth century British novelists, but later in a creative writing course at Brooklyn College she came across the book that influenced her most—*The Bluest Eye* (1970), by the African American novelist Toni Morrison. The example of Morrison inspired Naylor to write fiction and to focus on the lives of black women, who Naylor believed were underrepresented (if not ignored) in American literature. Naylor began work on *The Women of Brewster Place*, which was published the year after her graduation from Brooklyn College with a B.A. degree in English. By that time, Naylor was studying on a fellowship at Yale University, from which she received an M.A. degree in Afro-American studies in 1983.

Naylor's background and literary achievements have won for her numerous invitations for lectureships or other appointments in academia. She has held visiting posts at George Washington University, the University of Pennsylvania, Princeton University, New York University, Boston University, Brandeis University, and Cornell University.

Analysis

Naylor is a feminist writer who explores issues of African American identity and celebrates the lives and special powers of black women. White people do not appear often and are certainly never featured in the work of Gloria Naylor. Yet their presence can be felt like a white background noise or like the boulevard traffic on the other side of the wall from Brewster Place. White culture is simply another fact of life, like a nearby nuclear reactor or toxic waste dump, and the effects of racism and discrimination are omnipresent in Naylor's work. Against these stifling effects her characters live their lives and try to define their sense of black identity, from the ghetto women of Brewster Place to the social climbers of Linden Hills to the denizens of Willow Springs, a pristine Southern island relatively untouched by slavery and segregation.

Naylor began fulfilling her commitment to make black women more prominent in American fiction with *The Women of Brewster Place*, subtitled *A Novel in Seven Stories*. The seven stories, featuring seven women, can be read separately, but they are connected by their setting of Brewster Place and by characters who carry over from one story to another (at least by brief mention). The women arrive on the dead-end street by different routes that exhibit the variety of lives of black women, but on Brewster Place they unite into a community.

The middle-aged bastion of this community is Mattie Michael, who over the course of her life was betrayed by each of the three men she loved—her seducer, her father, and her son. She mothers Lucielia (Ciel) Louise Turner (whose grandmother once sheltered Mattie) when Ciel's abusive boyfriend destroys her life. In addition, Mattie welcomes her close friend Etta Mae Johnson, who also once gave Mattie refuge. Etta Mae is a fading beauty who has used men all her life but has now been used by a sleazy preacher for a one-night stand. The other women featured are the young unwed Cora Lee, a baby factory; Kiswana Browne, an aspiring social reformer who hails from the affluent suburb of Linden Hills; and Lorraine and Thersa, two lesbians seeking privacy for their love.

Few men are in evidence on Brewster Place, and these few inspire little confidence. C. C. Baker and his youth gang lurk about the alleyway and, in the novel's brutal climax, rape Lorraine. The crazed Lorraine in turn kills the wino Ben, the old janitor who earlier had befriended her. As these scenes suggest, Brewster Place is located in a ghetto plagued by social ills. The women must face these on a daily basis in addition to their personal tragedies and dislocations. Instead of being overcome by their sufferings, however, the women find within themselves a common fate and a basis for community. They gain strength and hope from their mutual caring and support. Besides their informal support system, they form a block association to address larger problems. The ability of women to unite in such a community inspires admiration for their courage and their special powers.

The community feelings of Brewster Place, from which the women gain a positive sense of identity, somehow make the ghetto's problems seem less awesome, paradoxically, than those of Linden Hills, an affluent suburb. If Brewster Place is a ghetto, Linden Hills is a hell. Naylor underlines this metaphor by deliberately modeling her novel *Linden Hills* after Dante's *Inferno*. Linden Hills is not a group of hills, but only a V-shaped area on a hillside intersected by eight streets. As one travels down the hill, the residents become richer but lower on the moral scale. Lester and Willie, two young unemployed poets who perform odd jobs for Christmas money (they are the modern counterparts of Vergil and Dante), take the reader on a guided tour.

The residents of Linden Hills have sold out for affluence: They suffer from a loss of black identity, or soul, as the result of adopting white attitudes, compromising their personal loyalties, and denying their kinship with other blacks. Lester's sister Roxanne deems black Africans in Zimbabwe unready for independence; one young executive, Maxwell Smyth, encourages another, Xavier Donnell, no longer to consider Roxanne as a prospective corporate bride; and Dr. Daniel Braithwaite has written the authorized twelve-volume history of Linden Hills without making a single moral judgment. Other sellouts are more personal: The young lawyer Winston Alcott leaves his homosexual lover to marry respectably, and Chester Parker is eager to bury his dead wife in order to remarry.

Significantly, Linden Hills is ruled over by men. The archfiend himself is Luther Nedeed, the local undertaker and real estate tycoon who occupies the lowest point in Linden Hills. Speaking against a low-income housing project planned for an adjacent poor black neighborhood, Nedeed urges outraged Linden Hills property owners to make common cause with the racist Wayne County Citizens Alliance. Most damning of all, however, is that Nedeed disowns his own wife and child and imprisons them in an old basement morgue; the child starves, but the wife climbs up to confront the archfiend on Christmas Eve.

It is clear that, while examining problems of middle-class black identity in *Linden Hills*, Naylor has not overlooked the plight of black women. In *Mama Day*, Naylor returns to a more celebratory mood on both subjects. The setting of *Mama Day* is a unique black American culture presided over by a woman with even more unique powers.

The coastal island of Willow Springs, located off South Carolina and Georgia but belonging to no state, has been largely bypassed by the tides of American history, particularly racism. The island was originally owned by a white man, Bascombe Wade, who also owned slaves. Bascombe married Sapphira, one of his slaves, however, who bore their seven sons. In 1823

Bascombe freed his other slaves and deeded the island to them, his sons, and their respective descendants in perpetuity (the land cannot be sold, only inherited). Bascombe was more or less assimilated, and a black culture grew up on the island that was closely tied to the land, to the culture's beginnings, and to African roots. In other words, Willow Springs is definitely a mythical island—a tiny but free black state flourishing unnoticed under the nose of the Confederacy. Naylor underlines the island's mythic qualities by drawing parallels between it and the magical isle of *The Tempest*.

If Prospero presides over Shakespeare's island, then Prospero's daughter, Miranda "Mama" Day (actually a great-granddaughter of the Wades), presides over Willow Springs. Known and respected locally as an old conjure woman, Mama Day is a repository and embodiment of the culture's wisdom. In particular, she is versed in herbs and other natural phenomena, but she also speaks with the island's spirits. Mama Day uses her powers to heal and aid new life, but other island people who have similar powers are not so benevolent. One such person is Ruby, who stirs her knowledge with hoodoo to kill any woman who might take her man.

Unhappily, Mama Day's grandniece Cocoa, down from New York on a visit with her husband George, arouses Ruby's jealousy. By pretending to be friendly, Ruby is able to give Cocoa a deadly nightshade rinse, scalp massage, and hairdo. Just as a big hurricane hits the island, Cocoa begins to feel the effects of the poison. George, an engineer, native New Yorker, and football fan, works frantically to save Cocoa, but he is over-matched. With his urbanized, masculine rationality, he cannot conceive of what he is up against or how to oppose it. Suffering from exhaustion and a weak heart, he is eventually killed in an encounter with a brooding hen.

Meanwhile, Mama Day has been working her powers. She confronts Ruby in a conjuring match, good magic versus bad magic, just as in Mali's oral epic tradition of the thirteenth century ruler Sundjata and in other traditions of Africa. Ruby is destroyed by lightning strikes, and Cocoa is saved. It is too late for George the doubter, however, who has learned about the mystical powers of women the hard way.

Mama Day provides Naylor's most advanced statements of her favorite themes, the assertion of black identity and the celebration of black women. There is much about her work that might ultimately prove self-limiting, mainly her doctrinaire feminism and her tendency to write in broad, sweeping gestures. Yet these same features give her work a mythic quality that is undeniably powerful.

Bibliography

Bell, Bernard W. *The Afro-American Novel and Its Tradition*. Amherst: University of Massachusetts Press, 1987.

Braxton, Joanne M., and Andrée Nicola McLaughlin, eds. *Wild Women in the Whirlwind: Afro-American Culture and the Contemporary Literary Renaissance*. New Brunswick, N.J.: Rutgers University Press, 1990.

Carby, Hazel V. *Reconstructing Womanhood: The Emergence of the Afro-American Woman Novelist*. New York: Oxford University Press, 1987.

Gates, Henry Louis, Jr. "Significant Others." *Contemporary Literature* 29 (Winter, 1988): 606-623.

Gates, Henry Louis, Jr., and K. A. Appiah, eds. *Gloria Naylor: Critical Perspectives Past and Present*. New York: Amistad, 1993.

Homans, Margaret. "The Women in the Cave: Recent Feminist Fictions and the Classical Underworld." *Contemporary Literature* 29 (Fall, 1988): 369-402.

Naylor, Gloria, and Toni Morrison. "A Conversation." *The Southern Review* 21 (Summer, 1985): 567-593.

ISHMAEL REED

Born: Chattanooga, Tennessee; February 22, 1938

Principal long fiction

The Free-Lance Pallbearers, 1967; *Yellow Back Radio Broke-Down*, 1969; *Mumbo Jumbo*, 1972; *The Last Days of Louisiana Red*, 1974; *Flight to Canada*, 1976; *The Terrible Twos*, 1982; *Reckless Eyeballing*, 1986; *The Terrible Threes*, 1989.

Other literary forms

Ishmael Reed may be best known as a satirical novelist, but he is also a respected poet, essayist, and editor. His poetry collections have established him as a major African American poet, and his poetry has been included in several important anthologies. In well-received collections of essays, Reed has forcefully presented his aesthetic and political theories. He has also proved to be an important editor and publisher. *19 Necromancers from Now* (1970) was a breakthrough anthology for several unknown black writers. *Yardbird Lives!* (1978), which Reed edited with Al Young, includes essays, fiction, and graphics from the pages of the *Yardbird Reader*, an innovative periodical that published the work of minority writers and artists. Reed's most ambitious editing project resulted in *Calafia: The California Poetry* (1979), an effort to gather together the forgotten minority poetry of California's past. He published a volume of short fiction in 1993.

Achievements

Reed has earned a place in the first rank of contemporary African American authors, but such recognition did not come immediately. Most established reviewers ignored Reed's first novel, *The Free-Lance Pallbearers*, and many of the reviews that were written dismissed the novel as offensive, childish, or self-absorbed. Although *Yellow Back Radio Broke-Down* was even less traditional than its predecessor, it received much more critical attention nd became the center of considerable critical debate. Some reviewers attacked the novel as overly clever, bitter, or obscure, but many praised its imaginative satire and technical innovation. Reed's increasing acceptance as a major black American author was demonstrated when his third novel, *Mumbo Jumbo*, was reviewed on the front page of *The New York Review of Books*. Both *Mumbo Jumbo* and *Conjure*, a poetry collection published in the same year, were nominated for the National Book Award.

Subsequent novels have maintained Reed's position in American letters. In 1975, Reed's *The Last Days of Louisiana Red* received the Rosenthal Foundation Award, and some reviewers viewed *Flight to Canada* as Reed's best novel. Yet his work has consistently been controversial. His novels have, for example, been called sexist, a critical accusation that is fueled by comparison of Reed's novels with the recent, powerful fiction written by African American women such as Alice Walker and Toni Morrison. The charge of sexism is further encouraged by Reed's satirical attack on feminists in *Reckless Eyeballing*. Reed has also been called a reactionary by some critics because of his uncomplimentary portrayals of black revolutionaries. His fiction has been translated into three languages, and his poetry has been included in *Poetry of the Negro*, *New Black Poetry*, *The Norton Anthology of Poetry*, and other anthologies.

Biography

Reed was born the son of Henry Lenoir and Thelma Coleman, but before he was two years old, his mother remarried autoworker Bennie Reed. When he was four years old, his mother moved the family to Buffalo, New York, where she found factory work. Reed was graduated from Buffalo's East High School in 1956 and began to attend Millard Fillmore College, the night division of the University of Buffalo, supporting himself by working in the Buffalo public library. A satirical short story, "Something Pure," which portrayed Christ's return as an advertising man, brought Reed the praise of an English professor and encouraged him to enroll in day classes. Reed attended the University of Buffalo until 1960, when he withdrew because of money problems and the social pressures that his financial situation created. He moved into the notorious Talbert Mall Projects, and the two years he spent there provided him with a painful but valuable experience of urban poverty and dependency. During these last years in Buffalo,

Reed wrote for the *Empire Star Weekly*, moderated a controversial radio program for station WVFO, and acted in several local stage productions.

From 1962 to 1967, Reed lived in New York City. As well as being involved with the Civil Rights and the Black Power movements, Reed served as editor of *Advance*, a weekly published in Newark, New Jersey. His work on the *Advance* was admired by Walter Bowart, and together they founded the *East Village Other*, one of the first and most successful "underground" newspapers. An early indication of Reed's commitment to encouraging the work of minority artists was his organization in 1965 of the American Festival of Negro Art.

In 1967, Reed moved to Berkeley, California, and began teaching at the University of California at Berkeley. Although he was turned down for tenure in 1977, he continued to teach there and at other universities: the University of Washington, the State University of New York at Buffalo, Yale University, and Dartmouth College. In 1971, with Al Young, Reed founded the Yardbird Publishing Company, which from 1971 to 1976 produced the *Yardbird Reader*, an innovative journal of ethnic writing and graphics. The Reed, Cannon, and Johnson Communications Company, which later became Ishmael Reed Books, was founded in 1973 and has published the work of William Demby, Bill Gunn, Mei Mei Bressenburge, and other ethnic writers. In 1976, Reed and Victor Cruz began the Before Columbus Foundation. In all of his publishing ventures, Reed has tried to expose readers to the work of Asian Americans, African Americans, Chicanos, and Native Americans in an effort to help build a truly representative and pluralistic national literature.

Analysis

Reed is consciously a part of the African American literary tradition that extends back to the first-person slave narratives, and the central purpose of his novels is to define a means of expressing the complexity of the black experience in a manner distinct from the dominant literary tradition. Until the middle of the twentieth century, African American fiction, although enriched by the lyricism of Jean Toomer and Zora Neale Hurston, concentrated on realistic portrayals of black life and employed familiar narrative structures. This tendency toward social realism peaked with Richard Wright's *Native Son* (1940) and *Black Boy* (1945), but it continued into the late twentieth century through authors such as James Baldwin. Reed belongs to a divergent tradition, inspired by Ralph Ellison's *Invisible Man* (1952),

a countertradition that includes the work of Leon Forrest, Ernest J. Gaines, James Alan McPherson, Toni Morrison, and Alice Walker. Reed argues that the special qualities of the black American experience cannot be adequately communicated through traditional literary forms. Henry Louis Gates, Jr., has compared Reed's fictional modifications of African American literary traditions to the black folk custom of "signifying," maintaining that Reed's novels present an ongoing process of "rhetorical self-definition."

Although Reed's novels are primarily efforts to define an appropriate African American aesthetic, his fiction vividly portrays the particular social condition of black Americans. Indeed, "Ishmael" seems to be an ironically appropriate name for this author of violent and darkly humorous attacks on American institutions and attitudes, for the sharpness and breadth of his satire sometimes make him appear to be a man whose hand is turned against all other men. His novels portray corrupt power brokers and their black and white sycophants operating in a dehumanized and materialistic society characterized by its prefabricated and ethnocentric culture. Yet Reed's novels are not hopeless explications of injustice, for against the forces of repression and conformity he sets gifted individuals who escape the limitations of their sterile culture by courageously penetrating the illusions that bind them.

It is in *Yellow Back Radio Broke-Down* that Reed first attempts to construct an alternative to social presumptions. The novel is set in a fantastic version of the Wild West of popular literature. Reed's protagonist, the Loop Garoo Kid, is a proponent of artistic freedom and an accomplished voodoo *houngan*. Armed with supernatural "connaissance" and aided by a white python and the hip, helicopter-flying Chief Showcase, the Kid battles the forces of realistic mimesis and political corruption. His villainous opponent is Drag Gibson, a degenerate cattle baron given to murdering his wives, who is called upon by the citizens of Yellow Back Radio to crush their rebellious children's effort "to create [their] own fictions."

Although *Yellow Back Radio Broke-Down* satirizes Americans' eagerness to suspend civil rights in response to student protests against the Vietnam War, its focus is literature, specifically the dialogue between realism and modernism. Through the Loop Garoo Kid, Reed takes a stand for imagination, intelligence, and fantasy against rhetoric, violence, and sentimentality. This theme is made explicit in a debate with Bo Shmo, a "neo-social realist" who maintains that "all art must be for the end of liberating the masses," for the Kid says that a novel "can be anything it wants to be, a vaudeville show, the six o'clock news, the mumblings of wild men saddled by demons."

Reed exhibits his antirealist theory of fiction in *Yellow Back Radio Broke-Down* through his free use of time, characters, and language. The novel ranges from the eighteenth century to the present, combining historical events and cowboy myths with modern technology and cultural detritus. His primary characters are comically exaggerated racial types: Drag Gibson represents the white's depraved materialism, Chief Showcase represents the Indian's spirituality, and the Loop Garoo Kid represents the African American's artistic soul. Reed explains the novel's title by suggesting that his book is the "dismantling of a genre done in an oral way like radio." "Yellow back" refers to the popular dime novels; "radio" refers to the novel's oral, discontinuous form; and a "broke-down" is a dismantling. Thus, Reed's first two novels assault America in an attempt to "dismantle" its cultural structure.

In *Mumbo Jumbo*, Reed expands on the neo-hoodooism of the Loop Garoo Kid in order to create and define an African American aesthetic based on voodoo, Egyptian mythology, and improvisational musical forms, an aesthetic to challenge the Judeo-Christian tradition, rationalism, and technology. Set in Harlem during the 1920's, *Mumbo Jumbo* is a tragicomical analysis of the Harlem Renaissance's failure to sustain its artistic promise. Reed's protagonist is PaPa LaBas, an aging hoodoo detective and cultural diagnostician, and LaBas' name, meaning "over there" in French, reveals that his purpose is to reconnect black Americans with their cultural heritage by reunifying the Text of Jes Grew, literally the Egyptian Book of Thoth. Reed takes the phrase Jes Grew from Harriet Beecher Stowe's Topsy and James Weldon Johnson's description of black music's unascribed development, but in the novel, Jes Grew is a contagion, connected with the improvisational spirit of ragtime and jazz, that begins to spread across America in the 1920's. Jes Grew is an irrational force that threatens to overwhelm the dominant, repressive traditions of established culture. LaBas' efforts to unify and direct this unpredictable force are opposed by the Wallflower Order of the Knights Templar, an organization dedicated to neutralizing the power of Jes Grew in order to protect their privileged status. LaBas fails to reunify the text, a parallel to the dissipation of the Harlem Renaissance's artistic potential, but the failure is seen as temporary; the novel's indeterminate

conclusion looks forward hopefully to a time when these artistic energies can be reignited.

The novel's title is double-edged. "Mumbo jumbo" is a racist, colonialist phrase used to describe the misunderstood customs and language of dark-skinned people, an approximation of some critics' description of Reed's unorthodox fictional method. Yet "mumbo jumbo" also refers to the power of imagination, the cultural alternative that can free black Americans. A text of and about texts, *Mumbo Jumbo* combines the formulas of detective fiction with the documentary paraphernalia of scholarship: footnotes, illustrations, and a bibliography. Thus, in the disclosure scene required of any good detective story, LaBas, acting the part of interlocutor, provides a lengthy and erudite explication of the development of Jes Grew that begins with a reinterpretation of the myth of Osiris. The parodic scholarship of *Mumbo Jumbo* undercuts the assumed primacy of the European tradition and implicitly argues that African American artists should attempt to discover their distinct cultural heritage.

In *The Last Days of Louisiana Red*, LaBas returns as Reed's protagonist and again functions as a connection with a non-European tradition of history and myth. In the novel, LaBas solves the murder of Ed Yellings, the founder of the Solid Gumbo Works. Yellings' business is dedicated to combating the effects of Louisiana Red, literally a popular hot sauce but figuratively an evil state of mind that divides African Americans. Yelling's gumbo, like Reed's fiction, is a mixture of disparate elements, and it has a powerful curative effect. In fact, LaBas discovers that Yellings is murdered when he gets close to developing a gumbo that will cure heroin addiction.

In *The Last Days of Louisiana Red*, Reed is examining the self-destructive forces that divide the black community so that its members fight one another "while above their heads . . . billionaires flew in custom-made jet planes." Reed shows how individuals' avarice leads them to conspire with the establishment, and he suggests that some of the most vocal and militant leaders are motivated by their egotistical need for power rather than by true concern for oppressed people. Set in Berkeley, California, *The Last Days of Louisiana Red* attacks the credibility of the black revolutionary movements that sprang up in the late 1960's and early 1970's.

Ishmael Reed's substantial body of fiction has established him as an important satirist. His innovative narrative techniques have stretched the limits of the American novel and dramatically broadened the scope of African American literature.

Other major works

POETRY: *Catechism of D Neoamerican Hoodoo Church*, 1970; *Conjure: Selected Poems, 1963-1970*, 1972; *Chattanooga*, 1973; *A Secretary to the Spirits*, 1977; *Cab Calloway Stands In for the Moon*, 1986; *New and Collected Poems*, 1988.

NONFICTION: *Shrovetide in Old New Orleans*, 1978; *God Made Alaska for the Indians*, 1982; *Writin' Is Fightin'*, 1988; *Airing Dirty Laundry*, 1993.

ANTHOLOGIES: *19 Necromancers from Now*, 1970; *Yardbird Lives!*, 1978 (with Al Young); *Calafia: The California Poetry*, 1979.

SHORT FICTION: *Japanese by Spring*, 1993.

Bibliography

Boyer, Jay. *Ishmael Reed*. Boise: Boise State University Press, 1993.

Fabre, Michel. "Postmodern Rhetoric in Ishmael Reed's *Yellow Back Radio Broke-Down*." In *The Afro-American Novel Since 1960*, edited by Peter Bruck and Wolfgang Karrer. Amsterdam: Gruener, 1982.

Fox, Robert Elliot. *Conscientious Sorcerers: The Black Post-Modern Fiction of LeRoi Jones/Amiri Baraka, Ishmael Reed, and Samuel R. Delaney*. New York: Greenwood Press, 1987.

Gates, Henry Louis, Jr. *The Signifying Monkey: A Theory of Afro-American Literary Criticism*. New York: Oxford University Press, 1988.

Lee, A. Robert, ed. *Black Fiction: New Studies in the Afro-American Novel Since 1945*. New York: Barnes & Noble Books, 1980.

Martin, Reginald. *Ishmael Reed and the New Black Aesthetic Critics*. New York: St. Martin's Press, 1988.

Review of Contemporary Fiction 4 (Summer, 1984). Special issue on Reed.

Settle, Elizabeth A., and Thomas A. Settle, eds. *Ishmael Reed: A Primary and Secondary Bibliography*. Boston: G. K. Hall, 1982.

JEAN TOOMER

Born: Washington, D.C.; December 26, 1894   **Died:** Doylestown, Pennsylvania; March 30, 1967

Principal poetry

"Banking Coal," in *Crisis*, 1922; *Cane*, 1923 (prose and poetry); "Blue Meridian," in *New American Caravan*, 1936; *The Wayward and the Seeking*, 1980 (prose and poetry; Darwin T. Turner, ed.); *The Collected Poems of Jean Toomer*, 1988.

Other literary forms

Most of Jean Toomer's work was in genres other than poetry. His one published volume of creative writing, *Cane*, contains only fifteen poems, mostly short, and fourteen pieces that appear to be in prose. Toomer published several pieces of fiction after *Cane*, generally quite experimental inasmuch as they lacked plot, often included philosophical meditations, and indeed often worked more like poetry, with impressionistic scenes and descriptions and an emphasis on developing a theme through juxtaposition of sections rather than an overall sequence of action. A previously unpublished story from 1930, "Withered Skin of Berries," appears in *The Wayward and the Seeking*.

Toomer published one short, fragmentary play during his lifetime and two of several other plays that he wrote in *The Wayward and the Seeking*.

Nonfiction predominates in Toomer's work, indicating his concerns with philosophical and spiritual goals. Portions of several versions of Toomer's autobiography appear in *The Wayward and the Seeking*. The rest of his many unpublished works, including many poems, remain in the Toomer Collection of the Fisk University Library.

Achievements

Cane is one of the most memorable and appealing books in African American literature, conveying a vivid sense of the life of Southern blacks around 1920 (though little changed since the time of slavery) and showing clearly the conflicts between the feelings of black people and the desensitizing and spirit-diminishing urban life they found in the North. Yet *Cane* is significant not merely for its content but also for its innovative form and style. Its combination of prose and verse, stories and poems, produces a unified impression, with poems foreshadowing or commenting on adjacent stories and the stories and sketches exploring a multitude of perspectives on black life, rural and urban.

Toomer's impressionistic style, his seductive but not mechanical rhythms, his brilliant imagery and figurative language, and his manipulation of language to produce a wide range of emotional and literary effects were refreshing to many African American writers during and after the Harlem Renaissance of the 1920's. Instead of adhering strictly to traditional European models of form and meter (as did his major black contemporaries Claude McKay and Countée Cullen) or the literary realism and straightforward narrative style of black fiction to that date, he joined the progression of revolutionary poets and fiction writers who were creating literary modernism, from Walt Whitman on through James Joyce, D. H. Lawrence, Gertrude Stein, Sherwood Anderson, and T. S. Eliot, up to Toomer's friend and contemporary Hart Crane.

Very few of Toomer's other works come even close to the towering achievement of *Cane*, but its poems and poetic prose provided later writers a successful means of evoking the African American experience. A reader can still sense echoes of its style in the evocative prose of novelist Toni Morrison.

Biography

Jean Toomer (born Eugene) spent most of his life resisting a specific racial label for himself. His childhood and youth were spent in white or racially mixed middle-class neighborhoods in Washington, D.C. Jean's father left shortly after his birth and his mother died after remarrying, so that the most potent adult influences on his life were his maternal grandparents, with whom he lived until his twenties. His grandfather, P. B. S. Pinchback, had been elected lieutenant governor in Reconstruction Louisiana and served as acting governor in 1873. Toomer believed that Pinchback's announcement of having black blood helped him get elected, although Toomer denied knowing whether it was true. One thing is clear: Pinchback had indeed served the Union cause in the Corps d'Afrique.

Later in life Toomer, whose family was light-skinned, denied that he was a Negro—in the sense of his own definition of "Negro" as one who identifies solely with the black race—for he, with certainly a great deal of nonblack ancestry, saw himself as not white, either, but "American," a member of a new race that would unify the heretofore conflicting racial groups through a mixture of racial strains. The attainment of such an "American" race remained his goal throughout most of his life after *Cane*.

Toomer's education after high school was varied, from University of Wisconsin, where he studied agriculture, to the American College of Physical Training in Chicago. Rather than completing courses toward a formal degree, however, he pursued his own reading in literature and social issues while working at assorted jobs until he decided to devote all his efforts to writing.

The real nudge came in the form of a three-month stint as substitute principal of a school in a small Georgia town in the fall of 1921. He returned to Washington in November with material for a whole book. He published several poems and stories in assorted periodicals the following year and then gathered most of them and many new ones into a carefully structured book called *Cane*, published in 1923 by Boni and Liveright. The book caused a considerable stir among the influential white literati with whom he associated (such as Waldo Frank, Sherwood Anderson, and Hart Crane) and among African American writers and intellectuals as well. Yet in its two printings (the second in 1927), it sold fewer than a thousand copies.

That same year, Toomer met the Russian mystic George Gurdjieff and embraced his philosophy of higher consciousness. After studying with him in France, Toomer returned to spread Gurdjieff's teachings in America. A ten-month marriage to a white poet, Margery Latimer, ended with her death in childbirth in 1932. Two years later Toomer married another white woman, Marjorie Content, and spent the rest of his life with her. This period in Toomer's life was largely devoted to lecturing and writing, primarily philosophical and spiritually oriented work. He continued to publish some literary works until 1936, when his career came virtually to an end, despite attempts to have other works published. He became a Quaker and maintained no further identity with the black race, dying in 1967 largely forgotten.

Analysis

Toomer emerged a major African American author and poet principally on the basis of *Cane*. It is an eccentric book, experimental and unclassifiable in its combination of poems and what is technically prose—pieces that are generally developed as short stories (somewhat like those of Anderson or Joyce) but that are occasionally "mere" sketches, sometimes prose-poems without plot encompassing no more than a few pages and conveying impressionistically the sense of a person's spirit. Some of the pieces approach drama, with conversation printed like dialogue, setting described as meticulously as for a stage designer, and action presented in the present tense.

Toomer's purpose in this work is to embody what he sees as the dying folk-spirit of the South by depicting the lives of its people and re-creating their feelings through language and rhythm. *Cane* achieves a vivid sense of the sensuality of its women, the alternating anguish and joy of life in the South, the toughness and beauty of the land of Georgia. These themes appear primarily in the first third of the book; the second third moves north into the city, where blacks from the South have difficulty fitting into the white-dominated social patterns while retaining roots in the South; in the final third, Ralph Kabnis, a Northern black man, comes South, and the focus is on his conflict with the South. Throughout the book, Toomer shows both attraction to the South and a sense of holding back from it—on the part of a narrator in the first third, of Kabnis in the last third, and of assorted Northern-based characters in the middle third, who are losing touch with their black roots. The book, however, is hardly a glorification of the way of life of Southern blacks: The South still hosts an occasional lynching, as Toomer several times reminds his readers. Still, Toomer appreciates a vitality in Southern blacks that disappears when they are removed from the land, a process that Toomer views as unfortunately inevitable in the modern world.

A close analysis of one of his pieces—"Karintha," the opening sketch in *Cane*—will illustrate Toomer's typical methods. Like other pieces in the book, "Karintha" opens with an epigraph, a songlike refrain of four lines that recurs throughout the sketch as a unifying device. The first of four paragraphs of varying lengths then introduces Karintha as a child, summing her up in the first sentence, which is poetically accretive rather than prosaically structured. Two sentences in parallel construction follow, dealing with the actions the old men and the young men take with her, followed by two sentences in response to these, describing their respective feelings about her. The final sentence sums up the paragraph and "this interest of the male," with a metaphoric interpretation of it and a note of foreboding.

The second paragraph re-creates her girlhood in terms of concrete actions and images: visual (color, shape, light), auditory (sounds of feet, voice, silence), kinetic (running, wind), tactile (stoning the cows, touching the earth). It sums up her sexual nature as well and ends with two sentences referring to the wishes of the old and young men from the first paragraph, regarding Karintha as she matures. Before Karintha is shown as a woman, the refrain of the epigraph is repeated, the first three lines each being cut by a few words. The new rhythm creates a pace appropriately faster than the wondering, more meditative earlier version.

The third paragraph makes assorted references to the subject matter and phrasing of earlier paragraphs. Repetitions of actual sentences and phrases and of sentence structure (in a series of short sentences showing what young men do for Karintha) evoke the sense of poetry, as does the second half of the paragraph, which, through indirection, reveals Karintha's murder of her infant. The birth is presented as a kind of emotionless miracle unconnected with Karintha herself, while the scene is given sensory richness. Juxtaposed, after ellipses, is the description of a nearby sawmill, its smoldering sawdust pile, and the heaviness of the smoke after Karintha's return. Ending this paragraph is a short song that someone makes up about smoke rising to "take my soul to Jesus," an unconsciously appropriate elegy for the unwanted baby.

The final paragraph of the piece begins as the third did—"Karintha is a woman"—and then echoes the last sentence of the first paragraph: "Men do not know that the soul of her was a growing thing ripened too soon." Toomer then suggests her unbreachable remoteness from men; the last sentence recalls the first in this sketch, describing her at twenty in the phrases used to describe her as a child. After a last repetition of her name, followed by ellipses, comes a repetition of the epigraph, followed by an ominous repetition of its last two words, "Goes down," and then more ellipses, hinting at the inevitable descent and defeat of this beautiful, vital creature, brought to maturity too soon through misuse by men.

Though printed as prose, this piece is essentially poetic; Toomer merely hints at the outer details of Karintha's life, but his poetic prose gives a full sense of Karintha's person and appeal through the precise sensory details of the second paragraph, the recurring patterns of the old and young men's responses to her, and the use of songs as commentary. The echoes and repetitions of images and phrases act as leitmotifs, and Toomer's careful arrangement of them gives the piece a satisfying structure and a strong sense of Karintha's doom, trapped in an unchanging pattern.

In the pieces clearly printed as poetry, Toomer is less experimental. Yet scarce as the poems in *Cane* are, they cover a variety of forms that few single books of poetry display. "Song of the Son," for example, is skillfully rhymed, beautifully evoking in five stanzas of flowing iambic pentameter the Southern music that the poet is trying to capture in literature—as he says in this poem, before it vanishes. There are poems of rhymed couplets and brief pieces such as the Imagists might produce. There is a "Cotton Song," such as the work songs that slaves or free but poor farmhands might sing. There is much free verse, notably in "Harvest Song." Toomer's choices are not arbitrary; they suit the moods and subjects of their respective poems, conveying the spectrum of feelings that the writer wishes to present, from joy and exaltation to bitterness and despair.

Toomer also varies style and tone, as well as form, to suit theme and mood. Grim and laconic irony flavors "Conversion," as the African succumbs to "a white-faced sardonic god." "Georgia Dusk" offers lush images both of Southern life and of the African past (a recurring motif throughout the book). "Portrait in Georgia," with its short free-verse lines, reads like a catalog of bodily parts, such as an auctioneer would have prepared. Each is described through images of Southern white violence: "lyncher's rope," "fagots," "scars," "blisters," "the ash of black flesh after flame." This poem makes no explicit statement, but the juxtaposition of human parts with these images, presented so simply and concisely, evokes a subtle sense of horror and sets up an appropriately ominous mood for the following story, "Blood-Burning Moon," which ends with an actual lynching. However attractive the Georgia of pines, red soil, sweet-smelling cane, and beauteous dusks may be, Toomer insists on reminding his reader of the dangers there as well, even without explicit condemnation of the bigoted whites or the oppressive social system. Toomer works by indirection, but without diminished effect.

Too often, unfortunately, Toomer's later poetry drops the effective device used in *Cane* and becomes didactic, explicitly philosophical, lacking *Cane's* brilliantly realized images of concrete reality or its sharp, often startling metaphors. Toomer was mightily inspired by his few months in Georgia, and his sojourn even affected his interpretations of his own more familiar Washington and New York life; but after he had said what he had to say about the South and about the North in relation to the South, he seems to have exhausted his inspiration, except for his more "universal" themes, with only a little sense of poetry left, to be used in "Blue Meridian" and his stories "Winter on Earth" and "Withered Skin of Berries." Toomer began to ignore stylistic and literary matters and in favor of expressing his spiritual and philosophical beliefs, urging a regeneration of humanity that would eliminate the differences imposed by racial and other categories and bring people close to God, one another, and the natural world. This is the point that he makes explicitly in his last major work, the long poem "Blue Meridian," which follows a structure much like that of Whitman's long poems, with recurring phrases or stanzas, often significantly altered. Its concerns, however, are more akin to those of T. S. Eliot's *The Waste Land* (1922) and Stephen Crane's *The Bridge* (1930), being an examination and criticism of the twentieth century world, achieving a multifaceted view by varying tone and form.

At his best, Toomer was a brilliant artist in words, a sensitive portrayer of the life he lived and observed, as well as a sincere and concerned member of the human race. *Cane* will forever keep his name alive and arouse an interest in his other work, however inferior most of it may be judged to be. The musical quality of his best poetry and prose will be admired, not for its mere beauty but for its aptness to its subjects: the beauty and appeal as well as the tragedy of the life of the South.

Other major works

FICTION: *Cane*, 1923 (prose and poetry); "Mr. Costyve Duditch," in *The Dial*, 1928; "York Beach," in *New American Caravan*, 1929; *The Wayward and the Seeking*, 1980 (prose and poetry; Darwin T. Turner, ed.).
PLAY: "Balo," in Alain Locke's *Plays of Negro Life*, 1927.
NONFICTION: "Winter on Earth," in *The Second American Caravan*, 1929; "Race Problems and Modern Society," 1929; *Essentials: Definitions and Aphorisms*, 1931; "The Flavor of Man," 1949.
MISCELLANEOUS: *A Jean Toomer Reader: Selected Unpublished Writings*, 1993.

Bibliography

Benson, Joseph, and Mabel Mayle Dillard. *Jean Toomer*. Boston: Twayne, 1980.
Byrd, Rudolph P. "Jean Toomer and the Writers of the Harlem Renaissance: Was He There with Them?" In *The Harlem Renaissance: Revaluations*, edited by Amritjit Singh, William S. Shiver, and Stanley Brodwin. New York: Garland, 1989.
Durham, Frank, ed. *The Merrill Studies in "Cane."* Columbus, Ohio: Charles E. Merrill, 1971.
Jones, Robert B. *Jean Toomer and the Prison-House of Thought: A Phenomenology of the Spirit*. Amherst: University of Massachusetts Press, 1993.
Kerman, Cynthia Earl, and Richard Eldridge. *The Lives of Jean Toomer: A Hunger for Wholeness*. Baton Rouge: Louisiana State University Press, 1987.
Larson, Charles R. *Invisible Darkness: Jean Toomer and Nella Larsen*. Iowa City: University of Iowa Press, 1993.
McKay, Nellie Y. *Jean Toomer, Artist: A Study of His Literary Life and Work, 1894-1936*. Chapel Hill: University of North Carolina Press, 1984.
O'Daniel, Therman B., ed. *Jean Toomer: A Critical Evaluation*. Washington, D.C.: Howard University Press, 1988.

ALICE WALKER

Born: Eatonton, Georgia; February 9, 1944

Principal long fiction

The Third Life of Grange Copeland, 1970; *Meridian*, 1976; *The Color Purple*, 1982; *The Temple of My Familiar*, 1989; *Possessing the Secret of Joy*, 1992.

Other literary forms

Alice Walker has published several volumes of short fiction, poetry, children's literature, and essays.

Achievements

Walker's literary reputation is based primarily on her fiction, although her second book of poetry, *Revolutionary Petunias and Other Poems* (1973), received the Lillian Smith Award and a nomination for a National Book Award. Her first short-story collection, *In Love and Trouble* (1973), won the Rosenthal Award of the National Institute of Arts and Letters. In addition, she has received a Charles Merrill writing fellowship, an award for fiction from the National Endowment for the Arts (NEA), and a Guggenheim Fellowship. She has also been a Bread Loaf Scholar and a fellow at the Radcliffe Institute. *The Third Life of Grange Copeland* was widely and enthusiastically reviewed in journals as varied as *The New Yorker*, *The New Republic*, and *The New York Times Book Review*, although journals aimed primarily at a black readership were often silent or critical of the violence and graphic depiction of rural black life. With the publication of *Meridian*, Walker's second novel, her work as a poet, novelist, essayist, editor, teacher, scholar, and political activist came together. *Meridian* was universally praised in scholarly journals, literary magazines, popular magazines, and black-oriented journals. Some critics, mainly black male reviewers, objected again to the honest, straightforward portrayals of black life in the South and to Walker's growing feminism, which they saw in conflict with her commitment to her race. Walker's third novel, *The Color Purple*, was very widely acclaimed. The accolades were substantiated when Walker received both the Pulitzer Prize and the American Book Award in fiction in 1983. The novel became a successful film, directed by Steven Spielberg, in 1985.

Biography

Alice Walker was born in Eatonton, Georgia, on February 9, 1944, the last of eight children of Willie Lee and Minnie Lou Grant Walker, sharecroppers in rural Georgia. Her relationship with her father, at first strong and valuable, became strained as she became involved in the Civil Rights and feminist movements. A moving depiction of her estrangement from her father occurs in her essay "My Father's Country Is the Poor," which appeared in *The New York Times* in 1977. For Walker, a loving and healthy mother-daughter relationship has endured over the years. An account of that relationship is central to her essays "In Search of Our Mothers' Gardens" and "Lulls—A Native Daughter Returns to the Black South" and in Mary Helen Washington's article "Her Mother's Gifts," in which Walker acknowledges that she often writes with her mother's voice: "Just as you have certain physical characteristics of your mother . . . when you're compelled to write her stories, it's because you recognize and prize those qualities of her in yourself."

One of the central events in Walker's childhood was a BB gun accident that left her, at age eight, blind in one eye. Scar tissue from that wound, both physical and psychological, seems to have left her with a compensating acuteness of vision, despite the conviction that she was permanently disfigured. Walker's partial blindness allowed her to attend Spelman College in Atlanta on a scholarship for the handicapped following her graduation from Butler-Baker High School in 1961. She left Spelman after two years—which included summer trips to the Soviet Union and to Africa as part of a group called Experiment in International Living—for Sarah Lawrence College, from which she was graduated in 1965.

Walker's political activity controlled her movements during the years immediately following her college graduation: She spent the summer of 1965 in the Soviet Union and also worked for civil rights in Liberty County, Georgia. The next year she was a caseworker for New York City's Department of Social Services and then a voter-registration worker in Mississippi. In 1967, she married Melvyn Leventhal, a civil rights lawyer, and moved to Jackson, Mississippi. There she continued her civil rights work, lived in the heart of the South as part of an interracial couple, and taught at Jackson State University, while continuing to write stories, poems, and essays. She taught at Tougaloo College in Mississippi for a year before returning to the East, where she was a lecturer in writing and literature at Wellesley College, an editor at *Ms.* magazine, and an instructor at the University of Massachusetts at Boston. By 1977, she had divorced her husband, accepted a position as associate professor of English at Yale University, and written more books.

Walker has continued to write, teach, edit, lecture, and read poetry across the nation from her base in rural Northern California.

Analysis

The story of Walker's childhood scar provides the most basic metaphor of her novels: the idea that radical change is possible even under the worst conditions. Although she was never able to regain the sight in one eye, Walker's disfigurement was considerably lessened:

> I used to pray every night that I would wake up and somehow it would be gone. I couldn't look at people directly because I thought I was ugly. . . . Then when I was fourteen, I visited my brother Bill [who] took me to a hospital where they removed most of the scar tissue—and I was a *changed person.* I promptly went home, scooped up the best-looking guy, and by the time I graduated from high school, I was valedictorian, voted "Most Popular," and crowned queen!

That change and personal triumph is possible, despite the odds, is central to all Walker's writing. Walker herself has defined her "preoccupations" as a novelist: "The survival, the survival *whole* of my people. But beyond that I am committed to exploring the oppressions, the insanities, the loyalties, and the triumphs of black women." Her work focuses directly or indirectly on the ways of survival adopted by black women, usually in the South, and is presented in a prose style characterized by a distinctive combination of lyricism and unflinching realism. Walker's women attempt not merely to survive but to survive completely with some sense of stability, despite the constant thread of family violence, physical and mental abuse, and a lack of responsibility on the part of the men in their lives. Walker is simultaneously a feminist and a supporter of civil rights, not only for black Americans but also for minorities everywhere.

Meridian describes the struggles of a young black woman, Meridian Hill, who comes to an awareness of power and feminism during the Civil Rights movement, and whose whole life's meaning is centered in the cycles of guilt, violence, hope, and change characteristic of that dramatic time. Thematically, *Meridian* adopts the theme of self-sacrificial murder as a way out of desperate political oppression in the form of the constant question that drives Meridian Hill—"Will you kill for the Revolution?" Meridian's lifelong attempt to answer that question affirmatively (as her college friends so easily do) while remaining true to her sense of responsibility to the past, her sense of ethics, and her sense of guilt of having given to her mother the child of her teenage pregnancy constitutes the section of the novel entitled "Meridian."

The second third of the novel, "Truman Held," is named for the major male character in the narrative. At one time, Meridian loves Truman, but his callous treatment of her and his desertion of her for Lynne Rabinowitz, a white civil rights volunteer from the North, causes their relationship to change. By the novel's end, Meridian has become teacher, confidante, and savior to both Truman and Lynne, whose eventual marriage is destroyed by the pressures of interracial tensions.

The third major section of the novel, "Ending," looks back at the turmoil of the movement from the perspective of the 1970's. Long after others have given up intellectual arguments about the morality of killing for revolution, Meridian is still debating the question, still actively involved in voter registration, political activism, and civil rights organization, as though the movement had never lost momentum. Worrying that her actions, now seen as eccentric rather than revolutionary, will cause her "to be left, listening to the old music, beside the highway." Meridian achieves release and atonement through the realization that her role will be to "come forward and sing from memory songs they will need once more to hear. For it is the song of the people, transformed by the experiences of each generation, that holds them together."

In 1978, Walker described her second novel, *Meridian,* as "a book 'about' the civil rights movement, feminism, socialism, the shakiness of revolutionaries and the radicalization of saints. . . ." Her word "about" is exact, for the novel revolves around such topics; the central point remains the protagonist, Meridian Hill. In some ways, Meridian is a saint; by the book's end she has sustained her belief in the Civil Rights movement without losing faith in feminism and socialism, despite family pressures, guilt, literally paralyzing self-doubts, the history of the movement, and the sexism of many of its leaders. In contrast, Truman Held represents those males who were reported to have said that "the only position for a woman in the movement is prone." Although Truman Held is Meridian's initial teacher in the movement, she eventually leaves him behind because of his inability to sustain his initial revolutionary fervor, and because of his misogyny. Later in the novel, Truman marries a white civil rights worker, whose rape by another black man produces disgust in him, as much at his wife as at the man. When Truman seeks Meridian out in a series of small Southern hamlets where she continues to persuade black people to register to vote and to struggle for civil rights, he tells her that the movement is ended and that he grieves in a different way than she. Meridian answers, "I know how you grieve by running away. By pretending you were never there." Like Grange Copeland, Truman Held refuses to take responsibility for his own problems, preferring to run away to the North.

Meridian's sacrificial dedication to the movement becomes a model for atonement and release, words that once formed the working title of the book. Meridian leads three lives: as an uneducated child in rural Georgia who follows the traditional pattern of early pregnancy and aimless marriage; as a college student actively participating in political demonstrations; and as an eccentric agitator—a performer, she calls herself—unaware that the movement is ended. Meridian Hill is solid proof of the ability of any human to change dramatically by sheer will and desire.

The writing is clear, powerful, violent, lyrical, and often symbolic. Spelman College, for example, is here called Saxon College. The large magnolia tree in the center of the campus, described with specific folkloric detail, is destroyed by angry students during a demonstration: "Though Meridian begged them to dismantle the president's house instead, in a fury of confusion and frustration they worked all night, and chopped and sawed down, level to the ground, that mighty, ancient, sheltering music tree." This tree (named "The Sojourner," perhaps for Sojourner Truth) expands symbolically to suggest both the senseless destruction of black ghettos by blacks during the turmoil of the 1960's and also Meridian Hill herself, who receives a photograph years later of The Sojourner, now "a gigantic tree stump" with "a tiny branch, no larger than a finger, growing out of one side." That picture, suggesting as it does the rebirth of hope despite despair, also evokes the last vision of Meridian expressed by the now-shamed Truman Held: "He would never see 'his' Meridian again. The new part had grown out of the old, though, and that was reassuring. This part of her, new, sure and ready, even eager, for the world, he knew he must meet again and recognize for its true value at some future time."

The Color Purple presents the author's familiar and yet fresh themes—survival and redemption—in epistolary form. Most of the novel's letters are written by Celie, an uneducated, unloved, black woman living in rural Georgia in the 1920's; Celie's letters are written in what Walker calls "black folk English," a language of wit, strength, and natural humor. Ashamed of having been raped by her stepfather, a man whom Celie thinks at the time is her father, she begins to send letters to God, in the way that children send letters to Santa Claus, because her rapist told her to tell nobody but God. Although her early letters tell of rape, degradation, and pain, of her stepfather's getting rid of the two children born of his cruelty, the tone is nevertheless captivating, ironic, and even humorous. Soon the despair turns into acceptance, then into understanding, anger, rebellion, and finally triumph and loving forgiveness as the fourteen-year-old Celie continues to write until she reaches an audience, some thirty years later. Like the author, who began writing at the age of eight, and who has turned her childhood experience in rural Georgia into three novels of violence, hatred, understanding, love, and profound hope for the future, Celie is a writer, a listener, a thinker, and a promoter of Walker's constant theme: "Love redeems, meanness kills."

Like Meridian Hill, Celie, compares herself to a tree. Following the rape, Celie is sold into a virtual state of slavery to a man who beats her, a man she neither knows, loves, nor talks to, a man she can never call anything but Mr. ——, an ironic throwback to the eighteenth century English epistolary novel. Celie tries to endure by withholding all emotion: "I make myself wood. I say to myself, Celie, you a tree. That's how come I know trees fear man."

Based on Walker's great-grandmother, a slave who was raped at twelve by her owner, Celie works her way from ignorance about her body and her living situation all the way through to an awakening of her self-worth, as well as to an understanding of the existence of God, the relations between men and women, and the power of forgiveness in uniting family and friends. Much of this transformation is brought about through the magic of blues singer Shug Avery, who guides Celie in understanding sexuality, men, and religion without causing her to lose her own fresh insights, naïve though they are.

The letters that make up the novel are something like the missives that the protagonist of Saul Bellow's novel *Herzog* (1964) writes but never sends, in that they are often addressed to God and written in an ironic but not self-conscious manner. Because of the combination of dark humor and despair, the letters also evoke memories of the desperate letters from the physically and spiritually maimed addressed to the hero of Nathanael West's *Miss Lonelyhearts* (1933). Although Celie is unlettered in a traditional sense, her ability to carry the complicated plot forward and to continue to write—first without an earthly audience, and then to her sister, whom she has not seen for more than twenty years—testifies to the human potential for self-transformation.

Discussing Celie's attempts to confirm her existence by writing to someone she is not certain exists, Gloria Steinem says, "Clearly, the author is telling us something about the origin of Gods: about when we need to invent them and when we don't." In a sense, Shug Avery becomes a god for Celie because of her ability to control the evil in the world and her power to change the sordid conditions of Celie's life. Early in the book, when Celie is worrying about survival, about rape, incest, beatings, and the murder of her children, her only source of hope is the name "Shug Avery," a name with a magical power to control Celie's husband. Not even aware that Shug is a person, Celie writes, "I ast our new mammy bout Shug Avery. What it is?" Finding a picture of Shug, Celie transfers her prayers to what is at that point only an image: "I see her there in furs. Her face rouge. Her hair like somethin tail. She grinning with her foot up on somebody motocar. Her eyes serious tho. Sad some. . . . An all night long I stare at it. An now when I dream, I dream of Shug Avery. She be dress to kill, whirling an laughing." Shug Avery becomes a god to Celie not only because she is pictured in the first photograph Celie has

ever seen but also because she is dressed in a style that shows a sense of pride and freedom.

Once return letters from Celie's missionary sister Nettie begin to appear, mailed from Africa, the ironic connection between the primitive animism of the Africans and Celie's equally primitive reaction to Shug's picture becomes clear. Although Nettie has crossed the ocean to minister to a tribe of primitive people, her own sister is living in inhuman conditions in Georgia: ignorance, disease, sexism, lack of control of the environment, and the ever-increasing march of white people. When Shug explains her own animistic religious beliefs—which include the notion that God is not a he or a she but an it (just as Celie once thought Shug Avery was an it)—Celie is converted to a pantheistic worship that makes her early identification with trees seem less naïve.

When the narrator of Herman Melville's "Bartleby the Scrivener" tries to explain Bartleby's withdrawal from life, he thinks of the dead letter office in which the scrivener was rumored to have worked, and says, "On errands of life, these letters speed to death." In contrast, Celie's and Nettie's letters, ostensibly written to people long thought to be dead, speed across the ocean on errands of life, where they grow to sustain, not merely the sisters in the book, but all those lucky enough to read them. There is no question that Alice Walker's name could be substituted for Celie's in a statement made by the author: "Let's hope people can hear Celie's voice. There are so many people like Celie who make it, who come out of nothing. People who triumph."

Walker once described herself as a "womanist": by her definition, a black feminist acutely concerned with the double oppression of racism and sexism in American society. Her literary themes are generally revolutionary and confront the modern experiences of all African Americans but particularly those of black women.

Other major works

SHORT FICTION: *In Love and Trouble: Stories of Black Women*, 1973; *You Can't Keep a Good Woman Down*, 1981.

POETRY: *Once: Poems*, 1968; *Five Poems*, 1972; *Revolutionary Petunias and Other Poems*, 1973; *Goodnight, Willie Lee, I'll See You in the Morning: Poems*, 1979; *Horses Make a Landscape Look More Beautiful*, 1984; *Her Blue Body Everything We Know: Earthling Poems, 1965-1990 Complete*, 1991.

NONFICTION: *I Love Myself When I Am Laughing . . . And Then Again When I Am Looking Mean and Impressive: A Zora Neale Hurston Reader*, 1979 (edited); *In Search of Our Mothers' Gardens: Womanist Prose*, 1983; *Living by the Word: Selected Writings, 1973-1987*, 1988; *Warrior Marks: Female Genital Mutilation and the Sexual Blinding of Women*, 1993 (with Pratibha Parmar).

CHILDREN'S LITERATURE: *Langston Hughes: American Poet*, 1974; *To Hell with Dying*, 1988; *Finding the Green Stone*, 1991.

Bibliography

Bloom, Harold, ed. *Alice Walker: Modern Critical Views*. New York: Chelsea House, 1989.

Christian, Barbara. *Black Feminist Criticism*. New York: Pergamon Press, 1985.

Davis, Thadious M., and Trudier Harris. *Afro-American Fiction Writers After 1955*. Vol. 33 in *Dictionary of Literary Biography*. Detroit: Gale Research, 1984.

Fairbanks, Carol, and Eugene A. Engeldinger. *Black American Fiction: A Bibliography*. Metuchen, N.J.: Scarecrow Press, 1978.

Gates, Henry Louis, Jr., and K. A. Appiah, eds. *Alice Walker: Critical Perspectives Past and Present*. New York: Amistad, 1993.

Howard, Lillie P., ed. *Alice Walker and Zora Neale Hurston: The Common Bond*. Westport, Conn.: Greenwood Press, 1993.

Pratt, Louis H., and Darrell D. Pratt. *Alice Malsenior Walker: An Annotated Bibliography, 1968-1986*. Westport, Conn.: Meckler, 1988.

Tate, Claudia. *Black Women Writers at Work*. New York: Continuum, 1983.

Winchell, Donna Haisty. *Alice Walker*. New York: Twayne, 1992.

JOHN EDGAR WIDEMAN

Born: Washington, D.C.; June 14, 1941

Principal long fiction

A Glance Away, 1967; *Hurry Home*, 1970; *The Lynchers*, 1973; *Hiding Place*, 1981; *Sent for You Yesterday*, 1983; *The Homewood Trilogy*, 1985 (includes *Damballah*, *Hiding Place*, and *Sent for You Yesterday); Reuben*, 1987; *Philadelphia Fire*, 1990.

Other literary forms

An intensely lyrical novelist, John Edgar Wideman has also published numerous short stories based upon family members, friends, and neighbors from his childhood community of Homewood, a long-standing all-black subdivision of Pittsburgh, Pennsylvania. Twelve of these pieces are presented as letters in his critically acclaimed collection *Damballah* (1981), which has also been published with two of his novels as *The Homewood Trilogy*. Wideman's autobiographical *Brothers and Keepers* (1984) blends facts with fictionalized characters and incidents as the author scrutinizes his own relationship to his brother, Robert Wideman, imprisoned for life in Pennsylvania's Western State Penitentiary. *Fever* (1989), a collection of twelve stories, combines themes of family and community with those of displacement, estrangement, and cultural loss. Uncollected poetry, reviews, and essays on African American literature by Wideman abound in the foremost scholarly journals and literary digests.

Achievements

When he emerged upon the literary scene in the late 1960's, Wideman stood out from his peers as an African American writer who did not address exclusively themes of racial conflict and militant nationalism. He concentrated instead on individual psychological struggles that transcend color lines. His earliest novels having been enthusiastically received, he was lauded as a successor to William Faulkner. Nevertheless, it can be argued that he really did not tap the depths of his talent until, influenced in part by slave narratives and African folklore, he initiated his Homewood series. Expressing the black American experience epitomized by Homewood's extensive French family and their fictive kin, *Sent for You Yesterday* received the 1984 Faulkner Award for Fiction from PEN, the International Association of Poets, Playwrights, Editors, Essayists, and Novelists. *Philadelphia Fire* earned the honor in 1991.

In spite of favorable reviews of his fiction, many people have accused Wideman of indulging in an unconventional style at the expense of theme. More often than not, though, his experimentation extends meaning by illustrating the impact of the past in addition to the inextricable bonds among generations. In fact, his autobiographical *Brothers and Keepers*, which displays some of his innovative techniques, earned a National Book Critics Circle Award nomination. Hailed as "the most authentic black blues voice since Billie Holiday," Wideman certainly merits consideration as one of the best American writers of his generation.

Biography

Born in Washington, D.C., on June 14, 1941, John Edgar Wideman initially aspired to be a professional basketball player. Consequently, he served as both a Benjamin Franklin Scholar at the University of Pennsylvania and captain of the school's championship basketball team. A member of Phi Beta Kappa, he was graduated from the University of Pennsylvania in 1963 with a B.A. degree in English. Promptly selected as only the second black Rhodes Scholar in history, he received his B.Ph. degree from Oxford University in 1966, specializing as a Thouron Fellow in the eighteenth century novel. He then spent one year as a Kent Fellow at the University of Iowa Writers' Workshop, subsequently returning to lecture at his alma mater, Pennsylvania. while writing and teaching literature at the University of Wyoming, he endured the conviction of his oldest son, Jacob, on charges of fatally stabbing another youth during a camping trip in Arizona. This tragedy recalls the imprisonment of his brother Robert for involvement in a robbery and killing. A professor of English at the University of Massachusetts, Amherst, since 1986, he has contributed articles and review essays to *The New York Times Book Review* and to popular magazines such as *TV Guide*, *Life*, and *Esquire*.

Analysis

Wideman's works use experimental literary techniques to explore African American themes concerning social injustice and the violence that it generates. He dramatizes the issues faced by black American males in a racist society, particularly the issue of cultural rootlessness and isolation.

The recurring thematic emphasis in Wideman's novels is placed upon history, both collective and personal. From homosexual college professors to ghetto junkies, Wideman's characters are often uncomfortable with their places in history and unsure that they even understand those few traditions that they do observe. Therefore, they shuttle between the imaginary and the real in order to rediscover the past, revive it, or at least preserve whatever parts they do recall. Despite Wideman's literary beginnings in the racially turbulent 1960's, when blacks in America articulated their estrangement from Africa, his white as well as black characters crave the rootedness that distinguishes those who have come to terms with their backgrounds. Shifting from the anonymous Northern cities of his first three novels to the clearly delineated Homewood of *Hiding Place* and *Sent for You Yesterday*, Wideman nevertheless consistently indicates that ignorance of heritage results in isolation and psychological turmoil.

Wideman forgoes strictly chronological plot development, adopting instead an intricate experimental style consisting of stream-of-consciousness narrative, long interior monologues, dream sequences, surrealistic descriptions, and abrupt shifts in time, diction, and points of view. Beginning each novel almost exclusively *in medias res*, he employs a technique influenced by the works of T. S. Eliot, James Joyce, and Jean Toomer yet indisputably original. In *The Lynchers*, for example, he illustrates the traditionally victimized status of black Americans with a preface that cites more than one hundred documented lynchings. Reeling between their own ravaged communities and impenetrable white ones, the black protagonists of his first two novels, *A Glance Away* and *Hurry Home*, occupy a jumbled landscape where blues clubs coexist with biblical icons. Similarly, in *Hiding Place* and *Sent for You Yesterday*, Wideman retells the stories of his ancestors until a shack or a cape acquires the same expressive quality as a cross.

Dedicated to "Homes," *A Glance Away* creates thematic excitement with its treatment of two drifting men coming to terms with their pasts. After a year spent at a rehabilitation center for drug addicts, Eddie Lawson, a disillusioned young black man, returns to his listless, decaying urban neighborhood. Rather than celebrating, however, he spends his gloomy homecoming confronting the goblins that drove him to the brink in the first place: his mother Martha Lawson's idealization of his dead older brother, his girlfriend Alice Smalls's rejection of him for sleeping with a white woman, and his own self-disgust over abandoning a secure postal job for menial, marginal employment. Dejected and defeated by nightfall, he drags himself to grimy Harry's Place in order to cloak his memories in a narcotic haze. There, he is reconciled by his albino friend, Brother Smalls, with another outcast, Robert Thurley, a white college professor struggling with his own record of divorce, alcoholism, and homosexuality. Though discrepancies between wealth and power divide the two homeless men, each manages to urge the other to maintain his faith in people despite his guilt-ridden history.

A Glance Away generated much favorable critical response in particular for Wideman's depiction of the alienated Thurley. In trying to disavow his personal past, this connoisseur of food and art embraces a surfeit of creeds and cultures. "In religion an aesthetic Catholic, in politics a passive Communist, in sex a resigned anarchist," he surrounds himself with treasures from both East and West and indulges in a smorgasbord of the globe's delicacies. Yet as a real measure of the displacement that these extravagances so futilely conceal, he quotes lines from T. S. Eliot's "The Love Song of J. Alfred Prufrock," in which a similarly solitary speaker searches for intimacy in a world bereft of its cultural moorings.

Emphasizing his protagonists' self-absorption and the estrangement of their family members and friends, Wideman abandons strictly chronological plot development in favor of lengthy interior monologues. Conversations tend to be short; more likely than not they are interrupted by unspoken flashbacks and asides. Using speech to measure isolation, the author portrays both Eddie and Thurley as incapable of communicating adequately. Eddie, for example, becomes tongue-tied around a group of Southern travelers, shuddering in his bus seat instead of warning them as he wishes of the reality of the Northern mecca that they seek. Similarly, despite the empowering qualities of a gulp of Southern Comfort, Thurley delivers a lecture on Sophocles' *Oedipus Tyrannus* (c. 429 B.C.) fraught with "futility and detachment, . . . introspection and blindness." In one brilliant play on this speechlessness, both men suddenly converse as if they were actors on a stage. This abrupt emphasis on what is spoken—to the exclusion of private thoughts—stresses each man's imprisonment within himself. Flowing from a weaker artist's pen, *A Glance Away* would have become a mere exercise in allusive technique and stream-of-consciousness style. On the contrary, it reads with the effortless ease of a masterfully crafted lyrical poem. Key to its success is Wideman's careful alliance of form and content, not to mention his insightful treatment of a rootlessness that transcends the barriers of race.

The same compact length as the novel that precedes it, *Hurry Home* similarly focuses upon the theme of rootlessness. Its ambitious protagonist, the honors graduate Cecil Otis Braithwaite, is in many ways an upscale Eddie Lawson with a wife and an advanced degree. After slaving through law school, supporting himself with a meager scholarship and his earnings as a janitor, Cecil has lost his aspirations and his love for his girlfriend, Esther Brown. In search of something more, he escapes from his wedding bed to Europe, where he roams indiscriminately for three years among its brothels as well as its art galleries. In the tradition of Robert Thurley of *A Glance Away*, two white men as displaced as Cecil attempt to guide him: Charles Webb, belatedly in search of an illegitimate son, and Albert, a mercenary in Webb's employ who has also abandoned a wife. Too lost to save themselves, however, this pair can offer no enduring words of solace to Cecil.

Hurry Home is more sophisticated than *A Glance Away* in its treatment of the isolation theme. It suggests, for example, that the upwardly mobile Cecil is not merely disturbed by his personal past; he is estranged as well from his African and European cultures of origin. Yet nowhere does *Hurry Home* convey the hope that pervades its predecessor. Cecil travels more extensively than does Eddie to reclaim his past, yet he gains no key to it to speak of. Confronting his European heritage merely confirms his status as "a stranger in all . . . tongues." He flees to the African continent by boat, "satisfied to be forever possessed," only to be forever rebuffed from a past that "melts like a wax casing as I am nearer . . . the flame." When he returns at last to his Washington, D.C., tenement, the fruitlessness of his journey is underscored. There, he finds all the same as when he first entered following his miserable nuptials. Symbolically limning his rootlessness, he switches vocations, abandoning the tradition-steeped protocol of the bar for the faddish repertoire of a hairdresser. Thus, "hurry home," the catchphrase for his odyssey, is an ironic one. Cecil really can claim no place where a

heritage nurtures and sustains him, no history that he can truly call his own.

Hurry Home displays a masterful style commensurate with that of the later Homewood novels. In addition to a more controlled stream-of-consciousness technique, recurring Christian symbols, icons of Renaissance art, and fragments from Moorish legend powerfully indicate Cecil's fractured lineage. This second novel being a more refined paradigm than the first, Wideman seemed next inclined to break new ground, to address intently the racial polarization that had unsettled American society by the early 1970's, producing that period's most influential published works.

After an eight-year interval during which he researched black American literature and culture, Wideman applied folk sources more fully than ever before in *Hiding Place*, one of the three works of fiction that make up *The Homewood Trilogy*. Challenged to enlarge his black readership without limiting the universal relevance of his themes, he chose to emphasize one black family based largely on his own Homewood clan. In this novel's swift, uncomplicated plot, Tommy Lawson, a tough, wisecracking youth from the black neighborhood of Homewood, is running from the police for his involvement in a robbery and killing. He seeks refuge among the weedy plots and garbage piles of desolate Bruston Hill, a once-fertile area to which his ancestor Sybela Owens fled from the South and slavery with Charlie Bell, her white owner's recalcitrant son. In the lone residence at the crest of the Hill, a rotting wooden shack sardonically known as "that doghouse," the reclusive "Mother" Bess Owens reluctantly offers her sister's great-grandson a temporary haven. After Tommy regains the courage to elude the authorities eager to convict him for a murder that he did not commit, Bess reaffirms her ties to her kin and ends her self-imposed isolation. Not knowing whether Tommy is dead, has escaped, or has been captured, she burns her shack and prepares to reenter Homewood to retell Tommy's tragic story so that another like it might never happen again.

Though Bess does not leave her longtime home until the novel's final chapter, *Hiding Place* is as much the story of her isolation from family as it is one of Tommy's. Just as Tommy has shirked his responsibilities as a husband, father, and son, Bess has turned her back upon the younger generations of kin whose ways are alien to her. Widowed and childless, she has retreated into an archaic lifestyle, shunning the twentieth century amenities of electricity and phones, in order to avoid intimacy with others. Physically rooting herself among Bruston Hill's ruins, she has been running from the present in her mind by focusing her thoughts on the past, especially the deaths of loved ones that have occurred. Only when she becomes involved in Tommy's affairs does she rekindle her active commitment to the family.

In *Hiding Place*, Wideman's style dramatically differs from those of the canonized white writers who were his early models. With a method many reviewers have compared to jazz, his characters unfold the histories of five generations of Lawsons and Frenches. Bess herself repeats certain key events in the family history several times; one of her favorites is the one in which Mary Hollinger revives her cousin Freeda French's stillborn baby by plunging it into the snow. Yet like a jazz improvisation, where instruments alternately play solo and play together, she retells the tale each time in a different way, varying her approach to it with different bits of superstition, mysticism, and folklore. Even Wideman's Clement, an inarticulate orphan similar to Benjy Compson in William Faulkner's *The Sound and the Fury* (1929), bears the unique stamp of the black American experience. As the author himself avows, Clement's assimilation into Homewood reflects the nature of the black community as a tolerant extended family.

Its legacy of songs, tales, and superstitions notwithstanding, the Homewood that finally draws Bess back is a model of urban blight, a "bombed out" no-man's-land of "pieces of buildings standing here and there and fire scars and places ripped and kicked down and cars stripped and dead at the curb." This dying landscape, and in a similar way Bess's ramshackle Bruston Hill homestead, proclaims the present descendants' dissociation from their ancestors and one another. In *Sent for You Yesterday*, the final installment of *The Homewood Trilogy* and the 1984 PEN Faulkner Award winner for outstanding fiction, this undercurrent becomes the novel's predominant theme. Carl French and his lover Lucy Tate relate the stories of a Homewood gone by to the latest generation of listeners, as if the recovery of the past is integral to the entire community's survival and solidarity.

Sent for You Yesterday cannot be divided easily into main story and subplots. All the episodes in it are major in scope and significance. The most memorable ones include the saga of the piano player Albert Wilkes, who slept with a white woman and murdered a white policeman; the tragedy of Samantha, whose college education could not shield her from grief and madness; and the bittersweet adventures of the resilient Brother Tate, an albino and best friend of Carl who communicates only with gestures and scat sounds. Retold by Carl's nephew Doot, a former Homewood resident modeled largely after Wideman himself, each tale conveys a lesson to a younger generation. More than mere example, however, the stories emphasize the cyclic nature of the human condition: Each generation rises to further, alter, and often reenact the accomplishments of its predecessors. Thus, Uncle Carl's street in Homewood becomes to Doot "a narrow, cobbled alley *teeming* with life. Like a wooden-walled ship in the middle of the city, like the ark on which Noah packed two of everything and prayed for land." This determination to survive that the ark imagery calls to mind impels Carl and Lucy to share Homewood's history. By remembering past lives, by preserving traditions, they ensure their own enduring places in the memories of their heirs.

Wideman's novels present black America from the perspectives of the enslaved and the descendants of the enslaved, as well as from the vantage of those whites who served as either tormentors and oppressors or benefactors and friends. These works warn of the potholes where our elders slipped before, and they expose the reader to the vistas that one often fails to notice and enjoy. They achieve Wideman's goal of ever "expanding our notions of reality, creating hard, crisp edges you can't swallow without a gulp."

Other major works

SHORT FICTION: *Damballah*, 1981; *Fever*, 1989; *The Stories of John Edgar Wideman*, 1992.
NONFICTION: *Brothers and Keepers*, 1984.

Bibliography

Berben, Jacqueline. "Beyond Discourse: The Unspoken Versus Words in the Fiction of John Edgar Wideman." *Callaloo* 8 (Fall, 1985): 525-534.
Coleman, James W. *Blackness and Modernism: The Literary Career of John Edgar Wideman*. Jackson: University Press of Mississippi, 1989.

_____ . "Going Back Home: The Literary Development of John Edgar Wideman." *CLA Journal* 27 (March, 1985): 326-343.

Frazier, Kermit. "The Novels of John Wideman: An Analysis." *Black World* 24 (June, 1975): 18-38.

O'Brien, John. *Interviews with Black Writers*. New York: Liveright, 1973.

Putnam, Linda. "Home Again at Last." *Rocky Mountain Magazine* (April 4, 1982): 74-76.

Samuels, Wilfred D. "Going Home: A Conversation with John Edgar Wideman." *Callaloo* 6 (February, 1983): 40-59.

Wideman, John Edgar. "The Black Writer and the Magic of the Word." *The New York Times Book Review* 113 (January 24, 1988): 1, 27-28.

_____ . "Fear in the Streets." *The American Scholar* 40 (Autumn, 1971): 611-622.

_____ . "Home: An Interview with John Edgar Wideman." Interview by Jessica Lustig. *African American Review* 26, no. 3 (Fall, 1992): 453.

Wilson, Matthew. "The Circles of History in John Edgar Wideman's *The Homewood Trilogy*." CLA Journal 33 (March, 1990): 239-259.

AUGUST WILSON

Born: Pittsburgh, Pennsylvania; April 27, 1945

Principal drama

Ma Rainey's Black Bottom, pr. 1984, pb. 1985; *Fences*, pr., pb. 1985; *Joe Turner's Come and Gone*, pr. 1986, pb. 1988; *The Piano Lesson*, pr. 1987, pb. 1990; *Three Plays*, 1991; *Two Trains Running*, pr. 1990, pb. 1992.

Other literary forms

Some of August Wilson's poetry was published in African American literary journals, such as *Black World*, in 1969. He is known primarily for his plays.

Achievements

Critics have hailed Wilson as an authentic voice of African American culture. His plays explore the black experience historically and in the context of deeper metaphysical roots in African culture. Between 1984 and 1992, his major plays have been successfully produced by regional theaters and on Broadway; in fact, he is the first African American playwright to have had two plays running on Broadway simultaneously.

Wilson has received an impressive array of fellowships and awards: the Jerome Fellowship in 1980, the Bush Foundation Fellowship in 1982, membership in the New Dramatists starting in 1983, and the Rockefeller Fellowship in 1984. He has also been an associate of Playwrights Center, Minneapolis, and received the McKnight Fellowship in 1985, the Guggenheim Fellowship in 1986, five New York Drama Critics Circle Awards from 1985 to 1990, the Whiting Foundation Award in 1986, the Pulitzer Prize in drama in 1987 (for *Fences*) and 1990 (for *The Piano Lesson*), the Tony Award by the League of New York Theatres and Producers (for *Fences*), the American Theatre Critics Award in 1986, the Outer Circle Award in 1987, and the Drama Desk Award and John Gassner Award in 1987.

Wilson's goals are "to concretize the black cultural response to the world, to place that response in loud action, so as to create a dramatic literature as powerful and sustaining as black American music." While the form of his plays breaks no new ground, the substance and language produce powerful emotional responses. Rooted in the black experience, Wilson's plays touch universal chords.

Biography

August Wilson was born in Pittsburgh, Pennsylvania, on April 27, 1945, in the Hill District, a black neighborhood. He was one of six children born to Daisy Wilson from North Carolina, and a German baker, Frederick August Kittel, who eventually abandoned the family. Wilson left school at fifteen when a teacher refused to take his word that a twenty-page paper on Napoleon was his own work. He spent the next few weeks in the library, pretending to be at school. It was through reading, especially all the books he could find in the "Negro" subject section, that Wilson educated himself.

Later, Wilson worked at odd jobs and spent time on street corners and at a cigar store called Pat's Place, listening to old men tell stories. Coming into adulthood during the Black Power movement of the 1960's, Wilson was influenced by it and participated in the Black Arts movement in Pittsburgh, writing and publishing poetry in black journals. With longtime friend Rob Penny, he founded the Black Horizons Theatre Company in Pittsburgh in 1968. He produced and directed plays, but his efforts at playwriting in those years failed, he later recalled, because he "didn't respect the way blacks talked" and thus "always tried to alter it." He formed a connection with the Penumbra company in St. Paul and moved there in 1978. It was in this much smaller black community that he learned to regard the "voices I had been brought up with all my life" with greater respect.

Married in 1981 to Judy Oliver (he has a daughter, Sakina Ansari, from an earlier marriage), Wilson began to write scripts for the children's theater of a local science museum. This effort led him to submit his scripts to the National Playwrights Conference at the Eugene O'Neill Center in Waterford, Connecticut. His work caught the attention of conference director Lloyd Richards, who was also the dean of the Yale School of Drama and the artistic director of the Yale Repertory Company. Under Richards' direction, a staged reading of *Ma Rainey's Black Bottom* was performed in 1982 at the Eugene O'Neill Center, followed by a production at

Yale and a Broadway success. The four succeeding plays by Wilson followed the same pattern, sometimes with intervening production at other regional theaters.

Divorced in 1990, Wilson moved to Seattle, Washington, where he continued to write another of his cycle of plays. He also participated as a dramaturge at the Eugene O'Neill Center when one of his own works was not being produced.

Analysis

Each of Wilson's major plays dramatizes the African American experience in a different decade of the twentieth century, and the action of each play is driven by the arrival or presence of a character who has what Wilson calls the "warrior spirit," the quality that makes an individual dissatisfied and determined to change or disrupt the status quo. Each of the plays is affected by Wilson's feeling for the blues, music that he calls the "flag bearer of self-definition" for African Americans. Characters sing the blues, music is called for in scene transitions, and the rhythms of the dialogue reflect the blues. His plays are written to be performed on a single setting with action that is chronological. While he writes within the genre of psychological realism, each play displays a different degree of adherence to structure and plotting. His characters, mostly men, are African Americans uncertain of their own places in the world.

One of Wilson's greatest strengths is with language: The authenticity and rhythms of the dialogue and the colorful vitality of metaphor and storytelling connect him to the oral tradition of the African American and African cultures. He discussed in an interview the indirect quality of black speech, with its circling of issues and answers that are not answers. Characters answer the question they think is intended, not necessarily the one that is expressed. This language, in fact, often becomes the unique poetry of his drama. The language is full of implied meanings and dependent on tonal quality for interpretation. Wilson also places increasing emphasis with each play on the superstitions and beliefs that affect his characters. These superstitions seem to come from a mixture of Christianity, ancient African religions, and street wisdom.

In *Ma Rainey's Black Bottom*, Wilson uses a historical figure, "Mother of the Blues" singer Ma Rainey, and invents a story around her. The setting is a simultaneous representation of a 1927 recording studio and a band-rehearsal room. Overlooking the studio from the control booth are Ma's white producer and white agent, their presence and location a graphic symbol of white society's control over black music.

The dialogue seems to meander through silly and inconsequential matters. The underlying seriousness of these matters becomes apparent as the characters reveal their ways of coping with the white world. Ma Rainey plays the prima donna (note the pun in the play's title) while she acknowledges to her band that, like all black artists, she is exploited. Her music is her "way of understanding life." Wilson centers her in the play, a dynamic and colorful presence, but the character central to the action is Levee.

Levee has the warrior spirit. The tragic irony is that when he lashes out and kills, he kills the only educated band member in the play. His urge for self-sufficiency (to have his own band and make his own music) becomes self-destructive. By implication, Wilson suggests that the misplaced rage of his race can result in self-destruction. The grimly serious resolution to this play does not describe the tone of lightness and humor in much that precedes it. It is Levee's appetite that drives the play, sometimes comically, and it is his frustrated hunger that causes an unnecessary death.

Wilson's second major work, *Fences*, won a Pulitzer Prize in drama as well as Tony Awards for Wilson, the director, and two actors. It centers on the dynamic, volatile character Troy Maxson and takes place primarily in 1957. Troy is the warrior character whose spirit disrupts his own life as well as those of his sons and wife. Often inviting comparison with Arthur Miller's *Death of a Salesman* (pr. 1949), *Fences* dramatizes the life of a baseball player prevented from realizing his big-league dreams by the color barrier, overcome too late for him. *Fences* is about a man's battle with life and his emotional, sometimes irrational way of facing unfairness, pain, love, hate. The fence that Troy built around his life, like that built around his home, could neither shut out the world's injustice nor protect his family or himself from his shortcomings. The final scene occurs after Troy's death in 1965, when others can express feelings about Troy that were not articulated before. This scene provides a quietly emotional contrast to the intensely alive Troy of the previous eight scenes. It is a necessary scene and points up the failure of father and son to express directly what they felt in their earlier confrontation.

Troy's brother, Gabriel, whose head injury from the war has made him believe himself to be God's angel Gabriel, provides a kind of mystical presence. Wilson uses his madness for a theatrically effective closing to the play. When Gabriel discovers that his horn will not blow to open the gates of heaven for Troy, he performs a weird "dance of atavistic signature and ritual" and howls a kind of song to open the gates. This marks the beginning of Wilson's increasing use of ritual, myth, and superstition in his plays.

In *Joe Turner's Come and Gone*, Wilson reaches further back into the historical black experience. As in the old blues song of the same title, the brother of the governor of Tennessee, Joe Turner, found and enslaved groups of black men. Herald Loomis, the mysterious central character in this play, was so enslaved in 1901 and not released for seven years. The play dramatizes his search for his wife, which is actually a search for himself. His arrival at a Pittsburgh boardinghouse in 1911 disrupts and disturbs, creating the tension and significance of the drama.

Another boardinghouse resident, Bynum, establishes his identity as a "conjure man" or "rootworker" early in the play. Bynum's search for his "shiny man" becomes a thematic and structural tie for the play. At the end of the first act, during a joyous African call-and-response dance, Loomis has a sort of ecstatic fit, ending with his being unable to stand and walk. Some kind of dramatic resolution must relate Bynum's vision and Loomis' quest. It comes in the final scene when wife Martha returns and Loomis learns that his quest is still unrealized. Wilson describes Loomis' transformation in actions rather than words. His wife does not restore him; her religion does not restore him. In desperation, he turns a knife on himself, rubs his hands and face in his own blood, looks down at his hands, and says, "I'm standing. My legs stood up! I'm standing now!" It is at this point that he has found his "song of self-sufficiency." Wilson's rather poetic stage directions articulate a redemption that Loomis cannot verbalize, risking audience misinterpretation.

Bynum's final line of the play recognizes Loomis as a shiny man, the shiny man who can tell him the meaning of life. The suggestion of a Christ figure is unmistakable, and yet Loomis' soul is not cleansed through religious belief. He has denied the Christ of the white man, despite Martha's pleading. His epiphany is in finding himself. Joe Turner has come but he has also gone. Herald Loomis finds his identity in his own African roots, not in the slave identity that the white Joe Turner had given him.

With his fourth major play, Wilson crafts a more tightly structured plot. In fact, *The Piano Lesson* is stronger thematically and structurally than it is in char-acter development. The characters serve to dramatize the conflict between the practical use of a family heritage to create a future, and a symbolic treasuring of that heritage to honor the past. The piano, which bears the blood of their slave ancestors, is the focus of the conflict between Boy Willie and his sister, Berniece. Its exotic carvings, made by their great grandfather, tell the story of their slave ancestors who were sold in exchange for the piano. Its presence in the northern home of Berniece and her Uncle Doaker represents the life of their father, who died stealing it back from Sutter.

Berniece is embittered and troubled not only by the piano and her father's death but also by her mother's blood and tears, which followed that death, and by the loss of her own husband. In contrast, Boy Willie is upbeat and funny, an optimistic, ambitious, and boyish man who is sure he is right in wanting to sell the piano to buy Sutter's land. He has the warrior spirit. Throughout the play, the presence of Sutter's ghost is seen or felt. Sutter's ghost seems to represent the control that the white man still exerts over this family in 1937. Boy Willie chooses to ignore the ghost, to accuse his sister of imagining it, but ultimately it is Boy Willie who must wrestle with the ghost. The conflict is indeed unresolved as Boy Willie leaves, telling Berniece that she had better keep playing that piano or he and Sutter could both come back.

Wilson has said that Berniece and boy Willie are both right. The lesson of the piano is twofold: Berniece has learned that she should use her heritage, rather than let it fester in bitterness, and Boy Willie has learned that he cannot ignore the significance of this piano, which symbolizes the pain and suffering of all of his ancestors. There is little in the play that deviates from the central conflict. The skill of Wilson's writing is seen in the interplay of characters bantering and arguing, in the indirect quality of questions that are not answered, and in the storytelling. While the characters may serve primarily as symbols and plot devices, they are nevertheless vivid and credible.

The disruptive character in Wilson's fifth play is Sterling, but the theme of *Two Trains Running*, set in 1969, is found in the character Memphis, the owner of the restaurant in which the action occurs. Memphis came north in 1936, driven away by white violence. He has always meant to return and reclaim his land. In the course of the play, he learns that he has to go back and "pick up the ball" so as not to arrive in the end zone empty-handed. He must catch one of those two trains running south every day. He must not surrender.

The major characters in the play represent varying degrees of tenacity. Wilson skillfully builds a plot around two threads: Memphis' determination to get the city to pay his price for his property, and Sterling's determination to find a place for himself and gain the love of Risa. Hambone is a crazy character, driven mad almost ten years before when the butcher Lutz across the street refused to pay him a ham for doing a good job of painting his fence. Hollaway, a commentator character, observes that Hambone may be the smartest of them all in his refusal to give up—each day going to Lutz and asking for his ham. The unfortunate fact is, though, that his life has been reduced to this one action; all he can say is "I want my ham. He gonna give me my ham." Risa, a woman determined not to be dependent on a sexual attachment, has scarred her own attractive legs to make herself less desirable. In spite of herself, she is attracted to the vitality and optimism of Sterling, and Sterling is most tenacious of all. His warrior spirit has landed him in prison and may do so again, but his zeal and good humor are compelling.

The constant reminders and presence of death give resonance to the lives and efforts of these people. When the play opens, the Prophet Samuel has already died, and the offstage mayhem surrounding the viewing of his body is evident. Characters talk about several other deaths, and no sooner is Prophet Samuel buried than Hambone is discovered dead (again offstage). The reactions to his death constitute the ending of the play. Memphis and Sterling, trusting in the prophecies of the 322-year-old seer Aunt Ester, both triumph. Sterling runs across the street, steals a ham, and presents it to Mr. West, the undertaker, to put in Hambone's coffin. This final flourish of the play is an assertion of character identity and life. *Two Trains Running* may be Wilson's most accomplished work in blending character, plot, and theme.

Clearly, Wilson is an important playwright whose language, characters, storytelling, and themes have placed him in the vanguard of dramatic artists exploring the lives of African Americans.

Bibliography

Bigsby, C. W. E. *Modern American Drama, 1945-1990*. Cambridge, England: Cambridge University Press, 1992.

Brustein, Robert. *Reimagining American Theatre*. New York: Hill & Wang, 1991.

Harrison, Paul Carter. "August Wilson's Blues Poetics." In *Three Plays*. Pittsburgh: University of Pittsburgh Press, 1991.

Hill, Holly. "Black Theatre into the Mainstream." In *Contemporary American Theatre*, edited by Bruce King. New York: St. Martin's Press, 1991.

Moyers, Bill. "August Wilson's America: A Conversation with Bill Moyers." *American Theatre* 6 (June, 1989): 12-17, 54-56.

Nadel, Alan, ed. *May All Your Fences Have Gates: Essays on the Drama of August Wilson*, Iowa City: University of Iowa Press, 1994.

Theater 9 (Summer/Fall, 1988). This special issue includes the script of *The Piano Lesson* with an earlier version of the ending, production photographs, and two informative essays.

Wilson, August. "Blues, History and Dramaturgy: An Interview with August Wilson." Interview by Sandra G. Shannon. *African American Review* 27, no. 4 (Winter, 1993): 539.

_____ . "A Song in Search of Itself." Interview by Hilary De Vries. *American Theatre* 3 (January, 1987): 22-25.

RICHARD WRIGHT

Born: Natchez, Mississippi; September 4, 1908   *Died:* Paris, France; November 28, 1960

Principal long fiction

Native Son, 1940; *The Outsider*, 1953; *Savage Holiday*, 1954; *The Long Dream*, 1958; *Lawd Today*, 1963.

Other literary forms

Richard Wright published collections of essays and short stories and two autobiographical volumes. Two collections of short stories, the early *Uncle Tom's Children* (1938) and the posthumously collected *Eight Men* (1961), represent some of Wright's finest fiction. Even more important than these two collections is the first volume of Wright's autobiography, the critically acclaimed best-seller *Black Boy* (1945). The record of his years in Chicago is found in the posthumously published second autobiographical volume, *American Hunger* (written in 1944, published in 1977). Other nonfiction writings include works that explore his Third World political concerns; examples are *Black Power* (1954), *The Color Curtain* (1956), and *White Man, Listen!* (1957). Wright coauthored the play version of *Native Son* (it was performed in 1941) as well as the screenplay for the novel's 1951 film adaptation, in which he played the role of Bigger Thomas.

Achievements

In his best work, Wright gives American literature its strongest statement of the existential theme of alienated humanity defining itself. Wright's use of the African American as archetypal outsider gives his work a double edge. No American writer has so carefully illuminated the black experience in America. The ambivalence of black feeling, the hypocrisies of the dominant culture, and the tension between them find concrete and original manifestation in Wright's work, a manifestation at once revealing and terrifying.

Biography

Born in Mississippi of sharecropper parents, Richard Wright had a lonely and troubled childhood. His father deserted the family early, and after his mother suffered a stroke, Wright was forced at a young age to work to help support the family, which moved frequently from one relative to another. His portrayal of his mother is of a stern but loving parent, unable to contend with the stronger personality of his extremely religious grandmother. Wright's grandmother believed that all fiction was "the devil's lies"; her chief goal was to force Wright into a religious conversion, a goal in which she was singularly unsuccessful.

Wright moved from school to school, attempting to make friends and make his talents known. Though both tasks were difficult, he became valedictorian of his ninth-grade class. Even this accomplishment was spoiled when the principal insisted that Wright read a speech that the principal himself had written, and Wright refused. An uncle told Richard, "They're going to break you," and society, both black and white, seemed intent on doing so. Wright was determined to resist, not to be claimed by his environment as he felt so many blacks around him were.

Wright left Mississippi for Memphis, Tennessee, had little luck there, and—with money stolen from the movie theater where he worked—moved to Chicago. When others stole, Wright disapproved—not for moral reasons but because he felt stealing did not change the fundamental relationship of a person to his environment. When, however, thievery offered a chance to change that environment, Wright accepted it.

In Chicago, Wright became involved with others who viewed the country as he did, first in a federal theater project and then with the Communist John Reed Club, which supported his writing until Wright's goals differed from its own. In 1937, he moved to New York City to become the editor of the *Daily Worker*. A year later, he published his first important work, *Uncle Tom's Children*, after which he won a Guggenheim Fellowship, which provided him with the time and funds to write *Native Son*. The novel was published to great acclaim and was followed by a second major work, *Black Boy*. Although his writing career was a success, Wright was arguing more frequently with the Communist Party, with which he finally broke in 1944, and was becoming less optimistic about the hope of racial progress in America.

In 1946, Wright moved to France, where he spent the rest of his life. Although he wrote a great deal there, nothing in his later work, with the possible exception of

The Outsider, approaches the strength of *Native Son* and *Black Boy*. The existentialism that was always implicit in his work became the dominant theme, but—displaced from his native environment—Wright never again found a convincing dramatic situation in which to work out his preoccupations. Wright died in France of a heart attack on November 28, 1960.

Analysis

Perhaps Wright's greatest accomplishment as a writer is his skill at depicting the particulars of racism in American society from the vantage point of those victimized by prejudice. Indicting all aspects of society, he powerfully chronicles the historical injustices that African Americans have endured. At the same time he views the black person's experience in America as a universal metaphor for the modern human condition.

Wright's best work is always the story of one man's struggle to define himself and by so doing make himself free and responsible, fully human, a character worthy not of pity but of admiration and horror simultaneously. Typically, the character is an outsider, and Wright uses blackness as a representation of that alienation, though his characters are never as interested in defining their blackness as in defining their humanity. Although many characters in Wright's works are outsiders without being aware of their condition, Wright is never interested in them except as foils. Many of them avoid confronting themselves by fleeing to dreams; religion and liquor are two avoidance-mechanisms for Wright's characters, narcotics that blind them to their surrounding world, to what they are and what they might be.

Even Wright's main characters must not think about that world too often: To let it touch them is to risk insanity or violence, and so his characters strive to keep the fire within in check, to keep the physical hunger satisfied. Thus, all Wright's protagonists are initially trapped by desire and by fear—fear of what might happen to them, what they might do if they risk venturing outside the confines of black life in America, and the desire to do so. The life outside may be glimpsed in movies; Bigger Thomas, for example, goes to a film and watches contrasting and artificial views of black and white society. Yet as untruthful as both views are, they remind Bigger of a reality beyond his present situation. Desire is often symbolized by fight; Bigger, like other Wright characters, dreams of flying above the world, unchained from its limitations.

Most of Wright's stories and novels examine what happens when the protagonist's fear is mastered for a

moment when desires are met. The manifestation of desire in Wright is almost always through violence. Violence is central to Wright's fiction, for as important as sex may be to his characters, power is much more so, and power is often achieved through violence. In Wright's world, beatings and murders are frequent acts—central and occasionally creative.

Once the character has acted, he finds himself trapped again in a new set of oppositions, for in acting, he has left the old sureties behind, has made himself free, and has begun to define and create himself. With that new freedom comes a new awareness of responsibility. He is without excuses, and that awareness is as terrifying as—though more liberating than—the fears he has previously known. Although Wright does not always elaborate on what may follow, the characters open up new possibilities for themselves. If one may create one's self by violence, perhaps, Wright sometimes suggests, there are other, less destructive ways as well.

Some of Wright's novels end on this note of optimism, the characters tragically happy: tragically because they have committed violent and repulsive acts, but happy because for the first time they have *chosen* to commit them. They have freed themselves from their constraints, and the future, however short it may be, lies open. Others end simply with tragedy, the destruction achieving no purpose, the characters attaining no illumination.

Lawd Today, written before *Native Son* but not published until after Wright's death, tells the story of Jake Jackson from his awakening on the morning of February 12, 1936, to that day's violent conclusion. Jackson is Wright's most inarticulate protagonist: He has a banal life, undefined dreams, and a vague sense of discontent that he is unable to explain. Violent and prejudiced, he speaks in clichés, a language as meaningless as his life.

Technically, the book incorporates a montage of radio broadcasts, newspaper articles, and religious and political pamphlets into the narration of Jake's day. Divided into three sections, *Lawd Today* opens with Jake's dream of running up an endless staircase in pursuit of a disappearing voice. That dream gives way to the reality of his life: hunger, anger, and recrimination. Tricked by Jake into an abortion for which Jake still owes five hundred dollars and now claiming to have a tumor that will cost another five hundred dollars to remove, Jake's wife represents his entrapment. In the first section, "Commonplace," Jake reveals his brutish and trivial character: his anger at his wife, a jealousy and resentment that lead him to bait her so he can hit her, a mock-battle straightening his hair, and a meeting with friends who work with him at the post office. As they play bridge to pass the time until work, Wright presents without comment their stupid, cliché-ridden conversation.

Section 2, "Squirrel Cage," shows the men at work. They are all alienated in meaningless, routine jobs, but Jake's position is the most desperate, for his wife has been to see his boss, and he is now threatened with the loss of his job. Falling deeper into debt by borrowing more money and making mistakes on the job, Jake is trapped by his work—despite his own protestations, as a self-proclaimed Republican and capitalist, that work is liberating. This section, too, ends with a long, rambling, and banal conversation among the men at work.

In the concluding section, "Rat's Alley," the men go to a brothel for a good time on some of Jake's borrowed money. There, Jake is robbed and then beaten for his threats of revenge. Finally, Jake drunkenly stumbles homeward, his day nearing an end. The February weather, pleasant when the book began, has turned bad. All of Jake's frustration and anger finally erupt; he beats his wife, whom he finds kneeling asleep by the bed in an attitude of prayer. As they struggle, he throws objects through the window. She grabs a shard of broken glass and slashes him three times. The book ends with Jake lying in a stupor, bleeding, while his wife is on her knees, also bleeding, praying for death. Outside, the wind blows mercilessly.

Lawd Today foreshadows the strengths of *Native Son*. Along with *Black Boy*, the latter is one of Wright's finest achievements: a brilliant portrayal of, as Wright put it, the way the environment provides the instrumentalities through which one expresses oneself and the way that self becomes whole despite the environment's conspiring to keep it divided. The book parallels Theodore Dreiser's *An American Tragedy* (1925): Both are three-part novels in which there is a murder, in part accidental, in part willed; an attempted flight; and a long concluding trial, in both cases somewhat anticlimactic. Both novels are concerned with the interplay of environment and heredity, of fate and accident, and both have protagonists who rebel against the world that would hold them back.

In the first part of *Native Son*, Bigger Thomas is a black man cut off from family and peers. Superficially like his friends, he is in fact possessed of a different consciousness. To engage that consciousness is for him to risk insanity or violence, so Bigger endeavors to keep

his fears and uncertainty at a preconscious level. On the day of the first section, however, he is required by welfare law to apply for a job as a menial at the home of the rich, white Dalton family. Mr. Dalton is a ghetto landlord who soothes his conscience by donating sums of money for recreational purposes. That it is a minuscule part of the money he is deriving from blacks is an irony he overlooks. Mrs. Dalton is blind, a fact that is necessary to the plot as well as being symbolic. Their daughter, Mary, is a member of the Communist Party, and from the moment she sees Bigger, who wants nothing more than to be left alone, she begins to enlist his support.

The first evening, Bigger is to drive Mary to a university class. In reality, she is going with Jan Erlone, her Communist boyfriend, to a party meeting. Afterward, they insist that Bigger take them to a bar in the black part of town. Jan and Mary are at this point satirized, for their attitudes toward blacks are as limited and stereotyped as any in the novel. Bigger does not want to be seen by his friends with whites, but that fact does not occur to Mary. After much drinking, Bigger must carry the drunken Mary to her bedroom. He puts her to bed, stands over her, attracted to the woman he sees. The door opens and Mrs. Dalton enters. When Mary makes drunken noises, Bigger becomes frightened that Mrs. Dalton will come close enough to discover him, so he puts a pillow over Mary's face to quiet her. By the time Mrs. Dalton leaves, Mary is dead.

Wright wanted to make Bigger a character it would be impossible to pity, and what follows is extremely grisly. Bigger tries to put Mary's body in the furnace and saws off her head to make her fit. However accidental Mary's death may appear to the reader, Bigger himself does not regard it as such. He has, he thinks, many times wanted to kill whites without ever having the opportunity to do so. This time there was the act without the desire, but rather than seeing himself as the victim of a chance occurrence, Bigger prefers to unite the earlier desire with the present act, to make himself whole by accepting responsibility for the killing. Indeed, not only will he accept the act, but also Bigger determines to capitalize on it by sending a ransom note. Later, accused of raping Mary as well, an act he considered but did not commit, he reverses the process, accepting responsibility for this, too, even though here there was desire but no act. His only sign of conscience is that he cannot bring himself to shake the ashes in the furnace; this guilt is not redemptive, but his undoing, for, in an implausible scene in the Dalton basement, the room fills with smoke, the murder is revealed to newspaper reporters gathered there, and Bigger is forced to flee.

He runs with his girlfriend, Bessie Mears. She, like Bigger, has a hunger for sensation, which has initially attracted him to her. Now, however, as they flee together, she becomes a threat and a burden; huddled with her in an abandoned tenement, Bigger wants only to be rid of her. He picks up a brick and smashes her face, dumping her body down an airshaft. His only regret is not that he has killed her but that he has forgotten to remove their money from her body.

The rest of the plot moves quickly: Bigger is soon arrested, the trial is turned into a political farce, and Bigger is convicted and sentenced to death. In the last part of the novel, after Bigger's arrest, the implications of the action are developed, largely through Bigger's relations to other characters. Some of the characters are worthy only of contempt, particularly the district attorney, who, in an attempt at reelection, is turning the trial into political capital. Bigger's mother relies on religion. In a scene in the jail cell, she falls on her knees in apology before Mrs. Dalton and urges Bigger to pray, but toughness is Bigger's code. He is embarrassed by his mother's self-abasement, and although he agrees to pray simply to end his discomfort, his attitude toward religion is shown when he throws away a cross a minister has given him and throws a cup of coffee in a priest's face. In his view, they want only to avoid the world and to force him to accept guilt without responsibility.

Bigger learns from two characters. The first is Boris Max, the lawyer the Communist Party provides. Max listens to Bigger, and for the first time in his life, Bigger exposes his ideas and feelings to another human. Max's plea to the court is that, even as Bigger must accept responsibility for what he has done, so must the society around him understand its responsibility for what Bigger has become and, if the court chooses to execute Bigger, understand the consequences that must flow from that action. Max does not argue—nor does Wright believe—that Bigger is a victim of injustice. There is no injustice, because that would presume a world in which Bigger could hope for justice, and such a world does not exist; more important, Bigger is not a victim, for he has chosen his own fate. Max argues rather that all people are entitled to happiness. Like all Wright's protagonists, Bigger has earlier been torn between the poles of dread and ecstasy. His ecstasy, his happiness, comes from the meaningfulness he creates in his existence, a product of self-realization. Unhappily for Bigger, he realizes himself through murder: It was, he feels, his highest creative act.

If Max articulates the intellectual presentation of Wright's beliefs about Bigger, it is Jan, Mary's lover, who is its dramatic representation. He visits Bigger in his cell and, having at last understood the futility and paucity of his own stereotypes, admits to Bigger that he too shares in the responsibility for what has happened. He, too, addresses Bigger as a human being, but from the unique position of being the one who is alive to remind Bigger of the consequences of his actions, for Bigger learns that Jan has suffered loss through what he has done and that, while Bigger has created himself, he has also destroyed another.

Native Son ends with the failure of Max's appeals on Bigger's behalf. He comes to the cell to confront Bigger before his execution, and the novel closes with Bigger Thomas smiling at Max as the prison door clangs shut. Bigger will die happy because he will die fulfilled, having, however terribly, created a self.

Native Son is Wright's most powerful work, because his theme, universal in nature, is given its fullest and most evocative embodiment. That novel and the autobiographical *Black Boy*, his two greatest works, are a lacerating challenge to contemporary readers and writers—a challenge to share the relentless integrity of Richard Wright's vision.

Other major works

SHORT FICTION: *Uncle Tom's Children*, 1938, 1940; *Eight Men*, 1961.
PLAY: *Native Son: The Biography of a Young American*, pr. 1941 (with Paul Green).
NONFICTION: *Twelve Million Black Voices*, 1941; *Black Boy*, 1945; *Black Power*, 1954; *The Color Curtain*, 1956; *Pagan Spain*, 1957; *White Man, Listen!*, 1957; *American Hunger*, 1977; *Conversations with Richard Wright*, 1993.
MISCELLANEOUS: *Works*, 1991.

Bibliography

Baldwin, James. *The Price of the Ticket: Collected Nonfiction, 1948-1985*. New York: St. Martin's Press/Marek, 1985.

Bloom, Harold, ed. *Richard Wright*. New York: Chelsea House, 1987.

Butler, Robert. *Native Son: The Emergence of a New Black Hero*. Boston: Twayne, 1991.

Fabre, Michel. *The Unfinished Quest of Richard Wright*. Translated by Isabel Barzun. New York: William Morrow, 1973.

——————— . *The World of Richard Wright*. Jackson: University Press of Mississippi, 1985.

Gates, Henry Louis, Jr., and K.A. Appiah. *Richard Wright: Critical Perspectives Past and Present*. New York: Amistad, 1993.

Gounard, Jean-François. *The Racial Problem in the Works of Richard Wright and James Baldwin*. Translated by Joseph J. Rodgers, Jr. Westport, Conn.: Greenwood Press, 1992.

Kinnamon, Keneth. *The Emergence of Richard Wright*. Urbana: University of Illinois Press, 1972.

Miller, Eugene E. *Voice of a Native Son: The Poetics of Richard Wright*. Jackson: University Press of Mississippi, 1990.

Walker, Ian. "Black Nightmare: The Fiction of Richard Wright." In *Black Fiction*, edited by A. Robert Lee. New York: Barnes & Noble Books, 1980.

Walker, Margaret. *Richard Wright: Daemonic Genius*. New York: Warner Books, 1988.

Webb, Constance. *Richard Wright: A Biography*. New York: Putnam, 1968.

VI

THROUGH WOMEN'S EYES
Re-Visions of America

. . . caring asks doing. It is a long baptism into the seas of humankind,
my daughter. Better immersion than to live untouched.
                                        —Tillie Olsen, "O Yes," 1961

Sigmund Freud asked, "What do women want?" For at least the first half of the twentieth century it was principally American male writers who explored this issue and provided the "answers." Since the resurgence of the American Women's Movement in the 1960's, however, American women writers have given their reflections on the needs, hopes, and concerns of American women. Not only do contemporary American women writers talk about who they are, but they also offer insightful and challenging reinterpretations of the ways in which American women and men interact, views that very often reflect what can be described only as a female consciousness. These new women writers explore America through a woman's eyes, offering powerful—and often uncomfortable—commentary on their culture and subcultures.

Contemporary American women write about what interests them; and, while it is fair to say that each writes her own "version" of being female and being American, it would be a gross exaggeration and do no justice to these women to assume that they, any more than their male counterparts, can be reduced to one generic stereotype. Like the voices of any "group," new American women writers resist simple categorization. These writers express a multitude of perceptions: African American, Native American, Euro-American, immigrant, lesbian, conservative, feminist, Asian American, "disabled," poor, privileged, twenty-something, octogenarian—the list of categories is as multifaceted as the population of the United States about which these women speak. Contemporary American women's lit-

erature represents difference with a capital *D*, voicing diverse, and often conflicting, concerns, points of view, and subcultures. Far from causing confusion or diminishing the value of their work, it is precisely their Differences that contribute to the provocative nature of contemporary American women writers' work. As we come to understand more fully that American identity is not homogeneous but challengingly diverse, we grow to appreciate, even welcome, the symphony of perspectives voiced by contemporary American women writers such as those discussed in this section: Ann Beattie, Mary Gordon, Barbara Kingsolver, Joyce Carol Oates, Tillie Olsen, Sylvia Plath, Jane Smiley, and Wendy Wasserstein.

Adding the issue of gender and female identity to the mixture of American multiculture serves only to enrich the possibilities available to contemporary American writers. Many American women have certainly made these aspects of their characters the central focus of their work. In this way, as at perhaps no other time, the issue of being female—and what that translates into for a particular writer and her characters—takes on a centrality in how these writers position themselves in the discussion of "who we are." When these writers explore what it means to be identified as American, the issue of gender is never ignored. For instance, for Sylvia Plath, and others sharing her European Jewish immigrant background as well as her family's place of relative economic privilege, identifying as an American meant finding ways to reconcile one's talent not only with the apparently rigid constraints of being female but also with traditional cultural expectations for women's behavior. In Plath's case, the combination resulted in powerfully expressed explorations of one woman's depression, anger, mixed feelings about fathers, husbands, and children, and literally as well as figuratively suicide. In the case of Ann Beattie, Mary Gordon, Joyce Carol Oates, or Wendy Wasserstein, we frequently see women trying to balance their own needs and those of their families within the often oppressive value system of the greater community. While these writers' heritage and that of their female characters could be described as mainstream, when the issue of gender is added to the discussion, it becomes clear that what it means to be female in late twentieth century America plays an important determining role in their idea of what shapes identity: who they are, who American women are, and what American women can or should expect to be and become.

Ann Beattie, Mary Gordon, Barbara Kingsolver, Joyce Carol Oates, Tillie Olsen, Sylvia Plath, Jane Smiley, and Wendy Wasserstein examine issues similar to those raised by Plath, yet no two women offer readers the "same" picture of American identity. Naturally, many explore relationships between women and men, in all their painful complexities, such as Wendy Wasserstein in *The Heidi Chronicles* or Ann Beattie in *Falling in Place*. Writers such as Mary Gordon deal with the frustration and despair that women experience when they attempt to move beyond the traditional limits set for them by American Irish Catholic community norms.

Not surprisingly, anger and violence—either overt or redirected—often contribute powerfully expressive elements to the work of these contemporary American women writers. Writers such as Kingsolver, Oates, and Plath frequently examine the personalities and struggles of those women and men caught up in webs of aggression, self-loathing, and emotional or physical abuse. A key identifying feature of the late twentieth century psychological landscapes created by these writers are worlds and relationships in which anger, emptiness, and terror of abandonment or punishment dominate. For many, this circle of anger, violence, and despair is firmly situated in their female characters' familial relationships. Often, as in the case of Beattie or Smiley, the violence and anger are so subtly masked that, at first glance, the aggression hardly seems like violence. Yet the hostilities and anger that underlie the passive-aggressive silences and withdrawals are as punishing and destructive as any slap or rape.

The other side of violence and anger is the courage expressed in the face of abuse, abandonment, and poverty. In the works of Kingsolver and Olsen, the nobility and strength manifest in their female characters comes as a result of those women's refusal to surrender to poverty, neglect, abuse, or abandonment. Unlike the frequently suicidal confessional voice of Plath's work, the frame for Kingsolver's and Olsen's characters is one of stubborn resistance. The personae these contemporary American women writers create are strong women, women on the outside of privilege and power: working-class women, abandoned women, women whose beauty comes from their inner fire and stubborn refusal to give in rather than form faces and bodies fit to adorn a fashion magazine. Contemporary American women writers often explore the lives of women and men on the margins rather than in positions of power. In some instances the class struggle does not resolve itself into a traditional "up-by-her-bootstraps" success story; rather, the main characters gain nobility and find depth and value to their lives far removed from the homes of the rich and famous. Kingsolver and Olsen return to this motif over and over. By contrast, Beattie persists in detailing the vapidity of the privileged class and the emotional vacuum that exists in the lives of the seemingly well-off, relationships in which neglect and alienation are more frequently to be found than compassion and community.

The diverse ways in which contemporary American women writers explore their worlds also reflect the multicultural nature of contemporary American life. For this reason, no one woman or group of women should be expected to speak for all women. Yet issues that apparently have an impact on shaping the identity of contemporary American women do come up with startling frequency among the work of the writers discussed in this section: pregnancy, abortion, childbirth, and mothering; gender roles, education, poverty, and work; beauty, disability, and aging; sexuality, sexual orientation, and social mores; empowerment, sisterhood, and "outsideredness" (the state of being shut out); rape, incest, and battering; love, marriage, divorce, and single parenting; the power inequities and struggles for dominance between women and men; and isolation, loneliness, or outsideredness, particularly for those women who seek more than traditional avenues to express their identities or who do not fit easily into traditional patterns.

New contemporary American women writers such as Ann Beattie, Mary Gordon, Barbara Kingsolver, Joyce Carol Oates, Tillie Olsen, Sylvia Plath, Jane Smiley, and

Wendy Wasserstein provide challenging, unsettling, and provocative reinterpretations of their culture and subcultures—a "re-visioning" process that cannot be ignored. These women's voices are controversial, painful, and challenging in their intensity and often intimidating in their honesty. The writers discussed in this section give voice to the full range of women's lives as well as to the multiplicities of contemporary American experience.

—*Melissa E. Barth*
Appalachian State University

ANN BEATTIE

Born: Washington, D.C.; September 8, 1947

Principal short fiction

Distortions, 1976; *Secrets and Surprises*, 1978; *Jacklighting*, 1981; *The Burning House*, 1982; *Where You'll Find Me*, 1986; *What Was Mine and Other Stories*, 1991.

Other literary forms

While Ann Beattie's reputation rests primarily on her short stories, particularly those that first appeared in *The New Yorker*, she has also written several novels. The first, *Chilly Scenes of Winter* (1976), appeared simultaneously with *Distortions*, a rare occurrence in the publishing world, especially for a first-time author. Her second novel, *Falling in Place* (1980), is her most ambitious and her best. In 1986 and 1987, she worked on her first nonfiction project, the text to accompany a monograph containing twenty-six color plates of the paintings of Alex Katz. She has also published children's books.

Achievements

Beattie was once called the most imitated short-story writer in the United States, an amazing claim for an author who at that time was in her thirties. Along with such writers as Raymond Carver, she is a premier practitioner of minimalism, the school of fiction-writing that John Barth has characterized as the "less is more" school. In 1977, she was named Briggs-Copeland Lecturer in English at Harvard. After receiving a Guggenheim grant, she left Harvard and moved to Connecticut, where she had attended graduate school. She received an award of excellence from the American Academy and Institute of Arts and Letters in 1980.

Biography

Born on September 8, 1947, Ann Beattie grew up with television, rock music, and all the other accoutrements of the baby boomers. The child of a retired Health, Education, and Welfare Department administrator, Beattie took a B.A. degree in English at American University in 1969 and completed her M.A. degree at the University of Connecticut in 1970. She began, but did not complete, work on her Ph.D. degree. In 1972 she was married to, and was later divorced from, David Gates, a writer for *Newsweek* and a singer. Together they had one son. Before her appointment at Harvard, Beattie taught at the University of Virginia in Charlottesville. After living in the Connecticut suburbs and in New York City, she returned to Charlottesville and the university in 1985. She appeared as a waitress in the film version of *Chilly Scenes of Winter* (released as *Head over Heels* in 1979) and, after her divorce, was named one of the most eligible single women in America. In 1985, Beattie met painter Lincoln Percy, whom she later married. The couple settled in Charlottesville.

Analysis

Beattie has been called the voice of a new "lost generation" of Americans, a sort of Ernest Hemingway for those who came of age during the 1960's and 1970's. Many of her themes and much about her style support the assertion that she, like Hemingway, voices a pervasive and universal feeling of despair and alienation, a lament for lost values and lost chances for constructive action. Yet to limit one's understanding of Beattie's work to this narrow interpretation is a mistake.

Beattie shares much with writers such as Jane Austen, who ironically portrayed the manners and social customs of her era, and with psychological realists such as Henry James, who delved into the meanings behind the subtle nuances of character and conflict. Her primary themes are loneliness and friendship, family life, love and death, materialism, art, and, for want of a better term, the contemporary scene. Her short fiction tends to be spare and straightforward. Her vocabulary and her sentence structure are quite accessible, or minimalist, to use a more literary label. Even when the stories contain symbols, their use is most often direct and self-reflexive.

Beattie's characters experience a profound longing for a different world. Despite the ennui that dominates the texture of their lives, they hold on to the hope of renewal and redemption, often with great fierceness. If members of the generation about which she writes are indeed lost, they have not accepted their condition, even though they recognize it. They are still searching for the way out, for a place in which to find themselves or to be found.

"Dwarf House," the first story in *Distortions*, establishes an interest in the grotesque, the bizarre, and the slightly askew that surfaces several times in this first of Beattie's collections. The main characters of the story are James and MacDonald, brothers who struggle to find understanding and respect for each other and to deal with their possessive and intrusive mother. Because James, the older of the two, is a dwarf, Beattie immediately plays upon the collection's title and places the story beyond the plane of realism.

The irony of the story develops as the reader realizes that MacDonald's supposedly normal life is as distorted as the life of his sibling. When MacDonald goes to visit James in the dwarf house where he lives, along with several other dwarfs and one giant, he finds himself repulsed by the foreign environment. Yet, when he gets home, he cannot face his own "normal" world without his martinis. He is as alienated and isolated at home and at work as he would be if he were a dwarf. Beattie uses the ludicrous, exaggerated scenario of James's life, complete with his wedding to a fellow dwarf, conducted by a hippie minister and culminating in the releasing of a caged parrot as a symbol of hope and the new freedom of married life, to bring into focus the less obvious distortions of regular American life.

MacDonald is typical of many Beattie characters. He is relatively young—in his late twenties—and well educated. He works, but his work provides little challenge or stimulation. He has enough money to live as he wants, but he struggles to define what it is he does want. His wife is his equal—young, well educated, hip—but they have less than nothing to talk about.

MacDonald wants to make his brother's life more normal—that is, get him out of the dwarf house, the one place where James has been happy, and back into their mother's home, where James and MacDonald will both be miserable. Macdonald is motivated not by malice toward James but by an overdeveloped sense of guilt and responsibility toward his mother, a trait he shares with many of Beattie's young male characters. By the story's end, the reader cannot say who is better off: James, whose life is distorted but productive and satisfying to him, or MacDonald, who has everything a man could want but still lacks an understanding of what it is he should do with what he has.

If *Distortions* emphasizes the outward manifestations of the disordered contemporary world, *Secrets and Surprises*, the second collection, turns inward, as its title suggests. "A Vintage Thunderbird" features a woman who comes to New York to have an abortion, against the wishes of her husband. The friends to whom she turns, Karen and Nick, have their own problems in love. By mirroring the sense of loss that follows the abortion with the sense of loss felt by Karen and Nick when she sells the vintage car of the title, Beattie addresses the connection between spiritual and emotional needs and material needs.

Very few of the people in Beattie's fiction suffer for want of material goods; almost all suffer from lack of spiritual and emotional fulfillment. The interesting aspect of this dichotomy is that the characters do not, as a rule, actively pursue material well-being. Their money is often inherited, as are their houses and many of their other possessions. The main character in "Shifting," for example, inherits an old Volvo from an uncle to whom she was never very close. The money earned by these characters is almost always earned halfheartedly, without conspicuous ambition or enthusiasm. These are not yuppies, who have substituted acquisition for all human emotion; they are people who, by accident of birth or circumstance, have not had to acquire material wealth; for whatever reason, wealth comes to them.

What does not come is peace, satisfaction, and contentment. When a material object does provide emotional pleasure, as the Thunderbird does for Karen and Nick, Beattie's characters tend to confuse the emotion with the symbol and to conclude, erroneously, that ridding themselves of the object will also rid them of the gnawing doubts that seem to accompany contentment and satisfaction. It is sometimes as frightening, Beattie seems to suggest, to be attached to things as to people.

In *The Burning House*, Beattie's third collection, she turns to the darker, more richly textured veins of her standard subject matter to produce stories that are less humorous but more humane, less ironic but wiser than those in the earlier collections. Infidelity, divorce, love gone bad—all standard Beattie themes—are connected to parenthood and its attendant responsibilities, to homosexuality, to death, and to birth defects. The affairs and the abortions that were entered into, if not concluded, with a 1970's "me-generation" bravado suddenly collide with more traditional values and goals.

Many of Beattie's characters, both married and single, have lovers. In fact, having a lover or having had one at some time during a marriage is almost standard. In "The Cinderella Waltz," Beattie adds a further complication to the *de rigueur* extramarital affair by making the husband's lover a male. Yet, in much the same way that she makes the unusual work in a story such as "Dwarf House," Beattie manages to make this story more about the pain and suffering of the people involved than about the nontraditional quality of the love relationship.

The wife in "The Cinderella Waltz," left to understand what has happened to her marriage and to help her young daughter to reach her own understanding, finds herself drawn into a quiet, resigned acceptance of her husband's relationship with his lover. She laments the loss of innocence in the world, for her child and for them all, but she chooses to go forward with the two men as part of her life and the child's. She rejects—really never even considers—the negative, destructive responses that many women would have.

"The Cinderella Waltz" ends with images of enormous fragility—glass elevators and glass slippers. Yet they are images that her characters embrace and cling to, recognizing that fragile hope is better than none. The cautious nature of such optimism is often mistaken for pessimism in Beattie's work, but her intention is clearly as affirmative as it is tentative.

Another story from *The Burning House*, "Winter: 1978," offers a glimpse of most of Beattie's concerns and techniques. An unusually long story for Beattie, "Winter: 1978" features a selfish mother who is hosting a wake for her younger son, who has drowned in a midwinter boating accident. His death is mystifying, for there were life preservers floating easily within his reach, a fact that suggests the ultimate despair and surrender often present in Beattie's characters. An older son blames the mother for placing too much guilt and responsibility on the dead son, but he himself has done nothing to assume some of that burden. His former wife, their child, his current girlfriend, and his best friend are all present at the wake. The best friend's girlfriend is alone back in California, having her uterus cauterized. His former wife seems inordinately grief-stricken until it is revealed that the dead man was her lover. During the course of the wake, which lasts several days, she becomes the lover of her former husband's best friend.

This extremely baroque and convoluted situation contains much that is ironically humorous, but it also reflects deep pain on the part of all the characters, not only the pain of having lost a loved one but also the pain of reexamining their own lives and measuring them against the idea of death. That sort of existential questioning, rarely overt but frequently suggested, contributes to the idea of a lost generation brought to life on the pages of Beattie's fiction.

Yet Beattie rarely leaves her characters in perpetual existential angst, as is the case in a Hemingway story such as "A Clean, Well-Lighted Place," an embodiment of the existential despair and the longing for some minute, self-created order and refuge typical of the original literary lost generation. Instead, Beattie often opts for a neoromantic, minimalist version of hope and redemption, of continued searching as opposed to acquiescence.

"Winter: 1978" concludes with the absentee father, the surviving son, taking his own child upstairs for a bedtime story. The little boy, like the daughter in "The Cinderella Waltz," is far too wise to take comfort from the imaginary world of the story: He has been exposed to far too much of the confused adult world of his parents. On this occasion, however, he pretends to believe, and he encourages his father's tale about the evolution of deer. According to the story, deer have such sad eyes because they were once dinosaurs and cannot escape the sadness that comes with having once been something else.

This story serves as a metaphor for the melancholy cast of characters in this and Beattie's other collections of short fiction. Almost all of her characters have a Keatsian longing to connect with a better, more sublime existence that seems to be part of their generational collective consciousness. Far too aware and too ironic to follow the feeling and thereby to transcend reality, they linger in their unsatisfactory lesser world and struggle to accommodate their longing to their reality.

The characters in *Where You'll Find Me*, the fourth collection, are generally older and wiser than their predecessors. They have, as a rule, survived an enormous loss and are still hoping for a richer, more rewarding life, or at least one in which they feel less out of place and alone.

Andrea, the real-estate agent who is the main character of "Janus," is typical. Safely married to a husband who is interesting and financially secure, she is also successful in her career. The two of them take great pleasure in the things that they have accumulated. Yet Andrea takes most pleasure in a relatively inexpensive and quite ordinary-looking ceramic bowl, a gift from a former lover who asked her to change her life, to live with him.

Although she has long since turned him down, Andrea finds herself growing increasingly obsessed with the bowl. She begins to believe that all of her career success comes from the bowl's being precisely placed in the homes that she shows to her clients. A mystery to her, the bowl seems to be connected to the most real, the most private parts of herself. She loves the bowl as she loves nothing else.

She fears for its safety. She is terrified at the thought that it might disappear. She has lost the chance that the lover represents, choosing instead stasis and comfort, remaining intransigent about honoring her previous commitments. Sometimes she goes into her living room late at night and sits alone contemplating the bowl. She thinks, "In its way, it was perfect; the world cut in half, deep and smoothly empty."

Such is the world that Beattie observes, but Beattie is, after all, an artist, not a real-estate agent. All that Andrea can do is contemplate. Beattie can fill the bowl, to use a metaphor, with whatever she chooses. She can capture, again and again, the story behind the "one small flash of blue, a vanishing point on the horizon,"

that Andrea can only watch disappear.

Barth's description of the impulse behind minimalism, the desire "to strip away the superfluous in order to reveal the necessary, the essential," is a fair assessment of Beattie's work. Yet it is equally important to recall what necessary and essential elements remain after the superfluous has been stripped away. They are love, friendship, family, children, art, and creativity. Beattie fills the bowl of her fiction with much the same fruits that other writers have used.

Beattie's fiction is a lesson in the psychological reality of a certain segment of American life: well-educated, upper-middle-class men and women of the baby-boom generation. Although she sometimes writes about other people, it is these with whom she is most often identified. While the scope of her short fiction may be somewhat narrow, her finely detailed canvases yield a rich reward.

Other major works

NOVELS: *Chilly Scenes of Winter*, 1976; *Falling in Place*, 1980; *Love Always*, 1985; *Picturing Will*, 1989.
NONFICTION: *Alex Katz*, 1987.
CHILDREN'S LITERATURE: *Goblin Tales*, 1975; *Spectacle*, 1985.

Bibliography

Atwood, Margaret. "Stories from the American Front." *The New York Times Book Review*, September 26, 1982, 1, 34.

Barth, John. "A Few Words About Minimalism." *The New York Times Book Review*, December 28, 1986, 1, 2, 25.

Beattie, Ann. "An Interview with Ann Beattie." Interview by Steven R. Centola. *Contemporary Literature* 31 (Winter, 1990): 405-422.

Gelfant, Blanche H. "Ann Beattie's Magic Slate: Or, The End of the Sixties." *New England Review* 1 (1979): 374-384.

Hansen, Ron. "Just Sitting There Scared to Death." *The New York Times Book Review*, May 26, 1991, 3, 14.

Montresor, Jaye Berman. *The Critical Response to Ann Beattie*. Westport, Conn.: Greenwood Press, 1993.

Opperman, Harry, and Christina Murphy. "Ann Beattie (1947-   ): A Checklist." *Bulletin of Bibliography* 44 (June, 1987): 111-118.

MARY GORDON

Born: Far Rockaway, New York; December 8, 1949

Principal long fiction

Final Payments, 1978; *The Company of Women*, 1980; *Men and Angels*, 1985; *The Other Side*, 1989; *The Rest of Life: Three Novellas*, 1993.

Other literary forms

In addition to her novels and novellas, Mary Gordon has published several collections of short stories. Many of her uncollected articles and essays on literature, the Catholic church, women's issues, and other subjects have appeared in numerous major American periodicals.

Achievements

With the publication of her first novel, *Final Payments*, in 1978, Gordon received instant critical acclaim as well as widespread popularity among general readers. She was immediately recognized as a notable Catholic writer of serious fiction; critics compared her to Flannery O'Connor and Walker Percy, both renowned Catholic writers. *Final Payments* was considered remarkable both for its unfashionable theme—spiritual hunger and obsessive self-sacrifice—and for the intensity and aptness of its language. Gordon was twenty-nine years old at the time.

Gordon's second novel, *The Company of Women*, also received serious attention. Writing in the *Saturday Review*, B. G. Harrison noted some flaws but commended its treatment of the conflicts between instinct and reason, submission and authority, its depiction of "the awesome power of love to diminish, enrich, and immortalize." *Men and Angels*, Gordon's third novel, moved away from the parochial Catholic world of her first two novels to explore the complexities of motherhood and family. Rosellen Brown called it Gordon's "finest book."

In 1989 a fourth novel appeared. *The Other Side* was again something of a departure. The complicated story of two Irish immigrants, the novel probes the lives of a large family, including the founding parents, their children, grandchildren, and even great-grandchildren. The critical reception was mixed, but again, as with her first three novels, this one quickly became a national bestseller. The Kafka Prize for Fiction was awarded to Gordon in 1979 and again in 1982.

Biography

Mary Catherine Gordon was born in Far Rockaway, New York, on December 8, 1949. Her mother, Anna Gagliano Gordon, was a Roman Catholic. Her Jewish father, David, a writer and publisher, had converted to Catholicism before Mary was born; he died when Mary was eight years old. Growing up in Queens, Mary was reared in a devoutly Catholic home, thereby acquiring a particular perspective that is reflected in much of her writing.

Educated in convent schools and at Barnard College (B.A., 1971) and Syracuse University (M.A., 1973), Gordon has taught English at Dutchess Community College, Poughkeepsie, New York; Amherst College, Amherst, Massachusetts; and Barnard College, New York.

In 1974 Gordon married James Brian, an anthropologist; the marriage ended in divorce. She was married to Arthur Cash, a professor of English, in 1979; the couple had two children.

Analysis

Although not quite all Gordon's writing concentrates on characters and situations related to the life of a Catholic, there is no question that her view of the world, her attitudes, and her values have been ineradicably affected by her rootedness in American Catholicism. Her first novel, *Final Payments*, instantly placed her, according to many critics, in the company of eminent contemporary Catholic writers. Her subsequent writings reinforced that initial impression. The critic Francine du Plessix Gray suggested that Gordon was "her generation's preeminent novelist of Roman Catholic mores and manners." Yet the Catholic influence in her novels is not so much a matter of dogma and doctrine as it is a way of looking at life through the eyes of one whose faith has colored her spiritual, intellectual, and emotional values.

Thus, what it means to be a Catholic, in faith or in revolt, whether priest or nun, schoolgirl or college student, wife or husband, mother or father, lawyer, psychiatrist, transit worker, teacher, bookkeeper, social worker—is what concerns Gordon. She tells the stories of such people with the special familiarity and understanding of an "insider," one who knows their lives from direct experience or close observation. Her aim seems to be to examine lives and relationships not only with precision and accuracy but also with candor and honesty. Gordon describes truth as she sees it; sympathy and compassion are sometimes present, but not always. Humor is very seldom present; her view precludes the light touch, the saving grace of wit. Gordon is an intensely serious writer; she has said she does not write of trivialities. The emotions that she depicts with devastating passion are anger, guilt, estrangement, and despair. Lovelessness and joylessness are the usual condition of many of her characters, with the result that the tone of her novels is one of gloom and sorrow.

What Gordon's characters seek is a reconciliation between the impulses and forces—spiritual, sexual, familial—that imbue the difficulties of living in the late twentieth century, with its changing, conflicting demands. With a Catholic background as context and framework, Gordon's fiction is rich with powerful imagery and allusions springing from her grounding in the Church.

In every work some characters are at war with others, in either subtle or obvious ways. *Final Payments* contains the seeds of much of the fiction that followed. In this work, Isabel Moore, dry-eyed at her father's funeral, reflects on the eleven years she spent caring for him as he became increasingly helpless from a series of strokes, increasingly demanding and dependent on her. These years of selfless, grim devotion take their toll as Isabel reenters the world and makes a disaster of her newly gained freedom. Two friends of her girlhood and an alcoholic priest somehow see her through. The novel ends with the suggestion of possible hope that Isabel will be able to reclaim her life, having made the "final payments" of guilt and rage.

The Company of Women extends the number of characters: Five women and the young daughter of one of them spend some weeks every summer spiritually renewing themselves in their devotion to Father Cyprian, a failed priest, who does his best to give them the guidance and understanding that they desperately need. The separate lives of the women play themselves out within the context of their disparate personalities and ordinary occupations. Again, at the end of the novel, there is a clear indication that the illegitimate daughter

of the youngest of them will keep the group together through her innocence and joy.

In *Men and Angels*, there is again a conflict between two characters, a young mother and a younger babysitter, who battle over who small children, a battle having its source in the mother's attempts to pursue scholarly interests as well as motherhood while a fanatically religious girl struggles for power that she confuses with love. This novel explores family relationships more deeply and complexly than do the parochial concerns of the earlier novels.

The Other Side exemplifies Gordon's growing ability to deal with an extensive range of character types in a family setting. The book opens on the day that eighty-eight-year-old Vincent MacNamara, the founder of the family, is to return home after recovering from an injury caused, perhaps unintentionally, by his wife, Ellen. The grown children, grandchildren, and great-grandchildren have gathered to welcome him home, where his ninety-year-old wife lies upstairs, totally incapacitated by several strokes and unable to speak or recognize anyone.

Using her favorite narrative method of presenting events out of sequence, switching back and forth from the present to the distant past to the near past again and again, Gordon weaves together all the strands of the family members' lives, revealing their characters and personalities through inner reflection and through conversations with one another in various situations, present and past.

"The other side" was how Irish immigrants to America referred to their new land. In a more symbolic sense, the novel's title can also be taken to refer to the stories of her characters, each of whom has more than one "side" or interpretation. (This view of her characters and their lives is applicable to most of Gordon's fiction; there is always more than one side to their stories. The classic discrepancy between appearance and reality is explored in various ways.)

The Irish immigrant experience in New York before World War I affected the generations that followed the first settlers in countless ways. Gradually, as layer after layer of family history is revealed, a few of the novel's characters begin to come to the forefront. Vincent and Ellen are the most fully realized and interesting, yet their stories are over when the novel opens, and one comes to know them only through Gordon's oscillating narration, with time and space shifting constantly. Vincent is shown to be a much misunderstood and undervalued man, whose gentleness and nobility have been seen as weakness and simplicity by many of the family members, especially Ellen. Her grief over the death of her only son stunted her life and deprived her two daughters of love, turning them into neurotic and unlovable women. The grandchildren, especially the cousins Cam and Dan, are in effect reared by their grandmother, are professionally successful, but are caught in tangled, loveless marriages and hopeless affairs.

In this novel Gordon's style is repetitive and unadorned, much leaner than in her previous novels. Critics differed considerably in their appraisal of this aspect of the novel, some finding it "lilting and rhapsodic," others calling it "disjointed, nervous, and lifeless." Feminist critics such as Melanie Kaye Kantrowitz saw in the book "a powerful steady feminist consciousness about the experiences and options of women."

Three novellas were published in 1993 under the title of the last one of the three, *The Rest of Life*. Each is told by a different woman, two of them unnamed. "Immaculate Man" is told by a non-Catholic social worker who falls in love with a priest. Sensing her fear that he will abandon her as she approaches middle age, he says that he will never leave her, and she believes him but not with conviction. This novella is a rambling rumination with no clear focus or theme. The second one, "Living at Home," presents another unnamed narrator who tells her story as if she were writing a journal full of questions that reveal her confusion and conflicted feelings about her lover, a foreign correspondent who enjoys covering revolutions and similar dangerous situations. Again, however, the narrator is so self-absorbed, humorless, and bewildered that the reader finds her story unrewarding and pointless, even though the main char-

acter has pondered deep and important questions.

The final novella is quite different from the other two. Here the woman who is the main character meditates on her long life of silence. Paola is seventy-eight years old and has lived in the United States since she was forced by her father to leave her home in Turin when she was fifteen. The facts of her life are unfolded in Gordon's characteristic nonsequential style. It is a sad and mysterious story. Paola was exiled because of the shame of having been the lover of a sixteen-year-old boy with whom she signed a suicide pact, never having intended, we gradually learn, to go through with it. The real source of the shame is never revealed. Paola has been totally silent about it, even as she has married and reared several children. Her son and his fiancée take her on a trip back to Turin, hoping that the scenes of her early life will give her pleasure. They do not. She is still frozen, unable to tell the young people of her lifelong sorrow. Finally, she goes alone to see the place where her young lover died and realizes that she can no longer remember his face. This moment is an epiphany to her. Released from the sorrow and shame in which she has lived so long, she feels joy as she returns to life—to colors, tastes, and smells.

This final novella represents Gordon at her best—elegant, spare, compassionate, and in complete control of her material. With this novella, she continued to impress serious and enthusiastic readers, who looked forward to enjoying her development as a writer who examines significant aspects of the American experience, especially those concerned with the spiritual state of her varied and troubled characters.

Other major works

SHORT FICTION: *Temporary Shelter*, 1987; *Good Boys and Dead Girls and Other Essays*, 1991.

Bibliography

Barker-Nunn, Jeanne Beverly. "A More Adequate Conception: American Women Writers' Quest for a Female Ethic." Ph.D. dissertation, University of Minnesota, 1985.

Baumann, Paul. "A Search for the 'Unfettered Self': Mary Gordon on Life and Literature." *Commonweal* 118 (May 17, 1991): 327.

Dudar, Helen. "Portrait of the Novelist as a Young Mom." *The Wall Street Journal*, April 1, 1985.

Iannone, Carol. "The Secret of Mary Gordon's Success." *Commentary* 79 (June, 1985): 62.

Morey, Ann-Janine. "Beyond Updike: Incarnated Love in the Novels of Mary Gordon." *The Christian Century* 102 (November 20, 1985): 1059.

Neary, John M. "Mary Gordon's *Final Payments*: A Romance of the One True Language." *Essays in Literature* 17 (Spring, 1990): 94.

Pierce, Judith. "Profile." *Belles Lettres: A Review of Books by Women* 9 (Fall, 1993): 8.

Suleiman, Susan Rubin. "On Maternal Splitting: A Propos of Mary Gordon's *Men and Angels*." *Signs* 14 (Autumn, 1988): 25.

BARBARA KINGSOLVER

Born: Annapolis, Maryland; April 8, 1955

Principal long fiction

The Bean Trees, 1988; *Animal Dreams*, 1990; *Pigs in Heaven*, 1993.

Other literary forms

Barbara Kingsolver's publications include *"Homeland" and Other Stories* (1989), a collection of short stories; *Holding the Line: Women in the Great Arizona Mine Strike of 1983* (1989), a nonfiction documentary; *Another America/Otra America* (1992), and a volume of poems. Various fiction and nonfiction pieces, reviews, and poems written by her have appeared in a number of newspapers and magazines.

Achievements

Kingsolver has achieved both a truly popular following and an estimable reputation among critics. Her first award was presented by the Arizona Press Club for outstanding feature writing in 1986. The American Library Association honored *The Bean Trees* in 1988 and *"Homeland" and Other Stories* in 1990. The United Nations National Council of Women awarded her a Citation of Accomplishment in 1989. *Animal Dreams* won a PEN Fiction Prize and an Edward Abbey Ecofiction Award, both in 1991. Kingsolver has also been nominated for several other awards, including multiple listings for the ABBY honors, given to the books that retailers most enjoy selling.

Biography

Barbara Kingsolver was born in Annapolis, Maryland, on April 8, 1955, the daughter of a country physician in Appalachian Kentucky. Like many native to that region, she early acquired a fascination with stories and storytelling, learning the lore of the hills and community values through folktales; tending garden and telling stories are among her earliest memories. Yet in spite of feeling deeply rooted in the land, she saw no future there, where the only options were to "be a farmer or a farmer's wife." Her first break came when she won a scholarship to DePauw University in Indiana, where she majored in biology. Graduating magna cum laude in 1977, she did graduate work through a research assistantship at the University of Arizona, where she earned a master's degree in biology and ecology in 1981.

During this period of her life, Kingsolver also lived in Greece and France for two years, supporting herself as an archaeologist's assistant, copy editor, X-ray technician, biological researcher, and translator of medical documents. She returned to Arizona to become a technical writer in the office of arid land studies. From there she began writing and submitting feature articles, first for local newspapers and magazines, then for such national publications as *The Nation*, *The New York Times*, and *Smithsonian*. She also met and married the chemist Joseph Hoffman, with whom she became active in humanitarian and ecological activities, especially the protection of Central American Indian refugees. She and Hoffman were later divorced. Meanwhile, while suffering from insomnia associated with pregnancy, she took to writing fiction to pass the time.

Intended at first as a sketch of the section of Tucson where she lived, Kingsolver's first efforts developed into *The Bean Trees*, which immediately found an enthusiastic audience. Women in particular found it easy to identify with the self-named Taylor Greer, a young woman who flees her native Kentucky to find an independent life, only to become saddled with an abandoned Native American infant while on her flight of liberation. Writing this work determined the direction of Kingsolver's life; since 1987 she has described herself as a full-time writer. Her next publication, however, was not fiction but an account of the first complete participation by women in a major mining union action, *Holding the Line: Women in the Great Arizona Mine Strike of 1983*. Because Kingsolver lived through part of the dispute with the Phelps Dodge Copper Company as an eyewitness and participant, she captures the event in striking detail and intensity. The same year saw the publication of *"Homeland" and Other Stories*, which expands on both of her previous successes, for its twelve stories combine and blend the imaginative creativity of the fiction and the vivid portraits of the documentary.

A second novel, *Animal Dreams*, staked out new territory, emphatically from a female perspective but without commitment to any specific doctrine or slant. It deals with a woman's return to her hometown after an absence of fourteen years; in the course of the story she reconciles her relationships with her father and her sister, learns how even protected lives can be affected by the political and moral outrages of the times, and discovers how to direct her own life. Kingsolver next published a dual-language volume of poetry, *Another America/Otra America*, with poems on facing pages in English and Spanish. Her third novel, *Pigs in Heaven*, continues the adventures of Taylor and Turtle Greer from *The Bean Trees* by considering what might transpire if the Cherokee Nation tried to recover Turtle. Like her earlier works, it develops from the real-life experiences of the author, who nevertheless insists that her fiction reflects but is not equivalent to her life.

Analysis

The first half-dozen years of Barbara Kingsolver's literary career were, at best, unlikely. She appeared out of nowhere; the standard references disagreed on her place of birth, and none identified her hometown. Writing fiction at first was merely a diversion, something done to distract her from the toils of pregnancy; she alleged astonishment when a friend informed her that her scribbling was a sketch of a novel. Still, she managed to elaborate the sketch into the full-blown novel; improbably, she even got it published, though with a hint that doing so was not her object. Then a miracle occurred. Reviews were uniformly positive; more important, people were buying and reading the book. She declared herself a full-time writer. Amazingly, she just happened to have a nonfiction documentary, a set of stories, a volume of poems, and another novel ready to publish within two years. Truth might be stranger than fiction, but this reads almost like a typical Kingsolver plot. It also adds up to the most conspicuous and least engineered literary debut since that of J. D. Salinger forty years previously.

The Bean Trees is an auspicious beginning. Its hero, Taylor Greer—she names herself in the course of the novel—may be an alter ego of the author, with whom Greer shares certain biographical coincidences. A role model for the self-motivated woman, Greer at the onset of maturity decides to cut herself free of the restrictive shackles of her upbringing in Appalachia in order to find more congenial settings "out there." She reaches this decision effortlessly; yet her action is epochal, if only because she is aware of no social or sexual—let alone gender—constraints on her movements. She can

leave because she is free. Not since Moll Flanders, perhaps, has a female protagonist been less conscious that being female may pose restrictions.

Taylor, at any rate, gives these possibilities little thought. Her only objective in setting out is to make a clean break—thus the reason for renaming herself—and to find a place to establish her identity. In doing this she is as little aware of following a cause or of hammering out a template for future generations, as Huckleberry Finn or Holden Caulfield did in their respective milieus, but her resiliency and knack for making the best out of the situations in which she finds herself are easily the equal of theirs. She heads west because it seems natural; her mother had often reminded her that their Cherokee heritage was their ace in the hole, offering them a way out of Kentucky, and so Greer sets out to see the Cherokee Nation in Oklahoma first. On the way there, her car loses its steering. Taylor is not yet up to repairing it herself, and it takes most of her money to get the car back on the road. At this point she nearly gives up but decides to play out her hand to the end. Immediately thereafter she is literally given a little Native American girl by a woman who begs her to take the child, telling her only that she is her dead sister's. Having no choice, Taylor checks into a motel, where she talks her way into a room in exchange for service.

Eventually, Greer makes her way to Tucson, where she meets and joins forces with two other women, each of whom is isolated in her own way. Lou Ann Ruiz and her young son were recently abandoned by her husband; Mattie runs Jesus Is Lord Used Tires and harbors illegal immigrants from Latin America. Taylor and Turtle, the child—so named by Taylor because she refuses to speak and hangs on with the deathlock of a snapping turtle—move in with Lou Ann while Taylor takes a job with Mattie across the street. The rest of the novel essentially details how the women learn to make lives for themselves by themselves, primarily by turning an old, rundown neighborhood into a community. Taylor learns that Turtle was mistreated, even sexually abused, before her "adoption," and that this trauma is responsible for her refusal to speak. When Turtle does finally speak, it is to pronounce the word "bean"—which modulates into the significance of the title. This discovery makes the bond between Taylor and Turtle even tighter, so that when Taylor realizes that she needs adoption papers to keep Turtle, she panics. The community provides a solution: Taylor will deliver two refugees, who have become friends, to a safe house in Oklahoma; while there she will try to trace Turtle's family and obtain papers. As it turns out, the refugees end up posing as Indians in order to get the necessary documents.

When Kingsolver returns to the problems of Taylor and Turtle in *Pigs in Heaven*, their situation has changed considerably. Turtle, now six and in kindergarten, is learning how to read, though she still speaks only reluctantly. She and Taylor, her mother, live with Jax Thibodeau, a rock musician, in a colony of stone houses on a former desert ranch outside Tucson. After receiving national publicity for helping rescue a mentally disabled man from a spillway at Hoover Dam, they are invited to visit Chicago for an appearance on Oprah Winfrey's show. As a result they come to the attention of Annawake Fourkiller, a lawyer interning at Cherokee Nation headquarters and specializing in finding Native American children who have been illegally given up for adoption into white families.

When Fourkiller intervenes to restore Turtle's contact with her heritage, Taylor panics and runs away to Seattle. Along the way her mother, Alice, joins her, having left her second husband; in Las Vegas they pick up a recently fired waitress, Barbie, whose name and morals mimic those of the famous doll. Before arriving in Seattle, Alice visits Sugar Hornbuckle, a cousin with whom she grew up, in Heaven, Oklahoma, hoping that her own Cherokee connections can rectify the problem. Subsequently, Taylor meets with Fourkiller, who hatches a plan to resolve the difficulties. The latter engineers a meeting between Alice and Cash Stillwater, a widowed Cherokee who has recently returned to his hometown from the Black Hills area. In the meantime Barbie has run off with Taylor's savings, and Taylor loses her bus-driving job because she cannot afford child care for Turtle.

Through Cash, Alice begins rediscovering her people and her culture. She plans to enroll in the Cherokee Nation. In Seattle, Taylor hangs on solely because to let go would be to admit to failure, to proving incapable of taking care of herself and Turtle. Finally, however, she is forced to take Turtle to a free clinic because of lingering digestive distress that is getting worse. Turtle, like many nonwhite people, turns out to be lactose-intolerant. While Taylor, in feeding the child milk products, thought she had been guarding Turtle's health, she had actually been hurting her. She faces Fourkiller's prediction squarely: What she does not know about Turtle's heritage can damage her child. She concludes that she must face Fourkiller and the Cherokee Nation.

Before Taylor can do so, Alice learns from Cash that he is Turtle's grandfather, and Alice realizes that Fourkiller had reached that conclusion earlier. Feeling used, Alice confronts Fourkiller, only to learn that he had been hoping that a natural solution would occur before the court dictated one: If Cash and Alice married, Cash could delegate the raising of Turtle to his new stepdaughter (Taylor) and provide the necessary cultural education himself. Turtle herself seems to call for a resolution of this kind when she first encounters Cash: She recognizes him as the grandfather she has not seen for nearly four years. Yet the matter is still unresolved when the hearing is convened in the council chamber, especially because Alice has told Cash she cannot marry someone who keeps a television in his kitchen for company. Her previous husband had communicated primarily with the television set.

Kingsolver relates Taylor and Turtle's experiences through a series of scenes, not all of which immediately concern her and which are not necessarily in chronological order. This approach to composition by apparently random scenes arranged intuitively rather than by comprehensive plot integration may link Kingsolver with other women writers of her generation—it is practiced by Louise Erdrich, Bobbie Jo Mason, and Alice Hoffman, for example. In any case it is more characteristic of short-story writers than of novelists. It has become standard practice with Kingsolver, even though her stories have become significantly longer and more complex.

Although not in any sense a thesis-dominant writer—in fact, the reader is likely to be more aware of her vivid characters and quirky situations—Kingsolver's thematic centers are emphatically feminist. Female characters outnumber males by striking numbers; the former are also significantly more idiosyncratic, less stereotyped. Her female characters are brilliantly sketched and are among the most striking in all of literature. Furthermore, Kingsolver promotes her cause by bringing them to life: She makes them emphatically female, yet keeps them sympathetic. She accomplishes the most difficult task of creating female characters with whom male readers can identify. Then she carries the process further by making her characters' reactions and feelings entirely natural while being consistently female. In this respect Kingsolver is perhaps the most effective presenter of the female perspective in fiction since Willa Cather.

Other major works

SHORT FICTION: *"Homeland" and Other Stories*, 1989.
NONFICTION: *Holding the Line: Women in the Great Arizona Mine Strike of 1983*, 1989.
POETRY: *Another America/Otra America*, 1992.

Bibliography

"Kingsolver, Barbara." In *Contemporary Authors*. Vol. 55. Detroit: Gale Research, 1989.

Kingsolver, Barbara. Interview by Mark Ferguson. *The Reader* (July, 1993): 1-3.

_____ . "An Interview with Barbara Kingsolver." Interview by Amy Pence. *Poets and Writers* 21, no. 4 (July, 1993): 14.

_____ . *"Publishers Weekly* Interviews Barbara Kingsolver." Interview by Lisa See. *Publishers Weekly* 237 (August 31, 1990): 46-47.

JOYCE CAROL OATES

Born: Lockport, New York; June 16, 1938

Principal long fiction

With Shuddering Fall, 1964; *A Garden of Earthly Delights*, 1967; *Expensive People*, 1968; *them*, 1969; *Wonderland*, 1971; *Do with Me What You Will*, 1973; *The Assassins: A Book of Hours*, 1975; *Childwold*, 1976; *The Triumph of the Spider Monkey*, 1976; *Son of the Morning*, 1978; *Unholy Loves*, 1979; *Cybele*, 1979; *Bellefleur*, 1980; *Angel of Light*, 1981; *A Bloodsmoor Romance*, 1982; *Mysteries of Winterthurn*, 1984; *Solstice*, 1985; *Marya: A Life*, 1986; *Lives of the Twins*, 1987 (as Rosamond Smith); *You Must Remember This*, 1987; *American Appetites*, 1989; *Soul/Mate*, 1989 (as Rosamond Smith); *Because It Is Bitter, and Because It Is My Heart*, 1990; *I Lock My Door upon Myself*, 1990; *The Rise of Life on Earth*, 1991; *Black Water*, 1992; *What I Lived For*, 1994.

Other literary forms

The extremely prolific Joyce Carol Oates has published volumes of short fiction, poetry, plays, and nonfiction. She has also edited several anthologies.

Achievements

As a writer who avidly embraces the contingencies of this world and a teacher who maintains her classroom along with an amazing proliferation of writing, Joyce Carol Oates has been awarded numerous and varied prizes. Among them are the 1967, 1969, and 1973 O. Henry Awards, the Richard and Hinda Rosenthal Award of the National Institute of Arts and Letters (1968), the National Book Award for 1970, and the Lotos Club Award of Merit (1975).

Biography

Joyce Carol Oates was born on June 16, 1938, in Lockport, New York. She received a modest education in a one-room schoolhouse and, as a child, had very little exposure to literature. This, however, did not quell her desire to write, and she spent much of her time as a child writing stories and short books. Even with all the writing and composing experience from her childhood, she would not publish her first story until 1959. While studying at Syracuse University, she won the *Mademoiselle* college fiction award for her short story "In the Old World." This would be her first in a series of public recognitions for her writing.

After receiving her B.A. degree from Syracuse in 1960, where she was valedictorian, she went on to receive her M.A. degree from the University of Wisconsin. During her term at Syracuse, she had met her future husband, Raymond J. Smith, and they married in 1961.

The Smiths then moved to Beaumont, Texas, and Oates began to work on her Ph.D. degree at Rice University. She would never accomplish this task; she and her husband moved to Michigan in 1962. While in Michigan, she taught English at the University of Detroit. This would continue until 1967, when she and her husband began teaching at the University of Windsor in Ontario. During their tenure at the university, Smith and Oates cofounded *The Windsor Review*. After leaving the university in 1978, she went on to join the Princeton University Creative Writing Program. While a member of this program, she wrote not only fiction but also some brilliant essays on writers ranging from William Shakespeare to Norman Mailer. She was eventually appointed to a professorship at Princeton.

Analysis

Oates chronicles the personal dislocation and troubled national identity of twentieth century America. Her fictional world often features characters whose will to control their lives, to force life to conform to their vision of it, is all-consuming and, in the end, ruinous. The experiences of such personalities become a candid depiction of the disintegration of the self. The setting for many of Oates's novels is the fictional Eden County—as the name suggests, a mythical paradise wherein she tracks the American loss of innocence. Her earliest works evidence a vision in which the expression of violence (the violence resting beneath the surface of American life) becomes, for her protagonists, a means of deliverance from their particular plight. Later works propose less violent resolutions in which these individuals transcend their personal horror to create a more acceptable life within the fabric of society.

Oates's poor, unimaginative characters typically ply their swords through a fogged-in existence inflicted upon them by a fatalistic creator. They cannot escape from the miasma they must breathe, and so they are poisoned by it, confused by muddled thoughts in an unkind world. The characters finally become enraged by their situation and so do bloody battle to extricate themselves from it.

In her first novel, *With Shuddering Fall*, Oates introduced a theme that would pervade almost all the rest of her fiction: the awful responsibility of freedom. Her characters struggle to divest themselves of their little lives in order to achieve personal freedom, but they are unable to cope with the consequences of their release from their former lives. They learn that they have abandoned not only their pasts but also their identities. Then they must struggle either to reclaim their selves or to forge new ones.

With Shuddering Fall is one character's reconciliation with her life, and this treaty gains for her a new appreciation of her history and that of her family. Karen must endure a sort of familial ritual at the hands of her father, Hert, and her lover, Shar. At first Karen rejects her father's values. He is a legendary figure who wields great power and enjoys a close relationship with Karen; however, this is destroyed by the arrival of the violent, virile Shar, who deposes Hert. Shar is not a new ruler, however, but an anarchist who wishes only to topple kings, not replace them. He leaves, and Karen follows, not because she believes in him but because she seeks to escape Hert and "a life dominated by fathers." Once free from her father, Karen begins to feel uprooted, aimless and nameless. Without Hert, she has "nothing of herself but a face, a body, a set of emotions." There is nothing of depth to her being. She discovers that she needs her familial history to add meaning to her identity and so finally refuses the history-less Shar and his attempts at nihilism.

Shar's proclivity for race-car driving leads to the lowland town of Cherry River. Cherry River is a town that seems to exist for the edification of the summer tourists and little else. It offers appreciation of self-gratification but not of history. The high point of the summer seems to be when Shar commits suicide on the race track. Oates seems to be saying that in a community with no shared history, the only communal ties that exist are shared acts of violence.

The spokesperson for the novel is Max, a self-centered businessman, who is the only one intelligent enough to share Oates's philosophy with the reader. He appears in many other novels as the maniacal oracle who tries to make Fate subservient to his will. He tries to cheat Karen of her birthright by confounding her with questions, but she eludes him and is, thus, saved. She returns to herself, her family.

It is not chance that Lewis Carroll's child adventure and Oates's novel *Wonderland* bear the same word in the title. Oates considers the work of this nineteenth century English mathematician to ask the pertinent questions of life: Can all life be merely a game, and am I the only one who is not cheating? Both protagonists in the novels—Alice and Jesse Harte—run and jump from square to square on a large, mostly unseen chessboard. Along the way they are both transmogrified into oddly sized versions of their original selves. Finally, in order to survive, Jesse and Alice regain their normal proportions and become resolved with their communities.

In the beginning of Oates's novel, the newly orphaned Jesse travels from his grandfather's farm to an orphanage and finally to the home of Dr. Pedersen, a brilliant but unbalanced surrogate father. He is the first of a triumvirate of adoptive fathers whom Jesse must survive. His biological father's initial attack has given Jesse the strength to deal with these surrogates. His father has slaughtered his wife and their unborn child and wounded Jesse before killing himself. Jesse escapes to his grandfather's farm, where he recuperates until he must start his strange odyssey. In the Pedersen family, Jesse learns of things small and fantastic. He studies cell life and becomes involved in Dr. Pedersen's cancer research. The more he learns, the more he is confused by his father's view of life, which is overshadowed by death. At last, Pedersen grows impatient with Jesse and dismisses him from the family, saying, "You have no existence. You are nothing." Jesse must seek another, more receptive, life-style.

Jesse enters medical school, is graduated, marries, and tries to forge a new family, a home, for himself. He keeps returning in his dreams, however, to the site of his father's tragic demise. His own children gradually start to shrink away like the Cheshire Cat. Michelle becomes Shelley and ultimately Shell, until Jesse can no longer grasp her—or the rest of his family—with any degree of certitude. Even Jesse's two father-figures, Drs. Cady and Perrault, become in turn distant and disdainful. Dr. Cady will now acknowledge anything but the ethereal, and Dr. Perrault will not admit that the mind is anything but actual. These two opposing views further succeed in alienating Jesse from a "real" life. To offset these unrealistic real people, Jesse creates an unreal friend, or series of friends, but she only promises disharmony and death, so he eventually rejects her, too.

In the end of the novel, the action picks up speed, racing toward the now of the narrative, 1971. Jesse finally returns to his father's psyche and discovers the final, perfect answer: "A clean, pure, empty being, a void." It is only through the total destruction of the universe that a peaceful existence (or nonexistence) can be enjoyed.

The setting of *Childwold* is again Eden Valley, scene of the action in *With Shuddering Fall* and *Wonderland*. The novel is peopled by a variety of characters and is narrated by several of them in turn, as each becomes the lover of the central figure's mother, Arlene Bartlett. Arlene's daughter, Laney Bartlett, is the unconscious catalyst for much of the violence in the novel.

The primary reaction between Laney and another character occurs between her and Fitz John Kasch, a fiftyish hermit who lives among the debris of his large but deceased family. In Laney, Kasch sees not only his failed marriage but also his repressed desires. She becomes for him both an icon and a Tantalus, love and passion. Unable to avail himself of her, Kasch woos and wins Arlene and becomes another in a lengthy retinue of lovers.

Arlene is a figure of the sex goddess, but, unlike so many untouchable figures, she is the small statue in the back of the church, worn down by the grasp of many hands. This, however, does not dismay her; indeed, it invigorates her. Where many single women would not welcome pregnancy, Arlene revels in it; her children reaffirm her existence in a world of many people. Kasch, by contrast, is unable to enjoy the company of others. He secrets himself in a small part of what was once the family manse, now a museum. He blames his self-imposed isolation on his divorce, brought on by his former wife's infidelity. Retiring into his hermitage, however, only amplifies his feelings of detachment from life. Although he seeks to redefine himself in various ways (as a voyeur, among others), he remains at one, in harmony with only himself. When he finally becomes reconciled to the Bartletts' violent way of life, he remains unfulfilled. He can satiate himself neither with the daughter nor with the mother.

Instead of an object of violence, of rape or murder, Laney becomes an object of Kasch's creation. It is at this point that *Childwold* most neatly resembles Vladimir Nabokov's *Lolita*: the story of a middle-aged man's obsession with a nubile, pubescent girl. As did Humbert, Humbert Kasch casts a spell about Laney, using art as a medium, but she eventually escapes, moving through the two-dimensional world of Kasch's photographs to the world of nature outside his museum/prison. She frees herself from the world he is doomed to inhabit.

It is a world that is of his own design. After Arlene has joined Kasch, her former lover, Earl Tuller, returns to threaten and bully her. In a rage, Kasch kills him and seals his fate as a prisoner. He has dreamed of being a murderer, but now that his fantasy has been accidentally granted, he is unable to bear the results. He has been defeated by his own desires mixed with the mindless tide of the universe. The novel ends with Arlene musing over the turn of events their lives have taken. Laney returns to Kasch's mansion, but he will not answer the door. Imagining that she sees him behind a curtained window, she calls out. She feels she is strong enough, has changed enough from the girl that she was, to save him, and so in a flush of anticipation she waits for "a sign, a sign," but it never comes. Oates demonstrates in *Childwold* the tragic consequences of the conflict between man's ambitions and the machinations of the world.

The gothic mystery novel *Mysteries of Winterthurn* has been hailed as a feminist dissertation, a charge that has not been denied by Oates. Although the main character is male and the action in the novel is seen through his eyes, most of the victims are women and children, and it is to their plight that the narrator and the reader grow sympathetic. In this novel Oates discusses the existence of women in a male-dominated society, and a pitiable existence it is.

Even though Oates owes much of her presentation of the situation of nineteenth century women and children to several other popular authors, her interpretation is uniquely her own. Her victims are disposable pawns in a society that is more than willing to sacrifice them for its own (male) devices. Oates inserts the supernatural into the novel to allow her women a modicum of revenge upon these perpetrators. If this seems to be impossible (the unreal attacking the real), Oates insists that once something is thought to be real, it becomes so whether it should be real or not. Thus, the view of women as passive, thoughtless beings is true for the males in her novel, even though it is a false concept. The women victims in the novel are freed by this misconception to react violently to those who misuse them because they (the women) cannot have acted in such a manner within the male scheme of things.

To drive this point home, Oates repeats it three times during the novel. The first story, "The Virgin in the Rose-Bower," deals with a sadistic husband and father, Erasmus Kilgarven, who has a hand in the brutal deaths of his two wives and commits incest for several years with his daughter, Georgina, causing her to become pregnant several times. Georgina kills her infants but claims that they have been destroyed by angels painted on the ceiling of her bedroom. The narrator, young Xavier Kilgarven, sees one painted angel bleed, and this leads to the discovery of several other infant corpses, silent witnesses to Erasmus Kilgarven's hideous habit. By claiming supernatural murder (and rape), Georgina is able to evade guilt and exact a small amount of revenge on her father.

In the persona of Iphigenia, her pen name, Georgina is also able to free her female family members by publishing her poetry. The money she receives from this enterprise, until her father forbids it as unseemly, is later used to finance even more unfeminine exploits by the young Perdita. Perdita needs no spectral avenger; she takes matters into her own hands, although she is never seen as a murderer by anyone but the reader. The only people who are capable of violent acts in *Mysteries of Winterthurn* are male; the females are those upon whom these acts are perpetrated. Thus, an invisible shield is created around Perdita, enabling her to murder several people in order to achieve her goal, union with young Xavier.

The third sister, Thérèse, is able to profit from her sisters' cloaked deeds, and, indeed, there are indications that she may be involved in Perdita's violent crimes in a peripheral manner. This is only hinted at; outwardly, Thérèse appears to be a happy, modern woman. It is here that Oates's use of paradox—the woman who is both angel and demon, visible and invisible—culminates. All the women in the novel have been so seduced by the theory of their own guilt that they must violently oppose it in order to free themselves.

Oates's novels explore the evolving American identity. Her major characters fight to gain control of their lives, often resorting to horrifying violence to achieve it. For Oates, the American loss of innocence is reflected in this all-consuming need for personal deliverance and the often-violent means by which it is attained.

Other major works

SHORT FICTION: *By the North Gate*, 1963; *Upon the Sweeping Flood*, 1966; *The Wheel of Love*, 1970; *Marriages and Infidelities*, 1972; *The Goddess and Other Women*, 1974; *The Hungry Ghosts*, 1974; *Where Are You Going, Where Have You Been?* 1974; *The Poisoned Kiss*, 1975; *The Seduction*, 1975; *Crossing the Border*, 1976; *Night-Side*, 1977; *All the Good People I've Left Behind*, 1978; *A Sentimental Education*, 1980; *Last Days*, 1984; *Raven's Wing*, 1986; *The Assignation*, 1988; *Heat, and Other Stories*, 1991; *Where Is Here?: Stories*, 1992; *Foxfire: Confessions of a Girl Gang*, 1993; *Haunted: Tales of the Grotesque*, 1994.

POETRY: *Women in Love*, 1968; *Anonymous Sins*, 1969; *Love and Its Derangements*, 1970; *Angel Fire*, 1973; *The Fabulous Beasts*, 1975; *Women Whose Lives are Food, Men Whose Lives Are Money*, 1978; *Invisible Woman: New and Selected Poems, 1970-1982*, 1982.

PLAYS: *Miracle Play*, 1974; *Three Plays*, 1980; *Twelve Plays*, 1991.

NONFICTION: *The Edge of Impossibility: Tragic Forms in Literature*, 1972; *The Hostile Sun: The Poetry of D. H. Lawrence*, 1973; *New Heaven, New Earth: The Visionary Experience in Literature*, 1974; *Contraries: Essays*, 1981; *The Profane Art: Essays and Reviews*, 1983; *On Boxing*, 1987; *(Woman) Writer: Occasions and Opportunities*, 1988.

ANTHOLOGIES: *Scenes from American Life: Contemporary Short Fiction*, 1972; *The Best American Short Stories of 1979*, 1979 (with Shannon Ravenel); *Night Walks: A Bedside Companion*, 1982; *First Person Singular: Writers on Their Craft*, 1983.

Bibliography

Chell, Cara. "Un-tricking the Eye: Joyce Carol Oates and the Feminist Ghost Story." *Arizona Quarterly* 41 (Spring, 1985): 5-23.

Creighton, Joanne V. *Joyce Carol Oates*. Boston: Twayne, 1979.

——————. *Joyce Carol Oates: Novels of the Middle Years*. New York: Twayne, 1992.

Friedman, Ellen G. *Joyce Carol Oates*. New York: Frederick Ungar, 1980.

Grant, Mary Kathryn. *The Tragic Vision of Joyce Carol Oates*. Durham, N.C.: Duke University Press, 1978.

Oates, Joyce Carol. *Conversations with Joyce Carol Oates*. Edited by Lee Milazzo. Jackson: University Press of Mississippi, 1989.

Waller, G. F. *Dreaming America*. Baton Rouge: Louisiana State University Press, 1979.

Wesley, Marilyn C. *Refusal and Transgression in Joyce Carol Oates' Fiction*. Westport, Conn.: Greenwood Press, 1993.

TILLIE OLSEN

Born: Omaha, Nebraska; January 14, 1913

Principal short fiction
Tell Me a Riddle, 1961.

Other literary forms

Tillie Olsen has published both long fiction and non-fiction. She composed a substantial biographical interpretation for a 1972 reprint of Rebecca Harding Davis' *Life in the Iron Mills*, which Olsen edited. In addition, Olsen has written uncollected magazine articles on women and writing and many uncollected poems, several of which have appeared in *Partisan Review*.

Achievements

Even though Olsen secured her literary reputation on the strength of one collection of short fiction, her voice as a humanist and feminist extends her influence beyond this small output. Olsen is also known as a leading feminist educator. Her courses have introduced students to forgotten writings, such as journals, to teach them about women's lives. The reading lists she developed have provided models for other women's studies courses throughout the United States. Besides the O. Henry Award for the best American short story of 1961 for "Tell Me a Riddle," Olsen has also won the Award for Distinguished Contribution to American Literature from the American Academy and the National Institute of Arts and Letters. Her short fiction appears in more than one hundred anthologies. She won the 1994 Rea Award for the Short Story.

Biography

The daughter of Jewish immigrant parents, Tillie L. Olsen spent her youth in Nebraska and Wyoming. Her parents were active union members, so political commitment as well as economic pressures accompanied her early years. In 1933, she moved to California, where, in 1936, she married printer Jack Olsen. Because she raised four daughters and worked at full-time clerical jobs, she did not publish her first book until she was in her late forties. Then, with the help of a Stanford University Creative Writing Fellowship and a Ford grant in literature, she put together *Tell Me a Riddle*, the title story of which received the O. Henry Award for the best American short story of 1961. There followed a fellowship at the Radcliffe Institute for Independent Study, grants from the National Endowment for the Arts, and a Guggenheim Fellowship. A grant from the MacDowell Colony allowed her to complete *Yonnondio: From the Thirties*, a novel she began in the 1930's. After its publication in 1974, Olsen continued writing essays and articles as well as editing collections of women's writings. She has taught at Amherst College, Stanford University, the Massachusetts Institute of Technology, and the University of Minnesota, among others.

Analysis

Olsen writes about working-class people who, because of class, race, or sex, have been denied the opportunity to develop their talents. Frequently, she focuses on the obstacles that women have experienced, the universal issues faced by women developing individual skills while combating socially imposed views.

Olsen's *Tell Me a Riddle* contains four stories arranged chronologically in the order in which they were written: "I Stand Here Ironing," "Hey Sailor, What Ship?," "O Yes," and "Tell Me a Riddle." All but the first story contain, as major or minor characters, members of the same family, whose parents emigrated from Russia.

"Hey Sailor, What Ship?" introduces Lennie and Helen and their children, Jeannie, Carol, and Allie; but the story is not so much about them as it is about Whitey (Michael Jackson, a sailor and friend of the family who seems more lost at sea than at home in any port or ship). Filtering through Whitey's consciousness, the story explores his frustrations and anger, pain and despair. At the same time, however, the living conditions of Lennie and Helen and their children and the relationships among the family and between various members of the family and Whitey are carefully delineated.

Whitey is a mariner, a perpetual wanderer whose only contact with family life is with Lennie, a boyhood friend. As the story opens, Whitey is drunk, a condition in which he increasingly finds himself, and with almost nothing left of his pay. His anguish, born of his desire to be with Lennie and the family and his reluctance to bear the pain of such a visit, is evident from the beginning, as is also the shame and degradation he feels associated with his lifestyle. What had started out as a dream, a life of adventure on the sea, with comrades who shared the good and the bad, has become a parade of gin mills and cathouses, clip joints, hockshops, skid rows, and, lately, hospitals. Lennie's dreams, however, have also been frustrated. Lennie is a worn likeness of his former self; Helen is graying and tired from holding a job as well as caring for house and home. They live in poverty in cramped quarters. Still, as Helen explains to her oldest daughter, Jeannie, this house is the only place where Whitey does not have to pay his way. The tragedy is that he feels he does. He comes bearing presents, distributing dollars and at the same time too drunk to share in meaningful interaction with the family he loves, where he is brother, lover, and father to a family not his own.

"O Yes" picks up the family several years later when Carol, the second daughter, is twelve and about to experience the pain of parting with a close friend, Parry, a black girl. Carol and her mother, Helen, have accompanied Parry and her mother, Alva, to a black church to witness Parry's baptism. Carol is uncomfortable, however, both with the surroundings and with Parry, who is growing away from her. As the services rise to a crescendo of passion, Carol asks her mother to take her home and then faints. Later Alva tries to explain to Carol that the religion is like a hope in the blood and bones and that the music offers a release from despair, but Carol will not listen.

Later Jeannie tries to explain to her mother that Carol and Parry are undergoing an inevitable "sorting out" process, a sorting out demanded by the culture—their environment, their peers, their teachers—a sorting out that "they" demand. The separation is hard on both girls. Nevertheless, Parry seems better equipped to handle the crisis, while Carol continues to suffer and question. Helen knows that Carol, too, has been baptized, immersed in the seas of humankind, and she suffers with her daughter. The irony is that white people have no means of catharsis through their religion; they are unable to cry "O Yes."

The most haunting story in the collection *Tell Me a Riddle* is the title story. Longer than the other stories, this one focuses on Lennie's mother and father while at the same time it brings to a culmination themes Olsen explores in the other stories: the frustration of dreams unrealized; the despair of never having enough money; the anger and hostility of women who have had to cope with too much with too little and who have lost themselves in the process; the search for meaning and explanation; the continuing hope of the young in spite of the tensions around them; the pain of mortality. "Tell me a riddle, granny," a grandchild demands. "I know no riddles, child," the grandmother answers; but she knows, and the reader knows, that the riddle is of existence itself. Why claw and scratch; why hold on? Aged and consumed by cancer, the grandmother's body will not let go.

Russian emigrants of Jewish extraction who have fled persecution to come to the American land of promise, the grandfather and grandmother have been married forty-seven years and have reared seven children, all of whom are married and have families of their own. Now the grandfather wants to sell the house and move to The Haven, a retirement community, where he will have freedom from responsibility, from fretting over money, and will be able to share in communal living, to fish or play cards to make jokes with convivial companions. The grandmother refuses, however, countering every argument her husband puts forth. She was the one who worked eighteen hours a day without sufficient money to keep the house together. Not once did he scrape a carrot or lift a dish towel or stay with the children. He is the one who needs companions; she lived a life of isolation. "You trained me well," she tells him. "I do not need others to enjoy." She is adamant: "Never again to be forced to move to the rhythms of others." The argument between them erupts continually, fanned by his desires and her anger and resentment.

The children do not understand. How can people married forty-seven years and now at a time of life when they should be happy get themselves into a power struggle that threatens to pull them apart? Unknowingly, the children take their father's side, considering their mother to be unreasonable or sick. They advise him to get her to a doctor. The doctor finds nothing seriously wrong and advises a diet and a change in lifestyle—"start living like a human being." The grandmother continues to deteriorate; more and more she keeps to herself, stays in bed, and turns her face to the wall. One night she realizes that although the doctor said she was not sick, she feels sick, and she asks her husband to stay home with her. He refuses, once again bringing up the old argument, and as he leaves she sobs curses at him. When he returns he finds that she has left their bed and retired to a cot. They do not speak to each other for a week until one night he finds her outside in the rain singing a love song of fifty years ago. The husband and the children bring her to a son-in-law who is a physician, and during surgery he finds cancer. The children advise their father to travel with her and visit all the children; and now begins an exodus of pain. She does not yet realize she is terminally ill, and the constant movement causes her utter despair when all she wants is to be at home. From house to house they carry her, but she refuses to participate, will not touch a baby grandchild, and retreats finally to sit in a closet when they believe she is napping. Once a granddaughter, herself upset, hauls her little body into the closet and finds her grandmother there—"Is this where you hide, too, Grammy?"

Finally, the grandfather brings her to a new apartment close to a seaside resort, but dismal in the off-season and filled with the impoverished aged. The grandmother, ill in bed for several days, is tended by her granddaughter, Jeannie, daughter of Lennie and Helen, and a visiting nurse. When she is better, the grandmother wants to go by the sea to sit in the sand. More

and more now she loses control of her conscious self, sings snatches of songs, remembers pieces of quotations, tries in herself to find meaning while noticing that death, decay, and deterioration are all around her. Then she realizes that she, too, is dying and knows that she cannot tell her husband of her realization because a fiction is necessary to him; and she wants to go home.

One day Jeannie brings her a cookie in the shape of a real little girl who has died and tells her of a Spanish custom of partying at funerals, singing songs, and picnicking by the graves. From this interaction Jeannie draws solace, from what she takes to be a promise from her grandmother that at death she will go back to when she first heard music, to a wedding dance, where the flutes "joyous and vibrant tremble in the air." For the others there is no comfort. "Too late to ask: and what did you learn with your living, Mother, and what do we need to know?"

Olsen's fiction affirms the individuality and complexity of women. It expresses the inner lives of her female characters—their richness, depth, and diversity—forcing readers to see life through a woman's eyes, and to see women as individuals.

Other major works

NOVEL: *Yonnondio: From the Thirties*, 1974

NONFICTION: *Silences*, 1979

EDITED TEXTS: *Life in the Iron Mills*, 1972; *Mother to Daughter, Daughter to Mother: A Daybook and Reader*, 1984; *Mothers and Daughters: That Essential Quality*, 1987.

Bibliography

Faulkner, Mara. *Protest and Possibility in the Writing of Tillie Olsen*. Charlottesville: University Press of Virginia, 1993.

Jacobs, Naomi. "Earth, Air, Fire, and Water in *Tell Me a Riddle*." *Studies in Short Fiction* 23 (Fall, 1986): 401-406.

Martin, Abigail. *Tillie Olsen*. Boise, Idaho: Boise State University Press, 1984.

Niehus, Edward L., and Teresa Jackson. "Polar Stars, Pyramids, and *Tell Me a Riddle*." *American Notes and Queries* 24 (January/February, 1986): 77-83.

Olsen, Tillie, "PW Interviews." Interview by Lisa See. *Publishers Weekly* 226 (November 23, 1984): 76.

Pearlman, Mickey, and Abby H. P. Werlock. *Tillie Olsen*. Boston: Twayne, 1991.

Staub, Michael. "The Struggle for 'Selfness' Through Speech in Olsen's *Yonnondio*." *Studies in American Fiction* 16 (Autumn, 1988): 131-139.

SYLVIA PLATH

Born: Boston, Massachusetts; October 27, 1932   **Died:** London, England; February 11, 1963

Principal poetry

The Colossus and Other Poems, 1960; *Three Women*, 1962; *Ariel*, 1965; *Uncollected Poems*, 1965; *Crossing the Water*, 1971; *Winter Trees*, 1971; *Fiesta Melons*, 1971; *Crystal Gazer*, 1971; *Lyonesse*, 1971; *Pursuit*, 1973; *The Collected Poems*, 1981; *Selected Poems*, 1985.

Other literary forms

Sylvia Plath was a prolific writer of poetry and prose. Her first publication was a short story, "Sunday at the Mintons'," which appeared in *Mademoiselle* in 1952. Throughout the remainder of her life, her stories and prose sketches appeared almost yearly in various journals and magazines. At her death Plath left behind extensive diaries, journals, and correspondence. Her work in other forms include a poetic drama, *Three Women*, that was aired by the British Broadcasting Corporation (BBC) on August 19, 1962; an autobiographical novel, *The Bell Jar* (1963); and a popular children's book.

Achievements

Plath's poetry, like that of Hart Crane, will be read, studied, and known for two reasons: for its intrinsic merit and for its bearing on her suicide. In spite of efforts to disentangle her poetry from her life and death, Plath's reputation and impact have fluctuated with public interest in her suicide. Almost immediately after her death, she was adopted by many members of the feminist movement as an emblem of the female in a male-dominated world; her death was lamented, condemned, criticized, and analyzed as a symbolic gesture as well as an inevitable consequence of her socialization. Explanations for her acute mental anguish were often subsumed in larger arguments about her archetypal sacrifice.

With the publication of *The Bell Jar* and the posthumous collections of poetry, however, her audience grew in diversity and appreciation. *The Collected Poems* (1981) was awarded the Pulitzer Prize in poetry in 1982. While she never lost her value to the feminist movement, she gained other sympathetic readers who attempted to place her in a social and cultural context that would help to explain, although certainly not definitively, her artistic success and her decision to end her life.

It is not difficult to understand why Plath has won the respect of a wider audience. Her poems transcend ideology. Vivid, immediate re-creations of mental collapse, they are remnants of a psyche torn by severely conflicting forces. Yet Plath's poems are not merely re-creations of nightmares; were they only that, they would hardly be distinguishable from reams of psychological case histories. Plath's great achievement was her ability to transform the experience into art without losing its nightmarish immediacy.

To retain that immediacy, Plath sometimes exceeded what many readers consider "good taste" or "aesthetic appropriateness"; she has even been convicted of trivializing universal suffering to the level of individual "bitchiness." For Plath, however, survival became paramount—and her poetry therefore became a kind of prayer, a ritual to remind her of her identity in a world gone mad. As a record of such experiences, Plath's poetry is unexcelled in any tradition.

Biography

Sylvia Plath was the daughter of a German father and an Austrian mother, both of whom were university-level teachers. Plath's father died when she was eight years old. Her early years were spent near the sea in her native Massachusetts, where she passed much of her time with her younger brother, Warren, exploring the beaches near their home. A very bright student, she consistently received high grades in virtually all of her subjects and won many awards.

In September, 1950, Plath began her freshman year at Smith College in Massachusetts, the recipient of a scholarship. She continued her brilliant academic record, and at the end of her third year she was named guest managing editor of *Mademoiselle* and given a month's "working vacation" in New York. In August, 1953, after returning from New York, she suffered a nervous breakdown and attempted suicide. She was hospitalized and given shock treatments and psychotherapy. She returned to Smith for her senior year in February, 1954.

After being graduated summa cum laude in 1955, she won a Fulbright Fellowship to study at Newnham College, Cambridge University, and sailed for England in September.

After one semester of study, Plath briefly toured London and then went to Paris to spend the Christmas break. Back in Cambridge, she met English poet Ted Hughes at a party on February 25, 1956. They were married on June 16 in London. That summer she and Hughes toured France and Spain. In June, 1957, she and Hughes sailed for the United States, where she became an instructor in freshman English at Smith College. She enjoyed teaching and was regarded as an excellent instructor, but the strain of grading essays led her to abandon the academic world after one year. She and Hughes remained in Boston for the following year, both trying to earn a living by writing and part-time work. In the spring of 1959 Hughes was given a Guggenheim Fellowship; meanwhile Plath was attending Robert Lowell's seminars on poetry at Boston University.

In December of 1959 the couple returned to England, settling in London after a brief visit to Hughes's Yorkshire home. During this time Plath was pregnant with her first child and also saw her first book of poems, *The Colossus*, published. On April 1, 1960, Plath gave birth to her daughter, Frieda. Her book was published in October, to generally favorable reviews.

In February, 1961, Plath suffered a miscarriage. That summer, Plath and Hughes purchased a house in Croton, Devon, and went to France for a brief vacation. In August they moved into their house in Devon, and in November, Plath was given a grant to enable her to work on *The Bell Jar*.

On January 17, 1962, Plath gave birth to her second child, Nicholas. Within a period of ten days in April she composed six poems, a sign of her growing desire to fit into the village life of Croton and of her returning poetic voice.

In July, Plath learned of Hughes's affair with Assia Gutman. On September 11, Plath and Hughes journeyed to Ireland; almost immediately Hughes left Plath and went to London to live with Gutman. Plath returned alone to Devon, where, with her children, she attempted to rebuild her life. She wrote extensively: twenty-three poems in October, ten in November. She decided, however, that she could not face another winter in Devon, so she found a flat in London and moved there with her children in the middle of December.

That winter proved to be one of the worst on record, and life in the flat became intolerable. The children were ill, the weather was cold, there was little heat, the pipes had frozen, and Plath was suffering extremes of depression over her separation from Hughes. On January 14, 1963, *The Bell Jar* was published to only lukewarm reviews. Her mood worsened, and on February 11, 1963, Plath committed suicide in the kitchen of her flat. She was thirty years old.

Analysis

Plath was a leading figure of the so-called confessional school of poetry that achieved popularity during the 1960's and 1970's. Her intensely candid and personal writings reveal an obsession with death and rebirth, pollution and purification. Assuming almost archetypal status following her premature death, she became for feminists a symbol of the female in a male-dominated society.

In many ways, Plath as a poet defies categorization. She has been described variously as a lyricist, a confessionalist, a symbolist, an imagist, and a mere diarist. While none of these terms can adequately convey the richness of approach and content of her work, they aptly describe the various modes of discourse that work effectively in her poetry and her prose. As Plath developed as a poet, she attempted to fuse these various modes, so that, by the end of her life, she was writing poems that combined any number of symbols and images into a quasi-lyrical confessional poem. What remains constant throughout her life and the assorted modes in which she wrote, however, is the rooting of the poems in her own experience. That is perhaps her greatest talent: her ability to transform everyday experiences—the kind that would be appropriate entries in a diary—into poems. Her poetry is a journal, recording not only full-fledged experiences but also acute perceptions and a wide range of moods.

Especially in her last years, Plath used the confessional mode frequently, personally, and often viciously. She seldom bothered to create a persona through whom she could project feelings; rather, she simply expressed her feelings in open, exposed, even raw ways, leaving herself equally exposed. One such poem is "The Jailer," written after her separation from Hughes. The focus is the authorial "I," which occurs twelve times (together with the pronouns "my" and "me," which occur thirteen times) within the poem's forty-five lines. This thinly disguised persona imagines herself captive of her lover/ husband (the jailer of the title), who has not only drugged her but also raped her; she has become, in her degradation, a "Lever of his wet dreams." She then imagines herself to be Prometheus; she has been dropped from great heights to be smashed and consumed by the "beaks of birds." She then projects herself in the role of an African American woman being burned by her captor with his cigarettes. Then she sees herself as a starved prisoner, her ribs showing after her meals of only "Lies and smiles." Then she sees herself as persecuted by him because of her rather frail religious belief (her "church of burnt matchsticks"). She is killed in several ways: "Hung, starved, burned, hooked." In her impotence to wish him the harm she feels he deserves, she retreats to slanders against his sexuality, making him impotent as well. She is, however, paralyzed in her inability to attain freedom through his death (by her wishes) and to escape her own imagination and her own psyche's fears.

Perhaps Plath's greatest talent lay in her ability to transform everyday experiences—the kind that would be appropriate entries in a diary—into poems. Her poetry is a journal, recording not only full-fledged experiences but also acute perceptions and a wide range of moods. One such poem based on an everyday happening is "Medallion," in which the persona tells of discovering a dead snake. In fact, if the lines of the poem were simply punctuated as prose, the piece would have very much the appearance of a diary entry. This style in no way lessens the value of the piece as poetry. It is, indeed, one of Plath's most successful works because it is elegantly easy and colloquial, exemplifying one more mode of expression in which the poet excelled.

As Plath developed as a poet, she attempted to fuse these various modes, so that, by the end of her life, she was writing poems that combined any number of symbols and images into a quasilyrical confessional poem. What remains constant throughout her life and the various modes in which she wrote, however, is the rooting of the poems in her own experience. If Plath is to be faulted, this quality is perhaps her greatest weakness: she was not able to project her personae a great distance from herself. Plath was aware of this limitation (she once wrote: "I shall perish if I can write about no one but myself"), and she attempted to turn it into an advantage. She tried to turn her personal experiences and feelings into a vision. Her vision was in no way comprehensive, nor did it ever receive any systematic expression in prose, but it did govern many of her finest creations, especially in her later poetry, and it does account for the "lapses of taste" that many readers find annoying in her.

One of her last poems will serve as an example of how this vision both limited and freed Plath's expression. "Mary's Song" is a complex of religious imagery and the language of war, combined to express feelings of persecution, betrayal, impending destruction, and, at the same time, defiant hope. The poem is very personal, even though its language works to drown the personal voice. An everyday, ordinary scene—a Sunday dinner in preparation, a lamb cooking in its own fat—suddenly provokes violent associations. It is the Sunday lamb whose fat, in the cooking process, sacrifices its opacity. The fire catches the poet's attention—fire that crystallizes window panes, that cooks the lamb, that burned the heretics, that burned the Jews in Poland. The poet recreates the associations as they occurred to her, as it was prompted by this everyday event of cooking. Her vision of the world—bleak, realistic, pessimistic—demands that the associations follow one another and that the poem then turn on the poet herself, which it does. The victims of the fire do not die, she says, implying that the process has somehow transformed them, purified them. She, however, is left to live, to have the ashes of these victims settle on her eye and in her mouth, forcing her to do a psychic penance, during which she sees the smokestacks of the ovens in Poland as a kind of Calvary. The final stanza returns the poet to her immediate plight: Her own heart is a holocaust through which she must travel; it too has been victimized by fathers, mothers, husbands, men, gods. She ends by turning to her own child—her golden child—and lamenting that he too will be "killed and eat[en]" by this same world.

This poem shows how Plath's vision worked to take a moment in her day and, rather than merely entering it mechanically in her journal, transform it into a statement on suffering. The horror of death by fire for heretics and Jews in Poland is no less horrible, she says, because her horror—a heart that is a holocaust—is as real as theirs was; nor is her horror any less horrible because other victims' horror was so great or so real. Plath's vision works to encapsulate this statement with its corollary in virtually all of her later confessional pieces.

Plath's poems are also rooted in her personality, which is capable of adopting numerous, almost infinite, masks. Plath played at many roles in her life: wronged daughter, brilliant student, coy lover, settled housewife, poet of promise, and mentally disturbed woman. Her life reflects her constant attempt to integrate these masks into what she could consider her identity—an irreproachable and independent psyche that needed no justification for its existence. Her life was spent in pursuit of this identity. She attempted to reassemble her shattered selves after her first suicide attempt, to exorcise selves that seemed to her too horrible, and to invent selves that she felt she should possess. Her poetry overwhelms its readers with its thematic consistency, drafted into this battle by Plath to help her survive another day, to continue the war against a world that seemed always on the verge of undoing the little progress she had made. Her personae were created from her and by her, but they were also created for her, with a very specific intent: survival of the self as an integrated whole.

In her quest for survival, Plath uncannily resembled Hedda Gabler, the title character of the 1890 Henrik Ibsen play. Like Hedda, Plath viewed the feminine self as a product created and manipulated by traditions and bindings far beyond the control of the individual woman. Also like Hedda, Plath believed that by rejecting the traditional demands placed on women, she could take one step toward assertion of an independent self. Yet the bulk of her poetry deals not so much with rejection of demands as with the whole process of establishing and maintaining identity. Masks, roles, charades, lies, and veils all enter Plath's quest, and all recur throughout her poems.

In "Channel Crossing," an early poem, Plath uses the excitement of a storm at sea to suspend temporarily the identity of the persona, who reassumes her identity when the poem ends and she picks up her luggage. Identity is depicted as a fragile, dispensable entity. The nature of identity is also a theme in "The Lady and the Earthenware Head," in which the head is a tangible mask, a physically separate self that the persona seeks unsuccessfully to destroy. Here, instead of fragility, Plath emphasizes the oppressive durability of a prefabricated self. Identity's endurance, if it violates one's personal sense of self, is a terrible burden. That quality is displayed in "The Bee Meeting." Here the persona is a naked, vulnerable self that assumes identity only when the villagers surrounding her recognize her need for clothing, give her the clothing, and respond to the new self. The poem ends with the implication that her perceived identity will prove to be permanent, despite any efforts she might make to alter these perceptions. Identity becomes a matter of perception, as is clearly stated in "Black Rook in Rainy Weather." In this poem the persona concedes to the artist's perception the very power to establish the artist's identity. The dynamic of power between perceived and perceiver is finely balanced in this poem. In "A Birthday Present," the balance

is tipped by the duplicity of veils and what they hide in identities that are established within personal relationships.

Toward the end of her life, Plath's concern with identity became defensively rebellious. In "Daddy," she openly declares her rebellion, severing the demands and ties of tradition that so strangled her earlier in her life and in her poetry. She adopts several methods to achieve her end of freedom: name-calling, new identities, scorn, humiliation, and transfer of aggression. Her freedom rings false, however; the ties are still there. "Lady Lazarus" reveals Plath's awareness of the lingering ties and stands as an encapsulation of her whole life's quest for identity—from passivity to passive resistance to active resistance and finally to the violently imagined destruction of those people who first gave and then shattered her self: men. This poem contains meaning within meaning and exposes much of Plath's feelings about where her identity arose. She saw herself as a product of a male society, molded by males to suit their particular whims or needs. Her contact with females in this context led inevitably to conflict and competition. This duality in her self was never overcome, never expelled, or, worse, never understood. Having failed to manipulate her manipulators, she tried to find identity by destroying her creators. Set free from the basis she had always known even if she despised it, she had nowhere else to go but to the destruction of the self as well.

Plath realized this quandary. In "Words," a poem written ten days before her death, she looked back:

> Years later I
> Encounter them on the road—
> Words dry and riderless,
> The indefatigable hoof-taps.
> While
> From the bottom of the pool, fixed stars
> Govern a life.

The words with which she had striven to create a self—a meaningful self that would integrate her various sides in a harmonious whole and not merely reflect "daddy's girl," "mommy's girl," "big sister," "sorority Sue," or "Mrs. Hughes"—these words had turned "dry and riderless." They too had failed her, even as her family, friends, husband, and her own self had failed her. She had sought identity in traditional places—parents, school, marriage, and work—but had not found enough strands to weave her various selves together. She had sought identity in unorthodox places—the mind, writing, Devon, and hope—but even these failed her.

Plath finally conceded her failure to create a self that would satisfy her and the world about her. She reviewed a life that she had tried to end earlier. Even then she had been forced to regroup, forced to continue inhaling and exhaling. The truth of the real world that had threatened to overwhelm her collection of masks throughout her life had finally yielded to her on one point. She asked ten days before her death: "Once one has seen God, what is the remedy?" The perfection of death that had haunted her throughout her life seemed the only answer. Her final act was her ultimate affirmation of self in a world that would not let her or her words assume their holistic role.

Other major works

LONG FICTION: *The Bell Jar*, 1963.
NONFICTION: *Letters Home*, 1975; *The Journals of Sylvia Plath*, 1982 (Ted Hughes, ed.).
CHILDREN'S LITERATURE: *The Bed Book*, 1976.
PLAY: *Three Women*, 1962.
MISCELLANEOUS: *Johnny Panic and the Bible of Dreams*, 1977, 1979 (Hughes, ed.).

Bibliography

Axelrod, Steven Gould. *Sylvia Plath: The Wound and the Cure of Words*. Baltimore: The Johns Hopkins University Press, 1990.

Barnard, Caroline King. *Sylvia Plath*. Boston: Twayne, 1978.

Bundtzen, Lynda. *Plath's Incarnations: Woman and the Creative Process*. Ann Arbor: University of Michigan Press, 1983.

Butscher, Edward. *Sylvia Plath: Method and Madness*. New York: Seabury Press, 1976.

Hayman, Ronald. *The Death and Life of Sylvia Plath*. Secaucus, N.J.: Carol, 1991.

Markey, Janice. *A Journey into the Red Eye: The Poetry of Sylvia Plath, a Critique*. London: The Women's Press, 1993.

Meyering, Sheryl L. *Sylvia Plath: A Reference Guide, 1973-1988*. Boston: G. K. Hall, 1990.

Newman, Charles, ed. *The Art of Sylvia Plath*. Bloomington: Indiana University Press, 1970.

Rose, Jacqueline. *The Haunting of Sylvia Plath*. Cambridge, Mass.: Harvard University Press, 1992.

Stevenson, Anne. *Bitter Fame: A Life of Sylvia Plath*. Boston: Houghton Mifflin, 1990.

Van Dyne, Susan R. *Revising Life: Sylvia Plath's "Ariel" Poems*. Chapel Hill: University of North Carolina Press, 1993.

Wagner-Martin, Linda. *Sylvia Plath: A Biography*. New York: St. Martin's Press, 1987.

JANE SMILEY

Born: Los Angeles, California; September 26, 1949

Principal short fiction
The Age of Grief, 1987; *Ordinary Love and Good Will*, 1989 (two novellas).

Other literary forms
Jane Smiley has published several novels. In addition to studies of family life, she has experimented with several novelistic subgenres, including a murder thriller (*Duplicate Keys*, 1984) and a historical epic (*The Greenlanders*, 1988).

Achievements
Smiley's short fiction has drawn consistent praise for its linguistic economy and incisive detail in the service of the complex mysteries of American family life. Her versatile experiments in character, voice, and plot line are well suited to short fictional forms. The psychological immediacy she achieves bespeaks a compassionate interest in decent people caught at dramatic crossroads, where they must assess the compromises and delusions that have shaped their lives. Having begun her career as what she calls a "devoted modernist" preoccupied with the nihilistic anomie dramatized in the great literature of the early twentieth century, Smiley found herself losing that alienated edge when she first became pregnant. In trying to resolve the ensuing creative challenge plaguing her—"Can mothers think and write?"—she discovered her true subject: the continually shifting dynamics of familial relationship. Her best work captures the intricate dance of need, love, retribution, and loss that entwines competing subjectivities within every family. *The Age of Grief*, which signaled a new gathering of creative force in Smiley's writing, was nominated for the National Book Critics Circle Award. *A Thousand Acres* (1991) earned both the Pulitzer Prize and the National Book Critics Circle Award in fiction in 1992.

Biography
Born to James La Verne Smiley and Frances Graves Nuelle in 1949, Jane Graves Smiley began life during her father's military tour of duty in California. She was transplanted early to the Midwest and grew up in St. Louis, Missouri. The daughter of a writer mother, she attended Vassar College and received her B.A. degree in English in 1971; she composed her first novel for her senior thesis and discovered that "this was for me, this creation of worlds." Smiley completed a master of fine arts at the University of Iowa in 1976, and in 1978 she received M.A. and Ph.D. degrees in medieval literature from the same institution. In 1981, she began teaching literature and creative writing as a member of the faculty at Iowa State University and became a full professor in 1989. In 1981 and 1987, she also served as a visiting professor at the University of Iowa. A Fulbright Fellowship in 1976-1977 allowed her to spend time in Iceland, where she continued a study of the Norse sagas that would later provide the framework for her novel *The Greenlanders*. Grants from the National Endowment for the Arts supported her writing in 1978 and 1987.

Smiley has commented that a childhood shadowed by the existence of the atomic bomb and an adolescence informed by the invention of "the Pill" have attuned her imagination to two major subjects: "sex and apocalypse." Her personal history reflects an intimate engagement with the tensions of family life that has inspired her best fiction. A first marriage to John Whiston in 1970 took place before her graduation from college and lasted until 1975. Her second marriage, to editor William Silag in 1978, produced two daughters, Phoebe and Lucy; it was with Phoebe's birth that she says her imagination was first "fully engaged." A third marriage, to Stephen Mark Mortensen, began in 1987. She lists her "avocations" as "cooking, swimming, playing piano, quilting."

Analysis
Smiley's short fiction plumbs the mysteries of family life in modern America. Taken together, her collections delineate the steady course of her imagination toward its true subject: the crisis of the adult who must confront not only the flawed and destructive nature of individual desire but also the unfathomable enormity of that individual's emotional power within the familial network both to create and to annihilate. In the first volume,

Smiley offers a series of glimpses at the potent appeal of the family idyll, her tone at times bordering on the satiric. Yet the hunger of the family romance is not, finally, a laughing matter but the very engine of bourgeois tragedy as Smiley portrays it. In her works, she examines the myth of familial ideality from various positions—that of insider and outsider, homebuilder and home-wrecker—proving the seductiveness of the dream of family and the anguish of its heartbreakingly predictable insufficiency.

Consisting of five short stories and a novella, *The Age of Grief* presents a seemingly wide array of characters who range from active aggressors to passive victims in the contemporary battles for and against emotional commitment raging among adults who are still not quite willing to see themselves in their parents' roles. While the stories do not provide the depth of insight offered in the volume's closing novella, they establish the cultural ambiance of fragmentation and insubstantiality through which the longed-for idyll of family life demolished in "The Age of Grief" achieves its tragic incandescence.

Thus *The Age of Grief* breaks essentially into two parts: The first section, composed of the short stories, allows Smiley to examine family life through a series of characters peripheral to its most immediate and intimate dynamics. In "Lily" and "The Pleasure of Her Company," the female protagonists are admiring outsiders to the marital relationships they observe, and both find themselves unprepared for the destruction they witness. Their limited notions about the violence of human emotions possible and all too probable within conventional frames result in part from the absence of such entanglements in their own lives. In Lily's case, her preference for an emotional "virginity" that permits the freedom needed for her work as a poet has led her to meddle unwittingly in the heart of marital darkness, whose capacity for long-borne compromise and truce she has failed to comprehend and for which she stands profoundly humbled at the end. Florence, the narrative consciousness of the other tale, is allowed a more graceful if ironically inflected exit; faced with the dissolution of a marriage that she had regarded as ideal, she rejects the cynic's conclusion that love is delusion and pursues her own blossoming relationship with the realist's admonition "that it's worth finding out for yourself." Florence differs from Lily in this willingness to attempt the risk of emotional involvement in the very face of its failures.

Smiley is most harshly disposed toward those who attempt to orchestrate their emotional destinies with the same kind of professional calculation that they apply to their stock portfolios, as in the case of the female letter-writer of "Jeffrey, Believe Me." Smiley wittily satirizes the narcissism and determined self-gratification of 1980's urbanites by presenting a protagonist so intent on satisfying her biological clock that she devises the seduction of a gay male friend to achieve pregnancy. Perhaps the most scathing element of this sketch is its absence of any glimmer of personal responsibility within the narrator for the emotional network of obligations and yearnings that she has brought into being with her fetus. Her opposite number in the collection is the male protagonist of "Long Distance," whose literal odyssey to join his brothers for the Christmas holidays necessitates a reassessment of the callous disregard he has shown a young Japanese woman with whom he has had an affair. Never having taken a good look at the continual negotiations that make possible the sustained family relationships he has traditionally scorned, he now recognizes that he has been more than eager to jettison all such complications in his own life and, as a result, has proven morally bankrupt when confronted with the cost to others of his self-serving actions.

Stock-taking of this kind is at the heart of Smiley's most deeply felt writing, and hence her narratives are most effective when they enter the unmediated psychological terrain of the first person. Her characteristic tone, a laconic meditative stillness, emerges for the first time in *The Age of Grief* in "Dynamite," a piece in which the outsiders of the earlier stories give way to the hybrid insider-outsider Sandy, a woman in her early middle age caught between lifelong conflicting impulses to connect and to disrupt. Oscillating between past and present, as well as the discrete identities into which Sandy's life has split as a result of a radical political commitment that has kept her underground for twenty years, the fiction traces her inescapable desire to recover ties with a mother whom she feels she has never truly known, alongside a still evident restlessness "to do the most unthought-of thing, the itch to destroy what is made—the firm shape of my life, whether unhappy, as it was, or happy, as it is *now*." The twin complications of memory and fantasy make the present an elaborate web of past and future longings that motivate her wild swings of behavior and shake them loose from the bourgeois stability they seem superficially to relish. Smiley offers, however, a glimpse inside the paradox of Sandy's character to illuminate the logic of its contradictions—mysteries of the human heart that defy tam-ing and that make Sandy emblematic of the struggle with self typical of Smiley's protagonists.

With "The Age of Grief," Smiley moves full force into that theme, shifting the angle of vision from the aggressor to the victim of a family crisis but in reality exposing the insufficiency of such categories to describe the emotional upheavals. The novella unfolds as first-person narrator, David Hurst, learns that his wife, Dana, his partner in a busy dentistry practice and the mother of their three daughters, has fallen in love with another man. At the real center of the drama, however, is David's struggle with his knowledge of the affair and his choice to remain silent about it. Smiley is familiar not only with the routines of parenting small children but also with the social changes that have necessitated that fathers become full participants in all the nuances of that routine. Thus she creates a poignant exactness around David's intimate involvement in the daily lives—including illnesses—of his young children, ages seven, five, and two. The emotional tyranny of Leah, a toddler who insistently demands all of her father's attention, mimics the jealous ownership of a lover that becomes all the more bittersweet in the face of the waning love between her parents. Neither spouse can speak to the other of the schism between them, and in his anguish David concludes:

> I am thirty-five years old, and it seems to me that I have arrived at the age of grief. . . . It is not only that we know that love ends, children are stolen, parents die feeling that their lives have been meaningless. . . . It is more that the barriers between the circumstances of oneself and of the rest of the world have broken down, after all—after all that schooling, all that care . . . it is the same cup of pain that every mortal drinks from.

The narrative moves right up to the edge of dissolution as Dana's obsession finally disrupts even her carefully orchestrated daily schedule and keeps her away from home for twenty-four hours. When she reappears, they agree not to discuss what has led her to relinquish her affair and resume her marriage. David—with a generosity of spirit, or failure of will, that is utterly convincing because of its profound sadness—offers by way of explanation his dearly bought insight that "marriage is a small container, after all. . . . Two inner lives, two lifelong meditations of whatever complexity, burst out of it and out of it, cracking it, deforming it." The tragic center of Smiley's fictions rests upon her illumination of the impossible burden placed on the emotional bonds of family and marriage, and the challenge of learning to live with the diminishment of faith in the future.

The first novella in *Ordinary Love and Good Will* offers another sustained examination into the disruption of a once idyllic homelife. Its theme is the loss of parental illusions about the real scope of one's protective power within the family circle and the potential compensatory wisdom of recognizing the mysterious otherness and inevitable falling from innocence—and into humanity—of one's children.

The first-person narrator of *Ordinary Love*, a fifty-two-year-old divorced Iowan mother of five adult children, typifies Smiley's clear-eyed rejection of sentimental pieties about the heartland matriarch. Rachel Kinsella does indeed attend to the baking of cakes and spoiling of grandchildren as she awaits the homecoming of a long-absent son. Rachel's story, however, matter-of-factly told in a voice that is both accepting and unrepentant, includes the jarring paradox of having proudly borne five children in five years with a doting, ambitious doctor husband, yet also having initiated a love affair that caused an ugly divorce, prolonged separation from her still young children, and ended in separation of the children in custody arrangements that divided even their twin sons. Rachel realizes that in yielding to the destructive power of desire, she acted on an unspoken but profoundly felt need to escape the suffocating control of her husband, Pat, a man aggressively committed to the bourgeois family fantasy in which all other subjectivities were subsumed with his own powerful optimism.

Rachel's perspective, however, is not self-serving. She admits the contradictions driving her emotional life: the allure of creating a timeless domestic haven free from the typical ravages of family life; her relief upon being freed from the marriage that lay as the cornerstone to that haven; her "terror" upon entering the void left when her family collapsed and her children disappeared for a time from her life. Smiley plots Rachel's history as an arc of emotional loss and recovery, and in late middle age she is self-possessed and steady, a mature woman who, because she has consciously made herself anew out of wildness, grief, and perseverance, now possesses the strength to confront the ongoing costs of the past within the present.

Rachel's more immediate story, while inseparable from the rupture of twenty years earlier, involves her effort to mediate the return of her son Michael from a two-year stint as a teacher in poverty-stricken areas in India. In a family where each separation recollects the primal rifts of mother from child and sibling from sibling, Michael's transformation overseas exposes once again the discontinuities afflicting even the most fundamental human ties. Within this atmosphere, a series of confidences delivers a powerful lesson about the tantalizing impenetrability of each family member's private reality. Rachel tells her children for the first time of the love affair that upended their lives; her elder daughter, Ellen, retaliates with a description of their neglect by a vengeful father who transplanted them to London; Michael reveals his destructive relationship with a married woman that produced an abortion and the loss of the woman he really loved. The shock created by each of these "secrets" is multiple, and Rachel registers them all. Unlike her ex-husband, she struggles to subordinate the possessive assumptions of a parent and instead tries "to accept the mystery of my children, of the inexplicable ways they diverge from parental expectations, of how, however much you know or remember of them, they don't quite add up." She muses on the disruptive irrationality of human desire and realizes that Michael's new maturity reflects his own discovery of that fact. The real fruit of knowledge, she concedes, lies not simply in one's own suffering but in learning one's potential to inflict suffering on others, especially those one holds most dear. With a fatalism balanced against faith in the human capacity for renewal, Rachel squarely confronts the fact that she cannot spare her children life's bitterest lesson—the perverse and unrelenting hunger of the heart for what it cannot have, and that given the destructive pressure of the inner life, a parent may unforgivably offer her children "the experience of perfect family happiness, and the certain knowledge that it could not last."

In her fictional preoccupation with the family, Smiley has decidedly not abandoned her early artistic attraction to the condition of modernist anomie that inspired her to become a writer. Rather, she has concentrated upon the innumerable ways in which the family, that bedrock of middle-class faith challenging nihilistic despair, dramatizes the unbridgeable chasm between the capacity for selflessness and self-love within the same individual, and the terrible grief to be had in experiencing that gap within oneself.

Other major works

NOVELS: *Barn Blind*, 1980; *At Paradise Gate*, 1981; *Duplicate Keys*, 1984; *The Greenlanders*, 1988; *A Thousand Acres*, 1991.

Bibliography

Bernays, Anne. "Toward More Perfect Unions." Review of *The Age of Grief*. *The New York Times Book Review*, September 6, 1987, 12.

Brown, Kurt, ed. *The True Subject: Writers on Life and Craft*. St. Paul, Minn.: Graywolf Press, 1993.

Carlson, Ron. "King Lear in Zebulon County." Review of *A Thousand Acres*. *The New York Times Book Review*, November 3, 1991, 12.

Humphreys, Josephine. "Perfect Family Self-Destructs." Review of *Ordinary Love and Good Will*. *The New York Times Book Review*, November 5, 1989, 1, 45.

Kakutani, Michiko. Review of *The Age of Grief*. *The New York Times*, August 26, 1987, C21.

Klinkenborg, Verlyn. "News from the Norse." Review of *The Greelanders*. *The New Republic* 198 (May 16, 1988): 36-39.

Leavitt, David. "Of Harm's Way and Farm Ways." *Mother Jones* 14 (December, 1989): 44-45.

WENDY WASSERSTEIN

Born: Brooklyn, New York; October 18, 1950

Principal drama

Any Woman Can't, pr. 1973; *Happy Birthday, Montpelier Pizz-zazz*, pr. 1974; *When Dinah Shore Ruled the Earth*, pr. 1975 (with Christopher Durang); *Uncommon Women and Others*, pr. 1975 (one act), pr. 1977 (two acts), pb. 1978; *Isn't It Romantic*, pr. 1981, pr. 1983 (revised version), pb. 1984; *Tender Offer*, pr. 1983 (one act); *The Man in a Case*, pr., pb. 1986 (one act; adapted from Anton Chekhov's short story of the same title); *Miami*, pr. 1986 (musical); *The Heidi Chronicles*, pr., pb. 1988; *The Sisters Rosensweig*, pr. 1992, pb. 1993.

Other literary forms

Wendy Wasserstein, though best known for her plays, is the author of several teleplays, including *The Sorrows of Gin* (1979), an adaptation of John Cheever's short story. She has written several film scripts, among them an adaptation of her play *The Heidi Chronicles*. Her essays, which have appeared in numerous periodicals, including *Esquire* and *New York Woman*, have also been published in a collection entitled *Bachelor Girls* (1990).

Achievements

Wasserstein has been hailed as the foremost theatrical chronicler of the lives of women of her generation. Her plays, steeped in her unique brand of humor, are nevertheless moving, sometimes wrenching explorations of women's struggle for identity and fulfillment in a world of rapidly shifting social, sexual, and political mores. Most often against the backdrop of the burgeoning feminist movement, her characters navigate through obstacle courses of expectations—those of their parents, their lovers, their siblings, their friends, and, ultimately, themselves. They seek answers to fundamental questions: how to find meaning in life, and how to strike a balance between the need to connect and the need to be true to oneself. Wasserstein's works, which deftly pair wit and pathos, satire and sensitivity, have garnered numerous honors for her work, including the Pulitzer Prize, the Tony (Antoinette Perry) Award, the New York Drama Critics Circle Award, the Outer Critics Circle Award, and the Susan Smith Blackburn Prize.

Biography

Wendy Wasserstein was born on October 18, 1950, in Brooklyn, New York. She was the fourth and youngest child of Morris W. Wasserstein, a successful textile manufacturer, and Lola (Schleifer) Wasserstein, a housewife and nonprofessional dancer, both Jewish émigrés from central Europe. When she was thirteen, Wasserstein's family moved to Manhattan, where she attended the Calhoun School, an all-girl academy at which she discovered that she could get excused from gym class by writing the annual mother-daughter fashion show. Some years later, at Mount Holyoke, an elite Massachusetts women's college, a friend persuaded Wasserstein, a history major, to take a playwriting course at nearby Smith College. Encouraged by her instructor, she devoted much of her junior year, which she spent at Amherst College, performing in campus musicals before returning to complete her B.A. degree at Mount Holyoke in 1971.

Upon graduating, Wasserstein moved back to New York City, where she studied playwriting with Israel Horovitz and Joseph Heller at City College (where she later earned an M.A. degree) and held a variety of odd jobs to pay her rent. In 1973, her play *Any Woman Can't* was produced Off-Broadway at Playwrights Horizons, prompting her to accept admission to the Yale School of Drama, turning down the Columbia Business School, which had simultaneously offered her admission.

It was at Yale University, where she earned her M.F.A. degree in 1976, that Wasserstein's first hit play, *Uncommon Women and Others*, was conceived as a one-act. Ultimately expanded, it was given a workshop production at the prestigious National Playwrights Conference at the O'Neill Theater Center in Connecticut, a well-known launching pad for many successful playwrights. Indeed, in 1977, the Phoenix Theater's production of *Uncommon Women and Others* opened Off-Broadway at the Marymount Manhattan Theater. Although some critics objected to the play's lack of traditional plot, most praised Wasserstein's gifts as a humorist and a social observer.

By 1980, Wasserstein, established as one of the United States' most promising young playwrights, was commissioned by the Phoenix Theater to write *Isn't It Romantic* for its 1980-1981 season. The play's mixed reviews prompted Wasserstein to rework it under the guidance of director Gerald Gutierrez and André Bishop, artistic director of Playwrights Horizons. There, with a stronger narrative line and more in-depth character development, it opened in 1983 to widespread praise.

In the meantime, Wasserstein had been at work on several new pieces—among them a one-act play, *Tender Offer*, which was produced at Ensemble Studio Theater, and, collaborating with Jack Feldman and Bruce Sussman, a musical, *Miami*, which was presented as a work-in-progress at Playwrights Horizons in 1986. In 1988, one of Wasserstein's most ambitious works, *The Heidi Chronicles*, which had been previously performed in workshop at the Seattle Repertory Theater, had its New York premiere at Playwrights Horizons. It moved quickly to the larger Plymouth Theater on Broadway, where it opened to mostly positive critical response. The play earned for Wasserstein the Pulitzer Prize, the Tony Award, and virtually every New York theater award. Wasserstein's eagerly awaited *The Sisters Rosensweig* opened at the Mitzi E. Newhouse Theater at Lincoln Center in the fall of 1992. Receiving widespread critical acclaim, the piece augmented her already prominent presence on the American dramatic scene.

Analysis

Wendy Wasserstein's plays are, for the most part, extremely consistent in their emphasis on character, their lack of classical structure, and their use of humor to explore or accompany serious, often poignant themes. Throughout her career, Wasserstein's central concern has been the role of women—particularly white, upper-middle-class, educated women—in contemporary American society. Though her plays are suffused with uproarious humor, her typical characters are individuals engaged in a struggle to carve out an identity and a place for themselves in a society that has left them feeling, at worst, stranded and desolate and, at best, disillusioned. This is not to say that Wasserstein's worldview is bleak. Rather, the note of slightly skewed optimism with which she characteristically ends her works, along with her prevailing wit, lends them an air of levity and exuberance that often transcends her sober themes.

These themes—loneliness, isolation, and a profound desire for meaning in life—are examined by Wasserstein chiefly through character. One of the playwright's great strengths is her ability to poke fun at her characters without subjecting them to ridicule or scorn. Her women and men, with all their faults and foibles, are warmly and affectionately rendered. They engage their audience's empathy as they make their way through the mazes of their lives, trying to connect and to be of consequence in the world.

Uncommon Women and Others, *Isn't It Romantic*, *The Heidi Chronicles*, and *The Sisters Rosensweig* are four of Wasserstein's most acclaimed works. The first three plays have in common their episodic structure and non-plot-driven narrative. In each of the three, scenes unfold to reveal aspects of character. *Uncommon Women and Others*, for example, begins with five former college friends assessing their lives as they reunite six years after graduation. The body of the play is a flashback to their earlier life together at a small women's college under the often conflicting influences of the school's traditional "feminine" rituals and etiquette and the iconoclasm of the blossoming women's movement. In each of the two time frames, events are largely contexts for discussions in which Wasserstein's women use one another as sounding boards, each one testing and weighing her hopes, fears, expectations, and achievements against those of her friends. Similarly, in *Isn't It Romantic*, two former college friends, Janie Blumberg, a free-lance writer, and Harriet Cornwall, a corporate M.B.A., move through their postcollege lives, weighing marriage and children against independence and the life choices of their mothers against their own. The play climaxes at the point where the two women diverge, Harriet, who has formerly decried marriage, accepting a suitor's proposal out of fear of being alone, Janie choosing to remain unattached and to seek happiness within herself.

The Heidi Chronicles, though more far-reaching in scope, is also a character-driven play. Here, Wasserstein narrows her focus to one woman, Heidi Holland, but through her reflects the changing social and political mores of more than two decades. From the mid-1960's to the late 1980's, Heidi, like Wasserstein's earlier characters, struggles to find her identity. Moving through settings ranging from women's consciousness-raising meetings and protests to power lunches in trendy restaurants and Yuppie baby showers, Wasserstein's Heidi functions as, in her words, a "highly-informed spectator" who never quite seems to be in step with the prescribed order of the day. In a pivotal scene, Heidi, now an art-history professor, delivers a luncheon lecture entitled "Women, Where Are We Going?" Her speech, which disintegrates into a seeming nervous breakdown, ends with Heidi confessing that she feels "stranded": "And I thought the whole point was that we wouldn't feel stranded," she concludes, "I thought the whole point was that we were in this together."

Isolation and loneliness and, contrastingly, friendship and family are themes that run throughout these three earlier plays. Heidi's wish, expressed in that luncheon speech, is for the kind of solidarity that exists among the women in *Uncommon Women and Others*, who, while constantly comparing their lives, are not competitive in the sense of putting one another down. On the contrary, they are fervent in their praise and support of one another, a family unto themselves. Janie and Harriet, in *Isn't It Romantic*, share a relationship that is much the same until something comes between them, Harriet's decision to marry a man she hardly knows because he makes her feel "like [she has] a family." Heidi, by contrast, at the point when she makes her speech, has no close women friends. Presumably, they are all off having babies and/or careers. Her decision, at the play's end, to adopt a Panamanian baby girl, thereby creating a family of her own, is much akin to Janie Blumberg's decision finally to unpack her crates in her empty apartment at *Isn't It Romantic*'s end and make a home for herself.

This desire on the part of Wasserstein's characters for a family and a place to belong has at its root the desire for self-affirmation. It is evident in the refrain that echoes throughout *Uncommon Women and Others*, "When we're twenty-five [thirty, forty, forty-five], we're going to be incredible," as well as in Janie Blumberg's invocation, "I am," borrowed from her mother, Tasha. Though failures by the standards of some, Janie, Heidi, and the others can be seen as heroic in their resilience and in the tenacity with which they cling to their ideals—however divergent from the reality at hand.

This aspect of Wasserstein's writing—that is, her tendency to create characters who resist change—can exasperate audiences, as her critics have noted. The women, in particular, who people her plays are often, like Janie with her unpacked crates of furniture, in a state of suspension, waiting for life to begin. In *Uncommon Women and Others*, there is a constant look toward the future for self-substantiation, as there is, to some extent, in Heidi's persistent state of unhappiness. Still,

Heidi does ultimately make a choice—to adopt a baby, a step toward the process of growing up, another of Wasserstein's recurrent themes.

One of Wasserstein's greatest gifts is her ability to find and depict the ironies of life. This is evident in each of the three plays' bittersweet final images: the "uncommon women," their arms wrapped around one another, repeating their by now slightly sardonic refrain; Janie, tap-dancing alone in her empty apartment; and Heidi, singing to her new daughter "You Send Me," the song to which she had previously danced with her old flame, Scoop, at his wedding reception. These images are pure Wasserstein. In face of the disappointment, even the disillusionment, of life, her characters manifest a triumph of the spirit and a strength from within that ultimately prevails.

Wasserstein's *The Sisters Rosensweig* is a departure from her earlier plays in a number of ways. Most overt among these differences are the play's international setting (the action takes place in Queen Anne's Gate, London) and its concern with global issues and events. Also of note is the playwright's uncharacteristic use, here, of classical, nonepisodic structure, maintaining unity of time and place: in this case, several days' events in the sitting room of Sara Goode, the play's main character and the eldest of the three sisters for whom the play is named.

Sara shares many of the characteristics of Wasserstein's earlier protagonists—that is, her gender (female), ethnic group (Jewish), social class (upper-middle to upper class), and intelligence quotient (uncommonly high). She is, however, considerably older than her forerunners. *The Sisters Rosensweig* centers on the celebration of Sara's fifty-fourth birthday. This is significant in that Sara, a hugely successful international banker who has been married and divorced several times, does not share the struggle for self-identity carried out by such Wasserstein heroines as Heidi Holland and Janie Blumberg. With a lucrative, challenging career (noteworthily, in a male-dominated field) and a daughter she loves, Sara has achieved, to some degree, the "meaning" in her life that those earlier characters found lacking and sought.

As the play progresses, however, it is revealed that Sara, despite her self-confidence and seeming self-sufficiency, shares with Heidi, Janie, and the others a deep need to connect—to find, create, or reclaim a family. As she fends off and at last gives in to a persistent suitor, Merv Kant, a false-fur dealer, and plays hostess to her two sisters (Pfeni Rosensweig, a sociopolitical journalist-turned-travel-writer, and "Dr." Gorgeous Teitelbaum, who hosts a radio call-in show), Sara manages, at last, to peel back the layers of defense and reserve that have seen her through two divorces and the rigors of her profession and to rediscover the joys of sisterhood and the revitalizing power of romantic love.

It is not Sara alone who serves Wasserstein in her exploration of her characteristic themes of loneliness, isolation, and the search for true happiness. Pfeni, forty years old, the play's most autobiographical character, a writer who has been temporarily diverted from her true calling, has been likewise diverted from pursuing "what any normal woman wants" by remaining in a relationship with Geoffrey, a former homosexual. Jilted, and distraught over the havoc that acquired immune deficiency syndrome (AIDS) has played with the lives of his friends, Geoffrey has wooed and won Pfeni, only to leave her in the end to follow his own true nature. Pfeni's ceaseless "wandering" as well as her self-confessed need to write about the hardships of others to fill the emptiness in her own life is much akin to Heidi Holland's position as a "highly informed spectator," waiting for her own life to begin.

The Sisters Rosensweig harks back to Wasserstein's *Isn't It Romantic* in its concerns with the profound role that both mothers and Judaism play in shaping women's lives. Here, Sara rejects, and attempts to cast off, the influences of both. An atheist expatriate in London, she has reinvented her life, purging all memories of her Jewish New York upbringing and her deceased mother's expectations as firmly as she has embraced the habits and speech patterns of her adopted home. Sara's eventual acquiescence to Merv, a New York Jew, along with the rekindling of her emotional attachment to her sisters, represents, at the play's end, an acceptance and embracing of the past that she has worked so hard to put behind her.

Like all Wasserstein's works, *The Sisters Rosensweig* presents characters whose spirit triumphs over their daily heartaches and heartbreaks. While they long to escape the tangled webs of their lives ("If I could only get to Moscow!" Pfeni laments, in one of the play's several nods to Anton Chekhov's *The Three Sisters*), they manage to find within themselves and in one another sufficient strength not only to endure but also to prevail.

As in *Uncommon Women and Others*, *Isn't It Romantic* and *The Heidi Chronicles*, there is a scene in *The Sisters Rosensweig* in which the women join together to share a toast, affirming and celebrating their sisterhood and themselves. Be they blood sisters, sorority sisters, or sisters of the world, Wasserstein has made sisters her province. With *The Sisters Rosensweig*, she adds three more portraits to her ever-growing gallery of uncommon women, painted, as always, with insight, wit, and compassion.

Wasserstein is a unique and important voice in contemporary American theater. As a woman writing plays about women, she has been a groundbreaker, though never self-consciously so. Despite her often thin plot lines, she finds and captures the drama inherent in the day-to-day choices confronting the women of her generation. As a humorist, too, Wasserstein is unquestionably a virtuoso. Her ability to see the absurdity of even her own most deeply held convictions, and to hold them deeply nevertheless, is perhaps the most engaging and distinctive of her writing's many strengths.

Other major works

NONFICTION: *Bachelor Girls*, 1990.
TELEPLAY: *The Sorrows of Gin*, 1979 (from the story by John Cheever).

Bibliography

Bennets, Leslie. "An Uncommon Dramatist Prepares Her New Work." *The New York Times*, May 24, 1981, p. C1.
Berman, Janice. "The Heidi Paradox." *Newsday*, December 22, 1988.
Hoban, Phoebe. "The Family Wasserstein." *New York* 26, no. 1 (January 4, 1993): 32.
Nightingale, Benedict. "There Really Is a World Beyond 'Diaper Drama.'" *The New York Times*, January 1, 1984, p. C2.
Rose, Phyllis Jane. "Dear Heidi—An Open Letter to Dr. Holland." *American Theater* 6 (October, 1989): 26.
Shapiro, Walter. "Chronicler of Frayed Feminism." *Time* 133 (March 27, 1989): 90-92.
Wallace, Carol. "A Kvetch for Our Time." *Sunday News Magazine*, August 19, 1984, 10.

VII

IN THE HEART OF THE COUNTRY
American Identities in the Midwest

Hog Butcher for the World,
Tool Maker, Stacker of Wheat,
Player with Railroads and the Nation's Freight Handler;
Stormy, husky, brawling,
City of the Big Shoulders. . . .

—Carl Sandburg, "Chicago," 1916

Even to the casual eye, the Midwestern Heartland presents a remarkably harmonious panorama of red barns, bountiful corn and wheat fields, neat farmhouses, and silver-capped silos. Once part of the Old Northwest Territory, the Heartland embraces a huge geographical landform of glacial moraines, river valleys, woodlands, and seemingly endless prairies—an area encompassing twelve states (from Ohio to Iowa and North Dakota to Kansas) and at least three major river valleys: the Ohio, Mississippi, and Missouri. The Heartland is the region habitually evoked by photographers and filmmakers to suggest the most enduring American values: honesty, generosity, love of land, and devotion to family. It is no accident, perhaps, that such quintessentially American artifacts as automobiles and hot dogs derive from this region. At its mythological heart is Abraham Lincoln of Illinois, the one president revered above all others because he somehow welded the nation together and emancipated the slaves. The Heartland is not so much a collection of geographical states, then, as it is a state of mind. Hence, Nick Carraway, the narrator of F. Scott Fitzgerald's *The Great Gatsby* (1925), is constantly drawing contrasts between the plain simplicity of Minneapolis and the sly duplicity of New York City.

Besides its abundant harvests of grain and cattle and its equally rich industrial production (in cities such as Detroit, Chicago, and St. Louis), the Heartland has been fertile in literary production. Some of the most important American authors—Samuel Clemens (Mark Twain), Ernest Hemingway, Carl Sandburg, and Gwen-

dolyn Brooks, among others—have their roots in the Heartland. Moreover, the Heartland is not restricted to its rural roots: The great city of Chicago is the focal point of Heartland literary life, having experienced a phenomenal outburst of cultural activity known as the Chicago Renaissance, a movement which flourished from about 1905 to 1925. At the center of that rebirth was *Poetry* magazine, which commenced publication in 1912 under the able editorship of Harriet Monroe. In its first five years, *Poetry* introduced such influential authors as Robert Frost, T. S. Eliot, Ezra Pound, and Carl Sandburg. It may be fairly said that modern American poetry began in the Heartland, and one single volume, Edgar Lee Masters' *Spoon River Anthology* (1915), a book that captures the vernacular speech of ordinary Americans, stands in the vanguard of that poetic revolution.

The Chicago Renaissance, fed by the cultural boosterism that lingered powerfully after the Columbian Exposition of 1893, acted as a kind of magnet that drew a plethora of talent into the city. Carl Sandburg, Theodore Dreiser, Sherwood Anderson, and many others gathered in and around the Loop in downtown Chicago; they collectively redefined the meaning of art. Experimentation, social relevance, ethnic concern, and uncensored language were much in evidence. Among those experimenters was a young organizer from the Socialist Party, a man who had begun to try his hand at poetry: Carl Sandburg.

Sandburg was born and reared in the Swedish immigrant neighborhood of Galesburg, Illinois, and did hard physical work all the time he was growing up and attending school irregularly. He worked as a traveling salesman for a while, and then he briefly attended Lombard College. His life, however, had already prepared him for the great themes of his poetry: the dignity of the common worker and the cultural diversity of American life. It was the publication of the poem "Chicago" in *Poetry* magazine (1914) that set his career in motion. "Chicago," with its bold free-verse format, its colloquial language, and its glorification of work and the energy of urban life, made possible much of the poetry of the 1920's and 1930's. Chicago, after all, was an utterly American city: It contained a rich diversity of ethnic enclaves, especially Irish, Italian, Jewish, and Polish neighborhoods, as well as other East European, African American, and Latino settlements. There was no typical Chicagoan, and the poet celebrated this diversity in his poetry at the same time that he praised the prairie, the smokestacks and the steel mills, and the new form of music, jazz, that was being played everywhere. The titles of books that Sandburg produced during the Chicago Renaissance are telling examples of his work as a whole: *Chicago Poems* (1916), *Cornhuskers* (1918), *Smoke and Steel* (1920), and *Slabs of the Sunburnt West* (1922). Sandburg's special veneration of the American worker became the motive for writing his magnificent epic composed during the Great Depression, *The People, Yes* (1936). Finally, it is most important to note that Sandburg devoted most of his creative life to a huge, six-volume biography of Abraham Lincoln. Sandburg's six volumes, *Abraham Lincoln: The Prairie Years* (1926, two volumes) and *Abraham Lincoln: The War Years* (1939, four volumes) offer eloquent proof of Sandburg's devotion to Lincoln, who thereby became a kind of patron saint of the Heartland.

With the exception of his writings on Lincoln, Sandburg tended to paint with a rather broad brush, creating two-dimensional, generic characters such as the worker-heroes he described in "Chicago" and in *The People, Yes*. Other Heartland writers, however, chose to create memorable and unique characters, with all their peculiarities and special traits, as Willa Cather did in her many novels of life on the prairie. Especially noteworthy in this connection is her classic tale of a heroic young woman growing up on the Nebraska frontier, *My Ántonia* (1918). In the character of Ántonia Shimerda, Cather is able to create an ideal immigrant type (here Bohemian) who successfully overcomes a variety of physical and social obstacles to take her proper place on the prairie. Ántonia does not entirely escape the wagging tongues and disapproving glances of conservative Black Hawk, Nebraska, nor do her Scandinavian chums, Lena Lingard and Tiny Soderball. It is Jim Burden, the Harvard-educated lawyer who serves as narrator, who best expresses this duality of attitudes toward the prairie and its people.

In fact, Jim Burden epitomizes the love-hate relationship that obtains between many writers and the Heartland. On one hand, he glories in the open country, the splendid sunsets, and the ubiquitous wildflowers; on the other hand, he detests the small-mindedness and smothering air of conformity that govern all social relations, especially in Black Hawk. He therefore leaves forever, establishing a tone and a pattern echoed in Sherwood Anderson's *Winesburg, Ohio* (1919), Sinclair Lewis' *Main Street* (1920) and *Babbitt* (1922), Theodore Dreiser's *An American Tragedy* (1925), James T. Farrell's *Studs Lonigan* trilogy (1932-1936), and J. F. Powers' *Morte d'Urban* (1962).

The modern manifestation of this bittersweet attitude toward the Heartland appears again and again in the work of a writer originally associated with the city of Chicago and *Poetry* magazine—Peter De Vries, whose sardonic wit and natural gift for social comedy often combine to create punsters like Anthony Thrasher, the unlikely hero of *Slouching Towards Kalamazoo* (1983). Thrasher, a precocious eighth-grader, has impregnated his teacher, Miss Molly Doubloon, an event that outrages the small town in North Dakota where the event takes place, all in the hilarious context of Miss Doubloon's improbable teaching of Hawthorne's *The Scarlet Letter*. De Vries produced nearly thirty novels before his death in 1993, including such classics as *The Tunnel of Love* (1954), *The Blood of the Lamb* (1962), and *Consenting Adults* (1980).

Larry Woiwode continues this tradition of close examination of rural Midwestern life, especially in his epic tale of the Neumiller family of North Dakota and Illinois, *Beyond the Bedroom Wall: A Family Album* (1975), a rich book whose documentary details recall another classic Heartland work, Wright Morris' *The Home Place* (1948). Thus, "in the heart of the heart of the country," to borrow a beautifully resonant phrase from novelist William Gass, one finds a paradoxical place containing beauty, pain, and that wonderfully complex identity that we call American.

—Dan Guillory
Millikin University

SHERWOOD ANDERSON

Born: Camden, Ohio; September 13, 1876

Died: Colón, Panama Canal Zone; March 8, 1941

Principal short fiction

Winesburg, Ohio, 1919; *The Triumph of the Egg*, 1921; *Horses and Men*, 1923; *Death in the Woods and Other Stories*, 1933; *The Sherwood Anderson Reader*, 1947.

Other literary forms

Sherwood Anderson published seven novels, collections of essays, memoirs, poetry, and dramatizations of *Winesburg, Ohio*, as well as other stories. He was a prolific article writer and for a time owned and edited both the Republican and Democratic newspapers in Marion, Virginia. In 1921, he received a two-thousand-dollar literary prize from *The Dial* magazine.

Achievements

Anderson, a protomodernist, is generally accepted as an innovator in the field of the short story despite having produced only one masterpiece, *Winesburg, Ohio*. In his work, he not only revolutionized the structure of short fiction by resisting the literary slickness of the contrived plot but also encouraged a simple and direct prose style, one that reflects the spare poetry of ordinary American speech. Anderson's thematic concerns were also innovative. He was one of the first writers to dramatize the artistic repudiation of the business world and to give the craft of the short story a decided push toward presenting a slice of life as a significant moment. His concern with the "grotesques" in society—the neurotics and eccentrics—is also innovative, as is the straightforward attention he pays to his characters' sexuality. Anderson's contemporaries Ernest Hemingway, William Faulkner, and John Steinbeck were influenced by his work, as were several later writers: Carson McCullers, Flannery O'Connor, Saul Bellow, Bobbie Ann Mason, and Raymond Carver.

Biography

Sherwood Anderson was the third of seven children of a father who was an itinerant harness maker and house painter and a mother of either German or Italian descent. His father was a Civil War veteran (a Southerner who fought with the Union), locally famed as a storyteller. His elder brother, Karl, became a prominent painter who later introduced Sherwood to Chicago's Bohemia, which gained him access to the literary world.

Declining fortunes caused the family to move repeatedly until they settled in Clyde, Ohio (the model for Winesburg), a village just south of Lake Erie. The young Anderson experienced a desultory schooling and worked as a newsboy, a housepainter, a stableboy, a farmhand, and a laborer in a bicycle factory.

After serving in Cuba during the Spanish-American War (he saw no combat), Anderson acquired a further year of schooling at Wittenberg Academy in Springfield, Ohio, but remained undereducated throughout his life. A job as an advertising copywriter gave him a first taste of writing, and he went on to a successful business career. In 1912, the central psychological event of his life occurred; he suffered a nervous breakdown, which led him to walk out of his paint factory in Elyria, Ohio. He moved to Chicago, where he began to meet writers such as Floyd Dell, Carl Sandburg, and Ben Hecht, a group known collectively as the "Chicago Renaissance." A significant nonliterary contact was Dr. Trigant Burrow of Baltimore, who operated a Freudian therapeutic camp in Lake Chateaugay, New York, during the summers of 1915 and 1916. It should be noted, however, that Anderson ultimately rejected scientific probing of the psyche, for he typically believed that the human mind is static and incapable of meaningful change for the better. Publication of *Winesburg, Ohio* catapulted him into first prominence, after which he traveled to Europe in 1921, where he became acquainted with Gertrude Stein, Ernest Hemingway, and James Joyce. In 1923, while living in New Orleans, he shared an apartment with William Faulkner.

Anderson married and divorced four times. He and his first wife had three children. His second wife, Tennessee Mitchell, had been a lover to Edgar Lee Masters, author of *Spoon River Anthology* (1915). His last wife, Eleanor Copenhaver, had an interest in the Southern labor movement, which drew Anderson somewhat out of his social primitivism, and, for a time in the 1930's, he became a favorite of communists and socialists. His death, in Colón, Panama Canal Zone, while on a voyage to South America, was notable for its unique circumstances: He died of peritonitis caused by a toothpick accidentally swallowed while eating hors d'oeuvres.

Analysis

Anderson's most acclaimed short stories are penetrating studies of the unfulfilled lives of residents of small-town America, a community of individuals perverted by the rise of industrialization and materialism in society. Like his contemporary Theodore Dreiser, he broke with the genteel tradition of American letters and embraced the tenets of naturalism, to which he added a new dimension by plumbing the psychological depths of his characters. His discovery of ordinary America as a fount of meaningful literary themes influenced other notable writers, as did his spare prose style, based on the common speech of ordinary individuals.

Anderson's best-known and most important work is the American classic *Winesburg, Ohio*. It is a collection of associated short stories set in the mythical town of Winesburg in the latter part of the nineteenth century. The stories catalog Anderson's negative reaction to the transformation of Ohio from a largely agricultural to an industrial society, which culminated about the time he was growing up in the village of Clyde in the 1880's. Its twenty-five stories are vignettes of the town doctor, the voluble baseball coach, the still attractive but aging-with-loneliness high school teacher, the prosperous and harsh farmer-turned-religious fanatic, the dirt laborer, the hotel keeper, the banker's daughter, her adolescent suitors, the Presbyterian minister struggling with temptation, the town drunk, the town rough, the town homosexual, and the town halfwit. The comparison to Edgar Lee Masters' *Spoon River Anthology* is obvious: Both works purport to reveal the secret lives of small-town Americans living in the Middle West, and ironically both owe their popular success to the elegiac recording of this era, which most Americans insist upon viewing idyllically. Anderson's work, however, differs by more directly relating sexuality to the bizarre behavior of many of his characters and by employing a coherent theme.

That theme is an exploration of psychological "grotesques"—the casualties of economic progress—and how these grotesques participate in the maturing of George Willard, the teenage reporter for the *Winesburg Eagle*, who at the end of the book departs for a bigger city to become a journalist. By then his sometimes callous ambition to get ahead has been tempered by a sense of what Anderson chooses to call "sophistication," the title of the penultimate story. The achievement of George's sophistication gives *Winesburg, Ohio* its artistic movement but makes it problematic for many critics and thoughtful Americans.

The prefacing story defines grotesques. A dying old writer hires a carpenter to build up his bed so that he can observe the trees outside without getting out of it (while living in Chicago in 1915 Anderson had his own bed similarly raised so that he could observe the Loop). After the carpenter leaves, the writer returns to his project—the writing of "The Book of the Grotesque," which grieves over the notion that in the beginning of the world there were a great many thoughts but no such thing as a "truth." Men turned these thoughts into many beautiful truths such as the truth of passion, wealthy, poverty, profligacy, carelessness, and others; a person could then appropriate a single one of these truths and try to live by it. It was thus that he or she would become a grotesque—a personality dominated by an overriding concern which in time squeezed out other facets of life.

A story such as "Hands" clearly illustrates what Anderson means by a grotesque. The hands belong to Wing Biddlebaum, formerly Adolph Myers, a teacher in a Pennsylvania village who was beaten and run out of town for caressing boys. Anderson is delicately oblique about Wing's homosexuality, for the thrust of the story demonstrates how a single traumatic event can forever after rule a person's life—Wing is now a fretful recluse whose only human contact occurs when George Willard visits him occasionally. George puzzles over Wing's expressive hands but never fathoms the reason for his suffering diffidence. "Hands," besides giving first flesh to the word "grotesque," makes the reader understand that a character's volition is not necessarily the factor that traps him into such an ideological straitjacket; sympathy can therefore be more readily extended.

"The Philosopher" provides a subtler illustration of a grotesque and introduces the idea that a grotesque need not be pitiable or tragic; in fact, he can be wildly humorous, as demonstrated at the beginning of the story with the philosopher's description:

> Doctor Parcival, the philosopher, was a large man with a drooping mouth covered by a yellow moustache. . . . he wore a dirty white waistcoat out of whose pocket protruded a number of black cigars. . . . there was something strange about his eyes: the lid of his left eye twitched; it fell down and it snapped up; it was exactly as though the lid of the eye were a window shade and someone stood inside playing with the cord.

It is George Willard's misfortune that Dr. Parcival likes him and uses him as a sounding board for his wacky pomposity. He wishes to convince the boy of the advisability of adopting a line of conduct that he himself is unable to define but amply illustrates with many "parables" that add up to the belief (as George begins to suspect) that all men are despicable. He tells George that his (Parcival's) father died in an insane asylum, and then he continues about a Dr. Cronin from Chicago who may have been murdered by several men, one of whom could have been yours truly, Dr. Parcival. He announces that he actually arrived in Winesburg to write a book. About to launch on the subject of the book, he is sidetracked into the story of his brother, who worked for the railroad as part of a roving paint crew (which painted everything orange), and who on payday would place his money on the kitchen table—daring any member of the family to touch it. The brother, while drunk, is run over by the rail car housing the other members of his crew.

One day George drops into Dr. Parcival's office for his customary morning visit and discovers him quaking with fear. Earlier a little girl had been thrown from her buggy, and the doctor had inexplicably refused to heed a passerby's call (perhaps because he is not a medical doctor). Other doctors, however, arrived on the scene, and no one noticed Dr. Parcival's absence. Not realizing this, the doctor shouts to George that he knows human nature and that soon a hanging party will be formed to hang him from the lamppost as punishment for his callous refusal to attend to the dying child. When his certainty dissipates, he whimpers to George, "If not now, sometime." He begs George to take him seriously and asks him to finish his book if something should happen to him; to this end he informs George of the subject of the book, which is: Everyone in the world is Christ, and they are all crucified.

Anderson exhibits a particular interest in the distorting effect that religious mania has upon the personality, and several stories in *Winesburg, Ohio* attack or ridicule examples of conspicuous religiosity. "Godliness," a tetralogy with a gothic flavor, follows the lives of Jesse Bentley, a wealthy, progressive farmer who poisons the lives of several generations of his relatives with his relentless harshness until he becomes inflamed by Old Testament stories and conceives the idea of replicating an act of animal sacrifice. Because of this behavior, he succeeds in terrifying his fifteen-year-old grandson, the only person he loves, who flees from him never to be heard from again, thus breaking the grandfather's spirit.

Two stories, "The Strength of God" and "The Teacher," are juxtaposed to mock cleverly a less extravagant example of piety. The Reverend Curtis Hartman espies Kate Swift, the worldly high school teacher, reading in bed and smoking a cigarette. The sight affronts and preoccupies him severely and plunges him into a prolonged moral struggle that is resolved when one night he observes her kneeling naked by her bed praying. He smashes the window through which he has been watching her and runs into George Willard's office shouting that Kate Swift is an instrument of God bearing a message of truth. Kate remains entirely oblivious of the Reverend, for she is preoccupied with George, in whom she has detected a spark of literary genius worthy of her cultivation. Her praying episode—an act of desperation that the Reverend mistook for a return to faith—was the result of her realization, while in George's arms, that her altruism had turned physical.

It is exposure to these disparate egoisms, the death of his mother and a poignant evening with Helen White, the banker's daughter, which are gathered into the components of George's "sophistication," the achievement of which causes him to leave town. George's departure, however, has a decidedly ambivalent meaning. Anderson as well as other writers before and after him have shown that American small-town life can be less than idyllic, but *Winesburg, Ohio* is problematic because it is not simply another example of "the revolt from the village." In the story "Paper Pills," the narrator states that apples picked from Winesburg orchards will be eaten in city apartments that are filled with books, magazines, furniture, and people. A few rejected apples, however, which have gathered all their sweetness in one corner and are delicious to eat, remain on the trees and are eaten by those who are not discouraged by their lack of cosmetic appeal. Thus the neuroses of Anderson's grotesques are sentimentalized and become part of his increasingly strident polemic against rationality, the idea of progress, mechanization, scientific innovation, urban culture, and other expressions of social potency. Anderson never wonders why pastorals are not written by pastors but rather by metropolitans whose consciousnesses are heightened by the advantages of urban life; his own version of a pastoral, *Winesburg, Ohio*, was itself written in Chicago.

Anderson published three other collections of short stories in his lifetime, and nearly all of those singled out by the critics for their high quality are first-person narratives. They are told in a rambling, reminiscent vein and are often preferred to those in *Winesburg, Ohio* because they lack a staged gravity. The grotesques are there, but less as syndromes than as atmospheric effects. The gothic nature of the later stories becomes more pronounced, and violence, desolation, and decay gain ascendancy in his best story, "Death in the Woods," from the collection of the same name. This work has another dimension: It is considered "to be among that wide and interesting mass of creative literature written about literature." Because Mrs. Grimes is such an unobtrusive and inarticulate character, the narrator is forced to tell her story, as well as how he gained each aspect of the story, until the reader's interest is awakened by the uncovering of the narrator's mental operations. This process leads the narrator to ponder further how literature itself is written and guides him to the final expansion: consciousness of his own creative processes. The transfer of interest from the uncanny circumstances of Mrs. Grimes's death to this awareness of human creativity lends some credibility to Sherwood Anderson's epitaph, "Life, Not Death, Is the Great Adventure."

Other major works

NOVELS: *Windy McPherson's Son*, 1916; *Marching Men*, 1917; *Poor White*, 1920; *Many Marriages*, 1923; *Dark Laughter*, 1925; *Beyond Desire*, 1932; *Kit Brandon*, 1936.

PLAYS: *Plays: Winesburg and Others*, 1937.

POETRY: *Mid-American Chants*, 1918; *A New Testament*, 1927.

NONFICTION: *A Story Teller's Story*, 1924; *The Modern Writer*, 1925; *Tar: A Midwest Childhood*, 1926; *Sherwood Anderson's Notebook*, 1926; *Hello Towns!*, 1929; *Perhaps Women*, 1931; *No Swank*, 1934; *Puzzled America*, 1935; *Home Town*, 1940; *Sherwood Anderson's Memoirs*, 1942; *The Letters of Sherwood Anderson*, 1953; *Sherwood Anderson: Selected Letters*, 1984; *Letters to Bab: Sherwood Anderson to Marietta D. Finley, 1916-1933*, 1985; *The Sherwood Anderson Diaries, 1936-1941*, 1987; *Sherwood Anderson's Love Letters to Eleanor Copenhaver Anderson*, 1989; *Sherwood Anderson's Secret Love Letters: For Eleanor, a Letter a Day*, 1991.

Bibliography

Anderson, David D. *Sherwood Anderson: An Introduction and Interpretation*. New York: Holt, Rinehart and Winston, 1967.

Appel, Paul P. *Homage to Sherwood Anderson: 1876-1941*. Mamaroneck, N.Y.: Paul P. Appel, 1970.

Campbell, Hilbert H., and Charles E. Modlin, eds. *Sherwood Anderson: Centennial Studies*. Troy, N.Y.: Whitston, 1976.

Howe, Irving. *Sherwood Anderson*. Toronto: William Sloane Associates, 1951.

Papinchak, Robert Allen. *Sherwood Anderson: A Study of the Short Fiction*. New York: Twayne, 1992.

Townsend, Kim. *Sherwood Anderson*. Boston: Houghton Mifflin, 1987.

WILLA CATHER

Born: Back Creek Valley, near Gore, Virginia; December 7, 1873

Died: New York, New York; April 24, 1947

Principal long fiction

Alexander's Bridge, 1912; *O Pioneers!*, 1913; *The Song of the Lark*, 1915; *My Ántonia*, 1918; *One of Ours*, 1922; *A Lost Lady*, 1923; *The Professor's House*, 1925; *My Mortal Enemy*, 1926; *Death Comes for the Archbishop*, 1927; *Shadows on the Rock*, 1931; *Lucy Gayheart*, 1935; *Sapphira and the Slave Girl*, 1940.

Other literary forms

Willa Cather was a prolific writer, especially as a young woman. By the time her first novel was published when she was thirty-eight, she had written more than forty short stories, at least five hundred columns and reviews, numerous magazine articles and essays, and a volume of poetry. A great many of her early newspaper columns and reviews have been collected in *The Kingdom of Art: Willa Cather's First Principles and Critical Statements, 1893-1896* (1966) and in *The World and the Parish: Willa Cather's Articles and Reviews, 1893-1902* (1970, 2 vols.). Her single volume of poetry, *April Twilights*, appeared in 1903, but Cather later spoke apologetically of that effort, even jokingly telling a friend that she had tried to buy up and destroy all extant copies so that no one would see them. Only one of Cather's novels, *A Lost Lady*, has been adapted for the screen. A second screen version of that novel was so distasteful to her that in her will she prohibited any such attempts in the future. One story, "Paul's Case," has been presented on PBS television. Cather's will also forbids the publication of her letters.

Achievements

Cather actually had at least two careers in her lifetime. Prior to becoming a novelist, she was a highly successful journalist and writer of short fiction, as well as a high school English teacher. As a columnist for the *Nebraska State Journal* and, later, the Lincoln *Courier*, she discussed books and authors and reviewed the many plays, operas, and concerts that came through Lincoln on tour. She gained an early reputation as an astute (and opinionated) critic. Even after she moved to Pittsburgh, the Lincoln papers continued to print her columns.

Over the years, Cather published stories in such national magazines as *Century, Collier's, Harper's, Ladies' Home Journal, Woman's Home Companion, Saturday Evening Post*, and *McClure's*, the popular journal for which she served as an editor for several years.

Among her major honors, she was awarded the 1923 Pulitzer Prize for *One of Ours*, and an ardent admirer, Sinclair Lewis, was heard to remark that she was more deserving than he of the Nobel Prize he won. Cather is particularly appealing to readers who like wholesome, value-centered art. She is held in increasingly high regard among critics and scholars of twentieth century literature and is recognized as one of the finest stylists in American letters. Time will surely accord her a lasting position in the first rank of American novelists.

Biography

Willa Cather was born in Back Creek Valley, Virginia, on December 7, 1873, the first of seven children of Charles and Mary Virginia Cather. In 1883, when Cather—named Wilella, nicknamed Willie, and later renamed Willa by her own decree—was nine years old, her family sold their holdings at Back Creek and moved to Webster County, Nebraska. In that move from a lush Virginia countryside to a virtually untamed prairie, Cather experienced what Eudora Welty has called a "wrench to the spirit" from which she never recovered. It proved to be the most significant single event in her young life, bringing her as it did face to face with a new landscape and an immigrant people who were to make a lasting impression on her imagination. The move was a shock, but a shock that was the beginning of love both for the land and the people, and for the rest of her life, Cather was to draw from this experience in creating her fiction.

Cather always had a special affection for her father; he was a gentle, quiet-mannered man who, after eighteen months on his parents' prairie homestead, moved his family into Red Cloud, sixteen miles away. There, he engaged in various business enterprises with no great success and reared his family. Unlike her husband,

Mary Cather was energetic and driving, a hard disciplinarian, but generous and life-loving. A good many scenes and people from Cather's years on the farm and in Red Cloud appear in her fiction.

At the university in Lincoln, Cather gratefully discovered the joys of the theater and of meeting people with broad interests and capabilities. At first she planned to study science but switched to the humanities, she later confessed, when she saw an essay of hers printed in the newspaper. While at the university, she was active in literary circles, serving as an editor for the *Lasso* and the *Hesperian*, two student literary magazines. Several of her stories appeared in those magazines and in others. She spent the year after her graduation, in 1895, in and around Red Cloud, where she began writing for the weekly Lincoln *Courier* as well as for the *Nebraska State Journal* and published her first story in a magazine of national circulation, the *Overland Monthly*. Then in June, 1896, she left Nebraska to take a position with the *Home Monthly*, a small, rather weak family magazine in Pittsburgh.

Later, Cather secured a position with the Pittsburgh *Daily Leader* and then taught high school English and Latin for five years. While in Pittsburgh, Cather continued to write short fiction while pursuing an active social life. It was there that she met Isabelle McClung, who was to become her dearest friend. For a time, Cather lived with Isabelle and her parents, and in their home she enjoyed the quiet seclusion she needed for her writing. Cather's big break in her journalistic career came in 1903 when S. S. McClure, the dynamic publisher of *McClure's* magazine, became aware of her work and summoned her to his office. That interview began an association that led to an important position with *McClure's* and eventually made it possible for Cather to leave the world of journalism and devote her full energies to the writing of fiction. The publication in 1905 of *The Troll Garden*, a collection of short stories, announced that a major new talent had arrived on the literary scene.

Cather's first novel, *Alexander's Bridge*, was written while she was still with *McClure's*, and it was first conceived as a serial for the magazine. It appeared as a novel in 1912, the year she left *McClure's* to try writing on her own. Still, it was not until *O Pioneers!* came to fruition the next year that Cather felt she had hit what she called "the home pasture" and discovered herself as a novelist. In this book, she turned to her memories of the Nebraska prairie and wrote powerfully of immigrant efforts to come to terms with the land. In 1920, she

began a long and satisfying professional relationship with Alfred A. Knopf, who became her publisher and remained so for the rest of her life.

Cather lived most of her professional life in New York City with a friend and literary associate, Edith Lewis. Her many trips to Europe confirmed her great admiration for France and the French people, an appreciation that receives repeated expression in her novels. She also visited the American West a number of times and drew upon her experiences there for some of her work. Prior to her death on April 24, 1947, Cather was working on a novel that was set in medieval France. After her death, the unfinished manuscript, as she had requested, was destroyed.

Analysis

Cather is noted for her portrayals of the settlers and frontier life on the plains of America. Her works exalt the American spirit and the conquest of material hardships in the New World. Cather once said in an interview that the Nebraska landscape was "the happiness and the curse" of her life. That statement points up the ambivalence in Cather that produced in her a lifelong tug-of-war between the East and the Western prairie. That ambivalence is the central tension in her novels.

As a young, burgeoning writer, Cather discovered that her very being was rooted in the landscape of her childhood. Thus, going back to it, even if only in memory, was essential and inescapable. In her "Nebraska works," it is not only Nebraska that Cather evokes; it is also what Nebraska symbolizes and means, for she is not simply a regional writer. The range of her work is as broad as the range of her experience, and Nebraska represents the westward necessity of her life. Wherever in her work the pull of the landscape is felt, there is Nebraska—whether the setting is Colorado, Kansas, New Mexico, or even rural Pennsylvania or frontier Quebec.

As has been suggested, her life had an eastward necessity too. The raw hardships of prairie life could sometimes mutilate the body and drain the spirit, and a human being often needed something else. Not only could the beloved land be killingly cruel, but it also failed to provide the environment of training, discipline, and appreciation so necessary for the growth and development of an artist. Yet while East and West, civilization (art) and the land—the very foundations of Cather's work—are sometimes at opposite poles in terms of the choices one must make, they are both positive values to her. The greatest threat to each is not the other; the greatest threat to each is an exploitative materialism that has no appreciation for the innate value of the land or of art.

In Cather's work, the same impulse that exploits the land is also destructive to art and the best qualities of civilization. The author's most despicable characters are those such as Ivy Peters in *A Lost Lady* and Bayliss Wheeler in *One of Ours*, who have no feeling for the land or for the past which it harbors. All that interests them is making money, as much as possible as fast as possible. Yet the lust for wealth and the acquisition of it are destructive to character. They subvert what are for Cather some of life's most positive values, a relationship with the earth and an aesthetic sensibility.

Cather's second novel, *O Pioneers!*, her first to use Nebraska materials, presents the conflict between the land and civilization and the threat of destructive materialism as its major concerns. The novel's principal character, Alexandra Bergson, is something of an earth mother, a being so closely linked with the soil and growing things that her very oneness with the earth seems to convert the harsh wild land into rich acreage that willingly yields its treasures. From the first, she believes in the land and loves it, even when her brothers and neighbors grow to despise and curse it. Two of Alexandra's brothers have such a fear of financial failure that they cannot see the land's potential.

Cather, however, does not simply present Alexandra's struggle and eventual triumph. There is another value, opposed to the land but equally important, with which Alexandra must contend. Her youngest brother, Emil, is sensitive in a way that does not lend itself to life on the continental divide, and she wants him to have opportunities that are available only in centers of civilization. His finely tuned spirit, though, leads him to disaster in a prairie environment where passions can run high, untempered by civilizing influences. Emil falls in love with Marie Shabata, a free, wild creature, and both of them are killed by her enraged husband. The book's final vision, however, returns to an affirmation of the enduring qualities of the land and the value of human union with it.

Something of an earth mother like Alexandra Bergson, yet more malleable and human, Ántonia Shimerda of *My Ántonia* is for many readers Cather's most appealing character. She becomes a total embodiment of the strength and generosity associated with those who are at one with the land and the forces of nature. Unlike Alexandra, her capacity for life finds expression not only in the trees and plants she tends but also in her many children, who seem to have sprung almost miraculously from the earth. It is in Jim Burden, who tells the story, and to some extent, in Ántonia's husband, Anton Cuzak, that the conflict between East and West occurs. Jim, like Cather, comes to Nebraska from Virginia as a youngster, and though he has to seek his professional life in Eastern cities, he never gets Nebraska out of his soul. Even as a student at the University of Nebraska in Lincoln, he gazes out his window and imagines there the landscape and figures of his childhood. Ántonia represents for Jim, even after twenty years of city life, all the positive values of the earth for which no amount of civilization can compensate. At the end of the book, he determines to revitalize his past association with the land and yet still tramp a few lighted streets with Cuzak, a city man at heart.

The conflict between the harshness of life on the prairie and the cultural advantages of civilization is also presented in Ántonia's father, who had been a gifted musician in Europe, but who now, poverty-stricken and overworked, no longer played the violin. Ántonia's deep appreciation for Cuzak's quality and for his gentle city ways and her pride in Jim's "city" accomplishments, bridges the gap between prairie and civilization.

Claude Wheeler, the main character of *One of Ours*, is torn, like so many of Cather's young people, by the need to go and the need to stay. Claude is filled with yearnings he does not completely understand. All he knows is that he is burning to fulfill some inner desire, and everything he does seems to go wrong. Much as he loves the rivers and groves of his own landscape, he feels like a misfit there. His father's hearty, nonchalant materialism is only slightly less distressing to him than the hard, grasping greed of his older brother Bayliss, the bloodless, pious parsimony of his wife Enid, and the cheerful selfishness of his younger brother Ralph. The world begins opening to him during the short period when he is allowed to attend the university at Lincoln, but Claude completely finds himself only when he enlists in the Army and begins fighting in France. There, he meets Lieutenant David Gerhardt, a musician, and encounters a gracious cultural climate to which he responds with all his heart.

Claude's real fulfillment comes in the midst of battle, surrounded by death and destruction. Only then does he feel at one with himself and his surroundings; only then is the old anguish gone, the tension released. In the end, he is killed, and his mother feels some sense of gratitude that at least he does not have to face the disillusionment of returning to a country that has given itself over to material pursuits. The novel is a poignant portrayal of the central tensions in Cather's work between the land and civilization, and it also describes the ever-present threat of spiritually damaging materialism.

In *A Lost Lady*, Cather again shows a character's need for civilization's amenities, in spite of the appeal of the Western landscape. The ruthless, materialistic mind-set that nearly always characterizes "the enemy" in Cather's work is graphically portrayed in the coarse figure of Ivy Peters. As a boy, Ivy cruelly blinded a bird and then set it free, and as a man he drained what was once the Forresters' lovely marshlands in order to make them yield a profit. Unscrupulous and shrewd, he manages to compromise the beautiful Marian Forrester with as little conscience as he showed toward the helpless bird.

Until her husband's decline, Mrs. Forrester managed to have the best of both worlds, East and West, spending her summers in the beautiful countryside outside Sweet Water, on the Burlington line, and her winters in the lively social atmosphere of Denver and Colorado Springs. Captain Forrester, much her elder, had made his fortune pioneering Western railroad development. When the novel opens, the Captain's failing health has already begun to limit Mrs. Forrester's social and cultural opportunities, though she still enjoys visits to the city and entertains important guests at Sweet Water. It becomes apparent, however, much to the dismay of Marian Forrester's young admirer, Niel Herbert, that Marian's passion for life and high living has led her into an affair with the opportunistic, if handsome, Frank Ellinger even before the death of the Captain. This affair foreshadows her later desperate sellout to Ivy Peters. It is significant, however, that Cather never judges Marian, though the prudish Niel does. It is not the life-loving Marian Forrester that Cather condemns, but the grasping Ivy Peters and the unprincipled Frank Ellinger—and perhaps even the unforgiving Niel Herbert. The novel's hero is Captain Forrester, who willingly relinquishes his fortune to preserve his honor.

Even though *Death Comes for the Archbishop* is not Cather's final novel, it is in a very real sense a culmina-

tion of her efforts at reconciling the central urges toward land and toward art, or civilization, that are the hallmark of her life and her work. Selfishness and greed are a threat in this book, too, but their influence is muted by Cather's concentration on Father Jean Latour as the shaping force of her narrative. He is Cather's ideal human being, by the end of the book a perfect blend of the virtues of the untamed landscape and the finest aspects of civilization.

As a young priest, Latour is sent from a highly cultivated environment in his beloved France to revitalize Catholicism in the rugged New Mexico Territory of the New World. Learned in the arts, genteel in manner, dedicated to his calling, this man of fine-textured intelligence is forced to work out his fate in a desolate, godforsaken land among, for the most part, simple people who have never known or have largely forgotten the sacraments of the civilized Church. His dearest friend, Father Joseph Vaillant, works with him—a wiry, lively man, Latour's complement in every way. Latour must bring a few greedy, unruly local priests into line, but his greatest struggle is internal as he works to convert himself, a product of European civilization, into the person needed to serve the Church in this vast desert land. In the end, his remarkable nature is imprinted indelibly on the barren landscape, and the landscape is imprinted indelibly on his nature. Instead of returning to France in his official retirement, he elects to remain in the New World. His total reconciliation with the land is symbolized in the fulfillment of his dream to build a European-style cathedral out of the golden rock of New Mexico. In that building, the art of civilization merges gracefully with the very soil of the Western landscape, just as Jean Latour's spirit had done.

Cather's work stands as something of an emotional autobiography, tracing the course of her deepest feelings about what is most valuable in human experience. For Cather, what endured best, and what helped one endure, were the values contained in the land, and in humanity's civilizing impulses, particularly the impulse to art. What is best in humanity responds to these things, and these things have the capacity to ennoble in return.

Other major works

SHORT FICTION: *The Troll Garden*, 1905; *Youth and the Bright Medusa*, 1920; *Obscure Destinies*, 1932; *The Old Beauty and Others*, 1948; *Willa Cather's Collected Short Fiction: 1892-1912*, 1965; *Uncle Valentine and Other Stories: Willa Cather's Collected Short Fiction, 1915-1929*, 1973.
POETRY: *April Twilights*, 1903.
NONFICTION: *Not Under Forty*, 1936; *Willa Cather on Writing*, 1949; *Willa Cather in Europe*, 1956; *The Kingdom*

of Art: Willa Cather's First Principles and Critical Statements, 1893-1896, 1966; *The World and the Parish: Willa Cather's Articles and Reviews, 1893-1902*, 1970 (2 vols.).

MISCELLANEOUS: *Writings from Willa Cather's Campus Years*, 1950.

Bibliography

Bloom, Edward A., and Lillian D. Bloom. *Willa Cather's Gift of Sympathy*. Carbondale: Southern Illinois University Press, 1962.

Bloom, Harold, ed. *Modern Critical Views: Willa Cather*. New York: Chelsea House, 1985.

Fryer, Judith. *Felicitous Space: The Imaginative Structures of Edith Wharton and Willa Cather*. Chapel Hill: University of North Carolina Press, 1986.

Gerber, Philip. *Willa Cather*. Boston: Twayne, 1975.

Harrell, David. *From Mesa Verde to "The Professor's House."* Albuquerque: University of New Mexico Press, 1992.

March, John. *A Reader's Companion to the Fiction of Willa Cather*. Westport, Conn.: Greenwood Press, 1993.

Middleton, Jo Ann. *Willa Cather's Modernism: A Study of Style and Technique*. Rutherford, N.J.: Fairleigh Dickenson University Press, 1990.

Murphy, John. *Critical Essays on Willa Cather*. Boston: G. K. Hall, 1984.

Shaw, Patrick W. *Willa Cather and the Art of Conflict: Re-visioning Her Creative Imagination*. Troy, N.Y.: Whitston, 1992.

Stouck, David. *Willa Cather's Imagination*. Lincoln: University of Nebraska Press, 1975.

Thomas, Susie. *Willa Cather*. Savage, Md.: Barnes & Noble Books, 1990.

Winters, Laura. *Willa Cather: Landscape and Exile*. Selinsgrove, Pa.: Susquehanna University Press, 1993.

Woodress, James. *Willa Cather: A Literary Life*. Lincoln: University of Nebraska Press, 1990.

PETER DE VRIES

Born: Chicago, Illinois; February 27, 1910   **Died:** Norwalk, Connecticut; September 28, 1993

Principal long fiction

But Who Wakes the Bugler?, 1940; *The Handsome Heart*, 1943; *Angels Can't Do Better*, 1944; *The Tunnel of Love*, 1954; *Comfort Me with Apples*, 1956; *The Mackerel Plaza*, 1958; *The Tents of Wickedness*, 1959; *Through the Fields of Clover*, 1961; *The Blood of the Lamb*, 1962; *Reuben, Reuben*, 1964; *Let Me Count the Ways*, 1965; *The Vale of Laughter*, 1967; *The Cat's Pajamas and Witch's Milk*, 1968; *Mrs. Wallop*, 1970; *Into Your Tent I'll Creep*, 1971; *Forever Panting*, 1973; *The Glory of the Hummingbird*, 1974; *I Hear America Swinging*, 1976; *Madder Music*, 1977; *Consenting Adults: Or, The Dutchess Will Be Furious*, 1980; *Sauce for the Goose*, 1981; *Slouching Towards Kalamazoo*, 1983; *The Prick of Noon*, 1985; *Peckham's Marbles*, 1986.

Other literary forms

Peter De Vries was also a short-story writer of some repute; a number of his stories have been collected. He collaborated with Joseph Fields in writing a stage version of one of his novels, *The Tunnel of Love*. Finally, he published a handful of essays and interviews.

Achievements

In the 1950's, Kingsley Amis called De Vries the "funniest serious writer to be found either side of the Atlantic." De Vries is certainly a brilliant writer of puns and epigrams, a master of situation comedy, and a devastating observer of the foibles of suburbia. His droll humor often involves the amorous adventures of the middle-aged suburban male, torn between the sophisticated mores of Connecticut suburbia and his simpler childhood roots, usually in the Dutch Reformed Church or his native Midwest.

The targets of De Vries' humor are the pretenses and absurdities of modern, affluent suburbia. His "Avalon" and "Decency" are the fictional counterparts of the wealthy, exclusive suburbs such as Greenwich, Stamford, and Westport along Connecticut's "Gold Coast." His characters—or sometimes caricatures—show all the vanities, postures, and affectations of wealth, education, and good breeding that might be expected of sophisticated suburbanites, yet De Vries is never harsh or satirical, commenting that the purpose of humor, unlike satire, is not to kill one's prey but to bring it back alive to be released. De Vries' humor is thus more charitable than satirical; he invites humankind "to laugh at itself."

Biography

Peter De Vries was born in Chicago, Illinois, on February 27, 1910. His parents, Joost and Henrietta De Vries, immigrated from Holland and settled in a closely knit Dutch Calvinist community on Chicago's South Side. De Vries' father was an iceman and furniture mover who started with "a one-horse outfit that he gradually built to a sizeable warehouse business." During De Vries' boyhood, the family lived in a three-room apartment behind his father's business office.

The De Vries family were members of the strict Dutch Reformed Church, and their domestic life was probably much like that described in the autobiographical *The Blood of the Lamb*: a large, contentious family with parents and in-laws forever arguing about some obscure point of theology or church doctrine. De Vries' parents were also strict about forbidding any form of worldliness: motion pictures and card-playing were forbidden, and instead Bible-reading and theological discussions were encouraged. During his adolescence, De Vries rebelled against these strictures, but he later expressed fond memories of the Dutch-language services and hymns of his childhood.

Young De Vries attended the Chicago Christian High School of the Dutch Reformed Church and then entered Calvin College in Grand Rapids, Michigan, a private liberal arts college founded by the same denomination. There he won a Michigan state extemporaneous speaking contest and was graduated with an English major in 1931. That summer he also studied briefly at Northwestern University. His family had hoped that he would enter the ministry after graduation, but instead he decided to become a writer and embarked upon a series of odd jobs in Chicago to support himself. He edited a community newspaper, tended vending machines, peddled candy apples, served as a radio actor, and spoke before women's clubs.

From 1938 to 1944, he served capably as an editor of *Poetry* magazine. There he met his future wife, Katinka Loeser, who was a poetry contributor and later became a short-story writer of some note. They were married on October 16, 1943. During this time, De Vries had published three early novels, *Who Wakes the Bugler?*, *Handsome Heart*, and *Angels Can't Do Better*, which earned him some critical notice but met with only limited financial success. In 1943, De Vries invited James Thurber to speak at a Chicago benefit for *Poetry* magazine and Thurber subsequently persuaded De Vries to go East and write for *The New Yorker*. De Vries joined the staff of *The New Yorker* in 1944 and served as a contributor and cartoon editor. At *The New Yorker*, he worked with editor Harold Ross and such famous humorists as E. B. White and James Thurber, on a staff that had once included Robert Benchley and S. J. Perelman.

De Vries settled with his wife in suburban Westport, Connecticut, in a ten-room house on one acre of land. They had three children—Jan, Peter Jon, and Derek. A fourth child, Emily, died of leukemia before adolescence, a deep personal loss registered in De Vries' most serious novel, *The Blood of the Lamb*, where a similar event occurs. Unlike the zany characters in many of his novels, De Vries was a man of conventional tastes, happily married and devoted to his family.

During his long career, De Vries published more than two dozen novels, along with his collections of short stories. He won wide critical acclaim for his humorous novels and was a member of the American Academy of Arts and Letters and the National Institute of Arts and Letters. He died September 28, 1993, in Norwalk, Connecticut.

Analysis

De Vries' protagonists are typically torn between a strict Calvinism in which they cannot believe and an exurban Vanity Fair of which they disapprove. Most of the novels are narrated in the first person by someone who displays an amused contempt for the primitive Protestantism he has left behind in the Midwest and yet is appalled by the shallow hypocrisy he finds among his Eastern neighbors. De Vries' defense is a humor attuned to the absurdity of their opinions and the ridiculousness of their fashions but always in a comic, lighthearted vein.

Eschewing the realistic novel, De Vries concentrates instead on entertaining his readers with witty and humorous works, filled with hilarious but highly improbable incidents. He is satisfied to write a good comic novel without aiming for any higher artistic qualities. Many of his novels are, arguably, not novels at all but rather loosely constructed narratives that simply provide a framework for his comic genius. Beyond the purpose of sheer entertainment, De Vries is ambiguous about the intent of his humor, minimizing the social commentary and underlying seriousness of his work so that it is difficult to categorize him as a comic novelist of manners or a satirist. Like his mentor, James Thurber, De Vries chooses to limit the scope of his humor and to evoke laughter through grotesque or absurd depictions of modern suburban life.

De Vries' first novel of note, and still perhaps his most popular, is *The Tunnel of Love*. Here one enters the affluent world of Connecticut suburbia as seen through the eyes of the first-person narrator, a New York magazine cartoon editor much like De Vries himself. The focus of the novel, however, is on the comic imbroglios of his next-door neighbors, Augie and Isolde Poole, a young, well-to-do, "artistic" couple who try to adopt a child to save their marriage. The novel alternates between Manhattan and Avalon, Connecticut, through a round of weekend cocktail parties and dinners that provide a backdrop for De Vries' wit and cleverness. De Vries peoples the book with a humorous collage of "artsy" types—would-be actresses and directors, abstract painters, mediocre illustrators, poets *manqués*, affected snobs, precious aesthetes, and other rarefied types. In short, one finds all the empty worldliness of "Vanity Fair," which De Vries is quick to mimic and satirize, yet one also feels the narrator's attraction to these values, which lends the novel a curiously mixed tone of admiration and ridicule. De Vries is a shrewd observer of suburban language and behavior, with a good ear for nuances of conversation, and he creates a wonderful satire of the pretentious cocktail chitchat about creativity and neuroses that the characters employ to boost their sagging egos and disguise from themselves the truth of their mediocrity.

The protagonist, Augie Poole, is a good gag writer though a poor cartoonist who cannot sell his work, so he turns to profligacy to salve his ego. A self-confessed "rotter," he is never quite as wicked as he pretends to be. Superficially a glib and literate ladies' man, he is basically shallow and conceited, though not beyond eventual redemption through the responsibilities of parenthood. The Pooles ironically adopt the illegitimate child of Augie and his artist mistress, but not before a comic series of mishaps during the adoption process. Augie is forced to compromise his "artistic integrity" and sells his gags without the cartoons to prove himself a responsible prospective parent with a steady income. Much of the humor is generated in the domestic life of the narrator, however, in a genial "battle of the sexes" with his wife and family. In conversations with his wife, the narrator of course defends Augie, while she defends Isolde, with predictable results.

In *The Tunnel of Love*, husbands and wives are torn between the routines of respectable suburban life and the allure of a self-indulgent and liberated "artistic" life, with its glamour and sophistication. De Vries contrasts the romantic myth of personal creativity and self-indulgence with the more staid world of middle-class marriage and commuter life. His characters enjoy all of the luxuries of suburban affluence, yet they seem to yearn for a vague "something more"—a vicarious excitement missing from their lives and beckoning from the bohemian life or from the narrator's vicarious dreamworld of "Moot Point," a Hollywood fantasy-world of cinema clichés. The comedy is generated by the clash of illusion and reality as Augie and the narrator slowly learn to accept the world as it is; "Moot Point" is eventually replaced by "Drowsy Dell," the summer cabin on a New Hampshire lake that both families enjoy. After De Vries' commercial success with *The Tunnel of Love*, he adapted the novel for stage and screen, and the play ran for a year on Broadway.

The Blood of the Lamb marked a sharp departure from the slapstick comedy of De Vries' earlier novels. In what is undoubtedly his finest book, he blends comedy and pathos in the story of Don Wanderhope, an obviously autobiographical character who breaks away from Chicago and his strict Dutch Calvinist background and goes East to work in a New York advertising agency. The focus of the novel is on the relationship between the protagonist and his daughter Carol, a graceful and precocious child who is stricken with leukemia. Her illness, suffering, and eventual death test Wanderhope's faith and, through the example of his daughter's courage, lead him back to grace. *The Blood of the Lamb* contains a depth and seriousness otherwise missing in De Vries' work, since it is based on the author's loss of his own daughter Emily to the same disease. Here De Vries finds a theme that permits him to move beyond cleverness for its own sake and create characters of substance and credibility.

"What people believe is a measure of what they suffer," remarks Don Wanderhope, who is himself tried by a series of misfortunes, including the death of his older brother Louie, his father's insanity, his wife's suicide, and finally his daughter's death. Since De Vries' characters are for the most part unable to accept the consolations of traditional belief, and since they are uneasy with modern, relativistic assumptions, their suffering often seems grotesque, and it is from this quality that De Vries extracts much of his humor. This "gallows humor" is what ultimately saves Wanderhope from despair, as when, in a scene of bitter poignancy after he learns of his daughter's death, he pitches her birthday cake at a statue of the suffering Christ. The theme of the novel seems to be that, contrary to received opinion, suffering does not teach one anything; hence, laughter is the best antidote to despair.

There are some very funny episodes in *The Blood of the Lamb*, such as when Wanderhope and his future wife, Greta, are caught in bed together by Greta's parents in a model home that her parents are showing to a client. The emotional center of the book, however, is Carol, especially after her mother's suicide. Carol is the most compelling and believable character in any of De Vries' books. She is, of course, the "Lamb," and her blood is shed gratuitously to a disease for which there is no cure. "The blood of the Lamb" does not redeem anything (except perhaps the protagonist, though that point remains deliberately ambiguous), and hence her suffering and that of the other children in the leukemia hospital remain meaningless. It recalls Herod's slaughter of the innocents. One's only defense against such realities is to laugh at the tragic absurdity of life; this tragicomic note is best illustrated by the birthday party in the hospital for the young leukemia patients. Once Carol's illness has been diagnosed, Wanderhope must race against time to cherish every moment with his daughter while sparing her the truth of her condition. As he observes, in such a case "the greatest experience open to man is the recovery of the commonplace." In another moment of bitter emotional truth, a parent remarks to Wanderhope that grief does not unite people but separates them. De Vries' personal credo may be reflected in the philosophical statement written by Wanderhope for his alma mater, which is read back to him in a tape recording by his daughter Carol: that humankind has only "Reason, Courage, and Grace" to see it through.

De Vries is a master of the humorous scene and the comic caricature. The theme of many of his novels (and hence the source of their humor) is the shallowness and superficiality of the sophisticated urban life.

Other major works

SHORT FICTION: *No, but I Saw the Movie*, 1952; *Without a Stitch in Time: A Selection of the Best Humorous Short Pieces*, 1972.

PLAY: *The Tunnel of Love: A Play*, 1957 (with Joseph Fields).

Bibliography

Bowden, Edwin T. *Peter De Vries*. Boston: Twayne, 1983.

David, Douglas M. "An Interview with Peter De Vries." *College English* 28 (April, 1967): 524-530.

Hasley, Louis. "The Hamlet of Peter De Vries: To Wit or Not to Wit." *South Atlantic Quarterly* 70 (1971): 467-476.

Higgins, William R. "Peter De Vries." In *American Novelists Since World War II*. Vol. 6 in *Dictionary of Literary Biography*. Detroit: Gale, 1980.

Jellema, Roderick. *Peter De Vries: A Critical Essay*. Grand Rapids, Mich.: Wm. B. Eerdmans, 1966.

Sale, Richard B. "An Interview in New York with Peter De Vries." *Studies in the Novel* 1 (1969): 364-369.

Wood, Ralph C. *The Comedy of Redemption: Christian Faith and Comic Vision in Four American Novelists*. Notre Dame, Ind.: University of Notre Dame Press, 1988.

Yagoda, Ben. "Being Seriously Funny." *The New York Times Magazine*, June 12, 1983, 42-44.

THEODORE DREISER

Born: Terre Haute, Indiana; August 27, 1871

Died: Hollywood, California; December 28, 1945

Principal long fiction

Sister Carrie, 1900; *Jennie Gerhardt*, 1911; *The Financier*, 1912, 1927; *The Titan*, 1914; *The "Genius,"* 1915; *An American Tragedy*, 1925; *The Bulwark*, 1946; *The Stoic*, 1947.

Other literary forms

The scope of Theodore Dreiser's literary accomplishment includes attempts in every major literary form, including autobiography, philosophy, short fiction, poetry, and drama.

Achievements

With the publication of *Sister Carrie* in 1900, Dreiser committed his literary force to opening the new ground of American naturalism. His heroes and heroines, his settings, his frank discussion, celebration, and humanization of sex, his clear dissection of the mechanistic brutality of American society—all were new and shocking to a reading public reared on genteel romances and adventure narratives. *Jennie Gerhardt*, the Cowperwood trilogy (at least the first two volumes), and *An American Tragedy* expand and clarify those themes introduced in *Sister Carrie*. Dreiser's genius was recognized and applauded by H. L. Mencken, who encouraged him, praised his works publicly, and was always a valued editorial confidant, but the general reaction to Dreiser has always been negative. He has been called "solemn and ponderous" and "the world's worst great writer," but his influence is evident in the works of Sherwood Anderson, Sinclair Lewis, Ernest Hemingway, and James T. Farrell, among others. Lewis refused the 1925 Pulitzer Prize, which probably should have gone to Dreiser for *An American Tragedy*, and in 1930 took the Nobel Prize committee to task for choosing him as the first American Nobelist for literature instead of Dreiser, a finalist for the honor. In 1944, the year preceding his death, Dreiser received the Award of Merit from the American Academy of Arts and Letters for extraordinary achievement in his field. Dreiser's political and social activism during the long hiatus between *An American Tragedy* and *The Bulwark*, and his never-ending battle against censors and censorship, kept him in the public eye, and the failure of *The Bulwark* and *The Stoic* consigned him to years of neglect after his death. His technical and stylistic faults have often obscured his real value, but the effects of Dreiser's work are still rippling through American fiction. He was the first to point out the fragile vulnerability of the façade that was understood to be the American Dream and to depict the awful but beautiful reality that supported the façade.

Biography

Theodore Herman Albert Dreiser was born in Terre Haute, Indiana, on August 27, 1871, into a family of German Americans. His father, John Paul Dreiser, was a weaver by trade, and from the time of his entry into the United States (in 1846), he had worked westward in an attempt to establish himself. He induced Sarah Schanab (later shortened to Shnepp), the daughter of an Ohio Moravian, to elope with him and they settled near Fort Wayne. John Paul became the manager in a woolen mill and soon amassed enough funds to build his own mill in Sullivan, Indiana. In 1870, the year before Theodore's birth, the mill burned, John Paul was seriously injured, Sarah was cheated out of the family property by unscrupulous "Yankee trickery," and the family was forced to move to Terre Haute, where Theodore was born the eleventh of twelve children, ten of whom survived to adulthood.

After the family misfortunes, John Paul never recovered physically and sank into a pattern of paternal despotism and narrow religious fervor, against which Theodore and the rest of the children could only express contempt and revolt and from which their only haven was the open, loving character of their mother.

In 1879, with the family teetering on the edge between poverty and penury, Sarah took Theodore and the youngest children to Vincennes, Indiana, and the girls stayed with John Paul in Terre Haute in an attempt to economize. There then followed a series of moves that took the two parts of the family, in succeeding moves, from Vincennes back to Sullivan, to Evansville to live with Theodore's brother Paul, who had succeeded in the vaudeville circuit, to Chicago, and finally to Warsaw, Indiana. This nomadic life could only deepen the destitution of the family and heighten the children's craving for the material part of life they never had. In 1887, after the move to Warsaw, sixteen-year-old Theodore announced that he was going back to Chicago; his mother, characteristically, gave him six dollars of her savings and her blessing, and Theodore went on his way back to the most wonderful city he had ever seen.

As a sixteen-year-old, alone in Chicago, Dreiser, like Carrie Meeber of *Sister Carrie*, could find only menial labor, first as a dishwasher, later working for a hardware company. In 1889, however, a former teacher who believed in his latent abilities encouraged him to enroll at Indiana University and subsidized his enrollment. After a year of frustrated attempts to break into the fraternity social life of Bloomington, Dreiser left Indiana University and returned to Chicago.

After another series of menial jobs, including driving a laundry delivery wagon, Dreiser managed to land a job with the Chicago *Globe* as a reporter. After a few months, he was invited to take a position on the St. Louis *Globe-Democrat* and *Republic* staff and moved to St. Louis. In St. Louis, he covered the usual types of news events and met Sara (Sallie) White, to whom he found himself unaccountably attracted. In 1895, after brief periods on newspaper staffs in St. Louis, Toledo, Cleveland, and Pittsburgh, Dreiser took up residence in New York City. Even after his newspaper success in St. Louis and Chicago, however, Dreiser could only find free-lance work in New York City until his brother Paul, by then a successful songwriter and publisher, persuaded his publishers to make Dreiser the editor of their newly established music periodical, *Ev'ry Month*, for which Dreiser wrote monthly editorial columns. This forum for Dreiser's talents was the beginning of a long editorial career that led him to editorships of *Smith's Magazine*, *Broadway Magazine*, and editorial positions with Street and Smith and Butterick. During this period he published *Sister Carrie*, separated from his wife, Sallie White, whom he had married in 1898, saw his brother Paul die, began work on *Jennie Gerhardt*, and quit his position at Butterick's to avoid scandal and to devote his time to fiction.

After his publication of *Jennie Gerhardt*, Dreiser's career is the story of one laboriously prepared publication after another. Even at the end, he was working on *The Stoic*, the last of the Cowperwood trilogy, almost as if it were unfinished business. He died in Hollywood, California, on December 28, 1945.

Analysis

Dreiser is the outstanding American exponent of the naturalist literary movement. Exhibiting a biting social conscience, a mechanistic and deterministic view of life as a fight for survival, and a transparent depiction of human sexuality, his fiction helped to shape a generation of American writers and to curb censorship in American culture. The underlying theme in Dreiser's work is the individual and society—in this case, an increasingly urban, industrialized America in which material wealth and status are the measurement of personal success and help to perpetuate a social class-system. The point of his fiction is the exposure of the fragility of the American Dream.

Dreiser's background offers powerful insights into his life's work. His unstable home life; the dichotomy established between a loving, permissive mother and a narrow, bigoted, dogmatic, penurious father; abject poverty; and his own desires for affluence, acceptance, sexual satisfaction, and recognition were all parts of his fictional commonplace book. His sisters' sexual promiscuity was reflected in Carrie and Jennie, and his own frustrations and desires found voice in, among others, Clyde Griffiths. The character of Frank Cowperwood was shaped in Dreiser's lengthy research into the life of C. T. Yerkes, but Cowperwood was also the incarnation of everything that Dreiser wanted to be—handsome, powerful, accepted, wealthy, and capable. Dreiser projected his own dreams on characters such as Griffiths and Cowperwood only to show that human dreams are never ultimately fulfilled. No matter for what man (or woman) contested, "his feet are in the trap of circumstances; his eyes are on an illusion." Dreiser did not condemn the effort; he chronicled the fragile nature of the pursued and the pursuer.

The publication of *Sister Carrie* did more to change modern American fiction than any novel since. The amatory adventures of Dreiser's sisters in Indiana and his own experiences in Chicago and in New York were the perfect materials for the story of a poor country girl who comes to the city to seek whatever she can find. The one thing she is certain of is that she does not wish to remain poor. Her goals are clothes, money, and fame, and the means by which she achieves them are relatively unimportant. More important, however, is that Carrie is a seeker and a lover. She cannot be satisfied. There must always be a new world to conquer, new goals to achieve. In New York, when she has finally acquired all that she has sought, Ames shows her that there is a world beyond the material—a world of literature and philosophy; it is an aesthetic world of which Carrie has not dreamed and which she recognizes as a new peak to conquer and a new level to achieve. There is a hint that this new level is more satisfying than any she has reached, just as Ames seems more interesting and satisfying than either of her previous lovers, Drouet and Hurstwood, but the novel ends with Carrie still contemplating her attack on his new world.

Carrie subordinates everything to her consuming ambition. She comes to understand the usefulness of sex, but she also understands the emotional commitment necessary to love, and she refuses to make that commitment. In the pursuit of the fullest expression and fulfillment of life she can achieve, human attachments are only transitory at best, and Drouet and Hurstwood are only means to an end for Carrie.

Drouet, the traveling salesman Carrie meets on the train to Chicago, becomes her first lover after she has had time to discover the frustration of joblessness and sweatshop employment and the despair of the poverty in which the relatives with whom she is staying live. Drouet ingratiates himself with Carrie by buying her dinner and then by slipping two ten-dollar bills into her hand. Not long thereafter, Drouet outfits a flat for her, and they set up housekeeping together. Drouet is, for Carrie, an escape. She does not love him, but his means are a source of amazement, and she recognizes that the relative opulence of his chambers and of the apartment he procures for her are the signs of that for which she is striving. She recognizes very early that Drouet is static, a dead end, but he is only an intermediary in her movement from poverty to affluence.

Hurstwood is the bartender and manager of a prominent Chicago tavern. As he watches Carrie perform in a cheap theatrical, he is smitten by her youth and her vitality. A middle-aged, married man, possessed of a virago of a wife, he is naturally attracted to Carrie. Carrie in turn recognizes the quality of Hurstwood's clothes, his style, and his bearing as distinct improvements on Drouet and makes it clear she will accept his advances. Hurstwood's wife uncovers the subsequent affair, a messy divorce threatens Hurstwood's stability and prestige in his job, fortuity brings him to embezzle ten thousand dollars from the bar safe, and he flees with Carrie first to Montreal and then to New York. Once in New York, the chronicle becomes the tale of Hurstwood's steady degeneration and Carrie's alternatively steady rise to stardom on the stage. Unable to find work, Hurstwood finally commits suicide. The counterpoint of Carrie's rise and Hurstwood's fall is the final irony of

the novel. Carrie and Hurstwood reach their final disappointments in almost the same basic terms. Hurstwood dies tired of the struggle and Carrie realizes that she has finally arrived and there is nothing more to conquer or achieve. Only the promise of an aesthetic world beyond material affluence offers hope for Carrie, and that hope seems illusory. The ubiquitous rocking chair is the perfect symbol for *Sister Carrie*. It is an instrument that forever moves but never goes anywhere and never truly achieves anything. Carrie's every success is ultimately unsatisfying and every new horizon offers only a hollow promise.

An American Tragedy is Dreiser's acknowledged masterpiece. In the work, Dreiser was interested in exposing the flaws in the seamless fabric of the American Dream. He had seen the destructive nature of the untempered drive for success and he understood that such a drive was an unavoidable result of the social temperament of the times. He also understood that the victims of that destructive urge were those who strove not fully understanding why they struggled or why they failed. Thus, his criticism is aimed both at those who struggle for an unattainable dream and at the society which urges them on and laughs when they fall. His research led Dreiser to the case of Chester Gillette and the narrative skeleton for *An American Tragedy*.

The events leading to Gillette's murder of Grace Brown in 1906 and the circumstances of his early life were amply documented in the sensational, yellow-press coverage of the Gillette trial, and they provide a circumstantial sketch of the events of Clyde Griffiths' life and times. Gillette and Griffiths also bear the marks of a common background with Dreiser. The poverty-stricken youth, the desire for success and material things, the sexual frustrations, and the attraction to beautiful, well-placed women are all parts of Dreiser's youth and young manhood. If one adds Dreiser's later unhappy marriage, his philandering, and his tense relationship with Helen Richardson, one has all the pieces that produced Dreiser's empathy for and attraction to Chester Gillette and, ultimately, Clyde Griffiths. Thus, in addition to the dramatic possibilities of the Gillette case, Dreiser felt a kinship with his protagonist which allowed him to portray him as a pitiable, arresting, trapped creature.

Clyde Griffiths, in Dreiser's vision, is trapped by forces over which he has little or no control. The "chemisms" of Clyde's life trap him: He no more has control over his desires for success, sex, and material goods than he has over the voice which urges him on during the accident/murder that kills Roberta. In short, Clyde has no control over the irresistible American Dream. Writing of the Gillette case, Dreiser observes that Chester Gillette, if he had not committed murder, "was really doing the kind of thing which Americans should and would have said was the wise and moral thing to do" by trying to better his social standing through a good marriage. Gillette did, however, commit murder; Clyde Griffiths, on the other hand, intends to commit murder but loses his nerve in the boat with Roberta. When she falls into the water after he accidentally hits her with the camera, she drowns only because of Clyde's inaction. Faced with the decision to save her or not, Clyde cannot or will not make the decision, and his inaction damns him. The evidence against him is circumstantial at best and objective examination allows doubt as to his guilt. That doubt intensifies Clyde's entrapment. It is a trap of his own making, but the reader is never sure if he deserves his fate.

In the trial scenes and the events surrounding the trial, Dreiser shows all the external forces which work against Clyde to seal that fate. Political pressures on the defense attorneys and the prosecutors, the prejudice of the rural jury impaneled to try Clyde, the haste with which his wealthy cousins disavow him in order to save their social standing, and Clyde's own ineptitude as a liar form a second box around him, enclosing the first box of his own desires and failures.

Clyde's inevitable conviction and death sentence place him in the final box—his prison cell. This final enclosure is the ultimate circumstance over which Clyde has no control. There is no exit after the governor is convinced of Clyde's guilt by Clyde's mother and his clergyman. When Clyde is finally executed, his inexorable fall is complete.

Clyde's doom is sealed in his tawdry youth, first as a member of an itinerant evangelist's family, later in his work at the Green-Davidson, and ultimately in his fatal liaison with his wealthy Lycurgus cousins. He is not clever enough to help himself, is not wealthy enough to pay anyone to help him (especially during Roberta's pregnancy), and his "chemisms" drive him on in spite of his limitations. When he has his goal of wealth and success in sight, the only obstacle in his path, the pregnant Roberta, must be discarded at any cost without a thought of the consequences. His dreams are the driving force and those dreams are the product of forces over which he has not a shred of control. When he attempts to force his dreams to fruition, he further commits himself into the hands of those forces and they lead him to his death.

Clyde commits the crime and he is punished, but Dreiser indicts all of society in Clyde's execution. Clyde's death sounds the knell for the romance of success and heralds the vacuum that takes its place. Clyde is not only the natural product of Dreiser's cast of tragic characters and of Dreiser's development but also the symbol of Dreiser's worldview: a relentless vision that permanently altered American literature as it set out to expose the cracks in the definition of success propagated by an emerging industrialized America.

Other major works

SHORT FICTION: *Free and Other Stores*, 1918; *Chains: Lesser Novels and Stories*, 1927; *Fine Furniture*, 1930; *The Best Short Stories of Theodore Dreiser*, 1947 (Howard Fast, ed.); *Best Short Stories*, 1956 (James T. Farrell, ed.).
PLAYS: *Plays of the Natural and Supernatural*, 1916; *The Hand of the Potter: A Tragedy in Four Acts*, 1918.
POETRY: *Moods: Cadenced and Declaimed*, 1926, 1928; *The Aspirant*, 1929; *Epitaph: A Poem*, 1929.
NONFICTION: *A Traveler at Forty*, 1913; *A Hoosier Holiday*, 1916; *Twelve Men*, 1919; *Hey, Rub-a-Dub-Dub!*, 1920; *A Book About Myself*, 1922 (rev. as *Newspaper Days*, 1931); *The Color of a Great City*, 1923; *My City*, 1929; *Dawn*, 1931; *Tragic America*, 1931; *America Is Worth Saving*, 1941; *Letters of Theodore Dreiser*, 1959; *Letters to Louise*, 1959; *American Diaries, 1902-1926*, 1982; *Selected Magazine Articles of Theodore Dreiser*, 1985; *Dreiser-Mencken Letters: The Correspondence of Theodore Dreiser and H. L. Mencken, 1907-1945*, 1986; *Theodore Dreiser's "Heard in the Corridors" Articles and Related Writings*, 1988.

Bibliography

Dudley, Dorothy, *Forgotten Frontiers: Dreiser and the Land of the Free*. 1932. Reprint. St. Clair Shores, Mich.: Scholarly Press, 1972.
Elias, Robert H. *Theodore Dreiser: Apostle of Nature*. Ithaca, N.Y.: Cornell University Press, 1970.
Gerber, Philip L. *Theodore Dreiser Revisited*. New York: Twayne, 1992.
Hakutani, Yoshinobu. *Young Dreiser: A Critical Study*. Madison, N.J.: Fairleigh Dickinson University Press, 1980.

Hussman, Lawrence E. *Dreiser and His Fiction: A Twentieth-Century Question.* Philadelphia: University of Pennsylvania Press, 1983.

Moers, Ellen. *Two Dreisers.* New York: Viking Press, 1969.

Mookerjee, Rabindra N. *Theodore Dreiser: His Thought and Social Criticism.* Delhi, India: National, 1974.

Pizer, Donald. *Critical Essays on Theodore Dreiser.* Boston: G. K. Hall, 1981.

Takeda, Miyoko. *The Quest for the Reality of Life: Dreiser's Spiritual and Esthetical Pilgrimage.* New York: P. Lang, 1991.

Zanine, Louis J. *Mechanism and Mysticism: The Influence of Science on the Thought and Work of Theodore Dreiser.* Philadelphia: University of Pennsylvania Press, 1993.

JAMES T. FARRELL

Born: Chicago, Illinois; February 27, 1904   **Died:** New York, New York; August 22, 1979

Principal long fiction

Young Lonigan: A Boyhood in Chicago Streets, 1932; *Gas-House McGinty*, 1933; *The Young Manhood of Studs Lonigan*, 1934; *Judgment Day*, 1935; *Studs Lonigan: A Trilogy*, 1935; *A World I Never Made*, 1936; *No Star Is Lost*, 1938; *Tommy Gallagher's Crusade*, 1939; *Father and Son*, 1940; *Ellen Rogers*, 1941; *My Days of Anger*, 1943; *Bernard Clare*, 1946; *The Road Between*, 1949; *This Man and This Woman*, 1951; *Yet Other Waters*, 1952; *The Face of Time*, 1953; *Boarding House Blues*, 1961; *The Silence of History*, 1963; *What Time Collects*, 1964; *When Time Was Born*, 1966; *Lonely for the Future*, 1966; *New Year's Eve/1929*, 1967; *A Brand New Life*, 1968; *Judith*, 1969; *Invisible Swords*, 1971; *The Dunne Family*, 1976; *The Death of Nora Ryan*, 1978; *Sam Holman: A Novel*, 1983.

Other literary forms

James T. Farrell wrote more than two hundred short stories. Most of them have been collected, but there are several stories and manuscript works that remain unpublished. Farrell also published drama and poetry as well as volumes of literary criticism, cultural criticism, and essays on a wide range of subjects. His letters remain to be collected, and his biography has yet to be completed.

Achievements

On the evidence of his three major complete works, the *Studs Lonigan* trilogy, the Danny O'Neill series (or the O'Neill-O'Flaherty series, as Farrell preferred to call it), and the Bernard Carr trilogy, Farrell presented urban America and the people who sprang from it with a brutal candor rarely equaled in American literature.

Farrell never achieved great popularity; his style was considered too flat and brusque, his language profane, and his methods inartistic. His fiction was considered basically plotless or merely photographic, and he was condemned, especially by the Marxists, for failing to be didactic. Since his death, however, the scope of his urban vision has been recognized; Farrell's fictional world has the breadth of conception associated with greatness and has been compared favorably to that of William Faulkner. Much like Theodore Dreiser, whom he admired, Farrell went his own way when it was extremely unpopular to do so, and his impact on modern fiction remains to be assessed.

Biography

James Thomas Farrell was born on February 27, 1904, in Chicago, where he lived continuously, except for a short sojourn in New York City during the 1920's,

until 1931. The son of a family of Irish teamsters and domestics, he was the product of a curious dual lifestyle in his youth. One of fifteen children, Farrell was taken, when he was three, to live with his maternal grandparents as the result of his own family's impoverished condition. His grandparents, John and Julia Daly, were of the same poor, hardworking stock as his father and mother, but they were somewhat more financially stable and lived a different, more affluent life. The difference in these two families was important in Farrell's development.

Living with the Dalys, Farrell found himself in a neighborhood of modern brick buildings which were a sharp contrast to the poor, wooden-shack neighborhood where his parents lived with the rest of their children. The personal confusion and divisions of loyalties caused by this unusual arrangements were only a part of Farrell's childhood problems. Living in one household and coming from another made Farrell the center of many family tensions and involved him in most of the family's disagreements.

Farrell entered Corpus Christi Parochial Grammar School in 1911 and through the course of his education was a loner and a dreamer. He became an excellent athlete, taking seven letters in sports at St. Cyril High School. He attended St. Cyril after giving up early plans to attend a seminary in preparation to become a priest. He excelled in his studies and was active on the St. Cyril *Oriflamme*, the school's monthly magazine, in addition to being an active member of the high school fraternity, Alpha Eta Beta. He was desperately in need of acceptance, but his classmates sensed that he was different and his social incapacity was another influence on his later life.

After high school, Farrell went to work full time for the Amalgamated Express Company, where he had worked summers while in school. After nearly two years with the express company, Farrell felt trapped by the routine and, in 1924, enrolled in night classes at De Paul University as a pre-law student. He first encountered political and economic theory there and first read Theodore Dreiser. The financial and mental strain eventually became too much for Farrell, and he left De Paul and the express company in 1925. He then took a job as a gas station attendant for the Sinclair Oil and Refining Company and saved part of his wages for tuition at the University of Chicago.

In eight quarters at the university, completed between 1925 and 1929, Farrell became a voracious reader, enjoyed an intellectual awakening that has been compared to Herman Melville's similar awakening in the 1840's, and discovered that he wanted to become a writer. In 1927, he dropped out of school and hitchhiked to New York City, determined to make it as a writer. He returned to Chicago in 1928, reentered the university, and began to write, placing critical articles and book reviews in campus publications and in Chicago and New York newspapers. By 1929, he had sold his first story, "Slob," to a little magazine, and his career was launched.

Farrell and Dorothy Patricia Butler were secretly married in 1931. (Farrell was to divorce Dorothy later, marry the actress Hortense Alden, whom he also divorced, and remarry Dorothy in 1955.) Also in 1931, Farrell and Dorothy sailed for France immediately after their wedding. In France, Farrell discovered that he had little in common with the American expatriates in Paris and that he had important admirers and supporters such as Samuel Putnam, James Henle, and Ezra Pound. The publication of *Young Lonigan* and *Gas-House McGinty* during this period established Farrell as a writer and confirmed his faith in his vision. He began to publish a great number of short stories, and by the time the Farrells returned to New York in 1932, his conceptions for the entire *Studs Lonigan* trilogy and the first Danny O'Neill novel, *A World I Never Made*, were outlined. His contribution to American letters included stormy confrontations with Marxist critics and novelists and a staunch defense of the integrity of art and the artist as opposed to the socialist demands that fiction, and all art, serve the party.

The 1930's were the end of the personal experiences that Farrell used as the material for his major fiction; the *Studs Lonigan* trilogy, the Danny O'Neill series, and the Bernard Carr trilogy are all drawn from the same well; in describing that world, Farrell was determined to "shake the sack of reality" until it was empty. In 1957, he completed his original life plan for twenty-five volumes that were to be "panels of one work" and had begun a second lifework, called *A Universe of Time*, of which he published seven volumes (*The Silence of History*, *What Time Collects*, *When Time Was Born*, *Lonely for the Future*, *A Brand New Life*, *Judith*, and *Invisible Swords*). Farrell died in New York on August 22, 1979, before this lifework was complete.

Analysis

Farrell's youth, spent in Irish atholic, lower- and middle-class Chicago, gave him the milieu from which a whole society could be examined and explained. His career began with his conscious decision to quit a steady job and become a writer and survived despite indifference, shock, bad reviews, prejudice, and ignorance. Farrell's social activism led him into and out of Marxist circles, sustained him through attacks by the Marxist critics who accused him of abandoning the cause, and gave him the focus necessary to show Americans an entire society that survived and prospered in spite of its environment.

Farrell did not write exclusively of Chicago or of Irish atholics, but it was on this home "turf" that he most effectively showed the effects of indifference and disintegration on an independent, stubborn, often ignorant urban subculture. He was at once appalled by and attracted to the spectacle of an entire people being strangled by the city and by their own incapacity to understand their position, and he was most successful when he embodied the society in the life and times of an archetypal individual.

While the *Studs Lonigan* trilogy, the five novels of the O'Neill-O'Flaherty series, and the Bernard Carr trilogy have different protagonists, they all share a common impulse and reflect Farrell's almost fanatical obsession with time, society, and the individual's response to both. Studs Lonigan, Danny O'Neill, and Bernard Carr are extensions or facets of Farrell's primal character, pitted against a hostile urban environment.

The *Studs Lonigan* trilogy, arguably Farrell's best and certainly his best-known work, is the story of the development and deterioration not only of the title character but also of the Depression-era, Irish Catholic Chicago society from which he springs. In the fifteen-year span of Lonigan's life portrayed in *Young Lonigan*, *The Young Manhood of Studs Lonigan*, and *Judgment Day*,

Farrell shows the total physical, moral, and spiritual degeneration of Studs Lonigan.

Studs is doomed from the moment he appears just prior to his graduation from grammar school. His announcement that he is "kissin' the old dump goodbye tonight" is ominously portentous. He drops out of high school, goes to work for his father, a painting contractor, and becomes a member and leading light of the gang that hangs out in Charlie Bathcellar's poolroom. The association with the gang is Studs's life—everything else is "plain crap." Through a swirl of "alky," "gang-shags," "craps," and "can-houses," Studs fights to prove himself to be the "real stuff" and ultimately finds himself a frail, thirty-year-old shell of the vigorous youth he once was. The physical ruin of Studs Lonigan, however, is only the result of larger deficiencies.

Studs is a sensitive, moral being who consciously rejects his innate morality as a weakness. He blindly accepts his Catholic upbringing without believing it. There is never a present for Studs Lonigan—there is only a future and a past. In *Young Lonigan*, the future is the vision of Studs standing triumphantly astride the fireplug at 58th and Prairie proclaiming his ascendancy to the brotherhood of the gang. The past is his rejection of juvenile harassment he suffered as the result of his one moment of ecstasy with Lucy Scanlan in Washington Park. He proclaims himself the "real stuff" and flees from human emotions and the potentialities of those experiences with Lucy.

Studs consistently refuses to allow his emotional sensitivity to mature. The spiritual stagnation that results confines him to dreams of future aggrandizement or of past glories. The future dies, and Studs is left with memories of his degeneracy. His affair with Catherine Banahan awakens new sensibilities in Studs, but he is unable to nurture them, and they die stillborn. His heart attack at the beach, his dehumanizing odyssey through the business offices of Chicago looking for work, his shockingly prurient behavior at the burlesque show, and his final delirium are simply the payment of accounts receivable.

As Studs dies, his world is dying with him. His father's bank has collapsed, the mortgage on his building is due, Studs's fiancée is pregnant, and the gang has generally dispersed. These are not the causes of Studs's failures, however; they are reflections of that failure. Studs is the product and the producer. He is not a blind victim of his environment. He makes conscious choices—all bad. He is bankrupt of all the impulses that could save him. He batters and abuses his body, he strangles his emotions, and he clings to the stultifying spirituality of a provincial Catholicism. As Lucy Scanlan dances through his final delirium and his family abuses his pregnant fiancé, Studs Lonigan's dying body becomes the prevailing metaphor for the empty world it created and abused and in which it suffered.

Danny O'Neill, of the O'Neill-O'Flaherty series, is the product of the same environment but recognizes that he controls his destiny in spite of overbearing environmental pressures and, by the end of the series, seems on the verge of success. If he succeeds, he does so because he refuses to fall into the trap that Studs builds for himself, and he thus escapes into the larger world that Studs never knows. In the five novels of the series, *A World I Never Made*, *No Star Is Lost*, *Father and Son*, *My Days of Anger*, and *The Face of Time*, Danny not only escapes the strictures of environment but also sloughs off the psychological and spiritual bondage of family and religion and creates his own freedom.

Farrell's most clearly autobiographical work, the O'Neill-O'Flaherty series, portrays Danny's growth from 1909 to 1927—from a five-year-old child to a man breaking from college and Chicago. Born to Jim and Lizz O'Neill, a poor, working-class Irish couple, he is taken to live with his grandparents, of the lace-curtain Irish variety, because his parents cannot support their already large family. Danny grows up alone in a world which he has difficulty understanding and which seems to engulf but reject him summarily. Only late in the series does he understand Jim, his father, and come to accept him for what he is, a hardworking, decent, poor Irish laborer, who loves his children desperately enough to thrust them into a better world than he can make for them.

By the end of the series, Danny finally seems to understand that his basic character is still that of the poor, hardworking Irishman that, with all its flaws, is at least pitiable rather than repugnant. As Danny prepares to escape his oppressive Chicago past to pursue success in New York City—the hub of the world—he escapes with a fuller appreciation and self-preserving understanding of his heritage and an ability to progress beyond his previous angry rejections. He displays a tolerance and acceptance of himself and his culture that are the foreground of promised success.

Bernard Carr seems to take up the story where Danny leaves it. The trilogy of *Bernard Clare* (Farrell changed the name to Carr in the second novel after a man named Bernard Clare brought libel proceedings against him),

The Road Between, and *Yet Other Waters* is Farrell's attempt to represent the lives of a generation of artists in New York during the Depression era and in the circles of politically radical activism.

Bernard is the last member of Farrell's Irish Catholic trinity—he is the embodiment of the whole man whom Studs could not become and Danny might well have become had his story been continued.

Bernard's New York is a world of struggling artists and of Communists, whom he later rejects. Bernard's marriage introduces him to family life, the wonder of birth and rearing a child, and is the spur in his attempt to recover and understand his family and his heritage. During all these events, Bernard is achieving a limited success from his writing, and by the end of the trilogy he has brought all the pieces together and has found himself, his vocation, and an enlightened ability to see life for what it is and make the most of it.

The dovetailing of the experiences and environments of his major characters is what ultimately makes Farrell's work live. Their stories make up a tapestry which mirrors the world from which they sprang and rivals it for true pathos and vitality.

Other major works

SHORT FICTION: *Calico Shoes and Other Stories*, 1934; *Guillotine Party and Other Stories*, 1935; *Can All This Grandeur Perish? and Other Stories*, 1937; *The Short Stories of James T. Farrell*, 1937; *$1,000 a Week and Other Stories*, 1942; *Fifteen Selected Stories*, 1943; *To Whom It May Concern and Other Stories*, 1944; *When Boyhood Dreams Come True*, 1946; *The Life Adventurous and Other Stories*, 1947; *A Hell of a Good Time*, 1948; *An American Dream Girl*, 1950; *French Girls Are Vicious and Other Stories*, 1955; *An Omnibus of Short Stories*, 1956; *A Dangerous Woman and Other Stories*, 1957; *Saturday Night and Other Stories*, 1958; *Side Street and Other Stories*, 1961; *Sound of a City*, 1962; *Childhood Is Not Forever*, 1969; *Judith and Other Stories*, 1973; *Olive and Mary Anne*, 1977.

PLAYS: *The Mowbray Family*, 1940 (with Hortense Alden Farrell); *A Lesson in History*, 1944.

POETRY: *The Collected Poems of James T. Farrell*, 1965.

NONFICTION: *A Note on Literary Criticism*, 1936; *The League of Frightened Philistines and Other Papers*, 1945; *The Fate of Writing in America*, 1946; *Literature and Morality*, 1947; *The Name Is Fogarty: Private Papers on Public Matters*, 1950; *Reflections at Fifty and Other Essays*, 1954; *My Baseball Diary*, 1957; *It Has Come to Pass*, 1958; *On Irish Themes*, 1982; *Hearing Out James T. Farrell: Selected Lectures*, 1985.

Bibliography

Bogardus, Ralph F., and Fred Hobson. *Literature at the Barricades: The American Writer in the 1930s*. Tuscaloosa: University of Alabama Press, 1982.

Branch, Edgar M. *James T. Farrell*. New York: Twayne, 1971.

Butler, Robert James. "Parks, Parties, and Pragmatism: Time and Setting in James T. Farrell's Major Novels." *Essays in Literature* 10 (Fall, 1983): 241-254.

Fried, Lewis F. *Makers of the City*. Amherst: University of Massachusetts Press, 1990.

Pizer, Donald. *Twentieth-Century American Literary Naturalism: An Interpretation*. Carbondale: Southern Illinois University Press, 1982.

Wald, Alan M. *James T. Farrell: The Revolutionary Socialist Years*. New York: New York University Press, 1978.

SINCLAIR LEWIS

Born: Sauk Centre, Minnesota; February 7, 1885   **Died:** Rome, Italy; January 10, 1951

Principal long fiction

Our Mr. Wrenn: The Romantic Adventures of a Gentle Man, 1914; *The Trail of the Hawk: A Comedy of the Seriousness of Life*, 1915; *The Innocents: A Story for Lovers*, 1917; *The Job: An American Novel*, 1917; *Free Air*, 1919; *Main Street: The Story of Carol Kennicott*, 1920; *Babbitt*, 1922; *Arrowsmith*, 1925; *Mantrap*, 1926; *Elmer Gantry*, 1927; *The Man Who Knew Coolidge: Being the Soul of Lowell Schmaltz, Constructive and Nordic Citizen*, 1928; *Dodsworth*, 1929; *Ann Vickers*, 1933; *Work of Art*, 1934; *It Can't Happen Here*, 1935; *The Prodigal Parents*, 1938; *Bethel Merriday*, 1940; *Gideon Planish*, 1943; *Cass Timberlane: A Novel of Husbands and Wives*, 1945; *Kingsblood Royal*, 1947; *The God-Seeker*, 1949; *World So Wide*, 1951.

Other literary forms

Sinclair Lewis started writing regularly during his freshman year at Yale. His stories and poems imitating the manner of Lord Tennyson and A. C. Swinburne appeared in the *Yale Literary Magazine*. His short stories began to appear in 1915 in the *Saturday Evening Post*. During his lifetime, there were numerous stage and screen adaptations of many of his novels. Lewis also wrote a play, and several volumes of his correspondence have been published.

Achievements

In 1930, Lewis received the Nobel Prize in Literature, the first American so honored. He acknowledged in his acceptance address that the Swedish Academy honored American literature with this prize. By awarding it to the novelist who not only added "Babbitt" to the American language but also enriched the European vocabulary with his "Main Street," Europe acknowledged America's coming-of-age.

Lewis wrote five novels before he achieved his first big success with *Main Street* in 1920. Although critics were divided, at the peak of Lewis' career his works found widespread acceptance among numerous esteemed writers on both sides of the Atlantic. Lewis himself was generous with others; he helped young writers such as Thomas Wolfe and was quick to praise novelists of his own generation. In his Nobel Prize acceptance speech, which came to be called "The American Fear of Literature," he repudiated the genteel tradition, in which he included William Dean Howells, and praised Theodore Dreiser, Sherwood Anderson, and a score of younger writers. Like all his writings, this speech was controversial.

Each novel renewed the controversy; some considered him unworthy of the attention and overrated; others denounced his aggressive criticism of American life, but after *Arrowsmith* he received favorable recognition even in *The Atlantic*, *The Nation*, *The New Republic*, *The New York Times*, the New York *Herald Tribune*, and the *Literary Review*. Indeed, his popularity in America reached unprecedented levels. In one decade, with the help of Harcourt, Brace and Co., he became the most widely known novelist in the country. An authentic interpreter of American life, he created self-awareness among the American people.

Biography

Harry Sinclair Lewis was born in Sauk Centre, Minnesota, on February 7, 1885. His father, Edwin J. Lewis, and his mother, Emma F. Kermorr, were both schoolteachers, but Edwin Lewis took a two-year medical course in Chicago and practiced as a country doctor, first in Wisconsin and later in Sauk Centre, a small Minnesota town with a population of 2,500. Harry Sinclair, nicknamed "Red" because of the color of his hair, was the third of three sons. His mother died of tuberculosis when he was three. Edwin Lewis remarried shortly after her death. The future novelist was an awkward, rather ugly, lonely child with little aptitude for sports or any type of physical exercise. He soon became an ardent reader; at an early age, he also started a diary and tried his hand at creative writing.

After a short preparation in the Oberlin Academy, Lewis became a freshman at Yale at the age of seventeen. There, too, he was a loner, even after he became a regular contributor of poems and short stories to the *Yale Literary Magazine*. In the summers of 1904 and 1906, he participated in cattle-boat trips to London, and in his senior year he left Yale. For a month, he worked as a janitor in Upton Sinclair's New Jersey commune, Helicon Hall. Since he had no financial support from his father at that time, he tried to make money, first in New York with his writing and then in Panama with work on the canal construction. Unsuccessful in both attempts, he returned to Yale and was graduated in 1908.

Between 1908 and 1915, Lewis traveled from New York to California in search of employment; he also sold story plots to other writers. From 1910 to 1915, he worked in New York for commercial publishers. In 1914, his first novel, *Our Mr. Wrenn*, was published, and on April 15, he married Grace Livingston Hegger. The couple settled in Long Island. In 1915, the *Saturday Evening Post* accepted one of Lewis' short stories for publication, the first of many to be published there. With some money at his disposal, he traveled around the country with Grace, publishing short stories and writing more novels.

The five novels following *Our Mr. Wrenn*, all published under pseudonyms, were unsuccessful, but *Main Street*, Lewis' first novel to be published by Harcourt, Brace and Co., suddenly made him famous. Never again did Lewis worry about money. With *Babbitt* his fame was firmly established. He went on a Caribbean tour in preparation for *Arrowsmith*, and from 1923 to 1925 he traveled with Grace in Europe. It is interesting to note that Lewis loved publicity. In 1925, while working on *Elmer Gantry*, he defied God from a pulpit in Kansas City, giving God fifteen minutes to strike him down. His refusal of the Pulitzer Prize in 1926—an obvious act of anger over a previous disappointment—became an internationally broadcast event.

In 1927, Lewis separated from Grace and spent much of the next year in Europe. After Grace had obtained a Reno divorce, Lewis married Dorothy Thompson, whom he had met in Berlin, on May 14, 1928. At that time, Thompson was the best-known American journalist in Europe; she also became the first American journalist to be expelled from Nazi Germany. *It Can't Happen Here*, Lewis' novel about the possibility of Fascism in America, was written under Thompson's influence. In 1929, Lewis published *Dodsworth*, a product of his long stay in Europe, which dealt with the American-in-Europe theme. In 1930, Lewis received the Nobel Prize and reached the peak of his fame.

After this period of renown, Lewis' life and career declined. A longtime drinking problem grew worse and his health rapidly deteriorated. One sign of his restlessness was his break with Harcourt, Brace and Co.; he switched to Doubleday and Co. The world around him was changing rapidly; he became increasingly confused, unhappy, and lonely. In 1937, he separated from his second wife, and they were divorced in 1942. Lewis attempted to find a new career in acting and simultaneously had an affair with a young actress. His obsession with the theater is documented in *Bethel Merriday*. With *Kingsblood Royal*, a novel about racism, he once more tried his hand at an urgent contemporary issue, but his energy was decreasing. After World War II, he spent most of his time in Europe. He died in Rome, Italy, on January 10, 1951. His last novel, *World So Wide*, dedicated to "memories in Italy," was published posthumously in 1951.

Analysis

The five novels that made Lewis famous, *Main Street*, *Babbitt*, *Arrowsmith*, *Elmer Gantry*, and *Dodsworth*, can be read as a series of variations on the same theme. Lewis exposed an America dominated by business and petty bourgeois mentality. His characters, still full of nostalgia for the excitement of the frontier, persuade themselves that what they have at the present represents the zenith, the summit of human potential. Descendants of pious pioneer Puritans, Lewis' wealthy Americans of the 1920's are in desperate need of a civilization they can call their own. This transitory stage of the American experience becomes the theme of Lewis' writings.

As Van Wyck Brooks described it, America's coming of age in the decade before World War I paved the way for a cultural and moral revolution, heralded by works such as Edgar Lee Masters' *Spoon River Anthology* (1915), Sherwood Anderson's *Winesburg, Ohio* (1919), and Lewis' *Main Street* (1920) and *Babbitt* (1922), with its bitter attacks on "boobus Americanus." *Civilization in the U.S.* (1921), edited by Harold Stearns, gave a rather bleak picture of the average American in the 1920's—materialistic, hypocritical, and suffering from emotional and aesthetic starvation. At his best, Lewis portrayed this same world and became himself part of "the revolt from the village."

Lewis' capacity for mimicry and for detailed observation made him a true "photographer" of life. Indeed, his novels are almost historical documents. He documented a fixed period in the American development, the frustrations and disillusionments of one generation. Unfortunately, Lewis never went beyond documentation; he re-created the symptoms but never analyzed them, never provided any formula for a meaningful life. The pattern in his books is always similar: There is a central character who—at any given moment—realizes the emptiness of his or her life and tries to break out of the mechanical boredom of the suffocating environment. The revolt is short-lived and leads nowhere. Unlike H. L. Mencken, who praised and encouraged him, Lewis was not a true iconoclast; deep down he remained attached to the values he exposed.

In the year when Warren Harding was successfully campaigning for the presidency with the pledge of a "return to normalcy," Lewis captured the reading public with his *Main Street*. The novel's theme is the "village virus." In fact, Lewis had originally intended to give this title to the book. The village-virus syndrome was a characteristic of a certain period of American life. Describing it with photographic accuracy, Lewis preserved the atmosphere of a short historical stage in the American development. Village novels were no rarity in literature before Lewis, but Lewis' sharp satirical approach marks a radical departure from that tradition.

The most popular book of 1920, *Main Street*, is deeply rooted in the author's life. Gopher Prairie, population three thousand, is modeled on Sauk Centre, Lewis' birthplace. Dr. William Kennicott is based in part on Lewis' father and on his brother Claude, who also became a doctor. Carol is partly Lewis himself, the romantic side of him. Born in Minnesota, she is not exactly a village girl when she first appears in the novel. It is 1906, and she is a student at Blodgett College near Minneapolis. Her studies in professional library work take her to Chicago, the center of a poetic revival in the twentieth century. There she is exposed to the benefits of America's coming-of-age: the Art Institute, classical music, intellectual discussions on Sigmund Freud, Romain Rolland, syndicates, feminism, radically new thinking in philosophy, politics, and art. She has a job at St. Paul's public library when she meets Dr. Kennicott. The bulk of the novel is about their married life in Gopher Prairie, where Will works as a country doctor; it covers the years 1912 to 1920, from World War I and the American participation in the war to 1920, the cynical decade of the jazz age. American was passing on to a new period in which the political and economic fiber of the country came to be shaped and determined in cities rather than rural communities. *Main Street* is not so much a chronicle of Carol Kennicott's life between 1912 and 1920 as it is a documentation of the national phenomenon of the village virus.

The village virus is best described by Gopher Prairie's frustrated liberal, Guy Pollock. He defines it as a vicious disease menacing ambitious people who stay too long in places such as Gopher Prairie. The small-town atmosphere breeds boredom, dullness, stupidity, complacency, and vulgarity, causing the inhabitants to wither away spiritually and become living dead men. Only a few of the inhabitants see Gopher Prairie as a menace. All the "important" people of the community—Ole Jensen, the grocer; Ezra Stowbody, the banker; Sam Clark, owner of a hardware store—take pride in Main Street. When she first sees Main Street, Carol is terrified by its repulsive ugliness, but to the others it constitutes the "climax of civilization."

All the people to whom Carol is drawn are outsiders in the community. Except for the resigned Guy Pollock, they all leave, disappointed and frustrated, or else die. Those who always triumph are the Bogarts and Stowbodys; they succeed in slowly killing all of Carol's romantic ambitions.

When Carol arrives in Gopher Prairie, she is determined to bring about changes for the better. Much of the novel is about her frustrated reform efforts. Again and again she tries to initiate new and fresh ideas and plans, but all of them fail because of the all-pervasive spiritual emptiness of Gopher Prairie. People there are not interested in poetry or theater or intellectual discussions.

Carol leaves Gopher Prairie with their son just as the war is ending. Will is there to wave good-bye as the train taking her to Washington, D.C., pulls out of the station. In the nation's capital, Carol is on her own; she tries to find her identity, tries to become a whole person, not simply a wife. She succeeds and enjoys the opportunity of a new life in which she can be active and in which she can use her brain once again, as she did in her girlhood, but she learns something else too: the radical changes in the behavior and attitudes of the young girls around her shock her as much as her behavior once had shocked a sleepy Gopher Prairie. In the end, she returns with Will to their home and settles down in Gopher Prairie, this time permanently. She still has dreams for her baby girl and likes to picture her as a future feminist or scientist; to the end, Carol remains a dreamer rather than a doer.

The last word in the novel belongs to the pragmatic Will Kennicott. He is Lewis' real favorite—the simple country doctor who performs acts of quiet heroism and worries about matters such as putting up storm windows. Lewis is unquestionably drawn to this stable, dependable, and reliable man, representing in his view the best of middle-class America. Lewis only half-heartedly endorses Carol's romantic attempts at beautifying Gopher Prairie because he himself was of divided mind whom to prefer: the artistically minded Carol or the always commonsensical though unsophisticated Will. If the cigarette-smoking modern young girls of the 1920's shocked Carol, Lewis, too, was unable to catch up with new trends. In this sense, *Main Street*, a novel about the village virus, is also an autobiography of Sinclair Lewis' spiritual development, or, rather, spiritual stagnation.

Even before he finished *Main Street*, Lewis had started work on *Babbitt*, a novel about a land speculator. From Main Street, U.S.A., "the climax of civilization," the novelist moved to an imaginary city in the Middle West, satirically named Zenith, symbolizing the average American city and its status-symbol-oriented population. Set in the boom decade of the 1920's, the novel concentrates on the new national disease, which came to be called "Babbittry," after the book's protagonist. Webster's dictionary now defines a Babbitt as "a business or professional man who conforms unthinkingly to prevailing middle-class standards." The book is thus a realistic, satirical look at middle-class America and its business culture. Predominantly, though, the almost photographic portrayal of Zenith prevails. While President Harding was hoping to plant a Rotary Club in every city and village in the country to ensure the propagation of American ideals, Lewis was provoking the anger of those very Rotary Clubs by holding up a mirror to their Tartuffe-like hypocrisy and their materialistic culture.

Just as *Main Street* killed the friendly village novel by concentrating on the village virus, so *Babbitt* undercut the traditional business novel. With *Babbitt*, Lewis demonstrated that the era of the independent, creative tycoon was over. The tycoon gave way to the joiner, the conformist relying on status symbols and good public relations rather than daring and creative initiative. Babbitt, positively no giant, is almost a pathetic figure in his desperate need for approval. Far from being a tycoon, he lacks any individual ideas. He is a Booster, an Elk, a Presbyterian, a member of the chamber of commerce, a family man—nothing more. Senators of the Republican Party prescribe his political beliefs; national advertisers dictate his preferences in consumer goods. Without all these accessories, he is nobody; Babbitt is spiritually empty. While he relies on the sham values that make him a "solid citizen," he becomes a pitiful victim of mechanical gadgets; his identity depends on having a car, the newest alarm clock, and a royal bathroom.

This apparent contentment, however, is one side of the novel; Babbitt only appears to be satisfied. In reality, this prosperous real estate agent passionately desires something more and different from mere material success. This desire leads to his unsuccessful, vague, romantic rebellion against the Zenith world. Babbitt escapes to Maine, but the escape does not help; his frustration remains, and he returns to Zenith.

In *Main Street*, Lewis made Carol Kennicott return to Gopher Prairie. In a similar spirit of compromise, he finds a convenient way for Babbitt to give up his empty rebellion. His wife Myra has to undergo emergency surgery; her hospitalization pulls Babbitt back to his duties as a solid citizen. To seal his return to normality, he joins the Good Citizens' League. At the end of the novel, he is taken by surprise by his younger son; Ted drops out of school and elopes. In a private, man-to-man talk with his son, Babbitt acknowledges that he admires him for doing what he wants. He, Babbitt, never did that at any time during his life. In *Main Street*, Carol Kennicott's rebellion dwindles to romantic dreams for her daughter; all that remains of Babbitt's rebellion is his pleasure in his son's defiance and an encouragement not to let himself be bullied by Zenith. At the moment, however, Ted does not hold out much promise; rather than going to college, he wants to be a mechanic at a factory.

The most obvious characteristic of *Elmer Gantry* is its brutality; there is no trace of the sympathy that mitigated the dark picture in *Main Street* or *Babbitt*; there is no trace of a love/hate relationship with Elmer Gantry. He as well as the novel's other major characters have few redeeming qualities. The novel, indeed, is an uncompromising indictment of American religious practices in the early twentieth century. The book's three main parts concern Elmer Gantry's involvement with three different women. In no other Lewis novel is the sexual element as important as in this one; it is Gantry's sexual desire that threatens his rise in religious circles.

The young Elmer Gantry attends a Baptist College and is ordained a minister. As soon as he receives his first pulpit, he becomes sexually involved with a young girl. He gets rid of Lulu by casting doubt on her character, revealing the depths of falsehood and villainy of which he is capable. In the second phase of his religious career, he becomes an evangelist, the partner (religious and sexual) of the female evangelist Sharon Falcon. They are two of a kind who never consider "their converts as human beings"; they regard them as a surgeon regards his patients or as a fisherman regards trout.

Sharon dies in a fire, and Elmer Gantry's adventures take him to the Methodist denomination. There, he rises fast and is promoted to pastorates in larger and larger communities. He is made a Doctor of Divinity, marries, becomes the first fundamentalist preacher whose sermons are broadcast, and tours Europe. Suddenly, his fame and position are almost destroyed by a new love affair. Hettie and her convict husband try to outwit Gantry; they set a trap for him. For a short time he is frightened, but influential and clever friends come to his rescue and he bounces back again. At the end of the novel, he is leading his congregation in prayer, determined "to make these United States a moral nation." Like all true hypocrites, Gantry convinces himself of his sincerity.

Lewis' novels are a stinging critique of American life. In an era of intense national self-consciousness following World War II, he punctured American complacency with his satirical depictions of the crass values, emotional shallowness, and spiritual emptiness of middle America. His biographer, Mark Schorer, describes him as a major force in the liberating of twentieth century American literature.

Other major works

SHORT FICTION: *Selected Short Stories of Sinclair Lewis*, 1935.

PLAY: *Jayhawker: A Play in Three Acts*, 1934 (with Lloyd Lewis).

NONFICTION: *From Main Street to Stockholm: Letters of Sinclair Lewis, 1919-1930*, 1952 (Harrison Smith, ed.); *The Man from Main Street: Selected Essays and Other Writings, 1904-1950*, 1953 (Harry E. Maule and Melville H. Crane, eds.).

Bibliography

Bloom, Harold, ed. *Modern Critical Views: Sinclair Lewis*. New York: Chelsea House, 1987.

Bucco, Martin. *Main Street: The Revolt of Carol Kennicott*. New York: Twayne, 1993.

Derleth, August. *Three Literary Men: A Memoir of Sinclair Lewis, Sherwood Anderson, Edgar Lee Masters*. New York: Candlelight Press, 1963.

Koblas, John J. *Sinclair Lewis: Home at Last*. Bloomington, Minn.: Voyageur Press, 1981.

Light, Martin. *The Quixotic Vision of Sinclair Lewis*. West Lafayette, Ind.: Purdue University Press, 1975.

Love, Glen A. *"Babbitt": An American Life*. New York: Twayne, 1993.

Parrington, Vernon Louis. *Sinclair Lewis: Our Own Diogenes*. Seattle: University of Washington Press, 1927. Reprint. New York: Haskell House, 1973.

Schorer, Mark, ed. *Sinclair Lewis: A Collection of Critical Essays*. Englewood Cliffs, N.J.: Prentice-Hall, 1962.

WRIGHT MORRIS

Born: Central City, Nebraska; January 6, 1910

Principal long fiction

My Uncle Dudley, 1942; *The Man Who Was There*, 1945; *The World in the Attic*, 1949; *Man and Boy*, 1951; *The Works of Love*, 1952; *The Deep Sleep*, 1953; *The Huge Season*, 1954; *The Field of Vision*, 1956; *Love Among the Cannibals*, 1957; *Ceremony in Lone Tree*, 1960; *What a Way to Go*, 1962; *Cause for Wonder*, 1963; *One Day*, 1965; *In Orbit*, 1967; *Fire Sermon*, 1971; *War Games*, 1972; *A Life*, 1973; *The Fork River Space Project*, 1977; *Plains Song, for Female Voices*, 1980.

Other literary forms

Wright Morris has been one of the most productive artists of his time, crafting novels, short stories, essays, criticism, and photographs that explore what it means to be an American. The his works include a memoir, *Will's Boy* (1981), and the autobiographical *Solo: An American Dreamer in Europe, 1933-1934* (1983), followed by *A Cloak of Light: Writing My Life* (1985).

Achievements

While a few of Morris' books have European settings, he is most effective when writing about his native Nebraska and picaresque characters returning home to try to recapture memories or relive the past. Morris is inevitably compared to both James Agee and Walker Evans because of his poetic, reflective prose about the dignity of rural life and because his photography is reminiscent of Evans' in *Let Us Now Praise Famous Men* (1960). Morris combines the talents of both men in his phototexts, conducting a search for the meaning of America through word and picture.

Although Morris has always received critical acclaim, he has not enjoyed popular success. Robert Knoll has suggested that the reason may be his failure to involve the reader in the exciting events of his fiction. Morris rather invites the reader casually, as did Robert Frost, to come along and clear the leaves away. His poetic style is as far removed as prose can be from the popular journalistic narrative mode. Although Morris himself knows that readers do not want fictive distance, he continues to write novels that create rather than confess, that disturb rather than reassure.

Morris has received three Guggenheim awards, two of them for photography and the third for fiction (*The Deep Sleep*), the National Book Award for *The Field of Vision* and *Plains Song, for Female Voices*, and the National Institute for Arts and Letters Award for *Ceremony in Lone Tree*. He received a National Institute Grant in 1960 and was fiction judge for the National Book Award in 1969.

Biography

After his birth in Central City, Nebraska, Wright Morris lived with his father in Schuyler, Kearney, and other small Nebraska towns along the Platte River before moving to Omaha. He worked for two summers on his uncle Harry's farm in Norfolk, Nebraska, but the move to Chicago in 1924 brought him a different kind of employment at the Young Men's Christian Association (YMCA). He attended Adventist College in California for five weeks, then worked for several months on the Texas ranch of his uncle Dwight Osborn. He entered Pomona College in Claremont, California, but withdrew to spend a year in Austria, Italy, Germany, and France. He had written some brief prose sketches while at Pomona, and he returned to California to begin his first novel.

Morris married Mary Ellen Finfrock of Cleveland, Ohio, in 1934. Between 1935 and 1938, he wrote two novels and the sketches for *The Inhabitants* (1946) and developed the interest in photography that flourished during two summers at Wellfleet, Massachusetts. In 1940-1941, he toured the United States, taking pictures to be used in *The Inhabitants*. He lived in California two more years before moving to Haverford, Pennsylvania, in 1944. In 1954, he began spending more time in Venice, Italy, Mexico, and Greece, returning intermittently to California. He has lectured at the University of Southern California and at Amherst College and taught at the California state universities in Los Angeles and San Francisco.

In 1961, Morris and his first wife were divorced, and he married Josephine Kantor. He was selected in 1983 to occupy the Visiting Writers' Chair at the University of Alabama.

Analysis

In his phototexts and his nonfiction, Morris revealed his abiding interest in and concern for the American scene and those components of the physical and cultural landscape that inform the American experience. Likewise, in his fiction, Morris explored the American character, particularly as manifested in the Midwest and California. He examined the legacies of heroism and nostalgia, the dreams and delusions examined by earlier twentieth century American writers. Another concern of Morris, whose novels seldom display violence, is the rise of violence in America. His narratives usually take place within a twenty-four-hour time period, suggesting the capture of a finite period of time as the photographer captures a finite space with his camera. This limitation of time unifies Morris' novels, which are more intimately related by the device of recurring characters.

The spirit of place, whether it be the central plains, a California beach, a Philadelphia suburb, or an Alpine chateau, is central to Morris' novels, and the impingement of objects or places upon the individual is a major facet of Morris' imagination, as it had been to Henry James, who believed that places gave out a "mystic meaning." Admittedly influenced by James and by D. H. Lawrence, Morris has been his own man for five prolific decades. Fortunate to have as his birthplace the "navel of the universe," the central United States, he has from that vantage point "salvaged" meaningful artifacts that represent an earlier American life and, concomitantly, the values of that life.

It is not easy to generalize about an oeuvre as varied as Morris', but he does frequently disregard chronology, an attempt to possess time and understand it being one of his obsessions. A recurring relationship, as David Madden points out, is that of the hero and his "witnesses"—the characters who are transformed because their lives have intersected his. The contact, strangely enough, is often more meaningful after the death of the hero. Wayne Booth notes that the novels of Morris begin with a problem or a misunderstanding and conclude with a solution or a clarification. While this statement could be made about most plots, it is not the beginnings and the endings that occupy Morris' inventive mind but what is in between. The resolutions that he works toward require especially appropriate intervening incidents that require "a lot of doing." Morris, adds Booth, thinks of his introductions not as promises to the reader but as problems to be solved by the author himself. What is important in this kind of plot progression is the quality of the middle, and here Morris excels.

Believing that the fiction-writer must do more than reproduce facts, Morris transmutes his raw material, particularly his experience of the Midwest, through his imagination into something that he sees as more real than life itself.

The pursuit of the American Dream, played out against the backdrop of the Great Plains, is the setting of *The Works of Love*. The protagonist, Will Brady, learns to love in a prodigious, self-conscious, almost methodical manner, even though he has not himself been loved or found suitable recipients for his own works of love. The self-centered women in his life have not appreciated his fumbling, inarticulate efforts at communication. Two of them have been prostitutes, one of whom laughed when he proposed marriage; the other ran away and mailed him another man's baby son to adopt. After his marriage to the widow Ethel Bassett, who sleeps like a mummy tightly wrapped in a sheet, he lies beside her listing in his incipiently loving mind her reasons for doing so. The last woman to whom he tries to become a father-husband is a cigar-counter girl turned alcoholic streetwalker. In an effort to understand and grow closer to his adopted son Willy, Will searches the pages of *Penrod* and *The Adventures of Tom Sawyer* for enlightenment. His final role, that of a department store Santa Claus, allows him to touch and love little children, at the same time distributing some of the works of his abundant love.

Will handles the eggs that he sells with the same gentle touch that he reserves for women, sensing perhaps that both species contain the miracle of life. He is more at home, however, with the eggs than with the women, always a stranger in his own house. In his pursuit of love, he finally cuts himself off from all Midwestern, rural roots and heads for Chicago on a quest to fill his emotional void. His incapacity to receive love, his failure to understand himself, and especially his inability to communicate his feelings have set up an almost insurmountable barrier between Will and his love-objects. Significantly more at home in a hotel than in his house, he has, for most of his life, failed to connect with the rest of humankind.

In *The Deep Sleep*, Morris again presents a hero who has died, this time Judge Howard Porter. Porter's "witnesses" include the hired man Parson, who has worked for the Porter family for thirty years and loves the almost unlovable Mrs. Porter; the judge's son-in-law Paul Webb, who gets to know him well just before the funeral, and the judge's mother, who communicates by tapping her cane and never became acquainted with her son at all. Mrs. Porter had known her husband twice—once in the biblical sense, when their first child was conceived, and a second time just before the funeral, when she told their daughter Katherine that she missed him.

Paul Webb discovers that Mrs. Porter had not ruled her husband as ironhandedly as she had thought. Like Violet Ormsby's husband, the judge had found a basement-toilet retreat where he stashed his whiskey. In addition, Paul discovers, Judge Porter had an attic hideout where he smoked cigars and admired his expensive Swiss watch, while he carried a cheap, loud, dollar watch in public. The artist Webb is objective enough to get a balanced picture of the Porter family as he studies the house, room by room. While his wife Katherine fears that he cannot show her mother the sympathy she deserves, the fact that the two finally arrive at the same conclusion about Judge and Mrs. Porter suggests that both are fair in their appraisal.

Webb takes on an additional characteristic of the dead man every time he gains a new insight. As Webb becomes the judge's spiritual son, he reaches a better understanding of Mrs. Porter. The two watches become the artifacts that connect Webb and his mother-in-law, whose sense of order ("Never go to bed with dirty dishes in the house") leads to an understanding with daughter Katherine. Webb finds satisfaction in a compassionate act: He places the gold watch in the cabinet, where Mrs. Porter will have the pleasure of finding it herself.

David Madden explains that the novel's title refers to the deep sleep into which American males of the twentieth century have allowed themselves to fall. Like the sleep induced in Adam before God created Eve from his rib, it is so deep that the man never awakens. Woman is born; she dominates, and man sleeps on. That this is a twentieth century phenomenon is demonstrated in Morris' 1980 novel *Plains Song, for Female Voices*, whose character Cora carries out her wifely duties with such distaste that she bites herself on her wedding night. Her husband Emerson feels obliged to explain to the frontier doctor that Cora suffers from the bite of a horse; the uncomplaining Cora finds most of her life as a Nebraska farmwife distasteful, but rebellion never occurs to her.

Another novel with a dead hero, *The Huge Season* is different because it is told from the single viewpoint of Peter Foley, a professor of classics in a small Pennsylvania college and himself a fully developed character. Foley attempts to escape the bondage of two experi-

ences from the past. The first took place at Colton College in California: Foley shared a suite with several other young men, among them Charles Lawrence, a would-be great tennis player who has since committed suicide. The second experience was a single day spent in New York after one of his other suitemates, Jesse Proctor, testified before the Senate Committee on Un-American Activities.

Lawrence, the hero who affects all the other men, is another Midwesterner with an audacious grandfather. Lawrence himself tries to be audacious, both in the bullring and on the tennis court. He succeeds at tennis, not because he plays well, but because he wills himself to win. As is to be expected, the hero strongly influences the lives of his witnesses—three of them actually write books about him.

Foley finally frees himself from captivity by recreating the past in his mind while wearing his hero's jacket around the house. As he achieves his own freedom, Foley at the same time understands more about America. The title of the novel refers to the past—the youth—that Foley realizes is over when he is released into the present. Lawrence, however, continues to live in the imagination of his witness, who has also acquired the tennis player's audacity.

The past, so important in *The Huge Season*, is missing in *Love Among the Cannibals*. Macgregor and Horter, two middle-aged Hollywood songwriters, take two girls to Acapulco, one a Memphis "chick" who reads Norman Vincent Peale, the other Eva the Greek. The story is about people who live to the tune of "What Next?," a song in progress when Horter and Eva meet. Their car, a fire-engine red convertible with green leather upholstery, has a built-in record player. Macgregor, a true Hollywood cliché and composer of sentimental popular music, insists that what he is looking for in a woman is "the real thing." Horter, who writes cliché lyrics because that is what Hollywood demands, persuades Billie, Eva, and Mac that they can write a Mexican musical if they have the proper setting. Mac and Billie find romance in Acapulco and swear to be true to each other, but Eva leaves with a ladybug-shaped biologist, Dr. Leggett.

The Hollywood beach with its suntan oil and portable radios symbolizes the artificial present with no traditions or values, the Mexican beach the real present, unspoiled, honest, and authentic. The two "artists" deal in clichés of the kind demanded by mass culture, but Horter recognizes that even clichés can be powerful. He is transformed in Mexico by the natural, physical powers of the Greek, who is unabashedly tanned all over. As he appreciates her vitality and audacity, he even considers returning to the life of a serious poet. He has been stripped to essentials and returned to a wholeness and a recognition of his past that bring with them a hope for the future.

After several decades of novels about women who dominated their men, lured them into sex, and left them or who married them and honeymooned shrouded in a sheet, Morris' *Plains Song, for Female Voices* should perhaps have redressed some grievances. Madge, however, the only happy wife in the novel, is content with being a bearer of children and smelling Fels-Naptha soap. Cora, a plain Ohio girl who marries Emerson to move to Nebraska, becomes Madge's mother. Cora's world is Emerson's farm, and although she finds enjoyment only with her chickens and her garden, she never considers widening her horizon. Sharon Rose, Madge's cousin, is the modern woman and artist who shuns men altogether, finding her happiness in fleeing Nebraska for Chicago and music study. Sharon cannot understand her past and why her relatives are content with their bleak lives, but she does attain a certain amount of self-knowledge.

Like so many of Morris' protagonists, Sharon tries to go home again. What startles her memory is not the paint scaling off Emerson's house but the absence of people. The dipper (a marvelous artifact) floats in a bucket of water, and Sharon smells scorched ironing. Displeased that Madge's husband Ned refers to his car as a "good girl," Sharon becomes ill when Avery, who plans to be a veterinarian, chips tartar off the teeth of a Maltese cat with his thumbnail while she is at the dinner table. On the train on the way back to Chicago, however, she is ashamed of disliking these friendly, decent people. She writes Madge's daughter to suggest that Blanche attend a private school for girls in Waukegan and spend her weekends in Chicago, because Sharon cannot bear the "thought of Blanche thick with child by some loutish youth."

When the pretty girl arrives, Sharon deliberately dresses her in a way to "emphasize her adolescence" so that the "idling males" will not be tempted to molest her. When she finds Blanche with a "beardless, oafish" young man, his arm about the girl's waist, she knows that her efforts to "citify" Blanche—actually, to make her independent—have been in vain, and she allows her to return home to her daddy, whom she missed a great deal.

Sharon finally teaches at Wellesley, more respected than liked by her students. On her last trip home for Cora's funeral, Madge's daughter Caroline assures Sharon that because of her example, the girls "don't get married anymore unless [they] want to." All that is left of her parents' farm is a pitted field of stumps. "There was nothing worth saving," says Caroline, who adds that she would never forgive Cora for her failure to complain about the hard farm life.

Funerals and eggs—an unlikely combination—continue to recur in Morris' fiction. Unlikely, until one realizes that, in a Morris novel, the dying will "connect" with and transform many characters, perhaps even achieving resurrection through them, and that eggs, important to Morris since his father sold them, represent not only a new and ongoing life but also the rural Midwest to which he returns again and again for his fictional world.

The wasteland motif, actually verbalized in some of the novels, is to be found in a society without imagination, as on the Los Angeles beach where women wear bathing caps that look like fake hair. The one who can deliver others from such a wasteland is a man or woman with a creative heart—an audacious artist who dares to transform the clichés of the past into the wonders of the present and future, who can convert the raw material of America into values that enable humankind to endure. Morris' works speak to that effort.

Other major works

SHORT FICTION: *Green Grass, Blue Sky, White House*, 1970; *Here Is Einbaum*, 1973; *Real Losses, Imaginary Gains*, 1976; *Collected Stories: 1948-1986*, 1986.
NONFICTION: *The Inhabitants*, 1946; *The Home Place*, 1948; *The Territory Ahead*, 1958, 1963; *A Bill of Rites, a Bill of Wrongs, a Bill of Goods*, 1968; *God's Country and My People*, 1968; *Love Affair: A Venetian Journal*, 1972; *Wright Morris: Structures and Artifacts, Photographs, 1933-1954*, 1975; *About Fiction: Reverent Reflections on the Nature of Fiction with Irreverent Observations on Writers, Readers, and Other Abuses*, 1975; *Earthly Delights, Unearthly Adornments*, 1978; *Will's Boy*, 1981; *Photographs and Words*, 1982; *Picture America*, 1982; *Solo: An American Dreamer in Europe, 1933-1934*, 1983; *A Cloak of Light: Writing My Life*, 1985.
MISCELLANEOUS: *Wright Morris: A Reader*, 1970; *Timepieces: Photographs, Writing, and Memory*, 1989.

Bibliography

Bird, Roy K. *Wright Morris: Memory and Imagination*. New York: Peter Lang, 1985.

Crump, G. B. *The Novels of Wright Morris: A Critical Interpretation*. Lincoln: University of Nebraska Press, 1978.

Hicks, Granville. Introduction to *Wright Morris: A Reader*. New York: Harper & Row, 1970.

Howard, Leon. *Wright Morris*. Minneapolis: University of Minnesota Press, 1968.

Knoll, Robert E., ed. *Conversations with Wright Morris: Critical Views and Responses*. Lincoln: University of Nebraska Press, 1977.

Madden, David. *Wright Morris*. New York: Twayne, 1964.

Wydeven, Joseph J. "Images and Icons: The Fiction and Photography of Wright Morris." In *Under the Sun: Myth and Realism in Western American Literature*, edited by Barbara Howard Meldrum. Troy, N.Y.: Whitston, 1985.

J. F. POWERS

Born: Jacksonville, Illinois; July 8, 1917

Principal long fiction

Morte d' Urban, 1962; *Wheat That Springeth Green*, 1988.

Other literary forms

J. F. Powers is highly regarded for his prowess as a short-story writer. "Lions, Harts, Leaping Does" (1943), only his second story to be published, appeared in the O. Henry and Martha Foley anthologies in 1944. Powers' stories appeared first in magazines such as *Accent, Collier's, Commonweal, The Nation, Kenyon Review, Partisan Review*, and *The New Yorker*. Powers has also written reviews of poetry and fiction, autobiographical pieces, and articles dealing with social issues. His nonfiction, like most of his fiction, is often satirical in tone.

Achievements

Powers is to be numbered among those American writers—others include Katherine Anne Porter and J. D. Salinger—who have produced a relatively small body of work distinguished by meticulous craftsmanship. Powers has been praised by critics and fellow writers such as Alfred Kazin, William Gass, Thomas Merton, and Stanley Edgar Hyman; the Irish master of the short story, Frank O'Connor, judged Powers to be "among the greatest of living story tellers." When Powers has drawn negative critical response, it has often been for what is deemed to be his overly parochial concerns, his narrow focus on the world of the Catholic church in America and, especially, the clergy. In fact, Powers' narrow focus is a source of strength; he writes about what he knows best, and, like excellent writers everywhere, he discovers the universal in the particular. He has a permanent place in American literature as one of the most accomplished short-story writers of the twentieth century.

Biography

James Farl Powers was born in Jacksonville, Illinois, on July 8, 1917, to James Ansbury and Zella Routzong Powers. He is one of three children. His father was a manager for Swift and Company, and the family lived in comfortable circumstances. Jacksonville was a predominantly Protestant community, and that made the Catholic Powers family part of a minority.

In 1924, the Powerses moved to Rockford, Illinois, where they lived for seven years and where James attended public schools. After another move, to Quincy, Illinois, in 1931, Powers became a student at the Franciscan-run Quincy Academy, from which he was graduated in 1935. He then moved to Chicago, where, over the next eight years, he held various jobs: insurance salesman, clerk at Marshall Field's, chauffeur, editor with Chicago Historical Records Survey, and clerk at Brentano's bookstore. From 1938 to 1940, he was taking night courses at Northwestern University. It was while he was working at Brentano's, in 1942, that he wrote his first story, "He Don't Plant Cotton," published the following year in *Accent* magazine. He was fired from Brentano's for refusing to buy war bonds.

In 1943, Powers experienced what J. V. Hagopian describes as a religious crisis. Since moving to Chicago, he had become increasingly sensitive to social issues; the status of African Americans and war were two issues with which he was particularly concerned. His moral revulsion at the injustices to which blacks were subjected was tellingly expressed in such stories as "He Don't Plant Cotton" and "The Trouble." Powers became a pacifist in 1943. Arrested two weeks after he failed to report to induction, he was, after pleading not guilty and waiving trial by jury, sentenced to serve three years in Sandstone Federal Prison in Minnesota. He was paroled in late 1944 after serving thirteen months of his sentence. In 1945, he met Elizabeth Alice Wahl at St. Benedict's College, St. Joseph's, Minnesota, and the following year they were married. Powers was a resident at the Yaddo artist's colony in 1947, the year in which *Prince of Darkness and Other Stories*, his first collection of stories, was published. The book met with very favorable critical response. In 1948, Powers received grants from the Guggenheim Foundation and the National Institute of Arts and Letters and taught at St. John's University of Collegeville, Minnesota. He continued teaching for several years, this time at Marquette University, and had another residency at Yaddo. Throughout the 1950's, Powers and his growing family (he has five children—Katherine, Mary, James, Hugh, and Jane) lived either in Minnesota or in Ireland. In 1956, when his second collection of stories, *The Presence of Grace*, was published, he taught at the University of Michigan.

Powers' first novel, *Morte d'Urban*, was published by Doubleday & Company in 1962. It won the 1963 National Book Award and the Thermod Monsen Award, given by the Chicago critics for the best book written by a Midwesterner. Powers was writer-in-residence at Smith College between 1965 and 1966. His third collection of stories, *Look How the Fish Live*, appeared in 1975. His second novel, *Wheat That Springeth Green*, was published in 1988. Besides receiving grants from the National Institute of Arts and Letters, of which he is a member, and the Guggenheim Foundation, Powers has received Rockefeller Fellowships on three occasions. He now lives in his adopted state of Minnesota.

Analysis

Powers' "world," his equivalent of William Faulkner's Yoknapatawpha County, is the American Catholic church, more particularly that church as it manifests itself in the Midwest, and more particularly still the clergy of that church. Unquestionably, Powers' best fiction is that written about Catholic priests. Choosing to write about priests was in itself an ingenious artistic ploy. The priest is by vocation, if not by disposition, an idealist and therefore presents an excellent focal point for examining the discrepancy between the ideal and the real. Powers' characters are drawn not from the common people but from a kind of scaled-down aristocracy, people from whom readers would be justified in expecting more because more has been given them.

Morte d'Urban is essentially a comic novel, not only in the sense that it is funny, which it certainly is, but also, and more important, in the sense that it is the obverse of tragic. It is the story of a priest who, though by no means a bad man, is not manifesting in his life the type of goodness of which he is capable and, more pointedly, to which he is dedicated by vows. Father Urban is a Roman Catholic priest, but on the basis of the attitudes that dominate his consciousness and the behavior in which he engages, he is more appropriately identifiable as the all-American boy. He is George F. Babbitt with a Roman collar, always on the lookout for the ecclesiastical main chance. He is intelligent, imaginative, witty, well spoken, and possessed of a seemingly inexhaustible fund of energy. He is doubtless sincere in his conviction that the various projects to which he dedicates his talents are eminently worthwhile—that is, for the good of the church and, ultimately, for the greater glory of God. Father Urban is an activist, and there is something almost intrinsically admirable in the activist, but he is a man for whom activity has become altogether too much. His "can do" attitude toward his vocation, which puts a premium on tangible results, has been nurtured over the years at the expense of his interior life. While ostensibly a man oriented toward the spiritual, he is in fact a materialist.

Father Urban is a member of the Order of St. Clement, the Clementines, of whom it has been said that their uniqueness consists in their being noted for nothing at all. He concurs in this cruel judgment, but if he belongs to a third-rate order, he takes consolation in the fact that he is its star, the scintillating exception in an organization composed, for the most part, of bland mediocrities. He behaves toward his confreres with *pro forma* charitableness, a disguise for condescension. He is in fact an accomplished preacher, and in much demand as a conductor of parish missions. When he is assigned to the Order's latest white elephant, then, a retreat house in rural Minnesota, his paranoid conviction that he is persecuted by his foolish superiors because they are jealous of his talents is only more firmly established.

In time Urban begins to see possibilities for the retreat house, St. Clement's Hill. With the financial backing of Billy Cosgrove, a wealthy Chicago layman and friend, he secures the permission of the Clementine Provincial Superior and the local bishop to build a nine-hole golf course at St. Clement's Hill. The idea behind the venture is to make the facility more attractive for the better sort of Catholic layperson, those who will not only come there to make a retreat but also leave behind them a generous donation. It would seem that Father Urban's characteristic modus operandi has stood him in good stead even in the backlands of Minnesota, but his streak of successes is put in jeopardy by the rumor that the bishop may take the retreat house away from the Clementine Order and turn it into a seminary for his diocese. The bishop visits St. Clement's Hill with a young priest of the diocese who is an expert golfer. They all take to the links together, and as the game progresses, it becomes evident to Father Urban that in his match with the young priest, the bishop's man, he has symbolically entered the lists and is involved in a trial of strength. Whatever might be the eventual fate of St. Clement's Hill, it becomes a point of honor for him that he win the golf match. Having made a nice approach shot to the final green, he is apparently on the verge of doing so when events are suddenly reversed: Father Urban is struck on the head and knocked unconscious by a golf ball hit by the bishop. This seemingly absurd incident marks the turning point of the novel.

After the accident on the golf course, as a result of which the bishop drops his plans to take over the retreat house, Father Urban's attitude toward life and toward his vocation slowly changes. His being felled by a golf ball, while not comparable to St. Paul's being knocked off his horse on the road to Damascus, precipitates a period of reassessment. During this period, Father Urban undergoes three trials, which are consonant with the Arthurian theme that is one of the informing elements of the novel. In one trial, he tries and fails to persuade Mrs. Thwaites, an elderly benefactress, with whom previously he had attempted to ingratiate himself, to restore to an innocent employee money which she had effectively stolen from her. His eyes are thus opened to the unpretty realities of Mrs. Thwaites's hypocrisy and stark avariciousness, which in the past he was inclined to overlook as supportable eccentricities. In the second trial, he goes on a fishing trip with his friend Billy Cosgrove, which results in the dissolution of the friendship. The experience proves to be painful but educative. He is made fully aware that Billy Cosgrove is not a noble human being. He is rich, yes, but he is also egotistical, childish, and pathologically cruel. In the third trial, Father Urban is put upon by Mrs. Thwaites's daughter, Sally Hopwood, rich, sophisticated, bored, and bereft of principles, who attempts to seduce him. She fails, but out of the ordeal, Father Urban comes to a new, and disturbing, consciousness of himself; he realizes that had he chosen to follow a vocation other than the priesthood, his outlook on life would not have been appreciably different from the one he entertains as a priest. He is brought to see that there is something fundamentally lacking in the quality of his priestly life.

The novel is brought to an abrupt and significant close after Father Urban is elected as the Provincial Superior of the Chicago Province of the Clementines. It is a position for which, when he was possessed of the consciousness of the "old man," he had often longed, as it would provide him with the power base to implement the kind of progressive reforms about which he had always dreamed. Here would be his chance to get the Clementines off dead-center, to shake them up, to move them toward becoming a first-rate order that had a reputation for gumption. Those who elect Father Urban

to the post have in mind the type of man who can make the right kind of friends for the order, people such as Billy Cosgrove, people who have the money to make things happen. The Father Urban who moves back to Chicago from Minnesota to become Father Provincial, however, is a radically changed man. He has undergone a conversion.

Father Urban does not die physically, but as the title *Morte d'Urban* suggests, a death does take place. Father Urban dies to the kind of life, superficial and meretricious, to which he had devoted the better part of his days, and turns to a life which, though less flamboyant, is decidedly more promising.

Powers' long-awaited second novel, *Wheat That Springeth Green*, was published in 1988. Although it was nominated for a National Book Award shortly after its publication, that honor was to elude Powers this time around. Like its predecessor, *Morte d'Urban*, this second novel is primarily the story of a priest. In this case, the protagonist is one Father Joe Hackett, who is a member of the presbyterate of an unnamed diocese in Minnesota. The world of the novel is essentially the world of the Catholic church. The novel might be described as a portrait of a modern priest, set against the background of a church, as well as a larger society, that finds itself in a state of disorientation and turmoil.

The reader encounters Joe as a young priest and watches as his tenuously founded idealism begins to give way to a spiritless pragmatism. Discovering that the daily life of a priest is often composed of prosaic and undramatic demands, he loses his initial fervor. He makes accommodations. Slowly and subtly, he becomes worldly, although his worldliness is not something of which he himself is fully aware.

The latter two-thirds of the novel takes place in the present, relative to the narrative. The year is 1968; Father Joe, now forty-four years old, is the comfortably established pastor of a well-to-do suburban parish. He fulfills his rather tightly circumscribed duties in a conscientious fashion and shows a lively alertness to the particulars of his situation. Significantly, he is guided by what has now become a conviction that his is the right way of doing things. He has developed a strong, although low-key, propensity to regard himself as somewhat the ecclesiastical "genuine article." On occasion, he seems to view himself as a lonely warrior for the right, engaged in constant battle on several fronts with several varieties of benighted bumblers and pretenders, both inside and outside the Church, by whom he is surrounded. By this time, he has become a habitual drinker, dependent upon alcohol to see him through the day. The novel ends abruptly, as if *in medias res*, after Father Joe seemingly undergoes a sort of conversion experience, which is as sudden as it is difficult to understand. In his final state, which is simply announced to the reader, Father Joe has given up drinking, as well as his suburban pastorate; he now ministers among the poor in the inner city. Somehow, the authenticity of this latest transformation is less than fully convincing. Has Father Joe finally found himself and his proper place in the Church and in the world, or is it but the stage to a further impetuous move?

It is possible to read *Wheat That Springeth Green* as an extended exercise in irony, the kind of thing one would expect from Powers. Clues to such a reading can be found, for example, in the parallels one can make between the objects of Father Joe's constant criticism and the patterns of his own behavior. He has what comes close to being an obsessive concern for what he regards as the church's preoccupation with money. He strives to present himself as the refreshing antithesis of the type of pastor who is absorbed with money, but it is debatable whether his own way of handling the finances of his parish does not in the end succeed in giving more, or at least as much, attention to money matters. The point is that the demands of a genuine poverty of spirit do not seem to be key factors in Father Joe's life.

Moreover, Father Joe scarcely comes across as a paragon of priestly virtue. He is not what would be identified as "pastoral" in his inclinations; he is anything but outgoing, and any thought to the continuing spiritual needs of his parishioners that he may have fails to manifest itself in his day-to-day activities. It is difficult to see how Father Joe's daily performance of the duties of his office stands as a marked improvement over the behavior he vigorously criticizes. Hence the irony. Father Joe falls far short of qualifying as the great Midwestern hope of a confused and blundering church.

Powers' priests embody the conflict between the ideal and the real. While posturing the ideal, the greater religious good, their behavior is dangerously real, driven by secular motives, providing the satire that enlivens Powers' work. The conflict is ultimately resolved by morality, in Powers' fictional world a morality clearly defined by Catholic theology. Powers is, however, a writer of comic fiction, and stops short of the moral answer. He recognizes that his subject is this world, not the hereafter.

Powers writes highly original tales about the toils of Roman Catholic priests in the American Midwest. Emanating from within the church, his fiction illuminates the philosophical positions and internal tensions within American Catholicism in the second half of the twentieth century.

Other major works

SHORT FICTION: *Prince of Darkness and Other Stories*, 1947; *The Presence of Grace*, 1956; *Lions, Harts, Leaping Does and Other Stories*, 1963; *Look How the Fish Live*, 1975.

Bibliography

Hagopian, John V. *J. F. Powers*. New York: Twayne, 1968.

Henault, Marie. "The Saving of Father Urban." *America* 108 (March 2, 1963): 290-292.

Iannone, Carol. "The Second Coming of J. F. Powers." *Commentary* 87, no. 1 (January, 1989): 62.

McInerny, Ralph. "The Darkness of J. F. Powers." *Crisis* 7 (March, 1989): 44-46.

Merton, Thomas. *"Morte d'Urban*: Two Celebrations." *Worship* 36 (November, 1962): 645-650.

Schmitz, Anthony. "The Alphabet God Uses." *Minnesota Monthly* (December, 1988): 35-39.

Wind, James P. "Clergy Lives: Portraits from Modern Fiction." *The Christian Century* 108, no. 25 (September 4, 1991): 805.

CARL SANDBURG

Born: Galesburg, Illinois; January 6, 1878   *Died:* Flat Rock, North Carolina; July 22, 1967

Principal poetry

Chicago Poems, 1916; *Cornhuskers*, 1918; *Smoke and Steel*, 1920; *Slabs of the Sunburnt West*, 1922; *Selected Poems of Carl Sandburg*, 1926; *Good Morning, America*, 1928; *Early Moon*, 1930; *The People, Yes*, 1936; *Chicago Poems: Poems of the Midwest*, 1946; *Complete Poems*, 1950; *Wind Song*, 1960; *Harvest Poems: 1910-1960*, 1960; *Honey and Salt*, 1963; *Breathing Tokens*, 1978 (Margaret Sandburg, ed.); *Ever the Winds of Chance*, 1983 (Margaret Sandburg and George Hendrick, eds.); *Billy Sunday and Other Poems*, 1993.

Other literary forms

Besides his poetry, Carl Sandburg wrote a multi-volume biography of Abraham Lincoln, composed children's stories, collected American folk songs, and worked for many years as a journalist. His only novel, *Remembrance Rock* (1948), summarizes the American experience from Plymouth Rock to World War II.

Achievements

Sandburg was a great communicator—as writer, poet, folk singer, and entertainer—whose poetry reaches out to millions of Americans, and he was, like his hero, Lincoln, a great spokesperson for the common American. Sandburg had a particular genius for reaching out to ordinary people and touching their lives through his poetry and song. In his public performances, one felt the power of a dynamic personality, which helped to establish the popularity of his poems.

During his lifetime, Sandburg published seven major volumes of poetry, and at his death he left enough uncollected verse for an additional posthumous volume, *Breathing Tokens*, which was edited by his daughter Margaret. Contained in these volumes are more than a thousand free-verse poems. In *The People, Yes*, he compiled a record of American folk wisdom, humor, and truisms that Willard Thorpe called "one of the great American books." Besides his six-volume Lincoln biography, he completed biographies of his brother-in-law, the photographer Edward Steichen, and of Mary Todd Lincoln. His delightful children's books, the most popular of which remains *Rootabaga Stories* (1922), were read and admired by many adults, including the architect Frank Lloyd Wright. For many years Sandburg was a regular columnist for the *Chicago Daily News*. In 1928, he was named Harvard Phi Beta Kappa poet, and twice he won the Pulitzer Prize: in 1940, in history, for his *Abraham Lincoln: The War Years* (1939) and, in 1950, in poetry, for his *Complete Poems*. Yet for many Americans he is best recalled as the genial, white-haired folk singer and poet, the embodiment of folksy Americana, who during his lifetime was called "America's best loved poet."

Chronologically, Sandburg belongs with Vachel Lindsay and Edgar Lee Masters as one of the poets of the "Chicago Renaissance." Like these other writers, he was one of the "sons of Walt Whitman." Early in his career, he adopted a style of loose, rhapsodic free verse, massive detail, a line pattern of parallelism and coordination, and the idiom and cadences of ordinary American speech. At his best, he is a verse reporter—a lyrical poet of the marketplace and the factory. More than the others of his generation, Sandburg was the poet of labor and the common individual.

Biography

Carl Sandburg was born on January 6, 1878, in Galesburg, Illinois, the second of five children in the family of August and Clara Sandburg, Swedish immigrants of peasant stock. August Sandburg was a blacksmith's helper with the Chicago, Burlington and Quincy Railroad, and his wife kept house with the children and later took in boarders. Carl had an older sister, Mary, a younger brother, Martin, and two younger sisters, Esther and Martha. Two other younger brothers died of diphtheria.

Sandburg's memories of Galesburg were of the close-knit, immigrant, working-class neighborhoods, the commemoration of the Lincoln-Douglas debate at Knox College, the pageant of General Grant's funeral procession, the excitement of the Blaine-Cleveland presidential campaign, and the tension during the railroad strike of 1888. In his childhood autobiography, *Always the Young Strangers* (1953), Sandburg recalls playing baseball in cow pastures, walking along dusty roads to the county fair, carrying water for the elephants at the circus, and swimming in the forbidden brickyard pond. He enjoyed a typical if not always carefree Midwestern boyhood. Sandburg left school at thirteen, after completing the eighth grade. He worked variously as a porter, newspaper boy, bootblack, bottlewasher, delivery boy, milkman, ice cutter, and housepainter. From these early experiences came much of Sandburg's sympathy for labor and his identification with the common person.

In 1898 Sandburg enrolled at Lombard College, a small Universalist liberal arts school, where he became active in basketball, debating, drama, the college newspaper, and the yearbook. A professor there, Philip Green Wright, encouraged Sandburg's writing interests and later arranged to publish privately several of his early poetry volumes. Although he apparently enjoyed college life, Sandburg was never graduated from Lombard; in the spring of his senior year the call of the road proved irresistible, and he left school to wander again as a hobo. This time he worked his way across the country selling stereoscopic slides and absorbing the language and folklore of the people.

In June, 1908, Sandburg married Lillian Steichen, sister of Edward Steichen (who later became a world-famous photographer). Lillian was a high school teacher and ardent idealist who shared Sandburg's socialist beliefs. They settled near Milwaukee, where he eventually worked as a reporter for the *Milwaukee Leader*. Their first daughter, Margaret, was born in 1911. A few years later he moved his family to Chicago and found a job with the *Chicago Daily News*, serving as a special correspondent and columnist for the next fifteen years.

Meanwhile, Sandburg was writing verses at night and assembling notes for what was to become his monumental Lincoln biography. On a hunch, he submitted some of his "Chicago Poems" to *Poetry* magazine, where they were published in the March, 1914, issue and won the Levinson Poetry Prize that same year. *Poetry* editor Harriet Monroe was at first disconcerted by the boldness of the opening lines of "Chicago," but she recognized their strength and championed their free verse. At the age of thirty-six, recognition had finally come to Sandburg for his poetry. The money from the Levinson prize went to pay the hospital bills for the birth of Sandburg's second daughter, Janet, but he was still not earning enough from his poetry to support his family without his newspaper work. He remained active in the socialist movement and, along with Jack London, contributed much of the copy for the *International Socialist Review* in 1915; he became disillusioned with the socialist position on World War I, however, and eventually left the party, even though he remained liberal in his politics.

A publisher's representative for Holt, Alfred Harcourt, was so impressed with Sandburg's verse in *Poetry* that he asked to examine additional poems and persuaded his firm to publish them as the *Chicago Poems* in 1916. This began a long and cordial relationship between Sandburg and Harcourt, who later founded his own publishing firm. In 1918, Sandburg was sent to New York to cover a labor convention and while there discovered he had been chosen to travel to Sweden as a special war correspondent. His knowledge of Swedish served him well there, and he was glad of the opportunity to learn more about his cultural roots. He spent the remainder of the war in Stockholm, and while he was abroad, Holt brought out his second volume of poetry, *Cornhuskers*.

Sandburg returned to the United States a seasoned reporter and a poet with a growing reputation. In 1920, Cornell College in Iowa invited him to read from his poetry, and Sandburg made his first of many visits there, entertaining the audience with a public reading and then taking out his guitar to sing folk songs for the rest of the evening. This combination of poetry recitation and folk song fest came to be the standard Sandburg repertory on his tours and won for him many admirers. Also in 1920, his third daughter, Helga, was born, and a third poetry volume, *Smoke and Steel*, was published. *Slabs of the Sunburnt West*, another collection of verse, followed in 1922, along with *Rootabaga Stories*, a collection of children's stories that Sandburg had originally written for his daughters.

By 1923, Sandburg was deeply involved in a project that would occupy much of his time for almost the next twenty years—his multivolume Lincoln biography. The plans for the book originally grew from a conversation with Alfred Harcourt about a proposed children's biography of Lincoln, although Sandburg had been interested in Lincoln since childhood and had for some years been storing up anecdotes, stories, books, articles, and clippings about him. As the manuscript progressed, it rapidly outgrew its juvenile format and Sandburg continued it as a full-scale adult biography, written in clear, concise language. The two-volume *Abraham Lincoln: The Prairie Years* met with such immediate success that Sandburg was inspired to continue his biographical portrait in the four-volume *Abraham Lincoln: The War Years*, which won for him the Pulitzer Prize for history in 1940. These same years had seen him publish a fifth volume of poetry, *Good Morning, America*, and *The People, Yes*, a compilation of American folk sayings, proverbs, clichés, and commonplaces.

More than anything else, Sandburg earned critical acclaim for his Lincoln biography, hailed as the "greatest biography by one American of another." Literary awards and honorary degrees were bestowed upon him, including doctorates from Yale and Harvard. In 1945, the Sandburgs moved from Michigan to Connemara, a picturesque mountain farm in Flat Rock, North Carolina, where Mrs. Sandburg continued to raise her prizewinning goats. The 1950's saw Sandburg reap the harvest of his long and successful career. He was honored by the states of Illinois and North Carolina and asked to give a joint address before both houses of Congress on February 12, 1959, the 150th anniversary of Lincoln's birth. During the last few years of his life, Sandburg spent more and more of his time at Connemara surrounded by his family and his grandchildren, who called him Buppong. He died at the age of eighty-nine on July 22, 1967, after a brief illness. After his death, tributes came from throughout the country, including a message from President Lyndon Johnson, who spoke for all Americans when he said that Sandburg "gave us the truest and most enduring vision of our own greatness."

Analysis

In "The American Scholar," Ralph Waldo Emerson foresaw the conditions from which American poetry would emerge when he remarked that "I embrace the common, I explore and sit at the feet of the familiar, the low." The American poet would have to sing of "the shop, the plough, and the ledger." His subject matter would come from the world of trade and commerce and his language would be that of the common man. The democratic muse would be prosaic; there would be no sublime flights of poesy. In many ways, Sandburg's poetry realized Emerson's vision. Sandburg makes clear his distaste for formal poetry in his "Notes for a Preface" to his *Complete Poems*. Instead, he is interested in the raw material for poetry, in the unpolished utterances and colloquial speech of Midwest American life. He is the poet of names and places, of trades and occupations.

Sandburg's concern for the common people is more than intellectual. Throughout his life he kept in close contact with the laboring classes and was motivated by his experiences with the populist movement. It is no coincidence that in addition to his many volumes of poetry he wrote a massive biography of Lincoln. He viewed Lincoln much the same way that he viewed the city of Chicago—as a folkloric figure of the people, standing for the average worker.

In *Chicago Poems*, which many critics believe to be the best of his early volumes, the vigorous lines of the opening apostrophe to the city itself are followed by a casual assemblage of character sketches, place descriptions, fleeting impressions, and renderings of urban life. For the most part, Sandburg employs the coarse, vigorous language of the common people to present a frank, honest portrayal of his city in all of its various moods. Poems such as "They Will Say" express a compassionate regard for the conditions of the working class. As Gay Wilson Allen, the most perceptive Sandburg critic, has observed, "A prominent theme in *Chicago Poems* is the longing of ordinary people for the beauty and happiness they have never known."

"Chicago" is one of Sandburg's most anthologized works and, according to many critics, one of his finest. The poem, written in the first person so that the poet addresses the reader directly, celebrates both the virtues and vices of the city. It begins with a staccato list of occupations found in Chicago (hog butcher, tool maker, stacker of wheat), followed by three adjectives that attach an emotion to those occupations. Carl Sandburg calls them "Stormy, husky, brawling," creating an aura of vitality. This first section of the poem is abrupt and rapid, like the city being portrayed.

The second section departs from the brief phrasing and turns to long, flowing, melodic sentences. Each of the first three sentences acknowledges a vice of the city in the first half of the sentence. It is wicked, corrupt, and brutal. The poet agrees to each accusation, supplying a specific detail that supports the charge in the second half of the sentence. There are "painted women," "gunmen," and "wanton hunger." The city does, in fact, have its failings.

The poet more than accepts the failings of his city, however; he answers in the remaining lines with a list of positive attributes. His city is singing and loud, "proud to be alive and coarse and strong and cunning." Sandburg celebrates this strength, and it is clear that the vices are a small enough price to pay for the overwhelming vitality and life the city contains.

In the last four lines, an important shift of perspective occurs. The poet personifies the city, saying it laughs as a young man does, laughs "as an ignorant fighter who has never lost a battle." This suggests a sense of innocence despite the previously mentioned corruption. Only youth laughs and feels confident regardless of circumstances. Only youth swaggers with the assurance of victory. Hence, a sense of immaturity mingles with the confidence and vitality.

"Chicago" is a celebration of America's vitality. It is about boundless energy, about love of life, about the zest and laughter that Sandburg found. Granted, the city has its dark side, but Sandburg's city laughs in the face of terrible destiny. This attitude is a prominent theme in American literature, especially in the latter half of the twentieth century.

In *Cornhuskers* and *Smoke and Steel*, Sandburg continued to explore the poetry of the Midwest, rural and urban. *Cornhuskers* includes a wider range of material than his first volume, and many of the poems reveal a new lyricism. Some of the most memorable titles evoke seasonal moods of the prairie landscape—"Prairie," "Prairie Water by Night," "Laughing Corn," "Falltime," and "Autumn Movement." Perhaps the most accomplished poem, "Prairie," shows Sandburg experimenting with variable lines and sprung rhythm. "Fire-Logs" offers a romantic treatment of a Lincoln legend, and "Southern Pacific" comments ironically on the fate of a railroad baron. In "Grass," a poem on the American war dead, Sandburg links America with the rest of the world in resignation over death's inevitability and nature's indifference to humankind. Unlike his better-known verse, "Grass" does not express faith in human capacity to transcend life's hardships. Its matter-of-fact tone is reminiscent more of Emily Dickinson than of Walt Whitman as it recognizes an unfortunate but immutable fact of life. In his mention of American battles and trains and conductors, the poet implies that even a confident America, with its brash democratic ideals, is not exempt from war, death, and nature's silent unresponsiveness.

Smoke and Steel extends the material of the previous volume, but on a less optimistic note. The title poem celebrates America's industrial prowess, but other selections reveal Sandburg's awareness of the darker side of American life in the 1920's—in the cynicism of "The Lawyers Know Too Much" and "Liars" and the gangland violence of "Killers" and "Hoodlums." Even with the inclusion of poems to his wife and daughters, *Smoke and Steel* is a less affirmative volume than Sandburg's earlier work.

With *Good Morning, America* and *The People, Yes*, Sandburg introduced a new direction in his work by reverting to the raw material of poetry in the slang and lingo of the people. Henceforth, as a poet of the people, he would take his material directly from them. At this point perhaps more folklorist than poet, Sandburg seems satisfied merely to collect and compile the words of the people rather than to exert artistic selection and control over his material. *The People, Yes* may have value as a collection of verbal portraits of the American people, but whether it is poetry in any traditional sense is debatable.

Two subsequent collections, *Complete Poems* and *Harvest Poems: 1910-1960*, each included new material and evinced a deepening of Sandburg's poetic talents. During the 1940's, he experimented with a new form of dramatized poetry or recitation—designed to be read publicly with musical accompaniment. Several of these occasional poems—"Mr. Longfellow and his Boy" and "The Long Shadow of Lincoln: A Litany" are notable for the new note of somber dignity in his free verse. Sandburg read his Lincoln litany as the Phi Beta Kappa poem at the College of William and Mary in 1944 and used the occasion to draw an implicit parallel between Lincoln's struggle during the Civil War and the nation's efforts during World War II. This same patriotic note was struck in his moving elegy on Franklin Delano Roosevelt, "When Death Came April Twelve 1945."

A major objection among Sandburg's critics has been his lack of development. Detractors point to the formulaic nature of his poems and their lack of intellectual content or complexity. They comment on his neglect of prosody and his disdain for the traditional poetic devices that make poetry a "heightened and intensified use of language." They also comment that Sandburg did not master the major poetic forms—the elegy, the ballad, the sonnet, or the lyric. The neglect of form in favor of expression is certainly a trait common to much of modern poetry, and one must ask, finally, whether Sandburg is any more deficient in this respect than his contemporaries. Certainly, in his subject matter, he spoke for a generation of Americans who witnessed their nation's move from a relatively insular, agrarian country to an industrialized, international power. The free-verse form of his poems is strangely appropriate to that subject matter.

Other major works

LONG FICTION: *Remembrance Rock*, 1948.
NONFICTION: *The Chicago Race Riots*, 1919; *Abraham Lincoln: The Prairie Years*, 1926 (2 vols.); *Steichen the*

Photographer, 1929; *Mary Lincoln: Wife and Widow*, 1932 (with Paul M. Angle); *A Lincoln and Whitman Miscellany*, 1938; *Abraham Lincoln: The War Years*, 1939 (4 vols.); *Storm over the Land: A Profile of the Civil War*, 1942; *The Photographs of Abraham Lincoln*, 1944; *Lincoln Collector: The Story of Oliver R. Barrett's Great Private Collection*, 1949; *Always the Young Strangers*, 1953; *Abraham Lincoln: The Prairie Years and the War Years*, 1954; *The Sandburg Range*, 1957; "Address Before a Joint Session of Congress, February 12, 1959," 1959; *The Letters of Carl Sandburg*, 1968 (Herbert Mitgang, ed.).

CHILDREN'S LITERATURE: *Rootabaga Stories*, 1922; *Rootabaga Pigeons*, 1923; *Abe Lincoln Grows Up*, 1928; *Potato Face*, 1930; *Prairie-Town Boy*, 1955; *The Wedding Procession of the Rag Doll and the Broom Handle and Who Was In It*, 1967; *More Rootabagas*, 1993.

ANTHOLOGIES: *The American Songbag*, 1927; *The New American Songbag*, 1950.

MISCELLANEOUS: *Home Front Memo*, 1943.

Bibliography

Allen, Gay Wilson. *Carl Sandburg*. Minneapolis: University of Minnesota Press, 1972.

Crowder, Richard. *Carl Sandburg*. New York: Twayne, 1964.

Durnell, Hazel. *The America of Carl Sandburg*. Washington, D.C.: University Press of Washington, D.C., 1965.

Golden, Harry Lewis. *Carl Sandburg*. Cleveland: World Publishing, 1961.

Hallwas, John E., and Dennis J. Reader, eds. *The Vision of This Land: Studies of Vachel Lindsay, Edgar Lee Masters, and Carl Sandburg*. Macomb: Western Illinois University Press, 1976.

Niven, Penelope. *Carl Sandburg: A Biography*. New York: Charles Scribner's Sons, 1991.

Salwak, Dale. *Carl Sandburg: A Reference Guide*. Boston: G. K. Hall, 1988.

LARRY WOIWODE

Born: Carrington, North Dakota; October 30, 1941

Principal long fiction

What I'm Going to Do, I Think, 1969; *Beyond the Bedroom Wall: A Family Album*, 1975; *Poppa John*, 1981; *Born Brothers*, 1988; *Indian Affairs*, 1991.

Other literary forms

Larry Woiwode is known primarily for his longer fiction, but he has frequently published short stories in such prominent literary periodicals as *The Atlantic* and *The New Yorker*; several of his stories have been chosen for anthologies of the year's best. *Even Tide* (1977), a book of poetry, was well received.

Achievements

Woiwode's first novel, *What I'm Going to Do, I Think*, won for him the prestigious William Faulkner Foundation Award for the "most notable first novel" of 1969 and brought him immediate critical attention. It reached the best-seller list and has been translated into several foreign languages. His second novel, *Beyond the Bedroom Wall*, actually begun before *What I'm Going to Do, I Think*, was nominated for both the National Book Award and the National Book Critics Circle Award. It became an even bigger commercial and critical success than his first novel.

Critics are quick to credit Woiwode's idiosyncratic, family-centered narratives with helping indirectly to rehabilitate the family chronicle, a genre long considered out of fashion. Woiwode's evolving canon of Neumiller narratives depicts prodigal sons and daughters who, no matter where they tread, fulfill their destiny in rediscovering their roots and the family relationships which nurtured them early in their lives. Woiwode unabashedly admires the traditional nuclear family, and his fiction underscores the value of finding one's way by retracing one's steps. His narrative strength is thus seen in the fact that, even among readers accustomed to despondent, "lost" protagonists preoccupied with discovering the mysteries of life in the squalor of the city of some illicit relationship, Woiwode can make such old-fashioned premises seem startlingly fresh and appealing.

Biography

Larry Alfred Woiwode (pronounced "why-woodee") was born in Carrington, North Dakota, October 30,

1941, and spent his early years in nearby Sykeston, a predominantly German settlement amid the rugged, often forbidding north-midwestern terrain. No doubt the beauty as well as the stark loneliness of this landscape heightened the author's appreciation for the effect of nature upon individual character. At the age of ten, he moved with his family to Manito, Illinois, another evocatively Midwestern environment capable of nurturing the descriptive powers of a budding fiction writer.

He attended the University of Illinois for five years but failed to complete a bachelor's degree, leaving the university in 1964 with an associate of arts in rhetoric. He met his future wife, Carol Ann Patterson, during this period and married her on May 21, 1965. After leaving Illinois, Woiwode moved to New York City and supported his family with free-lance writing, publishing in *The New Yorker* and other prestigious periodicals while working on two novels.

He has been a writer-in-residence at the University of Wisconsin, Madison, and has had extended teaching posts at Wheaton College (Illinois) and at the State University of New York at Binghamton. In 1977, he was awarded the doctor of letters degree from North Dakota State University. In 1988 he became Professor of English at Beth-El Institute for the Arts and Sciences, Carson, North Dakota.

Analysis

As a novelist, Larry Woiwode stands apart from most of his contemporaries in refusing to drown his characters in the angst-ridden excesses that have become so conventional in the modern American novel. His characters are not helpless victims of their times but participants in them; they are accountable not so much for what has happened to them but for what they do in response to their circumstances. Their conflicts, from Chris Van Eenanam's enigmatic search for manhood in *What I'm Going to Do, I Think* to Poppa John's drive to recover his self-identity, are not merely contrived psychological dramas played out inside their own consciousness, but compelling confrontations with the very concrete world of everyday life. This is a world that registers as authentic to the reader precisely because of Woiwode's gift for realism.

Woiwode's characters eventually recognize that the answer to their dilemmas is only partly in themselves. In the reestablishment of personal trust in friendships and the nostalgia of forgotten familial relationships, they recover a sense of balance and worth in themselves. However obliquely, the major Woiwode characters find themselves in a quest for a transcendent moral order, a renewed trust in God and humanity that will give them a reference point for their lives. This quest animates their rejection of narcissism and a search for a love and security that only marital and familial relationships can foster.

Woiwode's quirky, family-centered narratives mark the rehabilitation of the family chronicle. His fiction underscores the value of finding one's way in the modern world by retracing one's steps in his or her family legacy. Woiwode's willingness to affirm that family relationships are central to self-fulfillment and to the stability of American culture makes him unique among a generation of writers whose thematic concerns tend to focus on their characters' dehumanization in society and alienation from family life and marital fidelity. Woiwode thus belongs in the company of self-consciously moralistic writers such as Walker Percy and Saul Bellow, who are more interested in the ways human beings survive and thrive in a fallen world than in the ways they capitulate to it.

Woiwode's first novel, *What I'm Going to Do, I Think*, is an absorbing character study of two newly-weds, each of whom is originally drawn to the other as opposites proverbially attract. Chris Van Eenanam, the protagonist, is a listless mathematics graduate student, an unhappy agnostic unsure of his calling in life. The novel's title accentuates his self-doubt and indecision, echoing something Chris's father once said in observing his accident-prone son, "What I'm going to do, I think, is get a new kid." Ellen Strohe, his pregnant bride, is a tortured young woman, dominated by the overbearing grandparents who reared her after her parents' accidental death. Neither she nor Chris can abide their interference and meddling.

In this retreat from the decisions Chris elects not to make, the couple, now intimate, now isolated, confront a grim modern world, which has lost its faith in a supreme being fully in control of his created universe. This loss is exemplified most dramatically in the lives of Chris and Ellen as they try to sort out the meaning of affection and fidelity in their new relationship as husband and wife and as potential parents. Ellen's pregnancy is at first a sign of a beneficent nature's approval of their union, but later, as each has a premonition of their unborn child's death, it becomes a symbol of an ambivalent world's indifference to their marriage and its apparent fruitlessness.

In the absence of a compensatory faith even in humankind itself, a secondary faith arguably derived from faith in God, Chris and Ellen come to realize that they have lost their ability to navigate a hostile world with lasting, meaningful relationships. Neither mathematics nor nature can fill the vacuum left by an impotent faith whose incessant call is to fidelity and perseverance without passion or understanding. In a suspenseful epilogue that closes the novel with an explanation of what has happened to them in the seven years following their marriage, Chris and Ellen return to their honeymoon cabin. Chris retrieves the rifle he has not touched in many years, and, as the action builds toward what will apparently be his suicide, he repeats to himself the beginning of a letter (suicide note?) that he could not complete: *"Dear El, my wife. You're the only person I've ever been able to talk to and this is something I can't say. . . . "*

As he makes his way to the lake, he fires a round of ammunition into a plastic bleach container half-buried in the sand. In the novel's enigmatic final lines, Chris fires "the last round from his waist, sending the bullet out over the open lake." This curious ending seems intended by Woiwode to announce Chris's end of indecision—a recognition that his life can have transcendent meaning only in embracing fully his marriage commitment to Ellen.

The expansiveness and comic vitality of Woiwode's second novel, *Beyond the Bedroom Wall*, offer a marked contrast to *What I'm Going to Do, I Think*. In *Beyond the Bedroom Wall*, Woiwode parades sixty-three characters before the reader by the beginning of chapter 3. True to its subtitle, "A Family Album," *Beyond the Bedroom Wall* is a sprawling, gangly work of loosely connected snapshots of the Neumiller family. An engaging homage to the seemingly evaporating family unit at the end of the twentieth century, the novel's "plot" is nearly impossible to paraphrase, consisting as it does of some narrative, some diary entries, and even its protagonist Martin Neumiller's job application for a teaching position.

The novel opens in part 1 with the funeral of Charles

Neumiller, a German immigrant farmer who had brought his family to America before the war, and it continues, to part 5, closing with stories of the third generation of Neumillers in 1970, bringing the Neumiller family full circle from birth to life to death. Yet it is Martin Neumiller, Charles's son, a god-fearing, devoutly Catholic man and proud son of North Dakota, whose adventures and misadventures give the novel any unity it possesses. "My life is like a book," he says at one point. "There is one chapter, there is one story after another." The eccentric folks he encounters in and out of his extended family form a burlesque troupe of characters who boisterously sample both the joys and the sorrows of life on Earth. In the Neumiller "family album," Woiwode lends concreteness to his notion that reality is a fragile construction, one that sometimes cannot bear scrutiny "beyond the bedroom wall," that is, beyond the dreamy world of sleep, of its visions of what might be. Woiwode intimates that whatever hope there may be for fulfilling one's dreams, it is anchored in "walking by faith, and not by sight," by trusting in and actively nurturing family intimacy.

The rather sentimental, "old-fashioned" quality Woiwode achieves in this family chronicle, his evocation of once-embraced, now-lamented values, prompted critic and novelist John Gardner to place Woiwode in the company of literature's greatest epic novelists: "When self-doubt, alienation, and fashionable pessimism become a bore and, what's worse, a patent delusion, how does one get back to the big emotions, the large and fairly confident life affirmations of an Arnold Bennett, a Dickens, a Dostoevsky? *Beyond the Bedroom Wall* is a brilliant solution."

Woiwode's eye for the rich details of daily life enables him to move through vast stretches of time and space in executing the episodic structure in this novel. His appreciation for the cadences of Midwestern speech and his understanding of the distinctiveness of prairie life and landscape and its impact on the worldviews of its inhabitants recall other regional writers such as Rudy Wiebe and Garrison Keillor at their best.

In *Born Brothers*, Woiwode returns to the characters, setting, and moral center that brought him his greatest and most uniformly favorable critical attention. Woiwode begins what he calls not a sequel but a "companion volume" to *Beyond the Bedroom Wall* in the middle of the twentieth century, the narration filtered through the consciousness of Charles Neumiller, a lost soul searching his memories for a meaning to life and a purpose for living it. He finds both in exploring his relationship with his brother Jerome. Charles's fragmentary childhood memories in fact become the narrative building blocks for the often elliptical and multiperspectived chronicle that unravels before the reader in an even more challenging sequence than that of *Beyond the Bedroom Wall*. *Born Brothers* contains less a plot than a chain of remembrances; as family members and their ahistorical interactions with Charles are paraded before the reader in a kind of visual patchwork, one is compelled to enter Charles's consciousness and see the world through his convoluted epistemology.

Despite his outward sophistication and sense of being, Charles is obsessed with suicide; he seems incapable of conceiving of a meaningful order outside the family structure that had shaped his life and has now dissipated with the death of his mother and the collapse of his marriage. In part, it is Woiwode's intent to explain American society's apparent moral disintegration—rampant promiscuity, unwanted pregnancy, and divorce—by reference to the absence of strong family ties. Charles longs for the bond of brotherhood he once shared—or thinks he shared—with elder brother Jerome. That idyllic childhood in North Dakota, free from the cares and stresses of modern industrial life, impinges without provocation upon Charles's consciousness. Charles's strange career as a "radio personality" who is both the interviewer and the interviewee is somehow emblematic of his need for conversion, for freedom from self. He needs an "outside," a reference point, which, Woiwode hints, will come only from faith in the transcendent God whose eternal family Charles is invited to join.

Woiwode makes few compromises for the reader unwilling to attend to—or, perhaps eavesdrop upon—Charles Neumiller's open-ended musings. To refer to his ramblings as stream-of-consciousness narration is to give too precise a labeling, for not merely a consciousness is under consideration here but the history of a mind and a life as well.

To understand Woiwode's craft and achievement, one must finally recognize the essentially religious character of his narratives and their thematic structure. Woiwode believes that the most important human questions are religious in nature. He thus stands out as an advocate for restoring a moral, even religious, voice to modern letters and promises to become one of North America's more studied and imitated writers of regional narrative.

Other major works

SHORT FICTION: *The Neumiller Stories*, 1989; *Silent Passengers: Stories*, 1993.
POETRY: *Even Tide*, 1977.
NONFICTION: *Acts*, 1993.

Bibliography

Connaughton, Michael E. "Larry Woiwode." In *American Novelists Since World War II*, edited by James E. Kibler, Jr. 2d ser. Detroit: Gale Research, 1980.
Gardner, John. Review of *Beyond the Bedroom Wall*, by Larry Woiwode. *The New York Times Book Review* 125 (September 28, 1975): 1-2.
Pesetsky, Bette. Review of *Born Brothers*, by Larry Woiwode. *The New York Times Book Review* 93 (August 4, 1988): 13-14.
Woiwode, Larry. "An Interview with Larry Woiwode." *Christianity and Literature* 29 (1979): 11-18.

VIII

AMERICANS ABROAD
Identities Lost and Found

It's a complex fate, being an American. . . .
—Henry James, letter to Percy Lubbock, 1872

American writers have lived outside the United States and enriched their work with international perspectives since the earliest days of the Republic; witness Benjamin Franklin, Washington Irving, James Fenimore Cooper, and Nathaniel Hawthorne. After the Civil War, for the first time in U.S. history, Europe became not only an experience but, to use one of Henry James's favorite words, an "opportunity." Henry Wadsworth Longfellow spent three years of travel and study in Europe before becoming a professor of modern languages at Harvard. Having written Abraham Lincoln's campaign biography, William Dean Howells was rewarded with the consulship at Venice. He kept it for five years, writing travel sketches of Italy and essays on Italian comedy. Mark Twain was the darling of audiences not only throughout the United States but also on the Continent and in England. His first book, *The Innocents Abroad* (1869), had him play the Southwestern primitive in both Europe and the Middle East. For Henry James, on the contrary, Europe was the treasure house of tradition, art, manners—indeed, all of civilization—and enabled him to become a distinguished author.

No writer has ever pursued more persistently the cultural manifestations of not only the United States but also England, France, and Italy than Henry James. James's views on the art of fiction derive from America's Nathaniel Hawthorne, England's George Eliot, France's Honoré de Balzac, and Russia's Ivan Turgenev. His main focus as a writer is international: on the role of the American, as the New Man, in his relations with the Old World, Europe. His major fictional theme

is the New Man's—or Woman's—loss of innocence upon exposure to Europe's more alluring and profound but also more amoral and treacherous world.

As a youth, James frequently lived in Europe with his family, and he found himself dazzled by its splendid cities, with their glorious architecture, museums, music and theaters, and the stability and order of continental manners. He began his long expatriation in 1872, with trial residences in France and Italy. In 1876 he settled in England, making London his primary home; in 1898 he removed to an estate in Rye, Sussex; in 1915, in an act of allegiance to a Great Britain embattled in World War I, he became a British subject.

In his mature years, James came to view the Old World's civilization, despite his fascination with it, from a highly skeptical perspective. In his greatest novels, such as *The Portrait of a Lady* (1880-1881), *The Wings of the Dove* (1902), *The Ambassadors* (1903), and *The Golden Bowl* (1904), he narrates intricate dramas of differences between inexperienced Americans with an innate moral sense and experienced Europeans without it who often prove corrupt and conspiratorial. In contrast to such contemporary American authors as Mark Twain, who considered the frontier experience as their country's model, James regarded the United States not only as wealthy and energetic but also as eager to create a high civilization. His American protagonists, such as Isabel Archer and Lambert Strether, embody an innate goodness and sensitivity that triumph spiritually over both the crudeness of their own country and the ruthlessness of Europe.

In 1925, in a study of Henry James, the critic Van

Wyck Brooks warned that American writers like James who left their country to reside abroad risked blighting their art by separating themselves from native materials and audiences. Many authors chose to disregard this danger, particularly during and shortly after World War I. Some, like Archibald MacLeish, e. e. cummings, John Dos Passos, and F. Scott Fitzgerald, lived abroad for a limited number of years. Others, like Richard Wright, James Jones, and James Baldwin, made their reputations in America but moved to France in midlife. Still others made their careers permanently overseas; Ezra Pound, T. S. Eliot, and Gertrude Stein belong in this category.

In 1908 a twenty-two-year-old budding poet and scholar of Romance languages was dismissed from his teaching position at Wabash College, Indiana, for having sheltered an unemployed burlesque queen. Ezra Pound thereupon migrated briefly to Venice, then settled in London for a decade. In 1925 he moved to Rapallo, Italy. His espousal of Fascism and anti-Semitism made him notorious during World War II. Imprisoned in 1945 and returned to the United States for trial, he was declared insane and spent the years from 1946 to 1958 as a patient in St. Elizabeths Hospital, Washington, D.C. He then returned to Italy for the rest of his life, except for a lengthy visit to America in 1969.

Pound made his reputation in England and Italy not only as an important poet, critic, and translator but also as a remarkably energetic and generous booster of and publicist for the work of T. S. Eliot, Robert Frost, William Carlos Williams, and James Joyce. He and his friend Eliot achieved enormous influence in London's literary culture and pioneered the revolution that established such modernist poetic modes as Imagism, vorticism, and a new language based on the irregular rhythms of contemporary speech.

Yet Pound never lost his sense of his American identity. He despised his native land's provinciality, particularly "the thin milk of New York and New England." However, his autobiographical text, *Indiscretions* (1923), dwells proudly on the frontier life of his lumberjack grandfather and the reputation his mother's family had for horse stealing. He enjoyed using colloquial American idioms in his poetry and raw American slang in his letters and criticism. His reaction to what he scorned as America's lack of worldliness was to establish cosmopolitan and transnational standards of literary taste. Pound's insistence on a radically new poetic structure was Emersonian in its boldness and noncon-

formity. His major, not quite completed work, the *Cantos* (1915-1972), resembles Walt Whitman's *Song of Myself* (1855). To be sure, the *Cantos*' form and technique contradict those of Whitman's long poem: Where Whitman wanted to project his sense of self upon the world, Pound wanted to project the world upon his self. Still, Pound's poem amounts, like Whitman's, to a quest for an ideal social order. His historic/literary pantheon of heroes includes not only Homer and Dante but also John Adams and Thomas Jefferson, Henry James, and, yes, Walt Whitman.

Like Pound, Thomas Stearns Eliot longed for order and hierarchy and despised both democracy and industrial capitalism. Unlike the nonreligious, pagan Pound, however, he was to become a devout religionist as well as a royalist in politics. The two poets were to affect one another's work profoundly, with Pound shaping Eliot's mass of brilliant fragments into what may be the twentieth century's greatest poem, *The Waste Land* (1922).

Like James, Eliot was a transatlantic writer who established long residence in England and became a British subject yet retained a strong spiritual allegiance to his native America. Deeper parallels unite these writers: Whereas James became an influential critic of the craft of fiction, Eliot became the dominant theorist of the art of Anglo-American poetry for several decades. Both writers excelled in complex perceptions and technical virtuosities. Both were profoundly intellectual, erudite, and psychologically astute, filtering their feelings through intricate verbal structures. Both were products of the "genteel tradition," descended from white Anglo-Saxon Protestants in the northeastern United States.

Although Eliot was born in St. Louis, his ancestors had previously lived in Massachusetts since the seventeenth century. His undergraduate and most of his graduate studies, in poetry and philosophy, were at Harvard, where the professors deeply affected him: the neo-humanist Irving Babbitt, with his fondness for tradition in literature and philosophy, and George Santayana, whose interest in Dante stirred Eliot's lifelong veneration for that poet. In 1914 Eliot settled for what was to be the rest of his life in England, recovering roots there which he found even stronger than his American heritage. In 1927 he took both British citizenship and confirmation in the Anglican church.

The distinguished American critic Edmund Wilson wrote several essays on Eliot's poetry in the 1920's and early 1930's, which insisted on the importance of Eliot's American Puritan temperament in his work. Wilson stressed the American sources of Eliot's fastidiousness and fear of vulgarity, his focus on unexplored opportunities and inhibited passions in such poetic personae as Sweeney and Prufrock. The parallel was again drawn to Henry James, with his persistent theme of the life lived too cautiously and hence too sadly.

In his reevaluation and reshaping of poetic tradition, Eliot was in the American grain of Emerson, Thoreau, and Whitman in seeking to reconstitute the language of his craft. And in his depersonalized theory of literature, arguing that "the poet has, not a 'personality' to express, but a particular medium" and that "the emotion of art is impersonal," Eliot follows not only Gustave Flaubert's doctrines of the aesthetic autonomy of art but also Edgar Allan Poe's earlier insistence, in "The Philosophy of Composition," on purity of style and avoidance of didacticism. Paradoxically, the writer who left his native land at the age of twenty-six never forgot America's literary past and became the dominant American man of letters for the first half of the twentieth century.

While Pound and Eliot modernized and reoriented the twentieth century's poetry, Gertrude Stein helped to discipline its prose by instructing the many writers who visited her in the art of composing concisely, clearly, dryly, and precisely. Her significance as a mentor considerably exceeded her uneven achievement as an author.

Born into a prosperous German-Jewish family in Baltimore, Stein was first exposed to Europe when her family lived in Austria and France from 1875 to 1879. She followed her beloved brother Leo from the University of California at Berkeley to Harvard, where William James regarded her as the best female student he had ever taught. In 1902 she and Leo moved to Paris.

There Stein began her stylistic experiments in writing, stressing repetitions and recurrences to capture the essential qualities of people and perceptions, echoing American cadences in her calculatedly flat, simple diction. She claimed to have taught Sherwood Anderson and Ernest Hemingway to write according to the natural rhythms of speech as they frequented the famous salon she was to keep in Paris for her remaining life.

Stein's most popular novel, *Three Lives* (1909), includes a superb portrait of a black working woman, Melanctha Herbert, that constitutes perhaps the first successful treatment of a modern black character by a white author. In her most ambitious novel, *The Making of Americans* (1925), she narrates the history of several German-Jewish families, including her own, in prolix meditations that many readers found too fragmented to

follow. After the liberation of France in 1944, she renewed her native heritage by welcoming hundreds of American troops to her home. World War II had strengthened her identification of herself as an American.

In the 1920's, a large and talented group of young writers and artists from the United States became at least temporary expatriates living in Paris. What united them was the assumption that the Great War had irreparably damaged the spiritual and cultural values of Western society. "You are all a lost generation" was the characterization by Gertrude Stein that seemed to sum up their sense of emptiness, drift, apprehension, and despair. Ernest Hemingway, whose legs had been shattered by shrapnel while he was serving on the Italian front, used Stein's famous phrase as an epigraph to his first novel, *The Sun Also Rises* (1926). Themes of disillusionment, loss, and defeat pervade Hemingway's fiction, though his protagonists accept their wounds with tight-lipped fortitude and dignity, what he termed "grace under pressure."

The formative parent in the upscale Chicago suburb where Hemingway was reared was his father, a physician who took the boy hunting and fishing in the woods of northern Michigan. Ernest returned to these rituals in his Nick Adams stories, which dramatize his youth and young manhood, recounting events of brutal violence in the spare, terse prose that revolutionized American writing.

Hemingway lived and traveled abroad most of his life, beginning in 1918, when he volunteered for ambulance service in Italy. After a two-year return to the United States, he moved to Paris in 1921 with a letter of introduction to Gertrude Stein. He was to write about international settings in most of his stories, novels, and essays: France, Italy, Switzerland, Spain, Africa, Cuba. He simultaneously lived in these places, and the residences he chose in the United States were in places peripheral to American culture: Key West, Florida, and Ketchum, Idaho.

Nonetheless, Hemingway's cult of embattled individualism is deeply embedded in America's psyche. His heroes affirm qualities of compassion and loneliness, craftsmanship and decency, honor and endurance which also inform the myths of the American frontier. No wonder that Hemingway's most cherished literary model was Mark Twain, from whose *Huckleberry Finn*, he asserted in a hyperbolic moment, all modern American literature originates. His other mentors for his disciplined prose style were also native: the style sheet of the *Kansas City Star*, where he worked briefly as a cub reporter, which banned most adjectives and encouraged vigorous, short sentences, and the tutelage in France by Gertrude Stein, who taught him to evoke through diction and rhythm the essential physical quality of an experience or object. Yet the obsession with death and the tone of despairing irony with which his autobiographical heroes brood on its prospect are Hemingway's own patent. *Winner Take Nothing* (1933) was not only the title of one of his story collections; it was also the essence of Hemingway's tragic metaphysics.

The quintet of expatriate writers considered in the following section all exemplify the mind- and soul-expanding benefits of multiculturalism. All five crossed frontiers of language, chauvinism, and history without either prejudice or illusion, learning to live and work against the background of international settings. All five used both European and American sources for their literary inspiration and techniques. All five belonged, not to one country alone, but to a worldwide, cosmopolitan sphere that liberated their imagination and enriched their art. All five exiled themselves from their native land not to repudiate it but to redefine, strengthen, and deepen the definitions of what it means to be an American.

—Gerhard Brand
Seattle, Washington

T. S. ELIOT

Born: St. Louis, Missouri; September 26, 1888   **Died:** London, England; January 4, 1965

Principal poetry

Prufrock and Other Observations, 1917; *Poems*, 1919; *Ara Vos Prec*, 1920; *The Waste Land*, 1922; *Poems, 1909-1925*, 1925; *Ash Wednesday*, 1930; *Triumphal March*, 1931; *Sweeney Agonistes*, 1932; *Words for Music*, 1934; *Collected Poems, 1909-1935*, 1936; *Old Possum's Book of Practical Cats*, 1939; *Four Quartets*, 1943; *The Cultivation of Christmas Trees*, 1954; *Collected Poems, 1909-1962*, 1963; *Poems Written in Early Youth*, 1967; *The Complete Poems and Plays*, 1969.

Other literary forms

When he startled the poetic world with the publication of *Prufrock and Other Observations* in 1917, T. S. Eliot was already on his way to becoming a prolific, formidable, and renowned literary critic of extraordinary originality and depth. Between 1916 and 1920, for example, he contributed almost a hundred essays and reviews to several journals, some of which he helped to edit. He published thirty books and pamphlets and scores of essays, many of which remain uncollected. From the inception of *The Criterion* in 1922 until its last issue in 1939, Eliot was its editor and an important contributor to that and other journals concerned with literary, cultural, political, and religious matters. Eliot came to drama later than to poetry and criticism, though the seeds of drama are clearly in his early poetry, and the drama occupied much of his criticism. All of his dramatic work has as one of its objects the restoration of poetic drama to the popular theater.

The record of Eliot's achievement is by no means complete. Many of his essays are available only in the journals in which they were published, and his notebooks have not been fully mined. Eliot's thousand or so letters to Emily Hale have not been published; they are in the Princeton University Library and may be made public after January 1, 2020.

Achievements

The achievements of Eliot are such that he became the premier poet of his own generation and enlivened literary criticism by contributing such phrases as "objective correlative," "dissociation of sensibility," and "impersonal poetry." He fostered a resurgence of interest in Dante, in the Metaphysical poets of the seventeenth century, and in Elizabethan and Jacobean drama. He also provided a strong critical and poetic voice that chided the Victorian and Edwardian poets while furnishing a new poetry that served as a practical criticism of theirs.

Eliot's poetic originality, called into question in his early days by those who charged him with plagiarism, lies in the careful crafting and arrangement of lines and phrases, the introduction of literary, historical, and cultural allusions, and the elaboration of image and symbol in highly charged and often dramatic language that both describes and presents a personal emotion or experience and generalizes it. Eliot's careful husbanding of words, phrases, images, and symbols results in a recurrence of those elements and a continuity of subject matter from his juvenilia through his first and second masterpieces ("The Love Song of J. Alfred Prufrock" and *The Waste Land*) to his last (*Four Quartets*). The themes of his greater poems, like those of his lesser ones, involve identity, sexuality, the nature of love, religious belief (or its absence), and the telling of a tale/writing of a poem in language adequate to the emotion or state that the telling/writing seeks to express. Above all, Eliot expressed the angst of an entire generation of poets who, in the wake of World War I's failure to make the world "safe for democracy," articulated a loss of moral certitude. In many ways, Eliot led what Gertrude Stein called the "lost generation" in proclaiming this new world a moral and spiritual "waste land." The fact that he was an expatriate writer can be seen as a metaphor for a loss of faith in the innocence and idealism of pre-World War I America. Eliot's achievements have led at least one critic to state that in the area of humane letters the larger part of the twentieth century may be called the Age of Eliot.

No stranger to prizes and awards, Eliot may have valued, and needed, the *Dial* award of 1922 for *The Waste Land*. In the course of his long career he received doctoral degrees (*honoris causa*) from a score of British, European, and American universities; was Clark Lecturer at Trinity College, Cambridge (1926), and

Charles Eliot Norton Professor of Poetry at Harvard University (1932-1933); and won the Hanseatic Goethe Prize (1954), the Dante Gold Medal (Florence, 1959), the Emerson-Thoreau Medal (American Academy of Arts and Sciences, 1959), and the U.S. Medal of Freedom (1964). In 1948 he achieved a dual distinction: Not only was he awarded the British Order of Merit, but he also won the Nobel Prize in Literature for, he surmises, "the entire corpus."

Biography

Thomas Stearns Eliot's grandfather, the Reverend William Greenleaf Eliot, forsook his native New England and went with missionary zeal to the outpost of St. Louis, Missouri, in 1834. There he founded the (first) Unitarian church of the Messiah and later founded Washington University (originally, Eliot Seminary), where he became chancellor (1870-1887). In the year after William Eliot's death, on September 26, 1888, Thomas Stearns Eliot, the seventh child of a second son, was born to Henry and Charlotte (Stearns) Eliot. Eliot matriculated at Harvard College, where he received a B.A. degree (1909) and pursued graduate studies (1910-1914), completing but not defending a doctoral dissertation on the philosophy of F. H. Bradley (published, 1964).

During the years 1910 and 1917, Eliot spent time in Europe. A fellowship stipend allowed him to enroll at Merton College, Oxford, at the onset of World War I. On September 22, 1914, Eliot met Ezra Pound; it was an event that marked the forging of a spiritual bond that endured for the rest of Eliot's life. It was largely through Pound's influence that the poems of *Prufrock and Other Observations* were first published in American and English periodicals. Eliot's marriage to Vivien Haigh-Wood, on June 26, 1915, was followed by brief periods of teaching and lecturing.

Eliot's literary activity between 1916 and 1922 was prodigious: It was the time of his numerous essays and reviews for *The Egoist*, *The Dial*, *Athenaeum*, the *Times Literary Supplement*, and many other journals, of *Prufrock and Other Observations*, *Ara Vos Prec*, *Poems*, and his masterpiece, *The Waste Land*. That work would catapult him to a prominence attained by no other poet of the twentieth century. In 1922 he assumed the editorship of *The Criterion*. In 1927 Eliot experienced a sea change: He became a communicant in the Church of England (June 29) and then a British subject (November).

Before returning from his post as Norton Professor of Poetry at Harvard (1932-1933), Eliot obtained a legal separation from his wife (to whom he had dedicated *Ash Wednesday*) and lectured at the University of Virginia on Christian apologetics, a subject of increasing interest for him. His poetry of the 1930's centered on verse drama and on such disparate efforts as "Five Finger Exercises," "Triumphal March," and *Old Possum's Book of Practical Cats*; but the highlights of the decade are *Ash Wednesday*, *Murder in the Cathedral* (1935), and his best poem of those years, "Burnt Norton."

The first of the poems later to comprise *Four Quartets*, "Burnt Norton" was followed by "East Coker" (1940), "The Dry Salvages" (1941), and Eliot's own *Paradiso*, "Little Gidding" (1942). In the years following the publication of *Four Quartets*, Eliot wrote little poetry; he kept writing verse drama and began to enjoy generous recognition of his work; notably, he received the Nobel Prize in Literature in 1948, a year after the death of Vivien. His marriage to Valerie Fletcher (January 10, 1957) marked another of the many turning points of his life—this time a turn for the better in a happy marriage. Eliot truly became, in the 1940's, 1950's, and 1960's, the elder statesman of letters. His position in the history of modern poetry became unassailable.

Eliot died on January 4, 1965, survived by Valerie. His ashes were interred in the parish church at East Coker, Somerset, the church of his English ancestors, and a memorial was placed in the Poets' Corner, Westminster Abbey.

Analysis

Critic, dramatist, and Nobel laureate, Eliot became one of the twentieth century's leading poets, a writer squarely in the forefront of the modernist movement. In a literary career spanning more than fifty years, he was hailed as the premier poet of the age, acclaimed especially for "The Love Song of J. Alfred Prufrock," *The Waste Land*, and *Four Quartets*, his three masterworks. In his verse he explored the essentially modernist themes of anxiety, depersonalization, the quest for identity and meaning, and the search for meaning through language; he also examined the timeless theme of love, both erotic and divine, and the physical and spiritual dualities of human existence.

One useful approach to Eliot's poetry is to examine voices and fragments as they announce and illustrate themes. These fragments consist mainly of highly allusive phrases and quotations, of intricately wrought verbal symbols, of lines of direct simplicity and complex opacity, of passages of sheer beauty and crabbed commonality fixed in formulated phrases, arranged and rearranged until, in the best of the poetry, one finds the complete consort dancing together. The voice or voices in the poems are usually those that repeat formulas embedded in literary, cultural, and religious traditions—uncertain voices that often betray their speakers' lack of self-knowledge or clear identity. The voices speaking the fragments, even the unified voice of *Four Quartets*, are the voices of humanity (though often a special order of humanity) seeking, as they turn over the fragments and seek the sense of sounds, to understand, explain, and identify themselves in terms of the past, present, and future.

"The Love Song of J. Alfred Prufrock" forms the nucleus for Eliot's first volume of poetry, *Prufrock and Other Observations*, in which he may justly be said to have inaugurated modern poetry in English. The work is a dramatic, if static, monologue. It is heavily influenced by Jules Laforgue's poetic technique in that it presents an interior landscape of atomized consciousness. The male narrator (the voice) worries about the possibility of an erotic encounter as he puzzles over his own identity, his too-conscious sense of self, his meaning and place in a surreal and menacing universe of his own devising, and his observations (objective and subjective genitive, as James Joyce phrased it) while he confides to a reader (who is called upon to become part of Prufrock's divided self) the fragmented perceptions of himself and his situation. Prufrock does not, however, arrive at any conclusions about the encounter or about his own identity and meaning.

The epigraph (Dante, *Inferno*, XXVII) provides a key to the incongruous "love song" of an impossible lover and sets the reader squarely in Hell listening to a reluctant speaker (who cannot say what he means) who will confide in the auditor/reader as Guido did in the character Dante, "without fear of infamy," without fear that the secret will be revealed on earth (will become the subject of "observations"), particularly in the hearing of the perplexing women who "come and go" in the troublesome room or of the desirable but distant and somewhat fearsome recumbent woman. It is possible to exclude the "reader" as the addressee of this poem and to read it as an interior dialogue between "self" and "soul": Such a reading would heighten to a clinical level the disorder or identity that is sensed in Prufrock's divided self.

The voice that addresses the reader in scraps of experience remembered and fearfully anticipated and in fragments of historical- and self-consciousness does so in response to a question, presumably posed by the reader in a Dantesque role. As Hugh Kenner aptly points out, the reader enters a "zone of consciousness" in the poem, not a verifiable or constant "realistic" setting. Prufrock is not a "real" character who tells a logical or temporally sequential story. Indeed, the reader participates in the unfolding narrative by hearing and deciding what is part of the world of recognizable experience and what is intrinsic to a fragmented, disjointed, disordered, diseased consciousness that speaks familiarly ("you and I") of a shared boredom of social rounds and obligations, of the terror of rejection, and (the greater Prufrockian terror) of acceptance and surrender in sexual contact—all of which contribute to a sense of cognitive and emotional paralysis (accidia) for which Prufrock finds a disordered "objective correlative" in the "sky/ Like a patient etherised upon a table."

The literary fragments in the poem include the central situational analogue in the *Inferno*, the Polonian self-caricature, and grotesque visions of St. John the Baptist and Lazarus returned from the dead. None of the characters in the fragments belongs to the realm of the living, and all represent an inability "to say just what I mean."

The Waste Land preserves the pattern of monologue that Eliot established in his previous work. Structurally, the work is a series of five poems that constitute one poem. Eliot wrote (note to 1.218), "Tiresias, although a mere spectator and not indeed a 'character,' is yet the most important personage in the poem, uniting all the rest. . . . What Tiresias *sees*, in fact, is the substance of the poem." One may, on Eliot's authority, read the poem as an account of Tiresias' observations as he guides the reader through his own memory to various locations in *The Waste Land* as seen or remembered on a journey that is both in and out of time. Thus, many elements fall into place as Tiresias subsumes all the characters or speakers in a multilayered, cyclical ritual of death and rebirth. Alternatively, one may read the poem as a series of fragmented monologues, in the manner of "The Love Song of J. Alfred Prufrock," so that Tiresias' voice becomes only one among many voices.

Assuming that this is a Symbolist poem, perhaps the Symbolist poem of the twentieth century, the historical and cultural dimensions that many critics have so ably attributed to it (as being a poem about the disillusionment of a particular generation, about the 1920's, about London, and so on) recede. So, too, do the ubiquitous anthropological considerations of barren land, infertility, initiation rites, and the death of gods. Both sets of data may, then, be treated as "objective correlatives" for emotions that the poet seeks to express. What remain as underlying themes are sexual disorder (basic to the Grail and vegetation myths), the lack of and need for religious belief (accented negatively by the presence of Madam Sosostris and positively in "The Fire Sermon" and "What the Thunder Said"), and the process of poetic composition (fragments "shored against my ruins").

The diverse interpretations of what the poem is about have obvious implications for how one values the fragments of which it is composed and, to return to the question of voice, how one identifies the speaker and the burden of his speech. If, for example, one assumes that the blind, androgynous Tiresias speaks in many voices and does so with foreknowledge of all, one may conclude that the work stands as a monument to the disillusionment not of one generation but of many. One may also find that the slight progress of the Fisher King from the dull canal behind the gashouse (III) to the shore (V) has slight significance and that the question about setting his lands in order is, like shoring fragments against ruins, all that can be done before capitulating to the inevitable continuation of a condition in which the land will remain waste. Tiresias has, after all, foreseen this, too. If one assumes a multiplicity of voices, however, beginning with Marie, the Hyacinth Girl (or, in the epigraph, with the Sibyl's complaint and the voice speaking of it), and ending with the Fisher King, the Thunder, and a new voice (or many voices) speaking in the poem's last lines, one has a quite different experience of the poem. In the second reading one treats the work as a series of soliloquies or monologues all mixing memory with quite different desires, all commenting on various meanings (or lack of meaning) of love, and all concerned with hope or its opposite, hope negated in self-irony, hope centered on the release from individual prisons, hope tempered by trepidations attendant upon the "awful daring of a moment's surrender," and, possibly, hope that the Fisher King has finally thrown off accidia by asking himself the one needful question.

The poem's last verse paragraph displays little overt coherence once the Fisher King asks his question, but it does nevertheless offer a direct key to understanding the poem. That the Fisher King has traversed the arid plains, has put them behind him and now may have some power to set his kingdom in order, provides a sense of closure. In the next line (427), London Bridge, crossed by so many who had been undone by death in the unreal City (Part I), is falling down: This action will end the procession of dead commuters; in the nursery rhyme there is no adequate means to rebuild the bridge permanently. The next line is from Dante, who is a source for many of the attitudes, emotions, and possibly the situational contexts of many of the poem's speakers: Here Arnaut Daniel, suffering in Purgatory for sins of lust, leaps back into the refining fire of his own accord; this may be seen as a gloss on the "Fire Sermon" and as a cure for the various forms of lust in the entire poem. In "These fragments I have shored against my ruins" (430), "these fragments" are the preceding 429 lines, the immediately preceding seven lines, the fragmented speeches, the fragments of poetic and religious traditions, and the fragments of verses composed over many years to form the poem itself.

What do these keys unlock? Bernard Bergonzi, following C. K. Stead's analysis of the pattern and meaning of *Four Quartets*, provides an invaluable guide to the significance of each of the poem's five sections. "The Burial of the Dead" concerns movement in time (seasons, change, reluctant birth); "A Game of Chess" reveals patent dissatisfaction with worldly experience; "The Fire Sermon" leads through purgation in the world and a divesting of the soul of love for created things; "Death by Water" is a brief lyric containing a warning and an invocation; "What the Thunder Said" deals with the issues of spiritual health and artistic wholeness. To read the work as a poem about the artist's concern for artistic wholeness allied to spiritual health offers extraordinary and suggestive possibilities for revaluing it and the poetry that preceded it.

The assured masterpiece of his poetic maturity, *Four Quartets* is more immediately accessible than Eliot's early and middle work. The poems that constitute it, like his earlier poetry, grew incrementally from "Burnt Norton," which sprang from lines discarded from *Murder in the Cathedral*, to "Little Gidding," with "East Coker" and "The Dry Salvages" intervening. Unlike his earlier poetry, the poems of *Four Quartets* lack a dramatic character who speaks; instead, they are in the lyric tradition of direct poetic speech in which the speaker has a constant voice that may well be the poet's own. This shift in poetic style, away from masks and personae, is a new element in Eliot's verse.

Each of the poems adopts a musical and frequently iterative pattern, as if the reader is meant to hear the instrumental conversations endemic to musical quartets. In reading these poems, one is frequently reminded of Walter Pater's dictum that "all art continually aspires to the condition of music." The poems are set pieces in the eighteenth century tradition of verse inspired by a visit to a specific place. Taken together, they constitute some of Eliot's most beautiful (and, in places, most banal) poetry, as the lyricist adopts a consistent poetic voice that muses on the process of cognition and composition.

The essential structure of these poems, filled as they are with local references dear to Eliot, follows the five-part structure of *The Waste Land*. C. K. Stead admirably analyzes the fivefold structure of each of the sections of *Four Quartets* as follows: the movement of time, in which brief moments of eternity are caught; worldly experience, leading only to dissatisfaction; purgation in the world, divesting the soul of love of created things; a lyric prayer for, or affirmation of the need of,

Intercession; and the problems of attaining artistic wholeness, which become analogues for, and merge into, the problems of achieving spiritual health.

The poems of *Four Quartets* in some way negate, by their affirmations, the fragmented, disparate, and "unreal" elements in Eliot's earliest poems; on the whole, however, they present a synthesis of Eliot's poetic concerns and his varied statements about the problems and business of being a poet. They stand not at the end of his artistic career but at the summit of his career as a poet whose later work, in both bulk and intensity, is minimal. *Four Quarters* constitutes a compendium of the themes that Eliot pursued from his earliest days as a poet, but with the decided difference that sex has become part of love, belief has been ratified, and the word has become flesh again.

Other major works

PLAYS: *Sweeney Agonistes*, 1932; *The Rock: A Pageant Play*, 1934; *Murder in the Cathedral*, 1935; *The Family Reunion*, 1939; *The Cocktail Party*, 1949; *The Confidential Clerk*, 1953; *The Elder Statesman*, 1958; *Collected Plays*, 1962.

NONFICTION: *Ezra Pound: His Metric and Poetry*, 1917; *The Sacred Wood*, 1920; *Homage to John Dryden*, 1924; *Shakespeare and the Stoicism of Seneca*, 1927; *For Lancelot Andrewes*, 1928; *Dante*, 1929; *Thoughts After Lambeth*, 1931; *Charles Whibley: A Memoir*, 1931; *John Dryden: The Poet, the Dramatist, the Critic*, 1932; *Selected Essays*, 1932, 1950; *The Use of Poetry and the Use of Criticism*, 1933; *After Strange Gods*, 1934; *Elizabethan Essays*, 1934; *Essays Ancient and Modern*, 1936; *The Idea of a Christian Society*, 1939; *The Music of Poetry*, 1942; *The Classics and the Man of Letters*, 1942; *Notes Toward the Definition of Culture*, 1948; *Poetry and Drama*, 1951; *The Three Voices of Poetry*, 1953; *Religious Drama: Medieval and Modern*, 1954; *The Literature of Politics*, 1955; *The Frontiers of Criticism*, 1956; *On Poetry and Poets*, 1957; *Knowledge and Experience in the Philosophy of F. H. Bradley*, 1964; *To Criticize the Critic*, 1965; *The Letters of T. S. Eliot: Volume I, 1898-1922*, 1988; *The Varieties of Metaphysical Poetry*, 1994 (Clark and Turnbull lectures).

Bibliography

Ackroyd, Peter. *T. S. Eliot: A Life*. New York: Simon & Schuster, 1984.

Eliot, Valerie, ed. *The Letters of T. S. Eliot, 1898-1922*. Vol. 1. New York: Harcourt Brace Jovanovich, 1988.

Gordon, Lyndall. *Eliot's Early Years*. New York: Oxford University Press, 1977.

_____. *Eliot's New Life*. New York: Farrar, Straus & Giroux, 1988.

Kim, Dal-Yong. *Puritan Sensibility in T. S. Eliot's Poetry*. New York: P. Lang, 1993.

Litz, A. Walton, ed. *Eliot in His Time: Essays on the Occasion of the Fiftieth Anniversary of "The Waste Land."* Princeton, N.J.: Princeton University Press, 1973.

Matthews, T. S. *The Great Tom: Notes Toward a Definition of T. S. Eliot*. New York: Harper & Row, 1974.

Raffel, Burton. *T. S. Eliot*. New York: Continuum, 1991.

Sharpe, Tony. *T. S. Eliot: A Literary Life*. New York: St. Martin's Press, 1991.

ERNEST HEMINGWAY

Born: Oak Park, Illinois; July 21, 1899   ***Died:*** Ketchum, Idaho; July 2, 1961

Principal long fiction

The Sun Also Rises, 1926; *The Torrents of Spring*, 1926; *A Farewell to Arms*, 1929; *To Have and Have Not*, 1937; *For Whom the Bell Tolls*, 1940; *Across the River and into the Trees*, 1950; *The Old Man and the Sea*, 1952; *Islands in the Stream*, 1970; *The Garden of Eden*, 1986.

Other literary forms

Ernest Hemingway will be best remembered for his novels and short stories, although critical debate rages over whether his literary reputation rests more firmly on the former or the latter. In his own time he was also known to popular reading audiences for his newspaper dispatches and his essays in popular magazines. He composed plays and a number of nonfiction works as well. His treatise on bullfighting (*Death in the Afternoon*, 1932) is still considered the most authoritative treatment of the subject in English.

Achievements

There is little question that Hemingway will be remembered as one of the outstanding prose stylists in American literary history; his influence on the development of twentieth century American letters is incalculable, his spare style becoming a model for novelists and short-story writers. Hemingway will also be remembered as the explicator of a stoic attitude toward life and a style of living that influenced his readers during the mid-twentieth century and beyond. It was for his stylistic contributions, which reached their purest expression in *The Old Man and the Sea*, that he won the Nobel Prize in Literature in 1954. *For Whom the Bell Tolls* was a candidate for the Pulitzer Prize; *The Old Man and the Sea* won that award.

Biography

Ernest Miller Hemingway was the first son of an Oak Park, Illinois, physician, Clarence Edmonds Hemingway, and Grace Hemingway, a Christian Scientist. As a student in the Oak Park public schools, Hemingway received his first journalistic experience writing for *The Trapeze*, a student newspaper. After serving as a reporter for the Kansas City *Star* for less than a year, he enlisted as an ambulance driver for the American Red Cross and was sent in 1918 to serve on the Italian front during World War I. He received a leg wound that required that he be sent to an American hospital in Milan, and there he met and fell in love with Agnes Von Kurowski, who provided the basis for his characterization of Catherine Barkley in *A Farewell to Arms*. Hemingway was married in 1921 to Hadley Richardson. They moved to the Left Bank of Paris, lived on her income from a trust fund, and became friends of Gertrude Stein and other Left Bank literary figures. The Paris years provided Hemingway with material for the autobiographical sketches collected after his death in *A Moveable Feast* (1964). Also in the Paris years, he met the people who would become the major characters in his *roman à clef*, *The Sun Also Rises*. Hemingway dedicated the novel to Hadley, divorced her (in retrospect, one of the saddest experiences in his life), and married Pauline Pfeiffer in 1927. During the 1930's, Hemingway became attached to the Loyalist cause in Spain, and during the years of the Spanish Civil War (1936-1939), he traveled to that country several times as a war correspondent. His feelings about that war are recorded in *For Whom the Bell Tolls*, which was an enormous popular success. In 1940, he divorced Pauline and married the independent, free-spirited Martha Gellhorn, whom he divorced in 1945, marrying in that same year Mary Welsh, his fourth wife. The 1952 publication of *The Old Man and the Sea* is usually regarded as evidence that the writing slump, which Hemingway had suffered for nearly a decade, was ended. The last years of his life were marked by medical problems, resulting to a great extent from injuries which he had sustained in accidents and from years of heavy drinking. In 1961, after being released from the Mayo Clinic, Hemingway returned with his wife Mary to their home in Ketchum, Idaho. He died there on July 2, 1961, of a self-inflicted shotgun wound.

Analysis

The public persona of Hemingway as a macho risk-taker—a big-game hunter, hard drinker, woodsman, and fisherman—garnered almost as much attention as his fiction and established a role for American men (and, in its manifestation in his female characters, women) in the decades following World War I. He is often thought of now as the chronicler of the "lost generation" of the 1920's, a label applied by Gertrude Stein and used by Hemingway himself in *The Sun Also Rises* as one of the novel's epigraphs. The phrase applied to a generation of disaffected Americans who had lost faith, following the carnage of World War I, in the ideals represented by America and American democracy. In their place, Hemingway offered a "code," a prescription for living that demanded a stoic, pragmatic, and somewhat existential response to the harsh realities of the postwar world.

Hemingway's command of language and style revolutionized American letters. Hemingway stripped language to the bare essentials for expressing fundamental thoughts and ideas and rendering the most accurate descriptions possible. His works, crafted in his intensely masculine style, glorify male participation in bullfighting, big-game hunting, fishing, war, drinking, and brawling. His protagonists move from the hedonistic, self-centered "code" of the early novels to the transcendent, sacrificial view of humankind of the later works.

"All stories, if continued far enough, end in death, and he is no true story teller who would keep that from you," Ernest Hemingway wrote in *Death in the Afternoon*. He might have added that most of his own stories and novels, if traced back far enough, also begin in death. Indeed, in Hemingway's work, as Nelson Algren observes, it seems "as though a man must earn his death before he could win his life." Yet it would be a mistake to allow what may appear to be Hemingway's preoccupation—or, to some, obsession—with death to obscure the fact that he is, above all, concerned in his fiction with the quality of individual life, even though it must be granted that the quality and intensity of his characters' lives seem to increase in direct proportion to their awareness of the reality of death.

There is a danger, however, in making so general an observation as this. Hemingway's attitudes about life, about living it well and living it courageously in the face of death, changed in the course of his most productive years as a writer, those years between 1926 and 1952, which were marked by the creation of his three best novels and the novella *The Old Man and the Sea*. During this period, Hemingway shifted away from what many consider the hedonistic value system of early characters such as Jake, Brett, Frederic, and Catherine, a system often equated with the Hemingway code, to a concern with the collective, almost spiritual value of human life reflected in the actions of Robert Jordan and Santiago.

The life-in-death/death-in-life philosophy is presented in Hemingway's first major novel, *The Sun Also Rises*. On the face of it, the novel tells the story of Jake Barnes, whose war wound has left him physically incapable of making love, though it has done so without robbing him of sexual desire. Jake has the misfortune to fall in love with the beautiful Lady Brett Ashley, who loves Jake but must nevertheless make love to other men. Among these men is Robert Cohn, a hopeless romantic who, alone in the novel, believes in the concept of chivalric love. Hemingway explores the frustration of the doomed love affair between Jake and Brett as they wander from Paris and its moral invalids to Pamplona, where Jake and his lost-generation friends participate in the fiesta. Jake is the only one of the group to have become an *aficionado*, one who is passionate about bullfighting. In the end, though, he betrays his *aficion* by introducing Brett to Pedro Romero, one of the few remaining bullfighters who is true to the spirit of the sport—one who fights honestly and faces death with grace—and this Jake does with full knowledge that Brett will seduce Romero, perhaps corrupting his innocence by infecting him with the jaded philosophy that makes her "lost." Predictably, she does seduce Romero but, less predictably, lets him go, refusing to be "one of these bitches that ruins children." Finally, she and Jake are left where they started, she unrealistically musing that they "could have had such a damned good time together" (presumably if he had not been wounded) and he, perhaps a little wiser, responding, "Yes. . . . Isn't it pretty to think so."

Few will miss the sense of aimless wandering from country to country and bottle to bottle in *The Sun Also Rises*. The death with which *The Sun Also Rises* begins and ends is less a physical death than it is a living or waking death, which, granted, is most acute in Jake's case but which afflicts all the characters in the novel. They must establish rules for playing a kind of spiritual solitaire, and Jake is the character in the novel who most articulately expresses these rules, perhaps because he is the one who most needs them. "Enjoying living," he says, "was learning to get your money's worth and knowing when you had it." In a literal sense, Jake refers here to the practice of getting what one pays for with actual money, but in another sense, he is talking more abstractly about other kinds of economy—the economy of motion in a good bullfight, for example.

To see how thoroughly Hemingway weaves this idea of economy into the fabric of the novel, one need only look at his seemingly offhand joke about writing telegrams. On closer examination, the joke yields a valuable clue for understanding the Hemingway code. When Jake and Bill, his best friend, are fishing in Burguete, they receive a telegram from Cohn, addressed simply, "Barnes, Burguete": "Vengo Jueves Cohn" (I come Thursday Cohn). "What a lousy telegram!" Jake responds. "He could send ten words for the same price." Cohn thinks that he is being clever by writing in Spanish and saving a word, an assumption as naïve as the one that leads him to shorten the name and address to "Barnes, Burguete." The address was free, and Cohn could have included full name and address, thus increasing the probability that Jake would get the message. As a response to Cohn's telegram, Jake and Bill send one equally wasteful: "Arriving to-night." The point is that the price of the telegram includes a laugh at Cohn's expense, and they are willing to pay for it.

Unlike Cohn, both Brett and Jake send ten-word telegrams, thus presumably getting their money's worth. When Brett, in the last chapters of the novel, needs Jake, she wires him: "Could you come hotel Montana Madrid. Am rather in trouble. Brett"—TEN words followed by the signature. This telegram, which had been forwarded from Paris, is immediately followed by another one identical to it, forwarded from Pamplona. In turn, Jake responds with a telegram which also consists of ten words and the signature: "Lady Ashley Hotel Montana Madrid Arriving Sud Express tomorrow. Love Jake." Interestingly, he includes the address in the body of the telegram in order to obtain the ten-word limit. The sending of ten-word telegrams indicates that Jake and Brett are bonded by their adherence to the code; since they alone send such telegrams, the reader must see them as members of an exclusive society.

Yet ironically, to Jake and Brett, the code has become a formalized ritual, something superimposed over their emptiness. They have not learned to apply the code to every aspect of their lives, the most striking example of which is Brett's ten-word (excluding the signature) postcard at the beginning of Chapter 8: "Darling. Very quiet and healthy. Love to all the chaps. Brett." The postcard has no word limit, except that dictated by the size of one's handwriting. Brett, however, in the ab-

sence of clearly labeled values, must fall back on the only form she knows: in this case, that of the ten-word telegram, which is here an empty form, a ritual detached from its meaningful context.

Jake and Brett, then, come back full circle to their initial frustration and mark time with rituals to which they cling for not-so-dear life, looking in the meantime for physical pleasures that will get them through the night. Yet if this seems a low yield for their efforts, one should remember that Hemingway makes no pretense in *The Sun Also Rises* of finding a cure for "lostness." In fact, he heightens the sense of it in his juxtaposition of two epigraphs of the novel: "You are all a lost generation" from Gertrude Stein, and the long quotation from Ecclesiastes that begins "One generation passeth away, and another generation cometh; but the earth abideth forever. . . . The sun also ariseth, and the sun goeth down. . . ." As Hemingway maintained, the hero of *The Sun Also Rises* is the abiding earth; the best one can hope for while living on that earth, isolated from others and cut off from the procreative cycle, is a survival manual. Finally, that is what *The Sun Also Rises* is, and this is the prescription that it offers: One must accept the presence of death in life and face it stoically, one must learn to exhibit grace under pressure, and one must learn to get one's money's worth. In skeletal form, this is the foundation of the Hemingway code—the part of it, at least, that remains constant through all of his novels.

Many of the conditions that necessitated the forming of a code for Jake and Brett in *The Sun Also Rises* are still present in *A Farewell to Arms*, and there are obvious similarities between the two novels. Like Jake, Frederic Henry is wounded in the war and falls in love with a woman, Catherine Barkley, whose first love, like Brett's, has been killed before the main events of the novel begin. Yet there has been a subtle change from *The Sun Also Rises* to *A Farewell to Arms* in Hemingway's perception of the human dilemma. The most revealing hint of this change is in the nature of the wound that Frederic receives while serving as an ambulance driver on the Italian front. Unlike Jake's phallic wound, Frederic's is a less debilitating leg wound, and, ironically, it is the thing which brings him closer to Catherine, an English nurse who treats him in the field hospital in Milan. Though their relationship begins as a casual one, it evolves in the course of Catherine's nursing him into a love that is both spiritual and physical. Catherine's pregnancy affirms at least a partial healing of the maimed fisher king and the restoration of fertility to the wasteland that appeared in *The Sun Also Rises*. Knowing that Catherine is pregnant and knowing that he loves her, how can he continue to fight, even for a cause to which he feels duty-bound? Partly because Catherine has initiated him into the life of love, then, and partly because he needs to escape his own death, Frederic deserts the Italian army in one of the most celebrated baptismal rites in American literature: He dives into the Tagliamento River and washes away his anger "with any obligation," making what he terms a separate peace. No sooner have they escaped the life-in-death of war in Italy to the neutrality of Switzerland, where the reader could logically expect in a fifth and final chapter of the novel a brief, pleasant postscript, than does the double edge hidden in the title become clear. The arms to which Frederic must finally say farewell are those of Catherine, who dies in childbirth. "And this," Frederic observes, "is the price you paid for sleeping together. . . . This was what people get for loving each other."

In most ways, Catherine is a model of the code hero/heroine established in *The Sun Also Rises*: She stoically accepts life's difficulties, as evidenced by her acceptance of her fiancé's death, and she exhibits grace under pressure, as shown in her calm acceptance of her own death. In giving herself to Frederic, she adds a dimension to the code by breaking through the isolation and separateness felt by Jake and Brett; finally, even though she does not complete the re-creative cycle by giving birth to a child conceived in love, she at least brings the possibility within reach. The reader must decide whether Frederic will internalize the lessons he has learned through Catherine's life and allow his own initiation into the code, which now contains the possibility of loving, to be accomplished.

For Whom the Bell Tolls and *The Old Man and the Sea* show Hemingway's code characters moving toward a belief in the collective values of their own lives. The epigraph of *For Whom the Bell Tolls*, which was taken from a John Donne sermon and which gives the novel its title, points clearly to Hemingway's reevaluation of the role of death in life: "No man is an *Iland*, intire of it selfe; every man is a peece of the *Continent*, a part of the *maine*. . . . And therefore never send to know for whom the bell tolls; It tolls for thee." Regardless of the route by which Hemingway came to exchange the "separate peace" idea of *The Sun Also Rises* for the "part of the *maine*" philosophy embraced by Robert Jordan in *For Whom the Bell Tolls*, one can be sure that much of the impetus for his changing came from his strong

feelings about Spain's internal strife, particularly as this strife became an all-out conflict during the Spanish Civil War. This war provides the backdrop for the events of *For Whom the Bell Tolls*, and the novel's main character, like Hemingway, is a passionate supporter of the Loyalist cause. The thing that one immediately notices about Jordan is that he is an idealist, which sets him apart from Jake. Also, unlike Jake, who wanders randomly throughout Europe, Jordan has come to the Sierra de Guadaramas with the specific purpose of blowing up a bridge that would be used to transport ammunition in attacks against the Loyalists. Thrown in with the Loyalist guerrillas of Pablo's band at the beginning of the novel, Jordan is confronted with the nearly impossible task of accomplishing the demolition in three days, a task whose difficulty is compounded by Pablo's resistance to the idea and, finally, by increased Fascist activity near the bridge.

Potentially even more threatening to Jordan's mission is his meeting and falling in love with the beautiful and simple Maria, who is in the protection of Pablo's band after having been raped by the Falangists who killed her parents. Jordan, however, has no intention of declaring a separate peace and leaving his duty behind in pursuit of love. He sees no conflict between the two, and to the degree that Hemingway presents him as the rare individual who fulfills his obligations without losing his ability to love, Jordan represents a new version of the code hero: the whole man who respects himself, cares for others, and believes in the cause of individual freedom. Circumstances, though, conspire against Jordan. Seeing that his mission stands little hope of success and that the offensive planned by General Golz is doomed to failure by the presence of more and more Fascists, he attempts to get word through to Golz, but the message arrives too late. Although he manages successfully to demolish the bridge and almost escapes with Maria, his wounded horse falls, rolls over, and crushes Jordan's leg. He remains at the end of the novel in extreme pain, urging the others not to stay and be killed with him and waiting to shoot the first Fascist officer who comes into range, thus giving Maria and Pablo's group more time to escape.

Jordan is perhaps Hemingway's most ambitious creation, just as *For Whom the Bell Tolls* is his most elaborately conceived novel. Its various strands reflect not only what had become the standard Hemingway subjects of personal death, love, and war but also his growing concern with the broader social implications of individual action. One example of the many layers of meaning contained in the novel is the Civil War framework, which leads the reader not only to see the conflict of social forces in Spain but also to understand that its analogue is the "civil war" in Jordan's spirit: The reader is reminded periodically of the noble death of Jordan's grandfather in the American Civil War, compared to the "separate peace" suicide of Jordan's father. Jordan debates these alternatives until the last scene, when he decides to opt for an honorable death which gives others a chance to live. This, Hemingway seems finally to say, gives Jordan's life transcendent value.

If *For Whom the Bell Tolls* presents a "whole man" who recognizes the value of individual sacrifice for the survival of the human race, *The Old Man and the Sea* carries this principle to its final step and issues, through Santiago, a definitive statement about the role of life in death.

It is no surprise that *The Old Man and the Sea* takes the form of a parable and that its old man takes the form of the archetypal wise man or savior common to most cultures, mythologies, and religions. While others who surround Santiago depend on gadgets to catch their fish, Santiago relies only on his own endurance and courage. He goes eighty-four days before hooking the marlin, against whose strength he will pit his own for nearly two full days, until he is finally able to bring him to the boat and secure him there for the journey from the Gulf Stream. Numerous critics have noted the similarities between Santiago and Christ. Santiago goes farther out than most men, symbolically taking on a burden for humankind that most men could not or would not take on for themselves. When Santiago returns to land from his ordeal, secures his boat, and heads toward his shack, Hemingway describes his journey explicitly in terms of Christ's ascent to Calvary: "He started to climb again and at the top he fell and lay for some time with the mast across his shoulder." Moreover, Santiago talks with the boy Manolin about those who do not believe in him or his ways in terms that are unmistakably religious: Of the boy's father, who does not want his son to be with the old man, Santiago remarks, "He hasn't much faith." In all of this, Hemingway is leading the reader to see that some, in going out "too far," risk their lives in order to transmit to others the idea that "a man can be destroyed but not defeated." Finally, it is of little importance that sharks have reduced Santiago's great fish to a skeleton by the time he has reached land because the human spirit that has been tested in his battle with the fish has in the end prevailed; those who are genuinely interested in that spirit are rarely concerned with ocular proof of its existence. Santiago's legacy, which must stand as Hemingway's last major word on the human condition, will go to Manolin and the reader, since, as the old man tells him, "I know you did not leave me because you doubted"; he did not doubt that man's spirit can prevail.

Hemingway, then, traveled a great distance from the nihilistic philosophy and hedonistic code of *The Sun Also Rises* to the affirmative view of humankind expressed in *The Old Man and the Sea*. His four major works, if read chronologically, lead the reader on an odyssey through the seasonal cycle of the human spirit. "All stories, if continued far enough, end in death," and Hemingway never stops reminding the reader of that fact. He does add to it, though, in his later work, the hope of rebirth that waits at the end of the journey, a hope for which nature has historically provided the model.

Other major works

SHORT FICTION: *Three Stories and Ten Poems*, 1923; *In Our Time*, 1924, 1925; *Men Without Women*, 1927; *Winner Take Nothing*, 1933; *The Fifth Column and the First Forty-nine Stories*, 1938; *The Snows of Kilimanjaro and Other Stories*, 1961; *The Nick Adams Stories*, 1972.

PLAYS: *Today Is Friday*, 1926; *The Fifth Column*, 1938.

NONFICTION: *Death in the Afternoon*, 1932; *Green Hills of Africa*, 1935; *A Moveable Feast*, 1964; *By-Line: Ernest Hemingway, Selected Articles and Dispatches of Four Decades*, 1967; *Ernest Hemingway: Selected Letters, 1917-1961*, 1981; *The Dangerous Summer*, 1985; *Dateline, Toronto: The Complete "Toronto Star" Dispatches, 1920-1924*, 1985.

Bibliography

Benson, J. J. "The Life as Fiction and the Fiction as Life." *American Literature* 61 (October, 1989): 345-358.

Bloom, Harold, ed. *Ernest Hemingway: Modern Critical Views*. New York: Chelsea House, 1985.

Brenner, Gerry. *Concealments in Hemingway's Works*. Columbus: Ohio State University Press, 1983.

Bruccoli, Matthew Joseph. *Fitzgerald and Hemingway: A Dangerous Friendship*. New York: Carroll & Graf, 1994.

Donaldson, Scott. *By Force of Will: The Life and Art of Ernest Hemingway*. New York: Viking Press, 1977.

Harper, Michael. "Men Without Politics? Hemingway's Social Consciousness." *New Orleans Review* 12 (Spring, 1985): 15-26.

Hemingway, Ernest. *Conversations with Ernest Hemingway*. Edited by Matthew J. Bruccoli. Jackson: University Press of Mississippi, 1986.

Larson, Kelli A. *Ernest Hemingway: A Reference Guide, 1974-1989*. Boston: G. K. Hall, 1990.

Love, Glen A. "Hemingway's Indian Virtues: An Ecological Reconsideration." *Western American Literature* 22, no. 4 (1987): 201-223.

Mellow, James R. *Hemingway: A Life Without Consequences*. Boston: Houghton Mifflin, 1992.

Noble, Donald R. *Hemingway: A Revaluation*. Troy, N.Y.: Whitston, 1983.

Reynolds, Michael S. *Hemingway: The American Homecoming*. Cambridge, Mass.: Blackwell, 1992.

Scafella, Frank, ed. *Hemingway: Essays of Reassessment*. New York: Oxford University Press, 1991.

HENRY JAMES

Born: New York, New York; April 15, 1843   **Died:** London, England; February 28, 1916

Principal long fiction

Roderick Hudson, 1876; *The American*, 1876-1877; *The Europeans*, 1878; *Daisy Miller*, 1878; *An International Episode*, 1878-1879; *Confidence*, 1879-1880; *Washington Square*, 1880; *The Portrait of a Lady*, 1880-1881; *The Bostonians*, 1885-1886; *The Princess Casamassima*, 1885-1886; *The Reverberator*, 1888; *The Tragic Muse*, 1889-1890; *The Spoils of Poynton*, 1897; *What Maisie Knew*, 1897; *The Awkward Age*, 1897-1899; *In the Cage*, 1898; *The Turn of the Screw*, 1898; *The Sacred Fount*, 1901; *The Wings of the Dove*, 1902; *The Ambassadors*, 1903; *The Golden Bowl*, 1904; *The Outcry*, 1911; *The Ivory Tower*, 1917; *The Sense of the Past*, 1917.

Other literary forms

Fiction was assuredly where Henry James's essential talent and interest lay, and it was the form to which he devoted almost all of his literary efforts. For a five-year period, from 1890 to 1895, he concentrated on playwriting; during this time he wrote no novels but continued to publish short stories. He returned to fiction with what many scholars believe to be a stronger, more ambitious inspiration, resulting in what has been called the "major phase" of his writing.

Unlike many creative writers, James produced an enormous volume of critical writings, chiefly literary, in which he not only studied the works of other authors but also performed a detailed analysis of his own work. This latter effort appears primarily in the form of the prefaces to the New York edition (1907-1909) of his novels and tales. Inasmuch as the New York edition occupies twenty-six volumes, these prefaces provide a considerable body of critical material that has proved to be of great value to James scholars. His often reprinted essay "The Art of Fiction" (1884) presents his general theories on the art. Aside from his literary criticism, James wrote numerous studies and critiques on other subjects, such as painting (which greatly interested him) and travel.

James's travel sketches and books have attained critical admiration for their graceful style and penetrating insight into times that have gone and places that will never be the same. As might be expected, his studies of Italy, France, and England (the foreign countries that most intrigued him) are detailed and entertaining. More surprising is his finest work in this genre, *The American Scene* (1907). His account of America at the start of the twentieth century fuses the poignancy of a native's return with the distance and objectivity of a European perspective.

Achievements

James was the first American novelist to bring to the genre a sense of artistic vocation comparable to Gustave Flaubert's. Except for the wide popularity of *Daisy Miller*, which appealed to audiences both in Europe and in the United States, no work of James achieved a wide readership in his lifetime. This fact, though it caused him pain, did not impel this most discriminating of writers to lower his standards in order to appeal to a mass audience. Those who did appreciate his work tended to be the better educated, more sophisticated readers. With the growth of courses of study in modern American literature, James began to enjoy the wide readership that was denied him during his lifetime, and since World War II, critical studies and biographical works devoted to him have proliferated in staggering numbers.

As to James's influence on the subsequent course of the novel, there can be no question. He refined the novelistic art, purified it, and gave it directions never thought of before his time. Four areas of emphasis have especially attracted scholars in their attempts to isolate the essential contributions to the art of fiction with which James can be credited: point of view, psychological realism, style, and the connection of moral and aesthetic values. Throughout his career, James experimented with the varieties of "consciousness" (the word can be found everywhere in his fiction and criticism) through which stories can be told. The completely objective point of view, in which the reader is presented solely with what anyone present would see and hear, and the first-person point of view, in which a character tells the story as he perceives it, were both traditional, and James used them frequently. As his writing became more complex and dense, though, he endeavored to relate the action more in terms of what goes on in people's minds, the most impressive example of such a "center of consciousness" being Lambert Strether in *The Ambassadors*. James's experiments in viewpoint did two important things: They prepared the way for the stream-of-consciousness novel, and they deepened the psychological realism that was to be James's chief intellectual contribution to the novel form.

Biography

James was born in New York City on April 15, 1843, into a well-to-do, lively, and articulate family. Growing up, the future novelist enjoyed the benefits of instruction by tutors as well as in excellent European institutions (1855-1858). Though James was largely self-educated, it is generally agreed that he was one of the best informed of the major literary men of his time.

Apart from several later trips to Europe, which finally led him to the decision to move there in 1875 and to remain there for the rest of his life, James led, for his first thirty years, a largely domestic life in the family circle. In his early twenties he had decided to become a writer; his initial publication is thought to be an unsigned story, which appeared in 1864. This was the first of an endless stream of tales, reviews, essays, and novels. He was closely attached to his older brother William, a relationship that endured until William's death, in 1910, and to Alice and his cousin Mary ("Minny") Temple, whom James thought to be "the very heroine of our common scene." This charming young lady may have been the only real romantic love of James's life—it has been suggested that her death at twenty-four, in 1870, had much to do with James's resolution never to marry—and he immortalized her in Milly Theale, the ailing heroine of *The Wings of the Dove*, and perhaps in all the bright, appealing American girls who come to grief in his novels.

After James's removal to Europe, the rest of his life became chiefly a matter of hard work, important friendships with literary figures, and extraordinary ranges of travel. After a year in Paris, in 1875, James decided that his art would flourish more fully in England, where he took up residence, first in London, later in Rye, Sussex. It is plain that James's art was determined largely by the European experience. Abroad, James found what he believed to be lacking in America, at least for a novelist of manners interested in cultural phenomena. In his biography of Hawthorne, James listed, perhaps with tongue at least partly in cheek, those items that could be studied only in Europe, since they did not exist in

America: "No sovereign, no court . . . no aristocracy, no church, no clergy, no army, no diplomatic service, no country gentlemen, no palaces, no castles, nor manors, nor old country-houses . . . no literature, no novels, no museums, no pictures, no political society, no sporting class." Though this list offers some hint of James's sense of humor, the works themselves are sure evidence that he was convinced that Europe provided him with indispensable materials for his novels.

James never made a great deal of money from his writing, but he always lived comfortably. He was a generous friend, with both money and advice, to his many acquaintances and to young writers hoping to succeed. He had what some biographers call a genius for friendship, which his enormous correspondence attests. On James's seventieth birthday, April 15, 1913, some 270 friends presented him with a "golden bowl" and asked him to sit for a portrait by John Singer Sargent (which is now in the National Portrait Gallery, in London). More formal honors were an honorary degree from Harvard (1911) and one from Oxford (1912); perhaps the loftiest distinction was the Order of Merit, presented to James by King George V, in 1916, the year of the author's death (from heart trouble and pneumonia). This decoration was given in recognition of James's valued service to England during the opening years of World War I.

As death approached (James wrote of it, "So here it is at last, the distinguished thing!") he was still engaged in writing; he left two unfinished novels, *The Ivory Tower* and *The Sense of the Past*, and a number of unpublished essays and stories, all of which have since been printed.

Analysis

James was one of the nineteenth century's most important and influential writers in English. His examples and theoretical principles established the foundation of the modernist movement in twentieth century fiction and poetry, and his major novels constitute the greatest accomplishment in the literature of psychological realism. Through the publication of *The Portrait of a Lady*, in 1881, and then from about 1896 until the close of his career, James was chiefly interested in the now famous "international theme," the learning experiences and conflicts of Americans in Europe and Europeans in America. *Daisy Miller*, *The Portrait of a Lady*, and *The Ambassadors* are among the most articulate statements of this theme in American literature.

Daisy Miller, which established James's reputation

as a leading novelist in both England and the United States, announces several of his recurring themes and motifs. From the standpoint of plot, the story is an uncomplicated one. Frederick Winterbourne, a sophisticated young American who lives in Europe, meets Daisy Miller, a young woman from Schenectady, New York, who is visiting Europe with her mother and younger brother. The essence of the novella is the relationship that develops between the young, cosmopolitan expatriate and the pretty, naïve, and willful girl.

In *Daisy Miller* a central issue is whether Winterbourne could have prevented the tragedy that ends Daisy's life. As he gets to know her better and comes to like her, he becomes increasingly distressed at Daisy's refusal to heed the warnings of Mrs. Costello, his aunt, and Mrs. Walker, another Europeanized American society matron (it is significant that the people who most condemn Daisy are not native Europeans but expatriates). Daisy stubbornly continues to consort with the gigolo Giovanelli, who is seen with her all about Rome, much to the dismay of the society people, who are scandalized by such "loose" behavior—even the Romans joke about it in a subdued fashion, which only irritates Winterbourne more. He tries to warn Daisy that she is seen too much with Giovanelli—"Everyone thinks so"—but she refuses to take his cautions seriously: "I don't believe a word of it. They're only pretending to be shocked. They don't really care a straw what I do." This perverse attitude finally leads to Daisy's death, when she goes, against Winterbourne's urging, to the Colosseum at night (a place that, after dark, was reputed to have a miasma often fatal to foreigners) and contracts a mortal fever. When Winterbourne angrily asks Giovanelli why he took Daisy to such a dangerous place, the Italian answers, "*she*—she did what she liked."

The complexity of the moral nuances of the story is revealed when one remembers that Winterbourne, who is regarded as quite the perfect young gentleman and is welcomed in the best society, has a mistress back in Geneva. Clearly, in that "best" society what matters is not virtue (Daisy is quite guiltless of any actual wrongdoing) but the appearance of it—Winterbourne may not be virtuous, but he is discreet. The old theme of appearance versus reality thus emerges in this story, but with social implications not found in the work of other authors. To James, one of the most difficult problems for Americans trying to come to terms with Europe is that the appearance of virtue often counts for more than the reality.

James's realism is most evident in the close of the story. Winterbourne is remorseful over Daisy's death. He regrets that he did not try harder to understand her and correct her misconceptions. He tells his aunt, "She would have appreciated one's esteem." Then, he applies the lesson to himself: "I've lived too long in foreign parts." So far, the story has seemed to advance a moral thesis about the corruption of innocence and the valuable truths that can be learned. James closes the novella, however, on a note that proves how realistic his vision of human nature was: "Nevertheless he soon went back to live at Geneva, whence there continue to come the most contradictory accounts of his motives of sojourn: a report that he's 'studying' hard—an intimation that he's much interested in a very clever foreign lady." James had no illusions about people.

While *Daisy Miller* is told in the first person, from Winterbourne's consciousness, *The Portrait of a Lady*, a much longer and more complicated fiction, is related through the minds of a number of characters. This book is probably the most generally admired of all James's full-length novels. It carries the "international theme" to what some consider its highest level of expression, and it offers the reader one of the most impressive characters in James's work, the delightful Isabel Archer, the "lady" of the title. Again, James is psychologically realistic: While Isabel is honest, intelligent, and sensitive, she is not without fault; she does have "an unquenchable desire to think well of herself." She is an "innocent abroad" who is "affronting her destiny." This fate is to be given, first, the chance to visit Europe (offered by Mrs. Lydia Touchett, her wealthy aunt who lives in Europe) and, then, a great deal of money (provided by the will of Mr. Daniel Touchett, at the suggestion of his son Ralph, who becomes very fond of Isabel). This combination of high connections—Mr. Touchett associates with a number of prominent English families, most significantly that of Lord Warburton—opportunities for travel, and comfortable circumstances is common in James's novels.

In *The Portrait of a Lady*, James studies the relationships of the characters in great detail. When Lord Warburton proposes to Isabel, the situation is examined closely, and her rejection of him prepares for later plot developments and revelations of character. As is often the case in James, the money that Isabel inherits is both a blessing and a curse. It permits her to travel and to live almost lavishly, but it also attracts to her one of the few outright villains in James's fiction. Gilbert Osmond appears to be charming, modest, intelligent, and sensitive. He proves to be proud, arrogant, idle, and cruel. In a powerful enunciation of the international theme, Osmond courts Isabel cleverly, appealing to her sense of the artistic wonders of Europe, of which he seems to be a fine judge. He wins her hand, partly through the efforts of Madame Serena Merle, an American expatriate (as is Osmond) who, Isabel later discovers, was once Osmond's mistress (they could not marry, since neither was wealthy—the topic of marrying for money is one that James explored as thoroughly as any writer ever had and with greater insight). Mme. Merle is eager for Osmond to marry well, since they have a daughter, Pansy, whom she wishes to see well placed in the world.

Of course, the marriage is a failure. Osmond comes to resent Isabel, and eventually she despises him. In the famous chapter 42, Isabel examines the grim condition of her life. In an extended passage of what is clearly a precursor of the stream-of-consciousness technique, James causes Isabel to review the terrible errors she has made—"It was her deep distrust of her husband—this was what darkened her world"—and to consider how foolish her pride has made her: Ralph Touchett, among others, warned her against Osmond. Isabel's stubbornness and refusal to heed wise advice remind one of Daisy Miller's similar folly. The plot becomes more complex when Lord Warburton directs his affections to Pansy. Naturally, Osmond is highly in favor of such a marriage since Warburton is very rich. Isabel incurs her husband's even more intense hatred by discouraging the English peer with the simple argument that he and Pansy do not really love each other. Here, European corruption (expressed in an American expatriate, as is often the case in James's fiction) is opposed to native American innocence and emotional integrity.

The conclusion of this novel is among James's most subtle and ambiguous. Isabel returns to England to visit the deathbed of Ralph Touchett. Ralph is one of James's truly virtuous characters, as is shown by his renunciation of any thought of marrying Isabel, whom he loves, because of his failing physical condition. Isabel admits to Ralph that he was right and that she committed a monumental error in marrying Osmond. Ralph, typically, blames himself for having provided her with the money that tempted Gilbert; Isabel refuses this excuse, recognizing that the mistake was her own. The puzzling aspect of the last pages of the novel is that Isabel determines to go back to Osmond as his wife. What will become of her—whether she will remain with him—remains a mystery.

The Ambassadors is now generally rated as one of James's masterpieces (some critics believe it to be far and away the most accomplished work of the major phase). Middle-aged Lambert Strether, the hero of *The Ambassadors*, is indeed an "ambassador." He has been given the unenviable assignment (by his formidable patroness, Mrs. Abel Newsome) of persuading her son, Chadwick Newsome, to return to his family and commercial responsibilities in Woollett, Massachusetts (probably representing Worcester, Massachusetts). The primary subject of this novel is *joie de vivre*; this quality is just what Strether, finds when he arrives in Paris, where he has not been since he was a young man. It has been observed that one of the salient aspects of James's fiction is irony. Nowhere is the quality more in evidence than in *The Ambassadors*. Chad Newsome, Strether discovers, has been made a gracious gentleman by his life in Paris; Strether, charmed by the beauty and enchantment of the city, cannot in good conscience urge Chad to leave delightful Paris for dull Woollett. The irony lies in the fact that Chad is quite willing and, finally, eager to return home to make a great deal of money, while Strether longs to remain in Paris. Indeed, his delay in dispatching Chad home impels Mrs. Newsome to send her intimidating daughter, Mrs. Sarah Pocock, and her husband to take up the commission, since Strether has evidently failed.

This conflict is chiefly in the mind of Strether, since, in his novel, James undertook to employ the third-person limited point of view to its fullest effect. As usual, the situation is not so simple as it appears. It is not merely residence in Paris that has "civilized" Chad; it has also been his mistress, Mme. Marie de Vionnet. Strether, before he knows of the intimacy between his young friend and this sophisticated and charming lady, develops an intense admiration and affection for her. Even after he learns of the liaison, accidentally seeing the two rowing on a river near an inn where they are staying, Strether is still entranced by Marie de Vionnet. When Chad decides to return home and abandon his mistress, Strether recognizes her tragedy and is extremely sympathetic. He has, however, his own problems. Thanks to Mrs. Newsome's already aroused suspicions and Sarah Pocock's expected damning report, Strether sees that his comfortable position in Woollett (and possible eventual marriage to his widowed employer) is very likely gone.

The renunciation theme, so prominent in James's novels, is perhaps more powerfully formulated at the close of this novel than in any other of his books. Despite the appeal of Paris and the hinted offer of an agreeable marriage to Maria Gostrey, an American expatriate who had befriended Strether when he first landed in Europe, this highly moral and responsible man resolves to return to Woollett, where he believes his duty to lie. This sort of ethical resolution may seem foolish to modern readers, but it is believable in the novel, and the circumstances suggest James's belief that, in current terms, there is a price tag on everything, even happiness. The novel, then, is not only a tribute to Paris and the life of cultural elevation that it can provide but also an acknowledgment of the necessity of responsible and considerate action. The temptation of Strether is almost overwhelming, but his New England sense of duty compels him to conquer it.

James's contributions to the evolution of the modern novel are of staggering magnitude and diversity. Perhaps his greatest contribution was best summed up by Ezra Pound shortly after James's death: "Peace comes of communication. No man of our time has so labored to create means of communication as did the late Henry James. The whole of great art is a struggle for communication."

Other major works

SHORT FICTION: *A Passionate Pilgrim*, 1875; *The Madonna of the Future*, 1879; *The Siege of London*, 1883; *Tales of Three Cities*, 1884; *The Author of Beltraffio*, 1885; *The Aspern Papers*, 1888; *The Lesson of the Master*, 1892; *The Real Thing*, 1893; *Terminations*, 1895; *Embarrassments*, 1896; *The Two Magics: The Turn of the Screw and Covering End*, 1898; *The Soft Side*, 1900; *The Better Sort*, 1903; *The Novels and Tales of Henry James*, 1907-1909; *The Finer Grain*, 1910; *A Landscape Painter*, 1919; *Traveling Companions*, 1919; *Master Eustace*, 1920; *Henry James: Selected Short Stories*, 1950; *Henry James: Eight Tales from the Major Phase*, 1958; *The Complete Tales of Henry James*, 1962-1965; *Tales of Henry James*, 1984; *The Figure in the Carpet and Other Stories*, 1986; *The Jolly Corner and Other Tales*, 1990.

PLAYS: *The American*, 1891; *Guy Domville*, 1894; *Theatricals: Tenants and Disengaged*, 1894; *Theatricals, Second Series: The Album and The Reprobate*, 1895; *The Complete Plays of Henry James*, 1949.

NONFICTION: *Transatlantic Sketches*, 1875; *French Poets and Novelists*, 1878; *Hawthorne*, 1879; *Portraits of Places*, 1883; *A Little Tour in France*, 1884; *Partial Portraits*, 1888; *Essays in London*, 1893; *William Wetmore Story and His Friends*, 1903; *English Hours*, 1905; *The American Scene*, 1907; *Views and Reviews*, 1908; *Italian Hours*, 1909; *A Small Boy and Others*, 1913; *Notes of a Son and Brother*, 1914; *Notes on Novelists*, 1914; *The Middle Years*, 1917; *The Art of the Novel: Critical Prefaces*, 1934; *The Art of Criticism: Henry James on the Theory and Practice of Fiction*, 1986; *The Complete Notebooks of Henry James*, 1987; *Selected Letters of Henry James to Edmund Gosse, 1882-1915: A Literary Friendship*, 1988; *The Correspondence of Henry James and Henry Adams, 1877-1914*, 1992; *Collected Travel Writings*, 1993; *Traveling in Italy with Henry James: Essays*, 1994.

Bibliography

Anderson, Charles R. *Person, Place, and Thing in Henry James's Novels*. Durham, N.C.: Duke University Press, 1977.

Bloom, Harold, ed. *Modern Critical Views: Henry James*. New York: Chelsea House, 1987.

Cannon, Kelly. *Henry James and Masculinity: The Man at the Margins*. New York: St. Martin's Press, 1994.

Cargill, Oscar. *The Novels of Henry James*. New York: Macmillan, 1961.

Cross, Mary. *Henry James: The Contingencies of Style*. New York: St. Martin's Press, 1993.

Edel, Leon. *Henry James: A Life*. Rev. ed. New York: Harper & Row, 1985.

Fussell, Edwin Sill. *The Catholic Side of Henry James*. New York: Cambridge University Press, 1993.

Gale, Robert L. *A Henry James Encyclopedia*. New York: Greenwood Press, 1989.

Gargano, James W., ed. *Critical Essays on Henry James: The Early Novels*. Boston: G. K. Hall, 1987.

Hutchinson, Stuart. *Henry James: An American as Modernist*. Totowa, N.J.: Barnes & Noble Books, 1982.

Jolly, Roslyn. *Henry James: History, Narrative, Fiction*. New York: Oxford University Press, 1993.

Kaplan, Fred. *Henry James: The Imagination of Genius, A Biography*. New York: William Morrow, 1992.

Putt, Samuel P. *Henry James: A Reader's Guide*. Ithaca, N.Y.: Cornell University Press, 1966.

Woolf, Judith. *Henry James: The Major Novels*. New York: Cambridge University Press, 1991.

Yeazell, Ruth Bernard, ed. *Henry James: A Collection of Critical Essays*. Englewood Cliffs, N.J.: Prentice-Hall, 1994.

EZRA POUND

Born: Hailey, Idaho; October 30, 1885   **Died:** Venice, Italy; November 1, 1972

Principal poetry

A Lume Spento, 1908; *A Quinzaine for This Yule*, 1908; *Personae*, 1909; *Exultations*, 1909; *Provença*, 1910; *Canzoni*, 1911; *Ripostes*, 1912; *Cathay*, 1915 (translation); *Lustra*, 1916; *Quia Pauper Amavi*, 1919; *Hugh Selwyn Mauberley*, 1920; *Umbra*, 1920; *Poems 1918-1921*, 1921; *Indiscretions*, 1923; *A Draft of XVI Cantos*, 1925; *Personae: The Collected Poems of Ezra Pound*, 1926; *A Draft of the Cantos 17-27*, 1928; *Selected Poems*, 1928; *A Draft of XXX Cantos*, 1930; *Eleven New Cantos XXXI-XLI*, 1934; *Homage to Sextus Propertius*, 1934 (translation); *Alfred Venison's Poems: Social Credit Themes*, 1935; *The Fifth Decad of Cantos*, 1937; *Cantos LII-LXXI*, 1940; *A Selection of Poems*, 1940; *The Pisan Cantos*, 1948; *The Cantos of Ezra Pound*, 1948; *Selected Poems*, 1949; *The Translations of Ezra Pound*, 1953; *Section: Rock-Drill 85-95 de los cantares*, 1955; *Thrones: 96-109 de los cantares*, 1959; *Drafts and Fragments of Cantos CX-CXVII*, 1968; *Selected Cantos*, 1970; *The Cantos of Ezra Pound I-CXVII*, 1970; *Selected Poems: 1908-1959*, 1975; *Collected Early Poems*, 1976 (Michael J. King, ed.).

Other literary forms

Ezra Pound was the most influential translator of poetry in the twentieth century. He translated, sometimes with assistance, from Greek, Latin, Provençal, Italian, French, German, Old English, Chinese, and Japanese. *The Translations of Ezra Pound* (1953) contains most of his poetic translations; there are also two separate books of Chinese translations, *The Classic Anthology Defined by Confucius* (or *The Confucian Odes*, 1954) and *Confucius* (1969), which gathers together in one volume Pound's translations of *The Analects*, the *Chung Yung* (*The Unwobbling Pivot*), and the *Ta Hio* (*The Great Digest*).

Pound wrote a great deal of criticism. His music criticism has been collected in *Ezra Pound and Music* (1977); the best of his art criticism is found in *Gaudier-Brzeska: A Memoir* (1916), and his miscellaneous pieces have been brought together in *Ezra Pound and the Visual Arts* (1980). More important than either of these was his literary criticism, which, though more the notes of a working poet than a systematic body of doctrine, influenced many of the important poets of the century. *Literary Essays* (1954) and *ABC of Reading* (1934) contain the best of Pound's formal criticism, though the informal criticism found in *The Letters of Ezra Pound, 1907-1941* (1950) is at least as interesting.

Pound's translations and criticism have aroused controversy, but nothing in comparison with that aroused by his writings on social, political, and economic questions. These include *ABC of Economics* (1933), *Jefferson and/or Mussolini* (1935), *Guide to Kulchur* (1938), and *Impact: Essays on Ignorance and the Decline of American Civilization* (1960); Pound's *Selected Prose, 1909-1965* (1973) includes a generous sampling of his writing in this area.

The foregoing account far from exhausts Pound's work in other forms. He composed an opera, *The Testament of François Villon* (1926); one of his first books, *The Spirit of Romance* (1910), was an extended discussion of medieval literature; he translated Confucius into Italian as well as English; and his contributions to periodicals number in the thousands.

Achievements

There is more disagreement over Pound's achievements than over those of any other modern poet. There can be no disagreement, however, over Pound's extraordinary importance in the literary history of the twentieth century. Such importance derives in large measure from the close relationship that he enjoyed with so many of the twentieth century's leading writers. While serving as W. B. Yeats's secretary (from 1913 to 1915), he introduced Yeats to Japanese Nō drama, which served as a model for Yeats's subsequent plays for dancers. In the same period, he discovered, promoted, and found publishers for James Joyce and T. S. Eliot. Later, in 1922, he edited Eliot's masterpiece, *The Waste Land*, into final form. In 1914, he and Wyndham Lewis founded the Vorticist movement and the short-lived but seminal magazine *Blast*. During these years, he was actively involved with some of the most exciting literary journals of the period, including *Poetry*, *The Egoist*, *The Little Review*, and *The Dial*.

In the 1920's, as he began to write the *Cantos*, the long poem that would occupy him for fifty years, his pace of activity as a promoter of other writers declined. Nevertheless, he was an important influence on several generations of American poets, from his contemporaries William Carlos Williams and Marianne Moore to e. e. cummings, Louis Zukofsky, Charles Olson, and others. It is no exaggeration to say that the literary history of the twentieth century is unthinkable without Pound.

Pound's work as a translator was as multifarious and stimulating as his activities on behalf of other writers. With Pound's Chinese translations in mind, Eliot in his introduction to Pound's *Selected Poems* called Pound "the inventor of Chinese poetry for our time." His versions of Sextus Propertius, Arnaut Daniel, and Guido Cavalcanti did a great deal to increase interest in these poets. More important, Pound's example has redefined the art of translation and has influenced several generations of poets. The enormous importance of translation in contemporary poetry can largely be traced to Pound's groundbreaking work. Nevertheless, his translations have also been attacked as hopelessly inaccurate; his scholarship has been said to be nonexistent; and it must be granted that Pound's translations, in attempting to catch the spirit of the original, often do great violence to the letter.

The achievement of Pound's early verse (that written between 1908 and 1920) is, to put it simply, that he created, with Eliot, the modern poetic idiom in English and American poetry. Breaking free from the Victorian style in which he had begun, he began to write concise, laconic, austere poems in free verse, in which the line was the chief unit of composition. This style is usually called Imagism, a useful term as long as one remembers that Pound was the instigator of the style and movement, not simply one among equals. The best-known Imagist poem is Pound's famous two-line poem, "In a Station of the Metro" (1913), but Pound quickly outgrew the tight, haikulike style of his Imagist period (1912-1914), applying its concision and characteristically elliptical juxtapositions in longer, more complex, and more substantial poems.

This change quickly bore fruit in *Homage to Sextus Propertius* (first published in *Quia Pauper Amavi*, 1919), a kind of translation whose problematic status as a translation has diverted critical attention from its substance, and *Hugh Selwyn Mauberley*, one of the classics of modernism. Even before completing the dense, witty *Hugh Selwyn Mauberley*, Pound had begun what was to

be the work of a lifetime, the *Cantos*. He first published sections from the *Cantos* in 1917; the poem was left unfinished at his death in 1972. In 1949 he was awarded the prestigious Bollingen Prize for *The Pisan Cantos*, perhaps the best and most moving section of the long poem. The *Cantos* has been praised as the greatest long poem of the twentieth century, but it has also been vigorously attacked or simply dismissed without comment. For a number of reasons, the achievement of the *Cantos* remains a matter of great controversy and may not be settled soon.

Biography

It seems appropriate that Ezra Loomis Pound should have been born on the frontier (in Hailey, Idaho, in 1885) and then moved to Philadelphia at the age of two, to be reared in the suburb of Wyncote until his education at Hamilton College (Ph.B. 1905) and the University of Pennsylvania (M.A. 1906). Pound, though always presenting himself as the ultimate American, kept moving east, in search of culture, in a voyage that would lead him to England, then to France, finally to Italy, and in spirit all the way to China.

Wrong turnings in Pound's career always took the form of moving west. After his education in romance languages and philology—what today would be called comparative literature—he took a teaching position at Wabash College in Crawfordsville, Indiana. Given his scholarly bent, he might easily have become a teacher and a scholar, but a scandal involving Pound's offering a night's hospitality to a destitute woman ended his career at Wabash and, as it was to turn out, his academic career as well.

Pound left for Venice in 1908, published his first book of poems there, *A Lume Spento*, and then went to London, where he was to spend the next twelve years remaking literature. Tiring of London after World War I, he moved to Paris in 1921; in 1924 he moved again, to the lovely Italian seaside town of Rapallo. In his twenty years of residence there, he became increasingly enamored of the policies of Italy's Fascist ruler, Benito Mussolini. When war broke out between Italy and the United States in 1941, Pound stayed in Italy, either unable or unwilling to return home (the record is not entirely clear), and broadcast on Rome Radio throughout the war. In July, 1943, he was indicted for treason for his talks; in 1945 he was taken into custody by the American Army. Though returned to Washington for trial and in some danger of being executed for treason, Pound was never tried. He pleaded unfitness to stand trial by reason of insanity—he had suffered a complete breakdown from his harsh treatment after his capture in Italy—and was sent to Saint Elizabeths Hospital, where he was to remain until 1958. Finally, after a worldwide campaign on Pound's behalf, the indictment against him was dismissed. He immediately left for Italy and spent the remaining years of his life there, mostly in Venice. Deeply scarred by his experiences, convinced that his political activities had been a mistake, and unable to finish the *Cantos*, Pound refused to speak throughout most of the last ten years of his life.

Analysis

Pound remains one of the most important literary figures of the twentieth century. His influence in the development of the modern poetic idiom in English and American letters is unsurpassed. He was also a supremely discerning and energetic champion of arts and culture. His *Cantos* has become the preeminent example of modernism in contemporary times, perhaps the most ambitious didactic poem of the century and a fascinating intellectual argosy.

In 1926, Pound took the title of his third collection of verse, *Personae*, as the title for his collected shorter poems, which complicated his bibliography but afforded his readers a valuable cue. *Persona*, in Latin, means "mask," and in the 1909 volume *Personae*, there are a number of poems in which Pound takes on the persona, the mask, of an earlier poet and speaks in his voice. By calling his collected shorter poems *Personae*, Pound indicates that this device of the persona, far from being confined to a single volume, is central to his poetry.

Thus Pound's personality is not directly expressed in his poetry; it is found almost nowhere in his work. This clashes strongly with the Romantic notion that poetry is the expression of a poet's personality. One could say that, for Pound, poetry is the expression of someone else's personality. Pound's choice of personae, however, is never haphazard, and his own sensibility and voice come through in the choice of the persona. In Pound's best works, the mask that the poet assumes is a perfect fit: The original speaker is rendered so expertly that readers can take the poem as their own and see Pound as merely a poetic midwife; yet the reader can also view the poem as Pound's through and through and see the original speaker as a mask that Pound has donned for the occasion.

It was with the publication of *Cathay*, a book of translations from the Chinese, that Pound became a major poet and began to write the kind of poetry he had long wanted to write. The poems in *Cathay* are far more than beautiful translations, though they are that. Pound selected, translated, and published these poems—in 1915—as an indirect way of writing about Europe in the midst of World War I. In other words, Pound translated poems about war, exile, parting, and loss as a way of writing "war poetry." This was not, however, immediately recognized; the poems were regarded simply as translations, and readers missed or ignored the implicit relation between the world of the poems and the world of the translator.

Pound's first extended poem, *Homage to Sextus Propertius*, was called an homage in order to make Pound's presence in the poem clear. It works in the same way that *Cathay* does: It is a translation of Propertius, a very lively if not overly accurate one; but here too translation and original composition fuse. Pound is interested in Propertius because he sees an extraordinary parallel between Propertius' times and his own and between their respective situations. Both, according to Pound, are ironic sensualists surrounded by an imbecilic Empire, and the thrust of Pound's poem is to assert a parallel between Propertius' Rome and Pound's London. Despite the title, Pound's intention of using Propertius to make his own statement was not grasped, and the *Homage to Sextus Propertius* has never received its due as Pound's most important poem before the *Cantos*. It was attacked by classicists as a horrible mistranslation, and in places it is. Perhaps the most notorious phrase in the poem is Pound's reference to "a frigidaire patent." Pound put in such phrases deliberately to signal to the reader that this poem is about the London of frigidaire patents, not simply about Rome. Instead, these phrases were seen as Pound's crude attempt to modernize his idiom, and so what should have provided valuable clues to Pound's intention were rejected as tasteless excrescences.

Cathay and *Homage to Sextus Propertius* thus represent the main line of Pound's development toward the *Cantos* because they combine his poetic of the persona with an indirect way of commenting on the present by means of implicit parallels with the past. Pound's reconciliation of the split between translation and original composition in these poems, however, was beyond his audience. Even the most sophisticated of his readers did not get the point, and it is only with the perspective offered by the *Cantos*, which work in the mode of *Cathay* and *Homage to Sextus Propertius*, that one can see the return to the present implicit in these works.

In the wake of the stormy reception of *Homage to Sextus Propertius*, Pound wrote *Hugh Selwyn Mauberley*, which presents virtually the same perceptions about London as *Homage to Sextus Propertius*, but with the subtle temporal loop between Rome and London replaced by an ironic persona, Hugh Selwyn Mauberley. Mauberley's relation to Pound is problematic: He shares certain traits with him, yet the poem is only tangentially autobiographical. It is perhaps most accurate to say that Mauberley is a self that Pound sloughed off, or the kind of figure that Pound might have become had he stayed in England. Mauberley, though fighting the stupidity and crassness he finds in English literary life, will not win that fight, and, the reader feels, he knows it. The dominant mood of *Hugh Selwyn Mauberley* is a resigned acceptance of lesser hopes and aspirations. Written just after World War I, it clearly expresses Pound's disillusionment with the course of history and with the state of English civilization. For these reasons, it is often referred to as Pound's farewell to London. It is also Pound's farewell to poems using a persona alone, without the more complicated temporal loops of *Cathay* and *Homage to Sextus Propertius*, and his farewell to the short, independent poem. After 1920, aside from a few stray political poems written in the 1930's, Pound's work in poetry was confined to the *Cantos*, a massive, sprawling eight-hundred-page poem that dwarfs the early poetry discussed so far.

Pound had always wanted to write a long poem, in this, as in other ways, remaining faithful to the traditional model of the poetic career. According to this model, he actually began his "epic" very early, for sections of the *Cantos* began to appear as early as 1917, though the first section to be published in book form, *A Draft of XVI Cantos*, did not appear until 1925. The last section of the *Cantos* to be published, *Drafts and Fragments of Cantos CX-CXVII*, came out in 1968, fully fifty-one years after the first, and it marked not the completion of the poem but its abandonment, as Pound at the age of eighty-two realized that he could not finish it. This circumstance makes discussion of the *Cantos* extraordinarily difficult. Perhaps the difficulty is best expressed by asking a simple question: Does one refer to the poem in the singular or the plural? That in turn leads to another question, involving one's critical approach to the work: Is it one long, unified poem, or is it a collection of separate parts? It is not easy to describe what unifies the poem, aside from Pound's claim that it is one poem. The *Cantos*, in short, are probably more complicated than any other poem written since the Renaissance. The reader's difficulty in subsuming all these materials under one unifying scheme should not, however, blind one to the fact that Pound hoped that the reader would be able to discover such a design. He did set out to write a unified poem, even if he took unprecedented risks in doing so. What complicates the issue is that his ideas about the structure of the poem changed, which should come as no great surprise, given the fifty-odd years that the poem occupied him. To make sense of the *Cantos*, therefore, one must approach them historically, precisely as a poem written across fifty years.

The 115 cantos available in the collected edition are customarily divided into four sections: Cantos I-XXX are known as the Early Cantos; Cantos XXXI-LXXI are the Middle Cantos; Cantos LXXIV-LXXXIV are *The Pisan Cantos*; and Cantos LXXXV-CXVII are the Later Cantos. Although material in every section escapes any ready classification, the *Cantos* in any given section tend to gather around one common theme.

The theme of the Early Cantos is the Renaissance, as the two longest sequences in this section are about Sigismundo Malatesta and sixteenth century Venice. The one feature of the *Cantos* that never changes is that they are always, no matter how indirectly or obliquely, really about the present. The implicit return to the present in the Early Cantos is that Pound is wondering whether his own era can fulfill its potential to be a new Renaissance. It has the turbulence of Malatesta's time; has it the brilliance? Toward the end of the 1920's and the Early Cantos, Pound grows less optimistic about contemporary culture and more interested in the economic and political conditions that allow art to flourish. In an implicit contrast with Malatesta's support for the arts treated in the Malatesta Cantos, the Venetian Cantos relate how Titian failed to paint works the government had commissioned, in effect defrauding the state.

This change in Pound's focus and vision prepares the reader for the new direction taken by the Middle Cantos. The cultural and artistic material of the Early Cantos is replaced by political and economic material. Cantos XXXI-LXXI present a series of images of good and bad rulers and good and bad banks: mostly good rulers—Thomas Jefferson, John Adams, Martin Van Buren, Duke Pietro Leopoldo of Tuscany—and bad banks. For Pound there has been only one good bank in history, the Monte dei Paschi Bank in Siena, and modern banking practices are responsible for the growing disorder of the modern world. History for Pound at this point is a Manichaean struggle between the forces of order and disorder, and Cantos LII-LXI summarize twenty-five hundred years of Chinese history because this struggle between order and disorder can be seen most clearly there. According to Pound, the forces of order are the Confucians, and the ideas of Confucius are the most reliable guide to the creation of political order.

None of this would have excited much interest or controversy in itself, but Pound, as always, applies his vision to the present. The implicit thrust of the Middle Cantos is that Benito Mussolini, the Fascist ruler of Italy, is the modern embodiment of the Confucian will to order; the forces of disorder are modern banks and speculative capitalists. This perception led Pound toward anti-Semitism, as he identified the Jews with the usurious banking practices he deplored. Pound, as has already been discussed, attempted to put these political ideas into action as well as putting them in his poem. The resulting personal consequences and the collapse of Mussolini's regime in 1945 were obviously catastrophic for Pound, as his thirteen years in an insane asylum attest. The artistic consequences were disastrous as well, for the contemporary political implications of the *Cantos* were rendered hopelessly out of date and exposed as absurd. Mussolini had obviously not proved to be the twentieth century's Great Emperor; Pound's poem was in praise of a murderous buffoon.

This turn of events doomed Pound's poem to be unfinished and unfinishable, at least in the sense of having a single, articulated direction and structure. What resulted, however, was paradoxically the most brilliant section of the poem. Pound, writing in a prison camp, with all action blocked, no prospect beyond incarceration or execution, his beloved Italy and much of the rest of Europe in ruins, and his political vision and his poem in a similar state of ruin, could not continue to write the Confucian epic of the Middle Cantos. Forced into a fresh start, he wrote *The Pisan Cantos*, Cantos LXXIV-LXXXIV, which are in sharp contrast to what has come before in a number of respects.

First of all, *The Pisan Cantos* mark at least a temporary abandonment of the ordering and definition of universals so prominent in the Middle Cantos. This modification has broad implications, as Pound's formal imperative to order particulars had been linked to his Confucian politics of order. No longer is he exclusively concerned with defining what constitutes a good or a bad bank, or a good or a bad ruler. There is a new willingness on Pound's part to stay with the fragment or detail, to respect its concreteness, rather than to align it with other details for the purpose of defining a generality.

In *The Pisan Cantos*, consequently, Pound comes to accept a new measure of disorder, and this allows him to open the poem to new kinds of material. He includes elements that resist generalization, such as details from nature, snippets of conversation he overhears in the detention camp, personal memories, particularly of his first years in London, and selected images and passages of poetry. These details are set out page after page, in a bewildering if dazzling array, in many languages and on every conceivable subject, without any apparent plan or order. In the earlier cantos, one canto might be set in Homeric Greece and the next in Renaissance Greece, but in *The Pisan Cantos* this kind of juxtaposition occurs on the level of the line: A quotation from Mencius will follow a detail about how olive trees look in the wind, details about economics will follow a line of conversation overheard by Pound in the camp. In these cantos, Pound feels free to include whatever he wants, and he freely moves from particular to particular by means of haikulike juxtapositions.

Critics divide much more sharply on the Later Cantos. Pound returns to promoting his views on order and maintains much the same views on society, but he recognizes that he will not see his ideals realized in his lifetime and this lessens his messianic intensity. This recognition also leads him into extended lyric passages that move away from his social and political concerns. Cantos CXVI and CXVII contain confessions of failure similar to those found in a number of Pound's late statements and interviews. He believed not only that his political activities and his anti-Semitism had been stupid and shallow but also that the *Cantos* were a failure. Just as *The Pisan Cantos* began in tragedy but ended in triumph, here Pound abandons the poem in an act of humility that somehow goes a long way toward redeeming what has gone before.

In the literary history of modern times, few individuals have cast a wider shadow of influence than Pound. In masterworks such as the *Cantos*, he single-handedly made it again possible to express serious intellectual and political matters in verse.

Other major works

PLAY: *The Testament of François Villon*, 1926 (translation into opera).

NONFICTION: *The Spirit of Romance*, 1910; *Gaudier-Brzeska: A Memoir*, 1916; *The Chinese Written Character as a*

Medium for Poetry, 1920 (editor); *Instigations of Ezra Pound, Together with an Essay on the Chinese Written Character by Ernest Fenollosa*, 1920; *Antheil and the Treatise on Harmony*, 1924; *Imaginary Letters*, 1930; *How to Read*, 1931; *ABC of Economics*, 1933; *ABC of Reading*, 1934; *Make It New*, 1934; *Social Credit: An Impact*, 1935; *Jefferson and/or Mussolini*, 1935; *Polite Essays*, 1937; *Guide to Kulchur*, 1938; *Orientamenti*, 1938; *What Is Money For?*, 1939; *Carta da Visita*, 1942 (*A Visiting Card*, 1952); *Introduzione alla natura economica degli S.U.A.*, 1944 (*An Introduction to the Economic Nature of the United States*, 1950); *L'America, Roosevelt, e le cause della guerra presente*, 1944 (*America, Roosevelt, and the Causes of the Present War*, 1951); *Orro e lavoro*, 1944 (*Gold and Work*, 1952); "*If This Be Treason . . . ,*" 1948; *The Letters of Ezra Pound, 1907-1941*, 1950; *Lavoro ed usura*, 1954; *Literary Essays*, 1954; *Impact: Essays on Ignorance and the Decline of American Civilization*, 1960; *Nuova economia editoriale*, 1962; *Patria Mia and the Treatise on Harmony*, 1962; *Pound/Joyce:The Letters of Ezra Pound to James Joyce*, 1967; *Selected Prose, 1909-1965*, 1973; *Ezra Pound and Music: The Complete Criticism*, 1977; "*Ezra Pound Speaking*": *Radio Speeches of World War II*, 1978; *Letters to Ibbotson, 1935-1952*, 1979; *Ezra Pound and the Visual Arts*, 1980; *From Syria: The Worksheets, Proofs, and Text*, 1981; *Pound/Ford: The Story of a Literary Friendship*, 1982; *Ezra Pound and Dorothy Shakespear: Their Letters, 1909-1914*, 1984; *The Letters of Ezra Pound and Wyndham Lewis*, 1985; *The Selected Letters of Ezra Pound to John Quinn, 1915-1924*, 1991; *A Walking Tour in Southern France: Ezra Pound Among the Troubadours*, 1992; *The Letters of Ezra Pound to Alice Corbin Henderson*, 1993; *Ezra Pound and James Laughlin: Selected Letters*, 1994.

TRANSLATIONS: *The Sonnets and Ballate of Guido Cavalcanti*, 1912; *Cathay: Translations by Ezra Pound for the Most Part from the Chinese of Rihaku, from the Notes of the Late Ernest Fenollosa and the Decipherings of the Professors Mori and Ariga*, 1915; *'Noh' or Accomplishment*, 1916 (with Ernest Fenollosa); *The Natural Philosophy of Love*, 1922 (of Remy de Gourmont's work); *The Testament of François Villon*, 1926 (translation into opera); *Rime*, 1932 (of Guido Cavalcanti's poetry); *Homage to Sextus Propertius*, 1934; *Digest of the Analects*, 1937 (of Confucius' work); *Italy's Policy of Social Economics, 1930-1940*, 1941 (of Odon Por's work); *Confucius: The Unwobbling Pivot and the Great Digest*, 1947; *The Translations of Ezra Pound*, 1953; *The Classic Anthology Defined by Confucius*, 1954 (*The Confucian Odes*); *Women of Tranchis*, 1956 (of Sophocles' play); *Love Poems of Ancient Egypt*, 1964; *Confucius*, 1969.

ANTHOLOGIES: *Des Imagistes: An Anthology*, 1914; *Catholic Anthology 1914-1915*, 1915; *Active Anthology*, 1933; *Confucius to Cummings: An Anthology of Poetry*, 1964 (with Marcella Spann).

MISCELLANEOUS: *Ezra Pound's Poetry and Prose: Contributions to Periodicals*, 1991.

Bibliography

Carpenter, Humphrey. *A Serious Character: The Life of Ezra Pound*. Boston: Houghton Mifflin, 1988.

Froula, Christine. *A Guide to Ezra Pound's Selected Poems*. New York: New Directions, 1983.

Heymann, David. *Ezra Pound: The Last Rower*. New York: Viking Press, 1976.

Kenner, Hugh. *The Poetry of Ezra Pound*. London: Faber & Faber, 1951. Rev. ed. Lincoln: University of Nebraska Press, 1985.

Knapp, James F. *Ezra Pound*. Boston: Twayne, 1979.

Kuberski, Philip. *A Calculus of Ezra Pound: Vocations of the American Sign*. Gainesville: University Press of Florida, 1992.

Laughlin, James. *Pound as Wuz: Essays and Lectures on Ezra Pound*. Saint Paul, Minn.: Graywolf Press, 1987.

Sicari, Stephen. *Pound's Epic Ambition: Dante and the Modern World*. Albany: State University of New York Press, 1991.

Stock, Noel, ed. *Ezra Pound Perspectives: Essays in Honor of His Eightieth Birthday*. Chicago: H. Regnery, 1965.

Stock, Noel. *The Life of Ezra Pound*. 1970. Rev. ed. San Francisco: North Point Press, 1982.

GERTRUDE STEIN

Born: Allegheny, Pennsylvania; February 3, 1874   **Died:** Neuilly-sur-Seine, France; July 27, 1946

Principal long fiction

Three Lives, 1909; *The Making of Americans*, 1925; *Lucy Church Amiably*, 1930; *A Long Gay Book*, 1932; *Ida, a Novel*, 1941; *Brewsie and Willie*, 1946; *Blood on the Dining-Room Floor*, 1948; *Things As They Are*, 1950 (later as *Quod Erat Demonstrandum*, or *Q.E.D.*); *Mrs. Reynolds and Five Earlier Novelettes, 1931-1942*, 1952; *A Novel of Thank You*, 1958.

Other literary forms

Very few of Gertrude Stein's more than six hundred titles in more than forty books can be adequately classified into any traditional literary forms. Her philosophy of composition was so idiosyncratic, her prose style so seemingly nonrational, that her writing bears little resemblance to whatever genre it purports to represent. If references to literary forms are made very loosely, Stein's work can be divided into novels, autobiographies, portraits, poems, lectures, operas, plays, and explanations. Other than her novels, her best-known works are *The Autobiography of Alice B. Toklas* (1933), *Tender Buttons* (1914), *Four Saints in Three Acts* (1934), *Lectures in America* (1935), *Everybody's Autobiography* (1937), and *Portraits and Prayers* (1934).

Achievements

Whether towering or crouching, Stein is ubiquitous in contemporary literature. A child of the nineteenth century who staunchly adhered to many of its values halfway through the twentieth, she nevertheless dedicated her creative life to the destruction of nineteenth century concepts of artistic order and purpose. In her own words, she set out to do nothing less than to kill a century, to lay the old ways of literary convention to rest. She later boasted that "the most serious thinking about the nature of literature in the twentieth century has been done by a woman," and her claim has great merit. During the course of her career, Stein finally managed to convince almost everyone that there was indeed some point, if not profundity, in her aggressively enigmatic style. The ridicule and parody that frustrated so much of her early work had turned to grudging tolerance or outright lionizing by 1934, when Stein made her triumphant American lecture tour; for the last fifteen or so years of her life, she was published even if her editor had not the vaguest idea of what she was doing (as Bennett Cerf later admitted he had not). On

the most concrete level, Stein's distinctive prose style is remarkably significant even when its philosophical dimensions are ignored. William Gass has observed that Stein "did more with sentences, and understood them better, than any writer ever has."

More important was Stein's influence on other leaders in the development of modernism. As a student of William James and a friend of Alfred North Whitehead and Pablo Picasso, Stein lived at the center of the philosophical and artistic revolutions of the twentieth century. She was the natural emblem for modernism, and in her person, career, and legend, many of its salient issues converged. In the light of more recent developments in the novel and in literary theory, it has also been argued that Stein was the first postmodernist, the first writer to claim openly that the instance of language is itself as important as the reality to which it refers. Among major writers, Ernest Hemingway was most obviously influenced by his association with her, but her genius was freely acknowledged by F. Scott Fitzgerald, Sherwood Anderson, and Thornton Wilder. William Saroyan explained her influence most directly when he asserted that no American writer could keep from coming under it, a sentiment reluctantly echoed by Edmund Wilson in *Axel's Castle* (1931), even before Stein's great popular success in the mid-1930's.

Biography

Gertrude Stein was born on February 3, 1874, in Allegheny, Pennsylvania, but she was seven before her family settled into permanent residence in Oakland, California. Stein's early years were comfortably bourgeois and uneventful. Her father, a vice president of the Union Street Municipal Railway System in San Francisco, was authoritarian, moody, aggressive, but vacillating, and he may have helped foster her sense of independence, but he undoubtedly left her annoyed by him in particular and by fatherhood in general. Her mother barely figured in her life at all: A pale, withdrawn, ineffectual woman, she left most of the rearing of her children to governesses. By the time Stein was seventeen, both parents had died and she had grown even closer to her immediate older brother, Leo. In 1893, she entered Harvard Annex (renamed Radcliffe College the following year), thus rejoining Leo, who was a student at Harvard. There, Stein studied with William James and Hugo Munsterberg and became involved in research in psychology. Together with the great influence exerted on her thinking by William James, this early work in psychology was to provide her with both a subject and a style that would continue in many forms throughout her career. She was awarded her A.B. degree by Harvard in 1898, almost a year after she had entered medical school at The Johns Hopkins University. Her interest in medicine rapidly waned, and she left Johns Hopkins in 1901, failing four courses in her final semester.

After leaving medical school, Stein spent two years moving back and forth between Europe and America. During that time, she was involved in an agonizing love affair with another young woman student at Johns Hopkins, May Bookstaver. The affair was painfully complicated, first by Stein's naïveté, then by the presence of a more sophisticated rival for May's love, Mabel Haynes. The resulting lover's triangle led Stein, in an effort to understand May, to begin formulating the theories of personality that dominated her early writing. The frustration and eventual despair of this lesbian relationship profoundly influenced Stein's view of the psychology of personality and of love. Most directly, Stein's troubled affair with May Bookstaver provided her with many, if not most, of the concerns of three of her books, *Q.E.D.*, *The Making of Americans*, and *Three Lives*, the first two of which she began while living in New York in the winter of 1903.

After a brief stay in New York, Stein lived with Leo, first in Bloomsbury in London and then, beginning in 1903, in Paris at 27 rue de Fleurus, the address she was to make so well known in the world as a parlor for the exchange of ideas among American and European artists, including other expatriates. In Paris, Gertrude and Leo became more and more interested in painting, buying works by new artists such as Henri Matisse and Picasso.

In 1907, Stein met another young American woman in Paris, Alice Toklas. Alice learned to type so she could transcribe Stein's handwritten manuscripts, beginning with portions of *The Making of Americans* in 1908. In 1909, Alice moved in with Gertrude and Leo at 27 rue de Fleurus, and by 1913, Alice had replaced Leo as Gertrude's companion and as the manager of her household. Stein later referred to her relationship with Alice as a "marriage," and few, if any, personal relationships have ever influenced a literary career so profoundly. Apart from providing Stein with the persona for her best-known work, *The Autobiography of Alice B. Toklas* (1933), Alice typed, criticized, and valiantly worked to publish all Stein's work for the rest of her career and for the twenty years that she lived after Stein's death.

Modernism had burst on the American consciousness when the Armory Show opened in New York in 1913, and this show, which had confronted Americans with the first cubist paintings, also led to the association in the public mind of Stein's writing with this shockingly new art, particularly since Stein's first periodical publications had been "Matisse" and "Picasso" in *Camera Work*, the year before. Stein's mammoth, 925-page novel, *The Making of Americans*, was published in 1925, and in 1926, she lectured at Oxford and Cambridge, attempting to explain her idiosyncratic writing style. Her "landscape" novel, *Lucy Church Amiably*, appeared in 1930, but it was in 1933, with the publication of the best-selling *The Autobiography of Alice B. Toklas*, that Stein first captured the public's interest. She became front-page news the following year when her opera *Four Saints in Three Acts* (1934) was first performed and when she embarked on a nationwide lecture tour, later described in *Everybody's Autobiography* (1937) and *Lectures in America* (1935).

Stein died following an operation for cancer in the American Hospital in Neuilly-sur-Seine, France, on July 27, 1946. While Alice Toklas' account of Stein's last words may be apocryphal, it certainly is in keeping with the spirit of her life. As Alice later reconstructed their last conversation, Stein had asked her, "What is the answer?" Then, when Alice remained silent, Stein added, "In that case, what is the question?"

Analysis

While Gertrude Stein's persistence finally earned her access to readers, it could never guarantee her readers who would or could take her strange writing seriously. As a result, more confusing and contradictory information surrounds her career than that of any other twentieth century writer of comparable reputation. Usually responding in any of four basic ways, readers and critics alike seemed to view her as (1) a literary charlatan of the P.T. Barnum ilk, interested in publicity or money rather than in art; (2) something of a naïve child-woman incapable of comprehending the world around her; (3) a fiery-eyed literary revolutionary, den mother of the avant-garde; or (4) an ageless repository of wisdom and genius.

Starting from the assumption that no one can ever really understand what someone else says or writes because of the inherent ambiguity of language, Stein not only decided to force her readers to confront that ambiguity but also claimed it as a primary virtue of her writing. She announced triumphantly that "if you have vitality enough of knowing enough of what you mean, somebody and sometimes a great many will have to realize that you know what you mean and so they will agree that you mean what you know, which is as near as anybody can come to understanding any one."

Three central concerns underlie the development of Stein's writing style. These concerns are with the value of individual words, with repetition as the basic rhythm of existence, and with the related concept of "movement" in writing. Her articulations of these central concerns all run counter to her readers' expectations about the purpose and function of language and of literature. Her writing surprised her readers in much the same way that her penchant for playing only the black keys on a piano surprised and frustrated all but the most patient of her listeners.

One of Stein's goals was to return full meaning, value, and particularity to the words she used. "I took individual words and thought about them until I got their weight and volume complete and put them next to another word," she explained of seemingly nonsense phrases such as "toasted Susie is my ice cream." or "mouse and mountain and a quiver, a quaint statue and pain in an exterior and silence more silence louder shows salmon a mischief intender." She frequently chose to stress or focus on a part or aspect of the object of her description that the reader normally does not consider. The "things" Stein saw and wrote of were not the "things" with which readers are familiar: Where another observer might see a coin balanced on its edge, Stein might choose either of the descriptive extremes of seeing it literally as a thin rectangle, or figuratively as the essence of money.

Stein said she had learned from Paul Cézanne that everything in a painting was related to everything else and that each part of the painting was of equal importance—a blade of grass as important to the composition of the painting as a tree. She attempted to apply these two principles to the composition of her sentences, taking special delight in using normally "overlooked" words, arguing that articles, prepositions, and conjunctions—the transitive elements in grammar—are just as important and more interesting than substantives such as nouns and verbs. Her reassessment both of the value of words and of the conventions of description resulted in what Michael J. Hoffman has described as Stein's "abstractionism." It also resulted in her including in her writing totally unexpected information in perplexingly paratactic word-strings.

A second constant in Stein's style, influenced by cubism, is the pronounced repetition of words, phrases, and sentences, with no change or with only incremental progressions of sounds or associations. Works such as *The Making of Americans* and *Three Lives* contain long passages in which each sentence is a light variation on some core phrase, with great repetition of words even within a single sentence. Repetition is perhaps the central aspect of what has been called Stein's "cinema style," based on her claim that in writing *The Making of Americans* she was "doing what the cinema was doing." She added that her writing in that book was "like a cinema picture made up of succession and each moment having its own emphasis that is its own difference and so there was the moving and the existence of each moment as it was in me."

Stein's discussion of "what the cinema was doing" appears in her *Lectures in America* and also suggests the third basic concern of her writing: movement. By "movement," she referred not to the movement of a message to its conclusion or the movement of a plot or narrative but to "the essence of its going" of her prose, a timeless continuous present in the never-ending motion of consciousness. Stein also credits Cézanne with discovering this concern, "a feeling of movement inside the painting not a painting of a thing moving but the thing painted having inside it the existence of moving." She seemed to understand Cézanne's achievement in terms of William James's model of consciousness as an ever-flowing stream of thought. Accordingly, she used her writing not to record a scene or object or idea (products of thought) but to try to capture the sense of the process of perceiving such things. Stein's subject is almost always really two things at once: whatever attracted her attention—caught her eye, entered her ear, or crossed her mind—and the mobile nature of reality, particularly as it is perceived by human consciousness.

From James at Harvard and possibly from Henri Bergson in Paris, Stein had learned that the best model for human consciousness was one that stressed the processual, ever-flowing nature of experience. She added to this belief her assumption that the essence of any subject could be perceived and should be represented only through its motion, echoing Bergson's claim that "reality is mobility." While James would certainly have objected to Stein's sequential cinema model as an approximation of the stream of consciousness, her motion-obsessed writing probably suggests the flow of consciousness as well as does any literary style.

Three Lives is easily Stein's best-known and most respected piece of fiction. Technically three novellas, this work is unified by its three subjects, by its central concern with the nature of consciousness, and by its attempt to blend colloquial idioms with Stein's emerging style, here based largely on her understanding of Cézanne's principles of composition, particularly that "one thing was as important as another thing." "The Good Anna," "Melanctha," and "The Gentle Lena" are the three sections of this work. Anna and Lena are poor German immigrants who patiently work as servants in Bridgepoint, Baltimore; Melanctha is a young black woman who discovers sexuality and love, then turns from a frustrating relationship with a sincere young black doctor to a dissipative affair with a gambler. Since all three women are essentially victimized by their surroundings and die at the end of their stories, this work is deterministic in the naturalist tradition, but *Three Lives* marks the transition from naturalism to modernism as Stein departs from nineteenth century literary conventions. She abandons conventional syntax to try to follow the movement of a consciousness rather than of events, and she develops a new narrative style only partially tied to linear chronology. The result is an interior narrative of consciousness in which Stein's prose style serves as the primary carrier of knowledge. Through the rhythms of her characters' speech and the rhythms of her narration, Stein gives her reader a sense of the basic rhythms of consciousness for these three women—what Stein would elsewhere refer to as their "bottom natures."

Possibly Stein's most widely celebrated piece of writing, "Melanctha" has been praised by Richard Wright, among others, as one of the first realistic and sympathetic renderings of black life by a white American author. Melanctha's race is, however, incidental to Stein's central concerns with finding a style to express the rhythms of personality and the frustrating cycles of love.

While it was not published until 1925, Stein's *The Making of Americans* occupied her as early as 1903 and was in fact begun before *Q.E.D.* and *Three Lives*. This mammoth novel began as a description of the creation of Americans from a representative immigrant family: "The old people in a new world, the new people made out of the old, that is the story that I mean to tell, for that is what really is and what I really know." Stein's projected family chronicle soon lost its original focus, becoming first a history of everyone, then a study of character types rather than of characters. Leon Katz, who has worked with this book more than has anyone else, calls it "a massive description of the psychological landscape of human being in its totality." Although the book ostensibly continues to follow events in the lives of two central families, the Herslands and the Dehnings, its real concern is almost always both larger and smaller, ranging from Stein's questions about her own life and identity to questions about the various personality types of all of humanity. As Richard Bridgman suggests, this is "an improvised work of no identifiable genre in which the creator learned by doing," one "full of momentary wonders and botched long-range schemes, lyrical outbursts and anguished confessions." Accordingly, Bridgman concludes that *The Making of Americans* is best thought of "not as a fictional narrative nor a philosophic tract, but as a drama of self-education." In a way, the book chronicles the "making" of Gertrude Stein, presenting a phenomenology of her mind as it works its way through personal problems toward the distinctive "cinema style."

Underlying a great part of the writing in this book is Stein's belief that human personality consists of variations on a few basic "bottom natures" or kinds of identity which can be perceived through a character's repeated actions. "There are then many things every one has in them that come out of them in the repeating everything living have always in them, repeating with a little changing just enough to make of each one an individual being, to make of each repeating an individual thing that gives to such a one a feeling of themselves inside them." There are two basic personality types, "dependent independent" and "independent dependent," polarities identified in part by the way the person fights: the first kind by resisting, the second by attacking. Concerns with character-typing dominate the book's first two sections, "The Dehnings and the Herslands" and "Martha Hersland" (the character most closely modeled on Stein's own life), while the third section, "Alfred and Julia Hersland," contains mostly digressions about contemporary matters in Stein's life.

The fourth section, "David Hersland," becomes a meditation on the nature of aging and death ("He was dead when he was at the beginning of being in middle living"), and the final section, "History of a Family's Progress," is—even for Stein—an incredibly abstract and repetitive series of reflections on the concerns that had given rise to the novel. This final section contains no name, referring only to "some," "any," "every," or "very many."

Stein later described her efforts in this book as an attempt "to do what the cinema was doing," that is, to give a sense of motion and life through a series of highly repetitive statements, each statement only an incremental change from the preceding one, like frames in a strip of film. One of the main effects of this technique is to freeze all action into a "continuous present." Not only do Stein's sentences exist in overlapping clusters, depending more for their meaning on their relationships to one another than on individual semantic content, but also her verbs in *The Making of Americans* are almost exclusively present participles, suspending all action in the present progressive tense. As a result, while *The Making of Americans* does ostensibly present a history of four generations of the Hersland family, it conveys little or no sense of the passage of time. Instead, the book presents a sense of "existence suspended in time," a self-contained world existing quite independently of the "real world," a basic modernist goal that has also become one of the hallmarks of postmodernism. For all its difficulty, *The Making of Americans* is one of modernism's seminal works and an invaluable key to Stein's literary career.

However idiosyncratic Stein's writing may seem, it must be remembered that a very strong case can be made for its substantial philosophical underpinnings. To her way of thinking, language could refuse few things to Stein, and the limitations of language were exactly what she refused to accept. She bent the language to the very uses that process philosophers such as James and Bergson and Whitehead feared it could not be put. Her stubborn emphasis on the individual word—particularly on transitive elements—her insistent use of repetition, and her ever-present preoccupation with the essential motion of words were all part of Stein's monumental struggle with a language she felt was not accurately used to reflect the way people perceive reality or the motion of reality itself. In a narrow but profound sense, she is the most serious realist in literary history.

Other major works

PLAYS: *Geography and Plays*, 1922; *Operas and Plays*, 1932; *Four Saints in Three Acts*, 1934; *Lucretia Borgia*, 1939; *In Savoy: Or, Yes Is for a Very Young Man (A Play of the Resistance in France)*, 1946; *The Mother of Us All*, 1947; *Last Operas and Plays*, 1949; *In a Garden: An Opera in One Act*, 1951; *Selected Operas and Plays*, 1970.

POETRY: *Tender Buttons: Objects, Food, Rooms*, 1914; *Two (Hitherto Unpublished) Poems*, 1948; *Bee Time Vine and Other Pieces: 1913-1927*, 1953; *Stanzas in Meditation and Other Poems: 1929-1933*, 1956.

NONFICTION: *The Autobiography of Alice B. Toklas*, 1933; *Matisse, Picasso, and Gertrude Stein, with Two Shorter Stories*, 1933; *Portraits and Prayers*, 1934; *Lectures in America*, 1935; *Narration: Four Lectures*, 1935; *The Geographical History of America*, 1936; *Everybody's Autobiography*, 1937; *Picasso*, 1938; *What Are Masterpieces*, 1940; *Wars I Have Seen*, 1945; *Reflections on the Atomic Bomb*, 1973; *How Writing Is Written*, 1974; *The Letters of Gertrude Stein and Carl Van Vechten, 1913-1946*, 1986.

CHILDREN'S LITERATURE: *The World Is Round*, 1939.

MISCELLANEOUS: *The Gertrude Stein First Reader and Three Plays*, 1946; *The Yale Edition of the Unpublished Writings of Gertrude Stein*, 1951-1958 (8 vols.); *Selected Writings of Gertrude Stein*, 1962; *The Yale Gertrude Stein*, 1980; *A Stein Reader*, 1993.

Bibliography

Bridgman, Richard. *Gertrude Stein in Pieces*. New York: Oxford University Press, 1970.

Chessman, Harriet Scott. *The Public Is Invited to Dance: Representation, the Body, and Dialogue in Gertrude Stein*. Stanford, Calif.: Stanford University Press, 1989.

Doane, Janice L. *Silence and Narrative: The Early Novels of Gertrude Stein*. Westport, Conn.: Greenwood Press, 1986.

Dubnick, Randa. *The Structure of Obscurity: Gertrude Stein, Language, and Cubism*. Urbana: University of Illinois Press, 1984.

Hoffman, Michael J., ed. *Critical Essays on Gertrude Stein*. Boston: G. K. Hall, 1986.

——————— . *Gertrude Stein*. Boston: Twayne, 1976.

Knapp, Bettina Liebowitz. *Gertrude Stein*. New York: Continuum, 1990.

Mellow, James R. *Charmed Circle: Gertrude Stein and Company*. New York: Praeger, 1974.

Neuman, Shirley, and Ira B. Nadel, eds. *Gertrude Stein and the Making of Literature*. Boston: Northeastern University Press, 1988.

Ruddick, Lisa. *Reading Gertrude Stein: Body, Text, Gnosis*. Ithaca, N.Y.: Cornell University Press, 1990.

Steiner, Wendy. *Exact Resemblance to Exact Resemblance*. New Haven, Conn.: Yale University Press, 1978.

Walker, Jayne L. *The Making of a Modernist: Gertrude Stein from "Three Lives" to "Tender Buttons."* Amherst: University of Massachusetts, 1984.

IX

AMERICANS AT WAR
Defining Moments

One day one of their number would write a book about all this. . . .
—James Jones, *The Thin Red Line*, 1962

The writers in this section are not war novelists in any conventional sense of the term, though they did make their reputations writing of war. For them all war was at once an example and a metaphor. War loomed large over their lives, the Civil War for Stephen Crane, World War II and Vietnam for James Jones, Joseph Heller, Kurt Vonnegut, Jr., Thomas Pynchon, and Tim O'Brien. Each of them had some sort of military experience. All but Pynchon saw combat. As artists, as men, they could not escape the unprecedented violence of their times. More important, war came to embody for these authors profound processes molding their age. War was not an accident, or a disruption of modern life, but rather an expression of the true nature of contemporary society. War was the raw face of a mechanized, industrial order, stripped of any prettying mask. Moloch offered men and women a reeking mirror.

These writers criticized an America in which the individual was lost, submerged in bureaucracies that dehumanized, and urban landscapes that dwarfed, any man or woman attempting to breathe free. Their works were acts of rebellion. They called for resistance. Against the modern background of total war and mobilization for total war, these authors, from Crane to O'Brien, urged a more modest but also more meaningful battle, a struggle for individual autonomy and reverence for the human soul. Their restive hostility to urban, industrial society firmly anchored them to American cultural and literary tradition. Thematic and formal iconoclasm simply served as the badge of a deeper conformity. These men worshipped at the altar of American individualism, a recurrent ideal in American

intellectual history, eternally elastic but also eternally evocative. Their writings reverberate with echoes lingering from the days of the pioneers—or, more precisely, subsequent generations' imaginings of the heroic opening of America. The almost anarchic spirit of liberty celebrated by these authors shadows the resolute independence of frontiersmen like Daniel Boone, men supposedly so untrammeled by the bonds of civilization that they felt crowded by the appearance of a cabin within twenty miles of their own. Life, lived in all its richness, lay outside the constraints of society. It is one of the ironies of American history that, while resolutely building cities and industries, Americans have clung to the romance of forest and field. While the commercial vision of Alexander Hamilton captured Americans' heads, Thomas Jefferson's vision of an agrarian utopia won a lasting place in their hearts. Individual fulfillment was to be found in nature's embrace.

Such was the message of many early classics of American literature. James Fenimore Cooper created an enduring American archetype in his Leatherstocking novels. His character Natty Bumppo became the original American hero, a frontier woodsman who, because of his sylvan upbringing, was untouched by the vices of the settlements. Literally nature's nobleman, Natty Bumppo adumbrated a distinctly American literary persona, untroubled by the deadening hand of history and convention. As such, he was an American innocent, an Adamic figure, symbolically incarnating the lofty promise of a young nation happily cocooned in the New World. Other writers, such as Nathaniel Hawthorne and Herman Melville, picked up the theme of the American innocent and explored it with great subtlety. They and their nineteenth century peers produced a rich body of work, which in its celebration of American exceptionalism and American individualism reflected the essential optimism of a frontier nation still predominantly a rural land of small villages.

Stephen Crane, James Jones, Joseph Heller, Kurt Vonnegut, Jr., Thomas Pynchon, and Tim O'Brien all experimented brilliantly with the figure of the American innocent. But living in the shadow of a different history, their writings took on a more somber tone. The cold grandeur of the modern city, with its jagged skyline and belching smokestacks, had replaced the comfortable insularity of the nineteenth century village. With its continental boundaries secured by the displacement of the Indians and the intimidation of its neighbors, the United States pursued great power status across the oceans, leaving behind its once cherished isolation, playing again and again the bitter coin of imperial glory, a succession of wars, great and small. As both observers and participants, the writers discussed in this section had to make sense of this dramatic transformation of the United States. They had to record the drift of the American people away from the ideals of the nation's founding generations. And so, in their hands, the American innocent becomes a much more ambivalent figure, not simply an outsider but an outcast, with the purity of Natty Bumppo's life in the majestic forest little more than a wistful memory. The protagonists of these writers are rebels and grifters. They live perilously on the fringes of communities and institutions. They lurch, often blindly, through the treacherous shoals of modernity, seeking refuge from the impersonal forces that would destroy them, not daring to hope for more. Thus, it is not surprising that desertion becomes a central motif in the "war" novels of Crane, Jones, Heller, Pynchon, and O'Brien. Even Kurt Vonnegut, Jr.'s aptly named character Billy Pilgrim, though not technically a deserter, finds relief from the corruption of his world through his adventures on the planet Tralfamadore. For these authors the American innocent becomes the innocent antihero.

Fittingly, Stephen Crane created the innocent antihero in a novel about the Civil War, the first modern war, in which developments in military firepower began to negate storybook battlefield heroics. In *The Red Badge of Courage* (1895), a young soldier named Henry Fleming is thoroughly lost amid the awesome immensity of the Civil War. Running from his unit after a skirmish, he wanders aimlessly in the flotsam of battle. After Fleming receives a blow to the head, his comrades receive him back as a wounded hero, and he mechanically lives up to his fresh reputation in the next firefight. The novel ends ironically with the inadvertent hero convinced of his own manhood and insight into the nature of things. James Jones explored similar themes in his powerful trilogy *From Here to Eternity* (1951), *The Thin Red Line* (1962), and *Whistle* (1978), which traced the experiences of American soldiers in World War II, from the days before Pearl Harbor, through combat on Guadalcanal, and then to the agony of veterans' hospitals. Jones's most memorable character is the doomed bugler Robert Prewitt in *From Here to Eternity*, who struggles against the brutalities of the army only to be shot accidentally by his fellow Americans. Joseph Heller created a surreal fable of corporate authority run amok in his novel *Catch-22* (1961). His justly paranoid protagonist Yossarian desperately tries to evade both the horrors of more bombing missions over Germany and the dangerous enthusiasms of his compatriots, one of whom in a triumph of capitalist enterprise contracts with the Germans to have his own airfield bombed. Kurt Vonnegut, Jr., veers wildly through space and time in *Slaughterhouse-Five* (1969) as he explores Billy Pilgrim's unsuccessful quest to escape the grim memory of being caught in the Allies' unnecessary firebombing of Dresden. Thomas Pynchon's massive *Gravity's Rainbow* (1973) centers on the travails of Tyrone Slothrop, an American soldier sexually attuned to the German V-2 rocket attacks on London. Seeking an explanation for this bizarre trait, Slothrop literally loses himself in the backwash of World War II. Tim O'Brien's *Going After Cacciato* (1978) is a study of the power of imagination. Cacciato, an American soldier in Vietnam, decides to walk away from what seems a pointless war, marching overland across Eurasia to Paris. Another solider, Paul Berlin, follows this mad endeavor in his mind, imagining the adventures of his squad as they trail Cacciato to the banks of the Seine.

In keeping with the pattern established by Crane's *The Red Badge of Courage*, all these works share a dreamlike quality, reflecting the thwarted aspirations of their protagonists. War in these novels is not the orderly exercise of force analyzed in military histories. It is instead an industrial process. Men and women become cogs in a machine running increasingly out of control. Therein lies the moral of these authors and the terror of their antiheroes. In the bleak American realm of these novels, a realm spiritually far removed from the moral cosmos of Cooper, Hawthorne, and Melville, no one is in charge, not man, not God. People are trapped in a technological and corporate prison which has no keeper. The American antihero struggles to survive in an existential chaos. Most of these novels depict worlds as brilliantly confused as the interior of a funhouse hall of mirrors, with images endlessly reflected off each other. The soothing natural truths of Natty Bumppo are lost to the antihero. The modern descendants of the literary frontiersmen must dwell in uncertainty and doubt. Truth in these books is subjective, caught somewhere in the protagonists' minds. As James Jones elegantly put it in the last words of *The Thin Red Line*: "One day one of their number would write a book about all this, but none of them would believe it, because none of them would remember it that way."

—Daniel P. Murphy
Hanover College

STEPHEN CRANE

Born: Newark, New Jersey; November 1, 1871   **Died:** Badenweiler, Germany; June 5, 1900

Principal long fiction

Maggie: A Girl of the Streets, 1893; *The Red Badge of Courage: An Episode of the American Civil War*, 1895; *George's Mother*, 1896; *The Third Violet*, 1897; *Active Service*, 1899; *The Monster and Other Stories*, 1899; *The O'Ruddy: A Romance*, 1903 (with Robert Barr).

Other literary forms

Stephen Crane was an accomplished poet, short-story writer, and journalist as well as a novelist. His first collection of poems, *The Black Riders and Other Lines*, appeared in 1895; in 1896, a collection of seven poems and a sketch was published as *A Souvenir and a Medley*; and *War Is Kind*, another collection of poetry, was published in 1899. Crane's uncollected poems form part of the tenth volume of *The University Press of Virginia Edition of the Works of Stephen Crane* (1970). *The Blood of the Martyr*, a closet drama believed to have been written in 1898, was not published until 1940. One other play, *The Ghost* (1899), written for a Christmas party at Crane's home in England by Crane and others, has not survived in toto. Crane's short stories and sketches, of which there are many, began appearing in 1892 and have been discovered from time to time up to the present. His journalistic pieces occasionally have literary value.

Achievements

As one of the Impressionist writers—Joseph Conrad called him "The Impressionist"—Crane was among the first to express in writing a new way of looking at the world. A pivotal movement in the history of ideas, Impressionism grew out of scientific discoveries that showed how human physiology, particularly that of the eye, determines the way everything in the universe and everything outside the individual body and mind is perceived. People do not see the world as it is; the mind and the eye collaborate to interpret a chaotic universe as fundamentally unified, coherent, and explainable. The delusion is compounded when human beings agglomerate, for then they tend to create grander fabrications such as religion and history. Although Crane is also seen as one of the first American naturalistic writers, a symbolist, imagist, and even a nihilist, the achievements designated by these labels all derive from his impressionistic worldview.

Crane's major achievement, both as a fiction writer and as a poet, was that he unflinchingly fought his way through established assumptions about the nature of life, eventually overcoming them. His perceptions were the logical end to the ideas of a long line of American Puritans and Transcendentalists who believed in the individual pursuit of truth. The great and perhaps fitting irony of that logic is that Crane repudiated the truths in which his predecessors believed. Rejecting much that was conventional about fiction in his day—elaborate plots, numerous and usually middle- or upper-class characters, romantic settings, moralizing narrators—Crane also denied values of much greater significance: nationalism, patriotism, the greatness of individual and collective man, and the existence of supernatural powers that care, protect, and guide.

In his best fiction, as in his life, Crane squarely faced the horror of a meaningless universe by exposing the blindness and egotism of concepts that deny that meaninglessness. He was, unfortunately, unable to build a new and positive vision on the rubble of the old; he died at age twenty-eight, his accomplishments genuinely astounding.

Biography

Born on November 1, 1871, in the Methodist parsonage in Newark, New Jersey, Stephen Crane was the fourteenth and last child of Mary Peck Crane and the Reverend Jonathan Crane, whose family dated back more than two centuries on the American continent. On the Peck side, almost every male was a minister, and one became a bishop. By the time his father died in 1880, Crane had lived in several places in New York and New Jersey and had been thoroughly indoctrinated in the faith he was soon to reject. Also around this time, he wrote his first poem, "I'd Rather Have." His first short story, "Uncle Jake and the Bell Handle," was written in 1885, and the same year he enrolled in Pennington Seminary, where he stayed until 1887. Between 1888 and 1891, he attended Claverack College, Hudson River Institute, Lafayette College, and Syracuse University. He was never graduated from any of these, preferring baseball to study. In 1892, the New York *Tribune* published many of his New York City sketches and more than a dozen Sullivan County tales. Having apparently forgotten Miss Helen Trent, his first love, he fell in love with Mrs. Lily Brandon Munroe. That same year, the mechanics' union took exception to his article on their annual fete, which resulted in Crane's brother, Townley, being fired from the *Tribune*.

In 1893, Crane published at his own expense an early version of *Maggie: A Girl of the Streets*. William Dean Howells introduced him to Emily Dickinson's poetry, and in the next year he met Hamlin Garland. Also in 1894, the Philadelphia *Press* published an abridged version of *The Red Badge of Courage*.

During the first half of 1895, Crane traveled in the West, where he met Willa Cather, and in Mexico for the Bachellor Syndicate. *The Black Riders and Other Lines* was published in May; *The Red Badge of Courage* appeared in October. By December, he was famous, having just turned twenty-four. In 1896, he published *George's Mother*, *The Little Regiment and Other Episodes of the American Civil War*, and fell in love with Cora Stewart (Howarth), whom he never married but with whom he lived for the rest of his life.

In January, 1897, on the way to report the insurgency in Cuba, Crane was shipwrecked off the Florida coast. Four months later, he was in Greece, reporting on the Greco-Turkish War. Moving back to England, he became friends with Conrad, Henry James, Harold Frederic, H. G. Wells, and others. During that year, he wrote most of his great short stories: "The Open Boat," "The Bride Comes to Yellow Sky," and "The Blue Hotel."

Never very healthy, Crane began to weaken in 1898 as a result of malaria contracted in Cuba while he was reporting on the Spanish-American War. By 1899, Crane was back in England and living well above his means. Although he published *War Is Kind*, *Active Service*, and *The Monster and Other Stories*, he continued to fall more deeply in debt. By 1900, he was hopelessly debt-ridden and fatally ill. Exhausted from overwork, intestinal tuberculosis, malaria, and the experiences of an intense life, Crane died at the early age of twenty-eight, leaving works that fill ten sizable volumes.

Analysis

Crane's first novel, *Maggie: A Girl of the Streets*, is the first American novel to portray realistically the chaos of the slums without either providing the protagonist with a "way out" or moralizing on the subject of social injustice. *Maggie* is the story of a young Irish American girl who grows up in the Bowery slums of New York. The novel seems to belong to the tradition of the *Bildungsroman*, but its greatness lies in the irony that in this harsh environment, no one's quest is fulfilled, no one learns anything: The novel swings from chaos on the one side to complete illusion on the other side.

The form of the novel is that of a classical tragedy overlaid by nihilism that prevents the final optimism of tragedy from surfacing. The tragic "mistake," what the Greeks called *hamartia*, derives from a naturalistic credo: Maggie was unlucky enough to have been born a pretty girl in an environment she was unable to escape. Although she tries to make the best of her limited choices, she is inexorably driven to make choices that lead her to ruin and death. The novel's other characters are similarly trapped by their environment. Mary drinks herself into insensibility, drives her daughter into the street, and then, when Maggie kills herself, exclaims, "I fergive her!" The irony of this line, the novel's last, is nihilistic. This contrasts with classical tragedy, which ends on an optimistic note: Purged of sin by the sacrifice of the protagonist, humankind is given a reprieve by the gods, and life looks a little better for everyone. In *Maggie*, however, there is no optimism.

In his most famous novel, *The Red Badge of Courage*, Crane takes his themes of illusion and reality and his impressionistic method from the Bowery to a battlefield of the Civil War, usually considered to be the battle of Chancellorsville. A young farm boy, Henry Fleming, hears tales of great battles, dreams of "Homeric" glory, and joins the Union army. Published in 1895, the story of Henry Fleming's various trials took the literary world by storm, first in England and then in the United States. Crane became an immediate sensation, perhaps one of America's first media darlings. *The Red Badge of Courage* became a classic in its own time because it combined literary merit with a subject that captured the popular imagination. Never again did Crane reach the height of popularity that he had achieved with *The Red Badge of Courage*.

Structurally, the novel is divided into two parts. In the first half, Henry's illusions disappear when confronted by the reality of battle. During the first skirmish, he sees vague figures before him, but they are driven away. In the next skirmish, he becomes so frightened that he runs away, becoming one of the first heroes in literature actually to desert his fellow soldiers in the field.

Separated from his regiment, Henry wanders through the forest behind the lines. There he experiences the kinds of illusions that dominate Crane's writing. First, he convinces himself that nature is benevolent, that she does not blame him for running. Next, he finds himself in a part of the woods which he interprets as a kind of religious place—the insects are praying, and the forest has the appearance of a chapel. Comforted by this, Henry becomes satisfied with himself until he discovers a dead soldier in the very heart of the "chapel." In a beautiful passage—beautiful in the sense of conveying great emotion through minute detail—Henry sees an ant carrying a bundle across the face of the dead man. Shifting to a belief in nature as malevolent or indifferent, Henry moves back toward the front. He soon encounters a line of wounded soldiers, among whom is his friend Jim Conklin and another man called simply "the tattered man." Conklin, badly wounded, is dying. Trying to expiate his crime of desertion, Henry attempts to help Conklin but is rebuffed. After Conklin dies, the tattered man probes deeply into Henry's conscience by repeatedly asking the youth, "Where ya hit?" The tattered man himself appears to be wounded, but Henry cannot abide his questions. He deserts the tattered man as well.

When Henry tries to stop another Union soldier to ask the novel's ubiquitous question, "Why?," Henry is clubbed on the head for causing trouble. Ironically, this wound becomes his "red badge of courage." Guided back to his regiment by a "Cheery Soldier," who performs the same function as the ancient gods and goddesses who helped wandering heroes, Henry embarks on the novel's second half. Between receiving the lump on his head and returning to his regiment, Henry's internal wanderings are over. Not until the last chapter does Henry ask questions of the universe. Most of the repudiations are complete: Heroes do not always act like heroes; no one understands the purpose of life or death; nature may be malevolent, probably indifferent, but is certainly not the benevolent, pantheistic realm of the Transcendentalists; and God, at least the traditional Christian God, is simply nowhere to be found.

In the second half of the novel, Henry becomes a "war devil," the very Homeric hero he originally wanted to be. Wilson, his young friend, who was formally called "the loud soldier," has become a group leader, quiet, helpful, utterly devoted to the regiment. He becomes, in short, what Henry would have become had he not run from the battle. The idea of "brotherhood," so prevalent in Crane's works, is embodied by Wilson. Henry is another kind of hero, an individual owing allegiance to no group; he leads a successful charge against the enemy with the spirit of a primitive warrior.

When the battle is over, however, all that Henry has accomplished is negated. Many critics have found the last chapter confused and muddled, for Henry's feelings range from remorse for the "sin" for which he is not responsible to pride in his valor as a great and glorious hero. Finally, he feels that "the world was a world for him," and he looks forward to "a soft and eternal peace." The beautiful lyricism of the novel's last paragraphs is, like that of many of Crane's conclusions, completely ironic. No one lives "eternally peacefully"; the world is not a world for Henry. As John Berryman says, Crane's "sole illusion was the heroic one, and not even that escaped his irony."

Thus, the novel's conclusion is not at all inconsistent. During the course of his experiences, Henry learns at first hand of the indifference of the universe, the chaos of the world, the illusory nature of religion and patriotism and heroism, but he learns these lessons in the heat of the moment, when recognition is virtually forced on him. When the memory has an opportunity to apply itself to past experience, that experience is changed into what humanity wants it to be, not what it was. Henry, then, becomes representative of humankind. The individual memory becomes a metaphor for collective memory, history. Everything is a lie. Not even heroism can last.

Resisting conventional assumptions reflective of a benevolent natural world, Crane in his fiction probed the depths of a universe that he saw as meaningless, indifferent—if not malevolent—toward humanity, and devoid of the supernatural. As one of the first American naturalistic writers, he played a critical role in the development of modern psychological realism in literature. He therefore remains a crucial transitional figure in American fiction.

Other major works

SHORT FICTION: *The Little Regiment and Other Episodes of the American Civil War*, 1896; *The Open Boat and Other Tales of Adventure*, 1898; *Whilomville Stories*, 1900; *Wounds in the Rain: War Stories*, 1900; *Last Words*, 1902.

PLAYS: *The Ghost*, 1899 (with Henry James); *The Blood of the Martyr*, 1940.
POETRY: *The Black Riders and Other Lines*, 1895; *A Souvenir and a Medley*, 1896; *War Is Kind*, 1899; *The University Press of Virginia Edition of the Works of Stephen Crane*, 1970.
NONFICTION: *The Great Battles of the World*, 1901.

Bibliography

Beer, Thomas. *Stephen Crane: A Study in American Letters*. New York: Alfred A. Knopf, 1923.
Benfey, Christopher E. G. *The Double Life of Stephen Crane*. New York: Alfred A. Knopf, 1992.
Cady, Edwin Harrison. *Stephen Crane*. Rev. ed. Boston: Twayne, 1980.
Halliburton, David. *The Color of the Sky: A Study of Stephen Crane*. New York: Cambridge University Press, 1989.
Knapp, Bettina L. *Stephen Crane*. New York: Frederick Ungar, 1987.
Linson, Corwin K. *My Stephen Crane*. Edited by Edwin H. Cady. Syracuse, N.Y.: Syracuse University Press, 1958.

JOSEPH HELLER

Born: Brooklyn, New York; May 1, 1923

Principal long fiction

Catch-22, 1961; *Something Happened*, 1974; *Good as Gold*, 1979; *God Knows*, 1984; *Picture This*, 1988; *Closing Time: The Sequel to Catch-22*, 1994.

Other literary forms

Joseph Heller's first published piece was a short story in *Story Magazine* (1945), and in the late 1940's, he placed several other stories with *Esquire* and *The Atlantic*. He has written several plays, all of which deal directly or indirectly with the material he used in *Catch-22*; only *We Bombed in New Haven* (1968) enjoyed a modicum of critical and commercial success. Heller has also contributed to a number of motion-picture and television scripts, the best-known of which is *Sex and the Single Girl* (Warner Bros., 1964).

Achievements

Heller's reputation rests largely on his first novel, *Catch-22*, the publication of which vaulted Heller into the front ranks of postwar American novelists. Critics have hailed it as "the great representative document of our era" and "probably the finest novel published since World War II." The phrase "Catch-22" quickly entered the American lexicon; eight million copies of the novel have been printed; and it has been translated into more than a dozen languages. In 1970, Mike Nichols' movie adaptation of Heller's tale sparked renewed interest in the novel itself and launched it onto the best-seller lists.

Biography

Joseph Heller was born in Brooklyn, New York, on May 1, 1923, the son of Russian Jewish immigrants only recently arrived in America. His mother then barely spoke English; his father drove a delivery truck for a bakery until, when Heller was only five, he died unexpectedly during a routine ulcer operation. The denial of this death in particular and the bare fact of mortality in general were to color Heller's later life and work. The youngest of three children, Heller spent his boyhood in the Coney Island section of Brooklyn, an enclave of lower- and middle-class Jewish families, in the shadow of the famous amusement park. Both his family and his teachers recognized Heller as a bright but bored student; he tinkered with writing short stories while still in high school.

In 1942, at the age of nineteen, Heller joined the Army Air Corps. He spent one of the war years flying sixty missions as a wing bombardier in a squadron of B-25's stationed on Corsica. This proved to be the crucial year of his life; it provided him with the materials, and the bitterly sardonic attitude, out of which he forged his major work—*Catch-22*—as well as three of his plays. Moreover, his sixty missions, many of them brutal and bloody (including the series of raids on Bologna which form the core of *Catch-22*), profoundly affected the attitude toward death that informs all of his work.

Demobilized in 1945, having achieved the rank of first lieutenant, Heller married fellow Brooklynite Shirley Held, with whom he had two children. Heller spent the next seven years within academe. Under the G.I. Bill, he attended college, first the University of Southern California and then New York University, where he received his B.A. degree in 1948. Heller then traveled uptown to take a master's degree at Columbia University before receiving one of the first Fulbright scholarships to study at Oxford. He returned to the United States to teach English at Pennsylvania State University between 1950 and 1952.

During the remainder of the 1950's, Heller was employed in the advertising departments of *Time*, *Look*, and *McCall's* magazines successively. In 1954, he began writing, at night and during odd hours, the manuscript that would be published eight years later as *Catch-22*. Nearing forty when *Catch-22* finally appeared, Heller ironically referred to himself as an "aging prodigy."

Heller abandoned his successful advertising career during the 1960's and returned to teaching. His position as Distinguished Professor of English at the City University of New York (CUNY) afforded him both the salary to support his family and the free time to devote to his writing. In these years, he began work on a second novel, wrote several motion-picture and television scripts (usually adaptations of the work of others and often using a pseudonym), and completed his first play, *We Bombed in New Haven*.

Something Happened, Heller's second novel, took thirteen years to complete before appearing in 1974. Never fully at ease with academic life, Heller resigned his chair at CUNY in 1975 and in 1979 published his third novel, *Good as Gold*. Although he has occasionally lectured on the college circuit and has served as writer-in-residence at both Yale University and the University of Pennsylvania, Heller is basically a reclusive writer, uncomfortable at literary gatherings and suspicious of the trappings of literary success. His life and work seem guided by Ralph Waldo Emerson's dictum that "a foolish consistency is the hobgoblin of little minds."

In December, 1981, Heller was diagnosed as a victim of Guillain Barré syndrome, a sometimes fatal condition involving progressive paralysis. He was hospitalized for several months but eventually recovered. The experience resulted in a book, *No Laughing Matter* (1986), written with his friend Speed Vogel, describing Heller's condition and its resolution; the illness also led to his second marriage, to one of his nurses, Valerie Humphries, in 1987.

God Knows returns to the irreverence and defiance of logic that characterized *Catch-22*. Its narrator, the biblical King David, speaks in modern jargon and in his extended version of his life and career displays knowledge of events long after his own time. *Picture This* is a protracted meditation on the ironies of history and of human life, focusing on the Netherlands of Rembrandt's time and the Athens of Aristotle. The long-anticipated sequel to *Catch-22*, *Closing Time*, appeared in 1994.

Analysis

Catch-22 was one of the most widely read and discussed novels of the 1960's and early 1970's; its blend of humor and horror struck a responsive chord, particularly with the young, during the upheavals of the Vietnam era. The critic Josh Greenfield, writing in 1968, claimed that it had "all but become the chapbook of the sixties." Within the context of Vietnam, the novel seemed to be less about World War II than about that Asian war over which America was so furiously divided. *Catch-22*, then, remains the classic fictional statement of the antiwar sentiments of its time; indeed, one student of twentieth century American war literature has suggested that "*Catch-22* has probably contributed more than any other work to the literary apprehension of war during the last two decades."

Although some have compared *Catch-22* to Norman Mailer's *The Naked and the Dead* (1948), James Jones's *The Thin Red Line* (1962), and other essentially naturalistic war tales written by Heller's contemporaries, its conception of war in basically absurdist terms and its crazy-quilt structure suggest affinities rather with such works as Kurt Vonnegut's *Slaughterhouse-Five* (1969). Although he objects to the term and prefers to characterize his novels as "burlesques," Heller's fiction is frequently described as "black comedy." In the tradition of Nathanael West, Günter Grass, Ralph Ellison, and Thomas Pynchon, Heller stretches reality to the point of distortion.

While *Catch-22*'s most obvious features are its antiwar theme and its wild, often madhouse humor, the novel itself is exceedingly complex in both meaning and form. In brief, the plot concerns a squadron of American airmen stationed on the fictional Mediterranean island of Pianosa during World War II. More specifically, it concerns the futile attempts of Captain John Yossarian, a Syrian American bombardier, to be removed from flying status. Every time he approaches the number of missions necessary to complete a tour of duty, his ambitious commanding officers increase it. Yossarian tries a number of ploys to avoid combat. He malingers, feigns illness, and even poisons the squadron's food with laundry soap to abort one mission. Later, after the gunner Snowden dies in his arms during one particularly lethal mission, Yossarian refuses to fly again, goes naked, and takes to walking backward on the base, all in an attempt to have himself declared insane.

Yossarian is motivated by only one thing—the determination to stay alive. He sees his life threatened not only by the Germans who try to shoot him out of the sky but also by his superior officers, who seem just as intent to kill him off. "The enemy," he concludes at one point, "is anybody who's going to get you killed, no matter which side he's on." When Yossarian attempts to convince the camp's medical officer that his fear of death has driven him over the brink and thus made him unfit to fly, he first learns of the "catch" that will force him to keep flying: "There was only one catch and that was Catch-22, which specified that a concern for one's own safety in the face of dangers that were real and immediate was the process of a rational mind." As Doc Daneeka tells Yossarian, "Anyone who wants to get out of combat duty isn't really crazy."

Most of the large cast of characters surrounding Yossarian are, by any "reasonable" standard, quite mad. They include Colonel Cathcart, who keeps raising the number of missions his troops are required to fly not for the sake of the war effort but for his own personal glory; Major Major Major, who forges Washington Irving's name to official documents and who is pathologically terrified of command; and Milo Minderbinder, the mess officer and black marketeer who bombs his own base under contract with the Germans. These supporting characters most often fall into one of four categories. The ranking officers—Cathcart, Dreedle, Korn, Black, Cargill, and Scheisskopf—appear more concerned with promotion, neat bombing patterns, and their own petty jealousies than with the war itself or the welfare of their men. A second group, including Doc Daneeka, Minderbinder, and Wintergreen, are also concerned with pursuing the main chance. They are predatory, but also extremely comic and very much self-aware. Another group, including Nately, Chief Halfoat, McWatt, Hungry Joe, and Chaplain Tappman, are (like Yossarian himself) outsiders, good men caught within a malevolent system. The dead—Mudd, Snowden, Kraft, and "the soldier in white"—constitute a final group, one which is always present, at least in the background.

It is the military system—which promulgates such absurdly tautological rules as "Catch-22"—that is Yossarian's real enemy. He and the other "good" men of the squadron live in a world that is irrational and inexplicable. As the company's warrant officer explains, "There just doesn't seem to be any logic to their system of rewards and punishments. . . . They have the right to do anything we can't stop them from doing."

As the novel progresses, the victims, increasingly aware of the menace posed by this system, carry their gestures of rebellion to the point of open defiance. Yossarian is the most blatant in this regard: He moans loudly during the briefing for the Avignon mission; he insists that there is a dead man in his tent; he goes naked during the Avignon mission itself and then again during the medal ceremony afterward; he halts the Bologna raid by putting soap in the squadron's food and by moving the bomb-line; he requests that he be grounded and eventually refuses to fly. Finally, he deserts, hoping to reach sanctuary in neutral Sweden.

In the world of *Catch-22*, then, the reader is forced to question the very nature of sanity. Sanity is commonly defined as the ability to live within society and to act appropriately according to its rules. If those rules—such as Catch-22—are patently false, however, then adhering to them is in truth an act of insanity, for the end result may be death or the loss of freedom. The world of *Catch-22* is, to Yossarian, a spurious culture, as anthropologists would call it, one that does not meet the basic needs of its members—above all, the need to survive. Authority, duty, and patriotism are all called into question, and Heller demonstrates that when those in authority lack intelligence or respect for life, as is the case with Yossarian's commanding officers, obeying authority can only be self-defeating. Heller thus argues that in an absurd universe, the individual has the right to seek his or her own survival; he argues that life itself is infinitely more precious than any cause, however just. When Yossarian decides that he has done his part to defeat the Nazis (and after all, he has flown many more missions than most other airmen), his principal duty is to save himself. Yossarian's desertion, then, is a life-affirming act. As one critic noted, *Catch-22* "speaks solidly to those who are disaffected, discontented, and disaffiliated, and yet who want to react to life positively. With its occasional affirmations couched in terms of pain and cynical laughter, it makes nihilism seem natural, ordinary, even appealing." Thus the surface farce of *Catch-22*, when peeled away, reveals a purpose that is deadly serious.

If the basic plot of *Catch-22* is fairly simple, its narrative technique and structure most certainly are not. The novel appears to be a chronological jumble, flashing forward and backward from the central event—the death of Snowden—which marks Yossarian's final realization of the mortal threat posed by Catch-22. Time in the novel exists not as clock-time but rather as psychological time, and within Yossarian's stream-of-consciousness narrative, events in the present intermingle with cumulative repetitions and gradual clarifications of past actions. For example, in chapter 4, the bare facts of Snowden's death are revealed, that he was killed over Avignon when Dobbs, his copilot, went berserk and grabbed the plane's controls at a crucial moment. Yossarian returns to this incident throughout the novel, but it is not until the penultimate chapter that he reconstructs the story in full. In this fashion, Heller seeks to capture the real ways in which people apprehend the world, incompletely and in fragments.

Catch-22 is intricately structured despite its seeming shapelessness. Until chapter 19, almost everything is told in retrospect while Yossarian is in the hospital; chapter 19 itself begins the movement forward in time leading to Yossarian's desertion. The gradual unfolding of the details of Snowden's death provides another organizing device. Such structural devices as parallelism, doubling, and, most important, repetition force the reader to share Yossarian's perpetual sense of *déjà vu*, the illusion of having previously experienced something actually being encountered for the first time. The ultimate effect of such devices is to reinforce the novel's main themes: Yossarian is trapped in a static world, a world in which nothing seems to change and in which events seem to keep repeating themselves. He does not move through his experiences but rather seems condemned to a treadmill existence. The only way to resist this world is to escape it, to desert.

Other major works

PLAYS: *We Bombed in New Haven*, 1968; *Catch-22: A Dramatization*, 1971; *Clevinger's Trial*, 1973.

NONFICTION: *No Laughing Matter*, 1986 (with Speed Vogel).

SCREENPLAYS: *Sex and the Single Girl*, 1964 (with David R. Schwartz); *Casino Royale*, 1967 (uncredited); *Dirty Dingus Magee*, 1970 (with Tom and Frank Waldman).

Bibliography

Aldridge, John W. *The American Novel and the Way We Live Now*. New York: Oxford University Press, 1983.

Heller, Joseph. *Conversations with Joseph Heller*. Edited by Adam J. Sorkin. Jackson: University Press of Mississippi, 1993.

Klinkowitz, Jerome. *The American 1960's: Imaginative Acts in a Decade of Change*. Ames: Iowa State University Press, 1990.

LeClair, Thomas. "Joseph Heller, *Something Happened*, and the Art of Excess." *Studies in American Fiction* 9 (Autumn, 1981): 245-260.

Martine, James J., ed. *American Novelists*. Detroit, Mich.: Gale Research, 1986.

Merrill, Robert. *Joseph Heller*. Boston: Twayne, 1987.

_____ . "The Structure and Meaning of *Catch-22*." *Studies in American Fiction* 14 (Autumn, 1986): 139-152.

Pinsker, Sanford. *Understanding Joseph Heller*. Columbia: University of South Carolina Press, 1991.

Plimpton, George, ed. *Writers at Work*. Vol. 5. New York: Penguin Books, 1981.

Seed, David. *The Fiction of Joseph Heller: Against the Grain*. New York: St. Martin's Press, 1989.

JAMES JONES

Born: Robinson, Illinois; November 6, 1921   **Died:** Southampton, New York; May 9, 1977

Principal long fiction

From Here to Eternity, 1951; *Some Came Running,* 1957; *The Pistol,* 1959; *The Thin Red Line,* 1962; *Go to the Widow-Maker,* 1967; *The Merry Month of May,* 1971; *A Touch of Danger,* 1973; *Whistle,* 1978.

Other literary forms

James Jones published one much underrated collection of short fiction, *The Ice-Cream Headache and Other Stories,* in 1968. Despite the excellence of several of these stories, he did not return to short fiction, primarily because of the difficulty of writing openly about sex in mass circulation magazines. He wrote two book-length works of nonfiction, *Viet Journal* (1974) and *WWII* (1975). The first is an account of Jones's experiences and observations while a war correspondent in Vietnam. *WWII,* a much more important work, is an analysis of the graphic art produced during World War II. The book contains some of Jones's finest writing, as well as an extended analysis of the central concept underlying his best fiction, "the evolution of a soldier." Jones also contributed essays to *Esquire, Harper's,* and the *Saturday Evening Post,* among other journals; the subject matter of these pieces ranges widely, from theories of fiction to skin diving.

Achievements

Jones's first novel, *From Here to Eternity,* was a spectacular success, both with critics and with the popular reading audience. As several reviewers pointed out, its frank treatment of sexuality and military brutality broke important new ground for American literary naturalism. While the novel had its detractors, it won the National Book Award for Fiction. *From Here to Eternity* appeared just in time to ride the crest of the new wave in paperback publishing, and in November, 1953, *Newsweek* reported that the paperback reprint of Jones's novel had gone through the five printings of "1,700,000 copies . . . in the past six weeks." The popularity of the novel was augmented by its adaptation into one of the most highly regarded American films of the 1950's. Directed by Fred Zinnemann and with unforgettable performances by Montgomery Clift, Burt Lancaster, and Deborah Kerr among others, the film version won the Best Picture award from the Motion Picture Academy of Arts and Sciences and the New York Film Critics in 1953. Jones himself became an international celebrity.

During the next twenty-five years, Jones remained an enormously popular writer. He and Norman Mailer were sometimes praised for having inspired a revitalized American literary realism. Still, Jones never regained the critical acceptance he enjoyed with his first novel.

In part because of the time he devoted to civilian novels, the major achievement of Jones's career was unrecognized at the time of his death. *From Here to Eternity* and *The Thin Red Line* were always intended as the first two volumes in a highly innovative trilogy. *Whistle,* the concluding volume of the trilogy, was published posthumously in 1978 and inspired a reappraisal of Jones's lasting contribution to American literature. His army trilogy has at last begun to receive its proper recognition as the most important fictional treatment of American involvement in World War II. Moreover, *From Here to Eternity* has attained the status of a modern classic, and *The Thin Red Line* is frequently praised as the best American "combat novel." One can expect that a new appreciation of Jones's shorter fiction, especially *The Pistol,* will be forthcoming as well.

Biography

Born in Robinson, Illinois, on November 6, 1921, James Jones grew up in a proud and socially prominent family. When he was a junior in Robinson High School, however, the family's position abruptly deteriorated, largely because of the Samuel Insull stock scandal. Even though his father, Ramon, was never professionally successful and became an alcoholic before ultimately committing suicide, Jones was fond of him. In sharp contrast, he felt contemptuous of, and rejected by, his mother, Ada Blessing Jones.

After he was graduated from high school in 1939, Jones, on the advice of his father, joined the United States Air Force and was stationed in Hawaii, where he transferred to the infantry. His army career was not distinguished. Still, in more than one way, Jones's military experience was crucial in his development as an artist. Primarily, he developed a complex love-hate relationship with the United States Army which later gave his military fiction a unique tension. Moreover, he was present at Schofield Barracks, Hawaii, on December 7, 1941, when the Japanese bombed Pearl Harbor and witnessed the birth of a new and terrifying world. Later, Jones saw combat on Guadalcanal, the brutality of which inspired his concept of "the animal nature of man."

Wounded on Guadalcanal in 1943, Jones was sent back to the United States and, on July 6, 1944, received his military discharge. Greatly shaken both by the combat horror he had experienced and by the continuing dissolution of his family, Jones met Mrs. Lowney Handy of Marshall, Illinois, in late 1943 or early 1944, and began one of the strangest, and ultimately most publicized, apprenticeships in the history of American letters. She and her husband, Harry Handy, supported Jones during the seven-year period in which he worked at his ambition of becoming a writer.

The young soldier had discovered Thomas Wolfe at the Schofield Barracks Post Library and realized that he "had been a writer all his . . . life without knowing it or having written." With Lowney Handy's encouragement, Jones wrote a first novel, which he submitted to Maxwell Perkins, the legendary editor at Charles Scribner's Sons. Perkins rejected this first novel but encouraged Jones to concentrate on a work about the old peacetime army. After Perkins' death, Jones profited from the help and encouragement of editor Burroughs Mitchell, and when Scribner's published *From Here to Eternity* in 1951, its author became an instant celebrity. Initially, he used his new wealth to establish a writers' colony at Marshall. Lowney Handy assumed the directorship of the colony and imposed an iron discipline upon her new protégés.

Jones, however, grew bored and skeptical in Marshall, seeing the cynicism of some of the writers and the failure of Mrs. Handy's methods to create universally good writing or even cooperation among the writers. His introduction to the beautiful actress Gloria Mosolino made inevitable a bitter and painful break with the Handys. In 1957, Jones and Gloria Mosolino were married at the Olofson Hotel in Haiti. The couple lived for a few months in New York City before moving to Paris in 1958. For the next sixteen years, the Jones's were the center of the American expatriate community in Paris. Whether his books were critically praised or attacked made no difference to Jones's new status as international celebrity.

In 1973, Jones went to Vietnam as a war correspondent and, the following year, published *Viet Journal*, a nonfictional account of what he had seen in that tragic country. Also, in 1974, he and his wife and two children returned home to the United States. Jones was increasingly determined to complete what he had long envisioned as the central work of his career, a trilogy about the United States Army, of which *From Here to Eternity* and *The Thin Red Line* constituted the first two volumes.

On May 9, 1977, Jones died of congestive heart failure in Southampton, New York. He had not quite completed *Whistle*, the third volume of his trilogy. It was possible, however, for Willie Morris, a writer, editor, and longtime friend, to finish the manuscript from Jones's notes and tapes. When *Whistle* was published in February, 1978, Jones's army trilogy took its place as one of the most important American fictional treatments of World War II.

Analysis

As the term is most commonly used, Jones is not strictly a "war novelist." Of his eight novels, only one, *The Thin Red Line*, is devoted primarily to a description of military combat, while four have peacetime civilian settings. While it is true that army life provides the background of his best fiction and World War II its controlling event, his reactions to the army and the war exhibit the complexity and ambiguity essential to meaningful art.

Especially during the 1950's, Jones often permitted himself to be depicted as an advocate of masculine toughness in life and literature. A 1957 *Life* magazine "Close-Up" emphasized the novelist's devotion to knives and boxing and declared his prominence in the literary cult of violence. Yet a careful reader of Jones's fiction will discover an artist deeply concerned about humankind's capacity for self-destruction. The modern individual, Jones believed, is caught in both an external and an internal trap. Human strength, which has its source in the "animal nature of man," has been translated into an awesome technology that ironically threatens the extinction of human individuality, if not the actual obliteration of humankind. In his civilian novels, Jones's characters habitually seek the few remaining "frontiers" of individualism (for example, skin diving), only to discover the impossibility of escaping their own

484

"animal" heritage. An element of brutal and destructive competition is thereby introduced into the "frontier," which is perverted and ultimately doomed. It is in his army fiction, however, that Jones most memorably dramatizes the tragic vulnerability of contemporary humanity.

The thematic focus in all Jones's army fiction is upon the evolution of the soldier. In Jones's view, warfare constitutes humanity's total capitulation to its animal nature. The traditional concepts of the individual and the self must be discarded in combat: The army trains the soldier to function on a primitive, subhuman level of consciousness. This training is a reversal of evolution; it is a process by which the army systematically dehumanizes the enlisted soldier. Such dehumanization is necessary for the soldier's acceptance of anonymity and probable death in combat. In World War II's anonymous, technological warfare, the enlistee became more clearly expendable and anonymous than at any time in history. Throughout his military fiction, Jones is intent upon describing the manner in which the army, by using technology and its awareness of the enlisted man's inherent animalism, carried out the dehumanization process.

The three novels that constitute the army trilogy— *From Here to Eternity*, *The Thin Red Line*, and *Whistle*—depict three major stages in the evolution of a soldier. The army trilogy's most innovative feature is the presence of three character types in all three volumes. Of these three character types, two are of overriding importance. First Sergeant Milt Warden of *From Here to Eternity* is transformed into Sergeant "Mad" Welsh in *The Thin Red Line* and into Sergeant Mart Winch in *Whistle*. Private Robert E. Lee Prewitt of *From Here to Eternity* becomes Private Witt in *The Thin Red Line* and Private Bobby Prell in *Whistle*. John W. Aldridge, sometimes a perceptive critic of Jones's fiction, sees a more important reason than Prewitt's death in *From Here to Eternity* for the characters' different names in each of the novels: Increasingly brutal experiences, he writes, have "transformed [them] into altogether different people." In other words, as they reach new and more dehumanizing stages in the evolution of a soldier, their inner selves undergo transformation.

The central factor in the critical and popular success of *From Here to Eternity* was its vivid characterization. As Maxwell Perkins had anticipated, Sergeant Milt Warden and Private Robert E. Lee Prewitt are unforgettable figures. They are not, however, the novel's only memorable characters. Private Angelo Maggio and "the

women," Alma Schmidt and Karen Holmes, are also strong individuals determined to preserve their integrity in an anonymous, bureaucratic world. *From Here to Eternity* is easily Jones's most romantic novel. In it, he depicts a world that ceased to exist on December 7, 1941; the novel's setting is Hawaii, and its climax is the Japanese attack on Pearl Harbor. For most of the novel, modern technological destruction has not made its appearance, and individualism seems a vital concept that is to be preserved in spite of "old Army" corruption. On the surface, the novel's roster of unforgettable characters seems to guarantee the survival of this traditional Western value.

Because his individualism is related to much that is crucial to Western values, Prewitt does, in fact, emerge as the dominant character in the novel. In the beginning, his quarrel with the army is almost absurdly simple. His commanding officer, Dynamite Holmes, is determined that Prewitt will become a member of the regimental boxing team; the private is equally determined not to box, even if his refusal means that he must give up playing the bugle, his "calling." Prewitt undergoes prolonged and systematic mental and physical abuse without acquiescing to Holmes's insistence that he box. Ultimately, this vicious "treatment" does force him past his breaking point and into a mistake that enables Holmes to have him sentenced to the stockade, where he experiences further brutality at the hands of Sergeant Fatso Judson. Judson is one of the most unforgettable sadists in American literature, and Prewitt decides that he must be destroyed. The reader can hardly disagree with this decision; still, it assures Prewitt's own doom.

Much of *From Here to Eternity*'s unique power derives from the levels of symbolic meaning contained within the deceptively simple Prewitt-Holmes conflict. Boxing is a metaphor for humanity's animal nature, while Prewitt's "calling" to play the bugle comes to represent that uniquely individualistic integrity that makes possible artistic creation. Throughout the novel, Prewitt is something of a romantic folk hero; he is the personification of "the good soldier," the proud enlisted man. When he plays taps on the bugle or helps in the collective composition of "The Re-Enlistment Blues," he is also giving artistic expression to the enlisted man's pain and loneliness. His desire to play the bugle symbolizes the urge to create a distinctive proletarian art. Warden sees the army's destruction of Prewitt as an illustration of animalism negating man's potential for lasting creativity. Yet, because Prewitt's death occurs just after the Japanese attack on Pearl Harbor, the sergeant has no real opportunity to mourn him. Since Warden understands that December 7, 1941, represented the end of traditional individualism and self-expression, Prewitt's death seems to him almost anticlimactic.

The mood of doomed romanticism so vital to *From Here to Eternity* is completely missing from the second volume of Jones's army trilogy, *The Thin Red Line*, a grimly detailed account of brutal combat. The bolshevik private in this novel is Witt, whose defiance has no relevance to art or to any idealistic values. In a real sense, the novel's main character is "C-for-Charlie Company," all the members of which are forced to submerge themselves into an anonymous mass. *The Thin Red Line* has been called the best American combat novel, and such high praise is deserved. The novel offers an unforgettable account of the sheer animalism of war. The sexuality of all the men of Charlie Company is systematically translated into brutal aggression toward the enemy. In fact, the only meaningful difference among the characters is the degree to which they are aware that such a transformation is taking place.

The one most aware is the superficially cynical first sergeant, Edward "Mad" Welsh. Like Milt Warden in *From Here to Eternity*, "the First" continually wonders how much of his basic self can be denied without a resultant loss of sanity. He has come very close to finding an answer to this question; one source of Jones's title is an old Midwestern saying: "There's only a thin red line between the sane and the mad." Welsh's sanity is still intact, but it is being severely strained by his unrelenting awareness of the dehumanization process that he and his men are undergoing. They are threatened not only by the fanatical determination of the Japanese enemy and by the deadly accidents of warfare but also by the gross incompetence of their own officers. Writing out of a proletarian consciousness, Jones depicted the officer class as incompetent, if not actually corrupt, in all his army fiction.

The Thin Red Line is Jones's most structurally sound novel, focusing upon the American struggle to capture an area of Guadalcanal known as "The Dancing Elephant." The brutality of combat is documented in complete naturalistic detail. Still, a majority of the central characters are alive when the novel ends with Charlie Company preparing to invade New Georgia. It is only here that the reader comes to share with Mad Welsh an awful knowledge—for those men who did not die on Guadalcanal, another Japanese-occupied island awaits, and then another and another. Thus, ultimate survival

seems out of the question, and madness becomes a form of escape from too much awareness.

While no one individual American soldier could confidently expect to survive the war, the majority of the soldiers did survive to return home. Such men returned to a country that, Jones believed, was being irrevocably changed by an unprecedented wave of material prosperity. Thus, men who had accepted the inevitability of their own deaths and whose sexuality had been converted into unrestrained animalism returned to a vital, challenging economy that could not afford the time for their reorientation. They faced what Jones, in *WWII*, called "The De-Evolution of a Soldier," the final and most difficult stage of the soldier's evolution: the acceptance of life and healthy sexuality by men who, after a long and excruciating process, had been converted to death-dealing and death-accepting savagery. *Whistle* focuses on this last, and nearly impossible, transformation.

In large part because Jones was unable to finish it before his death in May, 1977, *Whistle* lacks the power of *From Here to Eternity* and *The Thin Red Line*. Still, as completed from Jones's notes, it stands as a memorable conclusion to the army trilogy. The novel focuses upon the return home of four characters, all members of Charlie Company and all veterans of the kind of brutal combat depicted in *The Thin Red Line*. The war is not yet over, but the stateside economic boom is well under way. In the person of the returning war veteran is the forced realization that modern technological combat negates the heroism assigned in romantic myth to warfare.

Jones's Bolshevik private in *Whistle* is Bobby Prell. Very seriously wounded, Prell is battling the army that wishes to give him the Congressional Medal of Honor—the army that also insists on amputating his leg. While not convinced that he deserves the medal, Prell is certain that he should keep his leg, even if refusing amputation means certain death. Certainly, his conflict is elemental and significant; still, Prell never attains a stature comparable to that of Prewitt. Given Jones's vision, Prell must, in fact, seem largely anachronistic. Pearl Harbor marked the death of the romantic rebel as hero.

The truly memorable figure in *Whistle* is Sergeant Mart Winch, the culmination of Jones's depiction of "the First." Throughout most of *Whistle*, Winch functions as Warden and Welsh did, secretly protecting his men by elaborate manipulation of army bureaucracy. He is forced to see, however, the severe limitations of his ability to protect anyone in a new and nightmarish world. After Landers and Prell are shattered by their inability to adjust to civilian society, Winch surrenders to insanity. Thus, he crosses "the thin red line" and is destroyed by the madness that had threatened to engulf Warden and Welsh.

The cumulative characterization of "the First" is the most brilliant achievement in Jones's fiction; it is the heart of the army trilogy. Jones called the vision underlying his trilogy "quite tragic" and talked of the impossibility of an affirmative contemporary literature. He described a world so thoroughly converted to dehumanizing bureaucracy and technology that it drives to insanity those men who still believe in such traditional Western values as the self and individualism.

Other major works

SHORT FICTION: *The Ice-Cream Headache and Other Stories*, 1968.
NONFICTION: *Viet Journal*, 1974; *WWII*, 1975; *To Reach Eternity: The Letters of James Jones*, 1989.

Bibliography

Aldrich, Nelson W., ed. *Writers at Work: The Paris Review Interviews*. 3d ser. New York: Viking Press, 1967.

Giles, James R. *James Jones*. Boston: Twayne, 1981.

Hassan, Ihab. *Radical Innocence*. Princeton, N.J.: Princeton University Press, 1961.

Jones, Peter G. *War and the Novelist*. Columbia: University of Missouri Press, 1976.

MacShane, Frank. *Into Eternity: The Life of James Jones, American Writer*. Boston: Houghton Mifflin, 1985.

Moore, Harry Thornton, ed. *Contemporary American Novelists*. Carbondale: Southern Illinois University Press, 1964.

Morris, Willie. *James Jones: A Friendship*. Garden City, N.Y.: Doubleday, 1978.

TIM O'BRIEN

Born: Austin, Minnesota; October 1, 1946

Principal long fiction

Northern Lights, 1975; *Going After Cacciato*, 1978; *The Nuclear Age*, 1985; *In the Lake of the Woods*, 1994.

Other literary forms

Tim O'Brien has also published a memoir of his Vietnam War experiences, *If I Die in a Combat Zone, Box Me up and Ship Me Home* (1973, rev. 1979), and a collection of short stories and essays, *The Things They Carried* (1990). He has also published numerous uncollected short stories, several of which have been incorporated, often in heavily revised versions, into his books.

Achievements

Three of O'Brien's books centering on the Vietnam War—*If I Die in a Combat Zone, Box Me up and Ship Me Home*, *Going After Cacciato*, and *The Things They Carried*—have earned him critical recognition as one of the most accomplished of the large number of talented American writers to have dealt with war. His short stories, which have been recognized with several awards, have been included in *Prize Stories: The O. Henry Awards* (1976, 1978, 1982), *The Best American Short Stories* (1977, 1987), and *The Pushcart Prize* (1977). His critically acclaimed novel *Going After Cacciato*, widely cited as among the finest novels to depict the experiences of American soldiers in Vietnam, won the National Book Award for Fiction in 1979. O'Brien has been the recipient of multiple awards from the National Endowment for the Arts and has taught at the Bread Loaf Writers' Conference at Middlebury College. Taken as a whole, his books have established him as an important voice in contemporary American fiction.

Biography

William Timothy O'Brien was born in Austin, Minnesota, to William T. O'Brien, an insurance salesman, and Ava E. Schultz O'Brien, a schoolteacher, on October 1, 1946. Ten years later the family moved to Worthington, Minnesota. After high school the younger O'Brien attended Macalester College in Saint Paul, where he became student body president in his senior year and graduated summa cum laude in 1968 with a bachelor's degree in political science.

O'Brien was drafted into the Army almost immediately after graduation. He had earned a reputation as something of a radical and activist in college and had personal misgivings about the morality of the war, reservations that led him to contemplate desertion. Nevertheless, he accepted his assignment to the infantry, largely out of concern for social pressures, a decision he analyzes in several of his more or less autobiographical stories and essays. O'Brien served a tour of duty in Vietnam, where he was awarded a Purple Heart after being wounded in action near My Lai, and was soon promoted to the rank of sergeant.

After his discharge in 1970, O'Brien entered graduate school at Harvard to pursue a doctorate in government. During his first year there he resumed work on a series of vignettes about his war experiences that he had begun writing back in Vietnam, publishing one of them in *Playboy* magazine and a few in various newspapers, including *The Washington Post*, where he worked as an intern during the summers of 1971 and 1972. In 1972 he finished writing his first book, *If I Die in a Combat Zone, Box Me up and Ship Me Home*, which brought together twenty-three of his brief sketches about the war, and published it in 1973. O'Brien took a leave of absence from Harvard to serve as a national affairs reporter for *The Washington Post* from 1973 to 1974, writing his second book, the novel *Northern Lights*, during his off-hours. He then returned to Harvard, where he continued his graduate work while beginning his third book, *Going After Cacciato*. He left Harvard to devote himself to his writing full-time in 1976.

Analysis

O'Brien intentionally directs his works at big issues, what he terms "the abstractions: what's courage and how do you get it? What's justice and how do you achieve it? How does one do right in an evil situation?" In this regard he distinguishes his own work from much contemporary literature, which he finds too often trivialized by its "tendency to examine purely personal concerns—the minutia of life." As O'Brien sees it, one of the goals of literature should be "to jar people into looking at important things. Much of our lives is spent thinking about clothing ourselves and our families and feeding ourselves and so on, so that we rarely try to grapple with philosophical issues. A good novel will seduce you into caring about those things." Not surprisingly, the bulk of his work thus far has centered on the Vietnam War, the dominant public event not only in his own life but also perhaps in the cultural life of his generation. This concern with public, even political, issues does not, however, result in a simplistically didactic body of work: "If you go through a cancer experience," O'Brien remarks in an apt analogy, "you don't come out of it with the lesson, 'don't get cancer.'" His works carefully avoid moralizing and focus instead on the imaginative re-creation of experiences that lead the reader into the contemplation of moral issues.

O'Brien's most widely admired book, the novel *Going After Cacciato*, has been called by Dean McWilliams "the most important literary consequence of the American involvement in Vietnam." Owen W. Gilman, Jr., has asserted that it is "one text certain to survive as a major document of the imagination in the late twentieth century." The novel's complex structure, which interweaves three distinct narrative orders, has drawn considerable critical attention. The narrative "present" of the book details the actions and reflections of Paul Berlin, the protagonist of the novel, who is on watch at an observation post in Quang Nai from midnight until dawn on November 20, 1968. During this night, the description of which is broken up into ten chapters (all entitled "Observation Post") scattered throughout the novel's forty-six chapters, Berlin meditates upon and attempts to come to terms with his feelings about his first six months in Vietnam. In particular, the reader comes to realize, Berlin's compulsion to reflect derives from two events, one a past event, the other a potential event.

The first concern is evidently over Berlin's role in the fate of his former platoon leader, Lieutenant Sidney Martin, who was apparently killed ("fragged") by his own men in late August out of fear that he would continue to order them into virtually suicidal explorations of booby-trapped and sometimes occupied enemy tunnels, a killing to which Berlin was at least a passive accomplice. This part of Berlin's night-long meditation drives another sixteen of the book's forty-six chapters (again, scattered throughout the book rather than presented in a block), which take place in the narrative "past" and are devoted to accounts of various experiences that he has had during his tour in Vietnam, from

his arrival on June 3 through late October, almost up to the night he is on watch.

Berlin's second concern is his hope of coming to terms with his half-acknowledged desire to desert the Army by following Cacciato, a member of his squad who has recently gone AWOL (absent without leave), apparently in an attempt to make his way from Vietnam to Paris. The remaining twenty chapters of the book, interspersed among those devoted to the narrative "present" and "past," present Berlin's imagined "future" narrative of his squad's pursuit of Cacciato from Vietnam all the way to Paris. In the course of their picaresque journey, along which they have a series of often wildly improbable adventures, they are joined by a young Chinese refugee, Sarkin Aung Wan, with whom Berlin falls in love and who comes to represent in some measure the various forces that lead him away from finishing his tour of duty and toward desertion.

O'Brien has described the novel's structure "as a teeter-totter, with the 'Observation Post' chapters as the fulcrum—the present of the book. The teeter-totter swings back and forth between reality—the war experience—and fantasy—the imagined trek to Paris." Each of the narrative streams is written in a different style, and the combination of grittily realistic combat scenes and lyrical, almost dreamlike fantasy has led several critics to identify in O'Brien's writing, at least in this novel, influences as disparate as Hemingway's deadpan objectivity, the absurdism of Joseph Heller's *Catch-22* (1961), and the Magical Realism associated with Gabriel García Márquez and Jorge Luis Borges.

Unlike the majority of novels written about the Vietnam experience, *Going After Cacciato* is not fundamentally an antiwar novel; the imaginary flight to Paris ends with a debate between Sarkin Aung Wan and Berlin at the Paris peace table (a mock version of the peace talks that were in fact being held at the time of the story) in which Berlin resolves his philosophical dilemma by rejecting her arguments and deciding that he is personally obliged to continue to fight. Although the setting and subject matter have to do with the war, O'Brien has always claimed that the book is not really a war novel (he has suggested the label "peace" novel might be better) but is instead concerned with issues more broadly relevant to readers' daily lives: "The central theme of the novel has to do with how we use our imaginations to deal with situations around us, not just to cope with them psychologically but, more importantly, to deal with them philosophically and morally."

Despite O'Brien's insistence that he does not think of

himself as a "Vietnam writer," those books that take the war as their subject have received substantially more attention than his second and fourth books, *Northern Lights* and *The Nuclear Age*. These appeared in the "gaps" between the war books and were perhaps undervalued because they did not meet popular and critical expectations that he would continue to mine the war genre. This relative neglect has more recently begun to be addressed, especially for *Northern Lights*, a novel that, as Milton J. Bates has demonstrated, is much closer to the Vietnam narratives in terms of both thematic concerns and literary quality than many early reviewers had recognized. Nevertheless, O'Brien's current literary reputation rests primarily on *Going After Cacciato*, *If I Die in a Combat Zone, Box Me up and Ship Me Home* and *The Things They Carried*.

If I Die in a Combat Zone, Box Me up and Ship Me Home has been difficult to label and has been treated by critics as an autobiography, as a collection of short stories, and as a novel. O'Brien has claimed that the book was "intended to be a straight autobiography" but that for some reason, probably "largely subconscious," "the book was written as a novel; that is, the form of the book is fictional." He casts the scenes in the book in what most readers think of as fictional form, with extensive realistic dialogue and chapterlike construction, with each episode having the internal integrity of a beginning, middle, and end. In fact, O'Brien used many of the stories from the "nonfictional" memoir in the "fictional" novel *Going After Cacciato*. *The Things They Carried*, sections of which have won a National Magazine Award and two O. Henry prizes and have been included in *The Best American Short Stories*, is even more difficult to classify generically. As Martin Naparsteck has noted, "It is part novel, part collection of stories, part essays, part journalism; it is, more significantly, all at the same time."

While the blurring of the fiction/nonfiction boundary may have occurred subconsciously in his first book, in the later work O'Brien set out quite consciously to conflate genres: "It's a new form, I think. I blended my own personality with the stories, and I'm writing about the stories, and yet everything is made up, including the commentary. . . . The point being, among others, that in fiction we not only transform reality, we sort of invent our own lives, invent our histories, our autobiographies." The narrator of many of the stories is a writer named "Tim O'Brien," and several of the names listed in the acknowledgments—conventionally the realm of extrafictional material—appear as the names of characters in various stories. He frequently follows a story with another story in which he discusses the writing and publication history of the preceding story, often commenting on the degree to which the "story-truth" of a given selection relates to the "happening-truth" of the autobiographic facts, and sometimes giving contradictory information about this degree of veracity, telling the reader on one page that "this is true," but then insisting a few pages later that "none of it happened. None of it." This reliance on the experimental techniques of metafiction, in which the writer comments on the processes of writing while writing, represents to some extent a new direction for O'Brien. It is, however, a device closely related to his use of the "Observation Post" chapters in *Going After Cacciato*, in which Berlin's process of imagining the story of the journey to Paris is similarly foregrounded.

O'Brien's interest in important ideas and issues, his unremitting attention to narrative structure and style, and his success at continually reinventing his subject matter and overcoming generic restraints have combined to earn him a place in the tradition of outstanding American war novelists, begun by such writers as Stephen Crane and Ernest Hemingway. O'Brien's standing as one of the more accomplished writers of contemporary American literature is well deserved.

Other major works

NONFICTION: *If I Die in a Combat Zone, Box Me up and Ship Me Home*, 1973, rev. 1979.
MISCELLANEOUS: *The Things They Carried*, 1990.

Bibliography

Bates, Milton J. "Tim O'Brien's Myth of Courage." *Modern Fiction Studies* 33, no. 2 (1987): 263-279.
Calloway, Catherine. "Pluralities of Vision: *Going After Cacciato* and Tim O'Brien's Short Fiction." In *America Rediscovered: Critical Essays on Literature and Film of the Vietnam War*, edited by Owen W. Gilman, Jr., and Lorrie Smith. New York: Garland, 1990.
Herzog, Toby C. "*Going After Cacciato*: The Soldier-Author-Character Seeking Control." *Critique* 24, no. 2 (1983): 88-96.

McCaffery, Larry. "Interview with Tim O'Brien." *Chicago Review* 33, no.2 (1982): 129-149.

McWilliams, Dean. "Time in O'Brien's *Going After Cacciato*." *Critique* 29, no. 4 (1988): 245-255.

Naparsteck, Martin. "An Interview with Tim O'Brien." *Contemporary Literature* 32, no. 1 (1991): 1-11.

Nelson, Marie. "Two Consciences: A Reading of Tim O'Brien's Vietnam Trilogy." In *Third Force Psychology and the Study of Literature*, edited by Bernard J. Paris. Rutherford, N.J.: Fairleigh Dickinson University Press, 1986.

Raymond, Michael W. "Imagined Responses to Vietnam: Tim O'Brien's *Going After Cacciato*." *Critique* 24, no. 2 (1983): 97-104.

Schroder, Eric James. "The Past and the Possible: Tim O'Brien's Dialectic of Memory and Imagination." In *Search and Clear: Critical Responses to Selected Literature and Films of the Vietnam War*, edited by William J. Searle. Bowling Green, Ohio: Bowling Green State University Popular Press, 1988.

——————— . "Two Interviews: Talks with Tim O'Brien and Robert Stone." *Modern Fiction Studies* 30, no. 1 (1984): 135-164.

Slabey, Robert M. "*Going After Cacciato*: Tim O'Brien's 'Separate Peace.'" In *America Rediscovered: Critical Essays on Literature and Film of the Vietnam War*, edited by Owen W. Gilman, Jr., and Lorrie Smith. New York: Garland, 1990. 205-212.

Vannatta, Dennis. "Theme and Structure in Tim O'Brien's *Going After Cacciato*." *Modern Fiction Studies* 28, no. 2 (1982): 242-246.

Vietnam, We've All Been There: Interviews with American Writers. Westport, Conn.: Praeger, 1992.

THOMAS PYNCHON

Born: Glen Cove, New York; May 8, 1937

Principal long fiction

V., 1963; *The Crying of Lot 49*, 1966; *Gravity's Rainbow*, 1973; *Vineland*, 1989.

Other literary forms

Before his novels began to come out, Thomas Pynchon published a handful of short stories. In addition to the odd review or introduction, Pynchon has published several articles, including "A Journey into the Mind of Watts" (1966) in *The New York Times Magazine* and "Is It O.K. to Be a Luddite?" (1984) in *The New York Times Book Review*.

Achievements

Among those contemporary novelists who enjoy both a popular and an academic following, Pynchon stands out as a virtual cult figure. His novels and stories stand up to the most rigorous critical analysis; they prove, like all great works of art, to be the product of a gifted sensibility and careful craftsmanship. At the same time, Dr. Samuel Johnson's "common reader" cheerfully wades through much abstruse matter because this author never fails to entertain—with bizarre plots, incandescent language, anarchic humor, and memorable characters.

Pynchon has an enormous, diverse, and fanatically loyal following. There are now approximately thirty books on his work, not to mention a triquarterly journal (*Pynchon Notes*, published at Wesleyan University) and special issues of other scholarly journals. Much of the fascination he holds for readers derives from his reclusive habits. He refuses to be interviewed, photographed, or otherwise made into a darling of the media. His residence, which probably changes frequently, is not a matter of public record.

Pynchon has been honored with a number of literary awards. He received the William Faulkner Foundation Award for *V.*, the 1967 Rosenthal Foundation Award of the National Institute of Arts and Letters for *The Crying of Lot 49*, and the National Book Award for *Gravity's Rainbow* in 1974. Though the judging committee unanimously voted to award the Pulitzer Prize in fiction to *Gravity's Rainbow*, the committee was overruled by an advisory board that found the novel immoral and "turgid." The Howells Medal, awarded once every five years, was offered to Pynchon in 1975, but he declined it. He was awarded a MacArthur Foundation Fellowship in 1988.

Pynchon remains, in the eyes of most followers of the fiction scene, in the front rank. More than one distinguished critic has declared him America's finest novelist, and few would deny him a place among the best American novelists of modern times.

Biography

Because of Thomas Pynchon's passion for privacy, little is known about his life. His father was an industrial surveyor, and the family lived in Glen Cove, East Norwich, and Oyster Bay—all on Long Island in New York. His father, a Republican, eventually served as town supervisor of Oyster Bay. Pynchon was sixteen when he was graduated from Oyster Bay High School in 1953. He was class salutatorian and winner of an award for the senior attaining the highest average in English. With a scholarship at Cornell University, he first majored in engineering physics but, though he was doing well academically, abandoned that curriculum after the first year. A year later, he decided to do a hitch in the Navy before completing his baccalaureate degree. He attended boot camp at Bainbridge, Maryland, and did advanced training as an electrician at Norfolk, Virginia. Two years in the Navy, partly spent in the Mediterranean, provided Pynchon with a number of comic situations and characters, which he has exploited in "Low-Lands," *V.*, and *Gravity's Rainbow*. Pynchon finished at Cornell as an English major and was graduated in 1959. While at Cornell, Pynchon took a class taught by Vladimir Nabokov: Nabokov's wife, Vera, who did her husband's grading, remembers Pynchon for his distinctive handwriting.

Pynchon lived briefly in Greenwich Village and in uptown Manhattan before taking a job with the Boeing Company and moving to Seattle. With Boeing for two and a half years (until September, 1962), he worked in the Minuteman Logistics Support Program and wrote for such intramural publications as *The Minuteman Field Service News* and *Aerospace Safety*. After leaving Boeing, he lived in California and Mexico and completed *V.*, which was published in 1963 and hailed as a major first novel.

Rumors of Pynchon's whereabouts circulate often, some indicating that he has been seen in California, Mexico, and Oregon; in the late 1970's, he made a trip to England that mysteriously got noted in the national newsmagazines. Otherwise, there are only apocryphal stories of Pynchon that accompany the novels that have followed *V.* Would-be biographers have been frustrated, and some have simply written articles about their search for Pynchon, a search as beguiling and as ultimately inconclusive as the guests that figure in each of Pynchon's novels.

Pynchon has supplied a few tantalizing autobiographical facts in the introduction to *Slow Learner* (1984) and in the introduction he wrote for the 1983 Penguin reprint of Richard Fariña's 1966 novel, *Been Down So Long It Looks Like Up to Me.*

Analysis

The quest would seem to be the one indispensable element in the fictions of Pynchon, for each of his novels proves to be a modern-dress version of the search for some grail to revive the wasteland. Pynchon's characters seek knowledge that will make sense of their unanchored lives and their fragmented times; Pynchon hints that questing has a value irrespective of the authenticity of that for which one quests. The quest lends purpose to life, enabling one to function, to see life as worthwhile. At the same time, however, Pynchon invites his more privileged reader to recognize that the ordering principle thus projected is factitious. What is real is the gathering dissolution, the passing of human beings and whole civilizations. All attempts to discover or create order and system are doomed.

Pynchon's works, except perhaps *Vineland*, have emphasized two basic themes. The first is the principle of entropy (the second law of thermodynamics, broadly defined as the gradual deterioration of the universe caused by irreversible thermodynamic equalization). Pynchon has applied this law of physics to human organizations, especially to political systems.

Pynchon's fictional world has also featured intricate labyrinths in which readers experience the paranoia that figures as the second prominent theme in his work. Paranoia is the conviction that mighty conspiracies exist, that all things are connected "in spheres joyful or

threatening about the central pulse of [one]self." Pynchon's protagonists come to believe in this infinite reticulation of conspiracy because it is preferable to the possibility that "nothing is connected to anything." Pynchon's readers, by the same token, encounter fictive structures that formally imitate the paranoid premise: All is connected in great, seamless webs of interdependent detail.

In his first novel, *V.*, Pynchon brilliantly interweaves two narratives, one in the present (mid-1950's), the other in the period 1880 to 1943. The historical narrative, presented obliquely, concerns an extraordinary woman who appears originally as Victoria Wren and subsequently under *noms de guerre* in which the letter *V* of the alphabet figures prominently: Veronica Manganese, Vera Meroving. This is V., who turns up whenever there is bloodshed in the course of the twentieth century. In 1898, for example, she appears at the periphery of the Fashoda crisis in Egypt, and the following year she gravitates to Florence, where the spies of several nations are jockeying for position, engaging in what Pynchon calls "premilitary" activity. In 1913, she is in Paris, involved in a bloody theater riot that, like the crisis in Egypt and Florence earlier, proves an earnest of World War I—a kind of fulfillment for V. in her early phase. When World War I ends with Western civilization intact, though permanently altered, V. begins to be involved with those elements that will figure in the more satisfying carnage of the century's real climacteric, World War II. In 1922, she is in German South-West Africa, where the massacre of the native Hereros reenacts the even greater massacre of two decades earlier and anticipates the really accomplished genocide in Europe between 1933 and 1945. On and off after 1918, she is on Malta, consorting with a group sympathetic to Benito Mussolini and his Fascists. V. dies in an air raid on Malta in 1943—just as the tide turns against the Fascist cause with which she has become increasingly identified.

V.'s affinity with Fascism complements a decadent religiosity, and she comes to personify the drift to extinction of Western culture and of life itself. She gradually loses parts of her body and becomes more and more the sum of inanimate parts: false eye, false hair, false foot, false navel. She is a brilliant metaphor for entrophy and the decline of civilization, and her baleful influence is projected in the novel's present in the decadence of the contemporary characters, most of whom are part of a group called the "Whole Sick Crew." The Crew is exemplified by its newest member, the winsome schlemiel Benny Profane. Profane is incapable of love and emotional involvement; he is also perennially at war with inanimate objects. His dread of the inanimate suggests that he intuits the cultural situation as the century wanes. Though he is no thinker, he realizes that he and his fellows are Eliot's hollow men, on the way to their whimpering end. His inability to love is presented in comic terms—though fat, he is doted on by various desirable women, including the Maltese Paola Maijstral and the beautiful Rachel Owlglass. The failure is that of his entire circle, for though there is much sex among the Whole Sick Crew, there is no commitment, no love, no hope. The one baby generated by all the sexual freedom is aborted.

The Whole Sick Crew is what Western civilization has become as a result of entropic processes that are utterly random and mindless. The meaninglessness of entropy is something difficult for the human mind to accept, however, and in Herbert Stencil, a marginal member of the Crew, Pynchon presents what becomes his standard character, a person who must discover conspiracy to deal with the fragmentation of life and culture. It is Stencil who does the mythmaking, the elevating of Victoria Wren from mere perverted adventures to something awesome and as multifaceted as Robert Graves's White Goddess. Nor is Stencil alone, for the undeniable desire for connectedness is quintessentially human. It is also shared by the sophisticated reader, who flings himself into the literary puzzle and becomes himself a Stencil, a quester for meaning in the convoluted plot of *V.* and in the identity of the mysterious personage who gives the novel its name. Pynchon's genius manifests itself in his ability to keep his readers suspended between his two mutually exclusive alternatives: that the clues to *V.*'s identity are the key to meaning and that *V.* is nothing more than a paranoid fantasy, the product of a mind that cannot deal with very much reality.

Pynchon's second novel, *The Crying of Lot 49*, seems slight set between *V.* and *Gravity's Rainbow*, and Pynchon himself seems to consider it something of a potboiler. Some readers, however, believe it to be his perfect work of art. It is the story of Oedipa Maas, who is named "executor, or she supposed executrix" of the estate of an ex-lover, the millionaire Pierce Inverarity. In carrying out her duties, she stumbles upon evidence of a conspiracy to circumvent the United States Postal Service. She discovers Tristero, a *sub rosa* postal system at war for centuries with all officially sanctioned postal services, first in the old world, then in the new.

Tristero subsumes an extraordinary number of revolutionary or simply alienated groups. In its new-world phase, it seems to bring together all those within the American system who are disenfranchised, disaffected, or disinherited—all those defrauded of the American Dream.

Oedipa, like Herbert Stencil, finds that the harder she looks, the more connections to Tristero she discovers, until the connections start revealing themselves in such number and variety that she begins to doubt her sanity. Though Pynchon does not resolve the question of Oedipa's sanity, he hints that becoming sensitized to the problems of twentieth century American culture (and to the horrors of the spiritual void contingent on certain twentieth century habits of mind) involves a necessary sacrifice of sanity or at least serenity. At the end, Oedipa is faced with a harrowing choice: Either she is insane, or Tristero, with its stupendous reticulation, really exists. When Oedipa attempts to rephrase the dilemma, she finds that the paranoia is somehow inescapable. Oedipa's experiences are almost certainly an imaginative version of Pynchon's own. At the time of the novel, 1964, Oedipa is twenty-eight years old—about the same age as Pynchon was in that year. Like Pynchon, she has attended Cornell and then gravitated to the West Coast. Like Pynchon, too, she comes to view herself as an "alien," unable to fit into the furrow of American success, prosperity, and complacency. Thus, one can read the novel as Pynchon's account of why he has gone underground.

All Pynchon's books are filled with bizarre characters and incidents, but *Gravity's Rainbow* is especially dense and demanding. The hero is Tyrone Slothrop, an American army lieutenant attached to an Allied intelligence unit in World War II. Slothrop's superiors become aware that the map of his sexual conquests (or his sexual fantasies; this is kept ambiguous) coincides with the distribution of German V-2 rockets falling in London. Significantly, the erection precedes the arrival of the rocket. This fact, which calls into question the usual mechanism of cause and effect (it complements the fact that the rocket, traveling faster than the speed of sound, is heard falling after it has exploded) is of central importance to the novel, for Pynchon means to pit two scientific models against each other. The older model, which few laypeople question, posits a mechanistic universe that operates according to the laws of cause and effect.

The character associated with this worldview is the sinister Dr. Pointsman, a diehard Pavlovian threatened by the new model, which posits a universe in which physical phenomena can be plotted and predicted only in terms of uncertainty and probability (Pynchon is on sound theoretical ground here; he is presenting the physics of Werner Heisenberg and Max Planck). The character who embraces the more up-to-date worldview is the sympathetic Roger Mexico, a statistician. Between these two, poor Slothrop—a kind of Everyman—tries to stay alive and, if possible, free. Pointsman and his minions concoct an experiment with Slothrop; they will provide him with the best information they have on the German rocket and then observe him closely for further revelations. Slothrop, aware that he is being used, goes AWOL to embark on a private quest to discover the truth of his personal destiny—and perhaps the destiny of his age as well.

Pynchon picks his historical moment carefully, for World War II was the moment when humanity came of age technologically. Technology offers humankind complete control of its environment and its destiny; it offers something very like transcendence—or it offers annihilation. Pynchon's novel is a meditation on the choice, which is seen nowhere more clearly than in the new rocket technology. Will humankind use the rocket transcendentally, to go to the stars, or will it use it to destroy itself? The answer has been taking shape since the German rocket scientists were sent East and West after World War II, and Pynchon concludes his great narrative with the split second before the ultimate cataclysm: The apocalyptic rocket plunges toward the "theatre" in which the film *Gravity's Rainbow* has unreeled before the reader. Critical opinion is split on the degree of bleakness in this ending. Figuratively, says Pynchon, the world is separated from its end only by "the last delta-t," the last infinitesimal unit of time and space between the rocket and its target. The delta-t, however, is a relative unit of measure. Modern humanity's folly has indeed set in motion the process of its own destruction, but the process might still be arrested by a reordering of priorities, human and technological. As for Slothrop, he simply fades away. Pynchon says he becomes "scattered," and his scattering coincides with the founding of the Counterforce, a group of enlightened, anarchic men and women devoted to reversing the technology of violence and death. The Counterforce, which has affinities with various countercultural movements waxing at the moment of this novel's composition, is not particularly powerful or effective, but it offers hope for a planet hurtling toward destruction.

In his long-awaited fourth novel, *Vineland*, Pynchon returns to the California setting of *The Crying of Lot 49*. As in *V.*, Pynchon sets up a dual historical focus. He imagines characters in the present—the portentous year 1984—trying to come to terms with the period, twenty years earlier, when they and the whole country underwent a searing passage. Pynchon reflects on the direction the country's history has taken—from anarchic but healthy self-indulgence to neo-Puritan repression. These poles are visible in the People's Republic of Rock and Roll, with its ethic of freedom, pleasure, dope, music, and self-expression, and in the Nixonian and Reaganite reaction that put an end to the polymorphous perversity of the 1960's and ushered in the return to materialism and political conservatism.

The novel is structured—somewhat more loosely than is usual with Pynchon—around the quest of a girl named Prairie for the mother, Frenesi Gates, who abandoned her shortly after her birth. Prairie's father, Zoyd Wheeler, still loves Frenesi, as does the man with whom she was involved before him—the sinister Brock Vond, a federal agent who had used her to infiltrate and subvert PR[3] and other radical causes. Zoyd accepts his misery, but Vond will stop at nothing to get Frenesi back in his clutches—not even kidnapping Prairie, who could be made into an instrument of renewed control. Also involved in the action are female Ninja Darryl Louise (DL), Chastain, an old friend of Frenesi, and DL's companion, the "karmic adjuster" Takeshi Fumimota, a kind of Zen private eye.

The centrality of Prairie, Frenesi, and DL, not to mention the narrational attention to Frenesi's mother and grandmother (Sasha Gates and Eula Traverse), make this essay Pynchon's first in feminist fiction. (Though a woman, V., was central to his first novel, it was really a parody of the kind of matriarchal vision associated with Robert Graves and the White Goddess.) It is in terms of this feminism that he is able in *Vineland* to move beyond the apocalyptic obsession that characterizes all three of his previous novels, as well as the stories "Mortality and Mercy in Vienna" and "Entropy." *Vineland* ends with a vision of familial harmony that is nothing less than mythic—an augury of what an America-wide family might be. Here the reader sees Prairie reunited with her mother and half-brother, as Zoyd and others are also integrated. Vond alone is excluded (his surname is an apocope of the Dutch word *vondeling*, a foundling—as if to hint at his inability to be integrated into family wholeness). The reunion of the Traverse-Becker clans, which seem to center in their women, is Pynchon's Vonnegut-like imagining of the

millennium, the era of peace and harmony that ironically succeeds the apocalyptic disruptions everywhere
expected in the novel. Beyond apocalypse is millennium, and *Vineland* announces what will be a trend in
fiction as the year 2000 approaches: It is a *fin de
millénaire* novel.

Herein, too, is the meaning of Pynchon's setting, the
imaginary community of Vineland that provides the
novel with its title. Vineland, of course, is the name
given to the American continent by the Vikings, its first
European visitors, at the end of the first millennium.
Pynchon's novel reminds American readers that their
land has been known to history for a thousand years.

Other major works
SHORT FICTION: *Slow Learner: Early Stories*, 1984.

Bibliography
Chambers, Judith. *Thomas Pynchon*. New York: Twayne, 1992.

Coward, David. *Thomas Pynchon: The Art of Allusion*. Carbondale: Southern Illinois University Press, 1980.

Dugdale, John. *Thomas Pynchon: Allusive Parables of Power*. New York: St. Martin's Press, 1990.

Hume, Kathryn. *Pynchon's Mythography: An Approach to "Gravity's Rainbow."* Carbondale: Southern Illinois University Press, 1987.

Levine, George, and David Leverenz, eds. *Mindful Pleasures: Essays on Thomas Pynchon*. Boston: Little, Brown, 1976.

McHoul, Alec, and David Wills. *Writing Pynchon: Strategies in Fictional Analysis*. Urbana: University of Illinois Press, 1990.

Madsen, Deborah L. *The Postmodernist Allegories of Thomas Pynchon*. New York: St. Martin's Press, 1991.

Mead, Clifford. *Thomas Pynchon: A Bibliography of Primary and Secondary Materials*. Elmwood Park, Ill.: Dalkey Archive Press, 1989.

Mendelson, Edward. *Pynchon: A Collection of Critical Essays*. Englewood Cliffs, N.J.: Prentice-Hall, 1978.

Newman, Robert D. *Understanding Thomas Pynchon*. Columbia: University of South Carolina Press, 1986.

Schaub, Thomas. *Pynchon: The Voice of Ambiguity*. Urbana: University of Illinois Press, 1981.

Seed, David. *The Fictional Labyrinths of Thomas Pynchon*. Iowa City: University of Iowa Press, 1988.

Slade, Joseph. *Thomas Pynchon*. New York: Warner Paperback Library, 1974.

Tanner, Tony. *Thomas Pynchon*. London: Methuen, 1982.

Weisenburger, S. C. *A "Gravity's Rainbow" Companion: Sources and Contexts for Pynchon's Novel*. Athens: University of Georgia Press, 1988.

KURT VONNEGUT, JR.

Born: Indianapolis, Indiana; November 11, 1922

Principal long fiction

Player Piano, 1952; *The Sirens of Titan*, 1959; *Mother Night*, 1961; *Cat's Cradle*, 1963; *God Bless You, Mr. Rosewater: Or, Pearls Before Swine*, 1965; *Slaughterhouse-Five: Or, The Children's Crusade, a Duty-Dance with Death*, 1969; *Breakfast of Champions: Or, Goodbye Blue Monday*, 1973; *Slapstick: Or, Lonesome No More!*, 1976; *Jailbird*, 1979; *Deadeye Dick*, 1982; *Galápagos*, 1985; *Bluebeard*, 1987; *Hocus Pocus*, 1990.

Other literary forms

Welcome to the Monkey House (1968) is a reprinting of all earlier short stories and twelve new ones. *Wampeters, Foma, and Granfalloons (Opinions)* (1974) is the first collection of essays. Kurt Vonnegut, Jr., has also written for Broadway and television and has published children's literature.

Achievements

Critical acclaim eluded Vonnegut until the publication of *Slaughterhouse-Five* in 1969. An immediate best-seller, it earned for Vonnegut respect from critics who had previously dismissed him as a mediocre science-fiction writer. Vonnegut has been honored as the Briggs-Copeland Lecturer at Harvard University, as a member of the National Institute of Arts and Letters, and as the Distinguished Professor of English Prose at the City University of New York. Through his insightful and sympathetic treatment of the psychologically and morally crippled victims of the modern world, Vonnegut has earned his reputation as one of the greatest humanist writers of his time.

Biography

Kurt Vonnegut, Jr., was born in Indianapolis, Indiana, in 1922. Both the location and the era of his birth helped shape his distinctive worldview, a worldview that informs all of his works. Growing up in the American heartland in the calm interval between World Wars I and II, Vonnegut had a brief vision of a middle-class world that embraced the values of honesty, decency, and human dignity. For Vonnegut, this was the world as it should be, a world unravaged by violence and war, a world untouched by technology. This period of childhood happiness was, however, merely the calm before the storm in this life that would be rocked by a series of personal and national disasters: the death of his mother by suicide on Mother's Day; his prisoner-of-war expe-

rience in World War II; the deaths of his sister and brother-in-law; the dissolution of his first marriage; the bombing of Dresden and Hiroshima; and the Kennedy and King assassinations. All the heartaches of his family and his nation reverberate through Vonnegut's work, while the artist, through his fiction, strives to create a saner, calmer world.

During the Depression years, Vonnegut's family suffered emotional and financial setbacks. When Vonnegut entered Cornell University in 1940, his father forbade him to study the arts and chose instead for his son a career in science, a career with guaranteed job security. In 1943 Vonnegut left Cornell to enlist in the Army, despite his own public opposition to the war. Less than one year later, he was captured by the Germans and, in 1945, survived one of the greatest massacres of the war, the Allied firebombing of Dresden. This horror pursued Vonnegut for twenty-three years, until he worked through the pain by writing *Slaughterhouse-Five*.

After the war, Vonnegut married and began studies in anthropology at the University of Chicago. After three years, he left college and took a job as a publicist with General Electric (GE), where his brother worked as a physicist. Vonnegut's background in science and his disillusionment at GE influenced his first two novels, *Player Piano* and *The Sirens of Titan*, both parables of dehumanization in a technological society.

Since 1952, Vonnegut has written more than a dozen novels, numerous essays, a Broadway play, and a musical work, *Requiem*, which was performed by the Buffalo Symphony. Despite his varied artistic talents, however, Vonnegut has always been known for his fiction.

Analysis

Vonnegut's writings constitute an unremitting protest against the horrors of the twentieth century: the unspeakable atrocities of war, the destruction of the environment, and the depersonalization of the individual in a society ruled by science and technology. The satiric bent of his short stories points up his primary concern: the alleviation of human suffering. Fantasy, black humor, and a keen sense of the absurd are the ingredients of his fiction.

In his novels, Vonnegut coaxes the reader toward greater sympathy for others and deeper understanding of the human condition. His arena is as expansive as the whole universe and as tiny as a single human soul. Part philosopher, part poet, Vonnegut, in his fictive world, tackles the core problem of modern life: How can the individual maintain dignity and exercise free will in a world overrun by death and destruction, a world in which both science and religion are powerless to provide a solution? The reader will find no ready answers in Vonnegut, only a friendly guide along the questioning path.

In *Mother Night* Vonnegut peers deeply into the human soul, exploring the roots of human alienation, probing the individual's search for his "real" identity, and uncovering the thin veil that separates reality from illusion. The story is told as the memoirs of Howard W. Campbell, Jr., a self-proclaimed "citizen of nowhere." He allows himself to be recruited by Major Frank Wirtanen to be an American double agent posing as a Nazi radio propagandist in Germany. Secretly, Campbell sends coded American messages in his propaganda broadcasts, but he does not understand the code and never comprehends the messages he transmits. Still unaware, he even transmits the news of his beloved wife's death.

Publicly, Campbell is reviled as a traitorous Nazi hatemonger, but he does not mind, because he enjoys being on the radio. Eventually, though, he begins to lose touch with his "real" self. Is he the sensitive artist, the cruel Nazi, or the American patriot? Campbell allows himself to be manipulated by those around him. With no will or identity of his own, Campbell is easy prey for those who would use him for their own ends.

American agents eventually arrest Campbell and two Russian spies who were planning to escape to freedom with him. The latter are detained, but Campbell is soon freed by Wirtanen. Gripped by existential fear at finding himself a free man, Campbell appeals to a Jewish couple in his apartment building, a doctor and his mother, both survivors of Auschwitz. Campbell begs to be tried for his crimes against the Jews and soon finds himself awaiting trial in a Jerusalem prison. Before Campbell goes to trial, Wirtanen sends a letter on his behalf,

explaining how he had recruited Campbell and honoring him as an American patriot. Yet Campbell can never be a truly free man until he purges his conscience. Upon his release from prison, he is nauseated by the prospect of his freedom, knowing that he is one of the many people "who served evil too openly and good too secretly." In his failure to resist evil and his openness to manipulation by others, Campbell gave up his free will and lost his ability to choose. Coming to this realization, he finally asserts his will to choose and, ironically, chooses to die, vowing to hang himself "for crimes against himself."

Vonnegut's efforts to touch the soul of humanity are most fully realized in *Slaughterhouse-Five*, his most touching and brilliant work. Incorporating all Vonnegut's common themes—the nature of reality and illusion, the question of free will and determinism, the horror of man's inhumanity to man, the vision of life as an ironic construct—*Slaughterhouse-Five* produces "an image of life that is beautiful and surprising and deep." This often-misunderstood novel leads the reader on a time-warped journey, as popular films say, "to hell and back." Emotionally suffocated by his experience in World War II, Vonnegut waited twenty-three years to tell the story of his capture by the Germans and his survival of the Allied firebombing of Dresden, the calculated annihilation of a quarter of a million refugees and civilians in an unguarded city.

As befits a tale of such distorted experience, *Slaughterhouse-Five* breaks all novelistic conventions. The story is divided into ten sections, spanning the years from 1944 to 1968. Opening with a simple, first-person narrative, Vonnegut describes his return to Dresden in 1967. He recounts his life after the war, discusses his wife and children, and relives a conversation with his old war buddy Bernard V. O'Hare, in which he reveals why *Slaughterhouse-Five* is subtitled *The Children's Crusade*. In the original Children's Crusade of 1213, Catholic monks raised a volunteer army of thirty thousand children who were intent on traveling to Palestine but instead were sent to North Africa to be sold as slaves. In the end, half the children drowned en route and the others were sold. For Vonnegut, this incident provides the perfect metaphor for all wars: hopeless ventures fought by deluded children. Thus Vonnegut prepares the reader for this personal statement about the tragedy of war. Nevertheless, the reader finds himself unprepared for the narrative shape of the tale.

To increase his emotional distance from the story, Vonnegut, the masked narrator, tells not his own story but the story of pathetic Billy Pilgrim, Vonnegut's mythical fellow soldier. The reader first sees Billy as a forty-six-year-old retired optometrist living in Ilium, New York. Billy's daughter, Barbara, thinks that he has lost his mind. Billy has given up interest in business and devotes all of his energies to telling the world about his travels to the planet Tralfamadore. Two years earlier, Billy had been captured by aliens from Tralfamadore and had spent six months on their planet. Billy's belief in Tralfamadorian philosophy is the great comfort of his life, and he is eager to share this philosophy with the world. The aliens taught Billy, the optometrist, a better way to "see." On Tralfamadore, time is not linear; all moments are structured and permanent; death is merely one moment out of many moments in a person's life. The Tralfamadorians do not mourn the dead, for even though one may be dead in one moment, he is alive and happy in many others. The Tralfamadorians respond to life's temporary bad moments with a verbal shrug, "So it goes." Their world is a world without free will, without human responsibility, without human sorrow. On an intellectual level, Billy hungrily embraces their philosophy. Yet deep inside him (as inside Vonnegut) stirs the need to reconstruct his life, to reconcile his past. So, armed with Tralfamadorian detachment, Billy steps back in time to where it all began.

It is 1944, and Billy, a night student at the Ilium School of Optometry, is drafted into action in World War II. No soldier is more unsuited to war than Billy. Timid and friendless, he is a chaplain's assistant, a hapless soul with a "meek faith in a loving Jesus which most soldiers found putrid." Billy's marching companion is Roland Weary, a savage young man even by military standards. Weary's father collects ancient instruments of torture, and Weary regales Billy with gruesome tales of cruelty, giving the gentle boy an unwanted view of a monstrous world. Weary, a callous, stupid killing machine, is the natural result of man's inhumanity to man. Although physically robust, he is morally depleted, a symbol of the spiritually bankrupt world into which poor Billy has been thrust. Billy—kind, sensitive, tenderhearted—has no natural defenses against the barbarity that surrounds him.

After a brief respite of time travel, Billy returns to the war. He and Weary have been captured behind German lines, taken prisoner by two toothless old men and two young boys. The Germans are accompanied by a guard dog, a female German shepherd, Princess, who had been stolen from a farmer. Princess and Billy are confused and shivering from the cold. Of the whole motley group, only the barbarous Weary belongs at war. Billy, Princess, the old men, and the young boys symbolize helpless humanity in the grip of military madness.

Billy and his fellow prisoners, including Vonnegut and Bernard V. O'Hare, are taken to a prisoner-of-war camp before their transport to Dresden. As Billy recalls these moments of his life, he is moved to time travel many times. He flashes forward to 1948, when, emotionally shattered by his war experience, he checks himself into a veterans' hospital for mental patients. Here the reader is introduced to Valencia Merble, Billy's unlovely fiancée, and Eliot Rosewater, his fellow mental patient. In the hospital, Eliot and Billy devour the science-fiction novels of Kilgore Trout. They are drawn to Trout's work for the same reason Billy is drawn to the philosophy of Tralfamadore: Human experience on earth has been too disturbing; life seems meaningless. Escaping to the world of science fiction relieves the pressure, enabling Eliot and Billy to "reinvent" themselves in a kinder universe.

When Billy returns to his war story, he and his fellow American soldiers are in Dresden, working in a factory producing vitamin syrup for pregnant women. Yet soon there will be no pregnant women in Dresden. The American soldiers are quartered underground in a former pig butchery—slaughterhouse number five. On the night of February 13, 1945, Billy (and Vonnegut) nestles safely in the shelter while the city is flattened by British and American firebombs. The next morning, the prisoners go aboveground, finding the city as lifeless as the surface of the moon. Only the one hundred American prisoners and their guards have survived.

In chapter 10 Vonnegut returns as narrator and eventually takes the reader back to Dresden. He and Billy are there, where the prisoners of war are digging for bodies, mining for corpses. Billy's digging companion dies of the dry heaves, unable to face the slaughter. Billy's friend Edgar Derby is executed for stealing a teapot. When the corpse mines are closed down, Billy, Vonnegut, and their companions are locked up in the suburbs to await the end of the war. When the war is over, the freed soldiers wander out into the street. The trees are blooming, and the birds are singing; springtime has finally arrived for Kurt Vonnegut. Even if Billy remains blankly ignorant of the connections between events in his life, both the reader and the author learn about emotional survival in the modern world. For Vonnegut, Billy's story is a parable and a warning to all humankind: a warning that people must resist the temptation to abandon free will, as Billy has, and an exhortation to keep one's dignity in the face of modern dehumanization.

Vonnegut has said that the writer functions like the canaries that coal miners took with them down into the mines "to detect gas before men got sick." He or she must serve society as an early-warning system so that society can work to improve the human condition while it is still possible to do so.

Other major works

SHORT FICTION: *Canary in a Cat House*, 1961; *Welcome to the Monkey House*, 1968.

PLAYS: *Happy Birthday, Wanda June*, 1970; *Between Time and Timbuktu: Or, Prometheus-5, a Space Fantasy*, 1972 (teleplay).

NONFICTION: *Wampeters, Foma, and Granfalloons (Opinions)*, 1974; *Palm Sunday, An Autobiographical Collage*, 1981.

CHILDREN'S LITERATURE: *Sun Moon Star*, 1980 (with Ivan Chermayeff).

Bibliography

Allen, William Rodney. *Understanding Kurt Vonnegut*. Columbia, S.C.: University of South Carolina Press, 1991.

Broer, Lawrence R. *Sanity Plea: Schizophrenia in the Novels of Kurt Vonnegut*. Ann Arbor: University of Michigan Press, 1989.

Giannone, Richard. *Vonnegut: A Preface to His Novels*. Port Washington, N.Y.: Kennikat Press, 1977.

Klinkowitz, Jerome. *"Slaughterhouse-Five": Reforming the Novel and the World*. Boston: Twayne, 1990.

_____ , ed. *The Vonnegut Statement*. New York: Delacorte Press, 1973.

Schatt, Stanley. *Kurt Vonnegut, Jr.* Boston: Twayne, 1976.

X

THE GEOGRAPHY OF HOPE
American Identities in the West

The West is a region of extraordinary variety within its abiding unity,
and of an iron immutability beneath its surface of change.
—Wallace Stegner, *The American West as Living Space*, 1987

The fundamental story of the West is the story of opportunity knocking on the gates of Paradise, the Big Rock Candy Mountain rediscovered, the Garden of Eden ripe for harvest—or as Huck Finn would have put it, "lighting out for the Territory." This is the story of America, the American Dream of ownership, of finding a place to call our own. We Americans are a people driven by the illusion that the grass is always greener in the place where we have never before been. We look to the West as a solace of wide-open spaces that we can come home to, a frontier of second chances where we can start over as the person we were meant to be. This is a heavy weight to saddle on the shoulders of the West. As Wallace Stegner points out, the West has been as "notable for mirages as for the realization of dreams." This is the gold-rush mystique of Jack London, that certain brand of steadfast self-reliance and rugged individualism that is a typically Western trait.

It is hard not to be seduced by the abundance of space out West, the untamed wildness of a world where wildlife translates into an excuse—a reason, even—to live each day as if it is our last. The writers of the "Old West" (London, Bret Harte, Louis L'Amour) romanticized the brutality of westward expansion; at times they even offered excuses for the acts of savage bloodletting committed in the name of the American Dream: the imperialist desire to own it all. The writers of the "New West" must own up to the brutality of Western mythology; they must struggle with the ghosts and roadside landmarks that constantly remind us, day after day, of how the West was really won. But this, too, is only one side

of the story, one version of the West. The voices of the West are as wide-ranging and dexterous as the landscape of the region itself: a world in which the big skies of Thomas McGuane and Wallace Stegner are diamond-studded by the stars of Joan Didion's coastal California; home also to Frank Norris' gritty turn-of-the-century stark realism; home too to John Steinbeck's Cannery Row and the Zen-grounded Big Sur poetics of Beat-naturalist Gary Snyder; home too to the out-of-work working-poor portraits of a domestic American West made to seem near-heroic in the hands of Raymond Carver.

Home: It is a word one encounters often in the literature of the American West. Home is both a place of comfort and a place that we cannot wait to leave. The writers of the West are constantly struggling with this tension—the sense of "lighting out for the Territory" while at the same time haunted, perhaps even paralyzed, by the notion that you can't go home again: the possibility that there will be nothing left to come home to. Larry McMurtry's *Leaving Cheyenne* (1963) and Thomas McGuane's *Keep the Change* (1989) both explore and dramatize the polarity of such a paradoxical impulse. A plot of land to claim as one's own was once the ideal of the American Dream. But now, as McGuane's protagonist Joe Starling points out, we are living in a West where "leaving a ranch to one's children was called child abuse." This is, perhaps, the postmodern dilemma of the American West. The frontier has disappeared. The gold-rush towns of the late eighteen hundreds have been replaced by two-bit tourist-trap towns inhabited by ghosts and nostalgia. The writers of the New West must live and write in a house of big sky that is in desperate need of revisioning and structural repair. McGuane, McMurtry, and Stegner, among a wealth of less-well-known, West-bred-and-West-based writers, have given us a new story to inhabit. For this we should all be thankful.

The writers of the "Old West" fulfill in us a basic need to light out for *new* territory. Americans are driven by the promise of mobility, of packing up all their belongings and "lighting out" in search of new ground and new worlds to conquer. Perhaps this is the result of our migratory heritage, the myopic American belief that we can go anywhere and do anything there that we damn well please. In John Steinbeck's *The Grapes of Wrath* (1939), the road out of the Depression, into the land of milk and honey, led west, where dreams were already beginning to dry up. Traditionally, the West has been defined by its emptiness and its long silences, those twin distances that separate town from town, neighbor from neighbor. It is not an easy place in which to live.

The land itself, like the folks who call the West home, can be dry and unforgiving. To make a living out West is to pray and wait for rain. Oftentimes, rain comes only when it is too late. Perhaps that is why the writers of the West are so obsessed with and fixated on the weather. Pick up a novel by Stegner, McMurtry, McGuane, and you will find long passages describing the beauty of rain, earth, and sky. Or look at the opening stanza from Gary Snyder's "Mid-August at Sourdough Mountain Lookout":

> Down valley a smoke haze
> Three days heat, after five days rain
> Pitch glows on the fir-cones
> Across rocks and meadows
> Swarms of new flies.

Consider, too, the cold, peopleless photographs of Ansel Adams and Russell Chatham's calmly churning landscapes of the rivers, breakwater valleys, and mountains of Montana. What we are seeing here, and what we should see, is a series of portraits of the West itself. Not surprisingly, then, the writers of the West, like their visual counterparts, generate works of art that are colored and mythically enlarged by a sense of grandeur and wonder for the natural world. When they are read collectively, the writers of the West paint for us a linked series of self-portraits of the American West.

In Stegner's *Big Rock Candy Mountain* (1943), for example, we witness the encroaching spread of community values slowly swallowing up Bo Mason, a bonanza man who still holds strong to the ideals of the Old Western frontier. Like the traditional headstrong heroes of "classic" Westerns (represented here by Louis L'Amour), Bo Mason is a man who steadfastly refuses to alter his often stubborn, violent ways. He is an anomaly who would not bide well in the world of the New West—a world increasingly domestic and inward-turning in its search for self and meaning.

It is possible that the spirit of Bo Mason lives on through the works of short-story-writer Raymond Carver, whose characters live displaced, inarticulate, often drunk in a world with which they have failed to keep pace. Carver's vision of the West, which he shares with playwright Sam Shepard, is a world of dimly lit kitchenettes and seedy, neon-bleeding motel rooms inside which people fight to go on living. It is a world in which even the mirage of hope no longer exists. It is the New West house of ozone skies shielded by vinyl siding, a world of strip malls and fast-food drive thrus—the American West of the way we live today. It is a world that Lewis and Clark, Crazy Horse, Jack London, and Bo Mason would have hated to see and could not have imagined.

The dominant mythology of the American West is also the story of our nation, the claiming of our national identity: the story of a disenfranchised populace headbent on building a new and much better world where all men and women not only were created equal and free but also are equal and free; where the dream of owning it all—house, land, and sky—is a God-granted birthright upheld by an American creed. Such a mythology is, of course, wrong and bull-headed, as luridly fictitious as the classic gunslinging pulp novel misnamed the "Western." This is the West of the imagination, the fairy-tale world of cowboys and Indians, where John Wayne and Shane come to save the day. The truth-telling literature of the American West, the literature that lasts, relates a different story. It tells a more private tale that takes us inside the quiet, routine lives of everyday Westerners. Everyday Americans. People like you and me.

—Peter Markus
Detroit, Michigan

RAYMOND CARVER

Born: Clatskanie, Oregon; May 25, 1938   **Died:** Port Angeles, Washington; August 2, 1988

Principal short fiction

Put Yourself in My Shoes, 1974; *Will You Please Be Quiet, Please?*, 1976; *Furious Seasons and Other Stories*, 1977; *What We Talk About When We Talk About Love*, 1981; *Cathedral*, 1984; *Where I'm Calling From*, 1988.

Other literary forms

Raymond Carver distinguished himself as a short-story writer and poet, and he wrote in both forms until his death.

Achievements

Carver's greatest achievement was overcoming his economically and culturally disadvantaged background to become an author of world renown. He made the short story a viable literary form; since Carver, short-story collections have again become a marketable commodity in the book trade. Both as a model and as a teacher, he had such an influence on younger fiction writers that author Jay McInerney could truthfully say (alluding to a famous statement that Fyodor Dostoevski made about Nikolai Gogol) that there is hardly a single American short-story writer younger than Carver who did not "come out of Carver's overcoat."

With only a bachelor's degree and mediocre grades, Carver was invited to teach at distinguished universities and became a professor of English at Syracuse University in 1980. He received many honors during his lifetime, including a Strauss Living Award, which guaranteed him an annual stipend of thirty-five thousand dollars and enabled him to devote full time to writing during the last years of his life. Shortly before his death, he received a doctorate of letters from the University of Hartford. In 1993, Robert Altman's acclaimed film *Short Cuts* brought further attention to Carver's short stories by interweaving storylines and bringing Carver's fictional world to the screen.

Biography

Raymond Carver grew up in a sparsely populated corner of the Pacific Northwest. This rustic environment had an indelible effect upon his character and writing. Like Ernest Hemingway, one of the writers who influenced him, he loved the purity and freedom of the American wilderness, and he also respected the simplicity, honesty, and directness of the men and women who earned meager and precarious livelihoods in that primitive setting. He married young and had two children to support by the time he was twenty. He had wanted to be a writer from the time he was in the third grade, but the responsibilities of parenthood made it extremely difficult for him to find time to write. His limited education forced him to take menial jobs for which he was temperamentally unsuited. He was unable to consider tackling anything as ambitious as a full-length novel, so he spent his odd free hours writing short stories and poetry. He managed to get some of his work published in small magazines, but these publications paid little or nothing for his work, so he was haunted by financial problems for much of his life.

One of the most important influences in Carver's life was John Gardner, who taught creative writing at California State University at Chico and said, "You cannot be a great writer unless you feel greatly." The idealistic Gardner introduced his students to the literary magazines that represented the cutting edge in contemporary American fiction and poetry, and he urged them to write honestly about what they knew, as opposed to turning out formula fiction in an attempt to make money. This is exactly what Carver did, and ironically, he found that the hardships and distractions that were preventing him from writing were the very things that provided him with material to write about. This may account for the characteristic stoical humor to be found in many of his stories.

Another profound influence in his life was alcohol. One of Carver's distinguishing traits as a writer is his astonishing candor, and anyone who reads a dozen of his short stories will get a good idea of what his life was like for nearly two decades. His drinking caused serious domestic and financial problems, which led to feelings of guilt and more drinking. Amazingly, his strong constitution and unwavering motivation enabled him to continue producing stories and poems.

With the publication of *What We Talk About When*

We Talk About Love in 1981, Carver achieved critical and popular fame. His financial problems were ameliorated because he was receiving valuable grants and teaching assignments and was also selling his work to high-paying magazines such as *Esquire, Harper's Bazaar, Playgirl,* and *The New Yorker.* Collections of his short stories sold well. He was earning money teaching creative writing courses and appearing as a featured attraction at many workshops and seminars.

By the late 1970's, Carver had separated from his first wife and was living with the poet and teacher Tess Gallagher. She helped him cope with his drinking problem and provided a much-needed stabilizing influence. Carver, always a heavy cigarette smoker, died of lung cancer in 1988. By that time, his works had been published all over the world in more than twenty foreign languages.

Analysis

Carver enjoyed a critical reputation as one of the most gifted and innovative short-fiction authors of his generation. He is also credited with reviving the short story as a genre in American literature. His hard-biting prose is peopled with characters—chiefly the working poor—from his native Pacific Northwest.

Nearly everything written about Carver begins with two observations: He is a minimalist, and he writes about working-class people. Their problems, however, are universal. Carver writes about divorce, infidelity, spiritual alienation, alcoholism, bankruptcy, rootlessness, and existential dread; none of these afflictions is peculiar to the working class, and in fact, all were once more common to members of the higher social classes.

Carver was a minimalist (although he never embraced that label) by preference and by necessity. His lifelong experience had been with working-class people. It would have been inappropriate to write about simple people in an ornate style, and furthermore, his limited education would have made it impossible for him to do so effectively. The spare, objective style that he admired in some of Hemingway's short stories, such as "The Killers" and "Hills Like White Elephants," was perfectly suited to Carver's needs. The advantage and appeal of minimalism in literature is that it draws readers into the story by forcing them to conceptualize missing details.

Carver also possessed a unique sense of humor. He was so constituted that he could not help seeing the humorous side of the tragic or the grotesque. It might be said that Carver's theme and thesis throughout his career was the human comedy.

Will You Please Be Quiet, Please? includes the tragicomic "Neighbors," the first of Carver's stories to appear in a slick magazine with a large circulation. Gordon Lish, editor of the venerable men's magazine *Esquire,* recognized Carver's talent early but did not immediately accept any of his submissions. Lish's welcome encouragement, painful rejections, and eventual acceptance represented a major influence in Carver's career. "Neighbors" deals with ordinary people but has a surrealistic humor, which was to become a Carver trademark.

Bill and Arlene Miller, a couple in their thirties, have agreed to feed their neighbors' cat and water the plants while they are away. The Stones' apartment holds a mysterious fascination, and they both find excuses to enter it more often than necessary. Bill helps himself to the Chivas Regal, eats food out of their refrigerator, and goes through their closets and dresser drawers. He tries on some of Jim Stone's clothes and lies on their bed masturbating. Then he goes so far as to try on Harriet Stone's brassiere and panties and then a skirt and blouse. Bill's wife also disappears into the neighbors' apartment on her own mysterious errands. They fantasize that they have assumed the identities of their neighbors, whom they regard as happier people leading fuller lives. The shared guilty adventure arouses both Bill and Arlene sexually, and they have better lovemaking than they have experienced in a long while. Then disaster strikes: Arlene discovers that she has inadvertently locked the Stones' key inside the apartment. The cat may starve; the plants may wither; the Stones may find evidence that they have been rummaging through their possessions. The story ends with the frightened Millers clinging to each other outside their lost garden of Eden.

This early story displays some of Carver's strengths: his sense of humor, his powers of description, and his ability to characterize people through what they do and say. It also has the two main qualities that editors look for: timeliness and universality. "Neighbors" portrays the alienated condition of many contemporary Americans of all social classes.

The publication of the collection titled *What We Talk About When We Talk About Love* made Carver famous. These short, rather ambiguous stories also got him permanently saddled with the term "minimalist." One of the best short stories of the collection is "Why Don't You Dance?" It is one of the most representative, the most Carveresque of all Carver's short stories. A man who is never given a name has placed all of his furniture and personal possessions outside on the front lawn and has whimsically arranged them as if they were still indoors. He has run an extension cord from the house and hooked up lamps, a television, and a record player. He is sitting outside drinking whiskey, totally indifferent to the amazement and curiosity of his neighbors. One feels as if the worst is over for him: He is the survivor of some great catastrophe, like a marooned sailor who has managed to salvage some flotsam and jetsam.

A young couple, referred to throughout the story as "the boy" and "the girl," drive by and assume that the man is holding a yard sale. They stop and inquire about prices. The man offers them drinks. The boy and girl get into a party spirit. They put old records on the turntable and start dancing in the driveway. The man is anxious to get rid of his possessions and accepts whatever they are willing to offer. He even makes them presents of things that they do not really want. Weeks later, the girl is still talking about the man, but she cannot find the words to express what she really feels about the incident. Perhaps she and her young friends will understand the incident much better after they have worked and worried and bickered and moved from one place to another for ten or twenty years.

"Why Don't You Dance?" is a humorous treatment of a serious subject, in characteristic Carver fashion. The man's tragedy is never spelled out, but the reader can piece the story together quite easily from the clues. Evidently, there has been a divorce or separation. Evidently, there were financial problems, which are so often associated with divorce, and the man has been evicted. Judging from the fact that he is doing so much drinking, alcoholism is either the cause or the effect of his other problems. The man has given up all hope and now sees hope only in other people, represented by this young couple starting out in life and trying to collect a few pieces of furniture for their rented apartment.

Divorce, infidelity, domestic strife, financial worry, bankruptcy, alcoholism, rootlessness, consumerism as a substitute for intimacy, and disillusionment with the American Dream are common themes throughout Carver's stories. The symbol of a man sitting outside on his front lawn drinking whiskey, with all of his worldly possessions placed around him but soon to be scattered to the four winds, is a striking symbol of modern human beings. It is easy to acquire possessions but nearly impossible to keep a real home.

On a different level, "Why Don't You Dance?" reflects Carver's maturation as a person and an author.

The responsibilities of parenthood as well as the experience of teaching young students were bringing home to him the fact that his personal problems could hold instructional utility for others. As a teacher of creative writing, placed more and more in the limelight, interacting with writers, editors, professors, and interviewers, he was being forced to formulate his own artistic credo. The older man in the story sees himself in his young yard-sale customers and wants to help them along in life; this is evidently a reflection of the author's own attitude. Consequently, the story itself is not merely an autobiographical protest or lament like some of Carver's earlier works but is designed to deliver a message—perhaps a warning—for the profit of others. The melancholy wisdom of Carver's protagonist reflects Carver's own mellowing as he began to appreciate the universally tragic nature of human existence.

"Where I'm Calling From" is a great American short story. It originally appeared in the prestigious *The New Yorker*, was reprinted in the collection titled *Cathedral*, and appears once again as the title story in the best and most comprehensive collection of Carver's stories, *Where I'm Calling From*. The story is narrated by an alcoholic staying at a "drying-out facility," an unpretentious boardinghouse where plain meals are served family-style and there is nothing to do but read, watch television, or talk.

The narrator in Carver's story tells about his drinking problems and interweaves his own biography with that of a friend he has made at the drying-out facilities, a man he refers to as "J. P." The only thing unusual about their stories is that J. P. is a chimney sweep and is married to a chimney sweep. Both J. P. and the narrator ruined their marriages through their compulsive drinking and are now terrified that they will be unable to control their craving once they get out of the facility. They have made vows of abstinence often enough before and have not kept them. They have dried out before and gone right back to the bottle.

Carver manages to convey all the feelings of guilt, remorse, terror, and helplessness experienced by people who are in the ultimate stages of alcoholism. It is noteworthy that, whereas his alcoholic protagonists of earlier stories were often isolated individuals, the protagonist-narrator of "Where I'm Calling From" not only is actively seeking help but also is surrounded by others with the same problem. This feature indicates that Carver had come to realize that the way to give his stories the point or meaning that they had previously often lacked was to suggest the existence of large-scale social problems of which his characters are victims. He had made what author Joan Didion called "the quantum leap" of realizing that his personal problems were actually social problems. The curse of alcoholism affects all social classes; even people who never touch a drop can have their lives ruined by it.

"The Bridle" first appeared in *The New Yorker* and was reprinted in *Cathedral*. It is an example of Carver's mature period, a highly artistic story fraught with social significance. The story is told from the point of view of one of Carver's *faux-naïf* narrators. Readers immediately feel that they know this good-natured soul, a woman named Marge who manages an apartment building in Arizona and "does hair" as a sideline. She tells about one of the many families who stayed a short while and then moved on like tumbleweeds being blown across the desert. Although Carver typically writes about Northern California and the Pacific Northwest, this part of Arizona is also "Carver Country," a world of freeways, fast-food restaurants, Laundromats, mindless television entertainment, and transient living accommodations, a homogenized world of strangers with minimum-wage jobs and tabloid mentalities.

Mr. Holits pays the rent in cash every month, suggesting that he recently went bankrupt and has neither a bank account nor credit cards. Carver, like minimalists in general, loves such subtle clues. Mrs. Holits confides to Marge that they had owned a farm in Minnesota. Her husband, who "knows everything there is about horses," still keeps one of his bridles, evidently symbolizing his hope that he may escape from Carver Country. Mrs. Holits proves more adaptable: She gets a job as a waitress, a favorite occupation among Carver characters. Her husband, however, cannot adjust to the service industry jobs, which are all that are available to a man his age with his limited experience. He handles the money, the two boys are his sons by a former marriage, and he has been accustomed to making the decisions, yet he finds that his wife is taking over the family leadership in this brave new postindustrial world.

Like many other Carver males, Holits becomes a heavy drinker. He eventually injures himself while trying to show off his strength at the swimming pool. One day the Holitses with their young sons, pack and drive off down the long, straight highway without a word of explanation. When Marge trudges upstairs to clean the empty apartment, she finds that Holits has left his bridle behind.

The naïve narrator does not understand the significance of the bridle, but the reader feels its poignancy as a symbol. The bridle is one of those useless objects that everyone carts around and is reluctant to part with because it represents a memory, a hope, or a dream. It is an especially appropriate symbol because it is so utterly out of place in one of those two-story, frame-stucco, look-alike apartment buildings that disfigure the landscape and are the dominant features of Carver Country. Gigantic economic forces beyond the comprehension of the narrator have driven this farm family from their home and turned them into the modern equivalent of the Joad family in John Steinbeck's classic novel *The Grapes of Wrath* (1939).

There is, however, a big difference between Carver and Steinbeck. Steinbeck believed in and prescribed the panacea of socialism; Carver has no prescriptions to offer. He seems to have no faith either in politicians or in preachers. His characters are more likely to go to church to play bingo than to say prayers or sing hymns. Like many of his contemporary minimalists, he seems to have gone beyond alienation, beyond existentialism, beyond despair. God is dead; so what else is new?

Carver's working-class characters are far more complicated than Steinbeck's Joad family. Americans have become more sophisticated in the past fifty years as a result of the influence of radio, motion pictures, television, more abundant educational opportunities, improved automobiles and highways, cheap air transportation, alcohol and drugs, more leisure time, and the fact that their work is less enervating because of the proliferation of labor-saving machinery. Many Americans have also lost their religious faith, their work ethic, their class consciousness, their family loyalty, their integrity, and their dreams. Steinbeck saw it happening and showed how the Joad family was splitting apart after being uprooted from the soil; Carver's people are the Joad family a half-century down the road. Oddly enough, Carver's mature stories do not seem nihilistic or despairing, because they contain the redeeming qualities of humor, compassion, and honesty.

Reprinted in *Where I'm Calling From* is "Boxes," which first appeared in *The New Yorker*. "Boxes" is written in Carver's characteristic tragicomic tone. It is a story in which the *faux-naïf* narrator, a favorite with Carver, complains about the eccentric behavior of his widowed mother, who, for one specious reason or another, is always changing her place of residence. She moves so frequently that she usually seems to have the bulk of her worldly possessions packed in boxes scattered about on the floor. One of her complaints is the attitude of her landlord, whom she calls "King Larry."

Larry Hadlock is a widower and a relatively affluent property owner. It is evident through Carver's unerring dialogue that what she is really bitter about is Larry's indifference to her own fading charms. In the end, she returns to California but telephones to complain about the traffic, the faulty air-conditioning unit in her apartment, and the indifference of management. Her son vaguely understands that what his mother really wants, though she may not realize it herself, is love and a real home and that she can never have these things again in her lifetime no matter where she moves.

What makes the story significant is its universality: It reflects the macrocosm in a microcosm. In "Boxes," the problem touched on is not only the rootlessness and anonymity of modern life but also the plight of millions of aging people, who are considered by some to be useless in their old age and a burden to their children. It was typical of Raymond Carver to find a metaphor for this important social phenomenon in a bunch of cardboard boxes.

Carver uses working-class people as his models, but he is not writing solely about the working class. The fact that all Americans can see themselves in his little, inarticulate, bewildered characters makes Carver an important writer in the dominant tradition of American realism, a worthy successor to Mark Twain, Stephen Crane, Sherwood Anderson, Theodore Dreiser, Willa Cather, John Steinbeck, and William Faulkner.

Other major works

SCREENPLAY: *Dostoevsky*, 1985.
POETRY: *Near Klamath*, 1968; *Winter Insomnia*, 1970; *At Night with Salmon Move*, 1976; *Two Poems*, 1982; *Fires: Essays, Poems, Stories*, 1983; *If It Please You*, 1984; *This Water*, 1985; *Where Water Comes Together with Other Water*, 1985; *Ultramarine*, 1986; *A New Path to the Waterfall*, 1989.
ANTHOLOGY: *American Short Story Pieces*, 1987 (with Tom Jenks).
MISCELLANEOUS: *No Heroics, Please: Uncollected Writings*, 1991.

Bibliography

Adelman, Bob, and Tess Gallagher. *Carver Country: The World of Raymond Carver*. Introduction by Tess Gallagher. New York: Charles Scribner's Sons, 1990.
Barth, John. "A Few Words About Minimalism." *The New York Times Book Review*, December 28, 1986, 2.
Bugeja, Michael. "Tarnish and Silver: An Analysis of Carver's Cathedral." *South Dakota Review* 24, no. 3 (1986): 73-87.
Campbell, Ewing. *Raymond Carver: A Study of the Short Fiction*. New York: Twayne, 1992.
Carver, Raymond. "A Storyteller's Shoptalk." *The New York Times Book Review*, February 15, 1981, 9.
Halpert, Sam, ed. *When We Talk About Raymond Carver*. Layton, Utah: Gibbs Smith, 1991.
Saltzman, Arthur M. *Understanding Raymond Carver*. Columbia: University of South Carolina Press, 1988.
Stull, William L., and Maureen P. Carroll, eds. *Remembering Ray: A Composite Biography of Raymond Carver*. Santa Barbara, Calif.: Capra Press, 1993.
Wolff, Tobias. "Raymond Carver Had His Cake and Ate It Too." *Esquire* 112 (September, 1989): 240-248.

JOAN DIDION

Born: Sacramento, California; December 5, 1934

Principal long fiction

Run River, 1963; *Play It As It Lays*, 1970; *A Book of Common Prayer*, 1977; *Democracy*, 1984.

Other literary forms

Joan Didion is respected as a novelist, but she has been even more highly acclaimed as an essayist. Didion achieved national recognition with her first collection of essays, *Slouching Towards Bethlehem* (1968); her second collection, *The White Album* (1979), was a best-seller. Her books *Salvador* (1983) and *Miami* (1987) are more overtly political and have aroused considerable controversy. Didion has also collaborated with her husband, John Gregory Dunne, on several screenplays.

Achievements

Didion's achievements are somewhat paradoxical. Despite her claims that she speaks only for herself, she has become a spokesperson for the anxiety-ridden generation of the late 1960's and early 1970's; as surely as F. Scott Fitzgerald became the chronicler of the jazz age, she has become the chronicler of a generation living, in her terms, "close to the edge." Didion has developed a reputation for cool, detached observation and for her syncopated but elegant style. Poet James Dickey has called her "the finest woman prose stylist writing in English today," and even some who dismiss her as intellectually shallow respect her craftsmanship. Her awards include a Bread Loaf Writers Conference Fellowship in 1963.

Biography

Joan Didion was born to Frank Reese and Eduene Jarret Didion on December 5, 1934, in Sacramento, California. Didion is a child of the West—not the West of Los Angeles but of the more pastoral Sacramento Valley. The land on which Didion lived had been in her family for five generations, and as a child, she was expected to absorb the myth that America was a new Eden. In *Slouching Towards Bethlehem*, Didion reports that her Episcopal Sunday school teacher used to ask the children, "In what ways does the Holy Land resemble the Sacramento Valley?" Didion explores—and largely explodes—the myth of the Sacramento Valley as Eden in her first novel, *Run River*. Eden, however, is not

lost—or rejected—without some sense of regret, and Didion's novel reflects a nostalgia for the lost paradise and the passing of innocence.

Didion's intellectual break from a more traditional world may have begun in high school, when she discovered literature, and it must have been accelerated by her studies at the University of California at Berkeley, where she majored in literature, read Ernest Hemingway, Joseph Conrad, Henry James, and Albert Camus, moved out of her sorority house, and did not, as she points out with some regret, make Phi Beta Kappa. She did, however, win first prize in *Vogue*'s Prix de Paris contest. Given as an award the choice of a trip to Paris or a job on the magazine, Didion chose the more practical option and moved to New York.

At *Vogue*, Didion learned to write for the general public, and she began writing for several other magazines as well. She also seriously began writing fiction, and *Run River* was published in 1963. Her time in New York, then, was important for her development as a writer, and, judging from her essay "Good-bye to All That," she enjoyed her first few years there. Unfortunately, as the essay continues, she began to believe that "it is distinctly possible to stay too long at the fair." Disenchantment turned to depression. In January, 1964, in lieu of seeing a psychiatrist, she married John Gregory Dunne, also a writer, and the couple moved to Los Angeles.

In Los Angeles, Didion's writing continued to go well—she published *Slouching Towards Bethlehem* in 1968, and she and Dunne wrote the screenplay for *The Panic in Needle Park* (1971)—but for some time, she continued to suffer from the depression and sense of disorientation she describes in *The White Album*. Her marital problems were publicized in her own essays and in Dunne's. In the 1970's, however, both her marriage and her emotional state improved, and her literary success continued to grow: *Play It As It Lays*, *The White Album*, and *A Book of Common Prayer* were all best-sellers. Financial success also came, not so much from the books as from Didion and Dunne's collaboration on screenplays. Besides *The Panic in Needle Park* and the 1981 film adaptation of Dunne's novel *True Confessions*, the couple worked on the script for *A Star Is Born* (1976). According to Dunne, that motion picture "made us a fortune." Dunne and Didion divided their time between Los Angeles and New York during the mid-1980's. They moved to New York in 1988.

Analysis

While very much a California writer, Didion is not provincial. She uses her immediate milieu to depict the loss of America's frontier values amid the signs of moral erosion that have triggered their demise. Her major characters struggle with a demoniac nihilism that has infected the individual, the family, and the social environment.

Almost all Didion's works are concerned with similar themes, and there is an interesting complementary relationship between her essays and her novels. Her essays generally seem intended to force the reader to strip away illusions about contemporary life and accept realities, even if they are bleak. The novels are generally explorations of characters crippled by illusions. To some extent, in each novel, the heroine is disabused of her illusions. The fragile hope that each novel holds out, however, is offered not in terms of this disillusionment but in terms of new illusions and almost meaningless gestures. Each novel ends with the heroine learning to care for others—for a husband, for children, for friends—and yet this caring is generally based on illusion and seems doomed to failure. Didion's final implication, then, seems to be that people need to strip away all illusions, except those that help them to care for others. Such illusions—even though they are doomed to lead to failure—are sacred. These sacred illusions might be fictional, as stories are fictional, but, as Didion has said, "We tell ourselves stories in order to live . . . or at least we do for a while."

Perhaps no setting could be more appropriate for an illusion-hunter than Los Angeles. In *Play It As It Lays*, Didion places her heroine Maria (pronounced "Mar-eye-ah") squarely in the fast lane of life in Southern California. The novel opens with Maria in a psychiatric ward. She has been placed there, presumably, for her failure to attempt to stop a friend from committing suicide in her presence. As the novel unfolds backwards into the past, however, the reader comes to realize that if Maria has become unhinged, it is probably a result of the cumulative effect of her abortion, her divorce, and

the miscellaneous acts of casual sex, drugs, and other perversities one might expect in a novel about Hollywood.

Didion does not condemn the fast lane from a traditional moral perspective; that would have been too easy, and probably not very convincing or interesting. Besides, Didion's target is not simply the sexual mores of contemporary culture. Rather, she explores the popular "philosophy" or worldview that so many have accepted since the collapse of the traditional morality—a "philosophy" that might be called sloppy existentialism, extreme relativism, or simply nihilism. Maria states the key tenet of this philosophy on the second page of the novel: "NOTHING APPLIES."

Maria herself was not reared with the traditional American values. Instead of the Puritan work ethic ("God helps those who help themselves"), she was taught the gambler's code: "My father advised me that life itself was a crap game." That view was infused with a faith in good luck: "I was raised to believe that what came in on the next roll would always be better than what went on the last." For a long time, Maria was content to wait for the rolls, to go with the flow, and to "play it as it lays."

Unfortunately, Maria's luck runs out. The bad roll is an unwanted pregnancy. She thinks, but is not sure, that Carter, her husband, is not the father. He demands that she have an abortion and threatens to take away Kate, their brain-damaged daughter, if she refuses. Maria acquiesces, and her mental deterioration begins.

If Maria could completely accept the mores of her set, she would have no problem; for them, neither abortion nor divorce is anything to lose one's composure over. Maria, however, does cling to one traditional dream; she wants a family. She fantasizes about living a simple life with Kate and some man; in almost identical fantasies, the man is either Ivan or Les, two of her steadier lovers. Abortion—the termination of another possible child—is almost more than Maria can contemplate, yet she undergoes it.

Maria's reaction to the abortion is not philosophical, moral, or religious: It is emotional, physical, and psychological. She cries; she hemorrhages; she reaches a point where she cannot easily use plumbing because she imagines pipes clogged with chopped-up pieces of flesh. Didion does not attempt to make an abstract moral issue out of abortion. Maria's reaction is almost primitive, in the sense of being immediate and unreflecting. In a real sense, however, to return to Didion's essay "On Morality," abortion is a denial of the most basic social responsibility, that of mother to child (it is hard here not to recall Didion's own traumatic miscarriage and her devotion to her adopted daughter). In *Play It As It Lays*, characters fail to fulfill their primal social responsibilities. Carter, Les (even Les's wife), Maria's friends, Helene and BZ, and a number of others all say that they are "seriously worried" about Maria as she slips more and more into self-destructive behavior; they say that they care, but none of them can reach her, none of them can take care of her. Some of their protestations are hard to take seriously; Carter humiliates Maria on a number of occasions, and Helene and BZ use her—while she is drunk and only half-conscious—for obscure and unpleasant sexual purposes.

Most of these characters profess not to be concerned with the sexual conduct of their spouses. When Helene, BZ's wife, drifts into an affair with Carter, BZ asks Maria if she cares. For a time, Maria tries to insist that she does care, but as the novel draws to a conclusion, BZ forces her more and more to a nihilistic position: "'Tell me what matters,' BZ said. 'Nothing,' Maria said." The "nothing" here is Ernest Hemingway's *nada*, and at the end of the novel, BZ, like Hemingway, kills himself. BZ, however, does not use a gun. He goes out with a bottle of vodka and a grain-and-a-half of Seconal. When Helene and Carter force their way into the room, BZ is dead and Maria is asleep next to him, holding his hand.

On the last page of the novel, Maria, from the psychiatric ward, affirms BZ's nihilism, if not his suicide: "I know what 'nothing' means, and keep on playing. Why, BZ would say. Why not, I say." That, however, is not all there is to it. Maria has already made it clear that she is playing for Kate. She wants to take Kate away from the hospital; she wants them to have a home by the sea where they can live a simple life. Given Kate's condition—to say nothing of Maria's—this future does not sound very likely. Despite her acceptance of nihilism, Maria holds on to one last romantic notion. Perhaps she realizes how illusory her hope is, but the illusion and the hope are necessary. They keep her in the game and away from the Seconal.

Play It As It Lays, then, demonstrates the failures both of traditional American myths and of more current nihilistic lifestyles. Maria Wyeth survives but is sustained by hopes that seem based largely on illusion. In Didion's third novel, *A Book of Common Prayer*, the reader is told on the first page that the protagonist, Charlotte Douglas, does not survive. The narrator, however, comments that "she died, hopeful." Whether Charlotte's hope is also illusory is a central question of the novel.

It is the question that the narrator, Grace Strasser-Mendana, née Tabor, is trying to answer throughout the novel. Grace, originally from the United States, "married into one of the three or four solvent families in Boca Grande," the small central American republic in which Charlotte Douglas is finally killed (or murdered; as Grace says, neither word seems to work). The death of Grace's husband has left her "in putative control of fifty-nine-point-eight percent of the arable land and about the same percentage of the decisionmaking process in La República." From this position of power, Grace observes the political scheming of her family. She also watches Charlotte walk barefooted into the scene and become caught up in it. Grace leaves the country before Charlotte dies, and the novel is her attempt to understand Charlotte.

Early on, Grace comments that Charlotte "dreamed her life," and much of what Grace says makes Charlotte seem a woman even more given to illusion than was Maria Wyeth. Grace insists that Charlotte was the "usual child of comfortable family in the temperate zone." She had been supplied with all the material benefits and easy optimism of an affluent American. As a child, she was given a carved Austrian angel that listened to her bedside prayers: "In these prayers the child Charlotte routinely asked that 'it' turn out all right, 'it' being unspecified and all-inclusive, and she had been an adult for some years before the possibility occurred to her that 'it' might not."

Like Maria, Charlotte loses some of the optimism; her luck runs out. The more traditional lifestyle fails her. Her first husband, Warren Bogart (perhaps the name is meant to be halfway between Warren Beatty and Humphrey Bogart), had been "raised to believe not in 'hard work' or 'self reliance' but in the infinite power of the personal appeal." He is also sadistic, sexually perverse, and alcoholic. Charlotte is not perfect, either; one Easter, while their child Marin is still a baby, Charlotte gets drunk and sleeps with a man she does not even like (she later conveniently forgets the episode). Warren hits her, and she finally walks away from the marriage.

Her second marriage is not unlike Maria's life in the fast lane, except that the game is no longer motion pictures but radical politics. Her husband is not a director but a radical chic lawyer who flies from one center of revolution to another. Leonard does seem genuinely to care for Charlotte, but there are complications. Marin, Charlotte's child by Warren, turns revolutionary;

she and her friends hijack a jetliner, burn it in the desert, and join the underground.

Charlotte's main illusion, like Maria's, is centered on her daughter. She later tells Grace that she and Marin were "inseparable" (a term she also uses to describe her relationship with Warren), and she spins out fantastic accounts of their visit to the Tivoli Gardens. As might be expected, the revolutionary Marin claims to have little use for her bourgeois mother.

After a disastrous reunion with Warren and after the birth and almost immediate death of her child by Leonard, Charlotte drifts to Boca Grande, where she meets Grace. At first, Charlotte gives Grace every reason to think that she is dreaming her life; for quite a while, she goes to the airport every day, on the off chance that Marin will pass through Central America; she drifts aimlessly into sexual relations with Victor, Grace's brother-in-law, and then with Gerardo, Grace's son; she seems not to notice the growing signs of revolution; she refuses the attempts of Gerardo, Leonard, and Grace to persuade her to leave. Finally, the revolution begins, and she is arrested and killed. Her body is dumped on the lawn of the American embassy.

Even though Grace has been trying to understand Charlotte throughout the novel, she is as much a victim of delusion as Charlotte is. For some time, Grace has realized the difficulty in understanding things, in trying to get the story straight. She abandoned her first discipline before the beginning of the novel: "I am an anthropologist who lost faith in her own method, who stopped believing that observable activity defined anthros." She turned to biochemistry, but that, too, failed: "Give me the molecular structure of the protein which defined Charlotte Douglas." When Leonard reveals to her that her husband, Edgar, had been involved with the guerrillas himself, Grace is finally forced to realize that her life, as much as Charlotte's, has been one of delusion.

Grace's statement, "We all remember what we need to remember," is one of the lessons of the novel; all people prefer to believe their own versions of the stories in which they are trapped; all people accept delusions. Grace finally realizes, "I am more like Charlotte Douglas than I thought I was." Perhaps Charlotte's death was something of a meaningless gesture, but beside her coffin, Grace can only make a small, meaningless gesture of love; she places a T-shirt painted like an American flag on the casket. By way of comment, she borrows a phrase from Charlotte and Leonard: "There were no real points in that either."

Neither Grace nor Charlotte—perhaps none of Didion's characters in any of her novels—scores any real points in the end. They try to take care of one another, but they fail. Grace and Leonard try to take care of Charlotte, but they fail. Charlotte would like to take care of Marin, but she cannot. Warren wants Charlotte to take care of him, but it does not work. As cynical as Warren is, he may have the final judgment in the novel: "It doesn't matter whether you take care of somebody or somebody takes care of you. . . . It's all the same in the end. It's all the same." Warren dies alone; Charlotte dies alone. Grace will die—as she says—very soon, and she will be alone. It is all the same in the end. At least Charlotte does to some degree shape her own life toward the end. The night she was arrested, she was, Grace imagines, "walking very deliberately."

The protagonist of Didion's fourth novel, *Democracy*, is Inez Christian Victor, the daughter of a prominent Honolulu family and the wife of a liberal California senator who narrowly lost the Democratic nomination for president in 1972. The love of her life, however, is a shadowy soldier of fortune named Jack Lovett. She follows him to Southeast Asia on the eve of the fall of Vietnam (to retrieve her daughter—a heroin addict who has drifted to Saigon because she hears that employment opportunities are good there) and sees him drown in a hotel pool in Jakarta. She brings the body back to Hawaii to be buried under a jacaranda tree at Schofield Barracks and returns to Kuala Lampur to work with refugees.

In *Democracy*, one finds evidence of two of Didion's most prominent characteristics as a writer—her acute sense of place and her fascination with the American West. While these twin aspects of her muse have always been evident in her writings about California, she has occasionally cast her glance farther westward to Hawaii. In *Slouching Towards Bethlehem*, she wrote: "I sat as a child on California beaches and imagined that I saw Hawaii, a certain shimmer in the sunset, a barely perceptible irregularity glimpsed intermittently through squinted eyes." In a column for *New West* magazine, written more than a decade later, she revealed that she kept a clock in her bedroom in Los Angeles, set at Honolulu time.

When Didion, however, tried to write a novel about feudal Hawaii (originally entitled *Pacific Distances*), she produced a book that is only marginally about that subject. In *Democracy*, Hawaii is less important as a society in transition than as a way station between the Mainland and America's ultimate western frontier, Southeast Asia. (In *Slouching Towards Bethlehem*, she speaks of sailors who got drunk in Honolulu because "they were no longer in Des Moines and not yet in Da Nang.") As Walt Whitman proclaimed more than a century earlier in his poem "Passage to India" (1871), the roundness of the Earth leads not to some apocalyptic West but back east whence we came. America's Manifest Destiny, however, has not even produced a mystical passage to India, but rather helicopters lifting off the roof of the American embassy in Saigon during the final days of the only war the United States has ever lost.

Other major works

SCREENPLAYS: *The Panic in Needle Park*, 1971 (with Dunne); *Play It As It Lays*, 1972 (with Dunne); *A Star Is Born*, 1976 (with Dunne and Frank Pierson); *True Confessions*, 1981 (with Dunne).

NONFICTION: *Slouching Towards Bethlehem*, 1968; *The White Album*, 1979; *Salvador*, 1983; *Miami*, 1987; *After Henry*, 1992.

SHORT FICTION: *Telling Stories*, 1978.

Bibliography

Felton, Sharon, ed. *The Critical Response to Joan Didion*. Westport, Conn.: Greenwood Press, 1994.

Friedman, Ellen G., ed. *Joan Didion: Essays and Conversations*. Princeton, N.J.: Ontario Review Press, 1984.

Henderson, Katherine Usher. *Joan Didion*. New York: Ungar, 1981.

Kasindorf, Martin. "New Directions for the First Family of Angst." *Saturday Review* 9 (April, 1982): 14-18.

Kazin, Alfred. "Joan Didion: Portrait of a Professional." *Harper's* 243 (December, 1971): 112-114.

Lahr, John. "Entrepreneurs of Anxiety." *Horizon* 24 (January, 1981): 36-39.

Olendorf, Donna. "Joan Didion: A Checklist, 1955-1980." *Bulletin of Bibliography* 32 (January-March, 1981): 32-44.

Stout, Janis P. *Strategies of Reticence: Silence and Meaning in the Works of Jane Austen, Willa Cather, Katherine Anne Porter, and Joan Didion*. Charlottesville: University Press of Virginia, 1990.

Winchell, Mark Royden. *Joan Didion*. Rev. ed. Boston: Twayne, 1989.

KEN KESEY

Born: La Junta, Colorado; September 17, 1935

Principal long fiction

One Flew over the Cuckoo's Nest, 1962; *Sometimes a Great Notion*, 1964; *Sailor Song*, 1992.

Other literary forms

When Stewart Brand was the editor of *The Last Whole Earth Catalog* in 1971, he asked Ken Kesey to edit *The Last Supplement to the Whole Earth Catalog* (1971). Somewhat reluctant, Kesey agreed if Paul Krassner would be the coeditor. Krassner accepted, and it took almost two months to write, edit, and lay out the five-hundred-page final issue, which contained the best selections from previous issues as well as some new writings by Kesey. The final issue had a total press run of 100,000 copies and is now out of print.

Viking Press and Intrepid Trips jointly published *Kesey's Garage Sale* (1973), a volume based on an American phenomenon: the rummage, yard, or garage sale. The book is a miscellany of essays, poetry, letters, drawings, interviews, prose fiction, and a film script. Although much of the writing was Kesey's, "Hot Item Number 4: Miscellaneous Section with Guest Leftovers" contained a letter by Neal Cassady and poems by Allen Ginsberg and Hugh Romney. Kesey's "Who Flew over What," "Over the Border," and "Tools from My Chest" supply interesting insights into Kesey's beliefs and personality, and more important, they supplement the biographical details in Tom Wolfe's *The Electric Kool-Aid Acid Test* (1968), an informative biographical account of Kesey's Merry Pranksters exploits.

Achievements

Tom Wolfe remarked that Kesey was one of the most charismatic men he had ever met, and others have likewise commented upon Kesey's charisma. In fact, social critics affirmed that there were two important leaders in the 1960 counterculture revolution: Timothy Leary and his devotees on the East Coast and Kesey and his Merry Pranksters on the West Coast. Leary and his Learyites took themselves seriously, advocated passively dropping out of society, and rejected much that was American, especially American gadgetry. In contrast, Kesey and his Merry Pranksters were pro-America, were more interested in the spontaneous fun of the twentieth century neon renaissance, and took LSD not to become societal dropouts but rather to lead society to new frontiers of social communality.

As a novelist, Kesey achieved both notoriety and distinction as a major voice of his generation. Yet some critics argue that his achievement goes further. They point to his complex characters, rollicking humor, and creative manipulation of point of view as Kesey's enduring contribution to American literature.

Biography

Ken Elton Kesey was born in La Junta, Colorado, on September 17, 1935, to Fred A. and Geneva Smith Kesey. Kesey's father shrewdly foresaw that the West Coast would be ideal for business ventures, and he moved his family to Springfield, Oregon, where he founded the Eugene Farmers Cooperative, the largest and most successful dairy cooperative in the Willamette Valley. The father taught his sons, Ken and Joe, how to box, wrestle, hunt, fish, swim, and float the Willamette and McKenzie rivers on inner-tube rafts.

After attending the Springfield public schools and being voted most likely to succeed, Kesey enrolled in the University of Oregon at Eugene. In 1956, he married his high school sweetheart, Faye Haxby. During his undergraduate years, Kesey was an adept actor and seriously considered pursuing that career. He was also a champion wrestler in the 174-pound division and almost qualified for the Olympics. He received his B.A. degree in 1957, then enrolled in the graduate school at Stanford University on a creative writing scholarship and studied under Malcolm Cowley, Wallace Stegner, Frank O'Connor, and James B. Hall.

During his graduate years, two important things occurred that would influence Kesey's life and writing. The first occurred when he moved his family into one of the cottages on Perry Lane, then the bohemian quarters of Stanford. He met other writers, including Larry McMurtry, Kenneth Babbs, Robert Stone, and Neal Cassady. The second event was that Kesey met Vic Lovell, to whom he would dedicate *One Flew over the*

Cuckoo's Nest. Lovell not only introduced Kesey to Freudian psychology but also told Kesey about the drug experiments at the veterans' hospital in Menlo Park, California. In 1960, Kesey volunteered, earned twenty dollars per session, and discovered mind-expanding drugs. Kesey thus experienced LSD two years before Timothy Leary and Richard Alpert began their experiment at Harvard. Lovell also suggested that Kesey become a night attendant on the Menlo Park Veterans Hospital psychiatric ward so that he could concentrate on his writing. Kesey became intensely interested, however, in the patients and their life on the ward, and he began writing *One Flew over the Cuckoo's Nest* during the summer of 1960 and completed it in the spring of 1961. More important, as a volunteer and an aide, Kesey stole all types of drugs—especially LSD—which he distributed to his Perry Lane friends.

One Flew over the Cuckoo's Nest was published in 1962 and was a critically acclaimed. In the late spring of 1962 the Kesey family returned to Perry Lane, where he began writing his second novel and where he renewed his drug experiments. When a developer bought the Perry Lane area for a housing development, Kesey purchased a home and land in La Honda, California, and invited a dozen or so of his closest Perry Lane friends to join him so that they could continue their drug experiments. This group would eventually become Kesey's famous Merry Pranksters, or the Day-Glo Crazies.

Sometimes a Great Notion was scheduled for publication in July, 1964, and Kesey and Ken Babbs, who had just returned from Vietnam, had planned a trip to the New York World's Fair to arrive there for the publication of Kesey's second novel. Kesey bought a converted 1939 International Harvester school bus for the trip; it had all the conveniences for on-the-road living. The trip mushroomed and was the final impetus for forming the Merry Pranksters. Besides painting the bus various psychedelic colors, the Pranksters wired it with microphones, amplifiers, speakers, recorders, and motion-picture equipment. Prior to departing for New York, Kesey established the only rules for the trip—everyone would "do his own thing," would "go with the flow," and would not condemn anyone else for being himself. As an adjunct to the trip, the Pranksters recorded their entire odyssey on tape and film, which would eventually become a film entitled "The Movie," the first acid film recorded live and spontaneously. When the journey ended, there were more than forty-five hours of color film, large portions of which were out of focus, an obvious effect of the drugs. Kesey

devoted much of the 1964 spring and the 1965 fall to editing the film.

Through the remainder of the decade, Kesey continued his drug experimentation, especially with LSD. He was arrested several times for possession; at one point he fled to Canada to escape arrest, returning to the United States later the same year. He eventually served time in prison, in 1967.

Late in 1971 the film version of *Sometimes a Great Notion* was released, followed in 1975 by the film version of *One Flew over the Cuckoo's Nest*. During the 1970's Kesey remained content to work on his Pleasant Hill, Oregon, farm and produce his yogurt, which was marketed in Oregon, Washington, and Northern California. In the 1980's, a three-term teaching assignment with graduate students in the creative writing program at the University of Oregon resulted in the collaborative novel *Caverns* (1990).

Analysis

To understand some of the ideas behind the counterculture revolution is to understand Kesey's fictional heroes and some of his themes. Originating with the 1950's Beat generation, the 1960's counterculture youth were disillusioned with the vast social injustices, the industrialization, and the mass society image in their parents' world; they questioned many values and practices—the Vietnam War, the goals of higher education, the value of owning property, and the traditional forms of work. They protested by experimenting with Eastern meditation, primitive communal living, unabashed nudity, and nonpossessive physical and spiritual love. At the core of the protest was the value of individual freedom. One of the main avenues to this new type of life and freedom was mind-expanding drugs, which allowed them to "grok," a word from Robert A. Heinlein's *Stranger in a Strange Land* (1961), which means to achieve a calm ecstasy, to contemplate the present moment. In that it emphasized some major problems in the United States, the counterculture had its merits, but it was, at best, a child's romantic dreamworld, inevitably doomed, because it did not consider answers to the ultimate question: "After the drugs, what is next?"

From Kesey's counterculture experiences, however, he learned at least two important lessons. First, he learned that drugs were not the answer to changing society and that one cannot passively drop out of life. Second, Kesey detested the mass society image that seemed to dominate life in twentieth century America. Although Kesey was pro-America and admired American democracy per se, he abhorred those things in society that seemed to deprive people of their individuality and freedom. For Kesey, mass society represents big business, government, labor, communication, and religion and thus subordinates the individual, who is stripped of dignity, significance, and freedom. One of the counterculture's protest slogans underscored this plight: "I am a human being. Do not fold, spindle, or mutilate." The system, preachments, and methodologies of the twentieth century had indeed betrayed humankind and left it with only two choices: It could either passively conform and thus lose individuality or find some way to exist in the modern wasteland without losing dignity and freedom.

Kesey believes that people must not and cannot isolate themselves from life; each individual must meet life on its own terms and discover his or her own saving grace. Having their archetypes in the comic book and Western heroes, Kesey's McMurphy in *One Flew over the Cuckoo's Nest* and Hank Stamper in *Sometimes a Great Notion* are vibrant personalities who defy the overwhelming forces of life by constantly asserting their dignity, significance, and freedom as human beings. Each one learns also that no victories are ever won by passively isolating oneself from life or by being self-centered. They therefore immerse themselves in life, ask no quarter, and remain self-reliant. McMurphy and Stamper may not be able to save the entire world, but, Kesey believes, they can save themselves and perhaps even part of the world. Their victories may be slight, but they are, nevertheless, victories.

In *One Flew over the Cuckoo's Nest*, the oppressive power of the mass society is evident in its setting—a mental ward dominated by the tyrannical Miss Ratched, the big nurse, whom Chief Bromden, the schizophrenic narrator, describes in mechanical metaphors. Her purse is shaped like a toolbox; her lipstick and fingernail polish are "funny orange" like a glowing soldering iron; her skin and face are like an expensively manufactured baby doll's; her ward is run like a computer. If a patient dares disrupt her smoothly running ward, Nurse Ratched has the ultimate threats—electroshock treatments—and if these fail, she has prefrontal lobotomy operations that turn men into vegetables. Bromden says that the ward is only a "factory for the Combine," a nebulous and ubiquitous force that ruthlessly destroyed Bromden's father and that is responsible for the stereotyped housing developments along the coast.

Kesey's metaphors are clear. The Combine, the macrocosm, and the hospital ward, the microcosm, are the twentieth century world gone berserk with power; it uses the miracles of modern science, not to free humanity and make its life better but to compel it to conform. It is the mass society that will not tolerate individuality and that will fold, spindle, or mutilate any person who fails to conform.

Into the ward boils McMurphy, the former Marine, logger, gambler, and free spirit who is intimidated by neither the nurse nor her ward attendants, and who immediately becomes a threat to Nurse Ratched and her ward policies. McMurphy has had himself committed for purely selfish reasons—he disliked the manual labor on the prison work farm, and he wants the easy gambling winnings from the patients, two facts that he candidly admits. Outraged at Ratched's power, McMurphy bets the other patients that he can get the best of her. Certain that he can win his wager, he sings and laughs on the ward, conducts poker games in the tub room, and disrupts the group therapy sessions. He finally succeeds in destroying her composure when he leads the men in watching the blank television screen after Nurse Ratched has cut the power source during the first game of the World Series.

Yet the Kesey hero must learn a further lesson. McMurphy has won his wager, but he has not yet won significant victory, because his actions are selfish ones. Several important incidents transform McMurphy into a champion of the patients. McMurphy is committed, which means that Ratched can keep him on the ward as long as she wishes. Instead of jeopardizing his relatively short sentence, McMurphy conforms and does not disrupt the therapy sessions or life on the ward. When Charles Cheswick argues with the nurse about the cigarette rationing, he gets no support from McMurphy, despairs, and drowns himself in the hospital swimming pool. Cheswick's death plagues McMurphy, even though he is not actually responsible. McMurphy cannot understand why the other patients, who are there voluntarily, do not leave the hospital. Billy Bibbit finally tells McMurphy that they are not big and strong like McMurphy, that they have no "g-guts," and that it is "n-no use." McMurphy begins to realize that he must do something to convert the patients into responsible men again. At the next group therapy session, when Ratched is supposed to win her final victory over him, McMurphy rams his hand through the glass partition in the nurses' station and thereby renews the struggle.

A key scene occurs earlier that not only summarizes Kesey's view of man in the modern world but also provides a clue to McMurphy's actions. Scanlon, who is also committed, says that it is a "hell of a life," and that people are damned if they do and damned if they do not. Scanlon adds that this fact puts man in a "confounded bind." At this point, McMurphy is damned either way. If he does nothing, then Ratched has the final victory and McMurphy will become another victim of the Combine, a non-entity like the other patients. If he renews the struggle, he must remain on the ward until the nurse discharges him or kills him. McMurphy chooses, however, the higher damnation, to give of himself selflessly, and in so doing, he also reaffirms his own dignity and significance.

Dedicated to the patients' cause, McMurphy continues to disrupt the ward and ward policy by using what can only be termed McMurphy's therapy. He continues the poker games and organizes basketball games and even a deep-sea fishing trip, during which the men finally learn to laugh at themselves, Nurse Ratched, and the world in general. He fights with an attendant who was bullying one of the patients, and as a result he is given a series of electroshock treatments. Finally, McMurphy physically attacks the nurse when she ironically accuses him of "playing" and "gambling" with the men's lives. When a prefrontal lobotomy turns McMur-

phy into a vegetable, Bromden sacrificially and mercifully smothers him with a pillow and then escapes from the hospital.

In Kesey's world, an individual may indeed be damned either way when he or she encounters the overwhelming forces of mass society, but through accepting responsibility and acting one can still win an important victory. McMurphy's death is not futile, because he has saved his soul by losing it to a higher cause. He did not save or even change the entire world, but he did save and change part of it: The other patients are no longer cowed and intimidated by Nurse Ratched, and several of them voluntarily check out of the hospital. Bromden, as McMurphy had promised, has been "blown back up" to his full size. There is, then, a slight but significant victory.

One Flew over the Cuckoo's Nest, the novel on which Kesey's fame primarily rests, contrasts the maverick frontier spirit of freedom and individuality with the repressive authoritarianism of mass society that devalues and dehumanizes the individual. The work serves to underscore the importance of preserving human dignity, freedom, and significance against the destructive forces of life.

Other major works

NONFICTION: *The Further Inquiry*, 1990.

MISCELLANEOUS: *The Last Supplement to the Whole Earth Catalog*, 1971 (ed. with Paul Krassner); *Kesey's Garage Sale*, 1973; *Demon Box*, 1986.

CHILDREN'S LITERATURE: *Little Tricker the Squirrel Meets Big Double the Bear*, 1990; *The Sea Lion: A Story of the Sea Cliff People*, 1991.

Bibliography

Kesey, Ken. Interview by Robert Faggin. *Paris Review* 35, (Spring, 1994).

Perry, Paul. *On the Bus: The Complete Guide to the Legendary Trip of Ken Kesey and the Merry Pranksters and the Birth of the Counterculture*. New York: Thunder Mouth's Press, 1990.

Porter, M. Gilbert. *The Art of Grit: Ken Kesey's Fiction*. Columbia: University of Missouri Press, 1982.

_____ . *"One Flew over the Cuckoo's Nest": Rising to Heroism*. Boston: Twayne, 1989.

Safer, Elaine B. *The Contemporary American Comic Epic: The Novels of Barth, Pynchon, Gaddis, and Kesey*. Detroit: Wayne State University Press, 1988.

Searles, George J., ed. *A Casebook on Ken Kesey's "One Flew over the Cuckoo's Nest."* Albuquerque: University of New Mexico Press, 1992.

Sherwood, Terry G. *"One Flew over the Cuckoo's Nest* and the Comic Strip." *Critique: Studies in Modern Fiction* 13, no. 1 (1971): 97-109.

Tanner, Stephen L. *Ken Kesey*. Boston: Twayne, 1983.

Vogler, Thomas A. "Ken Kesey." In *Contemporary Novelists*, edited by James Vinson. London: St. James Press, 1976.

Wolfe, Tom. *The Electric Kool-Aid Acid Test*. New York: Farrar, Straus & Giroux, 1968.

LOUIS L'AMOUR

Born: Jamestown, North Dakota; March 22, 1908   **Died:** Los Angeles, California; June 10, 1988

Principal long fiction

Westward the Tide, 1950; *Hondo*, 1953; *Sitka*, 1957; *Last Stand at Papago Wells*, 1957; *The First Fast Draw*, 1959; *The Daybreakers*, 1960; *Sackett*, 1961; *Shalako*, 1962; *Lando*, 1962; *Mojave Crossing*, 1964; *The Sackett Brand*, 1965; *The Broken Gun*, 1966; *Mustang Man*, 1966; *The Sky-Liners*, 1967; *Down the Long Hills*, 1968; *The Lonely Men*, 1969; *The Man Called Noon*, 1970; *Galloway*, 1970; *North to the Rails*, 1971; *Ride the Dark Trail*, 1972; *Treasure Mountain*, 1972; *The Ferguson Rifle*, 1973; *The Man from Skibbereen*, 1973; *Sackett's Land*, 1974; *Rivers West*, 1975; *The Man from the Broken Hills*, 1975; *Over on the Dry Side*, 1975; *To the Far Blue Mountains*, 1976; *Borden Chantry*, 1977; *Fair Blows the Wind*, 1978; *Bendigo Shafter*, 1979; *The Iron Marshal*, 1979; *The Warrior's Path*, 1980; *Lonely on the Mountain*, 1980; *Comstock Lode*, 1981; *Milo Talon*, 1981; *The Cherokee Trail*, 1982; *The Lonesome Gods*, 1983; *Ride the River*, 1983; *Son of a Wanted Man*, 1984; *The Walking Drum*, 1984; *Jubal Sackett*, 1985; *Last of the Breed*, 1986; *The Haunted Mesa*, 1987.

Other literary forms

Although Louis L'Amour has achieved his greatest success as a Western novelist, he began his career as a writer of short pulp fiction, later assembled in a number of collections. He also wrote some hard-boiled detective stories, and early in his career he issued a book of undistinguished poetry. In 1988, the year of his death, a collection of L'Amour quotations entitled *A Trail of Memories* was issued. The following year saw the publication of *Education of a Wandering Man*, an autobiographical work.

Achievements

L'Amour was one of the most prolific Western writers America has ever produced. Each of his eighty-five novels, mostly traditional Westerns, has sold at least a million copies; ten of his novels have doubled that figure. His books have been translated into more than a dozen foreign languages. More than thirty of his plots have been made into motion-picture and television dramas. In 1981, with *Comstock Lode*, L'Amour became a formidable presence in the hardbound-book market; he immediately made the best-seller list; all of his subsequent hardbound novels matched this performance. By 1977, L'Amour had sold fifty million copies of his books. In 1987, the figure was 175 million.

L'Amour also received important awards and honors. He won the Western Writers of America (WWA) Golden Spur Award in 1969 for *Down the Long Hills* and the WWA Golden Saddleman Award in 1981 for overall achievement and contributions to an understanding of the American West. When, in 1985, the WWA published a list of the twenty-six best Western novels of all time, L'Amour's *Hondo* made the list. In 1982, the United States Congress awarded him a National Gold Medal, and one year later, President Ronald Reagan awarded him the Medal of Freedom.

Biography

Louis L'Amour was born Louis Dearborn LaMoore in Jamestown, North Dakota, on March 22, 1908, into a rugged, French-Irish pioneering family. His father, Louis Charles LaMoore, reared by his paternal grandparents in Ontario, was a veterinarian, a Jamestown police chief, and a civic leader. The novelist's mother, Emily, whose father was a Civil War veteran and an Indian-fighter, attended the normal school at St. Cloud, Minnesota, and married L. C. LaMoore in 1892. Louis was the youngest of the couple's seven children, four of whom survived to distinguished maturity.

After a healthy early boyhood of outdoor activity and voracious reading, L'Amour moved in 1923 with his family to Oklahoma but soon struck out on his own. An incredible sequence of knockabout jobs followed: sailor, longshoreman, lumberjack, boxer, circus worker, cattle skinner, fruit picker, hay shocker, miner, friend of bandits in China, book reviewer in Oklahoma, lecturer there and in Texas, neophyte writer, and a United States Army tank-destroyer and transportation officer in World War II in France and Germany.

In 1946, L'Amour decided to live in Los Angeles and became a professional writer. Some of his short-story pulps and slicks into the mid-1950's were under the pen names Tex Burns and Jim Mayo. A turning point for L'Amour came with the publication of "The Gift of

Cochise" in *Collier's*, the story that formed the basis for *Hondo* a year later. This was not, however, L'Amour's first Western novel, which was the competent *Westward the Tide*, published in London in 1950.

With the publication of *Night over the Solomons* (a collection of old pre-war stories) in 1986, L'Amour saw his one hundredth book into print. Of the many films made from his fiction, the most notable are *Hondo* (1953), *The Burning Hills* (1956), *Apache Territory* (1958), *Heller in Pink Tights* (1960), *Shalako* (1968), and *Catlow* (1971). The best television adaptation from L'Amour fiction was *The Sacketts* (based on *The Daybreakers* and *Sackett*), which first aired in 1979. Beginning in 1960, L'Amour started the first of three family sagas, novels in multiple numbers featuring generations of families. *The Daybreakers* opened the ongoing Sackett saga, which by 1986 had grown to eighteen volumes. The 1971 publication of *North to the Rails* began another ongoing series, the Chantry family series. In 1975, *Rivers West* began the Talon family sequence.

Abetting L'Amour was the former Kathy Adams, who relinquished her career as an actress to marry him in 1956. In the 1960's, they had a daughter, Angelique, and then a son, Beau, and Kathy served as Louis' business manager, informal editor, and chauffeur. L'Amour wrote early in the morning, six hours a day, seven days a week. Throughout his long career, he lectured and traveled widely and personally scouted locales to make his work more authentic. L'Amour died in Los Angeles in 1988.

Analysis

L'Amour will be remembered for his action-filled Western novels, especially his family sagas. He is appreciated by readers from all walks of life who want to follow the exploits and suffering of heroic men, attractive and dutiful women, and manifestly evil villains, in exciting, well-knit plots, against a backdrop of accurately painted scenery. L'Amour extols the old American virtues of patriotism, respect for the land, go-it-alone courage, stoicism, and family loyalty. He offers his updated vision of the Old West as the locus of increasingly endangered humankind's last, best hope.

L'Amour was pleased to be put in the same company as James Fenimore Cooper, Honoré de Balzac, Émile Zola, Jules Romains, and William Faulkner. L'Amour's Tell Sackett bears comparison with Cooper's Natty Bumppo. L'Amour follows Balzac's habit of creating reappearing characters, who help produce both unified, multivolume fiction and loyal readers. The hero of

L'Amour's *Shalako*, between wars in Paris, meets Zola, whose Rougon-Macquart cycle may have inspired L'Amour to build his Sackett/Chantry/Talon series. Romains employed historical figures, real events, and even specific dates to augment the verisimilitude of his monumental *Les Hommes de bonne volonté* (1932-1946; *Men of Good Will*, 1933-1946); L'Amour, to be sure, deals with three centuries of American frontier Sacketts rather than France in a mere quarter-century, but in doing so he uses details reminiscent of Romains. Moreover, Faulkner's love of his native soil, his combination of different races together in weal and woe, his praise of the old virtues of enduring and prevailing, and his construction of interlocked families are echoed in L'Amour's novels.

In "Ride, You Tonto Raiders!" (*New Western Magazine*, August 6, 1949; reprinted in *Law of the Desert Born*, 1983), L'Amour prophetically introduced many of his books' most typical features. The broad-shouldered hero is a hard-bitten adventurer with a military, cosmopolitan, cattleman background, and he is now a gunslinger. He kills a bad man in Texas, then delivers the victim's money to his sweet widow and small son. She owns some Arizona land and is aided but also jeopardized by an assortment of L'Amouresque types: rich man, gunslinger, bumbling lawman, codger, literary drunk, Europe-trained pianist, and loyal ranch hand. Other ingredients include surrogate fatherhood, dawning love for a red-haired heroine, the taking of the law into one's own hands, hidden documents, place-names aplenty, the dating of the action by reference to historical events, cinematic alternation of close-up and wide-angle lens scenes, the use of key words (especially "alone," "eye," "home," "land," "patience," "shoulder," "silence," and "trouble"), and compositional infelicities.

The Daybreakers is the first volume of L'Amour's million-word Sackett sequence. It introduces the most famous Sacketts. They are five Tennessee-born brothers: William Tell, Orrin, Tyrel, Bob, and Joe Sackett. An 1866 feud with the evil Higgins family, during which a Higgins kills Orrin's fiancée and is hastily gunned down by narrator Tyrel, obliges both brothers to head out. They go West to gather wild cattle, in spite of dramatic adversities, along the Santa Fe Trail. Once in New Mexico, Orrin marries disastrously: His vicious wife is the daughter of a dishonest and anti-Latino politician and land grabber from New England. Tyrel, by contrast, while on the trail is taught to read by an ex-army officer who later turns alcoholic, jealous, and lethal; Tyrel becomes the gun-handy marshal of Mora and marries a lovely heiress of an old Spanish land grant there. Orrin and Tyrel send for their widowed Ma and younger brothers Bob and Joe. The plot is energized by much violence, though not involving the offstage Tell Sackett; having fought in the Civil War, he is now campaigning against the Sioux in the Northwest and is soon to leave Montana for Mora. L'Amour continued his narrative of these Sackett brothers in six more novels, which, not in order of publication (1961 to 1980) but in chronological order of events (1867 through 1878 or so), are *Lonely on the Mountain*, *Sackett*, *Mojave Crossing*, *The Sackett Brand*, *The Lonely Men*, and *Treasure Mountain*.

During this time, L'Amour was turning his Sackett clock back more than two centuries. In 1974, he published *Sackett's Land*, which introduces Barnabas Sackett of the Welsh fenlands, in 1599. The first of the Sackett dynasty, he and his wife Abigail, daughter of an Elizabethan sea captain, generate a wild brood in the Carolinas: sons Kin Ring, Brian, Yance, and Jubal Sackett and daughter Noelle Sackett. In the later novels, the three brothers, Kin, Yance, and Jubal (in *To the Far Blue Mountains*, *The Warrior's Path*, and *Jubal Sackett*, respectively), are shown to be different, and their stories shift from the Eastern seaboard, New England, and the Caribbean to the Far West and advance to the year 1630

or so. In 1983 came *Ride the River*, which tells how feisty Tennessee girl Echo Sackett (destined to become the aunt of Tell and his brothers) ventures to Philadelphia to claim an inheritance as Kin Sackett's youngest descendant and gets it home again.

L'Amour wrote six other Sackett novels (*Lando*, *Mustang Man*, *The Sky-Liners*, *Galloway*, *Ride the Dark Trail*, and *The Man from the Broken Hills*), which star a dusty array of cousins to Tell and his brothers and bring in still more Sacketts. These cousins, from different parts of Tennessee, Arizona, and New Mexico, include Lando, twins Logan and Nolan, brothers Flagan and Galloway, and Parmalee. The action, ranging through the Southwest and into Mexico, may be dated 1867-1878. There are about sixty Sacketts in the ambitious Sackett sequence, amid a gallery of more than 750 characters in all.

L'Amour's two most admirable traits were his troubadour wizardry as a narrator and his profound love of Mother Nature and American derring-do. His late-career ambition to broaden his fictive scope, while admirable, can never diminish the significance of what will probably remain his most lasting contribution—namely, his best Westerns, among which the Sackett saga retains a high place. It is certainly to those works that one can attribute his immense popularity.

Other major works

SHORT FICTION: *War Party*, 1975; *Bowdrie, 1983; The Hills of Homicide*, 1983; *Law of the Desert Born*, 1983; *Riding for the Brand*, 1986; *The Rider of the Ruby Hills*, 1986; *Night over the Solomons*, 1986; *The Outlaws of Mesquite*, 1990.

POETRY: *Smoke from This Altar*, 1939.

NONFICTION: *Frontier*, 1984 (with photographs by David Muench); *A Trail of Memories*, 1988; *Education of a Wandering Man*, 1989.

Bibliography

Gale, Robert L. *Louis L'Amour*. Rev. ed. Boston: Twayne, 1990.

Hall, Halbert W. *The Work of Louis L'Amour: An Annotated Bibliography and Guide*. San Bernardino, Calif.: Borgo Press, 1991.

Marsden, Michael T. "The Concept of the Family in the Fiction of Louis L'Amour." *North Dakota Quarterly* 46 (Summer, 1978): 12-21.

——————. "Louis L'Amour (1908-)." In *Fifty Western Writers: A Bio-Bibliographical Sourcebook*, edited by Fred Erisman and Richard Etulain. Westport, Conn.: Greenwood Press, 1982.

Marsden, Michael T. "The Modern Western." In *The American Literary West*, edited by Richard W. Etulain. Manhattan, Kans.: Sunflower University Press, 1980.

Nesbitt, John D. "Change of Purpose in the Novels of Louis L'Amour." *Western American Literature* 13 (Spring, 1978): 65-81. Reprinted in *Critical Essays on the Western American Novel*, edited by William T. Pilkington. Boston: G. K. Hall, 1980.

Nesbitt, John D. "Louis L'Amour: Papier-Mâché Homer?" *South Dakota Review* 19 (Autumn, 1981): 37-48.

Weinberg, Robert E. *The Louis L'Amour Companion*. Kansas City: Andrews and McMeel, 1992.

JACK LONDON

Born: San Francisco, California; January 12, 1876   **Died:** Glen Ellen, California; November 22, 1916

Principal long fiction

A Daughter of the Snows, 1902; *The Call of the Wild*, 1903; *The Sea-Wolf*, 1904; *The Game*, 1905; *White Fang*, 1906; *Before Adam*, 1906; *The Iron Heel*, 1907; *Martin Eden*, 1909; *Burning Daylight*, 1910; *Adventure*, 1911; *The Abysmal Brute*, 1913; *The Valley of the Moon*, 1913; *The Mutiny of the Elsinore*, 1914; *The Scarlet Plague*, 1915; *The Star Rover*, 1915; *The Little Lady of the Big House*, 1916; *Jerry of the Islands*, 1917; *Michael, Brother of Jerry*, 1917; *Hearts of Three*; *The Assassination Bureau, Ltd.*, 1963 (completed by Robert L. Fish).

Other literary forms

Jack London's prolific catalog of published works includes plays, children's fiction, sociological studies, essays, short stories, and novels. Although generally known as a writer of short fiction, London is also remembered for his pioneering work in tramp fiction (*The Road*, 1907, an autobiographical novel), screenwriting (*Hearts of Three*), and the science-fiction novel (*The Star Rover*). London was also a journalist, serving as a newspaper correspondent for the San Francisco *Examiner* during the Russo-Japanese War in 1904 and, later, during the Mexican conflict in Vera Cruz in 1915. His accounts of these wars were published in 1970 under the title *Jack London Reports*.

Achievements

Called at one time the "Kipling of the Klondike," London was in the forefront of the move toward naturalistic fiction and realism. His social fiction, which included the first sympathetic and realistic treatment of the convict and the tramp, gave him credence as a spokesman for the working class. As a folk hero, London has achieved a popularity that has made him, along with Mark Twain, a permanent figure in American mythology. London is also extremely popular abroad—especially in Europe and Russia. His work has been translated into more than fifty languages, and his stories appear in countless anthologies of short fiction. Complete editions of London's work have been published in French, German, and Russian. London's novels, especially *The Sea-Wolf* and *The Call of the Wild*, are taught each year in high school and college English courses; a number of his books remain in print year after year.

Biography

A sometime tramp, oyster pirate, seaman, socialist, laundryman, and miner, Jack (John Griffith) London is as famous for the life he lived and the myths he wove around it as he is for the short stories and novels he wrote. Largely self-educated, London was the product of California ranches and the working-class neighborhoods of Oakland. His rise to literary fame came as a result of the Klondike gold rush. Unsuccessful in his attempt to break into the magazine market, London joined the flood of men rushing toward instant riches in the Yukon. He found little gold but returned after the winter of 1897 with a wealth of memories and notes of the Northland, the gold rush, and the hardships of the trail. By 1900, London had firmly established himself as a major American writer.

Also in 1897, London married Elizabeth May Maddern. The couple settled in Oakland, soon adding two daughters to their family. In 1904, seeking new material for his stories and escape from his marriage, which by this time had gone sour, London signed with William Randolph Hearst to cover the impending Russo-Japanese War for Hearst's newspaper the San Francisco *Examiner*. His photographs and accounts of that war were among the first to be published, and he returned to California in triumph, only to face a divorce action.

London's next years were marked by further adventures and travels. In 1905, he journeyed across the United States, lecturing on the need for a socialist revolution. He married Clara Charmian Kittredge that same year, and together they planned a seven-year voyage around the world on a yacht they named *Snark* after Lewis Carroll's mock epic. Ill health forced abandonment of the adventure after only two years, however, and London returned once more to California, this time to create a large ranch complex in Sonoma County.

To support his travels and building program, as well as an extravagant lifestyle, London wrote at a furious pace, publishing fifty books by his fortieth year. His body could not withstand the brutal treatment it received, however, and shortly before his forty-first birthday, London died. His death, officially labeled uremic poisoning and renal colic, was widely rumored to have been suicide. The mysterious circumstances surrounding it have never been explained satisfactorily.

Analysis

London's success as a writer came about largely through his ability to interpret realistically humanity's struggle in a hostile environment. Early in his career, London realized that he had no talent for invention, that in his writing he would have to be an interpreter of things that are, rather than a creator of things that might be. Accordingly, he drew his plots, characters, themes, and settings from real-life experiences and published accounts.

London's novels characteristically contain at least one of three different settings: the Canadian Northland, where he began his literary apprenticeship; the primitive South Seas and Hawaii, where his career began anew following a short decline; and California—particularly the Sonoma Valley—to which London retreated during the last years of his life.

Each novel also generally contains a philosophical focus. Popular at the time were Charles Darwin's theory of evolution, as interpreted by Herbert Spencer; Friedrich Nietzsche's version of the superman; and, much later, the new psychology of Sigmund Freud and Carl Jung, as well as Karl Marx's theories of a new social order. All fired London's imagination and provided fuel for his characters and plots, and their presence, particularly London's version of the Darwinian "survival of the fittest" motif, lends credence to London's claim for membership in the naturalistic school of fiction.

London was at the height of his powers when he wrote *The Call of the Wild*. He was dealing with the kind of subject matter, theme, and setting with which he was most comfortable. The book was written shortly after his return from the slums of London. Wanting to escape the degradation and poverty he had witnessed there, London returned to the clean, frozen, beautiful world of the North, where the struggle for survival was elemental, uncomplicated, and fierce. The story is that of a dog, Buck, who is kidnapped from his home on a California ranch and taken to the Yukon, where he is forced to pull heavily laden sleds for inhuman masters. In order to survive, Buck must adapt, falling back on primitive instincts. With domesticity stripped from him, Buck learns the ways of his ancestors; he learns the law of the club: He will be beaten, but he will survive. Gradually, as he completes his initiation into the primitive, Buck

learns to respond. He learns the law of the fang: that he must be quick to use his own fangs, before others use theirs on him. By adapting to his new environment, Buck survives, learns the instincts of his forebears, and finally, hears the true call of the wild.

In *The Call of the Wild*, London incorporated to good advantage the popular notion of the fierce Darwinian struggle for survival of the fittest. Curiously, he modified the Darwinian theme slightly. Buck must struggle to survive, but his survival is not predicated upon ultimate triumph. He must learn how to use his instincts, he must learn to be a good sled dog, but he need not become the team leader in order to survive. Struggle for its own sake also appears in London novels such as *The Iron Heel*, *Martin Eden*, and *The Valley of the Moon*.

The Sea-Wolf drew on London's youthful adventures in the sealing grounds off Japan. The novel concerns the survival of upper-class Humphrey Van Weyden, a man who finds himself, through means beyond his control, aboard *The Ghost*, a sealing schooner on its way to Japan. Van Weyden soon finds that the captain of the schooner, Wolf Larsen, has created a hell-ship, filled with brutality and sordidness, where even the ship's practical purpose—to hunt seals—is lost in the misery of mere survival. Van Weyden survives this environment because, like Buck, he is able to adapt to it, learning new codes of survival, drawing upon unknown instincts, and using to best advantage all the benefits of his upbringing and status: intelligence, optimism, and a capacity to love. Van Weyden's growth is the focus of the novel.

If Van Weyden survives because he, too, has learned the law of the club and the fang, the ship's captain, Wolf Larsen, dies precisely because he cannot adapt. At least, that was London's intention, but it was lost upon many early critics. "I attacked Nietzsche and his super-man idea," London wrote. "Lots of people read *The Sea-Wolf*, [but] no one discovered that it was an attack upon the super-man philosophy."

The Sea-Wolf is a fine example of literary naturalism. Larsen, a sensitive, intelligent, domineering man, treats his crew with arrogance. He has no inhibitions and also no friends. Alone, his life lacks purpose and direction, and his aloneness and alienation from nature, from other people, and, in fact, from himself, lead to his inevitable destruction. Without Van Weyden's ability to adapt, Larsen dies.

The last third of the book is concerned not only with the powerful element of Larsen's degeneration (which Ambrose Bierce called "unforgettable") but also with the introduction of Maud Brewster. London generally had trouble with female characters in his fiction—his editors demanded strict Victorian morals, and London was happy to oblige—and following Maud's introduction, the book is reduced to a sentimental shambles. While the love story, in great part, ensured the critical failure of the book, it also ensured the book's popular success. As soon as Maud steps aboard, Van Weyden reverts to his earlier stature, as if wholly unaffected by the events that have transpired: His growth and adaptation are cast aside. The contradictions of *The Sea-Wolf* mirror the contradictions of London's own times. The novel is successful in depicting the early twentieth century society in which London lived, which was shaking off the morals and ways of the last century yet was still holding on to vestiges and customs of the earlier time.

While *The Sea-Wolf* may have failed to convey its point to the critics, it did not fail to capture the fancy of the reading public. Next to *The Call of the Wild*, it was (and is) London's most popular book, and it gave the author the financial security he so desperately needed.

If *The Call of the Wild* is a novel about a dog who reacquaints himself with his ancestral instincts and learns survival by adaptation, *White Fang* is both its sequel and reverse. *White Fang* is the story of a wolfdog brought from the Alaskan wilderness to Californian civilization. Just as Buck used his civilized intelligence to survive, so White Fang uses his primitive strength and endurance to survive in a new environment—the world of civilized man. Environment is London's primary focus in this novel, as he traces the changes in the animal's behavior as it moves first from the wolf pack to an Indian village, then to the white settler, and, finally, to the Santa Clara Valley in California. White Fang is tamed by love and successfully makes the transition from savage wolf to loving house pet. While the book does not have the power of *The Call of the Wild*, it does show White Fang's struggle with nature as represented by Indians, dogs, white men, and finally, after critical injuries suffered while defending his new benevolent master, death itself.

While sailing around the world on his yacht *Snark*, London attempted a novel to bolster his career, which, in 1907, was sagging badly. The result, *Martin Eden*, was a profoundly moving work of imaginative realism but also, as literary critic Franklin Walker would later note, a most puzzling novel. Called alternately London's finest and his worst novel, *Martin Eden* was meant as another attack on individualism and the Nietzschean superhero. As in *The Sea-Wolf*, London

was only partially able to convey this intention. The rags-to-riches motif runs so strongly through the book that the reader is compelled to identify and sympathize with Martin, a lowly seaman, who without education or culture is thrown into the world of the educated and cultured. His introduction to their world fires his mind, and he yearns for their sophisticated ways, their knowledge, and the woman who brings it to him. Like London himself, Martin decides that the path to social betterment lies through his writing talent, and the novel masterfully describes Martin's (and London's) literary apprenticeship, early failure, and final success.

Martin Eden is a *Bildungsroman*—a novel of education. It employs the potent cultural myth of rags-to-riches and masterfully depicts Martin's painful transition from the innocence of unknowing to the power of knowledge. As Martin grows and learns, he finds himself embroiled in a battle pitting individual against individual, oppressed against oppressor. London offers Martin the key to salvation, socialism, through the poet Brissenden, but Martin rejects it and, in so doing, seals his fate. By the time Martin's road to success ends, it is too late. Without a reason for living, Martin rejects all that he has sought and, finally, takes his own life.

Martin Eden was written aboard ship and is about a sailor. It is therefore not surprising that the paramount symbol in the novel is water. Beginning life as a sailor, coming from the ocean, Martin must return to his beginnings, and he does so by booking passage on an ocean liner and then committing suicide by drowning in he sea.

London returns to the theme of *The Call of the Wild* in *Martin Eden*, with one peculiar twist. Like Buck, Martin begins life unconscious of himself. He does not know that his grammar is imperfect, that his dress is slovenly, or that his manners are uncouth until Ruth Morse educates him. As he learns about himself, he becomes self-conscious. No longer do the instincts that Buck uses to adapt and survive work for Martin. Unable to adapt to his new environment, Martin returns to the only thing he knows best—the sea—and, fulfilling the paradox of knowing and unknowing, dies.

In a May, 1911, letter to editor Roland Phillips, London outlined his plan for *The Valley of the Moon*: The theme of the book would be back-to-the-land, a likely motif, for it paralleled London's own life story. The agrarian vision, London wrote, would be accomplished by a man and a woman, both wage earners, who meet and grow to love each other in the confines of a big city. Hard times befall them, and the woman, in an attempt to regain the good times they had had together, leads them both on a pilgrimage through California that ends, finally, in Jack London's own valley, the Valley of the Moon.

As London matured, he saw a return to the soil as the solution to the great economic problems of the age. He used this agrarian vision to advantage in his writings and also on the acres of his own expanding ranch. The theme runs through much of his work, including not only *The Valley of the Moon* but also *Burning Daylight* and *The Little Lady of the Big House.*

To solve the problems of the city, Saxon and Billy, the two characters in *The Valley of the Moon*, flee, as they must. London saw the strikes, the fierce struggles for economic and human survival, as symptomatic of the greater problem of humankind out of touch with itself. To return to the soil, to gain salvation, humanity must restore rural America. Billy and Saxon set out to do this, but first they must be reborn. London did not advocate an escape to the wilderness, but a return to the goodness of nature. To return to Eden, Billy and Saxon must first gain salvation so that they do not spoil Eden, as their ancestors once did.

Eden, of course, is London's own ranch, and once Billy and Saxon arrive they begin applying the principles of agrarian success London fancied himself to be applying. They bring with them the good intentions, motivation, good character, and knowledge necessary to treat the land gently. They do not make the same mistakes the old-style American farmer made. They do not use the land up or wear it out; they apply new methods they have learned from foreigners, Portuguese farmers, to restore the land to its former richness. London realized there was no longer a vast American West. The land beyond the horizon had long been conquered and ruined. It was up to enlightened men and women to restore the land for the reruralization of America that was to come.

London's best novels remain alive and vibrant even to this day. In them London offered a compelling vision of the human condition. The Darwinian struggle for survival was at the forefront of American thought at the start of the twentieth century; London's fiction mirrored his society, including its contradictions, and led his readers to the primitive arenas where the struggle for survival is best laid bare. London's contribution to the naturalistic tradition and his raw power as a storyteller ensure his place in the American literary heritage.

Other major works

SHORT FICTION: *The Son of the Wolf*, 1900; *The God of His Fathers and Other Stories*, 1901; *Children of the Frost*, 1902; *The Faith of Men and Other Stories*, 1904; *Moon-Face and Other Stories*, 1906; *Love of Life and Other Stories*, 1906; *Lost Face*, 1910; *When God Laughs and Other Stories*, 1911; *South Sea Tales*, 1911; *The House of Pride and Other Tales of Hawaii*, 1912; *Smoke Bellew Tales*, 1912; *A Son of the Sun*, 1912; *The Night-Born*, 1913; *The Strength of the Strong*, 1914; *The Turtles of Tasman*, 1916; *The Human Drift*, 1917; *The Red One*, 1918; *On the Makaloa Mat*, 1919; *Dutch Courage and Other Stories*, 1922; *The Complete Short Stories of Jack London*, 1993; *The Science Fiction Stories of Jack London*, 1993.

PLAYS: *Scorn of Women*, 1906; *Theft*, 1910; *The Acorn-Planter*, 1916.

SCREENPLAY: *Hearts of Three*, 1920.

NONFICTION: *The Kempton-Wace Letters*, 1903 (with Anna Strunsky); *The People of the Abyss*, 1903; *The War of the Classes*, 1905; *The Road*, 1907; *Revolution and Other Essays*, 1910; *The Cruise of the Snark*, 1911; *John Barleycorn*, 1913; *Letters from Jack London*, 1965 (King Hendricks and Irving Shepard, eds.); *Jack London Reports*, 1970.

CHILDREN'S LITERATURE: *The Cruise of the Dazzler*, 1902; *Tales of the Fish Patrol*, 1905.

MISCELLANEOUS: *The Portable Jack London*, 1994.

Bibliography

Hamilton, David Mike. *The Tools of My Trade: The Annotated Books in Jack London's Library*. Seattle: University of Washington Press, 1987.

Hedrick, Joan D. *Solitary Comrade: Jack London and His Work*. Chapel Hill: University of North Carolina Press, 1982.

Labor, Earle. *Jack London*. Rev. ed. New York: Twayne, 1994.

Stasz, Clarice. *American Dreamers: The Story of Charmain and Jack London*. New York: St. Martin's Press, 1988.

Watson, Charles N. *The Novels of Jack London: A Reappraisal*. Madison: University of Wisconsin Press, 1982.

THOMAS McGUANE

Born: Wyandotte, Michigan; December 11, 1939

Principal long fiction

The Sporting Club, 1969; *The Bushwhacked Piano*, 1971; *Ninety-two in the Shade*, 1973; *Panama*, 1978; *Nobody's Angel*, 1982; *Something to Be Desired*, 1984; *Keep the Change*, 1989; *Nothing but Blue Skies*, 1992.

Other literary forms

Thomas McGuane has produced work for motion pictures and for popular magazines. He wrote the screenplay and directed the film version of *Ninety-two in the Shade* (1975), wrote the scripts for *Rancho De-Luxe* (1973) and *The Missouri Breaks* (1975), and shared credit with Bud Shrake for *Tom Horn* (1980) and with Jim Harrison for *Cold Feet* (1989). *An Outside Chance: Essays on Sport* (rev. ed. 1990) contains many of his magazine pieces, and *To Skin a Cat* (1986) is a collection of short fiction.

Achievements

Early in his career, McGuane was heralded as one of the most promising writers of his generation, one with a good chance to become a major American writer. He appeared on the cover of *The New York Times Book Review* and was compared favorably with Ernest Hemingway, William Faulkner, and Saul Bellow. *The Bushwhacked Piano* won the Rosenthal Award, and *Ninety-two in the Shade* was nominated for a National Book Award. In the mid-1970's, however, when he began to devote the majority of his energies to writing for films, McGuane was dismissed as a sellout. In the late 1970's, his film career seemingly over, McGuane returned to publishing novels. Although Hollywood continued to option screenplays written in the 1970's, McGuane maintained that novels were his true calling, his goal to become "a true man of literature, . . . a professional." *Something to Be Desired* and *Keep the Change* reaffirmed his position as a contender for inclusion in the American canon. In 1989, McGuane received the Montana Centennial Award for Literature.

Biography

Thomas McGuane was born in Wyandotte, Michigan, on December 11, 1939. He was graduated with honors from Michigan State University in 1962, took an M.F.A. degree from the Yale Drama School in 1965, and spent 1966-1967 at Stanford on a Wallace Stegner Fellowship. His parents were New England Irish who migrated to the Midwest, where his father became an auto-parts tycoon. McGuane believes that he inherited his storytelling impulse from his mother's family, who loved verbal sparring and yarn-spinning. McGuane is a highly visible writer, articles about him appearing regularly in newspapers and slick magazines. These articles usually center on the manic behavior, heavy drinking, and drug use that marked his film years, and his eventual return to sobriety, family life, and hard work. McGuane has preferred to pursue a career as a writer apart from life in the academic world, believing that his chances of writing interesting novels would be diminished were he to confine himself to life in English departments.

Besides writing, McGuane supports himself by raising and training cutting horses. He is a champion horse cutter who competes regularly in rodeos and an accomplished sailor and fisherman.

Analysis

McGuane's works depict a degenerate and chaotic twentieth century America peopled by characters who recognize this condition and are determined to find a set of values that will enable them to endure.

His fictional universe is a "man's world." His protagonists appear to do whatever they do for sport and to escape ordinary reality. They seek a world where they can, without restraint, be whomever they choose to be. This goal puts them at odds with prevailing social customs and middle-class ideas of morality and achievement. Unfortunately, most of these quests end in frustration. Finding themselves quite apart from the normal flow of society, McGuane's protagonists must try all the harder to fulfill themselves. As a result, they easily become self-absorbed and further jeopardize whatever ties to conventional life they might once have had. Usually, this tie is to a woman, who, for her own self-fulfillment, in the end must forsake the protagonist.

Nobody's Angel is McGuane's first novel to be set entirely in the West, a West that McGuane characterizes as "wrecked." In Deadrock, Montana, farmers abuse the land, cowboys are lazy, and Indians are nowhere to be found. Returning to this damaged world is thirty-six-year-old Patrick Fitzpatrick. Patrick is as unconventional as earlier McGuane protagonists. As a whiskey addict and a professional soldier, he has been a tank captain in the army for all of his adult life, most recently in Europe, and the only place he feels secure is inside his womblike tank. Suffering from "sadness for no reason," he has returned to the family ranch, which he will someday own. He feels stranded on the ranch because becoming a property owner is not a meaningful achievement for him. Patrick appears to be in the worst shape of any McGuane protagonist. He is not only without goals but also without any sense of himself, conventional or unconventional.

The effect of the wrecked West is seen in the character of Patrick's grandfather. The old man has been a cowboy all of his life, has known real gunfighters, and has run the ranch like an old-time outfit. The West has changed, however, and everything from sonic booms to valleys cluttered with yard lights has got the old man down. In the end, the old man moves into town and takes an apartment from which he can see the local film theater, which plays old Westerns, and a little bar in which hangs the head of the best elk he ever shot. The open West has been reduced to one-bedroom apartments, yesterday's movies, and mounted animals, which serve only to remind him of a glorious past.

In *Nobody's Angel*, McGuane continued to work the theme of unfulfilled love. Patrick hopes to bring purpose into his life by means of a love affair with Claire Burnett. Claire and her husband, Tio, are second-generation nouveau-riche Oklahomans summering in Montana. Not a genuine stockman like Patrick's grandfather, Tio is mainly interested in oil, cattle futures, row crops, and running horses. Since Tio's main hobby is pretending to be a good old boy, Patrick sees him as a personification of the substanceless modern West.

Patrick believes that "Claire could change it all" and wishes theirs could be a sentimental love story, the kind found in romantic books. Claire, however, will not become a part of Patrick's dream. Even though she tells Patrick that she loves him, she never stops loving Tio, and Patrick's dream of a storybook romance crumbles. Even when Tio dies, Claire will not marry Patrick. She makes love to him one last time, explaining that love is "nothing you can do anything with." Patrick is not able to cope with Claire's pragmatic attitude about love and their relationship. She gives him a picture of herself, but he does not keep it with him because it reminds him of the frustrations of his romantic hopes.

In the end, Patrick survives, but not in the West. When he was a teenager, Patrick invented an imaginary girlfriend named Marion Easterly. Even though he was eventually discovered, the fantasy has remained a part of his consciousness. He had hoped that Claire would replace Marion, but a living woman will never become the woman of a man's imagination, and when Claire dismisses him, Patrick rejoins the army and finds fulfillment in his fantasy. Word filters back that he is now a blackout drinker in Madrid and that he is living with a woman named Marion Easterly. Patrick Fitzpatrick remains "at large"—in the sense that his heavy drinking and fantasy lover keep him outside the normal boundaries of life. The McGuane protagonist seemingly must find a way to accommodate himself, at least partially, to the concerns of conventional life.

In *Something to Be Desired*, the McGuane protagonist combines both unconventional and conventional goals. Lucien Taylor grows tired of normality and destroys his perfectly fine marriage with self-absorbed erratic behavior. Once his single life becomes empty, he tries to put it back together again by reuniting with his former wife, Suzanne, and their son, James. Lucien's plight is not entirely the result of his disenchantment with conformity; he is victimized by his capricious lust.

Lucien's sense of sexual discipline was broken in college by Emily, who slept with him on their first meeting. Emily was engaged to a medical student and continued to sleep with both young men at the same time. Lucien, however, married Suzanne, who "took the position that this was a decent world for an honest player." This basic decency is what Lucien eventually comes to value, but when he hears that Emily is free of her marriage, he thinks nothing of destroying his own and returning to Montana in quest of her. Lucien is troubled by the lack of romance in his life, an element that Suzanne and James cannot provide.

Through a series of exchanges, Lucien comes to own Emily's ranch and develops its sulfur spring into a thriving health spa. In short, he becomes rich. In this way Lucien remains unconventional, at the same time—new for a McGuane protagonist—gaining that which is admired by conventional society. Even though McGuane still maneuvers his protagonist through some outlandish paces because of the latter's peripatetic penis, McGuane at the same time imbues Lucien with a sense of purpose higher than sport or making the world tense. Lucien, once his new wealth requires him to bring a semblance of order into his life, begins to want to think of himself as a working man with a family to support.

What follows next is Lucien's attempt to reestablish his family, to recover his wife and bond with his son—because such a reestablishment would be better for all of them, not only for him alone. Lucien's is one of the few nonselfish acts committed by a McGuane protagonist. Suzanne, however, is too skeptical to welcome the sadder-but-wiser protagonist back into her arms. She tells him the truth about himself: He is self-absorbed, insensitive to those who love him, and not worth the effort of reconciliation. Lucien is going to have to recognize her as an independent and worthy person. Before the novel's end, she works through her sense of him as a totally selfish person, but even though she admits to loving Lucien, she is not sure if she is ready to trust him. As she and James drive away from the ranch, she does not look back. She is charting her own course, which may or may not include Lucien.

What is important here is that the McGuane protagonist has progressed through the state of self-absorption with adventure and sport. He has begun to understand that what matters about life is not being "at large" to commit glorious exploits but being a part of a larger whole that includes the other people in the world. The full life is lived not in furious battle with the forces of conventionality but in achieving deep and lasting relationships with human beings.

In *Keep the Change*, Joe Starling, Jr., an artist of limited talent, must come to understand this same truth. Chained by the ghost of his father, an overachiever who ultimately dies a failure, the young Starling's life is empty for no reason. He is not satisfied with his various successes as an artist, craftperson, cowboy, or lover, because everything pales in comparison with his expectations for himself. He ricochets between Montana, Florida, and New York City without fully realizing that individual human meaning is something created rather than found.

Two of McGuane's most fully realized female char-

acters offer Starling the possibility of a fully actualized life, but he is too full of himself to seize the opportunity. Ellen Overstreet, a rancher's daughter as wholesome as the new frontier, presents him with the vulnerability of awkward young love. The dynamic Cuban Astrid, whom Starling loves for her outlandishness, sticks by him until he is hopelessly lost in pointlessness. After she leaves him, Starling seems to be beginning to understand that sharing the routine concerns of daily life with Astrid may be the source of true meaning.

Keep the Change signals a new development in McGuane's perception of male competition. Games are no longer seen as means to make sport of conventionality. Joe Starling's rival here is Billy Kelton, an honest and simple, if luckless, cowboy, who marries Ellen Overstreet. Kelton is Starling's physical superior and twice humiliates him with beatings. Violence here is real, not comic, and because it is real, it is bewildering and confusing. Kelton understands that his physical prowess is dehumanizing, and, in facing the struggles of life with his wife and daughter, he shows Starling the importance of a deeper, if simpler, emotional life.

The key to the novel is found in a painting of Montana mountains, the white hills, which hangs in a decaying mansion that once belonged to the most powerful man in the territory. The work itself is indistinguishable: "It had seemed an unblemished canvas until the perplexity of shadows across its surface was seen to be part of the painting." Ultimately, Starling discovers that the shadows are in fact its only real feature. There is no painting; there never has been a painting. Yet "somewhere in the abyss something shone." That "something" is the meaning Starling seeks. He is the one who determined meaning in the painting and, by extension, in the hills themselves. He must then act to create a life for himself; he must determine his own meaning.

In McGuane's contemporary West, life is what you make it, nothing more, nothing less. His protagonists must work to fulfill hopes not by going against the grain of the conventional life but by partaking of its normal flow and by building useful foundations on its undramatic, but real, joys.

Other major works

SHORT FICTION: *To Skin a Cat*, 1986.
SCREENPLAYS: *Rancho DeLuxe*, 1973; *Ninety-two in the Shade*, 1975; *The Missouri Breaks*, 1975; *Tom Horn*, 1980 (with Bud Shrake); *Cold Feet*, 1989 (with Jim Harrison).
NONFICTION: *An Outside Chance: Essays on Sport*, 1990 (rev. ed.).

Bibliography

Carter, Albert Howard, III. "Thomas McGuane's First Three Novels: Games, Fun, Nemesis." *Critique* 17 (August, 1975): 91-104.

Grant, Kerry. "On and Off the Main Line: The Failure of Compromise in the Fiction of Thomas McGuane." *Mid-American Review* 3 (Spring, 1983): 167-184.

McCaffery, Larry. "On Turning Nothing into Something." *Fiction International* 4-5 (Fall/Winter, 1975): 123-129.

Masinton, Charles G. *"Nobody's Angel:* Thomas McGuane's Vision of the Contemporary West." *New Mexico Humanities Review* 6 (Fall, 1983): 49-55.

Wallace, Jon. "The Language Plot in Thomas McGuane's *Ninety-two in the Shade.*" *Critique* 29 (Winter, 1988): 111-120.

——————— . *The Politics of Style: Language as Theme in the Fiction of Berger, McGuane, and McPherson.* Durango, Colo.: Hollowbrook, 1992.

——————— . "Speaking Against the Dark: Style as Theme in Thomas McGuane's *Nobody's Angel.*" *Modern Fiction Studies* 33 (Summer, 1987): 289-298.

Welch, Dennis M. "Death and Fun in the Novels of Thomas McGuane." *Windsor Review* 14 (Fall/Winter, 1978): 14-20.

Westrum, Dexter. *Thomas McGuane*. Boston: Twayne, 1991.

LARRY McMURTRY

Born: Wichita Falls, Texas; June 3, 1936

Principal long fiction

Horseman, Pass By, 1961; *Leaving Cheyenne*, 1963; *The Last Picture Show*, 1966; *Moving On*, 1970; *All My Friends Are Going to Be Strangers*, 1972; *Terms of Endearment*, 1975; *Somebody's Darling*, 1978; *Cadillac Jack*, 1982; *The Desert Rose*, 1983; *Lonesome Dove*, 1985; *Texasville*, 1987; *Anything for Billy*, 1988; *Some Can Whistle*, 1989; *Buffalo Girls*, 1990; *The Evening Star*, 1992; *Streets of Laredo*, 1993.

Other literary forms

In a Narrow Grave (1968) is a collection of nine essays Larry McMurtry wrote for various periodicals, mostly concerning Texas. He collaborated on the script for the motion picture of his novel *The Last Picture Show* in 1971 and has written other scripts. In 1975-1976, he wrote monthly articles for *American Film* magazine, some of which are collected in *Film Flam: Essays on Hollywood* (1987).

Achievements

McMurtry's early reputation was based on his depiction of hard modern times in north Texas. *Horseman, Pass By*, *Leaving Cheyenne*, and *The Last Picture Show* are all located in that area, where the frontier and the old ranching way of life were disappearing while McMurtry was growing up. The second group of three novels, *Moving On*, *All My Friends Are Going to Be Strangers*, and *Terms of Endearment*, concerns an interrelated group of characters in the Houston area and focuses primarily on failed marriages. McMurtry's Pulitzer Prize and his greatest public success, however, came with his first venture into the traditional Western, his novel of the frontier past, *Lonesome Dove*, considered by many critics to be his finest achievement and the finest novel ever written in that form.

Biography

Larry Jeff McMurtry was born in Wichita Falls, Texas, in 1936, grandson of a pioneer cattleman in north Texas and one of four children of a ranching family. McMurtry grew up on the ranch, was graduated from high school in Archer City, Texas, the locale of much of his early fiction, in 1954, and after one semester at Rice University attended North Texas State University, from which he was graduated in 1958. He was married to Josephine Ballard in 1959; the marriage, which produced one son, ended in divorce in 1966.

McMurtry went back to Rice as a graduate student in English in 1958, beginning work on his first two novels. *Horseman, Pass By* was accepted for publication while he was at Rice and was published while he was a writing student at Stanford University in 1961. Between 1961 and 1969 he taught off and on at Texas Christian University and at Rice, while two more novels were published and he worked on his first long novel, *Moving On*. He had worked occasionally as a book scout for California bookstores while at Stanford, and in 1969 McMurtry left Houston and moved to Washington, D.C., where he became a partner in a bookstore. Since then he has divided his time between the store and his writing.

Many of McMurtry's books have been made into motion pictures, most notably *Hud* (1963; the screen name of *Horseman, Pass By*), *The Last Picture Show*, which was filmed by Peter Bogdanovich in Archer City, and *Terms of Endearment* (1983). Actors in all these films (Patricia Neal, Cloris Leachman, Shirley MacLaine, and Jack Nicholson) won Oscars for their performances. *Lonesome Dove* was made into a major miniseries for television, with Robert Duval and Tommy Lee Jones in the major roles. A film version of *Texasville* was released in 1990.

Analysis

McMurtry's best fiction has used the American Southwest as its location and the characters typical of that area for its subjects. In the early years of his career, he dealt with life in the dying towns and decaying ranches of north and west Texas, often using boys on the brink of manhood to provide perspective on a way of life that had reached a stage of corruption and betrayal. His trilogy, following these early novels, dealt with the tangled relationships among somewhat older characters and reflected McMurtry's own move from Archer City to Houston. Later, he invested the Western novel with new vigor in two novels, his classic *Lonesome Dove* and the satiric *Anything for Billy*, which holds the legend of Billy the Kid up to ridicule.

The Last Picture Show is set in the small, dying north Texas town of Thalia (there is a town with that name in Texas, but its geography does not fit the fictional town, which is clearly modeled on Archer City). Its central characters are Sonny Crawford and Duane Moore, two boys in their last year of high school. Neither is in fact an orphan, but neither lives with his surviving parent; they rent rooms in the town's rooming house, support themselves working in the oil fields, and hang out at the town's pool hall, run by their aging friend and mentor, Sam the Lion. In the course of about six months, Duane and Sonny learn hard lessons about life and love.

Sonny is the more sensitive of the two. He falls into a passionate affair with Ruth Popper, the frustrated and lonely wife of the high school athletic coach, a stock figure whose latent homosexuality is masked by an aggressive masculinity in the presence of his athletes. Ruth begins the affair in desperation and is startled by the depth of her feeling for Sonny, while the boy is surprised and gratified by the experience. Both realize that the affair cannot last, but Ruth is devastated when Sonny leaves her at the invitation of the town's reigning beauty, Jacy Farrow.

Jacy has been Duane's girlfriend, a monster of selfishness who plays games with both Sonny and Duane, almost destroying their friendship. She keeps putting off Duane's demands that she marry him and insists on seeing another young man and going with him to wild parties in Wichita Falls. When Duane leaves town to work in the fields, Jacy decides to take Sonny away from Ruth Popper. Duane finds out, fights with Sonny, and blinds his friend in one eye by hitting him with a beer bottle. Jacy convinces Sonny to elope with her as an adventure, arranging matters so that her father will stop them before they are actually married. Jacy's wise and experienced mother, Lois, offers Sonny brief consolation and shows him that he must make peace with Ruth Popper.

The boys' adventures have been made possible by the wise counsel and care of Sam the Lion. He has taught them about life, given them parental refuge, and showed them the limits of behavior by closing them out when they are involved in the mistreatment of his retarded ward, Billy. The safety of their world is shattered when Sam dies suddenly, leaving his pool hall and restaurant in the care of Sonny. The young man is forced to face the cruelty of the world when Billy, sweeping the streets of Thalia in his customary way, is hit and killed by a passing truck. The boys are reconciled when Duane leaves to join the army and fight in Korea.

The Last Picture Show, named for the film theater that is forced to close, symbolizing the decay of Thalia, is a compound of nostalgia, harsh realism, and tragedy. It deals with the inevitable loss of innocence of its central characters and with the hard realities of injury, loss, and death. It is frank about sex, but it makes clear the price Sonny and Ruth Popper pay for their affair. At the same time, its depiction of adolescence is often amusing and colorful. The boys take off on a wild adventure south through Texas and into Mexico, they enjoy playing bad basketball for an increasingly frustrated Coach Popper, and they enjoy earning their own livings. With the exception of the incident involving the joke played on Billy, they do harm only to themselves.

The Last Picture Show was McMurtry's sometimes bitter, sometimes nostalgic farewell to the North Texas setting of his early work. The next stage in his career focused on young people in the Houston area, beginning with *Moving On*, a long depiction of the damage wrought by a marriage that is falling apart, and a sad picture of university life and the lives of traveling rodeo performers. This second phase of McMurtry's career ended with *Terms of Endearment*, the story of a lively widow and her troubled daughter, who eventually dies of cancer. Typifying this stage is *All My Friends Are Going to Be Strangers*, a novel held together only by the central character and narrator, Danny Deck, who was introduced in *Moving On*.

McMurtry, in the group of novels which followed *All My Friends Are Going to Be Strangers*, seemed to be trying to demonstrate that he could write successful novels that had nothing to do with Texas or with the life of a writer. The brief satiric glimpse of Hollywood given in *All My Friends Are Going to Be Strangers* was expanded in *Somebody's Darling*, whose central character is a film director trying to cope with her early success and the demands of two men she loves. The world McMurtry entered as a bookstore owner is reflected obliquely in *Cadillac Jack*, whose protagonist is an itinerant antiques dealer and whose chief setting is Washington, D.C. The entertainment industry comes under further examination in *The Desert Rose*, which has as its heroine an aging topless dancer in Las Vegas. Each of these novels is entertaining and well written, but none did much to enhance McMurtry's reputation.

That had to wait until McMurtry decided to write a

novel in one of the oldest and most persistently popular of American fictional traditions, the Western. What McMurtry did in *Lonesome Dove* was to reinvent the Western novel by taking its basic elements and elevating them to the level of epic. The characters in *Lonesome Dove* are familiar to readers of Western fiction, here given new names: the silent hero, Woodrow Call, who cares more for horses than for women and who leads other men by example and by courage; the other hero, Gus McCrae, talkative and easygoing, always ready for emergencies; the prostitute with a heart of gold, Lorena (Lorie) Wood; the evil renegade half-breed, Blue Duck; the naïve but courageous boy, Newt; the strong almost-widow, Clara Allen; the handsome but weak gambler, destined to come to a bad end eventually, Jake Spoon; the unimaginative but dependable sheriff, July Johnson; the comic deputy, July's aide Roscoe; and a cast of thousands.

McMurtry's achievement in *Lonesome Dove* is two-fold. First, he puts his huge cast of characters into motion. Beginning with a rundown livery stable and cattle-trading business in a tiny Texas town south of San Antonio called Lonesome Dove, the former Texas Rangers Call and Gus put together a herd by rustling from Mexican ranches across the Rio Grande, hire enough cowboys to run the drive, and set out for Montana, where Jake Spoon has told them there is a world of grass unclaimed by white men. Their journey is difficult and tragic, lightened at times by comedy, but it is never dull or ordinary. Lorie, whose beauty has been the only relief to the boredom of Lonesome Dove, makes Jake take her along, to the great disgust of Call, the former Ranger captain who can see no use for women anywhere, much less on a cattle drive. She and Jake are not part of the drive, but they stay close to it; many of the cowboys, in love with Lorie, are kept in a state of agitation—especially the top hand, Dish, who desperately wants to marry her.

McMurtry's approach to his material is leisurely. More than two hundred pages at the beginning, exceeding one-fourth of the long novel, are devoted to preliminary events in Lonesome Dove and the first stages of the drive: the arrival of Jake, a former Ranger on the run from a murder charge, with his news of Montana; Call's sudden and uncharacteristic decision to go, after ten years of relative inactivity; the raids into Mexico to steal horses and cattle; the gathering of an outfit to supplement Newt, Pea Eye, and Deets, the Hat Creek crew; Lorie's instant love for Jake, even though she quickly sees his weakness. Most of this material is humorous,

largely because Gus is a man who refuses to take life seriously. The raid into Mexico is exciting and potentially dangerous, but even this adventure turns to comedy when the Hat Creek cowboys encounter two lost Irish brothers who left Ireland headed for Galveston and wound up missing their target by several hundred miles. The Irish brothers, despite their unfamiliarity with horses and cattle, are hired on.

The second major factor in McMurtry's success in *Lonesome Dove* is his ability to take stock characters and humanize them by making them recognizable and distinctive human beings while at the same time elevating them to mythic proportions. Call is a projection of the strong but silent type of frontiersman, quiet, self-contained, but restless and capable of angry outbursts. Despite his abilities, he is emotionally strangled. Gus McCrae is almost superhuman. When necessary, he can fight more effectively than other men, but he is also warm and sympathetic to women and to young boys in trouble, such as Call's unacknowledged bastard son, Newt. He brings Lorie out of her catatonic state and wins her love, but he is human enough to wish that he could have Clara instead. Newt Dobbs is the typical young man; subjected again and again to grief and strain, he grows and matures. The black scout, Deets, is everything a scout should be.

The pace of the novel accelerates once the herd is on the trail. As soon as the drive begins, disaster strikes. Two days out, the herd is hit by a storm, and the riders must stay up all night to keep the cattle from dispersing. The next day, crossing a stream roiled by the storm, the younger and sadder of the Irish brothers stirs up a nest of cottonmouth snakes and is horribly killed. It is the first of several deaths the men will encounter on their long odyssey.

Only late in this initial section does McMurtry introduce another set of characters: July Johnson, the sheriff of Fort Smith, Arkansas; his unhappy pregnant wife, Elmira, a former prostitute; her son, Joe; and the deputy Roscoe. In Fort Smith, July's brother, the town mayor, has been accidentally killed by a shot fired by Jake Spoon, and the mayor's widow is urging July to track down Jake and bring him back to hang. July, recovering from jaundice and convinced that the shooting was an accident, is reluctant to go, but eventually he sets out, at Elmira's insistence taking Joe along. Shortly thereafter, Elmira, pregnant with July's child, leaves town on a riverboat to seek out her former lover, the gambler Dee Boot, and July's sister-in-law insists that Roscoe track down July to tell him that his wife is gone.

All these characters, and others, eventually meet on the plains. Jake leaves Lorie to go to town to gamble, and while he is gone the Comanchero Blue Duck, a bitter, crafty, and resourceful renegade, kidnaps the terrified Lorie, takes her north to the plains, and keeps her barely alive only to sell her body to Kiowas and buffalo hunters, an experience that robs her of speech and very nearly of her sanity. She is rescued by Gus, but the cost of the rescue is high; July Johnson, still looking for Elmira, insists on helping Gus, and while they are dispatching the six Kiowas and two buffalo hunters who hold Lorie, Blue Duck sneaks into their small camp and murders Roscoe, July's stepson Joe, and a young girl who has been traveling with Roscoe.

Jake, in the meantime, has found himself entangled with the three Suggs brothers, hard cases who are getting harder. Jake accidentally kills another man and goes along with the Suggses, who kill several more, including the rancher Wilbarger, who has earlier befriended Gus. Call and Gus track down the Suggses and hang all three brothers; reluctantly, they also hang Jake.

Many of the elements of the plot resolve themselves in the Nebraska frontier town of Ogallala. Clara Allen, the only woman Gus has loved and lost, lives there with her comatose husband and two daughters. Elmira arrives first, has her baby, and departs with her buffalo-hunter escort, both soon to be killed by Sioux. Her lover, Dee Boot, is hanged. July Johnson comes next, sees his son, whom Clara has kept, and stays on as a hand at Clara's ranch. Gus and Call arrive with the herd, and Clara and Gus have a happy reunion, but she makes it clear that she will never marry him, even when her husband dies. Lorie finds herself welcomed by Clara, and she stays on when the herd moves north to Montana. Newt and the other young cowboys go to Ogallala and have their first experience with whores, and Newt decides to become a ladies' man like Gus.

In the final section, the herd moves north to Montana and encounters still-violent Indians. Deets is killed by a desperate young warrior who fails to comprehend that Deets is not hostile. Gus and the cowboy Pea Eye, scouting ahead for a ranch site, are cut off by a roving band and attacked. Pea Eye gets away, but Gus is wounded. He escapes from the Indians but dies in Miles City after refusing to allow the doctor to amputate both of his gangrenous legs.

Call finds the spot for a ranch, and the men build a ranch house and corrals and spend a hard winter there. When spring comes, Call leaves Newt in charge of the remaining men and the cattle, tacitly acknowledging

that he is Newt's father, but he cannot bring himself to call the boy his son. He fulfills his promise to take Gus's body and bury it in a Texas glen where Gus and Clara had picnicked years earlier. On his long and difficult journey, Call passes through Ogallala, where Clara's husband has died and she and Lorie are mourning for Gus. Later, he pauses long enough to witness Blue Duck's death. Call is shot and goes through numerous other trials, but he manages to bury Gus; at the end, he makes his way back to the deserted town of Lonesome Dove.

In *Lonesome Dove* McMurtry is at the height of his powers. The disparate strands of the plot are handled skillfully, as the story moves easily from the herd to July Johnson to Jake Spoon to Elmira and then back to the herd. McMurtry's ability to depict action comes into play often, in the violent scenes of the young Irishman's death, Gus's explosion into the Kiowa camp where Lorie is held, the sudden thunderstorms that batter the cowboys and scatter the herd, the sudden descent of a plague of grasshoppers, and many other scenes. He is equally skilled at depicting character, not only the major figures such as Call, Gus, Clara, and Lorie but also young Newt and such minor characters as the cook Po Campo, Roscoe, Wilbarger, and Elmira. There is a leavening of humor, some of it hilarious, not only in the early sections of the novel but also throughout. At the same time, there is no attempt to downplay the violence and hardship of the lives of these men and women; the long journey is marked by one violent death after another. The hard life of the frontier is represented not only by Lorie's terrible experience at the hands of Blue Duck and the sudden deaths among the cowboys but also by Clara's loss of three sons and a husband to the harsh conditions of life on the prairie.

It is entirely fitting that the ending is grim. The most powerful scene in the final section is Clara's condemnation of Call when he returns to Ogallala with Gus's body, bringing the final notes the dying Gus wrote to Clara and Lorie. Her scathing denunciation of his single-mindedness and the human sacrifice and misery the trip causes raises disturbing questions about the meaning of the heroic journey the men have accomplished. The surviving hands are left on the isolated ranch in Montana. Clara and Lorie remain on the ranch outside Ogallala, with July hoping to marry Clara and Dish hopelessly in love with Lorie. Call has no idea where to go after the trip back to Lonesome Dove is ended.

McMurtry is a highly prolific novelist who has

shown the ability to change his locales and his subject matter when he feels the need for novelty, and he has been willing to revive characters from earlier novels to suit new purposes. He has been most successful in exploring the past and present of his native Texas, a geographical state and a state of mind that provide seemingly inexhaustible material for his special blend of satire, romance, and tragedy. His most important achievement, *Lonesome Dove* has already attained the status of a classic of Western fiction.

Other major works

NONFICTION: *In a Narrow Grave: Essays on Texas*, 1968; *It's Always We Rambled: An Essay on Rodeo*, 1974; *Film Flam: Essays on Hollywood*, 1987.

Bibliography

Kingsolver, Barbara. "Across Texas by Non Sequitur." *The New York Times Book Review* 94 (October 22, 1989): 8.
Neinstein, Raymond. Afterword to *All My Friends Are Going to Be Strangers*, by Larry McMurtry. Albuquerque: University of New Mexico Press, 1982.
_____ . *The Ghost Country: The Novels of Larry McMurtry*. Houston: Creative Arts Book Co., 1976.
Nelson, Jane. "Larry McMurtry." In *A Literary History of the American West*, edited by Max Westbrook and James H. Maguire. Fort Worth: Texas Christian University Press, 1987.
Peavy, Charles D. *Larry McMurtry*. Boston: Twayne, 1977.
Reynolds, Clay. "Back Trailing to Glory: *Lonesome Dove* and Novels of Larry McMurtry." *The Texas Review* 8 (Fall/Winter, 1987): 22-29.
_____ , ed. *Taking Stock: A Larry McMurtry Casebook*. Dallas: Southern Methodist University Press, 1989.
Schmidt, Dorey, ed. *Larry McMurtry: Unredeemed Dreams*. Living Authors Series 1. Houston: Pan American Press, 1978.

FRANK NORRIS

Born: Chicago, Illinois; March 5, 1870

Died: San Francisco, California; October 25, 1902

Principal long fiction

Moran of the Lady Letty, 1898; *McTeague*, 1899; *Blix*, 1899; *A Man's Woman*, 1900; *The Octopus*, 1901; *The Pit*, 1903; *Vandover and the Brute*, 1914.

Other literary forms

Frank Norris' published work includes poems, short stories, essays, newspaper articles, novels, and literary criticism. Although he is best known today for his novels, Norris is also remembered for his popular short-story contributions to the San Francisco *Wave* and his insightful literary criticism, published in *The Responsibilities of the Novelist* (1903) and *The Literary Criticism of Frank Norris* (1964). Norris' success as a reporter was minimal. His reports on the Boer War were published in the San Francisco *Chronicle*, but his later writings on the Spanish-American War were not published for some time afterward, and never by *McClure's* magazine, which originally sent him there. The majority of Norris' writings were collected in a ten-volume *Complete Edition*, published by Doubleday, Doran and Company in 1928.

Achievements

Called by many (including himself) "the boy Zola" because his style was so reminiscent of the writings of French author Émile Zola, Norris spearheaded the naturalistic movement in American literature. Although Norris' contemporaries were, by and large, critical of his portrayal of the savage, seamy side of life, it is that very quality in his work that has helped to keep his fiction alive and readable. Even more than his challenge to the Victorian code, Norris' capacity to portray corruption and its evil effects upon humanity and his ability to make scenes and characters seem vibrant and real rank him high among twentieth century writers.

Norris never achieved the immense popularity of some of the other writers of his day, such as Jack London. He did not even live to see his most successful novel, *The Pit*, become a best-seller. Indeed, it was not until publication of *The Octopus* that he was able to enjoy even a modest financial success. His readers were simply not able to accept his preoccupation with sordid realities, including his treatment of sex, which by Vic-torian standards was quite shocking. Because of his unsavory choice of subject matter, Norris was ignored by reviewers who understood only the elegant prose and fine writing of an earlier era. Today, Norris' pioneering work in American naturalism is universally acknowledged.

Biography

Frank Norris was the son of Benjamin Franklin Norris, a successful businessman specializing in wholesale jewelry, and Gertrude Doggett. Born in 1870, Norris' early years were spent in Chicago. At fourteen, Norris moved with his family to California. They settled first in Oakland and then moved to a large house on Sacramento Street in San Francisco. Benjamin Norris began a real-estate-development business, building cheap houses for working-class people to rent, and enjoyed financial success. His son would later write about these houses in his first novel.

In 1885, Norris was enrolled in the Belmont Academy. This marked the beginning of a long, largely unsuccessful attempt at formal schooling. It was during this period that he made up his mind to pursue a career as an artist. After a short stint at Boys' High School, Norris convinced his parents to send him to the San Francisco Art Association School. His success there persuaded Benjamin Norris to send him to the finest art schools in Paris. While Norris did not learn how to paint in Paris, he did learn the fundamentals and principles of art and also the discipline that would later serve him well as a writer.

In the fall of 1890, Norris entered the University of California, determined to become a writer. Although his academic career at Berkeley was undistinguished, Norris' fraternity pranks were memorable.

Meanwhile his family was quickly breaking apart. Benjamin Norris left, alone, for Europe; while on the trip, he fell in love with another woman. Upon his return, he divorced Gertrude, married his new love, and moved to Chicago. Frank never saw his father again.

In 1894, Norris left the university without a degree. He enrolled at Harvard the following fall as a special student, taking courses in English and French. There, under Professor Lewis Gates's watchful eye, Norris began work on *Vandover and the Brute* and *McTeague*. After a year at Harvard, Norris returned to San Francisco, taking a job with the Chronicle as a special correspondent. He convinced the paper to send him to South Africa, where he covered the beginnings of the Boer War. There he contracted the tropical fever that would later contribute to his death.

Norris next joined the staff of the San Francisco Wave, where he wrote short stories, reviewed books and art exhibits, and composed feature stories. He also began publishing some of his work in magazines, a development that led to a job with Doubleday as a reader. While the position paid poorly and offered little status, it allowed him time to finish *Moran of the Lady Letty*. Norris left the firm in 1899 to join the newly founded firm of Doubleday, Page & Company, again as a part-time, poorly paid reader. He wrote *Blix* and *A Man's Woman* and began *The Octopus* during this time; he also married Jeannette Black. His major contribution to the firm came when Theodore Dreiser's Sister Carrie was submitted; Norris read the novel in manuscript and persuaded Doubleday, Page to publish it, in 1900.

As Norris' royalties grew from the sale of his own novels, he found the financial independence to return to California, and he made plans to purchase a ranch in the southern range of the Santa Cruz mountains. He completed *The Pit*, the second book in his projected trilogy of wheat novels, and planned a journey to the tropics with his wife. That journey was interrupted, however, when Jeannette underwent surgery to remove an inflamed appendix. While she was recovering in the hospital, Norris, too, began suffering stomach pains. Thinking it only a minor ailment, he refused to go to a doctor until he became seriously ill. Suffering from peritonitis and weakened by fever, Norris entered Mt. Zion hospital in San Francisco and died there on October 25, 1902, at the age of thirty-two.

Analysis

Frank Norris was one of a handful of writers at the start of the twentieth century who applied the literary naturalism of Émile Zola to American subjects and themes. As a writer in this tradition, Norris treated his subject matter brutally but sincerely. His characters are pawns, driven by outside forces over which they have no control. Devoid of souls, they are helpless creatures whose fates are determined by their heredity and environment. In Norris' most successful novels, these naturalistic ideas are employed with great faithfulness, and his depiction of human beings following a slow but inevitable course toward destruction has an enduring power.

In *McTeague* Norris focused his attention on the naturalistic novel of character, in which the title character proceeds slowly toward his inevitable destruction. In Norris' last two novels, *The Octopus* and *The Pit*, he again returned to naturalistic themes, but in a broader, more worldly sense, showing greater compassion and involvement with his characters. The progression from *McTeague*, a highly dispassionate view of a man's descent, to *The Pit*, which analyzes the social forces at work in the wheat industry, marks Norris' own maturation as both a writer and a man and illustrates his increasingly complex worldview.

McTeague emphasizes themes of chance, disintegration, and heredity. The novel is a study of the temperaments of two characters: McTeague, a scoundrel born in a California mining town, and Trina Sieppe, a working-class girl whose hoarding instincts eventually overcome her.

As the novel begins, McTeague is working with his father in the California mines. A traveling dentist arrives shortly after McTeague's father dies, and the young boy is apprenticed to the dentist so that he might learn a trade. McTeague is not bright enough to learn much—the result of his heredity—but he eventually learns enough to survive, and when his mother dies, he sets up dental parlors in San Francisco. The rich, descriptive detail with which Norris renders McTeague's surroundings greatly contributes to the success of the novel.

McTeague is well satisfied with his existence: The earnings from his practice keep him supplied with a daily glass of steam beer and allow him enough leisure time to practice his concertina and socialize infrequently with his friends, among them Marcus Schouler, who lives in the flat above McTeague. Chance, however, intervenes in McTeague's ordered existence when Marcus' girlfriend, Trina, breaks a tooth and Marcus brings her to McTeague for treatment. While they wait in the parlors, Trina buys a lottery ticket from the cleaning woman—a ticket that, later, will be worth five thousand dollars.

McTeague falls in love with Trina at first sight, and

Marcus, rather than fighting for his girl, aids McTeague in courting her, even to the point of introducing him to Trina's parents. The path paved, McTeague asks Trina to marry him, and, on the day the announcement is made public, Trina wins the money through the lottery. It is this chance event that sparks Trina's inherited passion for hoarding, first evident on the day of the lottery payment when Trina, to McTeague's dismay, decides not to spend her winnings on a nice apartment, but rather to save the money. This first clash of temperaments leads to others as McTeague and Trina continue toward their eventual disintegration.

At first, Trina and McTeague are happy; they move into a flat across from the dental parlors and live comfortably. McTeague's ambitions to live in more spacious quarters, however, conflict with Trina's thrifty attitudes. Marcus reenters their lives; embittered by McTeague's good fortune, he attacks McTeague with a knife. This first conflict arouses physical violence in both men only briefly, but during their second encounter, which begins as a friendly wrestling match at the park, Marcus bites off McTeague's earlobe and McTeague retaliates by breaking Marcus' arm. After the incident, Marcus leaves the city, but not before first notifying the authorities that McTeague is practicing dentistry without proper credentials.

Stripped of his profession, McTeague loses his income, thus exacerbating his conflict with Trina over the management of their money. The animal within him brought to the surface, McTeague is no longer able to cope with his environment or with Trina's hoarding, which has become obsessive. He deserts Trina and then comes back and steals her money. After he has spent all the money, McTeague returns to Trina for more. This time, however, he beats her so mercilessly that she dies. Taking her entire lottery winnings, McTeague flees the city for the gold mines and his birthplace. He is followed, however, and forced to flee again, to Death Valley, where he again meets Marcus. This time, however, the struggle their encounter precipitates is fatal to both.

A stark depiction of human degeneracy, *McTeague* shows how the interaction of two characters hastens their descent. Chance also plays an important part in the novel. Life itself is a gigantic lottery; Norris is emphatic when he labels the agent of the lottery a "man of the world."

By separating himself from his characters in *McTeague*, Norris was able to deal objectively with the impact of instinct and chance upon them. McTeague becomes an animal—a brute from the mines. Trina, too, crippled by her hoarding instinct both physically (her fingers are amputated) and mentally, becomes little more than an animal, defending her gold as a wolf might defend its kill. *McTeague* is Norris' most powerful and successful novel; his rendering of the seamy, bestial side of human life is masterful.

Norris' final novels were to constitute a projected trilogy on the wheat industry. In the first novel of the trilogy, *The Octopus*, Norris returned to naturalistic formulas. In *The Octopus*, the wheat is planted, grown, and harvested. In *The Pit*, the wheat is traded and taken to market. In "The Wolf," the planned but never written conclusion to the trilogy, the wheat was to be consumed by the hungry masses of Europe. Norris did not live to complete this third book. When he died in 1902, the second volume was only then being serialized.

The Octopus and *The Pit* both deal with the problems of society as a whole rather than with the individual. Jadwin, a weak, irresolute man, is a famous capitalist speculator. A taker of chances, he manages for a time to corner the wheat market and enjoy financial prosperity. His fortunes are wiped out, however, when the wheat crops of the West are harvested. Helpless in the face of vast economic forces that he cannot control—and helpless too in the face of his own heredity, which has forced upon him an uncontrollable urge to gamble—Jadwin is destroyed.

Norris is at his best when objectively and dispassionately analyzing his characters and allowing them to be subjected, like pawns, to the naturalistic forces of the universe. He was more, however, than a didactic sociologist in the guise of a novelist. His best work is characterized by a faithful reproduction of setting, by creative exuberance. Thus, one does not merely read about Polk Street in *McTeague* or the San Joaquin Valley in *The Octopus* or the Board of Trade in *The Pit*, but one also breathes the air of these places, smells their pungent smells. It is this fundamental sense of reality that gives Norris' fiction a lasting appeal.

Other major works

SHORT FICTION: *A Deal in Wheat and Other Stories of the New and Old West*, 1903; *The Joyous Miracle*, 1906; *The Third Circle*, 1909; *Frank Norris of "The Wave,"* 1931 (Oscar Lewis, ed.).
POETRY: *Yvernelle: A Tale of Feudal France*, 1892; *Two Poems and "Kim" Reviewed*, 1930.

NONFICTION: *The Responsibilities of the Novelist*, 1903; *The Surrender of Santiago*, 1917; *The Letters of Frank Norris*, 1956; *The Literary Criticism of Frank Norris*, 1964.
MISCELLANEOUS: *The Complete Edition of Frank Norris*, 1928 (10 vols.).

Bibliography

Boyd, Jennifer. *Frank Norris: Spatial Form and Narrative Time*. New York: P. Lang, 1993.

Dillingham, William B. *Frank Norris: Instinct and Art*. Lincoln: University of Nebraska Press, 1969.

French, Warren. *Frank Norris*. Boston: Twayne, 1962.

Graham, Don. *The Fiction of Frank Norris: The Aesthetic Context*. Columbia: University of Missouri Press, 1978.

McElrath, Joseph R. *Frank Norris: A Descriptive Bibliography*. Pittsburgh: University of Pittsburgh Press, 1992.

—————— . *Frank Norris Revisited*. New York: Twayne, 1992.

Marchand, Ernest. *Frank Norris: A Study*. New York: Octagon Books, 1964.

Pizer, Donald, ed. *The Literary Criticism of Frank Norris*. Austin: University of Texas Press, 1964.

—————— . *The Novels of Frank Norris*. Bloomington: Indiana University Press, 1966.

SAM SHEPARD
Samuel Shepard Rogers

Born: Fort Sheridan, Illinois; November 5, 1943

Principal drama

Cowboys, pr. 1964 (one act); *The Rock Garden*, pr. 1964, pb. 1971 (one act); *Chicago*, pr. 1965, pb. 1967; *Icarus's Mother*, pr. 1965, pb. 1967; *4-H Club*, pr. 1965, pb. 1972; *Fourteen Hundred Thousand*, pr. 1966, pb. 1967; *Melodrama Play*, pr. 1966, pb. 1967; *Red Cross*, pr. 1966, pb. 1967; *La Turista*, pr. 1966, pb. 1968; *Cowboys #2*, pr. 1967, pb. 1968; *Forensic and the Navigators*, pr. 1967, pb. 1969; *The Unseen Hand*, pr., pb. 1969; *Operation Sidewinder*, pb. 1969, pr. 1970; *Shaved Splits*, pr. 1969, pb. 1972; *The Holy Ghostly*, pr. 1970, pb. 1972; *Cowboy Mouth*, pr., pb. 1971 (with Patti Smith); *The Mad Dog Blues*, pr. 1971, pb. 1972; *The Tooth of Crime*, pr. 1972, pb. 1974; *Geography of a Horse Dreamer*, pr., pb. 1974; *Action*, pr. 1974, pb. 1975; *Angel City*, pr., pb. 1976; *Curse of the Starving Class*, pb. 1976, pr. 1977; *Suicide in B Flat*, pr. 1976, pb. 1979; *Buried Child*, pr. 1978, pb. 1979; *Seduced*, pr. 1978, pb. 1979; *True West*, pr. 1980, pb. 1981; *Fool for Love*, pr., pb. 1983; *A Lie of the Mind*, pr. 1985, pb. 1986; *States of Shock*, pr. 1991, pb. 1992.

Other literary forms

Sam Shepard has written a number of screenplays, including the ill-fated *Zabriskie Point* (1969) for Michelangelo Antonioni, the award-winning *Paris, Texas* (1984), and *Far North* (1988), which Shepard also directed. Shepard has also written poetry and short fiction, in *Hawk Moon* (1973) and *Motel Chronicles* (1982), and recorded the major events of Bob Dylan's Rolling Thunder Revue tour in a collection of essays titled *Rolling Thunder Logbook* (1977).

Achievements

Shepard is one of the United States' most prolific, most celebrated, and most honored playwrights. Writing exclusively for the Off-Broadway and Off-Off-Broadway theater, Shepard has nevertheless won eleven Obie Awards (for *Red Cross*, *Chicago*, *Icarus's Mother*, *Forensic and the Navigators*, *La Turista*, *Melodrama Play*, *Cowboys #2*, *The Tooth of Crime*, *Curse of the Starving Class*, *Buried Child*, and *Fool for Love*). In 1979, he received a Pulitzer Prize for *Buried Child*. His screenplay for Wim Wenders' film *Paris, Texas* won the Palme d'Or at the Cannes Film Festival, and Shepard himself received an Oscar nomination for his portrayal of Colonel Chuck Yeager in *The Right Stuff* (1983). *A Lie of the Mind* was named the outstanding new play of the 1985-1986 season by the Drama Desk.

Biography

Born Samuel Shepard Rogers, Jr., on an army base in Fort Sheridan, Illinois, on November 5, 1943, Sam Shepard's early years were marked by repeated moves from one place to another: South Dakota, Utah, Florida, Guam, and eventually Southern California. Shepard's father, Samuel Rogers VI, was severely wounded during World War II, became an alcoholic, and progressively withdrew from the family until he became a desert-dwelling, storytelling recluse; the playwright's father died after being struck by a car in 1983. Shepard recalls that his mother, Jane Schook Rogers, would fire her army-issued Luger pistol at the Japanese soldiers sneaking out of the jungle on Guam in the years following World War II. After Shepard's father retired from the Army, the family moved to an avocado ranch in the San Bernardino valley, in Southern California, where Shepard spent his adolescent years. In 1962, Shepard joined a barnstorming acting company with a religiously based repertory, the Bishop's Repertory Company. When the company reached New York, Shepard, nineteen years old, dropped out of the company and into the Lower East Side bohemian lifestyle, busing tables at the Village Gate, dabbling with acting, doing drugs, and running the streets with Charles Mingus, Jr., an old California friend.

In 1964, the twin bill of Shepard's first two plays, the original *Cowboys* and *The Rock Garden*, premiered at one of Off-Off-Broadway's most important theaters, Theater Genesis, and Shepard's career was launched. Shepard wrote prolifically for the Off-Off-Broadway theater during the last half of the 1960's, gaining recognition and critical acclaim with each play. By 1967, Shepard had gathered three Obie Awards, produced his first full-length play, and could boast of plays being produced on the West Coast, in New York, and in London. In 1969, Shepard married O-Lan Johnson (they had one son, Jesse Mojo), the actress who played the eponymous Oolan in *Forensic and the Navigators*. The following year, however, brought many difficulties for Shepard: *Operation Sidewinder* was produced at the Vivian Beaumont Theater at New York's Lincoln Center, but the frustrations posed by an expensive Broadway production and the generally unfavorable reaction to the play prompted Shepard to return to Off-Off-Broadway. Finally, losing patience with the New York theater scene, Shepard and his family moved to London in 1972. Upon his return to the United States in 1976, Shepard joined Bob Dylan on his Rolling Thunder Tour and then moved to San Francisco, where he began working with Joseph Chaikin and the Magic Theatre. The move to California also marks the beginning of Shepard's career as a film star; his portrayal of Colonel Chuck Yeager in *The Right Stuff* earned for him an Oscar nomination. While on the set of *Frances* (1982), Shepard met actress Jessica Lange; they later bought a ranch together in New Mexico and subsequently moved to Virginia.

Analysis

The settings of Shepard's plays, like the language used in the plays, contribute figurative significance to the dominant themes that appear. The action often unfolds against a backdrop composed of commonplace materials such as bathtubs, old wrecked cars, kitchen tables, refrigerators, living-room sofas, hotel beds, children's bedrooms, or hospital rooms, but these articles suggest an environment that is primarily metaphoric, not realistic. Shepard uses the icons of American pop culture to represent the mythic landscape of the American psyche, thereby demonstrating how personal identity is so often assembled out of the bits and pieces of the social iconography that dominates American culture. His figurative settings also underscore the predominant tensions dramatized, as in *Curse of the Starving Class*, where the lack of food in the refrigerator represents the lack of love and nurturing in the family. Because Shepard is primarily interested in depicting figurative conflicts and actions, he is free to draw on a wide variety of materials in the physical setting as well as the dialogue in order to create his mythic landscapes.

Hence, Shepard's plays are filled with borrowings from, and allusions to, what he sees as the core of the United States' mythology: rock and roll and country-western music, Hollywood and films of all kinds (Westerns in particular), the trappings of middle-class suburbia, the physical geography of the West (the desert in particular), science fiction, and the conflict between generations that shredded American society and culture during the Vietnam era.

Nearly all Shepard's plays examine the functions (and dysfunctions) of the relationships between individuals that constitute either family structures or social structures that approximate family structures—close friendships or tight-knit business alliances. The conflict between the two halves of what can be considered a single unit (brother and brother, father and son, husband and wife, boyfriend and girlfriend) as they struggle either for supremacy or for survival amid surrounding pressures can be found at the core of most of Shepard's plays. Further, his principal characters tend not only to be alienated from their immediate circumstances but also to be victimized by their drive toward a destructive self-isolation. The wake of devastation left by figures who are incapable of bridging the abysses they have created shapes the central conflict in many of Shepard's plays.

A cyclical pattern etched into the relationship between the generations provides the dominant structure for what have been called Shepard's "family" plays: *Curse of the Starving Class*, *Buried Child*, *True West*, *Fool for Love*, and *Lie of the Mind*. The "curse" in *Curse of the Starving Class* is quite clearly the curse of generational repetition: Children inevitably duplicate the actions of their parents. The natures of the parents are planted within the psyches of the children and emerge in actions that emphasize the familial curse passed down from generation to generation. Weston, the father, recalls the poison of his father's alcoholism; Wesley, the son, provides a chilling account of Weston's drunken attack on the home's locked front door; and in the third act, Wesley dons Weston's discarded clothes and admits that his father's essence is beginning to control him. Ella, the mother, passes on to her daughter Emma the curse of menstruation as well as the mother's desire to escape her family. The curse of starvation is overtly symbolized by the perpetually empty refrigerator, which underscores the family's physical, emotional, psychological, and spiritual starvation. Further, the curse of denial pervades all the play's relationships and colors almost every action. Clearly beset from within, this typical Shepardian family is also beset from without by those forces that Shepard believes threaten the mythic (and therefore true) West: the march of progress that wants to destroy the natural world and replace it with shopping malls, freeways, and tract housing developments. There is, obviously, no salvation for his family. Weston runs off to Mexico with the money he has received from the sale of the farm; Emma is blown up in Weston's car by thugs who are looking to extort money from Weston; Ella refuses to acknowledge what happens right in front of her and repeatedly addresses Wesley as "Weston"; Wesley completes the transformation into his father by adopting his father's attitudes and behaviors. The anecdote that Ella and Wesley jointly tell to close the play becomes the play's second great symbol: An eagle and a tomcat, tearing at each other in a midair struggle, crash to earth. Like that pair of animals, there is no salvation or escape that awaits the family in *Curse of the Starving Class*, only inevitable destruction.

Shepard's vision of the family in *Buried Child* is even darker; long and deeply buried familial secrets constitute the hereditary curse in Shepard's Pulitzer Prize winner. The family patriarch, Dodge, spends all of his time wrapped in an old blanket on the sofa, staring at the television. His wife, Halie, speaks at her husband (not to him) of trivial matters when she is not busy soliciting the local clergyman, Father Dewis. Their eldest son, Tilden, is a burned-out and mentally defective semi-mute who brings armload after armload of corn onto the stage. The second son, Bradley, had one leg cut off by a chain saw and now spends most of his time wrestling with Dodge for control of the blanket and television set or threatening to cut Dodge's hair. In a series of statements that recalls the pattern of denial that occurs in *Curse of the Starving Class*, Dodge refuses to acknowledge that Bradley is his own son, claiming that his flesh and blood are buried in the backyard. To complicate matters, Halie frequently mentions yet another son, Ansel, who (according to Halie and Halie alone) was a hero and basketball star. Into the midst of this dysfunctional home comes Vince, Tilden's son, who wants to reestablish his family ties, and Shelly, Vince's girlfriend. Tilden, however, refuses to recognize Vince, claiming that the son he once had is now dead and buried. The denial of family connections suggests both the physical and the emotional rejection that pervades the home in *Buried Child*. On a physical level, the dead child refers to Halie and Tilden's incestuously conceived child who was killed by Dodge and buried in the field behind the house. Metaphorically, the dead

child represents all the children in the family, all of whom are dead to their father and mother and to one another. Unable to gain recognition from any of his progenitors, Vince stomps out one evening and goes on an alcoholic binge, leaving Shelly at the mercy of Bradley, who menaces her sexually. When Vince returns the next morning, thoroughly drunk, his open violence provides Halie and Dodge with the clue to Vince's identity, once again suggesting that behavior is mechanically passed from generation to generation. When Dodge dies, Vince proclaims himself the family's new patriarch just as Tilden enters carrying the exhumed body of the buried child. The play's highly equivocal ending juxtaposes the hope symbolized by the rebirth of a new generation against despairing images of denial, disease, and death.

True West explores the conflict between two brothers: Lee, a reclusive and violent thief who has been living in the Mojave Desert, and Austin, a suburban Yuppie and screenwriter. Austin is trying to close a motion-picture deal with a Hollywood movie mogul, Saul Kimmer, but when Kimmer hears Lee's impromptu outline for a motion picture about two cowboys chasing each other across the plains of Texas, Kimmer decides to drop Austin's project and develop Lee's. *True West*, in addition to analyzing the fate of the artist in a manner that recalls *Angel City* and *Geography of a Horse Dreamer*, questions which version of the West is indeed true. Lee claims that the desert, with its brutally harsh environment that forces its denizens to live by their wits and strength, is the true West, while Austin claims that suburban California, with its shopping malls, highways, and tract housing, constitutes the real West. Further, the numerous references to famous Western films suggest that the only true West is Hollywood's West. The pressure of Kimmer's decision to pursue Lee's screenplay causes the brothers to switch roles: Austin, responding to Lee's taunts, steals a variety of toasters from the neighbors; Lee slaves over the typewriter, roughing out the dialogue. The reversal of roles indicates the fundamental similarities that bind the brothers. Upon their mother's abrupt return from Alaska (who, showing rare good sense for a Shepardian mother, claims to recognize nothing and immediately leaves), Lee and Austin square off in a physically violent but unresolved confrontation. *True West* not only questions the mythology that defines the American West but also probes the violence spawned by the fundamental psychological and behavioral equivalence of family members.

Shepard also examines the equivalency of siblings in *Fool for Love*, replacing the brother-brother conflict of *True West* with a love/hate relationship between half-brother and half-sister, Eddie and May. Reared in different towns by different mothers, Eddie and May meet, fall in love, and begin their incestuous relationship before discovering that they share the same father, the Old Man. Although the friction dramatized in Eddie and May's emotional and sexual relationship points toward Shepard's signature characterization of men and women as two opposite animals who cannot coexist, *Fool for Love* also examines how the same event is often shaped and reshaped by different individuals to create widely divergent memories and understandings of what happened. Eddie and May do not share the same recollection of their meeting and cannot come to terms with the implications of their relationship; moreover, none of their stories agrees with versions of the same incidents told by the Old Man, who at times seems to be Eddie's and May's mental projection but who at other times seems to be an independent character. Despite her attempt to establish a different lifestyle with Martin, the new man in her life, May is as inextricably bound to Eddie, as he is to her. Even though Eddie leaves at the end of the play and May believes that he is not coming back, the play suggests that the audience has witnessed but one episode in a continually repeating cycle in which Eddie and May are victimized by their repetitive actions just as surely as Wesley and Weston were by theirs in *Curse of the Starving Class*.

A Lie of the Mind explores the dysfunctional structure of the American family as well as the delusions that individuals impose on others and themselves. Beaten nearly to death by her husband Jake, Beth creates lies of the mind—fictions that permit her to survive. The play suggests that each character assembles a personal reality in his or her mind. For example, Jake's mother, Lorraine, blocks out the pain of being abandoned by her husband by pretending indifference; Beth's father, Baylor, hides from his family by erecting a façade of the crusty frontier hunter; Jake represses all of his memories of the race in Mexico that led to his father's death. Further, *A Lie of the Mind* suggests that the "two opposite animals," the male and the female, even when yoked together by an irresistible and consuming love, are torn apart by the violence of their fundamental incompatibility. Both Beth and Jake are trapped by their love—neither can be complete without the other—and their obsessive need to be reunited thrusts Beth into delusions of marriage and propels Jake to Montana to find Beth. Their drive for reunification, however, at last proves futile. After kissing Beth, Jake exits into the darkness, and Beth compulsively turns to Jake's wounded brother, Frankie. *A Lie of the Mind* suggests that the American family, like Beth, is fundamentally crippled.

Although Shepard has spoken of his personal aversion to the 1960's and early 1970's, the pulsing beat of his scintillating dramatic language, the resonant depth of the mythic images that permeate his plays, and the unwavering intensity of the conflicts that give his plays an unmatched toughness all have their ultimate source in the turmoil both caused and embraced by the sex, drugs, and rock-and-roll generation. The center of Shepard's work moves steadily and inexorably toward a distinctly American version of the domestic drama defined by his predecessors Henrik Ibsen, Anton Chekhov and Eugene O'Neill, but the conflicts between siblings, husbands and wives, or parents and children are consistently played out against the backdrop of the icons that created the American national identity during the Vietnam era.

Other major works

NONFICTION: *Rolling Thunder Logbook*, 1977.

SCREENPLAYS: *Me and My Brother*, 1967 (with Robert Frank); *Zabriskie Point*, 1969; *Ringaleevio*, 1971; *Paris, Texas*, 1984 (with L. M. Kit Carson); *Far North*, 1988; *Silent Tongue*, 1993.

MISCELLANEOUS: *Hawk Moon: A Book of Short Stories, Poems and Monologues*, 1973; *Motel Chronicles*, 1982.

Bibliography

Auerbach, Doris. *Shepard, Kopit, and the Off Broadway Theater*. Boston: Twayne, 1982.

DeRose, David J. *Sam Shepard*. New York: Twayne, 1992.

Hart, Lynda. *Sam Shepard's Metaphorical Stages*. Westport, Conn.: Greenwood Press, 1987.

King, Kimball, ed. *Sam Shepard: A Casebook*. New York: Garland, 1988.

Marranca, Bonnie, ed. *American Dreams: The Imagination of Sam Shepard*. New York: Performing Arts Journal Publications, 1981.

Mottram, Ron. *Inner Landscapes: The Theater of Sam Shepard*. Columbia: University of Missouri Press, 1984.

Oumano, Ellen. *Sam Shepard: The Life and Work of an American Dreamer*. New York: St. Martin's Press, 1986.

Tucker, Martin. *Sam Shepard*. New York: Continuum, 1992.

Wilcox, Leonard, ed. *Rereading Shepard: Contemporary Critical Essays on the Plays of Sam Shepard*. New York: St. Martin's Press, 1993.

GARY SNYDER

Born: San Francisco, California; May 8, 1930

Principal poetry

Riprap, 1959; *Myths and Texts*, 1960; *Hop, Skip, and Jump*, 1964; *Nanao Knows*, 1964; *The Firing*, 1964; *Riprap, and Cold Mountain Poems*, 1965; *Six Sections from Mountains and Rivers Without End*, 1965; *A Range of Poems*, 1966; *Three Worlds, Three Realms, Six Roads*, 1966; *The Back Country*, 1967; *The Blue Sky*, 1969; *Sours of the Hills*, 1969; *Regarding Wave*, 1970; *Manzanita*, 1972; *The Fudo Trilogy: Spell Against Demons, Smokey the Bear Sutra, The California Water Plan*, 1973; *Turtle Island*, 1974; *All in the Family*, 1975; *Axe Handles*, 1983; *Left Out in the Rain: New Poems 1947-1986*, 1986; *No Nature: New and Selected Poems*, 1992.

Other literary forms

Gary Snyder's pioneering journal of personal environmental discovery, *Earth House Hold* (1969), is subtitled "Technical Notes and Queries to Fellow Dharma Revolutionaries," a descriptive invitation to examine the treasure of the planet and to consider how it might be employed for the benefit of all living species. Its somewhat tentative, propositional format expresses the spirit of a movement that recognized the destructive aspects of modern industrial society and sought alternative approaches to the questions of planetary survival. His interest in the environment has proved to be as perceptive and enduring as his best poetry, and the publication of *The Practice of the Wild* (1990) has deepened the context of his interests, offering the wisdom and experience of a lifetime spent living in and thinking about the natural world.

Achievements

Before "ecology" had become a password of political correctness, Snyder was devising a program of study designed to create a language of environmental advocacy. After many trendy Westerners had long since recoiled from the rigors of Eastern thought, Snyder completed a curriculum of apprenticeship in Japan and went on to develop an American version of Zen applicable to his locality. As Native American life and lore gradually seeped into the area of academic interest, Snyder continued his examinations of the primal tribal communities that lived in harmony with the North American landmass for pre-Columbian millennia and worked to apply their successes to contemporary life. While hippies and dropouts returned to the button-down corporate culture after a brief dalliance with a counterculture, Snyder built his own home at the center of a small community that endures as an example of a

philosophical position in action. Most of all, while some of the other voices that arose during the post-"Howl" renaissance of the New American Poetry have become stale or quaint, Snyder's use of a clear, direct, colloquial but literature-responsive language made it possible for his concerns to reach, touch, and move a substantial audience through his poetry.

Snyder's varied interests have given him extensive material for his poems, but the appeal of his work is not dependent on a program calculated to educate or persuade. Much more than argument, the poetry is an outgrowth of the processes of Snyder's life—his work, his family, his intellectual and athletic interests, his cultural convictions, and his rapport with the landscape. He has been able to illustrate effectively how art and life can be intertwined in a reciprocal interchange that enriches and expands both realms, and in this he joins Herman Melville (the sailor), Henry David Thoreau (the naturalist), Ralph Waldo Emerson (the philosopher and teacher), and Walt Whitman (the celebrator) in a line of America artists whose work was, in a profound sense, the spiritual and aesthetic expression of their lives' focus. *Turtle Island* won the Pulitzer Prize in 1975.

Biography

Gary Snyder was born in San Francisco in 1930, the son of Harold Alton and Lois Wilkie Snyder. His parents moved back to their native Pacific Northwest in 1932, where they settled on a dairy farm near Puget Sound in Washington. Snyder's mother moved to Portland, Oregon, to work as a newspaperwoman when Snyder was twelve and reared Snyder and his younger sister Anthea as a single parent, insisting that Snyder commute downtown to attend Lincoln High, the most intellectually demanding school in the Portland system. In 1947, he received a scholarship to Reed College, where he devised a unique major in anthropology and literature. His first poems were published in the Reed College literary magazine. Upon graduation from Reed, Snyder began graduate studies at Indiana University before transferring to the University of California at Berkeley. During the summers of the years he pursued graduate work, he took a job first as a fire-watcher in the Cascade mountains and later, after he was fired in the McCarthy-era hysteria of 1954, as a choker-setter for the Warm Springs Lumber Company.

That fall, Snyder met Allen Ginsberg and Jack Kerouac and became involved in the exploding art scene in San Francisco, where he took part in the historic Six Gallery reading where Ginsberg read "Howl" in public for the first time. Snyder followed this extraordinary performance with his own poetry in a very different vein and was also successful in capturing the attention of the audience. He and Kerouac shared a cabin in Mill Valley, California, through that winter and spring, and then Snyder traveled to Kyoto, Japan, to take up residence in a Zen temple, beginning a twelve-year sojourn in Japan. His translations from the Chinese poet Hanshan, who lived in the seventh century, were published in the *Evergreen Review* in 1958 as "Cold Mountain Poems," and his first collection, *Riprap*, was published by Cid Corman's Origin Press in Japan in 1959.

Working as a part-time translator and researcher of Buddhist texts, Snyder eventually became a student of Rinzai Zen under Oda Sesso, Roshi (master), and established contacts with activist groups concerned with ecology, women's issues, and world peace. His next collection, *Myths and Texts*, was published in 1960, the same year he married the poet Joanne Kyger. In 1962, he traveled to India with Ginsberg, Peter Orlovsky, and Kyger, and his association with the poet Nanao Sakaki drew him into artistic circles in Tokyo in 1964. He returned to the United States to teach at Berkeley in 1965, won a Bollingen grant, and returned to Japan. His marriage with Kyger was over when he met Masa Uehara, a graduate student in English, and they were married in 1967.

With his wife and his son, Kai, who was born in Kyoto, Snyder returned to the Western Hemisphere, settling in the northern Sierra Nevada mountains, where he built a home (called "Kitkitdizze," meaning "mountain misery") in 1970 with a crew of friends. His first book of poems reflecting his commitment to his native country, *Turtle Island* (from an old Native American

name for the continent), was published in 1974 and won the Pulitzer Prize. During this time, Snyder was traveling to universities three or four months a year to read poetry, working on the needs of his immediate mountain community and serving the state of California as the chairman of its Arts Council. In 1985, he joined the English department at the University of California at Davis, where he taught literature and ecological matters, and he began to travel widely, visiting Hawaii, Alaska, China, and parts of Europe to speak "on the specifics of Buddhist meditation, ecological practice, language and poetics, and bioregional politics." In 1988, he was divorced from Masa Uehara and married Carole Koda, and in 1990, he completed a book that presented a program for personal renewal and planetary conservation called *The Practice of the Wild*. The following year, a compilation of comments, reminiscences, poems, and assorted other statements was published by the Sierra Club under the title *Gary Snyder: Dimensions of a Life* in celebration of the poet's sixtieth birthday. In his seventh decade, Snyder continued to work on his "poem of process," *Mountains and Rivers Without End*, and to train students at Davis to deal with environmental crises.

Analysis

Throughout his verse Snyder fuses elements of American transcendentalism, Native American culture, and Asian philosophy in an effort to express the spiritual and ecological unity of humankind and nature. The source of his love for Indian tribal culture and wilderness adventure is the American West. With his backwoods experience, gained through a variety of jobs in the forests of the Pacific Northwest, he is the modern-day equivalent of the American frontiersman who desires to live in harmony with the natural world.

Among many evocative statements about his life and work, a particularly crucial one is Snyder's claim that

> As a poet, I hold the most archaic values on earth. They go back to the late Paleolithic; the fertility of the soil, the magic of animals; the power-vision in solitude, the terrifying initiation and rebirth; the love and ecstasy of the dance, the common work of the tribe.

The social and philosophical principles he has expressed are the fundamental credo of his convictions as a man and an artist. He uses the word "archaic" to suggest "primal" or "original"—the archetype or first pattern from which others may evolve. His citation of the late Paleolithic era as source-ground stems from his belief that essential lessons concerning human consciousness have been learned and then lost. Thus Snyder devotes much time to the study of ancient (and primitive) cultures. The values he holds stand behind and direct his poetry, as it is drawn from his studies and experiences. His values include a respect for land as the source of life and the means of sustaining it; a respect for all sentient creatures and for the animalistic instincts of humans; a recognition of the necessity for the artist to resist social pressure in order to discover and develop power from within; an acknowledgment of the necessity for participation in both communal ritual and individual exploration of the depths of the subconscious to transcend the mundane and risk the extraordinary; an acceptance of the body and the senses—the physical capabilities, pleasures, and demands of the skin; and a feeling for the shared labor of the community, another version of "the real work" that unites the individual with a larger sense and source of meaning. The concept of poet as solitary singer or as enlightened visionary is insufficient without the complex of relationships that joins the local, the bioregional, and ultimately the planetary in an interdependent chain of reliance, support, and enlightened use of resources.

Snyder's first two collections, *Riprap* and *Cold Mountain Poems*—which were published together initially in 1965 and reached a "fourth incarnation" in 1990—are evidence of the writing and thinking that Snyder had been doing through the mid-1950's. *Riprap* took shape while Snyder was working on a back-country trail crew in 1955, and its title is at first a description of "stone laid on steep, slick rock to make a trail for horses in the mountains," then a symbol of the interlinkage of objects in a region and a figure for the placement of words in a poetic structure. It serves to connect language and action, reflective thought and the work that generates it. The poems in the collection are dedicated to the men with whom Snyder worked, the "community" of cohesion and effort he joined, men who knew the requirements of the land and who transmitted their skills through demonstration. *Riprap* includes elements of the oral tradition Snyder intersected, and the title "celebrates the work of the hands" while some of the poems "run the risk of invisibility" since they tried "for surface simplicity set with unsettling depths." Poems like "Above Pate Valley" and "Piute Creek" begin with direct description of landscape and move toward an almost cosmic perspective concerning the passage of time across the land over geological epochs. The specific and the eternal coalesce:

Hill beyond hill, folded and twisted
Tough trees crammed
In thin stone fractures
A huge moon on it all, is too much.
The mind wanders. A million
Summers, night air still and the rocks
Warm. Sky over endless mountains.
All the junk that goes with being human
Drops away, hard rock wavers.

Poetry, as Snyder put it in "Burning: No. 13" from *Myths and Texts*, is "a riprap on the slick road of metaphysics," helping one find meaning and explaining why one reads "Milton and Firelight" and finds new versions of hell and "the wheeling sky" in the Sierras.

The *Cold Mountain Poems* are "translations" (in the Poundian sense) from Han-shan, a hermit and poet of the T'ang dynasty, and they represent Snyder's identification with a kind of nature prophet at home in the wild as well as his inclination to isolate himself from those aspects of American (or Western) society he found abhorrent until he could fashion a program to combat the social ills he identified. As in most effective translations, there is a correspondence in sensibility between the two artists, and Snyder's comfort with the back country, as well as his growing sense of a cross-cultural and transepochal perspective, may be seen in lines like

Thin grass does for a mattress,
The blue sky makes a good quilt.
Happy with a stone underhead
Let heaven and earth go about their changes.

Calling Han-shan a "mountain madman" or "ragged hermit," Snyder expresses through the translations his admiration for a kind of independence, self-possession, and mindful alertness that he saw as a necessity for psychic survival in the Cold War era, a husbanding of strength to prepare for a return to the social struggle. "Mind solid and sharp," he says, he is gaining the vision to "honor this priceless natural treasure"—the world around him ("the whole clear cloudless sky")—and the insight ("sunk deep in the flesh") to understand the complementary wonder within.

Written at about the same time as *Riprap*, *Myths and Texts* is Snyder's first attempt to organize his ideas into an evolving, complex structural framework. In it, Snyder's wilderness experience is amplified by the use of Pacific Coast Indian texts, which are set as a kind of corrective for the exploitation and destruction of the environment that Snyder sees as the result of misguided American-European approaches to nature. The crux of the matter is the failure of Judeo-Christian culture to recognize the inherent sacredness of the land, and Snyder uses what he believes is a kind of Buddhist compassion and a Native American empathy as a corrective thrust. The three books of the collection are called "Logging," which uses the lumber industry as an example of "technological driveness" that destroys resources and shows no respect for the symbolic or ritualistic aspect of the living wilderness; "Hunting," which explores the intricate relationship between the hunter and the quarry (and between mind and body) in primitive societies; and "Burning," which is somewhat less accessible in its intriguing attempt to find or chart a symbolic synthesis that integrates the mythic material Snyder has been presenting into a universal vision of timeless cycles of destruction and rebirth.

As Snyder defines the terms, in a preliminary fashion, the myths and texts are the "two sources of human knowledge—symbols and sense-impressions." The larger context at which he aims—the "one whole thing"—is built on the power of individual poems, and among the best are ones like "Logging: No. 8," in which the logged ground is likened to a battlefield after a massacre; "Logging: No. 3," in which the lodgepole pine is treated as an emblem of nature's enduring vitality; "Logging: No. 13," in which a fire-watcher reports a fire ("T36N R16E S25/ Is burning. Far to the west") and seems more interested in the abstract beauty of the landscape than in any specific situation; and among several hunting songs, the exceptional "No. 6," which carries the dedication, "this poem is for bear."

Snyder read the original version of "The Woman Who Married a Bear" in an anthropology text and was fascinated by the interaction of the human and animal cultures. In *The Practice of the Wild*, he laments that "the bears are being killed, the humans are everywhere, and the green world is being unraveled and shredded and burned by the spreading of a gray world that seems to have no end." His poem is placed at the convergence of several cultures and is structured by the different speaking "voices"—not specifically identified but clear from tone and context. First, in a quotation from the anthropological text, the bear speaks: "As for me I am a child of the god of the mountains." Then, a field scientist, viewing the data, observes:

> You can see
> Huckleberries in bearshit if you
> Look, this time of year
> If I sneak up on the bear
> It will grunt and run.

This relatively matter-of-fact, outside position is replaced by a tale of the girl who married a bear: "In a house under the mountain/ She gave birth to slick dark children/ With sharp teeth, and lived in the hollow/ Mountain many years." A shift has been made to the Native American culture, and what follows is the burden of the legend, as the girl's tribe goes to reclaim her. The next voice is the hunter addressing the bear:

> honey-eater
> forest apple
> light-foot
> Old man in the fur coat, Bear! come out!
> Die of your own choice!

Now the poet enters, turning the tale (text) into poetry (myth): "Twelve species north of Mexico/ Sucking their paws in the long winter/ Tearing the high-strung caches down/ Whining, crying, jacking off." Then the tale continues, as the girl's brothers "cornered him in the rocks," and finally the "voice" of the bear-spirit speaks, as through a shaman perhaps, in the "Song of the snared bear":

> "Give me my belt.
> "I am near death.
> "I came from the mountain caves
> "At the headwaters,
> "The small streams there
> "Are all dried up.

In a deft conclusion, Snyder reduces the dramatic tension by the interposition of the disarmingly personal. As if inspired by the story, he begins to imagine himself a part of the Paleolithic hunter culture: "I think I'll go hunt bears." Yet he is too solidly grounded in reality to go beyond a reading of the text: "Why shit Snyder,/ You couldn't hit a bear in the ass/ with a handful of rice." The reader will note, however, that in the poem Snyder has hit the target squarely by assimilating the different voices (as different strands of culture) into his own modern version of the myth.

By then fully involved in the bioregional movement and committed to the local community of San Juan Ridge, where he had built a home, Snyder in the early 1970's followed a dual course in his poetry. The overarching theme of his work was to protect and preserve "Turtle Island—the old/new name for the continent, based on many creation myths," and it was expressed in poems that "speak of place, and the energy-pathways that sustain life" and in poems that decry the forces of destruction unleashed by the stupidity of "demonic kill-ers" who perpetuate "aimless executions and slaughter-ings."

These poems were published under the title *Turtle Island* (1974), which sold more than 100,000 copies and won the Pulitzer Prize. Among the most memorable poems Snyder has written, the ones that explore the "energy pathways" sustaining life include the unique "The Bath," a Whitmanesque rapture in appreciation of the body that challenges the latent Puritanism and fear of the skin in American society by describing in loving detail the physical wonder of his son, his wife, and himself in a bath. The sheer glory of the body glowing with health and the radiant reflection of the natural world around them build toward a feeling of immense physical satisfaction and then toward a complementary feeling of metaphysical well-being. The frankness of the language may be difficult for some readers, but Snyder's tasteful, delicate, and comfortable handling of it makes his declaration "this is our body," an echoing chorus, an assertion of religious appreciation. In an even more directly thankful mode, the translation of a Mohawk "Prayer for the Great Family" unites the basic elements of the cosmos in a linked series of gemlike depictions, concluding with one of Snyder's essential ideas: that there is an infinite space "beyond all powers and thoughts/ and yet is within us—/ Grandfather Space/ The Mind is his Wife."

In "The Call of the Wild," one of the more overtly political poems, Snyder's anger is projected in language purposefully charged with judgmental fervor. Avoiding easy partisanship, Snyder condemns, first, "ex acid-heads" who have opted for "forever blissful sexless highs" and have hidden in fear from what is interesting about life. His image of people missing the point of everything by living in trendy "Geodesic domes, that/ Were stuck like warts/ In the woods" is as devastating as his cartoon conception of advanced technology de-claring "a war against earth" waged by pilots with "their women beside them/ in bouffant hairdos/ putting nail-polish on the/ gunship cannon-buttons."

The poems in *Axe Handles* have a reflective tone, moving inward toward the life Snyder has been leading in his local community, to which he dedicated the col-lection. His concerns do not change, but in a return to the more spare, lyrical poems of *Riprap*, Snyder con-denses and focuses his ideas into "firm, clean lines of verse reminiscent of Ezra Pound's *Rock-Drill* cantos," according to critic Andrew Angyal. The title has a typi-cally dual meaning, referring to language as an instru-ment for shaping meaning and to the entire meaning of tools in human life. The theme of "cultural continuity" is presented in terms of Snyder's passing his knowledge on to his family, friends, and readers and is explicitly explained in the parable of the title poem. The book evokes an ethos of harmony in cycles of renewal and restoration, rebirth and reconsideration. Snyder moves beyond his specific criticism of human social organi-zations in the late twentieth century and toward, in Angyal's words, his "own alternative set of values in communal cooperation, conservation, and a nonexploi-tative way of life that shows respect for the land."

The pursuit of "relentless clarity" in everything char-acterizes Snyder's life and art. His verse remains firmly grounded in the human values he sees as the fundamen-tals of existence. It is with these values in mind that Snyder defines an ethical life as one that "is mindful, mannerly and has style," an attitude that is crucial to the accomplishment of "the real work." As he has said, "In a visionary way, what we would want poetry to do is guide lovers toward ecstasy, give witness to the dignity of old people, intensify human bonds, elevate the com-munity and improve the public spirit."

Other major works

NONFICTION: *Earth House Hold: Technical Notes and Queries to Fellow Dharma Revolutionaries*, 1969; *The Old Ways*, 1977; *He Who Hunted Birds in His Father's Village: The Dimensions of a Haida Myth*, 1979; *The Real Work: Interviews and Talks, 1964-1979*, 1980; *Passage Through India*, 1983; *The Practice of the Wild*, 1990.

Bibliography

Almon, Bert. *Gary Snyder*. Boise, Idaho: Boise State University Press, 1979.

Dean, Tim. *Gary Snyder and the American Unconscious: Inhabiting the Ground*. New York: St. Martin's Press, 1991.

Faas, Ekbert, ed. *Towards a New American Poetics*. Santa Barbara, Calif.: Black Sparrow Press, 1978.

Halper, Jon, ed. *Gary Snyder: Dimensions of a Life*. San Francisco: Sierra Club Books, 1991.

Molesworth, Charles. *Gary Snyder's Vision: Poetry and the Real Work*. Columbia: University of Missouri Press, 1983.

Murphy, Patrick, ed. *Critical Essays on Gary Snyder*. Boston: G. K. Hall, 1990.

——————— . *Understanding Gary Snyder*. Columbia: University of South Carolina Press, 1992.

Snyder, Gary. *The Real Work: Interviews and Talks, 1964-1979*. Edited by William Scott McLean. New York: New Directions, 1980.

Steuding, Bob. *Gary Snyder*. Boston: Twayne, 1976.

WALLACE STEGNER

Born: Lake Mills, Iowa; February 18, 1909   **Died:** Santa Fe, New Mexico; April 13, 1993

Principal long fiction

Remembering Laughter, 1937; *The Potter's House*, 1938; *On a Darkling Plain*, 1940; *Fire and Ice*, 1941; *The Big Rock Candy Mountain*, 1943; *Second Growth*, 1947; *The Preacher and the Slave*, 1950; *A Shooting Star*, 1961; *All the Little Live Things*, 1967; *Angle of Repose*, 1971; *The Spectator Bird*, 1976; *Recapitulation*, 1979; *Joe Hill*, 1980; *Crossing to Safety*, 1987.

Other literary forms

Wallace Stegner published two collections of short fiction, *The Women on the Wall* (1950) and *The City of the Living* (1956); two biographies, *Beyond the Hundredth Meridian: John Wesley Powell and the Second Opening of the West* (1954) and *The Uneasy Chair: A Biography of Bernard DeVoto* (1974); a collection of critical essays, *The Writer in America* (1951); a historical monograph, *The Gathering of Zion: The Story of the Mormon Trail* (1964); and two volumes of personal essays on the Western experience, *Wolf Willow: A History, a Story, and a Memory of the Last Plains Frontier* (1962) and *The Sound of Mountain Water* (1969). Stegner also published a number of edited works, both nonfiction and fiction.

Achievements

Stegner has had three distinct audiences since the start of his career: the popular magazine audience; readers interested in modern American literature; and a regional audience interested in the culture and history of the American West. He began publishing short stories in the 1930's; many of them have appeared in such magazines as *Harper's*, *Mademoiselle*, *Collier's*, *Cosmopolitan*, *Esquire*, *Redbook*, *The Atlantic*, *The Inter-Mountain Review*, and the *Virginia Quarterly*. Bernard DeVoto, was instrumental in encouraging Stegner to continue writing. Stegner enjoyed a solid critical reputation as a regional American writer concerned largely with the problems and themes of the Western American experience. As a master of narrative technique and a respected literary craftsman, Stegner in turn had the opportunity to influence many young writers associated with the Stanford University Creative Writing Program, where he taught from 1945 to 1971. His students included Eugene Burdick, one of the authors of *The Ugly American* (1958), Ken Kesey, and Thomas McGuane.

Stegner won numerous honors throughout his career.

He was elected to the American Academy of Arts and Sciences and the National Academy of Arts and Letters, and he was awarded fellowships by the Guggenheim and Rockefeller foundations. In 1937, he won the Little, Brown Novelette Prize for *Remembering Laughter*. He also won the O. Henry Memorial Award for short stories in 1942, 1948, and 1950, and in 1971 he won the Pulitzer Prize in fiction for *Angle of Repose*. In 1981, he became the first recipient of the Robert Kirsch Award for Life Achievement in the *Los Angeles Times* Book Awards.

Biography

Wallace Earle Stegner was born on February 18, 1909, in Lake Mills, Iowa, the second son of George and Hilda Paulson Stegner. He was descended from Norwegian farmers on his mother's side and unknown ancestors on his father's side. His father was a drifter and a resourceful gambler—a searcher for the main chance, the big bonanza. In Stegner's early years, the family moved often, following his father's dream of striking it rich, from Grand Forks, North Dakota, to Bellingham, Washington, to Redmond, Oregon, to East End, Saskatchewan, where they lived from 1914 to 1921. East End left him with memories of people and landscapes that played an important role in *The Big Rock Candy Mountain*. The family moved in 1921 to Salt Lake City, Utah, where Stegner attended high school and began college. There, Stegner went through the pains of adolescence, and, although not himself a Mormon, he developed a strong attachment to the land and a sympathy for Mormon culture and values that are reflected in his later books such as *Mormon Country* (1942), *The Gathering of Zion*, and *Recapitulation*.

From 1925 to 1930, Stegner attended the University of Utah. He studied freshman English with Vardis Fisher, then a budding novelist, and Fisher helped stimulate Stegner's growing interest in creative writing. In 1930, Stegner entered the graduate program at the University of Iowa, completing his M.A. in 1932 and his Ph.D. in 1935 with a dissertation on Utah naturalist Clarence Dutton, published as *Clarence Edward Dutton: An Appraisal* by the University of Utah in 1936. This work fed Stegner's interest in the history of the American West and the life of explorer John Wesley Powell, the subject of his *Beyond the Hundredth Meridian*. Teaching English and creative writing occupied him for several years, beginning with a one-year stint at tiny Augustana College in Illinois in 1934. Next, he taught at the University of Utah until 1937, moving from there to teach freshman English at the University of Wisconsin for two years. He also taught at the Bread Loaf School of English in Vermont for several summers and enjoyed the friendship of Robert Frost, Bernard DeVoto, and Theodore Morrison. In 1940, he accepted a part-time position at Harvard University in the English writing program. There, during the Depression, he was involved in literary debates between the conservative DeVoto and the literary left led by F. O. Matthiessen.

In 1945, Stegner accepted a professorship in creative writing at Stanford University, where he remained for twenty-six years until his retirement in 1971. The Stanford years were his most productive; he produced more than a dozen books in this period. In 1950, he made an around-the-world lecture tour, researched his family's past in Saskatchewan and Norway, and spent much of the year as writer-in-residence at the American Academy in Rome. He was also an active environmentalist long before ecology became fashionable. During the Kennedy Administration, he served as assistant to the secretary of the interior (1961) and as a member of the National Parks Advisory Board (1962).

Analysis

Stegner is a regional writer in the best sense. His settings, his characters, and his plots derive from the Western experience, but his primary concern is with the meaning of that experience. Geographically, Stegner's region runs from Minnesota and Grand Forks, North Dakota, through Utah and northern Colorado. It is the country where Stegner lived and experienced his youth. Scenes from this region appear frequently in his novels. East End, Saskatchewan, the place of his early boyhood, appears as Whitemud, Saskatchewan, in *The Big Rock Candy Mountain*, along with Grand Forks and Lake Mills, Iowa, his birthplace. Salt Lake City figures

prominently in *Recapitulation* and *The Preacher and the Slave*, the story of Joe Hill, a union martyr. *Wolf Willow*, furthermore, is historical fiction, a kind of history of East End, Saskatchewan, where Stegner spent his early boyhood, and *On a Darkling Plain* is the story of a much-decorated and seriously wounded veteran of World War I who withdraws from society in an isolated shack on the plains outside East End.

In a much larger sense, Stegner is concerned with the spiritual West—the West as an idea or a consciousness—and with the significance of Western values and traditions. He is also concerned with the basic American cultural conflict between East and West and with the importance of frontier values in American history. Modeled after Stegner's father, Bo Mason, the abusive head of the Mason family in *The Big Rock Candy Mountain*, is an atavism, a character who may have been at home on the early frontier, who searches for the elusive pot of gold—the main chance of the Western myth. Never content with domestic life or with stability, Bo Mason, like George Stegner, moves his family from town to town always looking for an easy fortune. As a man of mixed qualities—fierce pride, resourcefulness, self-reliance, and a short, violent temper—he is ill at ease in the post-frontier West, always chafing at the stability of community and family ties. He continually pursues the old Western myth of isolated individualism that preceded twentieth century domestication of the region. He might have made a good mountain man. Stegner stresses his impact on his family and community and shows the reader the basic tragedy of this frontier type trapped in a patterned world without easy bonanzas.

In *Angle of Repose*, Stegner explores the conflict between Western self-reliance, impermanence, and optimism and the Eastern sense of culture, stability, and tradition. In a way, this is the basic conflict between Ralph Waldo Emerson's party of hope (the West) and the party of the past (the East). He also explores the idea of community as a concept alien to the Western myth. Indeed, community as the close-knit cooperation between individuals is shown in Stegner's work as the thing that ended the frontier. In *The Big Rock Candy Mountain* and in *Recapitulation*, there is a longing for community and a pervasive feeling that the Mason family is always outside the culture in which it exists, particularly in Utah, where Mormon culture is portrayed as innocent, solid, stable, and therefore attractive. Mormon life is characterized by the absence of frontier individualism and by a belief in permanence and group experience, an anomaly in the Western experience.

A third major concern throughout Stegner's work is his own identity and the meaning of Western identity. Bruce Mason in *The Big Rock Candy Mountain* is much concerned with his relationship as an adolescent to the Utah culture and its sense of community.

Stegner's fifth novel, *The Big Rock Candy Mountain* is an obviously autobiographical account of his childhood and adolescence. A family saga, the novel follows the history of the rootless Mason family as it follows the dreams of Bo Mason, a thinly disguised version of Stegner's father, as he leads them to Grand Forks, North Dakota, to the lumber camps of Washington, then back to Iowa and up to Whitemud, Saskatchewan, and finally to Salt Lake City and Reno. Family identity problems are played out against the backdrop of an increasingly civilized and domesticated West against which the self-reliant and short-tempered character of Bo Mason stands out in stark relief. His qualities, which might have had virtues in the early settlement of the West, create family tensions and trauma that cause Bruce Mason (Stegner) to develop a hatred for his father only partially tempered by a grudging respect. Bo Mason relentlessly pursues the American Dream and the Western Myth of easy success rooted in the early frontier: He endlessly pursues the Big Rock Candy Mountain.

Throughout this odyssey, the family longs for stability and community, for a place to develop roots. Even in Salt Lake City, where Bruce spends his adolescence, Bo keeps the family changing houses to hide his bootlegging business during the Prohibition period. His activities in the midst of puritanical Mormon culture only highlight the contrast between the Masons and the dominant community. Even in his later years, Bo pursues his dream in Reno by operating a gambling house.

Stegner vividly illustrates how this rootless wandering affects family members. Else, Bo's wife, representing the feminine, domesticating impulse, is a saintly character—long-suffering, gentle, and protective of her two sons. She longs for a home with permanence but never finds it. Her initial good nature and mild optimism eventually give way to pessimism as resettlements continue. Three of the family members die: Else is destroyed by cancer; Chet, the other son, who is defeated by both marriage and career, dies young of pneumonia; and Bo, with all of his dreams shattered and involved with a prostitute after Else's death, shoots himself. Only Bruce is left to make sense of his family's experiences, and he attempts to understand his place in

the family saga as he strives to generalize his family's history. In the final philosophical and meditative chapters, Stegner tries to link Bruce (and therefore himself) to history, to some sense of continuity and tradition. His family history, with its crudeness and tensions, is made to represent the history of the frontier West with its similar tensions and rough edges. Bruce, who long sought solace and identity in books, excels in school and finally follows the civilized but ironic path of going to law school at the University of Minnesota. He has, finally, reached a higher level of culture than his family ever attained. *The Big Rock Candy Mountain* has achieved a reputation as a classic of American regionalism, while it also deals with broader national themes and myths.

Angle of Repose, awarded the Pulitzer Prize, is regarded by many critics as Stegner's most finely crafted novel. The metaphoric title is a mining and geological term designating the slope at which rocks cease to fall, the angle of rest. Stegner uses it to apply to the last thirty years of the marriage of Susan Burling and Oliver Ward, two opposite personalities, after their often chaotic early married years. This ambitious work, covering four generations, is a fictionalized biography of the writer and illustrator Mary Hallock Foote (1847-1930) and her marriage to Arthur De Wint Foote, an idealistic pioneer and self-educated mining engineer.

Lyman Ward, the narrator, was reared by his grandparents Susan Burling Ward and Oliver Ward, fictionalized versions of the Footes, and is a retired history professor from Berkeley who was crippled in middle age by a progressively arthritic condition. He has been transformed by the disease into a grotesque creature who loses first his leg and then his wife, Ellen, who runs off with the surgeon who amputated Lyman's leg. Bitter and disillusioned by his wife's behavior and his son Rodman's radical idealism and contempt for the past, he retires to Grass Valley, California, to write his grandparents' biography. There he is assisted by Shelly Hawkes, a Berkeley dropout who shares Rodman's attitude toward history.

As Lyman reads through his grandparents' correspondence, he simultaneously recounts the development of their marriage and discovers the dynamics of their personalities. Susan Ward, cultured, educated in the East, and artistically talented, marries Oliver Ward, an idealistic mining engineer, her second choice for a husband. Without having resolved her disappointment at his lack of culture and appreciation for the arts, she marries him and begins two decades of following him through the West as he looks for professional and financial success in the unstable mining industry. The years in New Almeden, California, Leadville, Colorado, Michoacán, Mexico, and southern Idaho increasingly wear Susan down, despite brief interludes of stability and the frequent company of other Eastern scientists and engineers during her Western exile.

In Boise Canyon, Idaho, as Oliver's grand irrigation project falls apart, Susan falls into infidelity with Frank Sargent, Oliver's colorful assistant, and steals away to the countryside under the pretext of taking five-year-old Agnes Ward for a walk. Soon, Agnes' body is found floating in a nearby canal, and the day after her funeral, Frank Sargent commits suicide. Suspecting the worst, Oliver leaves his wife for two years until persuaded to return. For the remaining fifty years of their marriage, Oliver treats her with a kind silence and lack of physical affection, never truly forgiving her infidelity. Lyman learns that his grandparents' angle of repose was not a time of harmony but a cold truce full of human weakness. His naïve image of his grandparents based on childhood memories is undercut as he comes to understand them in a more sophisticated way. He learns to respect their strength and complexity.

Lyman's discoveries are all the more poignant because of the similarities between his grandparents' experience and his own relationship with an unfaithful wife who has broken trust and who, it is implied, will seek a reconciliation. As in *The Big Rock Candy Mountain*, the two main characters symbolize two conflicting impulses in the settlement of the West: Oliver, the dreamer and idealist, pursuing his vision of success in a world with few amenities, and Susan, the finely cultured Easterner, yearning for stability and society. Lyman discovers links between his family's past and present and encounters universals of history such as suffering and infidelity, which are more poignant to him because he discovers them in his own family history. Finally, the novel suggests that frontier values and the civilizing impulses need their own angle of repose. In essence, American experience has not yet reached its angle of rest; frontier and domestic values lie instead in a kind of uneasy truce.

A continuation of the family saga played out in *The Big Rock Candy Mountain*, *Recapitulation* is the moving drama of Bruce Mason's return to Salt Lake City to face his past. Toward the end of a successful career as a diplomat in the United States Foreign Service, Mason returns to the scene of his turbulent adolescence and the death of his family. The visit reunites him with Joe Mulder, his best friend in high school and in college at the university of Utah. Bruce was virtually a member of Joe's family for three years during the time when his father's bootlegging business threatened to jeopardize his social life.

Bruce remembers the 1920's and his adolescence before the stock market crash. Trying to find himself, he slowly remembers the time when he was an outsider in Mormon country, a time when he found many of the values that sustained him after the death of his family. Throughout the narrative, he recounts the disintegration of his family during his adolescence.

Stegner stresses Bruce's close relationship with Joe, but Bruce is emotionally incapable of meeting Joe because Bruce hates being treated as "The Ambassador," a visiting dignitary—a title that would only exaggerate the changes and losses of the past forty-five years. In a sense, Bruce finds that he cannot go home again. He would have nothing in common with Joe except memories of adolescent love affairs and youthful myths. Their past could never be altered or renewed. Stegner ends the novel with Bruce, lonely, nostalgic, and emotionally incomplete, unable to make contact with Joe and with his past in a satisfying way. Even though the act of thinking through his past has served him therapeutically, he will continue as a diplomat, making formal contacts with people, living in the surface world of protocol, unable to connect emotionally with people. As a member of the Foreign Service, never developing roots and moving from one diplomatic post to another, Bruce carries on his family's tradition of rootlessness. He is, in the end, still a drifter like his father.

Crossing to Safety introduces a new set of characters but also is about coming to terms with the past. Larry and Sally Morgan are a young couple who have moved to Madison, Wisconsin, because Larry has been given a teaching post for a year at the university there. Almost magically, they meet a personable young couple like themselves, Sid and Charity Lang, who also turn out to be very generous. In these Depression days, security is the most sought-after item, and all the young academics vie furiously for tenure. Yet the Langs (though engaged as furiously in the contest as any) bestow on the Morgans a friendship rare in this backbiting atmosphere—wholehearted, sincere, giving, and free of envy.

Ultimately, Larry becomes a successful writer, while Sid never becomes successful either as an academic or as a poet. Belying her name—for she is a strong personality at best, harsh and unyielding at worst—Charity never really forgives Sid for his failure. Yet, Stegner concentrates on the love these people have for one another through the most harrowing of circumstances.

While described as a regional writer whose works express primarily the experience of the American West, Stegner also diversifies his themes and examines their widest cultural repercussions. His best books are an incisive appraisal of such major issues as the meaning of the frontier West, the East-West relationship in American history and culture, and the persistence of the past in personal and social life.

Other major works

SHORT FICTION: *The Women on the Wall*, 1950; *The City of the Living and Other Stories*, 1956; *Collected Stories of Wallace Stegner*, 1990.

NONFICTION: *Mormon Country*, 1942; *One Nation*, 1945 (with the editors of *Look*); *Look at America: The Central Northwest*, 1947; *The Writer in America*, 1951; *Beyond the Hundredth Meridian: John Wesley Powell and the Second Opening of the West*, 1954; *Wolf Willow: A History, a Story, and a Memory of the Last Plains Frontier*, 1962; *The Gathering of Zion: The Story of the Mormon Trail*, 1964; *The Sound of Mountain Water*, 1969; *The Uneasy Chair: A Biography of Bernard DeVoto*, 1974; *Ansel Adams: Images 1923-1974*, 1974; *One Way to Spell Man*, 1982; *The American West as Living Space*, 1987; *On the Teaching of Creative Writing: Responses to a Series of Questions*, 1988; *Where the Bluebird Sings to the Lemonade Springs: Living and Writing in the West*, 1992.

EDITED TEXTS: *An Exposition Workshop*, 1939; *Readings for Citizens at War*, 1941; *Stanford Short Stories, 1946*, 1947 (with Richard Scowcroft); *The Writer's Art: A Collection of Short Stories*, 1950 (with Richard Scowcroft and Boris Ilyin); *This Is Dinosaur: The Echo Park and Its Magic Rivers*, 1955; *The Exploration of the Colorado River of the West*, 1957; *Great American Short Stories*, 1957 (with Mary Stegner); *Selected American Prose: The Realistic Movement*, 1958; *Report on the Lands of the Arid Region of the United States*, 1962; *Modern Composition*, 1964 (4 vols.); *The American Novel: From Cooper to Faulkner*, 1965; *Twenty Years of Stanford Short Stories*, 1966; *The Letters of Bernard DeVoto*, 1975.

Bibliography

Burrows, Russell. "Wallace Stegner's Version of Pastoral." *Western American Literature* 25 (May, 1990): 15-25.

Colberg, Nancy. *Wallace Stegner: A Descriptive Bibliography*. Lewiston, Idaho: Confluence Press, 1990.

Mosher, Howard Frank. "The Mastery of Wallace Stegner." Review of *Crossing to Safety*, by Wallace Stegner. *The Washington Post*, October 4, 1987.

Robinson, Forrest Glen, and Margaret G. Robinson. *Wallace Stegner*. Boston: Twayne, 1977.

Stegner, Wallace. "The Art of Fiction: An Interview with Wallace Stegner." Interview by James R. Hepworth. *The Paris Review* 115 (Summer, 1990): 58-90.

_____ . "Back to Work After Bora-Bora." Interview by Eden Ross Lipson. *The New York Times Book Review* 92 (September 20, 1987): 14.

_____ . "Wallace Stegner." Interview by John F. Baker. *Publishers Weekly* 232 (September 25, 1987): 85-86.

Stegner, Wallace, and Richard Etulain. *Conversations with Wallace Stegner*. Rev. ed. Salt Lake City: University of Utah Press, 1990.

Willrich, Patricia Rowe. "A Perspective on Wallace Stegner." *The Virginia Quarterly Review* 67 (Spring, 1991): 240-258.

JOHN STEINBECK

Born: Salinas, California; February 27, 1902   *Died:* New York, New York; December 20, 1968

Principal long fiction

Cup of Gold, 1929; *The Pastures of Heaven*, 1932; *To a God Unknown*, 1933; *Tortilla Flat*, 1935; *In Dubious Battle*, 1936; *The Red Pony*, 1937, 1945; *Of Mice and Men*, 1937; *The Grapes of Wrath*, 1939; *The Moon Is Down*, 1942; *Cannery Row*, 1945; *The Wayward Bus*, 1947; *The Pearl*, 1947; *Burning Bright*, 1950; *East of Eden*, 1952; *Sweet Thursday*, 1954; *The Short Reign of Pippen IV*, 1957; *The Winter of Our Discontent*, 1961; *Acts of King Arthur and His Noble Knights*, 1976.

Other literary forms

John Steinbeck published two story collections and a few other uncollected or separately printed stories. His modern English translations of Sir Thomas Malory's Arthurian tales were published posthumously in 1976. Three plays he adapted from his novels were published as well as performed on Broadway: *Of Mice and Men* (pb. 1938), *The Moon Is Down* (pb. 1943), and *Burning Bright* (pb. 1951). Three of the six film treatments or screenplays he wrote also were produced as films: *Lifeboat* (1944), *The Pearl* (1945), and *The Red Pony* (1949). His nonfiction was voluminous, and much of it remains uncollected. The more important nonfiction books include *Sea of Cortez* (1941), *Bombs Away* (1942), *A Russian Journal* (1948), *Once There Was a War* (1958), *Travels with Charley* (1962), *America and Americans* (1966), *Journal of a Novel* (1969), and *Steinbeck: A Life in Letters* (1975).

Achievements

From the publication of his first best-seller, *Tortilla Flat*, Steinbeck was a popular and widely respected American writer. His three earlier novels were virtually ignored, but the five books of fiction published between 1935 and 1939 made him the most important literary spokesperson for the Depression decade. *In Dubious Battle*, *The Red Pony*, and *Of Mice and Men* established him as a serious writer, and his masterwork, *The Grapes of Wrath*, confirmed him as a major talent. During these years, his popular and critical success rivaled that of any of his contemporaries.

Although his immense popularity and public recognition and the impressive sales of his works persisted throughout his career, Steinbeck's critical success waned after *The Grapes of Wrath*, reaching a nadir at his death in 1968, despite his 1962 Nobel Prize in Literature. During World War II, his development as a novelist faltered for many reasons, and Steinbeck never recovered his artistic momentum. Even *East of Eden*, the work he thought his masterpiece, proved an artistic and critical failure though a popular success. Since his death, Steinbeck remains widely read, both in America and abroad, while his critical reputation has enjoyed a modest revival. Undoubtedly the appreciation of his considerable talents will continue to develop, as few writers have better celebrated the American Dream or traced the dark lineaments of the American "nightmare."

Biography

John Ernst Steinbeck was born on February 27, 1902, in Salinas, California. Steinbeck matured as an artist in his early thirties during the darkest days of the Depression, and his most important fictions are set in his beloved Salinas Valley. In one sense, Steinbeck's location in time and place may have made him a particularly American artist. Born shortly after the closing of the frontier, Steinbeck grew up with a frustrated modern America and, in the Depression, witnessed the most notable failure of the American Dream. He was a writer who inherited the great tradition of the American Renaissance of the nineteenth century and who was forced to reshape it in terms of the historical and literary imperatives of twentieth century modernism.

John Ernst Steinbeck and Olive Hamilton were the first-generation descendants of sturdy, successful, and Americanized immigrant farm families. They met and married in 1890, settling in Salinas, where the father was prominent in local business and government, and the mother stayed home to rear their four children—three daughters and a son, the third child named for his father. The Steinbecks were refined, intelligent, and ambitious people who lived a quiet middle-class life in the small agricultural service town of Salinas. Steinbeck seems to have enjoyed a happy childhood, and in fact he often asserted that he did. His father made enough money to indulge him in a small way, even to buy him a red pony. His mother encouraged him to read and to write, providing him with the classics of English and American literature. At school, he proved a popular and successful student and was elected president of his senior class.

After graduation from Salinas High School in 1919, Steinbeck enrolled at Stanford University. His subsequent history belies the picture of the happy, normal young man. He was soon in academic difficulties and dropped out of college several times to work on ranches in the Salinas Valley and observe "real life." His interests were varied, but he settled on novel-writing as his ambition, despite his family's insistence that he prepare for a more prosaic career. This traumatic rejection of middle-class values would prove a major force in shaping Steinbeck's fiction, both his social protest novels and his lighter entertainments such as *Cannery Row*.

Leaving Stanford without a degree in 1925, Steinbeck sojourned in New York for several months, where he worked as a laborer, a newspaper reporter, and a free-lance writer. Disillusioned in all his abortive pursuits, Steinbeck returned to California. In 1930, he married Carol Henning and moved with her to Los Angeles and later to Pacific Grove, a seaside resort near Monterey, where he lived in his parents' summer house. Still supported by his family and his wife, the ambitious young writer churned out the manuscripts of several novels.

A friend, Edward F. (Ed) Ricketts, a marine biologist trained at the University of Chicago, encouraged Steinbeck to treat his material more objectively. Under Ricketts' influence, Steinbeck modified his earlier commitment to satire, allegory, and romanticism and turned to modern accounts of the Salinas Valley. While Steinbeck's short story "The Murder" was selected as an O. Henry Prize story in 1934, popular and critical success as a novelist eluded him until *Tortilla Flat* in 1935. The novel's sales provided money to pay his debts, to travel to Mexico, and to continue writing seriously. His next novel, *In Dubious Battle*, established him as a serious literary artist and began the period of his greatest success, both critical and popular. *The Red Pony* and *Of Mice and Men* followed in 1937, *The Long Valley* in 1938, and his epic of the Okie migration to California, *The Grapes of Wrath*, in 1939. His own play version of *Of Mice and Men* won the Drama Critics Circle Award

in 1938, and *The Grapes of Wrath* received the Pulitzer Prize in 1940. Steinbeck had become one of the most popular and respected writers in the country, a spokesperson for an entire culture.

In 1941, Pearl Harbor changed the direction of American culture and of Steinbeck's literary development. During the war years, he seemed in a holding pattern, trying to adjust to his phenomenal success while absorbing the cataclysmic events around him. Steinbeck's career stalled for many reasons. He left the California subjects and realistic style of his finest novels, and he was unable to come to terms with a world at war, though he served for a few months as a frontline correspondent. Steinbeck divorced his first wife and married Gwen Conger, a young Hollywood starlet; no doubt she influenced his decision to move from California to New York. Steinbeck began to write with an eye on Broadway and Hollywood; the most important part of his career was finished. The war had changed the direction of his artistic development, and Steinbeck seemed powerless to reverse his decline.

Although Gwen presented Steinbeck with his only children—Tom, born in 1944, and John, born in 1946—they were divorced in 1948. Like his first divorce, this one was bitter and expensive. In the same year, his mentor Ricketts was killed in a car accident. Steinbeck traveled extensively, devoting himself to film and nonfiction projects. In 1950, he married Elaine Scott, establishing a supportive relationship which allowed him to finish his epic Salinas Valley novel *East of Eden*.

East of Eden, Steinbeck's major postwar novel, attempted another California epic to match the grandeur of *The Grapes of Wrath*. Although the book was a blockbuster best-seller, it was an artistic and critical failure. Steinbeck himself seemed to recognize his own decline, and in the last years he virtually abandoned fiction for journalism. He died in New York City on December 20, 1968.

Analysis

The Depression in the 1930's elicited a reevaluation of American culture, a reassessment of the American Dream: a harsh realism of observation balanced by a warm emphasis on human dignity. Literature and the other arts joined social, economic, and political thought in contrasting traditional American ideals with the bleak reality of breadlines and shantytowns. Perhaps the major symbol of dislocation was the Dust Bowl; the American garden became a wasteland from which its dispossessed farmers fled. The arts in the 1930's focused on these harsh images and tried to find in them the human dimensions that promised a new beginning.

The proletarian novel, documentary photography, and the documentary film stemmed from similar impulses; the radical novel put more emphasis on the inhuman conditions of the dislocated, while the films made more of the promising possibilities for a new day. Painting, music, and theater all responded to a new humanistic and realistic thrust. The best balance was struck by documentary photographers and filmmakers: Dorothea Lange, Walker Evans (James Agee's associate), and Arthur Rothstein in photography; Pare Lorentz, Willard Van Dyke, and Herbert Kline in film. As a novelist, Steinbeck shared this documentary impulse, and it refined his art.

Of Mice and Men was written in 1935 and 1936 and first published as a novel in 1937 at the height of the Depression. Steinbeck constructed the book around dramatic scenes so that he could easily rewrite it for the stage, which he did with the help of George S. Kaufman. The play opened late in 1937; a movie version appeared in 1939. The success of the play and film spurred sales of the novel and created a wide audience for Steinbeck's next book, *The Grapes of Wrath*.

Like his classic story of the "Okie" migration from the Dust Bowl to the promised land of California, *Of Mice and Men* is a dramatic presentation of the persistence of the American Dream and the tragedy of its failure. His characters are the little people, the uncommon "common people," disoriented and dispossessed by modern life yet still yearning for a little piece of land, that little particle of the Jeffersonian ideal. Lennie is the symbol of this visceral, inarticulate land-hunger, while George becomes the poet of this romantic vision. How their dream blossoms and then dies is Steinbeck's dramatic subject; how their fate represents that of America in the 1930's and after becomes his theme. His title, an allusion of the Scottish poet Robert Burns, suggests that the best-laid plans "of mice and men often gang a-gley"; so the American vision had gone astray in the Depression decade Steinbeck documented so movingly and realistically.

The Red Pony involves the maturation of Jody Tiflin, a boy of about ten when the action opens. The time is about 1910 and the setting is the Tiflin ranch in the Salinas Valley, where Jody lives with his father, Carl, his mother, Ruth, and the hired hand, a middle-aged cowboy named Billy Buck. From time to time, they are visited by Jody's grandfather, a venerable old man who led one of the first wagon trains to California. "The

Gift," the first section of the novel, concerns Jody's red pony, which he names Gabilan, after the nearby mountain range. The pony soon becomes a symbol of the boy's growing maturity and his developing knowledge of the natural world. Later, he carelessly leaves the pony out in the rain, and it takes cold and dies, despite Billy Buck's efforts to save it. Thus Jody learns of nature's cruel indifference to human wishes.

In the second part, "The Great Mountains," the Tiflin ranch is visited by a former resident, Gitano, an aged Chicano laborer reared in the now vanished hacienda. Old Gitano has come home to die. In a debate that recalls Robert Frost's poem "The Death of the Hired Man," Carl persuades Ruth that they cannot take Old Gitano in, but—as in Frost's poem—their dialogue proves pointless. Stealing a broken-down nag significantly named Easter, the old man rides off into the mountains to die in dignity. Again, Jody is faced with the complex, harsh reality of adult life.

In "The Promise," the third section, Jody learns more of nature's ambiguous promises when his father has one of the mares put to stud to give the boy another colt. The birth is complicated, however, and Billy Buck must kill the mare to save the colt, demonstrating that life and death are inextricably intertwined. The final section, "The Leader of the People," ends the sequence with another vision of death and change. Jody's grandfather comes to visit, retelling his timeworn stories of the great wagon crossing. Carl Tiflin cruelly hurts the old man by revealing that none of them except Jody is really interested in these repetitive tales. The grandfather realizes that Carl is right, but later he tells Jody that the adventurous stories were not the point, but that his message was "Westering" itself. For the grandfather, "Westering" was the source of American identity. With the close of the frontier, "Westering" has ended, and the rugged Westerners have been replaced by petty landholders such as Carl Tiflin and aging cowboys such as Billy Buck. In his grandfather's ramblings, Jody discovers a sense of mature purpose, and by the conclusion of the sequence, he too can hope to be a leader of the people.

Responding to a variety of social and artistic influences, Steinbeck's writing had evolved toward documentary realism throughout the 1930's. It is significant that Steinbeck first conceived of *The Grapes of Wrath* as a documentary book. In March, 1938, Steinbeck went into the California valleys with a *Life* magazine photographer to make a record of the harsh conditions in the migrant camps. The reality he encountered seemed too significant for nonfiction, however, and

Steinbeck began to reshape this material as a novel, an epic novel.

Although his first tentative attempts at fictionalizing the situation in the agricultural valleys were heavily satiric, as indicated by the early title "L'Affaire Lettuce-berg," Steinbeck soon realized that the Okie migration was the stuff of an American epic. Reworking his material, adding to it by research in government agency files and by more journeys into the camps and along the migrant routes, Steinbeck evolved his vision. A grand design emerged; he would follow one family from the Oklahoma Dust Bowl to California. Perhaps this methodology was suggested by the sociological case histories of the day, perhaps by the haunted faces of individual families which stared back at him as he researched in Farm Security Administration files.

In discussing his plans for his later documentary film *The Forgotten Village* (1941), Steinbeck remarked that most documentaries concerned large groups of people but that audiences could identify better with individuals. In *The Grapes of Wrath*, he made one family representative of general conditions. The larger groups and problems he treated in short interchapters which generalized the issues particularized in the Joad family. Perhaps the grand themes of change and movement were suggested by the documentary films of Pare Lorentz (later a personal friend), *The Plow That Broke the Plains* (1936) and *The River* (1938), with their panoramic geographical and historical visions. Drawing an archetypal theme from Sir Thomas Malory, John Bunyan, John Milton, and the Bible—the ultimate source of his pervasive religious symbolism—Steinbeck made the journey of the Joads into an allegorical pilgrimage as well as a desperate race along Route 66. During this journey, the Joad family disintegrates, but the larger human family emerges. Tom Joad makes a pilgrim's progress from a narrow, pessimistic view to a transcendental vision of American possibilities. The novel ends on a note of hope for a new American Dream.

The Grapes of Wrath was a sensational best-seller from the beginning. Some 430,000 copies were sold in a year, and in 1940, the novel received the Pulitzer Prize and the Award of the American Booksellers Association (later the National Book Award). Darryl F. Zanuck produced and John Ford directed a faithful adaptation starring Henry Fonda in 1940; the film, like the novel, has become a classic, and it gave Steinbeck's vision of America in the 1930's even wider currency.

Mexico always had been an important symbolic place for Steinbeck. As a native Californian, he had been aware of his state's Mexican heritage. For Steinbeck, Mexico was everything modern America was not; it possessed a primitive vitality, a harsh simplicity, and a romantic beauty—all of which are found in *The Pearl*. Mexico exhibits the same qualities in the works of other modern writers such as Malcolm Lowry, Aldous Huxley, Graham Greene, Hart Crane, and Katherine Anne Porter. All of them lived and worked there for some time, contrasting the traditional culture they discovered in Mexico with the emptiness of the modern world. Steinbeck also was fascinated by a Mexico still alive with social concern. The continued extension of the Revolution into the countryside had been his subject in *The Forgotten Village*, and it would be developed further in *Viva Zapata!* (1952). For Steinbeck, Mexico represented the purity of artistic and social purposes that he had lost after World War II.

This sense of the writer's personal involvement energizes *The Pearl*, making it Steinbeck's best work of fiction in the years following the success of *The Grapes of Wrath*. At the beginning of the novella, the storyteller states: "If this story is a parable, perhaps everyone takes his own meaning from it and reads his own life into it." Much like Ernest Hemingway's *The Old Man and the Sea* (1952), *The Pearl* uses the life of a simple fisherman to investigate symbolically an aging artist's difficult maturation.

Steinbeck was presented with the tale during his Sea of Cortez expedition in 1940. In his log, he recounts "an event which happened at La Paz in recent years." The story matches the basic outline of *The Pearl*, though Steinbeck made several major changes, changes significant in an autobiographical sense. In the original, the Mexican fisherman was a devil-may-care bachelor; in *The Pearl*, he becomes the sober young husband and father, Kino. Steinbeck himself had just become a father for the first time when he wrote the novella, and this change provides a clue to the autobiographical nature of the parable. The original bachelor thought the pearl a key to easy living; Kino sees it creating a better way of life for the people through an education for his baby son, Coyotito. If the child could read and write, then he could set his family and his people free from the social and economic bondage in which they toil. Kino is ignorant of the dangers of wealth, and *The Pearl* is the tale of how he matures by coming to understand them. Steinbeck, too, matured from his youthful innocence as he felt the pressures of success.

As in his best fiction of the 1930's Steinbeck fuses his universal allegory with documentary realism. Perhaps planning ahead for a screenplay, Steinbeck's prose in the novel often takes a cinematic point of view. Scenes are presented in terms of establishing shots, medium views, and close-ups. In particular, Steinbeck carefully examines the natural setting, often visually contrasting human behavior with natural phenomena. As in his best fiction, his naturalistic vision is inherent in the movement of his story; there is no extraneous philosophizing.

Steinbeck's characters in *The Pearl* are real people in a real world, but they are also universal types. Kino, the fisherman named for an early Jesuit explorer, Juana, his wife, and Coyotito, their baby, are almost an archetypal family, like the Holy Family in a medieval morality play. Kino's aspirations are the same universal drives to better himself and his family that took the Okies to the California valleys. Like the Joads, this symbolic family must struggle at once against an indifferent natural order and a corrupt social order. Unfortunately, aside

from the screenplay of *Viva Zapata!*, Steinbeck would never again achieve the fusion of parable and realism which energizes *The Pearl*.

In his Nobel Prize speech of 1962, Steinbeck indicated what he tried to accomplish in his work:

> The ancient commission of the writer has not changed. He is charged with exposing our many grievous faults and failures, with dredging up to the light our dark and dangerous dreams, for the purpose of improvement.

No writer has better exposed the dark underside of the American Dream, but few writers have so successfully celebrated the great hope symbolized in that dream—the hope of human development. Steinbeck's best fictions picture a paradise lost but also posit a future paradise to be regained. Steinbeck's best literary works demonstrate a greatness of heart and mind found only rarely in modern American literature.

Other major works

SHORT FICTION: *Saint Katy the Virgin*, 1936; *The Long Valley*, 1938.
PLAYS: *Of Mice and Men*, 1938; *The Moon Is Down*, 1943; *Burning Bright*, 1951.
SCREENPLAYS: *The Forgotten Village*, 1941; *Lifeboat*, 1944; *A Medal for Benny*, 1945; *The Pearl*, 1945; *The Red Pony*, 1949; *Viva Zapata!*, 1952.
NONFICTION: *Their Blood Is Strong*, 1938; *The Forgotten Village*, 1941; *Sea of Cortez*, 1941 (with Edward F. Ricketts); *Bombs Away*, 1942; *A Russian Journal*, 1948 (with Robert Capa); *Once There Was a War*, 1958; *Travels with Charley*, 1962; *Letters to Alicia*, 1965; *America and Americans*, 1966; *Journal of a Novel*, 1969; *Steinbeck: A Life in Letters*, 1975 (Elaine Steinbeck and Robert Wallsten, eds.).

Bibliography
French, Warren G. *John Steinbeck Revisited*. Boston: Twayne, 1994.
Fontenrose, Joseph. *John Steinbeck: An Introduction and Interpretation*. New York: Holt, Rinehart and Winston, 1963.
Hughes, R. S. *John Steinbeck: A Study of the Short Fiction*. Boston: Twayne, 1989.
Kiernan, Thomas. *The Intricate Music: A Biography of John Steinbeck*. Boston: Little, Brown, 1979.
Lisca, Peter. *The Wide World of John Steinbeck*. New York: Gordian Press, 1958.
McCarthy, Paul. *John Steinbeck*. New York: Frederick Ungar, 1980.
Noble, Donald R., ed. *The Steinbeck Question: New Essays in Criticism*. Troy, N.Y.: Whitston, 1993.
Timmerman, John H. *The Dramatic Landscape of Steinbeck's Short Stories*. Norman: University of Oklahoma Press, 1990.

XI

VOICES OF THE PEOPLE
Latino Writing and the American Experience

Family language: my family's sounds. The voices of my parents and sisters and brother. Their voices insisting: You belong here. We are family members. Related. Special to one another. Listen!
—Richard Rodriguez, "Aria," 1982

When we listen to the songs of America, that complex collection of tones both harmonious and dissonant and rhythms both regular and syncopated, we hear a music influenced increasingly and profoundly by Latino voices. Some of those voices belong to people newly arrived in the United States. Others belong to people whose roots in this land precede the existence of the United States itself. All of them accent American life in distinctive ways that make us Americans, a people of many peoples.

The writers whose lives and works are discussed in this chapter—Rudolfo A. Anaya, Jimmy Santiago Baca, Sandra Cisneros, Oscar Hijuelos, Rolando Hinojosa, Gary Soto, and Luis Miguel Valdez—have all made and continue to make lasting contributions to our national dialogue. One of the most important ways in which they do so is by showing how American culture contains a multiplicity of cultures. That multiplicity, moreover, includes great diversity even within the nation's varied Latino communities.

The contributions of these writers are documented and discussed in media as diverse as the journals that record the arcane debates of academicians, the bestseller lists and silver screens of popular culture, and the conferences at which schoolteachers, elected officials, and other community leaders are recognizing the importance of cultural diversity in the America of the next century. Latino literature wages a campaign for inclusion, not only on behalf of members of Latino communities but also on behalf of those of any group whose voices might not be heard. The Latino literary experience embraces all people: workers in the fields and factories, women in the home, the very young and the very old. At a time in our history when the American voice is finally concerning itself with the politics and the poetics of identity, we hear the Latino, the voice of the people, strong and clear within the choir, urging on our process of rediscovery.

Many analysts have noted the importance of coming-of-age stories, *Bildungsromane*, memoirs, and narratives of self in Latino literature. Fittingly, the theme of individual development reflects the Latino struggle for inclusion in the canon of American literature. Latino writers have long understood that individual members of any community need access to representations of their ethnicity to reinforce self-esteem as well as tolerance for others. Providing that access, however, is more complicated than simply sitting down to write a novel or a play that reflects the experiences of Chicanos, Cubans, or Puerto Ricans in America. Because of what Rudolfo Anaya terms the "censorship of neglect," the representations of Latino culture that do exist have had a difficult time finding their way to bookstores and libraries, let alone high school and college reading lists.

The scarcity of Latino representation, and the attempt by the writers discussed in this chapter to alleviate this poverty, speak to a skirmish in what Harold Augenbraum and Ilan Stavans, the editors of the collection *Growing up Latino: Reflections on Life in the United States* (1993), describe as America's fondness for "culture wars." The importance of a culture war for Latino writers, according to Augenbraum and Stavans, is the eradication of the perception that Latinos in America are a "monolithic" or even "amorphous" group. The coming-of-age story, in which the Latino or Latina protagonist undergoes a rite of passage that is grounded in the traditions and values of his or her own culture, helps to identify and reinforce the particular identities that come together to form the broader cultural category of "Latino." At the same time, however, the Latino in America must establish his or her relationship to the national value system.

This conflict between the goals of cultural retention and those of assimilation permeates Latino literature. Perhaps the paradox is best emblematized by the Cuban brothers who come to America to make their fame as musicians in Oscar Hijuelos' novel *The Mambo Kings Play Songs of Love* (1989). Cesar and Nestor Castillo's pursuit of the American Dream with Latin music is a quest that combines universal and unique passions. This is the American identity that Latino writers are helping to forge, one that accounts for the spirit of the individual, the community, the nation, and the history that binds these entities into a dynamic, expressive force.

The reclamation of Latino heritage is a major purpose of works of fiction such as Rudolfo Anaya's New Mexico trilogy, *Bless Me, Ultima* (1972), *Heart of Aztlán* (1976), and *Tortuga* (1979), and Rolando Hinojosa's Klail City Death Trip novels. These evocations of Southwestern homelands restore to Chicano history a sense of language, religion, and mythology. This work is at once literary and political, as is the strong portraiture of the individual in relationship to the Latino family provided by, among others, Hijuelos and Jimmy Santiago Baca, whose collection *Black Mesa Poems* (1989) includes a tribute to the poet's uncle ("Mi Tio Baca el Poeta de Socorro"), who recognized the link between words and action as weapons in the culture wars:

> Poet de Socorro
> whose poems roused *la gente*
> to demand their land rights back. . . .

For the Latino writer, words must equal action, the action of protecting one's ethnicity while joining it to the American identity. Latino literature that celebrates the history of family and place performs the double duty of engendering pride and tolerance by providing a source of self-definition for readers within the Latino community and helping to blend Latino ethnicity into the grain of our national understanding. In many cases, the lives and works of Latino authors have political importance that transcends the specificity of the literary mode in which they work. Luis Miguel Valdez's Teatro Campesino, for example, was founded in 1965 as an educational arm of the American labor movement. Through political theater, Valdez has been able to advance the causes of both Chicano nationalism and workers' rights. Similarly, Sandra Cisneros' work is invested with the triply political content of race, class, and gender.

Many of Cisneros' Latino compatriots successfully bring into focus the issues of cultural marginalization and economic distress. Cisneros, the only woman in the group of authors discussed in this section, has used her platform to describe the unique burdens and perspectives of the American Chicana. Her work is often mentioned in discussions that acknowledge the invaluable contributions of feminism to the politics of diversity. None of these significant historical, cultural, and political contributions would be possible, however, were the Latino writers who make them not masters of their respective literary forms. The politics of identity are advanced only through careful attention to the poetics of identity.

The writers discussed in this chapter represent the breadth of Latino literature's artistic accomplishment. Just as their works cover a vast range of thematic concerns, their use of form knows no boundary. The traditional narrative is represented by the novels of Anaya, Hinojosa, and Hijuelos, as well as the short stories of Gary Soto. Valdez's dramas have had political content (the *actos* performed in the very agricultural fields whose conditions Valdez sought to humanize), aesthetic virtuosity (Valdez won an Obie Award in 1969), and mass cultural appeal (La Bamba, 1987, was the first major motion picture to depict urban Latino culture). Baca's poetry has been recognized by peers and critics for its originality and passion. The work of Cisneros seems to combine elements of all these forms.

In *The House on Mango Street* (1989), Cisneros borrows drama's mode of direct address, the lyricality of poetry, and the storytelling power of narrative to create a hybrid form of expression and a piece of writing that, perhaps more than any other single work by a Latino writer, has captured the imagination of audiences across the many cultural divides and has taken up residence on the reading lists from which our high school and college students choose the texts that help them form their values. It is as if Cisneros, in the celebrated "Red Clowns," has created the kind of guiding voice tragically absent in the life of her heroine, Esperanza. Having been sexually abused by an older boy, the young Chicana woman wonders why there was never a voice of truth to prepare her for the moment when her world would lose its innocence:

> Sally, you lied. It wasn't what you said at all. What he did, where he touched me. I didn't want it, Sally. The way they said it, the way it's supposed to be, all the storybooks and movies, why did you lie to me?

Cisneros' bitter but poignant evocation of the need for role models to come from within the Latino community and from the information sources that document and shape our culture's disposition is a cause also taken up by Jimmy Santiago Baca, whose "Voz de la Gente" narrates the dream of a Latino voice that will unite the memory of the past and the promise of the future. In his reverie, Baca is that voice, a shaman drumming to summon his people to the river of redemption in which they will wash away the stains left by years of the censorship of neglect:

> I slapped harder, faster,
> wild weed doctor covering night with my cure . . .
> and my drum softened its speech to whisper
> sleeping to the shores
> singing us all together.
> > I heard rattling branches
> > crackle
> > as thousands of *la gente* pushed through the bosque,
> > lining the Rio Grande shore.
> Standing knee high in water, crowds swooped
> out into the shallows,
> drawn by the ancient voice of their beginnings.

The many Latino voices that sound within the American "shores singing us all together" have deepened Americans' sense of history, recalling our folk traditions, the importance of family, our connections to the land. These Latino voices remind us that an "American" identity is really one to which all classes and cultures belong, and one to which all must listen.

—*Nick David Smart*
New York University

RUDOLFO A. ANAYA

Born: Pastura, New Mexico; October 30, 1937

Principal long fiction

Bless Me, Ultima, 1972; *Heart of Aztlán*, 1976; *Tortuga*, 1979; *The Legend of La Llorona: A Short Novel*, 1984.

Other literary forms

Although Anaya is known best for his prose fiction, he is the author of several plays: *The Season of La Llorona* (pr. 1979), *Who Killed Don José?* (pr. 1987), *The Farolitos of Christmas* (pr. 1987), and "Rosa Linda," an unproduced work written for the Corporation for Public Broadcasting (CPB). He has also published short stories, poems, nonfiction, and children's fiction. His works as an editor and translator are extensive.

Achievements

Anaya has won a slew of honors and awards. *Bless Me, Ultima* received the Premio Quinto Sol literary award in 1971. *Tortuga* won the American Book Award of the Before Columbus Foundation in 1980. The Corporation for Public Broadcasting (CPB) Script Development award for the play "Rosa Linda" followed in 1982.

Biography

Rudolfo Anaya was born on October 30, 1937, in the small New Mexican village of Pastura. The harshness of the eastern plains of his birthplace—the windswept bleakness and desolation of the landscape—affected Anaya at an early age, and the influence was lasting. Later that landscape would have a powerful impact on his writing.

Anaya spent most of his life in New Mexico, the native state of his parents, Martin (a laborer) and Rafaelita (Mares) Anaya. His family instilled a strong sense of belonging in him and his brothers and sisters. The children grew up in an environment in which culture, tradition, and history were highly respected. When visitors came to the Anaya household, stories were often told. The elders would sit around the table playing cards or dominoes or merely talking, and the children would listen to their *cuentos* (stories), *dichos* (sayings), and *adivinanzas* (riddles). This oral tradition filled the children with a sense of pride in their history.

The family moved to Santa Rosa (which later be-

came the setting for *Bless Me, Ultima*) soon after Anaya's birth. Educated in the public schools of Santa Rosa and Albuquerque, Anaya received his bachelor's and master's degrees in English from the University of New Mexico in 1963 and 1968, respectively. He began to write seriously as an undergraduate student, although he never enrolled in any writing classes. He wrote three novels during this time—all of which he later destroyed. He received his master's degree in guidance and counseling from the university in 1972.

Anaya was a public school teacher in Albuquerque from 1963 to 1970, director of counseling at the University of Albuquerque from 1971 to 1973, and an associate professor of English at the University of New Mexico from 1974 to 1988, during which time he became a full professor of English.

Bless Me, Ultima received the Quinto Sol award in 1971, an award that brought him international recognition. This novel was followed by two others: *Heart of Aztlán* and *Tortuga*. Growing out of Anaya's abiding interest in oral literature was *Cuentos: Tales from the Hispanic Southwest, Based on Stories Originally Collected by Juan B. Rael*, an anthology that he translated for publication in 1980. Long interested in the short-story form, Anaya has also published a number of stories. He has written several plays.

Analysis

Anaya's writing stems from his New Mexican background and his fascination with the oral tradition of Spanish *cuentos*. The mystical nature of these folktales has had a significant impact on his novels, which portray the experiences of Latinos in the American Southwest. Yet the novels are also about faith and the loss of faith. As Anaya has explained, his education at the University of New Mexico caused him to question his faith in God, and this, in turn, led him to write poetry and prose in order to "fill the void."

Bless Me, Ultima leans heavily on Anaya's background in folklore in its depiction of the war between the evil Tenorio Trementina and the benevolent healer Ultima. In this work Anaya intersperses the legendary, folkloric, stylized, or allegorized material with detailed descriptions that help to create a density of realistic portrayal.

The novel is also a *Bildungsroman* (novel of development) about a young boy named Antonio Márez who grows up in a small village in New Mexico around the time of World War II. Most of Antonio's maturation is linked with a struggle with his religious faith and his trouble in choosing between the nomadic way of life of his father's family and the agricultural lifestyle of his mother's family.

The experiences that lead Antonio toward knowledge occur on both an external, objective plane and an internal, subjective one, and Ultima's presence hovers over both like an illuminating guardian spirit. Externally, the story contains elements familiar to many Chicano children growing up in the rural Southwest, with its tradition-bound Latino culture: the experience of a Spanish-speaking youth entering a monolingual English educational system, the religious questioning of a Catholic youth surrounded by a secular American society, and the conflicts experienced by a village youth whose aspirations seem partly oriented toward a more sophisticated urban setting. The protagonist of José Antonio Villarreal's *Pocho* (1959), for example, shares similar experiences in his rite of passage. Nevertheless, more traumatic events complicate Antonio's life and add complexity to the external plot structure of Anaya's novel.

For *Heart of Aztlán*, Anaya shifted to a third-person omniscient point of view, and this shift in turn parallels the more densely packed surface structure of the novel. While the focus of *Bless Me, Ultima* is on Antonio Márez, the narrative focus in this novel is on the Chávez family and the changes their move to the city brings to each family member. Beneath the surface, however, *Heart of Aztlán* shares the mythological themes and symbols of the earlier work.

The novel presents part of the first year of the Chávezes' life in Barelas, a *barrio* of Albuquerque, New Mexico. In that brief period the alien city ways and widespread unemployment force Clemente to shed his role as responsible provider for his family and to succumb to alcohol before he is able to tap the formidable moral center of his being and become the man the *barrio* people choose as leader in their fight for economic justice. That period sees the Chávezes' children trying to acclimate to their urban lives in microcosmic

reflections of the thousands whom technology has swept into the city.

While the changes wrought upon the family in their new environment constitute the plot of the novel, Clemente's development dominates much of its overall action. An adaptable man who leaves his village roots reluctantly but clearly knowing that economic forces beyond his control have removed the viability of their rural life, in Albuquerque Clemente Chávez faces the ultimate test of his manhood as husband, father, and man. Part of those economic forces relate to the unjust labor practices that force him and others like him into poverty, drink, and degradation. Yet Clemente's adaptability pulls through for him and his family, and, despite the hardships and near ruin he experiences, he struggles through darkness, reawakens his residual strength, and accepts the community's call for his leadership in opposing the vast sociopolitical power of their exploiters.

The exploiters are of three types: the technological giants who enslave the workers, embodied in the huge, steel water tank overlooking the railroad where most of the men in Barelas work; the Church, represented by Father Cayo who symbolizes not only the opium of the masses but their corrupter as well; and the capitalist system, with its most extreme narcissistic tendencies, captured by the owner of the *barrio* supermarket.

Ostensibly, the novel was an experiment that sought to combine mythic elements and a socioeconomic theme. It attempts to balance and to correlate the myth of Aztlán (presented in numerous symbols and archetypes) and *barrio* life in Albuquerque in the 1950's (presented in realistic details of socioeconomic conditions and the labor struggles of the time).

In attempting to weave together two discordant plots and themes, however, Anaya apparently placed himself in a difficult novelistic position. Although the novel was criticized as being "shallow" and "romantic," its redeeming features are its treatment of the urban experience and the problems therein, as well as in its attempt to define the mythic dimension of the Chicano experience.

Tortuga continues the mythic vein of the author's earlier works. It is a novel with a strong narrative line, striking realism, and a powerful theme. Critics have noted that there is an integrity and cohesiveness in *Tortuga* that were lacking in *Heart of Aztlán*. Apart from containing the rudiments of Anaya's fiction—a mythopoetic cluster of images and symbols—it discloses sharper insight and accommodation of realistic situations. Notably, Anaya returns to first-person narration,

Rudolfo A. Anaya

which seems to conform more precisely to his style. Anaya also returns to the exploration of memory and imagination, two elements that gave *Bless Me, Ultima* a magical resonance. Like the novelist's previous fiction, *Tortuga* is a story about growing up. In fact, *Bless Me, Ultima*, *Heart of Aztlán*, and *Tortuga* form a loosely tied trilogy that depicts the Latino experience in America over a period of several decades.

Tortuga is constructed around the mythic journey motif. It presents the rite of passage of a paralytic, sixteen-year-old boy identified only by the nickname Tortuga, given to him by his peers. Symbolically, the work is built around the same motif as the author's previous novels. It opens with the boy's trip to the Crippled Children and Orphan Hospital, and it traces his difficult struggle to health and eventual release from the prisonlike grip of the institution. Although his literal journey consists only of his travel from home across a stretch of New Mexican desert past the mountain to the hospital, Tortuga's passage to a physical, emotional, and spiritual health takes him through the agony of confinement within a plaster body cast (hence the nickname, which means "turtle"), painful therapy, and an anger nearly as immobilizing as his paralysis. Covering approximately a year's time, the novel also depicts his parallel passage from psychological immaturity to a wiser understanding of himself and his relation to others and, finally, to the fulfillment of his mystical destiny as the singer, the man who would not only feel the misery of the hell he lived in but also sing about it. The book's unified symbolic structure ends with Tortuga's bus ride away from the hospital, going "home."

The novel is relentless and graphic in its description of appalling diseases, amputations, and nerve-shattering cries of pain and despair. Appropriately, it also extensively explores the battered psyches of society's "throwaway children." By far, it is Anaya's most sober work and discloses a compelling tragic sense. Whereas the tragic sense is often weakened by obtrusive sentimentality in the earlier novels, in *Tortuga* it is sustained

and rivets a truth about the unconscionable disposal of human beings. Rather than being a tragic and pessimistic work, however, it exemplifies Anaya's faith in the regenerative power of love to deny victory to the forces of death. It exemplifies Anaya's compassion for human suffering and reflects his moral vision—which refuses to tolerate the absence of love and humanity in the world.

Tortuga, which received neither the popularity and critical acclaim of *Bless Me, Ultima* nor the diatribes leveled at *Heart of Aztlán*, is in several respects Anaya's most accomplished novel. Although there are rhetorical excesses and inconsistencies in the lyrical voice, when measured and used to enlarge a character's sensibility, the lyricism becomes effective.

Mythopoesis—myth and the art of mythmaking—is the crux of Anaya's philosophical and artistic vision. Precisely, Anaya's archetypical imagination is rooted in a reverence of the wisdom of the past and sees this ancient wisdom as a means toward the end of humanity's spiritual fulfillment. It is also informed by the conviction that myth is an eternal reservoir that nourishes the most creative and universal art. Anaya's conviction that harmony and the reconciliation of elemental forces are needed for spiritual fulfillment leads to the holistic philosophy that forms the thematic core of his three novels. The avenue for Anaya's accomplishment in expanding and invigorating the Chicano novel, therefore, has been myth and the mythopoetic art. His archetypal imagination richly mines indigenous materials, fuses them with poetic images and symbols, and connects the past and the present to make something new from the old.

All Anaya's novels attempt to find the answers to life's questions, doing so from the perspective of his own personal cultural background. In Anaya's view all literature reflects, in its more formal aspects, the mythos of the people, and his writings speak to the underlying philosophical assumptions that form the particular worldview of his culture.

Other major works

SHORT FICTION: *The Silence of the Llano*, 1982; *Albuquerque*, 1992.
POETRY: *The Adventures of Juan Chicaspatas*, 1985 (epic poem).
NONFICTION: *A Chicano in China*, 1986.
JUVENILE FICTION: *The Farolitos of Christmas: A New Mexico Christmas Story*, 1987 (with Richard C. Sandoval).
PLAYS: *The Season of La Llorona*, pr. 1979; *Who Killed Don José?*, pr. 1987; *The Farolitos of Christmas*, pr. 1987; "Rosa Linda" (unproduced).
EDITED TEXT: *Voices from the Rio Grande*, 1976; *Cuentos Chicanos: A Short Story Anthology*, 1980 (with Antonio Márquez); *A Ceremony of Brotherhood, 1680-1980*, 1981 (with Simon J. Ortiz); *Voces: An Anthology of Nuevo*

Mexicano Writers, 1987; *Aztlán: Essays on the Chicano Homeland*, 1989 (with Francisco Lomeli); *Tierra: Contemporary Short Fiction of New Mexico*, 1989.

TRANSLATION: *Cuentos: Tales from the Hispanic Southwest, Based on Stories Originally Collected by Juan B. Rael*, 1980 (José Griego y Maestas, ed.).

Bibliography

Anaya, Rudolfo. Interview by Feroza Jussawalla. In *Interviews with Writers of the Post-Colonial World*, edited by Feroza Jussawalla and Reed Way Dasenbrock. Jackson: University Press of Mississippi, 1992.

Bruce-Novoa, Juan. *Chicano Authors: Inquiry by Interview*. Austin: University of Texas Press, 1980.

Fisher, Dexter, ed. *Minority Language and Literature: Retrospective and Perspective*. New York: Modern Language Association of America, 1977.

Hinojosa, Rolando. "Mexican-American Literature: Toward an Identification." *Books Abroad* 49, nos. 3-4 (1975): 422-430.

Johnson, Richard S. "Rudolfo Anaya: A Vision of the Heroic." *Empire Magazine* (March 2, 1980): 24-29.

Leal, Luis, et al. *A Decade of Chicano Literature (1970-1979): Critical Essays and Bibliography*. Santa Barbara, Calif.: Editorial La Causa, 1982.

Mitchell, Carol. "Rudolfo Anaya's *Bless Me, Ultima*: Folk Culture in Literature." *Critique* 22, no. 1 (1980): 55-64.

Robinson, Cecil. "Chicano Literature." In *Mexico and the Hispanic Southwest in American Literature*. Rev. ed. Tucson: University of Arizona Press, 1977.

Testa, Daniel. "Extensive/Intensive Dimensionality in Anaya's *Bless Me, Ultima*." *Latin American Literary Review* 5 (Spring/Summer, 1977): 70-78.

Vassallo, Paul, ed. *The Magic of Words: Rudolfo A. Anaya and His Writings*. Albuquerque: University of New Mexico Press, 1982.

Waggoner, Amy. "Tony's Dreams: An Important Dimension in *Bless Me, Ultima*." *Southwestern American Literature* 4 (1974): 74-79.

JIMMY SANTIAGO BACA

Born: Santa Fe, New Mexico; January 2, 1952

Principal poetry

Fired up with You, 1979; *Immigrants in Our Own Land,* 1979; *Swords of Darkness,* 1981; *What's Happening,* 1982; *Poems Taken from My Yard,* 1986; *Martín; and, Meditations on the South Valley,* 1986; *Black Mesa Poems,* 1989; *Immigrants in Our Own Land and Selected Early Poems,* 1990.

Other literary forms

Jimmy Santiago Baca's *Working in the Dark: Reflections of a Poet of the Barrio* (1992) traces the author's development as a writer from the essentially illiterate angry convict who began keeping a journal in prison to the accomplished poet who has been invited to read his work at major American universities. Persistently probing and revealing, Baca's essays and poetic journal entries are a record of a difficult, uneven journey and a demonstration of the range and power of a mind formed through self-exploration and through experiments with varieties of self-expression. The energy and conviction that drive his works echo the "unconcealed passion" (as Denise Levertov puts it) of his poetry—qualities that are also essential features of the screenplay he cowrote for the film *Blood In, Blood Out* (1993), a brutally honest account of three young Chicanos living in a Los Angeles *barrio* in the 1980's. Baca also wrote a play, *Los tres hijos de Julia,* which was first produced in 1991.

Achievements

While Baca's poetry is very specifically centered on his own experiences, he locates himself within the ancient tradition of the poet as spokesperson for a cultural community—the Chicano Nation that has been largely ignored or submerged by mainstream media channels in the United States. Writing with an impressive command of the formal conventions and techniques of poetic expression while employing the speech patterns and vernacular rhythms of the South Valley settlements in New Mexico, where he grew up, Baca has been able to convey the conditions of life in prison and on mean streets. He has done so without losing his vision of a much more rewarding, enduring manner of living that includes the positive, inspirational aspects of a supportive family, a vital community, an artistic sensibility, a rapport with the natural world, and a connection to a historical heritage of some grandeur and accomplish-

ment. The success of his endeavors may be measured by such public recognition as a National Endowment for the Arts (NEA) Creative Writing Fellowship for Poetry (1987), the American Book Award from the Before Columbus Foundation (1988) for *Martín; and, Meditations on the South Valley,* a Wallace Stevens Fellowship at Yale University (1989), the Regents' Lecturer Award from the University of California at Berkeley (1989), the Pushcart Prize (1989), and the Border Region Library South-West Book Award for *Working in the Dark* in 1993.

Biography

Jimmy Santiago Baca was born in an adobe shack on the outskirts of Santa Fe, New Mexico, on January 2, 1952. His father, Damacio Baca, of Apache and Yaqui lineage, had moved to Santa Fe from the Estancia Pueblo to find work; his mother, Cecilia Padilla, had given birth to two other children prior to Jimmy's arrival, all before her eighteenth birthday. The family lived in ragged fashion, Baca's father often drunk and violent, his mother working, the children looked after by neighbors. Baca recalls a feeling of "this huge wave of catastrophe, carrying my family toward some unknown shore."

When Baca was two, his parents separated, and he was left with his *Indio* grandparents, Antonio and Petra Baca, until his grandmother's deteriorating eyesight required his placement in St. Anthony's Home for Boys in Albuquerque in 1957. Alternatively residing in the orphanage and on the streets of the South Valley *barrio,* Baca left the home permanently at the age of thirteen, dropping out of school as well. While working in the emergency room of St. Joseph's Hospital, Baca found a book in the reference library, *450 Years of Chicano History in Pictures.* Functionally illiterate at seventeen, he was attracted by the illustrations, and the pictures "confirmed" his identity as a Chicano. He continued to drift, eventually receiving a conviction for drug dealing and being sentenced to one of Arizona's toughest maximum security prisons. There, angry and resistant, he was subjected to lockdowns, solitary confinement, electroshock assaults, beatings, and other humiliations that reduced him to the point of "disintegration." Then, at the age of twenty, Baca stole a guard's textbook as a gesture of rebellion and discovered, in an anthology of Romantic poetry, "how sounds created music in me and happiness" even as he slowly pronounced the lines of a poem by William Wordsworth.

"A hunger for poetry possessed me," Baca recalls. He began to write with the stub of a pencil he whittled sharp with his teeth. He requested a grammar book from a friendly visitor and began to compose letters and poems for other inmates. Will Inman of *New Kauri* magazine encouraged him to send some work to Denise Levertov, then poetry editor of *Mother Jones* magazine, and Levertov accepted three poems, sending Baca a check for three hundred dollars and eventually helping him to find a publisher (Louisiana State University Press) for his first full-length book of poetry, *Immigrants in Our Own Land*, issued in 1979, shortly after Baca was released from prison.

Baca spent some time in North Carolina with a woman to whom he had written. He returned to New Mexico and worked as a night watchman, laborer, and janitor between periods of addiction to drugs and alcohol until he met Beatrice Narcisco, a therapist in a center for abused teenagers. They married after six months, and two sons, Antonio and Gabriel, were born during the mid-1980's while the Bacas renovated a small adobe home in Albuquerque's South Valley. His mother's return to Albuquerque and her murder in 1985, plus the loss of his home and all of his manuscripts in a fire, temporarily reawoke the demons of his psyche, and he found himself partially estranged from his writing and his family during the time when he was beginning to gain a degree of prominence as a writer.

The publication by New Directions of Baca's autobiographical, semiepic narrative sequence *Martín; and, Meditations on the South Valley* in 1987 convinced him that a career as a writer was possible. His relationship to his family, his neighbors, the land, and his cultural heritage is explored in *Black Mesa Poems*. In 1991, he spent some time in Hollywood while director Taylor Hackford filmed a screenplay Baca cowrote. The film was released in 1993 as *Blood In, Blood Out*, with Baca playing a small part. Other projects have included a documentary on Latino history, a trilogy of novels,

another screenplay, poetry, and essays. Baca continues to read his work and lecture at many universities.

Analysis

In his striking essay "Lock and Key," Baca describes his first effort as a writer at the age of twenty by likening his experience to the birth of his true self. "The child in me," he declares, "who had witnessed and endured unspeakable terrors cried out not just in impotent despair, but with the power of language." For Baca, the devastation and viciousness of his early life—which he has rendered with clarity and numbing force in *Immigrants in Our Own Land*—and his eventual escape from a series of "prisons" have resulted in a conception of poetic possibility that is at variance with many of the dominant modes of expression prominent in late twentieth century American writing. Baca's poetics operate from an unabashed romanticism built as a counterweight to the bleakness of his early life. Beginning with a sharply realistic assessment of what he has seen, Baca's work is guided by a vision of aesthetic revelation, cultural redemption, and social liberation. His love of the literal act of writing, which he sees as a genuinely religious experience ("Poetry sits in God's chair when God is absent") and his convictions about the exalting, ennobling aspects of a life structured by a language-shaping response to the phenomena of existence constitute a revival of the nineteenth century belief in the Romantic poet as (in Percy Shelley's words) an "unacknowledged legislator of mankind."

The pleasures Baca finds in the use of lyric language to convey emotional states, his trust in the accuracy of imagery to capture the vital essence of experience, and his insistence on the spiritual qualities inherent in the "magic" of poetry ("Image and song healing predates all medicine") suggest his deep faith in his craft, which he treats as a sacred gift, because it is more the result of a sudden discovery (or "prison epiphany") than an evolving educational process. This belief in an electric moment of inspiration akin to the Romantic's energizing "emotion" did not deter Baca from a program of self-education that has included a thorough investigation of the tradition of poetry in the English and the Spanish language. As a result, his incorporation of the vernacular speech patterns and rhythmic arrangements of the Chicano community in which he lives has given his poetic voice a singular, distinctive quality growing out of a fusion of technique, style, and subject.

While other writers have dealt with the conditions of imprisonment and its effect on psychic survival (notably François Villon, Jean Genet, and Breyten Breitenbach), Americans have generally approached the subject through film and prose fiction. Baca's early poems trace his efforts to gather the fragments of an identity that he began to salvage when he started writing poetry. His isolation in jail concentrated his attention, reversing his life on the run. In "A Song of Survival," Baca charts the path of a person who has been "losing touch with civilization" as he "traveled into oblivion, on a hunt for more/ oblivion," finally forced to look within as his life is reduced to "each particle of the cell's existence,/ the plain bed of gray steel." The realization that "all I was" had been reduced "to slave labor,/ to numbers, to dispensing with my name, a land/ without feeling" leads to a kind of existential awakening in which he accepts the necessity of applying the powers of the mind to every aspect of his imprisonment with a fierce joy that indicates his endurance and resilience. In a Whitmanesque declaration of self, "I Am Who I Am," Baca takes possession of his life by an assertion of being that recognizes the "vision I was offered." This enables him to find some grim satisfaction in his own responses to disappointment when he is turned down for parole in "I Applied for the Board" and to enjoy the minute particulars of his reactions in "Who Understand Me but Me," in which he enumerates "parts of myself never dreamed of by me." In his first book, *Immigrants in Our Own Land*, Baca begins to reclaim the community from which he has been estranged, resolving to sing "the freedom song of our Chicano dream" now that "poetry has lifted me to my feet."

As Harriet Slavitz states in her introduction to *Working in the Dark*, Baca "gives voice to the personal and inherited rage and pain of the dispossessed." By involving himself imaginatively in the lives of other convicts, he—a "detribalized Apache"—is able to reestablish connections to a cultural heritage he has glimpsed in tantalizing but incomplete fragments. Although he is held in relative isolation during the first years of imprisonment, he gradually becomes part of a convict network that includes many other Chicanos. Joining the life inside the prison to his experiences in the *barrio*, Baca suggests that "immigrants" or non-Anglo citizens are, in a sense, imprisoned by an actively hostile social structure, and he draws a striking parallel between Chicanos of the Southwest and the prisoners who will not "make it out of here as human/ as they came in." The shared strength of Baca and his "*celly*" (in "Joe"), the poise and self-composure of Stony (in "Stony, Fifteen Years in the Joint"), and the tactics for survival

listed in "When Life" present some reasons for hope in an unyielding, grim situation. In spite of these conditions, Baca's comic spirit is evident in the utopian vision of an ideal America depicted in "The New Warden." The latter stands at the opposite end of a spectrum of optimism from "On a September Day," which shows how close the abyss of despair is for everyone in the prison.

Baca's life after his release was very unstable. One way for him to begin to reassemble a life-pattern free of rage and discouragement was to begin the composition of two long, reflective, linked sequences of poems, *Martín; and, Meditations on the South Valley*. Using as a narrative consciousness the persona of Martín, a close approximation of himself, Baca gathers the events of his life as representative of mestizo experience into a modified epic of desert culture. Moving between vivid personal experience and the mythic resonance of a search for a way to come to terms with a hostile, external environment, Martín locates the home he has been looking for in the creation of a new family—his wife and children—which offers the possibility of replacing the mental torment of the past with a new series of memories fixed in poetic time. The quest Martín undertakes is marked by trial and reverses, as the recollective narrative of *Martín* shifts into an ongoing present in *Meditations on the South Valley*. In the latter the sections of the poem are framed by the loss in a fire of Martín's house (containing ten years' accumulation of manuscripts). The house is a figure for Martín's reconstructed life; the eventual rebuilding of the house is a demonstration of the power inherent in choosing to act to overcome the inertia of despair. The literal remaking of the house is drawn in an extended metaphor as akin to making a poem, and the entire process (section 27) is an emblem for a life-supporting creative act. The separate sections of *Meditations* show the flow of Martín's life in the South Valley as Baca develops a rich tableau containing neighbors, the land, the supernatural, and ancestors.

Baca includes two glossaries in *Martín; and, Meditations on the South Valley*, providing line translations of phrases and definitions of important words written in Spanish. He continues this practice in *Black Mesa Poems*, integrating the two languages so effortlessly that the hybrid culture he evokes does not seem unnatural or strained. The nonchalant mixture of disparate linguistic elements implies a tentative reconciliation for Baca, an acceptance of the coexistence of potentially volatile aspects of his life. In a poem that sets the direction of the collection, "Violence to Peace," Baca declares his desire to "diffuse the immutable core/ of vengeance in my heart." The poems that demonstrate his ability to work toward this goal shift their focus away from the specific events of his life to a more general view of the South Valley in what Baca calls "a gift of gratitude for keeping the culture alive." The poems are the work of a man drawing a breath, pausing, taking stock, weighing and measuring, and they develop a more reflective, contemplative mood. Now that he has settled in an "old adobe home" that fulfills his and his wife's dreams—a familiar motif for him of a structure as a source of psychic security—Baca has a real foundation for confronting the pain of dispossession in "Roots," the submersion of cultural exemplars in "Main Character," and the corrosive defilement of the land in "Invasion." Baca has always been able to capture the salient features of a person, and here his skills as a portraitist are highlighted in his depictions of friends and neighbors. The poems about "Perfecto Flores," about "BJ," about Juan in "Custom," and about "El Sapo" (the Frog King) are a gallery of Chicano vitality and variety. In a characteristically exuberant paean to "Green Chile," an emblematic tribute to a fundamental resource, Baca carries a pleasure with a cultural artifact into historical time.

Black Mesa Poems concludes with Baca's expression of commitment to the land of the Black Mesa, a union of the poet with a larger cosmos. Reconciled with his wild life to this point, ready for demands and necessities, Baca declares:

> I am here, scared, loving, helpful, brave,
> graying hair, meditative brown eyes, kind
> smile, angry eyes burning for equality.
> I am here

Other major works

NONFICTION: *Working in the Dark: Reflections of a Poet of the Barrio*, 1992.
SCREENPLAY: *Blood In, Blood Out*, 1993.
PLAY: *Los tres hijos de Julia*, pr. 1991.

Bibliography

Coppola, Vincent. "The Moon in Jimmy Baca." *Esquire* 119 (June, 1993): 48-56.
Crawford, John F., and Annie O. Eysturoy. "Jimmy Santiago Baca." In *This Is About Vision: Interviews with Southwestern Writers*, edited by William Balassi, John F. Crawford, and Annie O. Eysturoy. Albuquerque: University of New Mexico Press, 1990.
Levertov, Denise. Introduction to *Martín; and, Meditations on the South Valley*, by Jimmy Santiago Baca. New York: New Directions, 1986.
Olivares, Julian. "Two Contemporary Chicano Verse Chronicles." *Americas Review* 16 (Fall/Winter, 1988): 214-231.
Rector, Liam. "The Documentary of What Is." *Hudson Review* 42 (Summer, 1989): 393-400.
Rich, Adrienne. *What Is Found There: Notebooks on Politics and Poetry*. New York: W. W. Norton, 1993.

SANDRA CISNEROS

Born: Chicago, Illinois; 1954

Principal short fiction
The House on Mango Street, 1984; *Woman Hollering Creek and Other Stories*, 1991.

Other literary forms
Sandra Cisneros has published numerous uncollected poems and works of short prose as well as collections of poetry: *Bad Boys* (1980), *My Wicked, Wicked Ways* (1987), and *Loose Woman* (1994). Her writings also include literary criticism and children's fiction.

Achievements
Together with authors such as Ana Castillo, Denise Chávez, and Alma Villanueva, Cisneros is one of the literary voices that emerged in the 1980's and was responsible for securing for Chicana fiction a place in mainstream American literature. Her collection of short stories *Woman Hollering Creek and Other Stories* was the first work by and about Chicanas—that is, Mexican American women—to receive a contract with a major publishing house (Random House). Cisneros was awarded the American Book Award from the Before Columbus Foundation for her first collection of short fiction, *The House on Mango Street*.

Biography
Sandra Cisneros was born in 1954 into a working-class family in Chicago, Illinois. Her mother is Mexican American, her father Mexican. She is the only daughter in a family of six brothers, a fact that she describes as being similar to having seven fathers. Because of close familial and cultural ties with Mexico, the Cisneros family moved back and forth between a series of cramped apartments in Chicago and the paternal grandmother's home in Mexico City. The concept of home or the lack of one would later weigh heavily in Cisneros' writing. The combination of an uprooted lifestyle with an ever-changing circle of friends, schools, and neighborhoods, and the isolation that resulted from her brothers' unwillingness to let a "mere" girl join in on their play, led Cisneros to turn inward to a life of books. That time spent alone allowed an observant, creative voice to take root in the author.

Cisneros considers her career as a professional writer to have begun in 1974—the year in which she enrolled in a writing class as a junior at Loyola University of Chicago, where she would later receive her bachelor of arts degree in English. It was her tenure at the University of Iowa's Writers' Workshop, however, that proved an invaluable aid in the formation of her own literary voice. During a discussion of Gaston Bachelard's *La Bétique de l'espace* (1957; *The Poetics of Space*, 1964), in which her classmates spoke of the house as a literary symbol complete with attics, stairways, and cellars of imagination and childhood, Cisneros realized that her experience was different from that of her college classmates. Her background was that of a multiethnic, working-class neighborhood complete with drunken bums, families sleeping on crowded floors, and rats. She ceased trying to make her style fit that of the perfect, Anglo, and mostly male image that was foreign to her and, instead, undertook writing about that to which her classmates could not relate.

Cisneros' writing began to receive recognition in the 1980's. She is a two-time recipient of a National Endowment for the Arts (NEA) Fellowship for Creative Writers for her poetry and fiction. In the winter of 1982-1983, she was a resident poet at the Michael Karolyi Artists Foundation in Venice, Italy. In 1985, Cisneros received a Dobie-Paisano Fellowship.

Cisneros has used her education to foster change within the Chicano community. She taught high school dropouts for three years in a Chicano barrio. She has also worked as an administrative assistant at Loyola University, where she was involved in the recruitment of minority and disadvantaged students. In 1984, she was the literature director of the Guadalupe Cultural Arts Center of San Antonio.

Analysis
Cisneros has said that she writes about the memories that will not let her sleep at night—about the stories that are waiting to be told. Drawing on the memories of her childhood and her cultural identity—the run-down, crowded apartment, the double-edged sword of being

American yet not being considered American, the sight of women in her community closed in behind apartment windows—Cisneros' fiction avoids any romantic clichés of life in the barrio. Despite the sobering themes upon which Cisneros touches—poverty, sexism, and racism—she tells her stories with a voice that is at the same time strong, playful, and deceptively simple. Cisneros' distinctive style is marked by the grace with which Spanish words and phrases are woven into her stories. Central to her stories is a preoccupation with the house, the community, and the condition of women. Her images are vivid and lyrical. She acknowledges that she was influenced in style by the mix of poetry and fiction in Jorge Luis Borges' *El hacedor* (1960; *Dreamtigers*, 1964). Indeed, while Cisneros herself classifies her fiction as stories that read like poems, critics have not reached an agreement, labeling *The House on Mango Street* and *Woman Hollering Creek and Other Stories* alternatively as novels, short-story collections, series of vignettes, and prose poems.

The series of sketches in *The House on Mango Street* offers a bittersweet view of life in a Chicago barrio. Readers follow the young adolescent narrator Esperanza—whose name (as explained in the story "My Name") means "hope" in Spanish and also implies too many letters, sadness, and waiting—as she makes the discoveries associated with maturing. She introduces the reader to her neighbors and her neighborhood, making them as familiar to the reader as they are to her. In the title story, Esperanza explains how her family came to live on Mango Street. The family had hoped that the house on Mango Street would be like the ones they had always dreamed of—with real stairs and several washrooms and a great big yard with trees and grass.

Esperanza sadly explains, however, that their house does not fulfill this wish at all. She is ashamed of her red brick house, as she has been of all of her family's previous dwellings. She succinctly describes the embarrassment that she felt when the family was living on Loomis and she had to show her apartment to a nun from her school. She pointed to the family's third-floor flat, located above a boarded-up Laundromat, and suffered the blow of the nun's disbelieving response, "*There?*" From that moment, Esperanza knew that she had to have a house—one that she could show with pride to people as if it were a reflection of herself. She was sure the family would have such a house soon. Yet the house on Mango Street is not that house.

"Bums in the Attic" is a sketch resembling one of Cisneros' favorite stories, Virginia Lee Burton's 1978 storybook *The Little House*, in which the owners of a house on a country hill promise the house never to sell it. Esperanza again speaks of a house of her own. She speculates about the grand home on a hill that she will have someday. As much as she wants to leave Mango Street, she stresses that even in her country home she will not forget from where she came. Her house will not be a secured palace all her own; she will instead offer her attic to the homeless so that they too will have a home.

In "Those Who Don't," the young Esperanza discusses in a matter-of-fact tone the concept of being the "other" in society. She knows that people who pass through her neighborhood think that her community is dangerous, but she knows her neighbors by name and she knows their backgrounds. Among her Latino friends she feels safe. Yet Esperanza can understand the stranger's apprehension, for when she and her family venture out of the security of their neighborhood, their bodies get tense, and their eyes look straight ahead.

Cisneros' concern for the place women hold in Latino society is evident in the powerful story "Alicia Who Sees Mice." Alicia, Esperanza's friend, must rise early every morning "with the tortilla star" and the mice in the kitchen to make her father's lunch-box tortillas. Alicia's mother has died, and, Esperanza remarks, Alicia has inherited her mother's "rolling pin and sleepiness." Alicia has dreams of escaping this life, however, with a university education. She studies hard all night with the mice that her father says do not exist. With its precise imagery, "Alicia Who Sees Mice" is at once a criticism of patriarchal oppression of women and a beacon for those women who would struggle to break away from that oppression.

The theme of education and writing as a means whereby women can escape from the barrio is also found in "Minerva Writes Poems." Minerva is only a bit older than Esperanza, "but already she has two kids and a husband who left . . . and keeps leaving." Minerva's husband reappears sporadically, but their reunion usually ends in violence and abuse. Minerva cries every day over her bad situation and writes poems at night. In an act of artistic and sisterly solidarity, she and Esperanza read their poems to each other, yet at this point, Esperanza feels helpless, unable to stop the beatings. In her reply, "There is nothing *I* can do," there is a sense that Esperanza is inciting Minerva to take action for herself as well as the implication that society itself must change its attitudes.

Esperanza's passage into adulthood is not without

setbacks. In "Red Clowns," she goes to the amusement park with her friend Sally. When Sally goes off with her boyfriend and tells Esperanza to wait for them by the red clowns, Esperanza is abducted and raped by a man who tells her, "I love you Spanish girl, I love you." She is angry and sad and confused over the loss of her innocence. She cannot understand why everyone told her that sex would be so wonderful when, in fact, she found nothing pleasant about the man's dirty fingernails and sour breath. She wants to forget that degrading experience; she does not want to speak its horror. She yells at her friend Sally for leaving her, but she also directs her anger at a society that is partner to such an awful lie.

Likewise, the stories of *Woman Hollering Creek and Other Stories* offer a glimpse into the lives of women who must confront daily the triple bind of not being considered Mexican, not being considered American, and not being male. Cisneros has said that while the pieces of *Woman Hollering Creek and Other Stories* function individually, there is a single, unifying thread of vision and experience that runs through the collection. While the names of the narrators change with each work, each narrator retains a strong, determined, if not rebellious voice.

In "Eleven," eleven-year-old Rachel's birthday prompts her to consider what it means to grow older. The wisdom of her eleven years has taught her that it is the years "underneath" the birthday, like the rings inside a tree trunk, that make one a certain age. When people want to cry, she reasons, it is the part of them that is three that make them cry; when they are scared, it is attributable to the part in them that is five. For this reason, Rachel explains, she was not able to act eleven years old today in school when her teacher wrongly accused her of forgetting an ugly red sweater that had been in the coatroom for a month. All the years were welling up inside her, preventing Rachel from telling everyone that it was not her sweater. Instead, she was silent. She tried to be happy and remember that today she was eleven, and that her mother would have a cake for her when she got home. The part of Rachel that is three, however, came out in front of the class instead. She wished she were anything but eleven.

The narrator of the chilling "One Holy Night" is an adolescent girl who sells fruits and vegetables from her grandmother's pushcart. She meets a wanderer named Chaq who tells her that he is a descendant of a long line of Mayan kings. Intrigued by his story, the young woman begins to follow Chaq to his little room behind an automobile garage after she has sold each day's produce. Chaq spins mystic tales of the past and future greatness of his family's lineage as he entices the girl into her first sexual experience. She returns home to her grandmother and uncle a changed woman, barely able to contain her excitement. The young woman's secret, however, is soon discovered; she is pregnant. The family, in total disgrace, attempts to locate Chaq, who has since left town. Her uncle writes a letter in hopes of finding the man who could correct his niece's ruined life. A response arrives from Chaq's sister. She explains that her brother's name is actually Chato, which means "fat-face"; he is thirty-seven, not at all Mayan, and not at all royal. The girl's family sends her to Mexico to give birth and to avoid disgrace. It is later learned that Chato has been captured and charged with the deaths of eleven women. The girl appears unfazed by the news, however, and continues to plan her dreams of children. She becomes indifferent to love.

The collection's title story is one of its strongest. It is a story of Cleófilas, a woman reared in a small town in Mexico not far from the Texas border. Cleófilas dreams of the ubiquitous passion of the soap operas that she watches at her girlfriend's house. Her romantic fantasy is realized when she meets Juan Pedro, a Texan who wants to marry her right away, "without a long engagement since he can't take off too much time from work." Cleófilas is whisked away across the border to Seguin, Texas, a town like so many others, with nothing of interest to walk to, "built so that you have to depend on husbands."

Life on "the other side" is, at first, a blessing for Cleófilas. Texas is the land of Laundromats and dream homes. Running behind their new house is a creek that all call Woman Hollering. Cleófilas finds the name puzzling, since it is, like her, so ebullient and pretty. Her enthusiasm for her new life ends quickly, however, with a slap to her face by Juan Pedro. That slap will start a long line of abuse and cause Cleófilas to think flatly, "This is the man I have waited my whole life for." Although she always promised herself that she would not allow any man to hit her, Cleófilas, isolated at home, not allowed to correspond with her family, hindered by not knowing English, and afraid of Juan Pedro's rage, stays with him. When she begins to suspect that Juan Pedro is unfaithful, she thinks about returning to her native town but fears disgrace and does not act. Cleófilas always thought that her life would be like a soap opera, "only now the episodes got sadder and sadder. And there were no commercials in between for comic relief." She becomes pregnant with their second child but is almost too afraid to ask Juan Pedro to take her to the clinic for prenatal care. Once at the clinic, Cleófilas breaks down and tells her plight to a sympathetic doctor who arranges a ride for her and her son to the Greyhound station in San Antonio. The morning of their escape, Cleófilas is tense and frightened. As they pass over Woman Hollering Creek in a pickup truck, their spirited female driver lets out a Tarzan-like yell that startles her two passengers. On her way back to her father's home, Cleófilas catches a glimpse of what it is to be an autonomous woman.

Sandra Cisneros' refreshing style is enriched by Spanish-influenced images and phrases. In her fiction, she confronts issues of gender, race, nationality, religion, and economic status. Her characters may have come from a disadvantaged position in society, but Cisneros clearly empowers them and offers a means of confronting the status quo. She has an eye and ear for re-creating scenes particular to her Chicano heritage, yet her themes are universal and accessible to a wide variety of readers.

Other major works

POETRY: *Bad Boys*, 1980; *My Wicked, Wicked Ways*, 1987; *Loose Woman*, 1994.

Bibliography

Cisneros, Sandra. "From a Writer's Notebook"; "Ghosts and Voices: Writing from Obsession"; "Do You Know Me? I Wrote *The House on Mango Street*." *The Americas Review* 15, no. 1 (1987): 69-73, 77-79.

_____ . Interview by Jim Sagel. *Publishers Weekly* 238 (March 29, 1991): 74-75.

_____ . "On the Solitary Fate of Being Mexican, Female, Wicked, and Thirty-three: An Interview with Writer Sandra Cisneros." Interview by Pilar E. Rodríguez Aranda. *The Americas Review* 18, no. 1 (1990): 64-80.

McCracken, Ellen. "Sandra Cisneros' *The House on Mango Street*: Community-Oriented Introspection and the Demystification of Patriarchal Violence." In *Breaking Boundaries: Latina Writing and Critical Readings*, edited by Asunción Horno-Delgado et al. Amherst: University of Massachusetts Press, 1989.

Olivares, Julian. "Sandra Cisneros' *The House on Mango Street*, and the Poetics of Space." *The Americas Review* 15, nos. 3/4 (1987): 160-170.

OSCAR HIJUELOS

Born: New York, New York; August 24, 1951

Principal long fiction

Our House in the Last World, 1983; *The Mambo Kings Play Songs of Love*, 1989; *The Fourteen Sisters of Emilio Montez O'Brien*, 1993.

Other literary forms

Oscar Hijuelos is known principally for his novels.

Achievements

Oscar Hijuelos is generally regarded as one of the leading Cuban American writers. He won the Rome Fellowship in Literature from the American Academy and Institute of Arts and Letters in 1985 on the strength of his first novel, *Our House in the Last World*. His second novel, *The Mambo Kings Play Songs of Love*, won the Pulitzer Prize in fiction for 1990. That same year Hijuelos was awarded a prestigious Guggenheim Foundation grant to continue writing fiction. A feature film of *The Mambo Kings Play Songs of Love* was released in 1992 and met with modest success.

Biography

Oscar Hijuelos was born in New York August 24, 1951, the second son of Pascual and Magdalena Hijuelos. His parents had immigrated to the United States in the 1940's from Cuba's Oriente Province. Both of his parents were descended from Spanish immigrants to Cuba who had owned land and businesses. His father had an inheritance which he lost early in life. He spent his life in America working as a cook and waiter in a hotel.

When Hijuelos was three, he accompanied his parents and his older brother Joseph on a trip to Cuba. When the family returned, Oscar developed nephritis, a serious kidney disease that required his confinement in a hospital in Connecticut for two years, which created a difficult separation from his family and a loss of connection with his Cuban nature.

Hijuelos attended the City College of the City University of New York, from which he received both a B.A. and an M.A. degree. He was enrolled in the graduate writing program and studied with novelist and short-story writer Donald Barthelme. Karen Braziller, a classmate, invited him to submit a manuscript to Persea Books, a small press she had founded with her husband.

It was published in 1983 as *Our House in the Last World*; in 1990, Washington Square Press published the paperback edition.

This autobiographical first novel earned Hijuelos attention, and the fellowships and grants that followed made it possible for him to travel and write full-time. His second novel, *The Mambo Kings Play Songs of Love*, developed out of his study of Cuban immigrants in New York during the 1950's and a recurring character: the working-class immigrant whose artistic talents and ambitions force him to lead a double life. From this character sprang Cesar, the larger-than-life king of the musical and sexual arenas who works days as a building superintendent and plays music nights in Manhattan nightclubs.

Hijuelos' third novel, *The Fourteen Sisters of Emilio Montez O'Brien*, published in 1993, attracted considerable critical attention at the time of publication. However, it has not generated either the commercial or the critical success of his second novel.

Analysis

Hijuelos' fiction focuses on the ambitions of Cuban immigrants to the United States and the reality which keeps them from realizing their dreams. As a first-generation American, he confronts the conflict of being trapped between the passion and language of his immigrant parents and the demands of his new culture to make him one of its own, revealing the classic assimilation struggle of the American immigrant family through a Cuban American perspective. *Our House in the Last World*, the most clearly autobiographical of his novels, presents this dilemma through a young boy's coming of age.

Alejo and Mercedes meet and marry in Cuba, but a visit to Spanish Harlem in 1944 persuades them to leave their home for this new land. They have two sons, Horacio and Hector. On a visit to Cuba, Hector contracts a life-threatening illness; upon their return to the

United States, he must remain in a hospital in Connecticut for one year, seeing his mother only occasionally and his father not at all. The nurses force Hector to speak English, heightening his feeling of isolation from the only culture he has known. Eventually, the Spanish language and Cuba come to represent illness, the old ways, and superstition to Hector.

When he finally returns home, his isolation continues as his overprotective mother, fearful of illness, keeps him close to home. When he finally encounters the world on his own terms, he finds himself an outsider in both the Cuban and American worlds. He observes his relationship with his father deteriorate as his failure to live up to his father's macho code distances him emotionally from his father. He watches Alejo become an abusive husband, a drunk, and a dreamer looking back on his life with regrets. When Alejo dies suddenly of a heart attack, Mercedes' life falls apart. Hector is left unresolved about the attraction he has to his father's code of *machismo* and the alienation he feels from that world. Hector must sort out his dual identity and find a world in which he can be at home.

In *The Mambo Kings Play Songs of Love*, his second novel, Hijuelos continues to explore the cultural conflict experienced by Cuban immigrants to the United States. Again, his central characters are two generations of one Cuban American family. It is 1980, and Eugenio recalls a moment of glory for his father, Nestor, and his uncle, Cesar, the Mambo Kings. They appeared in 1954 on the *I Love Lucy* television program as Ricky's singing cousins from Cuba and sang their most successful song, "Beautiful Maria of My Soul." Yet this moment of triumph masks much sorrow. Nestor continues to long for his former girlfriend, Maria of the song, and is never able to be happy in America.

For carefree Cesar, who lives only for music, women, and drinking, sorrow comes in 1957 when Nestor is killed in an automobile accident. Cesar blames himself for Nestor's death and his life is overshadowed by sorrow. He gives up music but continues his womanizing and begins to drink more and more heavily. When he eventually dies, it is in the Hotel Splendour, the very apartment house where he lived with Nestor's family. The formerly fashionable hotel is now as worn out as Cesar himself.

Hijuelos successfully portrays the sadness and pain which accompany what appear to be pleasure and happiness. In this case, he has interwoven it with the experiences of the Cuban American trying to succeed in another country, another culture. To Hijuelos' credit, it is a pain that goes beyond the experience of one ethnic group and can be universally understood.

The Fourteen Sisters of Emilio Montez O'Brien is to date Hijuelos' longest and most ambitious novel. It is the story of an Irish immigrant photographer, Nelson O'Brien, who travels to Cuba during the Spanish American War. He meets beautiful Mariela Montez. They marry and return to the United States, where they settle in Pennsylvania's Amish country. Nelson takes photographs and runs the local movie theater. He also gradually loses his Irishness and becomes an assimilated American. Mariela, however, never abandons her Spanish roots. They produce fifteen children between 1902 and 1925.

The novel concentrates on Nelson, Mariela, the first-born, Margarita, and the only son, Emilio, covering much of the twentieth century in the process. The first part of the novel concerns Margarita, whose marriage to Lester Thompson ends in divorce after sixteen years. She finds fulfillment in teaching and travel, becomes the lover of a Cuban she meets in Spain, and marries a pilot and learns to fly at the age of ninety, the fulfillment of a youthful dream.

Emilio is born into a household of fourteen sisters and a father who has little time for him. He breaks free of these doting sisters only when World War II breaks out and he enlists in the Army. At the end of the war, Emilio decides to become an actor and eventually finds success as a star of B-films in Hollywood. Womanizing proves his downfall and he finds himself in Alaska, where his one meaningful romantic attachment ends with the death of his wife and baby. He finally returns to California, having overcome depression and alcoholism, to become a photographer to the stars, returning to the business that first brought his mother and father together.

In this family saga, Hijuelos creates an opportunity to continue his investigation of the process of assimilation into a new culture. As in his previous novels, the Cuban American does not assimilate without being tricked by ambition and desire into achieving conflict rather than happiness. By introducing a union of two immigrant cultures, Hijuelos comes closer to writing a novel of universal experience. The Cuban American writer edges closer to being the American writer, increasing the diversity of his unique American voice.

Bibliography

Birkerts, Sven. "The Haunted House." *The New Republic* 208 (March 22, 1993): 38-41.

Chavez, Lydia. "Cuban Riffs and Songs of Love." *Los Angeles Times Magazine* 112 (April 18, 1993): 22.

Jefferson, Margo. "Dancing into the Dream." *The New York Times Book Review*, August 27, 1989, pp. 1, 30.

Mallon, Thomas. "Ripening in Pennsylvania." *The New York Times Book Review*, March 7, 1993, p. 6.

Milton, Edith. "Newcomers in New York." *The New York Times Book Review*, October 21, 1984, p. 60.

Smith, Dinitia. "Sisters' Act." *New York* 26 (March 1, 1993): 46-51.

ROLANDO HINOJOSA

Born: Mercedes, Texas; January 21, 1929

Principal long fiction

Estampas del valle y otras obras/Sketches of the Valley and Other Works, 1973 (rev. in English as *The Valley*, 1983); *Klail City y sus alrededores*, 1976 (*Klail City: A Novel*, 1987); *Korean Love Songs from Klail City Death Trip*, 1978; *Mi querido Rafa*, 1981 (*Dear Rafe*, 1985); *Rites and Witnesses*, 1982; *Partners in Crime: A Rafe Buenrostro Mystery*, 1985; *Claros varones de Belken*, 1986 (*Fair Gentlemen of Belken*, 1986); *Becky and Her Friends*, 1990; *The Useless Servants*, 1993.

Other literary forms

Rolando Hinojosa collaborated with Gary D. Keller and Vernon E. Lattin on a biography, *Tomás Rivera, 1935-1984: The Man and His Work* (1988). He has also produced a collection of notes in both Spanish and English, *Generaciones, notas, y brechas/Generations, Notes, and Trails* (1978), about the generations of people who have lived on the Texas-Mexico border, and he wrote the essays for a pictorial book entitled *Agricultural Workers of the Rio Grande and Rio Bravo Valleys: A Portfolio* (1984). His articles, many of them in Spanish, have appeared in journals directed largely at Latino readers, although his "Mexican American Literature: Toward an Identification" (*Books Abroad*, Summer, 1975, pp. 422-430) trageted a broader audience.

Achievements

In his ambitious, multivolume "novel," the group of novels known collectively as *The Klail City Death Trip* (an ongoing work, of which several segments have been published), Hinojosa captures the ambience of the area in Texas, ten miles north of the Mexican border, where Mexican Americans, including many of his own family, have lived since the mid-1700's. Hinojosa establishes their identity as American citizens whose outlook is decidedly Mexican. Their first language is Spanish. Their allegiance is as much to Mexico as it is to the United States, although they serve in the armed forces of the latter country and pay taxes to it.

In a very real sense, Hinojosa demonstrates in his writing that the ethnic diversity of his native area is its major strength. The very texture of life in Klail City—based on Mercedes, Texas, where Hinojosa was born and reared—is derived from the cross-cultural nature of the community. Hinojosa himself is a part of both worlds, having had an Anglo mother and a Mexican American father.

Hinojosa, publishing always with small publishers, defies the usual conventions of literary production. He strives to communicate the community rather than individuals within it; therefore his writing is filled with contradictions and convolutions for which he does not apologize. He avoids the major publishers because he fears they might demand revisions that would undermine the philosophical premises on which his work is based.

Hinojosa has an encompassing aesthetic vision based upon understanding society through understanding its common people. Neither an idealist nor an ideologue, Hinojosa captures the pulse beat of a community that he depicts through the perceptions of a representative sampling of its members, defining in his writing what it is to be a Mexican American living in south Texas in the last half of the twentieth century.

Biography

Hinojosa's family lived a generation before the American Revolution in the area that eventually became Mercedes, Texas. From the 1740's, when they first appeared there, until 1845, when the boundary drawn between the United States and Mexico made them American citizens, the Hinojosas considered themselves Mexican. Hinojosa's father, Manuel Guzmán Hinojosa, like his parents and grandparents before him, was born in the United States, but his sympathies were always Mexican. Manuel fought in the Mexican Revolution. By contrast, Hinojosa's mother, Carrie Effie Smith, was the daughter of a Civil War veteran who, being from Illinois, fought in the Union Army. In 1887, he and his family moved to Mercedes. Carrie, then only six weeks old, was brought up in a wholly bicultural environment and was equally comfortable speaking English and Spanish.

Carrie became a schoolteacher and lived to be eighty-eight, long outliving Manuel, who succumbed to a stroke before he was fifty. Manuel, after trying his hand at farming, shepherding, dancing, and being a policeman, finally became the relatively successful owner of two dry-cleaning shops in Mercedes.

Rolando Hinojosa was Manuel and Carrie's youngest child. He had two sisters and two brothers, another brother having died before Rolando's birth. The young Hinojosa was sent to private schools in which Spanish was the language of instruction. His parents hoped that this sort of education would make him proud of his identity as a Mexican. This early education had a distinct bearing on the kind of writer Hinojosa would eventually become. When Hinojosa was a young boy, one of his favorite pastimes was listening to the old Mexicans in his community tell tales about the past. Through these people, he grew to understand how these border-town Mexican Americans lived, their identities and loyalties often divided between two adjoining nations.

In 1946, finishing his secondary education, Hinojosa joined the Army and, for the first time, left Mercedes for an extended period. His two-year hitch completed, he enrolled at the University of Texas at Austin. Before long, however, he was called back into service because of the Korean conflict and sent to Korea. This extended absence from Texas provided him with a view of his natural environment that he had not previously known.

His conscription behind him, Hinojosa returned to the university, which awarded him the bachelor's degree in Spanish in 1953. He returned to the border town of Brownsville as a high school teacher, whose responsibilities included teaching Spanish and Latin, along with government, history, and typewriting. Because the pay was low and the demands staggering, Hinojosa quit after a year to become a laborer in a local chemical plant, where he worked from 1954 until 1958.

In 1956, Hinojosa married and from that marriage, which ended in divorce, had one son, Robert Huddleston. During his four years as a laborer, Hinojosa devoured the classical literature of both Russia and the Spanish-speaking countries. Longing for a more intellectual existence, he returned to high school teaching in 1958. In 1962 a dean at New Mexico Highlands University in Las Vegas arranged for Hinojosa to enroll and work for a master's degree in Spanish, which he received in 1963, the year in which he married Patricia Louise Mandley, by whom he later had two daughters, Clarissa and Karen.

The newlyweds moved to Urbana, Illinois, where Hinojosa became a doctoral student in Spanish at the University of Illinois, from which he received the Ph.D. degree in 1969. Having finished his course work, he took a teaching position in 1968 at Trinity University in San Antonio, where he completed his doctoral dissertation on Benito Pérez Galdós.

Hinojosa knew that he did not wish to become a literary theorist, although his dissertation was theoretical. His chief wish at this point in his life was to write. He wanted to reflect his people by producing stories drawn from his background in Mercedes. At Trinity, Hinojosa met Tomás Rivera, a Latino novelist who had won a prize in fiction from Quinto del Sol Publications in 1970. Rivera urged Hinojosa to enter the latter's unpublished manuscript, in the Quinto del Sol contest, which Hinojosa won in 1972, resulting in Quinto del Sol's publishing his submission, *Estampas del valle y otras obras/Sketches of the Valley and Other Works*, the following year.

Few academics enjoy the dizzying advancement that Hinojosa did. He moved to Texas A&I University in 1970 as chair of the Department of Foreign Languages, a post he held until 1974, when he became dean of the College of Arts and Sciences. In 1976, he became vice president for academic affairs. He left that position in 1977 to become professor of English and chair of the Program in Chicano Studies at the University of Minnesota. In 1981, he returned to Texas to occupy the Ellen Clayton Garwood Chair in English at the University of Texas at Austin.

Patricia Hinojosa completed a law degree at the University of Minnesota while her husband taught there. In 1988, with her daughter Clarissa, she left Hinojosa and moved to California. Between 1973 and 1990, Hinojosa published nine major works of fiction, consistently resisting the temptation to show his writing to major publishers who asked to see it and publishing instead exclusively with small presses.

Analysis

To tell his stories effectively, Hinojosa has employed an unusual format. It is similar, however, to the multivolume formats that other writers have employed—notably William Faulkner, who, like Hinojosa, invented a county, Yoknapatawpha, and populated it with fictional characters drawn directly from life and depicting the community. In its conception, *The Klail City Death Trip* is not unlike Marcel Proust's *À la recherche du temps perdu* (1913-1927; *Remembrance of Things*

Past, 1922-1931, 1981). Proust's sprawling book consists of seven discrete novels, each part of the larger work. Hinojosa's still-to-be-completed work has assumed a similar format (but with something more than seven novels).

Hinojosa, however, is quite unlike Proust, whose seven novels essentially followed the conventions that readers have come to associate with the novel: sequential plot, identifiable major characters, sustained conflict. Whereas each of Proust's contributions to *Remembrance of Things Past* is written in French and in prose, Hinojosa has written some parts of *The Klail City Death Trip* in Spanish, others in English, most in prose, but one significant section, *Korean Love Songs from Klail City Death Trip*, largely in poetry.

Hinojosa's first two major contributions to his massive magnum opus, *Estampas del valle y otras obras* and *Klail City y sus alrededores*, were originally written in Spanish. Gustávo Valadáz and Rosaura Sánchez, respectively, translated them into English. Because his third book, *Korean Love Songs*, was set in the Orient, Hinojosa saw no justification for writing it in Spanish, so the book was written in English. His next novel, *Mi querido Rafa*, takes place around Mercedes, so Spanish is the appropriate language for it. Hinojosa himself, however, translated the English-language version of this novel.

Although *Rites and Witnesses* and *Partners in Crime: A Rafe Buenrostro Mystery* are set in Hinojosa's fictional Belken County, they are both in English, while his *Claros varones de Belken*, also set there, is written in both languages, with Spanish on one page and English on the facing page.

Hinojosa views *The Klail City Death Trip* as a single novel, although one has to redefine the term "novel" to classify the work in this way. Each element of the larger work is quite short, usually falling somewhere between 100 and 150 pages in length. Much of Hinojosa's writing employs a loosely conceived interview style. His chief motive is to present a community through its individual members. He shows his characters in different lights, often presenting them through different eyes. Some volumes, such as *Becky and Her Friends*, focus on one character, in this case Becky, as seen through twenty-seven pairs of eyes, including her own and those of her first husband, Ira Escobar, but, oddly enough, not of her second (and present) husband, Jehú Malacara. The latter is a major participant in the earlier *Dear Rafe*, where he is featured through the twenty-three letters he writes to Rafe Buenrostro during Rafe's imprisonment.

In *Becky and Her Friends*, which is essentially a group of interrelated tales ranging from a few lines to a few pages, each designed to present some aspect of Becky's personality and development, Hinojosa depicts the social fabric of a cohesive smalltown environment. In order to accomplish this, some of his works have more than a hundred characters in them but no protagonist. Readers do not come to know any of the characters in much psychological depth, but readers can glean quite successfully the sense of the Tex-Mex community Hinojosa re-creates.

This unique and unusual approach requires some adjustments on the part of most readers. Hinojosa's books, however, are quite easy to understand. His characters recur from book to book, so in tackling each new volume, readers encounter familiar characters. At times these characters are contradictory, but Hinojosa does not permit this to concern him. His explanation is that people and events are often contradictory. He, as author, does not attempt to manipulate his writing to make it consistent.

Realizing how bewildering his work might be to mainstream literary critics, Hinojosa has avoided them. Because his work is published by small presses, it has not been subjected to the kind of scrutiny that books published by major presses often receive. It has, however, been reviewed in the United States and abroad and has been quite well accepted by avant-garde readers in the United States and Europe, particularly in Germany.

A counterpoint of conflicting voices pervades much of Hinojosa's writing. It is from this counterpoint that he sustains the dramatic tensions that are vital artistically to the success of his work. The microcosm from and about which he writes is not a part of mainstream American literature, nor does Hinojosa wish it to be. Even when circumstances result in this author's taking his story outside his established microcosm, as he is forced to do in *Korean Love Songs*, he still writes largely about the people he knows best, the citizens of Belken County, some of them now transported to a foreign battleground.

In all of his fiction, Hinojosa is much more concerned with people and their communities than with ideologies. No more successful depictions of Mexican American life have been written than those found in *The Klail City Death Trip*. As the characters in Hinojosa's works interact, ideologies of community, loyalty, and inner conflict emerge, but it is not such ideologies that concern Hinojosa centrally in his fiction.

Other major works

NONFICTION: *Tomás Rivera, 1935-1984: The Man and His Work*, 1988 (with Gary D. Keller and Vernon E. Lattin).

ANTHOLOGY: *The Rolando Hinojosa Reader: Essays Historical and Critical*, 1985.

MISCELLANEOUS: *Generaciones, notas, y brechas/Generations, Notes, and Trails*, 1978; *Agricultural Workers of the Rio Grand and Rio Bravo Valleys: A Portfolio*, 1984 (essays by Hinojosa, photographs by Alan Pogue).

Bibliography

Calderón, Héctor. "On the Uses of Chronicle, Biography and Sketches in Rolando Hinojosa's *Generaciones y semblanzas*." In *The Rolando Hinojosa Reader: Essays Historical and Critical*, edited by José David Saldívar. Houston: Arte Público Press, 1985.

Hinojosa, Rolando. Interview by Feroza Jussawalla and Reed Way Dasenbrock. In *Interviews with Writers of the Post-Colonial World*, edited by Jussawalla and Dasenbrock. Jackson: University Press of Mississippi, 1992.

_____ . "Our Southwest: An Interview with Rolando Hinojosa." Interview by José David Saldívar. In *The Rolando Hinojosa Reader: Essays Historical and Critical*, edited by José David Saldívar. Houston: Arte Público Press, 1985.

Saldívar, José David. "Rolando Hinojosa's *Klail City Death Trip*: A Critical Introduction." In *The Rolando Hinojosa Reader: Essays Historical and Critical*, edited by José David Saldívar. Houston: Arte Público Press, 1985.

Saldívar, Ramón. "*Korean Love Song*: A Border Ballad and Its Heroes." In *The Rolando Hinojosa Reader: Essays Historical and Critical*, edited by José David Saldívar. Houston: Arte Público Press, 1985.

GARY SOTO

Born: Fresno, California; April 12, 1952

Principal poetry

The Elements of San Joaquin, 1977; *The Tale of Sunlight*, 1978; *Father Is a Pillow Tied to a Broom*, 1980; *Where Sparrows Work Hard*, 1981; *Black Hair*, 1985; *Who Will Know Us?*, 1990; *Home Course in Religion*, 1991; *A Fire in My Hands: A Book of Poems*, 1990; *Neighborhood Odes*, 1992.

Other literary forms

Included in Gary Soto's published poetry are two volumes written specifically for children and young adults, *A Fire in My Hands: A Book of Poems* and *Neighborhood Odes*. His other published works include prose memoir, *Living up the Street: Narrative Recollections* (1985), *Small Faces* (1986), and *A Summer Life* (1990); a collection of essays, *Lesser Evils: Ten Quartets* (1988); two collections of short stories for children and young adults, *Baseball in April: And Other Stories* (1990) and *Local News* (1993); and several novels for children and young adults, *Taking Sides* (1991), *The Skirt* (1992), *Pacific Crossing* (1992; a sequel to *Taking Sides*), *Pool Party* (1993), and *Too Many Tamales* (1993). Soto has edited a collection of prose memoirs, *California Childhood: Recollections and Stories of the Golden State* (1988), and a collection of short stories, *Pieces of the Heart: New Chicano Fiction* (1993). He has produced several short films for Mexican American children based on his stories. Poetry and articles by Soto have also been published in numerous magazines and journals.

Achievements

Soto's work was award-winning before his first volume of poetry was collected and published. He won an award from *The Nation* in 1975 for his poem "The Discovery." That same year Soto was awarded the Academy of American Poets prize. His first volume of poetry, *The Elements of San Joaquin*, was the winner of the United States Award of the International Poetry Forum for 1976. That year, he also received the Chicano Contest Literary Prize of the University of California at Irvine. In 1978, he was one of the first Chicano poets to be nominated for a Pulitzer Prize for his second volume of poems, *The Tale of Sunlight*. The book was also nominated for the National Book Award. Other prizes include the Bess Hokin Prize from *Poetry* (1978) and the Levinson Award from *Poetry* (1984). Soto's prose memoir *Living up the Street*, was awarded the American Book Award from the Before Columbus Foundation in 1985. His first collection of short stories for young people, *Baseball in April*, won the 1990 Beatty Award and *Parenting* magazine's Reading Magic Award and was named a Best Book for Young Adults by the American Library Association. Soto won a Guggenheim Fellowship for 1979-1980 and a creative writing fellowship from the National Education Association in 1982.

Biography

Gary Soto was born April 12, 1952, to working-class Mexican American parents Manuel and Angie Trevino Soto. Gary grew up poor in Fresno, California, next to a junkyard and across from a pickle factory. Fresno, the heart of the agricultural San Joaquin Valley, is a place Soto characterizes as a "frontier town, spreading and cannibalizing itself," where "neighborhoods are used up and abandoned." The city and his work as a migrant laborer during his childhood heavily influenced Soto's writings. Equally influential were two deaths in his family: his father's death in 1958 in an industrial accident and his uncle's death in 1957 from cancer.

Soto's early academic career was undistinguished. He had a 1.6 grade point average at Roosevelt High School. At first uninterested in higher education, Soto worked as a teen at car washes and in the fields picking grapes. Looking for direction, he enrolled at a community college and eventually at California State University at Fresno. Enrolled as a geography major, he came across the works of Beat poets Allen Ginsberg and Lawrence Ferlinghetti, as well as Donald Allen's anthology *New American Poetry*, and discovered, at age nineteen, what he wanted to do: write poetry. At Fresno State, Soto studied under the poet Philip Levine. Soto's poetry is similar in social concerns and stylistic aspects to Levine's work, which has led critics to associate Soto with the "Fresno school of poets." In 1974, Soto received his B.A. degree, graduating magna cum laude, and enrolled in graduate school at the University of California at Irvine in the M.F.A. Creative Writing Program. In 1975, Soto married Carolyn Oda, a Japanese American. In 1976, he received his M.F.A. degree, one of only four Mexican Americans (of six million living in California) to receive the degree. That year, he was also named Graduate Student of the Year in Humanities, 1976.

After graduation, Soto lived briefly in Mexico City before accepting a yearlong appointment as visiting writer at San Diego State University. In 1977, at age twenty-four, Soto published his first book of poems, *The Elements of San Joaquin*, which he had written to satisfy his M.F.A. thesis requirement. That same year, Soto accepted a teaching position in Chicano studies at the University of California at Berkeley. The birth of a child, Mariko, pushed Soto's career in another direction, toward children's literature, and was influential in his organizing a reading and writing program for children in the Puente program for Hispanic community college students. In 1985, Soto became associate professor of Chicano studies and English literature at Berkeley. In addition to his writing and teaching, Soto gives poetry readings around the United States.

Analysis

Soto was hailed by Tom D'Evelyn in the *Christian Science Monitor* as "not an important Chicano poet but an important American poet." This distinction is important to a critical understanding of Soto's work, which is grounded in the Mexican American experience but is always at odds with it, always comparing and contrasting it to the experience of mainstream America. The experience of Mexican Americans as detailed by Soto is a marginalized, alienated experience within the mainstream cultural forces—both intellectual and popular—that shape America.

In his first collection of poems, *The Elements of San Joaquin*, Soto presents a grim portrait of Mexican American life. He also establishes an image that recurs frequently not only in his poetical works but also in his short stories and prose recollections. This image is the street, a Chicano cultural marker. Soto uses it as a unifying image that provides a realistic background for the personae of his works and metaphorically represents their state of mind, as well as their oppressed existence.

In "San Fernando Road," the first poem of the book, the image of the street is one of a colorless road of gray factories that leads nowhere. The focus of the poem is

Leonard, a man among men "whose families/ Were a pain/ They could not/ Shrug off." The vision of humanity is dark and apocalyptic. The landscape is swept by dust. It is a place of waste, where toilets are not flushed and where young Mexicans are forced to work in factories that are likened to ovens. Even the beauty of the nighttime sky offers no hope. It does not allow Leonard to think about the problems of his cousin using cocaine or the woman suffering her first rape. Leonard's futile existence makes his life as barren as life on the San Fernando road, an industrial wasteland, a hopeless place that numbs the weakening body as it moves rapidly toward death. Instead of finding socioeconomic salvation in America, the land of opportunity, Mexican Americans find damnation to the lower strata of society.

In "Street," a poem in the second part of *The Elements of San Joaquin*, Soto presents a collage of realistic images that constitute a Mexican American's street, a street that the persona of the poem recalls from memory: "What I want to remember is a street,/ A wide street,/ And that it is cold." The cold refers not only to the temperature on the street but also to the street's almost hostile indifference. Soto piles up images of a fire in a gutter, stray cats running rampant, a woman with a cane tapping her way across tracks, an abandoned hotel with loud plumbing, and a forgotten jacket in a room of that hotel. The jacket is symbolic of the Mexican American Everyman, "forever without shadow/ And cold as the darkness it lies in." This Everyman is not as free as the birds that fly south, away from the cold. Instead, darkness descends, and this Everyman is posited as a Filipino standing "Under a neon, turning a coin/ in his pocket," this turning action as futile and stagnant as the position of the Mexican American on the American street where he or she lives.

The street in "Braly Street," the last poem in *The Elements of San Joaquin*, is the street on which Soto grew up in Fresno. The first stanza is a collection of memories of things discovered on Braly Street, that ants bite, matches flare, pinto beans unravel into plants, and aspirins do not cure dogs whose fur twitches. The place is a dumping ground of artifacts from the persona's past life and memories, a place covered with the blackness of soft, sticky asphalt, even as the mouths of the dead in the poem are covered with dirt. The images of blackness, death, and dirt set up in this stanza pervade the rest of the poem. Braly Street, sixteen years after the persona's childhood, is barren, a place where almond trees no longer produce fruit. Here, the persona recalls his uncle's death from cancer in 1957 and his father's death from an industrial accident in 1958. The final portrait of Braly Street is seen through adult eyes, still a place of death, neglect, and industrial despair. The persona of the poem, who has left his roots on Braly Street, comes to look upon a chinaberry tree, which still stands where his house once was, as a symbol of the poverty he knew in his early life. In this rooted tree of poverty, the uprooted persona defines the source of his dark poetic vision as the street.

The Elements of San Joaquin is a book bound by streets. "San Fernando Road" and "Street" are poems that express the oppression of the Mexican American; "Braly Street" is a more personal vision of this same oppression. All three poems deal with the elements that shape a life: youth and environment. In the final analysis, these elements can be left behind, but they are never forgotten.

In *Black Hair*, a book in two parts, Soto continues his recurring image of the street in three poems, "The Street as Frontier," "Morning on This Street," and "Under Trees." The street in these poems, however, represents Soto's changing vision and attitude, injecting hope and optimism not present in *The Elements of San Joaquin*. Critics have ascribed this change in Soto's worldview to his marriage and the birth of his child.

"The Street as Frontier" begins with a reference to "this good life," a world where the persona is "eager to/ Get down the street." The persona does not want to leave this street but is ready to take his place in it because he is looking for love: "I want—old girl,/ New girl, fired-up/ Bush to chase me/ Up the street,/ Back down, and up again." Love, even on one of Soto's streets, makes all things possible. Through love, the poem insists, one "can have it all."

"Morning on This Street" begins, like "San Fernando Road," with a gray, colorless image. Yet this is not a street of dust and despair. A falling rain damps down the dust. Inside his home on the street, the persona awakens to this rainy day in bunk beds with his brothers, one "Talking football, another/ Turning to the dreamed girl/ He'd jump from a tree to die for." On the street, the persona looks for something to do "In the absence of love." Then he sees Earl the Cartman, pulling a cart on which rides his wife, sitting under a "rough temple/ Of cardboard" he has cut for her. What is remarkable about this homeless pair is the love they share, despite the

hardships of their life: "It's for his wife/ That he lives and pulls a rope/ To its frayed end." The persona suggests that those who live in judgment of Earl and his wife are even less important to the couple than the raining sky. In love, in marriage, the persona finds hope, a reason to live: "This is marriage/ A man and a woman, in one kind of weather." The theme of these two poems in *Black Hair* is most succinctly stated in another poem from the collection, "Under Trees," where Soto writes, "Even on this street/. . . / Love is a way out."

The streets of Soto evolve as the writer evolves, still maintaining an important place in his work as he shifts from poetry to prose memoirs and short stories. In *Living up the Street*, Soto shifts his emphasis from the poverty and despair of childhood to the impact of popular culture and mass media upon the Mexican American experience in childhood as a force in direct contrast to this ethnic identity. Instead of focusing on the negative elements of the street—death, dust, and despair—Soto trains his vision on mainstream cultural forces—comics, sports, cars, fashion, and television—and explores how each shapes the socialization process of the Mexican American. These essays are a look at those on the street marginalized in other ways than merely their ethnic heritage, including young adults who are called "stupids," the victims of bigots and bullies, and children who must learn to deal with the world of work in a country where few children work.

In his poetry and prose, Soto returns to childhood in an effort to reconcile the streets of his past with his present. In The Elements of San Joaquin, the streets of childhood are hostile places that shape the Mexican American present. The streets are a hopeless place without salvation, a place that must be rejected for another place, another world. In Black Hair, the streets are tempered by love and less defined by minority-related circumstances. They become a place of hope, where people who understand their lessons can forge a future. Finally, in Living up the Street, the inescapable past is deemed escapable by a return to childhood through memory, which is used to create art, which ultimately creates stability. The efforts by Soto to live up to the past and to utilize self-help are common to Chicano writers, whose works both enrich and complicate a tradition. While the culture of Soto's work reflects the Mexican American experience, the struggles depicted are universal.

Other major works

NONFICTION: *Living up the Street: Narrative Recollections*, 1985; *Small Faces*, 1986; *Lesser Evils: Ten Quartets*, 1988; *A Summer Life*, 1990.

CHILDREN'S LITERATURE: *Baseball in April: And Other Stories*, 1990; *Taking Sides*, 1991; *The Skirt*, 1992; *Pacific Crossing*, 1992 (a sequel to *Taking Sides*); *Local News*, 1993; *Pool Party*, 1993; *Too Many Tamales*, 1993.
EDITED TEXT: *California Childhood: Recollections and Stories of the Golden State*, 1988; *Pieces of the Heart: New Chicano Fiction*, 1993.

Bibliography

Bruce-Novoa, Juan. "Patricide and Resurrection: Gary Soto." In *Chicano Poetry: A Response to Chaos*. Austin: University of Texas Press, 1982.

Bus, Heiner. "Sophisticated Spontaneity: The Art of Life in Gary Soto's *Living up the Street.*" *The Americas Review: A Review of Hispanic Literature and Art of the USA* 16 (Fall/Winter, 1988): 188-197.

De la Fuentes, Patricia. "Ambiguity in the Poetry of Gary Soto." *Revista Chicano-Riquena* 11 (1983): 34-39.

_____. "Entropy in the Poetry of Gary Soto: The Dialectics of Violence." *Discurso Literario: Revista de Temas Hispanicos* 5 (Autumn, 1987): 111-120.

_____. "Mutability and Stasis: Images of Time in Gary Soto's *Black Hair.*" *The Americas Review: A Review of Hispanic Literature and Art of the USA* 17 (Spring, 1989): 100-107.

Needham, Nancy. "Meet Gary Soto: Always Close to Home." *NEA Today* 11, no. 4 (November, 1992): 9.

Olivares, Julian. "The Streets of Gary Soto." *Latin American Literary Review* 18 (January-June, 1990): 32-49.

Soto, Gary. Interview by Ernesto Trejo. *Revista Chicano-Riquena* 11, no. 2 (Summer, 1983): 25-33.

Torres, Hector A. "Genre-Shifting, Political Discourse, and the Dialectics of Narrative Syntax in Gary Soto's *Living up the Street.*" *Critica: A Journal of Critical Essays* 2 (Spring, 1988): 39-57.

Varela-Ibarra, Jose. "Gary Soto." In *Chicano Literature: A Reference Guide*, edited by Julio A. Martinez and Francisco A. Lomeli. Westport, Conn.: Greenwood Press, 1985.

LUIS MIGUEL VALDEZ

Born: Delano, California; June 26, 1940

Principal drama

The Theft, pr. 1961; *The Shrunken Head of Pancho Villa*, pr. 1965, pb. 1967; *Las dos caras del patroncito*, pr. 1965, pb. 1971; *La quinta temporada*, pr. 1966, pb. 1971; *Los vendidos*, pr. 1967, pb. 1971; *Dark Root of a Scream*, pr. 1967, pb. 1973; *La conquista de México*, pr. 1968, pb. 1971 (puppet play); *No saco nada de la escuela*, pr. 1969, pb. 1971; *The Militants*, pr. 1969, pb. 1971; *Vietnam campesino*, pr. 1970, pb. 1971; *Huelguistas*, pr. 1970, pb. 1971; *Bernabé*, pr. 1970, pb. 1976; *Soldado razo*, pr., pb. 1971; *Actos*, pb. 1971 (includes *Las dos caras del patroncito*, *La quinta temporada*, *Los vendidos*, *La conquista de México*, *No saco nada de la escuela*, *The Militants*, *Vietnam campesino*, *Huelguistas*, and *Soldado razo*); *Las pastorelas*, pr. 1971 (adaptation of a sixteenth century Mexican shepherd's play); *La Virgen del Tepeyac*, pr. 1971 (adaptation of *Las cuatro apariciones de la Virgen de Guadalupe*); *Los endrogados*, pr. 1972; *Los olivos pits*, pr. 1972; *La gran carpa de los rasquachis*, pr. 1973; *Mundo*, pr. 1973; *El baille de los gigantes*, pr. 1973; *El fin del mundo*, pr. 1975; *Zoot Suit*, pr. 1978, pb. 1992; *Bandido!*, pr. 1981, pb. 1992; *Corridos*, pr. 1983; *"I Don't Have to Show You No Stinking Badges!,"* pr., pb. 1986; *Luis Valdez—Early Works: Actos, Bernabé, and Pensamiento Serpentino*, pb. 1990; *Zoot Suit and Other Plays*, pb. 1992.

Other literary forms

Although Luis Miguel Valdez is known primarily for his plays, his writing on Chicano culture has had a significant impact. In a number of essays in the 1960's and 1970's ("Theatre: El Teatro Campesino," "Notes on Chicano Theatre," and several others), he elaborated an aesthetic based on what he believed to be the special features of Chicano reality: bilingualism, *mestizaje* (mixed race), and cultural disinheritance. He is also the author of screenplays, teleplays, and other nontheatrical writings that underscore his commitment to Chicano nationalism.

Achievements

Without Valdez, the Chicano theater would not exist in its present vibrant form. At the age of twenty-five, in the fields of rural California, without financial backing and using farm laborers as actors, Valdez single-handedly created a movement that has since become international in scope, leading to the founding of Chicano theater troupes from Los Angeles, California, to Gary, Indiana. Although not usually mentioned in the company of revered American playwrights of his generation such as Sam Shepard, David Mamet, and Richard Foreman, Valdez is in many ways as distinguished and as well-known internationally, both in Europe and in Latin America. In one respect especially, Valdez has accomplished what no other American playwright has: the creation of a genuine workers' theater, completely indigenous and the work of neither university intellec-

tuals nor producers of a commercialized "mass culture." He has made "serious" drama popular, political drama entertaining, and ethnic drama universal.

A founding member of the California Arts Council, Valdez served on a congressional subcommittee of the National Endowment for the Arts and on the board of directors of the Theatre Communications Group, and he has acted in teleplays and films based on his own work. Winning an honorary Obie Award in 1968 for his work on the West Coast, he appropriately was the first, ten years later, to produce a Chicano play on Broadway, the highly acclaimed *Zoot Suit*.

Biography

Luis Miguel Valdez was born on June 26, 1940, in Delano, California, the second of ten brothers and sisters. His father and mother were migrant farmworkers. Already working in the fields by the age of six, Valdez spent his childhood traveling to the harvests in the agricultural centers of the San Joaquin Valley. Despite having little uninterrupted early schooling, he managed to win a scholarship to San Jose State College in 1960.

Soon after his arrival at college, Valdez won a regional playwriting contest for his first one-act play, *The Theft*. Encouraged by his teachers to write a full-length work, Valdez complied with *The Shrunken Head of Pancho Villa*, which was promptly produced by the San Jose State drama department. Graduating with a bachelor's degree in English in 1964, Valdez spent the next several months traveling in Cuba; upon his return, he joined the San Francisco Mime Troupe under Ron Davis, where he worked for one year, learning from the troupe's *commedia dell'arte* techniques, which he was later to adapt in new ways.

Partly as a result of the sense of solidarity that he gained from his experiences while in Cuba, Valdez returned home to Delano, where the United Farm Workers Union was then being formed under the leadership of César Chávez. Amid a strike for union recognition, the union officials responded enthusiastically to Valdez's offer to create an educational theater group. Using volunteer actors from among the strikers, he formed El Teatro Campesino (farmworkers' theater) in 1965. Traveling on a flatbed truck from field to field, the troupe produced a series of one-act political skits dubbed *actos* (actions, or gestures), performing them in churches, storefronts, and on the edges of the fields themselves.

Enormously successful, the plays soon won outside attention and led to a U.S. tour in the summer of 1967. Later that year, Valdez left the fields to found the Centro Campesino Cultural in Del Rey, California. Similar recognition followed, with an Obie Award in New York in 1968 for "creating a workers' theater to demonstrate the politics of survival" and an invitation to perform at the Théâtre des Nations festival in Nancy, France—one of four tours to Europe between 1969 and 1980. Later in 1969, Valdez and the troupe moved to Fresno, California, where they founded an annual Chicano theater festival, and Valdez began teaching drama at Fresno State College.

The Centro Campesino Cultural relocated once again in 1971 to San Juan Bautista, a small rural California town, where it would stay for the next several years, rooting itself in the community and transforming its dramaturgy to reflect local concerns—particularly through its adaptations of earlier devotional drama dating from the Spanish occupation. Teatro Campesino there underwent fundamental transformation. Living more or less in a commune, the group began increasingly to emphasize the spiritual side of its work, as derived not only from the prevalent Christianity of the typical Chicano community but also from their own newfound Aztec and Mayan roots. This shift from the agitational *actos* to a search for spiritual solutions was met with anger by formerly admiring audiences at the Quinto Festival de los Teatros Chicanos in Mexico City in 1974.

From its base in San Juan Bautista, the Centro Cam-

pesino Cultural continued to flourish, touring campuses and communities on a yearly basis; giving financial support, training, and advice to other theater troupes; and hosting visitors such as English director Peter Brook, who brought his actors from the International Centre of Theatre Research in 1973. After a career of refusing to participate in the commercial theater, Valdez determined finally, in 1978, to try reaching a middle-class audience. The result was *Zoot Suit*, a polished, full-length dance-musical based on the "Sleepy Lagoon" murder trial of 1943. It premiered at the Mark Taper Forum in Los Angeles in 1978 and ran for eleven months. The play opened at the Wintergarden Theatre on Broadway in 1979 but was forced to close after a month because of bad reviews. A film version of the play was made in 1981. In 1985, *Soldado razo* and *Dark Root of a Scream* were performed for the first time in New York at the Public Theater as part of a Latino theater festival.

Valdez brought Tony Curiel into the Teatro Campesino in 1985 to help run the company. Valdez's play *"I Don't Have to Show You No Stinking Badges!"* (a famous line from the 1948 film *The Treasure of the Sierra Madre*) was coproduced with the Los Angeles Theatre Center in 1986. The film *La Bamba* (1987), written and directed by Valdez, was the first major release to celebrate the urban Latino youth lifestyle. El Teatro Campesino began the process of restructuring in 1988, learning to work more independently of Valdez, although his commitment to it remained substantial.

Analysis

Valdez's genius has been to reach an audience both Chicano and working-class, not only with political farces about strikers, "scabs," and bosses in a familiar street-theater concept but also by incorporating the popular theatrical forms of Latino America itself—the *carpas* (traveling theater shows), *variedades* (Mexican vaudeville), *corridos* (traditional Mexican folk ballads), and others. It is a unique combination to which Valdez has added his own distinctive forms. Appraising Valdez's work is, however, different from appraising that of most other playwrights of his stature. By political conviction and by necessity, much of his oeuvre is a collective product. While he has always been Teatro Campesino's major creative inspiration, and although entire passages from the collective plays were written by him alone, Valdez's drama is largely a joint project under his guidance—a collective political and religious celebration.

The starting point for all Valdez's work is his evocation of what he calls *la plebe, el vulgo,* or simply *La Raza,* that is, the Chicano people. It is from this outlook that the first *actos* were created—a genre very close to the Brechtian *Lehrstück* (teaching piece), with its episodic structure, its use of broad social types, its indifference to all but the most minimal of props and scenery, and its direct involvement of the audience in the solving of its dramatized social problems. In Valdez's words, the *actos* "must be popular, subject to no other critics except the pueblo itself, but it must also educate the pueblo toward an appreciation of *social change,* on and off the stage."

According to various accounts, the form was first developed in a Delano storefront, where Valdez had assembled his would-be performers from among the strikers. He hung signs around their necks that read *huelguista* (striker), *esquirol* (scab), and *patroncito* (little boss) and then simply asked them to show what had happened that day on the picket line. After some hesitation, the actors performed an impromptu political play, alive with their own jargon and bawdy jokes and inspired by the passions of the labor dispute within which they found themselves.

One exemplary early *acto* is *Las dos caras del patroncito* (the two faces of the boss), in which a typical undocumented worker, recruited fresh from Mexico by a California landowner in order to scab on the strike, exchanges roles with his *patroncito.* Dressed in a pig mask and speaking in an absurd Texas drawl, the *patroncito* playfully suggests that he temporarily trade his own whip for the *esquirol's* pruning sheers. The two quickly assume the inner reality of these symbolic outward forms. The climactic moment occurs when the owner removes his mask, at which point the *esquirol* has the revelation that worker and boss look (and therefore are) the same. Calling now for help, the boss is mistaken by the police for a troublemaker and is hauled off-stage, shouting for César Chávez and declaring his support for *La huelga* (the strike). The social tensions and contradictions of this role-reversal are central to all the *actos.* If the boss is brought down to a vulnerable stature and the worker is shown to be capable of leadership, there is no simplistic identification of one or the other as totally good or evil.

In the next stage of his career, Valdez explored the legends and myths of the Chicano's *indio* past. *Bernabé* is perhaps Valdez's most fully realized *mito* (myth-play). The hero is a thirty-one-year-old village idiot who has never had sexual relations with a woman. At the same time, he is a symbolic embodiment of the Chicano who possesses what Valdez calls "divinity in madness." After a series of taunts by the village toughs and an embarrassing encounter with Consuela, the local prostitute, Bernabé flees to a favorite hiding place in the countryside, where he has dug a gravelike hole in which he frequently masturbates in a kind of ritual copulation with *La Tierra* (the earth).

The climactic scene occurs when the elemental surroundings take on the forms of an Aztec allegory. *La Luna* (the moon) appears dressed as a *pachuco* (an urban Chicano zoot-suiter), smoking marijuana and acting as a go-between for his sister *La Tierra,* who then enters in the costume of a Mexican revolutionary camp follower (the proverbial "Adelita"). In the interchange, *La Tierra* questions the extent of Bernabé's love for her—whether he is "Chicano" enough to kill and to die for her. It is precisely his status as *loco* (crazy) that gives him the courage finally to say yes, and *El Sol* (the sun), as father, is pleased. As if mimicking the sacrifices to the Aztec sun god, Huitzilopochtli, Bernabé offers his physical heart to *La Tierra* and immediately ceases being the village idiot he was before, buried now within the earth but living on as a lesson to his people.

Valdez was to refine further this allegorical (and less immediately political) approach to Chicano identity in his plays throughout the 1970's, particularly in *La gran carpa de los rasquachis* (the great tent of the underdogs) and *El fin del mundo* (the end of the world), which further developed the use of the Mexican *corrido* (musical ballad), the split-level staging designed to evoke a mythical and suprahistorical realm of action, and the traditional images from Spanish American religious drama—particularly the *calavera* (skeleton) costume. In *El fin del mundo,* his play had become a full-scale allegorical ballet—a great dance of death.

With his first deliberate turn to the commercial theater in 1978, Valdez incorporated the *mito, acto,* and *corrido* in the unlikely framework of a play about the urban Chicano of the 1940's. *Zoot Suit*—filled with stylized scenes from the Los Angeles barrio—was a drama about a celebrated murder trial and the racist hysteria surrounding it. A panorama of American life of the time, the play deliberately adopted many of the outward features of the "professional" theater, while transforming them for its purposes. It displayed immense photographic projections of newspaper headlines, slickly choreographed dances and songs, and the overpowering central image of the narrator himself, dressed in a zoot suit—the mythical *pachuco.* To an extent greater than in any other of his plays, the work addressed Americans as a whole, reviving for them a historical moment of which they had never been aware and bringing them face-to-face with their latent prejudices.

"I Don't Have to Show You No Stinking Badges!," Valdez's most celebrated play, concerns a middle-class Chicano family's attempts to blend into the American cultural mainstream. The family's parents, Buddy and Connie Villa, are middle-aged bit-part actors who play stereotyped Latino roles in television and films; their son, Sonny, is a law student who disapproves of his parents' work, which he finds demeaning. The play's mixture of the themes of generational and cultural con-

flict drew wide praise, and the work confirmed Valdez's standing as an important contemporary dramatist.

Valdez's theatrical vision is inseparable from the conditions under which he founded the Teatro Campesino in the farmworkers' strike of 1965. Born in struggle, his early plays all have a vitality, directness, and urgency that cannot be divorced from their lasting appeal. His achievement blossoms finally with his successful incorporation of the deep cultural roots of the Chicano Nation, which are found in the religious imagery of the *indio* past. Both facets of his career have been widely copied by other Chicano directors and playwrights and are admired widely outside the Chicano community as well.

Other major works

SCREENPLAYS: *Zoot Suit*, 1982; *La Bamba*, 1987.
TELEPLAYS: *Fort Figueroa*, 1988; *La Pastorela*, 1991; *The Cisco Kid*, 1994 (with Michael Kane).
ANTHOLOGY: *Aztlan: An Anthology of Mexican American Literature*, 1972 (with Stan Steiner).
MISCELLANEOUS: *Pensamiento Serpentino: A Chicano Approach to the Theatre of Reality*, 1973.

Bibliography

Flores, Arturo C. *El Teatro Campesino de Luis Valdez*. Madrid: Editorial Pliegos, 1990.
Huerta, Jorge A. *Chicano Theatre: Themes and Forms*. Ypsilanti, Mich.: Bilingual Press, 1982.
————————— . "Labor Theatre, Street Theatre, and Community Theatre in the Barrio, 1965-1983." In *Hispanic Theatre in the United States*, edited by Nicolas Kanellos. Houston: Arte Público Press, 1984.
Kanellos, Nicolas. *Mexican American Theater: Legacy and Reality*. Pittsburgh: Latin American Literary Review Press, 1987.
Morales, Ed. "Shadowing Valdez." *American Theatre* 9 (November, 1992): 14-19.
Pottlitzer, Joanne. *Hispanic Theater in the United States and Puerto Rico: A Report to the Ford Foundation*. New York: Ford Foundation, 1988.
Valdez, Luis. "*Zoot Suit* and the Pachuco Phenomenon: An Interview with Luis Valdez." Interview by Roberta Orona-Cordova. In *Mexican American Theatre: Then and Now*, edited by Nicolas Kanellos. Houston: Arte Público Press, 1983.

XII

MOTHER TONGUE, FATHER COUNTRY
Asian American Identities

Who is mother tongue, who is father country?
—Myung Mi Kim, "Into Such Assembly," 1989

In exploring how Asian influences have affected American identities, it is important to note that the development of Asian American literature can be divided into two periods. The first period lasted for more than a century. It started with first-generation Asian immigrants' using their native language to describe their experiences in the United States. Some of these writings were published in Asian-language newspapers and some were later translated, collected, and published in anthologies. Hamilton Holt's *The Life Stories of Undistinguished Americans* (1906), for example, is a collection of autobiographical information about a Japanese servant and a Chinatown merchant.

It was, however, the second-generation Asian American writers who introduced Asian American literature to the general reading public in America. Because American-born Asian writers did not have the kind of language problem their parents had struggled with, many of them adopted the role of "translator" for their ethnic cultural heritage. They not only told stories about their own lives but also served as bridges connecting their ethnic cultures with the mainstream culture in America. The literature produced by second-generation Asian American writers was marked as much by their demonstrated interest in using the autobiographical approach to define their experience as by a sensitivity sharpened by these writers' increased awareness of their own cultural heritage. Chinese American writer Pardee Lowe's *Father and Glorious Descendant* (1943), Jade Snow Wong's *The Fifth Chinese Daughter* (1945), Japanese American writer Daniel Inouye's *Journey to Washington* (1967), Monica Sone's *Nisei Daughter* (1953), and Filipino American writer Carlos Bulosan's *America Is in the Heart* (1943) use the genre of autobiography to describe the writers' struggle with not only inter- but also intra-cultural conflict. Chinese American writer Virginia Lee's *The House That Tai Ming Built* (1963), Chuang Hua's *Crossings* (1968), Maxine Hong Kingston's *The Woman Warrior* (1975) and *China Men* (1980), Shawn Wong's *Homebase* (1979), Japanese American writer Kazuo Miyamoto's *Hawaii: End of the Rainbow* (1964), and two short stories by Filipino American writers, Bienvenido Santos' "Scent of Apples" and Oscar Peñaranda's "The Price," are fictionalized memoirs that can also be read as semi-autobiographies.

In the same period, another group of writers made efforts to portray Asian American experiences in more creative ways. Chinese American writer Louis Chu's *Eat a Bowl of Tea* (1961) presents a satirical but accurate depiction of the bachelor society in Chinatown; it is one of few works in Asian American literature that deal with the struggle of lower-middle-class Asian Americans. Frank Chin's *The Chickencoop Chinaman* was produced by the American Place Theater of New York in 1972; his *The Year of the Dragon* (1974) was the first Asian American play on national television. Toshio Mori's *Yokohama, California* (1949) is acclaimed by the Japanese American critic and writer Lawson Fusao Inada as "the first real Japanese American book." The fictional community of Yokohama, California, establishes a stage for the author's exploration of the richness of Japanese American culture from the 1930's to the early 1940's.

Like *Yokohama, California*, John Okada's *No-No Boy* (1957) was initially rejected by the Japanese American community under the control of the Japanese American Citizens League (JACL), for the novel takes a realistic look at the complicated feelings behind a Japanese American's decision to refuse to join the army during the war and at the lingering effect that the relocation camps had on the Japanese American community.

The second period of Asian American literature started in the mid-1970's and eventually came to be known as the Asian American Renaissance. Heralded by Chinese American writer Maxine Hong Kingston's two celebrated autobiographical novels, *The Woman Warrior* (1975) and *China Men* (1980), this period witnessed two notable changes in Asian American literature; both are related to diversity. First, autobiography ended its reign as the predominant form of expression in Asian American literature. Asian American writers in this period became more interested in experimenting with various literary genres and styles in search of a medium that would reflect and depict their feelings accurately. This period was marked by an increase in the publication of short stories and poems. Both Japanese American writer Jessica Saiki's *Once, a Lotus Garden* (1987) and Hisaye Yamamoto's *Seventeen Syllables* (1988) are collections of short stories whose description of the Japanese American experience in Hawaii and the mainland is exquisite and smooth. In the spectrum of poetry, Japanese American writers Garrett Kaoru Hongo (in *Yellow Light*, 1982, and *The River of Heaven*, 1988) and David Mura (in *After We Lost Our Way*, 1988) intermingle the voice of anger with that of agony. Both poets nevertheless celebrate the triumph of the human spirit in dignified tones.

Second, writers from ethnic groups other than Chinese, Japanese, or Filipino started to make waves. Their writings have contributed to the democratization and canonization of Asian American voices. These writings also present a more colorful and pluralistic interpretation of Asian American experiences. Asian American writers of Korean, South Asian, and Southeast Asian descent became more productive and ready to take on the challenge to diversify both approach and voice in the portrayal of the Asian American experience. In *Clay Walls* (1986), Korean American writer Kim Ronyoung experiments expressionistically with the narrative point of view, describing a Korean couple's settlement in Los Angeles before World War II from three characters' perspectives. Another Korean American writer, Mary Paik Lee, depicts her family's struggle to adjust to American life in the her moving and inspiring autobiography, *The Quiet Odyssey: A Pioneer Korean Woman in America* (1990); the hardships the author underwent as a child in both Korea and the United States did not diminish her hope for a better future, nor did they shake her determination to fight for human dignity. In the late 1970's and early 1980's, Korean American writer Cathy Song demonstrated her talent as both a storyteller and a poet with short stories such as "Beginnings" (1976) and poems collected in *Picture Bride* (1983). Indian American writer Bharati Mukherjee's *Jasmine* and Vietnamese American writer Le Ly Hayslip's *When Heaven and Earth Changed Places* were published in 1989. *Jasmine* describes the metamorphosis of an Indian woman in America and how she helps change the ideological contours of the country. *When Heaven and Earth Changed Places* uses an autobiographical approach to examine the painful memory of the Vietnam War. Hayslip published her second autobiography, *A Child of War, a Woman of Peace*, in 1991. She is one of the first Asian American writers from Southeast Asia to be published in the United States.

Short stories and poems were not the only genres into which a new generation of Asian American writers poured their expression of the American experience. In 1988, *M. Butterfly* opened in Washington, D.C., at the National Theater, where *West Side Story* and *Amadeus* had premiered. The play won the Tony Award for the year's best play, the Outer Critics Circle Award for best Broadway play, the John Gassner Award for best play, and the Drama Desk Award for best new play. *M. Butterfly* marks the simultaneous coming-of-age of both Chinese American playwright David Henry Hwang and Asian American theater. In the play, Hwang dramatizes the pernicious effect of illusions built on stereotypes and false assumptions. The plot develops along the lines of the trickster tradition in African American folklore and literature.

The development of the Asian American Renaissance has not shown any sign of losing momentum. The huge success of Amy Tan's semi-autobiographical novel *The Joy Luck Club* and Japanese American writer Cynthia Kadohata's critically acclaimed novel *The*

Floating World in 1989 rekindled hopes in the hearts of many Asian American writers who were struggling with obscurity. The year 1991 alone saw publication by five Chinese American writers: Amy Tan's *The Kitchen God's Wife* was another success; Gish Jen's *Typical American* received rave reviews from both *People* magazine and *The New York Times Book Review*; David Wong Louie's *Pangs of Love* explores themes such as intercultural and intergenerational conflict; Frank Chin published his first long piece of work, *Donald Duk*; and Gus Lee, a lawyer from California, published his autobiographical novel, *China Boy*.

In Korean American poet Myung Mi Kim's poem "Into Such Assembly," the narrator discusses her ambivalent feelings about becoming a naturalized American citizen, for she does not know how to answer questions such as "Who is mother tongue, who is father country?" or "What is given, given over?" But the poem ends with the narrator envisioning the assembly of people from different cultures coming together in America; the rain dissolves land and ocean:

> One table laden with one crumb
> Every mouthful off a spoon whole
> Each drop strewn into such assembly

Asian American literature celebrates the culturally diverse nature of American society. It reclaims Asian Americans' sense of history and identity. It also democratizes American literary expression by (re)presenting what has been mis(sing)-represented and by giving voice to the voiceless. In these ways, Asian American literature is crucial for building the multicultural society that American identities are destined to create.

—Qun Wang
University of Wisconsin, River Falls

FRANK CHIN

Born: Berkeley, California; February 25, 1940

Principal drama

The Chickencoop Chinaman, pr. 1972, pb. 1981; *The Year of the Dragon*, pr. 1974, pb. 1981.

Other literary forms

Frank Chin has published a collection of short stories, longer fiction, and numerous essays and articles on Chinese American literature and culture. He coedited a breakthrough anthology of Asian American writing entitled *Aiiieeeee!* (1974), revised in 1991 as *The Big Aiiieeeee!* Chin has also published two novels, *Donald Duk* (1991) and *Gunga Din Highway* (1994).

Achievements

Chin is the first Chinese American playwright to have had serious drama produced on the New York stage (at the American Place Theater) and on national television (by the Public Broadcasting Service). Having come into prominence in the 1960's and 1970's, he represents the consciousness of Americans of Chinese descent—those born and reared in the United States, who thus have only tenuous ties to the language and culture of China.

Chin has sometimes been considered the John Osborne, the angry young man, of his generation of Chinese Americans. His plays turn on themes of identity—anguished and indignant probings into ethnic identity, gender identity, and self-identity. In them, Chin mirrors the issues and realities of Chinese American life and history as lived in Chinatown ghettos; his works seek to expose and explode generally held stereotypes of Chinese Americans as an emasculated model minority with a quaintly exotic culture. Painful truths told with exuberant verbal pyrotechnics are trademarks of Chin's theater, and the characteristic gamut of his language ranges from African American ghetto dialect to hipster talk to authentic Chinatown Cantonese (not Hollywood's "Charlie Chan-ese").

In addition to his achievement as a playwright, Chin is important as an editor of Asian American literature, a fiction writer, and an essayist. Chin's work has been recognized by many awards, among them prizes and grants from the Rockefeller Foundation, the American Place Theater (New York), and the National Endowment for the Arts.

Biography

Frank Chew Chin, Jr., was born a fifth-generation Californian of Chinese American parentage on February 25, 1940, in Berkeley, California, near Oakland, where his parents lived and worked. During his infancy, his family sent him to the Sierra, where he was cared for by retired vaudeville acrobat and a silent-film bit player. After World War II, he rejoined his family and grew up in the Chinatowns of Oakland and San Francisco, attending Chinese as well as English schools. During these years, he identified closely with his father, who was prominent in Chinatown governance and who became the president of the Six Companies (roughly the Chinatown equivalent of being elected mayor). Chin was graduated from the University of California at Berkeley, where he won several prizes for fiction writing; during his student years, he undertook the adventure of traveling to Fidel Castro's Cuba. In 1961, he was awarded a fellowship at the Writers' Workshop at the University of Iowa.

After leaving Iowa, Chin spent some time with the Southern Pacific Railroad, becoming the first Chinese American to work as a brakeman on the rails laid by his forefathers. Chin left the railroad company to become a writer-producer for KING-TV in Seattle, and several of his shows were aired by the Public Broadcasting Service (PBS) and on *Sesame Street*.

Chin left Seattle to teach Asian American studies at San Francisco State University and the University of California at Davis. With a group of scholars, he organized the Combined Asian American Resources Project (CARP), which collected literary, documentary, and oral history materials now kept in the Bancroft Library at Berkeley. CARP has since been responsible for the publication of key Asian American texts by the University of Washington Press. In 1972, Chin founded the Asian American Theater Workshop in San Francisco with the support of the American Conservatory Theater (where he has been a writer-in-residence). During the 1980's and early 1990's, Chin maintained his residence in Southern California (living with his third wife and third child), where he channeled his energies toward the writing of fiction and children's literature rather than drama. Meanwhile, his continuing research in Asian American folklore and history has been supported by several grants (including a Rockefeller Fellowship at the University of California, Los Angeles) and has borne fruit in several important exhibitions.

Analysis

Chin belongs to the vanguard of Asian American writers who began to publish in the 1960's and 1970's. Appearing on the literary scene in the wake of the Civil Rights and black arts movements, Asian American writers of Chin's generation differed from most of their Asian American predecessors in depicting characters, situations, and sentiments that shattered the majority of white stereotypes of Asian America. Chin and others of his generation sought to express a more realistic, less sentimentalized image of Asian Americans—their strengths and weaknesses unvarnished, their joys and sorrows revealed, their humanity unmitigated. Chin's plays center on a protagonist's confrontation with the problematics of identity. *The Chickencoop Chinaman* is a play that treats the theme of identity through dispelling stereotypes and myths. The play's action centers on Tam Lum, a Chinese American filmmaker who is making a documentary about an African American boxing champion, Ovaltine Jack Dancer. Tam comes to Pittsburgh from San Francisco in the 1960's in search of Dancer's father, Charley Popcorn, who was a quintessential formative figure for Dancer and who now runs a Pittsburgh theater. Allegorically, Tam's making a film about Dancer is an effort to express an identity for himself, and his search for Charley is his search for a father figure.

Before arriving in Pittsburgh, Tam is introduced in a surrealistic scene on his airliner from San Francisco. The flight attendant is transformed into a Hong Kong Dream Girl clad in a drill team uniform and twirling a baton (hence an American dream girl, too). Indeed, the woman represents the American stereotype of Asian women—attractive, compliant, trained to give pleasure. Although Tam scoffs at the Hong Kong Dream Girl's stereotypical identity, it becomes apparent that his own identity is problematic. For example, when asked what his mother tongue is, Tam can speak no Chinese but instead begins speaking in tongues, using a startling array of American dialects. Tam also points out that Chinese American identity is not one ordained by nature; Chinese Americans are not born to an identity but

must synthesize one out of the diverse experiences of living in crowded Chinatown tenements, metaphorical chickencoops. This opening sequence, then, poses the play's central theme: the problem of stereotyping and identity.

In Pittsburgh, Tam stays with a boyhood friend, a Japanese American dentist named "Blackjap" Kenji. Tam and Kenji, who grew up in the black ghetto of Oakland, California, talk in exuberant black dialect and express themselves by slapping skin; they have, to a great degree, adopted the style and expressiveness of a black identity. During their reunion scene in act 1, Tam and Kenji reenact a past obsession that they had with the figure of Helen Keller, imitating and parodying her. This may seem pointlessly cruel until one realizes that, in Chin's play, Keller symbolizes the myth of the disadvantaged person who overcomes all handicaps and pulls herself up by her own bootstraps. In other words, she epitomizes what American society fondly thinks that every disadvantaged minority group can do for itself. When Tam and Kenji mock and demythologize the figure of Helen Keller, they are, in particular, rejecting the popular American myth that Asian Americans are a model minority capable of miracles of self-help.

Tam and Kenji then track down Charley Popcorn. They are crushed, however, when Charley reveals that he is not, in fact, Dancer's father—that Dancer has constructed a myth around his memories of their association. Thus Tam's search for a surrogate and idolized father figure in an African American man ends in disillusionment.

Tam, however, appears to recover from his shattering disillusionment with Charley. In the surrealistic penultimate scene, he is shown being borne to Kenji's apartment on Charley's back, and in this position, Tam recalls the unmanning events when his wife left him on his birthday. In the play's last scene, however, Tam makes a great effort and stumbles into Kenji's apartment carrying Charley on his back. This reversal of position symbolically denotes Tam's freedom from his past reliance on an identity borrowed from African America and a new determination to find the wherewithal for a future identity from sources within himself. Before the curtain falls, Tam is shown in the kitchen unashamedly practicing the craft of his ethnic group par excellence. As he prepares the food, he reminisces about the Chinese American legend of the Iron Moonhunter, a mythic train that the Chinese railroaders supposedly created out of parts stolen from the railroad companies, and that wanders the West searching out the souls of dead Chinese to bear them home to their families. Chin seems to understand that people need myths, and in the end, his protagonist, disillusioned with the black myth that is unavailable to him and rejecting a white myth that he finds contemptible, shapes his own myth of identity in the heroism and craft of Chinese America.

Chin's second play, *The Year of the Dragon*, is more conventionally structured than its predecessor and was accorded a national audience in a television production on "PBS Theatre in America" in 1975. This play also treats the theme of identity, but it focuses more sharply and poignantly upon the question of self-worth: the worth of an individual self to loved ones (family) and the worth of a minority ethnic group to the majority society (white-dominated America). Again, stereotypes form the chief factor that obscures individual worth and identity—stereotypes about family relationships, stereotypes about ethnicity. These thematic strands are worked out in the exposition of the many psychological conflicts and confrontations in the well-established Eng family of San Francisco's Chinatown.

The exposition, and exposé, of ethnic stereotypes is presented chiefly through two elements of the play: the family business of providing tours of Chinatown and the new Anglo son-in-law whom their daughter has brought from Boston. The family owns Eng's Chinatown Tour and Travel agency, and the eldest son, forty-year-old Fred, conducts tours of San Francisco's Chinatown. For the sake of business, however, Fred cannot show Chinatown as it really is; rather, he must pander to the stereotypes of Chinatown held by the American public: that it is an exotic place of delicious foods, mysterious (but safe) goings-on, and incomprehensible (but happy) inhabitants composed of attractively available women, complaisant men, and harmonious families with above-average children. Fred knows that he is being false to himself and his people when he gives his happy tour-guide's spiel, and he mutters curses at his customers under his breath beneath his patter. In reality, Fred would like to tell the truths of Chinatown, which he sets down in short stories, but no one will publish his work. Through Fred's situation, then, Chin portrays the stifling effects of ethnic stereotypes.

The other element in the play that deals with ethnic stereotypes is presented through the character Ross, the Eng family's Boston-bred son-in-law on a honeymoon visit from the East. He is portrayed as a well-meaning but oafish Sinophile who has studied Chinese (although

in a dialect different from the Eng family's), admires Chinese culture and customs, and thinks of Chinese Americans as the only minority group that does not dislike white dominance. Such stereotypes prevent him from seeing the Chinese American realities that trip him up constantly.

In probing the stereotypes of familial relationships, Chin makes a painful but necessary criticism of stereotypes held by his own ethnic group. He also dispels the Charlie Chan-esque stereotype held by many Americans, that Chinese families are uniformly harmonious and hierarchical. Much of the conflict in the family swirls around its patriarch, Pa Eng, who came to the U.S. in 1935 accompanied only by his infant son Fred, for he was forced to leave his wife in China because United States immigration laws excluded Chinese women from entering America. It is in his relationship with Fred that Pa Eng's authoritarian role becomes most apparent.

Pa Eng's patriarchal dominance and his Chinese values have acted as long-standing denials of Fred's identity and self-worth. Fred aspired to be a writer, but his father scoffed at this: According to stereotypes he holds, if one is not a doctor or a lawyer, one is nothing at all. Pa Eng gives the job of editing his mayoral speech to Ross, not to Fred, who majored in English. Nevertheless, Fred is a dutiful son, nursing his father when he spits blood and even going through a daily ritual of accompanying him to the toilet and wiping him after a defecation, a viscerally affecting scene to stage. Fred has also sacrificed his own college career to work and provide for his sister's college expenses, but his father does not appreciate that, probably because his stereotypical values do not accord much importance to daughters. In attempting to impose his will on his son, Pa Eng resorts to violence and slaps him repeatedly. Yet the physical exertion is too much for the sick old man, and he dies in this pitiable moment of futile tyranny. Tragically, Pa Eng's death does not free Fred. The closing tableau of the play shows Fred being submerged by his milieu as he slips into the spiel of the Chinatown tour guide, and as the spotlight singles him out, Fred is shown dressed glaringly in white, the Chinese symbol of death.

Chin has pioneered in the field of Asian American literature. His daring and verbally exuberant theater has asserted the presence of the richly unique and deeply human complexities of Chinese American life, and his work has brought this presence to the attention of the American public. He has criticized the false myths and the deadening stereotypes of self and ethnicity held by Asians and whites alike. At a time when it was ripe and

necessary to do so, Chin proclaimed and proved that there is such an entity as Asian American literature.

Other major works

NOVEL: *Donald Duk*, 1991; *Gunga Din Highway, 1994.*

SHORT FICTION: *The Chinaman Pacific and Frisco R.R. Co.*, 1988.

TELEPLAYS: *S.R.T., Act Two*, 1966; *The Bel Canto Carols*, 1966; *A Man and His Music*, 1967; *Ed Sierer's New Zealand*, 1967; *Searfair Preview*, 1967; *The Year of the Ram*, 1967; *And Still Champion . . . .*, 1967; *The Report*, 1967; *Mary*, 1969; *Rainlight Rainvision*, 1969; *Chinaman's Chance*, 1971.

EDITED TEXT: *The Big Aiiieeeee! An Anthology of Chinese American and Japanese American Literature*, 1991.

Bibliography

Barnes, Clive. "Theater: Culture Study." *The New York Times*, June 3, 1974, p. 39.

Kim, Elaine H. *Asian American Literature: An Introduction to the Writings and Their Social Context*. Philadelphia: Temple University Press, 1982.

_____ . "Frank Chin: The Chinatown Cowboy and His Backtalk." *Midwest Quarterly* 20 (Autumn, 1978): 78-91.

Kroll, Jack. "Primary Color." *Newsweek*, June 19, 1972, 55.

McDonald, Dorothy Ritsuko. Introduction to *"The Chickencoop Chinaman" and "The Year of the Dragon": Two Plays by Frank Chin*. Seattle: University of Washington Press, 1981.

Oliver, Edith. "Off Broadway." *The New Yorker* 48 (June 24, 1972): 46.

GARRETT HONGO

Born: Volcano, Hawaii; May 30, 1951

Principal poetry
Yellow Light, 1982; *The River of Heaven*, 1988.

Other literary forms
Nisei Bar & Grill, a play, was written in 1976 and performed in Seattle and San Francisco. Its revised version became a workshop production at the Kilauea Theater (1992). The play depicts interactions among veterans of World War II and the Korean conflict. Garrett Hongo also has written literary essays appearing in *Agni Review*, *The New York Times Book Review*, *New England Review*, and *Ohio Review*.

Achievements
Hongo's poetry is notable for its immediacy of voice, clear evocation of place, and poignant negotiation of both ethnic and temporal boundaries. He typically employs memory to compile imagistic pastiches that recreate an emotional state. Many of his poems are quests—for a synthetic cultural identity, for a true personal history, for a unique and satisfactory voice. Traversing landscapes from the volcano of his birthplace to the volcanic experience of living in a mainland metropolis (primarily Los Angeles), Hongo explores the brutality of contemporary life as it assaults the tenderness of the spirit. Alienation, discrimination, cruelty, violence, loss, and isolation permeate the poems as insults to the soul.

Hongo has received high acclaim and support through several prizes and fellowships: the Thomas J. Watson Travelling Fellowship, 1973-1974; the Hopwood Poetry Prize, 1975; the Discovery/*The Nation* Award, 1981; National Endowment for the Arts fellowships, 1982 and 1988; Pushcart Prize selection, 1986; the Lamont Poetry Prize, 1987; and a Guggenheim Fellowship, 1990-1991. In 1989 he was a finalist for the Pulitzer Prize in poetry and the *Los Angeles Times* Book Award.

Biography
A fourth-generation Japanese American, Garrett Kaoru Hongo was born in Volcano, Hawaii, in 1951. His parents are Albert Kazuyoshi Hongo, who died in 1984, and Louise Tomiko Kubota Hongo. Until he was

six years old, he and his family lived in Kahuku and then Hauula on the island of Oahu. Hongo learned at this time to speak Pidgin English and Japanese. From the ages of six to eighteen, Hongo lived with his family in and around Los Angeles, where he began to experience the harshness of city life (in contrast to the easy rhythms of life in the rain forest) and the prejudices and injustices of a multicultural society. He attended an inner-city high school that piloted integration, combining whites, Asian Americans, African Americans, and Hispanic Americans in the same classes. Some of his poems, "Morro Rock" in particular, evoke conflicts experienced for the first time in his teenage years.

Hongo's beginnings as a poet came when he was eighteen and started writing love poems to a European American girl, celebrating a relationship that they felt pressured to keep secret. She awakened in him an intellectual camaraderie with "books about adolescent yearning and rebellion, about 'the system' not understanding you." His first serious poetry came when he was twenty and a student at Pomona College. There he read the works of James Joyce, Ezra Pound, and William Butler Yeats and attended readings by Philip Levine (who was to become a mentor), Gary Snyder, Seamus Heaney, and Galway Kinnell.

Hongo then returned to Hawaii and began to try to reclaim that portion of his own past, his heritage. There he discovered in a garage his father's library, consisting primarily of works of realistic fiction, and he established a connection with his uncle, Robert Hongo, who was a novelist. The first "real" poem Garrett Hongo wrote was called "Issei: First-Generation Japanese American." The poem relates an ancestral explanation of how he received his own middle name and thus reveals the close link between name and identity, between name and heritage. Writing the poem was a turning point for him, a moment that confirmed his calling.

After being graduated cum laude in 1973 from Pomona College, Hongo journeyed to Japan on a quest for an understanding of where he might belong; he spent a year there, traveling and writing poetry. He then commenced graduate study of Japanese language and literature at the University of Michigan. Returning to the West Coast, Hongo lived in Seattle from 1976 to 1979, where he worked as a professor and a poet. Ultimately, he returned to California to study and receive, in 1980, an M.F.A. in English from the University of California at Irvine, where he continued in doctoral study in critical theory for two more years.

Hongo found deconstructionist theory to be debilitating rather than enabling and thus left his doctoral program in 1984, taking a position as an assistant professor of English at the University of Missouri, where he was also poetry editor of *The Missouri Review*. Meanwhile Hongo had married Cynthia Thiessen, a violinist, and his first son, Alexander, was born (a second son is named Hudson). In Missouri, Hongo began daydreaming about Hawaii, about California, about his own and his family's past. Instead of producing a doctoral dissertation, he wrote *The River of Heaven*—a decision that salvaged his spirit in an alien landscape and confirmed his allegiance to creativity rather than to scholarship. After a year's sojourn at the University of Houston, Hongo accepted in 1989 a position as director of the creative writing program at the University of Oregon in Eugene, his wife's hometown; there he tries to instill in his students a poetic discipline analogous to that of the martial arts.

Hongo divides his time between Eugene and Volcano, a place for which his spirit hankers and where the ghost of his grandfather is evident. Hongo himself became an active literary presence in his hometown and the leader of a local theater group.

Analysis

Hongo belongs to a nucleus of younger American poets for whom the issue of ethnicity lends significant meaning and purpose to their work. In seeking to discover historical roots and their place in modern America, he expresses themes suggested by his Japanese American background as well as by the Hawaiian and Californian landscapes.

The collected volumes of Hongo's poetry—*Yellow Light* and *The River of Heaven*—offer a chronological narrative of his autobiography and his development as a poet. By reading the poems in the order of their collection, one becomes immersed in the external details of life in the modern metropolis, exotic locales, and a multicultural community, as well as in the resulting

internal emotions and reflections of the writer. A recurring theme in his work is the search for a personal identity that is unique, separate, and autonomous but also continuous with one's heritage. There is a sense of the need for separation and then return; the poems trace a journey of discovery.

The title poem of *Yellow Light* sets the tone for the rest of the collection. These earlier poems reflect the writer's concern with the sensibility of his father's soul, which was brutalized by his necessary manual labor and the hardship of making a living in an alien society. The sensations, the impressions, of his father's condition were indelibly etched on the consciousness of the poet as a young child. The conflict and compromise that he knew his father felt become abstracted into larger, less personal issues and then reparticularized into observable details of the environment and projections into the lives of observed people.

In "Yellow Light," a woman returns to her apartment after work and shopping. In her walk through the city, the poet juxtaposes images of nature to the trappings of city life. The contemporary urban environment has as its "natural" images children reenacting war games, sounds of domestic squabbles, noisy machinery, polluted air, and unsightly barriers separating yard from yard, protecting material property. These contrast with vivid sensations of a truly natural environment, appearing here as flowers that would be colorful, fragrant, and profuse.

The contrast continues in descriptions of the light the woman experiences. Light is often used in poetry to indicate truth or clarity of vision. The city offers only ugly, glaring, artificial light—false illumination. It is revealed in searchlights from car lots and the fluorescent and neon lights of commerce and trade. By offering as an alternative to this light the warm and mellow glow of a kitchen lamp, the poet hints that each individual may establish his or her own "natural" territory domestically: a place where one is in control and one's values and priorities are proper. Later poems indicate that poetry itself may be one's private territory, where a corrective vision can be offered as an alternative to the flawed world "out there." Hongo carries forth the kitchen image, and its associations with sustenance and nurturance, in the overpowering natural light of the moon, a larger version of the mellow kitchen lamp, here compared to the rich yellow of onions. The light of the moon proves ultimately victorious, as it blankets the horrors of the city and renders invisible the lesser metropolitan lights. The act of writing poetry, the poet suggests, may itself be redemptive.

Several of the works could be labeled "identity poems," as they reclaim the poet's personal heritage and ethnic history. "Roots" and "Issei: First-Generation Japanese American" are obviously in this vein. The poem "Stepchild" moves out of the concern with personal identity to retrace the troubled history of Asian Americans in the first half of the twentieth century. The form of this poem is also unique, for it actually incorporates accounts by other writers of life in the internment camps and after World War II. The suffering of others like him, the narrator implies, is also part of who he is.

A major work in this collection could be labeled a "quest poem." "Cruising 99" is a poetic version of the influential Beat-generation book *On the Road* (1955) by Jack Kerouac. In this poem, the narrator and two friends travel Highway 99 in California, looking for something to make sense of their lives but also simply content with movement, at least the illusion of making progress, of seeking, of "getting there." The poem chronicles the details observed on the trip, again juxtaposing the natural and the artificial, that made by nature and that produced by humankind. Separate sections in various experimental forms re-create the human sounds, the sights, and the events of the trip: a chant to pass the time; a dialogue; a philosophical meditation about the purpose of travel; a palm-reading incident; haikulike versions of postcard messages mailed home; an encounter in a café while the car is being repaired that leads to a realization of the fleeting nature of the travelers' youth; the surprising discovery of a Japanese community that brings them, ironically, back to themselves, back to where they began; and a final stanza on the patterns of running away and returning, patterns that can be remedied by a process of incorporation. By the end of this quest, the narrator realizes that one may become a landscape composed of all of one's heritage and experience: One becomes able to carry the journey within one rather than to move, constantly seeking something outside oneself.

Part of the quest in Hongo's case was to return to the ancestral homeland of Japan. Several of the poems recount the experience as "outsider poems." The visitor feels part of the culture yet alien to its sources. "Who Among You Knows the Essence of Garlic?" is an immersion into the culinary details of the Japanese ecosystem, ultimately becoming a microcosm of Japanese philosophy and culture that cannot include the American observer. In "To Matsuo Basho and Kawai Sora in Nirvana," the poet visits a site frequented by two of the most famous of Japanese poets and attempts to speak with their ghosts, to become part of their literary tradition. Even if he can recapture their vision for a moment, he still senses that time and his own distance from their realities will continue to separate them.

The other categories of poems contained in this volume are portraits, meditations, and love poems, as well as an important set of pieces that might be called "poems about art." "What For," in particular, reveals Hongo's concern with the value of capturing reality and giving it a name that occurs in writing poetry. This poem traces the child-poet's attraction to work rituals in his early life: the magic of incantation in Hawaiian natural mythology, family oral lore and storytelling, and singing. All of these contributed to the making of the poet, yet they are contrasted to the adult death of the spirit that the child perceives in his father. As he sees the exigencies of modern life drag his parent down, the child-poet desires to use his own word magic to soothe the pain and cure his father's suffering.

Hongo's second volume, *The River of Heaven*, takes its title from a line in "The Unreal Dwelling: My Years in Volcano," which is the death poem of the poet's grandfather. Here he imagines the last year of his ancestor's life in the town of Hongo's own birth. The title indicates the centrality of ancestral heritage and the image of the volcano itself in all the poems. Yet in this collection of poems, much of the restlessness of *Yellow Light* is gone. "Mendocino Rose," a poem of prologue to the collection, establishes a new tone of synthesis, wholeness, and peace. Indeed, the tenor of this poem is the harmonies that one can both find and impose on music, landscape, heritage, and a transplanted identity.

The collection is divided into two distinct parts, the first chronicling the poet's initial return to Hawaii after leaving at the age of six, and the second moving to mainland poems. There is a developmental movement to the first part. At the beginning the narrator simply tries to recapture the experience of coming home in all of its sensuous detail, as in "Nostalgic Catalogue." There follows an immersion into the memories that are stimulated by the new sensuous stimuli, as in "Village: Kahuku-*mura*." He begins to experience a reclaiming of authentic selfhood in poems such as "Ancestral Graves, Kahuku" and "Hilo: First Night Back" and recognizes his kinship to relatives who remained in Hawaii. Then there is the self-scrutiny that results when he writes poetic stories of his ancestors and applies the lessons to himself, as in "*Jigoku*: On the Glamour of Self-Hate." The center of this section is Volcano itself and its landscape, which is real, as the birthplace of the poet, but also metaphorical, as the representation of fragility, destruction, and re-creation, which occur in poetry as in life.

The mainland poems of the second section are introduced by a quotation from Albert Camus to establish their predominant tone. Camus speaks of "this desire for unity, this longing to solve, this need for clarity and cohesion," at which Hongo has already hinted as being the process of poetry. These poems are more intellectual and literary, such as "Portrait of a Lady" (a title used by other famous writers such as T. S. Eliot, Ezra Pound, and Henry James). Hongo modernizes and individualizes both the form and the content of the tradition, offering a portrait of a contemporary ethnic woman in a free-verse style that resembles a prose poem.

The elements present in both volumes of poetry remain, however they may be transformed or altered in tone. Hongo's persistent interests in identity, heritage, beauty and sadness, and the power of poetry lend a satisfying unity to the entire body of his work.

Other major works
PLAY: *Nisei Bar & Grill*, 1976, 1992.
EDITED TEXT: *The Open Boat: Poems from Asian America*, 1993.

Bibliography
Hongo, Garrett. "Ancestral Voices." Interview by Bill Moyers for *The Power of the Word*. Public Broadcasting Service, 1989.

Kaganoff, Penny. Review of *The River of Heaven*, by Garrett Hongo. *Publishers Weekly*, no. 233 (February 12, 1988): 81.

Muratori, Fred. Review of *The River of Heaven*, by Garrett Hongo. *Library Journal*, no. 113 (May 1, 1988): 81-82.

Pettingell, Phoebe. Review of *The River of Heaven*, by Garrett Hongo. *The New Leader*, no. 71 (June 13, 1988): 16.

DAVID HENRY HWANG

Born: Los Angeles, California; August 11, 1957

Principal drama

F.O.B., pr. 1978, pb. 1983; *The Dance and the Railroad*, pr. 1981, pb. 1983; *Family Devotions*, pr. 1981, pb. 1983; *Sound and Beauty*, pr. 1983 (two one-acts, *The House of Sleeping Beauties*, pb. 1983, and *The Sound of a Voice*, pb. 1984); *Broken Promises: Four Plays*, pb. 1983; *Rich Relations*, pr. 1986, pb. 1990; *As the Crow Flies*, pr. 1986; *Broken Promises*, pr. 1987 (includes *The Dance and the Railroad* and *The House of Sleeping Beauties*); *M. Butterfly*, pr. 1988, pb. 1988; *One Thousand Airplanes on the Roof*, pr. 1988, pb. 1989 (musical; music by Philip Glass); *F.O.B. and Other Plays*, pb. 1990; *Bondage*, pr. 1992 (one act); *Face Value*, pr. 1993.

Other literary forms

David Henry Hwang is known primarily for his plays.

Achievements

Hwang is the first Asian American playwright to bring specifically Asian and American themes to Broadway and Off-Broadway theater. Within the first decade of his career as a playwright, he staged six major productions in New York and abroad, garnering four Off-Broadway "Best Play" nominations and awards. *M. Butterfly*, his first Broadway play, won both the New York Drama Desk Award and the Tony Award for Best Play as well as a nomination for the Pulitzer Prize in drama. His plays explore issues of ethnic identity, gender, and imperialism, with often stunning theatrical flair.

Biography

David Henry Hwang was born in Los Angeles on August 11, 1957, the son of Henry Yuan Hwang, a banker, and Dorothy Huang Hwang, a professor of piano. His father grew up in Shanghai, China, and emigrated in the late 1940's to California, where he enrolled in the business program at the University of Southern California. His mother, born in southeastern China, had grown up in the Philippines.

Hwang received his A.B. degree from Stanford University in 1979, having majored in English, and he briefly taught writing in a high school in Menlo Park, California, before attending the Yale School of Drama in 1980 and 1981. His first play, *F.O.B.*, was performed at Stanford University before being accepted for production at the National Playwrights Conference at Connecticut's O'Neill Theatre Center in 1979, when he was twenty-one years old. The following year, Joseph Papp

brought it to the New York Shakespeare Festival's Public Theater, Off-Broadway. It won an Obie Award for the best new play of the season.

Like *F.O.B.*, Hwang's next two plays focused on the Chinese American experience. *The Dance and the Railroad* depicts two nineteenth century immigrants working on the transcontinental railroad, while *Family Devotions* is a bizarre farce set in contemporary California.

The next two plays, jointly titled *Sound and Beauty*, are stylized one-act plays set in contemporary Japan; they were produced Off-Broadway in 1983. The first, *The House of Sleeping Beauties*, reinvents a novella by Yasunari Kawabata, making the author a character in a version of his own work. The second, *The Sound of a Voice*, involves a conflict between a samurai warrior and a bewitching female hermit whom he intends to kill.

In 1983, Hwang received a Rockefeller playwright-in-residence award and a National Endowment for the Arts artistic associate fellowship. A Guggenheim Fellowship followed in 1984, as did fellowships from the National Endowment for the Arts and the New York State Council for the Arts in 1985. On September 25, 1985, he married Ophelia Y. M. Chong, an artist, from whom he was later divorced.

Rich Relations, produced Off-Broadway in 1986, was Hwang's first work not about the Asian experience and his first critical failure, though it recapitulated various themes from his earlier plays. Nevertheless, Hwang has termed this failure exhilarating, freeing him from undue concern about critical reaction.

M. Butterfly, produced in 1988, brought Hwang international renown, a Tony Award for the Best Play of 1988, the Outer Critics Circle Award, and a nomination for the Pulitzer Prize in 1989. Based on a true story of a French diplomat and his Chinese lover who turned out to be not only a spy but also a man, the play explores issues of gender, identity, racism, and political hegemony. *M. Butterfly* became a film in 1993. Also in 1988, Hwang collaborated with composer Philip Glass on *One Thousand Airplanes on the Roof*, a science-fiction work concerning a character who may have been kidnapped by visiting aliens.

In 1992, Hwang's one-act play *Bondage* premiered at the Humana Festival of New Plays at the Actors Theatre of Louisville, Kentucky. It was followed in 1993 by *Face Value*.

Analysis

Images of Asians and Asian Americans in modern culture have been relatively rare and often stereotypical; few have been created by Asian Americans themselves. On-screen stereotypes have ranged from Charlie Chan (performed by a white actor), an image of wise but humble, ultimately "knowing" inscrutability, to the cook Hop Sing on the television series *Bonanza* (1959-1973). Contact between Eastern and Western cultures had been depicted in such works as David Belasco's *Madam Butterfly* (pr. 1900, pb. 1935, the basis for Giacomo Puccini's opera *Madama Butterfly*), Richard Rodgers and Oscar Hammerstein II's *The King and I* (pr. 1951) and *Flower Drum Song* (pr. 1958), John Patrick's *The Teahouse of the August Moon* (pr. 1953, pb. 1954), and Paul Osborn's *The World of Suzie Wong* (pr. 1958, based on the novel by Richard Mason). Whatever their merits, however, none of these plays offered a genuinely Asian perspective on the events portrayed. By the early 1970's, literature by and about Asian Americans had begun to emerge; a decade later, Asian America's first critically acclaimed and commercially successful playwright was David Henry Hwang. From his earliest plays about the Chinese American experience to his Broadway hit *M. Butterfly* and subsequent plays, he has progressively explored issues of ethnic cultural identity, gender roles, the East/West relationship, and the effects of imperialism—and has done so with deftly constructed plots, a number of which incorporate elements of Chinese opera.

In his introduction to *F.O.B. and Other Plays*, Hwang identifies several phases "in attempting to define [his] place in America," and his early plays correspond to these. The first is an "assimilationist" phase, in which one tries to "out-white the whites" in order to fit in with the majority culture. Dale, the central character of his first play, *F.O.B.*, is a second-generation American of Chinese descent who dresses like a preppy and particularly disdains Chinese immigrants who are "Fresh Off the Boat," abbreviated "F.O.B." One such, named Steve, is the target of his scorn throughout the play, in part because he reminds Dale of his ancestry, the nonwhite, non-American past that Dale prefers to ignore, discard, or deny. Steve's cousin Grace, a first-generation Chinese American, functions as an intermediary between the two men, with insight into the plight of both the newly arrived and the all-too-assimilated "A.B.C.'s," meaning "American-Born Chinese." Steve announces himself as the great god Gwan Gung, the Chinese folk hero, the "god of warriors, writers, and prostitutes." Grace tells him that in the United States, Gwan Gung is dead; nevertheless, her contact with Steve reawakens her own fantasy, Fu Ma Lan, a great woman warrior. Dale repudiates both myths, having struggled for so long to overcome his Chineseness, but Steve's presence forces him to reexamine his values. Following Dale's attempt to humiliate the immigrant, Steve becomes in monologue the embodiment of "ChinaMan," the immigrant Everyman who helped build the American West, particularly its railroads. Such cultural kinship finally binds Steve and Grace, who transmutes him from dead god to living warrior. Dale is left behind at the end of the play, uncomprehending, unrepentant, and alone.

Gwan Gung also figures significantly in *The Dance and the Railroad*, Hwang's second play, a product of his "isolationist-nationalist" phase, in which he wrote primarily for other Asian Americans, having rejected "the assimilationist model" as "dangerous and self-defeating." Set in 1867, *The Dance and the Railroad* is a two-character, one-act play whose characters, Lone and Ma, are workers building the transcontinental railroad but are currently on a nine-day laborers' strike. Although conflicts between white management and Chinese labor underlie the action, personal differences between the characters and the traditions of Chinese opera and culture become increasingly prominent. Lone, a refugee from the Chinese opera, isolates himself from the other workers, practicing his art in solitude on the mountainside, above the strike and commercial toil. Ma, a gullible F.O.B. laborer who believes in the promises of the Gold Mountain in America, ascends in search of Lone, discovers Lone's austere artistic training regimen, and yearns to learn opera to "become" Gwan Gung in the new land. To learn the discipline that artistry requires, Ma maintains the locust position all night, a metaphor for immigrant experience. Finally worthy to study Gwan Gung, Ma rejects doing so and returns to the work below when the strike ends. The play's later scenes are performed in the style of Chinese opera. The actor playing Lone—his namesake, John Lone—had trained with the Peking Opera for eight years; he also directed the play, choreographed it, and provided its music.

Hwang's third play, *Family Devotions*, is a nine-character farce set in contemporary California. The action centers on three generations of a thoroughly "assimilated" Chinese American family satirically based on Hwang's own; they are visited by their "second brother" Di-gou, a doctor and former violinist who has lived for thirty years under the Communist Chinese regime. His sisters, ardent fundamentalist Christians, are shocked to find out that he is an atheist and that he rejects the legend of See-Goh-Poh, a Christian "Woman Warrior" who allegedly saved his soul at age eight. He, in turn, is baffled by the family's crass materialism and conspicuous consumption and has come to ask his sisters to renounce their faith and return home with him. The first act ends with one of them, Ama, delivering a fiery testimonial from a rolling, neon-lit pulpit as the "Hallelujah Chorus" blares away. In the second act, the sisters and their daughters tie Di-gou to a table, assailing him with the word of God and See-Goh-Poh. He breaks his bonds in a holy fit of possession, speaks in tongues, and exposes See-Goh-Poh as a fraud whose crusade was a ruse to conceal an unwanted pregnancy. As the grotesque exorcism proceeds, the sisters die in their chairs as Di-gou continues his vehement speech. Di-gou and the young child of the family depart, leaving the house a spiritual wreck, torn between the Chinese past and the California present, between myth and reality. The play shows the influence of American playwright Sam Shepard, to whom it is dedicated, but many of its thematic preoccupations—assimilation versus origins, lost ethnic awareness, a core conflict of incompatible values—are recognizably Hwang's own.

In the third phase of his writing, Hwang sought to move beyond his personal experience. *The House of Sleeping Beauties* is an adaptation of a story by Yasunari Kawabata, who is himself one of the play's two characters. The companion piece, *The Sound of a Voice*, is a fable of a samurai warrior who goes into a forest to kill a bewitching female hermit but instead falls in love with her. *Rich Relations* was Hwang's first play with all Caucasian characters and his first critical and commercial failure. Like *Family Devotions*, it lampooned Evangelical Christianity, deathbed resurrections, and crass materialism within a suburban Los Angeles family, but

it offered little that was new in technique or ideas.

M. Butterfly, seven years later, was a commercial and critical triumph on Broadway. The play is based on an article that appeared in *The New York Times* about the conviction of espionage of a French diplomat, who aided the Communist Chinese government by turning over embassy documents to his mistress of twenty years, a Chinese opera singer whom he had mistakenly believed to be an extremely modest woman. Hwang, however, sought no additional details from the actual case so as to avoid writing a docudrama; he was struck by the story as an inversion of the plot of the play and opera *Madama Butterfly*, in which a Japanese woman falls in love with a Caucasian man, is spurned, and commits suicide. In Hwang's play, the diplomat, René Gallimard, is the counterpart of Puccini's Westerner, Pinkerton. Gallimard falls in love with opera singer Song Liling, unaware that "she" is a Chinese male actor in the opera and an agent of the Communist government. The role of Song Liling is played by a man (B. D. Wong in the original production), though this fact is not revealed to the theater audience until the beginning of the third act when, in a moment of startling theatricality, Song Liling removes her makeup and changes clothes on stage, dispelling the illusion for the audience before disclosing her true gender and identity to Gallimard in a nude scene near the end of the play.

In many ways, *M. Butterfly* continues the devices and thematic preoccupations found in Hwang's earlier plays: the use of Chinese opera, the ambiguities of gender, the clash of Asian and Western values. Incorporating both Puccini's music and Chinese opera, *M. Butterfly* also explores issues of gender and racial stereotyping, of dominance and submission (political as well as sexual), and of the morality of the Western presence in Asia. Furthermore, the play audaciously questions the nature of love and illusion, undermining any certainty about the ultimate knowability of another person or, indeed, of the world itself. While that theme is not new in twentieth century literature—having been particularly prominent in Ford Madox Ford's novel *The Good Soldier* (1915), for example, seldom, if ever, has it been presented with such dramatic effectiveness and theatrical flair.

M. Butterfly also marks a considerable advance in Hwang's dramatic technique over the earlier plays, which were chronologically presented on realistic sets. The play begins with a retrospective monologue by Gallimard in his prison cell; many flashbacks to European and Asian locales are introduced throughout twenty-seven brief scenes in three acts. The stylized set, designed by Eiko Ishioka, is dominated by a gently sloping, curved ramp, enabling a flexible use of the stage space. The original title, "Monsieur Butterfly," was shortened to *M. Butterfly* (at Hwang's wife's suggestion) to reflect the play's ambiguity.

Following the phenomenal success of *M. Butterfly*, Hwang worried that whatever he did next would be considered a disappointment; accordingly, following a collaboration with the composer Philip Glass on a work entitled *One Thousand Airplanes on the Roof*, he worked on film scripts, including a planned screen adaptation of *M. Butterfly*. In 1992, his one-act play entitled *Bondage* opened in Louisville, Kentucky, fol-lowed in 1993 by the play *Face Value*. *Bondage*, like *The House of Sleeping Beauties*, is set in an exotic brothel: one that caters to sadomasochists, where a dominating female is paid to humiliate a male clientele. The play begins with Terri, the female dominatrix, in a session with Mark; both are covered from head to toe in black leather so that their faces as well as their ethnic identities are concealed from the audience. The play consists of a fantasy game in which their races continually change, further exploring themes of gender, racial, and political stereotyping, as well as the intricate power relationships that Hwang continues to dramatize with startling, provocative, and highly original theatrical effectiveness.

Other major works

TELEPLAY: *My American Son*, 1987.
SCREENPLAY: *M. Butterfly*, 1993.

Bibliography

Bernstein, Richard. "France Jails Two in Odd Case of Espionage." *The New York Times*, May 11, 1986, p. K7.

Gerard, Jeremy. "David Hwang: Riding on the Hyphen." *The New York Times Magazine*, March 13, 1988, 44, and 88-89.

Hwang, David Henry. "*M. Butterfly*: An Interview with David Henry Hwang." Interview by John Lewis DiGaetani. *The Drama Review: A Journal of Performance Studies*, 33, no. 3 (Fall, 1989): 141-153.

Pace, Eric. "I Write Plays to Claim a Place for Asian-Americans." *The New York Times*, July 12, 1981, p. D4.

Skloot, Robert. "Breaking the Butterfly: The Politics of David Henry Hwang." *Modern Drama* 33, no. 1 (March, 1990): 59-66.

Street, Douglas. *David Henry Hwang*. Boise, Idaho: Boise State University Press, 1989.

CYNTHIA KADOHATA

Born: Chicago, Illinois; July 2, 1956

Principal long fiction

The Floating World, 1989; *In the Heart of the Valley of Love*, 1992.

Other literary forms

Cynthia Kadohata is known mainly for her novels.

Achievements

The recipient of a 1991 Whiting Writer's Award and a grant from the National Endowment for the Arts (NEA), Kadohata has written short stories for *The New Yorker*, *Grand Street*, and *Pennsylvania Review*. Her novels, however, remain her major literary achievement and have earned for her comparisons to Mark Twain, Jack Kerouac, Raymond Carver, and William Faulkner. Her second novel was a finalist for the PEN West Awards.

Kadohata's narratives are simple and relatively unencumbered with subplots; her characters are good-natured despite living in a world that does not always treat them well. Her novels use narrators whose life experiences parallel Kadohata's in important ways. Her novels also show the redemptive power of familial and romantic love and trace the pursuit or fulfillment of that love within a journey motif. Kadohata has been hailed as a new voice on the Asian American scene, appearing in print subsequent to the success of more established female writers of Asian heritage such as Maxine Hong Kingston and Amy Tan.

Biography

Kadohata is a second-generation Japanese American who seems to be less conscious of her ethnicity than some critics would want or expect her to be. One critic, for example, took issue with the strong and aggressive portrayal of the Japanese grandmother in Kadohata's first novel because he thought that she intended to characterize all Japanese grandmothers as abusive. Kadohata emphasizes that she does not attempt to speak for all Asians when she writes. The fact that she happens to be Asian means that there will always be Asian elements in her writing because that is what she knows best. While there is no overt political agenda in her work, readers can see in her novels evidence of social and community reaction, some of which is negative, to

the presence of her Asian characters, which she has also experienced in her life. Her parents were born in Southern California. Her maternal grandfather was a graphic artist who moved his family to Hawaii. Kadohata's father's family worked as tenant farmers before World War II. His parents were born in Japan and immigrated to the United States in the 1920's.

Born in Chicago, Kadohata has a brother and a sister. Her family moved to Arkansas, Georgia, Michigan, and back to Chicago before finally settling in Los Angeles, the city that Kadohata has also called her home as an adult. She has said that writing and traveling are linked for her in important ways, that change and movement and transition make her happy because they show her ordinary things in surprising, new ways. Kadohata's parents divorced when she was eight years old, her mother and brother ultimately establishing homes in California, and her father, a private in the U.S. Army and a chicken-sexer like the father of the heroine in her first novel, returning permanently to small-town Arkansas. One formative influence on her childhood was the fact that she and her siblings lived in small towns rather than large cities for many years. She says that, although she has warm memories of Chicago, the serenity and wonder of living where she could clearly see the stars each night has stayed with her.

Kadohata's mother stayed at home while married. After the divorce, she worked clerical jobs and went to college to earn a sociology degree with a minor in philosophy. Growing up, Kadohata heard her frequently quoting lines from the Danish philosopher Søren Kierkegaard. In fact, Kadohata's father attributes the divorce to the fact that his wife began reading books.

Kadohata, an intense and competitive student, attended an alternative high school in Chicago and then transferred to Hollywood High, which did not accept many of her credits and where she never did gain a sense of belonging or identification. Although she says that she was shy as a teenager, she had jobs clerking in a department store and serving hamburgers in a fast-food restaurant before enrolling at Los Angeles City College. She transferred to the University of Southern California, from which she earned a degree in journalism. Kadohata lived for a time in Boston, where her sister lived before moving to Hong Kong, and honed her skills with writing classes at the University of Pittsburgh and Columbia University, though she did not complete programs at either institution. She counts traditional education as a less significant formative influence than the education that she and her family gleaned while traveling the country. In Los Angeles, where Kadohata makes her home with a musician husband and two large dogs, she feels more comfortable than in the East due to the slower pace and lack of obsession about writing, and there is also a substantial Asian community. She admits that her hyphenated heritage (Asian ethnicity coupled with American nurturing) brings with it issues that are complicated, and she explores some of these in her work.

When Kadohata was twenty-one, an accident convinced her that life was unpredictable. She was walking down a street in Los Angeles' affluent Hancock Park when a car with an elderly driver at the wheel jumped the curb and knocked her down, breaking her collarbone and crushing her right arm. Giving the narrator in her second novel the same misfortune was Kadohata's way of psychologically admitting a deformity and publicly working through its emotional scars.

Analysis

Kadohata's novels share significantly in major intentions, approach, and themes. Told by late-adolescent female narrators who are optimistic and a bit naïve, the novels are coming-of-age sagas that are cast within a journey motif and that rely in important ways on experiences from Kadohata's real life. Though devoid of important sociological or political agendas, the novels nevertheless glimpse, in varying degrees, the prevailing majority attitude toward minorities. Though *The Floating World* is set in the 1950's and *In the Heart of the Valley of Love* is set in the year 2052, both validate the place of discovery and the security of love in human relationships.

Differences between the novels are less significant but easily apparent. *The Floating World*, set some forty years before it was written, is nostalgic, almost wistful, and ends with an ancestral blessing. The language is uncomplicated, and the images and description are fresh. *In the Heart of the Valley of Love* is futuristic; darker, bleaker, confused, and threatening, its ending is

open-ended. The question posed in the first few pages—where did Uncle Rohn disappear to?—remains uncomfortably unresolved at the conclusion, despite the fact that the entire novel has been essentially a prolonged search for him. Living conditions have deteriorated rather than progressed. Inconveniences and depravation put the characters into a malaise, heat and pollution are stifling, and gun-brandishing is widespread. The reader's sense of being watched, of being stalked, of being threatened, is achieved in several ways. Futuristic inventions such as photographs that can be plugged in and "tubes" dispensing hallucinogenic drugs in a submarine sandwich shop, a disease that causes the skin to slough off black pearls, and the unquiet dreams of main character Francie are all foreboding. The environment has eroded: Where once were pastoral Pasadena homes and trees now exists an arid garbage dump. A smelly, massive, labyrinthine parking facility in the bowels of Los Angeles that confounds Francie may strike many readers as familiar territory, but neologisms such as "chirp," "creds," "richtown," and "that's dry" seem purposefully alienating.

In *The Floating World*, race is a tangential issue in a way that is obliterated in *In the Heart of the Valley of Love*. Olivia Ann's parents are so proud of her that they tell strangers, "If you couldn't see her, you wouldn't even know she was Japanese." The family is easily assimilated in Arkansas because they move into a Japanese community, and Olivia Ann is comfortable being bilingual because "Japanese and English . . . each contained thoughts you couldn't express exactly in the other." For most of the novel Olivia Ann stays so completely nestled in her family unit that race does not matter, and racism does not surface. *In the Heart of the Valley of Love* portrays a multicultural world both simpler and more complex. By the year 2052, nonwhites are the majority. Francie's mother was Japanese, but her father was half Chinese and half black. When she thumbs through her mother's high school yearbook, Francie comments about the past, that "strange period of transition in America" when white girls used lipstick to make their lips fuller like black girls' lips, when black girls straightened their hair to make it like Asians' hair, and when Asians used eye shadow to make their eyes seem rounder like those of white girls. In the work of other female writers of Asian heritage, notably Maxine Hong Kingston, Amy Tan, and Bharati Mukherjee, the challenges of reconciling Asian ethnicity with a white culture is a major theme, but Kadohata does not follow this trend.

Kadohata's selection of a nubile female voice for her tales is an effective choice, for the open-mindedness, vulnerability, and agreeable resilience in her narrators make for a convincing and appealing figure. Though two generations apart, Olivia Ann and Francie have strikingly similar personalities. They are both calm and questioning, amused or gently disgusted. In neither novel is the narrator jaded or cynical, although she has the hard luck of living with an abusive grandmother in the first and being oppressed by a restrictive and vigilant government in the second. Both narrators give love freely, and the concept of a closely bonded nuclear family is consistently their inspiration and their solace. Olivia Ann, protagonist in *The Floating World*, has a traditional family consisting of father, mother, three brothers, and a grandmother who is the bane of her existence, who dies in the course of the novel, but whose memory continues to haunt Olivia Ann. Francie in *In the Heart of the Valley of Love* has lost her parents to a curious disease but keeps with her in a pouch two stones representing them, which she likes to take out and talk to from time to time. Her family is her aunt and uncle, who reared her after her parents' death and with whom she lives. Although she says, "People became sick and died so abruptly that you hated to love anyone," Francie easily and sincerely loves family and friends.

In both novels, the heroine matures and becomes physically independent of family. After a childhood with her family spent more or less on the road, Olivia Ann's move into her own apartment in a different state marks the end of her adolescence. Francie, nineteen when the novel opens, seems mentally fixated at thirteen, her age when her parents died, and the ceremony and the finality of her burial of her parents' stones at the end of the novel is also a laying to rest of her dependence on them.

California, the setting of a good portion of *The Floating World* and all of *In the Heart of the Valley of Love*, is the region that Kadohata knows best. Her feeling of being more comfortable in Los Angeles than in any other place where she has lived makes that city the obvious choice for Olivia Ann's apartment and for the home that Francie makes with her aunt and uncle. On a more symbolic level, the Japanese *ukiyo-e*, or "floating world," depicts a nocturnal realm of pleasure, entertainment, and drink, while also referring to a dominant art form that flourished in Japan from the seventeenth through the nineteenth centuries. Olivia Ann glosses the term *ukiyo* by saying that it also implies "change and the pleasures and loneliness change brings." Her family literally "floats" from place to place, the children with open-eyed wonder, more or less enjoying themselves, while the parents struggle with a series of job losses and a rocky marriage. They are a world unto themselves, together exploring outward and nurturing one another inward. Like Olivia Ann, Kadohata has noted the pleasure of change and travel in her life, more important to her education than completion of an extended degree program.

Though the "heart" seems to have gone out of society by the year 2052, the principal characters exist in loving relationships. Francie notes frequently and contentedly how her aunt and uncle show love for each other. The fox-trotting and waltzing that they do in the living room make Francie "secretly optimistic about the world," because their lives were unhappy until they found each other. The love that Francie shares with her boyfriend, Mark, seems solid and mature beyond their years, and the carnival ride they enjoy on a whim in the middle of a snowstorm defies drought, riots, and the ubiquitous "they" to depress them. United in the valley between Los Angeles and the desert at the end of the novel, Francie and Mark ceremoniously bury effects of their childhood: the rocks that stand for Francie's mother and father and the bracelet Mark bought for himself at age fourteen, shortly after he had left his parents. Francie determines to replace the "sky" that she used to pray to with the inspiration she can draw from the here and now. Both people have become more realistic and self-possessed as the novel ends, and together they seem an oasis of human feeling in a wasteland of automated and malevolent, though ultimately ineffectual, forces.

Bibliography
"Bleakness and Brutality Beneath a Yellow-Blue Sky." *Miami Herald*, August 16, 1992, pp. F5+.
Caldwell, Gail. "A Japanese-American Family's Shifting World." *Boston Globe*, June 2, 1989, pp. A14+.
Hale, Mike. "Living the Bad Life in California." *San Jose Mercury News*, August 23, 1992, pp. F12+.
Innes, Charlotte. "Asian-American Family Finds a Life on the Road." *Philadelphia Inquirer*, July 30, 1989, pp. F12+.
Kadohata, Cynthia. "Cynthia Kadohata." Interview by Mickey Pearlman. In *Listen to Their Voices: Twenty Interviews with Women Who Write*. New York: W. W. Norton, 1993.

_____ . "Cynthia Kadohata: Her Second Novel Envisions the Decline—and Very Nearly the Fall—of L.A." Interview by Lisa See. *Publishers Weekly* 239 (August 3, 1992): 48-49.

O'Hehir, Diana. "On the Road with Grandmother's Magic." *The New York Times Book Review*, July 23, 1989, p. 16.

Quick, Barbara. Review of *In the Heart of the Valley of Love*, by Cynthia Kadohata. *The New York Times Book Review*, August 30, 1992, p. 14.

Yogi, Stan. Review of *The Floating World*, by Cynthia Kadohata. *Amerasia Journal* 16, no. 1 (1990): 261.

MAXINE HONG KINGSTON

Born: Stockton, California; October 27, 1940

Principal long fiction

The Woman Warrior: Memoirs of a Girlhood Among Ghosts, 1976; *China Men*, 1980; *Tripmaster Monkey: His Fake Book*, 1989.

Other literary forms

Maxine Hong Kingston has published both nonfiction, including essays, and short fiction. Her *Hawai'i One Summer, 1978* (1987) is a collection of twelve prose sketches with original woodblock prints and calligraphy.

Achievements

Kingston has played an instrumental role in introducing Asian American literature to the reading public in the United States and in bringing the country's attention to its achievement. In the middle of the 1970's, Kingston helped initiate a literary movement to reclaim Asian Americans' sense of history and identity by representing the "mis(sing)-represented" and by giving voice to the "voiceless." Kingston's writing style, use of language, and thematic preoccupations have not only strongly influenced the development of Asian American literature but also enriched the spectrum of American literature.

Kingston's first autobiographical novel, *The Woman Warrior*, won the National Book Critics Circle Award for nonfiction, as did her second book, *China Men*. Her many other accolades include the Anisfield-Wolf Race Relations Award (1978), a Living Treasure of Hawaii designation (1980), and inclusion of *The Woman Warrior* on *Time* magazine's 1979 list of the top ten nonfiction works of the decade. Kingston has also been the recipient of a National Education Association writing fellowship (1980) and a Guggenheim Fellowship (1981).

Biography

Kingston was born in Stockton, California, on October 27, 1940, to Tom and Ying Lan (Chew) Hong, both first-generation immigrants from China. Kingston grew up in a bilingual environment in which she learned how to appreciate her Chinese cultural heritage and deal with what W. E. B. Du Bois called the experience of "double consciousness."

Kingston demonstrated her interest in creative writing while attending the University of California at Berkeley. She practiced writing short stories in school. It was also Berkeley where Kingston met Earl Kingston, who was to become an actor. After receiving her B.A. degree from Berkeley in 1962, the two were married. Their son, Joseph Lawrence Chung Mei, was born in 1964. In the same year, Kingston returned to Berkeley to study for a teaching certificate.

From 1965 to 1977, Kingston taught high school in both California and Hawaii to finance her interest in creative writing. After the success of her first autobiographical novel, *The Woman Warrior*, in 1976, Kingston was invited by the University of Hawaii at Honolulu to teach English and writing as a visiting associate professor. During the period, Kingston also conducted a creative writing workshop at the University of Southern California and served as the Thelma McAndless Distinguished Professor in the Humanities at Eastern Michigan University in Ypsilanti.

In the mid-1980's, Kingston and her husband moved back to California. Kingston began working on her fourth novel and teaching courses at Berkeley. She and her husband have a home in the Rockridge section of Oakland.

Analysis

The development of Chinese American literature can be divided roughly into two periods. The first period lasted for about a century. It began with the publication of bilingual pamphlets and phrase books, such as Wong Sam's *An English-Chinese Phrase Book* (1875), and ended with Kingston's autobiographical novels *The Woman Warrior* and *China Men*.

The Woman Warrior and *China Men* are representative of the early development and achievement of Asian American literature in two aspects: first, both works use the autobiographical approach to describe their characters' struggle with their identity; second, both works display their characters' eagerness to reclaim their sense of history and identity through the study of family history.

Autobiography was used very effectively by early Asian American writers attempting to define the Asian American experience. Both Chinese American writer Pardee Lowe's *Father and Glorious Descendant* (1943) and Jade Snow Wong's *Fifth Chinese Daughter* (1945) use the genre of autobiography to describe the writer's struggle with not only inter-cultural but also intra-cultural conflict. Chinese American writer Virginia Lee's *The House That Tai Ming Built* (1963), Chuang Hua's *Crossings* (1968), and Shawn Wong's *Homebase* (1979) are fictionalized memoirs that can be read as semiautobiographies.

Of all the autobiographies and semiautobiographies that were produced in the first period of Asian American literature, *The Woman Warrior* and *China Men* were among the first to bring America's attention to the artistic and literary achievement of Chinese American culture. Both works use memories, talk-stories, and traditional Chinese legends, and both interweave the past and the present, fact and fiction, reality and imagination, and traditional Chinese and modern American culture.

The female narrator in *The Woman Warrior* is a second-generation Chinese American. The book, which describes the narrator's close relationship with her mother, also tells the story about the narrator's search for voice and identity, for the narrator believed that she had lost her voice when she had to speak English for the first time in kindergarten. Ever since, as the narrator recalls, "A dumbness—a shame—still cracks my voice in two, even when I want to say 'hello' casually, or ask an easy question in front of the check-out counter, or ask directions of a bus driver. I stand frozen, or I hold up the line with the complete, grammatical sentence that come squeaking out at impossible length. 'What did you say?' says the cab driver, or 'Speak up,' so I have to perform again, only weaker the second time."

The narrator's "silence" is apparently occasioned as much by her struggle with English as by her awareness of being different. In both cases, the traumatic feeling of alienation results from the narrator's having to deal with the clash of two cultural realities, an experience described by African American scholar W. E. B. Du Bois in *The Souls of Black Folk* (1903) as "double consciousness"—"the sense of always looking at one's self through the eyes of others, of measuring one's soul by the tape of a world that looks on in amused contempt

and pity." The narrator's early experiences obviously had a detrimental effect on her sense of identity as a child.

In her mother, the narrator found a strong role model. Brave Orchid "delivered babies in beds and pigsties" in China, the narrator tells the reader. "She yanked bones straight that had been crooked for years while relatives held the cripples down, and she did all this never dressed less elegantly than when she stepped out of the sedan chair." After Orchid immigrated to America, she protected her Chinese name the same way she valued her culture, for Orchid believed that professional women should "have the right to use their maiden names if they like" and decided to add "no American name nor holding one in reserve for American emergencies."

If the narrator has learned from her mother the importance of human dignity, her eagerness to identify with Fa Mu Lan, a legendary Chinese woman warrior, was what enabled the narrator to bridge the gap between the seemingly paradoxical duality of the past and the present, of the real and the imagined, of the visible and the invisible worlds, and of China and the United States. Such identification delineates and accentuates the process of cultural suture that helps give shape to the narrator's true identity.

Kingston's second autobiographical novel, *China Men*, chronicles the experience and sufferings of Chinese male immigrants in the United States. Ed, Woodrow, Roosevelt, and Worldster were first-generation Chinese immigrants who could barely speak English. Yet their eagerness to adapt to a new environment brought into question their relationship with their own cultural heritage. Worldster "had a thick moustache and tried to look like Clark Gable"; Ed dressed "like Fred Astaire"; Ed and Woodrow once "caught sight of themselves in windows and hubcaps" on Fifth Avenue in New York City and thought "they looked all the same American."

Woodrow, Roosevelt, and Worldster started their cultural transformation by trying to change their physical appearance. They completed the metamorphosis by leaving Ed out of the partnership contract for the Laundromat. In doing so, Woodrow, Roosevelt, and Worldster betrayed a well-honored traditional Chinese ethical code, which was once cheerfully chanted by Ed, the dupe in the money game: "Friends were fairer than brother; there was an equality." Woodrow, Roosevelt, and Worldster's betrayal of their friendship with Ed, thus, is juxtaposed with and corresponds to their betrayal of their own culture.

As Korean American critic Elaine Kim observes, Kingston first conceived *The Woman Warrior* and *China Men* as an interlocking story. According to Kim, Kingston decided to publish the two books separately out of fear that the men's stories "were anti-female and would undercut the feminist viewpoint." Indeed, even though the narrative point of view in *China Men* is similar to that in *The Woman Warrior*, the female narrator's detached voice in the latter suggests both a physical and an emotional distance between the daughter and her male ancestors.

In "Come All Ye Asian American Writers of the Real and the Fake," Chinese American writer and critic Frank Chin's introduction to *The Big Aiiieeeee! An Anthology of Chinese American and Japanese American Literature* (1991), Chin posits that Kingston and other Chinese American writers such as Amy Tan and David Henry Hwang "are the first writers of any race, and certainly the first writers of Asian ancestry, to so boldly fake the best-known works from the most universally known body of Asian literature lore in history." Chin argues that in *The Woman Warrior*, "Kingston takes a childhood chant, 'The Ballad of Mulan,' which is as popular today as 'London Bridge Is Falling Down,' and rewrites the heroine, Fa Mulan, to the specifications of the stereotype of the Chinese woman as a pathological white supremacist victimized and trapped in a hideous Chinese civilization. The tattoos Kingston gives Fa Mulan, to dramatize cruelty to women, actually belong to the hero Yue Fei, a man whose tomb is now a tourist attraction at West Lake, in Hanzhou city."

While Chin's arduous effort to defend the purity of Asian cultures in their reproductive forms in Asian American literature is admirable, his criticism of Kingston's use of materials from historical Asian literature and lore is too judgmental and arbitrary. What Kingston is able to accomplish by juxtaposing the legendary female character Fa Mulan and the historical male figure Yue Fei (a general who lived during the Song Dynasty) in *The Woman Warrior* is to destroy both the traditional gender line, which was ignominious in placing women at the bottom of the social strata in China,

and the line that separates imagination and reality. Hers, similar to what Anne Sexton and John Gardner had achieved in rewriting the fairy tale "Cinderella," is an effort to reveal the corroborative relationship between power and knowledge and, in doing so, make history not only responsive to but also responsible for a progressive society. Kingston's books thus epitomize the Asian American search for a literary voice that will best describe the Asian American experience.

The Woman Warrior and *China Men* brought the first period in the development of Asian American literature, which is dominated by the genre of autobiography, to an end. Kingston's success in blending autobiography and fiction heralded the beginning of the Asian American Renaissance, which has witnessed an increase in Asian American writers' interest in searching for approaches that can both democratize the canonization of the Asian American voice and present more colorful and more pluralistic portrayals of the Asian American experience.

Kingston's third book, *Tripmaster Monkey*, is her first attempt at straight fiction. The main character, Wittman Ah Sing, is a fifth-generation Chinese American who vacillates between the psychedelic culture of the 1960's and his interest in traditional Chinese culture. After Ah Sing loses his job as a salesperson, he devotes himself to introducing stories from Chinese classics into the American theater. In *Tripmaster Monkey*, Kingston continues her experiment with the use of language. She believes that the Chinese accents, cadence, and rhythm she uses in her books help enlarge and enrich American English.

Kingston's works represent an effort to celebrate consciously the writer's own cultural heritage, to reclaim Asian Americans' sense of history and identity by using a language whose power is generated by the writer's deep identification with her gender and race, and to democratize the American literary voice by giving a voice to the "voiceless." To understand Kingston's works is, therefore, to develop an appreciation for the culturally diverse nature of American society, to recognize the cause for the struggle behind her narrators' cracked voices, and to respond to their earnest call for understanding.

Other major works

MISCELLANEOUS: *Hawai'i One Summer, 1978*, 1987.

Bibliography

Kim, Elaine H. *Asian American Literature: An Introduction to the Writings and Their Social Context*. Philadelphia: Temple University Press, 1982.

Lim, Shirley Geok-lin. *Approaches to Teaching Kingston's "The Woman Warrior."* New York: Modern Language Association, 1991.

Lim, Shirley Geok-lin, and Amy Ling. *Reading the Literatures of Asian America*. Philadelphia: Temple University Press, 1992.

Ling, Amy. *Between Worlds: Women Writers of Chinese Ancestry*. Elmsford, N.Y.: Pergamon Press, 1990.

Wong, Sau-ling Cynthia. *Reading Asian American Literature: From Necessity to Extravagance*. Princeton, N.J.: Princeton University Press, 1993.

BHARATI MUKHERJEE

Born: Calcutta, India; July 27, 1940

Principal short fiction

Darkness, 1985; *The Middleman and Other Stories*, 1988.

Other literary forms

In addition to novels, essays, and articles, Bharati Mukherjee, along with Clark Blaise, is the author of *Days and Nights in Calcutta* (1977), a travel memoir, and *The Sorrow and the Terror: The Haunting Legacy of the Air India Tragedy* (1987), a documentary on the crash of Air India flight 182 in June of 1985. She also wrote *Kautilya's Concept of Diplomacy* (1976), a political treatise.

Achievements

Mukherjee occupies a distinctive place among first-generation North American writers of Indian origin. She has received a number of grants from the Canada Arts Council (1973-1974, 1977), the Shastri Indo-Canadian Institute (1976-1977), the Guggenheim Foundation (1978-1979), and the Canadian government (1982). In 1980, she won the first prize from the Periodical Distribution Association for her short story "Isolated Incidents." In 1981, she won second prize in the National Magazine Awards for her essay "An Invisible Woman." Her story "Angela" was selected for inclusion in *The Best American Short Stories* of 1985, and "The Tenant" was included in *The Best American Short Stories* of 1987. Her second collection of short stories, *The Middleman and Other Stories*, won for her the National Book Critics Circle Award in 1989.

Biography

Bharati Mukherjee was born into a well-to-do traditional Bengali Brahman family in Calcutta. Her father, Sudhir Lal Mukherjee, was the proprietor of a successful pharmaceutical company. She received her early education in Great Britain, in Switzerland, and at Loreto Convent School, Calcutta, and later joined Calcutta University, where she received a B.A. degree in English (with honors) in 1959. In 1961, having received a master's degree from the University of Baroda, she came to the United States to attend the Writers' Workshop at the University of Iowa, where she received her M.F.A. degree in 1963. At the University of Iowa, she met Clark Blaise, an American writer of Canadian descent, whom she married in 1963. In 1966, she moved with her husband to Montreal, Canada, where she obtained a teaching position in English at McGill University. In 1969, she received a Ph.D. degree in English from the University of Iowa. Her first novel, *The Tiger's Daughter*, which shows the influence of E. M. Forster, was published in 1971. In 1972, she became a Canadian citizen. During her stay in Canada, she became painfully conscious of the racial discrimination and harassment suffered by Indians and other Asian immigrants. She recorded her experience with racism in Canada in an article entitled "An Invisible Woman," and she also expressed it artistically in several of her short stories. After living in Canada for fourteen years and having established her career as a writer and teacher, she moved to the United States and became a permanent resident in 1980. She has taught at several American universities and colleges, including Emory University, Skidmore College, Columbia University, Queens College, and the Writers' Workshop at the University of Iowa. She has also become a distinguished professor of English at the University of California, Berkeley.

Analysis

In an interview published in *The Canadian Fiction Magazine*, Mukherjee stated: "My stories centre on a new breed and generation of North American pioneers." The "new pioneers" inhabiting her fictional world include a wide variety of immigrant characters—most of them India-born, and others, increasingly, from Third World countries—who pull up their traditional roots and arrive in the New World with dreams of wealth, success, and freedom. Her first collection of short stories, *Darkness*, focuses on immigrant Indians in North America and deals primarily with the problems of expatriation, immigration, and cross-cultural assimilation. Of the twelve stories in this collection, three reflect on the Canadian situation and the remaining are set in the United States. Mukherjee calls the Canadian stories "uneasy stories about expatriation," as they stem from the author's personal encounters with racial prejudice in Canada.

A notably painful and uneasy story about expatriation and racial prejudice, "The World According to Hsu" explores the diasporic consciousness of Ratna Clayton, an Indian woman married to a Canadian professor of psychology at McGill University, Montreal. Her husband, Graeme Clayton, has been offered the departmental chair at Toronto. Ratna dreads the thought of moving to Toronto. She ruminates, "In Toronto, she was not Canadian, not even Indian. She was something called, after the imported idiom of London, a Paki. And for Pakis, Toronto was hell." Hoping that a vacation would be the ideal setting to persuade his wife to move to Toronto, Graeme arranges a trip to a beautiful African island. Upon their arrival there, they find themselves caught in the midst of a revolution and a night curfew. The thought of surrounding violence unleashes memories of Toronto in Ratna's mind. "A week before their flight, a Bengali woman was beaten and nearly blinded on the street. And the week before that an eight-year-old Punjabi boy was struck by a car announcing on its bumper: KEEP CANADA GREEN. PAINT A PAKI." At the dinner table, when her husband reads to her an article by Kenneth J. Hsu about the geological collision of the continents, Ratna wonders why she had to move to Toronto to experience a different kind of collision—racial and cultural. Finally, she brings herself to accept her situation when she realizes that "No matter where she lived, she would never feel at home again."

Another painful story, "Tamurlane," attacks racism in Canada and dramatizes the precarious situation of illegal aliens who, lured by the dream of a better life, are smuggled into the country and are forced to lead an anonymous, subhuman, underground existence, sleeping in shifts and living in constant fear of being raided by immigration authorities. "Was this what I left Ludhiana for?" poignantly asks the narrator, an illegal Indian working as a waiter in a dingy Indian restaurant in Toronto. The title of the story (alluding to Tamerlane, a lame Mongol warrior) refers to the restaurant's lame chef, Gupta, who had been a victim of Canadian racism six years before and was thrown on the subway tracks to be maimed. During a raid on illegals at the restaurant, Gupta orders the Mounties to leave. When they refuse to do so and threaten to use force on him too, he picks up a cleaver and brings it down on the outstretched hand of a Mountie. He then defiantly holds his Canadian passport in front of his face. "That way," the story ends,

"he never saw the drawn gun, nor did he try to dodge the single bullet."

The immigrant experience dramatized in the American stories brings out the conflicts resulting from expatriation and cross-cultural assimilation. Dr. Manny Patel, in "Nostalgia," is an Indian psychiatrist working at a state hospital in Queens, New York. His American Dream has come true; he lives in an expensive home, drives a red Porsche, is married to an American nurse, and sends his son to Andover. Counting his manifold acquisitions and blessings, he regards himself "not an expatriate but a patriot." Yet he knows that, despite becoming an American citizen, he will forever continue to hover between the Old World and the New. Being the only child of his parents, he feels that it is his duty to return to India and look after them in their old age. In such a mood of remorse and longing, he drives one day into Manhattan and is smitten by the beauty of an Indian saleswoman, Padma. He is overwhelmed when Padma readily accepts his invitation for a date. He takes her to an Indian restaurant for dinner and then to bed in the expensive hotel above the restaurant. The whole experience makes him so nostalgic that he wishes "he had married an Indian woman," that "he had any life but the one he had chosen." As he prepares to get dressed, Padma's uncle enters the hotel room with a passkey and accuses Dr. Manny of the rape of his minor niece. To his great shock and humiliation, Dr. Manny discovers that the goddess of his dreams was nothing more than a common prostitute and that he had been conned by her and her uncle-pimp. The uncle extorts not only seven hundred dollars from Dr. Manny but also a physician's note on hospital stationery to secure immigration for his nephew. After the uncle-niece team leaves, Dr. Manny enters the bathroom, defecates into the sink, squatting the way he had done in his father's home, takes his own excrement in his hands, and writes "WHORE" all over the bathroom mirror and floor. Then, just before dawn, he drives home, thinking that he will somehow make up to his American wife for this night.

The conflict between tradition and modernity takes a different form in "A Father." Mr. Bhowmick, a traditional Bengali, works as a metallurgist with General Motors and lives in Detroit with his Americanized wife and a twenty-six-year-old engineer daughter. He worships the goddess Kali in his home shrine, believes in the sanctity of Hindu superstitions, and lives in constant awe of the presence of unseen powers that govern his destiny. Every day he finds himself frequently making compromises between his Old World beliefs and the

New World rationality. For example, when he discovers to his great shock that his unmarried daughter is pregnant, his first reaction is that she should get an abortion to save the family honor. For this unhappy situation, he blames his wife because coming to the United States was her idea. Then he tries to be reasonable. He thinks that maybe his daughter already got married secretly; he prays that his son-in-law should turn out to be a white American. He even secretly enjoys the thought of having a grandson.

He loses self-control, however, when his daughter reveals that she was impregnated by artificial insemination. As his daughter maniacally tirades against the Indian system of arranged marriages, he furiously lifts the rolling pin and strikes it hard against the dome of his daughter's stomach. His wife calls the police.

While *Darkness* focuses primarily on the experience of immigrants from the Indian subcontinent, Mukherjee's second collection, *The Middleman and Other Stories*, is broader in range and scope, as it explores the American experience of immigrants from India as well as from other countries such as Afghanistan, Iraq, the Philippines, Sri Lanka, Trinidad, Uganda, and Vietnam. Of the eleven stories in this volume, four have white American protagonists who view the immigrant situation from their perspective. The remaining stories are stories of survival, expediency, compromises, losses, and adjustment involved in the process of acculturation to American life. All the "new pioneers" in this collection are, in a metaphoric sense, middlemen and women caught between two worlds and cultures.

The title story, "The Middleman," is narrated by Alfred Judah from Baghdad, who is mistakenly regarded as an Arab by some and an Indian by others. He has lived in Flushing, Queens, and his first wife was an American. He feels, however, like an outsider. As he says, "There are aspects of American life I came too late for and will never understand." He now works for a smuggler, Clovis T. Ransome, and does the dirty job of delivering contraband as the middleman. Similarly, in "Danny's Girls," a young Ugandan boy living in Flushing works as a middleman for a hustler, Danny (originally, Dinesh, a Hindu from north India), whom he calls "a merchant of opportunity." Danny started out selling tickets for Indian concerts at Madison Square Garden, then fixed beauty contests, got into the business of arranging green cards (through proxy marriages) for Indians aspiring to become permanent residents in the United States, and later launched the racket of mail-order brides in partnership with the boy's aunt Lini,

selling Indian and other Asian girls to Americans. The young narrator always looked up to Danny and, like him, wanted to attain financial independence in the big world of the United States. When he falls in love, however, with a Nepali girl for whom Danny had arranged a green card, he determines to liberate her and himself from Danny's clutches.

"Jasmine" is the story of an ambitious Trinidadian girl of that name who, through a middleman, illegally enters Detroit from the Canadian border at Windsor and lands a job of cleaning and bookkeeping in the Plantations Motel in Southfield, run by the Daboos, a family of Trinidadian Indians. Later, she goes to Ann Arbor and finds a job as a live-in domestic worker with an easygoing American family: Bill Moffitt, a biology instructor, Lara Hatch-Moffitt, a performance artist, and their little girl, Muffin. After a few months, when Lara goes on the road with her performing group, Jasmine is happily seduced by her boss, Bill Moffitt. As they make love on the Turkish carpet, she thinks of herself as "a bright, pretty girl with no visa, no papers, and no birth certificate. No nothing other than what she wanted to invent and tell. She was a girl rushing wildly into the future." The story shows affinities with Mukherjee's novel *Jasmine* (1989).

"A Wife's Story" and "The Tenant" focus on well-educated Indian women. In "A Wife's Story," Mrs. Panna Bhatt, wife of a vice president of a textile mill in India, has come to New York on a two-year scholarship to get a Ph.D. degree in special education. Haunted by the memories of the oppressive roles of women played by her mother and grandmother, she believes that she is making something of her life. She even develops a friendship with a Hungarian man, with whom she goes to the theater. When an actor makes obscene jokes about Patel women, she feels insulted. She thinks: "It's the tyranny of the American dream that scares me. First, you don't exist. Then you are invisible. Then you are funny. Then you are disgusting. Insult, my American friends will tell me, is a kind of acceptance. No instant dignity here." When her husband comes for a short visit, she does not feel too enthusiastic. Though she shows him around and tries to make up to him for her years away, pretending that nothing has changed, she refuses to go back with him.

"The Tenant" goes to another extreme by showing how an attractive, middle-class, young Bengali woman becomes vulnerable when she breaks with her traditional ways and tries to become part of mainstream America. She is Maya Sanyal from Calcutta, who came to the United States ten years before, at nineteen, earned a Ph.D. degree, married an American, became a naturalized citizen, got divorced, and is now in Cedar Falls, Iowa, where she has come to teach comparative literature. Before coming to Cedar Falls, she indiscreetly slept with all kinds of men, except Indians. Now, afraid that her bachelor landlord might make sexual advances toward her, she calls the other Bengali professor on campus, a Dr. Chatterji, and gets invited to tea at his home. There, she feels unsettled to see everything so traditional. A newly awakened longing makes her respond to an *India Abroad* matrimonial advertisement from an Indian man, Ashoke Mehta. As she goes to meet him at the Chicago airport, she feels as if a "Hindu god" is descending to woo her. "She feels ugly and unworthy. Her adult life no longer seems miraculously rebellious; it is grim, it is perverse. She has accomplished nothing. She has changed her citizenship but she hasn't broken through into the light, the vigor, the hustle of the New World. She is stuck in dead space." On her return to Cedar Falls, when she learns that her landlord got married, she rents a new room from Fred, an armless man. Two months later, when Mehta tracks her down and invites her to come to Hartford, she has been sleeping with her armless landlord.

Conspicuously, both volumes contain some bizarre, melodramatic, and preposterous situations, and a streak of violence runs through most of the stories. Nevertheless, Mikherjee imparts a potent voice to these "new pioneers" and sheds light on their invisible world. She demonstrates how some of these latecomers to the New World become victims of racism and prejudice; others operate as middlemen in the shady underworld of sex, crime, and drugs; and some merely scramble for a living in their struggle for survival. To adapt to their new milieu, even professional men and women have to make compromises and trade-offs between their old belief systems and the New World ethos. In the process, they suffer from a sense of cultural disorientation and alienation and undergo traumatic changes—psychological, cultural, linguistic. Their main problem is how to snap ties with their native culture to become assimilated into the mainstream of their adopted country. In most cases, their adventures into the New World become, to use the author's own description, "stories of broken identities and discarded languages." In a broader sense, their rootlessness can be viewed as a symbol of the modern human condition.

Other major works

NOVELS: *The Tiger's Daughter*, 1971; *Wife*, 1975; *Jasmine*, 1989; *The Holder of the World*, 1993.
NONFICTION: *Kautilya's Concept of Diplomacy*, 1976; *Days and Nights in Calcutta*, 1977 (coauthored with Clark Blaise); *The Sorrow and the Terror: The Haunting Legacy of the Air India Tragedy*, 1987 (coauthored with Blaise).

Bibliography

Ascher, Carol. "After the Raj." Review of *The Middleman and Other Stories. Women's Review of Books* 6, no. 12 (1989): 17, 19.
Ispahani, Mahnaz. "A Passage from India." Review of *Darkness. The New Republic* 14 (April, 1986): 36-39.
Mukherjee, Bharati. "An Interview with Bharati Mukherjee." Interview by Geoff Hancock. *The Canadian Fiction Magazine* 59 (1987): 30-44.
Nazareth, Peter. "Total Vision." *Canadian Literature: A Quarterly of Criticism and Review* 110 (1986): 184-191.
Nelson, Emmanuel S., ed. *Bharati Mukherjee: Critical Perspectives*. New York: Garland, 1993.
Sivaramkrishna, M. "Bharati Mukherjee." In *Indian English Novelists: An Anthology of Critical Essays*, edited by Madhusudan Prasad. New Delhi: Sterling, 1982, 71-86.

CATHY SONG

Born: Honolulu, Hawaii; 1955

Principal poetry

Picture Bride, 1983; *Frameless Windows, Squares of Light*, 1988.

Other literary forms

Cathy Song is known principally for her poetry. She is coeditor (with Juliet S. Kono) of *Sister Stew: Fiction and Poetry by Women* (1991), which features Hawaiian writers.

Achievements

In 1982, poet Richard Hugo selected Song as the winner of the prestigious Yale Series of Younger Poets Award for *Picture Bride*, her first book-length manuscript. Upon its publication in 1983, the book was nominated for the National Book Critics Circle Award. Since then, her poetry has been widely anthologized in important collections such as *The Norton Anthology of Modern Poetry* (1988), in which she is the youngest poet represented. A winner of *Poetry* magazine's Frederick Bock Prize, Song has made a major breakthrough for Asian American poetry by giving it greater visibility.

Biography

Cathy Song was born in 1955 to a Korean American father and a Chinese American mother in Honolulu, Hawaii. She grew up in Wahiawa, a small town on the island of Oahu, which also serves as the setting for many of her poems. Because her ancestral roots can be traced to both China and Korea—the two countries where her maternal and paternal grandparents originated—and because she has spent most of her life in Hawaii, Song has at times been identified as a Hawaiian poet, and at others a Korean American or Chinese American poet, though in fact the three aspects of her heritage are essentially indivisible.

As a child, Song exercised her creative energy in the "pure fantasy" and "dream wishes" of fiction (her first story, written at the age of eleven, is a "spy novel"), romance (short stories about "beautiful blonde heroines on summer vacations"), and make-believe journalism ("imaginary interviews with movie stars"). It was after her schooling in Hawaii, when Song had left the University of Hawaii for Wellesley College in Massachusetts, that her talent in poetry began to blossom. While attending Wellesley, she came across the book *Georgia O'Keeffe* (1976), written by O'Keeffe herself, which so deeply impressed Song that it inspired her to write an entire sequence of poems (loosely known as the "O'Keeffe poems").

After receiving her B.A. degree from Wellesley in 1977, Song went on to study creative writing at Boston University, where she received an M.A. degree in 1981. She also attended the Advanced Poetry Workshop conducted by Kathleen Spivak, who offered suggestions on the divisions and subtitles of her first book manuscript. The manuscript, *Picture Bride*, which collects poems formerly published in journals and anthologies such as *Bambo Ridge*, *The Greenfield Review*, and *Hawaii Review*, was selected by poet Richard Hugo from among 625 manuscripts as the winner of the 1982 Yale Series of Younger Poets competition and was published by Yale University Press as volume 78 of the series in 1983. The series, which had once featured poets such as Adrienne Rich and John Ashbery, brought Song to prominence. The book was nominated for the National Book Critics Circle Award. Since then, her poetry has appeared in important anthologies such as *Breaking the Silence: An Anthology of Contemporary American Poets* (1983), *The Norton Anthology of Modern Poetry* (1988), *The Norton Anthology of American Literature* (1989), *The Heath Anthology of American Literature* (1990), and *The Open Boat: Poems from Asian America* (1993). Song's second collection of poems, *Frameless Windows, Squares of Light*, was published in 1988. She continues to publish in various journals, especially *Poetry*, which also awarded her the Frederick Bock Prize. She is also coeditor (with Juliet S. Kono) of *Sister Stew: Fiction and Poetry by Women* (1991).

Song has taught creative writing at various universities on the U.S. mainland and in Hawaii, where she maintains a permanent home. She is married to Douglass Davenport, a physician, and has a son and a daughter.

Analysis

Song's poetry generally deals with her personal experience as a woman with family roots in Hawaii and with ancestral and kinship ties to Korea and China. Although her subject matter revolves around regional, ethnic, and private experiences, it is expressed in idioms evidently inseparable from her formal training in Western culture. Her interest in art also comes through unmistakably in the visual qualities of her poems, especially in those inspired by family photographs, paintings by O'Keeffe, and Kitagawa Utamaro's *ukiyo-e* prints. In her poetry, Song often provides affectionate portraits and stories of family members in a language that is both contemplative and dramatic, both retrospective and prospective, moving freely between past and present and between observation and speculation. Because her memory of the past often merges with the reality of the present as if the two were indivisible, there is a lively immediacy to her poems. Many of her poems employ the second-person pronoun, thus stimulating a conversational style, which in turn is characterized by frequent understatements. Deceptively prosaic at times, the language has in store delightful surprises of images and a variety of emotions ranging from sadness to humor.

Song, despite (and because of) her initial success, has been faced with the same predicament that plagues many Asian American writers: Exploring their ethnicity explicitly often subjects them to criticism for exoticism (if the ethnic experience is noticed) and/or marginality (when such experience is assumed to be beneath notice). As Song warily told an interviewer, "I'll have to try not to write about the Asian-American theme" although "it is a way of exploring the past." Song's statement is essentially a reflection on the artificial dilemma, between ethnicity ("Asian") and the mainstream ("American") culture, that is deeply ingrained in the literature of the United States. As a poet, Song deserves special attention for her struggle to bridge the gap—not so much by circumventing ethnicity (which is impossible because the universal must derive from the particular), but rather by concentrating on her personal experience as a woman.

Picture Bride, a collection of thirty-one poems covering a range of topics including family history, life in Hawaii, childhood memories, sibling relationships, love, art, character studies, ethnic experience, and the quest of the self, exemplifies Song's struggle both as an Asian American and as a woman poet. "Picture Bride," the title poem with which the volume begins, serves as the seminal text of the collection, in a way defining the thematic direction of the book. In this poem, the persona, aged twenty-four, attempts to imagine what it was like for the maternal grandmother, at the age of twenty-three, to leave Korea to marry a sugar-mill laborer thirteen years her senior in Waialua, Hawaii, a man she had never before seen. The entire poem, except for the first three lines, consists of a series of questions intended to re-create not only the scenes of the departure, the journey, and the arrival but also the psychology and emotions of the picture bride throughout the process. The concluding question, which speculates on how willing she might have been with regard to her conjugal obligation ("did she politely untie/ the silk bow of her jacket,/ her tent-shaped dress"), focuses an entire economic and sociohistorical phenomenon on the question of sexuality, making the poem linger on a moment of truth in human terms. This ability to crystallize the general into the personal is characteristic of Song's poetry. Also characteristic of her approach is the way she attempts to negotiate for interaction between her subjectivity and her subject matter, in this case the interaction between two different generations whose cultural backgrounds and values are different and yet related.

The figure of the picture bride serves as a muse of sorts for the poet, in part because the questions raised in "Picture Bride" are either answered or contextualized in the other poems of the volume. For example, in "Untouched Photograph of Passenger," Song contemplates on the significance of the gaze of a man, dressed in a poorly tailored suit, into a camera. A likely portrait of the grandfather, which the picture bride could have turned in her hands, this photograph/poem captures the optimism with which the emigrant embraces the promises of a foreign land. The other poems in the volume, which loosely chronicle the proliferation of the first generation through two more generations, can be regarded as indirect answers to the question of sexuality raised in "Picture Bride." The extraordinarily big breasts that the woman (the picture bride as an older woman) jokes about, and that the poet describes as being like "walruses" and imagines to have been sucked by "six children and an old man," are symbols of her fecundity. Always keeping her focus on the personal dimension, when she finally writes about the death of the picture-bride grandmother in "Blue Lantern," Song makes it clear that what matters in the picture bride phenomenon is ultimately the human element. Prearranged marriages and love are not mutually exclusive under certain circumstances, as is evident from the way the grandfather mourns the death of his wife as witnessed by the grandchildren: "He played for her each night;/ her absence,/ the shape of his grief/ funneled through the bamboo flute."

Initially, readers such as Hugo tended to see Song's poems in *Picture Bride* as "flowers—colorful, sensual and quiet—offered almost shyly as bouquets." In his 1986 review, Stephen Sumida, however, cautions that "Song's poems seem especially liable to being appreciated or criticized for the wrong reasons" and suggests that her work requires an alternative approach. The fact that *Picture Bride* as a collection is organized according to two interrelated frameworks or principles hence deserves particular attention. To take the title poem as the seminal text, the book is apparently a collection of poems structured around the immigration and assimilation experience of the Song family, beginning with the arrival of her Korean grandparents—the grandmother in particular. Seen from this perspective, the book is essentially autobiographical in nature, with the poems serving as miniature memoirs and chronicles of the family's history and as memories of parents, relatives, and siblings. It is, however, important to note that such an ethnicized principle of organization was not Song's idea but her publisher's.

Even as it stands, the book, which Song originally intended to be titled "From the White Place," after a poem dedicated to Georgia O'Keeffe, also incorporates another framework of organization. This framework is derived from a five-part sequence, "Blue and White Lines After O'Keeffe," a poem placed at the center of the collection. The subtitles of the five divisions ("Black Iris," "Sunflower," "Orchids," "Red Poppy," and "The White Trumpet") of the volume, which were suggested to her by Kathleen Spivak, in fact come from this strategically positioned text; used as a structuring device, these subtitles imply that the book can be perceived as a poet's attempt, by way of visual art (the influence of O'Keeffe—and also Kitagawa Utamaro), to fashion personal experience into aesthetic experience, and thereby to define her vision as an artistic one. Reading the book according to this framework, however, would tend to deemphasize the ethnic elements of the poems, but the risk of the book's being treated like an ethnographic document would also be reduced.

Such an artist's framework is not without its problems, since it poses the danger of diminishing the peculiarity of Song's experience and her voice. Taken alone, neither one of the two frameworks is entirely satisfactory, but as Fujita-Sato explains, "What results . . . from the interlocked frameworks provided by the book's title and sections' titles, is a structure embodying synthesis." Corresponding to this synthesis, Fujita-Sato proposes, is the technique of "singing shapes" derived from O'Keeffe's paintings, by which two often dissimilar objects are juxtaposed and become mutually illuminated and transformed into "a fluid shaping and reshaping of energy."

As Patricia Wallace suggests, Song is among women poets of color who have to struggle between the literal (historical) and literary (aesthetic) dimensions of their experience. The struggle toward a synthesis of the two, already evident in *Picture Bride*, is further developed in *Frameless Windows*, Squares of Light, where Song concentrates on personal experiences in various stages of her life as a daughter, sister, wife, mother, and Hawaiian/Asian American woman. In this collection her voice as a poet who is not only a woman but also an artist also matures. The volume consists of twenty-six poems and is divided into four parts ("The Window and the Field," "A Small Light," "Shadow Figures," and "Frameless Windows, Squares of Light"), which are named after the title poems of each section. The organization here recalls but transcends that of *Picture Bride*; the aesthetic rendition of personal experience no longer relies on the appeal of ethnic elements or the authority of another artist but rather disseminates from the play and interplay of framed and frameless blocks and touches of light and shadow—vignettes of life as lived. The higher level of unity in this second collection also stems from Song's rather unique technique—related to that of "singing shapes"—of juxtaposing and transposing (or compressing) different segments of time, in the manner that a telescope is collapsed or expanded, so that memories of the past and realities of the present merge into one another. For example, whatever happened to the persona and her brother as children in the past would recur, with variations, in the present when she looks upon her son and daughter growing up. This unique approach to experience, by which the personal is merged with the familial and the mundane is elevated to the aesthetic, suggests that Song's attempt to bridge the gap, and hence resolve the dilemma confronting Asian American writers, is in fact feasible.

Song's struggle to be heard is tied to her experience as a woman artist with multiple cultural backgrounds. Her exploration of immigrants, family history, generational ties, Hawaiian culture, and personal visions of life and art is an integral part of the American experience. Confronted with the need to reconcile ethnicity and mainstream culture, Song has worked toward bridging the gap with creative means informed by her artistic sensibility. Her unfaltering interest in the primacy of the human and the personal, especially from the perspective of women without voices, is a distinct and dominant factor in her poetry.

Other major works

EDITED TEXT: *Sister Stew: Fiction and Poetry by Women*, 1991 (Song and Juliet S. Kono, eds.).

Bibliography

Fujita-Sato, Gayle K. "'Third World' as Place and Paradigm in Cathy Song's *Picture Bride*." *MELUS* 15, no. 1 (Spring, 1988): 49-72.

Hugo, Richard. Foreword to *Picture Bride*. New Haven, Conn.: Yale University Press, 1983.

Nomaguchi, Debbie Murakami. "Cathy Song: 'I'm a Poet Who Happens to Be Asian American.'" *International Examiner* 2 (May, 1984): 9.

Sumida, Stephen H. "Pictures of Art and Life." *Contact II* 7, nos. 38-40 (1986): 52-55.

Wallace, Patricia. "Divided Loyalties: Literal and Literary in the Poetry of Lorna Dee Cervantes, Cathy Song and Rita Dove." *MELUS* 18, no. 3 (Fall, 1993): 3-19.

AMY TAN

Born: Oakland, California; February 19, 1952

Principal long fiction

The Joy Luck Club, 1989; *The Kitchen God's Wife*, 1991.

Other literary forms

Excerpts from Amy Tan's long fiction have appeared in periodicals as short stories. She has also published noteworthy autobiographical essays. Of these, "Mother Tongue," published in *The Three Penny Review* (Fall, 1990), is an account of her fascination with language and the way she captured her immigrant mother's imperfect but vivid English for use in her own fiction writing. This essay was selected for inclusion in *The Best American Essays 1991* (1991), edited by Joyce Carol Oates.

Achievements

Amy Tan's work mines the literary vein of Chinese American women's experience, a rich vein that was first explored by works such as Jade Snow Wong's *Fifth Chinese Daughter* (1945) and Maxine Hong Kingston's *The Woman Warrior: Memoirs of a Girlhood Among Ghosts* (1976). Tan's first two novels have met with signal commercial success. Rave reviews greeted *The Joy Luck Club*, which remained on *The New York Times* best-seller list for nine months. Tan garnered a $1.23 million contract for the paperback rights. The book became a successful film, directed by Wayne Wang (1993) with a screenplay by Tan and Ronald Bass. *The Kitchen God's Wife* also received enthusiastic, if somewhat more restrained, reviews. Tan's first book was also a finalist for the National Book Award and was nominated for the National Book Critics Circle Award. It did win the (San Francisco) Bay Area Book Reviewers' Award for Fiction as well as the Commonwealth Club Gold Award.

Biography

Amy Tan was born of immigrant Chinese parents on February 19, 1952, in Oakland, California. Her Chinese name, An-mei, is homophonous with her American name and could be translated as "American tranquillity" or "beautiful peace." Her parents, John and Daisy Tan, emigrated to the United States in the 1940's shortly before the Communists took full control of the Chinese mainland. John Tan was an electrical engineer and Baptist minister educated in Peking (now Beijing); he also worked for the United States Information Service during World War II. Daisy Tan grew up near Shanghai in a well-to-do family, but she was in disfavor because her mother was considered a disgrace to her family. Daisy's mother had been widowed while young, was raped and forced into concubinage by a wealthy roué, and eventually committed suicide. Amy Tan has said (in a *Life* magazine article) that this grandmother, a victim unjustly blamed for her misfortune, has been a source of strength and an inspiring muse for her writing, especially for her second book. Daisy Tan had an unhappy first marriage with an abusive husband. Her second husband was a very different man, and they had two other children, sons born in California. The Tans moved often, residing in San Francisco, Oakland, Berkeley, Santa Clara, and Fresno, California. As is often the case with immigrants, Amy Tan's parents wanted their children to retain their internal Chinese character while assimilating external American attributes. Amy, however, grew up hating her Chinese physiognomy (for a time she slept with a clothespin on her too-Chinese nose) and preferring hot dogs and apple pie.

After winning an essay-writing contest at age eight, Tan dreamed of becoming a fiction writer although she believed (ironically, as it turned out) that writing was not financially rewarding. Her parents, especially her mother, also had high expectations for their daughter: They hoped that she would become a neurosurgeon with a supplementary career as a concert pianist. Although Tan felt the burden of her parents' aspirations, she also developed an independent and perhaps rebellious sense of what she wanted for herself.

Tan's teenage years were uneasy ones. When she was fourteen, her father and her elder brother died of brain tumors. Her mother decided to leave their unlucky house in Santa Clara and set sail for Europe with her two remaining children in 1968. The family settled in Montreux, Switzerland, where Tan completed high school. In Montreux, she fell in with a fast-paced crowd. She dated a German who had alleged connections with the drug underworld and had escaped from a mental institution. Tan's mother hired a private detective to help precipitate a drug bust that resulted in the daughter's being hauled before a local magistrate. The incident ended the relationship between Tan and her German friend.

In 1969, the Tans returned to the San Francisco Bay Area. Amy enrolled in Linfield College, a Baptist institution in McMinnville, Oregon. There she met her future husband, Louis DeMattei (they married in 1974). In 1970, Tan and DeMattei returned to California, where she enrolled at San Jose State University, from which she earned a B.A. degree in English and linguistics, followed by an M.A. degree in linguistics. She pursued further studies at the University of California, first at Santa Cruz, then at Berkeley, but decided to leave academia in 1976 for work at the Alameda County Association for Retarded Citizens. In the 1980's, she became a freelance business writer for companies such as International Business Machines Corporation (IBM), American Telephone & Telegraph (AT&T), and Apple Computer.

Becoming disenchanted with writing company reports and speeches for executives and sensing that she was becoming a ninety-hour-a-week workaholic, Tan embarked on a program of personal therapy in 1983: She taught herself jazz piano and read the fiction of women writers Eudora Welty, Flannery O'Connor, Alice Munro, and Louise Erdrich, whose *Love Medicine* (1984) became a potent influence. Tan then wrote her first short story, "Endgame" ("Rules of the Game" in *The Joy Luck Club*), and used it in 1985 to gain entrance to the Squaw Valley Community of Writers workshop. Since 1987, Tan has attended a writers' group headed by Molly Giles, a 1991 National Book Critics Circle Award winner. After completing a second story, "Waiting Between the Trees," Tan sought out a literary agent, who succeeded in selling her prospective book to G. P. Putnam for a $50,000 advance. Greeted by this news when she returned from a visit to her half-sisters in China (1987), Tan quit her business writing and completed fourteen other episodes of *The Joy Luck Club* in a prompt four months.

The resounding success of *The Joy Luck Club* exerted pressure on Tan to follow it with a worthy successor. Anguishing over this second book, Tan began and abandoned seven drafts before settling down to write *The Kitchen God's Wife*, which utilized her mother's life experience in China. *The Kitchen God's Wife*, contrary to Tan's angst, was also greeted with best-seller enthu-

siasm and garnered a paperback contract more lucrative than its predecessor's.

In San Francisco, where Tan lives with her tax-attorney husband, she has formed a variant of her fictional Joy Luck Club; named Fool and His Money, its members exchange investment leads. In the 1993 film version of *The Joy Luck Club*, she can be seen in a very brief walk-on scene.

Analysis

Two themes figure prominently in Tan's books: mother-daughter (mis)communication and women's empowerment. These two themes are frequently developed through a dramatic action involving a pattern of loss and/or recovery played out against a Chinese American or Chinese immigrant backdrop.

The theme of difficult communication is already apparent in the narrative structuring of her first two books. Both books are told through mother-daughter pairs of first-person narrators, one pair in *The Kitchen God's Wife* and four in *The Joy Luck Club*.

Structurally, *The Joy Luck Club*, like Chaucer's *The Canterbury Tales* (1387-1400) or Louise Erdrich's *Love Medicine* (one of Tan's immediate models), is a compilation of sixteen linked first-person narratives. Even as Geoffrey Chaucer, in *The Canterbury Tales*, employed for his narrative frame the social occasion of a pilgrimage as a metaphor for the journey of life, so Tan uses the occasion of a mah-jongg game as a metaphor for the game of life. An apposite paradigm for a narrative replete with voyages of immigration and clashes of cultures, mah-jongg is played by four persons seated figuratively at the four corners of the world. Indeed, spatial metaphors and spatial placement of selves and objects form a leitmotif in the book and are related to Chinese geomancy, or *fengshui* (literally, "wind and water," which, significantly, was the original draft title of the book). Consonant with this game-like four-sided structure, the contents of the book are symmetrically fourfold: There are four parts (like the rows of tiles forming each mah-jongg player's hand) tidily marked off by four italicized vignettes, each part containing precisely four episodes (like the tiles themselves). The four episodes of the first part are stories about the mothers, narrated by the mothers (although the first mother's story is embedded in the narrative that introduces the novel as a whole). The second four episodes are narrated by the daughters and concern their daughter-mother relationships during their childhood years. The third set of four episodes is again narrated by the daughters, who relate their adult experience of courtship, marriage, divorce, and work but who are also haunted by the influence of their experience of their mothers (the story about the last mother being embedded in the narrative that closes the novel as a whole). Structurally, then, *The Joy Luck Club* is almost mathematical in its intricate symmetry. This symmetry is, however, also decidedly and subtly nonlinear, for the narrators and narrative strands crisscross and flash back through time, intersecting characters and events as well as leitmotifs of imagery and symbolism. The intricacy and subtlety of the novel's structure is paradigmatic of the difficult communication between mothers and daughters, communication that is multilayered, many-angled, and open to multiple interpretations and misprisions.

The Kitchen God's Wife also employs the mother and her daughter as first-person narrators, the mother clearly dominating in length and interest. Both their narratives, addressed directly to the reader, have a performative quality, especially the mother's, who is telling the reader what she has told the daughter. Both narratives also take on the form of cathartic confessions that clarify a lifetime of mother-daughter miscommunications.

In both books, such mother-daughter miscommunications exist on several levels. On the fairly simple linguistic level, they highlight the generational differences between the immigrant and the native-born Chinese American and are often tragicomic in effect: When the daughter in *The Kitchen God's Wife* says "beach," the mother hears "bitch"; when the mother says that she has chosen the clothes and casket for a funeral, the daughter understands her to say that it will be a closed-casket ceremony. Such laughable misprisions, however, are indicators of this work's serious, overarching theme. When the novel begins, the mother-daughter miscommunications have calcified because of major secrets that the mother, Weili, and the daughter, Pearl, are hiding from each other and that poison their relationship like a tumor (images of potentially malignant growths appear noticeably in the book). Pearl's secret is that she suffers from multiple sclerosis. Weili's secret is her fear that Pearl is not the child of her loving second husband, Jimmy Louie, but of her heinous first husband, Wen Fu, who raped Weili the week before she left China to marry Jimmy in America. Once mother and daughter confess and communicate their secrets to each other, however, a catharsis is achieved and a reconciliation attained.

Similar kinds of linguistic miscommunications occur in *The Joy Luck Club*, although Tan has successfully concocted a tangy patois that allows her immigrant Chinese mothers to speak with winning individuality, humor, and irony. When Waverley Jong tells her mother, "I'm my own person," her mother thinks to herself: "How can she be her own person? When did I give her up?" Such instances of failed communication can become the presiding theme of entire episodes. "The Voice from the Wall," for example, contrasts the silent noncommunicativeness of the Chinese American mother and daughter with the noisy quarrelsomeness of their Italian American neighbors, whose apartment shares a wall with theirs. The Chinese American failure in communication results in paranoia and catatonia, whereas the Italian American outpouring of emotions leads through catharsis to mutuality—a difference not lost on the Chinese American daughter.

In addition to these difficult mother-daughter relationships, the other main theme of Tan's books is women's empowerment. In *The Joy Luck Club*, "The Red Candle" tells how Lindo Jong suffered a demeaning arranged marriage in pre-Communist China to an impotent husband, whose family then blames her for childlessness. Thus abused, Lindo empowers herself by playing on her mother-in-law's superstitions to annul her marriage and make a match between her hapless husband and a maid about to bear an illegitimate child. In this episode, the objective correlative for power is the wind (another image linked to mah-jongg), which Lindo observes blowing out the red candle's symbolic marital flame and which Lindo then adopts as a metaphor for her self-empowerment: "I was strong. . . . I was like the wind." Tan skillfully continues this metaphor for power in Lindo's Chinese American daughter Waverley, the chess prodigy of Chinatown, who describes a chess tournament as follows: "A light wind began blowing. . . . It whispered secrets only I could hear. . . . 'Check!' I said, as the wind roared with laughter. The wind had died down to little puffs, my own breath." Also, Lindo's self-empowerment evidently becomes a permanent character trait. After arriving in America, this victim of a failed marriage makes a marriage match for herself when she works in a fortune cookie factory and contrives an appropriate fortune to slip into a cookie for her intended man.

Similarly, the narrative of Weili, the mother in *The Kitchen God's Wife*, may be read as a gripping three-hundred-page account of her self-empowerment, a *Bildungsroman* of a girl with insecure feelings of self-worth growing into a woman capable of asserting her choice of a husband at gunpoint—a heartwarming variant of the shotgun wedding. Growing up as a tolerated and motherless daughter of a wealthy family in 1920's China, Weili gratefully marries the déclassé Wen Fu, her family's choice. She quickly discovers, however, that he is an entirely selfish man and an abusive sexual pervert. Wen Fu cheats, squanders Weili's dowry, gambles recklessly, rapes a servant who later dies in a botched abortion, beds a mistress in Weili's room, and beats his infant daughter into retardation and death. Crashing a Jeep (bought with Weili's money), Wen Fu loses an eye and metaphorically takes on his true aspect, a cannibalistic cyclops. During this brutalizing marriage, Weili endures the woes of a Griselda, but Weili is no unquestioning saint and consequently grows in awareness, independent judgment, and, finally, rebelliousness. After she realizes what a brutal father Wen Fu is, Weili exercises the choice of aborting the fetuses they conceive. She also discovers that men find her attractive, and she eventually meets and falls in love with Jimmy Louie, a considerate and loving Chinese American interpreter attached to the American forces in China. To exercise her choice of a new husband, an unthinkable act in her youth, she empowers herself by cunning and force, the very two instruments that Wen Fu has so often employed against her: She tricks him into signing their divorce papers, then uses his own revolver to extricate her airplane ticket to the United States from him. Thus Weili grows from a marginalized girl with no esteem and few options into a woman who chooses which child to bear and which man to marry, and who empowers herself by guile and gun to effect her choice.

The themes of mother-daughter communication and women's empowerment are played out through gripping dramas of loss and/or recovery. These losses and recoveries may be of several kinds. In *The Kitchen God's Wife*, Weili experiences a traumatic childhood loss of self-esteem because of the (to her) inexplicable way in which she is abandoned by her mother, a replacement secondary wife of a wealthy Shanghai merchant with a ménage of five concubines. Instead of being the apple of her mother's eye, as she was before this event, Weili has to grow up fostered by unloving aunts and marginalized in an island village away from her father's hearth in elegant Shanghai.

In *The Joy Luck Club*, Ying-Ying St. Clair experiences several variants of this pattern of loss and recovery. She suffers a childhood loss of self when she falls into a lake and becomes separated from her family in "The Moon Lady," though she is eventually recovered by them. In young adulthood, she is lost in an unhappy marriage to a philandering husband in China and can take power only by aborting their child. In her second marriage in America, she again loses herself to deep depression when she loses another child following a deformed stillbirth ("Voice from the Wall"). Her timid daughter, Lena, is losing her marriage when she lets herself be taken advantage of by a husband who nominally shares all their expenses but is actually making her pay more. When Ying-Ying sees Lena's situation, she determines to help her daughter recover her self and her marriage by giving her a greater measure of *chi* (Chinese for "spirit" or "breath," another wind-power metaphor).

Indeed, this pattern of loss and/or recovery forms a large part of the dramatic interest of all the mothers and daughters in *The Joy Luck Club*. An-Mei Hsu's mother loses her mother's favor until she returns to her mother's deathbed to nourish her with a soup made of her own flesh ("Scar"); An-Mei herself loses her son Bing in a drowning accident ("Half and Half"); and her daughter Rose is in danger of losing her home in divorce because she has become too malleable to assert her rights ("Without Wood"). Finally, the novel's framing narrative begins with a Chinese American daughter's (June's) loss of her mother through death and ends with her recovery of her Chinese sisters (whom her mother had lost in China during World War II) and, through them, a discovery of self and a recovery of the lost mother: "Now I . . . see what part of me is Chinese," says June, and then as a Polaroid photograph of her and her sisters develops, she realizes, "Together we look like our mother. Her same eyes, her same mouth, open in surprise to see, at last, her long-cherished wish" (her mother's name, Suyuan, being "long-cherished wish" in Chinese).

Immaculately structured, intricately narrated, Tan's lively fictions re-create the joys and sorrows that fill the hearts and lives of several generations of Chinese American mothers and daughters. Though the profundity and breadth of Tan's social vision may be debated, as may the representativeness of her portrayal of Asian men, her vast popular appeal and resounding commercial success are unquestionable. Unquestionable, too, is the narrative skill and craft with which she can mesmerize her readers by a well-told tale, tease their fancy with glimpses of sinologica, and tug at their heartstrings with the pathos of her women characters.

Other major works

NONFICTION: "Mother Tongue," 1990 (essay).

Bibliography

Chong, Denise. "Emotional Journeys Through East and West." *Quill and Quire* 55, no. 5 (May, 1989): 23.
Koenig, Rhoda. "Heirloom China." *New York* 22 (March 20, 1989): 82-83.
McAlister, Melanie. "(Mis) Reading *The Joy Luck Club*." *Asian America* 1 (Winter, 1992): 102-118.
Miner, Valerie. "The Daughters' Journeys." *Nation* 248 (April 24, 1989): 566-569.
Shear, Walter. "Generational Difference and the Diaspora in *The Joy Luck Club*." *Critique* 34, no. 3 (Spring, 1993): 193-199.
Tan, Amy. "Angst and the Second Novel." *Publishers Weekly* 238 (April 5, 1991): 4-7.

XIII
BALANCING ACTS
America's Gay and Lesbian Identities

America this is quite serious . . .
I'd better get right down to the job . . .
America I'm putting my queer shoulder to the wheel.
—Allen Ginsberg, "America," 1956

In the sea of identities that make up the social fabric of America, gays and lesbians reflect an American minority whose status is far different from ethnic, nationalistic, or religious minorities. These other minorities, like gays, face discrimination if not disdain from the dominant society; however, they are able to develop support systems within their families. Homosexuals have tended to grow up in families in which their sexual orientation is condemned, denied, or concealed. This separateness—even from other minorities—makes homosexuals a breed apart, with both visible and invisible members. With no support from the family, many gays choose to remain in the closet, invisible to their families and society. Others find support from an alternative form of family, an openly gay community, through the ritual of "coming out of the closet" and into visibility. Not surprisingly, the closet and coming out are common themes that weave in and out of the literature written by gays and lesbians.

No one is brought up to be gay. The moment an individual recognizes his or her difference, his or her otherness, the individual—in isolation—begins to account for it. As Edmund White writes, "'Coming out' is the rite that marks the passage from homosexual desire to gay identity, and this transition begins and ends in avowal." The coming-out experience is a very complex and individual rite of passage. Just as the attitudes of the majority inevitably affect minority cultures, most gays and lesbians are aware of and have absorbed homophobic attitudes long before they are able even secretly to acknowledge their sexual identity. For this reason, among others, self-realization is a preoccupation of gay and lesbian writings. This preoccupation is coupled with the search for and discovery of a cultural matrix in which homosexuality is accepted, valued, and nourished to stem the isolation and loneliness—the alienated sense of otherness—most coming-of-age homosexuals face. Gay and lesbian voices address these themes in literature to alleviate this sense of separateness.

The 1969 New York Stonewall Inn riots—violent clashes between gay men and the police at a Greenwich Village gay bar—ushered in the contemporary gay liberation movement. However, nearly a decade passed before a crop of fiction written by openly gay writers appeared. The year was 1978 and the novels were Larry Kramer's controversial *Faggots* and Andrew Holleran's portrait of contemporary Manhattan gay life *Dancer from the Dance*. The publication and popular critical reception of these books "legitimized" the works of gay men and women and marked the beginning of an impulse toward a fuller acceptance of the publication of representative texts that both reflect and effect the status of gay men and lesbians within the context of contemporary society.

When gay and lesbian writers perceived the marketability of their writings, a group of gay men met informally in the summer of 1979 to form New York's Violet Quill. Among the gay writers of this productive post-Stonewall workshop were Robert Ferro, Michael Grumley, Andrew Holleran, Felice Picano, Edmund White, George Stambolian, Christopher Cox, and George Whitmore. Building on the successes of *Dancer from the Dance*, White's *Nocturnes for the King of Naples* (1978), and Picano's *The Lure* (1979), these writers met to discuss the problems of autobiographical fiction and the literary coming-out process. Other writers of the same period, among them Rita Mae Brown, Richard Hall, Jane DeLynn, Audre Lorde, Larry Kramer, Armistead Maupin, and Bertha Harris, published texts that foisted the emerging, self-aware gay community upon America. As Stambolian notes, "Their novels and stories effectively moved the focus of gay literature away from the lonely homosexual figure doomed to unhappiness toward the elaboration of a world in which homosexuality was no longer an exclusively psychological issue shrouded in secrecy and guilt but a social reality."

Gay and lesbian writers are artists who must perform a balancing act, straddling the gap between public and private discourse about homosexuality as they struggle with questions of self, sexual identity, and the individual's relationship within his or her society. The representation of gay men and lesbians in literature is crucial in a world where the human rights of homosexuals are still disputed. The act of writing by gays and lesbians is a very influential part of the politics of social change, where the literature contributes to increasing understanding of the human condition, which is fundamental to social acceptance of homosexuals as well as personal liberation.

The fictional representations of homosexuals by gay male and lesbian writers since the Stonewall riots of 1969 have evolved, as have popular conceptions about homosexual identity. These texts are in no way identical in their approaches to homosexuality. The approaches are as individual as the writers themselves and their works are part of a growing body of literature that constructs, perpetuates, revises, and deconstructs the fictions—including defamations and stereotypes—about homosexuals and homosexuality.

Central to the development of an individual's gay identity is the individual's relationship to his or her dominant society. Gays and lesbians share the common cultural experience of living in a society that barely tolerates, but for the most part denies, the deep instincts and emotions that are the basis of a homosexual's sexual identity. While this intolerance and denial often lead gays and lesbians to seek a sense of solidarity with other homosexuals, it also forces the individual, especially the gay or lesbian writer, to evaluate his or her interactions with others as well as his or her perspective on the majority culture. Because the homosexual is forced to deal with the implications of his or her sexuality—much more so than any heterosexual as a member of the dominant culture must—the gay or lesbian writer's unusual relationship with society fosters a perspective that

bestows upon the homosexual writer the valuable role of social analyst and critic. As Claude Summers notes, "This ambiguous relationship may encourage many homosexuals to question received ideas about the larger society and develop insight into the arbitrariness and injustice of social forms and institutions generally."

Since the Stonewall Inn riots, the efforts of gay and lesbian writers have shifted homosexuality from an exclusively personal problem to a problem of human liberation and social justice. These writers explore the experience of otherness. Their unique relationship to society allows them to probe the depths of exclusion and the pain it brings. By portraying gays and lesbians as complete human beings who are part of faithful reflections of the human condition, homosexual writers are able to illuminate the rich, diverse, and complex human experience.

Gay and lesbian writers stand at the conceptual edge of human sexuality, posing questions of definition and identity: Who is a homosexual? What constitutes sexual identity? How do social forces influence sexuality? Is homosexuality a biological or psychological condition—or a mixture of both? If sexuality is not a matter of choice, how do categorizations such as homosexual, bisexual, or heterosexual affect individuals? Is there empowerment in epithets of stigmatization like "queer" and "dyke"? The relentless questioning about sexual identity that gay and lesbian writers must continually address has created a consciousness of difference that has made possible at least the acceptance, if not the tolerance, of otherness in America's multicultural society.

The gay and lesbian writers covered in this chapter are a diverse lot, whose individual experiences of self-discovery, self-avowal, and sexual affirmation are the impulses behind their fictions. Gay fiction often tells *Tales of the City*, to borrow the title of Armistead Maupin's series, because it is to cities that young gays and lesbians often move to find the sense of community and extended family they lack. Gay fiction also tells tales of confusion on coming out, as in Edmund White's *The Beautiful Room Is Empty* (1988), in which the protagonist emerges from youthful self-doubt and repression to maturity as he participates, somewhat bewildered, in the Stonewall Inn riots of 1969. Rita Mae Brown approaches a mixture of lesbianism with Southern humor in her works *Rubyfruit Jungle* (1973) and *Venus Envy* (1993). David Leavitt attempts to redefine the homosexual's relationship to the family and explores generational differences between young gays and closeted older gays in his novels *Equal Affections* (1989) and *The Lost Language of Cranes* (1986); he explores the self-avowed gay as integrated into society in his short-story collection *Family Dancing* (1984). Audre Lorde recounts the childhood incidents that influenced her developing sexuality in *Zami* (1982), an autobiographical work from a lesbian writer who is known principally for her poetry. Larry Kramer addresses the rhetoric of AIDS in polemics written specifically for gay men that address the dominant culture's contempt for homosexuals. Rounding out this section are Lisa Alther and Paul Monette, whose works, along with those of the aforementioned writers, demonstrate that gay and lesbian voices are just as indigenous and important as those of the Southern regionalists, urban Jewish writers, African American writers, and feminist writers, whose movements have enriched the literature of the twentieth century. These gay and lesbian writers have countered the dominant culture's negative and stereotypical representations of homosexuality with positive gay images through their own transforming use of language, tradition, and myth, allowing the love that once dared not speak its name to speak up loudly and proudly.

—*Thomas D. Petitjean, Jr.*
The University of Southwestern Louisiana

LISA ALTHER

Born: Kingsport, Tennessee; July 23, 1944

Principal long fiction

Kinflicks, 1975; *Original Sins*, 1981; *Other Women*, 1984; *Bedrock*, 1990.

Other literary forms

Lisa Alther has written articles on such subjects as cooking, gardening, and environmental issues, as well as reviews and essays about the art of writing. Her principal interest, however, is in writing fiction. Although she has written numerous short stories, only a few of them have appeared in print, and Alther continues to be known primarily as a novelist.

Achievements

With *Kinflicks*, Alther became one of the primary spokespersons for her generation. As the sales records of her novels suggest, Alther's disgust with the social and political establishment echoes the feelings of a great many Americans, particularly those who in the 1960's hoped for a better world, only to find that bigotry, intolerance, and callous selfishness are still in control as the century draws to an end. Alther also is regarded as an important spokesperson for her gender. Although she herself is not an activist, in her works she supports the women's movement, both through her attacks on gender stereotypes and in her insistence on the right of women to express their sexual natures and fulfill their sexual needs.

Biography

Lisa Alther was born on July 23, 1944, in Kingsport, Tennessee, one of five children of John Shelton Reed, a surgeon, and Alice Margaret Greene Reed, an English teacher. Lisa's father influenced her early interest in scientific subjects and science fiction, her mother her delight in reading, especially Southern women writers such as Eudora Welty, Flannery O'Connor, Katherine Anne Porter, and Carson McCullers. Although the family was always supportive, Alther herself did not write anything more than articles for her high school newspaper until, at age eighteen, she took a course in creative writing and attempted her first work of fiction.

At Wellesley College, though Alther did turn out some articles for the campus newspaper, she was preparing herself for a career in the publishing industry. After earning her B.A. degree in 1966, she moved to New York City, where she had obtained a position as secretary and editorial assistant for Atheneum Publishers. During the six months that she was employed by Atheneum, she began to write stories in her spare time. Meanwhile, on August 26, 1966, she married Richard Philip Alther, a painter, and shortly thereafter she settled down in rural Vermont, where for several years she was a freelance writer. On November 15, 1968, a daughter, Sara Halsey Alther, was born.

While Alther had considerable success in publishing her journalistic nonfiction articles, she found it more difficult to place her fiction, which was regularly rejected. After Sara's birth, Alther had to solve another problem common to women artists with children: how to find the uninterrupted time essential for creativity. In *Contemporary Fiction Writers of the South* (1993), Mary Anne Ferguson tells about one of Alther's solutions. During the first two years of Sara's life, every two months Alther would leave their daughter with Philip, move into a boardinghouse in Montreal, Canada, and work for as many hours a day as possible. In this way she managed to complete the first half of her novel *Kinflicks*. Later, life became easier. Alther simply disciplined herself to do her writing during her daughter's hours at school.

Although by 1970 *Kinflicks* was well under way, it was to be five more years before the novel was published. By then, in addition to her articles, Alther had been writing fiction for twelve years, turning out two unpublished novels and thirteen short stories and collecting some 250 rejection slips. Out of this experience came, almost necessarily, Alther's ability to find joy in the act of creation itself, as well as her emphasis on craftsmanship, which, though it has diminished her total output, ensures the high quality of her work.

To the surprise of the publishing world and of the author herself, Alther's first novel became a runaway best-seller. *Kinflicks* was a critical triumph as well. The author was praised for her wit, her skill in characterization, and her insight into the generation that came of age during the turbulent 1960's.

Despite her success, Alther continued to live quietly in Vermont, working at her own deliberate pace, recasting and revising each work until she considered it ready for publication. *Original Sins* came out six years after *Kinflicks*, and *Other Women* three years after that. Both novels did well commercially, but many critics thought that they lacked the comic verve of *Kinflicks*. During the six-year period that elapsed between the publication of *Other Women* and *Bedrock*, Alther may have decided that there was merit in these comments. At any rate, in *Bedrock* she is once again viewing the world from a comic perspective.

Analysis

In her first novel, Alther set the patterns and suggested the themes that are found in all of her later works. Her protagonists are women; each of them is involved in a search for identity and purpose; and each of them is torn between a fascination with death, even a desire for it, and a passionate longing for life, which seems to be most fully satisfied in the arms of a lesbian lover. What differentiates one novel from another is primarily the setting, the handling of plot, and the tone.

In *Kinflicks*, it is Ginny Babcock Bliss who, at age twenty-seven, is still confused about who she is and where she is going. After having been kicked out by her husband and refused access to her daughter, Ginny has flown home to Hullsport, Tennessee, to spend a month with her widowed mother, who is slowly but inexorably moving toward death. During this period, Ginny relives her adolescence, her college years, and her recent adventures, in the hope of finding some meaning in it all.

Growing up as a member of a prosperous family in a small Southern town might not seem particularly trying, but if one's parents are both obsessed with death, as Ginny's were, what might seem normal to others will have a peculiar twist of its own. After her father, the manager of a munitions plant, is nearly killed in an accident at the factory, he builds a bomb shelter; meanwhile, her mother demonstrates against nuclear tests, tours cemeteries, and continually revises her obituary. When Ginny enters high school, she finds another reason for bewilderment. In the back seat with Joe Bob Sparks, the football hero, Ginny tries in vain to understand why sex is considered so important, and she is no more impressed when she takes the final step and surrenders her virginity to the hood Clem Cloyd. Clem leaves her not only unfulfilled but also in traction, the

result of one ride too many on Clem's motorcycle. Ginny yearns for Clem only because he is forbidden, but she cannot honestly imagine being defined as the little wife of either of those good old boys.

In a women's college in Boston, however, Ginny believes that she has found her identity, first as the mirror image of her cerebral philosophy teacher, then, in a complete turnabout, as a sexual athlete, panting in the arms of Edna ("Eddie") Holzer. Having given up first on domesticity, then on scientific detachment, she is now drawn by Eddie into the movement and eventually finds herself in a women's commune in Starks Bay, Vermont. After Eddie dies in an accident that in fact resulted from her own plan to kill a few men, Ginny decides to try the role of wife and mother. In her husband's orderly world, however, where sex is carefully scheduled and performed with a guidebook, Ginny is miserable. Again, she reacts. This time she becomes involved with an army deserter, who entices her into peculiar sexual rituals designed to lead her to some kind of salvation, but as a consequence of her indiscretion, Ginny now must choose between making amends to her husband and leaving him, thereby losing her child.

So captivating is Alther's story that one might not notice the intricacies of her art. Yet the novel is structured not only for comic effect but also for thematic content. Clearly, during this odyssey in progress, Ginny has been vacillating between the physical and the intellectual, for example, between her lesbian lover and her rigidly controlled teacher. To represent the coldly rational approach toward life, Alther often uses references to scientific investigation; however, the fact that what Ginny studies is generally biological in nature, for example, her own blood, suggests that nothing and no one can actually be detached from existence, at least not until death.

There is also a movement between life, often expressed in sexual terms, and death, symbolic or real. Alther also shows how these polarities are often intertwined. The novel begins with Ginny's mother, much younger, already in love with death; it continues in alternating chapters, first a day in the present, devoted to Mrs. Babcock's dying, then months or years of the past, as Ginny seeks some guidance for the life still ahead of her. Nothing in this novel is simple. Ironically, death is as alive in Ginny's memories as it is in Mrs. Babcock's hospital room, and so, indeed, is love. Thus Ginny's sexual initiation is held in her father's bomb shelter, his bulwark against death; her seduction of Eddie is accomplished in the aftermath of another girl's attempted suicide; her involvement with the man she eventually marries seems to have evolved from Eddie's death; and at the end of the book, from her mother's long dying comes Ginny's decision to live her own life, wherever that may take her.

Technically, *Original Sins* is even more complicated than *Kinflicks*. Instead of a single protagonist, it has five, and the omniscient author undertakes not only to describe all five lives over a period of years but also to penetrate the minds of each of her major characters. There are some similarities to the earlier novel, for example, the New South setting and the pattern of departure and return: Like Ginny, three of the characters who have moved to the North come back home with new perspectives. The tone of *Original Sins*, however, is very different from that of *Kinflicks*. Abandoning her satirical approach, in this book Alther protests in no uncertain terms against what she sees as the hypocrisy, the corruption, the materialism, and the sexual stereotyping that cause such misery for those who have the misfortune of being reared in the South and, to an even greater degree, for those who remain in it. While she does admit that New York City is not perfect, in this novel Alther seems to equate death, or at least a spiritual death, with a region, rather than with the human condition.

Other Women represents still another departure in setting, plot, and tone. While the story is placed in New Hampshire, not much depends on that setting. The plot of this novel is also much simpler than that of the others, dealing primarily with only two characters, a psychotherapist, Hannah Burke, and her patient, Caroline Kelley, a nurse whom Hannah is trying to extricate from incapacitating despair. The work is serious in tone, not comic, but it lacks the anger that was evident in *Original Sins*. Even Caroline's parents, a pair of smug do-gooders who neglected their own family in order to aid strangers, are shown as more misguided than despicable.

Like Alther's other works, *Other Women* juxtaposes love and death. For example, had Caroline not loved her housemate so intensely, Caroline would not have begun to have death-dreams after being rejected by her. Moreover, as both Caroline and Hannah realize at the outset,

the very relationship between therapist and patient itself involves hate, attachment, perhaps even love, and, finally, separation. In this case, having so recently been deprived of a woman lover, Caroline naturally feels a passing attraction for her likable therapist; but, even aside from her ethical principles, Hannah is happily married. Nevertheless, Hannah does understand love and loss. Not a day goes by that she does not grieve for two of her children, who died in a senseless, unforeseeable accident.

With *Bedrock*, Alther returns to satirical comedy and a small-town setting, this time not in the South but in New England. The basic plotline is fairly straightforward. A middle-aged photographer, Clea Shawn, leaves New York City and buys a house in Roches Ridge, Vermont, where she expects to live in harmony with nature and her bucolic neighbors while she seeks direction for her life. By the end of the book, she realizes that her feelings for a woman sculptor are more intense than any she ever felt for her husband, and the two women decide to spend the rest of their lives together. Thus Clea discovers her identity and commits herself to love.

While Clea may be right about her lover, however, she is dead wrong about the townspeople of Roches Ridge. The citizens are not the noble peasants of Clea's vision but a set of scheming, lying, vengeful, brutal barbarians, who enjoy taking advantage of an outsider even more than they like cheating one another. In a real triumph of craftsmanship, Alther moves back and forth between the minds of a great many characters, systematically exposing the perfidious designs of the townspeople, while emphasizing the ironic contrast between their intentions and actions, on the one hand, and Clea's dependably erroneous reading of reality, on the other hand. The gullibility of urban sophisticates has rarely been so funny.

It is interesting to trace the development of Alther's characteristic themes through her novels, but it is even more fascinating to observe her technical virtuosity, particularly her use of point of view and her deft handling of narrative. If she is to be viewed as the spokesperson of a generation of women, one could hardly ask for a more effective or impressive voice.

Bibliography

Braendlin, Bonnie H. "Alther, Atwood, Ballantyne, and Gray: Secular Salvation in the Contemporary Feminist Bildungsroman." *Frontiers* 4 (1979): 18-21.

Braendlin, Bonnie H. "New Directions in the Contemporary Bildungsroman: Lisa Alther's *Kinflicks*." In *Gender and Literary Voice*, edited by Janet Todd. New York: Holmes & Meier, 1980.

Brown, Laurie L. "Interviews with Seven Contemporary Writers." In *Women Writers of the Contemporary South*, edited by Peggy Whitman Prenshaw. Jackson: University Press of Mississippi, 1984.

Cantwell, Mary. "Serious When Once She Was Funny." *The New York Times Book Review*, May 3, 1981, 9, 38.

Ferguson, Mary Anne. "Lisa Alther." In *Contemporary Fiction Writers of the South: A Bio-Bibliographical Sourcebook*, edited by Joseph M. Flora and Robert Bain. Westport, Conn.: Greenwood Press, 1993.

_____ . "Lisa Alther: The Irony of Return?" In *Women Writers of the Contemporary South*, edited by Peggy Whitman Prenshaw. Jackson: University Press of Mississippi, 1984.

Hall, Joan Lord. "Symbiosis and Separation in Lisa Alther's *Kinflicks*." *Arizona Quarterly* 38 (Winter, 1982): 336-346.

King, Francis. "Hannah and Caroline." *The Spectator* 254 (March 9, 1985): 23-24.

Schechner, Mark. "A Novel of the New South." *The New Republic* 184 (June 13, 1981): 34-36.

Waage, Frederick G. "Alther and Dillard: The Appalachian Universe." In *Appalachia/America: Proceedings of the 1980 Appalachian Studies Conference*, edited by Wilson Somerville. Johnson City, Tenn.: Appalachian Consortium Press, 1981.

RITA MAE BROWN

Born: Hanover, Pennsylvania; November 28, 1944

Principal long fiction

Rubyfruit Jungle, 1973; *In Her Day*, 1976; *Six of One*, 1978; *Southern Discomfort*, 1982; *Sudden Death*, 1983; *High Hearts*, 1986; *Bingo*, 1988; *Wish You Were Here*, 1990 (with Sneaky Pie Brown); *Rest in Pieces*, 1992 (with Sneaky Pie Brown); *Venus Envy*, 1993; *Dolley: A Novel of Dolley Madison in Love and War*, 1994.

Other literary forms

Although known primarily for her comic novels, with *Wish You Were Here*, supposedly coauthored by her feline companion Sneaky Pie Brown, Rita Mae Brown ventured into the mystery genre. *Rest in Pieces* is the second work in what is called the "Mrs. Murphy" series, after Brown's fictional cat-detective. Early in her career, Brown also produced a scholarly work, the translation entitled *Hrotsvitha: Six Medieval Latin Plays* (1971), and two volumes of poetry, *The Hand That Cradles the Rock* (1971) and *Songs to a Handsome Woman* (1973). *Poems* was published in 1987. Brown is also noted for her lively essays, collected in *A Plain Brown Rapper* (1976), and for *Starting from Scratch: A Different Kind of Writer's Manual* (1988), which contains biographical information as well as more general comments. Brown's film and television writing credits include *I Love Liberty* (1982), which she coauthored, the horror movie *The Slumber Party Massacre* (1982), both segments of *The Long Hot Summer* (1985), *My Two Loves* (1986), and *Rich Men, Single Women* (1989).

Achievements

Because of her outspoken espousal of women's causes and of sexual freedom, in particular the rights of lesbians, Brown was at first a cult figure, then, with her best-selling paperback novel *Rubyfruit Jungle*, a popular success. Although in 1974 she was awarded a Massachusetts Council on Arts and Humanities Fiction grant and National Endowment for the Arts Creative Writing Fellowship, it was only in the late 1980's that Brown began to receive the scholarly attention that she merits. In journal articles, in essays, and, most notably, in Carol M. Ward's book-length study in Twayne's United States Authors series (*Rita Mae Brown*, 1993), the novelist is now perceived not merely as an activist in minority causes or a creator of Southern eccentrics but as a writer who, like the Greek dramatist Aristo-

phanes, on whom she models her own work, uses comedy as a means of revealing universal truths.

Biography

Rita Mae Brown was born in Hanover, Pennsylvania, on November 28, 1944. Supposedly her mother was a Pennsylvanian, and her father was a member of the Venable family of Charlottesville, Virginia. After being left at an orphanage shortly after her birth, the baby girl was adopted by Ralph Brown, a butcher of Pennsylvania Dunkard stock, and Julia Ellen Buckingham Brown, who worked in a bakery and sometimes in a mill. Brown's adoptive mother was a Southerner, originally from Maryland, and a devout Lutheran. The couple had four natural sons.

Although Brown's parents gave the bright little girl unstinting love, careful moral guidance, and unfailing encouragement in her intellectual development, Brown soon discovered what it was to be an outsider. First she was taunted for her illegitimate birth; then, when in fourth grade she was transferred to a school filled with upper-middle-class children, she was snubbed because she belonged to a working-class family.

When Rita Mae was eleven, her family moved to Fort Lauderdale, Florida. Four years later, her adoptive father died. Despite this tragedy, for several years she led a happy, carefree life. By downplaying her academic interests, such as her enthusiasm for Latin literature, she managed to find acceptance among her peers, who admired her for her athletic ability, especially for her skill at tennis. Brown's sexual experimentation during her high school years, however, led eventually to her being branded a lesbian and becoming a social outcast.

After being graduated from high school, Brown went to the University of Florida on a scholarship, joined the Delta Delta Delta sorority, and once again moved in the social mainstream. Two years later, she found herself in trouble. After making an angry comment to a sorority officer who had warned her against involvement in the Civil Rights movement and, in particular, against association with African Americans, Brown was called in to the office of the dean of women, charged with promiscuity and lesbianism, and deprived of her scholarship. Without funds to continue at the university, Brown hitchhiked to New York. There she supported herself as a waitress until she could obtain a scholarship to New York University. In 1968, she graduated from NYU with a B.A. degree in English and the classics, and she also earned a certificate in cinematography from the School of Visual Arts in Manhattan, which enabled her to find a job as photography editor for the Sterling Publishing Company. In 1970, Brown moved to Washington, D.C., where she lectured at Federal City College and began graduate work at the Institute for Policy Studies, eventually earning her Ph.D. degree.

These were also years of political activism. While she was in New York, Brown had become a leader and an organizer of feminist, gay, and lesbian groups, but she often found herself at odds with their policies. In 1970, she resigned from the National Organization for Women (NOW), which she believed was intolerant of lesbian members, and worked instead through groups like Redstockings and Radicalesbians. In Washington, she helped to organize the lesbian separatist Furies Collective, but only a year later she was voted out of the group.

Disillusioned with feminist politics, Brown now decided to take the advice of her friend, the actress Alexis Smith, and voice her views through fiction. After being rejected by mainstream publishers, the autobiographical novel *Rubyfruit Jungle* was brought out by the feminist Daughters Press. Although the sales of the book were surprisingly high, Brown could not support herself by her writing as long as she remained outside the mainstream of literary production. With the aid of two grants, she was able to write a second novel, *In Her Day*; however, it was not successful either critically or financially. In 1977, when *Rubyfruit Jungle* was reprinted by Bantam Books and became a best-seller, Brown could at last become a full-time novelist.

in 1978, Brown moved to Charlottesville, Virginia. There she lived initially with the writer and actress Fannie Flagg, then with the woman she later called her first real love, tennis star Martina Navratilova. Their stormy, highly publicized relationship lasted until 1981, when Navratilova broke it off. Brown drew on her experiences with the women's tennis tour for the book *Sudden Death*, published in 1983. Immediately after the

end of her love affair, Brown lived for some months in Los Angeles, writing film and television scripts; she did not return to Charlottesville until 1982, when she bought a home and settled down, alone except for her beloved pets. After ten years of solitude, in 1992 she became romantically involved with Judy Nelson, an ex-lover of Navratilova. Although their life together proved to be harmonious, Brown insists that her greatest joy is still her writing, her greatest love the English language.

Analysis

While Brown makes no secret of the fact that her novels are written from the perspective of a feminist, a lesbian, and a Southerner, she has won a wide audience by dealing with such universal human problems as alienation, isolation, the quest for love, and the need for acceptance. Her protagonists find themselves in conflict with the community and its professed values; this conflict can be resolved either by their agreeing to conform or at least to conceal their nonconformity or, as Brown urges, by the community's agreeing to tolerate differences. Interestingly, it is to the conservative, traditional, Bible-haunted, small-town South, which has always made room for eccentrics who mind their manners, that Brown looks for her model society.

Brown is particularly sensitive to the feelings of those who feel themselves alienated from society. Brown's autobiographical first novel, *Rubyfruit Jungle*, shows the bewilderment of Molly Bolt when her own mother, Carrie Bolt, insists that as a "bastard," Molly is inferior to other children. Evidently, it is also bad to be a female. Other children tell her that she cannot be the doctor in the game they are playing, because girls have to be nurses. Later, Carrie opposes Molly's going to college, on the grounds that women stay home while men work.

Unlike the protagonists in other coming-of-age novels, Molly does not need to search for her identity. She has always known who she is. As for what she is, a bastard, a female, a lesbian, Molly sees such labels as threats to one's individuality.

In high school, however, she finds that others are not as secure about themselves as she is. For example, Molly's lover blithely insists that she (the lover) is too feminine to be a lesbian, whatever the boyish-looking, athletic Molly may be. Another friend turns away from Molly in horror, as if seeing Molly as a totally different person just because she has slept with a female.

Up to this point, Molly has been betrayed by individuals; not until she gets to the University of Florida does she experience the weight of community censure. When Molly and her female roommate fall in love, it soon becomes obvious to everyone that they are more than friends. Confronted by university officials, Molly admits the truth. As a result, she is first confined in a mental ward, then deprived of her scholarship, and thus, in effect, barred from the university.

After this disaster, one might expect Brown's protagonist to end her pursuit of happiness within an alternative society, where lesbianism is the norm. It is true that during the next period in her life, while she is in New York City, working first as a waitress and then as a secretary, Molly finds ample reason to side with women in their anger about sexual harassment and gender discrimination. She soon discovers, however, that men do not hold the patent on exploitation. Lesbians are just as likely as heterosexual men to regard their sexual partners as mere objects, to use and then discard them without a backward glance.

At the end of the novel, Molly has finished film school and is ready to conquer the world. Even more important, however, is her new capacity to accept others, with all of their faults, just as she hopes to be accepted by them. Molly can now come to terms with her past, and, specifically, with her adoptive mother, who has always diminished, discouraged, and rejected her. As her final school project, Molly films Carrie as she talks about her life. In the process, the two lifelong antagonists finally recognize each other's worth. Even though they will never agree about most things, Molly and Carrie can now admit their love for each other and accept their differences.

It is not in forced conformity, but in this kind of tolerance and compassion, that Brown sees hope for society as a whole. It is inevitable, she believes, that individuals will think and act in ways that other individuals find offensive. Unless a community is to end up with a single citizen, however, its members will have to overlook one another's peculiarities.

In *Southern Discomfort*, Brown shows one way that individual differences can be handled by society. It is called "hypocrisy." Everyone in Montgomery, Alabama, knows that the prostitutes of Water Street have regular customers among the most influential men in the city. As long as their wives can pretend ignorance, life in Montgomery will continue to run smoothly. The system can survive even when a woman who is married, white, and highly placed in society sleeps with a black man, just as long as no one is forced to recognize what

is going on. Problems arise only when the lovely Hortensia Reedmuller Banastre falls passionately in love with Hercules Jinks, then becomes pregnant by him. Brown solves one problem by having Hercules killed in an accident; Hortensia takes care of the other by having her devoted cook rear the baby as her own. Whatever the community suspects, it can pretend to believe the story. Both Hortensia and her little Catherine, however, have to live with unsatisfied yearnings; Hortensia needs to nurture her child, and Catherine needs to know who she is. Thus the author shows how individuals are forced to suffer when they live in a society based on appearances.

A better way of accommodating the differences between individuals is shown in *Six of One*, *Bingo*, and *Venus Envy*, as well as in the mysteries *Wish You Were Here* and *Rest in Pieces*. All these works are set in places so small that their inhabitants have no choice but to tolerate one another. The very fact that both *Six of One* and *Bingo* are set in a town that straddles the border between North and South, Pennsylvania and Maryland, makes the problems of other municipalities pale by comparison. In *Bingo*, the rival sheriffs quarrel constantly, but then so do the two elderly Hunsenmeier sisters, who are both pursuing the one available man in their age bracket. The fact that the protagonist, Nicole ("Nickel") Smith, and the male owner of the beauty shop are both openly gay is largely ignored; compared to some of the other inhabitants, those two seem rather staid. Like *Rubyfruit Jungle*, *Bingo* culminates in reconciliation. Yet while Brown's first novel ended with the mending of a single broken relationship, in the final chapters of *Bingo* the entire community takes part in a sort of love feast, which is occasioned by the coming into the world of two new lives.

Admittedly, the situation is not unusual, except for Nickel's professed lesbianism. After an affair with a married man, the young woman finds that she is pregnant. What is amazing is the community's response. There is very little criticism; instead, almost everyone comes to her aid. Her gay friend marries her and becomes the ecstatic father of twins; their own marriage revived, Nickel's former lover and her longtime friend, his wife, dote on the babies; the sisters concentrate on their new roles as grandmother and great-aunt; the dog is delirious, the cats at least tolerant. Even the departed are involved in the celebration, when Nickel releases a red kite with a note attached to inform her father that he has become a grandfather.

Where more strident demands for the rights of minorities may be ineffectual, Brown's tales have the force of fables. Brown is a realist; she does not ignore the existence of bigotry, prejudice, pettiness, or simple spite. Yet she is also an optimist, for she believes that it is possible to make life, if not perfect, at least pleasant. In an increasingly fragmented world, her works are a plea for good humor and goodwill and an invitation to find delight in diversity.

Other major works

NONFICTION: *A Plain Brown Rapper*, 1976; *Starting from Scratch: A Different Kind of Writer's Manual*, 1988.

POETRY: *The Hand That Cradles the Rock*, 1971; *Songs to a Handsome Woman*, 1973; *Poems*, 1987.

SCREENPLAY: *The Slumber Party Massacre*, 1982.

TELEPLAYS: *I Love Liberty*, 1982; *The Long Hot Summer*, 1985; *My Two Loves*, 1986; *Rich Men, Single Women*, 1989.

TRANSLATION: *Hrotsvitha: Six Medieval Latin Plays*, 1971.

Bibliography

Chew, Martha. "Rita Mae Brown: Feminist Theorist and Southern Novelist." In *Women Writers of the Contemporary South*, edited by Peggy Whitman Prenshaw. Jackson: University Press of Mississippi, 1984. Also published in *Southern Quarterly* 22, no. 1 (Fall, 1983): 61-80.

Davenport, Gary. "The Fugitive Hero in New Southern Fiction." *The Sewanee Review* 91, no. 3 (Summer, 1983): 439-445.

Fishbein, Leslie. "*Rubyfruit Jungle*: Lesbianism, Feminism, and Narcissism." *International Journal of Women's Studies* 7, no. 2 (March/April, 1984): 155-159.

Ladd, Barbara. "Rita Mae Brown." In *Contemporary Fiction Writers of the South: A Bio-Bibliographical Sourcebook*, edited by Joseph M. Flora and Robert Bain. Westport, Conn.: Greenwood Press, 1993.

Levine, Daniel B. "Uses of Classical Mythology in Rita Mae Brown's *Southern Discomfort*." *Classical and Modern Literature* 10, no. 1 (Fall, 1989): 51, 63-70.

Mandrell, James. "Questions of Genre and Gender: Contemporary American Versions of the Feminine Picaresque." *Novel* 29, no. 2 (Winter, 1987): 149-166.

Ward, Carol M. *Rita Mae Brown*. New York: Twayne, 1993.

LARRY KRAMER

Born: Bridgeport, Connecticut; June 25, 1935

Principal drama

The Normal Heart, pr., pb. 1985; *Just Say No*, pr. 1988, pb. 1989; *Sissies' Scrapbook*, pr. 1989; *The Furniture of Home*, pr. 1989; *The Destiny of Me*, pr. 1992, pb. 1993.

Other literary forms

Larry Kramer received initial acclaim from film critics for his screenplay *Women in Love* (1969), adapted from D. H. Lawrence's 1920 novel. He received wide publicity for his novel *Faggots* (1978). The versatile Kramer has also published a collection of his political writings, *Reports from the Holocaust: The Making of an AIDS Activist* (1989).

Achievements

Kramer has excelled in the various genres in which he has worked. In 1970, he received an Academy Award nomination for best screenplay for his adaptation of *Women in Love*. For *The Normal Heart*, he received the Dramatists Guild Marton Award, the City Lights Award for best play of the year, the Sarah Siddons Award for best play of the year, and a nomination for the Olivier Award for best play, all in 1986. He received an Arts and Communication Award from the Human Rights Campaign Fund in 1987 and an Obie Award in 1993 for *The Destiny of Me*.

Biography

Larry Kramer was born on June 25, 1935, to a middle-class family in Bridgeport, Connecticut. His father, George L. Kramer, was an attorney, his mother, Rea Wishengrad Kramer, a social worker. Finishing a B.A. degree at Yale University in 1957 and completing a tour of service in the U.S. Army the same year, Kramer desired a career in the theater. Realizing the difficulty that he would encounter in attempting to become an actor, he entered an Executive training Program at Columbia Pictures in 1958, where he ran a teletype machine. He later remembers bragging to fellow trainees that he would produce his first film by the time he was thirty.

Kramer was, in fact, an associate producer by that age, and he produced his first film at age thirty-three. His career in the movie industry was distinguished. Kramer worked for Columbia until 1965, serving as assistant story editor in New York City and production executive in London, England. In 1965, he became assistant to the president of United Artists. He worked as the associate producer of the motion picture *Here We Go Round the Mulberry Bush* (1968) and produced and wrote the screenplay for the motion picture *Women in Love*, which was released to great acclaim in 1969. For his adaptation of the Lawrence novel, Kramer was nominated for awards for best screenplay by the Academy of Motion Picture Arts and Sciences and the British Film Academy.

At this time Kramer was fully aware of his own homosexuality but had yet to integrate his professional and personal lives. He brought women with him to professional screenings to maintain the appearance of heterosexuality among his colleagues. After years of therapy and arguments with his family, however, he took the step of trying to deal honestly with his own sexuality in his writing. This resulted in the novel *Faggots*, which was published in 1978, a work immediately recognized for its anger and biting wit. Kramer was at work on a second novel when the AIDS crisis began in the early 1980's. He soon became an activist and critic of governmental inaction, cofounding the Gay Men's Health Crisis, a New York-based AIDS organization, in 1981, and ACT Up (AIDS Coalition To Unleash Power) in 1988. AIDS also motivated Kramer to write what became the most successful of his first five plays, *The Normal Heart*, which was produced in 1985 to great acclaim.

Kramer has continued to fight for AIDS-research funding. He is a vociferous critic of homophobia in the media and in governmental programs. While he once bristled when referred to as a "gay writer," he now happily embraces the term. An outspoken activist and commentator, he continues to challenge both gay and heterosexual readers through articles in *The New York Times* and *The Village Voice* and through his highly charged plays.

Analysis

Kramer's is an angry, some say cranky, voice, but one that clearly demands a response. Unifying all of his diverse works is a call to action, a plea for responsible behavior and a sympathetic treatment of others. Kramer is a harsh critic, both of traditional American institutions and of certain segments of the gay population in America. His characterizations and articulations are not always finely nuanced; they often border on caricature. Yet they clearly perform political work, even when their aesthetic qualities seem under-realized. Commentators have compared him favorably with Jonathan Swift, for like that great satirist of the eighteenth century, Kramer has a genius for holding up a mirror to society, reflecting back to it in unambiguous terms its own foibles and absurdities.

So what, one might ask, is Kramer trying to achieve through his harsh words and often heavy-handed parodies? In his afterword to *Reports from the Holocaust*, Kramer states simply that he wants everyone "to get off their butts and pitch in." While here he is speaking specifically about the fight against AIDS, the same impetus underlies all of his gay-relevant work, to communicate that only through self-aware and concerted social and political activity can a homophobic and disease-ridden world remedy its own ills. Kramer bristles slightly when he is termed an "activist," because it is a label that he believes is too often used pejoratively and as a way of obscuring the fact that he is first and foremost a writer. Kramer prefers the term "moralist," which accurately captures the didactic nature of most of his work. At times simply shocking, at other times berating or cajoling, Kramer time and again relays a simple truth to his audience, one that is the rallying cry of ACT UP, that silence equals death; it threatens not only the body but also the spirit. This theme has formed the nucleus of Kramer's literary concerns from the start, as indicated by his earliest published work, the successful and controversial novel *Faggots*. That book and two of his plays, *The Normal Heart* and *The Destiny of Me*, are perhaps the best realizations of these concerns.

Faggots is very much a product of, as well as a response to, gay urban culture of the 1970's, before the AIDS crisis. *Faggots* contains several thematic strands that concern the effects of silence and silencing. Kramer explores how traditional institutions such as the Church, the government, and medical establishments sequester and silence gay individuals. In *Faggots*, one finds a ghettoization of gay lives into the seediest parts of New York City: the squalid neighborhoods of the Lower East Side, the abandoned docks and piers of the Lower West Side, and the mean streets around Times Square. Furthermore, violence against gays is clearly and honestly represented: Families abandon their gay children, bars are raided needlessly and viciously, and jobs are threatened. Yet Kramer is equally interested in examining the damage that gay men can inflict upon themselves. Even as he reveals the oppressive context for most gay lives, Kramer decries the drug abuse, emotional sterility, and anti-intellectualism of some segments of the 1970's urban gay population. His narrative, often grim and always shocking, takes the reader into the sex clubs and hollow lives of men whose self-image is so low, whose mute acceptance of their own oppression is so thorough, that only in the most banal forms of physical excess can they find some sense of comfort. While Kramer has been criticized for his very broad condemnation of what others might call sexual liberation, his keen perception of self-destructive behavior patterns does demand that gay individuals examine their own lives and evaluate how and why they may be living "down to" the very stereotypes that are so often recognized as homophobic in media representations.

To bring the consequences of this tragic conformity into thematic relief, Kramer uses one character, a good-hearted and sympathetic Everyman named Fred Lemish, as his touchstone. Here Kramer explores the dilemmas of the individual who attempts to articulate his own system of values in an overwhelmingly corrupt world. Fred, too, has been promiscuous and emotionally insensitive, struggling to affirm his sexual orientation through promiscuity. Yet Fred, as he approaches his fortieth birthday, now seeks stability and love. While his (and Kramer's) ideal relationship comes suspiciously close to a traditional, suburban, heterosexual marriage for some critics, certainly the most interesting aspect of Fred's quest is the difficulty he had constructing a life that diverges from the norms of his only support group—his gay friends, acquaintances, and sex partners. That this quest does not end in unequivocal success is Kramer's acknowledgment of the powerful and continuing inducements toward conformity and silence within oppressed minority groups.

Finally, and further complicating the themes mentioned above, is Kramer's exploration of Jewish experience as it encounters and sometimes learns to coexist with gay experience. An important subplot of the novel concerns the Bronstein family, whose patriarch Abe discovers that many of his near relations are "fegalim," homosexuals. His earnest attempt to overcome his own homophobia, however, is threatened by the excesses he discovers in the gay community. Kramer's sympathy for Abe is tangible, even as Kramer acknowledges the oppressive nature of Abe's relationship with his own children and their mothers. Mirroring other aspects of the narrative, Kramer again indicates that Abe's enforcement of silence is deadening, even though vocalizing inanely, as some of Abe's relatives do, is hardly preferable and certainly counterproductive in the long run.

Similarly, the question of when to speak and when to remain silent is central to Kramer's drama. *The Normal Heart*, his best-known and most successful play, centers on the consequences of both silence and speech. Its central character, Ned Weeks, who strongly resembles Kramer himself, is moved to forceful articulation by the inactivity of individuals and governmental entities during the first years of the AIDS crisis. Intertwined with his desire to force the New York City municipal and the federal governments to acknowledge the presence and seriousness of the disease is his fight to raise the consciousness of the gay community. Echoing the themes of *Faggots*, *The Normal Heart* condemns self-destructive behaviors, including risky sexual activity and narcissistic disregard of one's responsibility to one's community. Kramer's messages are never veiled; he states them bluntly in the play through Ned: "I am sick of guys who can only think with their cocks. . . . I am sick of closeted gays." The play argues that thoughtful articulation and thoughtful action are the only possible hopes gay men have in the midst of a crisis that is killing them, as most of American society stands by unmoved or even smugly pleased.

Speaking out can, however, carry with it a high price, as Kramer himself discovered when he was fired from the board of directors of the Gay Men's Health Crisis, the organization he helped create. This parting of ways, which Kramer represents as a clear act of betrayal, is recounted in the play. Ned is expelled from his own action group because his temperament and brutal honesty threaten to undermine the organization's negotiations with the New York City mayor's office. While Kramer views Ned as a victim, whose tactics were simply too brave and forceful for many timid gay men, one must question the political wisdom of many of Ned/Kramer's confrontational tactics. Shrillness may lose its effectiveness if it is not balanced with understanding and quiet negotiation. "That's Larry," Kramer recounts hearing, "always screaming." A scream cer-

tainly serves notice to others of one's existence, but when repeated endlessly it can be perceived to be as lacking in nuance as the mindless behavior that Kramer decries so often. Ned is ostracized and self-tortured at the end of the play, a state of paralysis that is hardly better than the inactivity with which the play opened.

Kramer, in subsequent works, seems to have moved beyond the inertia of victimhood; his sequel to *The Normal Heart*, entitled *The Destiny of Me*, addresses many of the issues raised by the earlier play with far greater deftness and understanding. It is a play replete with nuances rather than ranting speeches. A memory play, *The Destiny of Me* might be compared to Tennessee Williams' *The Glass Menagerie* (pr. 1944, pb. 1945), though critics have also compared it to Eugene O'Neill's *Long Day's Journey into Night* (pr., pb. 1956), for both works deal with familial violence and oppression. In *The Destiny of Me*, a slightly older, but initially no wiser, Ned Weeks confronts AIDS researchers, whom he has viciously criticized in the past but to whom he now turns for help in his own battle against the disease. The play focuses, as well, on yet another but related struggle, with ghosts from Ned's childhood. Again, this is not unlike Kramer himself, who revealed his own HIV-positive status and continuing health problems in his afterword to *Reports from the Holocaust* and whose relationships with family members and national AIDS researchers have been stormy. *The Destiny of Me* is a play about healing and reconciliation, but one that remains true to Kramer's traditional themes. In Ned's struggles with demons past and present, one finds once again an attempt to understand the proper role of speech and the possible utility of silence in one's life. "The world can't be saved with our mouths shut," says Ned, but revealed in a series of flashbacks are the painful consequences of speaking out: rejection, violence, and misunderstanding. In fact, an older Ned cautions his younger self to remain silent to his family about his sexuality, a surprising piece of advice from a character and a playwright noted for their outspokenness.

AIDS is not merely a disease in *The Destiny of Me* but also a metaphor for a poison that remains in one's blood, that, while incurable, can be continually and successfully resisted. Ned's fight for life and health against a physiological opponent is mirrored in his fight for psychological health against a poisonous family and homophobic psychiatric establishment. After years of therapy that were designed to "cure" his homosexuality, Ned discovers that self-acceptance alone leads to peace and certainly should precede all attempts to communicate; healing begins with forgiving oneself and others. In his dialogues with the researchers whom he formerly condemned, Ned discovers the subtle shades of gray that inhabit the region between black and white; he learns to resist a simplistic designation of friend/enemy just as he comes to live with a disease that he had taken for a death sentence. Even his parents are finally forgiven; in his introduction, Kramer writes that *The Destiny of Me* was his attempt to understand "what in their lives made them the way they were" and that he came to realize that "their behavior [was] as destined as [his] own." The journey portrayed in the play ends on a note of hope and acceptance. "I want to stay a little longer," are Ned's last words; one senses that Kramer, too, has embraced the future and left behind the demons of the past.

Rarely subtle, but always energizing, Kramer is a brilliant polemicist. His ability to discern duplicity and decry hypocrisy is matched by few other contemporary writers. In his introduction to the play *Just Say No*, Kramer says that "theater should astonish, amaze, frighten, shock, purge, touch, and move." Certainly Kramer's works fulfill those requirements.

Other major works

SCREENPLAY: *Women in Love*, 1969.
NOVEL: *Faggots*, 1978.
NONFICTION: *Reports from the Holocaust: The Making of an AIDS Activist*, 1989.

Bibliography

Ben-Levi, Jack. "Kramer's Proposals." *The Minnesota Review* 40 (Spring, 1993): 126-132.

Bergman, David. "Larry Kramer and the Rhetoric of AIDS." In *AIDS: The Literary Response*, edited by Emmanuel S. Nelson. New York: Twayne, 1992.

Gross, Gregory D. "Coming Up for Air: Three AIDS Plays." *Journal of American Culture* 15 (Summer, 1992): 63-67.

Shatzky, Joel. "AIDS Enters the American Theater: *As Is* and *The Normal Heart*." *AIDS: The Literary Response*, edited by Emmanuel S. Nelson. New York: Twayne, 1992.

Shatzky, Joel. "Larry Kramer." In *Contemporary Gay American Novelists*, edited by Emmanuel S. Nelson. Westport, Conn.: Greenwood Press, 1993.

DAVID LEAVITT

Born: Pittsburgh, Pennsylvania; June 23, 1961

Principal long fiction

The Lost Language of Cranes, 1986; *Equal Affections*, 1989; *While England Sleeps*, 1993.

Other literary forms

David Leavitt began his career writing short stories. His first major sale came in the early 1980's, when *The New Yorker* published "Territory." This story was included in his first published book, *Family Dancing* (1984). In 1990, he published another story collection titled *A Place I've Never Been*. He has also written essays on books, art, travel, the gay lifestyle, and other subjects.

Achievements

From the beginning, Leavitt has impressed the literary world with his sophisticated prose style, poetic imagery, and effective dialogue. "Territory" won the Willets Prize for fiction from Yale University in 1982, while "Counting Months" received an O. Henry Award in 1984. *Family Dancing* received a nomination for best fiction from the National Book Critics Circle in 1984 and for a PEN/Faulkner Award in 1985. Translated editions of his books have received critical acclaim in such foreign countries as Italy and Spain.

Biography

David Leavitt was born in Pittsburgh, Pennsylvania, on June 23, 1961, but grew up in Palo Alto, California, in the stimulating cultural environment of Stanford University and nearby San Francisco. His father was a professor at Stanford and his mother a housewife. His brother and sister, who were considerably older, belonged to the revolutionary 1960's generation and involved Leavitt in protest demonstrations while he was only a child.

In his story "Counting Months," dealing with his mother's losing fight against cancer, Leavitt paints an unflattering portrait of himself as a seven-year-old child. Leavitt, who was stylistically influenced by the French novelist and homosexual Marcel Proust, was a timid, hypersensitive child, emotionally dependent upon his mother and subject to sudden outbursts of tears with little apparent provocation. His fiction is full of Proustian similes, such as the following from *Equal*

Affections: "Illness moved into their house like an elderly aunt in a back bedroom. It lived with them; it sat at the kitchen table with them; it became ordinary." Leavitt was an avid reader and also watched a considerable amount of television. Yet, his mother's lingering illness became the most important experience of his life. He has written about it in several novels and many stories, as if trying to exorcise the nightmare from his memory.

Leavitt attended Yale University, majoring in English and taking as many creative writing classes as the school would permit. He graduated with honors in 1983 and was elected to Phi Beta Kappa. On the strength of his scholastic achievements and collegiate literary experience, he obtained a job as editorial assistant at Viking-Penguin in New York City. Both at Yale and in the literary world of New York, he was able to meet important members of the Eastern publishing world. His work at Viking-Penguin helped him greatly in learning the business aspects of book publishing. His Yale education, his contacts with good teachers and important literary figures, and his experience in the American publishing capital help explain his early success; however, they would have been inconsequential without his own talents and motivation.

Leavitt's stories and novels reveal many details about his personal life. His main literary concern has been with homosexuality and all of its ramifications. One of the seminal events of his life occurred when he openly admitted to his parents that he was gay. Yet because he directs his work to the general market and not exclusively to the gay community, he does not believe he should be categorized as a "gay writer." In addition to short stories and novels, he occasionally publishes essays on assorted topics.

Analysis

Critically acclaimed Leavitt, acutely aware of the tension-filled conflicts of modern urban life in America, ably expresses the experiences a segment of American society that in the past has been underrepresented. His main literary concern is with the complex problems of being homosexual. These problems include accepting the fact that one is gay and learning how to live with it; finding social acceptance among other men who have accepted their sexual identity; "coming out" to one's parents, which involves the danger of hurting loved ones by making them feel guilty or ashamed; and finding a permanent love relationship with another male, something equivalent to marriage. If this last problem can be solved, then, according to Leavitt, the gay man can find as much happiness in life as the heterosexual; otherwise he is condemned to lifelong loneliness. Yet this issue is the most difficult of all for gay men to resolve, and none of the protagonists of Leavitt's first three novels manages to do it successfully.

The AIDS epidemic has put an end to the promiscuity and flamboyant effeminate mimicry called "camping" that used to be commonplace in the homosexual subculture. In *The Lost Language of Cranes*, Leavitt describes the strikingly modern phenomenon of gay monogamy:

> Men found themselves stranded in couples, reduced to a choice of living alone or continuing with a person who, if he was going to infect you at all, had already done it, so what was there to risk? Thus couples formed; fear had become an indirect route to monogamy and, sometimes, to happiness.

In *The Lost Language of Cranes*, Philip Benjamin has admitted his homosexuality to himself and found a lover, Eliot; however, Philip has not yet made the fateful step of coming out to his parents. The reader senses that Philip's unstable relationship with his lover is somehow rooted in the fact that he has not become mature enough to tell his parents he is gay. It seems impossible for two homosexuals to form a permanent love relationship unless they are both willing to admit it to the entire world.

Philip's father, Owen, represents an older generation who grew up in a world in which the attitude toward homosexuality was shaped by the biblical story of Sodom and Gomorrah and other fire-and-brimstone invective. Owen has never dared acknowledge his homosexuality to anyone and hardly dares admit it to himself. He frequents pornography theaters where furtive individuals indulge in masturbation or rudimentary sexual contact seated side by side in the dark.

The house of cards depicted in *The Lost Language of Cranes* comes tumbling down when Philip finally tells his parents he is gay. Owen feels responsible—not for somehow transmitting his homosexuality through his genes but for hiding his true identity from his whole family and thereby failing to become any kind of adequate role model for his son. As a final, desperate attempt to make amends, Owen comes out of the closet just far enough to make it obvious to his wife, Rose, who is the real victim of the family tragedy. Her disillusionment and despair are meant to dramatize Leavitt's moral that repression and concealment lead to suffering for everyone concerned. Philip's precarious relationship with his lover falls apart, but he finds another lover and starts building another house of cards.

In Leavitt's second novel, *Equal Affections*, the young protagonist, Danny Cooper, has come all the way out of the closet and is enjoying a satisfying love relationship with a man named Walter Bayles. The main problem in this story is Danny's feelings about the terminal cancer afflicting his mother, Louise. He would have found himself completely alone and unable to cope with this tragedy had it not been for Walter's moral support. When Louise finally dies at the hospital, the remaining family members—the father, Danny, and his older sister—immediately begin to drift apart, showing the dominant influence of Louise in the nuclear family. Without Walter, there is no telling what might have happened to Danny; he might, for example, have easily committed suicide.

The remarkable feature of *Equal Affections* is Leavitt's ability to enter into the consciousness of his own mother, portrayed in the novel. Critics have called Louise the book's most interesting character. It is because of Leavitt's unmistakably feminine orientation that he is able to describe his mother's suffering and death in such painful detail. Leavitt seems to take it for granted that his own homosexuality is attributable to identification with a strong mother figure rather than a weak father figure.

Danny has a much deeper relationship with Walter than did Philip with Eliot; nevertheless, there are many indications that their quasi-marriage is tearing at the seams. Just as Philip drove Eliot away by being too dependent, Danny is making Walter feel suffocated in their middle-class suburban monogamy. Walter reacts by communicating with other homosexuals by computer via a gay electronic-mail network. If homosexuals no longer dare to be promiscuous in the flesh, at least they can continue to be promiscuous over the phone lines.

The title *Equal Affections* is taken from lines written

by the English poet and homosexual W. H. Auden: "If equal affection cannot be,/ Let the more loving one be me." Both Philip in *The Lost Language of Cranes* and Danny in *Equal Affections* are the more loving ones and, consequently, suffer the most. While championing the cause of gay liberation, Leavitt takes a dim view of the prospects of gay domestic felicity.

Although Leavitt's third novel, *While England Sleeps*, deals squarely with homosexuality, it represents a radical change of artistic direction and started a great transatlantic literary controversy at a time when critics were complaining that no one was taking literature very seriously anymore. The novel's title alludes to a famous book titled *While England Slept* (1938), composed mainly of speeches by Tory statesman Winston Churchill warning against the growing menace of Fascism. Leavitt's novel is based on incidents recorded in another book, and it was this "springboarding" that caused the transatlantic tidal wave.

Eighty-four-year-old Sir Stephen Spender was outraged when it was brought to his attention that Leavitt's plot parallels incidents described in Spender's autobiography *World Within World*, published in 1948. Like Leavitt's hero, Spender had an intimate relationship with a working-class youth who ran off to fight in the Spanish Civil War. In February of 1994, Viking-Penguin announced that it was withdrawing *While England Sleeps* from worldwide sale as part of an out-of-court settlement of Spender's libel suit and that it planned to delete the objectionable sexually explicit sections in future editions. The uproar, gleefully reported in newspapers all over the world, not only brought more notoriety to Leavitt but also revived interest in the works of Spender.

The story is about a young British homosexual, Brian Botsford, who tries to follow his aunt's wishes by get-ting married. (The domineering Aunt Constance takes the place of the domineering mother in the two earlier novels.) Brian's courtship of sexually liberated young Phillipa Archibald grieves his lover, Edward Phelan, so deeply that Edward joins a volunteer brigade to fight for the Loyalists in Spain. Brian, relieved to be out of the relationship, proposes marriage, but Phillipa tells him she realizes he is a true homosexual and could never make a satisfactory husband. In the meantime, Edward finds that he hates fighting and wants to leave it. Brian goes to Spain to help him escape, but Edward dies of typhoid on the ship back to England. These events more or less parallel Spender's autobiography, although Spender, writing in a far less tolerant age, said nothing explicit about homosexual lovemaking.

In *While England Sleeps*, Leavitt depicts the underground homosexual world as it existed before World War II. Symbolically, Edward works for the London Underground subway system. Brian meets men in public lavatories and parks. Everyone is terrified of arrest and disgrace. Although *While England Sleeps* is set in a different time and part of the world, it echoes *The Lost Language of Cranes* in showing that it is not homosexuality but denial and criminalization of homosexuality that cause tragedy. Homosexuality, according to Leavitt, is not a matter of choice; it cannot be "cured"; it must be acknowledged and not denied or repressed; it should not be penalized; and it can lead to relationships that are meaningful, disappointing, or disastrous.

Leavitt's thematic concerns typically depict young gay men trapped by the damaging perceptions of homosexuality entertained by their society. In both his novels and his short fiction, he remains a spokesman for the underclass, for those whose stories have been largely suppressed.

Other major works

SHORT FICTION: *Family Dancing*, 1984; *A Place I've Never Been*, 1990.

Bibliography

Iannone, Carol. "Post Counterculture Tristesse." *Commentary* 83 (February, 1987): 57-61.

Klarer, Mario. "David Leavitt's 'Territory'": Rene Girard's Homoerotic 'Trigonometry' and Julia Kristeva's 'Semiotic Chora.'" *Studies in Short Fiction* 28 (Winter, 1991): 63-76.

Leavitt, David. "David Leavitt." Interview by Sam Staggs. *Publishers Weekly* 237 (August 24, 1990): 47-48.

_____ . "The New Lost Generation." *Esquire* 103 (May, 1985): 85-95.

Weir, John. "Fleeing the Fame Factory." *Advocate* 640 (October 19, 1993): 51-55.

AUDRE LORDE

Born: New York, New York; February 18, 1934

Died: Christiansted, St. Croix; November 17, 1992

Principal poetry

The First Cities, 1968; *Cables to Rage*, 1970; *From a Land Where Other People Live*, 1973; *New York Head Shop and Museum*, 1974; *Between Our Selves*, 1976; *Coal*, 1976; *The Black Unicorn*, 1978; *Chosen Poems, Old and New*, 1982; *Our Dead Behind Us*, 1986; *Undersong: Chosen Poems Old and New*, 1992; *The Marvelous Arithmetics of Distance: Poems 1987-1992*, 1993.

Other literary forms

The Cancer Journals (1980) is a personal account of Audre Lorde's struggles with breast cancer. *Zami: A New Spelling of My Name* (1982), which Lorde called a "biomythography," is a retrospective narrative of her emerging sexuality. *Sister Outsider* (1984) and *A Burst of Light* (1988) are collections of essays and speeches on poetry, feminism, lesbianism, and racism.

Achievements

Lorde received a National Endowment for the Arts (NEA) grant and was a poet-in-residence at Tougaloo College in Jackson, Mississippi, in 1968. Other recognitions included the Creative Artists Public Service grant (1972 and 1976) and the Broadside Poets Award (1975). She called herself a "black lesbian feminist warrior poet." At the heart of her work as poet, essayist, teacher, and lecturer lies an intense and relentless exploration of personal identity. Beyond the stunning portrayals of her deepest insights and emotions, her work is filled with powerful evocations of universal survival. The substance of her poetry and essays always reaches beyond the individual self into deep concerns for all humanity. Progressively, her work reveals an increasing awareness of her West Indian heritage in relation to her place in American society and its values.

Biography

Audre Lorde's parents emigrated from Grenada to New York City in 1924. Lorde, the youngest of three girls, was born in 1934. She has recounted many of her childhood memories in *Zami*, identifying particular incidents that had an influence or effect on her developing sexuality and her later work as a poet. She attended the University of Mexico (1954-1955) and received a B.A. degree from Hunter College (1959) and an M.L.S. degree from Columbia University (1961). In 1962, she was married to Edwin Rollins, with whom she had two

children before they were divorced in 1970.

Prior to 1968, when she gained public recognition for her poetry, Lorde supported herself through a variety of jobs, including low-paying factory work. She also served as a librarian in several institutions. After her first publication, *The First Cities*, Lorde worked primarily within American colleges and free presses. She was an instructor at City College of New York (1968-1970), an instructor and then lecturer at Lehman College (1969-1971), and a professor of English at John Jay College of Criminal Justice (1972-1981). In her forties, Lorde was diagnosed as having breast cancer, which gave rise to *The Cancer Journals* and her efforts on behalf of humanitarian concerns. In 1981, she became a professor of English at Hunter College and poetry editor of the magazine *Chrysalis*. She was a contributing editor of the journal *Black Scholar* and a founding member of Sisterhood in Support of Sisters in South Africa and Kitchen Table: Women of Color Press. She also served on the board of the National Coalition of Black Lesbians and Gays. Lorde died on November 17, 1992.

Analysis

All Lorde's poems, essays, and speeches are deeply personal renditions of a compassionate writer, thinker, and human being. Indeed, she draws much of her material from individual and multifaceted experience; she renders it in writing that seeks to reveal the complexity of being a black feminist lesbian poet. She expresses the feelings of being marginalized in an American society that is predominantly white, male, heterosexual, and middle-class. Her writings reflect the changing constitution and perspective of American life, but she never relents to an easy optimism, nor does she make uninformed dismissals of society's ills. Her personal experiences made her compassionate toward those who suffer under oppressive regimes all over the world. By drawing from the history and mythology of the West Indies, she is able to refer to the racism and sexism that exist in other cultures.

In her early collections of poetry, *The First Cities* and *Cables to Rage*, Lorde expresses a keen political disillusionment, noting the failure of American ideals of equality and justice for all. When Lorde uses the pronoun "we" in her poetry, she speaks for all who have been dispossessed. In "Anniversary," for example, she writes, "Our tears/ water an alien grass," expressing the separation between those who belong and those who do not. In poems such as "Sowing," the poet reveals the land's betrayal of its inhabitants by showing images of destruction juxtaposed to personal rage: "I have been to this place before/ where blood seething commanded/ my fingers fresh from the earth."

She also demonstrates a concern for the children of this earth in "Bloodbirth": Casting about to understand what it is in her that is raging to be born, she wonders how an opening will come "to show the true face of me/ lying exposed and together/ my children your children their children/ bent on our conjugating business." The image of the warrior, the one who must be prepared to go about the business of existing in an unjust world, signifies the need to take care of those not yet aware of unfulfilled promises.

If the rage in her early poems appears "unladylike," Lorde is setting out to explode sexual typecasting. Certainly, there is nothing dainty about her sharp images and powerful assessments of social conditions. As she confronts harsh realities, the portrayals must necessarily be clamorous. Yet the poet's rage does not lead to a blind rampage. In "Conversation in Crisis," the poet hopes to speak to her friend "for a clear meeting/ of self upon self/ in sight of our hearth/ but without fire." The poet must speak honestly and not out of false assumptions and pretenses so that real communication can occur. The reader and listener must heed the words as well as the tone in order to receive the meaning of the words. Communication, then, is a kind of contractual relationship between people.

In the collections *From a Land Where Other People Live* and *Between Our Selves*, Lorde uses a compassionate tone to tell people about the devastation that white racism has wreaked upon African Americans. She mixes historical fact with political reality, emphasizing the disjunction that sometimes occurs between the two. In "Equinox," Lorde observes her daughter's birth by remembering a series of events that also occurred that

year: She had "marched into Washington/ to a death knell of dreaming/ which 250,000 others mistook for a hope," for few at that time understood the victimization of children that was occurring not only in the American South but also in the Vietnam War. After she heard that Malcolm X had been shot, she reread all of his writings: "the dark mangled children/ came streaming out of the atlas/ Hanoi Angola Guinea-Bissau . . . / merged into Bedford-Stuyvesant and Hazelhurst Mississippi."

From the multiplicity of world horrors, the poet returns to her hometown in New York, exhausted but profoundly moved by the confrontation of history and the facts of her own existence. In "The Day They Eulogized Mahalia," another event is present in the background as the great singer Mahalia Jackson is memorialized: Six black children died in a fire at a day care center on the South Side; "firemen found their bodies/ like huddled lumps of charcoal/ with silent mouths and eyes wide open." Even as she mourns the dead in her poems, the poet is aware of both the power and the powerlessness of words to effect real changes. In the poem "Power," Lorde writes,

> The difference between poetry and rhetoric
> is being ready to kill
> yourself
> instead of your children.

Once the event has occurred, one can write about it or one can try to prevent a similar event from occurring; in either case, it is not possible to undo the first event. Therefore, as a society, people must learn from their errors and their failures to care for other people. Lorde even warns herself that she must discern and employ this crucial difference between poetry and rhetoric; if she does not, "my power too will run corrupt as poisonous mold/ or lie limp and useless as an unconnected wire."

For Lorde, the process of learning all over again how to transform thought into action begins with the awareness of her personal reality. In the collections *Coal*, *The Black Unicorn*, and *Our Dead Behind Us*, the poet addresses more specifically the individual human beings in her life, creating vignettes of her relationships with other people. In particular, she returns again and again to images of her mother, Linda Belmar Lorde, whose relatively light-colored skin is mentioned in many of the poems. In "Outside," she links her mother's lightness to the brutal faces of racism: "Nobody lynched my momma/ but what she'd never been/ had bleached her face of everything." When Lorde questions, "Who shall I curse that I grew up/ believing in my mother's face," she is echoing the anger that also appears in the poem "Sequelae." There she states explicitly the rage that evolved from the mother's lies, white lies: "I battle the shapes of you/ wearing old ghosts of me/ hating you for being/ black and not woman/ hating you for being white." (*Zami* elaborates many of the specific events to which Lorde refers in her poems about her mother.)

The return to childhood allows the poet to come to new terms with her mother. In several of her poems, she also returns to even deeper roots constituting her identity. In "Dahomey," she refers to the African goddess Seboulisa, "The Mother of us all," or the creator of the world. In embracing the mother goddess, the poet is able "to sharpen the knives of my tongue." Because the subjects of her poetry are painful ones, Lorde empowers her own speech by always calling attention to the dangers of remaining silent. In "A Song for Many Movements," she states simply and precisely the project of her poetry: "Our labor has become/ more important/ than our silence."

The title of one of Lorde's essays, "The Transformation of Silence into Language and Action," is especially appropriate to describing her work as a poet. As she wrote, "I became convinced, anti-academic though I am, that all poets must teach what they know, in order to continue being." Her insistent drive to exist according to the terms of her individual desires and powers is the focal point of many of her speeches and essays. Lorde, moreover, set out rigorously to combat racism, sexism, heterosexism, and homophobia in her work, perceiving that each of these stems from human blindness generally about the differences among people. Overtly political in intent and social in content, the essays and speeches ask all individuals to understand more deeply the ways in which human lives are organized. She then beckons people to take charge of their lives, to confront the tasks at hand, and to take responsibility for making changes.

Much of Lorde's mature work evolved from her identity as a black feminist lesbian poet. These terms are essential conjunctions that express her existence and her vision. In the essay "The Master's Tools Will Never Dismantle the Master's House," Lorde makes no apologies or defenses for her choices. She writes, "For women, the need and desire to nurture each other is not pathological but redemptive, and it is within that knowledge that our real power is rediscovered." For Lorde, the power to exist and be alive comes from her love—in all senses of the word—for women.

In her most often cited essay, "The Uses of the Erotic: The Erotic as Power" Lorde dislodges some of the negative assumptions that have sprung up around the terms "erotic" and "power" and offers new perspectives on how an individual must use her power and ability to love. For Lorde, the erotic is "a resource within each of us that lies in a deeply female and spiritual plane, firmly rooted in the power of our unexpressed or unrecognized feeling." Through a redefinition of the terms, Lorde shows how societal oppression numbs a woman's ability to feel and act deeply. Often the two—emotion and action—are in conflict with the values of a "racist, patriarchal, and anti-erotic society." Before individual human beings can come together as one society, each person must be in touch with his or her own feelings and be willing to express and share with others. These are the necessary first steps to effecting real political change.

Lorde contends that the need to share is a fundamental one that all people feel. Unfortunately, the prevailing attitudes of American society preclude true expression of individualism: If people do not fit into the norms or expectations of the dominant system of values, they are deemed "not normal" or deviant. Lorde argues against the hypocrisy of American values: Where is freedom if any forms of expression considered "unfit" are excluded? How might one such as herself, who is on the margins of all that is "normal," empower herself to take effective action?

These are the kinds of difficult questions Lorde has raised from the beginning of her work as a writer and poet. Always receptive to the notion of difference that exists among all people, Lorde sets out to consider the meaning of her own experiences first, before she attempts to convey to others what those experiences might mean in the larger context of existence. On the one hand, her work is intensely personal; it may even be considered self-absorbed at times. On the other hand, she has managed to transform her deeply private pains and joys into universal and timeless concerns.

Other major works

NONFICTION: *Uses of the Erotic: The Erotic as Power*, 1978; *The Cancer Journals*, 1980; *Zami: A New Spelling of My Name*, 1982; *Sister Outsider*, 1984; *A Burst of Light*, 1988.

Bibliography

Avi-Ram, Amitai F. "*Apo Koinou* in Lorde and the Moderns: Defining the Differences." *Callaloo* 9 (Winter, 1986): 193-208.

Brooks, Jerome. "In the Name of the Father: The Poetry of Audre Lorde." In *Black Women Writers (1950-1980): A Critical Evaluation*, edited by Mari Evans. Garden City, N.Y.: Doubleday, 1984.

Hull, Gloria, T. "Living on the Line: Audre Lorde and *Our Dead Behind Us*." In *Changing Our Own Words: Essays on Criticism, Theory, and Writing by Black Women*, edited by Cheryl A. Wall. New Brunswick, N.J.: Rutgers University Press, 1989.

Lorde, Audre. "Sadomasochism: Not About Condemnation." Interview by Susan Leigh Star. In *A Burst of Light*. Ithaca, N.Y.: Firebrand Books, 1988.

Lorde, Audre, and Adrienne Rich. "An Interview: Audre Lorde and Adrienne Rich." In *Sister Outsider: Essays and Speeches*. Trumansburg, N.Y.: Crossing Press, 1984.

Martin, Joan. "The Unicorn Is Black: Audre Lorde in Retrospect." In *Black Women Writers (1950-1980): A Critical Evaluation*, edited by Mari Evans. Garden City, N.Y.: Doubleday, 1984.

ARMISTEAD MAUPIN

Born: Washington, D.C.; May 13, 1944

Principal long fiction

Tales of the City, 1978; *More Tales of the City*, 1980; *Further Tales of the City*, 1982; *Babycakes*, 1984; *Significant Others*, 1987; *Sure of You*, 1989; *28 Barbary Lane: A Tales of the City Omnibus*, 1990 (contains *Tales of the City*, *More Tales of the City*, and *Further Tales of the City*); *Back to Barbary Lane: The Final Tales of the City Omnibus*, 1991 (contains *Babycakes*, *Significant Others*, and *Sure of You*); *Maybe the Moon*, 1992.

Other literary forms

Known primarily for his novels, Maupin has also written short stories, among them the acclaimed "Suddenly Home." Maupin adapted this short story for New York-based composer Glen Roven's musical about love in four different American cities, *Heart's Desire* (1990). Maupin wrote the dialogue for the stage show "Beach Blanket Babylon" and for a production of Jacques Offenbach's opera *La Périchole* (originally pr. 1868). A variety of periodicals, including *The Advocate*, the *Los Angeles Times*, *The New York Times*, and *The Village Voice*, have published his pieces. The autobiographical "Growing Up Gay in Old Raleigh" appeared in the June, 1988, issue of *The Independent*. He served as executive producer on Great Britain's Channel 4 television miniseries adaptation of *Tales of the City*, which aired on PBS in the United States in 1993.

Achievements

While official literary recognition of Maupin has placed him somewhere between a pop-culture translator and a serious satirist, the author is a worldwide success. His *Tales of the City* series has sold more than a million books and has been translated into German, Spanish, and Dutch. The last book of the series *Sure of You*, became not only a *New York Times* best-seller but also a best-seller in Great Britain and Australia. His works have been reviewed in a variety of publications, including Britain's *Punch*, *The New York Times Book Review*, *People*, *Publishers Weekly*, and *The Village Voice*. Maupin is highlighted in "The Castro" section of Frances FitzGerald's *Cities on a Hill* (1986), the best-selling examination of communities. In 1993, Maupin became the subject of a PBS documentary, *Armistead Maupin Is a Man I Dreamed Up*. Maupin was finally recognized as a serious literary talent when his short story "Suddenly Home" was included in *The Faber Book of Gay Short Fiction* (1991), which includes the works of such literary heavyweights as E. M. Forster, Henry James, Tennessee Williams, James Baldwin, William Burroughs, and Christopher Isherwood.

Biography

Armistead Maupin (pronounced "mop-pin") was born May 13, 1944, in Washington, D.C., the eldest of three children of Armistead Jones Maupin, a prominent lawyer, and Diana Jane Barton Maupin. Their son grew up in Raleigh, North Carolina, and attended the University of North Carolina at Chapel Hill, majoring in English. There, he wrote a column for the *Daily Tarheel*. He received his bachelor of arts degree in 1966. After graduation, he enrolled in the University of North Carolina Law School. Unhappy with this decision, he dropped out of law school after his first year and applied for naval officer candidate school. He was accepted and served from 1967 to 1970 in Vietnam as a lieutenant with the River Patrol Force. After his discharge, Maupin volunteered to return to Vietnam to build housing for disabled Vietnamese veterans. Upon his return to the United States, he was presented with the Freedom Leadership Award by the Freedom Foundation at Valley Forge and was invited to dine at the White House with President Richard Nixon, who categorized him as the model of a patriotic young Republican and awarded him a Presidential Commendation.

In 1970, Maupin began his professional career as a writer with the Charleston *News and Courier*, Charleston, South Carolina. He moved to San Francisco, California, in 1971 to work for the Associated Press. In 1973, Maupin worked as a public-relations account executive in San Francisco. A year later, he became a columnist for the city's edition of the *Pacific Sun*, the newspaper in which *Tales of the City* had an early dry run; the latter experience left Maupin confident he had created something that would appeal to people. While at the *Pacific Sun*, *San Francisco* magazine wanted to include Maupin in its list of the ten sexiest men in San Francisco. He agreed only if they would include the fact that he was gay. They did and Maupin's career as a gay rights advocate was born. After a stint as publicist for the San Francisco Opera in 1975, Maupin joined the *San Francisco Chronicle* as a columnist, where he began his *Tales of the City* series in a daily column format. He served as a commentator on KRON-TV, San Francisco, in 1979. In 1987, Maupin switched his column to the *San Francisco Examiner*. Although the column lost the "Tales of the City" label, *Significant Others* was serialized in the newspaper. *Sure of You* is the only novel of the series that was published without first being serialized. Frequently cited as a national spokesperson on gay matters, he serves as an adviser on the boards of numerous gay and lesbian organizations, working during his free time in fund-raising and advocating gay rights. Maupin lives in the San Francisco Mission district with his longtime companion, gay rights activist Terry Anderson.

Analysis

At the time Maupin started his eight-hundred-word daily column, "Tales of the City," in the *San Francisco Chronicle*, there was no such genre as gay and lesbian literature. Though there were writers who were rumored to be gay or who tackled gay themes in their writings, these writers did not identify themselves as "gay writers." Maupin was one of the first. As he said in a *Christopher Street* interview, "Tales of the City actually preceded by several years the noises being made by the Violet Quill in New York, and preceded them in a mainstream way. I was communicating gay themes and gay concerns to the readers of a so-called family newspaper." Already out of the closet and a gay rights advocate, Maupin decided to approach homosexuality in his fiction in a matter-of-fact way. The sexuality of the characters never comes into question; rarely is it a subject of angst or pain. As Maupin notes, "These people are living their lives and relating to their straight friends and getting on with life."

The central themes in Maupin's fiction are the notion of family, the conflict of appearance versus reality, and—as Maupin himself refers to it—"outsiderdom." These themes first surface in *Tales of the City*. All three converge in the central, pivotal character of Anna Madrigal, the transsexual proprietor of 28 Barbary Lane. Madrigal serves as a sort of earth mother to all who inhabit her apartment building, offering unconditional

love and setting up a sort of ironic paradigm that at once replicates and shatters the myth of the American family. Each of the characters in the first novel, especially Michael "Mouse" Tolliver, Mary Ann Singleton, and D'orothea, is alienated from his or her respective families. Brian Hawkins, in search of some semblance of family, is portrayed as the stereotypical heterosexual "stud" who courses through life in a series of one-night stands with no commitment. Michael comments on Brian's sexual proclivities: "Unwrapping the package is more fun than the package itself." Through the subtle machinations of Mrs. Madrigal and her Barbary Lane family, Maupin depicts an extended urban family that has all the love and support of the idealized, mythologized American family. In *More Tales of the City*, Madrigal is referred to as "the true mother of them all."

The theme of appearance versus reality is developed through several characters in *Tales of the City*. Anna Madrigal is not all she seems; she reveals to her lover, Edgar Halcyon, that she is a transsexual, but it does not change his love for her. Halcyon reveals that his father changed the family surname from Halstein "to be a Bohemian, I guess." D'orothea, an extremely successful African American model, is anything but African American. Because she could not make it as a white model in New York, she found a New Orleans dermatologist who gave her pills for vitiligo (to make body pigment darker) and ultraviolet treatments; she then returned to New York and became the most successful black model in the industry, the woman with the most sex appeal. She moves to San Francisco to become white once again. Beauchamp Day, an account executive at Edgar Halcyon's firm, is bisexual, carrying on liaisons with both men and women, all the while pretending to be at times a happily married man, a heterosexual looking for sex, or a homosexual in search of the same. Dr. Jon Fielding chooses his profession, obstetrics and gynecology, to maintain a heterosexual image. To keep the closet door shut, he maintains a sex life of anonymous encounters at bathhouses and a social life among an elitist group of wealthy gay men who isolate themselves from straight society. Sexuality and sexual image are the bottom lines in Maupin's use of the conflict between appearance and reality. Yet his interest in this issue lies deeper. Each conflicted character is in search of a mate, a lifetime companion. As Anna Madrigal notes in *Tales of the City*, "There are all kinds of marriages, dear . . . lots of things are more binding than sex. They last longer, too."

Maupin's notion of "outsiderdom" is best exemplified in the characters of Michael "Mouse" Tolliver and Mary Ann Singleton. Both come to San Francisco to "find themselves" and to escape family pressures to conform. Tolliver comes to San Francisco from Orlando, Florida, in search of sexual expression as a gay man. Mary Ann comes to escape Cleveland, Ohio. While Michael's affable Southern personality allows him to move freely among the residents of San Francisco, Mary Ann's more repressive nature causes many crises of faith for her in her choice of a new hometown. She complains about San Francisco and her "outsiderdom": "Michael, there's no stability here. Everything's too easy. Nobody sticks with anybody or anything, because there's always something just a little bit better waiting around the corner." For Michael, assimilation has a cost when he embarks upon an affair with Jon Fielding. Fielding spies Michael in a dance contest at a gay bar. The sight of Michael gyrating on stage in his jockey shorts is too much for Fielding, who storms out of the bar and roars down the street in a BMW with a pack of his snobby friends, all of whom are laughing at Michael. In his novels, the price Maupin put on "outsiderdom" is one of loneliness. As Barbara Bass writes, however, through this theme Maupin "stresses the conflicts that lie in sex and the more difficult but true answers found through family connectedness and love."

AIDS (acquired immune deficiency syndrome) does not appear as a theme in a Maupin novel until *Babycakes*. Notes Maupin, "*Babycakes*, as far as I know, was the first fiction anywhere to deal with the AIDS epidemic." Jon Fielding is revealed to be dead of AIDS at the beginning of the novel, and each character must come to grips with the young doctor's death in his or her own way. In Maupin's works, AIDS is not a gay disease. In *Significant Others*, Brian Hawkins, the series' promiscuous heterosexual, agonizes over whether or not the fatigue, illness, and sudden weight loss that afflict him are signs of AIDS. The disease continues to haunt the series, culminating in *Sure of You*. This novel, the sixth and final of the series, details a San Francisco haunted by the AIDS epidemic. Darker than the earlier novels, it is about the breakdown of relationships among Maupin's familiar characters. In this novel, the cast of characters breaks up and Maupin expounds on the theme that permeates his work: the closet and the hypocrisy it perpetuates.

Sure of You introduces Maupin's readers to Russell Rand, a successful fashion designer who is gay but married to a woman to camouflage his sexual identity.

Maupin's target as a satirist in this novel is gays who hide behind a heterosexual façade for the express purpose of monetary success. Michael Tolliver, the character in the series who seems closest to Maupin's alter ego, chides Rand: "You're just greedy. Keeping up a front while your friends drop dead. . . . You could've shown people that gay people are everywhere, and that we're no different." In his autobiographical piece "Growing Up Gay in Old Raleigh," Maupin speaks out about sexuality denied in a similar fashion: "The world won't change until gay people become visible and proud. We have our own dead to honor, and their blood is on the hands of the indifferent."

In 1992's *Maybe the Moon*, Cadence "Cady" Roth, the heroine, is a would-be actor whose most famous role was "Mr. Woods," an E.T.- or Yoda-like character who wears a rubberized costume in the film. She longs to be a famous film star, but the fact that she is a short, fat dwarf hinders even the most remote possibility of this happening. Cady is the ultimate denizen of "outsiderdom," a metaphor for all the downtrodden. In this novel, myths and stereotypes are the enemy. Cady meets an incredibly kind and handsome African American, Neil, and they embark on a sexual relationship. Cady, however, cautions herself: "Don't objectify this guy. The black man as superstud is a dehumanizing myth." Cady will not hear of Neil objectifying her: "[S]ome people see little people as . . . sort of enchanted. Like a good luck charm or something." Again, Maupin's prevalent theme of appearance versus reality enters the story. Neil does not tell his son about the true nature of his relationship with Cady. In failing to do so, Neil fails to deal realistically with the reality of Cady's appearance. The child, who speaks for the majority of society, says, "Cady grosses me out." The challenge Maupin poses for his readers in *Maybe the Moon* is for all people to see one another stripped of racial, sexual, and gender myths.

While Maupin is openly gay, he cannot be defined solely as a gay writer. He does not write exclusively about gay people because such works tend to evoke a rarefied atmosphere—a world only of gay men and women. Instead, Maupin shows both gay and straight people in the context of everyday, ordinary life. Even though the theme of the closet is critical in his novels, including *Maybe the Moon*, neither the closet nor homosexuality or gayness are the defining themes of the works. Instead, his works are appreciated for their themes of the liberating power of honesty and the humanizing treatment of marginalized characters—those who live in "outsiderdom." Maupin's ear for dialogue is keen; he tends to let characters speak for themselves, rather than have a narrator explain their actions through exposition. His works are also appreciated for their Dickensian plot twists and sharp satire. He places his work in the tradition of the nineteenth century serialists whose fiction brought social issues to life for the masses: "I try to celebrate difference through the books the way 19th century writers did, to show all the classes, the richness of humankind." In keeping with this tradition, Maupin follows the dictum of Dickens' contemporary, Wilkie Collins: "Make 'em cry, make 'em laugh, make 'em wait."

Other major works

PLAY: *Heart's Desire*, 1990 (with composer Glen Roven).

Bibliography

Allen, Chuck. "Armistead Maupin." *Frontiers* 10 (November, 1989): 18-21.

Bass, Barbara Kaplan. "Armistead Maupin." In *Contemporary Gay American Novelists: A Bio-Bibliographical Critical Sourcebook*, edited by Emmanuel S. Nelson. Westport, Conn.: Greenwood Press, 1993.

Block, Adam. "Teller of Tales." *Outweek* 1 (October 29, 1989): 42-45.

Clifton, Tony. "Mainstreaming a Cult Classic." *Newsweek* 114 (October 30, 1989): 77.

FitzGerald, Frances. *Cities on a Hill: A Journey Through Contemporary American Cultures*. New York: Simon & Schuster, 1986.

Maupin, Armistead. "An Interview with Armistead Maupin." Interview by Scott A. Hunt. *Christopher Street* 192 (November 23, 1992): 8-12.

_____. "A Talk with Armistead Maupin." Interview by Tom Spain. *Publishers Weekly* 237 (March 20, 1987): 53-54.

PAUL MONETTE

Born: Lawrence, Massachusetts; 1945

Principal long fiction

Taking Care of Mrs. Carroll, 1978; *The Gold Diggers*, 1979; *The Long Shot*, 1981; *Lightfall*, 1982; *Afterlife*, 1990; *Havana*, 1990 (with Judith Roscoe); *Halfway Home*, 1991.

Other literary forms

Paul Monette began his writing career as a poet, with the publication of *The Carpenter at the Asylum* (1975). While eventually shifting his attention to fiction, he has produced several more collections of poems. It was the loss of his longtime lover, Roger Horwitz, to AIDS (acquired immune deficiency syndrome) in 1986 that led Monette to publish his first work of nonfiction, *Borrowed Time: An AIDS Memoir* (1988). The volume is regarded by most critics as his most powerful piece of writing and one of the most affecting and memorable works in the growing canon of AIDS literature. The autobiographical *Becoming a Man: Half a Life Story* (1992) accounts for the years up to the time of his meeting Roger in 1974. *Last Watch of the Night* (1994) collects personal essays written between 1992 and 1993. Over the years, Monette has contributed articles to various gay and straight periodicals such as *The Advocate* and *Interview*.

Achievements

In spite of his distinctive string of novels, it seems clear that Monette's reputation as a writer will rest largely on the autobiographical works *Borrowed Time* and *Becoming a Man*. The first won the 1989 PEN West USA Literary Award for nonfiction and was nominated for the National Book Critics Circle Award in biography; the second won the prestigious National Book Award in nonfiction. In addition, his book of poems, *Love Alone: 18 Elegies for Rog* (1988), won the Words Project for AIDS Award in 1989. These books, along with the novels *Afterlife* and *Halfway Home*, both published after his HIV-positive diagnosis in 1986, have earned Monette universal praise for the passionate eloquence of his writing. He has unflinchingly recorded the lives of gay men courageously battling AIDS and probed the dark recesses of the "closet" to expose the pain of growing up homosexual in a homophobic culture. His provocative insistence on telling the crucial stories of his "tribe" during what he calls a "time of

war" has led to numerous civic awards for political activism and lifted him into national prominence in the fight to combat AIDS and to secure gay rights. For his work Monette has received several Lambda Literary Awards and the PEN Center West Freedom to Write Award, as well as honorary doctorates from Wesleyan University, the City University of New York, and the State University of New York at Oswego.

Biography

Paul Monette was born in Lawrence, Massachusetts, in 1945, the first-born son of Paul Monette, Sr., and Jackie Lamb. His parents were both twenty-three years old, former high school sweethearts who had been married for four years. Paul, Sr., had just returned from World War II service in the Air Force and was eager to relocate in New England. Shortly after Paul's birth they settled in Andover, where Paul, Sr., drove a truck for Cross Coal Company and where a second son, Bobby, was born with spina bifida. Having a brother who was an invalid had the effect of making Monette feel that he, too, had to deny the significance of his body. Monette has said in his autobiography that to compensate for Bobby's obvious physical imperfection, he became the perfect boy, well-mannered, self-effacing, a bodiless prig who tried to act the part of a normal, 1950's kid. He knew, however, that his secret sexual life made him anything but that.

Bright and artistically precocious, Monette made the difficult passage from the local grade school to Phillips Academy in Andover, where he spent four deeply unhappy years. In the rigid caste system of the school, he was a nobody: Ignored by the golden athletes whom he idolized, he avoided "misfits" like himself, fleeing in homosexual panic from any boy who recognized in him a trace of kindred feeling. Monette's sole refuge was writing poetry and performing Latin plays.

Monette went on to Yale University, reinventing himself first as a hearty, rock-climbing outdoorsman, then as a cultural gadfly, and, finally, with a clarifying sense of vocation, as a poet. He edited the school newspaper and a poetry magazine, administered the Yale Arts Festival, and graduated with a B.A. degree in English in 1967, having settled on a life of writing. When he confessed his homosexuality to the draft board, he secured a draft exemption that allowed him to take graduate courses at Harvard and to begin his teaching career, first at Milton Academy and then at Pine Manor College. As successful as Monette was in the classroom, however, and as popular as he was with colleagues, he became increasingly disturbed about his closeted existence, the denial of his gay nature, and so entered therapy in the early 1970's. Then at age twenty-eight he met Roger Horwitz, embraced his own sexuality, and embarked on the richly satisfying twelve-year relationship that ended only when Horwitz died from complications of AIDS in 1986.

In 1977, Monette and Horwitz moved from Boston to Los Angeles, where Horwitz practiced law and Monette began to write novels, television shows, and screenplays, and where both men became increasingly involved in the Los Angeles Gay and Lesbian Center. This growing intimacy with the Hollywood milieu—writers, agents, production people, closeted executives—provided Monette with enough background for several of his novels, from *Taking Care of Mrs. Carroll* to *The Long Shot* and *Afterlife*.

Confronted with Horwitz's death, the death in 1990 of his second life partner, Stephen Kolzak, and his own uncertain health and future, Monette turned to AIDS activism, connecting with ACT UP (AIDS Coalition To Unleash Power) and speaking on campuses and in cities across the country on issues of AIDS awareness, gay and lesbian rights, and censorship of the arts. His novels of the early 1990's have served to dramatize and reinforce the message of his nonfiction writing and his social activism: pride in being gay, courage and resilience in the face of AIDS, anger and resistance in the face of homophobic hatred.

Analysis

An early review described Monette's novels as being "naturalistic prose romances," a phrase that suggests not only how innovative the writing is but also how bold. Monette combines the tradition of realism (plausible setting and action, character and motive) with the tradition of romance (heightened depictions of human emotion, "love stories"). Attempting to blend these two traditions, a writer clearly risks jarring tonal and stylis-

tic shifts; but it may be even more of a risk to focus so intently and persistently on romance, to make love and the logic of the heart such unabashedly central concerns in an otherwise naturalistic novel. An author can seem to teeter on the verge of melodrama by insisting that the most heroic of quests is the pursuit of love. Yet Monette takes these risks and carries it all off successfully, often with real insight and always with verbal flair. The seams in the forced marriage of traditions seldom show; as for the romantic focus, it not only is integrated but also becomes a kind of signature, a key to Monette's vision of life. He has been quoted as saying that he would rather be remembered for loving well than writing well, and it is this romantic sentiment that informs his fiction.

From the beginning of his career as a novelist, Monette has insisted on presenting the reality of openly gay men loving one another. His central intent has been to show that healthy, functioning gay men, secure in their gay identities and generally blessed with an extended family of friends, are capable of creating and experiencing great and enduring relationships in which love and sex are not divorced, in which there is as much joy as there is suffering. He has insisted, in a word, on presenting richly dimensional human beings instead of reinscribing the pathological cartoons of homosexuals as furtive and self-loathing, sexually promiscuous and loveless. Monette has said that the single sustaining image that carried him through the "frozen years" from ages twelve to twenty-five was of "two men in love and laughing." That image of buoyant intimacy, of light and warmth and freedom, nourished him at a time when the only visible representations of homosexuality in the culture were of sad and isolated deviants. His fiction has consistently portrayed this belief in the possibility of gay men achieving love and happiness, and he has never shied away from pitching this portrait in terms of high romance.

In *Taking Care of Mrs. Carroll*, these characteristic features are immediately visible. The story takes place during one magical summer on the secluded beach estate of Mrs. Carroll, whose death triggers an amusingly far-fetched scheme designed to honor her wishes and to outwit avaricious developers and heartless family members. It involves an elaborate charade and reunites a collection of friends and lovers, all brought together in this pastoral world where their pasts will be reexamined, their lives revived, and their futures redirected. Though they launch the adventure with the understanding that they are simply "taking care" of some real estate business, it soon becomes apparent that the real story is the way they come to understand what it means to "take care" of one another.

The narrator, Rick, arrives with the legendary Madelaine Cosquer, a seventy-four-year-old movie queen and internationally celebrated chanteuse in the Piaf/Dietrich mold. Instead of finding Mrs. Carroll, they encounter Rick's former lover, David, who was Mrs. Carroll's housekeeper, and Phidias, the estate's overseer, who was Mrs. Carroll's lover and Madeleine's former husband. They are soon joined by Madeleine's Hollywood agent, the flamboyantly gay Aldo. Out of this complicated but wittily presented ensemble, full of piquant emotional possibilities, Monette creates, as he does in all of his novels, a sense of family—an alternative, certainly, to the traditional model, but a family nevertheless that triumphs over the callously self-absorbed members of Mrs. Carroll's actual brood.

For Rick, who since David's departure has become cynical about love and mechanical about sex, the summer presents an opportunity to revisit their relationship and begin to understand how a fierce determination to control his life, to monitor and protect his emotions, and to plan his future has effectively kept him from actually loving another person. Rick has been unable to give himself up to life in the present, to spontaneous desire. Offered this second chance with David, he is fearful but exhilarated, and he embarks on this transformative journey of self-discovery, emerging with a hard-won sense that taking care of someone does not mean controlling another life but committing to a shared life. It means accepting David's plea for "no rules" beyond taking their love out to face life together. It means steering clear of a fictionalized past, risking an uncertain future, and reveling in a complicated present.

Part of the joy of the present for Rick and David is their reestablished sexual relationship. Here, too, in this first novel, Monette introduces what will become a familiar feature in all of his work: lushly romantic love scenes. These are extraordinarily lyrical yet graphic depictions of passionate men, fearlessly celebrating their sexuality. Monette has admitted that, once he was finally able to accept his gay identity, he knew he wanted to tell what seemed to him the truth about gay desire, and he wanted to do this boldly, sensuously, regularly. The scene on the beach when David and Rick come together after five years apart is positively cinematic: the sea, the sun, the beneficent presence of the deer, the approach on horseback to the naked man standing on the sand. Their later lovemaking in the fragrant pine woods by the deep still pools of the quarry

has the same mythic quality. In less skillful hands these scenes could appear comically overblown or ridiculously clichéd, but Monette manages to avoid that trap. He knows the material (what one critic has described as the stuff of 1940's B movies) and reworks the formulas of romance to evoke moments of passion that have real power. The world of fantasy and fairy tale is never very far away at such moments, but it is a tribute to Monette's sureness of touch and mastery of tonal nuance that fantasy never completely overtakes the scene but only gives it added resonance.

It is also characteristic of Monette's fiction that he blends these privileged moments of high romance with witty scenes of acute observation and social criticism. In addition to its engagingly rendered meditations on time, loss, and memory, its reflections on morality and desire, *Taking Care of Mrs. Carroll* offers provocative views of Hollywood ethics, the seductions of materialism, and questions of gay sensibility and style. Between the savvy, extravagant Aldo and the sagely world-weary Madeleine, Monette provides an insider's look at the Hollywood scene from the 1930's to the 1970's. It is not always a pretty picture, but what is revealed about the interplay of glamor and illusion and human need suggests that the dream factories only heighten but do not seriously distort the complexity of life lived off-screen. This kind of witty exposé of the entertainment business in fact provides the main thrust of two later novels, *The Gold Diggers* and *The Long Shot*, in both of which the glittering façade of the City of Angels is stripped away to reveal the more unsavory workings of Los Angeles and the damage it can do, particularly to gay men who must endure an entrenched and industry-wide homophobia.

The plots of these next two novels again center on families constructed by gay men and their intimate friends. As is true in all Monette's books, these families include women, often in central roles: Madeleine in *Taking Care of Mrs. Carroll*, Rita in *The Gold Diggers*, Linda and Margaret in *Afterlife*, Aunt Foo and Mona in *Halfway Home*. In Monette's own life he has found women to be less afraid than men of candor and intimacy; in the novels women, lesbian or straight, are represented as strong, loyal, knowing, sexually experienced, and resistant to fiercely divided gender categories. They are as richly varied as the gay men whose lives Monette is principally interested in tracing. These variously constructed families are involved, in *The Gold Diggers*, with stolen art treasures and, in *The Long Shot*, with the murder of a closeted Hollywood leading man. As with *Taking Care of Mrs. Carroll*, the books are equal parts improbable but engaging plot, shrewd social commentary, and gay love story. Each pursues the theme of self-discovery through confrontation with the past. Yet what makes these early novels so distinctive is that this self-discovery is the character's recognition not of his homosexuality but of how best to live with that reality. They are not, therefore, typical "coming out" novels. The story Monette most wants to tell is how openly gay men go about living their lives and intersecting with the world in wide-ranging and meaningful ways. How do they fit into their families, perform their jobs, conduct their friendships, engage in their pleasures? What is refreshing is that the novels presume homosexual love is natural, something experienced by gay men without apology or remorse and accepted by friends as normal and satisfying.

To turn from Monette's fiction written before the AIDS crisis to that written after AIDS had become a grim fact of twentieth century life is to trace a clear development toward more pointed social criticism and overt political activism. In his two revelatory autobiographical works, but especially in *Borrowed Time*, he captures, with a fierce and disarming candor, the sense of what life is like for gay men living in the shadow of AIDS. Writing out of his own experience of loss and grief, Monette finds his way to a delicate balance between documenting the pain and articulating the strengths that come from great suffering; that personal resolution is reflected in *Afterlife* and *Halfway Home*. These two novels, while no less skillfully constructed and stylishly written than his earlier novels, seem more obviously dedicated to making the point that gay lives are at risk, that the concerted forces of deadly disease and bigoted fears imperil both individual gay men and the larger gay community and culture. Yet even with AIDS as the principal issue in his later work, Monette does not abandon the fictional territory staked out earlier. He still focuses on relationships and families, on how gay men can find happiness and fulfillment; that is to say, he still writes gay love stories, only now they unfold in the context of AIDS, which gives to the recurrent themes of love and loss an added gravity.

Afterlife is a novel about three AIDS widowers, men who have each lost a lover to the disease and who, having met at the hospital during those trying days, have met regularly during the year since to help one another through the difficult process of grief and recovery. Their responses to loss, however, have not exactly been the same. Steven, the novel's principal character,

has gotten fat, sees himself as terminally undesirable, and spends his time trying not to feel anything. Sonny, a Greek Adonis, has plunged deeper into bodybuilding and New Age spiritualism as a way of denying any threat to his health. Dell, one of Monette's few Hispanic characters, has become a late-night regular on the telephone sex lines and a secret terrorist waging a one-man guerrilla war against the gay-bashing televangelist Mother Evangeline.

This attack on religion's opposition to gays may not sound a new note in Monette's work, but it is now more insistent, more explicit. Here and in his nonfiction he suggests that the Church's smug demonization of "queers" and the blatant campaign to eradicate them amount to nothing less than genocide, something made increasingly possible by the alliance he sees between the Catholic hierarchy and the Fundamentalist Right. In the fact of this bigoted assault on human beings and human rights, Monette advocates open defiance; Dell most clearly embodies this posture of resistance. It is as if, in a time of war, there can be only collaborators and resistance fighters. Dell refuses to go the quiet way of collaboration. Yet though each character chooses to go a different way, they nevertheless all provide crucial testimony for the possibility of living on in this strange afterlife, the aftermath of loss. This may, in fact, be the most significant message of the novel: the assertion that even under the cloud of AIDS gay men can live productive lives and find fulfilling loves.

It is Steven who provides proof of that proposition. Overweight and concerned largely with monitoring his T-cell count, Steven has ruled out another serious relationship. Then he meets Mark, a handsome former television star, now a jaded but successful television executive who is HIV-positive; despite all the odds against them, they manage to cut through their protective layers of cynicism and doubt and fall in love. It is a circuitous but deeply rewarding journey, and Monette does not soften the account. It is romantic but hardly romanticized. That could be said for the entire novel. Its portrayal of love, anger, friendship, and commitment ends up blending the personal with the political in such a way that the love story is stiffened by the activist vision and the resistance politics are humanized by the deeply felt (and persuasively conveyed) personal affections. It is a new and powerful departure for Monette, but one clearly grounded in his previous practices.

Halfway Home marks a further development in Monette's AIDS fiction. The narrator, Tom Shaheen, a stage artist whose performance of Miss Jesus, the drag Messiah, won for him noisy fans among radical gays and irate foes among the radical Right, is now in the later stages of AIDS and has retreated to an isolated Malibu beach house to compose his life before dying. Surrounded by the quietly solicitous Gray, Gray's canny Aunt Foo, and his friend Mona, Tom seems to have removed himself from the business of living to brood about the past, particularly his troubled childhood and the humiliations he endured at the hands of his older brother, Brian, an athletic bully. Before long, however, Tom's exile is disrupted by Brian's arrival. The one-time poster boy for masculine privilege is now, however, anything but the picture of success: He is desperate, on the run, his marriage and business in ruins, and he has fled to this last remnant of family in a muddled attempt to redirect his life. The confrontation between Tom and Brian is difficult, disturbing, but ultimately liberating for both men. Tom is finally able to free himself of a traumatic past, while Brian comes to understand and accept his gay brother in a way he never has before.

The story turns on this moment of confrontation that leads to reconciliation. In defiance of limited time, Tom grows to discover new bonds of love, the filial bonds he had so longed for with his brother, the rich avuncular bonds with his sympathetic nephew, and the unexpected romantic bonds with the older man, Gray. Tom's chosen family and his blood family come together, and he turns from a deadly past to a future that though fraught with its own deadly realities of AIDS is also capable of bestowing great joy. With his health beginning to fail, Tom comes to realize that life can only be enjoyed moment by moment, in the present. There are lessons here, certainly for people with AIDS, but perhaps more important for the next generation of gay youth. Disease and discrimination kill, but even on the killing ground gay men can find their way to one another.

With this last novel Monette has once again written a love story, but one whose emotionally satisfying "happy ending" refuses to dismiss the ominously insistent realities of contemporary gay life. Romance does not blind him, but it obviously inspires and nourishes him. In a 1991 interview Monette explained: "I had to explore the love that it had taken me so long to find, the love that is my subject and has always been my subject and will always be my subject until I die." He is from first to last a romantic, and the novels shape this romantic vision in powerfully instructive ways.

Other major works

POETRY: *The Carpenter at the Asylum*, 1975; *No Witnesses*, 1981; *Love Alone: 18 Elegies for Rog*, 1988; *West of Yesterday, East of Summer: New and Selected Poems, 1973-1993*, 1994.

NONFICTION: *Borrowed Time: An AIDS Memoir*, 1988; *Becoming a Man: Half a Life Story*, 1992; *The Politics of Silence*, 1993; *Last Watch of the Night: Essays Too Personal and Otherwise*, 1994.

Bibliography

Clum, John. "'The Time Before the War': AIDS, Memory, and Desire." *American Literature* 62, no. 2 (December, 1990): 648-667.

Kaufman, David. "All in the Family." *The Nation* 253 (July 1, 1991): 21-25.

Roman, David. "Tropical Fruit? Latino Gay Men in Three Resistance Novels of the Americas." In *Tropicalizations*, edited by Francis Aparicio and Susan Chavez Silverman. Philadelphia: Temple University Press, 1993.

EDMUND WHITE

Born: Cincinnati, Ohio; January 13, 1940

Principal long fiction

Forgetting Elena, 1973; *Nocturnes for the King of Naples*, 1978; *A Boy's Own Story*, 1982; *Caracole*, 1985; *The Beautiful Room Is Empty*, 1988.

Other literary forms

Edmund White began his literary career in drama, writing *Blue Boy in Black* (pr. 1963). He has also written several works of nonfiction, including *States of Desire: Travels in Gay America* (1980) and *Genet: A Biography* (1993). With Adam Mars-Jones, he wrote *The Darker Proof: Stories from a Crisis* (1988), a short-story collection. In 1991, he edited *The Faber Book of Gay Short Fiction*.

Achievements

White's talent has been widely recognized. As a student at the University of Michigan, he received Hopwood Awards for fiction and drama (1961 and 1962). White was awarded Ingram Merrill grants in 1973 and 1978 and was named a Guggenheim Fellow in 1983. In 1983, he also received the American Academy and Institute of Arts and Letters award in fiction. For *The Beautiful Room is Empty*, he was honored with a citation for appeal and value to youth by the Enoch Pratt Free Library's Young Adult Advisory Board (1988). He added the Lambda Literary Award and the National Book Critics Circle Award in biography for his massive work *Genet: A Biography* (1993).

Biography

Edmund Valentine White III was born into a well-educated, upper-middle-class family on January 13, 1940, in Cincinnati, Ohio. His father, Edmund Valentine White II, was an engineer, while his mother, Delilah Teddlie White, was a psychologist. His parents divorced when White was seven, and he spent the next nine years with his mother in Chicago, with sporadic visits to his father and relatives in other states. White was sexually active at an early age and revealed his homosexuality to his parents at age fourteen; he then entered psychotherapy and spent many years attempting to become heterosexual. His painful early experiences with self-hatred form the basis of much of his later autobiographical fiction.

Even at a young age White was inquisitive and creative. His education culminated in a distinguished stay at the University of Michigan, where he garnered both drama and fiction awards and from which he received a B.A. degree in 1962. Over the protests of his father, he moved to New York and began to write in earnest, even as he continued to struggle to come to terms with his sexuality. White supported himself with a successful job as a staff writer for *Time* magazine. He also wrote, but could not find a publisher for, several novels during these early years; he claims they are still gathering dust in his files and are occasionally pirated for his current writing projects. White honed his skills as a novelist during the 1960's, but even more important was his establishment of a gradually more self-confident gay identity. His growing commitment to sexual liberation, as well as his artistic inclinations, brought him into contact with numerous other gay writers and activists. White was a member of the Violet Quill, a New York-based gay literary group that also included Felice Picano and Andrew Holleran. He was a participant in the Stonewall riots of June, 1969, in which harassed gay patrons of the Stonewall Inn bar battled police for two days. These were experiences that helped shape White's writing. While collaborating on nonfictional works for Time-Life, he finally found his own voice as a gay writer in the 1970's, conducting writing seminars at The Johns Hopkins University, publishing critically acclaimed novels and stories, and coauthoring *The Joy of Gay Sex* (1977) with Charles Silverstein.

White has been one of the most respected and visible gay authors in the years since then. Dividing his time between homes in Paris and New York, White has taught writing at Yale, New York, and George Mason universities, served as executive director of the New York Institute for the Humanities, and contributed articles and reviews to numerous popular magazines, while continuing his writing of novels, short stories, and gay-relevant nonfiction. He continues to explore fictionally and analytically the many forms of gay experience and to comment perceptively on homophobia in American society and within gay individuals.

Analysis

Linking all Edmund White's diverse writings from three decades is an earnest attempt to explore a range of gay experiences and lifestyles. He probes the stories that gay men tell themselves and that are told to them regarding a sexual orientation that is reviled by many Americans. He explained to an interviewer in 1988 that "writing, in its own way, is a rival to therapy." One might add that reading, too, can become therapeutic, and certainly White deserves enormous credit for his role in making gay fiction legitimate and providing gay readers with ways of understanding themselves and their unique experiences. White helped create a sense of gay culture and identity during the 1970's, values that may have had limitations but that served as rallying points for activism and self-affirmation. He asserts that writers "can use literature as a mirror held up to the world, or they can use writing as a consolation for life (in the sense that literature is preferable to reality). I prefer the second approach, although clearly there has to be a blend of both." That blend is masterful in White's best novels, which both reflect and help perfect the world surrounding them.

Many reviewers and critics have noted that White's fiction can be divided broadly into two categories. Jordan Elgrably classifies these as the "baroque, rather dreamlike" works, which would include *Forgetting Elena* and *Nocturnes for the King of Naples*, and the "autobiographical" pieces, such as *A Boy's Own Story* and *The Beautiful Room Is Empty*. Common to those four works, however, is a distinct sociopolitical thread exploring the way identity is formed and often deformed in an oppressive environment, whether that environment is the nuclear family or a rigidly defined social or cultural group. Thus while White clearly writes "gay fiction," in the sense that gay characters and aesthetic interests abound in his work, his writing also has a larger, one might even say universal, appeal, for it captures those processes that lead to self-definition, the honing down that occurs as individual personalities become bounded and defined through the influences of family, friends, and social belief systems. His readers are made to understand experience from another person's point of view, even while ethical judgments are gradually and masterfully encouraged, shaped, and driven home as his narratives draw to their conclusions.

This is clearly seen in White's first novel, *Forgetting Elena*, where the anonymous narrator, an amnesiac, is slowly revealed to be callous and morally bankrupt, but only after the reader feels a degree of interest in, even sympathy for, the narrator's awkward position in mysterious surroundings. *Forgetting Elena* is a rich aesthetic experience. It is a novel in code, not a work overtly about being gay but one that explores with considerable insight a closed community of snobbish aesthetes, whose island paradise closely resembles the 1970's gay community on Fire Island, New York. While the central relationship in the story is that of a man and woman, the unfolding action takes place against a backdrop of sexual hedonism and malicious gossip. The self-conscious and socially awkward narrator slowly discovers the rules and references that structure a rigid society, where one-upmanship and vicious backstabbing are part of a daily routine. The narrator, we finally learn, is not an innocent observer, is not a touchstone, but rather the most adept player of the game, whose morality is shaped by his environment and whose conscience disappears even as his consciousness returns. As social allegory, *Forgetting Elena* explores the evil that damaged individuals can perpetrate, the forces that mandate social conformity even among outcasts, and, finally, the central place that narcissism and egotism can play in an insecure person's strategy for operating in a hostile environment. All these themes had scathing implications for White's own social set, an elitist, hedonistic, and sometimes mean-spirited New York gay subculture of the 1970's.

Nocturnes for the King of Naples, White's next novel, while neither so veiled nor so unrelentingly critical as the first, again revolves around an insecure, anonymous narrator, whose unfolding tale both disturbs and enlightens the reader. Like *Forgetting Elena*, it is lushly detailed with sensations, colors, and aromas. White has asserted that "artists should be honest about the tremendous glamor and impact of physical beauty," an honesty that he brings to *Nocturnes*, which swirls around the memory and experience of an intense, but tragic, love affair between two men. White captures vividly the power and harsh beauty of desire, while remaining true to his purpose of revealing the harm that emotionally isolated, self-absorbed individuals can do to one another. As the narrative develops, he abandons all chronological linearity, preferring instead to arrange his novel around emotional progressions and linked sensations. At its center is a scared and scarred adult, whose affectionless childhood is revealed as a key to understanding his continuing problems relating to others. Hazy in its setting and time frame, *Nocturnes* is highly focused in its tone of regret and its psychological intensity. Like its predecessor, it finds that aesthetics can become a refuge from honest feelings for individuals whose emotionally messy childhoods were almost too painful to bear, and that for many gay men stylized performances can too easily replace sensitive interactions. The novel serves notice: The consequences of remaining defensive and aloof can be a life of loneliness and, finally, regret.

Both of White's early novels draw on the pain of his own childhood and young adulthood but can hardly be called autobiographical in a strict sense. Such is not the case for *A Boy's Own Story* and *The Beautiful Room Is Empty*, which represent explicit interventions in the coming-of-age tradition in fiction and effectively "hold a mirror up to life." *A Boy's Own Story* refines and foregrounds many of the themes that White explored in preceding novels. Once again its anonymous, first-person narration focuses explicitly on the sexual experimentations and fears of an adolescent boy, whose story resembles White's own in many ways. White has spoken often about his own sexual activity at an early age and candidly revealed his painful desires to be "cured" of his homosexuality. White's fictional narrator undergoes psychoanalysis, attempts heterosexual relationships, reviles himself and his desires, and acts out his self-hatred by treating others with contempt. This frank, sexually explicit story addresses forthrightly, yet gracefully, the difficult topics of sexual awakening and internalized homophobia. Like earlier novels, it probes how individuals can harm one another because they, themselves, have been harmed by a culture that hates sexual nonconformity. Its most painful scene is the concluding scene, in which the young narrator seduces and then betrays an older man, realizing in retrospect that "the complete cycle allowed me to have sex with a man then to disown him and it; this sequence was the ideal formulation of my impossible desire to love a man but not to be a homosexual." Like J. D. Salinger's *The Catcher in the Rye* (1951), *A Boy's Own Story* captures an excruciatingly painful transition from innocence to experience, from childish dreams to the hard realities of adult values and strictures.

This exploration is taken one step further in *The Beautiful Room Is Empty*, which White says is intended to reveal in the clearest terms possible "the puritanical oppression of sexual freedom." It operates as a sequel to *A Boy's Own Story* and picks up the narrator's journey as he leaves high school and enters college, where his experiences with homophobia, both external and internalized, are intensified. White's novel is a scathing critique of both society and the gay individual in society. The story follows the narrator into therapy sessions, through failed relationships, and into anonymous sexual encounters as it probes the intense psychological pain generated by self-hatred. The narrator has lost even the intermittent joys of childhood; he is wholly isolated, lonely, and self-destructive. His relationships with others are dishonest because he is unable to be honest with himself about a sexual orientation that will make him a social pariah. Elgrably says that White's narrator is "a man who yearns for beauty and love, yet who often lives at the edge of the society he so painstakingly observes."

The Beautiful Room Is Empty captures superbly a particular mindset, time, and place; much of the narrative is set in New York during the 1960's, before the beginning of the gay rights movement. It was a time when gay individuals had no immediate role models, no mechanism for affirmation. Yet the novel also ends with a glimmer of hope, for in its final paragraphs we experience firsthand the Stonewall riot, recounted with the accuracy of White's own personal memories. "It's really our Bastille Day," says one participant in the novel—even though the next day the narrator "couldn't find a single mention in the press of the turning point of our lives." This final sentence captures the hard reality of continuing social rejection and ignorance at the same time that it foregrounds the personal transformation and politicization experienced by the narrator, by White, and by a generation of gay individuals.

Here, as elsewhere, White carefully documents gay life; his novels and other writings serve not only as entertainment but also as social history. Perhaps his finest work of nonfiction, *States of Desire: Travels in Gay America*, was groundbreaking for its day and remains compelling and useful for its breadth of observation and insight into the many different lives lived by gay Americans; it presents case studies in courage and endurance, even as it incorporates White's critique of the self-destructive behavior patterns into which some gay men fall as they struggle with self-acceptance. These are patterns that White knows all too well; in an updated afterword to the book, he admits that during the late 1970's he, too, participated in activities that he finds extreme today; he "pumped iron, snorted coke, pigged out." Yet his firsthand knowledge of urban gay life and psychology gives his writing an immediacy and density of descriptive detail that is unparalleled. White says that "ordinary life is blah, whereas literature at its best is bristling with energy." Such is certainly the case with White's own writing, which bristles with the power of a keen aesthetic sense and an accurate eye for psychological and social truths.

Other major works

NONFICTION: *When Zeppelins Flew*, 1969 (with Peter Wood); *The First Men*, 1973 (with Dale Browne); *States of Desire: Travels in Gay America*, 1980; *Genet: A Biography*, 1993.

PLAY: *Blue Boy in Black*, pr. 1963.

SHORT FICTION: *The Darker Proof: Stories from a Crisis*, 1988 (with Adam Mars-Jones).

EDITED TEXT: *The Faber Book of Gay Short Fiction*, 1991.

Bibliography

Bergman, David. "Edmund White." In *Contemporary Gay American Novelists*, edited by Emmanuel S. Nelson. Westport, Conn.: Greenwood Press, 1993.

Elgrably, Jordan. "The Art of Fiction CV: Edmund White." *The Paris Review* 30 (Fall, 1988): 46-80.

McCaffery, Larry. *Alive and Writing: Interviews*. Urbana: University of Illinois Press, 1987.

White, Edmund. "An Interview with Edmund White." Interview by Kay Bonetti. *The Missouri Review* 13, no. 2 (1990): 89-110.

_____ . "Queer Fiction." *Brick* 47 (1993): 35-40.

EPILOGUE
Renewing Visions of America

I promised to show you a map you say but this is a mural
then yes let it be   these are small distinctions
where do we see it from is the question

—Adrienne Rich,
An Atlas of the Difficult World, 1991

No people would have become American without a place of their own. Nor would any place have become American without people who had visions of a nation in land that is now the United States. As the essays in *American Diversity, American Identity* show, persons and places conceive each other. Building on such conceptions, this epilogue's assessments of F. Scott Fitzgerald, Jack Kerouac, Toni Morrison, Adrienne Rich, Mark Twain, and Walt Whitman illustrate how journeys—figurative as well as literal—both separate and link persons and places. Such travels, including especially how and what we see through them, do much to focus visions of America that respond to the question "Who are we Americans?"

To contextualize these themes and, specifically, to set the scene for the essays on Fitzgerald, Kerouac, Morrison, Rich, Twain, and Whitman that follow, consider first an American writer named Bill Trogden. Better known as William Least Heat Moon, some years ago he chucked his Missouri routine on "the last night of winter," took to the back roads in a van named *Ghost Dancing*, and looped America "from the heartland out and around." Persuaded that there was no quick or inevitable fix for his "nearly desperate sense of isolation and a growing suspicion that I lived in an alien land," this part Anglo-Irish American, part American Osage Indian drove thirteen thousand miles on the "blue highways" (the back roads were marked that way on old maps) to search for clarity and a renewed sense of his own identity.

Returning to Missouri, Heat Moon eventually published a book about his journey, *Blue Highways* (1982), named for the American roads he had traveled. Though far from the same state he had been in when his journey began, Heat Moon wondered: "In a season on the blue roads, what had I accomplished?" To that question his travel log replied: "In my own country, I had gone out, had met, had shared. I had stood as witness." The blend of change and permanence he found was far from perfect. Yet its hope was enough to keep him going because he "sometimes heard *human* voices that showed the power not of visions but of revision, the power to see again and revise." Later, in an interview with Diane Dismuke published in the December 1993 issue of *NEA Today*, Heat Moon amplified what those visions and revisions suggested: "It's not that we're all part of one big family so much [as] that we all belong in an incredible web. Tracing our individual histories is like moving toward the bottom of a cone: As we go further and further back, the lines that separate us become fewer and fewer, and we realize how interlinked we all are."

To get where he was going, Heat Moon needed a map, even an atlas of maps, from time to time. His destinations, however, were not always the kind that conventional maps could locate. Heat Moon looked less for geographical sites than for places of self-discovery. If the destination of self-discovery was the answer to his quest, where he would see things from was the question. On the go and as it went along, Heat Moon's journey had to create its own maps of his country, maps that would turn out to be of himself and for his country as well. In these ways, his *Blue Highways* intersected with Walt Whitman's *Leaves of Grass* (1855). In that nineteenth century epic poem about American identity, Whitman said,

Not I, not any one else can travel that road for you,
You must travel it for yourself
. . . .
You are also asking me questions and I hear you,
I answer that I cannot answer, you must find out for
    yourself.

"Here is a map of our country," writes another American traveler, the contemporary poet Adrienne Rich. Her *Atlas of the Difficult World* (1991) explores poisoned environments and the divisions of race, class, and gender as it scans the illusion and disillusionment that have made American identities problematic. Rich's visions of America make her protest against the waste that forgets, ignores, or marginalizes "those who could bind, join, reweave, cohere, replenish . . . / those needed to teach, advise, persuade, weigh arguments/ those urgently needed for the work of perception." Versions of her concerns find expression in the writings of Fitzgerald, Kerouac, Morrison, Twain, Whitman, and all the others represented in *American Diversity, American Identity*. Like Rich, they show that when visions of America are at stake, "where do we see it from is the question."

To consider that question further, observe that national borders slice the globe. Typically we take such boundaries for granted, forgetting how recently they have become dominant within our planet's landscape. Although men and women are territorial creatures, human life itself is a newcomer on the cosmic scene. Today people think of themselves as Chinese or French, Russian, Mexican, or American, but there was a time when such distinctions were nonexistent. Millennia passed before those identities and their distinctive loyalties evolved. Nor have those identities and loyalties stayed the same. Mark Twain knew as much in the nineteenth century when he sent rafting down the Mississippi River a boy called Huckleberry Finn and a runaway slave named Jim. Just as Huck Finn concluded that he had to "light out for the Territory," American becoming is inescapable and constant.

Earth to earth, dust to dust, ashes to ashes—once born, each of us will perish. In time, most of us disappear without much trace, but what of the life we share by having a country that we call our own? Although national identities may also be destined ultimately for oblivion, their future is not ours to know completely in advance. Making the best of what we have is our lot instead. How we Americans cope with our identities affects the fate of humanity, if not the fate of the earth itself. The great American poet, Robert Frost, conveyed that insight when he favored John F. Kennedy's presidential inaugural with verse one January day in 1961. Frost presented from memory a poem he had written some twenty-five years before. "The Gift Outright" reminded Americans, first, that "the land was ours before we were the land's."

American identities are inconceivable without *the land*. Yet the land is a chief ingredient that renders an American fate complex, because how people think about and use the land puts them at odds. Created by no man or woman, the land was indeed a gift outright. Soon enough, though, it became a "gift" of another kind. The land was there for the taking. Taken it was, too. Long before it was called "American," the territory was home for hundreds of varied tribal cultures that most of us have come to know indiscriminately and insensitively as "Indian." The land granted visions of promise—economic, political, religious—but apparently not space enough to satisfy them all. If "this land is your land, this land is my land"—as Woody Guthrie's alternative national anthem puts it—*yours* and *mine* have excluded, and in many cases shattered, the ways of those now called Native Americans. Robert Frost's words add dissonant notes to Woody Guthrie's chorus—"this land was made for you and me"—by remembering that "the deed of gift was many deeds of war."

Nonetheless, the land, in a word, meant *possibility*. Reality may be frustrating, disappointing, even crushing, but in America the lure of new beginnings seems able to transcend all of those. So restless folks, their overseas bags and overland trunks packed with hope, entered what Frost called "the land vaguely realizing westward." What they found was strange, if not unmapped. The new space was so distant from what they left behind, its future as uncertain as it was unknown. Their home remained *there*, not *here*. Complicated by the land's problematic development, possibility was a fickle thing. As Toni Morrison's African American, Nobel-Prize-winning writing shows, the land's development and its possibilities included involuntary as well as voluntary arrival, enslavement as well as equality, oppression as well as opportunity, destruction as well as democracy. So it is and shall remain.

Frost's poem called the land "unstoried, artless, unenhanced." It was scarcely that for the many Indian tribes who witnessed the European colonization and its aftermath. But for those who, comparatively speaking, were newcomers by choice or by compulsion, and also for the vast majority of us who trace our roots to their arrivals, the land would be less than "our land of living" until the *irony* of being in it was discovered. That irony consisted of the incongruity that grew when people intended one thing and unintentionally produced another, which still happens as often as not. The newcomers—many of them, as Frost says, "still colonials"—would create and tell stories about the land, enhance it with arts and crafts. While thinking that the United States was "such as she was," Americans old and new would discover that this place was becoming—sometimes worse than we knew, sometimes better than we thought. As Jack Kerouac would put the point in his 1957 novel, *On the Road*, "the things that were to come are too fantastic not to tell." Such becoming and telling would have much to do—and still does—with American identities.

Things too important not to tell fill the record of a renewing relationship between a father and a son in Robert M. Pirsig's widely read *Zen and the Art of Motorcycle Maintenance* (1974). Driving home vital points about American identities, it provides an autobiographical parable about caring. As Chris and his dad figuratively bike their way toward each other (even though they are literally heading in the same direction), their journey within and across the land involves coming to grips with possibility and irony.

Pirsig says his concern is less with "What's new?" and more with "What's best?" His meditations survey the land and its spirit. Traveling with spare parts and instruction books on motorcycle repair, he does not want to get stranded or caught unprepared—if he can help it, which is not always possible. Yet, ironically, "it occurred to me," Pirsig writes, "there *is* no manual that deals with the *real* business of motorcycle maintenance, the most important aspect of all. Caring about what you are doing is considered either unimportant or taken for granted." In that environment, motorcycles are hardware: run by fuel, not by fidelity; sparked by plugs, not by perseverance. Attitudes toward them are inconsequential. No fiction, of course, could be further from the truth, and that is Pirsig's point. If it applies to motorcycles, it applies to American identities even more, a point that the writings of Fitzgerald, Kerouac, Morrison, Rich, Twain, and Whitman underscore in their distinctive ways.

Toward the end of *Zen and the Art of Motorcycle Maintenance*, Chris asks if he can have his own motorcycle some day. Pirsig tells the boy he can, if he will take care of it. Chris's questioning continues: What will he have to do? Will his father show him? Will those things be hard? Chris's father replies: Of course he will show and help his son. And what needs to be done won't be so hard—at least, as Pirsig puts it, "not if you have the right attitudes. It's having the right attitudes that's hard."

Chris's father expresses confidence that his son will have the right attitudes. Indeed, as San Francisco Bay looms ahead, Pirsig concludes: "Trials never end, of course. Unhappiness and misfortune are bound to occur as long as people live, but there is a feeling now, that was not here before, and is not just on the surface of things, but penetrates all the way through: We've won it. It's going to get better now. You can sort of tell these things."

Less than five years after Robert Pirsig's still popular narrative first appeared, the *San Francisco Chronicle* carried a story about his family: "The 23-year-old son of the author of *Zen and the Art of Motorcycle Maintenance*," its lead paragraph announced, "was stabbed to death Saturday night two blocks from the Zen Center where he lived, police said yesterday." The article continued by noting that the Pirsig family was scattered. Chris Pirsig had lived at the Zen Center since 1975. His mother was in Minneapolis. It was uncertain whether his father, who was then living on a boat off the English coast and writing about Zen and the art of sailing, would be able to attend the funeral.

Being an American is a complex fate because trials do have a way of never ending, even when things seem to be getting better. We Americans prefer, of course, to dwell on success stories. We thrive on hopes for the future, too. Hence we are partly truth, but we are also partly fiction insofar as we slight the contradictory character of our nation, which both is and is not what it wants to be and could become.

At the end of *The Great Gatsby* (1925), F. Scott Fitzgerald's best-known novel, Nick Carraway thinks how Long Island must have looked —"a fresh, green breast of the new world"—to the first Dutch voyagers who landed there centuries ago. As those explorers met "something commensurate to [their] capacity for wonder," he envisions, for a moment at least, that they "must have held [their] breath in the presence of this continent." Does the land, this place we call America, still make us hold our breath? What do we see as we envision America, and where do we see it from? Those are good questions, and so they will remain.

Visions of America produce maps and murals. Their sites and insights contain scenes of epic proportions. They have that quality not only because of optimistic dreams and their accomplishments but also because adversity and failure identify us. All of those realities reveal our American identities as they test our fundamental spirit. Mapping the land, plotting its possibilities, scouting the irony it contains, and reckoning with ourselves—having set the stage, the visions and revisions of America offered by Heat Moon, Frost, and

Pirsig, now give way to discussions of Fitzgerald and Kerouac, Morrison and Rich, Twain and Whitman. Each and all, those writers' American journeys, the visions they include and the identities they fashion, provide stories to enhance the appreciation that our complex American fate is worth having, artful, a gift to share and possess with care.

—John K. Roth
Claremont McKenna College

F. SCOTT FITZGERALD

Born: St. Paul, Minnesota; September 24, 1896   **Died:** Hollywood, California; December 21, 1940

Principal long fiction

This Side of Paradise, 1920; *The Beautiful and Damned*, 1922; *The Great Gatsby*, 1925; *Tender Is the Night*, 1934; *The Last Tycoon*, 1941.

Other literary forms

Charles Scribner's Sons published nine books by F. Scott Fitzgerald during Fitzgerald's lifetime. In addition to the first four novels, there were four volumes of short stories and one play. Fitzgerald also wrote essays and autobiographical pieces, many of which appeared in the late 1930's in *Esquire* and are now collected, among other places, in *The Crack-Up* (1945). Fitzgerald's Hollywood writing consisted mainly of collaborative efforts on scripts for films such as *Gone with the Wind* (1939). Fitzgerald's notebooks, scrapbooks, and letters have been published, and the record of his literary achievement is now nearly complete.

Achievements

Fitzgerald was the most representative American novelist of the storied 1920's—the "jazz age"—a decade rich in literary talent. An incomparable stylist and an acute social observer, he achieved fame for his depictions of American life during that period of history.

Curiously, Fitzgerald has appealed to two diverse audiences since the beginning of his career: the popular magazine audience and the elite of the literary establishment. His work appeared regularly in the 1920's and 1930's in such mass circulation magazines as the *Saturday Evening Post*, *Hearst's*, *International*, *Collier's*, and *Redbook*. The readers of these magazines came to ask for Fitzgerald's flapper stories by name, expecting to find in them rich, young, and glamorous heroes and heroines involved in exciting adventures. Popular magazines in the 1920's billed Fitzgerald stories on the cover, often using them inside as lead stories. Long after Fitzgerald lost the knack of writing the kind of popular stories that made him famous as the creator of the flapper in fiction and as the poet laureate of the jazz age, magazine headnotes to his stories identified him as such.

Many of Fitzgerald's critical opinions went into the public domain when he published his *Crack-Up* essays in *Esquire* in the late 1930's. These essays are now often anthologized and widely quoted for the ideas and theories about literature and life that they contain. At the time of his death, Fitzgerald seemed nearly forgotten by his popular readers and greatly neglected by literary critics. After his death and the posthumous publication of his incomplete *The Last Tycoon*, a Fitzgerald revival, still in progress, began. With this revival, Fitzgerald's reputation as a novelist (principally on the strength of *The Great Gatsby* and *Tender Is the Night*), short-story writer, and essayist has been solidly established.

Biography

Francis Scott Key Fitzgerald was born in St. Paul, Minnesota, on September 24, 1896. His mother's side of the family (the McQuillan side) was what Fitzgerald referred to as "straight 1850 potato famine Irish," but by the time of his maternal grandfather's death at the age of forty-four, the McQuillan fortune, earned in the grocery business, was in excess of $300,000. Fitzgerald's father was a poor but well-bred descendant of the old Maryland Scott and Key families. Always an ineffectual businessman, Edward Fitzgerald had met Mary McQuillan when he had come to St. Paul to open a wicker furniture business, which shortly went out of business. In search of a job by which he could support the family, Edward Fitzgerald moved his family from St. Paul to Buffalo, New York, in 1898—then to Syracuse and back to Buffalo. When Fitzgerald was eleven, the family returned to St. Paul and the security of the McQuillan wealth.

With McQuillan money Fitzgerald was sent for two painfully lonely years to private school, the Newman School in Hackensack, New Jersey. Discovering there a flair for writing musical comedy, Fitzgerald decided that he would attend Princeton, whose Triangle Club produced a musical comedy each year. At Princeton, Fitzgerald compensated for his feelings of social inferiority by excelling in the thing he did best, writing for the Triangle Club and the *Nassau Literary Magazine*.

During a Christmas vacation spent in St. Paul, Fitzgerald met Ginevra King, a wealthy Chicago debutante whose initial acceptance of Fitzgerald was for him a supreme social triumph; her later rejection of him became one of the most devastating blows of his life. He kept her letters, which he had typed and bound and which ran to more than two hundred pages, until his death.

In 1917, Fitzgerald left Princeton without a degree, accepted a commission in the Army, and wrote the first draft of what was to become his first novel, *This Side of Paradise*. During the summer of 1918, Fitzgerald met Zelda Sayre while he was stationed near Montgomery, Alabama, and, having recently received word of Ginevra King's engagement, he fell in love with Zelda. Zelda, however, although willing to become engaged to Fitzgerald, did not finally agree to marry him until he could demonstrate his ability to support her. Fitzgerald returned to New York, worked for an advertising firm, and revised his novel, including in it details from his courtship with Zelda. When Charles Scribner's Sons agreed in September, 1919, to publish the novel, Fitzgerald was able to claim Zelda, and they were married in April of the following year.

The first two years of their marriage were marked by wild parties, the self-destructive mood of which formed the basis for some of the scenes in Fitzgerald's second novel, *The Beautiful and Damned*. After a trip to Europe, the Fitzgeralds returned first to St. Paul and then to Great Neck, New York, where they lived among the Astors and Vanderbilts while Fitzgerald accumulated material that would figure in *The Great Gatsby*.

In the decade that followed the publication of that novel, the Fitzgeralds lived, among other places, on the French Riviera, which would provide the background for *Tender Is the Night*. Zelda headed toward a mental collapse, a fictionalized version of which appears in the novel; Fitzgerald sank into alcoholism. In 1930, Zelda was institutionalized for treatment of her mental condition. The rest of Fitzgerald's life was spent writing stories and screenplays that would pay for her treatment, both in and out of institutions. In 1937, Fitzgerald went to Hollywood, met Sheila Graham, worked under contract for M-G-M, and accumulated material for his last novel, while Zelda remained in the East. Fitzgerald died of a heart attack on December 21, 1940, while working on his unfinished novel, *The Last Tycoon*.

Analysis

Through his novels and short stories, Fitzgerald cap-

tured the essence of American life in the period between World Wars I and II. *The Great Gatsby* is the pinnacle of his achievement. In it he was able to bring together the themes that concerned him the most: failed dreams and lost hope, the power of money to corrupt the innocent, and the impossibility of recapturing the past.

At his best—in *The Great Gatsby*, in parts of *Tender Is the Night*, in the unfinished *The Last Tycoon*, and in parts of his first two novels, *This Side of Paradise* and *The Beautiful and Damned*—Fitzgerald demonstrates the aesthetic principle of "double vision." An understanding of this phrase (coined and first applied to Fitzgerald's art by Malcolm Cowley) is central to any discussion of Fitzgerald's novels. "Double vision" denotes two ways of seeing. It implies the tension involved when Fitzgerald sets things in opposition such that readers can sensually experience the event about which Fitzgerald is writing, immersing themselves emotionally in it, and yet at the same time retain the objectivity to stand back and intellectually criticize it. The foundation of double vision is polarity—the setting of extremes against each other; the result in a novel is dramatic tension.

The major themes of Fitzgerald's novels derive from the resolution of tension when one idea (usually embodied in a character) triumphs over another. Amory Blaine, the protagonist of *This Side of Paradise*, is a questing hero armed with youth, intelligence, and good looks. Anthony Patch in *The Beautiful and Damned* has a multimillionaire grandfather, a beautiful wife, and youth. Jay Gatsby in *The Great Gatsby* possesses power, newly made money, and good looks. Finally, Dick Diver in *Tender Is the Night* has a medical degree, an overabundance of charm, and a wealthy wife. The common denominators here are the subjects with which Fitzgerald deals in all of his novels: youth, physical beauty, wealth, and potential or "romantic readiness"— all of which are ideals to Fitzgerald. Set against these subjects are their polar opposites: age, ugliness, poverty, squandered potential. It is Fitzgerald's main gift that he can draw readers into a web of emotional attachment to a character, as he does to Daisy through Gatsby, while simultaneously allowing them to inspect the complexity of the web, as he does through Nick.

From the beginning of his career as a novelist, Fitzgerald stayed with the subjects and themes that he knew well and that were close to him: wealth, youth, and beauty. What did change between the creation of *This Side of Paradise* and *The Great Gatsby* was Fitzgerald's perspective on his material and his ability to objectify his attitudes toward it. In 1925, Fitzgerald was more than five years removed from his affair with Ginevra King, which gave him the distance to be Nick Carraway, the novel's "objective" narrator. Yet Fitzgerald was also near enough in memory that he could recall, even relive, the seductiveness of her world; that is, he was still able to be the romantic hero, Jay Gatsby. In effect, he had reached the pivotal point in his life that allowed him to see clearly through the eyes of both Gatsby and Nick; for the time of the creation of *The Great Gatsby*, he possessed double vision.

The success of the novel depends on Fitzgerald's ability to transfer to the reader the same kind of vision that he himself had: the ability to believe in the possibilities of several opposite ideas at various levels of abstraction. On the most concrete level, the reader must believe that Gatsby will and will not win Daisy, the novel's heroine and symbol of the American ideal. On a more general level, the reader must believe that anyone in America, through hard work and perseverance, can and cannot gain access to the best that America has to offer. Until Daisy's final rejection of Gatsby in the penultimate chapter of the novel, readers can, indeed, believe in both alternatives because they have seen them both from the perspective of Gatsby (who believes) and from the point of view of Nick (who wants to believe but intellectually cannot).

The central scene in *The Great Gatsby* nicely illustrates how Fitzgerald is able to present his material in such a way as to create dramatic tension through the use of double vision. This scene, which occupies the first part of chapter 5, is built around the reunion of Gatsby and Daisy after a five-year separation. The years, for Gatsby, have been devoted to the obsessive pursuit of wealth, which he wants only because he believes it will win Daisy for him. Daisy, who has married Tom Buchanan, seems to have given little thought to Gatsby since her marriage. The moment of their reunion, then, means everything to Gatsby and very little to Daisy, except as a diversion from the luxurious idling of her daily existence. In this meeting scene, as Gatsby stands nervously talking to Daisy and Nick, Fitzgerald calls the reader's attention to a defunct clock on Nick's mantelpiece. When Gatsby leans against the mantle, the clock teeters on the edge, deciding finally not to fall. The three stare at the floor as if the clock has, in fact, shattered to pieces in front of them. Gatsby apologizes and Nick replies, "It's an old clock."

The clock, a focal point of the room in which Gatsby and Daisy meet, represents the past time that Gatsby wants to repeat in order to recapture Daisy's love for him. That this clock, which has stopped at some past moment, can be suspended on a mantlepiece in front of them affirms the possibility of bringing the past into the present. Yet, the fact that they all envision the clock shattered on the floor suggests that all three are aware of the fragility of this past moment brought into the present. The fact that the clock does not work hints at the underlying flaw in Gatsby's dream of a relationship with Daisy.

The scene foreshadows the brutal and tragic events that follow: the brief and intense renewal of a courtship that takes place behind the closed doors of Gatsby's mansion and ends abruptly after a confrontation between Gatsby and Tom; the death of Myrtle, Tom's mistress; Gatsby's murder by Myrtle's husband; Daisy and Tom's "vacation" until the confusion abates; and Gatsby's funeral, arranged by Nick—each inexorably following upon the other in the last two chapters of the novel. Nick alone is left to tell the story of the dreamer whose dreams were corrupted by the "foul dust" that floated in their wake and of the reckless rich who "smashed up things and people and then retreated back into their vast carelessness, or whatever it was that kept them together, and let other people clean up the mess they had made."

At this end-point, the reader will recall the ominous foreshadowing of the broken clock: Gatsby cannot, as Nick has told him, repeat the past. He cannot have Daisy, because as Nick knows, "poor guys shouldn't think of marrying rich girls." Gatsby cannot have what he imagined to be the best America had to offer, which Nick realizes is not Daisy. Yet, the fault does not lie in Gatsby's capacity to dream, only in "the foul dust" which floated in the wake of his dreams—a belief in the money-god, for example—that makes him mistake a counterfeit (Daisy) for the true romantic vision. "No— Gatsby turned out all right at the end," Nick says in a kind of preface to the novel, a statement that keeps Fitzgerald's double vision intact in spite of Gatsby's loss of Daisy and his life. At the highest level of abstraction, the novel suggests that an idealist unwilling to compromise can and cannot survive in a materialistic world, an ambivalent and quintessentially American point of view that Fitzgerald held until his death. No longer did he need to write what he thought he should write; he was writing from the vantage point of one who saw that he had endowed the world of Ginevra King with a sanctity it did not deserve. Part of him, like Gatsby, died with the realization. The other part, like

Nick, lived on to make sense of what he had lost and to find a better dream.

For the nine years that followed the publication of *The Great Gatsby* (sometimes referred to as "the barren years"), Fitzgerald published no novels. During the first five of these years, the Fitzgeralds made four trips to Europe, where they met Ernest Hemingway in 1925 and where they lived for a time on the French Riviera, near Gerald and Sara Murphy, prototypes for Dick and Nicole Diver in Fitzgerald's last complete novel, *Tender Is the Night*. In 1930, Zelda had her first mental breakdown and was hospitalized in Switzerland. Two years later she had a second one. For Fitzgerald, the years from 1930 to 1933 were years during which he was compelled to write short stories for popular magazines, primarily the *Saturday Evening Post*, to enable Zelda to be treated in expensive mental institutions. All of the years were devoted to developing a perspective on his experiences: his feelings about Zelda's affair with a French aviator, Édouard Jozan; his own retaliatory relationship with a young film star, Lois Moran; his attraction to the lifestyle of the Murphys; Zelda's mental illness; his own alcoholism and emotional bankruptcy. He carried the perspective he gained through seventeen complete drafts, fully documented by Matthew J. Bruccoli in *The Composition of Tender Is the Night* (1963), to its completion in his novel.

Partly because it attempts to bring together so many subjects, partly because it deals with so complex a theme as the decline of Western civilization, and partly because of its experimentation with multiple points of view, *Tender Is the Night* is usually regarded as Fitzgerald's most ambitious novel. The story line of the novel is straightforward and has the recognizable Fitzgerald stamp. Its hero, Dick Diver, is a gifted young American in Europe who studies psychiatry with Sigmund Freud, writes a textbook for psychiatrists, marries a wealthy American mental patient, and over a period of years makes her well, while sinking himself into an emotional and physical decline that leads him away from Europe to wander aimlessly in an obscure part of upstate New York. The plot rendered chronologically can be represented as two *v*'s placed point-to-point to form an *X*. The lower *v* is Dick's story, which follows him from a relatively low social and economic position to achieve the American Dream, exceeding the bounds of class to become a doctor and scientist. From there he sinks back again to the low point of emotional bankruptcy. The story of his wife, Nicole, can be represented by the upper *v*, since Nicole starts life in America's upper

class, falls into mental illness (caused by an incestuous relationship with her father), and then rises again to a height of stability and self-sufficiency.

Fitzgerald, however, does not choose to tell the story in chronological sequence, electing instead to focus first on Dick Diver at the high point of his career, following him through his training in a flashback, and ending the novel with his collapse into anonymity. Nicole's story, secondary to Dick's, is woven into that of Dick's decline, with the implication that she has helped to speed it along. Nor does Fitzgerald select for the novel a single focus of narration, as he does in *The Great Gatsby*. Instead, book 1 of the novel shows Dick in June and July of 1925 at the high point of his life, shortly before the beginning of his decline, from the viewpoint of Rosemary Hoyt, an innocent eighteen-year-old film star whose innocence Dick will finally betray at his low point by making love to her. Book 2 contains four chronological shifts covering more than a decade, beginning in 1917, and is presented variously from Dick's and then Nicole's perspective. Book 3 brings the story forward one and a half years from the close of book 2 to Dick's departure from the Riviera and Nicole's marriage to Tommy Barban, and it is told from the point of view of the survivor, Nicole.

The complicated shifts in viewpoint and chronological sequence are grounded in the complexity of Fitzgerald's purposes. First, he is attempting to document both the external and internal forces that bring about the decline of a gifted individual. In Dick Diver's case, the inward flaw is rooted in an excess of charm and in a self-destructive need to be used, which the reader can best see from Dick's own perspective. From without, Nicole's money weakens his resistance and serves as a catalyst for the breaking down of his willpower, a process more clearly observable in the sections from Nicole's point of view. The value of seeing Dick at a high point early in book 1 through Rosemary's eyes is that it emphasizes how attractive and desirable he could be; by contrast, the fact of his emotional bankruptcy at the end of the novel gains power. Fitzgerald, however, is also attempting to equate Dick's decline with the decline of Western—and by extension, a young and idealistic American—society. This theme runs throughout Fitzgerald's work, from *The Great Gatsby* to *Tender Is the Night*: Both are stories of a decline of Western society and the downfall of American idealism in the face of American materialism. This decay of the good life, of beauty, wealth, and social status, and its corruption into illness and moral bankruptcy, concerned

Fitzgerald throughout his art as much as it consumed him in life. Fitzgerald's novels document one of the most complex and fascinating periods of American history, its coming-of-age and its loss of innocence. It was a time of unparalleled frivolity (during the "roaring" twenties) and subsequent national despondency (with the advent of the Great Depression), and it shaped the nation's sense of self. That heady rise and sober fall are mirrored in Fitzgerald's characters.

Other major works

SHORT FICTION: *Flappers and Philosophers*, 1920; *Tales of the Jazz Age*, 1922; *All the Sad Young Men*, 1926; *Taps at Reveille*, 1935; *The Stories of F. Scott Fitzgerald*, 1951; *Babylon Revisited and Other Stories*, 1960; *The Pat Hobby Stories*, 1962; *The Apprentice Fiction of F. Scott Fitzgerald, 1907-1917*, 1965; *The Basil and Josephine Stories*, 1973; *Bits of Paradise*, 1974; *The Price Was High: The Last Uncollected Stories of F. Scott Fitzgerald*, 1979.

PLAY: *The Vegetable: Or, From President to Postman*, 1923.

NONFICTION: *The Crack-Up*, 1945; *The Letters of F. Scott Fitzgerald*, 1963; *Letters to His Daughter*, 1965; *Thoughtbook of Francis Scott Fitzgerald*, 1965; *Dear Scott/Dear Max: The Fitzgerald-Perkins Correspondence*, 1971; *As Ever, Scott Fitzgerald*, 1972; *F. Scott Fitzgerald's Ledger*, 1972; *The Notebooks of F. Scott Fitzgerald*, 1978; *A Life in Letters*, 1994.

MISCELLANEOUS: *Afternoon of an Author: A Selection of Uncollected Stories and Essays*, 1958.

SCREENPLAY: *Babylon Revisited: The Screenplay*, 1993.

Bibliography

Bloom, Harold, ed. *F. Scott Fitzgerald*. New York: Chelsea House, 1985.

Bruccoli, Matthew J. *Fitzgerald and Hemingway: A Dangerous Friendship*. New York: Carroll & Graf, 1994.

―――――― , ed. *A Life in Letters*. New York: Scribner, 1994.

―――――― , ed. *New Essays on "The Great Gatsby."* Cambridge, England: Cambridge University Press, 1985.

―――――― . *Some Sort of Epic Grandeur*. New York: Harcourt Brace Jovanovich, 1981.

Eble, Kenneth. *F. Scott Fitzgerald*. New York: Twayne, 1963.

Gervais, Ronald J. "The Socialist and the Silk Stockings: Fitzgerald's Double Allegiance." *Mosaic* 15 (June, 1982): 79-82.

Kuehl, John. *F. Scott Fitzgerald: A Study of the Short Fiction*. Boston: Twayne, 1991.

Lee, A. Robert, ed. *Scott Fitzgerald: The Promises of Life*. New York: St. Martin's Press, 1989.

Meyers, Jeffrey, *Scott Fitzgerald: A Biography*. New York: HarperCollins, 1994.

Tytell, John. *Passionate Lives: D. H. Lawrence, F. Scott Fitzgerald, Henry Miller, Dylan Thomas, Sylvia Plath—in Love*. Secaucus, N.J.: Carol, 1991.

JACK KEROUAC

Born: Lowell, Massachusetts; March 12, 1922   **Died:** St. Petersburg, Florida; October 21, 1969

Principal long fiction

The Town and the City, 1950; *On the Road*, 1957; *The Dharma Bums*, 1958; *The Subterraneans*, 1958; *Doctor Sax*, 1959; *Maggie Cassidy*, 1959; *Tristessa*, 1960; *Visions of Cody*, 1960, 1972; *Big Sur*, 1962; *Visions of Gerard*, 1963; *Desolation Angels*, 1965; *Vanity of Duluoz*, 1968; *Pic*, 1971.

Other literary forms

In addition to his novels, Jack Kerouac published *Mexico City Blues* (1959), a poetry collection intended to imitate the techniques of jazz soloists, *Scattered Poems* (1971), and *Old Angel Midnight* (1976), a prose poem; the latter two were published posthumously. His nonfiction prose includes *The Scripture of the Golden Eternity* (1960), a homemade sutra written to Gary Snyder; *Book of Dreams* (1961), sketches that recorded Kerouac's dreams; *Lonesome Traveler* (1960), travel sketches; and *Pull My Daisy* (1961), a screenplay based on his abandoned play "The Beat Generation."

Achievements

While some critics have condemned Kerouac as an incoherent, unstructured, and unsound writer, the prophet of a nihilistic movement, his books have continued to be read. The very qualities for which he has been criticized—wildness, sensationalism, and irresponsibility—have been sources of charm to other commentators. He has been described on one hand as pessimistic and bizarre and on the other as optimistic and fresh.

Kerouac's unofficial and unwanted title, "King of the Beats," brought him a great deal of the publicity he shunned. Kerouac's friend Gary Snyder has described the Beats as a group of writers who gathered together the myths of freedom espoused by Henry David Thoreau and Walt Whitman, adding some of the notions of Buddhism. To Kerouac, who is generally credited with the invention of the term, "Beat" meant "beatific"—holy and compassionate. He declared that the Beats did not fear death and that they wanted to lose themselves as Christ had advised. In *Pageant* magazine, Kerouac wrote that the Beats believed that honesty and freedom would lead to a vision of a God of Ecstasy. In a public forum, Kerouac declared that America was changing for the better, and he warned those who wanted to spit on the Beat Generation that the wind would blow the spit back on them. The media developed the image of a bearded beatnik who wore sweat shirts and jeans, played bongo drums, never bathed, and used the word "like" as a ubiquitous conjunction. Even though the beatniks were a far cry from the intellectual Beats, the former became associated with the latter in the public eye.

Although Kerouac's public image endangered his critical reception, recent critics have recognized him as a powerful and talented writer. His work, as he intended it to be, is one long opus.

Biography

Jean Louis Lebris de Kerouac was born in Lowell, Massachusetts, on March 12, 1922. His mother, Gabrielle Ange Levesque Kerouac, and his father, Leo Alcide Kerouac, were both French Canadians whose families had emigrated from Quebec. Gabrielle's father, a mill worker and an owner of a small tavern, had died when she was fourteen, and she then went to work as a machine operator in a Nashua shoe shop. From this moment, and for the rest of her life, "Memere" fought for a higher social status. Leo was an insurance salesman who became a job printer. At the time of Kerouac's birth, his sister Caroline ("Nin") was three, and Gerard, the brother who had been weakened by rheumatic fever, was five. The family was very close.

At the age of nine, Gerard became so ill that he was forced to remain in bed. As Gerard grew weaker, he grew more angelic in the eyes of everyone in the family, and the lively young Kerouac suffered by comparison. As Gerard's pain grew worse, Kerouac began to feel that he, Jean, was somehow responsible. After Gerard's death, Kerouac tried futilely to replace him by being especially pious and sensitive.

As he grew older, Kerouac went frequently to the

movies on passes given to Leo. The public library also became a favorite haunt, but the biggest outside influence on Kerouac's childhood was the Roman Catholic church of his forefathers. He attended parochial school, had visions of Christ and the Virgin Mary, memorized the catechism, and worried about his sins and purgatory. When he became an altar boy, his Jesuit teachers thought that he might become a priest, but when he entered a public junior high school, Jean Kerouac became "Jacky," who could write and whose favorite radio program was *The Shadow*—the forerunner of Dr. Sax.

Kerouac attended Horace Mann Preparatory School prior to enrolling at Columbia University. At Horace Mann, Jack wrote papers for his classmates for pay, some of which he spent on his first prostitute. He published short stories in the *Horace Mann Quarterly*, discovered the jazz world in Harlem, and adopted Walt Whitman as his personal bard.

At Columbia, Kerouac studied William Shakespeare under Mark Van Doren, registered for the draft, found another mentor in the works of Thomas Wolfe, and broke his leg in a freshman football game. One day Kerouac left Columbia for Washington, D.C., New Haven and Hartford, Connecticut, and a series of short-lived jobs, including sportswriter for the *Lowell Sun* and merchant seaman on a ship out of Boston. In 1944, he met Allen Ginsberg, a Columbia student until he was banned from campus, and William S. Burroughs, with whom Kerouac wrote a detective story. Kerouac also met Edie Parker, whom he married but from whom he separated shortly thereafter.

After his father died of cancer in 1946, Kerouac started taking Benzedrine and writing *The Town and the City*. He also met Neal Cassady, the "brother" he had been seeking since Gerard's death. After Cassady returned to Denver, Kerouac set out to see America, stopping in Denver, San Francisco, Los Angeles, and Pittsburgh. Cassady came East again, and he, Kerouac, and Cassady's first wife, Lu Anne, made their famous "on the road" trip. In 1950, Kerouac married Joan Haverty and began writing *On the Road*, typing it on rolls of teletype paper.

After several rejections, *On the Road* was published in 1957 and was hailed by *New York Times* critic Gilberg Millstein as a major novel. Within the next six years, Kerouac published a number of other books.

While Kerouac was in New York, he fell in love with Mardou Fox, whose American Indian and African American ancestry Memere could never accept. After losing Mardou to the poet Gregory Corso, Kerouac wrote about the affair in *The Subterraneans*. In response to William Burroughs' request, Kerouac typed out "The Essentials of Spontaneous Prose," explaining the writing method he had used.

Kerouac found solace in *Walden: Or, Life in the Woods* (1854), by Henry David Thoreau, with whom he shared a rejection of civilization, and he also began to study Buddhism as part of his search for peace from the carping of Memere and the disappointments engendered by nonsympathetic editors. He meditated daily in an effort to reach Nirvana. When he met poet Gary Snyder, a Zen Buddhist whose approach was prayerful, Kerouac felt a harmony he had not known, even with Cassady.

By the time Kerouac married Stella Sampas, the sister of an old friend who was killed in the war, and settled down again in Lowell, he was suffering from three problems: recurring phlebitis, a dependency upon alcohol, particularly wine, and the adulation of youngsters who invaded his privacy and made him feel old. They expected him to be Dean Moriarty of *On the Road*, but his aging, alcoholic body rebelled.

Meanwhile, Cassady had been arrested for possession of marijuana and sentenced to San Quentin, after which he complained about Kerouac's lack of attention. After his release, Cassady drank tequila and swallowed Seconals at a Mexican wedding party; the combination caused his death. Kerouac never allowed himself to believe that Cassady was actually dead. In October, 1969, Kerouac's years of heavy drinking caused him to begin to bleed internally, and he died hours later.

Analysis

Jack Kerouac described himself as a "great rememberer redeeming life from darkness." He claimed on more than one occasion that his books were actually one book about his entire life. He had intentions to consolidate them, but these plans were not carried out before his death. The areas of life that he remembered and celebrated include the dichotomy between his family and friends in Lowell, Massachusetts, and the Beat friends with whom he carried on such a frenzied, peripatetic relationship.

Kerouac used the label "the Beat Generation" in reference to the small circle of individuals (largely poets and assorted other friends) who were his close companions through the late 1940's and into the 1950's. Their governing beliefs were clearly spelled out in *On the Road*: distrust of authority and social conventions, which were viewed as obstacles to self-knowledge and honest, meaningful communication; sexual liberation; and experience, including drug experimentation, for its own sake. The book is not, however, merely a manifesto of the Beat Generation. It is, rather, a truly American novel with roots in the works of Walt Whitman, Herman Melville, and Mark Twain. More than any other literary work, *On the Road* was the one that shaped Americans' perceptions of the Beat movement.

Both the title and the novel were incubating in Kerouac's mind for four years before he sat down to write *On the Road* on a one-hundred-foot roll of paper, in one 120,000-word, single-spaced paragraph. Six more years passed before its publication, and in the decade between conception and birth, America had changed, and so had the writer.

Sal Paradise, the narrator and the Kerouac figure, received his name when Ginsberg wrote a poem containing the line, "Sad paradise it is I imitate." The carelessly written *d* caused "Sad" to look like "Sal." Sal, whose ideals are both romantic and personal, sets out near the beginning of the tale to search for an Eden. He is at the same time leaving behind all intimacy and responsibility associated with home and family.

Like Geoffrey Chaucer's pilgrims, everyone Sal meets is described with superlatives: He hears "the greatest laugh in the world"; he observes the most smiling, cheerful face in the world, and he watches a tall Mexican roll the biggest bomber anybody ever saw. While observing these fellow pilgrims, he thinks of himself and his friends as seeking salvation and the promised land. In going "on the road," Sal expects to find direction and purpose.

Sal has studied maps of the West, and when he begins his trip, he wants to repeat as closely as possible the path of the old wagon trains. He glories in the names of such cities as Platte and Cimarron and imagines that the unbroken red line that represents Route 6 on his map duplicates the trail of the early American settlers. After a false start on a rainy day, Sal returns to New York, where he had started, and buys a bus ticket to Chicago; the bus is a mode of travel he uses more than once. In Des Moines, Sal awakens nameless and reborn at what seems to be a turning point in his life. This moment that divides his youth from his future occurs, fittingly enough, in mid-America. He goes from Denver to California, where he meets Dean Moriarty, the central figure of the book and the figure that made Neal Cassady a legend.

Moriarty becomes a part of Sal's life, an extension of his personality, his alter ego; he even insists on sharing his wife with Sal. Three become a crowd, however, and Sal, after several digressions, goes back to the East and his aunt. On the last lap of the journey, he meets a shriveled old man with a paper suitcase who is called "Ghost of the Susquehanna." Sal sees him as an aging reflection of what he himself will become—a bum.

The energy of the book derives from Moriarty, who is never far out of Sal's mind. Dean's accomplishments include skillful driving—often of cars he has stolen for a joyride; talking his way out of any tight situation; seducing women, frequently two at a time; and appreciating jazz. The friends Dean has met in pool halls become the minor heroes of this epic.

In Kerouac's mind, Cassady and America were one entity—vibrant, carefree, and admirable. Through Moriarty, Kerouac chronicles a new kind of existence in postwar America—suggesting a life less dependent upon place and family and more tolerant of impropriety. The hedonist Moriarty loves and leaves his women in the manner of the stereotyped cowboy who rides off into the sunset. Moriarty, never complacent, ever free, can be characterized by the fact that he goes to answer his door completely naked. Even when he is employed and has a home address, he seems to be on the move; he is always planning a break from entanglements, often represented by whomever his current wife might be.

Sal sees himself as a discipline to the saint, Moriarty, and he exults in Dean's uniqueness and eccentricity. Dean's mysticism consists of belief in his father, in God, and IT, which can be communicated by jazz musicians and which has somehow been communicated to Dean through his missing father, who was a drunk. The search for Dean's father is one of the book's themes, along with the search for God. The roaders are seeking someone to shelter them from life and responsibility, and they approve of those pilgrims (Montana Slim and Remi Boncoeur) who are respectful toward their own fathers.

Most of the characters Sal meets on the road are attractive in some way; as Huck Finn found people on the river to be sympathetic, Sal feels a communion with the hobos, who reject competition and jobs for a sense of brotherhood and a simple life. He is disappointed, however, when he sees his first cowboy, whose apparel is his only claim to authenticity. Like Stephen Crane before him, Sal sees that the West is merely trying to perpetuate dead traditions and that Central City is simply a tourist attraction. Nothing can be as fine as his dreams of the West, and he eventually begins to conclude that the East, after all, may be the place to find contentment and salvation. He returns home in his favorite month of October, realizing that he has acted out an adventure but has experienced no rebirth.

The point of view of *On the Road* is consistently that of Sal, but as he tells the reader about his experiences as they occurred at the time, he also comments on the same events as he sees them now, with a more mature, more disillusioned, more objective eye. Saddened by the realization that the road itself is all-important to Dean, Sal repudiates the idea of movement with no purpose.

Recognizing the vastness and shapelessness of the experience he was about to put on paper, Kerouac sought a suitable form and style. He began to write the book in a conscious imitation of Thomas Wolfe, but he finally decided to emulate Cassady's amorphous, joyous style. He added to that a new, free-association method that he called "sketching," suggested to him by Ed White, who thought it possible to paint with words. Sketching, comparable in Kerouac's view to the improvisation of the jazz musicians he greatly admired, was new, but the story he told was a repetition of the ageless initiation theme. *On the Road* is, however, not simply another *Tom Jones* (Henry Fielding, 1749) or *The Adventures of Huckleberry Finn* (Mark Twain, 1884); it reflects the confusion, the sense of search, and the troubled spirit of the Kerouac generation.

The title of *The Subterraneans* comes from Ginsberg's name for Greenwich Villagers; its setting is New York, disguised with San Francisco place-names. Kerouac claimed that the book is a full confession of the incidents surrounding his love affair with Mardou Fox, a part African American, part American Indian subterranean who had been associating with junkies and musicians. Kerouac fell in love with her, he said, even before they were introduced.

The book, consciously modeled after Fyodor Dostoevski's *Notes from the Underground* (1864), contains Mardou's private thoughts as she has whispered them to Leo Percipied (the Kerouac figure). She imagines herself walking naked in the Village, crouching like a feline on a fence experiencing a private epiphany, and then borrowing clothes and money to buy herself a symbolic brooch.

Leo (as Kerouac himself always did) sympathizes with minority races and listens to Mardou's thoughts about blacks, Indians, and America with a keen perception. The story carries Leo and Mardou on their frenzied movements through the Village in scenes that include meetings with bop musicians, poets, and novelists. A central scene describes the theft of a vendor's pushcart by a character named Yuri Gligoric (modeled after poet Gregory Corso); in this pushcart, Yuri transports his friends to the home of Adam Moorad (Allen Ginsberg), who is angry at Yuri because of the prank.

Both Mardou and Leo become dissatisfied with their life together, and when Yuri and Leo bicker over her, Leo chooses the incident as an excuse to separate from Mardou. Afterward, he wanders alone to a freight yard, where he has a vision of his mother. Leo finally admits that he felt inadequate sexually in the presence of Mardou, and he concludes, "I go home, having lost her love, and write this book."

The Dharma Bums, a book that Kerouac himself once described as a potboiler, is perhaps the most representative expression of the Beat sensibility in a work of fiction. Its focus is the close intellectual and religious relationship of Ray Smith (Kerouac) and Japhy Ryder (Gary Snyder). Snyder called *The Dharma Bums* a real statement of synthesis, through Kerouac, of the available models and myths of freedom in America: Whitman, Thoreau, and the bums—with Buddhism added as a catalyst.

The picture of Ryder is painted through faithful reproduction of Gary Snyder's speech and recollections of his poetry. The haiku Ryder composes on the mountainside are repeated verbatim. The way of life to which Ryder introduces Smith is a religious way, punctuated with prayer, laughter, and poetry, and it is espoused by the social minority who belong to the rucksack revolution. Both Smith and Ryder long to explain the Dharma, or the truth of religion and life, to others. The Dharma is associated with a nobility of body, mind, spirit, and speech that is surely worthy of their missionary zeal, if it can be attained. Through Ryder, Smith learns of ecology and earth consciousness. The two discuss their own private religious beliefs. After he learns about the lifestyle of the "rucksack saints" through observation and listening, Smith delineates the mode of living for any would-be followers, listing the spiritual and physical equipment necessary: submission, acceptance, expectancy, rucksacks, tents, and sleeping bags.

These three books—*On the Road*, *The Subterraneans*, and *The Dharma Bums*—shaped Kerouac's public image and eventually transformed him into an icon of the American Beat Generation, the individual questing for identity in postwar America. Each of them centers on a close relationship between a Kerouac figure and another person, and in each case an intense dependency is involved. All are testaments of love, and all suggest an opportunity to develop emotional maturity. Finally, all document a subculture open to new and often controversial experiences, anticipating the counterculture of the 1960's and the redefinition of American values that followed that era.

Other major works

POETRY: *Mexico City Blues*, 1959; *Scattered Poems*, 1971; *Old Angel Midnight*, 1976.

NONFICTION: *Lonesome Traveler*, 1960; *The Scripture of the Golden Eternity*, 1960; *Book of Dreams*, 1961; *Satori in Paris*, 1966.

Bibliography

Cassady, Carolyn. *Heart Beat: My Life with Jack and Neal*. Berkeley, Calif. Creative Arts, 1976.

——————— . *Off the Road: My Years with Cassady, Kerouac, and Ginsberg*. New York: William Morrow, 1990.

Hart, John E. "Future Hero in Paradise: Kerouac's *The Dharma Bums.*" *Critique: Studies in Modern Fiction* 14, no. 3 (1973): 52-62.

Jones, James T. *A Map of "Mexico City Blues": Jack Kerouac as Poet*. Carbondale: Southern Illinois University Press, 1992.

Montgomery, John. *Jack Kerouac*. Fresno, Calif.: Giligia Press, 1970.

Nicosia, Gerald. *Memory Babe: A Critical Biography of Jack Kerouac*. New York: Grove Press, 1983.

TONI MORRISON

Born: Lorain, Ohio; February 18, 1931

Principal long fiction

The Bluest Eye, 1970; *Sula*, 1973; *Song of Solomon*, 1977; *Tar Baby*, 1981; *Beloved*, 1987; *Jazz*, 1992.

Other literary forms

Toni Morrison is primarily a novelist. She has published a short story, "Big Box," in *Ms.* magazine (1980), essays, and a volume of literary criticism.

Achievements

Morrison is generally regarded as one of the most significant African American novelists to have emerged in the 1970's. Her novel *Sula* was nominated for the National Book Award in 1975. In 1977, *Song of Solomon* won the National Book Critics Circle Award. The former was a Book-of-the-Month Club alternate and the latter a main selection. In 1988, *Beloved* was awarded the Pulitzer Prize.

Morrison's fiction, especially *Song of Solomon*, has been compared to Ralph Ellison's *Invisible Man* (1952) for its mixture of the literal and the fantastic, the real and the surreal. Morrison has been praised for her use of language and for the sense of voice that emerges not only in her dialogue but also in the movement of her narratives. Morrison's novels are also remarkable for their sense of place, for the detailed, coherent physical worlds she creates. Finally, her fiction is noteworthy for its depiction of the deep psychic realities of women's experience. She was awarded the Nobel Prize in Literature in 1993, the first African American woman to be so honored.

Biography

Toni Morrison, daughter of George and Ramah (Willis) Wofford, was born Chloe Anthony Wofford on February 18, 1931, in Lorain, Ohio. Her father, a laborer, simultaneously held three jobs to take care of his family. Morrison was graduated from high school with honors and entered Howard University in Washington, D.C., where she received a B.A. degree in 1953. In 1955, Morrison earned a master's degree at Cornell University. She subsequently taught undergraduate English at Texas Southern University, and in 1957, she joined the faculty of Howard University. While there, she married Harold Morrison, an architect originally from Jamaica.

Morrison became the mother of two sons, Ford and Slade, before being divorced. While in Washington, Morrison joined a writer's group and began the story that became her first novel, *The Bluest Eye*. In 1965, Morrison became an editor for Random House, first in Syracuse and later in Manhattan, where she became a senior editor. Beginning in 1967, she also taught as a visiting lecturer at Yale University and has lectured at many other universities as well. She was appointed Goheen Professor of the Humanities at Princeton University in 1989.

Analysis

Morrison has advanced the canon of African American literature by constructing fiction that examines the black American experience for a black audience. The core concerns of her work remain the history of violence perpetrated upon black Americans, the damage that such violence brings to black cultural traditions, and the means by which blacks must act to preserve their heritage. Morrison's novels typically concern the experiences of black American women, although her explorations of the lives of black men are also powerful.

In all of her fiction, Morrison shows how the individual who defies social pressures can forge a self by drawing on the resources of the natural world, on a sense of continuity within the family and within the history of a people, and on dreams and other unaccountable sources of psychic power.

Sula explores the oppressive nature of white society, evident in the very name of the "Bottom," a hillside community that had its origin in the duplicitous white treatment of an emancipated black slave who was promised fertile "bottom land" along with his freedom. In a bitterly ironic twist, the whites take over the hillside again when they want suburban houses that will catch the breeze. In taking back the Bottom, they destroy a place, a community with its own identity. In turn, the black community, corrupted by white society, rejects Sula for her experimenting with her life, for trying to live free like a man instead of accepting the restrictions of the traditional female role.

Sula provokes the reader to question socially accepted concepts of good and evil. As Sula is dying, she asks her girlhood friend Nel, "How do you know that you were the good one?" Although considered morally loose and a witch by the townspeople, the unconventional Sula cannot believe herself to be an inferior individual. Contrasting the traditional role of mother and church woman that Nel has embraced, Sula's individuality is refreshing and intriguing. Despite her death, Sula maintains an independence that ultimately stands in proud opposition to the established network of relationships that exist within conventional society.

The novel shows that the Bottom society encompasses both good and evil. The people are accustomed to suffering and enduring evil. In varying degrees, they accept Eva's murder of her drug-addict son, Plum, and Hannah's seduction of their husbands, one after another. The community, nevertheless, cannot encompass Sula, a woman who thinks for herself without conforming to their sensibilities. They have to turn her into a witch, so that they can mobilize themselves against her "evil" and cherish their goodness. Without the witch, their goodness grows faint again. Like Pecola, Sula is made a scapegoat.

Growing up in the Bottom, Sula creates an identity for herself, first from the reality of physical experience. When she sees her mother Hannah burning up in front of her eyes, she feels curiosity. Her curiosity is as honest as Hannah's admission that she loves her daughter Sula the way any mother would, but that she does not like her. Hearing her mother reject her individuality, Sula concludes that there is no one to count on except herself.

In forging a self, Sula also draws on sexual experience as a means of joy, as a means of feeling sadness, and as a means of feeling her own power. Sula does not substitute a romantic dream for the reality of that physical experience. She does finally desire a widening of that sexual experience into a continuing relationship with Ajax, but the role of nurturing and possession is fatal to her. Ajax leaves, and Sula sickens and dies.

A closeness to the elemental processes of nature gives a depth to the lives of the Bottom-dwellers, although nature does not act with benevolence or even with consistency. Plum and Hannah, two of Eva's children, die by fire, one sacrificed by Eva and one ignited by capricious accident. Chicken Little and several of those who follow Shadrack on National Suicide Day drown because acts of play go wrong and inexplicably lead to their destruction. Sula's supposed identity as a witch is connected to the plague of robins that coincides with her return to the Bottom. The people of the Bottom live within Nature and try to make some sense of it, even though their constructions are strained and self-serving.

On one level, Sula refuses any connection to history and family continuity. Her grandmother Eva says that Sula should get a man and make babies, but Sula says that she would rather make herself. On another level, Sula is a descendant of the independent women Eva and Hannah, both of whom did what they had to do. It is at least rumored that Eva let her leg be cut off by a train so that she could get insurance money to take care of her three children when BoyBoy, her husband, abandoned her. When her husband died, Hannah needed "man-love," and she got it from her neighbors' husbands, despite community disapproval. In their mold, Sula is independent enough to threaten Eva with fire and to assert her own right to live, even if her grandmother does not like Sula's way of living.

To flourish, Morrison suggests, conventional society needs an opposite pole. A richness comes from the opposition and the balance—from the difference—and an acceptance of that difference would make scapegoats unnecessary. The world of the Bottom is poorer with Sula dead and out of it.

In *Song of Solomon*, Morrison again traces the making of a self. The novel is a departure for Morrison in that the protagonist is not a female but a young man, Milkman Dead. Milkman grows up in a comfortable, insulated, middle-class family, the grandson of a doctor on his mother's side and the son of a businessman, whose father owned his own farm. Son of a doting mother, Milkman is nursed a long time, the reason for his nickname, and is sent to school in velvet knickers. Guitar Baines, a Southside black, becomes Milkman's friend and an ally against the other children's teasing.

As the novel progresses, though, and as Milkman discovers the reality of his family and friends as separate people with their own griefs and torments, Milkman comes to feel that everyone wants him dead. Ironically, Milkman's last name actually is "Dead," the result of a drunken clerk's error when Milkman's grandfather was registering with the Freedmen's Bureau.

Milkman learns that his mere existence is extraordinary, since even before his birth, his father tried to kill him. Milkman survived that threat through the intercession of his mother and, especially, of his aunt, Pilate, a woman with no navel. After having been conjured by

Pilate into making love to his wife again, years after he had turned against her, Macon Dead wanted the resulting baby aborted. Ruth, the baby's mother, out of fear of her husband, took measures to bring about an abortion, but Pilate intervened again and helped Ruth to find the courage to save the child and bear him.

In the present action of the novel, Hagar, Milkman's cousin, his first love and his first lover, pursues him month after month with whatever weapon she can find to kill him. Hagar wants Milkman's living life, not his dead life, but Milkman has rejected her, out of boredom and fear that he will be maneuvered into marrying her. At this point, he does not want to be tied down: He wants freedom and escape.

Hagar feels unlovely and unloved, rejected because Milkman does not like her black, curly hair. Pilate says that Milkman cannot not love her hair without not loving himself because it is the same hair that grows from his own body. Hagar is a victim of an absolutely univocal standard of beauty, and she is a character who needs a supporting society, a chorus of aunts and cousins and sisters to surround her with advice and protection. Instead, she has only Pilate and Reba, grandmother and mother, two women so strong and independent that they do not understand her weakness. Unhinged by Milkman's rejection of her, Hagar chases Milkman with various weapons, is repeatedly disarmed, and finally dies in total discouragement.

Trying to find out about his family's past, Milkman travels to Virginia, to Shalimar, a black town, where the men in the general store challenge him to fight, and one attacks him with a knife. Milkman does not understand why these people want his life, but they think he has insulted and denied their masculinity with his powerful northern money and his brusque treatment of them, by not asking their names and not offering his own.

The most serious threat to Milkman's life, however, turns out to be Guitar, Milkman's friend and spiritual brother. When Guitar tries to kill Milkman, he is betraying the reality of their friendship for the idea of revenge against whites and compensation for the personal deprivation he has suffered. Guitar thinks that Milkman has a cache of gold that he is not sharing with him, so he decides to kill him. Guitar rationalizes his decision by saying that the money is for the cause, for the work of the Seven Days, a group of seven black men sworn to avenge the deaths of innocent blacks at the hands of the whites.

Milkman's being alive at all, then, is a triumph, a victory that he slowly comes to appreciate after coming out of his comfortable shell of self-involvement. Unwillingly, Milkman comes to know the suffering and griefs of his mother and father and even his sisters Magdalene and Corinthians. The decisive experience in his self-making, however, is the quest for Pilate's gold on which his father sets him. In the first stage, the men are convinced that Pilate's gold hangs in a green sack from the ceiling of her house, and Guitar and Milkman attempt to steal it. The two friends succeed in taking the sack because the women in the house are simply puzzled, wondering why the men want a sack which is really full of old bones. In leaving the house, though, the two men are arrested, and Pilate must rescue them and the bones by doing an Aunt Jemima act for the white policemen. Milkman's father, Macon, is convinced that gold still exists somewhere, and Milkman sets out to find it by going back to Pennsylvania, where Macon and Pilate grew up, and later to Virginia, where the previous generation lived.

Like Sula, too, Milkman creates a self from the reality of physical experience, the processes of nature, a connection to history and family continuity, and springs of human possibility through myth, dreams, legends, and other sources of psychic power. Milkman reaches an understanding of physical experience and the processes of nature in a struggle against the physical environment. As a rich city boy, Milkman was insulated from nature, but in his trip south to try to get the gold, he overcomes a series of physical obstacles to reach the cave where Macon and Pilate in their youth encountered the white man and the gold. Milkman gets there only after falling into the river and climbing up twenty feet of rock, splitting his shoes and the clothes that mark him as a city man. During the trip, Milkman loses his possessions—trunk, clothes, and whiskey—and he makes it on his own, in a place where his father's name and father's money do not protect him. Milkman succeeds in finding Circe, who years ago sheltered Pilate and Macon when their father was killed, and he reaches the cave where there is no longer any gold.

Milkman also encounters nature as an obstacle to be overcome when, after the knife-fight in Shalimar, he is invited to go on a coon hunt into the woods with the older men of Shalimar. Again, Milkman undergoes a test, having to move through the woods in the dark, having to show the courage and physical endurance necessary to be one of the hunters. Milkman also experiences the music of the hunt, the communication between the men and the dogs, the language before language, of a time when men were so close to their physical reality that they were in harmony with all creatures.

Milkman also creates himself in searching for his origins. In searching for his fathers, he discovers himself; like Telemachus and Stephen Dedalus, Milkman must find the reality of his fathers to know his own potential. Milkman's original pursuit of the gold seems to be an impulse he gets from his father, the man of business, and even from his father's father, who was a lover of property. The quest, however, changes as Milkman pursues it, finding the thread of his family's history. Stopping in Pennsylvania, Milkman hears the stories of the men who knew his father and grandfather and who rejoice in their successes. The story of the Dead family dramatizes the dream and the failure of that dream for blacks in America. When Macon Dead was killed by white men for his flourishing farm, the possibilities of his neighbors were narrowed and their lives scarred. Seeing his father and grandfather through their former neighbor's eyes helps Milkman to understand better the pride that Macon had when he said that his father had let Macon work side by side with him and trusted him to share in his achievements.

In Shalimar, Milkman also learns about his great-grandfather by piecing together the memories of people there and by deciphering the children's game and song, a song about Solomon and Rynah that seems to be interspersed with nonsense words. Milkman matches this song to a song that he had heard Pilate sing about Sugarman. He solves the riddle of the song, and he even figures out what the ghost of Pilate's father meant when he said "Sing" and when he told Pilate to go get the bones. Finally, he discovers that his grandmother was an American Indian, Singing Bird, and that his great-grandfather, Solomon, was one of the legendary flying Africans, the father of twenty-one sons, a slave who one day flew back to Africa. His grandfather Jake had fallen through the branches of a tree when Solomon dropped him, trying to take his last baby son back with him. Learning about that magic enables Milkman himself to fly when he surrenders to the air and lets himself be upheld.

Milkman creates a self so that he can share it and even sacrifice it for a friend. With Pilate, Milkman buries the bones of Jake, his grandfather, on Solomon's Leap. Guitar, who has continued to stalk Milkman, shoots and kills Pilate, but Milkman, says to Guitar, "Do you want my life? Take it if it is any good to you," leaps into the air and flies. Guitar is free to kill his friend, but Milkman soars.

The ending of the novel shows the transcendence of the spirit, as the hero achieves his destiny. The satisfaction of the ending, which also soars into legend, comes from the triumph of the human spirit, the triumph that even death cannot destroy. *Song of Solomon* is a beautiful, serious, funny novel that moves beyond the social to the mythic.

In her fifth novel, *Beloved*, Morrison confronts directly for the first time the institution of slavery. Morrison's intention is immediately apparent in the novel's dedication to the "Sixty Million and more" victims of slavery—a figure that is provocative not only in its sheer magnitude but also in its relation to the oft-cited "six million," that is, the number of Jews who perished in the Holocaust.

Spanning the period from 1855 to 1874, *Beloved* is at one level a powerful account of the slave experience, an intimate re-creation of suffering and struggle. Nevertheless, as readers of her previous novels might expect, to get at the deeper truth of her subject Morrison has created a lyrical, mythic narrative. At the heart of *Beloved* is a single terrible act: Sethe, a young slave, kills one of her children, a daughter not yet two years old. Much of the novel is devoted to making that act of murder comprehensible, not as an instance of insane cruelty but as an image of the legacy of slavery. That Morrison is thinking of that still-enduring legacy, a malign presence even in the late twentieth century, becomes clear when Sethe's murdered daughter, Beloved, appears as a young woman eighteen years after her death. A ghost story with echoes of Greek tragedy, an anguished, angry testament, *Beloved* is a significant addition to Morrison's body of work.

Morrison evocatively depicts the black American experience. Her novels underscore the need for present generations to come to terms with the past in order to understand the present. Re-creation of authentic black folklore enables her to forge the link joining the generations.

Other major works

NONFICTION: *Playing in the Dark: Whiteness and the Literary Imagination*, 1992.

EDITED TEXT: *Race-ing Justice, En-gendering Power: Essays on Anita Hill, Clarence Thomas, and the Construction of Social Reality*, 1992.

Bibliography

Bloom, Harold, ed. *Toni Morrison: Modern Critical Views*. New York: Chelsea House, 1990.

Bruck, Peter, and Wolfgange Karrer, eds. *The Afro-American Novel Since 1960*. Amsterdam, The Netherlands: B. R. Gruener, 1982.

Davis, Thadious M., and Trudier Harris, eds. *Afro-American Fiction Writers After 1955*. Vol. 3 in *Dictionary of Literary Biography*. Detroit: Gale Research, 1984.

Holloway, Karen F. C., and Stephanie A. Demetrakopoulos. *New Dimensions of Spirituality: The Novels of Toni Morrison*. New York: Greenwood Press, 1987.

McKay, Nellie Y., ed. *Critical Essays on Toni Morrison*. Boston: G. K. Hall, 1988.

Middleton, David L. *Toni Morrison: An Annotated Bibliography*. New York: Garland, 1987.

Otten, Terry. *The Crime of Innocence in the Fiction of Toni Morrison*. Columbia: University of Missouri Press, 1989.

Samuels, Wilfred D., and Clenora Hudson-Weems. *Toni Morrison*. Boston: Twayne, 1990.

ADRIENNE RICH

Born: Baltimore, Maryland; May 16, 1929

Principal poetry

A Change of World, 1951; *The Diamond Cutters and Other Poems*, 1955; *Snapshots of a Daughter-in-Law*, 1963; *Necessities of Life*, 1966; *Selected Poems*, 1967; *Leaflets*, 1969; *The Will to Change*, 1971; *Diving into the Wreck*, 1973; *Poems: Selected and New, 1950-1974*, 1975; *Twenty-one Love Poems*, 1975; *The Dream of a Common Language*, 1978; *A Wild Patience Has Taken Me This Far*, 1981; *Sources*, 1983; *The Fact of a Doorframe: Poems Selected and New, 1950-1984*, 1984; *Your Native Land, Your Life*, 1986; *Time's Power*, 1989; *An Atlas of the Difficult World: Poems, 1988-1991*, 1991; *Collected Early Poems, 1950-1970*, 1993.

Other literary forms

Of Woman Born: Motherhood as Experience and Institution (1976) is an analysis of the changing meanings of childbirth and motherhood in Anglo-American culture. Adrienne Rich draws upon personal experience as well as sources in mythology, sociology, economics, the history of medicine, and literature to develop her analysis. *On Lies, Secrets, and Silences: Selected Prose 1966-1978* (1979) is a collection of essays on women writers (including Anne Bradstreet, Anne Sexton, Charlotte Brontë, and Emily Dickinson) and feminism. *Blood, Bread, and Poetry: Selected Prose 1979-1985* (1986) followed with further essays on women writers and feminist criticism.

Achievements

Rich's work has been at the vanguard of the women's movement in America. Her poems and essays explore her own experience and seek to develop a "common language" for women to communicate their values and perceptions. She has received numerous awards, including two Guggenheim Fellowships, the National Institute of Arts and Letters award for poetry (1960), several prizes from *Poetry* magazine, the first annual Ruth Lilly Poetry Prize (1986), the Shelley Memorial Award of the Poetry Society of America (1971), and the National Book Award for *Diving into the Wreck* (1974). For several years she coedited (with Michelle Cliff) the lesbian feminist journal *Sinister Wisdom*. Rich won the 1992 Bill Whitehead Award for Lifetime Achievement in Lesbian and Gay Literature.

Biography

Adrienne Cecil Rich was born in 1929, into a white, middle-class Southern family. Her father, Arnold Rice Rich, taught medicine at The Johns Hopkins University.

Her mother, Helen Jones Rich, was trained as a composer and concert pianist but gave up her career to devote herself to her husband and two daughters. She carried out their early education at home, until the girls began to attend school in fourth grade. Arnold Rich encouraged his daughter to read and to write poetry. From his library, she read the work of such writers as Matthew Arnold, William Blake, Thomas Carlyle, John Keats, Dante Gabriel Rossetti, and Alfred, Lord Tennyson. Rich was graduated from Radcliffe College in 1951, the year she won the Yales Series of Younger Poets Award and the year her first volume of poetry was published. She traveled in Europe and England on a Guggenheim Fellowship in 1952-1953.

Rich married Alfred H. Conrad in 1953 and in the next few years gave birth to three sons, David (1955), Paul (1957), and Jacob (1959). She lived with her family in Cambridge, Massachusetts, from 1953 to 1966 but spent 1961-1962 in the Netherlands on another Guggenheim Fellowship. In 1964, Rich began her involvement in the New Left, initiating a period of personal and political growth and crisis. In 1966, the family moved to New York, where Conrad taught at City College of New York. Rich also began to teach at City College, where she worked for the first time with disadvantaged students. Conrad died tragically in 1970. Rich continued teaching at City College and then Rutgers University until 1979, when she moved to western Massachusetts.

Rich eventually moved to California and has continued her active career as poet, essayist, and speaker. Her earliest work is a notable contribution to modern poetry. Her later work has broken new ground as she redefines and reimagines women's lives to create a female myth of self-discovery.

Analysis

Rich has been reshaping poetic conventions to develop her own themes and to create her own voice, often a radical (and sometimes a jarring) one. Central concerns of Rich's poetry include the uses of history and language, the relationship of the individual to society, and the individual's quest for identity and meaning. The home is often a site for the working out of these themes. Above all, in her highly regarded feminist verse and essays, Rich articulates the concerns of a generation of American women.

Rich's early training at her father's hands reinforced her allegiance to a literary tradition of meticulous craft, of "beauty" and "perfection." Accordingly, these poems are objective, carefully crafted, and rhymed, with echoes of W. H. Auden, T. S. Eliot, and Robert Frost. A recurring image is that of the home as a refuge that is threatened by social instability or natural forces. The women in these poems remain at home, occupied with women's tasks and caring for their families.

Snapshots of a Daughter-in-Law and *Necessities of Life* are Rich's earliest attempts to move away from conventional poetic forms, to develop her own style, and to deal more directly with personal experience. Her attitudes toward literary tradition, history, and the home have changed markedly. She questions traditional attitudes toward home and family. As she found the patriarchal definitions of human relationships inadequate, her work became more personal and more urgent. The title poem of *Snapshots of a Daughter-in-Law* is a series of vignettes of women's experiences. It fairly bristles with quotations drawn from Rich's wide-ranging reading. According to the poem, male authorities have always defined women in myths and literature. Thus, women lacked a literature of their own in which to define themselves. Rich wrote that she composed the poem "in fragments during children's naps, brief hours in a library, or at 3:00 A.M. after rising with a wakeful child." Because of these interruptions, she wrote the poem over a two-year period. In this poem, she wrote, for the first time, directly about experiencing myself as woman" rather than striving to be "universal." As the indicates, these are static, fixed vignettes: The men are trapped, denied scope for action and choice. *Necessities of Life* continues Rich's movement toward a freer poetic line and toward subjectivity. Where formerly spoke of history in terms of objects, products tradition, she now identifies with historical persons, Emily Dickinson, and others). A struggle between death and life, between winter and spring,

is in process. Indoor-outdoor imagery carries the weight of these tensions. Poems of death and disappearance take place indoors; the expansive, life-enhancing experiences occur outdoors.

These poems are a retreat from the angry stance of "Snapshots of a Daughter-in-Law." Because at the time of *Necessities of Life* Rich feels oppressed by the human world, she turns to nature for sustenance. *Necessities of Life* establishes a deep relationship with the world of nature; it is one of the "bare essentials" that preserve the heroine in her difficulties. Through a bond with the vegetable and animal world, the world of warmth and light, the book is able to bring life to bear against death and darkness. Nature's cyclical pattern provides clues for survival. Plants move from winter's icy grip into spring's renewal by learning to exist on little. In order to achieve similar rebirth, humans must consciously will change and force themselves into action. This is the pattern of death and rebirth that structures the book.

Prompted by her increasing social concern and the leftist political critique evolving in the middle and later 1960's, Rich turned from personal malaise to political struggle, from private meditation to public discourse. Her jarring tone reflects her anger and impatience with language. Rhythms are broken, speech is fragmented. The poems suggest hurried diary entries. Images of violence, guerilla warfare, and global human suffering suggest an embattled society. Yet anger is close kin to hope: It asserts the wish to effect change. Therefore, alongside the destruction, symbols of fertility and rebirth appear. Rich writes of an old tradition dying and a new one struggling to be born. The poems of this period describe Rich's heroines casting off traditional roles and preparing for journeys.

Rich's poetry revises the heroic myth to reflect women's experiences. *Diving into the Wreck* (1973) presents questing female heroes for the first time in her work. On their quests, they reconnect with lost parts of themselves, discover their own power, and build commonality with other women. Women's lives are the central focus as Rich's project becomes that of giving voice to women's experience, developing a "common language" that will bring the "dark country" of women's lives into the common light of day. Yet Rich also claims another task for women: They must struggle to redeem an endangered society. She argues that patriarchy's exaggerated aggressiveness, competition, and repression of feeling have led Western civilization to the brink of extinction. The task of reconstruction must be taken up by women. Working for change, the women in this book seek to turn civilization from its destructive paths by persuasion, creation of new myths, or redirection of anger.

In order to understand and overcome patriarchy's suicidal impulses, Rich attempts to open a dialogue. Almost all the poems in *Diving into the Wreck* are cast as dialogue. Conversation is the book's central metaphor for poetry. The book begins with "Trying to Talk with a Man," a poem that deals with the dangers of an accelerating arms race but also has a deeper subject: the creation of a dialogue between men and women. Perceiving gender as a political issue, Rich calls upon men to join her in rethinking gender questions.

Yet the book comes to question the possibility of real communication. "Translations" examines the gulf between the languages spoken by women and men. In "Meditations for a Savage Child," the concluding poem, scientists cannot teach the child to speak.

Poems: Selected and New, 1950-1974 includes early unpublished poems and several new ones. In the final poem of this book, "From an Old House in America," Rich uses the hoe image as a starting point for a reconsideration of American history from a woman's point of view. She reimagines the lives of women, from immigrants to pioneers to the new generation of feminist activists. All are journeying. Simple and direct in language, written in stanzas of open couplets, the poem is a stream-of-consciousness meditation that builds in force as it imagines the unwritten history of American women and reaches a profound celebration of sisterhood. Thus, by the end of Rich's ninth book, the woman at home is transformed from the cautious door-closer of "Storm Warnings" (*A Change of World*) into the active participant in history and the questing adventurer eager to define herself by exploration and new experience.

Transformation is the cornerstone of *The Dream of a Common Language*. The poet wishes to effect fundamental changes in social arrangements, in concepts of selfhood, in governmental politics, in the meanings of sexuality, and in language. To that end, transformation supplants her earlier idea of revolution.

The title *The Dream of a Common Language* suggests vision, community, and above all a language in which visions and shared experience may be conceived and expressed. Dream is the voice of the nocturnal, unconscious self breaking into daytime existence. The terrain Rich explores here is the unknown country of the self, discovered in dream, myth, vision, ritual. Like dreams, the poems telescope time and space to make new connections among past, present, and future, be-

tween home and world. "Common" signifies that which is communal, habitual, shared, widely used, ordinary. Rich sets great value on the common, choosing it over the extraordinary.

In *The Dream of a Common Language*, the poet affirms that poetry stems from "the drive/ to connect. The dream of a common language." The book's central section, "Twenty-One Love Poems," orchestrates the controlling themes of women's love, power, language, world. Images of light and dark, dream and reality, speech and silence, home and wanderer structure the sequence. There are in fact twenty-two poems, for Rich has included an unnumbered "Floating Poem." The sequence records a particular lesbian relationship, its joyous beginnings, the difficulties encountered, and the termination of the affair. The poems ask questions about the meanings of self, language, and love between women, and about the possibilities of sustaining love in a hostile world. Rich insists upon grounding her explorations in the quotidian as well as the oneiric world. To be "at home" in the world requires coming to terms with the ugliness and brutality of the city, the pain and wounds, as well as the beauty of love and poetry. Deliberately, Rich situates the first sonnet of her sequence "in this city," with its "rainsoaked garbage."

Because Rich wishes to escape false romanticism, she seeks to connect the poems firmly to the world of daily life, to avoid sentimentality, and to speak honestly of her feelings. Because she wishes to transform th self-effacing behavior that has typically characteriz women in love, she stresses self-awareness and deli' ate choice. Caves and circles—images of round completeness, wholeness—are dominant. Li' homes of Rich's earlier work, they are enclosur ever, the meaning of encirclement has be formed, for in her new vision the poet no lon from the world in her narrow room but re' include the world, to bring it within her pr

Particularly in the last three poems of is a sacramental quality, as Rich affirm a world of women working together Weaving, cooking, caring for childre beautiful and utilitarian objects suc quilts, and clothing. Through the mementos of their lives and c making a world.

"Transcendental Etude" is great richness and power. It death, and rebirth through in the natural world and' begins in the pastoral imagery of an August evening and ranges over the realms of nature and of human life. Rich's vision here transforms the poet's craft. As a poet, she need not be, as she had once feared, an egocentric artist seeking undying fame at the expense of those she loves. Instead, through participation in the life of the physical universe, she articulates the patterns of her own being, of life itself. Thus, Rich's new metaphor of the poet is at once the most daring and the most simple: the poet is a common woman.

Achieving a selfhood that encompasses both creative work and human relationships, egotism and altruism, Rich and her women heal their psychic split in the symbolic return to home, to the full self represented by the circle. The voyage into history, the unconsciousness, the mind is completed in the return.

A Wild Patience Has Taken Me This Far is to a large extent a dialogue with nineteenth century women writers and thinkers: the Brontës, Susan B. Anthony, Elizabeth Barrett Browning. Rich celebrates a world of women's work, both verbal and nonverbal. Growing and cooking vegetables, responding to nature's seasonal rhythms, the simple tasks of women's lives, form a valuable cultural matrix out of which arise the heroic actions of individual women.

Rich's successive volumes of poetry reveal her development as poet and as woman. As she breaks out from restrictive traditions her voice is achieving power and authenticity. From a poet of isolation and withdrawal, of constraint and despair, she has become a seer of wide-ranging communal sympathy and great imaginative possibility. She is redefining in her life and poetry the meanings of language, poetry, love, power, and home. In the early poems the home was entrapping, because patriarchal voices defined women's roles. As Rich's women became more self-defining, the old relationships were abandoned or modified to fit the real needs of the persons involved. Achieving selfhood, Rich's female heroes came to seize control of their homes, their lives. Through metaphorical journeys exploring the world, women's history, and their own psychic heights and depths, they struggle for knowledge and self-mastery. Healing their tormenting self-division, they grow more "at home" in the world. They recognize and cherish their links to a women's tradition of great power and beauty and to the natural world. In this process the idea of home has acquired new significance: From frail shelter or painful trap it has grown to a gateway, the starting point for journeys of self-exploration, and the magic circle to which women return so that they may participate in the work of "making and remaking" the world.

Other major works

NONFICTION: *Of Woman Born: Motherhood as Experience and Institution*, 1976; *On Lies, Secrets, and Silence: Selected Prose 1966-1978*, 1979; *Blood, Bread, and Poetry: Selected Prose 1979-1985*, 1986; *What Is Found There: Notebooks on Poetry and Politics*, 1993.

MISCELLANEOUS: *Adrienne Rich's Poetry and Prose: Poems, Prose, Reviews, and Criticism*, 1993.

Bibliography

Altieri, Charles. "Self-Reflection as Action: The Recent Work of Adrienne Rich." In *Self and Sensibility in Contemporary American Poetry*. Cambridge, England: Cambridge University Press, 1984.

Cooper, Jane Roberta, ed. *Reading Adrienne Rich: Review and Re-Visions, 1951-1981*. Ann Arbor: University of Michigan Press, 1984.

Gelpi, Barbara Charlesworth, and Albert Gelpi. *Adrienne Rich's Poetry*. New York: W. W. Norton, 1975.

Juhasz, Suzanne. *Naked and Fiery Forms: Modern American Poetry by Women, a New Tradition*. New York: Harper & Row, 1976.

Keyes, Claire. *The Aesthetics of Power: The Poetry of Adrienne Rich*. Athens: University of Georgia Press, 1986.

Werner, Craig Hansen. *Adrienne Rich: The Poet and Her Critics*. Chicago: American Library Association, 1988.

MARK TWAIN
Samuel Langhorne Clemens

Born: Florida, Missouri; November 30, 1835　　　　　　**Died:** Redding, Connecticut; April 21, 1910

Principal long fiction

The Gilded Age, 1873 (with Charles Dudley Warner); *The Adventures of Tom Sawyer*, 1876; *The Prince and the Pauper*, 1881; *Adventures of Huckleberry Finn*, 1884; *A Connecticut Yankee in King Arthur's Court*, 1889; *The American Claimant*, 1892; *Tom Sawyer Abroad*, 1894; *The Tragedy of Pudd'nhead Wilson*, 1894; *Personal Recollections of Joan of Arc*, 1896; *Tom Sawyer, Detective*, 1896; *Mark Twain's Mysterious Stranger Manuscripts*, 1969 (William M. Gibson, ed.).

Other literary forms

In addition to his novels, Mark Twain wrote short fiction, speeches, and essays, the latter both humorous and critical. Early in his career, he wrote the travel sketches and impressions *The Innocents Abroad* (1869) and *A Tramp Abroad* (1880) and, later, *Following the Equator* (1897). Two of his most important books are the autobiographical *Life on the Mississippi* (1883) and *Mark Twain's Autobiography*, published after his death in various editions in 1924.

Achievements

At the heart of Twain's achievement is his creation of Tom Sawyer and Huck Finn, who embody that mythic America midway between the frontier American wilderness that produced so much of the national mythology and the emerging urban, industrial giant of the twentieth century. Tom and Huck, two of the nation's most enduring characters, give particular focus to Twain's turbulent, sprawling, complex career as journalist, humorist, entrepreneur, and novelist. The focus is in part symbolic because of the fundamental dualism which the two characters can be seen to represent on the personal, the literary, and the historical planes.

On the personal plane, Tom and Huck represent aspirations so fundamental to Twain's life as to make them seem rather the two halves of his psyche. Like good and bad angels, they have been taken to represent the contending desires in his life: a strong desire for the security and status of material success, on one hand, set against the deeply ingrained desire for freedom from conventional social and moral restraints, on the other. On the literary plane, the two may also be seen as representing contending forces, those of the two principal literary schools of the period, the Romantic and the realistic. Twain was both Romantic and realist, and Tom and Huck emerge almost allegorically as symbols of the two major literary schools of the late nineteenth century.

Tom as the embodiment of socially conforming respectability and as a disciple of Romantic literature contrasts illustratively with Huck as the embodiment of the naturally free spirit, who is "realistic" in part because of his adolescent honesty about such things as art, royalty, and the efficacy of prayer. It is the symbolic dualism on the historical plane, however, that brings into sharpest focus the nature of Twain's central and most enduring achievement. On the historical plane, his two central characters reflect most clearly Twain's principal legacy to posterity: the embodiment in fiction of that moment in time, a moment both real and imaginary, given some historical particularity by the driving of the golden spike at Promontory Point in 1869, when America was poised between the wilderness and the modern, technological state. In this context, Tom represents the settlements that were to become the towns and cities of the new century, and Huck represents the human spirit, freer, at least in the imagination, in the wilderness out of which the settlements were springing. At the end of *Adventures of Huckleberry Finn*, Twain sends Huck on that impossible mission that has been central to the American experience for centuries, when he has him decide to "light out for the territory" before Aunt Sally can "adopt" and "civilize" him.

Twain the humorist and satirist, Twain the silvermining, Paige-typesetting entrepreneur, Twain the journalist, the family man, the anguished, skeptical seeker after religious faith—all must be taken into consideration in accounts of the nature of his achievements. Without Tom Sawyer and Huck Finn, he would have made his mark as a man of his time, a man of various and rich talents. Most likely, his reputation would rest today largely upon his talents as a humorist and satirist, and that reputation still figures in the assessment of his overall achievement. With Tom and Huck, however, he made a central contribution to the national mythology. Huck's "voice" is frequently compared to the voice of Walt Whitman's "Song of Myself." Such comparisons rest in part upon rhetorical similarities between the two voices, similarities in what has been called the "vernacular mode." More significantly, they derive from the similarities of the achievements of the poet and the novelist in the establishing of historically and culturally distinctive American "voices" in poetry and fiction. Tom Sawyer and Huck Finn loom large on the nineteenth century literary horizon. They stand, along with James Fenimore Cooper's Natty Bumppo and Chingachgook, Nathaniel Hawthorne's Hester Prynne and Arthur Dimmesdale, and Whitman's persona in "Song of Myself," as the principal characters of the emerging national literature. Twain's contribution to that body of literature is at the deepest center of his achievement as a major American writer.

Biography

Mark Twain was born Samuel Langhorne Clemens in Florida, Missouri, in 1835. He first used the pen name Mark Twain, taken from the riverboat men's cry for two fathoms of water, in February, 1863.

A Virginian by birth, Twain's father was a lawyer, and the family was of poor but respectable Southern stock. In 1839, the family moved to Hannibal, Missouri, the Mississippi River town that would provide the source material and background for some of Twain's best-known fiction. After his father died in 1847, Twain left school to become an apprentice in the printing shop of his brother, Orion. From 1853 to 1857, Twain worked as a journeyman printer in St. Louis, New York, Philadelphia, Keokuk, and Cincinnati. Between 1857 and 1861, he acquired much of his knowledge of the Mississippi River as a steamboat pilot, beginning that short though richly productive career under the tutelage of a master pilot, Horace Bixby. Twain was a Confederate volunteer for several weeks after the Civil War began. In 1861, he left for the Nevada Territory with Orion, where he drifted into prospecting and journalism, beginning his career as a reporter with the Virginia City *Territorial Enterprise* and continuing it with the San Francisco *Morning Call*.

Twain's literary career and the beginning of his fame might be said to have begun in 1865 with the publication in the *New York Saturday Press* of "Jim Smiley and His Jumping Frog" (later published as "The Celebrated Jumping Frog of Calaveras County"). As a journalist, he went to the Sandwich Islands (Hawaii) in 1866 and to Europe and the Middle East in 1867. These latter travels provided him with the experiences that he shaped into his first major book, *The Innocents Abroad*. *Roughing It*, his highly embellished account of his experiences on the West Coast, appeared in 1872, and his first novel-length fiction, *The Gilded Age*, written with Charles Dudley Warner, came in 1873.

In 1870, Twain married Olivia Langdon. After an unhappy period in Buffalo, they settled in Hartford in 1871. Their infant son Langdon died in 1872, the year Susy, their first daughter, was born. Her sisters, Clara and Jean, followed in 1874 and 1880. Twain's most productive years as a novelist came in this middle period, when his daughters were young and he was prospering. *The Adventures of Tom Sawyer*, *The Prince and the Pauper*, *Adventures of Huckleberry Finn*, and *A Connecticut Yankee in King Arthur's Court* were all written during this period, when he did much of his productive writing during long summer visits to Elmira, New York.

By 1890, Twain's financial fortunes were crumbling, owing mostly to bad investments in his own publishing firm and in the Paige typesetter. In 1891, Twain closed his Hartford mansion and took his family to Europe to economize. After a round-the-world lecture tour in 1896-1897, Twain was in England when his daughter Susy died in Harford. Around this same time his daughter Jean was diagnosed as an epileptic. His wife, Livy, shortly afterward suffered a nervous collapse from which she never recovered. Twain blamed himself for bringing on his beloved family the circumstances that led to these and other disasters. His abiding skepticism about human nature deepened to cynicism and found expression in those dark stories of his last years, "The Man That Corrupted Hadleyburg," "The Mysterious Stranger," and the essay "What Is Man?" He died in 1910 at the age of seventy-four in Redding, Connecticut.

Analysis

Nearly everyone agrees that *The Adventures of Tom Sawyer*, Twain's second novel, is an American classic. It is at the same time a novel of the utmost simplicity and of deep complexity. The novel is a marvelous boy's adventure story, a fact given perspective by Twain's observation that "it will be read only by adults." That is, the essence of childhood can be savored only after the fact, only after one has passed through it and can look back upon it. Popularizations of Tom's adventures are produced for children, but the continuing vitality of the novel depends upon the adult sensibility and its capacity and need for nostalgic recollection. Twain plays on all the strings of that sensibility as he guides the reader through Tom's encounters with the adult world, represented by Aunt Polly and Judge Thatcher, through Tom's romance with Becky, and finally to the adventurous triumph over evil in the person of Injun Joe.

Aunt Polly is the perfect adult foil for a perfect boyhood. Not only does she provide the emotional security that comes from being loved in one's place, but she also serves as an adult whom Tom can challenge through his wits, thereby deepening his self-confidence about his place in the adult world. The fence whitewashing episode is surely one of the best known in American literature. In it, Tom not only outwits his friends, whom he dupes into whitewashing the fence for him, but also successfully challenges the adult world, which, through Aunt Polly, assigned the "boy's chore" to him in the first place. The episode also provides Twain an opportunity to exercise his irony, which, in contrast to much that was to come in the later fiction, is serenely gentle here. Judge Thatcher represents the secure, if somewhat pompous, authority of the adult world beyond the domestic circle. The much-desired recognition of that authority is achieved with decisive pomp when the judge rules the treasure found in the cave legally Tom's and Huck's.

The romance with Becky is almost pure idyll, although the young lovers' descent into the cave inevitably raises speculations about deeper implications. While Injun Joe as evil incarnate is believable enough to raise the hair on the necks of adults as well as children, especially when his torch appears in the cave, there is never any doubt that Tom and Becky will be saved, that good will triumph—never any doubt, that is, for the adult sensibility, secure beyond the trials and tribulations of adolescent infatuation and terror.

Adventures of Huckleberry Finn is almost universally hailed as Twain's best book, as well as one of the half dozen or so American classics of the nineteenth century. The novel continues the mythic idyll of American boyhood begun with *The Adventures of Tom Sawyer*. That connection and that continuation by itself would have ensured the book a place in the national archives if not the national heart. Most agree, however,

that its success derives from even deeper currents. *Adventures of Huckleberry Finn* is Twain's best book because, for whatever reasons, he brought together in it, with the highest degree of artistic balance, those most fundamental dualities running through his work and life from start to finish. The potentially destructive dualities of youth and age, of the need for both security and freedom, of the wilderness and civilization, of innocence and corruption, are all reconciled by means of an aesthetic transformation.

Huck's relationship with Jim, the runaway slave, is central to the novel's narrative, to its structure, and to its theme. Escaping "down" the river, a cruel irony in itself, provides the episodic structure, which is the narrative thread that holds together the developing relationship between the two runaways on the raft. The escape, the quest for freedom, is literal for both Huck and Jim as they flee from Pap and Miss Watson. It may also be seen as symbolic on several planes: historical, philosophical, and moral. The historical setting of the novel is that pivotal era in American history when the new nation was being carved out of the wilderness. The flight down the river is a flight from the complexities of the ever-expanding, westward-moving settlements of the new civilization. The continuing vitality of the novel depends in part upon the survival in the twentieth century of the need for that imaginative escape. Like Henry David Thoreau's Walden Pond, Huck's Mississippi River, originally an escape from what may now seem some of the simpler strictures of society, continues to serve the American psyche as an imaginative alternative to modern civilization.

The philosophical dimensions of the rapidly disappearing frontier are those of nineteenth century Romanticism. Celebrating their freedom on the raft from the legal and social strictures of the town along the river, Huck and Jim are at the same time affirming the central Romantic thesis concerning humanity's need to return to nature and to the natural self. There are two kinds of Romanticism in the novel: that which Tom espouses in his adolescent preoccupation with adventure, and that which Huck practices on the river under the stars and, most significantly, in the final resolution of the problem of Jim as a runaway slave. Twain holds up Tom's bookish Romanticism as childish at best and, for the most part, as silly. This attack on Romanticism—a secondary theme in *Adventures of Huckleberry Finn*, where Twain sends the derelict steamer, the *Walter Scott*, to its destruction on rocks—was one of Twain's lifelong preoccupations. It was continued with a vehemence later in *A*

Connecticut Yankee in King Arthur's Court, but its deep-running, destructive potential for Twain is harnessed in *Adventures of Huckleberry Finn*. The satire is there, but it is in the largely playful terms of the antics of the King and the Duke, their mangling of Shakespeare, and the obituary poetry art of Emmeline Grangerford. This playful treatment of one of his serious themes results in part from the fact that Twain is here working a deeper vein of Romanticism in the person of his supreme fictional creation, Huck.

The moral climax of the novel comes in chapter 31, when Huck decides that he will "go to hell" rather than turn Jim in to his legal master. Twain embodies in Huck and dramatizes in his decision a principle line of Ameri-can political and moral thought that has its roots in Thomas Jefferson and Thomas Paine, its "philosophical" development in Ralph Waldo Emerson and Thoreau, and its aesthetic transformation at the hands of Twain and Walt Whitman. Huck is the embodiment of both the political and the Romantic ideals of the common individual, with no past or roots, whose principal guide is experience rather than tradition. Huck is one of the principal literary symbols of that fundamental American mythical dream of moral rejuvenation in the edenic wilderness of the "new" continent. He stands at the center of nineteenth century American literature and at the center of Twain's achievements.

Other major works

SHORT FICTION: *The Celebrated Jumping Frog of Calaveras County, and Other Sketches*, 1867; *Mark Twain's Sketches: New and Old*, 1875; *The Stolen White Elephant and Other Stories*, 1882; *The £1,000,000 Bank-Note and Other New Stories*, 1893; *The Man That Corrupted Hadleyburg and Other Stories and Essays*, 1900; *A Double-Barrelled Detective Story*, 1902; *Extracts from Adam's Diary*, 1904; *King Leopold's Soliloquy: A Defense of His Congo Rule*, 1905; *Eve's Diary, Translated from the Original Ms*, 1906; *The $30,000 Bequest and Other Stories*, 1906; *A Horse's Tale*, 1907; *Extract from Captain Stormfield's Visit to Heaven*, 1909; *The Curious Republic of Gondour and Other Whimsical Sketches*, 1919; *Letters from the Earth*, 1962.

PLAYS: *Colonel Sellers*, 1874; *Ah Sin, the Heathen Chinee*, 1877 (with Bret Harte).

NONFICTION: *The Innocents Abroad*, 1869; *Roughing It*, 1872; *A Tramp Abroad*, 1880; *Life on the Mississippi*, 1883; *Following the Equator*, 1897; *How to Tell a Story and Other Essays*, 1897; *My Debut as a Literary Person*, 1903; *What Is Man?*, 1906; *Christian Science*, 1907; *Is Shakespeare Dead?*, 1909; *Mark Twain's Speeches*, 1910; *Mark Twain's Letters*, 1917 (2 vols.); *Europe and Elsewhere*, 1923 (Albert Bigelow Paine, ed.); *Mark Twain's Autobiography*, 1924 (2 vols.); *Sketches of the Sixties*, 1926 (with Bret Harte); *The Adventures of Thomas Jefferson Snodgrass*, 1926; *Mark Twain's Notebook*, 1935 (Albert Bigelow Paine, ed.); *Letters from the Sandwich Islands, Written for the Sacramento Union*, 1937; *Letters from Honolulu, Written for the Sacramento Union*, 1939; *Mark Twain in Eruption*, 1940 (Bernard DeVoto, ed.); *Mark Twain's Travels with Mr. Brown*, 1940; *Washington in 1868*, 1943; *The Love Letters of Mark Twain*, 1949; *Mark Twain to Mrs. Fairbanks*, 1949; *Mark Twain of the Enterprise, 1862-1864*, 1957; *Mark Twain-Howells Letters*, 1960; *Mark Twain's Letters to Mary*, 1961; *Mark Twain's Letters to His Publishers, 1867-1894*, 1967; *Clemens of the Call: Mark Twain in San Francisco*, 1969; *Mark Twain's Correspondence with Henry Huttleston Rogers, 1893-1909*, 1969; *A Pen Warmed-Up in Hell: Mark Twain in Protest*, 1972; *Mark Twain's Notebooks and Journals 1975-1979*; *Mark Twain Speaking*, 1976 (Paul Fatout, ed.); *Mark Twain's Letters*, 1988- (Edgar Marquess Branch, Michael B. Frank, and Kenneth M. Sanderson, eds. 3 vols. to date).

Bibliography

Clemens, Susy. *Papa: An Intimate Biography of Mark Twain*. Garden City, N.Y.: Doubleday, 1985.

Giddings, Robert, ed. *Mark Twain: A Sumptuous Variety*. Totowa, N.J.: Barnes & Noble Books, 1985.

Kaplan, Justin. *Mr. Clemens and Mr. Twain*. New York: Simon & Schuster, 1966.

Lauber, John. *The Inventions of Mark Twain*. New York: Hill & Wang, 1990.

LeMaster, J. R., and James D. Wilson, eds. *The Mark Twain Encyclopedia*. New York: Garland, 1993.

Long, E. Hudson, and J. R. LeMaster. *The New Mark Twain Handbook*. New York: Garland, 1985.

Miller, Robert Keith. *Mark Twain*. New York: Frederick Ungar, 1983.

Paine, Albert Bigelow. *Mark Twain: A Biography*. 3 vols. New York: Harper and Brothers, 1912.

Stoneley, Peter. *Mark Twain and the Feminine Aesthetic*. Cambridge, England: Cambridge University Press, 1992.

WALT WHITMAN

Born: West Hills, New York; May 31, 1819   **Died:** Camden, New Jersey; March 26, 1892

Principal poetry

Leaves of Grass, 1855, 1856, 1860, 1867, 1871, 1876, 1881-1882, 1889, 1891-1892; *Drum-Taps*, 1865; *Passage to India*, 1871; *After All, Not to Create Only*, 1871; *As a Strong Bird on Pinions Free*, 1872; *Two Rivulets*, 1876; *November Boughs*, 1888; *Good-bye My Fancy*, 1891; *Complete Poetry and Selected Prose*, 1959 (James E. Miller, ed.).

Other literary forms

Walt Whitman published several important essays and studies during his lifetime. *Democratic Vistas* (1871), *Memoranda During the War* (1875-1876), *Specimen Days and Collect* (1882-1883, autobiographical sketches), and *Complete Prose Works* (1892) are the most significant. He also tried his hand at short fiction and a novel. Many of his letters and journals have appeared either in early editions or as parts of the New York University Press edition of *The Collected Writings of Walt Whitman* (1961-1984, 22 vols.).

Achievements

Whitman's stature rests largely on two major contributions to the literature of the United States. First, although detractors are numerous and the poet's organizing principle is sometimes blurred, *Leaves of Grass* stands as the most fully realized American epic poem. Written in the midst of natural grandeur and burgeoning materialism, Whitman's book traces the geographical, social, and spiritual contours of an expanding nation. It embraces the science and commercialism of industrial America while trying to direct these practical energies toward the "higher mind" of literature, culture, and the soul. In his preface to the first edition of *Leaves of Grass*, Whitman referred to the United States itself as "essentially the greatest poem." He saw the self-esteem, sympathy, candor, and deathless attachment to freedom of the common people as "unrhymed poetry," which awaited the "gigantic and generous treatment worthy of it." *Leaves of Grass* was to be that treatment.

As James E. Miller points out in his edition of Whitman's *Complete Poetry and Selected Prose* (1959), the poet's second achievement was in language and poetic technique. Readers take for granted the modern American poet's emphasis on free verse and ordinary diction, forgetting Whitman's revolutionary impact. His free-verse form departed from stanzaic patterns and regular lines, taking its power instead from individual, rolling, oratorical lines of cadenced speech. He subordinated traditional poetic techniques, such as alliteration, repetition, inversion, and conventional meter, to this expansive form. He also violated popular rules of poetic diction by extracting a rich vocabulary from foreign languages, science, opera, various trades, and the ordinary language of town and country. Finally, Whitman broke taboos with his extensive use of sexual imagery, incorporated not to titillate or shock but to portray life in its wholeness. He determined to be the poet of procreation, to celebrate the elemental and primal life force that permeates humanity and nature. Thus, "forbidden voices" are unveiled, clarified, and transfigured by the poet's vision of their place in an organic universe.

Biography

Walter Whitman was born in West Hills, Long Island, New York, on May 31, 1819. His mother, Louisa Van Velsor, was descended from a long line of New York Dutch farmers, and his father, Walter Whitman, was a Long Island farmer and carpenter. In 1823, the father moved his family to Brooklyn in search of work. One of nine children in an undistinguished family, Whitman received only a meager formal education between 1825 and 1830, when he turned to the printing trade for the next five years. At the age of seventeen he began teaching at various Long Island schools and continued to teach until he went to New York City to be a printer for the *New World* and a reporter for the *Democratic Review* in 1841. From then on, Whitman generally made a living at journalism. Besides reporting and freelance writing, he edited several Brooklyn newspapers, including the *Daily Eagle* (1846-1848), the *Freeman* (1848-1849), and the *Times* (1857-1859). Some of Whitman's experiences during this period influenced the poetry that seemed to burst into print in

1855. While in New York, Whitman frequented the opera and the public library, both of which furnished him with a sense of heritage, of connection with the bards and singers of the past. In 1848, Whitman met and was hired by a representative of the New Orleans *Crescent*. Although the job lasted only a few months, the journey by train, stagecoach, and steamboat through what Whitman always referred to as "inland America" certainly helped to stimulate his vision of the country's democratic future. Perhaps most obviously influential was Whitman's trade itself. His flair for action and vignette, as well as descriptive detail, surely was sharpened by his journalistic writing. The reporter's keen eye for the daily scene is everywhere evident in *Leaves of Grass*.

When the first edition of his poems appeared, Whitman received little money but some attention from reviewers. Included among the responses was a famous letter from Ralph Waldo Emerson, who praised Whitman for his brave thought and greeted him at the beginning of a great career. Whitman continued to write and edit but was unemployed during the winter of 1859-1860, when he began to frequent Pfaff's bohemian restaurant. There he may have established the "manly love" relationships which inspired the "Calamus" poems of the 1860 edition of *Leaves of Grass*. Again, this third edition created a stir with readers, but the outbreak of the American Civil War soon turned everyone's attention to more pressing matters. Whitman himself was too old for military service, but he did experience the war by caring for wounded soldiers in Washington, D.C., hospitals. While in Washington as a government clerk, Whitman witnessed Lincoln's second inauguration, mourned over the President's assassination in April, printed *Drum-Taps* in May, and later added to these Civil War lyrics a sequel, which contained "When Lilacs Last in the Dooryard Bloom'd."

The postwar years saw Whitman's reputation steadily increasing in England, thanks to William Rossetti's *Selections* in 1868, Algernon Swinburne's praise, and a long, admiring review of his work by Anne Gilchrist in 1870. In fact, Gilchrist fell in love with the poet after reading *Leaves of Grass* and even moved to Philadelphia in 1876 to be near him, but her hopes of marrying Whitman died with her in 1885. Because of books by William D. O'Connor and John Burroughs, Whitman also became better known in America, but any satisfaction he may have derived from this recognition was tempered by two severe blows in 1873. He suffered a paralytic stroke in January, and his mother, to whom he

was very devoted, died in May. Unable to work, Whitman returned to stay with his brother George at Camden, New Jersey, spending summers on a farm at Timber Creek.

Although Whitman recuperated sufficiently to take trips to New York or Boston, and even to Colorado and Canada in 1879-1880, he was never again to be the robust man he had so proudly described in early editions of *Leaves of Grass*. His declining years, however, gave him time to revise and establish the structure of his book. When the seventh edition of *Leaves of Grass* was published in Philadelphia in 1881, Whitman had achieved a total vision of his work. With the money from a centennial edition (1876) and an occasional lecture on Lincoln, Whitman was able by 1884 to purchase a small house on Mickle Street in Camden, New Jersey. Although he was determined not to be housebound, a sunstroke in 1885 and another paralytic stroke in 1888 made him increasingly dependent on friends. He found especially gratifying the friendship of his secretary and companion, Horace Traubel, who recorded the poet's life and opinions during these last years. Despite the care of Traubel and several doctors and nurses, Whitman died of complications from a stroke on March 26, 1892.

Analysis

That democratic principles are at the root of Whitman's views becomes immediately clear in "One's-Self I Sing," the first poem in *Leaves of Grass*. Here, Whitman refers to the self as a "simple separate person" yet utters the "word Democratic, the word En-Masse." Citizens of America alternately assert their individuality— obey little, resist often—and yet see themselves as a brotherhood of the future, inextricably bound by the vision of a great new society of and for the masses. This encompassing vision requires a sense of "the Form complete," rejecting neither body nor soul, singing equally of the Female and Male, embracing both realistic, scientific, modern humanity and the infinite, eternal life of the spirit.

"Song of Myself," Whitman's great lyric poem, exemplifies his democratic "programs" without diminishing the intense feeling that so startled his first readers. It successfully combines paeans to the individual, the nation, and life at large, including nature, sexuality, and death. Above all, "Song of Myself" is a poem of incessant motion as though Whitman's energy is spontaneously bursting into lines. Even in the contemplative sections of the poem, when Whitman leans and loafs at his ease observing a spear of summer grass, his senses of hearing, taste, and sight are working at fever pitch. In the opening section he calls himself "nature without check with original energy." Having once begun to speak, he hopes "to cease not till death." Whitman says that although others may talk of the beginning and the end, he finds his subject in the now—in the "urge and urge and urge" of the procreant world. One method by which Whitman's energy escapes boundaries is the poet's ability to "become" other people and things. He will not be measured by time and space, nor by physical form. Rather, he effuses his flesh in eddies and drifts it in lacy jags, taking on new identities with every line. His opening lines show that he is speaking not of himself alone but of all selves. What he assumes, the reader shall assume; every atom of him, and therefore of the world, belongs to the reader as well.

This unchecked energy and empathy carry over into Whitman's ebullient imagery to help capture the physical power of human bodies in procreant motion. At one point Whitman calls himself "hankering, gross, mystical, nude." He finds no sweeter flesh than that which sticks to his own bones or the bones of others. Sexual imagery, including vividly suggestive descriptions of the male and female bodies, is central to the poem. Although the soul must take its equal place with the body, neither abasing itself before the other, Whitman's mystical union of soul and body is a sexual experience as well.

Because of its position near the beginning of *Leaves of Grass* and its encompassing of Whitman's major themes, "Song of Myself" is a foundation for the volume. The "self" in this poem is a replica of the nation as self, and its delineation in the cosmos is akin to the growth of the United States in the world.

The passionate celebration of the self and of sexuality is Whitman's great revolutionary theme. In "Children of Adam" he is the procreative father of multitudes, a champion of heterosexual love and the "body electric." In "From Pent-Up Aching Rivers," he sings of the need for superb children, brought forth by the "muscular urge" of "stalwart lions." In "I Sing the Body Electric," he celebrates the perfection of well-made male and female bodies. Sections 5 and 9 are explicit descriptions of sexual intercourse and physical "apparatus," respectively. Whitman does not shy away from the fierce attraction of the female form, or the ebb and flow of "limitless limpid jets of love hot and enormous" that undulate into the willing and yielding "gates of the body." Because he sees the body as sacred, as imbued

with divine power, he considers these enumerations to be poems of the soul as much as of the body. Indeed, "A Woman Waits for Me" specifically states that sex contains all—bodies and souls. Thus, the poet seeks warm-blooded and sufficient women to receive the pent-up rivers of himself, to start new sons and daughters fit for the great nation that will be these United States. The procreative urge operates on more than one level in "Children of Adam"—it is physical sex and birthing, the union of body and soul, and the metaphorical insemination of the poet's words and spirit into national life. In several ways, then, words are to become flesh. Try as some early Whitman apologists might to explain them away, raw sexual impulses are the driving force of these poems.

Whitman's contemporaries were shocked by the explicit sexual content of "Children of Adam," but modern readers and critics have been much more intrigued by the apparent homosexuality of "Calamus." Although it is ultimately impossible to say whether these poems reflect Whitman's homosexual associations in New York, it is obvious that comradeship extends here to both spiritual and physical contact between men. "In Paths Untrodden" states the poet's intention to sing of "manly attachment" or types of "athletic love," to celebrate the need of comrades. "I Saw in Louisiana a Live-Oak Growing" is a poignant contrast between the live oak's ability to "utter joyous leaves" while it stands in solitude, without companions, and the poet's inability to live without a friend or lover near. Other short poems in "Calamus," such as "For You O Democracy," "The Prairie Grass Dividing," or "A Promise to California," extend passionate friendship between men to the larger ideal of democratic unity. Even as procreative love has its metaphorical implications for the nation, so too does Whitman promise to make the continent indissoluble and cities inseparable, arms about one another's necks, with companionship and the "manly love of comrades."

The short section of *Leaves of Grass* entitled "Sea-Drift" contains the first real signs of a more somber Whitman, who must come to terms with hardship, sorrow, and death. In one way, this resignation and accommodation follow the natural progression of the self from active, perhaps callow, youth to contemplative old age. They are also an outgrowth of Whitman's belief that life and death are a continuum, that life is a symphony of both sonatas and dirges, which the true poet of nature must capture fully on the page.

"Out of the Cradle Endlessly Rocking" is a fuller, finally more optimistic, treatment of the poet's confrontation with loss. Central to the poem is Whitman's seaside reminiscence of a bird and his mate, who build and tend a nest of eggs. When the female fails to return one evening, never to appear again, the male becomes a solitary singer of his sorrows, whose notes are "translated" by the listening boy-poet. The bird's song is an aria of lonesome love, an outpouring carol of yearning, hope, and, finally, death. As the boy absorbs the bird's song, his soul awakens in sympathy. Whitman then fuses the bird's song and his own with death, which the sea, "like some old crone rocking the cradle," has whispered to him. This final image of the sea as old crone soothing an infant underscores the central point of "Out of the Cradle Endlessly Rocking": Old age and death are part of a natural flux. Against the threat of darkness, one must live and sing.

Like the tone of "Sea-Drift," darker hues permeate Whitman's Civil War lyrics. As a wound dresser he saw firsthand the destruction of healthy young bodies and minds. These spectacles were in part a test of Whitman's own courage and comradeship, but they were also a test of the nation's ability to survive and grow. As Whitman says in "Long, Too Long America," the country had long traveled roads "all even and peaceful," learning only from joys and prosperity, but now it must face "crises of anguish" without recoiling and show the world what its "children enmasse really are."

In "When Lilacs Last in the Dooryard Bloom'd," another of Whitman's acknowledged masterpieces, the poet must come to terms with the loss of one he loves—in this case, the slain President Lincoln. Death and mourning must eventually give way to consolation and hope for the future. To objectify his emotional struggle between grief on the one hand and spiritual reconciliation with death on the other, Whitman employs several vivid symbols. The lilac blooming perennially, with its heart-shaped leaves, represents the poet's perpetual mourning and love. The "powerful fallen star," which now lies in a "harsh surrounding cloud" of black night, is Lincoln, fallen and shrouded in his coffin. The solitary hermit thrush that warbles "death's outlet song of life" from a secluded swamp is the soul or spiritual world. Initially, Whitman is held powerless by the death of his departing comrade. Although he can hear the bashful notes of the thrush and will come to understand them, he thinks only of showering the coffin with sprigs

of lilac to commemorate his love for Lincoln. Eventually, as he sits amid the teeming daily activities described in section 14, he is struck by the "sacred knowledge of death," and the bird's carol thus becomes intelligible to him. Death is lovely, soothing, and delicate. It is a "strong deliveress" who comes to nestle the grateful body in her flood of bliss. Rapt with the charm of the bird's song, Whitman sees myriad corpses in a vision—the debris of all the slain soldiers of the war—yet realizes that they are fully at rest and unsuffering. The power of this realization gives him strength to loose the hand of his comrade. An ever-blooming lilac now signifies renewal, just as death takes its rightful place as the harbinger of new life, the life of the eternal soul.

Whitman's deepening concern with matters of the spirit permeates the last sections of *Leaves of Grass*. Having passed the test of Civil War and having done his part to reunite the United States, Whitman turned his attention to America's place in the world and his own place in God's design. In "Passage to India," the poet is a "true son of God," who will soothe the hearts of restlessly exploring, never-happy humanity. He will link all human affections, justify the "cold, impassive, voiceless earth," and absolutely fuse nature and humanity. This fusion takes place not in the material world but in the swelling of the soul toward God, who is a mighty "centre of the true, the good, the loving." Passage to these superior universes transcends time and space and death. It is a "passage to more than India." through the deep waters that no mariner has traveled, and for which the poet must "risk the ship, ourselves and all."

The grand design of *Leaves of Grass* appears to trace self and nation neatly through sensuous youth, crises of maturity, and soul-searching old age. Although this philosophical or psychological reading of Whitman's work is certainly encouraged by the poet's tinkering with its structure, many fine lyrics do not fit into neat patterns, or even under topical headings. Whitman's reputation rests more on the startling freshness of his language, images, and democratic treatment of the common American citizen than on his success as epic bard. Common to all his poetry, however, are certain major themes: reconciliation of body and soul, purity and unity of physical nature, death as the "mother of beauty," and above all, comradeship or love, which binds and transcends all else.

Other major works

LONG FICTION: *Franklin Evans*, 1842.
SHORT FICTION: *The Half-Breed and Other Stories*, 1927.

NONFICTION: *Democratic Vistas*, 1871; *Memoranda During the War*, 1875-1876; *Specimen Days and Collect*, 1882-1883; *Complete Prose Works*, 1892; *Calamus*, 1897 (letters, Richard M. Bucke, ed.); *The Wound Dresser*, 1898 (Richard M. Bucke, ed.); *Letters Written by Walt Whitman to His Mother, 1866-1872*, 1902 (Thomas B. Harned, ed.); *An American Primer*, 1904; *Walt Whitman's Diary in Canada*, 1904 (William S. Kennedy, ed.); *The Letters of Anne Gilchrist and Walt Whitman*, 1918 (Thomas B. Harned, ed.).

MISCELLANEOUS: *The Collected Writings of Walt Whitman*, 1961-1984 (22 vols.); *The Neglected Walt Whitman: Vital Texts*, 1993.

Bibliography

Allen, Gay Wilson. *The Solitary Singer: A Critical Biography of Walt Whitman*. Rev. ed. New York: New York University Press, 1967.

Dougherty, James. *Walt Whitman and the Citizen's Eye*. Baton Rouge: Louisiana State University Press, 1993.

Folsom, Ed, ed. *Walt Whitman: The Centennial Essays*. Iowa City: University of Iowa Press, 1994.

Folsom, Ed. *Walt Whitman's Native Representations*. New York: Cambridge University Press, 1994.

Gold, Arthur, ed. *Walt Whitman: A Collection of Criticism*. New York: McGraw-Hill, 1974.

Kaplan, Justin. *Walt Whitman: A Life*. New York: Simon & Schuster, 1980.

Knapp, Bettina. *Walt Whitman*. New York: Continuum, 1993.

Miller, James E., Jr. *Walt Whitman*. Rev. ed. Boston: Twayne, 1990.

Myerson, Joel. *Walt Whitman: A Descriptive Bibliography*. Pittsburgh: University of Pittsburgh Press, 1993.

Nathanson, Tenney. *Whitman's Presence: Body, Voice, and Writing in "Leaves of Grass."* New York: New York University Press, 1992.

Pearce, Roy Harvey, ed. *Whitman: A Collection of Critical Essays*. Englewood Cliffs, N.J.: Prentice-Hall, 1962.

Woodress, James, ed. *Critical Essays on Walt Whitman*. Boston: G. K. Hall, 1983.

Zweig, Paul. *Walt Whitman: The Making of a Poet*. New York: Basic Books, 1984.

A CATEGORIZED LISTING OF WRITERS

The following categorized list of writers is intended as a resource for readers who may be interested in exploring the works of other writers associated with a particular American identity or identities. All of the writers discussed in this book appear here, along with additional writers. In the spirit of this publication—which recognizes that not all writers are easily relegated to one category but rather may be seen as representing more than one voice—the editors have placed writers in various categories with which they might be affiliated. This listing furthermore represents only some of the many writers who are expanding the notion of what it means to be "American."

African Americans
Maya Angelou
James Baldwin
Toni Cade Bambara
Amiri Baraka (LeRoi Jones)
Arna Bontemps
Gwendolyn Brooks
Claude Brown
William Wells Brown
Bebe Moore Campbell
Countée Cullen
Frederick Douglass
Rita Dove
W. E. B. Du Bois
Paul Laurence Dunbar
Ralph Ellison
Ernest J. Gaines
Nikki Giovanni
Alex Haley
Lorraine Hansberry
Robert Hayden
Chester Himes
Bell Hooks
Langston Hughes
Zora Neale Hurston
Charles Johnson
James Weldon Johnson
Martin Luther King, Jr.
Audre Lorde
Terry McMillan
James Alan McPherson
Malcolm X
Paule Marshall
Toni Morrison
Walter Mosely
Gloria Naylor
Ann Petry
Ishmael Reed

Jessica Saiki
Ntozake Shange
Jean Toomer
Alice Walker
Margaret Walker
Booker T. Washington
Phillis Wheatley
John Edgar Wideman
August Wilson
Richard Wright
Al Young

American Indians
Sherman Alexie
Paula Gunn Allen
Betty Louise Bell
Michael Dorris
Louise Erdrich
Joy Harjo
William Least Heat Moon
Linda Hogan
Thomas King
N. Scott Momaday
Louis Owens
Lynn Riggs
Leslie Marmon Silko
Gerald Vizenor
James Welch

Americans Abroad
James Baldwin
Paul Bowles
Kay Boyle
William Burroughs
J. P. Donleavy
John Dos Passos
T. S. Eliot
H. D. (Hilda Doolittle)

Ernest Hemingway
Henry James
Henry Miller
Ezra Pound
Evelyn Scott
Gertrude Stein
Richard Wright

Asian Americans
Carlos Bulosan
Frank Chin
Louis Chu
Jessica Hagedorn
Le Ly Hayslip
Garrett Hongo
Jeanne Wakatsuki Houston
David Henry Hwang
Gish Jen
Cynthia Kadohata
Myung Mi Kim
Maxine Hong Kingston
Virginia Lee
David Wong Louie
Pardee Lowe
Toshio Mori
Bharati Mukherjee
David Mura
Monica Sone
Cathy Song
Amy Tan
Jade Snow Wong
Mitsuye Yamada
Hisaye Yamamoto

Gay and Lesbian Americans
Dorothy Allison
Lisa Alther
Rita Mae Brown

Robert Ferro
Allen Ginsberg
Michael Grumley
Andrew Holleran
Larry Kramer
David Leavitt
Audre Lorde
Armistead Maupin
Paul Monette
Mary Oliver
Jane Anne Phillips
Felice Picano
E. Annie Proulx
John Rechy
Adrienne Rich
George Stambolian
Mona Simpson
May Swenson
Mona Van Duyn
Edmund White
Walt Whitman

Jewish Americans
Nelson Algren
Woody Allen
Mary Antin
Sholem Asch
Saul Bellow
Richard Elman
Allen Ginsberg
William Goldman
Emma Lazarus
Norman Mailer
Bernard Malamud
Arthur Miller
Cynthia Ozick
Grace Paley
Marge Piercy
Chaim Potok
Henry Roth
Philip Roth
Susan Schaeffer
Delmore Schwartz
Karl Shapiro
Irwin Shaw
Sholom Aleichem
Isaac Bashevis Singer
Lionel Trilling
Leon Uris
Edward Lewis Wallant

Nathanael West
Elie Wiesel
Herman Wouk
Anzia Yezierska

Latinos
A. Alvarez
Julia Alvarez
Rudolfo A. Anaya
Jimmy Santiago Baca
Nash Candelaria
Denise Chávez
Sandra Cisneros
Oscar Hijuelos
Rolando Hinojosa
Nicholasa Mohr
Americo Paredes
John Rechy
Tomás Rivera
Richard Rodriguez
Gary Soto
Luis Miguel Valdez
Alma Villanueva
José Antonio Villarreal
Helena María Viramontes

Midwesterners
Sherwood Anderson
Saul Bellow
John Berryman
Ambrose Bierce
Robert Bly
Gwendolyn Brooks
Willa Cather
Robert Coover
Hart Crane
Peter De Vries
John Dewey
E. L. Doctorow
John Dos Passos
Theodore Dreiser
Edward Eggleston
James T. Farrell
F. Scott Fitzgerald
Hamlin Garland
William H. Gass
Jon Hassler
William Least Heat Moon
Ernest Hemingway
William Dean Howells

William Inge
Garrison Keillor
Ring Lardner
Sinclair Lewis
Abraham Lincoln
Vachel Lindsay
Edgar Lee Masters
Marianne Moore
Wright Morris
H. Richard Niebuhr
Reinhold Niebuhr
Robert M. Pirsig
J. F. Powers
James Whitcomb Riley
Theodore Roethke
O. E. Rölvaag
Carl Sandburg
Mari Sandoz
Upton Sinclair
Booth Tarkington
Studs Terkel
James Thurber
Frederick Jackson Turner
Mark Twain (Samuel
 Langhorne Clemens)
Carl Van Vechten
Robert James Waller
Glenway Wescott
Jessamyn West
Laura Ingalls Wilder
Thornton Wilder
Larry Woiwode
James Wright
Richard Wright

Northeasterners
Henry Adams
James Truslow Adams
Conrad Aiken
Edward Albee
Louisa May Alcott
Horatio Alger
Maxwell Anderson
Louis Auchincloss
Paul Auster
George Bancroft
Joel Barlow
John Barth
Donald Barthelme
Charles A. Beard

Mary R. Beard
Edward Bellamy
Stephen Vincent Benét
John Berryman
Elizabeth Bishop
Hugh Henry Brackenridge
William Bradford
Anne Bradstreet
Van Wyck Brooks
William Cullen Bryant
Frederick Buechner
John Cheever
James Fenimore Cooper
John Cotton
James Gould Cozzens
Hart Crane
Stephen Crane
J. Hector St. John de Crèvecoeur
e. e. cummings
Richard Henry Dana, Jr.
Don Delillo
John Dewey
Emily Dickinson
Annie Dillard
E. L. Doctorow
John Dos Passos
Jonathan Edwards
Bret Easton Ellis
Ralph Waldo Emerson
F. Scott Fitzgerald
Benjamin Franklin
Philip Freneau
Robert Frost
Margaret Fuller
William Gaddis
John Gardner
Charlotte Perkins Gilman
Allen Ginsberg
Edward Everett Hale
Alexander Hamilton
Dashiell Hammett
Nathaniel Hawthorne
Lillian Hellman
William Dean Howells
John Irving
Washington Irving
Henry James
William James
Thomas Jefferson
Sarah Orne Jewett

William Kennedy
Jack Kerouac
Kenneth Koch
Abraham Lincoln
Henry Wadsworth Longfellow
James Russell Lowell
Robert Lowell
Mary McCarthy
Archibald MacLeish
James Madison
John P. Marquand
Cotton Mather
Herman Melville
H. L. Mencken
James Merrill
W. S. Merwin
James A. Michener
Edna St. Vincent Millay
Arthur Miller
Marianne Moore
H. Richard Niebuhr
Reinhold Niebuhr
O. Henry (William Sidney Porter)
John O'Hara
Eugene O'Neill
Thomas Paine
Dorothy Parker
Francis Parkman
Chaim Potok
Jacob August Riis
Edwin Arlington Robinson
Henry Roth
Philip Roth
Josiah Royce
Muriel Rukeyser
J. D. Salinger
George Santayana
May Sarton
Catharine Maria Sedgwick
Hubert Selby, Jr.
Anne Sexton
Wallace Stevens
Harriet Beecher Stowe
Edward Taylor
Henry David Thoreau
Lionel Trilling
Mark Twain (Samuel
    Langhorne Clemens)
John Updike
Carl Van Vechten

Peter Viereck
Mary Heaton Vorse
Nathanael West
Edith Wharton
Walt Whitman
John Greenleaf Whittier
Richard Wilbur
Thornton Wilder
William Carlos Williams
Edmund Wilson
John Winthrop
Owen Wister
Tom Wolfe

Southerners

James Agee
Conrad Aiken
A. R. Ammons
Maya Angelou
Wendell Berry
Doris Betts
James Branch Cabell
Erskine Caldwell
Truman Capote
Kate Chopin
Pat Conroy
Donald Davidson
James Dickey
Annie Dillard
William Faulkner
Shelby Foote
Ellen Glasgow
Gail Godwin
Alex Haley
Joel Chandler Harris
Lillian Hellman
Zora Neale Hurston
Randall Jarrell
Thomas Jefferson
Sidney Lanier
Harper Lee
Cormac McCarthy
Carson McCullers
James Madison
James Alan McPherson
H. L. Mencken
Margaret Mitchell
Flannery O'Connor
Walker Percy
Edgar Allan Poe

Katherine Anne Porter
Reynolds Price
John Crowe Ransom
Anne Rice
William Styron
Allen Tate
John Kennedy Toole
Anne Tyler
Alice Walker
Margaret Walker
Robert Penn Warren
Booker T. Washington
Eudora Welty
Tennessee Williams
Thomas Wolfe
Tom Wolfe

War Writers

Robert Olen Butler
Stephen Crane
John Dos Passos
Joseph Heller
John Hersey
James Jones
Czesław Miłosz
Tim O'Brien
Thomas Pynchon
Michael Joseph Shaara
Irwin Shaw
Robert Stone
Leon Uris
Kurt Vonnegut, Jr.
Elie Wiesel
Herman Wouk

Westerners

Edward Abbey
Mary Austin
Ambrose Bierce
Ray Bradbury
Richard Brautigan
Raymond Carver
Raymond Chandler
Walter Van Tilburg Clark
Joan Didion
Annie Dillard
John Gregory Dunne
Edna Ferber
Lawrence Ferlinghetti
M. F. K. Fisher

F. Scott Fitzgerald
Mary Halleck Foote
Hamlin Garland
Allen Ginsberg
Zane Grey
Bret Harte
Helen Hunt Jackson
Robinson Jeffers
Jack Kerouac
Ken Kesey
Louis L'Amour
Jack London
Thomas McGuane
Norman Maclean
Larry McMurtry
John McPhee
Czesław Miłosz
Margaret Mitchell
N. Scott Momaday
Toni Morrison
John Muir
Frank Norris
O. Henry (William Sidney Porter)
Francis Parkman
Robert M. Pirsig
Kenneth Rexroth
Adrienne Rich
Richard Rodriguez
Josiah Royce
William Saroyan
Sam Shepard
Upton Sinclair
Gary Snyder
Wallace Stegner
John Steinbeck
George R. Stewart
Irving Stone
Frederick Jackson Turner
Mark Twain (Samuel
    Langhorne Clemens)
Margaret Walker
James Welch
Jessamyn West
Nathanael West
Owen Wister
Mitsuye Yamada

Women

Louisa May Alcott
Dorothy Allison

Paula Gunn Allen
Lisa Alther
Maya Angelou
Mary Antin
Mary Austin
Toni Cade Bambara
Mary R. Beard
Ann Beattie
Betty Louise Bell
Elizabeth Bishop
Kay Boyle
Anne Bradstreet
Gwendolyn Brooks
Rita Mae Brown
Pearl S. Buck
Bebe Moore Campbell
Willa Cather
Denise Chávez
Kate Chopin
Sandra Cisneros
Emily Dickinson
Joan Didion
Annie Dillard
Rita Dove
Louise Erdrich
Edna Ferber
M. F. K. Fisher
Mary Halleck Foote
Carolyn Forché
Betty Friedan
Margaret Fuller
Charlotte Perkins Gilman
Nikki Giovanni
Ellen Glasgow
Susan Glaspell
Gail Godwin
Mary Gordon
Lorraine Hansberry
Joy Harjo
Le Ly Hayslip
Lillian Hellman
Linda Hogan
Bell Hooks
Jeanne Wakatsuki Houston
Zora Neale Hurston
Helen Hunt Jackson
Shirley Jackson
Gish Jen
Sarah Orne Jewett
Erica Jong

Cynthia Kadohata
Barbara Kingsolver
Maxine Hong Kingston
Emma Lazarus
Harper Lee
Virginia Lee
Ursula K. Le Guin
Doris Lessing
Denise Levertov
Audre Lorde
Amy Lowell
Alison Lurie
Mary McCarthy
Carson McCullers
Paule Marshall
Bobbie Ann Mason
Edna St. Vincent Millay
Nicholasa Mohr
Marianne Moore
Toni Morrison

Gloria Naylor
Flannery O'Connor
Joyce Carol Oates
Tillie Olsen
Cynthia Ozick
Grace Paley
Marge Piercy
Sylvia Plath
Katherine Anne Porter
Ayn Rand
Muriel Rukeyser
Jessica Saiki
Mari Sandoz
May Sarton
Susan Schaeffer
Evelyn Scott
Catharine Maria Sedgwick
Anne Sexton
Leslie Marmon Silko
Jane Smiley
Monica Sone

Cathy Song
Susan Sontag
Gertrude Stein
Gloria Steinem
Harriet Beecher Stowe
Amy Tan
Jean Toomer
Anne Tyler
Alma Villanueva
Helena María Viramontes
Mary Heaton Vorse
Alice Walker
Wendy Wasserstein
Jessamyn West
Edith Wharton
Phillis Wheatley
Laura Ingalls Wilder
Jade Snow Wong
Mitsuye Yamada
Anzia Yezierska

Index